THE HUMAN PARADOX

The Human Paradox

Rediscovering the Nature
of the Human

An essay on the metaphysics of the virtues

RALPH HEINTZMAN

UNIVERSITY OF TORONTO PRESS
Toronto Buffalo London

ISBN 978-1-4875-4151-4 (cloth)
ISBN 978-1-4875-4153-8 (EPUB)
ISBN 978-1-4875-4152-1 (PDF)

Library and Archives Canada Cataloguing in Publication

Title: The human paradox : rediscovering the nature of the human : an essay
on the metaphysics of the virtues / Ralph Heintzman.
Names: Heintzman, Ralph, author.
Description: Includes bibliographical references and index.
Identifiers: Canadiana (print) 20220220123 | Canadiana (ebook) 20220220204 |
ISBN 9781487541514 (cloth) | ISBN 9781487541538 (EPUB) |
ISBN 9781487541521 (PDF)
Subjects: LCSH: Virtues. | LCSH: Ontology.
Classification: LCC BJ1521 .H45 2022 | DDC 171/.3 – dc23

We wish to acknowledge the land on which the University of Toronto Press
operates. This land is the traditional territory of the Wendat, the Anishnaabeg,
the Haudenosaunee, the Métis, and the Mississaugas of the Credit First
Nation.

This book has been published with the help of a grant from the Federation
for the Humanities and Social Sciences, through the Awards to Scholarly
Publications Program, using funds provided by the Social Sciences and
Humanities Research Council of Canada.

University of Toronto Press acknowledges the financial support of the
Government of Canada, the Canada Council for the Arts, and the Ontario Arts
Council, an agency of the Government of Ontario, for its publishing activities.

Canada Council   Conseil des Arts
for the Arts   du Canada

ONTARIO ARTS COUNCIL
CONSEIL DES ARTS DE L'ONTARIO
an Ontario government agency
un organisme du gouvernement de l'Ontario

Funded by the   Financé par le
Government   gouvernement
of Canada   du Canada

For Jane
sine qua non

The wolf shall dwell with the lamb, and the leopard shall lie down with the kid; and the calf and the young lion and the fatling together.

Isaiah[1]

[S]urely smallness is the most inapt quality for a soul which is always yearning to reach out after the divine and the human in its wholeness and its totality.

Plato[2]

[A]ll things are either contraries or composed of contraries, and unity and plurality are the starting points of all contraries.

Aristotle[3]

The Master said: "Virtue never stands alone. It is bound to have neighbours."

Confucius[4]

How can one soul contain within itself so much at variance, in such conflict with each other? How does it balance them in the scale?

Augustine of Hippo[5]

Earthly creatures have a fourfold nature.

Thomas Aquinas[6]

[I]l y a deux vérités générales absolues, c'est-à-dire qui parlent de l'existence actuelle des choses ... [D'une part] nous sommes, de l'autre ... il y a quelque autre chose que nous.

G.W. Leibniz[7]

Life is the union of union and non-union.

G.W.F. Hegel[8]

Did philosophy commence with an it is, instead of an I am, Spinoza would be altogether true.

Samuel Taylor Coleridge[9]

A table of virtues hangs over every people ... The love that wants to rule and the love that wants to obey created together such tables as these.

Friedrich Nietzsche[10]

[I]f metaphysics is to stand, it must, I think, take account of all sides of our being.

F.H. Bradley[11]

[The] paradox of the parallel passions ... We must have in us enough reverence for all things outside us ... We must also have enough disdain for all things outside us.

G.K. Chesterton[12]

[T]he knowable is the complete nature of the knower.

Alfred North Whitehead[13]

The unity of the four lingers in the gift of the pouring.

Martin Heidegger[14]

"I am" is an active verb. ... "it is" ultimately points out, not that which the thing is, but the primitive existential act which causes it both to be and to be precisely that which it is.

Étienne Gilson[15]

[À] l'infinie vertu unificatrice ... correspond l'infinie séparation dont elle triomphe.

Simone Weil[16]

[S]ocial and ethical life must exist in people's dispositions.

Bernard Williams[17]

The moral (or spiritual) life is both one and not one. ... We have to live a single moral existence, and also retain the separate force of various kinds of moral vision.

Iris Murdoch[18]

La multiplicité des moi's n'est pas le hasard, mais la structure de la créature.

Emmanuel Levinas[19]

[L]'être est originairement dialectique.

Paul Ricœur[20]

[W]e might perhaps change our picture of modern culture. ... we might rather see it as a free-for-all, the scene of a three-cornered – perhaps ultimately, a four-cornered battle.

Charles Taylor[21]

[I]t is actually perfectly possible to be from the north and the south and the east and the west all at once. ... It's as if they're in a conversation, but a conversation made of stance.

Ali Smith[22]

[A]t the intersection of those four directions, is right where we stand as humans, trying to find a balance among them.

Robin Wall Kimmerer[23]

Heaven doth with us as we with torches do,
Not light them for themselves; for if our virtues
Did not go forth of us, 'twere all alike
As if we had them not.

William Shakespeare[24]

Contents

Part Two: The Human Paradox in a Human World

Figures and Tables

Figures

Tables

Preface

In the language of the movies, this book might be called a "prequel." That is to say, it comes after. But, logically, it should have come before.

A few years ago I wrote a book called *Rediscovering Reverence*.[1] It was based on some assumptions about the nature of the human, which were sketched out in the first two chapters. But they couldn't be fully developed there. They were just the starting point, so I could get on to other things. When I finished that earlier book, I had a persistent feeling I should go back to the starting point, and explain myself more fully. I sensed a need to explore, in more depth, the assumptions of my previous book about the nature of the human.

It seemed important to do this for several reasons.

The first is simply the obligation arising from unfinished business. I'd asked the readers of the previous book to accept certain premises without fully justifying them. I had also referred repeatedly to two basic families of virtues, but without describing them in detail or listing them, except in the index. Readers of the previous book had to take these two families somewhat on faith, as it were, described only in rather general terms. It seemed to me important to make up both of these deficits.

Another reason is that *Rediscovering Reverence* was necessarily unbalanced. Because I was trying to reintroduce my readers to a side of themselves the post-modern world neglects or even denies, I had to give more attention to one side of the human than to the other. But both sides are essential. Without both, there is nothing we can call fully or genuinely human. So, it seemed important to start again, at the beginning, and give both of them the equal attention they deserve.

A third reason is that the nature of the human is much more complex and self-contradictory than a simple emphasis on two basic poles of the human would suggest. Without a supplement, the argument of the previous book might appear to over-simplify the nature of the human. Readers might be misled or might not be able to recognize or explain the infinite complexity and endless self-contradictions they find within themselves.

And finally, explaining the nature of the human is just as important as the subject of the previous book. In fact, as I suggest in the introduction to this book, and again in the final chapters, the fate of the world seems to hang on it. If we don't understand the human, in its fullness and complexity and contradiction, we can't construct a human world. In fact, we may *de*construct a human world.

That may be what we are already doing.

⁓

This, then, is the book I should have written first.

But that means it, too, has been very long in coming to birth. In fact, even more than its predecessor, the whole shape of this book, from beginning to end, was already sketched out in an essay, published fifty years ago. Indeed, the fifty-year gestation of this book has made me appreciate Bradley's warning that "to be earnest in metaphysics is not the affair of perhaps one or two years; nor did any one ever do anything with such a subject without giving himself up to it."[2] Although this book has been written, once again, in response to an immediate need, I can see that I've also been writing it, like the earlier one, all my life.

That means I have acquired many of the same debts. The first is, again, to Denis Smith and Tom Symons. Between them, they gave me my first opportunity to develop a writer's voice and try out the ideas in this book. Denis published that first essay fifty years ago and made it possible for me to explore its themes over the following decade.[3] Without his and Tom's confidence in me then, and since, there might be no book today. One of my great regrets is that, although Tom followed the progress of this book with keen interest, he did not live to see it print, as he longed to do.

To Denis and Tom, I must now add my debt to Dick Sadleir. It was Dick who introduced me to them and gave me the chance to work with all three, an opportunity that shaped my whole life. Before that, as a teacher, he had already provided me with the model of civil human discourse this book celebrates and strives to embody. The ideas of the human paradox and the educational contract explored here have roots in the dialogical spirit Dick showed and taught us. It is another sadness that he did not live to see his gifts to me, and to many others, reborn in this form.

Gordon Watson was another teacher who knew how to create dialogue and engagement. His courses at Trinity College in the University of Toronto introduced the history and language student I then was to philosophical ideas, and stimulated a lifelong appetite for more of the same. I am happy now to be able to acknowledge my debt to him.

I must again thank Alan Toff and Ted Chamberlin for helping me, long ago, to pursue the philosophical education Gordon launched. Alan encouraged me to deepen my acquaintance with the works of R.G. Collingwood, who proved to be a decisive influence on my nascent thinking. Ted fed my interest in aesthetic theory by pointing me to the work of Ernst Cassirer and Susanne Langer, another decisive influence. I must also say thanks again to André Burelle who not only shares my interest in Étienne Gilson, but introduced me to Thomas Gilby, the best translator and interpreter of Thomas Aquinas in the English language. And I want to acknowledge, again, my debt to the late Kenneth Windsor, who first put to me the question that lies behind this book. The first essay of which this book is merely a longer version was itself an interim answer to the puzzle Ken had set going in my head five years earlier.

I am deeply grateful to the late Robert Bellah for his support and encouragement when I had finished the previous leg of my journey, and was just setting out on this one. His spontaneous, warm feedback provided an infusion of confidence at a critical moment, and helped sustain me to the finish line. He was then starting the second leg of his own large project, and I deeply regret we were unable to finish together. I am similarly grateful to Merlin Donald and William M. Sullivan, who both read drafts of the book, provided helpful comments, and gave very welcome encouragement. Robert Vipond and Donald Savoie gave much appreciated support at vital turning points on the road to publication.

Many people assisted me in the writing of this book by pointing me to books and thinkers I might otherwise have missed. I feel I have been constantly blessed over the past decade by the sudden appearance of some decisive work, thanks to the suggestions of a small army of helpers. At the risk of omitting someone, I want to begin by acknowledging and thanking the following for their role in directing me to some important source: Thaïs Donald, Clara Fraser, Leo Groarke, Andrew Heintzman, John Lownsbrough, Catherine MacQuarrie, Tom McMillan, Charles Meanwell, Marc Ozon, Guy Peters, Boaz Schumann, Roger Scott-Douglas, Colin Talbot, and John Thorp. I owe special thanks to Maurice Demers and the other members of *le Cercle de Chelsea*: Gilles Cazabon, Ghyslain Charron, and Guy Côté. They not only drew my attention to several key works but also welcomed me into a model of warm but robust fellowship, in the spirit of Plato's *Symposium*, and awaited the appearance of the book with friendly interest and patience. I am likewise grateful to Brian Bitar for several stimulating conversations at Massey College, especially about Thomas Hobbes.

I also want to thank Keith Banting, Tony Campbell, and Jim Lahey for opportunities to try out some of the ideas in this book before audiences at the School of Policy Studies, Queen's University; the Canadian Centre for Management Development; and the Centre for Public Management in the Graduate School of Public and International Affairs, University of Ottawa, respectively.

The Graduate School of Public and International Affairs, University of Ottawa, provided research help over several years, and I thank especially Maria Chedrese for research assistance related to chapter 13. Elaine Nadeau, Geneviève Lépine, and Amy VanTorre of AN Design Communications helped make the most complex figures in the book suitable for publication. I thank Rosa Lopes for her invaluable help and support over many years.

I am grateful to the University of Toronto Press, and to Len Husband and Leah Connor in particular, for welcoming my book proposal and providing excellent support through the assessment and publication process. Perrin Lindelauf was a sensitive and thoughtful editor. The cover the Press proposed for the book aptly recalls the words of Immanuel Kant: "Two things fill the mind with ever new and increasing admiration and awe: the starry heavens above me and the moral law within."[4] This book is about both: about the reality that "It is" and the equal reality that "I am."

I obviously owe one of my greatest debts to the peer reviewers for the Press. Jack Mitchell's assessment was gracious well beyond any reasonable hope, and I am deeply grateful for his insight and generosity. David Cameron has long been a model for me as a leader, as a writer, and as a man. To be linked in this way is a special gift.

Stephen Bonnycastle has been a companion for sixty-five years and was a powerful influence on this book by introducing me to two of its key protagonists. Samuel Taylor Coleridge has been at the centre of my thinking ever since Stephen gave us *The Friend*, as a wedding gift, fifty years ago. I hope this book shows once again that Coleridge deserves to be regarded not just as one of the greatest poets in the English language but as one of the greatest thinkers in any language, a thinker who combines, in an unequalled degree, an unusually keen perception of the external and internal worlds and an ability to think (as so few can) with his gut and his heart. More recently, Stephen insisted I pay attention to Richard Rorty, for which I am almost equally grateful. Coleridge and

Rorty turn out to be the two polar figures of this book, concrete embod-iments of the human paradox. Coleridge is the personification of what I will call the virtues of reverence. And Rorty is a paradigmatic repre-sentative of the opposite stance of self-assertion, especially in one of its cultural forms most prominent today. I owe both, and much, much more, to Stephen.

John Fraser has been part of my moral universe for even longer. His gifts to me in that time are innumerable, thankfully always mixed with his teasing wit and all the untrue stories he refuses to revise. John followed the course of this book, like its predecessor, from the start, gave me several key sources – including a truly special one – read a full draft, and gave invaluable feedback and encouragement. His generous friendship is another of the blessings of my life.

Tony Campbell has been a friend in work, play, and spiritual pilgrim-age for five decades, and made an immense contribution to this book. I long ago lost track of all the books he gave or pointed me to, books which became essential building blocks of the story told by this one. He really ought to have an official credit here as bibliographer. It was a bonus that we were both pursuing large intellectual projects at the same time. Together with our common interest in the work of Charles Taylor, they provided ample material for many spirited conversations over the past decade, over many a good Tempranillo. Like Stephen and John, Tony is a constant reminder of Aristotle's insight that a true friend is almost "another self."[5] A sacred self, as I will put it in chapter 17.

Although – or perhaps because – I have received so much help in writ-ing this book, I want to make here an avowal of modesty in two ways.

First, I want to acknowledge how imperfect this book is and must be. And how much I look forward to it being perfected by others. By its very nature and ambition, the reach of a book like this one must exceed its grasp. For one thing, I have trespassed into many disciplines where I am an amateur at best, and where specialists will and should set me straight. For another, even in the fields I know better, I am acutely con-scious of all the books I haven't read, and all the things I don't know or understand. The pile of unread books grows higher daily, and each of them contains insights that might enrich, refine, or correct something in this one. In that circumstance, the prudent course might be silence. But that's no solution, either. An imperfect contribution to the conversation may still be useful, even if its reach *does* exceed its grasp – especially if its reach is great enough to justify the gap. I draw comfort from another of my heroes, Samuel Johnson, who had no patience with scholarly "scrupulosity" and timidity. "Let it be always remembered," he said, "that life is short, that knowledge is endless, and that many doubts deserve not to be cleared. Let those whom nature and study have qualified to teach mankind tell us what they have learned while they are yet able to tell it, and trust their reputation only to themselves."[6] I have now more reason than most to appreciate that life is short. So, while I am yet able to tell it, despite all its necessary limitations, here is what I have learned. The eventual test will not be whether it contains errors or omissions. It does. The real test will be whether it helps someone else to think about the nature of the human. And whether it helps some people to *be* human. To be more *fully* human.

Second, I want to caution you not to assume I am more certain than I really am. The writer of a book like this one is always at risk of speaking more forcefully than they intend. But, no matter how it may sound to you, nothing here is intended to be the last word. Everything here is up for discussion, correction, amendment, or improvement, including by myself. I subscribe wholeheartedly to Alfred North Whitehead's dictum that "In philosophical discussion, the merest hint of dogmatic certainty as to finality of statement is an exhibition of folly."[7] This book embraces a vision of the human as a conversation, a conversation made of stance. Each of us is constituted, I will argue, by a permanent dialogue between contrasting stances and families of virtues. And so is the human world we live in. Both can and should be held together, in creative unity, by what this book calls an educational contract. That contract starts here. In the following pages, you are invited not to a lecture or a sermon, but to participate in a conversation, a conversation that began long ago and will never end. That conversation has to take place within you before it can take place with others. But if you listen carefully and honestly to the different voices of the contending stances and virtues within you, I'm sure you will find it has already begun, in your own heart.

I dedicate this book, informally, to the memory of my parents and of my two exceptional brothers. I am not sure what any of them would have made of it. But their examples, their love, and the experience of family life I shared with them taught me most of what I have tried to say here. It took me much of what is now a pretty long lifetime to understand fully what they showed and gave me. Their absence now, like that of Tom Symons, Dick Sadleir, and many others, brings to mind another keen but melancholy insight of the great Samuel Johnson: that a scholar who reaches his objective after a lifetime of effort may look round in vain for those with whom he "should be most pleased to share it."[8]

I also dedicate this book to my beloved sons, Geoffrey and David. They are partly responsible for it, since it is a prequel to the book I was challenged to write for them. Without that challenge and its result, I would never have had the nerve to attempt something even more ambitious. They also influenced its conversational style because I consciously wrote, once again, as if I were speaking directly to them, rather than to specialists. I have deliberately chosen my words and graphical approach in the hope that, without too much effort, they, and readers like them, will be able to understand what I think it means to be a human being.

The book is formally dedicated to their wonderful mother, and the dedication means all it says, and much more. Without Jane, there would certainly be no book. She not only created the conditions which made it possible to write such a book, but also provided much of the raw material. Jane has an uncanny ability to come up with just the right source at just the right time. But the dedication means much more than that. She has been the necessary centre of my life since that sunny August day in 1966, when she walked into it, across a green lawn, smiling. Publication of this book happily coincides with our fiftieth wedding anniversary, and all the shared joys of a family extending now to a third generation, with its promise of future possibilities. The book's completion also coincides with a season of renewed hope, and the promise that love is stronger than anything. May our grandchildren and their children someday find here an explanation of the eternal possibilities within themselves, the possibilities that structure the whole nature of their humanity. And may they also discover here a testimony to the love in which their own lives are rooted, a love which draws them forward too, calling to them, out of the future.

Ralph Heintzman
Burnside, New Edinburgh
Ottawa, Ontario
Easter, 2021

Acknowledgments

The author and publisher are grateful to the following for permission to reproduce figures in this book:

Figure 33: John Wiley & Sons.
Figures 34, 35, and 37: Edward Elgar Publishing.
Figure 43: Paul & Peter Fritz AG. © 2007 Foundation of the Works of C.G. Jung, Zürich.
Figure 53: Oxford Publishing.
Figure 58: Harvard University Press. © 1991 by the President and Fellows of Harvard College.
Figure 70: Yale University Press.

THE HUMAN PARADOX

Introduction

What is a human being?

What does it mean to be human? And how can you lead your life in ways that best fulfil your own nature?

Those are the kinds of questions this book seeks, if not to answer, at least to explore. It aims to describe the nature of the human. And also to suggest how that nature is reflected in several important areas of our shared human life.

I begin from two assumptions. First, that the nature of the human is not now well understood.[1] In fact, many people today deny there is any such thing.[2] If they do take human nature seriously, they may think, like some sociobiologists – especially the "neo-Darwinian Hardliners" – that we don't have much choice about it: that it's largely determined by our genetic and evolutionary inheritance.[3] Or, like some of their critics, that our nature is entirely "up to humans to decide."[4] Or, that it's defined simply by human "consciousness."[5] While some of these options contain grains of truth, none of them, by itself, seems satisfactory. Or close to the whole truth.

My second assumption is that this denial and lack of understanding now block human progress in many ways. They may even be dragging us backward. Our lack of a shared understanding of the nature of the human prevents us from developing, cherishing, and protecting our full humanity. It stands in the way of developing greater human civility, and even threatens the idea of civilization itself.

But before I go any further, I need to distinguish what I'm calling the *nature of the human* from what is normally called *human nature*.[6] I take *human nature* to be something shaped by biology, psychology, evolution, and culture: something that can be studied by the human sciences. The *nature of the human* includes all this but goes deeper. It starts before culture, and even before biology. It's the way we humans are shaped not only by these realities but also by the very nature of reality.

To put this distinction in the kind of technical language I will usually try to avoid in this book, I might say that human nature is an anthropological concept, whereas the nature of the human is an *ontological* concept.[7] That is to say, the nature of the human is shaped by the structure of being itself.[8]

One of the many paradoxes of this book, however, is that we humans have our deepest encounter with being through our *own* being. So any genuine ontology must also be an "anthropology," in the broadest – and least technical, academic, or scientific – sense of that word. The two cannot, in the end, be separated.[9] We encounter being by encountering our own nature.[10] And it is in appreciating and expressing our nature, *in its fullness*, that we can also come to see how it's shaped by the structure of being.[11]

Perhaps even by something beyond being.

This is the part we have forgotten. We're so focussed on the foreground that we've forgotten the background. And this forgetting isn't harmless. It mutilates our idea of the human and prevents us from acting in ways more consistent with our full humanity. Worse, it leads us and our societies into ways of thinking and acting that do us harm – maybe even threaten our survival. If we are to do anything about this, we need to begin by relearning who we are. And how our nature is shaped by much more than we can see around us, in our everyday world.

One way to do that is to reflect again – as humankind did for thousands of years prior to our own era – on the human virtues.

Exploring the human through the lens of the virtues: in three parts

This book explores the nature of the human through the lens of the virtues.

Since the middle of the twentieth century there has been a slow revival of interest in the human virtues, beginning with thinkers in the field of ethics. Dissatisfied with the outcome of modern ethical theory – based on Immanuel Kant's (1724–1804) exclusive appeal to rational reflection on abstract ethical principles – philosophers such as Alasdair MacIntyre (b. 1929), Iris Murdoch (1919–99), and Bernard Williams (1929–2003) shifted attention back to the much older tradition of ethical thought based on the human virtues. Their work helped overcome the bad name "virtue" had acquired in the twentieth century, sparked a revival of interest in "virtue ethics," and initiated a rich vein of contemporary thought and writing in this and related fields, such as psychology and anthropology.[12]

Although I have been greatly assisted by these recent developments, this book takes a somewhat different tack. It runs parallel to the contemporary revival of interest in the virtues, and sometimes draws upon it. But it is not a contribution to "virtue ethics," as such. My focus is wider. I want to use reflection on the human virtues not to advance ethical thought *per se*, but rather to explore the wider human reality, of which ethics (at least as we use that word in everyday speech) is merely one expression.[13]

There are three parts to this exploration. The first part (chapters 1 and 2) aims to uncover the paradoxical structure of reality, the contradictory but unbreakable partnership between opposites that structures not only the human world but the world itself. The second stage (chapters 3 to 10) uses the lens of the virtues to explore how our encounter with this basic polarity of being shapes what I have called the nature of the human. Examining the polar structure of being through the lens of the virtues will help me explore and "map" the structure of the human spirit.[14] Although Clifford Geertz (1926–2006) offers the discouraging word that this part of the book looks for something that cannot be found, its objective might nevertheless be described, in his words, as "discovering the Continent of [Human] Meaning and mapping out its bodiless landscape."[15] Or, in Jonathan Haidt's (b. 1963) words: as creating a "map of moral space."[16] If G.W.F. Hegel (1770–1831) hadn't already used the title, this book might thus have been called a phenomenology of the spirit.[17]

The third leg of the journey (chapters 11 to 17) uses this map as a guide for further exploration of a number of areas of contemporary Western life.[18] In other words, once I have constructed a map of the human spirit, I will "apply" it.[19] The practical application of my map to several dimensions of contemporary Western life should help to do two things. First, it will help to test the map: to see whether it holds up or is supported and confirmed. Second, it should also shed some new light on these various domains of our human life. It may help you to see how a partial idea of the human has limited or diminished both our understanding and our practice in some of these areas. It may show you how we can do better, through a fuller understanding of how and why they are rooted in the paradoxical dynamics of the human spirit.

In other words, if it's sound, a map of the human should do more than merely improve your understanding. It should help you to go beyond understanding to action. It can help you not just to *understand* these dimensions of human life better but – far more important – to *act* within them in ways that are more consistent with the realities of the human spirit. My aim is thus to go beyond ideas and concepts to practice: beyond a virtues social science or philosophy, to a virtues *praxis*. A way of *living*.[20] I hope to help you *think* in the categories in which we actually *live* – so you don't have to go on living merely in the limited categories in which the Western world has become accustomed to think.[21]

Rather than an exercise in virtue ethics, this book might thus be described instead – in philosophical language – as a sort of "virtues ontology."[22] Somewhat to my surprise, I seem to have written an essay in what might be called virtue metaphysics.[23]

The big picture: seeing our humanity whole

In our contemporary world, metaphysics has an even worse name than virtue.[24]

In fact, twentieth-century Western philosophy – especially the logical positivist and analytic stream I will come back to in chapter 15 – spent much of its time ruling metaphysics out of court. The best human thought can hope for, it asserted, is to be a handmaid of the sciences, helping to tidy them up or clarify some of the tools and language they employ. Anything more is to overreach what human thinking can legitimately accomplish, and to force-fit reality into some partial and misleading framework.[25]

"Metaphysical statements are neither true nor false, because they assert nothing," said the logical positivist Rudolf Carnap (1891–1970) in 1935, "they contain neither knowledge nor error. They lie completely outside the field of knowledge, of theory, outside the discussion of truth and falsehood. ... The danger lies in the *deceptive* character of metaphysics; it gives the illusion of knowledge without actually giving any knowledge."[26] Four years later, American philosopher Sidney Hook (1902–89) said: "Traditional metaphysics has always been a violent and logically impossible attempt to impose some parochial scheme of values upon the cosmos in order to justify or undermine a set of existing social institutions by a pretended deduction from the nature of Reality. ... But once crack the shell of any metaphysical doctrine, what appears is not verifiable knowledge but a directing bias."[27]

Slightly more than a decade later, British philosopher Stuart Hampshire (1914–2004) made the same assessment – and, in the process, showed his own bias (the bias of the "linguistic turn" taken by analytic philosophy in the middle of the twentieth century):

> It is characteristic of metaphysical systems, and particularly of the greatest of them, that they can often be shown to rest on the exaggeration, or the taking very seriously, of one or two simple logical doctrines and linguistic analogies; as soon as the underlying logical assumptions are laid bare, the purely intellectual motives of the whole construction become clear. ... [M]ost metaphysical systems can be in part interpreted as exaggerated

projections upon reality of some obsessive difficulty of logic and of the interpretation of the forms of language. They generally show an obsession with a particular form of expression, or type of discourse, and a determination to assimilate all forms of expression and types of discourse to this single model, whatever it may be.[28]

There was some truth in these assessments, and this book certainly doesn't escape the pitfalls they identified. Like any exercise of thought, it necessarily reflects the outlook, the experience, the times – and, yes, the biases – of its author. But where's the harm in that? And what's the alternative?

My own initial, academic training was as an historian. The historical profession long ago accepted that bias is an unavoidable – perhaps even a positive – feature of the historical craft. Every step in the development of an historical work – from the choice of a period and a topic or problem, to the selection of the evidence, to the construction of the narrative – is determined and shaped by the historian's own outlook, personality, values, and perspective.[29] It cannot be otherwise. History is a dialogue between the present and the past, and, in such a dialogue, the present has as much of a role to play as the past.[30] The idea that we could ever step outside the present, or outside our world, or outside ourselves, and somehow discover the past "as it really was," is a pure illusion.[31] We are *inside* history, just as we are inside our world and our times.[32] History "does not belong to us," as Hans-Georg Gadamer (1900–2002) remarks, "we belong to it." So one of the most counter-productive forms of prejudice is the "prejudice against prejudice itself."[33] We simply have to accept ourselves as the time-bound and culture-bound creatures that we are.[34]

If that's the case, what should we do?

Just because thinkers are necessarily biased, or locked in the assumptions of their culture or their time, does that really mean we should refuse to think about human reality in a systematic way? Because metaphysical speculation (like any enterprise of thought, or, indeed, like anything *human*) inevitably reflects the partial and imperfect perspective of its perpetrator – and is therefore never final, but constantly challenged and evolving – does that mean we should give up the effort to see human life as a whole? Or to trace human life back to its foundations? To its roots?

Where would that get us? How could it profit us, if we were to decline the effort to see how things connect? To see the big picture?

The ancient Greek philosopher Aristotle (384–22 BCE) invented the genre of metaphysics, but not the name. The name came from his first ancient editor (possibly Andronicus of Rhodes [first century BCE]), and simply means "the books after the *Physics*."[35] What we now call (thanks to Andronicus) metaphysics, Aristotle himself called (among other things) Wisdom. And Wisdom, for Aristotle, was the enquiry into "the first causes and the principles of things." He himself recognized that it could not be done perfectly because it involves knowledge of ultimate things, the mysteries of existence that can be known only to God. Indeed, he referred to metaphysics, at least once, as "theology" because, he said, "if the divine is present anywhere, it is present in things of this sort." But for that very reason, it was for Aristotle, the "most divine science" and the "most honourable," the one "more to be desired" than any other kind of knowledge. Because it was the "highest science" or "first philosophy," the one that grounds and links all the others.[36]

Metaphysics is a fancy word. But you shouldn't let it intimidate you. For me, metaphysics is simply the big picture.[37] The biggest we can perceive or sketch. Not in detail, but in form and shape. Metaphysics doesn't seek to capture all the complexity and variety of the human – other disciplines are needed for that – but rather the structure or architecture of the human in its most elemental outline. The big picture of metaphysics isn't the biggest in detail but the most encompassing, at the highest, most abstract level. The bird's eye view. The map. It's the attempt to see reality, especially our human reality, whole.[38] To see it with the biggest lens we can employ, the one that links everything up, in as complete or systematic a way as we can achieve.

Metaphysics tries to make explicit what, for most people, remains implicit. Just because you don't make your big picture explicit, doesn't mean you don't have one. All of us operate with assumptions or presuppositions about the nature of reality – about the meaning of life or the lack of it – even if we don't examine them or take the trouble to bring them into the light of day, in a systematic way.[39] From that point of view, twentieth-century analytic philosophy's rejection of metaphysical system has been rightly called a kind of "covert dogmatism," because its own methods contain an implicit metaphysical outlook it simply declines to declare. The claim not to be doing metaphysics is merely a refusal to make its own metaphysical assumptions explicit, "while assuming their truth and sufficiency."[40]

"But it is not possible to escape metaphysics," as Hegel rightly says. "The real question is not whether we shall apply metaphysics, but whether our metaphysics are of the right kind."[41] Not doing metaphysics doesn't exempt you from having a metaphysical posture, whether you recognize it or not.[42] Since you can't *not* have one, you might as well be explicit about it, and think about it as carefully and as systematically as you can.[43]

Being both explicit and systematic has several advantages.

The first advantage is that it opens the door to criticism, to dialogue, and to further progress. Another twentieth-century knock against metaphysics – besides the accusation of bias – was that it allegedly claims a certainty and finality it can never achieve. But by its very nature, no thought can ever be final. Because to live, it must be *re*thought in another mind. The words on this page are dead until they are rethought in your own mind.[44] And, in the process of rethinking, thought is changed.[45] Because the new mind – your mind – brings to it a different range of experience and perception, perhaps even a different time or culture.[46] For change and progress to take place, however, there must first be something to change. One of the reasons for publishing a book like this one is so others can criticize it and go beyond it. You need to sum up your thinking, in a systematic way, if someone else is to improve it or go beyond it. Systematic thinking is the condition of progress, not its enemy.[47]

Another advantage of trying to see things as a whole is that it allows you to see how they connect. Viewed in isolation, a single truth may not really be true, or not as true as you think it is. Because your isolated truth doesn't take account of other things connected to it. Things it influences or that influence it. Or things that balance it. Things to which it must be connected, to be really true, or not to do harm. A truth pursued without awareness of other truths can be a false truth, or a dangerous truth. Even an evil truth.

Seeing connections also enables you to see contradictions and conflicts, both the good ones and the bad ones. The bad ones are the places where you're involved in a genuine contradiction: where some aspect of your thinking doesn't fit with something else. Unless you try to see the biggest picture, you may not notice this, and may be able to get away with something that doesn't really stand up, when looked at in a wider context. You'll see a few examples of that failing in this book.

The more important contradictions, however, are the good ones. Because of a deep bias in our Western culture I'll consider in chapter 1, we're inclined to think that, if two things contradict each other, only one of them can be true. The other must be false. But – in the immortal words of Ira Gershwin (1896–1983) – it ain't necessarily so. In fact, as you will see in chapter 2, it often isn't. And so our natural Western inclination toward binary choices allows and encourages us to deny or neglect large portions of our own humanity. Because we are deeply committed to one or to several dimensions of the human, we're tempted to ignore – or deny or oppose, or even fight – other equally important dimensions of our nature that *contradict* it, or them. We can do great harm, in this way, to ourselves and to our world.

So, another advantage of a systematic approach is that it can help you find a place for more of the human. Without a wide-enough lens, you may be tempted to dismiss or discard something that, from a wider perspective, is an essential part of the whole. If your picture isn't big enough, you may end up with an image or idea that leaves out some important feature or dimension of the human, and thus falls far short of the truth.[48] You may even end up mutilating the human, as so many contemporary accounts do.

That points to a fourth incentive for getting the big picture right, or at least trying to do so. There's much more than thought or thinking at stake here. The really important issue is how our partial or diminished image of the human limits us, as human and social beings. Limits us not just in our mental lives but in our real, everyday lives. Limits us as individual human beings. And also limits our societies and our civilization. Perhaps even threatens their future. If we want to escape those limits – and avoid the self-destruction to the brink of which we may already have brought ourselves – we need to regain a better idea of who we are, as whole human beings.[49]

If that be thought insufficient reason to aim for the big picture, I can only plead a personal inability to do otherwise. When the American sociologist Robert Bellah (1927–2013) was asked why he had bothered to write his magnum opus on religion in human evolution, his (no doubt, ironic) answer was a perfect expression of the metaphysical impulse: "Deep desire to know everything: what the universe is and where we are in it."[50]

That's my excuse too. I've always suffered from an unanswerable desire to see the whole picture. To understand how everything fits together, why things are the way they are, how they relate to each other, and what they mean. I suspect I'm not alone.[51] Many others may suffer from the same deformation, even though our contemporary world frowns on it, and discourages it.[52]

I suspect it may even be an indelible part of the nature of the human.[53]

Searching for agreement: the educational contract

The subtitle of this book is "Rediscovering the Nature of the Human." And I'd like to emphasize the *Re*. Because there's nothing new here. Or not very much. Just a new way of telling a very old story, with, perhaps, a few new tools.[54]

In his charming book, *Orthodoxy*, G.K. Chesterton (1874–1936) describes his acute embarrassment upon discovering he had undertaken a long spiritual journey, only to end up at the very place his own religious tradition had already revealed, some two thousand years earlier![55] I feel some of the same chagrin. Most of what I have to say here about the nature of the human has already been said by others, beginning some three thousand years ago.[56] This book aims only "to say once more, in words suited to our generation, something that everybody has always known."[57] But if there is some embarrassment in this, there's also comfort and reassurance.

Many a contemporary thinker, like Richard Rorty (1931–2007), has come to the conclusion that human beings have never been able to agree on anything important. Especially not on something as difficult and important as the nature of the human. Therefore, the task is impossible. The fruitless search for anything that could be called "truth" – including, or especially, the truth about the human – should now be given up. And we should simply agree to disagree.[58]

My conclusion, for what it's worth, is exactly the opposite.

It seems to me that, whether they recognize it or not, the greatest thinkers about the nature of the human are all in agreement. They have all been saying more or less the same thing, in their own way. Or from their own perspective.[59]

It all depends on whether you pay attention to what they assert, or to what they deny.[60] In all the great disagreements of the human past, as John Stuart Mill (1806–73) puts it, "both sides were in the right in what they affirmed, though wrong in what they denied."[61] So, if you listen only, or primarily, to what they reject or what they contradict, you will hear only cacophony. You will encounter only error and disagreement. But, if you listen carefully – and with genuine respect – to what they affirm, you will hear, instead, a surprising harmony.[62]

Taken as a whole, the great thinkers of the Western tradition seem to offer a remarkable unanimity about the nature of the human. But only if you take them seriously. And if you take them *as a whole*. As if each of them was *right*, in what they affirmed. As if each great thinker was a spokesperson for some necessary, enduring dimension of the human.

Even Richard Rorty has his own role to play here. He says exactly what he *should* say. He's a star witness for a permanent and necessary corner of the human paradox. But it's only when you put *all* the witnesses together that you can begin to get a better, more complete picture of the nature of the human than any one of them can give alone.[63]

That's one of the reasons why deep thinking about something like the nature of the human must always have an historical dimension.[64] Every genuine thinker must recapitulate the thinking of his or her predecessors. Not trying to refute them, but trying to *listen* to them. So their truth can emerge again, in a new context, and be reincorporated into the evolving wisdom of humankind.[65] *Listen* to them – as if each one of them had a necessary part to play, or sing, in the "choir" of the virtues[66]: in the great "concert"[67] or "symphony"[68] of civilization.

Indeed, as I will argue in chapter 17, the very idea of civilization seems to require the search for this kind of harmony. One of the characteristic marks of a genuine civilization – a community or culture we would call "civilized," or rather, "civilizing" – is the search for agreement. The assumption that we are all searching – genuinely and sincerely – for the truth about the universe and about ourselves. And that, behind all our disagreements, we are therefore actually in agreement, or wish to be. Because to act on any other assumption is to leave out something important.

Or worse.

Perhaps even to exclude it, or trample on it, or persecute it. And the result is not redeemed even if the processes by which you do so are called "democratic."[69] Democracy cannot be just a means for one faction to dominate the others and impose its arbitrary views.[70] It must have a deeper moral dimension, through which we seek to educate and persuade. To listen and learn. To embrace and include. And, over time, to agree.

All of our social, cultural, and political processes are therefore, essentially, learning processes, in which we are both teaching others and also reaching out to their own insights, listening carefully and sincerely seeking to understand them. In this book I am going to call the social contract that underpins this kind of process of civilization an "educational contract."[71]

This kind of contract or outlook is essential to our public life but also to our internal, mental, and moral life. As you will discover, the nature of the human is such that we have our own internal democracy.[72] There are contending, conflicting voices and perspectives in our own nature, just as in political life.[73] Indeed, the contending forces of political life are simply a mirror of those within ourselves. Rediscovering the nature of the human involves listening carefully to all of them. And establishing a respectful, attentive conversation between them.[74]

Establishing your own internal, educational contract.

The deep past and the deep future

In this book, I'm going to employ two perspectives on time that may be new to you. I will call them the concepts of the "deep past" and the "deep future." I'll have more to say about these two key ideas later. But here, I'd just like to introduce them to you. To help start you thinking in a new way.

When we begin to think about the nature of the human, our time horizon is normally too short, both backward and forward. And these limits inevitably distort our idea of the human. For example, we Westerners often start our thinking about what it means to be human from the emergence of ancient Greek civilization and culture, about 2,500 to 3,000 years ago. That's when the features we associate with our own "humanistic" culture began to develop, and so we assume that's when the real story of the human begins.[75] Anything else is simply "before."[76] It helps to prepare the story. But it isn't part of the story. If you want to know what it really means to be genuinely human – in any sense that could be relevant today or tomorrow – the last 3,000 years is what you need to consider.

But this way of thinking about the nature of the human isn't good enough. It biases your conclusions from the start. For one thing, it encourages you to adopt the focus of much Greek culture on the rational mind. Implicitly and unobtrusively, it embraces an assumption that the nature of the human – that which makes humans human, and distinguishes them from other forms of life – is the human capacity for rational thought. Without recognizing what you're doing, you've already closed off the possibility of defining the nature of the human in other ways, or from a wider or deeper perspective.

For another thing, the last 3,000 years are only a tiny fragment of the human story. Our hominid ancestors have been living on this planet for well over two million years. And our own immediate human family – homo sapiens – has been around for about 500,000 years.[77] So the last 3,000 years are only about 0.5 per cent of the second, and only about 0.125 per cent of the first! They aren't much to rely on, if you're looking for the enduring nature of the human.[78] And, as I just mentioned, they're biased by their roots in a rationalistic Greek culture. If you want to get some perspective on that bias, you need to take at least some account of the other 99 per cent of human life to date. That's what made us the human beings we are today.[79]

The same thing can be said about our human future. Our perspective on the time ahead is normally far too short. Even the greatest thinkers in the Western tradition (Hegel, for example) have often written as if the past were just a preparation for the present. As if the present age were, in some sense or other, "the end of history." That for which all past history is simply preparation, and toward which it has been leading us.[80] Historians sometimes call this the "Whig interpretation of history," the assumption that the past is simply a record of triumphant and inevitable progress toward a present that is its natural and, possibly, final culmination.[81] Even if Western thinkers do cast their minds forward, they are unlikely to do so very far, maybe a few hundred years at most.

But once again, this isn't good enough. The depth of the potential future ahead of us is not only far more than a few hundred years: it's almost unimaginably long. When you really start to get a handle on it, you may even feel a certain dizziness or vertigo, the way you do when you look down from a very great height, or when you try to think about the infinite depth of outer space. Even if you take the full 2.4–2.5 million years of human-type existence as our "deep past," that only represents a *tiny fraction of the time still to come.* If you were to imagine the whole history of our planet – from the Big Bang to the future extinction of life on earth – compressed into a single day, the entire span of human history since the emergence of our very first human-type ancestors would barely represent even *one minute on the clock*! And there are at least *eight hours* still to go, until life on earth perishes.[82] There are still at least a potential billion years left to go in the human story. And possibly more than two billion.[83] In other words, we don't just have hundreds or even thousands but millions of centuries still ahead of us. *Hundreds of millions,* in fact. So, unless we bring life on earth to an end prematurely, as we might well do (through nuclear war, climate change, environmental pollution, resource depletion, a global pandemic, or something else),[84] the time ahead for the human race is vastly greater than all our "deep past": than all the time elapsed since the first emergence of hominids on earth.

The human future is even "deeper" – much deeper – than our "deep past." That means we aren't anywhere near the end of the story, as we so often assume, implicitly. *We're barely even at the beginning.* When we think about our human future, we need to avoid assuming it will be an infinite extension of the present, or of our contemporary culture and outlook. Of our present virtues. They are just a very early moment in the whole human story, and will no doubt look as strange to our infinitely distant descendants as the prehistoric ancestors of our deep past now look to us.[85]

That doesn't mean that our distinctive Western achievements and virtues will or should be lost. With any luck, they can and will be retained, in some form, in the deep human future. In any case, we should certainly act on that assumption and with that intent. We should act as responsible stewards of our own accomplishments and values. But our current assumptions about the nature of the human will probably be preserved, if at all, within very different future cultures, with assumptions and outlooks altogether different from our own.

In trying to imagine what the cultural forms or stages of this "deep" human future might look like, however, you may be able to draw some insight from our "deep" past. Hegel suggested – rather plausibly, as you will see – that human experience (both individual and collective) takes a shape somewhat like that of a spiral staircase: a circular pattern of development in which human beings move through familiar forms or stages, but at successively higher levels or perspectives.[86] And he also suggested that each of these stages of human development is an image of the whole pattern, the whole nature of the human.[87] The whole circular or spiral pattern of human development is fully present and visible, in a "simplified" or "abbreviated" form, in any one of the human stages or cultures along this road.[88] If Hegel was right, or even close to the truth, rediscovering the full nature of the human, in our own time, may give you some clues to the possible shapes and stages of the "deep" human future ahead. I'll come back to that possibility in the final chapters of this book.

Mental pictures

Exploring the nature of the human raises some very big questions, questions that have puzzled and challenged the best minds of the Western intellectual tradition. And one of the biggest challenges in addressing these kinds of big questions is clarity.

As you will see in the first chapters, these kinds of large questions seem to involve us in an endless series of apparent contradictions. The way we *think* about reality even seems to contradict the very *nature* of reality. That's one of the reasons deep thinking can easily lead to obscurity, especially for ordinary readers, and even for specialists. Sometimes thinkers like Hegel and Martin Heidegger (1889–1976) – two of the deepest thinkers about this puzzle – almost seem to relish this obscurity.[89] But even when writers are trying to be clear, the very nature of these contradictions often makes it hard for ordinary people to follow what they're talking about.

I'm writing a book for those general readers – for you. So I'm going to tackle the problem of obscurity that plagues much thought and writing about the paradoxical nature of reality in two ways. First, by using ordinary, everyday speech as much as possible, and avoiding, where I can, technical terms or language.[90] And second, by using some pictures to illustrate what I'm trying to say. I do so with some trepidation, conscious of the estimable Thomas Gilby's (1902–75) warning that "the foundations of a realist philosophy are not to be exposed in a succession of diagrams."[91] But I can think of no other way to accomplish this difficult task. And in choosing this path, I'm comforted by the knowledge that, as discussed in chapter 6, I am going back to an approach adopted by some of the earliest Greek philosophers, at the very beginning of Western thought.[92]

By putting some of these realities into a concrete, visible form, I hope you'll be able to see exactly what I'm trying to describe, even when it gets quite complicated, as the very contradictions guarantee that it must. If you rely on words alone to express these complications, the meaning can eventually become very hard for most readers to follow. Most people – as even Hegel recognized – aren't used to "abstract thinking": they feel lost in a world of pure thought and long for (as he said) a "mental picture" to make the thought clearer to them.[93] So I'm going to try to help you by supplying some of those "mental pictures."[94] A picture, we say, is worth a thousand words. I hope that, in a subject as complex as the one I'm about to explore, a few pictures may be worth a *hundred* thousand words. Or maybe more.[95]

In fact, if you want to use it that way, this could almost become a picture book for you. If you simply flip through the figures and tables, you should be able to get the gist of what I'm trying to say, even without reading the text. I hope these visual tools help you understand the nature of the human I'm trying to describe: a nature both startlingly simple and infinitely complex and self-contradictory, at the same time.

Of course, if you flip through the figures and tables, I hope you'll also come back and read what I have to say about them. I think a great deal hangs upon it. Both for you, and for our world.

I hope you'll come to see that what's at stake here is much more than intellectual truth, or something in the mind. What's at stake is the meaning of your whole life, and how you live it. And not just how you live, but how others do too. What's at stake is the future of our whole civilization. Or rather, not just the future of *our* civilization.

The future of civilization itself.

PART ONE

The Human Paradox

1

Where to Begin?

If you want to think about the nature of the human, where should you begin?

This is an important question to ask. Because whenever you try to think about something, much depends on your starting point. Once you've embraced an assumption, or chosen a vantage point from which to begin, almost everything else flows from it. It doesn't matter whether the choice was a conscious one or an unconscious one. You're locked in. And may have great difficulty getting out.

So it pays to think carefully about where to begin, or what you may simply take for granted in your thinking.

The law of non-contradiction

Let's consider one possible starting point, or assumption, for thinking about the human.

A natural place from which to begin your thinking would be with what, in the Western tradition, we call the principle or law of non-contradiction. Or what (in a related form) is sometimes called the law of the excluded middle. Even if you didn't start your thinking from this so-called "law," consciously, you would almost certainly do so *unconsciously*. Because it's built right into our Western culture and is normally taken for granted. It's part of our common mental furniture – so common that we don't even notice it. Or think to question it.

A common way to put the law of non-contradiction is to say that something can't be both x and not-x at the same time.[1] It's the flip side or corollary of the other pillar of rational thought and logic, the principle of identity: "this is that." The principle of identity is often expressed as: $A=A$.[2] These two principles seem straightforward enough, don't they? They're the basis of all logic and of Western science, at least until the unsettling discoveries of quantum physics. Together with the principle of identity, the principle of non-contradiction "remain[s] fundamental to the pursuit and articulation of knowledge in the West today."[3] It's the basis of all common sense and of our everyday thinking. If something is true, it can't contradict itself. It can't be both something *and* its opposite, at the same time.

The principle of non-contradiction was first expressed by Aristotle, who seems to have offered at least three different versions of it. He said it was the most certain of all principles of thought and must be accepted by everyone who understands anything. You can't say something is both x and not-x, at the same time.[4]

What could be more obvious than that?

Thomas Aquinas (1225–74), one of the deepest thinkers of all time, said the law of non-contradiction is the "first indemonstrable principle" of all human thought.[5] Maimonides (Moses ben Maimon, 1138–1204), the great Jewish philosopher, said that all philosophers agree on the "impossibility of two opposite properties coexisting at the same time in one substance. This is impossible; reason would not admit this possibility."[6] Thomas Hobbes (1588–1679) agreed that "both parts of a contradiction cannot possibly be true, and therefore to enjoin the belief of them is an argument of ignorance."[7] G.W. Leibniz (1646–1716) – a mind almost as capacious as that of Aquinas – said that the law of non-contradiction is the first of the truths of reason.[8] John Locke (1632–1704) said it is the "first act of the mind ... without it there could be no knowledge, no reasoning, no imagination, no distinct thoughts at all."[9] Immanuel Kant – with Locke, one of the founders of modern thought – said that the law of non-contradiction is the universal "criterion of all truth."[10] "Ultimate reality," said F.H. Bradley (1846–1924), "is such that it does not contradict itself; here is an absolute criterion."[11] Étienne Gilson (1884–1978) said the principle of non-contradiction is "the first principle of all judgments."[12] W.V. Quine (1908–2000), an influential twentieth-century philosopher, held that someone who thinks both sides of a contradiction can be true simply doesn't know what they're talking about. Indeed, it has been suggested that challenging the law of non-contradiction is "outrageous to the sensibility of modern philosophers."[13]

So, everyone agrees. The law of non-contradiction is clearly something you can simply take for granted. And now get on with your task of thinking about the nature of the human.[14]

And yet. And yet ...

What if an assumption like this wasn't actually true? Or was only true in a partial or limited way, or in certain circumstances, or for certain purposes?[15] What if it didn't capture the deepest realities? Or didn't really describe the human situation at all? What if it were, in fact, an obstacle to really understanding what it means to be human?

If that were the case, your very way of *thinking* about reality would make it impossible for you actually to *see* our human reality. Before going any further, you need to make sure this common assumption of our everyday thinking really does help you to think about what it means to be human.

Let's take a moment to think about this a little more carefully.

Testing non-contradiction: the case of the family

One good place to begin to test this basic assumption of Western thought is in the everyday experience of family life.

Family is a good place to start because it's something we've all experienced, in some way or another. And it's one of the places where certain realities – little noticed or even denied elsewhere in contemporary life and thought – are still very much alive. The family is, as Aristotle says, the oldest human institution, "an older and more necessary thing than the state."[16] It's not only pre-modern. It's prehistoric. So it's a good place to start looking for some of the deepest facts about the human – especially those that are hard to find elsewhere today.

One of the things that makes a family so very *un*modern is that it has little to do with our own free will. With the single exception of our partner (and in some cultures, even that exception doesn't apply), we don't choose the members of our family. We don't choose our parents, or our children, or our grandparents, or our cousins, or our aunts and uncles. They're simply *given* to us. We are, as it were, *thrown* arbitrarily into their midst.[17]

We may not even *like* some of the members of our family very much. We may not find them pleasant, amusing, or charming. In fact, we may find some of them tiresome, boring, or downright annoying and exasperating, or even offensive. Sometimes they're simply inconvenient, burdensome, or exhausting. But sometimes they make us angry. Even very angry.

And yet, despite the fact that our families have nothing to do with our free will – or maybe even with our own tastes, or our pleasures – they create – and always have created – the deepest and most powerful sense of moral obligation. Often much more powerful than in the case of relationships we've chosen more freely. Throughout human history – and in Eastern as well as Western cultures – it's always been considered the deepest form of human virtue to feel a profound sense of connection to, and responsibility for, the members of our families. You may not respect your parents, but you are still obliged to "honour" them. You may not like your brother, but you are still his "keeper." You aren't obliged to like him. But you *are* obliged to "love" him. To assume your responsibility for him. And for all the other members of your family, too.

This primary sense of moral responsibility toward our families seems to be the source and model for all the other human moral virtues that develop out of them, as you will see in later chapters of this book.[18]

But, powerful though it is, your responsibility for your family doesn't cancel out your own obligations to yourself, your own free will. If a family smothered you, to the point where you felt *only* the obligations of family life – where you weren't able to assert your own will, your own desires, needs, ambitions, or purposes – then it wouldn't be a good or healthy family, would it? One of the purposes of a family is to provide the structure within which you can learn to be a person, a strong individual, in your own right, capable of making your own judgments, and assuming your own responsibilities, freely and maturely. Able to play your own roles, effectively, not only in the family but in your wider community and society, and in the world of work.[19]

If you didn't become a strong individual, then you wouldn't even be able to assume your moral responsibility for your brother, or your parents, or for anyone else. These two things go together. To be any good at honouring, respecting, helping, or loving your family, you have to become the kind of strong individual who can do all that, consistently and effectively.[20]

Family life seems, then, to involve two realities. We are both individuals *and* part of a wider family. *At the same time.* You can't have family without its individual members. And you can't have individuals without the families that make them who they are.

But these two realities are often in conflict. They *contradict* each other. In order to become ourselves we often have to assert ourselves *against* our families in order to develop and grow, to make the necessary space for our own lives and desires. That's what makes adolescence such a difficult stage of life, and, also, what often makes our adult life a delicate balancing act.

Very few of us ever assert ourselves so aggressively, however, as to break completely our ongoing bond with our families. We continue to love and cherish our families, and to feel obligations toward them, obligations which can often override our own desires or preferences, our own sense of well-being. And these feelings of love and obligation toward our families are an important part of our individual human identities. They've always been considered as among the deepest human virtues, one of the things that make humans most *human*.

In the test case of family life, you can see that what it means to be human seems to involve two contradictory things, at the same time. The love and the conflict go together. You can't get rid of them. Being human seems to involve an ineradicable paradox. In a paradox (or, in philosophical language, a "dialectic"*), two opposites are joined together in an unbreakable partnership. Though they seem to contradict each other, you can't have one without the other.[21] A paradox is the *opposite* of the law of non-contradiction: in a paradox, "what is, is and is not."[22] At the same time.

That's what human life seems to be like. We are both individuals and *not* individuals. We're both x and not-x, *at the same time*.[23]

Think of your two names: your first name and your last name.

Your first name designates the specific individual person you are. There's only one Jane in your immediate family. Jane is the specific, unique individual that you are. It's your most intimate identifier. But it's not the whole story about you. Because you also have a second name. And, without the second, the first wouldn't make sense. It wouldn't tell the whole story about you.

Your second name indicates the wider family unit within which you have your identity, and which made you what you are. There were other Smiths in your family, and you're only one of them. You're not just Jane. You're Jane Smith. Without the Smith there could be no Jane. And, even if there were, she couldn't be the specific Jane that you are. The Jane and the Smith go together.

But they don't always go together easily. Sometimes there's a lot of tension, maybe even opposition, between the Jane and the Smith. You may occasionally become so frustrated, annoyed, angered, or burdened by your family that you wish you could get rid of the Smith part of your name altogether. But without both the Jane and the Smith, you wouldn't be *you*. And if somehow you really *did* try to get rid of the Smith part altogether, you almost certainly wouldn't be a *good* you. Not someone we would admire or offer as a human model to others.

From this first test case of family life, it appears that the law of non-contradiction may not help you very much to understand what

---

* Because I'm writing this book for non-specialists, I have used the word "paradox" throughout, rather than "dialectic." But philosophically minded readers are welcome to substitute the word dialectic every time they encounter the word paradox. Other synonyms found in the literatures of various academic disciplines (some of which I will also employ) include contradiction, contrary, polarity, duality, dilemma, ambiguity, and so on. See note 21 above for a warning about these synonyms.

it means to be a human being. It may even be an obstacle or barrier to your objective. Being human seems to involve the very contradictions the law of non-contradiction tries to exclude. When it comes to being human, contraries can, it seems, be true of the same thing at the same time.

Some other tests

You will find the same contradictions when you widen your lens from the family to the community, and to ethical life in general. Here, again, you encounter the same paradox. Living as an ethical person in your community and society also seems to require you to be both x and not-x at the same time. As long ago as 1605, the English philosopher and statesman Francis Bacon (1561–1626) noted that the common proverbs of ethical conduct seem to contradict each other. In fact, he was able to construct a list of commonplace maxims by arranging them in contradictory pairs. In this way, he could show that, for almost any proverb, there's an equal and opposite one that contradicts it. And, though the two sides of each pair *contradict* each other, both are *true*. Many other writers have noted the same thing since Bacon's time.[24]

The contradictory truths of common moral proverbs reveal the same tension or conflict in our ethical and social existence you already saw in the family. On the one hand, human beings are individuals who need to assert themselves *against* their surrounding environment in order to grow and develop, perhaps even to survive. But at the same time, they're *part* of that wider environment and can't escape it, no matter how hard they try. Even if you think of yourself as a completely autonomous individual, your community has, in reality, helped make you the very independent individual you've become. And you'll continue to depend on it, in many ways, throughout the rest of your life.[25] You can only assert yourself as an autonomous individual in the context of your *involvement* with the world around you. The very process of self-assertion (or what psychologists and philosophers call "individuation") normally leads, paradoxically, to new forms of involvement. Think of an antisocial teenage rebel, for example, who angrily rejects their own family, only to fall into the even tighter embrace of a peer group or gang. Or an individualistic, independent-minded, buccaneering entrepreneur, who must create a tightly disciplined commercial, financial, or industrial organization to achieve her business goals. Or a self-consciously sceptical, critical, academic scholar who nevertheless wholeheartedly embraces the standards, conventions, and even the common technical jargon of her professional discipline.

A person who did nothing but assert their own needs and wishes wouldn't be a full or genuine human being. They wouldn't embody or express the full nature of the human. What makes us most fully human – that is, what makes us most fully *ourselves* – turns out, paradoxically, to be what connects us to *others*, and to the wider universe.[26] We are both individuals and *not* individuals, both x and not-x, at the same time.

The law of non-contradiction doesn't seem to work very well in human life. But it doesn't work very well even in the natural and biological life from which human life emerged.[27] Biological processes are all paradoxical: in fact, paradox is the "the basic biophysical pattern." Biological life is a dynamic, forward-moving *union of contraries*.[28] What we call life, even biological life, is a process of acts or actions. But these biological acts can only take place within a wider biological situation or environment. Biological life is a necessary, unbreakable relationship between the acts and processes of which it is composed, and the context or environment in which they occur.[29] You can't have one without the other. Even as these acts start to cluster into individual organisms, the higher forms of life which emerge from more primitive organisms still function within a larger environment. And they are themselves nothing more than a context or environment for countless *internal* organic processes or actions. Whether considered internally (within themselves) or externally (within the surrounding environment), forms of biological life are both x and not-x, at the same time. Both individual and not individual. Both separate and connected. A unity and a plurality, at the same time. And the more they separate, the more *integrated* they become internally, and also more connected to, or "involved" with, their environment and other creatures, in new, complex, and evolving ways. Think about the outer surface of the higher animals, like your own skin. It has a fundamentally *contradictory* function. To hold your body *apart* from the surrounding environment. But also to *connect* you to your environment. *At the same time.* Simultaneous separation and connection, detachment and attachment, individuation and integration – x and not-x, *at the same time* – are the inseparable, paradoxical (or "dialectical") poles of the great process of biological evolution.[30]

Finally, I could expand my test of the law of non-contradiction even further, beyond human and biological life, to the basic structure of the universe itself. Because everything – living or not living – is the *individual* thing that it is, yet, at the same time, is connected to everything else, and can only be the thing that it is as part of this wider *whole*. If there were no universe, no whole, there could be no part, no individual thing. Anything that exists is both separate and connected, both individual and *not*-individual. The modern ecological and environmental movements have rediscovered this truth, but it has fascinated philoso-phers as long as human beings have thought about the nature of reality, as you will see again in the next chapter.[31] Everything in the known universe is both x and not-x at the same time.

Paradox – *not* the law of non-contradiction – seems to be the logic of truth. The logic of the *real* world.

Starting over

The lesson of this chapter is that the normal, everyday way we *think* about the world – based on the law of non-contradiction – doesn't help you very much to understand the very *nature* of that world, let alone what it means to be human. If you want to explore the nature of the human, you'll need to set aside some of your normal, common-sense ways of thinking. You need a better or deeper vantage point from which to begin.[32]

You need to start all over again.

2

Union and Non-Union

The law of non-contradiction didn't turn out to be a very helpful place to start thinking about the nature of reality, let alone about the nature of the human.

In our ordinary, common sense way of thinking, it may be true and useful (I'll come back to that) to say that something can't contradict itself, it can't be both x and not-x at the same time. But this useful tool for *thinking* shouldn't be confused with a description of *reality*.[1] When you try to understand the nature of reality, you can't rule out contradiction in this way. If you do, you're creating an obstacle to understanding the nature of the human without recognizing what you're doing. Contradiction seems, instead, to be built right into the structure of the universe and, even more, of human life.

So you need a new starting point. But how are you to get it? How can you start to think about the world in a way that takes account of this contradictory or paradoxical nature of reality, and of the human? And, even more important, how can you explain it? How can you ground your thinking about the human in a more adequate or realistic picture of the larger reality within which human beings exist? If you want to fit all these contradictory pieces together in a way you can understand, what would a map of the human spirit look like?

As I explained in the Introduction, one of the challenges in trying to understand a paradoxical or self-contradictory world is clarity. The contradictions that structure our world – even a contradiction between the *nature* of reality and the way we *think* about it – make talking about them very difficult. And they make *understanding* that talk even more difficult.

That's why I'm going to tackle this challenge by using some "mental pictures" to illustrate what I'm trying to say. By putting some of these realities into the form of figures and tables, I hope, as I said in the

Introduction, that you'll be able to grasp more easily what I'm trying to describe, even when it heaps contradiction upon contradiction.

Something and other things

In order to begin constructing a visual image that will help you understand both a paradoxical world and the paradoxical nature of the human, let's start by thinking about something. Some individual thing.

Look about you, wherever you are. In a room, or on your porch, or in your garden, or in a library, or on a beach or a dock, or somewhere else. And choose some individual thing to focus on. Anything at all will do.[2]

What is it? What have you chosen?

I want you to keep that individual thing in your mind as we proceed in this chapter. Whatever it is, I'm now going to create an image that stands for it. I can symbolize the thing you're looking at or thinking about as I've done in Figure 1 on page 29.

To tell the truth, this starting point already biases your exploration of reality. Because you're thinking about an individual thing, you've already begun to construct a certain kind of world: a world made up of individual *things*. That's the way we normally think of the world, and have been thinking about it in the Western world, ever since the time of Aristotle.[3] And the more "modern" you are – that is to say, the more Western, educated, industrialized, rich, and democratic: that is, WEIRD! – the more likely you are to see the world this way.[4] "The WEIRDer you are," as Jonathan Haidt puts it, "the more you see a world full of separate objects rather than relationships."[5] And thinking about the world that way makes some of its most important features – especially those most important for human beings – very difficult to understand.

However, that's a problem we'll have to face later on. You sometimes have to unlearn some of your most natural, most instinctive ways of seeing and understanding the world. But you can only do that when you've begun to see some of the limits of thinking about the world in that way. You have to start where you are. All learning proceeds in this way, as Aristotle himself says: "[O]ne must start from what is barely knowable but knowable to oneself."[6] In our contemporary Western world, that means starting from a world of individual things.[7]

Let's continue thinking about this something.

While you're still focussing on the one individual thing you're looking at, try now, at the same time, to look at, or to be aware of, *all* the

Figure 1. Something

other things that surround it, *all* the other things in the room, or in the outdoor scenery, or wherever you are right now.

Have you tried?

You can't do it, can you?

You can't really look at one thing *and* all the other things around it – everything else, by which it and you are surrounded – at the same time.

And yet both are essential to each other. The thing you're looking at is only one thing in a world of other things. Beyond it are all the other things that surround it. When you look at or think about some individual thing, there's always a background of other surrounding things within which the individual thing you're looking at, or thinking about, exists, and without which, as I pointed out at the end of the previous chapter, it couldn't exist. Edmund Husserl (1859–1938) – one of those who have thought most deeply about our perception of things – calls this the inner "horizon" or "zone," the "indistinct *co-present* margin, which forms a continuous ring around the field of perception."[8]

Individual things can't exist by themselves. They take their place among other existing things. In a sense, then, all the individual things we see or think about are pointers or signposts to other things: they "refer beyond" themselves to the *other* things that surround them, the things you aren't focussing on right now but are nevertheless there – in your room, or your garden – to be experienced if you simply turn your head or change your focus.[9] You're intuitively aware of this background of other objects that surround the one you're looking at. But they don't emerge from that background, or become real, distinct objects for you, until you turn your attention to focus on them.[10] If you

Figure 2. Something and other things

want to think deeply about anything, you need to keep in mind this larger reality: the background of *other* things that the individual things you focus on, at any time, are actually reaching out to, or pointing silently toward.[11]

I can picture this duality as in Figure 2 above.

Figure 2 begins to give you a more adequate picture of reality because it takes account not just of the individual thing you're looking at or thinking about, but also the surrounding background of other existing things within which your individual thing takes its place, and without which, as I noted at the end of the previous chapter, it couldn't exist.[12] Figure 2 looks more like the tests I used for the law of non-contradiction in chapter 1. It seems to be a better image of something like a family, for example, where the individual takes his or her place within a larger unity. It begins to suggest to you that the structure of reality, of real life, has two poles, the poles of something and other things, or self and world. The structure of our world seems to be a logic of polarity or duality: something *and* other.[13]

But there's a problem with this second figure.

It gives you the mistaken impression that those other things – the things beyond the something you're thinking about – are part of the white space that surrounds it. But they're actually *other* "somethings," just like your first something, in your room or your garden. To give you a more accurate picture of reality, I would need instead to have added many more circles, or "somethings," inside the larger circle.

I can't really do that here. There isn't enough space inside the outer circle. And, if I tried, it would give you an image too complex to be helpful in your ongoing journey. Instead, throughout the rest of this book, the one grey dot in this figure will have to stand not only for the something you're thinking about but also for all those *other* individual things, in your room or garden, that surround the thing you're looking at or thinking about. My one grey dot stands for all those other imaginary grey dots, too.

That means my picture still isn't quite good enough. And it isn't yet good enough for another, bigger reason. The other reason my picture isn't yet good enough is that beyond the other things that surround the something you're thinking about is *everything else*. Not just everything else in the room or in your outdoor scene, but the *whole* background of *all* the other things that make up "the world," or even the *total* physical universe within which the individual thing you're looking at or thinking about exists.[14] The something you're looking at is only one of the infinite number of individual things that make up the physical universe. Without that surrounding totality of existing things, the thing you're looking at couldn't even exist, or be the thing that it is. Husserl calls this the outer "horizon," or background (*hintergrund*, in German), the "limitless beyond ... a *dimly apprehended depth or fringe of indeterminate reality* ... an empty mist of dim indeterminacy."[15]

If the universe didn't exist – with *all* the things of which it's constituted – your individual thing couldn't exist either, could it? There's an intimate relationship between the *totality* made up of *every* existing thing in the universe, and the one *individual* thing you're looking at.[16]

That makes my challenge even greater than the one I just identified. Because, to include *all* the other individual things, I would need a circle as large as the universe itself, a space whose boundaries we don't yet know – if there are any. It certainly wouldn't fit inside a book! So, the one grey circle has to stand here for *all* the other individual things in the universe. Though it will change shape, I'm going to keep that grey object constant in all the figures in this book. But whatever shape it takes, you need to remember that the grey space stands in for *all* the individual, visible things – insomuch as they are *individual* – that exist within the totality of existence.

Now I want you to consider a new version of the basic image I've been developing, in Figure 3, on page 32.

This version of my evolving figure is intended to help you recognize that the individual things you *can* see, or can think about, aren't just pointers or signposts to *some* other surrounding things. They point us to *everything else*, too.[17] They silently "reach out beyond" themselves, to *all* the other things that make up the whole reality of the physical world, the totality of existing things you *can't* see.[18] If you want to think

Figure 3. Something and everything

deeply about things, you also need to keep in mind this other even
larger reality: the unseen background of *all* the other things the individual things are reaching out to, or pointing silently toward.[19]

The revised image in Figure 3 gives you a better picture than the
preceding images because it includes not just the individual thing you're
thinking about, and the other things that surround it, but *everything else*
too: the whole background of existing things within which the individual thing takes its place, and without which it couldn't exist.[20]

But this picture still isn't quite good enough.

To give a more accurate picture of reality, I need to alter Figure 3
again, in at least two more ways.

The first way I need to alter my figure has to do with the visibility of
"everything." The whole point about the background of "everything
else" that exists is that it's completely invisible to us. You can only see
individual things, or maybe (if you stop focussing for a moment) a blur
of several or many individual things at the same time. A blur of the
individual thing and a few of the other things that surround it. But you
can never see the totality within which these few individual things exist. That's always hidden from us, always beyond our sight, and even
beyond our imagining. It's the invisible background or "horizon" that
surrounds us, within which every individual thing you can see or do
know exists. By rights, "everything" in my picture ought to be invisible.
But that would defeat the whole purpose of trying to create a visual
image of reality! I need to portray it visually, but in a way that reminds
you the background of "everything" is really invisible.

Figure 4 on page 33 tries to do this.

Figure 4. Something and everything (2)

I've altered Figure 4, so the faded letters of "Everything" can help remind you that the totality of everything, as a whole, is really invisible.

But there's a remaining problem with this picture. The dark line of the outer circle might make you think this wider space of everything else – in which all individual things exist – is really a finite space, with a clear, definable limit. But we don't know that to be the case. We can't see to the edge of everything. And, even if we could, what would be beyond it?! As far as we know, the expanding physical universe could go on forever.

So I need to make another change in my picture, to show that the frontier of "everything" doesn't really exist. For the purposes of our picture, we need *something* – some line, or defining limit – to indicate the domain or reality of everything, within which individual things take their own place. But that's just an illustrative device. The outer line of the circle *isn't really there*. In principle, it should be just as "invisible" – or at least faded, in my picture – as "everything." Maybe more so, because it's not only invisible, but potentially infinite too. It doesn't really exist, as I said. For that reason, I'm going to change the dark line of the outer circle in Figure 4 to a faded and dotted line, as a symbolic device to remind you that this apparent "limit" is really infinite.

You can see that revised picture in Figure 5 on page 34.

Figure 5 is beginning to get us somewhere. It shows you that the only things you can see are individual things like the grey dot, with sharp, definable features. But all these individual things you *can* see exist within a larger reality made up of everything else, a larger background you can't see, which is invisible to you and – as far as we know – has no limit.

Figure 5. Something and everything (3)

The paradox of the one and the many: union and non-union

We're making progress.

But the progress we've made so far has actually taken us backward! Back, paradoxically, to the very dawn of Western thought.

The contradictions you've been exploring in the first pages of this book are some of the very same things the first Greek thinkers thought about in the fifth and sixth centuries BCE. And the steps you've taken so far are also, more or less, the way they began to think about them. Especially the group of early Greek thinkers known as the Pythagoreans (named after the founder of the school, Pythagoras of Samos [ca. 570–495 BCE], whose name is also preserved in the "Pythagorean theorem" about "the square on the hypotenuse" you may have learned in your high school geometry class). According to Aristotle (whose accounts provide much of what we know about them), these ancient thinkers "said the elements of nature were more than one" (i.e., separate, individual things), yet at the same time they "spoke of the universe as if it were one entity" (i.e., the totality of everything).[21] The world, they said, is, paradoxically, both "one" and "many," at the same time.

The Pythagoreans sometimes expressed this same paradox by using the language of the "limited" (individual things) and the "unlimited" (the infinity of the totality).[22] The opening sentence of the first surviving book written by a Pythagorean – Philolaus of Croton (ca. 470–385 BCE) – reads: "Nature in the world order [the cosmos] was fitted together harmoniously from unlimited things and also limiting ones, both the world order as a whole and all the [individual] things within it." "Harmony" reconciles these two opposing principles, uniting unity and multiplicity.[23]

In these words, the Pythagoreans introduced a theme that haunted all Greek thought thereafter, and has remained an underground question for all subsequent Western thought: the fundamental paradox of "the one and the many." *How can things be both one and many, at the same time?* It's a paradox. A paradox central to the whole Greek philosophical tradition.[24]

The paradox of the one and the many is especially important for Plato (428/427–348/347 BCE), and it lurks in the background of almost all his doctrines and dialogues. The true nature of the human soul, as described metaphorically in *The Republic*, for example, is to strive to be *one*, despite all its apparent *multiplicity*. Whether the soul is to be one or many – a "many-headed monstrosity" – is the central question for human moral life, and the healthy soul must constantly and consciously aim to maintain itself in unity. Plato's famous doctrine of the "idea" is also propelled by the same question of how "the one can be many and many, one." The relation between an idea and its many appearances has the structure of a multiplicity bound together in one idea. And Plato's distinctive "dialectical" or dialogical method is inspired by his convictions about the interconnection of the ideas themselves, a unity which human dialogue, and only human dialogue, can reveal. In all these ways Plato, like the Pythagoreans, believed the divergent multiplicity of the human and natural worlds can and must be held together in a unified "harmony."[25]

Aristotle was somewhat more down-to-earth than Plato in his philosophical concerns and methods. But he, too, wrestled with the implications of the paradox of "the one and the many" for the structure of reality. It led him to conclusions that can seem, at first, to be the opposite of – or even to overturn – his famous law of non-contradiction. For Aristotle, the law of non-contradiction had a more limited application than it did for much of the later Western cultural tradition he influenced. For him, it was primarily about "statements" or about how we talk. You can't both assert and deny a truth at the same time, he argued. If you could, speech about reality would become meaningless.[26] But when you look at reality itself – the reality about which statements are made – another quite different law seems to prevail. Reality is structured instead by the Pythagorean paradox. It's both one and many, at the same time. The "logic" of the real world is very different from the logic of statements or of arguments. In fact, *it's the reverse.* After reviewing the thought of his Pythagorean predecessors, Aristotle himself asserted (only one page before introducing his law of non-contradiction) that "all things are either contraries or composed of contraries, and unity and plurality are the starting-points of all contraries."[27]

Aristotle's startling insight is so important, so fundamental for an accurate understanding of the world, that it's worth pausing here to underline it. What Aristotle is saying is that everything you can see or apprehend in the human or natural worlds – *absolutely everything* – is structured by contradiction, by a tension or conflict between opposites. Opposites like one and many, which are the starting point or origin of all the other tensions and contradictions. You can't understand anything, and especially not the nature of the human, unless you first comprehend it as a union of opposites, which are in tension or conflict with each other. Unlike our own speech or thinking, the logic of the *real* world isn't the law of non-contradiction: it's the logic of paradox.[28]

This same theme was later taken up by the Roman philosopher Plotinus (204/205–270), who was much influenced by Plato (therefore often called "Neoplatonic") and was the last great philosopher of the ancient world. Plotinus said that when you start to think deeply about things, you can't help recognizing the existence of "difference [i.e., something, or plurality] as well as identity [i.e., everything, or unity]," and from this basic duality "as from originating principles, everything else proceeds."[29]

The recognition of the simultaneous existence of the "one and the many," of unity and plurality, accomplished by these Greek and Roman philosophers, was the beginning of a paradoxical or contradictory interpretation of reality that rivalled the alternative outlook based on the law of non-contradiction for almost two thousand years, and has begun to do so again since the nineteenth century. The basic paradox of something and everything became the starting point for recognizing an endless series of other contradictions, paradoxes, or dualities that flow from these first two, and that structure the world we live in.

Partly because of the prestigious influence of Plotinus and Neoplatonism, the contradictory structure of reality – and of the human experience of reality – became a common theme of Christian spiritual writing for a thousand years, from the anonymous fifth-century writer known as "Pseudo-Dionysius" to the great fourteenth-century Dominican preacher, Meister Eckhart (ca. 1260–1327) and the sixteenth-century Spanish "mystic," John of the Cross (1542–91).[30] A paradoxical (or "dialectical") form of reasoning was also fundamental to many of the central theoretical works of medieval Christianity, such as Peter Lombard's (1100–60) *Sentences*, the standard theological textbook of the Middle Ages, Peter Abelard's (1079–1142) *Sic et Non* (*Yes and No*), Gratian's (mid-12th century) compendium of canon law, the *Decretum – A*

Concordance of Discordant Canons, and Thomas Aquinas' *Summa The-ologiæ*. Contradiction was also a structuring principle of the discipline of theological debates or "Disputations" in the theological schools of medieval universities.[31] This Christian emphasis on paradox and con-tradiction as the underlying structure of reality – and the way humans experience reality – reached one of its high points in the thought of Nicholas of Cusa (1400–64), a remarkable fifteenth-century thinker and cardinal of the Catholic Church, who suggested that human beings ex-perience reality – especially the deepest realities – not according to the law of non-contradiction but rather as a "coincidence of opposites" (in Latin, *coincidentia oppositorum*).[32]

Though paradox enjoyed a literary vogue in the Renaissance – Mar-tin Luther (1483–1546) himself framed the theses for his "Heidelberg Disputation" in 1518 as a set of "theological paradoxes"[33] – paradox-ical thinking was ultimately driven underground by the literalism of the Reformation, the scientific revolution of the seventeenth century, and the European Enlightenment of the eighteenth century, which all embraced the law of non-contradiction, in one form or other.[34] Galileo (1564–1642), for example, "rejected outright the validity of paradox as a method or criterion of truth."[35] However, paradoxical ways of thinking re-emerged once again at the end of the eighteenth century. Immanuel Kant started the process by noting that both sides of Ar-istotle's "contrary" of unity and plurality can be and are combined within a larger "allness or totality."[36] With a further push from J.G. Fichte (1762–1814), Hegel turned Kant's somewhat casual aside into the basis of a new way of thinking that challenged the exclusive reign of the law of non-contradiction. "Life," he declared, echoing Philo-laus of Croton and the other Pythagoreans, "is the union of union and non-union."[37]

Here we have perhaps the perfect expression of the view opposite to that of the law of non-contradiction. In this succinct formula, Hegel brilliantly captured the contrary view that contradiction is built right into the structure of life and of the universe. "Contradiction is the root of all movement and life," he said, "and it is only in so far as it contains a Contradiction that anything moves and has impulse and activity."[38] Not only *can* something be both x and not-x at the same time: it cannot be otherwise![39]

Although Hegel's words – the union of union and non-union – are typically abstract, your own exploration of the paradox of something and everything, in the previous pages, should help make clear at least part of what he meant. As Figure 5 on page 34 shows, reality is the union of individual things (i.e., non-union, since they are separate and

Figure 6. Union and non-union

distinct, in their individuality) with the greater whole (or union) of which they are only a part.[40] It's a union of union and non-union!

In fact, Hegel's brilliant formula allows me to revise my picture once more, in order to show you, even more clearly, the dynamic which underlies or structures it, as in Figure 6 above.

Figure 6 maintains the same basic image as Figure 5 to show the continuity with the previous concepts. But it wouldn't necessarily require the faded, dotted outer line I used in the previous image. Hegel's paradox of union and non-union can be found at all levels of reality, not just at the highest or widest level, that is, the level of "everything" I was exploring and expressing in Figure 5. So it works for Figure 2 just as well as for Figures 4 and 5. If you go back to the three tests of the law of non-contradiction I performed in chapter 1, you saw that this law didn't work very well in family life, ethical or community life, or even in biological life. The reason it didn't work there is that those realities – like all other realities – are structured instead by what Hegel calls the union of union and non-union. The *non*-union that is your individual self is inseparably connected – or united – to the *union* of your family.

Families are a union of union and non-union. And so are communities and societies and clubs and corporations and countries, and even our own physical bodies and the natural environment we live in. Their members are both x and not-x at the same time. Both separate, individual elements (non-union), and yet fully included in a greater whole (union), without which they couldn't be what they are. In fact, they couldn't even *be*![41]

Sometimes the domain or space of union (within which non-union occurs) is a clear, identifiable space, with a known boundary, like your body, or a family, a neighbourhood, a college, a team, a company, a pond, or the Georgian Bay. And sometimes it isn't – especially at the highest level of all reality, or the total universe. I'll come back to these other, lower levels in later chapters. But for the moment, let's continue our exploration at this highest level of reality, the level of "everything."

Being and beings

We've now made some more progress.

Hegel's "union of union and non-union" has allowed you to identify the underlying polar dynamic that structures the relationship between the individual thing you're looking at in your garden or room and the other things that surround it. The relationship between something and other things. And, even more, between something and everything, or what Aristotle calls unity and plurality. Any really deep thought about reality leads you to encounter this kind of "unity of opposites."[42] The union of union and non-union.

But my picture still isn't good enough. The Everything portrayed in Figure 5 may well be every *thing*, but it still isn't really *everything*. If I'm really going to develop an accurate image of reality for you, I need to expand your notion of it, in two more ways.

First, I've so far included all visible, physical things. But I also need to include all the things you *can't* see. Like the ancient cultures from which they emerged, the earliest Greek philosophers, such as the Pythagoreans, still didn't always distinguish sharply between the physical and the non-physical.[43] But by the time of Plato and Aristotle, Greek thinkers began to make a more consistent distinction between the physical cosmos and other important realities of a human world that *don't* have physical existence – the ideas of justice or goodness, for example. Or your dream of becoming a famous writer, architect, or broadcaster, or the prime minister, or a billionaire. Or the love your parents gave you. These things can't be seen. But they're just as real as the things that *can* be seen, maybe *more* real in some ways because they can change your whole life. They can also change the material or visible world, as an architect's vision brings a building into existence, or a journalist's idea of what's newsworthy or important makes a news story, or the story in a novelist's head becomes a book. Aristotle calls these ideas, purposes, and aspirations – the intangible, invisible things that *pull* us human beings forward, into the future – "final causes." And final causes are just as real as the physical causes recognized and studied – the only ones that *can* be studied – by the techniques of modern science.[44]

I need to make room in my picture for these unseen realities. But I also need to expand it in another way. Leibniz noted that you can't take the existence of existing things for granted. Instead of existing, they might well *not* exist. In fact, when you think about it for a moment, why should there be *anything at all* – rather than nothing?[45] Why does anything exist? That's still the first and the big, unanswered question in all human thought. Why do existing things exist, and what makes them exist? Why isn't there just *nothing* instead?

Nobody can answer that question. But we all know that existing things do, in fact, exist. So I also need to make room in my picture for whatever it is that makes existing things – both visible and invisible – exist, whatever it is that makes their existence possible, whatever creates the very possibility of existence and gives them the power and reality of existence. I have to include whatever it means for anything to actually *be*.

What then, shall I call this expanded notion of Everything, something that includes not just every *thing*, but truly *everything*? As you already saw, some twentieth century thinkers, such as Edmund Husserl, simply called it the "horizon" or the "background." Karl Jaspers (1883–1969), another twentieth century philosopher, called it the "Encompassing" or the "Comprehensive."[46] Writers of the Romantic era at the beginning of the nineteenth century often called it the Infinite or the Absolute. Many ancient thinkers (as you also saw) called it the One. But the word that has been used most consistently throughout the whole history of Western thought is the word "being."[47]

The word "being" has many potential meanings. In its narrowest sense, it can mean simply *one* of the existing things in the universe: "a" being, such as a human "being." In another wider sense – the initial sense in which I'm going to use it here – it can mean the *totality* of existing beings, the totality of existence. All beings and all being.[48]

But hidden within these first two meanings are at least two others. One of them is the process or action that makes beings – or all being – *be*. What do we mean when we say that something exists? What does it mean for something *to be*? The fact that we use the verb "to be" suggests that we assume being isn't just a noun – a thing – but also a verb, a process, an action or act, the action that makes a being *be*.[49] Thomas Aquinas says that "to be is the very act whereby [something] is."[50] So being has a dynamic overtone, the sense of an action or act, not just a thing or the totality of things. This is an important feature of being. Perhaps the most important.[51] I'll come back to it because it makes the background of being even harder to see or to grasp.

Figure 7. Being and beings

A fourth potential meaning hidden in the word "being," especially in the widest sense I'm using it here – as an expanded and improved version of "everything" – is the source or ground of being. What is it that makes it possible for things to *be*, either as a noun or as a verb, either as things or as acts or actions? Why do things exist, and what makes them exist? Why is there something rather than nothing, as Leibniz asked? Even if we can't answer that question very easily – or even at all, even if the answer must ultimately remain a mystery to us – our idea of "everything" needs to make room for it. If it is truly *everything*, it needs to include the ground or source of everything, whatever it is that makes things exist, that allows or enables them to *be*.[52]

With the expansion of "everything" to include both visible and invisible realities and also the process or action that makes both visible and invisible things exist, I'm now in a position to revise my picture once again. You can see the result in Figure 7 above.

Figure 7 now shows the background of "being" which not only includes everything, visible or invisible, but also causes all things to exist, or is the process or action through which they exist. The faded letters of "being" and the faded dotted line of the circle are intended to remind you that both the totality and the action of being are completely invisible to you, and have no limit or boundary. The revised label for the grey dot now shows once more that it stands for all the individual things that exist in the world, all the individual somethings within the larger sphere of "everything." And it will continue to stand for them in later chapters, even when the dot changes shape.

You need to remember, however, that although I've changed its label once again, the grey dot continues to express the *action* portrayed in Figure 6 that makes individual things what they are (i.e., separate and distinct, *not* just part of something else). It still stands for the dynamic by which individual things exist within that invisible background, by standing out *against it* – as the individual things that they are – by what Hegel calls "the power of negativity," by a defiant stance of *non*-union with the larger whole.[53]

But there's something else going on here, too, something you need to keep equally in mind. The individual things represented by the grey dot are what they are by the assertion of their own separateness. But at the same time, despite all their self-assertion, they can't escape the whole in which they find themselves. If only because, without it, they themselves couldn't exist, and wouldn't be the individual things that they are. From this point of view, you could even say the whole – the totality of everything – isn't just something *in which* individual things find themselves, but also something they find *in themselves*.[54]

Every single, individual point of being carries, within itself, the full "weight" of the *whole* of being. The degree to which it *feels* that weight seems to make all the difference. Especially, as you will see, where human beings are concerned.[55]

The polarity of being

From the starting point of thinking about one individual thing – the thing you started thinking about, in your own room or garden – I've now developed a simple picture of all reality, and of the fundamental polarity of being that structures our human world.[56]

But if the background of being against which all individual things exist is completely invisible and unknowable, how does this help you? How can you hope to understand something you can't see and can't know? And how does this simple picture of reality help you to understand what it is to be human?

Those two questions are closely related, and I'll begin to explore them both in the next chapter.

3

The Lens of the Virtues

At first glance, I seem to have constructed an image of reality that leads nowhere.

All I've done, so far, is to show you how the individual, separate things you *can* see exist against a background of everything else, an encompassing background of being that, by its very nature, you *can't* see and can't know.

It's a mystery.

Where does that get you? It seems only to lead you to a dead-end. How can you know something unknowable? And, even if you could – which seems impossible by definition – how does such a simple image of reality, that includes the unknowable, help you to explore the human?

Choosing a lens for the nature of the human

These two questions are closely related and are, in fact, the keys to answering each other. The relationship between the human and the unknowable background of being works in two directions.

First, the human is a potential pathway to the unknowable. Since the background of being (in which every individual, separate thing exists) is invisible, one of the few ways we can explore it or try to penetrate its mystery – perhaps the only way – is by considering how it seems to affect us, how it influences or shapes us. In other words, since the invisible background of being can't be known directly, perhaps we can come at it *in*directly, through the human. By considering how we respond to it, and how it's reflected in human life, that is to say, in our human behaviour. One of the few ways to explore the surrounding, invisible, unknowable reality of being, as Thomas Aquinas says, is to consider its effects "which are known to us," especially its effects in human life.[1]

The relationship between the human and the unknowable works the other way too. The human may be a potential pathway to the unknowable background, but our behavioural response to both the knowable and the unknowable is also an important key to understanding the human. After all, human beings are and must be shaped by the larger realities in which they find themselves. We have to explore and understand the human *within* this wider situation or context. If we don't do so, we can't understand what it means to be human – which seems to be the dilemma of much modern and post-modern* thought. The wider reality of all being – and of being itself – structures human reality. To understand the human, we need to explore it within the polarity of being that gives the human its distinctive shape.

In other words, it's a two-way street, or a two-for-one deal. The polar structure of being shapes human behaviour. And human behaviour may be one of the best ways – or even the only way – to explore the otherwise unknowable background of being.

If so, what kind of human behaviour or behaviours shall we consider? There are many possibilities, and most of them would be good ones. We could explore human behaviour from the point of view of psychology, or anthropology, or biology, or sociology, or aesthetics, or literature, or from some other angle. And each one of these can and has made important contributions to understanding human behaviour. They all shed light on the nature of the human, within the wider structure of being. And thus they also shed light backward on the structure of being itself. I will come back to some of these alternative lenses for looking at the human later, in the second part of this book.

Each one of these alternative ways of exploring the human would be partial. They interpret the human through their own specific lens. Is there a way to link them up, in a bigger, wider, or deeper picture? After all, each one of them is a form of human knowing or action. Where do each of these various forms of knowing – or acting – fit in the whole geography or architecture of human action? Many of these alternative lenses could probably stake a reasonable claim to do that job. They could claim – and often have claimed – to be the best or most reliable lens through which to view and integrate all the others. I don't want to challenge any of those claims. But clearly any really useful approach

---

* The normal way to spell this word is postmodern. But spelled that way, it refers to cultural developments only since the 1960s, or even since the 1980s. As I will explain in chapter 15, I want to refer instead to developments since the first decades of the nineteenth century. So I will spell this term with a hyphen, to distinguish my own meaning in this book from the normal one.

to the nature of the human should be able to meet this test. It should offer a map of the human spirit that helps you see where each of these different lenses or forms of human life and action fit into or embody the overall nature of the human.

Another important criterion for the lens you should choose is the question of what makes humans genuinely *human*. What is it that makes us different from other animals or other forms of life? Or from things that aren't alive, but have many human characteristics, like computers, robots, and artificial intelligence (AI)? Many of the potential lenses describe the human from a functional or empirical perspective. They can describe the human objectively. But they don't necessarily get at human values, or what social scientists call the "normative" dimension of human life. In fact, they sometimes even pride themselves on *not* doing so, as if that might sully their scientific "objectivity." As a result, some of the alternative lenses may describe human beings, but they don't necessarily describe our "humanity" – that is, what makes us truly *humane*. They don't get at the "truth" of the human, in the sense we intend when we talk about someone or something being "true" to a commitment, or a mission, or a vocation, or a vow. Or when we say (with William Shakespeare [1564–1616]), "To thine own self be true."[2] Or when we talk about someone being a "true" gentleman, or a true hero, or a true saint, or a true genius, that is, the ideal or essence or standard that allows us to identify the genuine article, to distinguish it from something that falls short, or is only a facsimile, parody, or counterfeit of the real thing.[3] To be "true" in this sense, you need to look for the qualities that can distinguish the human from something else. Even from something that looks like or *appears* to be human.

You may think that "human" is a neutral word, with no built-in values or normative content: simply an empty container into which you can put anything you like. But consider the word "*in*human." It's a word familiar to all of us, and we spontaneously recognize its meaning. We know what it means to call an action or an outcome "inhuman." And when we do so, we're implicitly asserting that to be "human" involves meeting a standard of some kind. You can fall short of the standard of being human.[4] What's the standard of the human – "the idea of humanity" – we take for granted when we describe something as inhuman?[5]

Ever since the ancient Greeks, many, if not most, Western definitions of the human have emphasized the human capacity for reason. They have defined our distinctive human nature in terms of rational consciousness.[6] The human capacity for rational thought, these definitions assume, is what distinguishes humans from other animals. But if you approach the human from a purely cognitive perspective, from the point of view of the mind, intellect, or rational consciousness alone, you will have no means to exclude human monsters from your definition of the human. Hitler, Stalin, Mao, Pol Pot, Al Capone, and Jack the Ripper would count as fully human. Yet we know that their behaviour was, in a very important sense, *in*human. If we lose sight of that inhumanity, we also lose sight of the human. Our definition of the human must make it clear why and how the actions of people like these, who are technically human beings, are nevertheless *in*human. They fall short of being "truly" or fully "human." Identifying the nature of the human exclusively with rationality is no help here.

The choice of lens for exploring the nature of the human in this book must also be guided by its purpose. In the Introduction, I said my aim is to help you not just to *understand* human life better but also to *act* in ways that are more consistent with the nature of the human. My aim, I said, is to go beyond ideas and concepts to practice: beyond social science or philosophy, to a way of *living*.

If I want to aim for this goal, I need to choose a lens that offers at least some chance of getting you there. That suggests two things. The first is that I need to focus on human action, on human behaviours. On the things you can *do*, the ways you can *act*, in your own life. The second thing my goal suggests is that I need to focus not just on any or all human behaviours, but on the *good* ones.[7] The ones that prevent you from being inhuman. The ones you already want to adopt in your own life – or should want to adopt, at least in some degree, if you aspire to be fully or genuinely human.

In other words, if I want to construct a picture of the human that will be helpful in your daily life, the best way to do that is through the lens of your own highest aspirations and values. The best way to explore the human – and, through the human, the wider structure of being within which human beings exist – is to do so from the perspective of what humans have always thought the best and most admirable human behaviours. The ones that make humans most human: that define what it is to be genuinely human.[8]

The lens of the virtues

The question of what to call these good human behaviours is a tricky one. The word that has been most commonly used for these behaviours over the last three thousand years of Western culture is the word "virtue." This word has at least three potential drawbacks, however. The first is that it's derived from a Latin word, itself a translation of an earlier Greek word, and therefore comes with built-in overtones from ancient Greek and Roman cultures. The linguistic root of our word "virtue" is the Latin word *vir*, or man. That means the word "virtue" carries overtones of Roman "manliness." It comes loaded with some of the snobbish, elitist, aristocratic, self-regarding, self-assertive, and militaristic elements of ancient Greek and Roman civic culture. These cultures paid little attention to, or even looked down upon, some of the best and most important human values and behaviours. Those that are most essential for making humans "truly" human.[9]

A second drawback is that, over the last three hundred years or so, our own Western notion of "virtue" has become equally narrow in another direction. It's become associated with sexual purity and self-restraint, acquiring overtones of prudishness. Partly for that reason, it has fallen very much out of favour in popular culture, especially in our sexually liberated Western culture of the late twentieth and early twenty-first centuries.[10] A third drawback is that it has also fallen out of favour in intellectual culture. At the end of the eighteenth century, the concept of "virtue" was displaced, in ethical thinking, by Immanuel Kant's notion of the "moral law." Kant replaced virtue with a kind of reasoning about morality, a form of ethical rationality. As I already noted in the Introduction, dissatisfaction with the results of Kant's revolution in moral theory has led to a post-war academic revival of interest in "virtue ethics." But this revival hasn't yet had a deep impact on popular culture.

Because our contemporary Western culture is uncomfortable with the word "virtue," it employs many substitutes or euphemisms for the same idea. Thus, James Q. Wilson (1931–2012), for example, prefers to call the virtues the "moral senses" (or feelings or sentiments).[11] Another term of art to replace virtue, for many current writers, is "character." Christopher Peterson (1950–2012) and Martin Seligman (b. 1942) normally speak about "character strengths" rather than virtues.[12] What I've called a "map" of the human virtues, Peterson calls the "structure of character."[13] David Brooks (b. 1961) describes the "road to character."[14] James Davison Hunter (b. 1955) laments the "death of character."[15] And so on.

Despite its drawbacks and the contemporary squeamishness about it, the word "virtue" still seems the best word to convey the good human behaviours that define the nature of the human. It's the one most deeply rooted in our Western culture. The greatest minds of the Western tradition have been reflecting on the virtues for almost three thousand years. That means any discussion of the virtues has a very deep well to draw from. And the fact that many of the greatest Western thinkers have taken the virtues to be at the core of the human is a powerful inducement to think they are. So "virtue" is the word I'll use in this book to designate the good behaviours that make humans truly human. But you shouldn't get hung up on the word itself, but look beyond it, to the good human acts or actions I'm talking about.

What makes humans human is our capacity for good human behaviour, which I'm going to call virtue. It is our capacity for the kind of behaviour that makes us genuinely or fully human, the behaviour that makes us the best we can be, as human beings. It is also the parallel ability to feel regret, shame, remorse, or guilt when we fall short of our own human standards, or contradict them by our actions.

Virtues are habits of behaviour we approve of, that we consider good.[16] But the goodness or "value" of the virtues isn't "known." It's *felt*.[17] It's not the product of a rational cognition, or deduction, or syllogism. It's not a proposition. The goodness of the virtues is simply *encountered*, in the immediate, intuitive, felt experience of a human life.[18] It is then confirmed as good through the experience of a whole human lifetime. And not just an individual lifetime. It's confirmed in the experience of the whole human race, in its many cultures, over tens of thousands of years.

Aristotle defines a virtue as a "state of character" or a "disposition" (depending on the translation), the kind of disposition that "makes one a good man and causes him to perform his function well."[19] Paul of Tarsus (ca. 5–67 CE) calls the virtues "weapons (or "the armour") of righteousness."[20] Thomas Aquinas defines a virtue as "a good habit": "a habit of choice, that is, a habit making us choose well."[21] Hegel describes virtue (singular) as "the ethical order reflected in the individual character" and virtues (plural) as "ethical principles applied to the particular."[22] Max Scheler (1874–1928) defines virtue (singular) as "the immediately experienced *power* to do something that ought to be done," and virtues (plural) as the "properties of the person that vary (according to rules) with the *goodness of the person*."[23] Bernard Williams defines a virtue as "an ethically admirable disposition of character." Virtues, he says, "involve characteristic patterns of desire and motivation."[24] Alasdair MacIntyre defines a virtue as "an acquired human quality the possession and exercise of which tends to enable us to achieve those goods that are internal to practices and the lack of which effectively prevents us from achieving any such goods."[25] Robert Adams (b. 1937) defines virtue (singular) as "persisting excellence in being for the good," and virtues (plural) as "an excellent way of being for and against things, a way whose excellence can be part of the excellence" of virtue (singular).[26] Roger Scruton (b. 1944) says virtues are "dispositions that we praise, and their absence is an object of shame."[27] Julia Annas

(b. 1946) defines a virtue as a disposition "to be a certain way, a disposition which expresses itself in acting, reasoning and feeling in certain ways ... which are not only admirable but which we find *inspiring* and take as *ideals* to aspire to, precisely because of the commitment to goodness which they embody."[28] Christine Swanton (b. 1947) defines a virtue as "a good quality of character, more specifically a disposition to respond to, or acknowledge, items within its field or fields in an excellent or good way."[29] N.T. Wright (b. 1948) defines virtue as "what happens when wise and courageous choices have become 'second nature.'"[30] André Comte-Sponville (b. 1952) describes virtue as "the power to be human," and the virtues as the "dispositions of heart, mind and character ... whose presence in an individual tends to increase my moral regard for him and whose absence tends to diminish it."[31] Paul Bloomfield (b. 1962) describes the virtues as "character traits tied to human nature, the possession of which, at least partly, constitutes a well-lived human life."[32] Of these definitions, Aquinas' seems the simplest and the best. A virtue is a good habit.[33]

But for Aquinas (and for his great mentor, Aristotle) the good habits known as virtues don't stand alone, or emerge already fully grown, like Athena from the forehead of Zeus. On the contrary, virtues are the end point of a deep human or anthropological process: they are the end point of a continuum of human development, structured by what they called powers (or potencies), dispositions, actions, and habits. "Powers" are the natural human capacities we inherit as human and animal beings – the basic genetic materials of our bodies and psyches. The existence of these inherited powers or capacities already gives us some innate tendencies. They allow us, and encourage – or "dispose" – us, to do specific things.[34] This inherited genetic material gives us certain basic "dispositions": we are already genetically "programmed," if you like, to behave in certain basic ways. But these basic "dispositions" are merely the human inclination or *potential*. They must be expressed through concrete human acts or actions if they are to become real features of the human or to have an impact on the human world. As our initial "dispositions" (derived from inherited human "powers") begin to interact with our natural and human environments, they translate into certain broad patterns of repeated acts or actions. Once an action has been performed, it tends to be repeated. And repeated actions become habitual. They become the "habits" which structure the nature of the human and of individual human beings.[35]

This classical Aristotelian and Thomistic account of the emergence of the human is remarkably consistent with contemporary evolutionary anthropology and psychology, and with cognitive science. The language has sometimes been altered. "Powers" may now be called capacities, competencies, or capabilities. Dispositions may sometimes be called propensities, proclivities, "memes," algorithms, or even (paradoxically) "demons." But the basic understanding remains the same. The story of human evolution told by the social and cognitive sciences is the development of human dispositions and habits under the twin (and mutually reinforcing) pressures of genetic selection and human culture.[36] For the contemporary human sciences, human beings still remain "an amazingly complex chain of habit systems" or "metasystems."[37]

It's our habits that make us who we are, as humans and as individual human beings. They structure our human nature. Our habits become, as Aristotle says, our "second nature."[38] Habits can be good or bad. A good habit, like courage, can allow you to do difficult things. A bad habit, like laziness, can prevent you from doing very much at all. A bad habit, like drug addiction, can destroy you. The good habits are what we call "virtues."[39] The bad habits are sometimes called vices.

Dispositions, habits, and virtues are both similar and different. They can be compared, but also contrasted. They have the same basic form, and they develop out of each other. But they're also different, or different stages or forms, of the human. A disposition is an initial, genetic inclination to behave in a certain way. But it has not yet become a habit. A habit is a disposition which, through repeated actions, has become habitual. A disposition can and often does turn into a habit. And a habit can become a virtue – or it can become the opposite: a destructive vice.

A virtue is a good habit. But this apparently simple definition contains three important elements that deserve some more attention. One is habit. A virtue is a habit. It's something we regularly and habitually do.[40] We don't have to think about it. Because it's a habit, we do it instinctively or naturally, without having to reflect on each action. As contemporary cognitive science puts it, the behaviour has become "automatized."[41] Except that habits aren't really "natural" at all. Most of them are acquired through behaviour itself: actions produce dispositions for more activity of the same kind.[42] Every act motivated by a disposition leaves a "trace" that strengthens the disposition.[43] Once acquired, habits are very hard – sometimes impossible – to change or to shed.[44] As Aristotle says, we only control the beginning of our dispositions. After that, they control us. It's very difficult to change our habits because they have become our "second nature." We are our habits. And they are us.[45]

There are two sides to the kinds of habit we call virtues. An inside and an outside. The *inside* is a habit of feeling, a good habit of feeling.[46]

Today, we often call these internal habits of feeling "values."[47] The *outside* is an action or activity, a habit of behaviour.[48] These two sides – virtues and values, action and feeling – go together and support each other.[49] But even though they support each other, it's very important to distinguish between them.[50]

A value, or a good habit of feeling is *not* – or not yet – a virtue.[51] Even if it's a habit of feeling, it's still just a feeling, and may never turn into anything else. It may never turn into an action or behaviour, let alone the kind of habit of good action we call a virtue.[52] A feeling of empathy, for example, is not a virtue, even though many people in our contemporary, wired world assume that it is. It's only a value, a habit of *feeling*. It's not yet a good habit of *behaviour* or a virtue.[53] The kind of empathy you find widely displayed on social media may never turn into a real virtue and may even be a kind of self-regarding narcissism.[54] Empathy only becomes a virtue when it turns into *acts* of empathy: acts of kindness, mercy, benevolence, generosity, and so on.[55] I'll have more to say about these kinds of virtues in chapter 5.

Though they need to be carefully distinguished, habits of feeling and behaviour are, nevertheless, essential to each other. They're two sides of the same coin. The habitual behaviours create habitual feelings about the actions.[56] And the habits of feeling support and nourish an inclination for other actions of the same kind.[57] Because of our feelings, it's often very difficult for us to imagine behaving in any other way than that in which our habitual feelings incline us to do. That's one of the strengths of a virtue. We don't have to think about it. We don't have to deliberate and debate about the pros and cons of a certain kind of action. We just do it. Because it's what we're disposed to do, and we can't really imagine doing anything else. To act otherwise would run completely against the grain of our *character*, the character our habits have created for us.[58] A virtuous person behaves virtuously naturally or instinctively – or, rather, habitually.[59]

A second thing you should note about Aquinas' definition of virtue is that virtues are not just any kind of habit. They are *good* habits, the habits humankind has always been disposed to consider the best that humans can be. Individual opinions about these things can vary, and so can the consensus of a particular age or culture. But the best guide in these kinds of matters is the settled view of humanity over the long haul. In judgment about something like human conduct, which is not based "upon principles demonstrative and scientific" but rather on "observation and experience," Samuel Johnson (1709–84) remarked (in a different context), "no other test can be applied than length of duration and continuance of esteem. What mankind have long possessed

they have often examined and compared; and if they persist to value
the possession, it is because frequent comparisons have confirmed
opinion in its favour."[60]

This doesn't mean virtues and values can't evolve, or even, in a sense,
be "created."[61] As you will see in this book, our Western civilization has
developed through different cultural stages, when new virtues, or families of virtues, emerged or appeared in a new light, or with a new emphasis or priority.[62] They became a new, dominant lens through which
all the other virtues were then interpreted.[63] Each of these cultural stages
developed its own "inner disposition" that gave "colours and directions"
to the overall "organization of life."[64] But I will argue that, even when
virtues and values seem to be "created" anew in this way, such a birth is
really a rebirth: a rediscovery, reinterpretation, reconfiguration, reprior-
itization, heightening, widening, or "universalization" of something that
is a permanent and necessary part of the nature of the human, something
without which humans wouldn't be fully or truly human.[65]

A third thing to note about Aquinas' definition of virtue is that the
good at the heart of a good habit or virtue, and of its corresponding
feeling or value, is not *separate* from the virtue or its inner feeling. They
aren't just habits of behaviour or feeling *about something else*. The two
cannot be separated. In fact, that's how we come to know the good. The
good is known *in* the virtues and the values themselves.[66] You don't
reason *to* the virtues. You reason *from* them.[67]

So, the best guide to what can be considered good in human conduct
is not the prevailing mood or fashion in a particular era or place, but
rather what humankind has persisted in thinking good over much of its
history, and in most of its various cultures – "not the particular but the
general inclination of mankind."[68] And that, as I said, is another advantage of the lens of the virtues. Because reflection on the virtues has been
going on almost as long as human life itself.

In fact, for most of human history, thinking about what it means to
be human has taken the form of thinking about the virtues. That's the
way the ancient Greek and Chinese thinkers, such as Aristotle and Confucius (551–479 BCE), thought about the human condition. And it's the
way Jewish, Christian, and Islamic thinkers reflected on the nature of
the human for over a thousand years. It's a very significant fact that
two-thirds of Thomas Aquinas' masterpiece, the *Summa Theologiæ*, one
of the greatest achievements of human thought, was devoted to a very
detailed discussion of the human virtues.[69] For Aquinas, reflection on
the human virtues was the key to understanding the bigger picture
within which human beings exist, an essential key to thinking about
the larger framework of reality and truth.

Even the Renaissance didn't initially change the focus on the virtues because it revived attention on Roman thinkers like Cicero (106–43 BCE) and Seneca (ca. 4–65 CE), whose "Stoic" outlook, influenced by Aristotle, was also based on the human virtues. It wasn't until the seventeenth and eighteenth centuries that the writings of thinkers such as Thomas Hobbes, Baruch (or Benedict) Spinoza (1632–77) and, especially, Immanuel Kant began to shift Western understanding of the human away from the virtues toward other sources of human conduct such as power, pleasure, will, social conditions, and abstract reasoning.[70] This trend was reinforced in the nineteenth and twentieth centuries by the emerging social and human sciences – from Jeremy Bentham (1748–1842) and Auguste Comte (1798–1857) to Sigmund Freud (1856–1939) – with their exclusive focus on material, physical, economic, and psychological causes (what Aristotle calls "efficient" causes, as you saw in chapter 3), often to the exclusion of human purposes, goals, and values (or what Aristotle calls "final" causes): the *motivations* for human action. Although there was a revival of interest in human "values" in the first half of the twentieth century (as you will see in chapter 15), it wasn't until later in the last century (as I mentioned in the Introduction) that dissatisfaction with the results of post-Kantian ethics began to shift attention back to the earlier and much longer tradition of thought based on the virtues, initiating a great deal of contemporary work in the field of "virtue ethics."

Are the virtues real?

That brings us back to the present. But before I introduce you to the virtues in more detail, let's pause here for a moment. Let's consider, a little more carefully, some of the implications of what I've just said, and some of the objections, or contrary views, that might be put forward.

Are the virtues really "real"?[71] Do they have any "objective" or permanent reality? Or are they just cultural artefacts? Do we live in a human world that is shaped or guided by real human virtues, as I've suggested? Or do we live, instead, in a world of "moral relativism," where values and virtues are just the product of specific circumstances, and where they can and do differ completely across different cultures and times?

Many, perhaps most contemporary social scientists would probably lean, explicitly or implicitly, to the second view.[72] They would say, like anthropologist Webb Keane (b. 1955), that "there are no categories of action simply out there in the world," that virtue words are "embedded within the vocabulary and grammar of a particular language and linked to a host of other ideas and practices." So we "should not assume they denote distinct entities that exist independently of the larger conceptual and linguistic contexts."[73]

Social scientists generally lean toward some form of moral relativism for at least two reasons. One reason is the discovery of modern anthropology that cultures can and do vary radically, in different times and places, and that what's commanded in some cultures is reviled, condemned, or incomprehensible in another time and/or place.[74] Until the late 1950s, for example, the Kaulong people on the island of New Britain, just east of New Guinea, practised the ritualized strangling of widows.[75] This kind of custom is so far from our post-modern ideas about good human behaviour that it's easy to think that virtues must be purely time and culture specific, entirely relative. Another example is the contemporary controversy over female "circumcision," or genital modification. In many parts of East and West Africa, and in Ethiopia, Somalia, Sudan, and Egypt, female (like male) circumcision is still widely practised and strongly endorsed by both men and women. Yet in the Western world, it is loudly and strongly condemned. It's described as brutal, barbaric, disgusting, and oppressive. Western feminists and their allies have successfully enlisted international human rights organizations and world health bodies in the campaign to eradicate this allegedly coercive and mutilating practice. When different cultures can disagree so profoundly about something that is so personal and arouses such strong feelings of approval or disgust, it casts into doubt, for many people, whether there can be any universal values or virtues.

In a counter example, hierarchy is maintained in Samoa by the display of *fa'aaloalo* (respect), composed of a prefix *fa'a* (to make) and the term *alo* (to face), thereby expressing "a bodily and social orientation toward others."[76] This kind of deep, culturally structured respect is almost as far removed from our post-modern values as widow-strangling, at the other end of the spectrum. Closer to home – but now equally distant, culturally speaking – nineteenth-century English culture developed the code of the "gentleman." This moral code has been called "the most successful extralegal mechanism ever invented for adapting male behaviour to the requirements of modern life."[77] But many contemporary Westerners would now call it sexist, elitist, paternalistic, patronizing or worse. The cultural world of the nineteenth-century English gentleman is now almost as far from contemporary Western culture as that of New Guinea and Samoa.

When cultures, customs, and conventions can be shown to differ so greatly, it's easy to think they have little in common, and that their values are simply a cultural artefact: they're all purely relative and culture-specific. But I think this widespread contemporary assumption confuses virtues with the customs and practices in which they're embedded, and by which they're expressed in a specific culture. Human beings are profoundly "enculturated" creatures, for better and for worse. The achievements, insights, practices, and institutions of our cultures vastly extend human capabilities and potential: practical, technological, intellectual, and moral. It's hard to state this strongly enough. Without culture we would simply be animals again. It's our cultures that make us human.[78] But our cultures also limit us: they limit what we can see and know. Our culture comes to us with assumptions and presuppositions that are built right into it, so deeply and invisibly, that we can't even see most of them, and certainly can't see around them, or through them.[79]

But, just because cultural practices, customs, and assumptions differ so dramatically, that doesn't mean the human goods at the heart of them – the human goods they're all trying (in such different ways) to express – are equally different. Though sometimes hard to do, it's important to distinguish the virtues from the specific customs, practices, or concepts in which they're embedded or by which they're expressed in a particular culture. You can look beneath the surface of specific cultural practices to discover the common human goods and virtues they express or embody, or are trying to embody. The virtues toward which they point.[80] Even the extreme case of widow-strangling (the origin of which no one can really explain) was apparently associated with, and maintained by, virtues like duty, honour, chastity, and courage, and their opposites, such as shame. And it's not hard to see links between this practice and the abandonment, exposure, or ritual killing of the sick or elderly in other pre-modern cultures.[81] In these similar or related practices, so different from traditional Western values, you can discern the same virtues at work, and others too, such as mercy, kindness, reverence, community, and self-preservation. At a time when many Western cultures are debating the virtues of assisted suicide, insight into the virtues embedded in these earlier or alien cultural practices may now be easier to achieve.

In the case of female genital modification, the virtues are easier to see, if Westerners take the time and care to do so. For the cultures in which it's practised, circumcised genitalia are considered more beautiful, pure, honourable, dignified, mature, and civilized than uncircumcised.[82] In other words, they're valued in those cultures because they are thought to express universal human virtues. Many of the same virtues traditionally valued by the very Western cultures that are now so loud in condemning this practice.

We can parse each one of the specific customs, practices, and concepts embedded in a particular, historical culture in the same way: to uncover the eternal virtues that are embedded or expressed in them. That's often how moral or social change proceeds: by identifying better or more virtuous ways to express a virtue previously enmeshed with other unnecessary, undesirable, or even immoral practices. For thousands of years, slavery, for example, was thought to be a social practice consistent with human virtue. But in the last three hundred years, we have come to see that human servitude is, in fact, incompatible with true human virtue.[83] In fact, the abolition of slavery was accomplished in little more than one lifetime "by appeal simply to virtue."[84] Without an eternal standard of that kind, this fundamental change in human attitudes would never have come about.

The second reason many contemporary social scientists lean toward moral relativism is their awkward relationship with what Aristotle calls (as you already saw, in chapter 2) "final causes."[85] Most social scientists want to think of themselves as just that: as "scientists."[86] So they adopt the assumptions and methodologies of the natural sciences in order to share in the prestige and authority – the aura of certainty – that "science" enjoys in the contemporary Western world.[87] This inclination presents social scientists with a big problem, however.[88] Modern scientific method was invented in the seventeenth and eighteenth centuries largely by excluding final causes from the natural sciences.[89] The scientific revolution of the seventeenth century (which actually began centuries earlier, with the medieval "nominalists," as you'll see in chapter 15) was based on the assumption that, henceforth, scientific explanations could and should be based exclusively on what Aristotle had called "efficient" causes.[90] Efficient causes make an event happen through the impact of another preceding event, like a chemical reaction, an electrochemical event in the brain, the impact of one billiard ball on another, or a person who advises someone else. Final causes, on the other hand, are those things for the sake of which something is done: the motivations, ideas, purposes, and aspirations that cause animals and humans to seek some purpose, goal, or "end." Efficient causes are the causes that *push* from behind, or below, as it were: they push us by the impact of some *preceding* event. Final causes are those that *pull* us, as it were, from ahead, or above. They pull us or draw us forward – toward some *future* action – through our own aims, goals, values, and desires.[91] The good ends we want to achieve or obtain.[92]

The problem for the social sciences is that final causes are what make humans human.[93] They are what turn an "event" into a voluntary "act" or action.[94] Aristotle's efficient causes can only explain human behaviour as physico-chemical or animal processes, or as the result of impersonal evolutionary, social, or economic "forces."[95] But humans, as humans, are essentially aspirational beings, "prone to evaluate themselves, others, and their circumstances."[96] If you really want to understand humans as humans, you have to take some account of the values, desires, purposes, and intentions for the sake of which they act: the values and desires that make them human. The goods, ends, or final causes that make them more than organisms or animals.[97] If you've excluded final causes from your explanations, you have only two options: you can either deny they exist and assert that human actions are merely physico-chemical events, or the result of purely impersonal forces.[98] Or you can admit that values, virtues, and intentions really do exist, after all, but try to explain them – or even explain them *away* – by showing how they're really just the indirect result of efficient causes – just efficient causes in disguise – by calling them simply a "psychological mechanism," a "proximate" cause, one of the "environmental forces," in a larger evolutionary process.[99] Thus, some anthropologists seek to show that the virtues are merely the product of gene pools and natural selection.[100] Others want to find the explanation, source, or authenticity of the virtues in the "natural," instinctive, unformed, moral reflexes of toddlers and very young children.[101] But in order to protect their "scientific" standing, few are inclined to seek an explanation of the virtues in the rightness and goodness of the virtues themselves, or in what Samuel Johnson calls the "naked dignity" of virtue.[102] "Perhaps the day will come," psychologists Christopher Peterson and Martin Seligman speculate hopefully, when the virtues will be regarded by most social scientists as traits worth cultivating simply "because they are good."[103] But that day has not yet arrived.

When you say (like Webb Keane) that "there are no categories of action simply out there in the world," everything depends on what you mean by "categories of action," and what you mean by "world." If, by "categories of action," you mean practices and customs, the statement is almost certainly true. But if you mean the virtues, I think the statement cannot be true. Every human action or behaviour "must have some effect on value and meaning." If its effect isn't positive, then it will be negative. It simply isn't possible "to eliminate the reference to value, meaning, or some evaluative dimension."[104] If by "world" you mean the historical, cultural, and social world, the statement may well be true. But if you include the moral and metaphysical world, shaped by final causes, I think the statement is not true. It simply isn't possible to imagine a human world in which courage, justice, honesty, generosity, and so on were not real human goods.[105] It's possible to imagine a world that denied them, or that expressed them in practices and customs that others would condemn. But they would condemn them on the basis of the virtues themselves. They would condemn them because the practices were not truly just, fair, compassionate, merciful, and so on. They would condemn them because they weren't truly human. Or because they were, in some sense, *inhuman*. Because they were not truly *humane*. Because they weren't truly good.

Webb Keane acknowledges that the virtues (or virtue words) aren't "simply cultural inventions created from scratch." They "direct attention and give specificity," he says, "to aspects of experiences based on objective sources whose meanings are undetermined." As I already mentioned in chapter 2, he calls these specific, objective aspects of experience "affordances." The virtues or virtue categories are the "outcomes of processes of objectification that respond to the affordances that cognition, the emotions and interaction offer."[106] This is certainly true. The virtues can only be encountered and discovered in specific events, processes, and features of the physical, psychic, historical, and social world. But what do these "affordances" *afford*? They afford a cause, a condition, or an "occasion" (as Hegel puts it) to encounter something: something real, some real feature of the human world.[107] You shouldn't make the common error of mistaking "the causes, the conditions and the occasions of our becoming conscious of certain truths and realities *for the truths and realities themselves*."[108] You shouldn't collapse the final cause into the efficient cause.[109] "Human nature" can perhaps be described or defined by efficient causes. When we talk about human nature, we're unconsciously putting the emphasis on *nature*, and on natural or efficient causation. But, in this book, I've spoken deliberately about the "nature of the human" instead, in order to put the emphasis on *human*. And the nature of the human – the *idea of humanity* – can only be defined by final causes.[110]

If you insist on explaining everything by efficient causes alone, you're implicitly accepting the implausible premise that human beings are simply *"driven by the past rather than drawn by the future."*[111] "[T]o be ethical," as Webb Keane himself says, "is to have some freedom of action and, so, to discover the ethical is to reveal some fundamental distinction between the causal determinations [i.e., the efficient causes] of behaviour (whether those be biological, psychological, or socioeconomic in origin) and people's capacity to act [i.e., their final causes]."[112] In other words, human behaviour "enjoys *motivational autonomy*."[113] "Affordances" are merely efficient causes which afford an opportunity to encounter or discover a final cause.[114] To discover a truth about the nature of the human.

The virtues are derived from the "affordances" of the real, human world.[115] They are the product of both our natural and social histories.[116] Though recognized, in some form, in all human cultures, they're combined, emphasized, prioritized, and interpreted quite differently in different cultural contexts, and at different stopping places in the process of human cultural evolution. Later in this book (as I mentioned in the previous section) you'll see how our own Western culture has evolved through different stages and cultures: cultures in which different families of virtues were successively highlighted or served as the primary lens from which to view, interpret, or apply all the rest. A similar variety of emphasis, among the families of virtues, can still be observed in the range of cultures across the world today.[117] But despite such deep cultural change and diversity, courage, duty, dignity, mercy, kindness, self-control, justice, equity, giving, generosity, sharing, and so on remain as constants, real components, goals, or ideals of a truly human world. Though expressed and emphasized in different ways, at different times, and in different places, the virtues are not only true, they are the truest truth about the human.[118] Because a culture that *didn't* recognize or express the virtues, in some manner or other, wouldn't be a genuinely or fully human culture.[119]

Thus it's possible to be *both* a cultural pluralist *and* a moral universalist, at the same time.[120] It's not only possible, but essential, if you want to live in a genuinely human world. If you want to achieve "any genuine understanding of the human condition."[121] The way to do it is through the virtues, as you will see in the rest of this book. The virtues provide the ingredients: the cultures provide the recipes.[122] The virtues make us both culturally diverse and universally human – both x and not-x – *at the same time.*

One of the reasons the virtues can make us both culturally diverse and universally human is that, as values (or good habits of feeling – the *inside* of a virtue), they're necessarily somewhat abstract.[123] They have something in common with what Plato calls an "idea," and Aristotle calls a "form."[124] You can't really define an idea or a form – a human value, like "justice" or "goodness" – in advance (or *a priori*), though many people (including Plato and Aristotle) have tried to do so.[125] You can only search or look for these kinds of human goods: pursue them, identify them, and practice them (i.e., turn them into real habits of behaviour, or virtues) in a specific context or setting, in the concrete circumstances of real, everyday life.[126] In that sense, the virtues are rather like English common law: something that can only be determined in a specific, concrete circumstance.[127] A value turns into a real virtue, a habit of behaviour, only in the context of a specific, concrete, individual circumstance, or culture.[128] Before that, a virtue is like the biblical pillar of fire by night and pillar of cloud by day: something that goes ahead of you and draws you on, in pursuit of it, in your effort to define it, and make it become a lived reality, in your own life, in your own culture, and in your own time.[129] Something to which, "by many different paths, we endeavour to approximate": "a sought beyond and an unattained goal," an ideal of "what ought to be."[130] The virtues are final causes, or what Leibniz calls forms of "eternal possibility."[131]

Because they're forms of "possibility," final causes such as virtues show themselves – in the visible, concrete, everyday world – only when we choose to turn them into realities of behaviour, in our own lives and cultures.[132] Values, like the cultures that give them life, are "ideas, premises, by which people guide their lives, and only to the extent that people live them [i.e., turn them into virtues] do they have force."[133] If the virtues don't "go forth of us," as Shakespeare says, it's "as if we had them not."[134] So it's very easy for people to think we don't, or that the virtues aren't "real." In fact, there have always been two ways to think about human nature, as Blaise Pascal (1623–62) and Immanuel Kant both noted. One is to deny that final causes, like the virtues, have any genuine reality because they're contradicted by so much human behaviour and so many human practices. But the other way is to see that when people behave that way – even if they are the majority, in some time or place – they're simply turning away from their true "end," from their true "humanity." From that which makes humans genuinely human.[135] The first way of thinking leads you to the concept we now call human nature. The second, to what I'm calling the nature of the human.[136]

The fact that the virtues are only forms of "eternal possibility" doesn't mean they aren't real.[137] They aren't just an "empty, logical possibility," as Martin Heidegger puts it. They aren't just a "free-floating potentiality of being," something "less than reality and necessity," or simply "chance possibilities." On the contrary, they are what Heidegger calls "definite, factical possibilities," the *real* possibilities within you that define what it is to be a human being. You can ignore them or embrace them, grasp them or fail to grasp them. But that doesn't show they aren't real. It only shows the real nature of the human is something "entrusted" to you. You are the trustee of your own *real* possibilities, as a human being.[138] They "belong" to you – or in you – even when they are lacking or not yet realized.[139]

When you use words like "reality" or "truth" in relation to the virtues and to the nature of the human, you mean something different than when you talk about "scientific," experimental, or empirical "truth" about the physical or phenomenal world. In the "scientific" or empirical case, you can see or agree to truths about the natural world because new "facts" about it have been uncovered or "explained" according to efficient causes. You say "yes" to a scientific or empirical reality because some efficient cause or statistical pattern has been demonstrated or verified "out there," as it were. To moral truth, however, you can only say "yes" when it corresponds to something "in here" – inside yourself, and your own nature. Of course, the something "in here" can also be – indeed *must* be – something "out there," in another sense: a standard that's "outside" or independent of your own ego and its wishes for power and pleasure. Something external that "calls" you and makes demands on you. But this second kind of "out there" can only be found "in here": not in the external, visible, or phenomenal world, but inside yourself.[140] You can only say "yes" to a moral insight when it "rings true" to you. That is to say, when it connects, or corroborates, or "rings" in harmony with your own deepest moral feelings and intuitions, when it brings into focus or expresses something true or real about yourself, something you already knew, but could not yet say.[141]

For that reason, acknowledging a truth about the demands of the virtues is not just an act of cognition, as it is for a scientific or natural truth. It is also an act of *re*cognition, a truth you accept because you *recognize* it as true. You can recognize it because you already knew it but did not yet know you knew it, or could not express it properly. Or you did not yet recognize its claim upon you, in new circumstances, or in a new form. You can say "yes" to a moral truth because you now recognize it expresses something true *about yourself*: a call, a claim, or possibility that's deep "inside" you, something that was *already there*, in your deepest moral feeling or intuition – in the deepest or "truest" definition of your own nature, your own humanity – but not yet fully present to consciousness, in that way, or in this new form.[142] You can acknowledge the claim or demand a virtue makes upon you because you recognize it as something real, a real fact about the human world, a reality without which the human world wouldn't be truly or genuinely human – and couldn't even be described properly. You couldn't properly describe a human world without using categories like courage, wisdom, justice, love, generosity, kindness, fairness, and so on. Something a human world can't do without is "real" – it is a real feature of a human world.[143] A real part of the nature of the human. And not just real. It is more than that: the litmus test or criterion of a genuinely human world.[144] The *nature of the human* is "something to live *up* to" – not, as in many accounts of *human nature*, "something to live down to instead."[145]

Virtues like courage, justice, or temperance aren't "invented," says Leibniz: they're just as real or true as other forms humans discover, encounter, or perceive in the natural world – forms like a triangle, for example, or a circle, or a square.[146] "[N]o principle of the human mind," David Hume (1711–76) says, "is more natural than a sense of virtue." The virtues are as much a part of a truly human world as the ground under your feet, or the air you breathe: "inseparable," as Hume puts it, "from the species."[147] Without them, humans wouldn't be human. For Hegel, to be a bad or immoral person is the same thing as to be untrue. A bad person is an "untrue" person, someone who isn't true to the nature of the human, "who does not behave as his notion or vocation requires."[148] Values and goods have exactly the "same immediacy" for us, Edmund Husserl suggests, as a "mere world of facts."[149] Isaiah Berlin (1909–97) agrees. "There is a world of objective values," he says. "By this I mean those ends that men pursue for their own sakes, to which other things are means. ... Forms of life differ. Ends, moral principles, are many. But not infinitely many: they must be within the human horizon. If they are not, then they are outside the human sphere."[150]

"Moral and political philosophy must begin with a statement about human nature," James Q. Wilson argues.

> We may disagree about what is natural, but we cannot escape the fact that we have a nature – that is, a set of traits and predispositions that set limits to what we may do and suggest guides to what we must do. That nature is mixed. ... It is a nature that cannot be described by any single disposition ... The incomplete and partial guidance provided by our moral senses [Wilson's term for the virtues] can lead the unwary philosopher to one or both of two errors: to suppose that if a sentiment does not settle everything it cannot settle anything, or to infer that if people differ in their practical choices [i.e., cultures] they must do so on the basis of different sentiments [i.e., virtues]. The first error leads to logical positivism, the second to cultural relativism, the two together to modern nihilism. A proper understanding of human nature can rarely provide us with rules for action, but it can supply what Aristotle intended: a grasp of what is good in human life and a rough ranking of those goods.[151]

The nature of the human isn't something to be invented. It's something to be discovered. Or *re*discovered.[152] The virtues which define the human – "the values we take as binding" – are "rooted in what we are," as Charles Taylor (b. 1931) puts it. "[T]hey need to be sought after, discovered, better defined, rather than being endorsed."[153] Or, maybe invention and discovery don't have to be as sharply distinguished as we commonly think.[154] Maybe the word "invent" (as Paul Ricœur

[1913–2005] suggests) can harbour the two meanings of discovering *and* creating, at the same time.[155] Perhaps (as Hans Joas [b. 1948] proposes) the concept of "genesis" can also bridge the gap between invention and discovery, by pointing us to the way in which values can have a *history*, and yet still be *unconditional*.[156] In this case, discovering – or *re*discovering – a virtue might be (in Ernst Troeltsch's [1865–1923] words) like an "act of generation that recognizes itself as obedience."[157] The human virtues can be "invented" yet, at the same time, be real, permanent and necessary features of the nature of the human. What I call the nature of the human "already exists," as Martin Heidegger puts it, "in such a way that its not yet [its potential] *belongs* to it."[158] Even when the virtues are (or were) "not yet," they nevertheless "belong" to us. Discovering them is also a kind of *re*discovering – a "coming back" to the true nature of the human. Because we already *are* what we may or may not become, we can say to ourselves, with Heidegger (and Augustine): "become what you are!"[159]

Whatever may be the right way to express the relationship between invention and discovery, doing your own thing is only good (as the prophetess Diotima points out, in Plato's *Symposium*), if you make the good your own – and not your own the good.[160] What I'm looking for in this book is what Jonathan Haidt calls a "map of moral space."[161] Or what Christopher Peterson calls "the structure of character."[162] Or what Samuel Taylor Coleridge (1772–1834) calls, even more aptly, the "structure of our proper humanity." And that can only be discerned (as Coleridge says) by discovering – or rediscovering – the structure of "the proper virtues of humanity."[163] By discovering and creating what Iris Murdoch calls "an 'order' of virtues."[164]

So the virtues are the right, even necessary, starting place to explore the nature of the human. In fact, judgments about human goods, about the virtues, go so deep in human history, they go to the very roots of our perceptions and of our languages. When we talk about human actions, as I mentioned, it's very hard to do so without reference to the virtues. Our everyday language and conversations are filled with constant, instinctive reference to the virtues, whether we notice it or not.[165] And, when we see human acts such as bravery or cowardice, we see acts of bravery and cowardice – or virtues. We can't really untangle the "facts" from the "values." The seeing and the evaluation aren't separate, and our language wouldn't allow us to separate the two easily, even if we wanted to.[166] It's "very difficult to observe without valuing" because "any experience has an immediate and intuitive nuance of value in 'feeling.'"[167] The perception and the valuing seem to go together, inseparably.[168]

You can't avoid starting a quest for the nature of the human from the virtues because they condition how you know anything at all, or how knowledge becomes reliable. And because, wherever else you might start, the virtues would still be the final place to which you must eventually come in your quest for insight. Before I end this section, let's consider both of these.

First: how you know. The important thing to note here is that the world isn't just *given* to you in an objective way, as we often assume. It isn't simply lying open and waiting for your senses to discover it. It isn't a direct and pure product of your "sense data," as so many modern thinkers have assumed since the seventeenth century. It's also *constructed* by you, by your mind, by your imagination, and by your culture.[169] Even what you can see or perceive is determined by the questions you ask.[170] Edmund Husserl calls this feature of human consciousness "intentionality." Human awareness is always awareness "*of* something": it has the quality of "directedness."[171] You can't see what you aren't looking for. Your perceptions are limited and shaped by the assumptions and even by the habits you bring to the task. The way you approach the world makes a difference. The stance you adopt *within* it helps to determine what *kind* of a world it will be for you.[172]

That means it makes a difference what kind of people we are if we're going to be reliable observers and reporters of reality. People of differing character or outlook, or who adopt different stances in the world, will see and live in different worlds. It makes a difference who you are, or whose views you rely on, or how you assess those on whom you *should* rely. Aristotle says that "the good man's view is the true one." That is to say, "the standard by which we measure everything is goodness, or the good man qua [as being] good." We don't get to the most fundamental kind of knowledge "by logical means: it is virtue, whether natural or acquired by habituation that enables us to think rightly about the first principle."[173] In other words, virtue comes *before* knowledge and shapes it. In order to *see* certain things, you have to *be* certain things.[174] Beneath and before your knowledge of the world lie the virtues. They shape your knowing even before you begin to know. So it makes sense to start there. At the beginning. Where the human starts to be human.

You may well have to end there, too. That's my second point. What will be your final arbiter of knowledge? When all is said and done, what or where does all your knowing come back to? Bernard Williams suggests that, ultimately, you have to come back to the virtues. That's true for ethics because, if you ask what needs to exist in the world for a certain ethical point of view to exist, the answer "can only be 'people's dispositions.'" The virtues must be "the ultimate supports of ethical value."[175]

And when you widen your perspective to the level of society itself, the "primacy" of the virtues remains a "necessary truth," even there. Because all social theories,

> whatever they may say, suppose there to be individuals who acquire certain dispositions and express them in action. In this sense, social or ethical life must exist in people's dispositions. It is the content of the dispositions, their intelligibility and their degree of particularity, that differs between societies and is at issue between different interpretations of modern society.[176]

In the course of this book, you'll have several opportunities to see that Bernard Williams was right in suggesting both how much cultures can differ, by the emphasis and interpretation they give to the various virtues, and how often contemporary thinkers are obliged to come back – even though they aren't conscious of doing so – to the bedrock of the virtues, when all their other arguments or evidence are exhausted. The same thing is true for ordinary people, too. When all the grand, "integrating narratives" of post-modern life fail or fall away, real people, in the real world, must and do come back, as Michael Ignatieff (b. 1947) says, to "the daily practice of the ordinary virtues."[177]

For all these reasons, the lens of the virtues is a good – maybe even the best – way to explore not just human nature but what I've called the nature of the human. And by exploring the nature of the human you may find your way back to the nature of reality itself: the reality by which your own nature is shaped.[178]

In other words, the virtues don't just have *practical* importance for your own daily life. They even have (as Bernard Williams puts it) "metaphysical significance."[179] They may be your best route to the big picture.[180]

What are the virtues? A sample list

What, then, are the virtues? What are these good habits of behaviour that define the nature of the human? What, exactly, am I talking about?

Here we run into a problem – or even a series of problems. But the first problem is also an advantage. An indication or confirmation that the virtues are a good lens through which to define the human.

The first problem is that there are so many words to define these good *external* habits of behaviour we call virtues – and so many more to define the inside of the virtues, the *internal* habits of feeling we call values. Aristotle mentioned at least eleven virtues. Thomas Aquinas mentioned about forty.[181] André Comte-Sponville starts from a list of some thirty virtues he winnows down to eighteen.[182] In another contemporary inventory of the virtues, Christopher Peterson and Martin Seligman start from a basic or "High Six," then expand their focus to twenty-four core virtues, and ultimately refer to over sixty virtues.[183] But in fact, the number of words for these things, in any language, is almost without limit.[184] The words for the virtues and the values are almost as rich as our language itself and could fill an entire dictionary or thesaurus of the virtues.[185]

That's a problem for me and for this book. But it's also a confirmation that the virtues are a good lens to use to define the human. If the language of the virtues is so large – if it's almost as large as our language itself – chances are it captures, as well as anything could, the richness, variety, and complexity of what it is to be a human being.[186] In fact, that very variety and complexity of the virtues is what can allow you to be both a pluralist *and* a universalist, at the same time.

My problem thus has a good side. And it has other good sides, as you'll see in a moment. But it's still a problem. A dictionary of the virtues might be a very worthwhile project, but it's not what I'm aiming for in this book. It wouldn't get me closer to my objective of developing a map of the human spirit. I need to stop short of a dictionary, so we'll have a manageable domain whose contours and structure I can explore and map.

That means I have to make a selection. My initial list can't be too long, or it will be unmanageable for the tasks I still have to perform in the rest of this book. The classical and medieval Western tradition got around this problem by focussing on seven key virtues: four from Greek thought, originally highlighted by Plato[187] – the so-called "cardinal" virtues: courage, justice, prudence, and temperance – and three from the Christian tradition, the so-called "theological" virtues: faith, hope, and love.[*] These are very important virtues, and they can help me greatly to accomplish my goal. But these seven classical virtues are too few in number to furnish a good starting point for our journey. They'll help to confirm that I've reached the right destination when we get there. But they aren't enough, at the outset. My list has to be long enough to capture the almost infinite richness and complexity of the human – but not too long. Not so long that you can't take it all in, or that I can't make use of it in the following chapters.

---

[*] "Theological" is a misleading term in English and encourages the assumption that these three virtues have something to do with "theology." I discuss this problem below, on page 205.

To give you an idea – a manageable idea – of the universe of virtues (and their related values) I'm talking about in this book, I'm going to introduce another visual aid. But now I need to change the picture. I need a different kind of image to show the many ways and words in which the human virtues have been expressed. The circular figure I've been using so far – to give a concrete, visual form to what might otherwise be merely abstract concepts – doesn't lend itself very well to something that can have so many different labels or forms of expression. Hence it may be helpful here to introduce another kind of illustration: a table. The format of a table will prove useful not only for this first overview of the virtues, but also, later, for mapping their contours and geography. You can see my initial sample list of the human virtues in Table 1 on pages 68–9.

As you look at this initial list, there are several things you should keep in mind and some others that may occur to you. The first is that this initial list can only be a sample of the virtues, for the reasons I already discussed. A full list might be almost as long as this book itself. That wouldn't be helpful or practical, so you should keep in mind that the virtues in Table 1 are just an arbitrary selection. Some virtues mentioned by the classical writers on the virtues, such as Aristotle (magnificence, amiability, etc.[188]) or Thomas Aquinas (deliberation, sagacity, docility, etc.[189]), don't appear here. You may be able to think of many other virtues I haven't included. I keep thinking of new ones as I write, and I expect you will too.

This is only a selection. But it's a pretty big selection. Over 200 virtues (and some values). More than 200 words that describe not just human behaviour, but *good* human behaviours or ways of being, or their related values. Even as a sample, it's a pretty good overview of the nature of the human. A pretty good menu from which to choose in order to describe what human beings are, and what they should be. It gives you a good idea of what human beings are like, when they are being most human. Being truly human – being true to the human – means being something like this. Or some selection from this list, or from another like it.

The kind of human being you would like to be, or should like to be, will be a person constructed from a list of virtues very like this one. You can't have all of these virtues. And you certainly can't have all those you *do* have in the same degree.[190] You will exhibit some of these virtues more strongly and consistently than others. The selection and emphasis among these virtues is what makes your individual personality, or character – and our diverse cultures.[191] But this sample list should capture the range of virtues you admire and may want to acquire or strengthen in yourself. Or that you hope your children may acquire.[192]

Table 1. The virtues: a sample list

acceptance	contrition	fairness	insight
accountability	control	faith(ful)(ness)	integrity
adaptability	conviction	fidelity	intensity
admira(ble)(tion)	cooperation	firmness	joy(ful)(ness)
ador(able)(ation)	courage	flexibility	judgment
agape	courtesy	flourishing	justice
agency	creativity	forbearance	kindness
altruism	curiosity	forgiveness	knowledge
appetite	decency	formality	law(-abiding)
appreciation	decisiveness	fortitude	(-enforcing)
assertiveness	deference	freedom	liberality
attachment	desire	friend(liness)(ship)	liberty
authenticity	detachment	frugality	love
autonomy	determination	fullness/fulfilment	loyalty
awe	devotion	generosity	meaning(ful)
beauty	dignity	gentleness	(ness)
belief	diligence	giving	meekness
benevolence	discern(ment)(ing)	glory	mercy
boldness	discretion	goodness	merit
bravery	dominance	grace	mindfulness
calmness	duty/dutiful(ness)	gratitude	moderation
caring	economy	happiness	modesty
caution	effectiveness	harmony	mutuality
certainty/certitude	efficiency	helpfulness	nobility
change	effort	heroism	non-union
charity	empathy	honesty	objectivity
chastity	empowerment	honour(able)(ing)	openness
cheerfulness	endurance	(-seeking)	optimism
cleanliness	energ(y)(etic)	hope	orderliness
commitment	enjoyment	human(ity)(eness)	originality
communion/	enlightenment	humility	partiality
community	enterpris(e)(ing)	humour	participation
compassion	enthusiasm	idealism	passion
competence	entitlement	identity	patience
competit(ion)	entrepreneur(ial)	imagination	peace(ful)(ness)
(iveness)	(ship)	impartiality	penitence
concern	equality	independence	perceptiveness
confidence	equanimity	individualism/	perseverance
connectedness	equity	individuation	piety
consideration	eros	informality	pity
consistency	esteem	ingenuity	play(ful)(ness)
contentment	excellence	initiative	pleasure
continence	expressivism	innovation	power

(Continued)

Table 1. The virtues: a sample list (*Continued*)

praise	right(s)(-giving)	separat(e)(ion)	tolerance
pride	(-seeking)	serenity	tranquil(ity)
prudence	righteous(ness)	service	transcendence
purity	risk-taking	sharing	trust(ing)(-seeking)
purposefulness	rite/ritual	shrewdness	trust(worthy)
rational(ism)(ity)	sacrifice	simplicity	(ness)
reason	science/scientific	sincerity	truth(ful)(ness)
reason(able)(ness)	seeking	skill(ful)(ness)	understanding
receiving/	self-assertion	solemnity	union/unity
receptivity	self-control	solidarity	unknowing
reciprocity	self-determination	spontaneity	utility/usefulness
reliability	self-development	steadfastness	valu(e)(able)(ing)
remorse	self-discipline	strength	wholeness
resilience	self-expression	subjectivity	will
resourceful(ness)	self-giving	success(ful)	wisdom
respect(able)(ful)	selfless(ness)/	sympathy	wonder
(-seeking)	unselfing	tact	work
responsibility	self-realization	technique	worship
responsiveness	self-reliance	temperance	worth(y)(iness)
revelation	self-respect	thankfulness	zeal
reverence	self-seeking	thoughtfulness	zest

Some of these virtues are more important than others. Some are probably essential to the human, like love or justice, for example. Some are more optional: nice to have but not indispensable for being recognizably human, such as ingenuity or innovation, for example.[193] For that reason, it's usually been found necessary to organize such lists into smaller groups, clusters, or families, under the headings of these more important virtues. You'll see a variety of ways that can and must be done in later chapters of this book.

If a person lacked a significant number of these virtues altogether or was completely unable to recognize them as virtues or goods, it would be hard to think of them as fully human. Of course, that would be even truer for the really important or essential virtues, the ones we might use as headings or names for groups of other virtues. Being genuinely or authentically human seems to require at least some kind of positive response to most of these virtues and values, especially the key ones. To have them in your moral and emotional vocabulary, at the very least. To recognize them and their place in the nature of the human. If someone had nothing but blanks for many of these virtues, they would seem to fall short of what it means to be "truly" human, in the sense I already discussed earlier in the chapter, that is, truly *humane*. They would lack some essential part of the nature of the human.

If you can't bring yourself to see some of these sample virtues in Table 1 as virtues, you could simply take them off the list. But you can't take all the virtues off the list, or you would abolish our humanity. You'd be left with something – or a nothing – that couldn't be human. When you've finished taking your non-virtues off the list, there would still be a substantial residue. Those remaining virtues, whatever they are, will still have the structure or geography I'm going to show you in this book. To understand the nature of the human, the important thing isn't any *individual* virtue, but the *architecture* of the virtues, as a whole.

But you shouldn't be in too much of a hurry to delete any virtues from this initial sample list. Even if you don't spontaneously recognize some of these human qualities to be virtues, you need to keep in mind that a great many people over much of human history have considered them to be good human behaviours. That's a strong clue they need to be included in any adequate picture of the human. Our post-modern Western culture doesn't currently attach a lot of value to virtues like modesty, chastity, and deference, for example. But you should consider that, in the premodern and non-Western cultures where they're very highly valued, they're associated with a sense of empowerment, agency, energy, strength, integrity, purpose, responsibility, authority, dignity, goodness, and meaning.[194] So if you're looking for the nature of the human, you shouldn't write them off too quickly. As I suggested earlier in the chapter, you need to take the long view. You shouldn't be restricted by the current mood or fashion, in a particular time or place. You should give due attention to what the human race has persisted in thinking good over most of its history and in its various cultures. If our age or culture doesn't recognize some of these virtues, that may say more about our age or culture than it says about the nature of the human. It may suggest we're missing out on or neglecting some important parts of the human. We may need to rediscover and reinterpret some virtues and values, whose "genesis" or rebirth might be part of the moral and cultural challenge of our "deep future."[195]

Another thing that may occur to you, as you look over this sample list of virtues, is that they don't seem to go together very well. In fact, they seem to be at odds with each other. They seem to be full of contradictions. Some of the contradictions are obvious. Objectivity and subjectivity are clearly opposites, but they both appear here as virtues.

Boldness is a virtue; but so is meekness, its opposite. Change and inno-vation are proposed. But so are patience and perseverance. The virtue of confidence seems contradicted by humility. Detachment seems to be the opposite of desire. And so on.

At this point you may throw up your hands in frustration and decide that the virtues aren't a very clear path to anywhere. But if you've read the previous chapters of this book, you may also begin to recognize exactly the same contradictions, the unity of opposites, that the Pythag-oreans and Aristotle found in all reality. Remember what Aristotle says: "All things are either contraries or composed of contraries, and unity and plurality are the starting-points of all contraries." In this first sam-ple list of the virtues, you seem to have found a striking confirmation of Aristotle's insight. The human virtues seem to be a series of contraries or composed of contraries.

In fact, that will turn out to be one of their strengths, as a lens for exploring the nature of the human. They show us how our nature is structured by contradiction: how the nature of the human is structured as a union of opposites. The virtues are contradictory because they are forms of human good, and there are two contradictory kinds of good human actions: the good of union and the good of non-union, the goods of both separation and connection, of freedom and attachment. We *feel* human behaviours are "good" because they promote some valuable di-mension or expression of these two contradictory poles of our being. To be human is to be a union of these contradictory human goods. A union of union and non-union.

But before I begin to explore the contradictions between the virtues, I want to warn you about a potential misunderstanding that could be created by my discussion of the virtues so far, and in the rest of this book.

The social and cultural dimensions of the virtues

Because this book explores the nature of the human through the lens of the virtues – and because I'm writing it for individual readers like you – I may sometimes appear to focus largely or exclusively on indi-vidual human beings. If so, that would lead to a wrong impression of the overall implications of this book. So it's important for me to say a few words of caution here about that potential misunderstanding be-fore I begin to look at the virtues and their contradictions in more detail.

In a discussion of the virtues, some emphasis or focus on the indi-vidual is natural, and even desirable. After all, the virtues can only be exercised by individuals. When you think about a virtue or try to visualize it, you have to think about the actions of an individual human being. If virtue is to occur in the world, it can only do so if somebody – some individual person, or group of persons – acts or behaves in a virtuous way.[196] Sometimes a virtuous action (or pattern of actions), exemplified even by a single human being, can have a momentous impact: an individual role model or example can change a whole culture or give rise to a new one. If great – or even small – evils are to be resisted, that can only occur when some individual chooses to take a stand against them.[197] So the individual perspective should never be discounted or discarded. In fact, one of the purposes of this book is to invite you to reflect on your own life and behaviours, and on the degree to which they reflect or express the whole nature of the human.

But virtue is also inherently social or interpersonal, not just individual. For one thing, the virtues can only be expressed in relation to other persons or things. Even virtues that seem to be largely inner-directed – virtues such as courage, prudence, and temperance, for example – require a wider social and environmental context for their exercise. You can be brave, or prudent, or temperate only in a context of relations with other human beings, and with the world. *Other* virtues (such as justice) are expressly about how you treat other people. The quality of your relationship with others is what makes them virtuous. That means you shouldn't think about virtue as something purely or even largely individual. As soon as you begin to think about the virtues, or acting virtuously, your outlook and action are necessarily and inherently social or interpersonal, not just individual. As David Hume says, the human qualities we call virtues are those that make us "a proper member of society."[198]

For another thing, virtue can only be exercised or observed within a specific human culture. Virtues *create* cultures, but they're also shaped and coloured *by* the cultures they create. And they also *evolve* with those cultures, just as they *cause* those cultures to evolve. In both cases, it's a two-way street.[199] Let's briefly review these three dimensions of the close relationship between virtue and culture: creating, shaping, and changing.

First, creation. Cultures are patterns of human behaviour, the behaviours a specific culture endorses, those it considers good or desirable.[200] They're patterns of virtues and of values (the good habits of feeling that are inside of a virtue). Cultures are constructed from the virtues. As I said earlier in this chapter, virtues are the "ingredients" of culture. Virtues and their related values – habits both of behaviour and of feeling – are what make a culture a culture.

But cultures also shape the exercise of the virtues. Each culture is a specific, distinctive pattern of virtues and values. Cultures select, emphasize, and prioritize the virtues. They colour and combine them in distinctive ways. If the virtues provide the ingredients, as I already said, cultures provide the recipes. Cultures also establish the customs, practices, traditions, rituals, and institutions in which their own distinctive "recipe" of the virtues is embodied and given life. The virtues highlighted or emphasized by a culture are embedded, expressed, and given their distinctive slant in the cultural practices specific to that culture. As you already saw in my discussion of the reality of the virtues earlier in this chapter, we can abstract and identify the universal values embedded in specific cultural practices and customs. But the practices remain the vehicle for them in that particular culture, giving the virtues a distinctive cultural form, character, and coloration. The practices shape the virtues and determine how they can or should be expressed in that culture.

Finally, the virtues are both the agents and the artefacts of cultural change. Agents, because cultural change often takes place partly as a result of tensions between conflicting virtues and values, in concrete historical circumstances and challenges (such as the abolition of slavery). Artefacts, because cultural evolution also changes the way virtues are practised, highlighted, or recognized. Cultural change can bring new virtues to the fore, and alter the way others are understood, or how they should now be practised. Later, in chapters 7 and 15, you'll see how human and Western culture has evolved, over the last 250,000 years or so, through successive cultures or stages, each of which had its own distinctive "recipe" of virtues, its own particular stance toward the human and natural worlds. Each one of these stages revealed new forms of human possibility, new forms of human good, new virtues, or priorities among the virtues. It's unlikely that this process of cultural evolution will cease in our "deep" future ahead. Human beings can look forward to learning more about the forms of "eternal possibility" we call virtues, as cultural change deepens our insight or widens our perspective about the nature of the human.

So, in the following chapters, as I explore the conflicts between the virtues and the way these contradictions structure and determine the nature of the human, keep in mind that virtues aren't merely aspects of *individual* human behaviour. They're also, and essentially, *social and cultural*. They can't be practised except in a social context. And they both shape, and are shaped by, that surrounding social and cultural environment. The virtues exhibit and express both sides of the human paradox: both union and non-union.

That's also why they're inherently contradictory.

The human stances of "*I am*" and "I *am*"

Before I explore the contradictions between the virtues in Table 1 in more detail, I need to return to my earlier circular figure and complete the work I began in the previous chapter. To illustrate these contradictions, and get on with the task of looking at the nature of the human through the lens of the virtues, I need to reshape the circular image of reality I've been constructing in this book so far. And I need to reconsider it from a human perspective.

First of all, I propose to alter my basic circular figure in order to make it more useful for the remainder of your journey. The grey dot will continue to stand for all the individual things in the universe. But I'll now change its shape in order to make it more usable in the next chapters, as an image for the paradoxical or dual structure of reality you've begun to discover: the polar structure of being created by unity and plurality, by something and other things, by something and everything, by self and world, by the one and the many, by diversity and unity, or by union and non-union.

You can see that new shape in Figure 8 on page 75.

I want to point out two important features of this new picture to you. First, although the grey dot has changed shape and has become a semicircle, you need to remember that, no matter what its shape, it still represents *all* the individual things of which the universe is composed. Although it appears to be only one grey semicircle, it still stands for the innumerable other (invisible!) grey dots that represent all those other individual things and beings.

Second, the altered shape and size of what is now a grey semicircle might encourage you to forget another important feature of this image: the grey shape representing all the individual things in the universe is fully *inside* the larger circle. It's both inside and surrounded by the larger, invisible universe of being, the domain of everything. The domain of "something" or of non-union can't exist outside the universe of other things and of everything else, or outside the power and process of being, whatever that may be. It's inside the background of being and can only exist, or be the thing that it is, *because* of the background. It will be very important for you to keep this feature of my basic image fully in your mind as we go forward.

Now you have a basic image of reality to work with in your exploration of the nature of the human through the lens of the virtues. But before you can begin the journey itself, I need to change the image once again to reflect not just what *is*, but how human beings *respond* to what is: how, as humans, we respond to this fundamental paradox. How is

Figure 8. Being and beings (2)

this larger polar structure of being – within which we exist – reflected in the nature of the human?

Union and non-union – or being and beings – are the kind of "objective sources" of experience that Hegel calls "occasions" and Webb Keane calls "affordances."[201] That is to say, they're objective and universal realities that can become causes, conditions, or occasions for human beings (and human cultures) to experience them, to respond to them, to interpret them, and to attach value to them. They are also occasions and opportunities to articulate those values in the form of behaviours the culture considers good or desirable: good human ways of responding to these unavoidable realities of human experience. So, how can I begin to describe the ways in which humans respond to this fundamental polarity of being?

Let's begin with the grey semicircle because it now represents all the individual things in the world or the universe, including all the individual human beings. The grey semicircle represents you and it represents me, and it represents all of the other individual human beings on the planet. And it represents us in our individuality, the fact that we really exist as individuals and are not just part of some wider unity of being. All the individual things and human beings are what they are by virtue of being distinct, separate, individual. Part of the wider universe of being maybe, but not *just* part of it. That's what "non-union" means or expresses. As individuals we are, by definition, *not* swallowed up in the larger whole. We are *individual*.

But how should I capture what non-union means for human beings, and for their mode of being in the world? What form or shape does it take in human life? What spirit does it express? How can I express the basic *stance* toward the world implied in our condition as an individual human being? In keeping with a long line of Western thinking, I'm going to suggest that the best or most fundamental way to express this basic stance of our individual existence is with the words "I am."

"I am" is the first of what, in this book, I'm going to call the fundamental human "stances." A "stance" is a way of being in the world. As the word itself expresses, a stance is an orientation, a way of standing in or toward the world. But it is not – or not only – a conscious or rational orientation. A stance necessarily includes a perspective, an outlook, a way of seeing and interpreting the world. But it is much more and much deeper than that. It comes first, long before conscious perception. By the time you are aware of it – if you ever *are* aware – you are already standing toward the world in a certain way. A stance is a way of acting in the world, a way of *feeling* the world, a way of participating in it, a way of owning it. A stance expresses *our* world, the world that is ours, the world in which we stand, and therefore the only world we know or perhaps can know.[202] The world in which we live, and move, and have our being. A stance is expressed in human life through a family of virtues, a constellation of related ways of acting in the world which are *felt* to be good. Felt to be good, in part, because they are the means to express the stance.[203]

The first and fundamental human stance is "I am." Thinkers from Leibniz and Kant to Martin Heidegger and Paul Ricœur have agreed that "I am" is the "first" or "primitive" truth for human beings.[204] You can understand why "I am" has to be the first truth for human beings by considering how you would respond to everyday questions such as "How are you?" or "Where are you going?" or "What do you do for a living?" To questions like these you would probably answer something like "I'm well, thank you." Or "I'm going to the store." Or "I'm a lawyer." What do all these statements have in common? They all start with "I am." Any statement about yourself includes (implicitly or, in these English cases, explicitly) the statement "I am." It presupposes that "I am." If you didn't exist, you couldn't be or do any of these things. So being has to come first. It comes before any fact or action or truth about yourself. Any kind of true statement is, first and foremost, a statement about being: its truth is "convertible" with being.[205] "I am" is therefore the first and fundamental truth for human beings.

But you should notice that the phrase "I am" is composed of two words: "I" and "am." It makes a difference which one of these you focus on, or which one you emphasize. Whether you emphasize the subject, or the verb. In fact, it makes *all* the difference. It makes a whole *world* – or even *worlds* – of difference, as the rest of this book will show you.

In the human stance of non-union represented by the grey semicircle, "I am" isn't just "I am." Rather, it is "*I* am," with the emphasis on the first word, on *I*. The basic expression of individuality is the stance that *I* am: not just somebody or something else, but *me*. My own individual ego. *I* am.[206]

So now I can make my first change to the basic image, to reflect this individual stance or mode of being, in Figure 9 on page 78.

Figure 9 gives you a picture of the human stance implicit in non-union, or what it means to exist as a distinct individual human being within the larger universe of everything (and everybody) else that exists, the larger background or reality of being.

But this is only half the picture. And it's only half of what it means to be an individual human being. We're shaped not just by non-union but also by union: shaped not just by assertion of our *own* individuality but also by the reality that we're part of, by something larger, something we didn't create and that we don't control, or can never completely control. Something we can never fully grasp, perceive, or understand. We're shaped by our relationship to the background of being, by which we are surrounded, and without which we couldn't even exist, or be what we are.[207] That's the reality I called "union." What's this other contradictory human stance or mode of being, the one that acknowledges or expresses "union," the one that expresses the wider reality of being within which an individual exists, and without which they couldn't exist? What's the human stance "union" implies? How can it be expressed in human terms?

I suggest the human stance of union is very similar to that of self-assertion, but also different in one decisive way. This second stance is one that expresses (explicitly or implicitly) the underlying background of being, of existence: it expresses the astounding fact that "I am."[208] Because "*I* am," it must also be true that "I am." The emphasis is no longer on the first word but on the second. Not "*I* am," but rather "I *am*," with the emphasis on *am*. Because I *exist*, I'm not just my isolated, individual self. I'm part of something larger than myself: the whole background and miracle of being, without which I wouldn't be myself because I wouldn't even *be*. But I really do *exist*, even though I might not have existed. I might not have been born. My parents might never have met or might never have had children. I might not have come into being. In fact, the world itself might never have come into existence. There might have been nothing at all, rather than something. But for reasons

Figure 9. Being and *I* am

we can't comprehend, the world really *does* exist, after all.[209] *And I share or participate in its existence.* I exist – only and simply – *because it exists.* I'm not just me. I'm also part of something larger than myself. Part of being itself. I *am*.

This gives you a new image, one that shows the relationship between two basic but fundamentally different human *stances* toward the polarity of being, the underlying realities of union and non-union.[210] You can see these two stances in Figure 10 on page 79.

As you'll see in the later chapters of this book, the addition of the new stance of "I *am*" to the initial human stance of "*I* am" is a crucial step in the construction of the nature of the human, in the development and identification of what makes humans truly human. It's the moment or stage at which human beings first appreciate that they aren't just isolated, egotistical atoms but that they participate instead in a wider reality on which their very life, their very *existence* depends. They are creatures not just of *non*-union, but also of union. They share something in common with all other living creatures and with everything else that exists. They share their *being*. And they owe that being to this wider reality. They share and *must* share, to go on living. They share a common identity, the identity of being. They don't just observe or see or control what surrounds them: they *participate* in it. They're not just a part: they're a *member*.[211] They have duties and responsibilities as well as needs and desires.[212] They are dependent as well as autonomous.[213] The experience and knowledge – and pure *assertion* – that *I* am, *depends on a prior reality*. It depends on the fact that I exist. It depends on the fact that I *am*.[214]

Figure 10. The stances of *I* am and I *am*

In Figure 10 you now have not only a basic image of the polar structure of reality but also an image of the two contrasting human stances
toward the underlying polarity of being: the paradox of union and
non-union. You're now ready to explore this basic human paradox, using the lens of the virtues.

I'll begin to consider the human virtues entailed in the human stance
of non-union or "*I* am" in chapter 4, and the virtues related to the stance
of union or "I *am*" in chapter 5.

4

The Virtues of Self-Assertion

In the last chapter you saw how human beings respond to the paradox of union and non-union – unity and plurality, something and everything, self and world, and so on – in two characteristic ways, two corresponding human stances toward the polarity of being, stances which I called "*I* am" and "I *am*." In the next two chapters, you'll start to look at these two basic human stances or modes of being through the lens of the virtues, beginning with the virtues of non-union, or "*I* am."

The stance of self-assertion

How can I describe the stance of "*I* am" as a general mode of being in the world and as a corresponding category of good behaviours or virtues?

Let's think again, about what it means to say "*I* am," with the emphasis on *I*. Recall what I said about this stance in the last chapter. As individuals we are, by definition, *not* swallowed up in the larger whole. We may be part of the wider universe of everything, but we aren't *just* part of it. We insist on our own individuality, our own distinctness, our own separate existence and identity. That's what "non-union" means. "*I* am" is the stance that expresses non-union in human life. It's a refusal to be absorbed and cancelled out in the larger scheme or union of things, a defiant *assertion* of my own existence and my own individual destiny. A pushing back against the rest of the universe. A power of negativity, as Hegel says.[1] I'm *not* just somebody or something else, but *me*. I am myself, with my own needs, appetites, and desires. My own individual ego. My own *self*.

Remember also what I said about family life in chapter 1 when I was testing the law of non-contradiction. In order to become ourselves we often have to assert ourselves against our families, to develop and grow, and to make the necessary space for our own lives and desires. And that makes our families not just places of love but, inevitably, scenes of conflict too.

The experience of being an individual person or thing, distinct from the surrounding whole, seems to be a process of self-assertion. The stance toward the world entailed in being a distinct individual or an individual something, the stance that says "*I* am" – with the emphasis on "I" – is a stance of *self-assertion*.[2]

This discovery takes us back, once again, to the beginning of Western thought, to the Pythagorean philosophers you already encountered in chapter 2. They expressed this same insight – the role of self-assertion in making or sustaining a world of individuals and of individual things, separate and distinct from the larger whole by which they are surrounded – in the form of a theory or mythology about the creation of the visible, physical universe. The way the first Pythagoreans put it was that what they called the "limited" (or what we might call the "finite" world) emerged from the "unlimited" (or what we might call the infinite).[3] Why or how it emerged was explained by later Pythagorean thinkers who attributed the emergence of the physical universe (out of the unlimited infinite) to what, in Greek, they called *tolma*, or self-assertion.[4]

This Pythagorean concept of *tolma*, or self-assertion, became a central theme in the writing of Plotinus, who described the emergence of the visible, physical world of things as a "descent" of being from the One, a descent initiated and sustained through all its various stages by *tolma*, a primal spirit of self-assertion. In Plotinus' thought, the "descent" of being proceeds through various stages or levels before emerging into the material universe.[5] But all of these stages are animated and pushed forward by a spirit of self-assertion, an innate desire for self-determination, an inherent impulse to stand apart, a drive toward otherness. And all of these levels exhibit the fundamental Pythagorean paradox of unity and plurality.[6]

Plotinus' account of the emergence of being through self-assertion is interesting enough, as it stands. But you can also read it backward. Rather than simply hearing it as a straightforward account of the "descent" of being from the One, you can also interpret it as an imaginative way to come to grips with three facts simultaneously: first, with the mystery of existence, the mystery that there is anything rather than nothing. Second, with the fundamental paradox of something and everything, of unity and plurality, of union and non-union, from which this book began (and which Plotinus himself recognized – as you saw in chapter 2 – as the source "from which everything else proceeds").

And third, with the stance of self-assertion implicit in non-union and in the existence of individual things and creatures: in their standing apart from the larger whole, in the principle of difference and differentiation. The will to otherness and the drive for self-determination that are observable facts of the human and natural worlds. Plotinus' myth of the descent of being is a way to express the reality of self-assertion inherent in individuality, while reconciling all this particularity – all these multiple, individual things – with the paradox that they can only exist within a single reality, a totality of being. As Plotinus himself says, his myth is just a way "to express our own experience"[7] – our own experience of living as self-assertive individuals, in a larger context of being.

For much of the subsequent history of Western thought, self-assertion enjoyed an ambiguous reputation, as it did in the thought of Plotinus himself.[8] On the one hand, self-assertion was held to be a good and necessary impulse in the human breast because all action comes from self-assertion, even – or especially – the good actions of a holy person. The function of self-assertion, as Thomas Aquinas puts it, is "to move all powers to act."[9] Yet on the other hand, self-assertion is also, for that very reason, the source of all sin and evil.[10] Much of the history of Western spirituality can be interpreted as a struggle to get these two views of self-assertion in some kind of proper perspective or balance. But in all three Western spiritual traditions – Judaism, Christianity, and Islam – the positive view normally had the edge because for them the world is God's creation, and humankind has an active role to play in bringing about God's plan for it. Human beings' freedom to assert themselves is part of the plan. Freedom has a positive as well as a negative connotation.

Gradually, at the beginning of the modern era, the positive view increasingly gained the upper hand. As you will see again, in chapter 15, the thought of writers like Thomas Hobbes and Baruch Spinoza, who helped to lay the intellectual foundations of the modern and postmodern worlds, gave primacy to self-assertion in the definition of the human, and even of the non-human.[11] This primacy was later taken for granted by the thinkers of the eighteenth and nineteenth centuries. Hegel, for example, like Hobbes and Spinoza, assumed that the existence of *individual* things and people implies or entails the spirit of *non*-union: a "spirit of *self-affirmation* in strict opposition to everything."[12]

Since Hegel's time, our Western culture has increasingly celebrated the feelings and behaviours associated with this assertive side of our nature. In the contemporary world, the virtues of self-assertion now entirely dominate our thinking and assumptions about the good life. They haven't yet eliminated all the other virtues because those other virtues are an equally important part of the nature of the human. Without them, humans wouldn't be human. But for the time being, the virtues of self-assertion have pushed others to the side, or covered them up, or renamed them, and given them a new orientation. With a few important exceptions, the virtues of self-assertion are the defining feature of our contemporary Western world.[13] When we say something is modern or post-modern, we're referring to these virtues of self-assertion, whether we recognize them or not.

As a result, the values that are the "inside" of these virtues – the values implicit in our inner habits of positive feeling – are very familiar to us. They're expressed for us by iconic words like liberty, equality, and the pursuit of happiness, words that have become the touchstones for contemporary culture and political life. These are the core values we acknowledge today, and others are usually related to them. Our contemporary language of self-assertion is the language of freedom: it's expressed in words like liberation, autonomy, separation, independence, individualism, empowerment, self-determination, self-development, self-expression, self-realization, self-respect, and so on. In the last fifty years, words and concepts like these have become the dominant language of our public, media, and intellectual discourse, the only language we normally feel able to use in public discussion.[14] Behind them and supporting them is an implicit social vision, a vision of individuals joining freely together to obtain certain benefits for ourselves. Individuals come first, our modern outlook assumes. They then agree to put aside some portion of their "natural" freedom in order to secure the benefits of living in society. The overwhelming importance we now give to freedom is closely linked to an implicit "cost-benefit" calculation for ourselves, or, at best, to a calculation of "mutual benefit," as you will see again in chapters 8 and 15.[15]

The virtues of self-assertion: a sample list

What, exactly, are these so-called virtues of self-assertion?[16]

Once again, as in the previous chapter, it would be impossible to give you a definitive list, even if I wanted to. The number of words in our language to describe these virtues obviously isn't as great as the number of all the virtues. But it's still very large. It would fill about half of the dictionary of virtues I imagined in chapter 3. So, the best I can do is offer you a representative sample from my previous sample list of all the virtues.

If human life is a union of union and non-union, the trick here is to identify all the virtues in Table 1 that seem to express the spirit of *non*-union: a tendency to separateness or individuality; a stance that stands back from things and views them coolly, analytically, or "objectively" – or wants to dominate and control them; a demand for answers; a drive to satisfy desires, to achieve purposes, and to get things done in the world. Above all: an impulse to assert the self and its needs, wishes, or purposes. At this highest level, each of the virtues in Table 1 has a tendency to lean *either* toward union *or* toward non-union, the two poles of the polarity of being. (At other levels, the same virtues can lean in the *other* direction, as you will see.) Which of them do you think lean initially toward *non*-union? You can see my own provisional attempt to sort out the virtues of self-assertion from the larger list of virtues, in a new sample list in Table 2 on page 85.

Once again, there are some things you should keep in mind, and some things that may come to mind as you look at this sample list of the virtues of self-assertion in Table 2. The thing to keep in mind is that this is obviously only a sample, an arbitrary selection. No list of the virtues of self-assertion could ever be complete because there would always be some new dimension of the human that could come to mind and be added to the list. You may be able to think of some additional candidates right away. I've been doing that myself, as I go along, so you may too. My sample is intended to be representative and suggestive, but not complete.

Something you may notice about this list is that, like my previous list, it still seems to contain contradictions and conflicts. In fact, it still contains some of those I already pointed out. Subjectivity and objectivity are still here. So are detachment and desire. Boldness is still here, but how can it go together with prudence? Autonomy seems to be in tension with cooperation. How does zeal fit with tolerance? Or self-expression with tact? Or desire with temperance? Or change, innovation, and originality, on the one hand, with perseverance, steadfastness, orderliness, and reliability, on the other? The list seems to be filled with opposites.

Obviously, shortening my list to only one set of virtues hasn't got rid of the conflicts and tensions I noted in the first sample list of all the virtues. That feature of the virtues seems to be constant, even as you divide the field. If these are really the virtues of self-assertion, then there seems to be more than one kind of self-assertion, to say the least.

But are these really virtues of self-assertion? Some of them don't sound, at first, very much like self-assertion. Reason, for example. Why would you describe reason as a virtue of self-assertion? Isn't it the opposite?

Table 2. The virtues of self-assertion: a sample list

acceptance (as tolerance/ reasonableness)	enterpris(e)(ing)	patience (as self-control)
adaptability	enthusiasm	perseverance
agency	entitlement	play(ful)(ness)
appetite	entrepreneur(ial)(ship)	pleasure
appreciation	equality	power
assertiveness	equanimity	pride
attachment (as pride/desire)	equity (as fairness)	prudence
autonomy	eros	purposefulness
beauty (as pleasure)	expressivism	rationality/rationalism
belief (that)	fairness (as equality)	reason
boldness	firmness	reasonableness
bravery	flexibility	reciprocity
calmness	flourishing	reliability
caution	forbearance (as self-control)	resilience
certitude/certainty	fortitude	resourceful(ness)
change	freedom *to*/*of*	respect(-seeking)
cleanliness (as self-control)	frugality	responsibility (as prudence)
community (as cooperation/reciprocity)	glory (as heroism)	responsiveness
competence	grace (as self-control)	rights(-seeking)
competit(ion)(iveness)	happiness	risk-taking
confidence	harmony (as reciprocity)	science/scientific
consideration	heroism	seeking
consistency	honour(-seeking)	self-assertion
contentment	humour	self-control
continence	identity (as self-assertion)	self-determination
control (external/instrumental)	imagination	self-development
conviction	impartiality	self-discipline
cooperation	independence	self-expression
courage	individualism/individuation	self-realization
creativity	informality	self-reliance
decisiveness	ingenuity	self-respect
desire	initiative	self-seeking
detachment (as objectivity/ equanimity)	innovation	separat(e)(ness)(ion)
determination	integrity (as self-control)	skill(ful)(ness)
dignity (as respect/ rights[seeking]/self-control)	intensity	spontaneity
diligence	judgment (as reason)	steadfastness
discretion	knowledge (as reason)	strength
dominance	law(-enforcing)	subjectivity
economy	liberality	success(ful)
effectiveness	liberty	tact
efficiency	moderation	technique
effort	mutuality (as reciprocity)	temperance
empowerment	non-union	tolerance
endurance	objectivity	tranquil(ity) (as equanimity)
enjoyment	openness (as confidence/ reasonableness)	trust(-seeking)
enlightenment (as knowledge/ reason)	optimism	utility/usefulness
	orderliness	will
	originality	work
	partiality	zeal
	passion	zest

Since the time of Aristotle, but especially since the European Enlightenment of the eighteenth century, we Westerners have been increasingly inclined to think that human beings are defined by reason, that reason is the standard of everything human. This is one of the distinctive features of our Western civilization. It's one of the things of which we are, justifiably, most proud. Even if, in many areas of our twenty-first century life, we respect reason less and less *in practice*, we still pay homage to it *in principle* or in theory. We think (or claim to think, especially when it suits us to do so) that everything should meet its test.[17]

Because of the importance Western culture has traditionally attached to reason in our definition of the human, it's hard for us to see rational thought isn't the neutral, transparent cognitive lens we think it is. It comes to us loaded with its own baggage. It always comes with a built-in, hidden agenda of domination and control. It's an attempt by our rational minds to grab hold of the world, to wrest meaning out of it, and control it.[18] As Aristotle says, "thinking is a process towards *assertion*."[19] The principle of identity (A=A) – which (together with its flipside, the law of non-contradiction) is the basis of all Western rational thought – is a pure *assertion*, assertion in one of its purest forms. The exercise of human reason (as in this book, for example) is an assertive demand for an explanation or argument that will satisfy our rational minds, for knowledge and know-how that will accomplish our purposes and desires. Rational consciousness, as Bernard Lonergan (1904–84) puts it, is a "self-assertive spontaneity." That is to say, our rational mind assertively "demands" explanations for everything "but offers no justification for its own demanding."[20] It doesn't have to because it's simply an expression of self-assertion itself. "[I]nstead of being the opposite of force, and an antidote to it, as much of our modern world thinks," pure human reason (in the words of a Shakespeare scholar) "*is force functioning on another plane*."[21] The assertive stance we adopt toward the world is deeper than the rational consciousness by which we know it. Reason – at least in its everyday, modern form – is merely one of the manifestations of the underlying stance of self-assertion we had already adopted before we started to think.[22] Reason is only one among the human virtues. And, as a virtue, it belongs among the virtues of self-assertion. Reason is an unseen, unacknowledged virtue of self-assertion.[23]

In addition to reason, you may also have difficulty at this point, in seeing some of the other virtues on my sample list as virtues of self-assertion. You may have questioned them too. If so, there are at least two good reasons why you did. First, in the contemporary Western world, it's very hard for us to see *beyond* the world of self-assertion.

Since self-assertion has created our modern and post-modern worlds, that's the only world we can see. And since we can't see what's *outside* this world, we obviously can't see what must be *inside* it either. Just as visiting some other part of the world is the only way to get perspective on your own country, you have to have a point of contrast – another stance – before you can see what belongs in the virtues of self-assertion.

Second, because we normally assume the world is governed by the law of non-contradiction, it's hard for us to see there's more than one kind of self-assertion. Since we normally assume something can't contradict itself and still be true, we also assume that human impulses that seem to *conflict* with pure self-assertion must be something *different* from self-assertion. They must be *other* than self-assertion. That can be true of course. In the next chapter I'll explore some of those virtues. But it's not the whole truth. As you will discover in later chapters, the house of self-assertion is also divided against itself. As you will see there, the self can assert itself *even against its own self-assertion*.

Patterns of self-assertion in today's world

If there's more than one kind of self-assertion, I will need to break my initial list down again, into some further subsets. My initial sample is interesting, but it's a bit unwieldy. In order to think more carefully about the virtues of self-assertion, it will be necessary to analyse them more precisely, separating them into their own clusters or sub-families of virtues. That will help you see why they're virtues of self-assertion. And where they fit in the overall nature of the human. That's something I'll come back to – identifying those sub-families will be a large part of the work of this book.[24]

Before I get to that work in later chapters, it may be helpful, first, to note some of the large, characteristic patterns in which the virtues of self-assertion express themselves in our contemporary world. Some of the ways you may encounter them in your everyday life. In the first decades of the twenty-first century, you can and do encounter the virtues of self-assertion in public discourse – in the language of public debate and of the internet, social media, television, radio, newspapers, magazines – in at least five typical ways.

The first is the language of human rights.[25] Almost all social claims are now expressed as some kind of "right," human or animal. Unless you express your ideas this way – unless you *assert* a right of some kind – you may have great difficulty in getting anyone to pay attention.[26] As Brad Gregory (b. 1963) says, "virtually all moral discourse in contemporary Western society takes the form of *assertive* and confrontational 'rights talk.'"[27] We live in "the age of rights."[28] Rights have become a "conceptual pass key" in contemporary political culture, serving to "unlock any door."[29] Modern values rooted in virtues other than those of self-assertion – benevolence or empathy, for example – values like these must often adopt the language of rights or freedoms, the language of self-assertion, to become effective. Because that's how our contemporary world expresses what we owe to other people. The one kind of unfairness, inequity, or harm to which we now respond spontaneously is an alleged denial of some fundamental human "rights."[30]

Another way we practise the virtues of self-assertion today is in the degree of importance and attention we give to physical pleasure. We now attach enormous value to anything and everything that pleases our bodies and our senses, and much of our economic and business life is dedicated to serving them. You have only to look at the lifestyle, food, wine, travel, decorating, or fashion websites, apps, and blogs, or to the newspaper sections and magazines dedicated to these and similar themes, to get an idea of how important these things now are for us. The pursuit of pleasure itself isn't new. It's as old as the human race and essential to us, a permanent part of our nature. What's new is the relative absence of anything – any contrary virtues – to counterbalance it, on the other side. Alexis de Tocqueville (1805–59), thought this new, unbalanced "passion" for comfort and sensual pleasure was typically modern and a potential threat to the future of democracy.[31] Tocqueville couldn't foresee how far the pursuit of pleasure, especially sexual pleasure, would go in the twentieth and twenty-first centuries.[32] But he was prescient in foreseeing how a consumer society and authoritarian government can, and do, go hand-in-hand.

A third way the virtues of self-assertion are expressed today is in competitive, market-based, economic self-assertion. In the late twentieth century, a free-market model of economic life achieved a decisive victory over all other models, for the time being at least. The values of the market now penetrate most other areas of human life in the contemporary Western world.[33] As a result, we now live in a deeply materialistic culture which attaches great value to entrepreneurship, to the acquisition of wealth, and the ownership of things, to the values of consumerism and "conspicuous consumption." Again, this is nothing very new, in itself. What's new is the lack of any equally powerful, countervailing forces. As a result of financial and business deregulation at the end of the twentieth century, the explosion and prestige of enormous wealth, and of what it can purchase, has surpassed even the "Gilded Age" at the end of the nineteenth century. In the first half of the twenty-first century, we live in a Western culture deeply shaped by what C.B. MacPherson (1911–87) calls "possessive individualism."[34]

In the last fifty years or so, this powerful consumer culture has contributed to the emergence of yet another large pattern the virtues of self-assertion assume today. It has transformed the way we see and relate to our own individual selves. It has led to what might be called the "aestheticization" of the self, in which each of us becomes an artistic object for ourselves. Even the body – perhaps especially the body – becomes a personal canvas on which to celebrate, explore, fulfil and, in some sense, even *create* our own unique, individual selves. Charles Taylor has called the self-conscious and even self-indulgent expressiveness of contemporary popular culture "expressivism."[35] Possessive individualism has combined with consumerism, communication technology, mass media, advertising, music, fashion, the internet, social media, smart phones, "selfies" – and many other technological and cultural influences – to create a mass culture of narcissism,[36] or "expressive individualism." Expressive individualism "holds that each person has a unique core of feeling and intuition that should unfold or be expressed if individuality is to be realized."[37] It's closely linked to the "therapeutic" outlook, which is another form self-assertion assumes in contemporary, post-modern life.[38] Because it emphasizes personal feelings, many people assume expressive individualism can balance or remedy the dehumanizing downsides of the very possessive individualism from which it emerged. Many people live in the latter in their public and professional lives, but they try to escape into the former in their personal and private lives: "A simplified expressivism infiltrates everywhere. Therapies multiply which promise to help you find yourself, realize yourself, release your true self, and so on."[39]

In the second half of the twentieth century, possessive and expressive individualism were supported and encouraged by a trend in the social sciences which has been called "theoretical" or "methodological individualism." Many scholars in fields such as economics, sociology, and psychology accept the "dogma that all human social group processes are to be explained by laws of individual behaviour – that groups and social organizations have no ontological reality – and that, where used, references to organizations, etc. are but convenient summaries of individual behavior."[40] Social sciences that start out from these kinds of (often hidden) premises are very likely to end up describing a world that corresponds to them. The very way we study and understand our post-modern world helps, in a circular way, to reinforce the very patterns of human behaviour it takes for granted.

These five – human rights, physical pleasure, and possessive, expressive, and methodological individualism – are some of the large cultural

patterns or forms in which we encounter and express the virtues of
self-assertion today.

All human action is self-assertion

It's very difficult today for us to see beyond the world that has been
created for us by these virtues of self-assertion.

One reason why this is so hard is that *everything* human is a form
of self-assertion. That makes human reality complex, confusing, and
hard to understand. Because even the virtues *other* than those of self-
assertion – even those *opposed* to self-assertion – are, ultimately, forms
of self-assertion.[41]

That sounds strange – maybe even impossible, doesn't it? But think
about it for a moment. *All* human action is self-assertion, by definition.
You can't *do* anything except as a form of self-assertion.[42] Self-assertion,
as primatologist Frans de Waal (b. 1948) says, "enters into everything
we do."[43] To act is to assert yourself. Hence there can be no action of any
kind that isn't some form of self-assertion.[44] Even the virtues genuinely
opposed to self-assertion (as I'll explain again, later) *are themselves acts
of self-assertion.*[45] Everything human – we might even say everything,
period – begins in the grey semicircle. And that can make it seem like
that's all there is.

Once you're living in it, the impression that the grey semicircle is
everything is reinforced by the close link between self-assertion and the
visible world by which we're surrounded – including the individual
thing on which I asked you to focus in chapter 2. The world self-assertion
creates is a world of those individual things. When you focussed on the
individual thing in your room or garden – *as* an individual thing – you
were unconsciously exercising a virtue of self-assertion. Aristotle himself – precisely because he helped to create our self-assertive Western
ideal of rational thought – was already living in a world of things, a
world constituted of individual "facts," things, and "substances." His
very stance toward the world, the stance of which he was such a sterling
model, made it inevitable that he would find himself in such a world of
individual things, of objects, and help to create it for us.[46]

Self-assertion is the mode of being of individual beings and things,
the expression of their individuality, their separateness and distinctness, their refusal to be absorbed into a larger whole. All of the individual things in the world are individual, self-asserting grey dots. But
the virtues of self-assertion also push human beings toward *seeing* a
world of this kind, a world made up of separate individual things or
objects. That's what the world looks like to the individual self-asserting

ego. It looks like an "objective" world, a world of individual, separate objects.[47] By asserting herself against the world, the individual separates herself from the other things and beings in such a world, which now appear to be something "other" than herself. The individual ego confronts and "creates" (i.e., perceives the otherness of) an objective world.[48] But this creation now works the other way, too. An objective world confronts and creates (i.e., causes human beings to feel the reality – or illusion – of) their own individual egos. It's a two-way street. A vicious or a virtuous circle, depending on your point of view. Or maybe both, at the same time. The virtues of self-assertion create a separate, objective world, standing over against, or confronting, the ego. But this objective world then, in turn, reinforces self-assertion. It creates a separate, independent ego, standing over against the world.[49] The virtues of self-assertion and the perception of an objective world go hand in hand, for better and for worse.[50]

Because of the way they push back against things, the virtues of self-assertion have an inherent tendency to atomism[51] – both in how we human beings see the natural world, and how we see ourselves. For self-assertion, the physical world is made up of individual things. And the human world is made up of individual human beings. In the modern Western world, human beings have therefore become – and can only imagine themselves as – the autonomous, self-determining individuals so influentially described at the end of the seventeenth century by John Locke.[52] Charles Taylor uses the expression the "punctual self" to describe the utter isolation, separateness, and distinctness of the Lockean self, which has become the modern and post-modern self, the only one we can readily imagine in a world shaped by the virtues of self-assertion.[53]

The difficulty of seeing beyond that world is increased by self-assertion's deep negativity. Remember the "non-" in non-union. As you just saw, the spirit of self-assertion is (in Hegel's words) "in strict opposition to everything." The virtues of self-assertion embody "a confrontational posture toward things as they are," "a transformative non-acceptance of things," a "constitutive power of negation."[54] So resistance, scepticism, and doubt are some of its main characteristics.[55]

Transcending self-assertion

But this isn't the whole story.

It isn't the whole story about the world, as you will see again in the next chapter. And it isn't the whole story about reason and self-assertion, either. Because, fortunately for us, self-assertion has the capacity to transcend itself. To go beyond itself. And so, therefore, does reason.

There are, in fact, at least two kinds of reason.[56] One of them is the normal discursive, calculating, everyday kind of reason. The models for this kind of reason are mathematics and empirical argument, the kind of thinking that seeks to know and control the physical world. It's based on "facts" and on inferences from the facts. In the contemporary world, we tend to think this is the only kind of reason.[57] But throughout human history the deepest thinkers have usually recognized a quite different kind of reason, a reason that recognizes its own limits and seeks to go beyond them by means other than itself. Aristotle calls this other kind of thinking contemplation.[58] Thomas Aquinas calls it "wisdom," a sub-division of a higher reasoning power he and many other medieval philosophers called "intellect."[59] Blaise Pascal calls it the "heart," or thinking with judgment, discrimination, or "finesse," in contrast to the "geometric mind" of discursive, calculating reason.[60] Many thinkers of the Enlightenment and its Romantic aftermath called it, confusingly, "Reason," in contrast to "Understanding" – which is what they called discursive, calculating reason (reversing common sense usage).[61] Martin Heidegger again calls it understanding – "undifferentiated " or "heedful understanding," or "attuned understanding" (B1) – and distinguishes it from "merely presentational [i.e., explanatory] thought," "thematic interpretation," or "theoretical propositional statements" (B2).[62]

The difference between these two types of thinking is the distinction between "the intuition of things which arises when we possess ourselves, as *one with the whole* ... and that which presents itself when ... we think of ourselves as *separated beings*, and place nature in antithesis to the mind, as subject to object."[63] One kind of thinking is rooted in our sense of union, the other in our feelings of non-union. One "discloses" a "totality of relevance" or a "totality of significance," the other makes that relevance "explicit," so its "conceptuality" can be "explicitly grasped."[64] One works by chains of reasoning, from "things" or facts, and abstract principles, the other more by feeling, insight, and sudden intuition about the whole.[65] However you describe it, the ancient distinction between two different types of reason points to a kind of thinking unfamiliar to our modern minds. This other kind of thinking goes right up to the limits of our ordinary, everyday reason – the limits imposed by the virtues of self-assertion that underpin it – and then seeks to go beyond those limits by transcending or subverting itself, pointing beyond the limits, "gesturing toward what it cannot know."[66]

This only stands to reason, after all. If the virtues of self-assertion are the human response to the knowable world – the world of the grey semicircle, the world of "*I* am" – and if human reason is one of those virtues, it can't expect, by itself, to look beyond that world, to the unknowable world of everything that surrounds it, and without which it couldn't exist. But if the virtue of self-assertion we call "reason" is a spontaneous, unquenchable "demand" to explain everything, its own demand will push it to go beyond itself. The characteristic mood of reason is one of "perpetual dissatisfaction."[67] So it can't be satisfied with its own limits. Its own self-assertion will require it to subvert or transcend itself in order to go further. Its own demand will oblige it to adopt or embrace another kind of virtue, the virtues that are the human response to the *un*knowable world of being, the virtues that belong to the human mode of being I called "I *am*."

But these virtues will transform reason and lead to a new kind of self. Assertion will remain – because everything human, all human action, is a form of self-assertion – but it will no longer be the primary way of relating to the world. Self-assertion will turn itself into its own opposite.[68]

I will explore these other virtues in the next chapter.

5

The Virtues of Reverence

In chapter 3 you saw that human beings respond to the paradox of union and non-union – unity and plurality, something and other, something and everything, self and world, and so on – in two characteristic ways: two corresponding human stances toward the polarity of being, stances I called "*I* am" and "I *am*," the two necessary and ineradicable sides of what it is to be a human being. In the previous chapter I began to explore the virtues of self-assertion: the virtues that express the mode of being of non-union, or the stance of "*I* am." In this chapter I'm going to use the lens of the virtues again, this time to explore the *other* half of the nature of the human, the virtues of union: the good behaviours that express the human stance I called "I *am*."

The virtues of union: the case of the family, again

As in chapter 4, let's begin by considering how to describe the mode of being of union or "I *am*" as a stance toward the world, and as a corresponding family of virtues.

This isn't as easy a question to answer here. The stance and its virtues were easier to identify in chapter 4 because the virtues of self-assertion created the modern and post-modern worlds – because these virtues are what it means to be modern. We use the language of self-assertion all the time. We're accustomed to appealing to things like liberty and equality and the pursuit of happiness. In the first decades of the twenty-first century, we spontaneously talk in terms of human rights, entrepreneurship, lifestyles, and "doing your own thing." These all come to us naturally.

But, if you were asked to identify another universe of virtues that's in conflict or some kind of tension with these values – other virtues that express the impulse to participation and sharing of the stance of "I *am*," rather than the separation and individualism of "*I* am" – you might have some difficulty doing so. You might even feel an understandable puzzlement, or perhaps even reluctance to do so. If pressed, you might come up with something negative, maybe something that isn't a virtue at all, even the opposite of virtue. Because this other way of being is in *conflict* with many of our most precious modern and post-modern values, you might even be tempted to describe it as something bad, rather than something good. The very power of our contemporary Western culture makes it very hard to see the good that stands outside it – or is even opposed to it. Because our own world is self-evident to us, anything else can seem simply illusory, irrational, or nonsensical at best – threatening, or even evil at worst.

Because this other way of being is so hard for us post-moderns to think about, let's try an indirect method of getting there. Let's go back to the case of family life I used in chapter 1, when I was testing the law of non-contradiction. As I already remarked, families are a good testing ground because they're one of the oldest forms of human life – much older "and more necessary" than the state, as Aristotle says[1] – and they show us forms of human behaviour that are very deep in our nature, but little noticed or even devalued in contemporary life. In order to identify the other side of the human paradox – so I can give it a name – let's think then, about some of the virtues we normally associate with family life, especially the life of a family you admire. That is to say, a good or successful family.

One quality that should strike you right away, in *this* kind of family, is respect. A traditional rule of family life is "honour thy father and thy mother." But, in a successful family, respect should go well beyond parent-child relationships. It's the way every member of the family should treat all other members. For parents and older members of the family, respect may well go even further: it may be more like deference, for example, or an explicit acknowledgment of superiority, authority, or primacy of the elder person. In ancient and Eastern cultures, deference toward elders and ancestors was almost always considered the highest form of virtue, the root of all other virtues, and it still is in North American Indigenous cultures. Even in our own Western cultures, until the last few decades, this deference or acknowledgment of superiority for age was openly expressed by symbolic gestures such as calling older males "sir," by standing up when adults came into the room, or by holding the door or a chair for an older family member, and so on.[2]

In chapter 4, you already saw that respect (in one of its forms) can be a virtue of self-assertion. But (like some other virtues) it can also be found among the second family of virtues, the virtues of "I

am," which I want to explore in this chapter. However, respect looks
different in these two different families of virtues. As a virtue of self-
assertion, it takes the form of claiming respect or respect-*seeking*. It's
seen from the point of view of the person by whom respect is claimed
or to whom it is shown.[3] As another kind of virtue, the kind to be
explored in this chapter, it's seen, instead, from the point of view
of the person *showing* the respect, and the good that person experiences or perceives, *in showing it*.[4] So it takes the form either of being
respect*ful*, or, in the second case, of being respect*able*, that is, worthy
of respect.

Another virtue of family life, similar to respect, is the virtue of trust.
In a good family, a family we admire, its members can trust other family members: to be there for them in times of need; to care for them
when they're young or old; to provide a home or shelter; to look after
their estate after death; to look after their children; and so on. Trust is
another virtue, like respect, that works two ways: from the point of
view of the giver and the receiver. For the latter, it means trust-seeking,
a virtue of self-assertion. But for the former, the giver of trust, it means
trust*ing* or trust*worthy*.

One reason the members of a good family can trust each other is the
existence of another related virtue of family life, the virtue of "commitment." Commitment is what makes a family a family. If you're fully
human, you won't discard your parents or your children, even when it
might suit your convenience, comfort, or peace of mind to do so. You
won't abandon them just because they become sick, disabled, tiresome,
or burdensome. You're committed to go on caring for them and about
them, even when that kind of commitment goes against your own
self-interest.

For this obvious reason, another virtue you may associate with a
good family is "care" or "concern." The members of a genuine family
aren't emotionally or morally detached from the welfare of other family members. The struggles or successes of some family members are
shared by all the others. They care for each other. They're concerned
about each other. And this concern frequently takes priority over their
own needs or satisfactions. It comes first.

Concern, care, and willing commitment to the welfare of other family members are forms of another family virtue we call "love," in the
proper sense of that word. (As distinct from erotic desire, which belongs, as you saw in my sample list in chapter 4, to the virtues of self-
assertion). Love, in this sense, is something you *do*, not something you
have, or fall into, or that happens *to* you. It means taking responsibility
for others and putting their needs and interests ahead of your own.

Virtues like love are self-*giving*, rather than (as in the virtues of self-assertion, including erotic desire) self-*seeking*.

Another virtue closely linked to commitment is "duty." Duty is the opposite of self-assertion. It's a conviction of absolute obligation "toward an other than yourself," an obligation that trumps your own personal preference.[5] Duty can be a solemn virtue. In fact, solemnity itself is a virtue, in this second large family of virtues. But families aren't always or even usually solemn. In fact, another virtue we normally associate with family life is "joy." We often come together as families to celebrate something – a birth, a marriage, a seasonal or personal milestone – and celebrations are usually joyous. To express our shared joy, we usually have favourite family rituals and ceremonies. But not all family rituals are joyous. Our families are also the place where we share that most profound mystery of life, the mystery of death. In death, the virtues of sharing and ritual help us to endure the most painful experience of our lives.

Naming the virtues of union

Let's review some of the virtues I've already collected from our Western culture's experience of family life: virtues such as respect, deference, trust, commitment, concern, love, duty, solemnity, joy, sharing, ritual, and so on. How would you sum up these virtues, feelings, and practices associated with the *other* side of the human paradox, the side that doesn't express autonomy and freedom but rather your union with something like a family, something larger than your individual self, to which you belong, and to which you have obligations, even though it's not the result of your own free choice? How would you describe the virtues that aren't inspired by self-assertion, or self-*seeking*, but rather by self-*giving*?

Have you thought of an obvious word or name for all these other virtues?

Chances are it wasn't easy or obvious. There probably isn't a word that comes naturally or spontaneously to your mind to describe this whole universe of virtues and values, the other side of the human paradox. And that's actually a very significant fact about our modern world. It shows how much we have lost sight of this second family of virtues, and how hard it is to recover.

One word that might come to mind is the word "altruism." It's a very popular word in the contemporary social and human sciences, there's substantial literature devoted to it, and there are lively debates about it. (Another word social scientists sometimes use, as a sort of synonym for altruism, is "prosociality.") There's much to be said for altruism as a term to convey the generous, self-giving human behaviours that are the opposite of the virtues of self-assertion. For example, David Sloan Wilson (b. 1949), a biologist and evolutionary theorist, describes altruism as "a concern for the welfare of others as an end in itself."[6] That's pretty close to the meaning I'm looking for, as a label for the second half of the human paradox.

But, despite its prevalence in the social sciences today, altruism doesn't seem to me to have quite the right overtones and nuances I'm seeking for the name of this second family of virtues. And it comes with some unwelcome undertone, too. To my ear, it has a slightly patronizing or sceptical undertone in everyday English. In ordinary usage, it implies an unnatural overcoming of a more natural human egotism.[7] In the social and biological sciences, especially evolutionary theory – where the concept of altruism plays a prominent role – this tendency increases. Anthropologist Christopher Boehm (b. 1931), for example, distinguishes altruism from other virtues in the same family, such as generosity and sympathy. For him, the meaning of altruism is restricted to "costly generosity that is extrafamilial." Altruism "merely involves a measure of beneficence as this affects gene frequencies."[8] Similarly (despite defining altruism in the way I just quoted), David Sloan Wilson says a behaviour is altruistic "when it increases the fitness of the group" in a process of natural selection: "altruism evolves whenever between-group selection prevails over within-group selection."[9] In other words, altruism involves self-assertion, and the overcoming of self-assertion, for essentially self-focussed reasons – such as survival and reproduction. In fact, evolutionary theory explicitly aims to remove all reference to motivation from the concept of altruism.[10] But even in its more general usage, altruism sounds less wholehearted, more calculating, more mechanical, more like a fallback or insurance policy, or an overcoming, less central and essential to the nature of the human, than the word I'm looking for.[11] For me, the issue of motivation, and the links to other virtues, are very important for understanding the nature of the human.[12] Altruism certainly points toward the family of virtues I want to describe. But it seems to point there from the *opposite* direction: from the perspective of self-assertion. Not from the perspective of the *other* stance itself, the one for which I'm seeking a name. Altruism seems to be a label for the virtues I want to name, but a label they acquire when seen from a point of view *opposite* to their own: when seen *from the point of view of the virtues of self-assertion*.

Even if it did capture the self-giving behaviours that are at the heart of this second family of virtues, altruism doesn't have a rich enough

secondary resonance to capture, point to, or link all the *other* virtues
of this second family, those that begin or are rooted in something like
altruism, but move beyond it, toward related forms of knowing and
evaluating. Human beings are evaluating and judging creatures, too.[13]
And, as you'll see, the evaluating and judging grow naturally out of
the self-giving. Altruism doesn't seem to capture or suggest this other
important side of the second family of human virtues, the family of union or "I *am*." It doesn't point beyond itself, to the other side of its own
paradox, to its necessary partners, internal to this same second family
of virtues I want to name.[14]

A third consideration – which is really just another way of putting
the second – is that altruism is a very recent word. It was coined in the
nineteenth century by the French founder of positivism and sociology,
Auguste Comte, then imported into English by his first translators. As a
recent coinage of the social sciences, it lacks the rich, suggestive historic
and linguistic associations of older words. Contrary to the assumptions
of Descartes, Hobbes, Spinoza, and many contemporary thinkers, the
strength and usefulness of a word doesn't stem from its precision but
rather, from its ambiguity and resonance: from the myriad overtones,
nuances, and shadings (even contradictions) of meaning it has acquired
from the countless variety of contexts and ways in which it's been used
over the whole history of the language, and of the earlier languages
from which ours was formed.[15] When you find the right word, it's like
striking a note on a piano, or plucking a string on a guitar: all the other
strings – or words in the language – vibrate with it, even if you can't
hear them.[16] Altruism is a technical term, a made-up word. It's a "thin"
word, or a flat word. It hasn't been used for thousands of years in poetry, song, and story, so it hasn't acquired the deep resonance and broad
connections this kind of history can give a word.

When altruism first appeared in English, about 150 years ago, an early
critic complained about the relative thinness of this new coinage: "[I]s
altruism a sweeter or better word," he asked, "than charity?"[17] Charity
is, of course, the traditional Christian word for selfless, self-giving love.
And love may be another word that occurred to you, as a possible label
for this second family of virtues. It would certainly be a better candi-
date than altruism, as a name for this second family, for the reasons I
just suggested. If I were to call this second family the virtues of love,
you probably wouldn't have much difficulty agreeing with my choice.
And it would be a natural choice. Love certainly is the highest of the
virtues of union or "I *am*," as you will see. And love and charity have
all the historic, linguistic, and moral resonance that altruism lacks. But
even though they come first in the family of virtues I want to name, I

still think they suffer from the same drawback I already identified in the case of altruism. The name for a family of virtues, as Thomas Aquinas points out, should strike a note that can be heard or found in all of the virtues of that family, a note that harmonizes them and links them all together.[18] From that point of view, love still isn't the best word to link *all* the virtues of this second side of the human paradox, the other side of our nature. It doesn't have the overtones I need to capture the full range of these virtues, including the kind of deference, respect, and humility we feel and practice, not just in relation to our families but also in relation to many other things of highest value, such as truth, goodness, and justice.

The same drawbacks apply to other words you might have thought of to describe this family of virtues, such as sympathy and empathy. The first has played an important role in modern moral theory, and the second is widely used by contemporary social scientists to describe attitudes of concern and generosity similar to altruism.[19] Sympathy and empathy are also important members of this second family of virtues. But like altruism and love, I don't think they have all the overtones I need to link all the virtues of this second family I want to name.

Another word that might come to mind is the word "fraternity." It's the third word in the motto of the French Republic, and it helps there to balance the two key modern values of self-assertion – liberty and equality – that I already began to discuss in the previous chapter. Perhaps partly for that reason, fraternity (or its synonym, brotherhood) has been evoked as a necessary component of the nature of the human by many modern thinkers, from the Swiss economist Léon Walras (1834–1910), one of the founders of modern economics (for whom it's one of the three foundational "principles" of the human "as he can and should be") to the American political philosopher John Rawls (1921–2002), as you will see again in chapter 12.[20] Fraternity is another good word, and certainly belongs in this second family of virtues I want to name. But like altruism, love, sympathy, and empathy, I don't think it has the overtones required to serve as the bridge between all of them, and between the many other virtues of this second family.

Altruism, love, sympathy, empathy, and fraternity are all part of this second family of virtues. But they aren't the best words to bind them all together. I think the English word that can best serve as the hinge or link between virtues like love, on the one hand, and values such as truth, justice, and goodness, on the other, is the word "reverence." You probably didn't think of this word. And now that I've proposed it, you may perhaps be inclined to resist or reject it. Possibly because you associate reverence exclusively with religion, something of which (if you are a typical citizen of the contemporary, Western world) you may have a rather dim view.

But that's backward. Reverence doesn't come from religion. It's the other way around. Religious practice emerged from human experience of the virtues of reverence.[21] And *both* of them came, originally, from the experience of family, tribal, and community life.[22] Human beings didn't become reverent because they were already religious. They developed religious practices because they had already experienced the human virtues of reverence.[23] Religious life is simply a further development of the human virtues and practices of reverence they learned first in their families, hunting bands, tribes, and ancient communities.[24] When Thomas Aquinas used the word "piety" he still thought, first, of what we owe to our family or community, not primarily about what we now think of as *religious* piety.[25] This older meaning of reverence or piety is still preserved in the traditional English expression "filial piety," which is used to express the virtue of devotion to one's parents. So the use of the word reverence in this way, to express "family" virtues, among others, is deeply established in the history of the English language.[26] Even John Locke, the father of modern liberalism, still spontaneously used the word reverence to describe some of the key virtues of family life, and those that a family should teach children.[27]

Since Locke's time, the idea of reverence gradually retreated – in modern and, especially, post-modern Western culture – from the whole of life to what we now think of as religion, alone. But if you really want to rediscover the full nature of the human, I think you need to recover its meaning for much more than that: for one half of the whole human paradox.[28] If you don't like the word reverence, you might want to consider what other word "you would rather use to speak about things that are elevated and have worth," a word that "gestures toward higher ways of living and being."[29]

In this book, I want you to turn the common, contemporary understanding of the word "reverence" upside-down. Instead of thinking of it as something essentially "religious" that may also have other human manifestations, I invite you to think of reverence as something fundamental to the nature of the human, but which may also have religious manifestations – or lead to them. The fact we now spontaneously associate the virtues of reverence specifically with religious practices can even be an advantage, rather than a disadvantage, for my purposes in this book. In the second half of the book, I want to show you how some of the large patterns and familiar forms of human life – social, political, organizational, and so on – are related to or rooted in the nature of the human. Religious practice is one of those cultural forms. We now have a lot of difficulty understanding where it fits in the economy or geography of the human. Exploring the virtues of "I *am*" will help me to show you where the human religious impulse comes from, as a form of expression for some of the deepest forces in our nature.

For all these reasons, I propose to use the word "reverence" to name the second family of virtues, the virtues of union or "I *am*" – which are in tension with the first family, or self-assertion. Reverence is the word that best captures the essence, core, or spirit of these essential human virtues. It's the golden thread running through and uniting all of them.[30] Reverence connects together the virtues which arise from our natural human impulse to attachment, to union with others and with the surrounding environment, and with the greater whole of which we are only a part.[31] In chapter 17, I'll show you a surprising case which I think illustrates why reverence works better as a name for this second family of virtues than any of the alternatives.

Reverence grows from our connection, and our *sense* of connection, to something larger than ourselves, something we didn't create, and over which we have little, if any, free choice. Reverence connects us to the world around us, but also to the past from which our present world emerged, and to the future into which it is already moving. For reverence, past, present, and future are one seamless continuity, for which we should be grateful, and for which we are responsible. "[T]he foundation of reverence," says Alfred North Whitehead (1861–1947), "is this perception that the present holds within itself the complete sum of existence, backwards and forwards, that whole amplitude of time, which is eternity."[32] When we "see" someone reverently, we see them not just as they are now – with all their current physical characteristics (attractive or unattractive) – but as they have been at all times in the past, and as they may be – or could be, or perhaps *should* be – in the future.

Reverence expresses a human attitude of respect, deference, and obligation, or responsibility.[33] It acknowledges something larger or higher in priority than our own individual selves, something that commands our admiration and our loyalty, and may imply obligations or duties on our part.[34] In acts of reverence, either physical or mental, *we acknowledge superior worth*, our relationship with it, and our obligations and responsibility toward it.[35]

These reverent virtues of "union" stand in contrast to the virtues of self-assertion that emerge from the equally natural human impulse to freedom, autonomy, and "non-union." "Reverence results from humility," a Jewish text says.[36] That means reverence comes from the human impulse that's the very *opposite* of self-assertion. In fact, reverence is a form or mode of what might be called *un*selfing or selflessness.[37]

*Un*selfing is a term I'll use quite frequently in this book as a synonym for or illustration of reverence. It can lead to some confusion. It might make you think I mean the destruction or obliteration of the self.[38] Actually, it's the opposite. True reverence requires a very strong self.[39] As you'll see in this book, the highest acts of reverence are the highest form of self-assertion. And the reverse: the highest acts of self-assertion are acts of reverence.[40] By the image of *un*selfing, I mean that reverence is the way you feel and the way you act when you recognize your existence and well-being depend not just or even primarily on yourself, and your own self-assertion, but on other people and other things, the whole surrounding community or environment.[41] You feel, or should feel, humble when you recognize that you're not just an isolated, self-asserting individual but are also connected to something larger – and perhaps more important – than yourself. When you acknowledge, deeply and fully, that there's a larger reality on which you yourself depend. And which therefore comes *before* you, in the order of priorities. Which must be put *first*. Ahead of your own precious ego and its needs or desires.[42] But this kind of *un*selfing requires a strong self, not a weak self. It requires a very strong self to put others and other things first, ahead of your own ego and its powerful desires.[43] The larger reality that can be put first may simply be other things, as in Figure 2: a family, or a community, or a culture, or a country. Or it may be the whole fragile, global ecosystem, on which all life depends. Or it may, at the limit, be the unknowable totality of everything, as in Figure 3. You can feel especially humble when you come upon the limits of the knowable world and recognize that it's surrounded by a larger unknowable reality of being to which you're inseparably connected, and without which you couldn't exist, or be what you are.[44]

Reverence starts in the family. But, by its *own* nature, it doesn't stop there. Because it comes from the principle of unity or connectedness built into all human experience – from the union that precedes and encloses non-union – reverence doesn't naturally stop at the boundaries of the family or the community beyond the family.[45] It often *does* stop there, at one of those levels. But it stops there *because it's blocked or hijacked by the virtues of self-assertion*.[46] Reverence "at one level of a multitier social hierarchy," as David Sloan Wilson notes, can become "part of the problem at higher levels" because it bonds the social group but leaves it still *self-assertive toward the rest*. In this kind of reverence, self-assertion is just kicked up a notch: to the town, region, nation, or an ethnic, racial, linguistic, or religious group.[47] But when undisturbed by self-assertion in this way, the pure spirit of reverence links humans outward, from the family, to the surrounding tribe, community, culture, nation, and even to humanity as a whole.[48] The "essence" of reverence is "to unite and join together."[49] It "reaches out through kinsmen, friends, acquaintances, through all the bonds – cultural, social, civil, economic, technological – of human cooperation to unite ever more members of the human race in the acceptance of a common lot, in sharing a burden to be borne by all, in the building of a common future for themselves and future generations."[50] One of the greatest achievements of our self-assertive modern and post-modern world, paradoxically, is that we have come closer to this vision of reverence than ever before in human history. The boundaries of our concern can now extend to the whole human race. We're all universalists now, Charles Taylor remarks – perhaps a little optimistically.[51] This is, indeed, another marvellous human paradox! An important paradox to which I'll return, later in this book.

Unless it's ambushed and hijacked by self-assertion, the impulse of reverence reaches out even beyond our human community. It connects us to the natural and physical world we inhabit, starting with our own bodies. As an impulse of union, or connectedness, reverence necessarily embraces mind, body, and spirit as one, single whole. Unlike self-assertion, reverence sees no "mind-body" problem or dichotomy. Virtues like empathy or charity aren't rooted just in the mind, but in the body – in the guts, or even in the bowels.[52] The feeling of "communion" in the higher animals and early humans wasn't – and still isn't – just something in the "mind." Instead, it's "almost a *physiological* condition, a felt communion of action and emotion and desire."[53] For reverence, the human being is an embodied spirit.[54] And through your physical body you can experience a sense of connectedness to your surrounding physical and natural environment.[55] Through the body, reverence continues its outward journey of union, reaching out to nature in general, and, eventually, to the universe as a whole. One of the most important ways in which reverence is experienced and practised today is in the widespread contemporary concern about the environment and global climate change. When post-modern people feel concern for the global environment, and when they take action or change their behaviours to protect it or to combat global climate warming, they're practising the virtues of reverence without knowing it. I'll come back to this in chapter 17.

The virtues of reverence: a sample list

What, exactly, are these virtues of reverence?

The trick here is the opposite of the challenge in the previous chapter. If life is the union of union and non-union, the virtues of reverence will be all those in Table 1 which lean, initially, toward *union*. (At later stages or levels, they may lean another way, as you will see.) The virtues of reverence will be those from the first list that express the deep human disposition for attachment, rather than self-assertion – the behaviours that embody the human necessity and inclination for union with others, with the surrounding environment, and with both the past and the future. The "generous virtues."[56] The virtues that put others or other things first, and are broadly self-*giving* rather than self-*seeking*.

Once again, as in the previous two chapters, I can't give you a complete list of these virtues. No list could ever be complete because you could probably always find another English word to add to the list. And even if I could compile a "complete" list, it wouldn't fit in the structure of this book. It wouldn't be helpful or useful to you, or for the work I still have to do in later chapters.

So, again, I can offer you only a representative or suggestive sample. A sample *from* a sample. The virtues of reverence that I discern in Table 1 are shown in Table 3, on page 106.

You may notice right away that Table 3 exhibits some partial overlaps with Table 2. As I already pointed out earlier in this chapter, virtues like respect and trust can be both virtues of self-assertion and of reverence. But they have a different emphasis, in either case. As virtues of self-assertion, they're about *seeking* or claiming respect or trust. As virtues of reverence, they're about *giving* or *meriting* them. The same can be said about honour. As a virtue of self-assertion, it means desiring or seeking honour.[57] As a virtue of reverence it means giving or deserving it.

Freedom is another virtue that overlaps the virtues of reverence and self-assertion. But in the former it takes the shape of freedom *from*, especially freedom from the vices (the opposite of the virtues) that block the virtues, especially the virtues of reverence[58] – or freedom *for*: freedom for others, freedom for mercy and compassion, freedom for love, freedom for all four stances and families of virtues.[59] These were the original ways the language of freedom entered our Western vocabulary, through the people of Israel and their bible. As a virtue of self-assertion, on the other hand, freedom normally takes the form of freedom *of* (freedom of the self, the freedom of some human activity, like freedom of speech, assembly, or religion) – the characteristic Enlightenment value – or freedom *to*: the absence of any constraint to do whatever you feel like doing, the most assertive of the virtues – indeed almost the purest form of self-assertion – and the most typical way in which freedom is understood or defended today.[60]

Belief is another virtue to be found in both my lists of the virtues, both of reverence and of self-assertion. In the latter, it means belief *that* – a

Table 3. The virtues of reverence: a sample list

acceptance (as gratitude/ respectfulness)	fairness (as what is *due*)	patience (as kindness)
accountability	faith(ful)(ness)fidelity	peacefulness
admira(ble)(tion)	forbearance (as forgiveness)	piety
ador(able)(ation)	forgiveness	pity
agape	formality	praise
altruism	freedom (from)	purity
attachment (as commitment/communion)	friend(liness)(ship)	receiving/receptivity
authenticity	fullness/fulfilment	remorse
awe	generosity	respect(able)(ful)
beauty (as goodness/ truth)	gentleness	responsibility (as duty/love)
belief (in)	giving	revelation
benevolence	goodness	reverence
caring	grace	righteousness
charity	gratitude	rights(-giving)
chastity	harmony	ritual/rite
cheerfulness	helpfulness	sacrifice
cleanliness (as purity)	honesty	self-giving
commitment	honour(able)(ing)	selflessness
communion	hope	serenity
community	human(ity)(eness)	service
compassion	humility	sharing
concern	identity (as communion)	simplicity
connectedness/ connection	idealism	sincerity
contrition	insight	solemnity
courtesy	integrity (as wholeness)	solidarity
decency	joy/joyfulness	sympathy
deference	judgment (as wisdom)	thankfulness
detachment (as unselfing)	justice	thoughtfulness
devotion	kindness	tranquil(ity) (as peacefulness/unselfing)
dignity (as worthiness/ reverence)	knowledge (as wisdom)	transcendence
discernment	law/rule(-abiding)	trust(ing)(worthy)
duty/dutiful(ness)	love	truth(ful)(ness)
empathy	loyalty	understanding
enlightenment (as wisdom/unselfing)	meaning(ful)(ness)	union/unity
equity (as what is *due*)	meekness	unknowing
esteem/estimable	mercy	unselfing
excellence	merit(orious)	valu(e)(able)(ing)
	mindfulness	wholeness
	modesty	wisdom
	nobility	wonder
	openness (as charity/ honesty/trust[ing])	worship
	participation	worth(y)(iness)

cognitive virtue. In the former, it means belief *in*, a virtue closer to trust, commitment, or loyalty than to cognition.[61] Similarly, knowledge appears in both lists. But as a virtue of self-assertion, knowledge is another form of reason, a rational form of knowing, empirical and scientific. As a virtue of reverence, it's closer to wisdom: an intuitive, holistic form of understanding, as in the biblical virtues of "wisdom and understanding." And what this kind of wisdom understands is, primarily, the whole nature of the human and its various, contending possibilities.

These overlaps between the virtues of reverence and self-assertion are important to notice right away because they show how difficult it can be to grasp the nuances lurking at the heart of the virtues, nuances that can shift a virtue in one direction or another, or that can even turn it upside down, or into its opposite. The human paradox goes all the way down, turning almost any virtue either in an assertive or a reverent direction, depending on the situation or context. Fidelity, for example, harbours the two quite different virtues of devotion and loyalty. Loyalty itself can be either a duty, or a form of devotion. And knowledge or judgment can be virtues either of self-assertion or of reverence, depending on whether you see them as virtues of rationality, or of wisdom and understanding. As you just saw, simply adding the suffixes *-seeking* or *-giving* to virtues like respect, trust, or honour can turn them toward self-assertion or toward reverence. In our contemporary world, we don't notice that we usually mean the former, not the latter, when we use such words without a suffix. It can take long and deep reflection on a virtue to tease out these nuances and get the distinctions right, or assign a virtue to its right place in the scheme of things.[62]

Consider, for example, the quintessential post-modern value of human "rights." In chapter 4, I identified the demand for human "rights" as one of the most important contemporary expressions of the virtues of self-assertion. And that's correct. *As a demand.* As rights-*seeking*. But there's another side of the contemporary concern for human rights, which is rights-*giving*: the spontaneous recognition of the dignity and value of the human person – of *another* person or another class of persons. Or, indeed, in our post-modern Western outlook: of *all* human persons. This alternative stance – rights-*giving*, *not* rights-*seeking* – is a virtue of reverence, not a virtue of self-assertion.[63] It's one of the most important, subterranean ways in which the virtues of reverence (unnoticed, as such) are still practised – or even flourishing – in our post-modern Western world.[64]

These overlaps between the two main families of virtues also show that my attempt to distinguish between different categories of virtues, while necessary – and an accurate reflection of our human reality – is also somewhat artificial. That is to say, these virtues are all ultimately part of *one* single nature of the human. They are inseparably linked to each other within this whole, and carry on their subtle, ceaseless conversation in our hearts. We can, and should, distinguish them. But only in order to unite them once again, within the nature of the human.[65]

As in chapters 3 and 4, you may also notice the contradictions or conflicts in Table 3. Or maybe you won't because they aren't quite as obvious, to our post-modern eyes, as were those in the previous two chapters. They're more subtle here. But they're just as real. There's a fairly obvious (and classic) conflict between justice and mercy, for example. A real conflict our court and justice systems encounter every day, to say nothing of its constant presence in our own roles as parents, friends, and professionals. Getting the right balance between justice and mercy is one of biggest challenges we face in our private lives, and in the world of politics, social and economic policy, and international affairs. Mercy without justice would not be right; and justice without mercy would not be good.[66]

There's another obvious tension between truth and love. When we love someone, we don't always want to tell them the whole truth: *to* them or *about* them. Conversely, a zeal for absolute truth-telling can often be very *un*loving, whatever it may pretend to be. There's yet another tension between excellence, on the one hand, and humility or meekness, on the other. It's hard to be really excellent in some activity or endeavour, and also be really or genuinely humble or meek about it. In our ordinary lives, meekness seems almost to preclude the achievement of real or outstanding excellence. Think of a really outstanding, world-class athlete or musician, and ask yourself whether they could have achieved that level of excellence if they were very meek. (This paradox should encourage you to think more deeply about what we mean by excellence and by meekness. Is this kind of technical excellence what we *really* mean by excellence? Or is there a much deeper kind of goodness? Similarly, does meekness really mean an absence of self-assertion? Or could it actually be a very high *form* of self-assertion?)

There also seems to be a big difference between virtues like sharing, generosity, service, forgiveness, and forbearance, where the accent is on a kind of giving, and other virtues like deference, merit, goodness, and purity, where the accent seems to be, instead, on meeting or acknowledging some kind of standard. In fact, the first group seems to be partly about *overlooking* the very standards the second group wants to impose or respect!

So, once again, narrowing the field doesn't seem to have eliminated the conflicts and contradictions. They seem to go all the way down. They seem to be an inherent feature of the virtues. And if the virtues are really the right way to define the nature of the human, then our nature must also be defined by its internal contradictions and conflicts.

As in the previous case of self-assertion, we don't seem to be able to get rid of the conflicts and contradictions among the virtues of reverence, either. It begins to look, again, as if I'm eventually going to have to break down my initial sample list of the virtues of reverence into some further subsets, clusters, or sub-families of virtues. If I do it properly, that should help you see how the virtues of reverence are internally structured and how they relate to other virtues, within the overall nature of the human. I'll come back to that task in later chapters. Because, as I said, identifying those sub-families is an important part of the work of this book.

Patterns of reverence in today's world

To prepare for that work in later chapters, it may again be helpful to point out some of the characteristic ways in which you can still encounter the virtues of reverence, even in our post-modern Western world. The fact that we can no longer spontaneously name this half of the nature of the human, and therefore have difficulty talking about it, doesn't mean it has disappeared from our own lives. That would be impossible, since we're still both connected and free, at the same time: both one and many, both individuals and part of a larger whole. Our post-modern culture has changed. But reality hasn't. And neither have we. So we go on practising the virtues of reverence without being conscious of doing so. As you already saw in Table 3, some of the highest values held by the citizens of Western countries today – values like compassion or honesty – are virtues of reverence.[67] But we don't usually recognize them for what they are.

Some of the most common daily actions of your life are – if you think about it carefully enough – acts of reverence. Even saying hello or goodbye, or shaking hands, or holding a door for someone are ritual acts of courtesy that express respect, kindness, perhaps even deference, and are an elementary form of self-giving to another. Saying a simple thank you or "You're welcome" is also a reverent action, a virtue of gratitude or generosity.[68] Even the act of speech itself, quite apart from what is actually said, is something offered or given to someone other than yourself. In the same quiet, invisible way, you're practising the virtues of reverence whenever you celebrate a family birthday or anniversary; or whenever you comfort a friend; or whenever you help a neighbour; or whenever you vote, or willingly obey the laws, or pay your taxes; or whenever you volunteer to help your community or a worthy cause; or whenever you make a charitable donation; or whenever you observe the code of sportsmanship; or whenever you pay attention to your table manners or your language; or whenever you tell a truth inconvenient for yourself; or whenever you are civil in the face of rudeness; or whenever you get dressed up, for a formal party; or whenever you participate in a graduation or award ceremony; or whenever you are genuinely concerned for the welfare of others, for those you lead, for example, or for whom you are responsible; or whenever you commit yourself to the goals or welfare of an organization, a team, a college, a club, or a firm; and so on. Whenever you're *self-giving* rather than self-*seeking*, even in your ordinary, daily life, you're already practising the virtues of reverence, without knowing it.[69]

Reverence also expresses itself today in more colourful or dramatic – even alarming – ways. In fact, because it's stifled or starved elsewhere, our innate human instinct for reverence can risk flipping over into a kind of reverse caricature of the real thing. Rock concerts, mosh pits, and raves, for example, are all expressions of a hungry search for connectedness and ritual that aren't currently satisfied in other ways. So are big media events – like the Olympics, the World Cup, Princess Diana's funeral, William and Kate's marriage, or a natural or human disaster – events that can rivet millions to their TV screens for days on end.[70] In all these ways, isolated citizens of Western countries seek out the kind of communal, ritualized experiences our Western culture, on the whole, no longer provides.[71] Sometimes this unsatisfied hunger goes well beyond caricature, to assume radically evil forms, as in the Nuremberg rallies of Nazi Germany in the 1930s.

Another way the virtues of reverence are practised today is in the explosion of secular or quasi-secular practices and disciplines of "spirituality" that's occurred in the West over the past forty years. There are now storefront yoga practitioners on many streets in Western countries. Instruction in secular forms of meditation is widely available. Practices from Chinese spiritual traditions including Tai Chi and Feng Shui have become mainstream. Our Western societies have recently spawned an enormous variety of secular spiritual industries the products of which can be found in our pharmacies, gift shops, and bookstores under titles such as wellness, "new age," and self-help. Some of these, like "*self*-help," show you the lengths to which the virtues of reverence must now go – how they must often disguise themselves in the contemporary language of self-assertion – in order to get your attention.

You may yourself have explored some of these contemporary practices of reverence. You may have begun to regulate your diet, conscious of how what you eat can affect the unbreakable unity of your body and spirit. You may have experimented with yoga and meditation or read some of the popular books on "spirituality."

Or you may not have done any of these, but simply seek nourishment in art, music, or nature. These are some other ways the virtues of reverence are explored and practised today. They're one of our many inheritances from the Romantic movement of the nineteenth century, which highlighted nature and art as sources that could provide an antidote to the allegedly dehumanizing rationalism of the Enlightenment. Since the beginning of the nineteenth century, many people in Western societies have tried to meet their need for reverence in the productions of high art and culture.[72] This new respect – even reverence – for artistic expression, for its own sake, is one of the characteristic features of modern and post-modern culture.[73] Many people in our Western societies now find they can give meaning and depth to their lives in the experience and enjoyment of classical music, painting, sculpture, theatre, dance, and so on.[74] For others, popular culture, music, and film play a similar role. Many people now wear earphones, even in public places, to connect themselves at all times to a private world of music.[75] Music is one of the most natural forms for the expression and experience of reverence.[76]

Another way you can still experience the virtues of reverence today is in your encounters with nature. The natural world can make you feel emotions like wonder and admiration, leading often to feelings of oneness, communion, harmony, and peace, but also gratitude, generosity, responsibility, relationship, and even love – some of the typical values and virtues of reverence.[77] This is another of our legacies from nineteenth-century Romanticism. Much of English lyric poetry since the beginning of the nineteenth century has aimed to express the feelings of reverence inspired by such encounters with nature. A first encounter with a dramatic natural phenomenon like the Grand Canyon, the Rockies, the Great Lakes, or the ocean can fill you with the feelings of awe and wonder, which are also characteristic virtues of reverence. Awe is what you feel when you encounter someone or something that exceeds anything in your normal life, and in which you see, or sense, qualities of excellence, beauty, or some kind of power or authority, qualities you can't help deeply admiring. Maybe even something or someone to which, in some way or other, you feel spontaneously inclined to submit or devote yourself. Awe is "an acknowledgement of the surpassing value" of something.[78] It's a natural component or source of reverence and a very important human emotion because it's a critical source of human motivation. It often provides the energy and the drive that causes people to act: to commit or devote themselves to something, to stand up for something, or to take a stand against something else – or just to go on living. Awe can overwhelm you. But it can also motivate and empower you.[79]

As I already noted, the environmental movement is one of the most significant ways the virtues of reverence are practised today. It shows you just how motivating the virtues of reverence can be. And the environment itself also shows you why the virtues of reverence must, in the end, take priority over, or come before, the virtues of self-assertion. Self-assertion can only take place within a larger whole. Your first obligation is, therefore, to ensure the health and well-being of the larger whole, without which self-assertion is pointless, impossible, or suicidal. To survive the global climate crisis, it will therefore be essential to rediscover the virtues of reverence our Western culture still practices in everyday ways, but of which it's no longer consciously aware. I'll come back to this in chapter 17.

The lost language of reverence

As Paul Woodruff (b. 1943) remarks, what our post-modern Western societies have lost isn't reverence itself, but rather the *idea* of reverence.[80] In reality, in our everyday lives, we go on living by the virtues of reverence, and we know, intuitively, how to blend and reconcile these other virtues with the virtues of self-assertion. Or rather, I should put that the other way around: in our daily lives, we know how to blend and reconcile the virtues of self-assertion with the *other* virtues which are the ground and precondition for both of them. But because we've lost a language for these other prior virtues, they have little or no official place in our modern public culture, and receive little public support, even for their practice as private virtues. If they survive at all, it is only as a kind of "second language," taking a back seat to the "first language" of self-assertion.[81]

That doesn't mean the virtues of reverence are absent from our contemporary public culture. On the contrary. In fact, much of political life and public policy in the twentieth century was driven and shaped by the virtues of reverence. The construction of welfare states and national healthcare systems was a work of benevolence and compassion. As I just mentioned, the growing recognition of human rights and the protection of minorities are works of mercy and respect. The growing acceptance of multiculturalism or interculturalism – in fact, and even sometimes in theory – is the same. Commitment by developed countries to international development aid is a virtue of generosity and concern. And so on. As claims, demands, expectations, or entitlements, all of these are virtues of self-assertion. But as granted or given, they're virtues of reverence.[82] In these and in countless other ways, our contemporary public cultures still express the virtues of reverence. But we don't recognize them for what they are. Instead, as I remarked in chapter 4, we're often obliged to dress them up in the accepted public language of self-assertion, the language of freedom.

In our private lives, we also go on practising the virtues of reverence and craving the inner feelings associated with them. We don't have much choice about that because they constitute one half of our nature. But they don't get much support from our public language, the language of self-assertion, which normally excludes any reference to the connecting thread that runs through them: the idea, or concept – or reality – of reverence itself. "As householders, housekeepers, parents we maintain allegiance to it in practice, possibly even in diffident principle," says Lionel Trilling (1905–75). "But as … participants in the conscious, formulating part of our life in society, we incline to the antagonistic position."[83] This makes it very hard for you consciously to nourish or develop the virtues of reverence, so essential to your own nature and to the kind of society you want to live in.

But it looks as if the twenty-first century will be one in which we must learn again to live by the virtues of reverence, to live in a spirit of respect for the larger whole on which we depend. This experience is almost certain to reshape our way of relating to the world, our moral and spiritual outlooks, just as the great age of discovery and European expansion – from the fifteenth to the nineteenth centuries – fostered the virtues of self-assertion that shaped the modern and post-modern world. When all the signposts around you are pointing in the same direction, you eventually turn your head to look in that same direction, whether you want to or not.

6

The Human Paradox

The virtues of self-assertion and the virtues of reverence are the two sides of the human paradox you began to encounter in Chapter 2. They are the two necessary and complementary halves of the totality that is a full human being. When you do anything at all, both ways of being are always present in your action, even if you can't see it. Though they are in conflict or at least in tension with each other, you can't have one without the other.

And they have a natural order of priority in their relationship. As my basic image shows, the virtues of self-assertion nestle *inside* the virtues of reverence.

Self-assertion and reverence

Let's look again at the basic circular figure I've been using so far. At this point, I'm going to replace the initial stances of "*I* am" and "I *am*" (from Figure 10) with "self-assertion" and "reverence," the names I've now given to the two families of virtues through which they are expressed. My image will now illustrate the relationship between the two inter-connected, inseparable families of virtues that express those two basic human stances in our human lives. And I'm also going to make another visual change to this basic image, to make it easier to use in my ongoing exploration of the human paradox. You can see that change in Figure 11 on page 115.

In Figure 11, you can see that I've once again made the outer circumference of the circle a solid line. I've done this for several reasons. One is purely practical. I want to make this basic circular image my tool for the rest of the book and the image is easier to see and work with in this form. Another practical reason is that it's important for you to

Figure 11. Self-assertion and reverence

remember that the virtues of self-assertion can only operate within the larger field of reverence. With a solid outer line, you can more readily see that the grey semicircle is fully *inside* the larger white circle.

Another reason is that the virtues of reverence operate at several levels. As you saw in Figures 2 and 3, the virtues of reverence connect you outward, first to other things and other people (things like your family, community, a club, a team, a country, a pond, the Georgian Bay, etc.), as well as – at the end of their outward journey of reverence – to the invisible totality of Everything or being. The solid line I've restored to the outer circle can help to remind you of these first levels of reverence, toward concrete things, persons, and communities.

But you should also remember two additional things. First, that those other things to which you're connected are actually other grey dots or semicircles. They, too, exist within the wider sphere of reverence and maintain themselves, through self-assertion, as the separate, distinct things or individuals that they are. To think of them as part of the white space would be to confuse the issue. They're also grey semicircles like ourselves. We're connected to them through the virtues of reverence.

The other thing you should keep in mind is that, although the outer line is now solid for the practical and visual reasons I just explained, in reality it's still the invisible, indefinite, infinite boundary I portrayed in Figures 5 to 10. The outward journey of reverence eventually takes us to the invisible, unknowable totality of being within which we exist, and, without which, we couldn't continue to exist.

Figure 12. Two basic human stances

Two human stances: a table of opposites

Figure 11 portrays the polar structure of the human spirit, a structure dictated by the polarity of being: the duality of unity and plurality, something and other things, something and everything, self and other, or self and world.

Because they're so fundamental to the structure of the human, these dual, conflicting but interconnected and inseparable sides of the human spirit have been recognized by innumerable thinkers and writers from the Pythagoreans, Aristotle, and Plotinus to those of the present day.[1]

Ancient and medieval thinkers tried to convey this dual character of human life by using contrasting words like being and becoming, identity and difference, or rest and movement. From Aristotle and Plotinus to Thomas Aquinas, philosophers made a corresponding distinction between the "contemplative life" of reverence and the "active life" of self-assertion.[2] In Figure 12 above, you can see another image that helps to expand the basic categories of reverence and self-assertion to include some of these other traditional words or expressions that have been used to describe or designate the two basic human stances.

In the modern and post-modern worlds, many thinkers have expressed this same human duality in other ways. One of the clearest (though incomplete) modern descriptions of the human paradox was given by Friedrich Schleiermacher (1768–1834):

The human soul has its existence in two opposing impulses. Following the one impulse it strives to establish itself as an individual. ... The other impulse is ... the longing to surrender oneself and be absorbed in a greater, to be taken hold of and determined. ... [E]very soul shares in the two original tendencies of spiritual nature. At the extremes one impulse may preponderate almost to the exclusion of the other, but the perfection of the living world consists in this, that between these opposite ends all combinations are actually present in humanity.[3]

Hegel put this same human duality in a variety of ways. For example, he said the "nature of human beings" is "twofold": "at one extreme, explicit individuality," "at the other extreme, universality." The human spirit is "not something single, but is the unity of the single and the universal."[4] Since Hegel's time, many (if not most) serious thinkers have recognized this dual nature of the human. Here are some examples:

- Auguste Comte, the founder of modern social science, distinguished between two sides of human culture he called egoism and altruism.[5]
- Emile Durkheim (1858–1917), the French pioneer sociologist, recognized that the nature of the human is to be *Homo duplex*, both an individual *and* part of a something larger than the individual, with two corresponding sets of "social sentiments."[6]
- F.H. Bradley said the "essential nature" of the human is "equally to assert and, at the same time, to pass beyond itself." These "two great divergent forms of moral goodness" or "two partially conflicting methods" for realizing human goodness he called "self-sacrifice" (or "self-denial" or "benevolence") and "self-assertion" (or "self-seeking").[7]
- William James (1842–1910) described human beings as possessing a "dual nature": a "private, convulsive self," the sphere of desire and "egotism," and a "wider" or "greater self," the sphere where "our ideal impulses originate" and "through which saving experiences come."[8]
- Friedrich Nietzsche (1844–1900) called these two sides of the human the "love that wants to rule and the love that wants to obey."[9]
- G.K. Chesterton calls them the "paradox of the parallel passions." Human beings have to have "enough reverence for all things outside us," he says. But they also have to have enough self-assertion "to make us, on due occasion, spit at the stars."[10]
- Max Scheler says there are "two tendencies" in human beings: on the one hand a "power-striving," a "principle of struggle founded on the egoism of the preservation of existence" and, on the other, a "tendency toward mutual solidarity and support, dedication and sacrifice." The challenge or "problem" of human existence is

to determine the "proportion" between these two sides of the human, or the relationship which underlies their necessary "union."[11]

- Martin Buber (1878–1965) calls these two sides of the human "the two primary metacosmical movements of the world": the "expansion" of individuals' own being, on the one hand, and the "turning to connexion," on the other. These are the "two poles of humanity": "The one is the spiritual form of natural detachment, the other the spiritual form of natural solidarity of connexion."[12]
- Franz Rosenzweig (1886–1929), Buber's contemporary and collaborator, also recognizes the "inner contradictoriness of life," and the "struggle between the two urges of [the human] heart." He calls it (among other things) the "contradiction between creative power and revealing love."[13]
- For Alfred North Whitehead, the human world is also structured by a "paradox" of "ideal opposites," a "complex structure of harmony," uniting "disjunction and conjunction"; that is to say: uniting non-union and union.[14]
- Maurice Blondel (1861–1949) recognizes the same "dialectic" of being and of beings, the two sides of which he calls (among other things) "egocentricity" (or "singularity") – an atomistic impulse seeking "domination" – and "universal solidarity," expressed in "self-giving."[15]
- For Jacques Maritain (1882–1973), the nature of the human is "double": both "liberty" and "love."[16]
- Emmanuel Levinas (1906–95) also describes the human person as defined by a "duality written into its very essence," contradictions which "tear" humanity apart, but which "have their source in the nature of the human, and in Nature, period." For Levinas, we are "[a]t one and the same time, part of the totality, and yet resisting or separated from it."[17]
- For Paul Tillich (1886–1965), the "first polar elements" of the polar structure of being are "individualization and participation."[18]
- Susanne Langer (1895–1985) also identifies the "dialectic" of "individuation" and "involvement" as the "basic pattern of life." These two poles are "the great rhythm of evolution."[19]
- Iris Murdoch describes the human being as defined by opposite but "interdependent," "interpenetrating," and "overlapping" virtues, which are structured by the human's "obligations which belong to his environment" and the obligations which "belong to himself."[20]
- Paul Ricœur identifies "two fundamental directions" of the human "social imaginary." One tends toward union; the other toward

non-union. But you can't have one without the other. In the truly human self, this takes the form of a "dialectic" of self-assertion and self-"effacement." The nature of the human has an inherently "dialogical structure."[21]

- Psychologist Ernest Becker (1924–74) identifies the same two poles as the basic "motives of the human condition": "the need to surrender oneself in full to the rest of nature, to become a part of it by laying down one's whole existence to some higher meaning; and the need to expand oneself as an individual heroic personality."[22]
- Irvin Yalom (b. 1931) describes the contradictory or paradoxical character of human beings, defined by a "dialectic" between "two diametrically opposed responses to the human situation": "The human being either asserts autonomy by heroic self-assertion or seeks safety through fusing with a superior force: that is, one either emerges or merges, separates or embeds."[23]
- Primatologist Frans de Waal says there is "both a social and a selfish side to our species."[24]
- Anthropologist Richard Shweder (b. 1945) suggests these two sides of the human are reflected in "two major alternative conceptualizations of the individual-social relationship": the "egocentric contractual" outlook characteristic of our Western culture, and the "sociocentric organic" outlook characteristic of almost all non-Western and premodern cultures.[25]
- James Q. Wilson agrees the human is a composite of "self-regarding" and "other-regarding" virtues. Humans struggle to reconcile "the desire for survival and sustenance with the desire for companionship and approval." From the latter comes a human "disposition to attachment." From the former comes the "radical individualism" of modern and post-modern Western culture.[26]
- For Marcel Gauchet (b. 1946), human history and culture are shaped by two "founding dimensions" or "basic possibilities," a "primeval double-sidedness": either "submission to an order ... determined before and outside our wills" or assertion of "an order accepted as originating in the will of individuals."[27]
- Susan Neiman (b. 1955) calls these "two moral paradigms" the "two Abrahams," based on two contrasting stories about the biblical Abraham: Abraham at Mount Moriah and Abraham at Sodom – the Abraham who "submits" and the Abraham who "questions."[28]
- In a similar biblical image, Rabbi Joseph Soloveitchik (1903–93) calls the two opposing sides of our nature Adam I and Adam II, based on the two different accounts of creation in Genesis: Adam I wants to dominate the world; Adam II wants to serve it.[29]

- Jean Vanier (1928–2019) describes human nature as "a real paradox," based on "two competing impulses": "the drive to belong, to fit in and be part of something bigger than ourselves, and the drive to let our deepest selves rise up, to walk alone." He acknowledges the "need for community," but also "the need to be fully oneself."[30]
- Roger Scruton agrees that humans are defined by a "tension that exists between our nature as free individuals and our membership of the communities on which our fulfilment depends." These two perspectives "each give one-half of the truth."[31]
- Christine Swanton recognizes the "potential tension" between "two broad components of the good life": "personal satisfaction and thriving," on the one hand, and "appropriate responsiveness to the demands of the world," on the other.[32]
- Anthropologist Christopher Boehm describes a human nature that is "ambivalent": "at the same time, significantly generous and immensely selfish."[33]
- Evolutionary psychologist Jonathan Haidt also identifies this "dual nature" of human beings: "we are selfish primates who long to be part of something larger and nobler than ourselves."[34]
- Sociologist David Martin (b. 1929) also sees human experience as defined by a "dialectic between the transforming vision of peace and harmony," on the one hand, and the "social realities of power and violence," on the other.[35]
- Another sociologist, Robert Bellah, calls these two sides of the human paradox the "culture of separation" and the "culture of coherence" or, alternatively, the "disposition to dominate" and the "disposition to nurture."[36]
- David Brooks calls them the "culture of self-promotion" and the "culture of self-effacement," or the "culture of humility" and the culture of the "Big Me."[37]
- Charles Taylor describes the human situation as "defined" by "two solicitations": an "immanence perspective" that sees only the knowable world of something, and a "transformation perspective" that seeks to go beyond it to the *un*knowable world of being on which the knowable world depends.[38]

I want to capture some of these various ways of expressing the human paradox. But, as Figure 12 shows, I've almost reached the limits that this kind of circular image can accommodate. For something that can be expressed in so many different ways, I need to go back to something more like the table format I already used for the virtues, in the last three chapters.

But the structure of the human paradox suggests I now need a slightly different kind of table. My first three tables were just lists. They didn't have the kind of internal structure of opposites my circular figure has been able to show you. That suggests I now need something in between the two visual images I've used so far. Something that incorporates the advantages of both of them. I need a "table of opposites."

Recognizing the need for a table of opposites takes you back, once again, to the very beginning of Western thought. The first Pythagoreans I talked about in chapter 2 recognized the same need. They developed the first table of opposites, to describe the dualities that flow from the basic paradox of unity and plurality, of something and everything. The Pythagorean table of opposites was composed of ten principles arranged in two columns of opposites: limit and unlimited, odd and even, unity and plurality, right and left, male and female, rest and motion, straight and crooked, light and darkness, good and bad, square and oblong.[39] You can see the Pythagorean table of opposites in Table 4, on page 122.

Aristotle was obviously much taken with the Pythagorean concept of a table of opposites. As you've already seen, he followed the Pythagoreans in recognizing that "all things are either contraries or composed of contraries, and unity and plurality are the starting-points of all contraries."[40] But he also thought there was something fundamentally wrong with the Pythagorean table of opposites. He devoted much of the *Metaphysics* to trying to explain what the problem was. In fact, it sometimes looks as if Aristotle wrote much of what Andronicus later assembled into the *Metaphysics* precisely to clear up what he thought were the errors and distortions of the Pythagorean table of opposites. He wanted to do that because getting these kinds of contraries right was, in his view, an important key to the very deepest kind of thought – the thinking about "being *as* being."[41]

From Aristotle's point of view, one of the problems with the Pythagorean table was that it confused contraries and contradictions, which "are not the same."[42] In fact, he appears to have developed his law of non-contradiction partly to explain the difference between these two so he could correct the Pythagoreans' table of opposites. Contradictions, he suggested, are genuine opposites like being and non-being, or true and false, or good and evil. Genuine contradictions of this kind can't both be asserted at the same time. You can't say that something is true *and* false, at the same time.[43] Or, if you do, speech ceases to have

Table 4. The Pythagorean table of opposites

unlimited	limit
even	odd
plurality	unity
left	right
female	male
motion	rest
crooked	straight
darkness	light
bad	good
oblong	square

any meaning at all. Contradictions are a feature of human thought or speech.[44]

But contraries, on the other hand, aren't features of speech or thought, but real things, in the real world. These kinds of real contraries, like union and non-union, are "related" and don't cancel each other out.[45] In a pair of contraries (as Thomas Aquinas put it later), "one, in a manner, includes the other." They're both "known through the same notion, for one is known by means of the other."[46] You've already seen this, in the case of union and non-union, which imply – and are therefore necessary to – each other. Contraries are features of the real world, the world about which human speech is spoken, and to which human thoughts refer.

For Aristotle, a flaw in the Pythagorean table was that it mixed up contradictions and contraries.[47] That wasn't the only problem, however. It also presented one column of the table as if it were good, and the other bad.[48] But union and non-union are both goods. Just as you can't say one side of a contrary is true and the other false, you also can't say one side is good and the other bad. They're both permanent and necessary features of the human, and of the human world. The Pythagorean table was based on a sound intuition – the insight that all things are composed of "contraries" (with their ultimate root in the primary contrary of unity and plurality). But it was mistaken about what that insight means or how to express it. Both sides of a true contrary represent "a productive and moving principle."[49] So both sides of a genuine table of opposites must be true *and* good.

This is an insight that's especially important if you want to apply the lens of the virtues to the basic polarity of being, the duality of something and everything. For one thing, it confirms the usefulness of the lens itself. If the basic dualities out of which the world is formed are opposite forms of the good, looking at the nature of the human through the lens of what we consider good behaviour or good habits makes all the more sense. If the contraries which structure our world are contrasting forms of the good, the best way to think about *the human* is probably through conflicting forms of *human* good.

For another thing, it suggests I can begin to construct a map of the human by assembling some of the various ways of expressing the human paradox I just discussed – including some of the modern ones, from Schleiermacher to Charles Taylor – in the kind of corrected table of opposites Aristotle proposed. You can see my initial table of opposites, for the two basic human stances or modes of being, in Table 5, on page 124.

Table 5 shows you how the human world and the humans in it are constructed from a basic contradiction, a duality or contrary – two basic human stances responding to the polarity of being – which has been expressed in a great many different ways (unity and plurality, union and non-union, and so on) from Aristotle and the Pythagoreans, to the present day. But in order to translate this basic human paradox into a more finely grained description of the nature of the human, I need to translate this basic paradox into the specific human behaviours through which it's expressed, and in which it becomes concrete or real, in our human lives. To achieve the kind of map of the human spirit I set out to develop for you in this book, I'll need to create another kind of table of opposites.

Two families of virtues: a table of opposites

Table 5 is a table of the two basic human stances or general modes of being, displayed in contrasting pairs. Now I need to do the same thing for the specific human virtues you began to explore in the last three chapters. I need to translate the basic human stances of Table 5 into the human virtues by which they are expressed in human life. But my exploration of the virtues will need to reflect the same structuring principle. When we consider the virtues, our picture of them will need to reflect both the basic polar structure of being, and also the insight that all contraries are forms of the good. A map of the nature of the human needs to be constructed from pairs of contrasting or conflicting human virtues.[50]

From one point of view, that shouldn't be too hard to do. You already explored the two basic but contrary families of contrary virtues in chapters 4 and 5. And in those two chapters, as in chapter 3, you already saw how often the virtues seem to contradict each other. So putting those contrary virtues together doesn't look, at first, like much of a challenge.

Table 5. The human paradox: two basic human stances

self-assertion	reverence
"*I* am"	"I *am*"
non-union	union
plurality	unity
non-identity/difference	identity
becoming/doing	being
movement/motion	rest
seeking	dwelling
profane	sacred
"active life"	"contemplative life"
immanence	transcendence
happiness/flourishing	fullness/fulfilment
"establish [oneself] as an individual"	"surrender oneself and be absorbed"
"the love that wants to rule"	"the love that wants to obey"
"spit at the stars"	"reverence for all things"
"effecting/winning/overcoming"	"suffering/succumbing/yielding"
"natural detachment"	"natural solidarity of connection"
"creative power"	"revealing love"
"disjunction"	"conjunction"
"liberty"	"love"
"resisting or separated"	"part of the totality"
"individualization"	"participation"
"individuation"	"involvement"
"expand oneself"	"surrender oneself"
"heroic self-assertion"	"fusing with a superior force"
"emerges/separates"	"merges/embeds"
obligations to the "self"	obligations to the "environment"
"selfish"	"social"
"egocentric contractual"	"sociocentric organic"
"self-regarding"	"other-regarding"
"radical individualism"	"disposition to attachment"
"the will of individuals"	"submission to an order"
"the Abraham who questions"	"the Abraham who submits"
"Adam I": dominate the world	"Adam II": serve the world
"drive to walk alone"	"drive to belong"
"need to be fully oneself"	"need for community"
"personal satisfaction and thriving"	"responsiveness to the world"
"immensely selfish"	"significantly generous"
"selfish primates"	"long to be part of something"
"power and violence"	"peace and harmony"
"culture of separation"	"culture of coherence"
"disposition to dominate"	"disposition to nurture"
"culture of self-promotion/Big Me"	"culture of self-effacement/humility"
"immanence perspective"	"transformation perspective"

But, from another point of view, it *is* a real challenge – one of the biggest challenges in this book. Just because two opposite-but-linked virtues contradict each other, that *doesn't* mean *one* particular paradox is the same, or the same kind, as another one. As you'll see later, there are different kinds or levels of contrary virtues. The contradictions I already pointed out in the last three chapters weren't all of the same kind, or at the same level, in the architecture of the human spirit. The paradox of justice and mercy doesn't belong in my first table of opposites, for example. Nor do boldness and prudence, or passion and self-control, or subjective and objective. You'll see later where these paradoxes fit in the geography of the human. If I mix up these different kinds or levels of paradox, my map of the human won't be accurate. It will match up paradoxes which don't belong together – which don't occur or arise at the same level of the human. It will mislead you or miss something important. That's one of the biggest challenges in mapping the human. In the second half of this book, you'll see some examples where otherwise excellent and useful maps of the human make the error of assuming that all contradictions are of the same kind or at the same level in the architecture of the human. And so they aren't entirely accurate or complete.[51]

With that in mind, you can see the first table of opposite virtues – my first map of the human paradox – in Table 6 on pages 126–7.

I want to underline, again, that this table is only another sample list. Even though my lists of virtues in chapters 3, 4, and 5 were only samples, too, they were still very long. If I tried to include all of those virtues, a table of opposites would be too long for a page in this book. Once again, I have to make a selection. A selection from a selection. The left-hand and right-hand columns of this table are only illustrative. Later on, I'll provide you with tables of all the virtues from the previous lists, arranged in their respective families and sub-families of virtues. When you get to the fuller lists, you can work out other potential pairs and contradictions for yourself. But my initial table of opposite virtues, like those in the following chapters, is only representative and suggestive. It is just enough to show you how the virtues balance each other. How they come to us in contrasting pairs, or paradoxes, which, though conflicting, or contrasting, still make their dual claims on us. Claims we can't refuse if we are to be fully, or genuinely, or authentically human.

The virtues in this first table of opposites are, inevitably, somewhat personal, that is, important to me. Other writers have created lists of virtues for their own purposes. James Q. Wilson, for example, focuses on four virtues – sympathy, fairness, self-control, and duty – but

Table 6. The human paradox: two basic families of virtues

self-assertion	reverence
acceptance (as tolerance)	acceptance (as gratitude/respectfulness)
agency/self-reliance	faith(ful)(ness)/hope/trust
attachment (as desire/pride)	detachment (as unselfing)
autonomy	solidarity
belief *that*	belief *in*
belief *that*/conviction	truth
boldness/decisiveness	patience
bravery/courage/heroism	humility/peacefulness/meekness
caution/prudence	hope
certainty/conviction	hope/insight/trust/wisdom
community (as reciprocity/cooperation)	community (as communion, duty)
confidence	awe/trust/faith(ful)(ness)
control/self-reliance/self-realization	devotion/service
cooperation	communion
courage/entitlement/power/strength	humility/modesty
desire	benevolence/devotion/duty
detachment (as objectivity/self-seeking)	attachment (as commitment/communion)
dignity (as respect/rights(-seeking)/ self-control)	dignity (as worthiness/reverence)
economy/frugality	generosity
effort	acceptance/deference/receptivity
entitlement/rights/seeking	giving
equality	deference
equality/fairness	excellence/merit
equanimity	peace(ful)(ness)
eros	agape
expressivism/rationalism	self-giving/unselfing
fairness	forgiveness
forbearance (as self-control)	forbearance (as forgiveness)
freedom/liberty/self-determination	duty/loyalty
freedom *of/to*	freedom *from*
glory (as heroism/honour-*seeking*)	glory (as goodness)
happiness/flourishing	fullness/fulfilment
happiness	joy
happiness/pleasure/intensity	goodness
heroism	benevolence
honour-*seeking*	honour*able*/honour*ing*
impartiality/objectivity	love/devotion
independence/separation	commitment/communion
individualism/individuation	communion/community/solidarity
informality	formality
innovation/change	commitment/loyalty
judgment (as reason/reasonableness)	judgment (as justice/wisdom)
liberality	generosity
liberty/freedom	commitment

(Continued)

Table 6. The human paradox: two basic families of virtues (*Continued*)

self-assertion	reverence
moderation/temperance/self-reliance	generosity
objectivity/subjectivity	identity (as communion)/participation
optimism	hope
patience (as self-control)	patience (as kindness)
pleasure/power	righteousness
pleasure	chastity/purity
power	justice/love
rationalism/rationality/reason/science	wisdom/understanding
reciprocity/rights/self-reliance	charity
respect-*seeking*	respect*able*/respect*ful*
responsibility (as prudence)	responsibility (as duty/love)
rights/entitlement	duty/responsibility
rights-*seeking*	rights-*giving*
self-expression/strength	modesty
self-realization/reliance	benevolence/charity/compassion/concern
self-*seeking*	self-*giving*/selflessness/unselfing
spontaneity	solemnity
tolerance	benevolence
trust-*seeking*	trust*ing*/trust*worthy*

acknowledges that his is an arbitrary selection (chosen "because I have something to say about them"), and that it leaves out many other virtues, such as integrity, courage, and modesty.[52] From his original list of thirty virtues, André Comte-Sponville eliminates those that seem to be covered by other virtues until he gets to his basic list of eighteen, the order of which is determined "by something like intuition" and the "demands of pedagogy, ethics, or aesthetics" rather than by "any deductive or hierarchical scheme."[53] William J. Bennett (b. 1943) structures his *Book of Virtues* according to ten virtues: self-discipline, compassion, responsibility, friendship, work, courage, perseverance, honesty, loyalty, and faith.[54] N.T. Wright focuses on seven virtues that he claims are recognized "by more or less all societies at all times in history" – five of which are virtues of reverence (justice, love, spirituality, beauty, and truth) and two of which are virtues of self-assertion (freedom and power).[55] Deirdre McCloskey (b. 1942) constructs two families of contrasting virtues somewhat similar to mine. But because of McCloskey's literary device of only including words beginning with the letters "P and S," the lists are necessarily incomplete lists of the virtues of self-assertion and of reverence. The "P" list lacks courage, for example. And the "S" list lacks justice and even reverence itself.[56] So neither her two lists nor the two in Table 6 are or could be complete. Hers, like mine, are merely suggestive and illustrative, and serve our particular purposes, even though they point toward exactly the same human realities.

Another thing to keep in mind about Table 6 is that the virtues in the left-hand column are all (in some form or other) manifestations of the human impulse to separation and autonomy (or "non-union"), while the virtues in the right-hand column are all manifestations of the corresponding impulse to attachment and connection (or "union"). In the nature of the human, "non-union" translates into human virtues of *seeking*. "Union" translates into human virtues of *giving*. Every virtue of individualism and autonomy has its corresponding opposite, a virtue of connection and commitment. This is how human behaviour reflects or responds to the basic polarity of being you discovered in chapter 2 – in pairs of contrasting virtues. For every virtue of self-assertion there are one or more virtues of reverence that contradict it, or are in some kind of tension or contrast with it. And vice versa.

The right-hand column in Table 6 (as in Table 5) reflects the reality that, whether we like it or not, we are part of something larger than ourselves, something we did not create and do not control. Our welfare and even our very existence depend on this larger frame.[57] The left-hand column, on the other hand, reflects the fact that, within this larger frame, each of us is still an individual, with our own individual needs and desires, and our individual drive for autonomy and self-development.

I'm going to maintain this left-right structure in *all* the tables and figures in the rest of this book. Whenever you see a table or figure in this book, the more self-asserting side of any pair (i.e., non-union) will be on the left, and the more "reverential" side (i.e., union) will be on the right.[58] That will be true even when I'm talking, primarily, about the virtues of one kind or the other, or some subset of either of them. Because, as you will see, even among the virtues of self-assertion, some are more "reverential" than others. And even among the virtues of reverence, some are more assertive than others. The human paradox goes all the way down.

Another thing to remember about Table 6 is that the table format is helpful, but also slightly misleading. It's helpful because, as you already saw (starting in chapter 3), it allows me to display much longer lists than I can in my circular figures. But it's also misleading because the two columns look the same, and so they also look equal in status. But, from the previous discussion, you know this can't be true. The two families of human virtues aren't "equal," and can't be equal, because one nestles *inside* the other.

The virtues of reverence are the virtues of "union," the habits of human feeling and behaviour associated with a deep awareness of the unity and connectedness of all things. The virtues of self-assertion are the virtues of "non-union," the habits of feeling and behaviour associated with our impulse to freedom, expansion, and self-development. Both are necessary to life, even to biological life, and especially to human life. But only the impulse to union, by definition, can provide a ground to link and nurture them both. Only the virtues of union can unite. The virtues of non-union divide. Yet human reality is a *union* of union and non-union. That's why, both logically and in reality – in our real lives, even if we can't see it or express it – the virtues of reverence have priority over the virtues of self-assertion. They come first because they establish the frame. Self-assertion can only take place within a larger frame. Without that larger frame, there wouldn't be any virtues at all. Because there wouldn't be anything.[59]

Look again at my basic circular image in Figure 11, at the beginning of this chapter. The grey semicircle of self-assertion (which stands for every *something*) is located *inside* the larger circle of reverence because individual things (like ourselves) can only exist within a wider whole. Without that wider, invisible background of other things and being itself, there wouldn't even be a self to assert.

There are two sides to this important insight: external and internal. Externally, the virtues of reverence must come first because, as in my examples of family life or the environment, you can see that nothing individual can come into existence, or be sustained in existence, if there isn't already a larger reality within which to exist.

But the virtues of reverence have the same priority *internally*, within the very self itself. Because self-assertion, by itself – if not balanced or moderated by any shade or hint of reverence (something that's impossible) – would necessarily dissolve the self into conflicting acts of self-assertion.[60] Pure self-assertion or absolute freedom would only lead you to what Hegel called the "disintegrated" self because you wouldn't any longer have a genuine self to which you could be true – just a lot of random acts of self-assertion.[61] In pure self-assertion, paradoxically, "selfhood is lost, and all that remains is different roles played in different situations."[62] In fact, a good image of where pure self-assertion would lead you, on its own, is the symbol placed over the doors of temples dedicated to the Hindu God Shiva: an image of the demon of pure hunger, eating itself up. Or Shakespeare's similar image of pure self-assertion as "a universal wolf" which must turn the whole world into "a universal prey, and last eat up himself."[63]

By themselves, your virtues of self-assertion turn out to be "empty."[64] Because, self-assertion, by itself, can't tell you what to assert yourself *for*. What do you want to use your freedom *for*? What do you want to be equal *for*? Self-assertion, alone, can't tell you.[65] To answer that question, you have to be able to put *value* on something, in order to give yourself a goal or objective for which to use your freedom and your equality. And value can only come from your relationship to something else: to your surrounding community or context, to other people and other things, and to the whole world.[66] "What we want liberty *for*," as Adam Gopnik (b. 1956) puts it, "is the power *to connect with others* as we choose."[67] The true value comes from the connection. It comes from "the working of the human spirit in the morass of existence in which it always at every moment finds itself immersed."[68] From some broader "horizon" or objective.[69] When you *give* yourself to others and to goals and values, your virtues of self-assertion have turned into virtues of reverence. And, in the practice of these virtues, you can begin to give your own self some internal coherence and consistency. You will no longer be just a random assembly of conflicting acts of self-assertion, but a genuine self, capable of committing yourself to people, things, and habits – and therefore able to put them ahead of your random impulses of self-assertion. Able to become a consistent self.[70]

This is perhaps the ultimate human paradox. Even for the creation of the self, the virtues of reverence must have priority. Without them the ego may be able assert itself. It can seek its own power and pleasure. But it can't do so in the coherent or consistent way that might justify us in speaking of a genuine "self."[71] So it turns out that your "unattached will" can't be "a prime source of value" for you.[72] Genuine self-assertion requires a "self." And to construct such a self, you'll need the virtues of reverence.[73]

Both internally and externally – in the construction of the very "self" itself, as well as in its relationship to other things and people, and to the totality of being – the virtues of reverence must have priority over the virtues of self-assertion. Union must come before non-union. The grey semicircle of self-assertion finds itself *inside* the broader circle of reverence.

Only the first step

By applying the lens of the virtues to the initial polarity of being, my exploration of the nature of the human has now given you both a basic circular image of the human, three initial lists of human virtues, and two first-level tables of opposites – two basic human stances and two families of virtues through which the stances are expressed – my first, high-level maps of the human. Two tables that reflects the paradox from which we began: the paradox of unity and plurality, of something and everything.

But this is only a first step in a much more complex story. Because that initial paradox doesn't stop working here. As you began to see in chapters 4 and 5, it goes all the way down.

In the next chapter I'll start to explore how the polar structure of being yields a much more complicated map of the human.

7

Paradox Breeds Paradox

In the last chapter, I used the lens of the human virtues to show how the polarity of being shapes the nature of the human. This approach made it possible to develop both a basic image of the human and a sample list of human virtues arranged in a table of opposites. A table that reflects the polar structure of reality from which we began: the paradox of unity and plurality, of union and non-union, of something and everything, of self and world.

But this isn't the end of the story. As far as the geography of the human is concerned, it's only the beginning. Because the initial paradox keeps on working. It keeps on working for one simple reason: because of the polarity of being. If all reality is shaped by a basic polarity of being, the same polarity must be reflected in everything real: *including the original paradox itself*. In other words, the two poles of the paradox should *themselves* have two poles. And so should *their* two poles. And so on. *Ad infinitum.*

In his typically abstract language, Hegel summed up this process in a single, famous sentence: "Something becomes an other; this other is itself somewhat; therefore it likewise becomes an other, and so on *ad infinitum.*"[1] You may find this sentence pretty dense. But don't worry – I'm going to unpack it over the rest of this book, starting in this chapter.

Separative projection

Hegel calls the process his terse sentence aims to describe "intro-Reflection." It's a process by which the two contrary sides inherent in everything strive to make themselves independent from each other. Yet these two (independent) sides inevitably end up retaining the original opposition "in themselves."[2] Bradley's name for the "process of intestine division" that Hegel calls "intro-Reflection" is external and internal "relation."[3] Whitehead's term for the same thing is "coordinate division."[4] But in this book, I'm going to use the expression "separative projection," associated with Samuel Taylor Coleridge, one of the greatest writers and thinkers of the English language.[5] All reality is structured, Coleridge argued, by an "essential dualism" or "polarity": by the tendency "at once to individuate and to connect, to detach, but so as either to retain or to reproduce attachment."[6] All reality is structured, that is to say, by the twin dynamics of separation and connection (or individuation and involvement) I've already identified in this book, starting in chapter 2. The poles of each duality appear at first to be a unity. But, on closer inspection, each of them splits apart, generating its own internal poles.[7] And these new polarities are themselves polarized in turn, producing their own two poles. This pattern continues, in an exponential or unending process of self-division or "separative projection." It is "separative" because of the tendency of each pole of a duality to "separate" into its *own* two poles. It is a "projection" because this process goes on indefinitely, continually expanding and "projecting" itself into the future, widening the range of dualities at every successive level of the process.[8] By this potentially infinite process, Coleridge suggests, nature and life rise through stages of increasing complexity, as if by "concentric circles," through the "perpetual reconciliation" and, *at the same time*, "perpetual resurgency of the primary contradiction, of which universal polarity is the result and exponent."[9]

The concept of "separative projection" is one of the few "technical" terms I'm going to use in this book, so it's important for me to give you a pretty good idea of how it works.

Think of a family tree. At each generation, a family tree splits apart into new families. But these new families still remain parts or branches of the original family. "Separative projection" works just like that. It's the tendency of everything to split apart, externally and internally, in a way that nonetheless preserves attachment, at each new level of separation. Just like a family tree. A family tree doesn't always exhibit the regular, balanced parallelism you'll see in this book, as "separative projection" works its way through the human virtues. But it's a helpful visual representation of a very similar process, in which each successive level divides itself, while remaining part of the original unity.

R.G. Collingwood (1889–1943) offers another concrete illustration of how this process works:

Hold up a stick, and distinguish its top and its bottom: there you have a concrete synthesis of opposites in an individual whole. Take a knife and cut it in two in the middle, into a top half and a bottom half. You have now

separated the opposites. But the instant the separation is complete, the top
half has its own bottom and the bottom half its own top. The top half is no
longer simply a top and the bottom half no longer simply a bottom; each is
at once a top and a bottom, each is indistinguishable from the other. Your
opposites have now coincided.[10]

Hegel himself offers a very similar illustration, using the image of a
magnet: "The north pole of a magnet cannot be without the south pole,
and vice versa. If we cut a magnet in two, we have not a north pole in
one piece and a south pole in the other."[11] The two halves of the original
magnet now have their own two poles. And if we were to split these
two, we would now have four, each with its own two poles. The human
paradox is simply a very high form of this process.

And since the human paradox shapes everything human, the two
basic families of human virtues I've identified so far should themselves
be subject to the same paradox. That is to say, each of the two initial
poles of the human paradox ought to generate its own internal poles.
And those four poles should, in turn, generate still more poles.

And, in fact, they do.[12]

From "*I* am" to "I *am*": the great reversal

I can begin to map how the initial human paradox breeds still more
paradoxes, by looking again at my basic circular figure, in the form of
Figure 10 on page 79. In that image, you saw that the polar structure of
being generates two basic human stances or modes of being, of which
the virtues of reverence and the virtues of self-assertion are the expression in human behaviour: the stances of "*I* am" and "I *am*." These two
stances express the fundamental reality that I am an individual person,
yet I also *share* my being with the world that surrounds me. I'm part of
something else, and even of *everything* else, part of a wider totality and
mystery of being without which I couldn't exist.

This way of putting it seems to give priority to the human stance of
"I *am*," and that is ultimately the right way to think about it, as you saw
at the end of the previous chapter. It appropriately reflects the prior
condition – of being – without which I could not *be*.

But in real life, the story seems to be much more complicated than
that. It's complicated because, from the human point of view, the process begins the other way around. And because it also reverses itself,
more than once.

The starting point for the human wasn't, and isn't, the human stance
of "I *am*," but rather, "*I* am." But then, in the early stages both of human

civilization and of our own individual human lives, this first human stance got – and gets – quickly covered up and is only gradually redis- covered. Once the original human stance is rediscovered, however, it can, and often does, seem to take over almost completely, in conscious- ness at least, if not completely in behaviour. When this happens, it can be a huge challenge to rediscover the logically (and "existentially") prior stance of "I *am*," the underlying reality that makes everything possible.

Let's see if I can unravel this very complicated story in an under- standable way, with the help of some schematic images. I'm going to be using some quite abstract words and concepts in this chapter. I want to sketch for you the enduring structural and dynamic relationships between the various stances that constitute the nature of the human, as well as how each of these stances may have provided the dominant lens for stages in the evolution of human and Western culture. Each stance is a way of *being human*. To see the "logic" of their relationships requires a high level of abstraction. But I hope the figures can provide a clearer idea of the realities I'm trying to describe. Although the words may be abstract, the human stances they aim to express are the fundamental pillars of the nature of the human. As a result, they have also been de- cisive in the evolution of human culture, and they continue to have a profound impact on our contemporary Western world and on our own individual lives.

First of all, the human story – our story – has to start from the human stance I called "*I* am," rather than from the stance of "I *am*." The emphasis is on *I*, in this first human stance, rather than on *am*. Be- cause everything human – *all* human action – is, by definition, a form of self-assertion. To act is to assert yourself, or the self, so you can't do *anything* – not even live or breathe – except, in the first instance, as acts of self-assertion.[13] Everything human – or even animal – begins with "*I* am."[14]

This is very important to bear clearly in mind at the start, because many things can work to obscure it or to confuse the picture. In the last three chapters, I've introduced you to two primary families of virtues, which I called the virtues of self-assertion and the virtues of reverence. This way of putting it makes it sound as if these two families of human behaviours were completely separate: as if you could act, at one time, according to the virtues of self-assertion, and, at another, according to a completely different and opposite set of virtues, the virtues of rever- ence. But, if *all* human action is a form of self-assertion, that can't be true. Or not quite the right way to think about it or express it. Rever- ence can't be an *alternative* to self-assertion. It must instead be a *kind* of

self-assertion. *Even the virtues of reverence must be forms of self-assertion.*[15]
I'll come back to what this means and its significance in a moment. But
here, the point I want to emphasize – and that is so important to get
clear – is that everything starts in the grey semicircle. Everything human starts from the stance of "*I am.*"[16]

But for humans, as you saw at the end of Chapter 3, that's just the beginning. Somewhere, very early in the history of the human race, and in
an individual life, action in the world – acts of self-assertion – teach human beings that they aren't just isolated selves. They are, instead, part
of a larger reality on which their welfare and even their very existence
depend: a family, a hunting band, a tribe, a clan, a community, a village,
a kingdom, a country, a planet, everything. This happens so early in our
own lives and in human history that the initial stance of self-assertion
seems to become rapidly obscured. Instead, the dominant early awareness, in both individual lives and human history, is probably of belonging to something larger than the individual, something on which the
survival of the individual depends, and which, at the earliest stages of
human life, may not even be distinguished from the individual at all.
I'm not just an isolated individual but part of something larger to which
I belong, something that creates even the possibility of a "me."

In the case of an infant, for example, despite the fact that its first
acts – its first cry, the first intake of air into the lungs – are *already* acts of
self-assertion,[17] "the first components of a sense of self do not emerge
until late in the second year."[18] Prior to that, its first awareness or state
of consciousness seems to be one of "attachment" or "connectedness."[19]
As a child grows, she has to learn to differentiate herself from others
before she can learn to relate to them.[20] Very young children can even
attribute to themselves, in retrospect, actions that were, in reality, performed by someone else. So one of the earliest processes of our human
lives is the "emergence of a sense of self from an initial condition lacking distinctiveness."[21]

The earliest humans seem to have gone through a similar shift, analogous to infants and toddlers. The culture of the higher primates from
which we emerged was a culture of self-assertion, a culture of domination by alpha males, and of submission by others to their domination.
You can still see this culture today in an unneutered dog pack. Of course,
that doesn't make dogs simply "brutes." If they were, we wouldn't love
them as we do. We love them because they also display many other behaviours, many of which resemble us at our best. Like dogs, our animal
ancestors (especially the primates) already exhibit many behaviours –
such as nurturing, care, concern, empathy, and play – that became the
foundation for important human virtues that, together, establish a

second side to our nature.[22] But in the animal world, these are still expressed within an overall culture of self-assertion and domination.[23] This is the human stance of "*I* am," what Hegel calls the "natural man" of appetite and pure "self-seeking."[24] But somewhere, perhaps around 250,000 BCE, early humans began to hunt large mammals in groups or bands, and to do this effectively – and therefore cooperatively – they had to develop a new kind of band or (later) tribal culture: no longer the self-assertive culture of hierarchy and domination, but a new culture that emphasized and enhanced some of the *contrary* dispositions of the higher primates – a culture of community, based on "sharing" the spoils of the hunt. They had to develop a culture of "I *am*."

In the evolution of human culture from prehistoric foraging cultures to hunting bands and, later, tribal societies and smaller chiefdoms, the initial self-assertive domination by individuals gave way to the dominance of the group itself. Those groups that developed higher levels of cooperation, sharing, and even generosity were more likely to survive than those that didn't. Natural selection by *individual* self-assertion was now balanced by natural selection at the *group* level. This process of "multilevel" selection altered the nature of the human – or revealed its true potential, inherited from our animal ancestors. The evolutionary process of natural selection now selected not just for self-assertion but also for social interaction, cooperation, and even self-sacrifice.[25] Between 250,000 BCE and about 50,000 BCE, some 7–8,000 generations of genetic selection seem to have gradually built a new disposition into the biological nature of the human: a disposition for attachment, belonging, loyalty, nurture, and generosity, generosity not only to family members but even to non-kin – a disposition for self-*giving*, or for what I have called reverence. This new disposition didn't eliminate our original disposition for self-*seeking* or self-assertion, but balanced and controlled it – sometimes even suppressed or submerged it – within the primacy of the group.[26] This new human disposition amounted to a shift in emphasis – from the original human stance of "*I* am" to a new stance of "I *am*."

Both the infant and the early human have the sense not just of being "me" but – even more – of simply "being," a state in which self and world are the same or share in the same being. Part of the same mysterious reality.[27] I can picture the logic of this process as in Figure 13 on page 138.

Some writers have called this second human stance an "I/Thou" or "I-and-Thou" relationship. And this isn't wrong. That's certainly where it leads or points. But beneath this kind of relationship is an even deeper awareness of a shared being or life: the emerging awareness not

Figure 13. *I* am to I *am*

only that "*I* am" – the outlook from which human beings started their evolutionary journey – but also that "I *am*."[28] That I am a living being in a world of being, and hence of other living beings. This crucial, early transition in the nature of the human has been rightly called "a confrontation *of life with life*."[29]

This second human stance is associated with impulses to sharing, participation, belonging, and identity. And these impulses are what set the stage, both in adults and in early human societies, for the virtues of reverence. As you've already seen, reverence is the habit of feeling and behaviour that expresses awareness and acceptance of our place in this larger whole, or oneness. Reverence is the spirit – the attitude, feeling, or purpose – that accompanies some actions, some acts of self-assertion, and transforms these acts of self-assertion into acts of reverence, also.

Reverence doesn't eliminate self-assertion. There might well be virtues of self-assertion with only very little reverence. But there can be no virtues of reverence *at all* without self-assertion.[30] Reverence is a quality which is *added to*, and hence *modifies*, what are still virtues of self-assertion. The inside, the moving power, of these human acts remains self-assertion. Without self-assertion, there would be no act at all. But what the self is now asserting itself *toward*, or *for*, is reverence.[31] Depending on the degree of its presence, reverence gradually turns these virtues of self-assertion *into their opposite*. The highest acts of self-assertion are acts of reverence. And the highest acts of reverence are heroic acts of self-assertion.[32]

In its cultural and adult (though not its infant) forms, this second human stance toward the world involves a sense of belonging to something, something to which I give myself. The movement from the human stance of "*I* am" to the stance of "I *am*" is a move from a world of self-*seeking* to a world of self-*giving*.[33] I do not give for a reason but simply *for the sake of giving itself.* Because "I *am.*" Because I share in, and am part of, or a member of, or related to, or participate in something *other* than me, but which nevertheless makes me *me.*[34] Indeed, for much of human history a sense of the priority of the whole seems to have largely obliterated or obscured the reality of the individual, even though self-assertion remains the unseen, subterranean source or form of all human action.[35]

The shift of emphasis from "I" to "am" – in both infant and prehistoric life – may seem like a tiny difference, a mere difference of emphasis. And yet it makes a whole world of difference. A difference between cultures, between civilizations, between periods of human history, between different ways of thinking and living, between different ways of being human.

From "I *am*" to 'It *is*"

This tiny shift of emphasis, making a whole world of difference, repeats itself once again in another mode. The initial movement – from the stance of "*I* am" to the stance of "I *am*" – leads eventually to a much more complex picture.

In the story of the human, this is where the process of "separative projection" really begins to kick in. It kicks in because continued experience of the wider mystery to which we belong – which is *ours* – inevitably suggests to human beings that this larger mystery to which we belong may have what could be called (a little prematurely) "objective" features.[36] It's not just that things *are*, and are *ours*. But they also have desirable or meritorious features *of their own.* They are also true or good or beautiful. The goodness of belonging to my family or tribe makes me implicitly aware of *goodness itself.*[37] My own acts of nurture, sharing, and self-giving, and those of my family, tribe, or clan, suggest to me not just the goodness of my giving or theirs, but even the idea of *giving itself*, of which mine is only a distant imitation or approximation. We don't have to give ourselves to this wider or other reality simply because I *am*, but also because "It *is*."[38] Because this wider reality has its *own* reality, its own existence, its own *being.*[39] A being that *deserves* my giving. It merits and earns it. There is something *due*. There is an external standard of excellence to which I not only belong but also willingly *give* or devote myself.[40] Because of its own value, its own *excellence*.

I can picture this second movement – the second stage of "separative projection," in the nature of the human – as in Figure 14 on page 140.

In Figure 14, you can see that the human stance of "I *am*" – which sprang, inevitably or necessarily, from the initial and opposite stance of

Figure 14. I *am* to It *is*

"*I* am" – has now begun to reveal its *own* internal polarities. Because of what Coleridge calls the tendency "to detach, but so as either to retain or to reproduce attachment" (or what Hegel calls "intro-Reflection"), the polarity of being, the paradox of separation and connection, now begins to reproduce itself at this new level. And will go on reproducing itself, all the way down.

I call this next human stance "It *is*." If the first or primitive truth for human beings is "I am," the second is "It is." You can understand why "It is" must be the second truth for human beings in the same way you saw it for "I am." Consider how you would respond to everyday questions about the world, such as "What's the weather like today?" Or "How do you like your dinner?" Or "How far is it to the next town?" Or "Is our flight on time?" To questions like these you would probably answer: "It's raining." Or "It's delicious." Or "It's about twenty-five miles." Or "It's going to be late." And what do these answers all have in common? Once again, they all start with a premise: "It is." Any statement about the world includes (implicitly or, in these English cases, explicitly) the statement "It is." It presupposes that "It is." If the world didn't exist, it couldn't have or exhibit any of these qualities or realities. So being has to come first, again. It comes before any fact, or action, or truth about the world. Any kind of true statement is, first and foremost, a statement about being: its truth is still "convertible" with being. "It is" is therefore the second fundamental truth for human beings.

But notice that "It is" has two words, like "I am." And, as in the case of "I am," it makes a difference which one you emphasize: whether you stress the noun or the verb. If you stress the verb, you are, once again, emphasizing the being of the world and the things in it, the mysterious fact that there is something, rather than nothing: "It *is*." If you put the accent on the noun rather than the verb, you focus instead on the thingness of the thing, on its very itness: "*It* is." At this second stage of separative projection, the accent is still, for the time being, on the verb: on being rather than on what is.

It's very important to grasp this second manifestation of "separative projection" because it introduces a new tension that plays a critical role in the development of the human, a tension that's very easy to overlook or to misunderstand. Many of the conflicts in the world today are rooted in our failure to notice and appreciate both the inevitability and the importance of this tension. The human stance of "I *am*" (reflected and expressed in human life through the virtues of reverence) has its own *internal* paradox: a tension between the initial impulse of reverence itself, on the one hand, and the excellence or goodness to which reverence is directed, on the other: a tension between "I *am*" and "It *is*." The existence of this tension explains a great deal about the nature and reasons for conflict within and between different religious traditions, and between religious and non-religious ways of life. I'll come back to this important tension in chapter 16.

For the moment, however, let's continue exploring how the polar structure of being continues to work through the process of "separative projection," introducing further contradictions and tensions in the nature of the human.

If the initial shift from the human stance of "*I* am" to the stance of "I *am*" occurred because of the emergence of band and tribal cultures, the cultural change that brought about a shift from the stance of "I *am*" to "It *is*" was the emergence of the first hierarchical societies – larger chiefdoms, kingdoms, and states – and the new religious traditions they spawned.

In the new human stance of these hierarchical cultures – the stance of "It *is*" – the emphasis is still on the action or the verb, on "*is*": on the act of existence or being. The emphasis is still on being and belonging. But what now emerges is not just the fact of existence but also the independent reality of being, its external otherness and goodness, an independent standard of excellence which commands my admiration and allegiance, excellence to which something is *due*.[41] A new, "objective" otherness has begun to be introduced, an external source of authority, truth, and value. A standard to be met or a law to which we are subject.[42]

The emergence of this new element – an external "It" – is a fateful shift in the development of the human, ripe with new possibilities.

For one thing, it introduces a principle of *otherness*, which makes possible the emergence of the later religions, especially the Western religious traditions. The God who announces Himself to Moses on Mount Sinai calls Himself "I AM," reflecting the human stance of "I *am*" and its associated virtues of self-*giving*: the virtues He demands of His people.[43] But His very majestic *otherness* and uniqueness, and His casting these virtues in the form of the Law, make clear that He appears to them, now, within a new cultural stage: a new cultural stage I call "It *is*."[44]

This fateful discovery of a new human stance – beyond "I *am*" to "It *is*" – was even more clearly announced, at the very beginning of Greek civilization, by the early Greek thinker, Parmenides of Elea (ca. 515–450 BCE). In the third line of Parmenides' *Way of Truth* – the earliest Greek example of sustained philosophical reasoning[45] — you will find a momentous new declaration about reality: "*it is*."[46] Parmenides' new human stance – based on the starting point of "It is" – shows that Greek culture had moved beyond – or skipped over – the "I AM" of the people of Israel. This new culture of "It *is*" became the default culture of the ancient world, including Greek and Roman cultures, and remained the heart of Western culture until the end of the Middle Ages.

From "It *is*" to "*It* is"

In medieval culture, the otherness Parmenides had discovered in the human stance of "It *is*" prepared the ground for the movement of Western culture, beyond its ancient and medieval forms, to the modern and post-modern world. The human stance of "It *is*" opened the door to yet another cultural stage. Just as an awareness of the goodness inherent in the family or tribe could make human beings aware of goodness itself, now awareness of the *otherness* of goodness makes them aware – increasingly aware – of *otherness itself*. The awareness of otherness – awareness of an independent reality that first developed when the mystery of *being* was dominant – prepares a new stance toward the world, a stance in which attention is focussed no longer on the *being* or existence of this otherness, but on the otherness itself, on the independent reality of things. Not their being, but their *thingness*.[47]

In terms of the human stances it implies or entails, this new cultural shift is equivalent, schematically, to yet another shift of emphasis between subject and verb. "It *is*," like "I *am*," is composed of two words with the emphasis on the second. But, just as the stance of "I *am*" emerged from the earlier stance of "*I* am" by what amounted, culturally, to a shift of emphasis from the noun to the verb, the emergence of

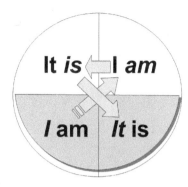

Figure 15. It *is* to *It* is

the human stance of "It *is*" in Western culture opened the door to yet another shift of emphasis. The cultural equivalent of a shift backward, from the verb to the noun: from "It *is*" to "*It* is."[48] The otherness implicit in the human stance of "It *is*" led, eventually, to a new stance of "*It* is."[49]

The culture of this new human stance of "*It* is" is the culture that developed, in the Western world, between the end of the Middle Ages and the beginning of the nineteenth century, the culture we especially associate with the scientific revolution of the seventeenth century and the European Enlightenment of the eighteenth century, the culture that culminates in Isaac Newton (1643–1727), Kant, and Hegel.

In this culture, the primary perception that "*It* is" heralds and expresses a new stance toward the physical world. The natural world is no longer simply the expression of being but assumes a separate life of its own. Nature becomes an *object*, not a *subject*, an object that can be studied objectively. It can be separated from the background of being and looked at objectively, that is to say, as an object – an "it" – not just as an expression of being.[50] But the same thing works in reverse, too: confronted with an objective nature, human beings are now free to discover themselves as potential natural *objects*.[51] The "I," too, becomes an "it" – merely an element in a proposition or in a natural process.[52]

I can picture the discovery of the fourth human stance as in Figure 15 above.

This new, distinctively Western stance of "*It* is" is a hugely important development, both for itself and for what it eventually spawns, by way of reaction. The cultural shift pictured schematically in Figure 15 is only the first step to something else. Both conceptually and historically, this process puts Western culture on a fateful path back toward its original human starting point.[53]

Figure 16. *It* is to *I* am

From "*It* is" to "*I* am"

The new Western Enlightenment stance of "*It* is" opens the door to yet another dramatic shift in the Western outlook, similar to the earlier shift from "*I am*" to "It *is*," but in reverse. The fourth stance of "*It* is" – which emerges from the prior human stance of "It *is*" – can now work its way forward to another human stance – taking Western culture "back" to the place where human life emerged from its animal origins: to something resembling the initial human stance of "*I* am."

This latest shift occurs because, in the stance of "*It* is," Westerners are confronted by an "objective" nature and come face to face with their *own* otherness, not just as objects but also as individual *subjects*. They rediscover their *own* independent reality, their own individuality, and their own assertive power. The stance of "*It* is" leads back – or forward – to "*I* am." The emergence of the objective otherness of the physical world prepares the way for a fourth shift: back to the human starting point, back to the original human stance in the world – or to something like it. This is the post-modern culture in which we are now beginning to live.

I can picture this latest discovery – the fourth step in the evolution of the Western human spirit – as in Figure 16 above.

The two human stances of "*It* is" and "*I* am" go together and reinforce each other. As I already pointed out in chapter 4, an objective nature confronts and creates (i.e., causes human beings to feel the reality – or illusion – of their own) individual egos. The individual ego confronts and "creates" (i.e., perceives the otherness of) an objective nature. The virtues of self-assertion and the emergence of an objective natural world go hand in hand, for better and for worse. The discovery of an objective world in ancient Greece and Rome – filtered through and augmented by Christianity's own discovery of the individual soul – prepared the way for the scientific revolution of the seventeenth century and the rationalism of the Enlightenment. But both of these also prepared the way for the newly assertive, possessive, and expressive individualism of the post-modern anti-Enlightenment.

The four human stances

I have now constructed a map of the four basic human stances. As I mentioned in the Introduction, I've been able to do that because the process of Western cultural evolution I've just described in these figures also reveals a basic truth about the human. It reveals the basic structure, the four possible stances of human beings toward the polarity of being, the four different ways of being human, in a human world.[54] It shows us the whole nature of the human, which can be found in every age and in each one of us.[55]

The four human stances toward the polarity of being are structured by two different modes of "I am" and two modes of "It is." In philosophical language, I could call the first two the "existential" stances, and the second two the "ontological" stances. In other words, the first two reflect and express, primarily, the being of the *self*. The second two reflect and express, primarily, the being of the *world*.

To help you intuitively grasp the underlying difference between the two linked stances of "I am" and the two of "It is," consider the different stances you can adopt toward your own body. You can approach your own body as a physical reality, a thing among things ("It is"), or you can approach it as your *own*, as "mine" ("I am"). Your body is at one and the same time both a "fact" of the world ("It is") and also the living, feeling expression of a unique subject ("I am") who doesn't belong merely to the objects you may perceive or toward which you may act ("It is"). You can think of your body as "mine" ("I am") or as merely a body among other bodies ("It is"). If the only stance available to you were the stance of "It is," you would reduce yourself to nothing more than a thing among things. The "who" of who you *really* are ("I am") would be completely captured and submerged by the "what" ("It is"). But that wouldn't do justice to the unique, living, feeling, loving, responsible person you are. In order to do justice to yourself as an individual, irreplaceable person – in order to be fully human – you can't just approach your body from the stance of "It is." You also require the alternative human stance of "I am."[56]

In chapter 17, I'll come back to these two necessary ways of being human: the "existential" stances of "I am" and the "ontological" stances of "It is." The important point here – to prepare the way for the next few chapters – is that, because of separative projection, they each have their own two internal forms: "*I* am" and "I *am*," on the one hand, and "*It* is" and "It *is*," on the other. Now, obviously, I don't mean, here or elsewhere, that someone, somewhere, actually parsed these simple, two-word statements, at various points in historical time, and consciously decided to shift the emphasis from the subject to the verb, then to change subject, and then to shift the emphasis, again, from the verb to the subject. These are just shorthand ways of expressing both the "logical" relationships between permanent realities of being – the four corners of the nature of the human – and deep, complex, social, and cultural processes. "I am" and "It is," with their four potential emphases, are merely verbal devices or labels. But they also identify genuine human realities: the four possible human stances toward the polarity of being. What the deep historic processes of Western cultural evolution added up to, or signified, was precisely the shifts between these four possible human stances.[57]

As you will see in later chapters, this map can become – and indeed must become – much more complex, as the dynamic of separative projection works its way down through the various levels of being, spawning paradox upon paradox. But this four-part schema will furnish my basic image of the human, reflecting the four basic stances that inevitably arise as we encounter ourselves *and* the reality by which we are encompassed, both visible and invisible, both seen and unseen.

I can now fix the first form of this basic image, as in Figure 17 on page 147.

In Figure 17, you'll notice that I've now given each of the four quadrants a designation: A1 and A2, B1 and B2. This will help me to do several things as the book proceeds. It will help me to remind you that, regardless of the language or the labels I may use at different times or in different chapters, I'm still referring to these four quadrants, these four basic human stances. The elements or names to be included in the quadrants will change, for different purposes, or for different arguments, or in different contexts. But they will always refer to – or take their place within – these four human stances, the four basic ways of being human, which emerge from the polar structure of being: from the paradox of unity and plurality, of something and everything, of self and other, or self and world. That's the purpose of my graphical approach.

Figure 17. Four human stances

The four quadrants of the basic figure (with their constant labels of A1, A2, B1, and B2) will show you how this same fourfold nature of the human is reproduced and reflected in many diverse forms of human life. If I tried to do it in words alone, you'd find the continuity between many frameworks and fields much harder to grasp. These labels give me a shorthand way of referring to the four corners of the human – the four basic human stances – and will allow me to point them out when they crop up in other contexts or in the thought and writing of other thinkers through the ages.

The short-form labels for the four quadrants will also help to highlight the links between the top quadrants and the bottom quadrants. Because of the form of my circular figure – the grey semicircle against a white background – and because of the natural unity of the two stances (self-assertion and reverence) it portrays – it would be very easy to see the horizontal linkages between the top (white) quadrants and the bottom (grey) ones and overlook the potential vertical or the diagonal links. I want to emphasize all three in this book. In some chapters the vertical links will be just as important as the horizontal links. And in others I'll highlight the diagonal links. The labels of A1 and A2 and of B1 and B2 will help me illustrate the diagonal unities within the stances of "I am" and of "It is," as well as the two types of linkages between reverence and self-assertion: both horizontal and vertical.

They will also help remind you of the order in which you discovered them in this chapter: the dynamic that starts from the initial human stance of "I am" and leads through "I *am*" to "It *is*," then to "*It* is," and thus back to the starting point of "*I* am." Hegel calls this dynamic progression the "procession of spirit."[58] Other thinkers have used similar or other terms for it.[59] But because I'm using the lens of the virtues to describe the nature of the human, I'm going to call this pattern (the shape of a figure of eight, in Figure 16) the "arrow of virtue."[60] The letters and numbers assigned to the four quadrants in Figure 17 should help you to keep the flight of this arrow – its direction – in mind.

Double vision: the four human stances from two perspectives

The flight of the arrow of virtue I've just described – with its movement from the initial human stance of "*I* am" (A1) to "I *am*" (A2) to "It *is*" (B1) to "*It* is" (B2), and finally back to "*I* am" (A1) – introduces a new wrinkle in my story of the human. It creates both the potential and the need for a sort of "double vision." A double vision that's very important for this book – and for understanding the full nature of the human – but can be confusing, and difficult to grasp. In order to describe the nature of the human, I need to make this double vision clear to you, with the help of a new image.

The complicating feature I call "double vision" arises from the fact that the four human stances described in this chapter can be seen from two different perspectives. They can be regarded either historically or metaphysically. The four human stances toward the polarity of being have both a historical *and* a permanent character. That is to say, each of them serves as the primary mode – the dominant lens – of the human during a specific period in the evolution of Western civilization. But all of them are permanent and enduring aspects of the human, present and available to human beings in every age. Each stance can be viewed as a phase or stage in the development of our Western idea of the human. But they aren't *just* stages. They also have a permanent reality, both then and now.[61] All four stances were available, as part of the full repertoire of the human, in each of those stages or phases along the way. And they still are today. They are the four enduring modes or corners of the human.[62]

Without something additional, Figure 16 on page 144 could give you a wrong impression. It could encourage you to think that, in each successive stage in the progress of the arrow of virtue, only one cultural lens or human stance is available. And it could also allow you to think that, when the arrow of virtue moves on to a new phase, the previous stances are over and done with. Nothing could be further from the truth about the nature of the human.

In the Introduction, I mentioned that Hegel describes human cultural evolution as a spiral: a circular pattern of development in which human beings move through familiar forms or stages, but at progressively higher levels or perspectives.[63] At each turn of the spiral, says Hegel, the process I've called the arrow of virtue "begins all over again." But it begins again, this time, "at a higher level," just like a spiral staircase.[64] And Hegel also suggested that each of these stages – or landings on the spiral staircase – is an image of the whole pattern, the whole nature of the human.[65] The whole circular or spiral pattern of human development is fully present and visible, in a "simplified" or "abbreviated" form, in any one of the human stages or cultures along this road.[66]

That's very similar to the process I've described in this book (but not identical, as you'll see in chapter 15).[67] So, in order to give you an idea of how Western cultural development follows the flight of the arrow of virtue – yet *all four* human stances toward the polarity of being can still be present and available *at every step* along the way – I need to offer you an image of that historical, spiral process Hegel identified. I need to turn Figure 16 into something more like a 3D image. The added third dimension should show you how *all the content* of Figure 16 can be present and available in *all of its constituent stages* or stances.

You can see a first spiral image in Figure 18 on page 150. (I'll show you others later, in chapters 10 and 15.)

As you look at Figure 18, notice, first, that the spiral represents a temporal progression, so the top images of the four human stances come later in the sequence, at higher levels of the spiral staircase. Notice also that the arrow pierces the circular disk of the human paradox in different places at each level. It passes through different quadrants, in succession: *I* am (A1), I *am* (A2), It *is* (B1), *It* is (B2), and back to *I* am (A1). This feature of Figure 18 is meant to express that one corner of the human is highlighted or dominant at each level of the spiral: it's the lens through which humans see *all four* basic human stances, which remain fully present and available at that time (or at that stage in the process), even if one of them is the primary lens for the others.[68]

This tendency to view all four corners of the human through only one lens isn't something that only happens historically. It also happens in today's world. When contemporary thinkers seek to "explain" everything according to material or (what Aristotle called) efficient causes, or when they assume – or even assert – that Enlightenment rationalism is the final word in human understanding, for example, they

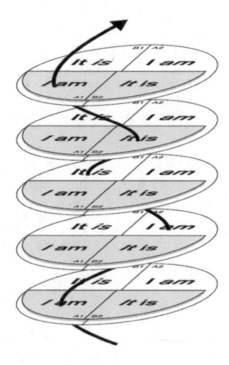

Figure 18. The four human stances as a temporal spiral

are simply viewing the human world through one kind of "double vision." They are viewing the whole nature of the human – all four corners of the human – through only one lens: from the stance of "*It* is" (B2). They are viewing the world from the point of view of the second highest level in Figure 18.[69]

To balance this contemporary kind of "double vision," you should keep in mind that, at the higher or later levels of the spiral, you can now "see" all the others, just the way you can look down from the top of a spiral staircase and see all its lower landings. That's another reason a spiral image of human evolution is helpful. It expresses, visually, that when the arrow of virtue restarts its upward climb from a new level, it doesn't have to start again just the way it did the first time. A culture which has reached this point has already progressed through previous human stances, so it should be able to advance with a widened awareness. Though a new stance may now be dominant, it doesn't rule alone. It carries the memory and experience – not to mention the current reality – of the others. The cycle can start again, as Hegel says, at a higher level, with a richer, fuller idea of human potential. A culture can move forward with awareness of the increasing range of the human, and of the other previous stances that are also part of the repertoire of the human.

Hegel's vision of the "spiral" of Western cultural development raises the question of what happens when the arrow of virtue has worked its way through all four human stances toward the polarity of being. Does the whole spiral process begin all over again? Hegel sometimes seems to suggest (or imply) that it does. Sometimes he appears to assume it doesn't. I'll come back to the question of where the Western story may go next in later chapters of the book.

The invisible background of being

Now that I've identified four basic human stances toward the polarity of being – and suggested how they may have shifted through the evolution of Western culture – my next task is to explore how they are reflected within the two families of virtues I discussed in chapters 4 and 5: how these stances launch a cascading series of polarities within both of them.[70] I'll begin to do that in the next chapter. But before I turn to that challenge, I want to take a moment to remind you of something that's crucial for understanding the journey ahead.

Look again at Figure 17 on page 147. As I discussed, the grey semicircle stands for you and me and every individual person or thing in the universe. You will also remember that the grey semicircle is entirely *inside* the surrounding white circle, which stands for the background of *everything else*, the invisible background of being within which every individual thing or person exists. And remember – everything really does mean *every*thing. Not just everything visible but also everything *in*visible too: all beings and all being, even the very possibility or source or ground of being. Whatever it is that makes it possible for things to be, and to be what they are.

This invisible background to every individual existing thing must remain a mystery to us. We can never see it or explain it. Because every individual thing we can perceive or control is always encompassed by a totality that remains elusively beyond our understanding.[71] No explanation could ever include everything, and the details of any explanation would always be influenced by what we've left out.[72] Look again at Figure 8 on page 75, which is the same image of reality with different labels. As Figure 8 suggests, the whole background of being *within* which everything exists – and without which nothing *could* exist – is, and must be, entirely invisible to us. Always and every-where present, but invisible.[73] It must remain a mystery.[74]

Although it's a mystery, this invisible background of being plays a critical role in structuring the human. Without it, humans would not be, and they would certainly not be human. And although it must remain an unknowable mystery, we can gain some insight into it through the ways in which humans *respond* to it in their behaviour. In their virtues.

But before we get to that, I want you to look, first, at how humans re-spond to the world they can see and can know. The world not of being but of beings.

The world as it is perceived from within the grey semicircle.

8

The Paradoxes of Self-Assertion

My task in the next two chapters is twofold.

I will continue to trace how the process of separative projection you discovered in the last chapter goes on working itself out, through the various levels of being, breeding polarities upon polarities, paradoxes upon paradoxes. But I'll do so, from here on, by returning to the lens of the virtues. Starting with the virtues of self-assertion, you'll see how the two basic families of virtues I described in chapters 4 and 5 – and yoked together in a table of opposites in chapter 6 – breed their own *internal* paradoxes. And these paradoxes inevitably breed still *other* paradoxes. As I said in chapter 7, this process could, theoretically, go on *ad inifinitum*. But in this book, I'll explore it only through the first three levels of separative projection (with one exception in chapter 14).

The paradox of "*I* am" and "*It* is"

The virtues of self-assertion aren't the only ones you can employ toward the visible and physical world, the world of beings. But they have a special relationship with it. As I pointed out in the previous chapter, the virtues of self-assertion and the emergence of an "objective" world go hand in hand, for better and for worse. The individual, self-asserting, controlling ego (*I* am) confronts and "creates" (i.e., perceives the otherness of) an objective world. But once the ego has begun to perceive an independent, objective world (*It* is), that very objective world now stands over against the ego and causes human beings to feel, even more acutely, the reality (or illusion) of their own individual egos.[1] It's a two-way street. The two human stances of "*I* am" and "*It* is" go together and reinforce each other, especially in our modern and post-modern world which, together, they have largely created.

But the tensions between these two stances also help to explain why the process of separative projection pursues its course *within* the family of self-assertive virtues, giving birth to two sub-families, and within them to four more, and so on *ad infinitum*. Separative projection goes all the way down.

What names do you think I should give to the first two of these sub-families of assertive virtues, the sub-families of virtues that give expression to the two contrasting stances of "*I am*" and "*It is*" *within* the virtues of self-assertion themselves? What should I call the two sides of the first paradox of self-assertion? How would you designate the two contrasting families which make up the virtues of self-assertion (A1 and B2 in Figure 17)?

There are many words you could use as headings or labels for the first two families of virtues that emerge from the internal tension or paradox inherent in the virtues of self-assertion: the tension between "*I* am" and "*It* is." These two families of virtues have long been recognized in Western culture, including by Aristotle and Thomas Aquinas, for example. They called self-assertion the "appetite" or the "appetitive power." And so they called the two opposing sides of self-assertion the "sense appetite" (*I* am) and the "rational [or intellectual] appetite" (*It* is).[2] But I want to choose names for these two families of virtues that have real resonance in our contemporary world – a world they have shaped and structured. In chapter 4, I already pointed out that the "goods" associated with these virtues are very familiar to us. They're expressed by words we hear and use all the time, words such as "liberty" and "equality." Liberty and equality are particularly useful words because of their familiarity and because, together, they sum up the leading ideal of the modern and post-Western world, the ideal that makes it both modern and Western, the ideal of freedom.[3] Liberty and equality are the two sides of that ideal of self-assertion.

That's why, in this book, I'm going to use Liberty and Equality as the names for the two contrasting families of virtues *within* the virtues of self-assertion. But don't get hung up on my labels: you should always look *behind* them, to see the real families of virtues they simply represent.[4] I think they're good labels for these two families of self-assertion because in asserting ourselves, we demand to be *free*, free to act as we choose, *and* we also demand to be *equal* in our freedom. But they're not the only labels you could choose. And I want you to focus as much as possible on the realities, *not* the labels.

For my purpose, what makes the labels of Liberty and Equality – the two ideals of freedom – especially helpful in this chapter, is the fact that, while they have the same source – self-assertion – they're also in tension or conflict with each other. Liberty and Equality reveal the paradox of self-assertion. If your impulse of self-assertion demands complete and unconstrained liberty, you aren't going to get equality or even anything approaching equality, as many "capitalist" countries show. If you demand absolute equality, you aren't going to get liberty, or even anything approaching liberty, as all the genuine experiments in "communism" show.

Liberty and equality are the two sides of the modern and postmodern ideal of freedom, but they're also a paradox.[5] They're what Aristotle called "contraries." They are two sides of the same thing but are in conflict or tension with each other. And they're in tension precisely because they embody the two contrasting stances of self-assertion: "*I am*" and "*It is*." Liberty is the demand of the pure, self-asserting ego that proclaims: "*I am*."[6] Equality is the demand of that same self-asserting ego whose very self-assertion has run up against the reality of an "objective," surrounding world of other *equally* self-asserting persons and things, an ego that is therefore obliged to acknowledge: "*It is*."[7]

For their familiarity to modern ears, for the way in which they capture the modern self-assertive ideal of freedom, and for the tensions between them that reflect the two basic human stances of self-assertion – for all these reasons – Liberty and Equality seem tailor-made to serve as headings or labels for the first two contrasting families of virtues that constitute the paradox of self-assertion (the same ones Aristotle and Aquinas called the "sense appetite" and the "rational appetite"). But remember: they're just names. Other people have used other names for these same families.[8] Here and elsewhere in this book, you should always look behind the names, for the full families of virtues they merely name, or represent.

How should I display the contrasting families of virtues that cluster round these two paradoxical human impulses of self-assertion? Obviously, for such a complex task, the circular image I used again in Figure 17 isn't very well suited. I need something that can accommodate rather long lists of virtues – something more like the table format I used in chapters 4–6. But I also want to show you the inherent tensions and conflicts between these virtues, the paradoxes they embody. So, as in chapter 6, I propose to take another leaf out of the ancient Pythagoreans' book and construct another "table of opposites." Later, at the end of this chapter, you'll find a table (Table 10) listing all the virtues of self-assertion you saw in Table 2 on page 85 but now assigned to the various sub-families within the virtues of self-assertion. But before you get there, I want to show you how all these families of virtues are constructed, and why they are therefore real features or continents in

the map of the human. To do that, I'll first construct some more tables of opposites, to show you the conflicting dynamics by which those
sub-families are shaped and determined.

In chapter 6 I was careful to distinguish between stances and virtues
proper. I put them in two separate tables of opposites. As we pursue
the journey of separative projection, this becomes a little harder to
do because, unless I started with a *very* long list – longer than I have
space for in this book – I'd soon start to run out of words. More important, the absence of certain words makes the overall stance or paradox
harder for you to grasp. From here on, I'll take the liberty of being
less discriminating. I'll include in the table of opposites not just the
virtues proper but also some other modes of being and some of the
"values" (like liberty and equality) associated with these virtues. (I'm
comforted in doing so by Aristotle's own somewhat eclectic approach
to the virtues!)

My initial table of opposite, the first paradox of self-assertion, can be
found in Table 7 on pages 157–8.

The left-hand column of this table includes virtues, values, and
modes of being which are, as it were, *pure* self-assertion. In this
stance, the ego knows no constraint at all. It seeks its own ends without taking account of anything other than its own drive to self-assertion, its own pursuit of power or pleasure, or whatever may be its
end. In this mood, the ego recognizes no rules or regularity. It wants
to be able to do whatever it wants to do, and whenever it wants to do
it. It is bold, spontaneous, and impulsive; it seeks its own advantage
and wants to dominate, to control things. Taken all together this may
not sound like a very attractive mix to you. It may remind you of
some tiresome teenagers you know or some obnoxious, irresponsible
adults who never grew up! Maybe a hated, abusive boss you would
rather forget.

That would be a reasonable point of view, if we ever met these virtues all by themselves, which we rarely do (except in some pathological or sociopathic cases or, as I mentioned, some cases of aggravated
adolescence or severely delayed maturity).[9] But dismissing such virtues as disagreeable or even dangerous would be to miss their crucial importance for human life: why they really *are* virtues, though
virtues we never want to stand alone. The virtues I can now call the
virtues of "Liberty" (A1) are what I will call the "engine room" for all
the other virtues.[10] They provide the energy and drive for all the others, including even the virtues of reverence, their opposite.[11] What

Table 7. The paradox of self-assertion

Liberty (A1) *External* control	Equality (B2) *Self*-control
agency	prudence/reason
agency	happiness/flourishing
(sense) appetite	(rational) appetite
art	science
attachment (as identity/desire)	detachment (as equanimity/objectivity)
boldness/bravery/courage	caution/judgment (as reason)/prudence
confidence	competence
creativity	competence/consistency
curiosity	certainty/conviction
desire	continence/moderation/temperance
desire	frugality
detachment (as individualism/liberty)	detachment (as equanimity/objectivity)
determination	prudence/judgment (as reason)
dominance	equality
effort	caution/moderation/prudence
enterprise/entrepreneurship	entitlement/rights
individuation/self-reliance	fairness/equity
expressivism	rationalism
firmness	flexibility
freedom	law-enforcing
freedom	happiness
freedom *to*	freedom *of*
heroism	caution/prudence
honour (-seeking)	respect (-seeking)
imagination	reason
individuation	equality/equity
ingenuity	shrewdness
innovation	caution/consistency/prudence
intensity	impartiality
liberality	frugality
liberty	order(liness)
openness (as confidence/curiosity)	openness (as reasonableness)
optimism	caution/judgment (as reason)/prudence
originality	consistency/impartiality
partiality	impartiality
passion	moderation/reason/temperance
perseverance	prudence/judgment (as reason)
playfulness	purposefulness
pleasure/enjoyment	temperance/happiness
power	rights/reciprocity
power	competence/knowledge (as reason)
risk-taking	caution/judgment (as reason)/prudence

(Continued)

Table 7. The paradox of self-assertion (*Continued*)

	Liberty (A1) *External* control	Equality (B2) *Self*-control
	self-reliance	entitlement/rights
	self-seeking	fairness/reciprocity
	self-seeking	self-discipline
	spontaneity	consistency/purposefulness
	subjectivity	objectivity
	utility (as agency)	utility (as effectiveness)
	pure will	rational will

we mean by life, even physical life, is nothing more than acts, acts of self-assertion. Without the energy, drive, motion, desire that come from the virtues of self-assertion, and especially from the virtues of "Liberty" (A1) – the purest form of self-assertion – there would be no other virtues, and there would not even be anything we could call life.[12] As Thomas Hobbes puts it, succinctly, "to have no desire is to be dead."[13] There's an old saying that the best race horses are the hardest to break. That's because, to do anything or to accomplish anything, especially anything hard or difficult, we need the pure impulse of self-assertion that comes from these virtues. The way Aquinas and Aristotle put it is that the proper function of self-assertion (or what they called "appetite") is "to move to action."[14] As Plato says, it's only when the self-assertive virtue of courage (including perseverance, determination, and all the rest) is combined with virtues like prudence and temperance that "you get [a virtue like] justice."[15] Even the highest forms of goodness, or even saintliness, find their root, their base here.

The reason the "virtues of Liberty" (A1) rarely remain alone is that, as you saw in the previous chapter, their own impulse of self-assertion brings them into contact with other realities, realities which don't eliminate them but balance and reshape them. Self-assertion leads to the encounter with other persons and the things of the physical world, and thus to other virtues, including other virtues of self-assertion, those found in the right-hand column, the virtues belonging to what I have called the category of "Equality" (B2). In these virtues, self-assertion is no longer "pure" because the self-asserting ego confronts a surrounding, "objective" world of which it is required to take account.[16] They are still self-regarding virtues, but they serve the self in a more "objective," rational, calculating way. Indeed, reason itself – the "self-assertive spontaneity" that demands explanations for everything – is one of the virtues that belong in this group. (That's why Aristotle and Aquinas called it the "rational" or "intellectual" appetite.)

Approaching the world in a more objective, rational, observant way – spontaneously demanding explanations for everything – leads the ego to seek no longer just its momentary pleasure, or its own spontaneous will to power, but to seek, instead, a more balanced, sustained kind of "happiness" or flourishing. The virtues in the right-hand column are *calculating* virtues.[17] They still seek the self-satisfaction of the ego, but they do so in a more calculating, deliberate, deliberat*ive* way. If the world is to be controlled and made subject to the will, it must be carefully observed and understood. This leads to a new notion, a new form of the virtue of "control."

Pure self-assertion makes it difficult to observe the world coolly and accurately. It can get in the way. Passionate desire can create obstacles to accurate calculation, including the calculation of genuine personal advantage, or real self-interest. So the self-assertive drive to control must now include a new object: the "self" itself. The virtues of Liberty (A1) are extroverted virtues, aiming at instrumental control of the *external* world outside the ego.[18] The virtues of Equality (B2) are the same controlling and assertive impulse, but directed *inward* toward the ego itself. The virtues of Equality are an "internalized" form of self-assertion, *within* self-assertion itself: a self-assertion "sent back to where it came from" – directed at the self itself, supplementing the drive for external or instrumental control with a parallel drive for *self-control*.[19]

The distinction between *external* or instrumental control and *self-control* is one of the important differences between the two sides of the paradox of self-assertion.[20] Another is their two different notions of freedom. The virtues of Liberty (A1) emphasize "freedom *to*," the unconstrained freedom of the ego to work its own will, simply because "*I* am." The virtues of Equality (B2), on the other hand, are rooted in the stance of "*It* is," the recognition that there is an objective external world of other persons and things of which due account must be taken if the self is to be properly served. They tend to emphasize not freedom *to* but rather "freedom *of*": freedom of speech, freedom of the press, freedom of assembly, freedom of religion, freedom of conscience, and so on. Freedom *of* the self. These virtues were the ones that gave rise to the first widespread use of the language of human "rights" in the eighteenth century.[21] They emphasize fairness, equity, impartiality, universality, and entitlement, rather than the opportunistic creativity and innovation celebrated by the virtues of Liberty (A1). The virtues of Equality (B2) assert the consistent, the regular, the repeated, the average, and the norm, rather than the exceptional and heroic – the drive to dominate, to master and acquire – which are the hallmarks of the virtues of Liberty (A1), the other side of self-assertion.

Separative projection: a reminder

I've now developed a picture of the paradox of self-assertion and its two contrasting families of virtues – the virtues I've linked with the twin goods of Liberty (A1) and Equality (B2). Human beings assert themselves through and in these two contrasting but inseparable families of good human behaviours, or virtues, the two sides of the paradox of self-assertion.

But at this point I should remind you of two things. The first is that *all* the virtues in Table 7 are virtues (or goods, or values – the inside of a virtue) of self-assertion. They may be in tension with each other, but they're all part of one single family of virtues, one half of what it means to be human. The virtues of Liberty (A1) and Equality (B2) may have separate families of their own. But they're all part of the larger family of self-assertion.

Think of your own family or another. The brothers Joe and Bill Smith may each have their own families. But the members of both families are all Smiths. It's the same thing here. The two contrasting families of Liberty (A1) and Equality (B2) are all part of the larger family of self-assertion.

The analogy with a human family can also help with the second thing you need to remember here. Just as the children in Joe's and Bill's families will have families of their own – thus extending the family tree into more generations – something similar happens to the families of virtues. And the reason it happens is *separative projection*. Because self-assertion can only take place in a context of prior *involvement* with the surrounding world, the self can only be asserted against its surroundings in a way that *either retains or reproduces attachment to that wider whole.*[22] So the original contrasting dynamics of separation and connection, of unity and plurality, of union and non-union keep reappearing at each level, introducing the same contrasts and the same tensions. The same paradox.[23]

The virtues of self-assertion split, first, into two contrasting, secondary families of Liberty (A1) and Equality (B2), perpetually in conflict and tension with each other, but also inseparable and necessary to each other. You can't have one without the other. A true paradox. But that's just the beginning because separative projection goes on working. The same dynamic that split self-assertion into two families must now split each of these second-level families into four more families: two new pairs, in which the two sides of each pair are in the same kind of contrast or tension, the same paradoxical relationship.

The paradox of Liberty (A1)

Let's consider, first, the virtues of Liberty (A1). Among these virtues, in the left-hand column of Table 7, there's one obvious tension that may have struck you immediately: the conflict between power and pleasure.

Building on insights of Plato and Aristotle, Thomas Aquinas recognized these two distinct sides of the paradox of Liberty (A1), and he called them the "irascible" and the "concupiscible" appetites.[24] Paul Ricœur calls these two sides of the original human stance of "*I* am" (A1) "effort" and "desire."[25] But I think the range of meanings intended by Aquinas (and by Plato, Aristotle, and Ricœur) can best be expressed today by the two contrasting words, "power" and "pleasure." They are the words I will use as headings for the two new families of virtues which, together, constitute the paradox of Liberty (A1). But here, as elsewhere, the names are far less important than the families of virtues they represent, and for which they are merely shorthand labels. Don't get hung up on the names: focus on the families instead. You can see a new "table of opposites" to illustrate the two "contrary" sides of this paradox, in Table 8 on page 162.

Even if you start with a very long, initial list of virtues, a table of opposites must necessarily become somewhat shorter at this third level of separative projection, as you drill down farther into the depths of the human paradox. Identifying the contraries within it also requires much finer discernment. At the highest level, they were obvious. But, as you drill down, the virtues are more and more closely related, and the differences between them are increasingly subtle. After all, at a higher level they were part of the same family, so they had much in common and were perhaps even synonyms. But at a lower level, subtle differences begin to emerge. The two sides of a paradoxical pair are no longer outright contradictions or conflicts, but *contrasts*: very subtle ways in which one side leans more toward union, and the other leans more toward non-union – especially when contrasted with each other, rather than with something else. As a result, there's more room for error, uncertainty, and legitimate, helpful debate. As I've already pointed out – and as you will see again in the second part of this book – one of the trickiest challenges in mapping the human

Table 8. The paradox of Liberty (A1)

Power (A1a)	Pleasure (A1b)
agency	autonomy
assertiveness	eros
attachment (as identity/pride)	attachment (as desire)
boldness	enjoyment
bravery	beauty
confidence	creativity
control	freedom *to*
control	change/innovation
control	competition/competitiveness
control	creativity/imagination
control	informality/spontaneity
control	risk-taking
control/power	individualism/individuation
courage	creativity/imagination
courage	desire/passion
decisiveness	playfulness
determination	change/spontaneity
determination	imagination/originality
diligence	play(ful)(ness)
dominance	creativity/initiative
effort	desire
endurance	enjoyment
enthusiasm	desire/play(ul)(ness)
energy	ingenuity
firmness	intensity
firmness/fortitude	desire/eros/pleasure
firmness/fortitude	enterprise/initiative
glory/heroism	enjoyment/eros/playfulness/pleasure
heroism	expressivism
honour-*seeking*	enterprise/risk-taking
identity (as pride/self-assertion)	imagination
liberality (as dominance/honour-*seeking*/pride)	liberality (as playfulness/pleasure)
openness (as confidence/optimism)	openness (as creativity/imagination)
optimism	intensity/passion
perseverance	change/spontaneity
power	liberty
pride	humour/play(ful)(ness)
resilience	imagination/originality
self-reliance	creativity/initiative/resourcefulness
self-seeking	risk-taking
steadfastness	change/creativity/initiative
strength	intensity/passion/self-expression
(pure) will	(sense) appetite
work	play
zeal	zest

paradox is determining the correct level at which a given contrary actually occurs, and where it should thus be located in a map of the human spirit.

The paradox of Power (A1a) and Pleasure (A1b) helps you to see how the dynamics of union and non-union keep reproducing themselves at each successive level of the human paradox. The pursuit and exercise of power is the most primitive and characteristic form of self-assertion because it's nothing *but* self-assertion. It aims simply to assert itself against the world, to impose itself upon the world, bending the world to its will, to its own pure impulse of self-assertion.[26] Although it can lead to great evil, this basic human impulse is essential to human life because it is, as I said, the engine that drives everything else. Effort, or agency, is what makes everything happen in the world. Self-assertion – or what Aristotle and Aquinas call the "appetite" – is what moves all other human powers to action.[27] Without self-assertion there is nothing human, and no human virtues. All human action is self-assertion, by definition.

The virtues of Power (A1a) are the purest form of self-assertion. A pure impulse of *agency*.[28] These are the quintessential military virtues. They are rank-seeking, status-seeking, and honour-seeking. They want to rule and command. To impose their will, and their power. Through force, if necessary. The virtues of Power (A1a) are the virtues of boldness, bravery, courage, heroism, and glory. As I just mentioned, Aquinas calls the virtues of Power(A1a) the "irascible" virtues, and he thought their great purpose was the overcoming of "obstacles" to human action.[29]

The pure self-assertion of the virtues of Power (A1a) is especially apparent when contrasted with the virtues of Pleasure (A1b), the other side of the paradox of Liberty (A1). Though it's also very much a virtue of self-assertion, the pursuit of pleasure – by contrast to power – has very strong overtones of union, almost of reverence. To take pleasure in something can almost be a sort of bond with it, the beginnings of a kind of love. As Thomas Aquinas says, "he who desires is borne *towards* the desirable thing."[30] Michael Oakeshott (1901–90) suggests a capacity for pleasure is a disposition to "enjoy what is present," a disposition "to enjoy rather than to exploit."[31] This is almost the beginning of a kind of respect. A willingness to let be, and to cherish. Indeed, says Oakeshott, "the condition of enjoyment is a ready acceptance of what *is*."[32] This side of enjoyment and pleasure seems to point, potentially, beyond the virtues of self-assertion to the virtues of reverence.

Aristotle notes that pleasure almost seems to be the "supreme good" because all humans and animals pursue it. They may not all seem to be pursuing the *same* pleasure but, without knowing it, they are in fact pursuing the same thing: "because everything contains by nature something divine" – the being that makes it be, and makes it be the thing that it is – and that something is the pleasure they ultimately seek.[33] This line of thinking became a commonplace of later Christian thought. Blaise Pascal for example, argues that the human will seeks only that which pleases it the most, and nothing can please it as much as the one unique good "that includes all the other goods."[34] This suggests one of the powerful reasons why the arrow of virtue leads from the first human stance of "*I* am" to the stance of "I *am*." Thomas Aquinas is getting at this first movement from "I am" (A1) to "I am" (A2), when he suggests that the *first* inclination of the will is to love.[35]

Power and pleasure are in conflict because if you want to pursue power in a single-minded way, you're going to have to curtail your pleasures. Otherwise, they will get in the way of obtaining, wielding, and retaining power. If, on the other hand, you make pleasure your primary goal, you will soon make yourself unfit or unable to hold power over others. If you don't have power now, you're unlikely to get it. And if you do, you're almost certain to lose it.

The will to power and the will to pleasure are two different kinds of self-assertion, not just one. They're intimately, inseparably connected, and yet distinct at the same time. Thomas Aquinas points out, for example, that the inclination to "fight against obstacles" (characteristic of what I've called the virtues of "power") can require you to confront some "unpleasant things."[36] So power and pleasure aren't always aligned. They can interfere with each other, since the drive to power, when roused, drives away, for the moment, your preoccupation with pleasure; while the desire for pleasure, when roused, can lower your aggressive impulses.

But the will to power and to pleasure are also intimately, inseparably connected, in the paradox of Liberty (A1). They support and fuel each other: the assertive virtues are what we use to obtain pleasure for ourselves or to protect us from its opposite: pain or harm. The pursuit of pleasure is also the source of much aggressive behaviour, and its goal or end point. As Aquinas puts it, in a specific example: "anger arises from sadness, and having wrought vengeance, terminates in joy."[37]

In the paradox of Power (A1a) and Pleasure (A1b), we can see the same dynamics of union and non-union very much present and at work, even at this tertiary-level remove from the original paradox of self-assertion and reverence, or from the stances of *I am* and I *am*. At this third level of separative projection, power seems to embody the self-assertive impulse to non-union, while pleasure leans more toward the principle of union. But even power itself retains overtones of union (reflecting the basic human paradox) because it requires some kind of link to others for its exercise. Power isn't power if there isn't something else or somebody else against which or over which to assert yourself. And while pleasure may well lean more to union than power does, the pursuit of pleasure is still a self-assertive pursuit. The pursuit of pleasure can lead you to assert yourself over others: to use them, exploit them, or even abuse them in some way. So, a discerning mind should be able to tease out the next level of paradox beyond even this tertiary level.

Another equally important contrary structuring the paradox of Liberty (A1) is the conflict between agency and control (A1a), on the one hand, and autonomy and freedom *to* (A1b), on the other. This is one of the most significant paradoxes within the larger, overall human paradox, and one of the most subtle, offering insight into the ambiguity of our modern value of freedom.

You might be inclined to think the human impulse to freedom is a pure and disinterested one, something that can be taken at its face value. But the virtues of Power (A1a) – the left-hand column in Table 7 – show you that the inner, central kernel or core of the virtues of Liberty (A1) is, in fact, the spirit of pure self-assertion alone, our pure disposition to dominate and control the surrounding environment and those around us.[38] It seeks freedom but, initially, this is only the freedom to dominate.[39] The free, untrammelled, unimpeded exercise of our own self-assertion. Freedom *as a value*, the freedom which gives a name to the virtues of Liberty (A1) is only, in a sense, secondary: it arises when our original, pure disposition to dominate (A1a) – the disposition we inherited from our animal origins – is blocked somehow. The demand for freedom *as a principle* then emerges as a demand to remove these impediments to our own self-assertion.[40] The virtues of Liberty, the most *assertive* form of self-assertion, are thus already at war *with themselves*. And the pursuit of freedom – especially absolute or radical freedom *to* – is haunted (and, in a sense, tainted at the source) by this fundamental ambiguity. It explains why so many radical "freedom-fighters," revolutionaries, and populists are transformed by the achievement of power into tyrants even worse than those they overthrew. They are only being consistent. Their radical fight for "freedom" was always secondary to removing all obstacles to their own self-assertion.[41]

From the point of view of the private sector, it's also revealing to point out another tension in the virtues of Liberty (A1): the paradoxical contrast between control (A1a) and competitiveness (A1b). As you will see again in later chapters, the virtues of Liberty (A1) are the primary virtues of the marketplace. This family of virtues is where market relationships and behaviour are most at home, the corner of the human where they are primarily rooted. This is the family of human virtues where everything can be given a price and can be bought and sold.[42] We often associate this with competition and assume that competition and competitiveness are core values of the market. The left-hand and right-hand columns of Table 8 show you that's true, but again, only in a secondary way. Competition and competitiveness don't find themselves in the same family as agency, decisiveness, diligence, self-reliance, and work (A1a), where you might expect. Rather, they are in the same family as creativity, innovation, and play (A1b). Competition and competitiveness are different from the pure disposition to dominate. For real competition to occur, there have to be rules, self-restraint, a level playing field, and even a sense of fair play – the things you need to make a game a game, or a sport a sport.

Even dogs know the difference between the two sides of the paradox of Liberty (A1). In dog *play*, dogs know and observe the rules, they respect the spirit of reciprocity that will keep the game going, even giving the ball back to a companion in order to keep it in play, to keep the game and the pleasure (A1b) going. But in a dog *fight*, there are no rules or limits. The only goal is victory, power, and domination (A1a).

In competition, there's already an implicit social or moral contract between the competitors. Competition is a form of self-assertion but with an overlay of reverence already in place.[43] It points beyond itself: beyond self-assertion to the virtues of reverence. But the virtues of Power (A1a) – the pure spirit of self-assertion, and of agency – have no time for such things as rules, unless forced to do so, either by external forces and virtues, or by their own internal self-contradictions. Power (A1) simply wants to dominate and control.[44] To assert itself. That helps to explain why business voices that publicly trumpet the values of a competitive market, are, in practice, very happy for the market to be managed in such a way as to reduce their competition (by mergers and acquisitions, or by government regulations and barriers to competition), or to help them achieve a monopoly or oligopoly, or to let them corner the market.[45]

There is no part of the human paradox that isn't in conflict with itself. No part of ourselves that is not, in fact, a human paradox.

The paradox of Equality (B2)

In Table 7 on pages 157–8, I called the other half of the paradox of "self-assertion" the virtues of "Equality" (B2). These virtues embody some of the most characteristic values of the eighteenth-century Western Enlightenment. Later, in the nineteenth and twentieth centuries, the anti-Enlightenment virtues of Power (A1a) and Pleasure (A1b) – the two sides of the paradox of Liberty (A1) – revolted against these Enlightenment virtues of Equality (B2). This revolt still continues today, in the twenty-first century. The paradox of self-assertion contains within itself the debate or conflict which has made us what we are, the debate between the Enlightenment and the anti-Enlightenment. Our modern and post-modern world can be seen as the product of an unending conversation – even argument or dispute – between our own virtues of Liberty (A1) and Equality (B2), the two conflicting sides of the paradox of self-assertion.[46]

But since polarity breeds polarities, the virtues of Equality (B2) – the quintessential Enlightenment virtues – harbour their own paradox. Like the virtues of Liberty (A1), they not only *are* one half of the paradox of self-assertion, but they also exhibit their *own* internal paradox. Separative projection is at work here, too. In the case of the paradox of Liberty (A1), its two sides were relatively easy to identify because, as you just saw, they have been recognized and named since ancient times. But the two sides of the paradox of Equality (B2) may seem harder, initially, both to discern and to name.

One way to tease them out is to consider the conflict between my self-assertion and yours, between my virtues of Liberty (A1) and your own. My self-assertion is as *equally real* as your self-assertion. But *your* pursuit of power and pleasure may well constrain or limit *mine*. In order for my self-assertion, my virtues of Power (A1a) and Pleasure (A1b), to operate as freely as their own assertiveness demands, I have also to *assert* the *equal* reality of my own self-assertion. Because my self-assertion is as equally real as yours, I assert myself as equal to you, or to anyone else. The demand for equality is a demand for recognition that my own self-assertion is as *equally real* as your self-assertion. I assert my *right* or entitlement to the recognition of my equality to you, as well as recognition for the other conditions or "rights" required for the achievement or maintenance of that equality.

The assertion of an entitlement or "right" of some kind is a quintessential virtue of Equality (B2). Liberty (A1) itself doesn't seek rights as spontaneously as Equality (B2) because *your* rights may constrain *my* liberty – your *right* to property may constrain *my* liberty to do what I want with my own. We can see this resistance at work in the contemporary libertarian agendas that seek to resist or roll back the protections for human rights that have been gradually built up since the eighteenth-century Enlightenment. But if Liberty (A1) by itself doesn't give rights the highest priority, Equality (A2) does. I demand recognition of *my* equal "rights" despite – or indeed *because* of – the limits they will impose on *your* freedom to abuse or exploit me.

However, the pursuit of my *equal* rights – that is a natural expression of our own self-assertion – also implicitly recognizes the rights of other people, too. If I am to secure the very equal rights the assertiveness of my own self-assertion demands, there must be a *reciprocal* relationship between your rights and mine: a reciprocal recognition of our own equal desire – and need – to assert ourselves. If I don't recognize your rights – if we don't work for each other's good on the basis of some kind of reciprocity – you won't recognize mine.[47]

Since rights and mutual recognition seem to be inseparable poles of the natural human pursuit of equality, I'm going to call the two poles of the paradox of Equality (B2) the virtues of "Rights" (B2a) and "Reciprocity" (B2b).[48] These two dynamics can pull *against* each other because the assertion of my *own* rights may well put me in conflict with yours: it often does. I may insist on some form of right or entitlement which doesn't seem fair to you, or which you don't think I deserve. The virtues of Rights (B2a) "lean" toward Liberty (A1), while the virtues of Reciprocity (B2b) lean toward Reverence (A2). But rights and reciprocity are also *necessary* to each other and – like every other level of the human paradox – can't exist alone, without their polar opposite. Because without reciprocity, rights can't be recognized.[49] And without rights, equality is replaced by domination and submission. The virtues of Liberty (A1) win.

You can see some of the potential ways we commonly express these two poles of the paradox of Equality (B2) in Table 9 on page 169.

The basic paradox of reverence and self-assertion, of union and non-union, keeps reproducing itself at each new level of the human paradox. And it does so again here, as you can see in Table 9. As in all my other tables and figures, the left-hand column groups the more assertive virtues in the family, and the right-hand the more "reverential." The pursuit of "Rights" (B2a) seems to reflect the more

Table 9. The paradox of Equality (B2)

Rights (B2a)	Reciprocity (B2b)
(rational) appetite	(rational) will
belief *that*	openness (as reasonableness)
certainty/conviction	acceptance/tolerance
certainty/conviction	caution
certainty/conviction	flexibility/reasonableness
competence	caution/prudence
consistency	adaptability/discretion/flexibility
consistency	impartiality
effectiveness/efficiency	cooperation/empowerment
effectiveness/efficiency	fairness/flexibility
efficiency	economy/frugality
enlightenment (as reason)	judgment/shrewdness
entitlement	contentment/reasonableness
entitlement	fairness/impartiality/reciprocity
equality	consideration/discretion
equality	equity
equality	fairness/reciprocity
detachment (as objectivity)	detachment (as equanimity)
dignity (as respect/rights(-seeking)	dignity (as equanimity/self-control)
flourishing/happiness	contentment/reasonableness
fairness (as equality)	fairness (as equity)
flourishing/happiness	frugality/prudence/temperance
flourishing/happiness	self-control/self-discipline
freedom *of*	cooperation/reciprocity
freedom *of*	moderation/prudence
freedom *of*	responsibility (as prudence)
freedom *of*	self-control/self-discipline
judgment (as reason)	acceptance/openness
judgment (as reason)	forbearance/tolerance
judgment (as reason)	appreciation/consideration
knowledge (as reason)	appreciation/prudence
law/rule(-enforcing)	equity/empowerment
law/rule(-enforcing)	self-control/self-discipline
objectivity	appreciation/reciprocity
purposefulness	flexibility/empowerment
rational(ity)(ism)/reason	reasonableness
respect(-seeking)	acceptance/appreciation
respect(-seeking)	reciprocity
rights(-seeking)	acceptance/tolerance
science/scientific	judgment/shrewdness
skil(l)(ful)(ness)/technique	caution/prudence
trust(-seeking)	appreciation/consideration

assertive side (*I* am) of the paradox of Equality (B2), while the family of virtues identified with "Reciprocity" (B2b) makes more room for the realities of union and for consideration of the other (I *am*). The virtues of Rights (B2a) advance and *assert* beliefs, certainties, claims, and rational convictions, judgments, and knowledge about the world. The virtues of Reciprocity (B2b) balance those certainties, claims, and convictions with virtues of acceptance, appreciation, cooperation, flexibility, reciprocity, tolerance, and so on, virtues which reach out or acknowledge the presence and legitimacy of other people and things, which make room for them, by controlling and moderating my own self-assertion.[50]

The pursuit of equality, as you saw, arises from our encounter with an objective world (*It* is), and the recognition that other things and beings in this world have an existence of their own for which even my pure asserting ego (*I* am) must make room or take into account. In the paradox of Equality (B2), this inevitable acknowledgment of otherness – by the self-assertive ego that encounters an objective, re-sisting world – finds expression in three important ways, which appear on both sides of Table 9.

The first is the theme of self-control. As I already noted in Table 7, one of the important contraries in the paradox of self-assertion is the tension between instrumental control of the *external* world (which belongs to the family of Liberty [A1]) and *self*-control (which belongs to the family of Equality [B2]). There's a tension between them because they constrain each other: if you have a strong drive to control the world, you are less likely to attach high value to self-control. If you aim at self-control, you relinquish, by definition, *some* measure of control over the external world (though you may get it back in other ways). But both are forms of self-assertion: the first is simply directed *outward* and the second *inward*. For the virtues of Equality (B2), the self *itself* becomes an "other": the self is split and the virtues of Equality seek to control the *other* self, especially the one embodied in the virtues of Liberty (A1).[51]

In the paradox of Equality (B2), overtones of *self*-control are inevitably found on both sides of the ledger. But these virtues are more obviously at home on the side of Reciprocity (B2b). The virtues of Reciprocity (B2b) are where we find not only self-control and self-discipline themselves, but also related virtues such as the classical virtues of prudence and temperance, as well as more contemporary virtues such as cooperation, empowerment, tolerance, and so on. Reciprocity (B2b) is thus the home of that subset of the virtues of self-assertion we sometimes call the "will" (which Thomas Aquinas called the "rational [or intellectual] appetite") that controls the "passions" of power (A1a) and pleasure (A1b).

Though it's a little less obvious there, self-control is also very important for the virtues of Rights (B2a), the other side of the paradox of Equality (B2), where we find virtues such as knowledge, reason, science, skilfulness, technique, and so on. These virtues are more assertive than the virtues of Reciprocity (B2b) because they're directed outward, toward the external world, which they seek to know and control. In fact, these virtues of Rights (B2a) provide the rational knowledge and techniques to support the instrumental control of the *external* world at which the virtues of Liberty (A1) aim. Without *self*-control – unless the energies, desires, and passions of the virtues of Liberty (A1) are well harnessed and disciplined – the external world can't be accurately observed, and objectively recorded. The subjective desires, drives, and pure self-assertion of Liberty (A1) are essential to the human if the ego is to have any kind of agency in the world, or even to be alive. But without the virtues of self-control (B2), they will get in the way of accurate observation and calculation. And, without the knowledge and technique provided by accurate observation and calculation, the external world can't be controlled in the way self-assertion ultimately seeks to do. Without these more calculating virtues, the pure self-asserting ego (A1) won't even be able to calculate accurately its own self-interest.[52] So the virtues of Equality (B2) are the home of the intellectual virtues of reason and science, those virtues of the mind that seek to understand the objective world, so that it can be made subject to the control of the assertive ego.[53] Because of their overtones of self-control, they take their place in the virtues of Equality (B2). But because of their close connection with the virtues of Liberty (A1), they find their place on the more assertive side of the paradox of Equality (B2), with the virtues of Rights (B2a).

Maybe I can bring out this distinction a little more clearly by drawing your attention to two virtues that may sound very similar to you, but which, on closer examination, turn out to harbour implicit distinctions or contrasts that place them on opposite sides of the virtues of Equality (B2). Consistency and impartiality sound very alike, or at least very compatible, don't they? And they are. They're both virtues of Equality (B2). But consistency (B2a) is a more assertive virtue, like entitlement, reason, and respect-seeking. It *insists* on being consistent. Whereas impartiality (B2b) is a more "reverential" virtue, involving stronger tones of self-control or *un*-selfing. Partiality is a virtue of Liberty (A1), a virtue of desire. To be *im*partial, you have consciously to *restrain* or control your partiality, your own self-assertion.

You should also note that some virtues appear among the virtues of Equality (B2), which, in Table 3 on page 106, you already saw among the virtues of reverence. Responsibility appears here in its modes of prudence and reciprocity, but as a virtue of reverence it can take the form of duty, or even of love. Similarly, judgment and knowledge appear here as virtues of reason and rationality. But as virtues of reverence, they already appeared (and will appear) as forms of wisdom and understanding.[54] You will encounter these virtues again, in their other forms, in the next chapter. They are good examples of the subtleties, nuances, and varieties of meaning that lurk deep in the virtues, and in all language about them. Indeed, in all language.

As you will see again in the second part of this book, the virtues of Equality (B2) are the special virtues of modern and post-modern civil society. As post-modern citizens of Western countries, we particularly cherish the virtues of Rights (B2a) with their emphasis on goods such as entitlement, equality, freedom, happiness, law, reason, respect, and trust. The paradox of Equality (B2) is also the home of what I might call the "bureaucratic" virtues, the special values of public administration. Civil (or public) servants identify, strongly and spontaneously, with virtues such as competence, expertise, objectivity, discipline, rules, consistency, and impartiality. If Power (A1a) is the natural home of the entrepreneurial virtues[55] and Pleasure (A1b) the home of artistic creativity and innovation,[56] the virtues of Equality (B2) are the primary home of the professional public servant. I will come back to this in chapter 13.

Encountering two kinds of otherness

I've now sketched out the two primary sub-families and the four sub-sub-families of virtues that, together, comprise the virtues of self-assertion. In Table 10 on pages 174–5, at the end of this chapter, you can find an alphabetical list of all the virtues of self-assertion you saw in Table 2, arranged, now, both in the two sub-families of Liberty (A1) and Equality (B2), and also in the four sub-sub-families of Power (A1a) and Pleasure (A1b), and of Rights (B2a) and Reciprocity (B2b).

If I wanted to do so – and had the necessary patience and discernment – I could go on pursuing this process of "separative projection" to still further levels of paradox within this same family of self-assertion, as the contrary impulses of union and non-union – the two stances of "*I* am" and "*It* is" – go on reproducing themselves within each new family or level of virtue.

But I propose, instead, to draw your attention now to the other side of the human paradox. And, if I needed a prod to do so, my discussion of the virtues of Equality (B2) has just given me one. You saw that the virtues of Equality emerge as "contraries" to the corresponding virtues of Liberty (A1) because of the self-asserting ego's encounter with the otherness of an objective world that confronts and resists it. But the encounter with an objective world beyond the ego can't stop with the physical world. It can't stop there because of the very experience of self-assertion itself.

Self-assertion eventually leads human beings to an encounter with a different kind of otherness, an otherness implicit in the virtues themselves. In practising the virtues, human beings can't help being brought into an "encounter with an (unassimilable) external other" (as Iris Murdoch puts it): an encounter with whatever it is that "like a light shines through all the virtues," as Plotinus says.[57] So discussion of the virtues of self-assertion – especially our concluding discussion of the virtues of Equality – invites and beckons us to continue our backward journey, following the arrow of virtue in reverse direction. Here you will also encounter an otherness. But it will no longer be an otherness of the physical world that confronts the ego. It will be an otherness of the spirit.

Table 10. The paradoxes of self-assertion: a sample list of virtues Two sub-families and four sub-sub-families of the virtues of self-assertion

The paradox of Liberty (A1) *External* control		The paradox of Equality (B2) *Self*-control	
Power (A1a)	Pleasure (A1b)	Rights (B2a)	Reciprocity (B2b)
1. activity	1. (sense) appetite	1. (rational) appetite	1. acceptance (as tolerance)
2. agency	2. attachment (as desire)	2. belief *that*	2. adaptability
3. assertiveness	3. autonomy	3. certainty/ certitude	3. appreciation
4. attachment (as identity/pride)	4. beauty (as pleasure)	4. competence	4. calmness
5. boldness	5. change	5. consistency	5. caution
6. bravery	6. competit(ion) (iveness)	6. conviction	6. cleanliness (as self-control)
7. confidence	7. creativity	7. detachment (as objectivity)	7. community (as cooperation)
8. (external) control	8. curiosity	8. dignity (as respect/ rights(-seeking)	8. consideration
9. courage	9. desire	9. effectiveness	9. contentment
10. decisiveness	10. enjoyment	10. efficiency	10. continence
11. determination	11. enterprise(ing)	11. enlightenment (as knowledge/ reason)	11. cooperation
12. diligence	12. entrepreneur(ial) (ship)	12. entitlement	12. discretion
13. dominance	13. eros	13. equality	13. detachment (as equanimity)
14. effort	14. expressivism	14. fairness (as equality)	14. dignity (as self-control)
15. endurance	15. freedom *to*	15. flourishing	15. economy
16. energy(y)(etic)	16. humour	16. freedom *of*	16. empowerment
17. enthusiasm	17. imagination	17. happiness	17. equanimity
18. firmness	18. independence	18. judgment (as reason)	18. equity
19. fortitude	19. individualism/ individuation	19. knowledge (as reason)	19. fairness (as equity)
20. glory (as heroism)	20. informality	20. law(-enforcing)	20. flexibility
21. heroism	21. ingenuity	21. objectivity	21. forbearance (as self-control/ tolerance)
22. honour (-seeking)	22. initiative	22. purposefulness	22. frugality
23. identity (as self-assertion)	23. innovation	23. rationality/ rationalism	23. grace (as self-control)
24. liberality (as dominance/ pride)	24. intensity	24. reason	24. harmony (as reciprocity)
25. openness (as confidence/ optimism)	25. liberality (as playfulness/ pleasure)	25. respect (-seeking)	25. impartiality
26. optimism	26. liberty	26. rights(-seeking)	26. integrity (as self-control)
27. partiality (as power)	27. non-union	27. science/ scientific	27. judgment (as shrewdness)
28. perseverance	28. openness (as curiosity/desire)	28. skil(l)(ful)(ness)	28. moderation
29. power	29. originality		
30. pride	30. partiality (as pleasure)		
31. resilience	31. passion		
32. seeking	32. play(ful)(ness)		

(*Continued*)

Table 10. The paradoxes of self-assertion: a sample list of virtues Two sub-families and four sub-sub-families of the virtues of self-assertion (*Continued*)

The paradox of Liberty (A1) *External* control		The paradox of Equality (B2) *Self*-control	
Power (A1a)	Pleasure (A1b)	Rights (B2a)	Reciprocity (B2b)
33. self-assertion	33. pleasure	29. technique	29. mutuality (as
34. self-reliance	34. receptivity (as	30. trust(-seeking)	reciprocity)
35. self-seeking	pleasure)	31. utility (as	30. openness (as
36. steadfastness	35. resourceful(ness)	effectiveness)	reasonableness)
37. strength	36. risk-taking		31. order(liness)
38. success(ful)	37. self-determination		32. patience (as
39. utility (as	38. self-development		self-control)
agency, control)	39. self-expression		33. prudence
40. (pure) will	40. self-realization		34. reasonableness
41. work	41. separat(eness)		35. reciprocity
42. zeal	(ion)		36. reliability
	42. spontaneity		37. responsibility
	43. subjectivity		(as prudence)
	44. zest		38. responsiveness
			39. self-control
			40. self-discipline
			41. self-respect
			42. shrewdness
			43. tact
			44. temperance
			45. tolerance
			46. tranquil(ity) (as
			equanimity)
			47. (rational) will

9

The Paradoxes of Reverence

In chapter 3 you saw how human beings respond to the paradox of something and everything in two characteristic ways, two corresponding human stances I called "*I* am" and "I *am*." In chapters 4 and 5 I began to explore the two families of virtues that express these two fundamental human stances. And in chapter 6, I put these two families of virtues together, as the two sides of the human paradox. In chapter 8, you saw how the process of *separative projection* you encountered in chapter 7 works its way down through one side of that paradox – the virtues of self-assertion – breeding paradox upon paradox.

My task in this chapter is the same as in the last. I now want to show you how that same dynamic of separative projection – reflecting the underlying polarity of being – works itself out in the other main family of virtues, the virtues which are *not* self-assertive but instead acknowledge our necessary involvement in a larger reality we did not make and did not choose: the virtues of reverence.

The paradox of "It *is*" and "I *am*"

The first tasks, then, as in the previous chapter, are to consider how the human paradox expresses itself within the virtues of reverence and what to call the two sides of the initial paradox of reverence: the two families of virtues that express the contrasting stances of "It *is*" and "I *am*."

This is not as straightforward a task as it proved to be in chapter 8 because neither the ancient thinkers nor our modern language provides ready-made labels, as they did there. It will take a little more work this time to identify the tension lurking within the virtues of reverence, and to select names for the two sides of the initial paradox of reverence.

One way to begin the task is to return to my definitions of reverence in chapter 5. I there suggested that an obvious difference between reverence and self-assertion is that, in the first, you are self-*giving* while in the second you are (by definition) self-*seeking*. But I also suggested that reverence acknowledges something larger or higher in priority than our own individual selves, something that commands our admiration and our loyalty, and may imply obligations or duties on our part. In a gesture of reverence, either physical or mental, I argued, we acknowledge superior *worth*, our relationship with it, and our potential obligations toward it.

Now, there appears to be a tension between these two approaches to reverence. The first seems to entail pure self-giving, without any condition or qualification. But the second is an acknowledgment of worth. In the second case, there is an element of evaluation. Human beings, as Webb Keane puts it, are "the kind of creatures that are prone to evaluate themselves, others, and their circumstances."[1] And acknowledgment of worth is the primary place where that tendency finds expression in the nature of the human. But to make such an assessment of quality or excellence there is a necessary element of *self-assertion*.[2] Evaluation implies standing back from something and *judging* it objectively. Even within the virtues of reverence, we can see the basic human paradox already rearing its head. One side of reverence is *more self-assertive than the other*. One side seems to be purely self-giving – giving merely for the sake of giving – without any judgment of what is due. The other is also self-giving, but in this case, *because* of an (assertive) judgement of merit or excellence. Because something – some obligation, respect or reverence – *is due*.[3] As your new awareness of separative projection prepared you to anticipate, there seems to be a tension between reverence and self-assertion *even within reverence itself*.[4]

Another way to come at this same question is through the arrow of virtue I described in chapter 7. You will recall that I suggested the nature of the human begins in a stance of "*I* am" toward the world, a stance which then quickly shifts into "I *am*" as the powerful, early immediacy of being surrounds the ego. But I also suggested this early awareness – of the larger reality to which you belong – shifts again to reveal more "objective" qualities. It's not just that things *are* and are yours. They also have desirable or meritorious features *of their own*. They're also true or good or beautiful. You don't have to give yourself to this wider reality simply because "I *am*," but also because "It *is*."[5] Because this wider reality has its own reality, its own existence, its own *being*, a being that deserves your self-giving. It merits and earns it. There is something *due*.[6] There is an external standard of excellence to which you not only belong but also willingly *give* or devote yourself, no longer purely for the sake of self-giving itself, but because of its own excellence. The arrow of virtue thus confirms that the virtues of reverence (expressing the stance of "I *am*") have their own internal paradox: a tension between the impulse of reverence *itself*, and the excellence to which reverence is directed: a tension between the stances of "I *am*" and "It *is*."

Both of these approaches to the paradox of reverence suggest that one of its sides – the side in which something is *due* – has to do with goodness or excellence. So let me call it Excellence.[7] What shall I call the *other* side, the virtues that express the stance of "I *am*," in which self-giving is pure and unconcerned with what is due? Where self-giving is simply for the sake of giving? Because this is the purest form of reverence, I will call this family simply Reverence, with a capital, to distinguish this sub-family from the larger family of reverence. Reverence seems to be a quality that goes all the way down, and it doesn't need another label at the different levels of separative projection. But in order to distinguish it at its different levels, I will add, first, a capital – and, at the next level, a superscript. As I have been doing throughout this book, I will also normally add my shorthand designation for each of these families of virtues (A2, B1, etc.), just to make sure you always know exactly which sub-family or sub-sub-family I'm talking about.

Let me then call the two sides of the paradox of reverence Excellence (B1) and Reverence (A2).[8] Table 11 on page 179 shows you what these two families of virtues look like.

I want to point out several things about this new "table of opposites" to you. The first thing is that, like the previous tables, it's not exhaustive. The lists are only illustrative or suggestive, a sample, and not in any sense complete. A second thing to notice about Table 11 is that, as in all my previous tables and figures, the more assertive virtues of reverence are all on the left-hand side of the table, and the more "reverential" are on the right. Almost all the virtues on the left-hand side seem to involve some kind of standard that must be met or which can be judged. A judgment which is, by definition, an act of self-assertion, or an act with assertive overtones.

But none of the virtues on the right-hand side of Table 11 require this kind of proto-assertive judgment. In fact, the *absence* of a standard seems to be an important feature of all the right-hand virtues. In this mode (of almost pure reverence) the self is self-giving *regardless* of the merits of the person or object to which the self is given. The important thing seems to be the giving itself and the good the person experiences (or in which she participates) *through* the act of self-giving. On the left-hand side, you are moved to reverence because that is what is due to

Table 11. The paradox of reverence

Excellence (B1) Something is *due*	Reverence (A2) Giving for the *sake* of giving
accountability	compassion/concern
beauty (as truth or goodness)	kindness
belief *in*	faith(ful)(ness)/trust(ing)
chastity	empathy/generosity
community (as duty)	community (as communion)
contrition	forgiveness
courtesy	agape
deference	devotion
dignity (as worthiness)	dignity (as reverence)
discernment/insight	empathy/forbearance
duty	love/service
freedom (*from*)	freedom (*for*)
goodness/merit	praise
goodness/merit	humility/modesty (as humility)
grace (as beauty)	grace (as gratitude or giving)
honesty/sincerity	compassion
honour*able*	honour*ing*
integrity	generosity
judgment (as wisdom)	forgiveness/hope/praise
justice	gratitude/mercy
knowledge (as wisdom)	faith/hope
law/rule(-abiding)	love
loyalty (as duty)/commitment	concern/devotion/faith(ful)(ness)
merit	benevolence
mindfulness/thoughtfulness	charity
modesty (as purity)	modesty (as humility)
purity	benevolence/compassion
respect*able*	respect*ful*
responsibility (as duty)	responsibility (as love)
righteousness	forgiveness
serenity	friendliness/kindness
solidarity (as community)	solidarity (as love)
truth(ful)(ness)	generosity/praise
trust*worthy*	trust*ing*
valu*able*	valu*ing*
wisdom/understanding	awe/benevolence/wonder

excellence. But, on the right-hand side, reverence is spontaneous. Nothing is due, except reverence itself. The self gives itself for the sheer joy and fulfilment of giving. For the very sake of giving itself.

When Marilynne Robinson (b. 1943) says, "There is no justice in love, no proportion in it," she is describing the boundary between the virtues of Reverence (A2) and the virtues of Excellence (B1).[9] There is no justice or proportion in a virtue like love because, in the virtues of Reverence

(A2), giving is for its own sake, for the sake of giving itself. There is no limit and no proportion. You can never give enough. There is no standard, no bottom line, no justice. But, in the virtues of Excellence (B1), giving is motivated because something is due, there *is* a standard to be met, a due proportion to be assessed or judged. This is where the virtue of justice is at home. In crossing the line from love to justice, you have crossed the line from the virtues of Reverence (A2) to the virtues of Excellence (B1).[10]

Another thing to note about Table 11 is that several virtues appear on both sides of the paradox but in slightly different forms. "Freedom" appears on both sides of the line, for example, but in the virtues Excellence (B1) it takes the form of "freedom *from*" (freedom *from* all the things that block or defile goodness and truth) while, in the virtues of Reverence (A2), it takes the form of "freedom *for*": freedom for mercy, compassion, and generosity, freedom for devotion and communion, freedom for love, freedom to give oneself freely, freedom for others. "Trust" also appears on both sides of the line, but in the family of Reverence (A2) it takes the form of trust*ing* whereas in the family of Excellence (B1) it takes the form of trust*worthy*. Similarly, "respect" and "honour" appear as respect*ful* and honour*ing* in Reverence (A2) but as respect*able* and honour*able* in Excellence (B1); and "value" takes the form of valu*ing* as a virtue of Reverence (A2) but of valu*able* as a virtue of Excellence (B1). The reason for this difference is obviously connected to the previous point. In the family of Excellence (B1), what counts is a standard of some kind. A judgment of quality is to be made. The dimensions of trust, respect, and value that are highlighted in Excellence (B1) are whether something is *deserving* of the trust, respect, and valu*ing* that are inherent to reverence. In Reverence (A2), however, no such judgment is to be made. What counts are the very *actions* of trusting, respecting, and valuing themselves.[11] As I already pointed out, in chapter 5, the virtues of Reverence (A2) seem to be partly about *overlooking* the very standards the virtues of Excellence (B1) want to impose or establish. I'll come back to this again in chapters 10 and 16.

A fourth point, connected to the previous two, is that many of the virtues in the left-hand column of Table 11 seem to involve a form of knowledge, the kind of knowledge necessary to make the judgments of quality and excellence required in this family of virtues (B1). But the virtues in the right-hand column (A2) don't seem to have the same requirement for knowledge. In fact, some of them seem almost to be incompatible with knowledge or to go beyond it. If Excellence (B1) demands truth, pure Reverence (A2) is fully at home with mystery, which excludes clear or full knowledge by definition. If judgments about respectability, trustworthiness, integrity, and honour seem to require a kind of knowledge, the virtues of respecting, trusting, and honouring don't seem to have the same requirement: they seem to be justified *by the virtuous actions themselves*, quite apart from the merits of those to whom they are shown. If wisdom and understanding seem to entail some kind of knowledge, awe and wonder seem to be struck dumb, and to stand silent before something too large to comprehend. If justice requires knowledge for judgments to be rendered, love, mercy, forgiveness, compassion, benevolence, and generosity don't seem to have knowledge at their core but something else instead, for which knowledge seems almost superfluous or beside the point. Hope, faith, and trust could not be what they are if knowledge were possible, or central, to this family of virtues.

Another way to put this is to say that these two families of virtues seem to call upon or mobilize different dimensions of the human person.[12] Many, if not most of the virtues in the left-hand column involve thought or the conscious mind. The virtues of Reverence (A2) on the right-hand side seem to require little reflection: they seem to be almost spontaneous, proceeding directly from the body, or from some wellspring deep inside the human spirit, or our genetic dispositions.[13] They involve awareness and consciousness, otherwise they wouldn't be human. But it is not yet a fully *rational* consciousness – more an intuitive physical and moral *awareness*.[14] The virtues of Excellence (B2), by contrast, involve a shift from the body or the psyche toward the conscious, rational mind. Not all the way, yet. That will only come when the arrow of virtue I described in chapter 7 gets to the virtues of Equality (B2), which we explored in the previous chapter. The virtues of Excellence (B1) are those of the stance of "It *is*." At this stage, the human spirit has begun to confront an external otherness. An "It." No longer just an "I." And so, the human mind is swinging into action in these virtues of Excellence (B1), which all involve forms of human thought and conscious reflection. But this is still the otherness of being itself. The human spirit has yet to confront the fully "objective" otherness of an alien world, as it will do in the stance of "*It* is" (B2). The virtues of Excellence (B1) are virtues of wisdom and understanding – not yet the virtues of reason and rationalism they will become in the virtues of Equality (B2), when the arrow of virtue has crossed the line from reverence to self-assertion: from the stance of "It *is*" (B1) to "*It* is" (B2).[15]

I'll come back to those links in chapter 10 and in the second part of this book.

The paradox of Excellence (B1)

In chapter 8 you saw that the initial human paradox reproduces itself in the paradox of self-assertion, dividing each of its poles into paradoxes of their own. That same process of separative projection also occurs, inevitably, within the paradox of reverence, ensuring that Excellence (B1) and Reverence (A2) are themselves split into their own conflicting dualities. I'll now introduce you to each of these, starting with the paradox of Excellence (B1).

Look again at the left-hand side of Table 11, on page 179. Can you see how the competing dynamics of reverence and self-assertion – of "I am" and "It is," of union and non-union – can be found hidden, once again, within this family of the virtues of Excellence (B1)? Can you apply the distinctions I just made between the two columns of Table 11 to the left-hand column alone? Can you see some virtues in the left-hand column that are more assertive than others, and some that are more reverent? Are there some where a judgment has to be made according to a standard? And others where the self seems to give itself more spontaneously, almost for the sake of giving, rather than for the sake of an external standard? Some that imply an otherness ("It *is*"), others an innerness ("I *am*")? Which virtues or goods on the left-hand-side of Table 11 seem to be closer in spirit to either of these two stances?

One of the virtues of Excellence (B1) that clearly seems to imply an *external* standard is truth and truthfulness. When you say something is true, you're making a judgment about reality, about the way things *are*. About the facts of the matter.[16] If you look again at the left-hand side of Table 11, you can see that many of the virtues listed there – knowledge, justice, law – seem to imply or entail some kind of judgment about truth, about the way things are. So one side of the new paradox of Excellence (B1) might be connected by the theme of "truth."

While some of the other virtues in the left-hand column share this same feature (otherwise they wouldn't be virtues of Excellence), they seem to emphasize rather more the inner state or reality about which, or by which, or in which judgments of truth are made. They seem to be *inner* as well as – or maybe even more than – *other*. They seem to partake more of that general quality you saw in Reverence (A2), where something exists or is done for its *own* sake. Justice makes judgments, but it does so according to some standard of goodness.[17] In these other virtues within the paradox of Excellence (B1), it's a not just a question of something being due, but of the very goodness *to* which, or *through* which, or *in* which it's due. Obviously, I could put goodness in this camp, but also wisdom, sincerity, purity, integrity, and so on. Here the common link seems to be some kind of inherent goodness rather than the truth *about* the goodness. To distinguish this new family of virtues from its larger parent family, I'll call it Goodness.[18]

Truth (B1a) and Goodness (B1b) can serve, then, as labels for these next two families of virtues that, together, constitute the paradox of Excellence (B1).[19] You can see what this new paradox looks like in Table 12 on page 184.

Once again, it's important to emphasize that Table 12, like all my other tables so far, is illustrative and suggestive rather than complete, or in any way definitive. It's merely a sample, to give you an idea of how the virtues of Truth (B1a) and Goodness (B1b) contradict each other, or are in some kind of tension, or pull in different directions. How every virtue of Truth (B1a) has a corresponding virtue, or virtues, of Goodness (B1b) by which it is balanced, contrasted, or moderated. And vice versa.

The virtues in the left-hand column of Table 12 render judgments of truth. The importance of thought or mind I noted in the left-hand column of Table 11 has now moved down to the left-hand column (B1a) of Table 12, more than to the right-hand column (B1b). The virtues in the right-hand column, like those on the right-hand of Table 11, embody or express more the inner *spirit* of what is judged in the left-hand column: the standard or spirit of goodness by which judgments of truth are to be made.

I can perhaps bring out this distinction more clearly by, again, pointing out some pairs of virtues that sound very similar. Virtues which looked like synonyms, or as if they were virtually interchangeable, when they were ranged against a contrary in the paradox of reverence, now appear in a different light when they are considered at a deeper level in the paradox of Excellence (B1). This is just like your own experience of family life. You and your sister may stand together as one when facing someone from outside the family, especially if that person differs radically from yourselves, or is even hostile. But, inside your own family, your differences become much more obvious. The same thing happens in the various families of virtues. The slight nuances of meaning or emphasis, which were disguised in a higher or external contrast, suddenly become more apparent when that external contrast is removed.

Honesty and sincerity, for example, sound like very similar virtues. And they are. They're clearly both virtues of reverence. And they're equally clearly virtues of Excellence, or of "It *is*" (B1). But, at this third level, some of their different nuances start to emerge. Honesty has

Table 12. The paradox of Excellence (B1)

Truth (B1a)	Goodness (B1b)
accountability	responsibility (as duty)
beauty (as truth)	beauty (as goodness)
belief *in*	loyalty
commitment	community/loyalty (as duty)
contrition (as honesty)	contrition (as penitence)
dignity	courtesy/deference
discernment	duty
freedom *from* (error)	freedom *from* (evil)
honesty	integrity
honesty	sincerity
insight	integrity/purity
judgment	integrity/purity
judgment	solidarity (as community)
justice	merit
justice	righteousness
knowledge (as understanding)	community/deference
knowledge (as understanding)	duty/righteousness
knowledge (as understanding)	modesty (as purity)
law/rule(-abiding)	duty/integrity/righteousness
law/rule(-abiding)	honour*able*
law/rule(-abiding)	freedom *from*
mindfulness	righteousness
perceptiveness	integrity
remorse	penitence
respect*able*	admir*able*/esteem
serenity	purity
thoughtfulness (as knowledge)	righteousness
thoughtfulness (as knowledge)	honour*able*/trust*worthy*
truth(ful)(ness)	sincerity
truth(ful)(ness)	integrity/righteousness
understanding/wisdom	honourable/trust*worthy*
understanding/wisdom	responsibility (as duty)

a more dispassionate, factual, or empirical connotation, very much in the spirit of "It *is*." Sincerity, on the other hand, seems to express a spirit or impulse that is even more spontaneously, generously, or genuinely self-*giving*. If, in the spirit of "It *is*" (B1), honesty points forward to the rational virtues of Equality, or "*It* is" (B2), sincerity seems to pull in the other direction, back toward the virtues of Reverence, or "I *am*" (A2).

The virtues of loyalty and commitment also sound much the same, at first. They, too, certainly belong together in the family of reverence, and in its sub-family of Excellence (B1). But, at this third level of separative projection, you can again begin to detect nuances which pull in different directions. Commitment seems a more cerebral, rational virtue. You often make a commitment because of some process of thought or reflection. Loyalty is a deeper, more visceral, almost pre-rational virtue. We are born into many of our loyalties, or learn them in our families, very early in our lives. Indeed, as you saw in chapter 1, family itself is, in some ways, simply the virtue of loyalty, in its deepest or most primitive form. Loyalty is also a fundamental virtue because you couldn't have virtues (or good habits) at all, if you couldn't be *loyal to goodness or to the good*.[20] Habits themselves *are* a kind of loyalty: loyalty to a certain kind or type of behaviour. And virtuous behaviour is another higher kind of loyalty. Loyalty to the good.[21] Loyalty has a very close connection with goodness (B1b), and thus pulls in a different direction from commitment, which, like honesty, points forward to the more assertive virtues of Equality (B2).

Similarly, accountability and responsibility look alike when contrasted with other virtues. But, compared to each other, their slight but significant differences emerge. Like honesty and commitment, accountability seems to be the objective response to a concrete condition, or set of facts. And, like sincerity and loyalty, responsibility seems to be the spirit of goodness which animates it, which gives it life, and makes accountability real. You already saw responsibility as a virtue of self-assertion, in the virtues of Equality (B2), where it was related to virtues like prudence and reciprocity. Here, in the virtues of Goodness (B1b), responsibility has a quality more like duty. And, in the next paradox, it will be more like love.[22]

Respectable and admirable also sound very similar. But Paul Ricœur argues that respectable goes with the family of law-abiding (B1a), whereas admirable goes with the family of Goodness (B2b).[23]

You can see this same pattern – synonyms turning into contraries – in the other families of virtues that, together, defines the nature of the human. And you would see it again if I followed the progress of separative projection down one more level. At the next level, you would find, for example, that wisdom and understanding themselves split apart. Understanding turns out to be more concerned about *certainty* than wisdom, which yearns, instead, to *participate* in something only *imperfectly known*.[24] Separative projection goes all the way down.

Or does this split, between wisdom and understanding, occur already, at this level, in the paradox of Excellence (B1)? Should I have put understanding in the family of Truth (B1a), but wisdom in the family of Goodness (B1b)? That's something I invite you to ponder. It will help show you how attention to nuance is needed to judge where the levels occur and to attribute the virtues to their proper families. It will show you how open-ended and debatable many of these judgments are.

Justice is one of the most important among the virtues of Truth (B1a), and one of the most important human virtues of all. In fact, Aristotle says justice is so important that, considered as a "certain kind of moral state," it seems to be virtue itself.[25] It was one of the four ancient, so-called "cardinal virtues," and is the primary virtue of the state. I'll have more to say about justice in chapter 10 because it's a hinge between the virtues of self-assertion and the virtues of reverence: the place where the virtues turn outward, from the self to others. As Aristotle put it, justice is "the good of others,"[26] So it has very close ties with goodness. But it is essentially a virtue of truth because it involves making "accurate" judgments not only about the good, but about proportion, facts, and "circumstances."[27] In matters of justice, everything depends on the truth of the circumstances. Justice makes judgments about the truth of goodness, and thus about how to apply it in specific circumstances. Justice shows how closely Truth and Goodness are connected within the virtues of Excellence (B1).

I should also draw your attention to some virtues – like beauty and contrition – that appear in both columns of Table 12, depending on the emphasis given to one side of them or another.[28] You can bring out the two sides of contrition by considering the contrasting virtues of remorse and penitence. Remorse is a kind of regret, acknowledging the *truth* of a bad action. Penitence focuses more on the *good* action or actions to which, as a result, you now aspire.

And you should note the presence here of another virtue you've already met, in slightly different forms, and will meet again later, in others. You already met freedom as a virtue of self-assertion, in the forms of freedom *to* (A1) and freedom *of* (B2). In the family of Excellence (B1), and in the sub-family of Goodness (B1b), freedom appears now as freedom *from*. Both freedom from error or untruth and freedom from all the vices which block virtue: freedom *from* the *bad* habits that prevent you from developing and maintaining the *good* habits that define the nature of the human. "Deliver us *from* evil," says the Lord's Prayer. That's what freedom means here. As I mentioned in chapter 5, this was one important way the language of freedom entered our Western vocabulary. In the virtues of reverence, freedom means no longer (as it did in the virtues of self-assertion) the liberation *of* the self. It now means freedom *from* the self: freedom from the self's own self-assertion.

The paradox of Reverence (A2)

By now you should have become accustomed to the dynamic of separative projection and be able to anticipate how the right-hand side of the paradox of reverence will also yield its own internal paradox – which I will call the paradox of Reverence (A2). Look again at Table 11 on page 179. Can you see how the conflicting dynamics of reverence and self-assertion – of union and non-union, of "I am" and "It is" – might again divide this field of virtues into yet another paradox?

Consider the two virtues of gratitude and generosity, for example. Gratitude is the virtuous attitude to adopt toward some benefit received from another. But generosity is the very virtue for which one should be grateful. Generosity and gratitude are the "two poles of a single relation."[29] Generosity is, as it were, the virtue gratitude is pointing us toward. The first is responsive and, in a sense, still somewhat self-regarding. After all, you are grateful for something *you* have received. The other is a spontaneous overflowing of virtue.

Similarly, respect*ful*ness and trust are virtues we should show to another we value, but gentleness, kindness, and mercy seem to be the kind of virtues that would justify such respect and trust. Humility and modesty are the proper attitudes to adopt toward something of greater worth, but forgiveness, benevolence, and compassion are the responses they seek. Devotion and selflessness seem to be consequences of virtues such as concern and self-giving. In each case the first virtues seem to point us to the second.

Can you discern threads or themes connecting the first and the second sets of virtues? In each case the difference seems to be a slightly different balance between self-*seeking* and self-*giving*. In the first there seems still to be a trace of self-assertion, if only in the consciousness of the gap that exists between yourself and something else of far greater worth. In the second set of virtues, it would be a mistake to say that the self has disappeared altogether because virtue would then be impossible, since there would then be no self to carry it out. But here the self is even more actively involved in giving itself away to others. The second virtues are all forms of spontaneous self-emptying and self-*giving*.

What should I call this second set of virtues? The answer is obvious. Because the highest form of self-giving, as we all know, is love. So I'll call one side of this new paradox: Love (A2b).

What shall I call the other side? This isn't quite as easy. In fact, it's one of the most difficult choices I've faced in this book. One good word is "communion." It's a very important word in contemporary thought, one that captures many of the characteristic features of this family of virtues, especially such virtues as solidarity, participation, harmony, devotion, and attachment.[30] Another good word is "transcendence." This excellent word links well to virtues of this family such as awe, wonder, hope, joy, praise, worship, and so on.[31] "Transcendence" also captures the way in which the virtues of this family form a kind of bridge between the pure self-giving of the virtues of Love (A2b) and recognition of the objective goodness and truth implicit *in* these virtues: between the virtues of Reverence (A2) and the virtues of Excellence (B1). "Transcendence" captures the growing recognition of an objective otherness beyond the self, an otherness of highest worth: the transition from "I *am*" (A2) to "It *is*" (B1). In this family, "transcendence" still signifies primarily unselfing: that is, the transcending of the self. But it points forward to another kind of transcendence: transcendence as wisdom, truth, enlightenment, or revelation, in the virtues of Excellence (B1).

Communion and transcendence are both excellent words, and I could easily choose either of them as the name for this sub-sub-family of virtues. But, to my ear, neither of them fully captures what Aquinas calls the distinctive "note" that can be heard throughout this (or any other) family of virtues. And, in ordinary English, they both seem to be better for expressing an end point or result, rather than the human stance, action, or virtue that *gets* you there. The common thread connecting virtues or modes of being such as awe, faithfulness, gratitude, humility, praise, respectfulness, ritual, solemnity, and worship seems to be that same acknowledgment of superior *worth* (the literal meaning of "worship") – our relationship with it, and our potential obligations toward it – that (in chapter 5, and again at the beginning of this chapter) I identified as a core characteristic of reverence. Reverence still seems to be the connecting thread or hinge between love, on the one hand, and truth and goodness, on the other.[32] As I already said, it seems to go all the way down. I think George Eliot (1819–80) gets the two sides of the paradox of Reverence (A2) exactly right, when she says: "The first condition of human goodness is something to love [A2b]; the second, something to reverence [A2a]."[33] For these reasons, I'm going to use the name reverence once again, for the other side of this paradox. But, to distinguish it from the first level of separative projection, I'll capitalize it again. And to distinguish it from the second level, the larger family (A2) to which it belongs, I'll add a superscript and make it Reverence[3] to indicate that it occurs at this third level of separative projection. If you feel uncomfortable with my decision to use the word "reverence" for a third time, feel free to substitute "communion" or "transcendence" or any other word you think best captures the common "note" of this important family of virtues. Here and elsewhere, please keep in mind that the name for a family of virtues isn't what really matters, but rather the virtues themselves that compose it. Look beyond the name to the family itself.[34]

Table 13 on page 190 shows what this second paradox of reverence looks like.

I've found this final table of opposites particularly challenging to construct. The two families of Reverence[3] (A2a) and Love (A2b) are clear enough.[35] And, fortunately for me, that's the really important thing in this book. Getting everything in its right place is less crucial. The containers are more important than the contained. Nonetheless, figuring out which virtues belong to which side of the paradox of Reverence (A2) at this level has been tricky, and I've changed my mind more than once. I'm even less sure here than elsewhere, that I've got it right. There's lots of room for you to make your own judgments here, as in all the paradoxes, at this third level.

For example, the proper location of virtues like hope and joy has not been easy for me. Hope and joy seem to have some of that exuberant, outward impulse I associated with the virtues of Love (A2b). But they're also states of mind, character, or spirit. They seem to be about the virtuous person *herself*, rather than about her self-giving to *others*. They seem to be the outside of a virtue, of which love is the inside. They seem to refer, beyond themselves, to something else, or to be pointing toward it. I think that, like devotion, humility, modesty, and selflessness, they're pointing toward the even more purely self-*giving* virtues of Love (A2b). The latter seem to be what you would be hopeful or joyous *about*. So, in this version, I decided, in the end, that hope and joy are virtues of Reverence[3] (A2a). But I might well be wrong.

Awe and wonder are another puzzle, not unlike wisdom and understanding in the virtues of Excellence (B1), that is, synonyms that can split apart as soon as their previous contrary is removed. They look more or less equivalent when contrasted with the virtues of Excellence (B1), the other family of reverence. They also seem more cerebral, more self-focussed and self-aware, less wholeheartedly self-giving than the virtues of Love (A2b) like benevolence, compassion, forgiveness, and generosity. Therefore, in this version I've kept them together in the family I've called Reverence[3] (A2a). But, when you look at them by themselves, they have quite different overtones and will clearly separate, if not at this level of separative projection, then at the next. "Wonder and awe are akin, but distinct," says Martha Nussbaum (b. 1947): "wonder is outward-moving, exuberant, whereas awe is linked with bending or making oneself small. In wonder I want to leap or run, in awe to kneel."[36] Nussbaum's description of the difference between awe and wonder sounds a lot like the contrast I just identified between the virtues of Love (A2b) and of Reverence[3] (A2a). Have I got it wrong? Does wonder belong to the virtues of Love (A2b), at this level? Or does the

Table 13. The paradox of Reverence (A2)

Reverence[3] (A2a)	Love (A2b)
acceptance	giving/sharing
admiration/esteem	forgiveness/patience
attachment (as communion)	forbearance/forgiveness
awe	agape/empathy/mercy/sympathy
communion	care, concern
connectedness	kindness
detachment (as unselfing)	generosity/giving
devotion	benevolence
dignity (as reverence)/formality	cheerfulness/kindness
enlightenment (as unselfing)	agape
faith	generosity
fidelity/loyalty (as devotion)	agape/charity
freedom *for* (unselfing, gratitude)	freedom *for* (self-giving, love)
fullness/fulfilment	forgiveness
grace (as gratitude)	grace (as giving)
gratitude	benevolence/generosity
honou*ring*	giving
hope	gentleness/helpfulness/kindness
hope	patience
humility	benevolence
humility	forgiveness
identity/participation	kindness/peacefulness/sharing
joy	cheerfulness/friendliness
meekness	mercy
modesty (as humility)	compassion/empathy
openness	giving/sharing
participation	peacefulness
patience (as unselfing)	patience (as kindness)
piety	service
praise	service
receiving/receptivity	giving/sharing
respect*ful*	love/patience
reverence	love
ritual	benevolence
sacrifice	sharing
selflessness/unselfing	self-giving
simplicity	generosity
solemnity	self-giving
solidarity (as communion)	solidarity (as love)
transcendence (as unselfing)	self-giving
trust(ing)	giving
union/unity	compassion
wonder	responsibility (as love)
worship	love

split occur at the next? That's something for you to think about. And, once again, it helps to show you how much discernment is required to get everything in its proper place as separative projection works its way down through the virtues of the human paradox.

I should also point out two other features of the paradox of Reverence (A2) in Table 13. The first is that freedom appears again here. Whereas freedom took the form of "freedom *to*" in the virtues of Liberty (A1), "freedom *of*" in the virtues of Equality (B2), and "freedom *from*" in the virtues of Excellence (B1), here it takes the form of "freedom *for*": both freedom *for* unselfing, gratitude, and devotion (A2a) and freedom *for* self-giving and love (A2b).

Another thing to note is that "reverence" appears, for the first time, on the left-hand rather than the right-hand side of the table. Why should that be so? The reason is that the left-hand side of all these tables is the more assertive, and the right-hand side more self-giving. Hitherto "reverence" signified the side of the paradox which was less assertive and more self-giving, the side that highlighted union rather than non-union, "I am" rather than "It is." So it was always on the right. Now, for the first time, it's the reverse. The highest form of the "virtues of reverence" turns out to be love, whereas reverence itself retains overtones suggesting it wants to humble itself before an otherness of superior worth, overtones that link it back to an "It *is*." In comparison to Love (A2b), the virtues of Reverence[3] (A2a) seem to lean "backward" (or forward, in the arrow of virtue) toward the other side of the first-level paradox of reverence, that is to say, toward the virtues of Excellence (B1). This seems to confirm that "reverence" is the right name for the overall family of virtues that constitutes one side of the human paradox. Reverence seems to be a quality unifying all four families on one side of that basic paradox: linking love to goodness and to truth.

Unity in complexity

I've now sketched out fourteen families of virtues that, together, constitute the first three levels of the human paradox: two initial families, reflecting the basic human paradox; four sub-families into which the first two divide; and, finally, at the third level, eight sub-sub-families of virtues resulting from the division of the four sub-families identified at the second level.

The process, at all three levels, reflects the polar structure of being, the basic duality of unity and plurality, something and other, or self and world. It's the inevitable result of the process of *separative projection* (or what Hegel calls "intro-Reflection"). Because of the polarity of being, division is inevitable at each level. But it can only take place *within* a larger whole. At each stage, division occurs in such a manner as to reproduce attachment at the next. Polarity breeds polarities. Paradox breeds paradox. Non-union goes on reproducing itself *and* its opposite, all the way down.

I've now created an inventory of the human spirit in its most complete form – or as complete as I'm going to try to make it in this book. We don't yet have a map of the human spirit. But we have the content *for* the map. Constructing the map is one of the tasks for chapter 10.

At the end of this chapter, as in chapter 8, you can find Table 14, which shows all the virtues of reverence from Tables 1 and 3 on pages 68–9 and 106, now listed alphabetically in the four sub-sub-families of the virtues of reverence. But before concluding this chapter, I need to make, or repeat, several points about this table, and about all the others in this book.

First of all, as I've said already, none of the tables or lists in this book is intended to be complete, or in any way definitive. They could all go on for pages. In fact, they could fill a whole book. You may be able to think of many other virtues I haven't included.

You may also be able to think of alternative ways of presenting or arranging them. You may think some virtues belong in different families than those to which I've assigned them. That's fine with me because I'm not absolutely certain I've got everything right here, especially the attribution of some of the individual virtues to their proper families.

The really important thing to grasp is not so much the content of these tables as what's going on here: how the polarity of being manifests itself in the nature of the human, spinning increasing depth, complexity, and conflict from a simple initial duality. What's important for my purposes in this book are the containers, even more than the contained. The virtues themselves are very important. Without them, there would be nothing human, and there would certainly be no book here, either. Each of them deserves deep and lengthy reflection, the kind Aristotle gave some of them in his *Nicomachean Ethics*, and Thomas Aquinas gave to even more of them in his *Summa Theologiæ*.[37] But that isn't my objective in this book. I'm more interested, here, in the *architecture* of all the virtues than in the specific content of each one of them.[38] My goal is to construct a map of the human virtues that will help you to understand better the nature of the human, and thus your own nature, too. And not just to understand it, but to live your life in a more humane way, in harmony with the full nature of the human.

The process of deriving new and deeper levels of paradox could go on indefinitely. But in a book the process is limited by the length of the original list of virtues. No matter how many virtues I started with, they would eventually winnow down to only two contrasting virtues from my original list. I won't try to go that far. I'll stop here so I can get on with the other tasks I want to accomplish in this book.

Another point to underline is the unity in all this complexity. Although the polar structure of being and the resulting process of separative projection go on producing division, the new poles don't stand alone. In fact, they might even be said to "lean" *toward* each other[39] – as you just saw, in case of the virtues of Reverence[3] (A2a), which seem to "lean" toward the virtues of Excellence (B1). The various families of virtues "lean" in more than one direction, depending on the perspective from which you view them. Compared to *another* paradox, the two sides of a paradox seem to lean toward each other. But compared with their partner *within* a paradox, the eight sub-sub-families of virtues at the third level seem to lean toward *another* duality. Compared with Love (A2b), for example, Reverence[3] (A2a) seems to "lean" toward Excellence (B1), as you just saw. But compared with Goodness (B1b), Truth (B1a) seems to "lean" toward Equality (B2); and compared with Truth, Goodness (B1b) seems to "lean" toward Reverence (A2). I'll come back to some of these important links in other chapters.

The story of the human paradox is one of unity and simplicity as well as of division and complexity. Yet another paradox! And it's very important to do adequate justice to both sides of this one. As you've seen in the last two chapters, the nature of the human is infinitely complex, a vast, expanding "kaleidoscope" of virtues, all of them in some degree of conflict or tension with each other.[40] Human beings live, by definition, in a world of "conflicting values": that is the very "condition of their humanity."[41] The human spirit is "a 'parliament' of competing instincts,"[42] a "great cauldron of conflicting ideas and motives ... an inner landscape so rich it seems to defy reduction."[43] That makes the nature of the human almost impossible to encompass, describe, or pin down, especially in any kind of linear thought process or ordinary prose. The only way to do justice to this kind of riotous complexity of the human is through something like the vaulting imagination of a Shakespeare, or the sprawling variety of the Jewish scriptures and the Talmud. The overflowing richness of their *contradictions* is the source of their incomparable truth.[44]

Yet all of this complexity and conflict emerges from a relatively simple framework, a framework established by the simple initial opposition of unity and plurality, something and everything, self and world. This original paradox is, to the expanding human universe of virtues, what the Big Bang is to the physical universe.[45]

In the last few chapters I've been emphasizing the variety, complexity, and conflicts of the human. In the next chapter I'll try to restore some of the original simplicity and clarity. Having distinguished, I'll now try to unite.

Table 14. The paradoxes of reverence: a sample list of virtues
Two sub-families and four sub-sub-families of the virtues of reverence

The paradox of Excellence (B1) Something is *due*		The paradox of Reverence (A2) Giving for the *sake* of giving	
Truth (B1a)	Goodness (B1b)	Reverence[3] (A2a)	Love (A2b)
1. accountability	1. admirable	1. acceptance	1. agape
2. attachment	2. adorable	(as gratitude/	2. altruism
(as commitment)	3. beauty	respectfulness)	3. benevolence
3. authenticity	(as goodness)	2. admiration	4. car(e)(ing)
4. beauty (as truth)	4. cleanliness	3. adoration	5. charity
5. belief *in*	(as purity)	4. attachment	6. cheerfulness
6. commitment	5. chastity	(as communion)	7. compassion
7. contrition	6. community	5. awe	8. concern
(as honesty)	(as duty)	6. communion	9. empathy
8. dignity (as serenity,	7. contrition	7. community	10. forbearance
wisdom)	(as goodness)	(as communion)	(as forgiveness)
9. discernment	8. courtesy	8. connectedness	11. forgiveness
10. enlightenment	9. decency	9. detachment	12. freedom *for*
(as wisdom)	10. deference	(as unselfing)	(love)
11. equity (as what	11. dignity	10. devotion	13. friend(liness)
is due)	(as worthiness)	11. dignity	(ship)
12. fairness (as what	12. duty/dutiful(ness)	(as reverence)	14. generosity
is due)	13. estimable	12. enlightenment	15. gentleness
13. freedom *from*	14. excellence	(as unselfing)	16. giving
(error)	15. fidelity (as duty)	13. esteem	17. grace
14. grace (as beauty)	16. freedom *from*	(as respectful)	(as giving/
15. harmony	(evil)	14. faith(ful)(ness)	mercy)
(as beauty/	17. glory	15. fidelity	18. harmony
grace)	(as goodness)	(as devotion)	(as peace)
16. honesty	18. goodness	16. formality	19. helpfulness
17. idealism	19. grace (as dignity/	17. freedom *for*	20. human(ity)
18. insight	goodness)	(unselfing)	(eness)
19. judgment	20. harmony	18. fullness/fulfilment	21. kindness
(as wisdom)	(as goodness)	19. grace (as gratitude)	22. love
20. justice	21. honour(able)	20. gratitude	23. mercy
21. knowledge	22. integrity	21. harmony	24. openness
(as wisdom)	(as wholeness)	(as communion)	(as charity/
22. law/rule (-abiding)	23. loyalty (as duty)	22. honour(ing)	mercy)
23. meaning (ful)(ness)	24. merit(orious)	23. hope	25. patience
24. mindfulness	25. modesty	24. humility	(as kindness)
25. openness	(as purity)	25. identity	
(as honesty)		(as communion)	

(*Continued*)

Table 14. The paradoxes of reverence: a sample list of virtues
Two sub-families and four sub-sub-families of the virtues of reverence (*Continued*)

The paradox of Excellence (B1) Something is *due*		The paradox of Reverence (A2) Giving for the *sake* of giving	
Truth (B1a)	Goodness (B1b)	Reverence[3] (A2a)	Love (A2b)
26. perceptiveness	26. nobility	26. joy/joyful(ness)	26. peace(ful)(ness)
27. remorse	27. penitence	27. loyalty	27. pity
28. respect(able)	28. purity	(as devotion)	28. responsibility
29. revelation	29. responsibility	28. meekness	(as love)
30. right (as justice/	(as duty)	29. modesty	29. self-giving
law)	30. righteousness	(as humility)	30. service
31. rights(-giving)	31. solidarity	30. mutuality	31. sharing
32. serenity	(as duty)	(as communion)	32. solidarity
33. sincerity	32. transcendence	31. openness	(as love)
34. thoughtfulness	(as goodness)	(as trusting)	33. sympathy
(as wisdom)	33. trust(worthy)	32. participation	34. thoughtfulness
35. transcendence	34. valu(e)(able)	33. patience	(as kindness)
(as revelation)	35. wholeness	(as unselfing)	35. tranquility
36. truth(ful)(ness)	36. worth(y)(iness)	34. piety	(as peaceful-
37. understanding		35. praise	ness)
38. wisdom		36. receiving/receptiv-	
		ity (as communion,	
		gratitude)	
		37. respect(ful)	
		38. reticence	
		39. reverence	
		40. ritual/rite	
		41. sacrifice	
		42. selflessness/	
		unselfing	
		43. simplicity	
		44. solemnity	
		45. solidarity	
		(as communion)	
		46. thankfulness	
		47. tranquility	
		(as unselfing)	
		48. transcendence	
		(as unselfing)	
		49. trust(ing)	
		50. union/unity	
		51. unknowing	
		52. valuing	
		53. wonder	
		54. worship	

10

Four Families of Virtues

In the last two chapters, you've seen how the initial paradox – of something and everything, unity and plurality, or self and world – gives life to an expanding universe of human virtues, all of them in some degree of conflict or tension with each other. Since the manifestations of human behaviour are virtually endless, this process of expansion and increasing complexity could go on almost indefinitely. The dynamic of separative projection ensures that each new pole will divide again into its own two poles, and so on, *ad infinitum*.[1]

I have traced the process only down to its third level, but already I've identified some fourteen families of virtues across these three different levels. At the next level I would have to add another sixteen and, at the next, another thirty-two, and so on. The question for me now is: where to stop? What configuration would make a map of the nature of the human most useful and usable? Is the optimum number two? Or four? Or eight? Or sixteen?

The duality of the original human paradox is very important because its dynamic determines all the rest. The conflicting virtues of reverence and self-assertion define the very nature of the human, so you should never lose sight of them. Their simultaneous opposition and union are the human paradox which serves as the title of this book. While this original duality is fundamental, it's also, in a way, too simple. It doesn't help you to see the tensions and conflicts lurking within those two initial families, or the way in which their tensions will explode into a vast, expanding, complex, and contradictory universe of the human virtues. Nor does it help you see how these new, emerging poles can recombine in surprising ways – across the boundaries of their own initial families of virtues – to spawn unexpected combinations and mutations. This potential is fundamental to the arrow of virtue and will be especially important in some areas of human behaviour, such as political life.[2]

Two isn't enough to be really useful for my ongoing exploration of the nature of the human. But if two is too few, eight – or sixteen or thirty-two – seems too many. I'll need to show you eight or more families from time to time, in the following chapters. But as a basic tool or framework, a field of eight or more would yield a map too large and complex to be easily remembered or used in operational ways.

Four seems, then, to be the right number. A map of four basic families of human virtues is sufficiently complex to be suggestive about its potential further developments, yet simple enough to be memorable and usable. It has enough detail to show internal tensions and potential external links, but it won't overwhelm with excess detail.

Toward a map of the virtues

To display these four families in a memorable image offering both simplicity and complexity, the table format I've been using in the last two chapters isn't ideal. Tables are useful for displaying rather long lists of contraries, as the Pythagoreans first showed us. But they aren't as useful for showing multiple relationships, as well as foreground and background. To do that, I need to return instead to the circular figure I employed in the first chapters and in Chapter 7. Figure 17 on page 147 gave you a basic image of the human in its fullest form to that point in the book. But I now need to show how its four quadrants, the four human stances (of "*I* am," "I *am*," "It *is*," and "*It* is") correspond to the four basic families of virtues. I need to import into that image all the insights you've gained along the way about the nature of the human virtues.

Based on the basic image developed in Figure 17, you can see an initial simple map of the nature of the human, in Figure 19 on page 198.

In Figure 19 you can see the placement and relationship between the four basic families of human virtues, here designated by the four key words of Reverence and Excellence, Liberty, and Equality (but for which other words might well be chosen). There are several things to be noted about this first image, which will recur in different versions later in this book.

The first thing to note is that Figure 19 retains the shorthand labels (A1, A2, B1, and B2) for each of the four quadrants that I introduced in Figure 17, on page 147. And, in Figure 19, these shorthand labels still have all the purposes and uses I mentioned there: they're intended to remind you that, regardless of the language or the titles I may use at different times or in different chapters, I'm still referring to these four basic human stances; the shorthand labels help to highlight the links

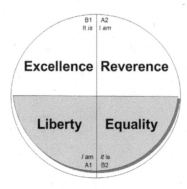

Figure 19. Four families of virtues

between the top quadrants and the bottom quadrants; they should also help remind you about what I called the "arrow of virtue," the dynamic that starts from the human stance of "*I* am" and leads through "*I* am" to "*It* is," and "*It* is" back to the starting point of "*I* am." The labels of A1, A2, B1, and B2 will also give me a shorthand way of showing how these four basic human stances crop up in many contexts, and in the thought and writing of thinkers through the ages.

But, from now on, these four shorthand labels have another important additional function. They should also serve as a reminder that the names I've chosen for each of the four sub-families of virtues (and their sub-sub-families) are merely titles for the larger families of virtues that stand behind them: the sub-families and sub-sub-families you can see in Tables 10 and 14. *And it's the family that's important, not the name.* From now on, whenever I refer to one of the families of virtues, I will add its shorthand label as follows: the virtues of Liberty (A1), the virtues of Reverence (A2), the virtues of Excellence (B1), and the virtues of Equality (B2). Sometimes I'll just use the even shorter form: Liberty (A1), Equality (B2), etc. When I use this shorter form, I'm not referring to only one virtue. The silent words "the virtues of" are always understood. The consistent shorthand label (A1, etc.) can help remind you of the many other virtues in the family designated by its title virtue (or value). The consistent inclusion of the shorthand label may seem repetitive. But remember: its purpose is to signify that I'm *never* referring to a single virtue, but rather, to *a whole family of virtues*, of which the title virtue (or value) is merely one.

A second thing to notice about Figure 19 is that two of the families – Liberty (A1) and Equality (B2) – are located on the grey semicircle which nestles within and above the wider white circle. You will remember from the first chapters that the grey semicircle (originally a round dot) stands for all the individual, physical things we can see, including ourselves and other people. So the placement of these two families of virtues on the grey semicircle indicates that the families of Liberty (A1) and Equality (B2) are the families of virtues we exercise especially in relation to that physical world, or when we think of ourselves primarily as separate, individual, physical beings located in a concrete, physical world of other things, one that can be explained by material and efficient causes alone. Since that is the kind of world we have been living in increasingly since the seventeenth century, it's not surprising that these virtues are the dominant ones in our contemporary world – indeed, they are almost the only ones now to be found in our public and political conversations.

A third thing to notice about Figure 19 is that the other two families – Excellence (B1) and Reverence (A2) – are located, instead, within the white circle which, you will recall, designates the invisible background of everything else – or of being – that surrounds and encompasses the individual, physical things we can see and manipulate, including ourselves and our bodies. Nothing can stand alone. Those individual things couldn't exist without that background. We can't see it. But it's as much a part of our everyday reality as the visible things we *can* see and control. And our response to it is as much a part of what it means to be human as the more familiar modern virtues found in the families of Liberty (A1) and Equality (B2). Our response to it is also one of our important sources of knowledge – perhaps our most important source – about the nature of the background itself.

You will also notice that, in the version of my basic image found in Figure 19, I have again capitalized Reverence (A2). This is to remind you that I've used the word "reverence" at all three levels of the human virtues examined so far. Reverence, as I suggested, is a quality that seems to go all the way down. At the first level – the simple duality of reverence and self-assertion – no capital was necessary for reverence. But at the next two levels I need to make changes that will distinguish them from other levels. So, at the second level, I have put a capital on Reverence, to signify the whole sub-family of virtues belonging to the quadrant A2. And at the third level of separative projection, I added a superscript. These changes of form are designed to distinguish the "lower" (or later) families of reverence from the "higher" (or earlier) ones, out of which they emerged as new polarities. Whenever you see some future version of this four-part image of Figure 19, remember that Reverence (with a capital) stands for only one half of the virtues of reverence (lower case), the half that is in tension with the other side of reverence, the virtues of Excellence (B1).

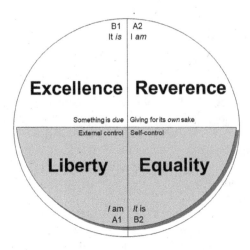

Figure 20. Four families of virtues (2)

Another thing to notice about Figure 19 is both the horizontal *and* the vertical relationships between the four quadrants. The horizontal relationships are visually obvious because of the different background colours I've used for the top and bottom pairs. They're also conceptually obvious because Liberty (A1) and Equality (B2) are the two sides of the virtues of self-assertion, just as Excellence (B1) and Reverence (A2) are the two sides of the virtues of reverence. The two pairs are parts of two larger unities. They're distinct and in tension with each other, but they're also two sides of the same coin, two sides of two larger wholes. I can show you some of the things that simultaneously distinguish and unite the horizontal pairs, by making some first additions to this basic image, as in Figure 20 above.

Figure 20 reminds you that the virtues of self-assertion are united by their common impulse to exercise some kind of control. But in the case of the virtues in the family of Liberty (A1), the emphasis is on instrumental control and domination of *others* and of the external environment, while the contrasting family of Equality (B2) introduces the notion of *self*-control. The bottom right-hand quadrant is the home of what Thomas Aquinas called the "rational appetite" or the "will," which seeks to control the impulses to Power (A1a) and Pleasure (A1b) (the "passions" of the "irascible" and "concupiscible" appetites) that, in Chapter 8, you saw to be the two sides of the virtues of Liberty (A1).

Figure 20 also reminds you that the two families of the virtues of reverence are united by relinquishing control, by their common recognition that an equally important part of what it is to be human is to acknowledge the importance – maybe even the primacy – of something other than our-selves – hence the necessity of being self-giving as well as self-seeking. But, at the same time, these next two families are also distinguished by their contrary takes on why we should be self-giving. For the family of Excellence (B1), it's because of what is due to the other. For this family, there's an external standard – truth or goodness – to which some kind of deference is due. But for the family of Reverence (A2), self-giving is no longer motivated solely by what's due. It's because of the very goodness and fullness of giving itself. Giving for the very sake of giving. Giving for its own sake.[3] Thomas Aquinas says that a virtue of Reverence (A2) (such as forgiveness) is "like giving a present."[4]

These important horizontal relationships are balanced and comple-mented by equally important vertical relationships between the quad-rants. I'll come back to some of these later in this chapter, and also in later chapters. But, for the moment, notice that the notations at the top or bottom of the four quadrants remind you that the virtues to be found in each of them express four different human stances toward the world. The *emphasis* – either on the subject or the verb (I *am* and It *is* vs. I am and It is) – indicates the *horizontal* links. But the common *subjects* (I am and I *am* vs. It *is* and It is) indicate equally important *diagonal* relationships. Later, I'll discuss some other more directly vertical links. But the two I want you to notice here are diagonal, forming an X. As I mentioned, that's one of the reasons I've given them the short-hand labels of A1 and A2, or B1 and B2: to emphasize the organic unities between the bottom left and top right quadrants, and between the top left and bottom right quadrants.

The diagonal pair of A1 and A2, ending in "am," reflects and expresses the being – the miraculous fact of existence – that underlies our human life. In fact, the two sides of this pair – I am and I *am* – are the expression (the lived experience) of that life itself, the life without which nothing else human would be possible, and on which everything human de-pends. These are the two "existential" stances. The diagonal pair of B1 and B2, beginning with "It," are the "ontological" stances, which reflect and express the inevitable encounter between human life and the *world*: the reality that surrounds and encompasses the self, a reality that is *other* than itself. A reality which can therefore become an "it," separate from the life that encounters it. Because the human encounter with this ex-ternal other or "it" involves *awareness* – an awareness that can develop from an affective or emotional awareness into a conscious or rational awareness – the axis of B1 and B2 (the virtues of Excellence and Equality) can also be called the axis of cognition or reason, while the axis of A1 and A2 (the virtues of Liberty and Reverence) is the axis of life or exist-ence.[5] The combination of the four families of virtues in two contrasting,

diagonal axes defines the nature of the human just as much as the horizontal alignment between the virtues of self-assertion and of reverence,
respectively. Understanding this "other" human paradox – of "I am" (A1
and A2) and "It is" (B1 and B2) – is one of the most urgent challenges for
our contemporary world, and I'll come back to it in chapter 17.

These diagonal relationships can be viewed as static and conceptual,
or dynamic and even historical. There's an obvious logical or conceptual link between human stances with common subjects ("I" or "It").
But, as you saw in Chapter 7, there also seems to be a natural – even
temporal – progression among them: a progression that leads from
A1 to A2 to B1 to B2, and then back to A1. In chapter 7, I called this
"figure-of-eight" movement the "arrow of virtue." In some later chapters, you'll see how the arrow of virtue seems to be found in human
evolution and in the history of Western thought, among other places.[6]

Mapping other approaches

At this point in our exploration, it may help you to see how this basic
map of the human stacks up against some other traditional approaches,
including classical Western and Eastern thinking about the virtues, as
well as North American Indigenous traditions.

As you saw in chapter 3, the lens of the virtues is one of the oldest ways
humans have employed to think about the nature of the human. For Confucius, Plato, Aristotle, Thomas Aquinas, and for almost all serious thinkers until the modern era, the virtues were the natural and necessary way
to think about the nature of the human. The Western traditions identified
seven classical virtues: four from Greek thought, originally highlighted by
Plato[7] – the so-called "cardinal" virtues: courage, justice, prudence, and
temperance – and three from the Christian tradition, the so-called "theological"* virtues: faith, hope, and love.[8] As I noted at the end of the previous chapter, these seven weren't the only virtues discussed by the classical
authors. Aristotle mentioned at least eleven virtues. Thomas Aquinas
mentioned about forty, but he thought all of them could be grouped under
the "family" headings of the cardinal or theological virtues.[9]

In Figure 21 on page 203 you can see how these seven classical virtues correspond to the four families of virtues I've identified so far.

As you can see here, the seven classical virtues seem to fit rather well
inside the four families of virtues identified in this book and correspond

---

* "Theological" is a misleading term in English and encourages the natural, but mistaken, assumption that these virtues have something to do with "theology." I address
this problem below, on page 205.

Figure 21. The seven classical virtues

to their defining characteristics. Before going any further, it may be helpful to say a little more about these key virtues.

As you've already seen, courage (or fortitude) is not only the key virtue of self-assertion, it's also the "engine room" of all the other virtues. Without the energy, drive, and sheer *unadulterated self-assertion* that come from the virtues of Liberty (A1) – from the stance of "*I* am" – there would be no virtues at all. It's courage and the other virtues of this family that make everything else that is human possible. Compared to pure self-assertion, "even the external world is secondary," says C.G. Jung (1875–1961), "for what does the world matter if the endogenous impulse to grasp it and manipulate it is lacking?"[10]

But, for the same reasons, the pure self-assertion expressed by courage is also the source of much, if not most, of evil. That's why the virtues of temperance and prudence are necessary. They're also a form of self-assertion, but their object of assertion is the self itself.[11] These virtues of self-control ensure the virtues of courage don't go off the rails, veering from virtue to vice. They constrain and guide the "irascible" and "concupiscible" appetites of Power (A1a) and Pleasure (A1b) – into which, as you saw in Chapter 8, the virtues of Liberty (A1) divide at the third level of separative projection. Aristotle's and Aquinas' idea of prudence was much more expansive than what our modern word conveys to us. To our post-modern ears, prudence sounds like a rather fussy, cautious virtue.[12] But for them it was "practical wisdom" (*phronēsis*), and was, for Aquinas, the "principal" moral virtue, directing and controlling the others. However, it was still a calculating, self-assertive virtue, turned inward, to control the "passions."[13]

Justice has a quite different character. While the other "cardinal" virtues look inward, toward the self, justice looks outward, toward others. It is, as Aristotle says, "the good of others."[14] While the other moral virtues are about the "interior passions," justice is about "external things," and about rendering each one, as Aquinas says, "what is due, neither more nor less." Through justice "man establishes order not only in himself but in relation to another."[15] For this reason, Aristotle considers justice to be the "complete" or "sovereign" virtue. For him it is "not a part of virtue, but the whole of it."[16]

Justice in this expansive sense has three key notions. One is the principle I identified earlier, of "what is due." Another is the notion of equity. But equity doesn't mean – or doesn't yet mean – equal.[17] Justice as "fairness," in the sense of equality, belongs in the bottom right quadrant, not in the top left. The full meaning of justice includes the broader idea of "appropriate," "fitting," or "proportional" which makes distinctions between things based on merit or value.[18] So this larger concept of justice – the kind Aristotle has in mind when he calls it the "sovereign" virtue – implies an external standard of some kind. "[F]or justice especially, in comparison with other virtues," says Aquinas, "an impersonal, objective interest is fixed."[19] To be just, you can't simply make it up, or do what you like, or even treat everyone exactly the same. If you're going to render what's due to things and to people, you need to know what *is* due. You need some standard of goodness or excellence. You can't know the "good of others" unless you have some idea of the good. And you also need to know how to compare or rank the various goods, in order to judge what might be due to them. The idea of the good implies a potential *hierarchy* of goods. So the idea of justice necessarily includes the idea that human beings aren't always sovereign, but can also be subject to something "superior."[20]

If you can't simply do what you want, if you have to think about the good of others, if you need some objective standards, external to yourself, and if you have to pay attention to what ranks higher than something else, you've clearly moved beyond the virtues of self-assertion. Because the classical virtue of justice involves all of these elements, it's rightly located in the virtues of reverence. It's an expression of the human stance of "It *is*" (B1).

But justice is only the first of the classical virtues of reverence. It expresses only "what is due" according to some external standard of goodness or truth. It doesn't yet go *beyond* what is due: beyond it to those virtues in which giving seems to be good for its *own* sake, not merely for the sake of what's due. The virtue of reverence we know as justice must be complemented and completed by the three virtues of faith, hope, and love, the virtues of reverence Aquinas referred to as the "theological" virtues.

It's important to emphasize that, in this context, the English word "theological" doesn't have its usual, modern meaning, referring to "theology," a kind of thought or academic discipline. In relation to the virtues, the word "theological" refers instead to the fact that these three additional virtues seem to go well beyond the usual capacities of human beings: they require some extra strength beyond what we normally think of as human. For that reason, Aquinas also called these three higher virtues the "heroic" virtues. "Theological," in the context of the virtues, simply means "godlike" or divine. But when Aquinas calls them "godlike" or "divine," he doesn't mean that "*by* them God is virtuous," but rather that "*by* them God makes *us* virtuous."[21] If I may put this in yet another paradox: the cardinal virtues are those of *human nature*, but the "theological" virtues are an important part – perhaps the most important part – of the *nature of the human*.[22]

Another tradition influenced by Greek philosophical thought is the tradition of Islam. Muslim law has been shaped by "universal and necessary values of human society": "*dīn*" (see below), life (*nafs*), intellect (*'aql*) family (*nasl*), property (*māl*), and honour (*'ird*, which is sometimes linked to *dīn* or family, and sometimes stands alone).[23] In addition, some fields of Muslim law (especially state legislation rather than jurists' jurisprudence) are also strongly (or even primarily) shaped by the related values of justice (*'adāla*) and human welfare (*maṣlaḥah*).[24]

Some of these eight Islamic legal values are easy to assign to one of the families of virtues. You've already seen where values like justice, honour, family, and intellect belong in my map of the human paradox. To pin down some others takes a little more thought. For reasons explained in the notes, I tentatively identify *dīn* with the virtues of reverence as a whole,[25] and life and welfare with the virtues of self-assertion.[26]

With these linkages in mind, you can see where these eight Islamic values may be located on the map of the human virtues, in Figure 22 on page 206.

As you can see in Figure 22, the eight Islamic legal values show a balance between self-assertion and reverence – and among the four families of virtues – similar to the one you saw in the seven classical virtues in Figure 21. That may be partly because the Christian and Islamic traditions were (and are) equally influenced and shaped by the Greek culture of self-assertive rationalism. You can get some perspective on that Greek influence by comparing the classical virtues and the eight Islamic legal values to two other traditions where the Greek

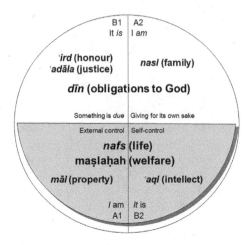

Figure 22. Eight Islamic values

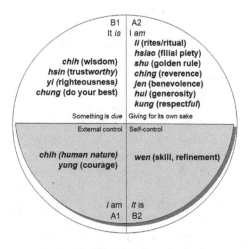

Figure 23. The Confucian virtues

influence (which still shapes our modern and post-modern Western culture) is absent.

The first of those two traditions is the Chinese tradition of Confucius. In Figure 23 above, you can see how the virtues taught by the Confucian tradition seem to be located on the map of the human paradox.

The interesting thing to observe about Figure 23 is the weighting across the four families of virtues. The number of virtues located in the top half

Figure 24. The Seven Grandfathers

of the circle – and in the top right-hand quadrant (A2) in particular – makes clear how much importance a non-Western tradition like that of Confucianism gives to the virtues of reverence in general, and to what I've called the virtues of Reverence (A2), in particular.

I can illustrate the same thing by showing you a similar emphasis in Indigenous North American ideas about the virtues. The Indigenous cultures of North America are a rich source of insight into the nature of the human, expressed, as in almost all pre-modern cultures, in the form of the virtues, or the best kinds of human behaviours. The key human virtues for many North American Indigenous peoples – and especially the Anishinaabe of north-eastern North America – are often called the seven "teachings of the Grandfathers," or, simply, the "Seven Grandfathers." There are some minor variations in the sources,[27] but the Seven Grandfathers, which define the best kind of human life – or the highest and most important human virtues – are usually identified as courage, honesty, humility, love, respect, truth, and wisdom.[28] By now, you should easily be able to identify where each of these virtues fits in the map of the human. You can see where I think they are properly located in the nature of the human, in Figure 24 above.

The striking thing about Figure 24, like Figure 23, is the weighting of the virtues toward reverence. With the single exception of courage or bravery, *all* of the other six "Grandfathers" are virtues of reverence. For the Indigenous peoples of North America – as for most pre-modern (and almost all tribal) cultures – the nature of the human is defined, overwhelmingly, by the virtues of reverence. Not, as the modern and post-modern world takes for granted, by the virtues of self-assertion.

I can underline this in two other ways. First, by pointing out that the bottom right-hand quadrant of Figure 24 is blank. The virtues I've called the virtues of Equality (B2) – the quintessential Enlightenment virtues – are absent and unaccounted for among the Seven Grandfathers. Second, the Seven Grandfathers make clear that "Truth," in its initial and fundamental meaning, is a virtue of reverence, not, as for the modern and post-modern worlds, a virtue of self-assertion. It belongs among the virtues of Excellence (B1), not the virtues of Equality (B2), where it fits now, in our contemporary world. For the Indigenous cultures of North America, truth isn't "scientific" truth. It isn't the truth of things, or phenomena, or of "*It* is," but rather the truth of goodness: the truth of "It *is*." It is the truth of the Grandfathers themselves: that is, the truth of the virtues.[29] In its original and deepest form, Truth – the Seven Grandfathers testify – is the truth about the nature of human: the truth about what makes humans *most* human. The truth to which we should strive to be true. This kind of truth doesn't owe something to you. You owe something *to it*.[30]

The overwhelming importance both the Confucian and Indigenous North American traditions give to the virtues of reverence is another confirmation of how important they are to any adequate survey of the nature of the human. You'll see some other ways their importance is confirmed, in later chapters.

A map of the human virtues: unities and contrasts

I'm now ready to develop my final image of the human paradox, the map of the human virtues that I'll use as an operational tool for looking at the world through various lenses – and in different areas of human life – in the second half of this book.

My map should show the four families of virtues, but it should also have just enough detail to show some of their most important members. I can't show the whole family: I'd need a table for that – like Tables 10 and 14. But even those tables don't include every virtue.

And I can't show all the contradictions either. You know, from chapters 8 and 9, that the four families will subdivide into eight families, and those eight will split into sixteen, and so on. But I've already decided to stop at the level of four to make my basic image of the nature of the human simple, memorable, and usable. So I now need to display the four families with just enough of their key members to be suggestive, and to show both some of the conflicts *and* some of the links between and across the four families.

Figure 25. Four families of virtues (3)

With all this in mind, the basic map of the human spirit I've been working toward, since the beginning of the book, can be found in Figure 25 above.

As noted earlier, I've capitalized Reverence (A2) in the top right-hand quadrant. But you should keep in mind that, in this visual image of the four families of virtues, the large word Reverence (A2) in the top right-hand quadrant signifies only one half of the virtues of reverence, not the larger family of reverence (lower case) which embraces *both* top quadrants, including the virtues of Excellence (B1).

The underlying dynamic which structures the nature of the human – given visual form in Figure 25 – is the union of union and non-union. On the one hand, everything pushes toward division, the unending process of separative projection I traced through three levels in Chapters 8 and 9. Tables 10 and 14 give you the details and show separative projection at work. Yet, at the same time, all of these conflicting virtues are all part of one unity, which is the nature of the human. Figure 25 shows you the unity and the relationships. Even in their conflicts, everything ultimately coheres. As you saw in Chapter 9, the four families of virtues – and their eight sub-sub-families – "lean" outward as well as inward: they lean toward adjacent, external families of virtues just as much as they do toward the other contrary side of their own family.

In chapters 8 and 9, you saw how some virtues create links, but also tensions and conflicts, *between* the families of virtues, as well as *within* them. Virtues such as respect, trust, and honour, for example, show different sides of themselves, depending on how they are lived in the four families of virtues. In the family of Reverence (A2), they take the form of respecting, trusting, and honouring, while in the family of Excellence, they are judged to be respec*tful*, trust*worthy*, and honour*able*. But they also show up in the virtues of self-assertion. If you look back at Table 10 on pages 174–5, you'll see that respect and honour also appeared there, but in that setting they took the form of *seeking* respect, trust, and honour. Respect implies a standard that isn't arbitrary but rational, and also an element of reciprocity, so it belongs on the right-hand side of the virtues of self-assertion, those of Equality (B2). Reciprocal respect is what "rights" seem to require. But honour-seeking is a more assertive, more arbitrary, and less rational virtue, so it seems to belong on the left-hand side, with what I've called the virtues of Liberty (A1). Aristotle's discussion of honour is mostly about *seeking* honour, and he seems to associate it with the pursuit of Power (A1a) in political or public life, while Aquinas seems to link it instead to the pursuit of Pleasure (A1b). Nevertheless, both views confirm that the family of the virtues I call Liberty (A1) is the right home for this virtue.[31]

Responsibility is another virtue that takes different forms in at least three different families of virtues, depending on whether it takes a form like prudence (B2), duty (B1), or love (A2).

The multiform character of these virtues helps show how the arrow of virtue leads across the families of virtues and links them together, in their differences and disagreements. It shows that the nature of the human is a four-cornered dialogue.

You can see some other links between reverence and self-assertion in the role that knowledge plays (and doesn't play) in both of them. If you compare Table 14 on pages 194–5 with Table 10 on pages 174–5, you'll notice that knowledge seems to be a virtue both of reverence and of self-assertion. But the knowledge that is valued seems to be different in the two cases. As a virtue of self-assertion, knowledge is called reason or science, the kind of knowledge that *demands* an explanation of things and that *seeks* clarity. The knowledge that is a virtue of reverence is called wisdom, and this kind of knowledge – the kind on which the other more rational kind of knowledge ultimately depends – is much more comfortable with ambiguity, uncertainty, contingency, and mystery. Not just the mystery of being, but also the mystery and uncertainty of the virtues. After all, what do we mean when we say someone is wise? We mean they have deep insight into the mystery of *life*, into the mysteries of living, of living *well*. That is to say, they have insight into the mysteries of the human virtues. Wisdom is, originally and primarily, an intuitive understanding of the human stances and virtues, and their eternal possibilities, as the Seven Grandfathers remind us. Insight into the whole nature of the human. It cannot therefore have the precision and clarity of knowledge about the physical world or the past because it is insight into something potential, always yet to come, always shrouded in the unknowable future. It must therefore always have an element of unknowing, and the "mysterious."[32] Wisdom has an ineffable, intuitive quality that is itself mysterious. If it were not so, we wouldn't call it wisdom. We would call it something else.

There is yet another kind of knowledge which has often been called understanding. Understanding seems to stand somewhere between wisdom and reason. It may have some of the certainty or clarity that reason demands, but it reaches out to the kind of insight that only wisdom provides, out of the possibilities of the virtues and the yet-to-come of the future. It seems to serve as a bridge between wisdom and reason, bringing clarity to wisdom, and wisdom to reason.[33]

You might say, then, that there are at least four forms of knowledge, two of which (reason and science) may be counted as virtues of self-assertion, and two others (wisdom and understanding) which may be considered virtues of reverence. The first two can be located in the family I've called the virtues of Equality (B2) and the second two are in the family of Excellence (B1).[34] The way in which the "knowledge" virtues span these two distinct families of reverence and self-assertion shows the important links between them, which is why I have labelled them B1 and B2. Both place high value on the mind, and on those kinds of virtues that emphasize mental knowledge or understanding. The virtues of Equality (B2) reach out to the physical world we can see, those of Excellence (B1) to the invisible, enveloping world of being we can't see, gesturing toward what they cannot know. These two families of virtues are the families of "It *is*" and "*It* is." Because they are both oriented toward an objective "It," they seem to "lean" toward each other, as I suggested.[35]

The same unities – across the divide between reverence and self-assertion – can be shown in parallel by the families of Liberty (A1) and Reverence (A2). Because the families of Excellence (B1) and Equality

(B2) emphasize knowledge, they seem to reside in the mind, or at least to focus on the life of the mind. But the corresponding families of Liberty (A1) and Reverence (A2) seem to reside elsewhere, or at least to find their primary source in other regions of the human. For them spirit, movement, energy, and life are more important than, or come before, mind or knowledge. Many names have been given to these other dimensions of the human. They might be called "feeling,"[36] or the "gut," or even the "bowels."[37] Another evocative term used frequently throughout the history of thought – and which we still use spontaneously in our everyday speech – is what Blaise Pascal calls the "heart."[38] If the virtues of Excellence and Equality call upon the human mind, the virtues of Liberty and Reverence seem to spring more directly and spontaneously from the human heart. As I already suggested, the families of "*I* am" and "I *am*" are the "existential" virtues. They express the realities of life and being themselves, the life and being within which, alone, thought and mind can occur. The life or being that is the necessary but paradoxical partner of human cognition and reason. For that reason, Liberty (A1) and Reverence (A2) also "lean" toward each other. Their common emphasis on the "existential" source and goals of the self serves to unify the nature of the human, just as the emphasis on the mental or cognitive does in the other two families of virtues.

You can see some of the links as well as the contrasts between the virtues of Liberty (A1) and the virtues of Reverence (A2) by comparing the virtues of optimism and hope, which are often confused or conflated.[39] Optimism and hope are good examples of the subtle distinctions between virtues that are closely related, and can sound, initially, quite similar – subtle distinctions which turn them, however, in quite different directions. Hope is a virtue of Reverence (A2), but optimism is a virtue of Liberty (A1), a virtue of self-assertion. Optimism is the virtue of the athlete or entrepreneur who thinks that, with enough hard work and a little luck, things will turn out OK – who assumes that, with enough self-assertion, the world will yield favourable outcomes. That fortune favours the bold. Hope is, if not the opposite, at least quite different. It is the attitude which – with full knowledge of the frequently overwhelming power of evil in the world – chooses goodness anyway. It is a *decision* for goodness, in the face of all the probabilities of evil. It is the hope *against* hope.[40] Optimism is a virtue of confidence. Hope is a virtue of trust. Optimism is a belief *that*. Hope is a belief *in*. Optimism implies "because of." Hope implies "*in spite of*."[41] Hope is a virtue of "faith" – understood (as faith should be) as faith*fulness* or loyalty. Not just loyalty to the good (B1) – essential though that is – but also loyalty for its *own* sake (A2). For the sake of being a loyal person.

Another theme which unifies the nature of the human is the role of freedom in all four quadrants. In Chapter 8, I noted the two different dimensions of freedom in the two sides of the virtues of self-assertion. The virtues of Liberty (A1) emphasize "freedom *to*," the unconstrained freedom of the ego to work its own will, simply because "*I am.*" The virtues of Equality (B2), on the other hand, emphasize not freedom *to* but rather "freedom *of*": freedom of speech, freedom of assembly, freedom of religion, and so on. The freedom *of* the self. The freedoms that go with Rights (B2a) and Reciprocity (B2b). But freedom, as you saw in Chapter 9, is also found among the virtues of reverence, both in the family of Excellence (B1) – where it takes the form of freedom *from*: freedom from error (B1a), from vice (B1b), and from everything that blocks human vision of ultimate truth, or that impedes the human heart – freedom *from* the self – and in the family of Reverence (A2), where it takes the form of freedom *for*: freedom for unselfing, humility, and devotion (A2a) and for self-giving generosity, compassion, and love (A2b). The unconstrained freedom *to* do whatever we want, so characteristic of the modern world (A1), began its modern career as freedom *of* (B2), which was rooted, in turn, in the ancient longings for freedom *from* all the things that turn the human spirit away from its highest aspirations (B1), and freedom *for* its own true nature (A2).

The presence of freedom in all four basic families of virtues illustrates, again, the unity of the nature of the human. It suggests that the arrow of virtue does indeed lead from the stance of *I* am (A1) to the stance of I *am* (A2), then to the stance of It *is* (B1), then to the stance of *It* is (B2), and, ultimately, back to its starting point in the stance of *I* am (A1). It also confirms that, while the nature of the human may be divided against itself, it is ultimately a unity: a four-way conversation.[42]

However, if the nature of the human is to be a dialogue, it's an unending dialogue between opposites. The four corners of the human cohere only in their disagreement. All of the virtues in Figure 25 must be treated as if they were what Iris Murdoch and Max Scheler call moral "axioms," or "axioms of values."[43] They must be regarded as separate and utterly distinct.[44] They not only seem to stand alone, they actually pull *against* each other, or even "fight each other."[45] They make claims upon us that may be very difficult to reconcile – perhaps ultimately *ir*reconcilable – at least in human terms. For example, in some circumstances we can't easily reconcile the claims of love and mercy with the competing claims of justice and truth, no matter how hard we struggle to do so. The experience of the virtues teaches us that such starkly contradictory claims can't be steamrollered into agreement by any rational formula or system. The mind can recognize their contradictory claims on us, as I've been doing in this book. But it can't smooth out, much less eliminate, the contradictions.[46] The virtues can only be reconciled, if at all, by living out their contradictory demands, to the full. The coherence comes not so much in our *minds*, as in the striving of our full *lives*, as complete human beings, in the messiness and confusion of the everyday.[47]

The contradictions of the human paradox are what make us human.

The virtues and the unity of the self

Understanding the dynamics of union and non-union that underlie and unify the nature of the human is important for you, not merely as abstract knowledge, or as something in your mind alone. It's even more important for you in your real, concrete life: for leading an authentically human life in the everyday. On their own, the virtues of self-assertion – the virtues of non-union – have a surprising result, the very opposite of what you would expect. *Self*-assertion should lead to the strengthening of the self, shouldn't it? Isn't that the logical or obvious outcome from self-assertion? Isn't that what you'd naturally expect? If you assert yourself, you're affirming and therefore solidifying and developing that very same self, aren't you?

But think about it for a minute. If your only principle is to assert yourself, there's nothing to make your acts of self-assertion coherent or even compatible. Your own self-assertion will lead you to satisfy this craving at one moment, some other drive at another. As I already pointed out in chapter 6, pure self-assertion can only dissolve the self into conflicting acts of self-assertion. There's nothing to hold the self together.[48] That's why Hegel called the self of pure self-assertion the "disintegrated" self.[49] Because, with pure self-assertion, there's no self left at all. There's no centre. Just a series of contradictory acts of self-assertion. Just "different roles played in different situations."[50] There's no "there" there – nothing to give you a real identity or character. There's nothing to which you can be loyal, faithful, or committed. Indeed the virtues of loyalty, faithfulness, or commitment don't even have any place in the virtues of self-assertion, as you can see in Table 10, and Figure 25. They don't belong there. If you want a real self – something to which you could actually be loyal – you have to look for it elsewhere than in the virtues of self-assertion. You have to look for it among the virtues where loyalty itself can be found.

This is completely counter-intuitive. In fact, it's a paradox. The human paradox. In asserting ourselves, we don't develop or enhance the self. We dissolve it. Because the virtues of self-assertion are "empty."[51]

They don't have any positive content of their own. They can tell you to assert your right to liberty or equality. But they can't tell you what to do it *for*. They can't set out a goal or standard that liberty or equality might be used to achieve. They can't tell you very much about the kind of life within which these virtues might have dignity or value.[52]

In order to ensure that Liberty (A1) is not just an ignoble liberty, pure self-assertion has to reach beyond itself to equality. But in order to ensure that Equality (B2) is not just a sordid, squalid, or brutal equality, self-assertion has to reach beyond itself to excellence, to the initial virtues of reverence. And in order to ensure Excellence (B1) is really true or just, reverence has to reach beyond excellence to the highest virtues, those of mercy, and of Love (A2).

Only reverence can construct a consistent self, the kind to which one could be loyal, faithful, or committed, because only reverence can supply those kinds of virtues. Or, to put it the other way around: once you've begun to feel the need for them or to exercise these other virtues, you've already passed beyond the virtues of self-assertion, to those of reverence.

Think for a moment about the meaning of integrity. Like the rest of us, I'm pretty sure you'd like to live a life that could be said to have integrity. But the English word integrity has its root in the Latin word *integer*, meaning "whole." Integrity means the state of being whole, undivided, unified, consistent. When you say someone has "integrity," you mean they behave in a way that's consistent, unvaried: what you see is what you get. You can count on them to act in a certain way. You can't have "integrity," if some part of you or your life is in flagrant contradiction with some other part. If you really want to live with integrity, you're putting a value on "union," whether you recognize it or not. You're saying the randomness or "non-union" of self-assertion isn't enough. You've committed yourself, in some degree or other, to the virtues of union, or of reverence. And once you *commit* yourself to living with integrity, you've also gone one step further and committed yourself, in some degree, to goodness and truth. Because without goodness and truth, human acts contradict each other.[53] Avoiding contradiction in human acts is one of the things we *mean* by goodness and truth, or that leads to them.

Conceptually, the arrow of virtue runs backward as well as forward. The very impulse of self-assertion leads us to reverence because only reverence can construct the self. Only reverence can give content to the self because it expresses the impulse to union, to connection with the "other." And content can only come from otherness, from our relationship to something other than ourselves. Not just the otherness of the physical world, as in the virtues of Equality (B2), though that's important too. But also another kind of otherness: the otherness of justice, truth, and goodness, the otherness of Excellence (B1). An otherness that points beyond itself to the otherness of Reverence, and of Love (A2). To the whole. And to the whole nature of the human.

Paradoxes of language

What a paradox, or series of paradoxes, each more paradoxical than the last! The self can't construct the self? Only reverence or "unselfing" can lead to the authentic self? Stated baldly or abstractly in this way, such statements can sound like self-contradictory nonsense, as they often do to many people. But Figure 25 can help you to see what they mean, concretely, for the nature of the human. And why they are the simple, unavoidable truth about the human.

The nature of the human is structured by paradox, the initial paradox of unity and plurality, of something and other, of union and non-union. Paradox runs all the way through it. Paradox, not the law of the excluded middle, is the logic of human truth. Paradox affects and infuses everything human, even our language. That's one of the things that makes the human so hard to talk about. Because words face two ways. They can mean one thing in one context, and another thing in another. They are always paradoxical.

Take words like "attachment" and "detachment," for example. There is a detachment – the detachment advocated in Buddhism, Christian mysticism, and the tradition of the Tao, for example – which is pure reverence. In this kind of detachment "selfish concerns vanish."[54] But there is another kind of detachment – the self-regarding isolation of the ego, pursuing its own freedom and equality – which is pure self-assertion. There is an attachment – the attachment of concern, connectedness, and selflessness – that is pure reverence, indeed the very condition of reverence. But there is also another kind of attachment – the attachment which is a craving for mastery and enjoyment – that is pure self-assertion.

Or take a word like "objectivity." The objectivity which is so important for reason and science always has a hidden agenda of understanding, mastery, and control, seeking the "empire of man over things," as Bacon said. This kind of scientific objectivity is a virtue of self-assertion, though we may not be inclined to see it that way. But there is another, quite different kind of "objectivity" that is instead a virtue of reverence. This kind of objectivity, the objectivity of "letting go," is the other side of spiritual detachment. This second kind of objectivity is not "the severing of desire's relation with its object but the restoration of desire to a proper relation of objectivity; as we might say, of *reverence* for its object."[55] Purely scientific objectivity can be aggressive, controlling, ultimately hostile – a principle of negation. This kind of objectivity can harm the subject as much as the object. "The subject is degraded," says Iris Murdoch, "by lack of reverence for the object."[56] Only reverence can restore a *true* objectivity, one that really cherishes the other for itself. Murdoch calls this kind of objectivity the "realism of compassion": "The direction of attention is contrary to nature, outward, away from self ... and the ability so to direct attention is love."[57]

In a world that takes due account of the whole nature of the human, language itself reflects the paradoxical realities it tries, often in vain, to express. Indeed, the more it becomes paradoxical, the more likely it will be able to express truth – the *whole* truth – about the human, and about the world human beings inhabit. Our reason – especially what we think of as scientific or "objective" reason – is rooted in our senses, as Aristotle and Aquinas argued – and in the physical world we can see. But the nature of the human – as Figure 25 reminds you – is structured not just by the physical world you can see but by the invisible world of being, truth, and love that you can't see, and can't even express very well. To which we can only respond. Which is expressed – if it is expressed at all – in our human behaviour, in our virtues.

Language that expresses the whole truth about the human has to take account of both sides of this human reality, even though one of them ends in the inexpressible mysteries of being, love, and self-giving. Even though – or especially because – they so often seem to contradict each other. The nature of the human *is* that contradiction. And our language has to reflect it to tell the truth about us. One of the tests for genuine truth, as Samuel Taylor Coleridge suggests – and as Figure 25 confirms – is that it occurs to our human reason "only in the disguise of two contradictory conceptions, each of which are partially true, and the conjunction of both conceptions becomes the representative or expression ... of a truth beyond conception and inexpressible."[58]

The virtuous "mean" vs. the "bottomless" virtues

My reflections on detachment, objectivity, and language suggest some important differences between the four quadrants of Figure 25, my basic image for the nature of the human.

Experience of the virtues of self-assertion – the virtues of Liberty (A1) and Equality (B2) – seems to show us that, in these families of virtues, there is a kind of "floor." We are on solid ground here. We're in the world of things and know the limits or boundaries. That's partly, I think, what Aristotle and Confucius mean when they talk about virtues having a "mean": a kind of rational limit beyond which a virtue becomes excessive or exaggerated, or tumbles over into a vice.[59] With these kinds of virtues you can easily go too far. But when you shift upward, to the virtues of Excellence (B1), this floor seems to start falling away.[60]

What's the limit for truth or goodness or justice? Can you have too much of them? At first, it doesn't seem that you could. Truth and goodness are absolutes, aren't they? Well, maybe not. Maybe not *absolute* absolutes. For example, you shouldn't tell the whole truth in circumstances where it isn't necessary and may be wounding. If you tell Aunt Mary her hat is ugly, or if you tell cousin David he's looking paunchy, truth may not be such a great virtue after all. It may be a kind of self-indulgent cruelty. It may be self-seeking rather than self-giving.[61] Even here, in the virtues of Excellence (B1), the idea of the mean may still have some lingering relevance. You may still be able to go too far in these virtues, at least in the way you express them.[62] But for goodness, truth, wisdom, and justice, the mean doesn't seem quite as relevant as it obviously is for Power (A1a), Pleasure (A1b), Rights (B2a), or even Reciprocity (B2b). The "floor" you found in the virtues of self-assertion seems already to be falling away from under your feet.[63]

And when you move up still further, to the virtues of Reverence (A2), the "floor" seems to fall away altogether. For these kinds of virtues – virtues like love, hope, and reverence itself – there doesn't seem to be any kind of limit or "mean." The more you have of them, the better. "Extravagance is impossible" for these kinds of virtues, Thomas Aquinas suggests. "Here is no virtuous moderation, no reasonable mean; the more extreme our activity, the better we are."[64]

There seems to be a qualitative difference between the virtues of Reverence (A2) and those of the other families, especially Liberty (A1) and Equality (B2). In the virtues of self-assertion there's a floor. But for pure reverence there doesn't seem to be one. Instead of a floor, the virtues of Reverence (A2) seem instead to have a secret trap door, through which you can tumble into something that doesn't seem to have any bottom at all. A trap door through which you can fall forever, without any end. The experience of this "bottomless" quality to the virtues of Reverence (A2) is what has led many people and traditions to think of them as having a quality that can be called "infinite" or "eternal." Indeed, the experience of the virtues in this quadrant, especially, seems to be what led humankind to conceive of things like "eternity" or the "infinite" in the first place.[65] I'll come back to this in Chapter 16.

Double vision: the arrow of virtue as a temporal spiral

Now that I've constructed my basic four-part image of the human, in Figure 25, I've created the same potential problem I faced at the end of chapter 7. Just like Figure 16 on page 144, Figure 25 risks giving you a mistaken impression. It could lead you to think that, in each successive stage of human cultural (and personal) development, human beings, and human culture are limited to only one family of virtues. It could also make you think that, when the arrow of virtue moves on to a new phase, the previous stages are over and done with.

In a particular stage of Western cultural development, one family of virtues does seem to be dominant – it serves as the primary lens through which all the others are interpreted and applied. But even though one is dominant in a specific culture and filters all the others, all four families of virtues are still present and available, as permanent and necessary dimensions of what it is to be a human being. We can't get rid of them, even if we want to. When we ignore, overlook, or deny them, they simply go underground, beneath our field of cultural vision. But they continue to operate in human life, often in surprising ways. As I already pointed out in chapter 5, when we think we've put some essential part of the human out at the front door, it sneaks right back in, through the back door.

So, before I move on, I need to help you develop the same kind of "double vision" for the four families of human virtues that (in chapter 7) I already illustrated for the four basic human stances they reflect and express, in human life. You should think of the four families of human virtues in two ways, or view them with two different lenses, at the same time. You can think of them as both historical phases and permanent and enduring features of the human. At the same time. Without all of them, human beings wouldn't be human – or wouldn't be fully human. They would lack some essential characteristic of what it means to be truly human. Yet the arrow of virtue never seems to rest. Because of the tensions and contradictions inherent in all the families of virtues, it keeps moving on to some new cultural stage and outlook. And when it does, the way we understand the virtues – and the nature of the human – changes too.

The need to view the four families of virtues through a "double lens" – both historical and permanent (or universal) – suggests that I should offer you a new version of Figure 18, with the four basic families of virtues replacing the four underlying human stances toward the polarity of being. You can see that revised image in Figure 26 on page 220 As you look at Figure 26, I need to remind you of some important features of this image, that I already pointed out about Figure 18, my

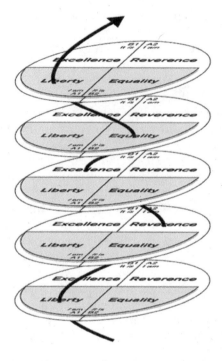

Figure 26. The arrow of virtue as a temporal spiral

earlier version. You should remember that my spiral image represents a temporal progression, so the higher images of the four families of virtues come later in the sequence of the spiral. Remember also that, in Figure 26, the arrow of virtue pierces a different family of virtues at each level: it passes through each of the four families of human virtues in succession: Liberty (A1), Reverence (A2), Excellence (B1), Equality (B2), and back to Liberty (A1). This pattern is again meant to illustrate that one family of virtues is highlighted, or dominant, at each level of the spiral: it's the lens through which humans view *all four* families – which nevertheless remain fully present in the human repertoire, at that time or at that historical or cultural stage, even if one (or more) of them is, for the time being, the lens for interpreting all the others.[66]

Third, remember that another reason for a spiral image is that, at the higher or later levels of the spiral, you can now "see" the earlier ones, just the way you can look down from the top of a spiral staircase and see all its lower landings.[67] That's another reason a spiral image of human evolution is helpful. It expresses visually that when the arrow of virtue restarts its upward climb from a new level, it doesn't have to start again just the way it did the first time. A culture which has reached this point has already progressed through other families of virtues. It can now advance with a widened awareness. Though a new family may now provide the primary lens, it isn't the only one. It's coloured by the memory and experience – not to mention the current reality – of the others.[68] All four families of virtues remain present and available, and any one of them can serve as the lens through which all the others are viewed and interpreted.[69] The arrow can start again, as Hegel says, at a higher level, with a richer, fuller idea of human potential. It should be able to start again with greater awareness of the increasing range of the human, and of other families of virtues that are also part of the full nature of the human.[70]

As I mentioned in chapter 7, Hegel's vision of the "spiral" of Western cultural development raises the question of what happens when the arrow of virtue has worked its way through all four families of virtues. Does the whole spiral process begin all over again? Hegel sometimes seems to suggest (or imply) that it does. Sometimes he appears to assume it doesn't. I'll come back to the question of where the arrow of virtue may go next in later chapters of the book. All we can perhaps be reasonably confident about, at this stage, is that the polarity of being and the resulting process of separative projection have already shown us the architecture of the virtues that define the nature of the human, and many, if not most, of its component virtues. They have shown us the geography of the virtues, the map or structure of the human.

But that doesn't mean the work is over. It doesn't mean the work of rediscovery – or creation, or invention – is completed. Or ever can be completed. Even if we *had* already discovered or identified all the main human virtues, they will go on, nevertheless, being forever rediscovered, recombined, re-emphasized, reinterpreted – "created," invented, or understood anew – in all the evolving cultural stages of our "deep future" ahead.

Eight sub-sub-families of virtues

Your journey to this point in the book seems to suggest that the best way to think of the nature of the human is as a four-way conversation. A four-way dialogue between different human stances or families of virtues: opposite, contradictory, but inseparable and ineradicable forms of the human spirit.

However, there's nothing final about the number four. The story didn't start there, and it doesn't end there either. Like the nature of the

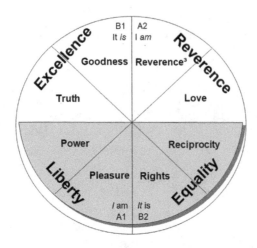

Figure 27. Four families of virtues and eight sub-sub-families

human itself, each family of virtues contains – and is structured by – an essential conflict, or paradox.[71] It's always in a state of tension between its two sides, reflecting the underlying polarity of being. A tension which can split it in two, through the process of separative projection. The original dynamic of union and non-union goes on dividing the first four families of values (as you saw in chapters 8 and 9) into eight, sixteen, thirty-two, and so on.

To ensure you aren't tempted to think of the four basic sub-families of virtues as real "things," or as being more final than they really are, it may now be helpful to add another image to your repertoire, one that also shows the four basic sub-families together with their eight sub-sub-families. You saw these eight sub-sub-families, in more detail, in Tables 8, 9, and 10, and in Tables 12, 13, and 14. But now I can display them conceptually in the same format as Figure 25. You can see both levels together – the four basic sub-families and the eight sub-sub-families they spawn (in the next or third level of separative projection) – in Figure 27 above.

Figure 27 will be useful to me later in this book. It's very easy to confuse the different levels of separative projection, and to mistake dualities on one level (the first four) for dualities on another (the next eight). In chapters 8 and 9, you already saw me struggling with this problem, in the cases of wisdom and understanding, and of awe and wonder, among others. Figure 27 will help me sort out some of this potential confusion later, especially in chapters 13, 14, and 15. But for practical reasons – in order to apply the framework in the rest of the book – I'm going to focus primarily on the level of the initial four-way conversation between the four sub-families of Excellence (B1) and Reverence (A2), on the one hand, and those of Liberty (A1) and Equality (B2), on the other, as depicted in Figure 25 on page 209.

Together with Figure 25, Figure 27 confirms that my evolving map of the human spirit captures some of the deepest and oldest wisdom about the nature of the human. In fact, the image of the human in Figures 25 and 27 – a circle divided into four (or eight) parts – is one of the oldest human ideas. It can be traced back to the Mesolithic and Palaeolithic ages, before the invention of the wheel.[72] For example, the "medicine wheel" (an ancient symbol used by almost all the Indigenous people of North and South America) takes the same form as Figure 25: a circle divided into four quadrants.[73] I'll come back to this in chapter 16.

But look again at Figure 25. The form it takes is not incidental. The families of Liberty (A1) and Equality (B2) are depicted on the grey semicircle located within and above the larger white circle. Remember, too, that the grey semicircle was originally the grey dot in Figure 1 on page 29, the grey dot that stood for the first individual thing you thought about in your room or garden, the one from which we started our journey of discovery together in this book.

Later, it also stood for *all* the other individual things in the universe, as in Figure 7 on page 41. Thus Figures 7 and 25 show us two things. First, that these two families of self-assertion are the human response to a world of individual things or objects. But, if you look again at Figure 7, you'll also be reminded that these individual things, and the virtues that respond to them, exist within a background of being which is largely invisible to us, a background that has its own corresponding virtues, the virtues of reverence.

Figure 25 could make you think the background to these other virtues is just as concrete, visible, and apparent to us as the visible world of things in which the virtues of self-assertion are at home. But Figure 25 is just another form of Figure 7. You need to keep in mind that the virtues of self-assertion, so familiar to us in the modern world – so familiar we're sometimes inclined to think they're the only virtues at all – can only exist within a much larger but invisible background. We can't see it. And so we can't talk about it very well. Much of it can only be a mystery for us. The only way we know very much about it is through our own response to it. Through the other two families of virtues – the virtues of Excellence (B1) and of Reverence (A2) – which are equally important parts of the four-way conversation that defines the nature of the human.

The nature of the human: "a conversation made of stance"

You have now come to the end of the first part of this book.

Starting from the simple act of thinking about a single thing – any individual thing – I've gradually constructed an image for the nature of the human. Focussing, first, on one single thing helped you to realize that we can't think about anything without taking account of the *other* things that surround it. In fact, we can't think about it deeply without reckoning with *all* the other things, visible and invisible, which furnish the background to that first thing, the background which makes its very existence possible. Which makes even existence *itself* possible.

Reality turned out to be not just a world of individual things but, at the same time, a single world of being within which these individual things connect, and without which none of them could exist. It turned out to be a world structured by a fundamental polarity of being: a world not just of many but of one; not just of plurality, but also of unity; not just of self, but also of world; not just of separation and individuality, but also of connection and of union. It turned out, in fact, to be the combination or union of these two opposite realities. It turned out to be a union of union and non-union.

You then saw how these two contraries are reflected in human behaviour, especially the good human habits we call virtues. The two opposing dynamics of union and non-union call forth two different human responses, two kinds of good human behaviours, or virtues: the virtues of reverence and the virtues of self-assertion. In good human behaviour, union translates into acts of reverence, and non-union into acts of self-assertion. But those same dynamics divide these two initial families of virtues into four more, reflecting the four basic stances of the human toward the polarity of being. I called those four stances *I* am, I *am*, It *is*, and *It* is. The nature of the human is an endless conversation between these four poles of the human. It is (as Ali Smith [b. 1962] puts it) "a conversation made of stance."[74]

The first stance – "*I* am" – reflects the pure, primitive self-assertion of the ego, without any acknowledgment of other realties or their potential claims upon us. The second – which springs inevitably from the first – is the recognition that we can't say "*I* am" unless I *am*. There's no self-assertion if there's no self. Existence is prior to self-assertion. And the unavoidable encounter with being forces us to recognize that our *own* being is just an expression of *being itself*, which seems to have objective features of its own.[75] Features like goodness, justice, or truth: features we can acknowledge, but which seem to have an existence independent of ours. If "I *am*," then, necessarily, "It *is*" too. But the encounter with this initial otherness of being inevitably leads to a recognition of the otherness of beings, the separate existence of other people and things, their existence as *objects* standing over against the *subjects* that we ourselves have now become. "It *is*" necessarily implies that "*It* is."

The second and third stances go together, as the virtues of reverence, and provide the unseen background for our daily lives: two distinct families of virtues which express our awareness of the priority of being. The priority of a world we did not create, did not agree to, and do not control, but which *calls* upon us in a variety of ways, creating obligations and responsibilities. We can't experience the fullness of the human if we don't hear, and respond, to that call.

The first and the last stances go together too, as the virtues of self-assertion, two distinct families of virtue that express the human stances of "*I* am" and "*It* is." These two families of virtues must also be understood together, as two side of the same coin. The individual ego confronts and "creates" (i.e., perceives the otherness of) an objective nature. An objective nature confronts and creates (i.e., causes human beings to feel the reality – or illusion – of their own) individual egos. The virtues of self-assertion and an "objective" natural world go hand in hand, for better and for worse. They reinforce each other, obscuring the unseen background within which they exist, and leading us to think this foreground of our post-modern lives is all there is. But it's not. The foreground only provides us with, at best, two of the four poles of the human, only two sides of a larger, four-way conversation that defines the nature of the human.

If the nature of the human is a four-way conversation between different human stances or families of virtues, we should expect to find that conversation reflected in the various forms of human life that make up our human world. In fact, it's logical to think that we won't be able to understand – and, more important, *act* in – many areas of human life if we don't see, and pay enough attention to, all four families of virtues.[76]

So now that I've developed a framework for understanding the nature of the human, my remaining task in this book is to apply it. To consider whether and how the nature of the human is at work in a human world. And determine what that means for us and for our world.

PART TWO

The Human Paradox in a Human World

11

Society

In the first part of the book, I developed a map of the nature of the human based on four human stances and their related families of virtues (Figures 20 and 25).

These four families are neither the first nor the last word about the human. They're not the first word because they are sub-families of an even more basic human duality – the paradox of reverence and self-assertion, the paradox of I *am* and *I* am (Tables 2, 3 and 6) – each of whose two poles produces its own dualities (Tables 7 and 11), thus yielding the basic four-part framework, the four sub-families of virtues. And they're not the last word either because these four basic poles in turn beget their own poles (Tables 8, 9, and 10; and 12, 13, and 14), initiating an endless process of polarization and division.

But the four basic sub-families of virtues are a good vantage point from which to explore the nature of the human because they are both simple and complex at the same time. Simple: because not yet far removed from the initial human paradox and from the polar structure of being it reflects. Complex: because they show how this initial paradox breeds further paradoxes, and how these subsequent paradoxes immensely complicate the nature of the human, opening the door to an infinite variety both of combinations and of conflicts. So the four stances and their four basic sub-families of virtues can serve as a framework for the task that still lies ahead in the second part of the book.

My task in the second half is to explore how the nature of the human is reflected in our human world: how the human paradox finds expression in some of the most important areas of our common human life. By exploring some of the concrete forms of human life, and how they are interpreted by various disciplines, I hope to help you put some flesh on the somewhat abstract outline of the nature of the human I sketched in the first half. I hope you will see how the four corners of the human paradox also structure our human world. When we look outward at our human world, what we find is our own human paradox reflected back at us. We can and must gain self-knowledge about our paradoxical selves, not just by looking inward at ourselves, but also by looking outward at our human world.[1]

In this chapter, I will begin the task of searching for the human paradox in our human world by looking at the largest frame, which is society itself.

Social sciences and the human paradox

Like science, the "scientific" study of human society has developed since the eighteenth century in parallel with the rise of the virtues of self-assertion. The virtues of self-assertion and what we now call "science" are two sides of the same coin.

As I pointed out at the end of the previous chapter, objectivity, subjectivity, and self-assertion go together. The self-asserting ego confronts and "creates" an objective nature. An objective nature in turn confronts and "creates" individual egos. The self-assertive spontaneity of the ego in the form of rational consciousness first makes the world appear as separate objects and then seeks to subdue it by means both of "objective" knowledge and of instrumental control. The steady rise of the virtues of self-assertion since the fifteenth century provided fertile ground for the parallel rise of modern science and technology. And vice versa. The triumphs of science and technology also fuelled and legitimized the growing dominance of the virtues of self-assertion in modern culture.

The decline of religious explanations based on final causes also opened the door for "scientific" explanations based purely on material and efficient causes. The banishing of final causes from explanations was a defining part of the scientific revolution of the seventeenth century. That was what made modern science both modern and "scientific." Explanations of phenomena were now to be given exclusively in terms of material and efficient causes.[2]

In a culture of self-assertion, it was inevitable that this same "scientific" spirit should eventually be applied even to the study of human society, giving rise to the development of the new social "sciences."[3] Although the roots of modern social science go back to the eighteenth century, the ambition to achieve what John Stuart Mill called a "general science of society" fully took hold in the nineteenth century.[4] The name most commonly associated with this grand objective is that of the French writer Auguste Comte, who coined the term "sociology" for the proposed new social science. Stripped of Comte's rather far-reaching ambitions, the discipline of sociology was developed in the later nineteenth century by theorists such as the French scholars Frédéric LePlay (1806–82) and Émile Durkheim, and the German Max Weber (1864–1920), and in the twentieth century by academic sociologists such as the Americans George Herbert Mead (1863–1931), Charles Horton Cooley (1864–1929), and Talcott Parsons (1902–79). "Scientific" understanding of social structure and processes was augmented by new, parallel disciplines such as anthropology – the study of human society through the lens of culture, especially pre-modern cultures – and of social psychology: the application of psychological perspectives to the life of groups and communities. These three modern social sciences offer "alternative descriptions of the same phenomenon from the perspectives of three different kinds of analysis."[5]

Not surprisingly, all three identified two basic forms of social relations early on. Comte himself identified two categories of "affective forces" in human culture: egoism or "personality," and (as I mentioned in chapter 5) altruism or "sociability."[6] In his wake (as I mentioned in chapter 6), Durkheim also recognized that the nature of the human is to be *Homo duplex*, both an individual *and* part of a something larger than the individual, with two corresponding sets of "social sentiments."[7] What Durkheim called organic and mechanical modes of social relations, Ferdinand Tönnies (1855–1936), a German sociologist, famously called *gemeinschaft* (informal community) and *gesellschaft* (civil society).[8] Another German sociologist, Georg Simmel (1858–1918), said that human beings strive for a "synthesis of restraint and expansion … of spontaneous will and dependence, of giving and receiving": they seek to achieve a whole that reconciles both "independence and unity."[9] Margaret Mead (1901–78), an American anthropologist, classified various cultures as either competitive or cooperative.[10] Other social scientists have given a variety of names to these same two poles of human social life: solidarity and dominance; solidarity and power; deference and dominance; interconnection and independence; commitment and individualism; beneficence and reciprocity; communion and agency; and so on.[11] Whatever language is used in the various social science disciplines, it isn't difficult to see that they are all ways of expressing the same basic duality that Hegel called union and non-union. And so, they are also ways of expressing the human responses *to* this duality which, in this book, I've called reverence and self-assertion.[12]

Sometimes, social scientists have gone beyond these two basic human impulses to identify three or even four variants of the basic two. Weber, for example, identified two bases of social relations: traditional (union/reverence) and rational-legal (non-union/self-assertion), but then added a third, within which he distinguished two sub-categories, thus pointing to a potential four-part framework.[13] Claude Lévi-Strauss (1908–2009), a French anthropologist and ethnologist, also identified four basic relational attitudes underlying all kinship systems.[14]

Fortunately for me, an American social scientist, Alan Page Fiske (b. 1947), has surveyed 150 years of this kind of social science literature, in all three disciplines. Fiske concludes that, taken as a whole, they suggest that human life is structured by four elementary forms of social relations. He calls these four: Communal Sharing, Authority Ranking, Equality Matching, and Market Pricing. He proposes that these four basic "models" provide the "psychological foundations of social relations and of society." This idea has come to be known as Relational Models Theory (RMT).[15]

I will have more to say about Fiske's conclusions and will, in fact, use them as the framework for the rest of this chapter and for my discussion of the way the human paradox is reflected in human social life. I think that Relational Models Theory (RMT) is true. Or true as far as it goes. Or true up to a point. My purpose here is constructive, not critical. I want to show how close RMT comes to the truth about the nature of the human, and what separates it from the goal. Even the ways in which it may not be the whole truth can help in rediscovering how important that truth is for us, and why.

Relational Models Theory and the four models of social relations

We can start by looking at the four "models" of social relations that Relational Models Theory (RMT) finds emerging from 150 years of social science.[16]

Communal Sharing is a social relationship "in which people are merged (for the purposes at hand) so that the boundaries of individual selves are indistinct. ... People have a sense of solidarity, unity and belonging and identify with the collectivity: they think of themselves as being all the same in some significant respect, not as individuals but as 'we.'" Communal Sharing is a relationship "based on duties and sentiments generating kindness and generosity among people conceived to be of the same kind, especially kin."[17]

Authority Ranking is described as a social relationship in which people "construe each other as differing in social importance or status. ... Characteristically, inferiors are deferential, loyal, and obedient, giving obeisance and paying homage to their betters." While ranking is central to this pattern of social relations, it is not a pure power relationship. "More typically, subordinates believe their subordination is legitimate."[18]

Equality Matching is an "egalitarian relationship among peers who are distinct but coequal individuals. People are separate but equal." Reciprocity is very important to this kind of social relationship, "such that people receive and give back what they construe as the 'same' thing in return." In an Equality Matching relationship, people "conceive of each other – or the rights, duties, or actions involved in the relationship – as distinct, but as balancing each other. Aligning or substituting, so they are interchangeable ... everyone is equal and things come out even."[19]

Finally, *Market Pricing* is described as a relationship "mediated by values determined by a market system." In this kind of social relation, the participants "typically value other people's actions, services, and products according to the rates at which they can be exchanged for other commodities." In a Market Pricing relationship, "people structure their interaction with reference to rates whose numerator is a common standard. ... People give and get, influence and exert themselves in proportion to the standard."[20]

These four models don't stand alone. They are combined in various ways to generate human social relations. Any actual social relation is "typically built out of a combination of these four basic psychological models." As groups and societies grow increasingly complex, "people generally construct large-scale social entities by putting together two or more basic models in various combinations and at various levels."[21]

There's more to Relational Models Theory (RMT) than simply the models themselves. It has much to say about the cultural protocols (now called "preos") which determine the recipes and etiquette by which the models are combined in different cultures, times, and places. It also describes the processes (now called "conformation systems") through which the four kinds of social relations are constituted or expressed.[22] But the four models are the heart of the theory and the feature that's of interest to me in this book.

RMT suggests these four models of social relationships are fundamental, general, elementary, and universal. Fundamental, because "they are the lowest or most basic-level 'grammars' for social relations." General, because they give "order to most forms of social interaction, thought and affect." Elementary, because "they are the basic constituents for all higher order social forms." And universal, because they are "the basis for social relations among all people in all cultures and the essential foundation for cross-cultural understanding and intercultural engagement."[23]

These are very large claims. But if you look back at Tables 7 and 11 (on pages 41 and 115) and at Figure 25 (on page 209), you will see that, from the perspective of this book, such claims are not at all implausible. In fact, at first glance, there's a remarkable convergence between

Figure 28. Relational Models Theory's four models of social relations

the four "models" of social relations proposed by Relational Models Theory (RMT) and the four families of virtues already identified in this book. Equality Matching obviously corresponds to the family of the virtues of Equality (B2). Communal Sharing matches to the virtues of Reverence (A2). Authority Ranking fits with the virtues of Excellence (B1). And Market Pricing (as Tables 7, 8, and 10 indicate) certainly finds its proper place among the virtues I've called the virtues of Liberty (A1).

So it would be entirely appropriate to recast Figure 20 to show how the human paradox manifests itself in the structures of human social life. The basic image developed in this book to describe the nature of the human also works very well to display the elementary forms of social relations identified by Relational Models Theory. You can see RMT's four models as they correspond to the four stances and families of virtues, in Figure 28 above.

Models of social relations and the families of virtues

When you compare RMT's models and the four families of virtues identified in this book, the fit or correspondence that's immediately obvious is the one between RMT's model of Equality Matching and what I've called the virtues of Equality (B2). RMT's emphasis on the reciprocal nature of Equality Matching corresponds to what I have called the virtues of Reciprocity (B2b). And the expectation not only to give but to receive in an equal, matching fashion implicitly reflects the family of virtues I call the virtues of Rights (B2a).

There's also a very close fit between Communal Sharing and the virtues of Reverence (A2). The emphasis in this model on the merging of the self in a wider sphere of unity and belonging – and the central role it gives to feelings of kindness, generosity, and sharing – clearly correspond to the virtues of union and self-giving associated with this side of the virtues of reverence.

But in RMT's discussion of this model, an important issue emerges, an issue that will become even more acute in the remaining two models.

Although RMT accurately reflects the inclusive and self-giving character of Communal Sharing, it's often inclined to emphasize the other side: its boundary-making and excluding features. A family or group has boundaries. And so those outside the boundary are excluded – sometimes rigidly excluded – from the communal feeling and from the sharing that goes with it. In a Communal Sharing relationship, inclusion is "binary. Either you are in, or you are out." An in-group creates an out-group that's excluded. Communal Sharing may well be "an idea of unity and identity," but, in practice, "people may opt to mark the unity between themselves and any given subset of others, contrasting 'we' and 'they' by drawing exclusionary boundaries where they wish." So RMT gradually redefines Communal Sharing as a "system of discrete social identities": the foundation of Communal Sharing is said to be "the categorization of people into discrete groups or classes" and the "essence" of Communal Sharing is said to be "the binary contrast between in and out." It "consists of making binary discriminations among people."[24]

There are two possible sources for this shift of emphasis. The first is that RMT is a theory of social relations, so it naturally looks at *both* sides of the relation, or the impact of the relationship on others.[25] The second is that much of the anthropological evidence for this model of social relations has been gathered from tribal societies where the consequences of strong family and tribal boundaries are obvious to the external observer.

Regardless of the source, it's also clear that two quite different – even opposite – human impulses are combined within this particular model of social relations. Of course, every human community has a "Janus face," both inclusive and exclusive.[26] But, from the point of view of the human virtues, it's essential to disentangle the exclusion from the inclusion. The idea of unity and sharing is not only different from but *opposite to* the instinct of division and exclusion. The first embodies the principle of union, the second of non-union. The first is an expression of reverence, the second an expression of self-assertion. So the exclusionary, boundary-drawing, "we/they" dimension of Communal Sharing can't be the essence or the "foundation" of Communal Sharing. The essence is clearly the idea of community and sharing, the human impulse to be self-*giving*. The exclusionary feature of the relationship results from an *interference* of self-assertion in a social relationship based on – or in – reverence.[27] When communal sharing becomes exclusive, reverence is being ambushed or hijacked by self-assertion. Reverence creates the *bonds*; self-assertion creates the *boundaries*. This is a good, concrete example of the blocking and hijacking of reverence by self-assertion that I already mentioned in chapter 5.[28] Self-assertion is just *moved up a notch*: to the family, community, tribe, ethnic or religious group, or nation.

The description of Communal Sharing, as one of the four models of social relations, can be refined and deepened through greater recognition of the human paradox and the tension or conflict it introduces into all human relations. *Every* human mode of being is a paradox. It's a tension between opposites. A tension between union and non-union. Between reverence and self-assertion. That's just as true of all the sub-families of virtues as it is of the initial human paradox. And it's why they continually divide and subdivide, in the unending process of separative projection.

So Communal Sharing is also a paradox – a paradox of inclusion and exclusion, of union and non-union – a paradox which RMT normally seems to overlook. I'll come back to this issue, more generally, in a moment. But, first, let's look at the third "model" of Authority Ranking where the paradox becomes more acute, as even the name suggests.

As you already saw, RMT fully recognizes the *voluntary* aspect of Authority Ranking, the human impulse to deference, obedience, and loyalty: the fact that, in this kind of relationship, subordinates normally believe their subordination is legitimate. But in practice, RMT seems more often inclined to emphasize instead the *other* side of Authority Ranking: the "power and rank" dimensions of these relations, the degree to which superiors seek higher rank and strive to exercise authority over their subordinates. Authority Ranking is formally defined as a "linear ordering in which everyone's rank can be compared to every one else's," and domination turns out, in RMT, to be even more important to linear ordering than deference. Authority Ranking "involves the realization of the self in superiority over others," and so both Machiavelli and Nietzsche can be taken to "represent a philosophy" of Authority Ranking.[29]

As in the case of Communal Sharing, this model of social relations seems to involve a deliberate combination of two quite distinct things: a hierarchy of "value" on the one hand, and a hierarchy of "power" and "control" on the other.[30] But these aren't at all the same. The distinctive essence of what RMT calls Authority Ranking is clearly ranking and value, *not* authority and control. Its essence isn't power and control (which are rooted elsewhere in the nature of the human) but rather the human impulse to acknowledge a hierarchy of goodness and truth, to distinguish the superior from the inferior.[31] The spontaneous recognition of quality and value is an essential part of reverence, what I have called the virtues of Excellence (B1). This dimension of the human is what explains the "eagerness" of people in so many cultures to take on subordinate roles.[32] Reverence *willingly* acknowledges higher worth. It's self-assertion that seeks power and control. These two go together in all human actions, and in all social relation, but they're distinct and also in tension with each other.

"It is part of the central paradox of human society that dominance and hierarchy have gone together from the beginning," says Robert Bellah. But "[e]ven though they always go together it is important that we separate them analytically."[33] You can see the importance of Bellah's observation here. To understand the social relationship RMT calls Authority Ranking, you need to distinguish the dominance from the hierarchy.[34] As a social relationship, Authority Ranking is the result of an *interference* of self-assertion with one half of the human impulse to reverence (Excellence [B1]). Reverence eagerly acknowledges a subordinate ranking to a higher power; self-assertion *asserts* authority and dominance.[35] (I'll come back to this crucial distinction in the next chapter.)

As you saw with Communal Sharing, the concept of Authority Ranking can be refined and deepened by recognizing the human paradox and the conflict or duality it introduces into this model of social relations.

The Market Pricing model and the virtues of Liberty (A1)

This same issue comes to a head in the fourth model.

Market Pricing (MP) certainly finds its proper location in the bottom-left corner (A1) of my map of the human, in Figure 25 on page 209. That's the home of utility, benefit-seeking, and all the market virtues. The question, if there is one, isn't whether it belongs there, but whether RMT's label is the right one. And if so, how to explain where this particular form of social relation fits into the evolution of the human.

If you look back at Figure 25 (on page 209) or at Tables 7, 8, and 10 (on pages 157–8, 162, and 174–5), the first thing you'll notice is that, while A1 is certainly the right location for Market Pricing, it's also the home of so much more. Market Pricing seems a very limited name for human social relations based on the virtues of Liberty (A1). The home of courage, boldness, and fortitude. The home of the military virtues, but also of art, imagination, creativity, innovation, and enjoyment. The home of pleasure and the true home of power. Now you might answer that these don't all require *social* relations, or that they involve forms of social relations already covered by the other three "models." And there may be some truth in that. But as I pointed out in the Introduction, performing most of these assertive virtues requires some kind of social context. Power is certainly a social relation. And what about other virtues in this family, such as play? Play normally (though not always) requires two or more people. And it's a fundamental human characteristic, one of the *most* fundamental. Where does it fit into a form of human relations called Market Pricing?

I may be in a better position to suggest one possible answer to this question in a moment. But first, I'd like to return to the larger issue I mentioned in the case of Communal Sharing. The main issue with Market Pricing – as you also saw in the cases of Communal Sharing and Authority Ranking – is a lack of reference to the human paradox, and especially to self-assertion as a fundamental part of the nature of the human. This omission is even more problematic in the case of Market Pricing because this is the very model where self-assertion would naturally be anticipated. But in fact, RMT even goes out of its way to *deny* any necessary link between self-assertion and market-based forms of human relations. It tries to neutralize market-based behaviour by defining this model exclusively in terms of "ratios," "rates," and "proportion."[36] This seems to put all the emphasis on "pricing" rather than on the human and moral implications of the concept of "market." As in the case of Authority Ranking, one half of the model's name seems eventually to squeeze out the other.

It would be unfair to say that RMT completely ignores the human paradox. On occasion it does acknowledge a kind of human duality, a duality between "compassion and morality" on the one hand, and "aggression" on the other. Aggression and conflict, it suggests, are "the obverse of kindness, respect and responsibility, equality and market rationality." RMT "depicts people as naturally aggressive in the same four ways that they are naturally sociable." It suggests that aggression and conflict occur when people fail to apply any of the models; or when they initiate or justify injurious acts in the name of principles derived from the models; or, most often, "when they feel wronged, punishing someone whom they perceive to have transgressed against one of the four fundamental social relationships."[37]

There is obviously much truth in this. But this way of putting it points to a more fundamental question. Something important seems to be missing from the theory. RMT isn't inclined to see self-assertion as something positive, as a human *virtue*, indeed, the most basic human virtue from which all the others proceed, and without which no virtue and no human relationships are possible. Instead of describing it positively, RMT describes self-assertion negatively, as "aggression and conflict." Or else as a "Null" or "Asocial" case. The latter is a very interesting and revealing element in the theory. When people act "without regard to any social relationship," or when they pursue "pure power," treating others "as a mere impersonal object, a mean to an end," RMT calls these Null or Asocial cases, and dismisses them (especially the latter) as merely a kind of "sociopathy."[38] RMT confuses the pursuit of "agency," in which (as Margaret Mead puts it) "the individual strives toward his goal without reference to others," with these so-called Null or Asocial orientations,[39] instead of seeing it as pure self-assertion – what Aristotle and Aquinas called "sense appetite" – the engine room for all human action and thus for all virtues and all human relationships. Without self-assertion there is no kind of human action at all. Self-assertion is where everything human – all human action – starts. Omitting it from the map of human relations introduces the distortions I already pointed out in Communal Sharing and Authority Ranking. And with Market Pricing the problem comes to a head because this model is rooted in that very part of the map of the human where the purest form of self-assertion – what I called the virtues of Liberty (A1) – finds its home.

RMT sometimes seems to recognize that what it calls Market Pricing (MP) points to something wider than a category of human relations based merely on rates and ratios. At one point, for example, it identifies exploitative sexual relations with this model. Elsewhere it correctly identifies the human need for "achievement," the striving "to do something difficult as well and quickly as possible"[40] with MP too. MP is also occasionally equated, significantly, with the individualism of "liberal moralities" or "contract individualism," with the "autonomy norm" of modern (especially American) culture, and even with the "libertarian ideology of absolute freedom of rational choice."[41] But these seem to be exceptions. More typically, RMT is inclined to argue that, while autonomous individualism, competitive striving, freedom, and contractualism may be "loosely associated with the idea of Market Pricing," there is nevertheless "no theoretically necessary or empirically invariable connection between any of these features and the core relational structure of the MP model," which RMT takes, instead, to be "an orientation toward ratios," rates, and proportion – thus mistaking the means for the motive.[42] RMT suggests that individualism, competition, and self-maximization can also occur in other models such as Communal Sharing and Authority Ranking.[43] While obviously true, this only compounds the issue I already noted: failing to see how, in these other models, self-assertion *interferes* with or hijacks the basic core of reverence to produce their dominating or excluding features.

Why is RMT so eager to distance its Market Pricing model from the core virtues of self-assertion? Part of the answer seems to be the motivational origins of the theory. It was developed "partly as an antidote to the asocial, selfish economic behaviourist or Machiavellian views of human sociality."[44] It aimed to demonstrate that "there is no intrinsic reason why we should suppose with Thomas Hobbes that normal people are fundamentally selfish, inherently competitive or individualistic by nature."[45] It wanted to show that these kinds of assumptions were merely prejudices or "artifacts" of modern Western culture.[46] That "calculative individualism is hardly the universal social logic it is sometimes taken to be within strands of Western social science."[47] So the assertive features of the human were characterized negatively and dismissed as the Null or Asocial cases, or else dissolved into all four models. This prevents RMT from seeing, more clearly, how each of its four models is structured, a question to which I'll return in a moment.

RMT itself seems to have some misgivings about its own Market Pricing (MP) model. MP doesn't seem to be a model quite like the others. It may even be a "unique case."[48] It's the model "most readily explicable in verbal form," for example, the one most readily represented in abstract symbolic forms or language-like propositions. And, unlike the other models, it seems to require a kind of conscious, shared understanding among participants in order to operate. It isn't "natural" because no other animal species has markets or makes rational cost-benefit calculations. And even for human societies, it has rarely been "an ideological and philosophical keystone" outside modern Western societies: elsewhere "one or another of the other three models generally has occupied that place."[49] Perhaps for these reasons, RMT sometimes seems unsure about whether Market Pricing really is a model at all, or simply "becoming" one, a work in progress, now only in an "intermediate stage," but gradually being assimilated, as a widespread pattern, into the fourfold structure of human social relations.[50]

This "evolutionary" perspective is very suggestive and can help me address the question I left unanswered earlier, about the narrowness of Market Pricing as a name for social relations based on the virtues of Liberty (A1): why Market Pricing might well be a reasonable name for RMT's fourth model, even though the kinds of social relations it describes emerge from a family of virtues (A1) which includes so many other facets of the human.

To approach this question, let me begin by noting that, on the basis of its broad survey of social science literature, RMT supports and confirms what I earlier called the "arrow of virtue." The various branches of social science, it suggests, show "how one mode of social relationship succeeds another ... Communal Sharing evolves into Authority Ranking, which transforms into Equality Matching which ultimately develops into Market Pricing." RMT argues this directional arrow can be observed in individual lives and child development (ontogenesis), as well as in the historical evolution of human societies (phylogenesis). At both the individual and evolutionary levels, the four models are "an ordered set, each one in turn encompassing and elaborating on the preceding structure."[51]

This is a very interesting suggestion, entirely consistent with Hegel's description of the evolution of the human. But it can also be tweaked, or augmented, in two ways. First of all, if you look again at Figure 16 on page 144, you'll see that the arrow of virtue doesn't begin, as RMT suggests, with Communal Sharing (A2). It starts instead with the stance of "*I* am" (A1). Of course, the initial human stance of "*I* am" almost immediately transforms itself – both in individual lives in and in the earliest tribal cultures – into the stance of "I *am*" (A2). So it's easy to think the sequence begins with Communal Sharing. But, without that very first step, you don't have any kind of human action or life, and certainly no social life. Before tribal cultures emerged, humans lived (as I already mentioned in chapter 7) in a culture of domination by alpha males, and of submission by others to their domination, the culture of our animal origins, as higher primates. A culture of self-assertion. Self-assertion is the motor of all human activity. The pure self-assertion of A1 (or what Aristotle and Aquinas call "appetite") is the source of all human action.[52] All human acts of any kind are acts of self-assertion.[53] Without it there is nothing human at all. The arrow of virtue doesn't start with Communal Sharing. It starts in the virtues of Liberty (A1), not the virtues of Reverence (A2).

But if so, that raises yet another intriguing possibility, a possibility to which I will return later in this book. If the arrow of virtue is not a linear progression as RMT argues, but rather, as Hegel suggested (and as I explored in chapters 7 and 10), something more like a spiral staircase – ultimately coming back to the same place in the spiral, but from a "higher" or more evolved perspective – it would help explain why quite different forms of social relations can emerge from the *same* family of virtues, at *different* times and *different* stages of development or evolution. Play, for example, emerged in the *earliest* stages of human development – both of individuals and societies – but is never superseded or lost, and remains an essential part of the human repertoire.[54] Rational or even "logical" thought was fully available to human beings long before it began to take centre stage in Greek culture.[55] Human beings knew what it meant to be individuals long before individualism became the central theme of Western culture, starting in the seventeenth century.[56] Similarly, Market Pricing has many early manifestations – at every stage of human development – but only emerges, as a full-blown form of social relations, at a *later* stage of individual and social development, at a later turn in the spiral staircase. It is one of the forms social relations assume when the virtues of Liberty (A1) take centre stage for the *second* time in human affairs.

This points to a key question which, in its eagerness to neutralize MP, RMT seems to avoid. Why is the Market Pricing model only now emerging as a fully-fledged and widely generalized model of human relations?[57] Why has it never formed the core of any previous society in the history of humankind?[58] And yet, for the first time in history, it is now suddenly the one we Westerners can explain most easily to each other, the one with which we are most familiar (at least consciously – real life is a different story) – and which we now expect to find or use in all manner of places, even where it doesn't belong.

The answer is obvious. It is because of the rise of the virtues of self-assertion since the seventeenth century, and their general dominance in contemporary, post-modern Western societies. Markets and market behaviour are among the purest contemporary expressions of the virtues of self-assertion, as you saw in chapter 4. The new prominence of Market Pricing as a form of social relations and the rise of self-assertion are two sides of the same coin. They are rooted in the same dimension of the nature of the human.[59]

So "market reasoning" isn't the value neutral outlook it claims to be in the contemporary Western world. Under the cover of neutrality, it "smuggles in" its own values and virtues, potentially at the expense of all the others.[60] It is the way you view the world when you are practising the virtues of self-assertion, and, more specifically, the virtues of Liberty (A1). Its values are important. But they are rooted in only one of the four families of human values – and don't even account for all the virtues of its own corner of the human. If allowed to rule alone, the market mentality can crowd out all the other vital dimensions that make humans most human. Like the human paradox itself, RMT helps to put the corner of the human it calls Market Pricing into necessary moral perspective, within the overall nature of the human.

The models as dispositions

The suggestion that the structures of social life may have an evolutionary character invites us to reconsider the status and nature of RMT's models themselves. What exactly are they?

RMT seems to be somewhat uncertain about this. In its original form, the theory was eager to present them as well-defined and fully developed patterns of human behaviour built right into human biology. These "shared psychological models" were "endogenous," that is to say "abstract empty forms" already determined "prior to any social experience." They were thus said to be "innate" and "unlearned."[61] Like the goddess Athena, they were said to emerge already full-grown, if not from the head of Zeus, then from the human genome: "built into the human genotype and the operation of the brain in such a way that it is practically impossible to block completely [their] expression in human interaction."[62] The models were not the result of the "'internalization' of norms" but rather were "intrinsically" motivated, that is to say "imposed" on the social world, not simply learned or internalized "from raw experience."[63]

The obvious problem of deriving patterns of social relations directly from human biology seems to have led, over the following decade, to a modification of RMT.[64] The later version takes evolution more seriously. It now concedes the "universality and pervasiveness" of the four basic models of human relations do not necessarily "imply they are innate." So RMT is now prepared to entertain the alternative possibility that they are *not* "built in to our neural architecture" but shaped instead by the evolutionary processes of "natural selection." The models can thus be reconceived as "emergent arrangements," "mental adaptations" to "relational niches." In this new, updated version of RMT, natural selection has evolved four basic "relational capacities" that "facilitate adaptive social coordination across diverse domains in diverse environments."[65]

Perhaps as a result of this shift of perspective, the language of RMT has shifted too. It's now more often inclined to describe the four models as human "proclivities." This vocabulary was by no means absent from the initial version of the theory.[66] But it seems to have become more central to the later version, used more regularly and consistently, reflecting the overall shift to a more evolutionary perspective.[67]

But what is a "proclivity"? Another word for a "proclivity" is a "disposition." A "proclivity" is an inclination or disposition to behave in a certain way. RMT itself sometimes uses the word "disposition" as a synonym for "proclivity."[68] But disposition is exactly the word that Aristotle and Aquinas also used (or their translators often use) to designate the large patterns of human behaviour (like reverence and self-assertion) that begin as powers (or potencies), then become habits, and, finally, virtues. A habit is simply a more settled disposition. A disposition can thus be defined in "two ways": as the "genus" or family of which habit is a member; or, "in another way, as opposed to" or distinguished from habit, that is to say, as a tendency (or inclination or potentiality) for a certain kind of human behaviour, but one that hasn't yet become a habit.[69] The latter is an original disposition to act in a certain way, a disposition that becomes a habit through repeated acts that gradually reinforce the disposition into a habit. And a virtue (as you saw in chapter 3) is simply a good habit. But a virtue is still a kind of disposition: a disposition that, through repetition, has become a settled habit, a good habit. A virtue is a habitual disposition for a certain kind of act: a good act.

In rediscovering the four "models" of human social relations as four families of human "proclivities," RMT seems to have worked its way back to a view of the human based on human dispositions, habits, and virtues. Its description of these families is entirely or largely consistent with the nature of the human developed in this book and helps to confirm it. The four families of virtues that define the nature of the human, RMT suggests, are found not just in the behaviour of *individuals* but in the life and culture of human *societies* as a whole. The structures of social life are determined by – and also determine – the nature of the human.

The models of social relations and the human paradox

RMT's survey of more than a century of modern social science confirms the nature of the human described in this book so far. But a perspective based on the human virtues can also help supply two things Relational Models Theory so far seems to lack. In doing this, it can also help to explain the "structure of the structures" of social life.

Even in its more "evolutionary" form, RMT is still inclined to describe the four "models" of human social relations as monolithic wholes. It cannot – or at least doesn't yet – explain the dynamic internal structure that shapes each one of the four models. As a result, it can't yet tell us where they have come from, or where they might be going, or why.

What seems to be missing from RMT's persuasive discovery of four kinds of social relations, as I already suggested, is recognition of the human paradox, and the tension or conflict this paradox necessarily introduces into all four forms of human relations. Each of the four models is structured by a tension between its two sides: between the virtues (or dispositions or proclivities or propensities) of reverence and self-assertion. Two of the models (Communal Sharing and

Authority Ranking) are rooted in the virtues of reverence, modified by self-assertion, while the other two (Equality Matching and Market Pricing) are rooted in the virtues of self-assertion, modified by reverence.

The "in and out" conflict of Communal Sharing, for example, is a reflection of this basic human duality. As I said earlier, reverence creates the bonds; self-assertion creates the boundaries. Similarly, the "deference/dominance" tension of Authority Ranking reflects the same paradox. Reverence "eagerly" seeks a hierarchy of "value" or excellence it can revere. Self-assertion exploits that eagerness to establish a hierarchy of dominance and power.

In the same manner, Equality Matching's assertive demand for separate but equal status and treatment is modified by a reverential willingness to match equality with reciprocity. And Market Pricing's assertive emphasis on utilitarian exchange is modified by the recognition (sometimes grudging, consistent with self-assertion) that such exchange can only take place within a larger social framework, within a larger whole.

The four models of RMT don't emerge into human social life spontaneously, as monolithic wholes, let alone as imprinted in the human genome. They are the result of a dynamic process rooted in the nature of the human. The four models are the evolutionary development in social life of the two basic human impulses – or dispositions, or "proclivities" – of reverence and self-assertion.

But reverence and self-assertion are themselves the human expression of something deeper still. Something very important that RMT has so far overlooked or even rejected as implausible. "Sociability," it declared, in its original formulation, "has no unique ultimate source or essence." There is no evidence, it suggested, of "any matrix determining the arrangement of all the components and giving society an overall form."[70] That conviction led to the original assumption that the four basic models must be "endogenous" or "innate," "phylogenetically situated," "represented in the human genome." "What constraints on everyday interaction and thought could generate the same basic forms in so many diverse cultures around the world?" RMT asked. "Does any one have any substantive proposals for such constraints?"[71]

Well, yes. One such constraint is the polar structure of being itself: the polarity of unity and plurality, of something and everything, of being and beings, of self and world, of union and non-union, of "I am" and "It is" (Figures 5, 6, 7, and 15 on pages 34, 38, 41, and 143). The initial duality of reverence and self-assertion, as you have seen, is the human response to this basic polar structure of being. And the encounter with this same polar structure also breeds still further levels of paradox, beginning (in social relations) with the emergence of RMT's four models – composed of two contrasting pairs (CS/AR and EM/MP) – as the basic structures of social life.

Within each of these two pairs, the two sides are polarized from each other by this same basic structure: the contrasting human stances of "I am" and "It is." The distinction between the two "reverential" social models of Communal Sharing and Authority Ranking, for example, is the distinction between the stances of "I *am*" and "It *is*." The stance of "I *am*" expressed in Communal Sharing emphasizes the shared being that binds the members of the group, reverently, into a single whole, a "we" in which it can even be difficult at times to distinguish individual identities. The stance of "It *is*" expressed by Authority Ranking acknowledges the objective features of being that establish a hierarchy of value, a hierarchy in which some things or some people turn out to be truer or more valuable, more worthy of reverence, than others.

By the same token, the distinction between the two "assertive" models of Equality Matching and Market Pricing is the distinction between the contrasting stances of "*It* is" and "*I* am." The human stance of "*It* is" emphasizes the objective reality of the things to be done or shared, and the separateness of the person who claims an equal share (EM). The stance of "*I* am" seeks an outcome of greater benefit and utility for *me* than strict equality (MP).

So the structures of social life aren't wholly endogenous or innate. They are the result of human evolution and experience. They have certainly been bred into us and our genetic inheritance through 250,000 years of evolution. But that evolutionary process is the natural result of the human encounter with the polar structure of being, an experience that is ultimately moral, as the encounter with being, and with the *otherness* of being, inevitably calls upon us to make distinctions of value and of worth. The four forms of human social relations correspond to the four possible human stances toward the polarity of being and their related families of virtues: four families which determine and define the nature of the human.

A perspective based in the human virtues can thus help you see where the structures of social life have come from. But maybe it can help you see where they're going, too.[72] After all, if the structures of social life, like the nature of the human, are the result of a dynamic process in which paradox breeds paradox, the four forms of social relations may not be the last word, at least in their current forms. Maybe the spiral staircase I described in chapters 7 and 10 keeps beckoning us higher?

That's a possibility I'll come back to. But first I'll look at another form of social life, another way in which the human paradox manifests itself in a human world: the world of politics.

12

Politics

Political life is a contradiction. Or a series of contradictions.

Before I explore them, I need to point out that the main kind of politics I'll be discussing in this chapter is *democratic* politics. There are other kinds of political regimes, and I'll refer to them, especially in the political map of the human I'll develop in this chapter. But the focus, in this chapter, will be on democratic politics, not only because that's the form most widely practised and endorsed in our contemporary Western world, but also because, as I will argue, it's the only one fully consistent with the human paradox, with the full and highest development of the nature of the human. The free and democratic contest between contradictory definitions of the good is the necessary public expression of the human paradox in political life.

The kind of democratic politics to be discussed here is the politics that arises when the arrow of virtue has already arrived at the virtues of Equality (B2) on the spiral staircase of Western cultural evolution I pictured in chapters 7 and 10 (Figures 18 and 26). Democratic politics is a form of political life *as viewed through the lenses of self-assertion*. All four families of virtues and values are still available to us, as our full human repertoire. But we now view and interpret them all through the lens of the virtues of Equality (B2), and, increasingly (in our post-modern world) through the lens of the virtues of Liberty (A1). As you will see in this chapter, even the language we now use to describe the basic political outlooks – words like "liberalism" and "conservatism" – emerged in the first half of the nineteenth century precisely to take account of the new phase of Western culture that had begun in the seventeenth century: the crossing of the arrow of virtue from the virtues of Excellence (B1), first, to the virtues of Equality (B2), and second, to the virtues of Liberty (A1). As a result, all political options are viewed and interpreted in a democratic state through these two lenses. In the language of this chapter, we are all "liberals" now – even the so-called "conservatives" are liberals. The only question is what we combine with our liberalism – and how much, and in what ways.[1]

That's one of the contradictions in the geography of democratic politics I'll explore in this chapter.[2] But before I get to the geography, there's another kind of paradox I'd like to point out first.

The paradox of politics

The first paradox of political life I want to point out to you is an *existential* one. It has to do with the very paradoxical *nature* of politics itself, not just its paradoxical *geography*.

On the one hand, politics is a struggle for power, sometimes a vicious – and even ruthless – struggle between different groups or interests, with enormous stakes not just for the winners and losers but for all citizens. In a civilized and democratic country this struggle is contained and moderated by laws, conventions, and public opinion, and – in a truly democratic country – by the self-restraint of the political actors themselves. But it's still, at bottom, a struggle. The civilized alternative to civil war, perhaps. But a kind of warfare or struggle, nevertheless. We don't improve our understanding of politics when we neglect or underestimate this necessary underside of political life.[3]

Yet if politics is a struggle for power between competing interests, that's not all it is. Because, at the very same time, politics is also, paradoxically, the moral life of the community. In at least two ways.

First, politics is a struggle not just between interests but also between goods. Democratic politics is a contest not just between factions but also between different ideas and conceptions of the public good. It's the way we choose between competing public goods. Political life is the means through which we define the social good for ourselves. That's what we do in a democratic election: we decide which party or leader offers the best current definition of the public good and should therefore have the democratic right to determine the public good, at least until the next election. In a democratic election, political parties appeal not just to our interests but also to our aspirations toward the good. They invite us to rise above our own immediate and personal interests and to consider the good of the political community as a whole. Elections are not just a series of low blows, insults, dirty tricks, and shameless appeals to self-interest (though there are more of those than we might wish): they are also a contest of ideas and values.[4]

Second, politics and politicians don't only argue about values, they also, in some sense, *embody* them. This is a dimension of political life too often overlooked or undervalued. One reason there aren't even more low blows, insults, and dirty tricks is that political leaders know, consciously or unconsciously, that they must appeal not only to our self-interest but also to the better angels of our nature. When we choose political leaders, we do so partly because we admire them: they seem to embody or express values and qualities of character we cherish, and wish to see expressed in our public life. In our political leaders we usually want to see an expression and reflection of the best *in us*, and in our communities. Political leaders and institutions thus have a symbolic and expressive role that's just as important as their functional, legislative, administrative, regulatory, and public policy roles. We want our political leaders and institutions to *embody* the best in us and to *express* it for us: to lift us up, to make us aim higher, make us better than we would otherwise be.[5]

In political life, the struggle for power is what Aristotle called the efficient cause – the force that's driving or pushing, from behind or below, as it were. And the moral life of the community is the final cause, the end or goal or good we're trying to achieve, that pulls us forward into the future, from ahead or above. In other words, politics – like everything else that's human – is a blend of efficient and final causes, of self-assertion and reverence, of union and non-union.[6] Self-assertion drives humans to seek power and to exercise mastery in human affairs. Or rather, self-assertion *is* that raw human drive. But political self-assertion can only take place within a wider frame of community, within a social contract or setting of some kind. And the encounter with others and with otherness leads, again, to encounters with the hierarchy of goods, with the fact that some things have more value than other things. And that, in a true community, sometimes the good of others must come before our own. The virtues of reverence we first encounter in family life are a necessary feature of all community and social life (as you saw in the previous chapter), and therefore of democratic politics too.

So I can use the basic image developed in this book to portray this fundamental or "existential" contradiction of political life. Figure 29 on page 250 illustrates the basic "paradox of politics."[7]

However, it's important to remind you, right away, that the bottom half of this figure doesn't convey something bad and the top half something good. They're both good. Without self-assertion, you don't have anything human. All action is, by definition, self-assertion. To *act* is to assert yourself. Even acts of reverence are acts of self-assertion: self-assertion that has turned into its opposite. But without the kernel of self-assertion there can be no reverence at all: no *acts* of reverence.

Figure 29. The paradox of politics

Similarly, without the struggle for power there would be no political life. There would be no contest. No competing visions of society and of the public good. No competition for political office and for the right to define the good. No struggle, no politics. No humanity.[8]

The struggle for power is not the shame of democracy – though it *can* be, if carried to excess. It's the essence of democracy. The free contest for power is what makes democracy democratic. When you suppress democracy, you don't suppress the struggle for power. Quite the contrary. You drive it underground and make it more vicious and corrupt.[9] The struggle for power re-emerges as court, bureaucratic, or internal party politics, as you can see in all totalitarian states. In China today, for example, as one senior Chinese official puts it: "The bureaucracy is political, and politics are bureaucratized."[10] Something very similar could be said about Iran or the Soviet Union, or pre-revolutionary and contemporary Russia, or the Ancien Régime in France. Or even in nominally democratic countries when there is no regular alternation of political power.

Self-assertion is essential to all things human, and democratic politics is one of the highest forms of the human. So the self-assertion which expresses itself in political life, as a struggle for political power, is the essence and starting point of democratic politics. That's why, in parliamentary democracies on the Westminster model, the leader of the second largest party in parliament is sometimes styled the Leader of the "Loyal" Opposition. To emphasize that the struggle for political power – political *opposition* to the current government – is just as important, just as legitimate, and just as central to democratic life, as government itself.

Indeed the emergence of this principle in the seventeenth and eighteenth centuries was what led to the establishment of our modern democracies. And it eventually gave a name to the virtues of self-assertion as they manifest themselves in democratic political life: the name of liberalism.

The paradox of liberalism

The basic liberal value is freedom.[11]

That's what "liberal" means, in a modern and post-modern political context. It means a political outlook founded on *liberty* as the highest human good.[12] Most of the causes for which liberalism (under various names) has striven since the seventeenth century involved the enlargement of some kind of freedom. Freedom of religion. Freedom of assembly. Freedom of speech. Freedom to elect one's own government. Free enterprise. And so on. The history of "specifically *liberal* activism" is, as Adam Gopnik says, a "story of human self-liberation."[13] Even the earlier, pre-modern meaning of "liberal" (as in the "liberal" arts or "liberal" education) was also rooted in an ideal of freedom. It described the education worthy of a free man and a gentleman (i.e., not a slave): "liberation from vulgarity."[14] "We call those studies liberal," said the Renaissance humanist Pier Paolo Vergerio (1370–1444), "which are worthy of a free man."[15] The "liberal arts" are still said to be those studies which, in some sense or other, "set one free."[16]

But freedom is only one half of liberalism. John Locke, one of the fathers of modern liberalism, began his famous *Second Treatise on Civil Government* by declaring that "all men are naturally in ... a state of perfect freedom," but they are in a "state also of equality ... there being nothing more evident than that creatures of the same species and rank ... should also be equal one amongst another, without subordination or subjection."[17]

Liberalism, as Locke shows, has always linked liberty and equality, historically.[18] But they are also linked logically, or metaphysically. As you already saw in the first part of this book, the pursuit of freedom immediately introduces a tension or contradiction within liberalism itself. The same spirit of self-assertion that demands freedom also demands equality. I want to be free because I am as good or as worthy or as deserving as anyone else. I want to be free simply because I am *me*. I don't need anyone else telling me what to do, or how to do it, or preventing me from doing it. At least not unless I have chosen them myself, or participated in choosing them. Unless I have somehow agreed or given my own consent. I assert my right to freedom, and thus, necessarily, to self-government also.

But so does everyone else. Every human being asserts the same claim. And if we all think we are as good or as worthy or as deserving of freedom (and hence self-government) as anyone else, then we claim our right to freedom *equally*. Raw self-assertion would be quite happy to dominate. It is, in fact, the natural human disposition to dominate.[19] But self-assertion, by definition, doesn't want to *be* dominated. It spontaneously resists domination. It *asserts* itself *against* its own disposition to dominate.[20] And because everyone's self-assertion *resists* domination just as much as it seeks to dominate, our natural human self-assertion can't help asserting a right not only to freedom but, in some sense or another, *to equal amounts of it*.[21] Our own self-assertion inevitably leads, then, to a principle of equal human desert. It leads us to a principle of equality.[22]

But these two claims are in conflict with each other. The more a society or a group favours liberty, the less equality is likely to flourish. Complete freedom will give some people the opportunity to acquire more power – or more wealth, or knowledge, or skill, or influence, or fame, and so on – than others. Societies that insist on absolute freedom end up as tyrannies of one kind or another – tyrannies of wealth (plutocracy) or influence (oligarchy) – with vast inequalities between citizens.

And the more equality is asserted, the less is liberty likely to flourish. To ensure or maintain some measure of equality, you will have to intervene in various ways to limit liberty, to limit the tendency of unfettered liberty to permit or foster inequality. To promote equality, you will have to make people less "free." And the more you do it, the less free they will be. (At least technically or legally. Many limitations of *individual* freedom would actually make *most* people "freer" in some other senses: freer from want, fear, misery, or sickness, for example.) Societies that claim to stand for absolute equality end up as another form of tyranny, a "dictatorship of the (so-called) proletariat," or something of that nature.

Liberty and equality contradict each other, and yet are necessary to each other. Without liberty, there would eventually be no equality. And, without equality, there would eventually be no liberty, either. This is the basic paradox of liberalism, as it was the basic paradox of self-assertion itself. Indeed, that's one of the reasons why, in chapter 8, I chose "Equality" and "Liberty" as the names for the two families of virtues that Aristotle and Aquinas called the "rational" and "sense" appetites. So that you would easily recognize them in their modern dress, in the language we now spontaneously use to express the two sides of the paradox of self-assertion. These two families of virtues – two of the four basic poles that define the nature of the human – are the two poles of what together we now know, in modern political life and thought, under the name of liberalism.[23]

John Rawls and the limits of liberalism

One of the best-known contemporary theorists of liberalism is the American philosopher John Rawls. Rawls argues that the only fair or just way to think about the fundamental principles of political life is to imagine yourself in what he calls an "original position," that is to say, you must put yourself behind a deliberate "veil of ignorance" about any existing community, and without any knowledge of the place you would occupy in the political society you are designing, or the resources that might be available to you in such a society.[24]

In this kind of abstract, utopian, or "original" position, Rawls argues, you would in fact choose to base your ideal society upon some kind of balance between the principles of liberty and equality.[25] You would want to ensure that, in this future society, you would be free to enjoy certain "basic liberties," such as political liberty (right to vote and stand for political office), freedom of speech, freedom from arbitrary arrest, and so on.[26] And you would also want to ensure that the society offered some genuine social equality: because you wouldn't know where you might end up in it – whether at the top or at the bottom – and would naturally want to make sure that, wherever you did land, you wouldn't be too badly off.

Although Rawls argues explicitly for the "priority" of liberty, he actually gives more emphasis (or attention) to equality. He suggests that neither inherited social position, nor merit, nor an entirely free market is an adequate basis for establishing the kind of equality necessary for a just society. He argues instead for a "difference principle." The idea behind this principle is that the social order should not advantage "those better off unless doing so is to the advantage of those less fortunate."[27] This means some kind of redistribution of the gains enjoyed, earned, or achieved by the more fortunate: redistribution in education, training, or in other activities or initiatives that "improve the situation of those who have lost out."[28]

Rawls' pursuit of liberal equality turns on those families of liberal virtues to which I gave the names of Rights (B2a) and of Reciprocity (B2b). The "difference" principle is a "principle of mutual benefit." It is a kind of tacit agreement "to regard the distribution of natural talents as a *common asset* and to *share* in the benefits of this distribution, whatever it turns out to be."[29]

In an outlook structured largely around the liberty and equality of individuals, this sudden reference to the "common" good and to a principle of "sharing" seems surprising. The "original position," remember, was a calculation of pure self-interest. Beyond an abstract thought exercise, why should we regard our own assets as "common," and not just as ours alone? What would move us actually to "share" them? These kinds of questions seem to point beyond Rawls' own liberalism to something else, something without which neither liberty nor equality can make much sense, or perhaps even come into existence. They seem to point to a prior framework of community.

Michael Sandel: beyond liberalism

Michael Sandel (b. 1953) is another American political philosopher who has explored some of the questions raised by Rawls' kind of liberalism. For Sandel, this liberal account of the human is "too thin."[30]

For one thing, it doesn't seem to pay enough attention to the prior framework of community. Can individuals exist outside of a community? Are individuals really prior to their community? Or is community prior to individuals, and even to their rights? For Sandel, the liberal version can't really explain the moral force of the loyalties and responsibilities we began to explore in chapter 4, those that arise, not abstractly, but concretely: because we are "members of *this* family or nation or people."[31]

To understand the moral force of these concrete ties we need another way to approach political and social obligation: we need to approach it from somewhere other than from behind a deliberate "veil of ignorance" about any concrete, existing community, or real life. Another way to do that is to start from the *inside* rather than the outside, from the concrete reality of the existing community and its culture. Instead of abstract principles, this alternative stance has its starting point in the moral obligations that arise from and sustain a specific, existing community. Hegel called this alternative moral outlook *sittlichkeit*.[32] The critical feature of *sittlichkeit* is that it "enjoins us to bring about what already is."[33] It expresses the inner moral idea of the community in whose life we already participate, and which makes us what we are. *Sittlichkeit* is a culture not of moral reasoning about abstract rational principles but rather of customary, habitual virtue. The institutions, practices, customs, habits, and traditions of a given society, in this alternative view, are the bearers of implicit norms which call upon us to develop and live them out, not in abstract theory but in practice. In this perspective, we start not from the universal but from "our own."

Rawls himself seems to recognize, implicitly, not only the force of these concrete ties but even their indispensable role in underpinning his own liberalism. Because, when he wants to justify his sudden leap from individual liberty and equality to a notion of the "common good" and of "sharing" – when he wants to explain why in practice we should share what is ours – he is forced to appeal to an external and additional principle, something beyond liberty and equality, a principle of "fraternity." But fraternity is clearly a very different kind of virtue than the self-*seeking* virtues of liberty and equality.[34] Fraternity is another name for the self-*giving* virtues we encounter first and most powerfully, as Rawls himself acknowledges (and as you saw in chapter 4), in our own families. "The family, in its ideal conception and often in practice," Rawls admits, "is one place where the principle of maximizing the sum of advantages is rejected. Members of a family commonly do not wish to gain unless they can do so in ways that further the interests of the rest."[35]

In other words, even to make liberalism work, you have to infuse it with something else. You have to go beyond liberty and equality to the very different virtues we find exhibited in families, where liberty and equality don't have priority: those I called the virtues of reverence, especially the specific set of virtues I called Reverence (A2).[36] Acknowledging the existence and necessity of these quite different and even prior virtues seems to be a first step toward achieving a "thicker" and more convincing account of how the nature of the human expresses itself in political form.

But this can only be a first step. As you saw in chapters 7 and 9, the virtues we encounter first in our families inevitably point beyond themselves to the second thing that seems to be missing from Rawls' liberalism. They point to the objective good.

This is a step Rawls himself tries hard to avoid. In fact (like his predecessor, Immanuel Kant), he argues that political life doesn't and can't permit decisions, laws, policies, or social arrangements to be based on ideas of the ultimate good or the final ends of life. Decisions about these may be necessary and appropriate for individual persons. But they can have no place in political life because we will disagree about them. Politics, as modern liberalism conceives it, can only legitimately deal with the "background conditions under which these aims are to be formed and the manner in which they are to be pursued" by individuals. "We should not attempt to give form to our life by first looking to the good independently defined," Rawls argues. "... For the self is prior to the ends which are affirmed by it ... We should therefore reverse the relation between the right and the good ... and view the right as prior."[37]

For Michael Sandel, the idea that the right is prior to the good is unconvincing. "The attempt to detach arguments about justice and rights from arguments about the good life is mistaken," he responds, "for two reasons: First, it is not always possible to decide questions of justice and rights without resolving substantive moral questions; and second, even where it's possible, it may not be desirable."[38]

It's not possible because the good is what, as Charles Taylor puts it, "gives the point of the rules which define the right."[39] It also isn't possible because that's not what human beings, or their world, are like. You can't expect people to park their deepest moral intuitions and commitments at the door of politics in order to gain entry. That would be a kind of amputation or mutilation of the human. It would amount to imposing a devious kind of moral uniformity, but exclusively "around a liberal social agenda."[40] A model of public dialogue based on a supposedly "neutral" public space, from which religious or other values and ideas are excluded, isn't really neutral at all. Just like logical positivism, which (as you saw in the Introduction) tried to banish metaphysics from philosophy, this kind of alleged "neutrality" really "presupposes a moral and political epistemology" of its own, while hiding it behind the claim of neutrality.[41] So this model of public space wouldn't even be genuinely "liberal," as Alan Wolfe (b. 1942) points out, because it would contradict liberalism's own commitment to the virtues of Equality (B2). A society that allows some people (say, atheists or secularists) to bring their deepest convictions into the public square but denies the same right to others (say, religious people) wouldn't be a liberal society, whatever it might claim about itself. Because it would treat people "unequally."[42]

In addition to being unjust, it would be a recipe for trouble. "Deciding important public questions while pretending to a neutrality that cannot be achieved is a recipe for backlash and resentment," Sandel warns. "… It is also an open invitation to narrow intolerant moralisms. Fundamentalists rush in where liberals fear to tread."[43]

Banishing ideas about the good from political discussion isn't desirable, even if it were possible, because it would radically impoverish political life. The problem with contemporary politics isn't "too much moral argument but too little. Our politics is overheated because it is mostly vacant, empty of moral and spiritual content. It fails to engage with the big questions that people care about."[44] And banishing arguments about the good biases political outcomes from the start. "A just society can't be achieved simply by maximizing utility or securing freedom of choice," says Sandel. "To achieve a just society we have to reason together about the meaning of the good life. And to create a public culture hospitable to the disagreements that will inevitably arise."[45]

Disagreements about desirable political outcomes are shot through with differing ideas about the hierarchy of goods. Which public goods are *more* good than other goods? Liberty and equality are themselves powerful moral goods. But they aren't the only ones. You just saw how John Rawls had to sneak in the additional and quite different idea of "fraternity" (or reverence) in order to grease the wheels of a liberal political order and make it work. But fraternity isn't the only additional good that will be needed.

Liberty and equality may be powerful goods, but, by themselves, they're also "empty," as Hegel pointed out.[46] They can't tell us what to do with our freedom. They can't tell us how to lead our lives. To have any value content, they must have some context, goal, or objective.[47]

Consider justice itself. Justice is the rendering of what is due. But what is due? That depends on the hierarchy of goods. There are gradations of the good. "[A] lesser good can be a kind of evil," says Leibniz, "if it becomes an obstacle to a greater good."[48] While justice is clearly closely bound up with the idea of equality,[49] it must mean more than that. Because some goods are higher than other goods, justice can sometimes also mean "subjection" or submission to another, or to some kind of higher good.[50]

Every political decision is a decision about the hierarchy of goods and about the just trade-offs that must be made within it: trade-offs made, in concrete situations, between different values. "Justice is not only about the right way to *distribute* things," Michael Sandel concludes. "It is also about the right way to *value* things."[51] So justice *itself* is powerfully connected to our ideas about the good, especially the ultimate good: to notions about the good life. In fact, as you saw in Tables 11, 12, and 14, and in Figure 25 (on pages 115, 116, 140, and 209) justice is just another word for it. It is merely another form or expression of "excellence" or the good.[52]

The political paradox

The contrasting views of John Rawls and Michael Sandel suggest two things missing from liberalism – or even, in some sense, opposed to, or in tension with it. The two things seem to be excellence and reverence. And these two other poles of the human paradox belong instead to liberalism's opposite. To what, in the modern world, we call (or used to call) conservatism.

In the history of Western political thought, it is a remarkable fact that, in the very first paragraphs of his *Second Treatise on Civil Government* – a

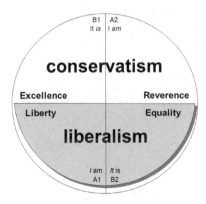

Figure 30. The political paradox: liberalism and conservatism

foundational text of liberalism – John Locke acknowledged all four poles of the human paradox. Right after setting out the virtues of self-assertion – freedom (A1) and equality (B2) – as the twin poles of the human in the "state of nature" – he immediately joined them to their opposites, the two poles of the virtues of reverence: "the great maxims of justice [B1] and charity [A2]."[53]

So, my basic image of the human in Figure 20 (on page 200) can also be made to serve, with only slight adjustment, for the basic political paradox.[54] You can see that paradox in Figure 30 above.

As Figure 30 suggests, the two main outlooks of democratic politics are both structured by an internal tension or paradox between competing and conflicting goods. Liberalism, as you saw in the second section of this chapter, is a tension between liberty and equality. That's one of the reasons why there can be so many kinds of liberals. Those who give higher value to liberty will be somewhat different in outlook from those who give priority to equality. And that's just the start. Because, as you saw in chapter 8, the virtues of Liberty (A1) and Equality (B2) have many sub-families and sub-sub-families. So, giving emphasis to any of these, or to some combination of them, enormously expands the potential varieties of liberalism. And that's still only the beginning. Because liberalism (like the self-assertion it expresses) is only one half of what it is to be a human being. As a human, a liberal must, inevitably, attach value to the virtues of reverence, or to some of them.[55] When all the families of reverence are taken into account, that creates the possibility of an almost endless range of flavours or colours of liberalism.[56]

Although it builds on the eternal virtues of self-assertion, liberalism is a quintessentially modern outlook. Of course, the eternal virtues of self-assertion played an essential role in the premodern world, too. But there, they formed the background, not the foreground. They expressed themselves in and through the context created by the foreground virtues of reverence. In the modern and post-modern worlds, they have become the foreground. The two poles of self-assertion – the liberal values of liberty and equality – have become the core values of the modern and post-modern worlds.

Conservatism, on the other hand, is the modern and post-modern version of an essentially *pre*modern political outlook. It's the survival of premodern political values in the new context established by the dominant modern and post-modern virtues of self-assertion. What was once the foreground has receded to the background. Conservatism is the premodern political values of reverence, now viewed through a liberal lens.[57]

For that reason, liberalism and conservatism stand in a somewhat different relationship to democracy. And the arrow of virtue explains why. Democracy didn't emerge as a working form of self-government in Western political cultures until the arrow of virtue had crossed the line from the virtues of Excellence (B1) to the liberal virtues of Equality, or the human stance of "*It* is" (B2), in the seventeenth and eighteenth centuries.[58] Thus, liberalism is *both* the precondition or framework *of* democracy *and* one of the contending options *within* democracy. There is no tension between liberalism and democracy. Liberalism and democracy are one. That is why we speak, quite properly and legitimately, of *liberal* democracy. If it isn't a liberal democracy, a democracy can't be genuinely democratic, just a pretend democracy, tyranny by another name. Its liberal side keeps democracy on track, and ensures the constraints, the diffusion of power, the checks and balances, the freedom of expression, and due process that make a democracy authentic and liberating.

There *is* a tension between conservatism and democracy, however. Because, while conservatism is another contending strand *within* democracy, it also expresses human stances that are *prior* to, or older than, democracy. It expresses dimensions of the human that are deeper, higher, or other than the modern and post-modern virtues of self-assertion. For that reason, conservatism can be a standing threat to democracy unless it consciously tames itself. For democracy to work, a conservative must make up her mind to *be* a democrat. To be, that is to say, a *liberal* conservative.

But liberalism can also be a threat to democracy through its own blindness and one-sidedness, its inclination to conflate liberalism and democracy. A liberal must therefore make a conscious effort to recognize that democracy emerges from – and depends on – deeper, higher, or older strands in the human than modern, liberal self-assertion.[59] For democracy and the educational contract to work, liberals must make up their minds to be *conservative* liberals. They must recognize the human paradox at work within democracy – the paradox or conversation that makes democracy genuinely democratic. If it is to be a *good* democracy, it must transcend its liberal roots and make room for the other, older side of the human spirit. Without the virtues of reverence, a democracy might be democratic, but it would not be fully human.

The paradox of conservatism

In chapters 2, 5, and 8, you saw that reverence is a virtue of union. In a political context, conservatism expresses this core impulse of union as a devotion to community – which can and does take a variety of forms, as you will see again in a moment. For an authentic conservative, the common good of the community and the state comes before – and is the prior condition for – the private good and liberties of individuals.[60] "[T]rue conservatives," as Leo Tolstoy (1828–1910) puts it, are animated by "the one purpose of the common good and the common security."[61] For a conservative, the state or government isn't something alien, standing over against the individual ego – something which threatens individual freedom, against which permanent vigilance and resistance are therefore required – but is, instead, an end in itself, an organic expression of the community in which the citizen shares and participates, and which gives her her very being and identity.[62] But this devotion to community is balanced and constrained by a contrasting devotion to excellence.[63] For a genuine conservative, quality matters: there's a hierarchy of goods, and so all things can't just be equal. Judgments and distinctions about relative value will have to be made.

The value conservatives attach to excellence is part of the conservative attachment to authority, or to what is authoritative. "It is through an ideal of authority," says Roger Scruton, "that conservatives experience the political world."[64] But, as soon as someone uses the word "authority," you have to guard against a potential (and widespread) confusion. When you hear the word "authority," your first impulse is probably to think of it *from above*: from the perspective of the person *in* authority, or who holds authority. As you saw in the previous chapter, it's very easy and common to confuse "authority" with power, rank, and domination. But these are virtues of self-assertion, more specifically, virtues of

Power (A1a). They aren't what an authentic conservative has in mind when she talks about authority. The properly conservative view of authority is the opposite. It's the view *from below*: the view of those, in so many cultures, who are "eager" (as Relational Models Theory recognizes) to acknowledge a hierarchy of goodness and truth, to distinguish the superior from the inferior. What distinguishes the conservative outlook isn't an attitude *by* authority, but an attitude *to* authority. Conservatism isn't the stance of the one who *wields* authority but rather, of the one who feels a duty or obligation *to* authority, or to what is authoritative. The conservative idea of political power is an extension of the power experienced in a good family: a power that is authoritative, a power toward which you feel a spontaneous "inner reverence" and loyalty, and for which you may be ready to sacrifice something important, perhaps even your own life.[65] When Anthony Trollope (1815–82) refers to the "benefits accruing" to a country from "established marks of reverence," he isn't thinking of the benefit just to those in authority, but rather to the whole society, including to those who *show* the reverence.[66] The conservative attitude isn't a disposition to dominate, but a recognition that *something is due*: due to truth (B1a), to goodness, and to justice (B1b) – and to the community and institutions by which they are upheld and maintained. The authority and hierarchy conservatives value is the hierarchy of excellence. The hierarchy of goods.

Because conservatism is a tension between the virtues of Excellence (B1) and of Reverence (A2), there can be many kinds of conservatives, just as there are many kinds of liberals. Those who give more importance to Excellence (B1) will be different in outlook than those who give priority to Reverence (A2). And when you add in all their sub-families and sub-sub-families – and all the contrasting virtues of self-assertion no human being (even a conservative) can ignore – the range of possibilities for conservatives (as you saw for liberals) is almost endless.[67]

The fact that the virtues of reverence can't be entirely ignored by liberalism, nor the virtues of self-assertion by conservatism, should help remind you that "conservatism" and "liberalism," as I've pictured them in Figure 30, are ideal or abstract political outlooks. No one is, or should ever be, a pure conservative or a pure liberal, any more than they can live by the virtues of reverence alone, or exclusively by those of self-assertion. They couldn't do it, even if they tried.

Remember that the basic image above is also an image of the nature of the human. And the nature of the human is nothing less than *all* four poles of the human, all four families of virtues, taken together. Whatever we do, all four dimensions of the human are always present – in some way, and to some degree – in our action, even if we can't see it. Which, normally, we don't.

Remember, also, the "spiral" shape of the arrow of virtue: Western culture has moved successively through each of the families of virtues, emphasizing each of them in turn, and viewing *all four* through that specific lens. Our post-modern Western culture has now evolved back to the virtues of self-assertion, where the human story began. And so it now views all four families through the lens of the virtues of Equality (B2) and of Liberty (A1), the lenses of liberalism.

Think again about John Rawls, and the way his own argument about equality couldn't work without a prior human impulse of sharing, and without a commitment to the common good. The need for these instincts obliges him to appeal to a principle of "fraternity," a principle which obviously comes from a quite different source than the self-assertive values of liberty and equality – the self-maximizing calculation of the "original position" – in which his liberalism is rooted. He goes even further, to describe a "well-ordered society" (in strikingly Hegelian language) as a "social union of social unions." He also acknowledges that unless social attachment goes beyond a merely "instrumental" outlook (A1) – in which we treat each other simply as means to our own ends – unless it is "fused with elements of affection and friendship [A2], it will not exhibit the characteristic features of a social union."[68] It's not easy to see how Rawls leaps to these important insights from what he himself admits to be the "individualistic features" of his starting point – how he gets from non-union to union.[69] But the fact that he's compelled to do so illustrates that, no matter where you begin, any adequate description of political life will eventually have to bring in all four stances of the human. They're what define the nature of the human. They are what human beings *are*.

Even as individuals, it's impossible for us to live in all four stances of the human equally, or at the same time. The four families of virtues are always competing for our attention, and we have to make choices or achieve balances between them in concrete situations.[70] Because of our biological make-up, social and cultural background, upbringing, temperament, personality type, education, experience, convictions, and so on, we tend to give priority to one or more of them – or even to some part of them, such as the sub-sub-families of Power (A1a) or Pleasure (A1b) – more often than to others, in the complex circumstances of our daily lives.

In politics, it's even more difficult to be all things at all times. And maybe even undesirable too. Because politics, as you saw at the beginning of the chapter, is simultaneously both a struggle for power *and* the moral life of the community. Both efficient and final causes, both self-assertion and reverence, at the same time. In both of these forms – as a contest both of *interests* and of *values* (the inside of the virtues) – it's essential for political leaders and parties to project and represent these same contending goods upon the public stage. If they don't do so, or don't do so completely or effectively, then the whole human paradox won't be represented in the sum of political life. The ideal objective may be a perfect union of all public goods. But that's only the *ideal* destination. It's not the human journey. We live our eternal journey *toward* that goal in non-union, in the separate strands that make up the whole.

The origin and evolution of conservatism

As I pointed out a moment ago, understanding how the human paradox takes political form is enormously complicated by the way political labels have evolved since the eighteenth century, and have even become reversed in popular usage.

The word "conservative," as a political label, for example, seems to have been coined by the French writer François-René de Chateaubriand (1768–1848) at the beginning of the nineteenth century. It had already been used, as an adjective, by Louis de Bonald (1754–1840), a political apologist for the *ancien régime* in France, who used it to describe the communitarian virtues of monarchical government: the alleged capacity of the monarch to "conserve" or preserve the organic unity and strength of society, as an undivided whole.[71] But in 1818, by choosing to call his new political journal *Le Conservateur*, Chateaubriand turned Bonald's adjective into a noun and a label for a new political outlook.[72] This new outlook aimed to renovate earlier French monarchical thought – the pre-modern political values of reverence – by reconciling it with the ideas of popular liberty and constitutional self-government that had emerged from the Revolution.[73] On the one hand, this new "conservatism" still harked back to the virtues of reverence and to the medieval Christian view that the common good of the community comes before the good and liberties of individuals.[74]

But at the same time, it also defended the cause of liberty – especially freedom of the press – and of constitutional monarchy, a monarchy reconciled with the principle of democracy. To Bonald's absolutism, Chateaubriand responded: "You reject the norms of our day to return to times we cannot even recognize."[75] His new conservatism looked forward as well as backward, trying to make a bridge between the past and the future, between modern and premodern, between union and non-union.

For this reason, the "conservative" label was soon adopted in Britain by those who were trying to do the same thing for what had previously been known as Toryism. The "Tories" (originally a term of abuse) started out as the "court" party in the seventeenth century, supporting the restored monarchy of the House of Stuart after the Civil War, and opposed to the exclusion of Charles II's Catholic brother from the succession to the Throne. After the Glorious Revolution of 1689 removed the Stuarts and assured the ascendancy of the largest landholders and a new merchant and banking class, the Tories became instead the "country" party, defending the interests of the lesser landed gentry and the Church of England against "Whig" reformers. Lord Bolingbroke (1678–1751), the great eighteenth-century Tory leader and theorist, described Toryism as motivated by "reverence for government."[76] This initial Tory reverence for government had deep roots, going back (like French "conservatism") to medieval Christianity, and its view of the "common good" – the assumption that the community comes before the individual.[77] This older view was exactly the outlook that the Tories' eighteenth-century opponents, the Whigs (also, originally, a term of abuse), were intent upon overthrowing. They were the political expression of the new monied interests, who sought to sweep away any remaining vestiges of medieval institutions, attitudes, practices, and communitarian restraints that might stand in the way of trade, finance, and individual enterprise.

By the beginning of the nineteenth century, however, the time had come, in Britain as in France, for a reconciliation of old and new. The political way to reconcile the premodern virtues of reverence with the modern liberal virtues of self-assertion had already been shown, at the end of the eighteenth century, by a Whig, Edmund Burke (1729–97). Against the rational individualism of the Enlightenment, Burke maintained the claims of the organic community and the state. Changes to them should never be considered, he argued, in anything but a spirit of appropriate "reverence," because they embodied a contract "not only between those who are living, but between the living, those who are dead, and those who are to be born," "the great primeval contract of eternal society."[78] It has been said of Burke that he "more than any other thinker in the eighteenth century approached the political tradition with a sense of religious reverence."[79]

Some forty years later a Tory prime minister, Robert Peel (1788–1850), applied this same spirit to a new era of reform. In his Tamworth Manifesto of 1834, Peel declared his aim was to reconcile the traditional Tory "respect for ancient rights, and the deference to prescriptive authority" with the new reforming spirit heralded by the

1832 Reform Act: "combining, with the firm maintenance of established rights, the correction of proved abuses and the redress of real
grievances." In the spirit of Bolingbroke, Peel said that his cause was
the "cause of good government."[80] It was in this spirit – both organic
and reforming at the same time – that the Tories soon came to be
known, in the spirit of Chateaubriand, as "conservatives." The new
Conservative party continued to combine these two themes through
subsequent decades, especially under Prime Minister Benjamin Disraeli (1804–81). "I see no other remedy," said Disraeli, "... but an
earnest return to a system which may be described as one of loyalty
and reverence, of popular rights and social sympathies."[81] His second
Reform Act of 1867 extended the vote to most of the British working
class, and his ministry of 1874–80 was responsible for the most nota-
ble program of social reform carried out by any British government
of the nineteenth century.[82] Disraeli's social conservatism was a "step
toward the welfare state."[83] Yet in these same decades, the British
Conservative party (especially under the leadership of Lord Salis-
bury, prime minister for three terms and twenty-one years at the end
of the nineteenth century) was already enlarging its base of electoral
support from the landed class to all owners of property, including
the new urban middle class and business interests.[84] For most of the
twentieth century, the Conservative Party in Britain (like conservative
parties elsewhere) continued to balance, sometimes uneasily, both its
initial, communitarian roots and its increasingly self-assertive, individualistic, urban clienteles, notably in the administrations of Stanley
Baldwin, Winston Churchill, Harold Macmillan, and Edward Heath.
But by the 1970s, the post-war, self-assertive reaction against the welfare state began to tell, culminating eventually in the deep hostility to
community and public values exhibited by Prime Minister Margaret
Thatcher (1925–2013) in the 1980s.[85] The same neoliberal takeover of
conservative parties occurred in the United States (where the "progressive" outlook of Theodore Roosevelt, Herbert Hoover, Dwight
Eisenhower, Richard Nixon, and Gerald Ford was overtaken by the
neoliberalism of Ronald Reagan) and in Canada (where the progressive conservatism of Robert Borden, R.B. Bennett, John Diefenbaker,
and Brian Mulroney – not to mention provincial progressive conservatives such as Leslie Frost, John Robarts, Duff Roblin, Richard
Hatfield, and Robert Stanfield – was replaced by the neoliberalism of
Stephen Harper).[86]

By the beginning of the twenty-first century – both in Britain and
in North America – the word "conservative" had come full circle. In
popular usage, "conservative" now means the opposite of its original

meaning. Instead of an organic view of society – in which "reverence for government" is the basis for securing the "common good," the welfare of the whole community[87] – the adjective "conservative" now often describes someone who seeks individual freedom above all and who is therefore hostile to government or to state intervention in economic, social, and cultural affairs.[88] By the end of 2015, Canada's "national newspaper" could simply take for granted that conservatism "focuses on individual liberties, limited government and support for free markets."[89] For many contemporary "conservatives" individual good now takes priority over the common good.[90]

This usage isn't consistent, however. Because many people who now call themselves conservative want to retain the *old* meaning in social policy and are in favour of state action to maintain standards of "excellence" in morality and behaviour, or to promote appropriate values in education and social policy.[91]

This contradiction and the broader reversal in the meaning of conservatism can both be explained, at least in part, by a similar shift that had taken place, over the same period, in the meaning of the word "liberal."

The origin and evolution of liberalism

The adjective "liberal," as I already noted, goes back to ancient times, where it described the qualities of a free man, that is, not a slave. This connection with the root meaning of liberty or freedom gave new life to the word in the seventeenth and eighteenth centuries, when it became associated with the Enlightenment ideals of liberty and equality. The adjective was first used, in a political sense, in 1750 by the Marquis d'Argenson (1694–1757), a French statesman and writer.[92] Napoleon liked to call himself a "liberal" and may have been the first important political leader to use the word this way. But it was first used as a label for a political movement in Spain, by those who resisted the Napoleonic occupation of their country and then defended the constitution of 1812 against encroachment by the restored Bourbon monarchy.[93] By 1818, the same year Chateaubriand coined the term "conservative," another French author, Maine de Biran (1766–1824) introduced the noun "liberalism" into French. Within five years it had found its way into a French dictionary, and *The Liberal* had even become the title of a short-lived magazine edited by Byron, Shelley, and Leigh Hunt.[94] As British Whigs searched for a new label that would modernize their own political movement – just as "conservatism" had done for the Tories – they also embraced a continental term, and the British Liberal party was eventually born, as a fusion of Whigs, Radicals, and Peelite Tories, on 6 June 1859.[95]

In the mid-nineteenth century, British liberalism was still closely connected with its root meaning. It had many strands, but all of them asserted "the need to protect [human projects and capacities] from cramping or controlling power."[96] Liberalism signified the pursuit of liberty, in all its forms. An "overarching thought" for nineteenth-century liberals – as for their eighteenth-century Whig predecessors – was that whatever "obstructed" initiative, innovation, originality, and enterprise was simply to be "swept away."[97] Liberalism meant free enterprise, and the sweeping away of practices, laws, privileges, or community institutions that stood in the way both of individual freedom and, it was alleged, of economic progress.[98] The successful campaign by two politicians, Richard Cobden (1804–65) and John Bright (1811–89), which led to the abolition of the British Corn Laws in 1846, was perhaps the high point of this kind of classical liberalism.[99]

However, liberalism itself then began an evolution which, like conservatism, has almost succeeded in reversing its original meaning. Alan Ryan (b. 1940) has called this the "great reversal in the history of liberalism."[100] This happened for at least three reasons. The first is that, through its initial association with political reform, liberalism came, for many, to mean simply a principle of change, or an openness to change. For these kinds of people liberalism meant change, and conservatism simply signified resistance to change. The Canadian Liberal leader Wilfrid Laurier (later prime minister of Canada) was typical of this new outlook. In 1877, he defined a Liberal as "one of those who think that everywhere, in human things, there are abuses to be reformed, new horizons to be opened up, and new forces to be developed."[101] There is some justification for this claim, metaphysically speaking. As you have seen (in Table 10, for example), the virtues of self-assertion *are* the part of the human most open to innovation and change. But in political life, as you can see in our own day, it makes much less sense. Conservatives can favour change quite as much as liberals. Indeed, in the countries where (so-called) "conservatives" have held power in recent decades, they have often favoured (though not always accomplished) rather radical change. It all depends on what *kind* of change you want.[102] But a liberalism that had come to think of itself as simply a principle of change and reform was ripe for changing the meaning of liberalism itself.

A second reason for the shift was a widening meaning of liberty. The first or classical phase of liberalism had emphasized what might be called "negative" liberty: removing old obstacles to free action. A second phase, in the second half of the nineteenth century, began to draw attention to a more "positive" definition, and to new reforms which, in the words of British philosopher T.H. Green (1836–82), "involve an action of the state in the way of promoting conditions favourable to moral life."[103] If the first or classical phase of liberalism had been largely anti-statist in its outlook – holding the view that the only proper role for government is "to prevent interference with the liberty of the individual" – the second was increasingly favourable to government intervention in economic and social life. It was inclined to take the view that the real cause of "advancing civilisation brings with it more and more interference with the liberty of the individual to do as he likes."[104] In other words, the Liberals of this second phase were in the process of becoming the new "Tories" – which is exactly what sociologist Herbert Spencer (1820–1903) – a defender of the old, classical liberalism – called them, in his hostile book, *The New Toryism*.[105]

Spencer wasn't wrong. The Liberals' greatest leader in the nineteenth century was, in point of fact, an old Tory. William Ewart Gladstone (1809–98) had begun his political career as a reforming Conservative, a disciple of Robert Peel, before beginning a gradual political transition which eventually took him to the leadership of the new Liberal Party. Gladstone was very much a liberal conservative, and a conservative liberal: he spoke "a language of rights [B2a], but also a language of sympathy [A2b]."[106] In his new political family he therefore found himself more at home with "the moral-force politics of the left of the Liberal party than he was with the more casual and less ideological outlook of the Whigs. This paradox was of much importance for British politics in the last forty years of the nineteenth century."[107] It led, in the first instance, to the very active legislative program of the second Gladstone ministry (1880–85), the very measures which prompted Spencer's book. In the 1880s, the role of government in Britain "was growing in ways the first liberals could scarcely imagine, and liberals had done much to bring government's new powers about."[108] Between 1888 and 1913, the social expenditures of the British state increased sixfold.[109]

This shift in the liberal outlook reflected and was encouraged by the growing support of the working class for the British Liberal Party, which undertook another ambitious program of social welfare in the first years of the twentieth century, including sickness, accident, old-age, and unemployment insurance and a minimum wage law.[110] Similar social reform programs were undertaken in France and Germany in the last decades of the nineteenth century and the first years of the twentieth. People who called themselves Liberals or liberals continued to promote such "conservative" reforms throughout most of the twentieth century in Britain, Europe, and North America. Following the Depression of the 1930s, they led the way to the introduction of the full-scale welfare state, from the 1940s to the 1970s, in the wake of Franklin Roosevelt's New Deal in the United States, the Beveridge Report in Britain (1942), and the Rowell-Sirois and Marsh Reports in Canada (1940 and 1943).[111]

The successes and failures of these efforts created a reaction that gathered steam in the 1960s and 1970s and became a powerful political countermovement by the 1980s, with the elections of Margaret Thatcher in the UK and Ronald Reagan in the US. On the European continent (where the "liberal" label never entirely lost its original, primary focus on individual liberty) the political vocabulary is somewhat different. But in the Western, English-speaking world, by the beginning of the twentieth-first century, many people who identify themselves as "liberals" have, as Herbert Spencer predicted, come to resemble the original Tories – fighting a rear-guard action against the dismantling of the welfare state, just as the Tories resisted the Whigs' dismantling of the protective (or "preservative"), premodern social institutions, beginning in the seventeenth century.[112] Contemporary political liberalism has become a liberalism of "conservation."[113] Conversely, many of those who today call themselves "conservatives" are really classical liberals or "neoliberals," having more in common with Cobden and Bright than with anything that might be described as genuine conservatism.[114] Thatcher herself has been called a "Cobdenite through and through."[115] If neoliberals have started to call themselves "conservatives," it's partly to contrast themselves with a "liberalism" that now means the opposite of its original meaning. Since most "liberals" have repositioned themselves as the guardians of community, the "conservative" label has been taken over, in reaction, by many of those who care only for individual freedom.[116]

But today's "liberals" are no more consistent than contemporary "conservatives." Just as many "social" conservatives – though they reject all *other* forms of government intervention – still want to hold onto the old meaning of conservatism in matters affecting morality and religion, for example, most people who identify as "liberals" have the same contradictory attitude to the old meaning of liberalism. Although they may favour government action to promote all kinds of other social goods, they normally see no need for the state to maintain standards of "excellence" in behaviour or expression, or to promote moral or public values in education and social policy. In these areas they remain classic liberals, just as, in the same areas, many of today's ersatz "conservatives" remain classically conservative.[117]

Socialism and libertarianism

The reversal of roles that has taken place between those who call themselves "liberals" and "conservatives" today can partly be explained by
the influence of additional political outlooks that have also emerged
from the human paradox. After all, liberalism and conservatism aren't
the only possible combinations. The four corners of the political paradox (Figure 30) can also be combined in other ways.

As I pointed out in chapters 8 and 9, the four poles of the human
paradox (and their sub-sub-poles) seem to "lean" in two opposite directions, simultaneously. Compared to the *other* half of a specific paradox,
the two poles of *each* half "lean" *toward* each other. But compared to
each other, they seem to lean *away*, toward another pole or sub-pole.
Compared to the pure self-assertion of Power (A1a), for example, its
partner, Pleasure (A1b), can seem to "lean" more toward union or reverence. When contrasted to Love (A2b), its partner, Reverence[3] (A2a),
appears to "lean" backward toward Excellence (B1). And compared to
Truth (B1a), its partner, Goodness (B1b), seems to "lean" toward Reverence (A2).

We can see this same process at work in the political paradox. There's
a very close link, for example, between Equality (B2) and Reverence
(A2). Attaching a very high value to equality shows a concern for the
social condition of the whole community, a concern that pulls this impulse *away* from the other side of the virtues of self-assertion, the pure,
individual self-assertion of Liberty (A1). There's a tension, as Edmund
Fawcett puts it, "between the virtues of liberalism [B2] and the virtues
of liberal capitalism [A1]."[118] This tension can therefore align the virtues
of Equality (B2), instead, with their neighbour (immediately above, in
Figure 30), the virtues of Reverence (A2). This tendency becomes even
clearer when you dig a little deeper, to the sub-sub-families of virtues.
As you saw in the case of John Rawls, Reciprocity (B2b) has very close
ties with Love (A2b). The kind of liberal reciprocity Rawls argues for
can't really be made to work (as he himself recognizes) unless it is infused with the "fraternal" or self-giving spirit, of which family love is
the prime example. Unless there is already a strong sense of belonging
to a prior shared community. Unless there is a reverential "we," not just
a self-asserting "I."

There's obviously, then, a strong potential link between the virtues
of Equality (B2) and the principle of union or reverence as a whole,
and with the virtues of Reverence (A2) in particular.[119] In fact, these
two families of virtues can be combined, and have been combined, to
produce a third political outlook, which is called "socialism" or "social

Figure 31. The political paradox (2): socialism and libertarianism

democracy." This political outlook combines an emphasis on equality (B2), with the sympathy, compassion, generosity, and concern of the virtues of Reverence (A2).

Similarly, the virtues of Liberty (A1) aren't necessarily linked exclusively with Equality (B2). In fact, compared to Equality (B2) – with its pull toward the whole community or the common good – Liberty (A1) almost seems to "lean" more toward Excellence (B1), its own near neighbour (immediately above, in Figure 30). Indeed, many of those who attach the highest value to liberty justify that priority on the basis of excellence (or justice, another form of excellence). Industrialists like John D. Rockefeller and Andrew Carnegie embraced Social Darwinism and rugged individualism in the late nineteenth century because they believed unregulated competition led to the betterment of humankind and to higher forms of life: they were the necessary conditions of the human "march to perfection."[120] So the virtues of Liberty (A1) can be and have been combined instead with those of Excellence (B1), and this combination yields the political outlook opposite to socialism, known as "libertarianism."[121]

With these alternative combinations in mind, I am now in a position to construct a second image of the political paradox displaying these two additional political perspectives, as in Figure 31 above.

The socialist (or social democratic) perspective combines conservatism's concern for union – for the whole society, or the common good – with liberalism's emphasis on equality. Because it attaches overriding importance to the values of Equality (B2), the socialist outlook downplays the other side of liberalism – its equal emphasis on Liberty (A1) – and joins equality instead with the compassionate or merciful side of reverence: that is, with the virtues of Reverence (A2). Socialism thus spans the liberal and conservative outlooks, combining partial elements (A2 and B2) of both.[122]

This explains why some conservatives have much in common with social democrats, and can often make common cause with them.[123] In authentic conservatism, there's always at least a strain of that old Tory reverence that resisted Whig laissez-faire and the dismantling of premodern social institutions in the eighteenth century – institutions and practices that had served and protected popular welfare for centuries.[124] William Pitt the Younger (1759–1806), a Tory prime minister, was the first to introduce an income tax in Britain, and Robert Peel, the first "conservative" prime minister, was the one who made it permanent.[125] I've already noted that Conservative Prime Minister Benjamin Disraeli's government implemented one of the most ambitious packages of social measures in nineteenth-century Britain. And, in the 1880s the very conservative German Chancellor, Otto von Bismarck (1815–98), was responsible for an even more ambitious program of social legislation, including sickness, accident, and old-age insurance for German workers, a social insurance scheme that was "years ahead" of more liberal countries, such as England and France.[126]

The same things have occurred in Canada in the twentieth century under Conservative Party governments, both at the federal and provincial levels. In Canada we have even invented a term for this kind of socially-minded conservative with a powerful sense of the common good, the conservatives who have much in common with social democrats. We call them "Red Tories." Until very recently these Red Tories were the dominant force in Canadian conservatism, which even styled itself "Liberal Conservative" in the nineteenth century and "Progressive Conservative" (after 1942) in the twentieth.[127]

These conservative (and liberal) social reforms were partly motivated by a desire to stave off the growing appeal of "socialism" to many voters in the nineteenth and twentieth centuries. But they could not have been implemented had they not appealed to something authentic in conservatism (and liberalism) itself.

The libertarian perspective instead combines the other side of liberalism – its emphasis on Liberty (A1) – with the conservative concern for Excellence (B1). A powerful commitment to individual freedom, libertarians commonly argue, is the best guarantee of excellence (or justice, another form of excellence). A contemporary libertarian like Peter Thiel (b. 1967), the co-founder of PayPal, argues, like Rockefeller and Carnegie before him, that absolute freedom is a "precondition for the highest good."[128] Too much emphasis on equality, compassion, or the common good leads instead, libertarians believe, to lower standards and mediocrity – mediocrity in health care, education, research, creativity, innovation, entrepreneurship, economic growth, or in something else.

Libertarianism, like socialism, thus spans the liberal and conservative outlooks combining partial elements (A1 and B1) of both. That explains why libertarians can have something in common with some conservatives: especially with those conservatives who give far more importance to excellence than to mercy or compassion, or the common good. In our day, many libertarians call themselves "conservatives," even though their libertarianism acknowledges only one side of authentic conservatism. They do this usually out of reaction (as I pointed out): to distinguish themselves from what they now think of (mistakenly) as "liberalism."

Both socialism and libertarianism seem to be political outlooks of reaction, reaction to the conditions of modern society since the eighteenth century. They are both reactions to social change. Socialism developed in the first half of the nineteenth century (the term seems to have been invented in 1832 by a Frenchman, Pierre Leroux, a follower of socialism's real intellectual founder, the Comte de Saint-Simon) as a reaction against the conditions of early European industrialism.[129] It called for the powers of the community, especially the state, to be used in defence of social equality. Libertarianism (though certainly foreshadowed by "classical" liberalism) seems to have been coined in the twentieth century (indeed even after the Second World War), largely in reaction to the progress of the welfare state in Britain (after the Beveridge Report) and in the US, after the New Deal.[130] Libertarians argue, in response, that the powers of the state should be reduced to a strict minimum in order to establish the maximum possible space for individual liberty.[131]

The fact that these two political outlooks are relatively recent and "reactionary" makes it plausible to suggest they are also more superficial and "derivative," more specifically "political" and less deeply rooted in the nature of the human than their legitimate parents, liberalism and conservatism, the initial poles of the political paradox – itself merely the political reflection of the even deeper human paradox.

These two "derivative" political outlooks – socialism and libertarianism – are essentially modern, even post-modern (in the sense in which I am using that word in this book). They are both, primarily, expressions of self-assertion, the dominant modern family of virtues. While both socialism and libertarianism include elements of conservatism, it seems nevertheless to be the liberal side that dominates in both of them. In libertarianism, the exclusive focus on freedom or liberty (as the name suggests) is the real driving force. In socialism the pursuit of equality is the same. In both cases, though a strand of conservatism is essential to their rationale, their political agendas are overwhelmingly liberal.

But the dominant focus in socialism and libertarianism – on either liberty or equality – can also lead to paradoxical results, results that seem to contradict the liberal starting point. An excessive emphasis on certain kinds of liberty – freedom from government intervention or taxation, for example – can lead to a decline in other kinds of liberty, such as the freedom of economic opportunity or economic mobility. Canadians, for example, are up to three times more economically mobile than Americans, and this difference is almost entirely the result of more interventionist Canadian public policies and a more progressive tax system. An American is far less "free" to escape from the economic class into which she was born than a Canadian. The American dream of economic opportunity is still alive, but it's alive *in Canada* – because of Canadians' more interventionist approach to government.[132]

Pure libertarianism leads back, paradoxically, to a more stratified, elitist, class-bound society. It leads back to a "plutocracy," which is a kind of "aristocracy," an aristocracy of wealth. This result, though paradoxical, isn't really surprising, given libertarianism's embrace of the conservative principle of excellence. "Excellence" was also the traditional principle of aristocracy, whose literal meaning was rule by the "best."[133] But traditional, pre-modern aristocracies claimed to recognize many other forms of excellence, especially moral excellence.[134] Whereas this new kind of "libertarian" aristocracy is based exclusively on money. In the contemporary world, extreme libertarians can and do make common cause with brutal autocrats – confirming that the virtues of Liberty (A1), on their own, are a form of unadulterated self-assertion.[135] The pure libertarian is a tyrant in disguise, rejecting the constraints and obligations of democratic community and civil society, and denying the claims of the other three families of virtues, without which humans cannot be genuinely or fully human. Giving priority to only *one half of liberalism* can lead to a very *un*liberal result.

Socialism focuses on equality rather than liberty. But it can lead to a similar paradox. Like libertarianism, it shows how you can end up sharing an outlook that, at first glance, might seem very different – or even opposite – to the one you started from. Putting all your emphasis on social equality can lead, ironically, to various new kinds of "despotism," as Tocqueville was among the first to argue.[136] Giving such a high value to equality can lead you to sacrifice liberty and allow the community or the state to interfere in many areas of human life, or to dictate its conditions, sometimes in very intrusive ways.[137]

Given the unequal natural endowments of human beings in talent, intelligence, appearance, character, temperament, and energy – and given the historical results: given, that is to say, how such inequalities play out in families, organizations, and societies – equality is a very "unnatural" state.[138] A society that wants to maintain a rough equality of status has to invest a lot of energy in fighting against these kinds of personal and historical "contingencies."[139] Equality is so unnatural, that it requires constant intervention – by a tribal community or by the modern state – to prevent "upstarts" and "free riders" from acquiring more than their fair share of power, wealth, influence, prestige, control, and so on.[140] When you make equality your highest value, you necessarily sacrifice some degree of liberty, and thus lead back, paradoxically, to some form of the very controlling community or authoritarian state, against which the eighteenth century claimed to rebel. Keeping both halves of liberalism in balance seems to be essential for keeping the spirit of self-assertion under control. Once again, giving priority to only one side of liberalism leads to a very unliberal result.

Left- and right-wing populism

If liberalism and conservatism can be called the legitimate offspring of the political paradox, and libertarianism and socialism its derivative outlooks, left-wing and right-wing populisms are – from the perspective of the human paradox – "illegitimate" developments.

However, I need to make a distinction between the precise way I'm using the word "populist" here and the more general way it's sometimes used. Democratic activists who fight for a cause they feel is unjustly neglected in mainstream politics are sometimes called "populists" because they claim to speak and work for some overlooked portion of the "people," and perhaps use their language or defend their cause in strong terms. That's not what I mean by populism. These activists aren't trying to undermine democracy. They simply want to take their rightful place within it. They may be upsetting the current political apple cart, but they don't want to get rid of the apple cart, just get into it. Both their views and those of their opponents are (as David Goodhart says) "decent and legitimate,"[141] so they can both find a place somewhere on the political map of the human I've already been constructing.[142]

The new point of view that needs to be added to my map is different. These second, more genuine "populists" (in the sense I'm using the term here) don't just speak for an unjustly neglected portion of the people, they claim to *be* the people – the *whole* people, or the only part of it that should be taken into account. The way Jan-Werner Müller (b. 1970) puts it is that democratic activists (or so-called "decent populists"[143]) say, "We are *also* the people." Whereas genuine populists (in my sense) say, "We *and only we* are the people."[144]

You can also distinguish between democratic activism and populism by the motivations and actions of populist leaders. Populist leaders deliberately feed and exploit popular prejudices, fears, and hostilities for purposes that run counter to the true, long-term interests of ordinary people, and serve, instead, the interests of some kind of authoritarian elite, while deliberately undermining authentic democratic institutions. In the case of "right-wing" populism, the prejudices exploited are usually ethnic, cultural, religious, and national feelings and hatreds.[145] In the case of "left-wing" populism, the prejudices are usually economic and class-based hatreds, but ethnic and national animosities can be exploited for left-wing purposes too. Because their objective is power rather than democratic justice, populist leaders are normally shameless and brazen liars who readily employ propaganda and misinformation to achieve their goals. In fact, that is one of the distinguishing marks of the populist: the deliberate and flagrant use of language that says the opposite of what it means (for example, calling an election law designed to favour the governing party a "Fair Elections Act," calling factual reporting of public mendacity and wrongdoing "fake news," calling an exemplary electoral process a "stolen" election, or calling a totalitarian dictatorship a "whole-process people's democracy").

In both right- and left-wing versions, populism is an "exclusionary form of identity politics."[146] Its deep vice is its claim that the populist faction, *and only the populist faction*, can speak for "the people."[147] But neither right- nor left-wing populism serves the real interests of the people whose emotions and identities they exploit. They serve instead the objective interests of the political leaders who exploit them to further their own authoritarian ambitions. "Right-wing" populism can also serve the hidden agendas of economic elites and the wealthy. But so does left-wing populism, in the disguised form of party elites. The two bleed into each other and can easily slide from one to the other – as Russia and China have both shifted easily, in recent decades, from official "communism" – the most extreme, authoritarian form of left-wing populism – to shades of right-wing populism, or even, in the case of China, almost a brand of "fascism," the most extreme, authoritarian form of right-wing populism. The anti-elitist posture of populism is thus a sham: it merely favours its *own* elites, at the expense of all the others.[148]

Liberalism and conservatism combine the four quadrants of the human paradox horizontally. Libertarianism and socialism combine them vertically. The two populisms seem to point *diagonally*. Like libertarianism and socialism, they both take an otherwise legitimate aspect of the virtues of self-assertion to an extreme. In these cases, an illegitimate extreme. And again, with paradoxical results.

Left-wing populism, for example, makes the socialist bias for equality an absolute, especially in its most extreme, authoritarian form, as communism. Communism's original objective was "summed up in the single sentence: Abolition of private property."[149] It aims to eliminate *all* contingencies and achieve a complete equality of status among citizens. At least in theory. Practice is a different matter altogether. This goal is such an unnatural one that it can only be pursued, even rhetorically, by establishing a complete despotism, a so-called "dictatorship of the proletariat."[150] Which means a dictatorship of the Communist Party and its leaders, who then transform themselves into a brutal new form of oligarchy. Whether in the Soviet Union, the so-called People's Republic of China, Cuba, or Venezuela, an extreme left-wing populist or communist regime simply replaces one form of aristocracy with another, an aristocracy based on the party hierarchy and the whim of the rulers. In China, the privileged offspring of the Party élite are even referred to as "princelings," which, in fact, they are.[151] So even a rhetorical commitment to the espoused goals of communism leads back, in practice, not to genuine equality (B2) but, diagonally, to the aristocratic principle (B1).

Right-wing populism, on the other hand, is the political expression of the single-minded pursuit of political power for its own sake – especially in its most extreme, authoritarian form as fascism, but in all its other forms too.[152] It's the illegitimate political expression of raw self-assertion (A1) – illegitimate because it undermines the very basis of authentic democracy. To be legitimate, democratic politicians must be not only contestants *in* a democratic process, with all its necessary constraints, but also careful, responsible stewards *of* that democratic process. And they must be able to tell the difference. Populists fail both tests.

It may seem curious to locate the roots of right-wing populism in the family of values I've called the virtues of Liberty (A1). But it's puzzling only if you forget where the demand for liberty comes from. The demand for liberty, for freedom – as the discussion of libertarianism just confirmed – is the purest form of self-assertion. It's an expression of pure self-assertion – the elemental human pursuit of "power after power"[153] – the disposition to dominate and control. Unless it's balanced by something else, that same demand – or rather the self-assertive spirit *behind* that demand – can and does take the form of unfettered domination and control. If you look back at Table 10 on pages 174–5, you will be reminded that the virtues of Liberty (A1) include the pursuit of Power (A1a) just as much as the pursuit of Pleasure (A1b) and freedom. They are the home of what Aristotle and Aquinas called the "irascible" and "concupiscible" appetites. The pursuit of liberty is the self-assertion of the self. It's the pursuit of *my* liberty, my liberty to dominate and control. To control my *own* life certainly, without interference. But that may be just the start. Unless these virtues are balanced by one or more of the three other families of virtues, this same spirit of self-assertion will seek to control other lives too. Perhaps our whole world. Even the physical world.

The virtues of Liberty (A1) can't be separated from the disposition to dominate. The disposition to assert yourself simply for the sake of self-assertion: for the sheer pleasure and gratification of nothing more than self-assertion itself. To fight and overcome obstacles. To win. To exercise power and control. To triumph. To enjoy the triumph of the will.

This is the spirit of right-wing populism, especially in the forms of German, Italian, and Spanish fascism, but also in all the forms of populist authoritarian states with "democratic" facades, as in Russia, Hungary, Turkey, Egypt, Myanmar, or Zimbabwe. It's the pure will to power. The pure political form of what Thomas Aquinas calls the "irascible" virtues.[154]

But here there is a curious twist. In order for this triumph of "power for the sake of power" to fulfil itself, it needs willing subjects. Populist *leaders* embody the modern and post-modern virtues of self-assertion, the disposition to dominate, in a raw form.[155] But populist *followers* exhibit a hankering for the pre-modern virtues of reverence, the disposition to lose themselves in a greater whole, the "eagerness" to subordinate themselves to a greater cause, good, or leader that Relational Models Theory (RMT) associates with the social relations model of "Authority Ranking" (B1). And they also have a longing for the "we/they" inclusion/exclusion dynamic RMT associates with its "Communal Sharing" model (A2).[156] (But remember the "exclusion" side of this dynamic really comes from self-assertion.)

In its more extreme forms, right-wing populism thus requires followers who are willing – or even eager – to adopt a deeply reverential attitude toward absolute power: people who are willing to *give* themselves to its purposes merely for the sake of giving. In this way, right-wing populism points, diagonally, from the virtues of Power (A1a) to the virtues of Reverence (A2). In its extreme, fascist form, it even transforms itself – through ritual, symbols, uniforms, propaganda, and so on – into a kind of secular theocracy. Theocracy is rule by a religious élite, as in present-day Iran. A theocracy can echo some of the features of fascism, as it does in Iran. And fascism also echoes some of the features of a theocracy.[157]

As a result of anxieties fuelled by economic globalism, population migration, and media-driven cultural change, among other things, the right- and left-wing populisms which ravaged Western countries in the 1920s and 1930s have enjoyed an astonishing revival in the second and third decades of the twenty-first century, mostly in their right-wing (Russia, Hungary, Poland, Turkey, and even, since 2016, the US) but also left-wing forms (Greece, Spain, Venezuela). At the same time, China's "communist-turned-fascist" dictatorship has emerged as the second largest economy in the world, and a competing "model" for stable economic and social development – as well as a frightening blueprint for comprehensive surveillance and repression in a digital age.[158]

The sudden re-emergence of populism in the first half of the twenty-first century suggests that some human energies and impulses the modern and post-modern worlds had overlooked or thought to banish are still lurking underground, waiting to be exploited by unscrupulous demagogues. Populism is the "permanent shadow" of modern representative democracy, not just because it challenges democracy's founding assumption that the "people" can and must have a variety of contending representatives to reflect the variety of contradictory human virtues and values,[159] but also because it harks back to some pre-modern instincts and impulses – including human yearnings for unity, wholeness, and the hierarchy of goods – that the post-modern world had thought to bury and forget.

Even though it may help remind us of some forgotten dimensions of the human, populism (in the sense I'm using here) poses a potentially mortal threat to Western democracy because it has no time for the human paradox. It is antipluralist by definition – not just demographically or culturally, but morally and humanly. It denies the very contradictions – the contending virtues and values – that structure both the nature of the human and democratic life. Rooted, as it is, in fear of the other, it takes pride in spurning the contradictions and deliberative dialogue that are the lifeblood of democracy and of the human. Populism has no room for the educational contract.

A political map of the human

Two populist orientations (right and left) must be added, then, to the initial horizontal combinations from the political paradox (liberalism

Figure 32. A political map of the human

and conservatism) and the derivative vertical pairings (socialism and libertarianism). These additions now allow me to construct a more complete map of the various ways the nature of the human expresses itself in political form. You can see that map in Figure 32 on page 280 above.

You will notice that four of the words on this map end in "y" and the others all end in "ism." The first four describe premodern political regimes, types of government already known to the ancient world, so they have either the suffix "-racy" (from a Greek word meaning "to govern") or the suffix "-archy" (from a Greek word meaning "leader"). The other six are all modern and post-modern words. The political "-isms" were almost all products of the first half of the nineteenth century, except libertarianism, which was a product of the second half of the twentieth.[160] Though their suffix, "-ism," is also Greek (from words meaning an action, condition, or thing done), this has become the common modern word-form for a doctrine, outlook, belief, school (of thought or art), or ideology.

It's a significant fact that three of the four words in the first category are associated primarily with the virtues of reverence. And five of the six words in the second group are associated with the virtues of self-assertion, while the sixth ("conservatism") is a modern word whose express purpose (as you saw, earlier in this chapter) was to reconcile both the modern and premodern outlooks: to reconcile monarchy and democracy, union and non-union, reverence and self-assertion.

Another thing you will notice is that I've placed the words "liberalism" and "conservatism" differently than the other words, especially the other "-isms." I could have put liberalism and conservatism around the *outside* of the circle: where the words monarchy and democracy are now located, for example. But instead I have placed them *inside* the circle, spanning the two families of virtues they each combine to form their complete outlooks.

I've done this for two reasons. First, I believe they're more fundamental. The other four modern political outlooks are derivative from them or "illegitimate" distortions of their basic values. And second – perhaps another way of saying the same thing – the liberal and conservative outlooks are the ones that link back most convincingly to the basic human paradox. With the four distinct poles they combine in two separate pairs, they are the nature of the human in its democratic political form.

These two political perspectives reflect the eternal human paradox at work in political life. Self-assertion begins, after all, as the assertion of the individual self (though it can also move up a notch or two, to express itself in group forms: such as tribalism, nationalism, racism, ethnic exclusion, xenophobia, or class distinctions). It's the spirit of division and of non-union. Reverence is the opposite human impulse: to acknowledge the connectedness of individual things, their fundamental unity.

A liberal, properly so-called, starts from the individual.[161] "Liberal" stands for liberty. For a liberal, the community is composed of free individuals who have entered into a social contract based on a cost-benefit calculation: free individuals agree to limit their own absolute freedom in order to secure the benefits from living in society. For a liberal, the individual comes before the community and should only surrender to that community the minimum of freedom necessary for a common life.[162] A "good liberal can be a good communitarian," as Alan Ryan suggests.[163] But, to the extent she does so, to that same extent she becomes a conservative, or embraces conservative values.[164]

A conservative, properly so-called, starts instead from the community.[165] As you have seen, that's where the name "conservative" came from, and what conservatives seek to "conserve." Conservatism is the political expression of the human impulse to union and connectedness, which is the basis (and literal meaning) of comm*unity*. Human connectedness takes the form of family, friendship, and all other kinds of community – including all the groups, clubs, and local associations that stand between the individual and the state. For a conservative, liberties come from a concrete community and can only be understood or enjoyed within that community, within its traditions, institutions, practices, and well-being.[166] For a conservative, the community comes *before* the individual and creates the possibility for individual liberty and fulfilment.[167] A good conservative can *and should* also be a believer in individual liberty. But to the extent she does so, to that same extent she becomes a liberal, or embraces liberal values.

It's important to remember, however, that, as Aquinas and Edmund Burke point out, there are two different kinds of community.[168] I might call them "horizontal" and "vertical." The horizontal community is the community of today, in all its current manifestations: our families, friendships, neighbourhoods, professions, churches, clubs, associations, peer groups, online virtual communities, cities, regions, countries, and ultimately the global community.

But there's another kind of community, the vertical community, which is instead a "community of memory."[169] This community is the historical experience out of which the horizontal communities of today have emerged, and without which they could not be what they are, the traditions that help us understand the "future possibilities which the past has made available to the present."[170] It is, in Burke's words, "an idea of continuity, which extends in time as well as in numbers and in space."[171] This kind of community is what G.K. Chesterton called "the democracy of the dead." Why, he asked (in effect), should the community only include "those who merely happen to be walking about"?[172]

So the conservative bias for union and community carries with it a distinctive attitude to time. Embracing not just their own communities of today but also their own communities of memory, conservatives are inclined to live in what has been called "gathered time."[173] This view of time, as you saw in chapter 5, means that the past, present, and future can be and should be seen as *united in the present*. It results from the inclination to see and value the *connectedness* of things, one of the conservative virtues.[174] That doesn't mean that conservatives want to live in the past, any more than they want to live in the future. It doesn't mean they are by nature reactionary, or resist change, just because it's change. It doesn't mean they want to hold on, irrationally, to the past, any more than they want to hold on to the future. It means they can see both the past *and* future contained in the present, deserving the same kind of respect. Respect for future generations is part of respect for those that have gone before. And vice versa.[175]

The natural liberal attitude to time is rather different. As you also saw in chapter 5, a self-assertive "bias for action"[176] – the "can do" attitude of modern culture, expressed in the impatient advertising and management slogan "just do it" – isn't naturally inclined to give a lot of thought to the past or the future. It wants to act *now*, without being unduly constrained by concern for the past or future. Building a heavy oil extraction plant or pipeline *now* – with all its short-term economic (not to mention political) benefits – is more important than worrying about the potential long-term consequences for the biosphere and climate change, or for ancient land rights and sacred places. The liberal attitude to time is the same as the liberal attitude to the self and to the material world: it divides them all up into separate, individual, analysable, manipulable units.[177]

The paradox of individual and community is the basis of political life. But exploring how the human paradox expresses itself in political life is enormously complicated by the fact that, as you saw earlier in the chapter, the labels of modern political parties have been reversed. In the twentieth and twenty-first centuries, Conservative parties have often (or even usually) been liberal parties, and Liberal parties (except in continental Europe) have often been conservative.

In the US today most of those who call themselves "conservative" (usually Republicans) are – or were, until the populist takeover of the Republican Party by Donald Trump in 2016 – classical liberals, or even libertarians. While US "liberals" (mostly Democrats) are actually conservatives, striving to protect the common good of the whole community against the strident, anti-government individualism of the so-called "conservatives." In the UK, the same reversal has taken place. Especially since Margaret Thatcher, who famously said that there is "no such thing as society," a sentiment to which no genuine conservative could subscribe.[178] Thatcher put an end to the neo-Disraelian conservatism of post-war Conservative governments and took the British Conservative Party sharply back to the anti-state individualism of classical liberalism. The Labour Party is now in many respects the voice of British conservatism, as it has been since it inherited that mantle from the Liberal Party after the First World War.

In Canada, the same reversal has taken place. The Liberal and New Democratic (social democratic) Parties are the "conservatives," while the Conservative Party (now shorn of its "Progressive" label, at least at the federal level) stands for a low-tax, small state, individualist liberalism, similar in many respects to the classical liberalism of many US Republicans. Because the communitarian cause was taken up in France and continental Europe by "radical" and "socialist" rather than by "liberal" parties, they are among the few places where "liberal" has retained its original meaning. Indeed, what in North America is sometimes called "neo-conservatism" – a hard, right-wing opposition to the post-Second World War consensus in support of the welfare state – is, more properly, called "neoliberalism" in France.

Liberals start from the individual, and conservatives from the community. But both of these are necessary to each other. You can't have individuals without community, as John Rawls discovered. And you can't have community without individuals, as Margaret Thatcher rightly implied. They go together. You can't have one without the other. But if so, they should never be isolated from each other, or regarded as enemies. They are necessary to each other. A political perspective shaped by only one of them is incomplete and ultimately antisocial, contrary to the good.

Civilized politics must eventually recognize the full nature of the human, and should aim, as a whole, for political and social outcomes that respond to and enhance all four of its dimensions. It is not the case that "conservatives," properly so called, are motivated exclusively by the virtues of Excellence (B1) and the virtues of Reverence (A2), nor that "liberals," properly so called, are animated only by the virtues of Liberty (A1) and of Equality (B2). It is a matter of emphasis. Both liberals and conservatives are human beings. So they should be open to, and respond to, all four human stances and their families (and sub-families) of virtues. A true conservative will often give somewhat higher priority to Excellence (B1) and Reverence (A2), and a liberal will normally give more importance to the virtues of Liberty (A1) and Equality (B2). But since the perspectives of the individual and of community are both legitimate – both necessary to each other – the only really reasonable thing to be is a conservative liberal or a liberal conservative. Anything less is a denial – or even an amputation – of some important part of what it means to be human. Wisdom should eventually make us either very conservative liberals or very liberal conservatives.

Of course, it makes a difference which is the adjective and which the noun. The order is important. And unavoidable. The world is "incomplete if seen from any one point of view, incoherent if seen from all points of view at once, and empty if seen from nowhere in particular."[179] Each of us must decide which is to be the noun and which the adjective. Both our own natures and the demands of political life will make us one or the other: either liberals or conservatives. (Or some other combination of the four basic poles of the human, as you saw.) Sometimes without even knowing it. We need political parties that embody these two principles in different ways and with different emphases. But we don't need political factions that want to serve only the one, without caring for the other.

In the political paradox, as in the larger human paradox, opposites don't cancel each other out. They reach out to embrace each other. Monarchy and democracy, for example, may be opposites, but they also go together admirably. Monarchies can be democracies, and many of the world's most successful democracies are constitutional monarchies. Indeed, the 2018 World Happiness Report shows that seven of the ten "happiest" countries in the world are constitutional monarchies.[180]

Legitimate opposites don't cancel each other out because they are contraries, not true contradictions. They represent legitimate and necessary facets of the whole nature of the human. Because human beings, if they are genuinely human, seek wholeness, one of the tests for legitimacy in the political paradox is precisely the degree to which the various outlooks can reach out to embrace their opposite.

To the extent to which it has any integrity at all, a robust political (or philosophical) position will turn out to be an unstable paradox, contradiction, or dialectic, the two poles of which are some form of union and non-union, or of reverence and self-assertion.[181] One of the sources of uncivilized or uncivil conflict between opposing political (or philosophical) positions or views is the failure of the participants to see the inner contradictions in their *own* outlook, and how it mirrors the conflict between their views and those of their opponents. They therefore fail to see that the "educational contract" I described in the Introduction, between themselves and their opponents, is just as important or essential as the same educational contract between the opposing (but overlooked) poles of their own position.

To the extent that any political (or philosophical) position does *not* exhibit an inner contradiction – a contradiction that makes it internally unstable – to that same extent it is also *not* authentically human, and does not make a genuine claim on us, or on our allegiance. It's likely to turn out to be some form of human evil. That is to say, a destructive and harmful force in human affairs. *It is our very contradictions that make us genuinely human.* An excessive effort to achieve "logical" consistency or eliminate contradiction is bound therefore to lead to something or somewhere *in*humane, contrary to genuine human civilization or well-being.[182]

Both right- and left-wing populisms were ruled out as illegitimate because they don't have or recognize enough internal contradiction, enough of the genuine human paradox. They are antipluralist by definition. Populists "speak and act *as if* the people were one – with any opposition, if its existence is acknowledged at all, soon to disappear."[183] And so they can't reach out to embrace their opposite. As pure expressions of only *one* side of self-assertion, despotism and destruction of the other are written into their DNA. That's why they can merge so easily into each other, as both Russia and China have shifted, without turning a hair, and in only a few years, from self-proclaimed communist states to de facto right-wing populist or even fascist ones.

Socialism and libertarianism are more legitimate because they acknowledge more of the human. The internal contradictions between their liberal and conservative elements help keep them honest and capable of operating within the rule of law, which makes at least grudging room for the other. But the assertive, liberal half of each of them dominates, and makes cohabitation difficult and bellicose. An excessive devotion to liberty can make concern for equality seem like an enemy of the good. And an equally excessive devotion to equality can make concern for liberty seem the same. Elections are likely to become bitter, or even ugly, and political transitions difficult.

The two basic political stances of liberalism and conservatism seem to be those that can embrace each other more easily, and, together, express the full nature of the human. That is partly because of the strength of their own internal contradictions: liberty and equality for one; excellence and reverence for the other. The contrary pull between the two poles of each of these dualities moderates the claims of both: liberty must be balanced by equality, and justice softened by mercy. That makes it easier for both of them to recognize the competing claims of the individual and the community. Liberty and equality can't flourish without fraternity. And no fraternity is genuine that doesn't promote freedom and equality for its members, together with truth, justice, and honour.[184]

The human paradox should help you see that what we often think of as competing, contradictory, and possibly irreconcilable political outlooks are really expressions of complementary and inseparable families of human virtues. The political outlooks, like the virtues they express, are contraries – but they can't exist or flourish without each other. In every political contest, and in every public policy debate, the four families of virtues (and their sub-sub-families) stand in the background, shaping the outlooks and purposes of the participants, even when they can't (or won't) see or articulate them. As you saw in the previous chapter, our contemporary policy debates over the role of the market, and of markets, for example, is simply a reflection of the virtues of self-assertion – to which the arrow of virtue has returned in Western culture – and the growing dominance of the virtues of Liberty (A1) in the first decades of the twenty-first century. Market reasoning and values have their primary home in one corner of the human, though they have powerful defenders and supporters elsewhere (especially in the science of economics, with its roots in the rational and self-controlling virtues of Equality [B2]). They are a very important expression of the human. But they aren't everything. They are in tension with the other three families of virtues. The instrumental virtues of the market are in tension not only with equality, fairness, and reciprocity – virtues of Equality (B2), the other side of the virtues of self-assertion – but also with all the virtues of reverence such as care, concern, respect, justice, gratitude, sacrifice, responsibility, sympathy, generosity, thoughtfulness, friendship, love, and the disposition to nurture – virtues that make up at least half the nature of the human. It's not just that "market reasoning is incomplete without moral reasoning."[185] "Market reasoning" is, in fact, without recognizing it, a covert *form* of moral reasoning, masquerading (like analytic philosophy) behind a disguise of value-neutrality. But it's only one form of morality, among many. It's the practical expression of a subset of the virtues of Liberty (A1). Even for markets themselves to work effectively, they need to be completed and supported by all the other virtues that constitute the nature of the human.[186] When we participate in a political discussion and in public policy debates, that's what we're doing, usually without recognizing it. We're bringing the four families of virtues into the public forum and requiring them to confront, accept, and embrace each other.

Reconciling the competing political claims of the four families of virtues should be easier now that we all live in a post-modern world. A world in which the virtues of self-assertion have triumphed. As I said at the beginning of this chapter, the arrow of virtue has brought modern and post-modern Western culture back to the virtues of self-assertion. All four families of virtues are available to us, as in every age. But now we see them all and express them from the vantage point of self-assertion. The spiral staircase I described in chapters 7 and 10 (Figures 18 and 26) has reached the virtues of self-assertion again, so we see the *whole* human and political paradox through their twin lenses: the lens of Equality (B2), and, increasingly, the lens of Liberty (A1).

It *should* be easier. But suddenly it isn't. Even a short decade ago it seemed possible to think we Westerners were all now liberals of one kind or another: liberal conservatives or conservative liberals, even if we had reversed the meaning of those words in our common usage. The old battle between the modern world and the *ancien régime* seemed to be over.[187] Except for a handful of extremists, nobody in the Western world is fighting today for the principles of aristocracy or theocracy.[188] So it looked as if liberals and conservatives could now meet and contend within the common, shared space of liberal democracy. Even if some of the most successful of those liberal democracies are still monarchies.

But the sudden re-emergence of both right- and left-wing populisms has thrown such premature optimism into question. The continued advance of the arrow of virtue, back into the virtues of Liberty (A1), now seems to have a serious cost, one that threatens many of the achievements of democratic constitutionalism since the end of the eighteenth century. In the last half century, Western democracies (led by the United States) have undergone what Mark Lilla (b. 1956) calls a "subliminal revolution" in which "the needs and desires of *individuals* [A1] were given near-absolute priority over those of *society* [B2]."[189] This shift from the virtues of Rights (B2a) and Reciprocity (B2b) – the virtues of self-control – back toward the virtues of Power (A1a) and Pleasure (A1b) now threatens the very conditions of a genuinely democratic life. In some cases, the new populisms preserve the façade of democratic elections, at least for the time being. But because populism's unbridled pursuit of power hijacks the state and media, undermines every form of institutional and judicial independence, and brands all democratic opposition as illegitimate, if not treasonous, elections aren't much more than window-dressing for new forms of tyranny.

The triumph of the virtues of self-assertion has another downside, too. It means that we now have great difficulty in seeing beyond them – seeing that they offer us only one side of the human. And not the most important one. Not the one that makes humans genuinely human. Our contemporary political and public policy debates are largely confined to the virtues of Liberty (A1) and the virtues of Equality (B2). When we debate public goods, we're usually trying to reconcile the competing claims of these two families of virtues. Even the contest between populism and genuine democracy takes place largely (though not exclusively) between them, between rights and reciprocity on the one hand and pure power on the other. The tensions between Liberty (A1) and Equality (B2) define the contours of contemporary Western politics.[190] We may sometimes sense that these two families don't really express the full nature of the human. But when we do, even contemporary "conservatives" often feel obliged to translate the missing virtues into the language of self-assertion. When we sense that there might be a larger moral universe of the human beyond self-assertion, our contemporary Western political discourse is usually compelled to translate these larger claims and human potential into the language of self-assertion, such as Rights (B2a) or Reciprocity (B2b).

So even if the old battle between the *ancien régime* and modernity is now happily over, maybe some of the issues that were at its heart should still be important for us. Maybe there are some features of the enduring human paradox, as Michael Sandel implies, that have slipped too far out of sight, and need to be brought back into view.

We now live in a world shaped by and for the individual self, the one that was discovered and liberated by the Enlightenment and the upheavals of the seventeenth and eighteenth centuries. But individuals still need community. And we need perhaps to relearn the importance, the sources, and the conditions of community – something the populist impulse may point toward, if often in illegitimate ways. Democratic politics, as David Goodhart puts it, "must be able to combine individual and minority rights on the one hand and a strong sense of belonging and group attachment on the other."[191]

One way you could approach this challenge of individual and community – "the two halves of humanity's political soul"[192] – would be to consider what degree of priority or precedence an individual should give to a community she expects to protect her individual rights.[193] But that would be to approach the question of community, implicitly, from a liberal, individual, or atomistic perspective. How would this challenge look if you were to turn the problem around and approach it from a genuinely conservative lens? Then the question wouldn't just be the liberal question turned upside down, asking how much liberty or how many "rights" a community can afford to grant to individuals before it loses its own viability as a community. That's a legitimate question. But the more genuine conservative questions would be quite different. They would be something more like this: How do all the various forms of community (family, neighbourhood, civil society, government) contribute to the development of good human beings? How do they nourish the very virtues we depend on, not just for trust in our individual human lives but also for our democratic and legal institutions to work and be sustained, and for our neighbourhoods and workplaces to be places full of human potential? And how can the institutions and practices of our civil and democratic communities be designed (or protected) to nourish the essential human virtues that contribute both to strong communities and to good human lives?[194]

The individual and the community don't cancel each other out. They embrace each other in the spirit of what Russian writer A.S. Khomiakov (1804–60) called *sobornost* or "conciliation." For Khomiakov this word expressed the idea that unity and freedom ultimately coincide. A rational society, he argued, is the result of "two different and concordant forces." One of these is the organic force of life "inherent in the whole body and the entire past life of the society." And the other is the force of the "individual intellect." These two are and must be linked together. The community and the individual are not opposed to each other. They are parts of the same whole. They go together. You can't have one without the other. You can't have union without non-union, or non-union without union. Unity and freedom are "indissolubly joined together," Khomiakov argued, "in the moral law of mutual love."[195]

In political life, as in our own individual lives, we need to rediscover the human paradox. That's something I'll come back to in the last chapters of this book. But first we need to look at how the human paradox expresses itself in some other areas of human life, beginning with the world of organizations.

13

Organizations

Organizational life – just like society and politics – is structured by the cascading polarities of the human paradox.

It would be surprising if it were otherwise. All corners of human life necessarily bear some imprint of the nature of the human. And none more so than those where we come together within common, shared structures and activities. Most of us spend most of our lives in some kind (or kinds) of organization. That's where we're employed or earn a living. And when we're not at work, we spend much of the rest of our lives in some other kinds of organizations: a club, team, charity, choir, church, interest or lobby group, professional association, community organization, and so on.

Because organizations bring us together, they are places where all the sides of the human are constantly on display.[1] As individuals, each of us may be able to give priority, most of the time, to some part or parts of our nature: to one or more of the contending families of virtues. But when we come together in organizations, the sum of *all* our natures, and the needs of organizational life itself, inevitably bring out the full potential of the human, the full spectrum of the human paradox.

Paradox in organizational life

The curious thing is how long it took to notice this.

Those who study the management and leadership of business organizations, for example, did not really twig to the role of the human paradox in organizational life until the last three decades or so. In the early stages of organizational theory at the beginning of the twentieth century, much attention was given to rational management and organizational efficiency, and then to the human dimensions of organizations, especially leadership and motivation. In the 1950s, organizational structure was often a focus of management theory, and in the 1960s and 1970s the issues of strategic planning and organizational "fit" were driving concerns, often encouraging organizations to make clear choices between contending options or possibilities: choices often of an "either/or" nature.

But in the 1980s, it began to dawn on scholars of business management that these either/or choices are often destructive, and lead to constant, destabilizing pendulum swings between contending opposites. Instead of an "either/or" approach to management, organizational theorists began to see the potential – or even the necessity – of a "both/and" approach.

Among the first to identify the role of paradox in organizational life was an organizational psychologist, Manfred Kets de Vries (b. 1942), who noted in 1980 that organizational life seemed to be structured by paradoxes that weren't reflected in the prevailing "rational" model of organizational management.[2] This hint was soon picked up by Tom Peters (b. 1942) and Robert Waterman (b. 1936), authors of the most popular management book of the 1980s, *In Search of Excellence*. One of the problems with earlier theories of organization, they suggested, was that they were based on "rational" or linear assumptions, whereas in reality human beings are a "study in conflict and paradox." The dualities embedded in human nature, Peters and Waterman argued, are reflected in a series of enduring organizational paradoxes, paradoxes that can never be resolved in an either/or fashion, but must be managed instead as permanent, contending dualities.[3]

As a result of Peters and Waterman's wide impact, the theme of paradox was soon taken up by a variety of other authors and scholars, many of whom developed their own lists of organizational paradoxes,[4] and their own imaginative, graphical ways of displaying them.[5] They, too, suggested that the essence of good organizational leadership and management is understanding and managing these organizational paradoxes – not making clear choices between contending polarities but respecting, balancing, and reconciling them all over time. By 1994, management guru Charles Handy (b. 1932) suggested that the theme of paradox had "almost become the cliché of our times."[6]

The volume of academic literature on organizational paradox over the last two decades would almost seem to confirm Handy's diagnosis.[7] But not all of this enormous output is of uniform quality. The most thoughtful and consistent application of this paradoxical perspective to organizational life has been developed by Robert E. Quinn (b. 1946), at the University of Michigan, together with a variety of colleagues, especially Kim S. Cameron (b. 1946). From the 1980s to the present, they have published an impressive series of books and articles developing a theory of organizations based on the concept of competing dualities.

Quinn and his colleagues observed that the various schools of thought about organizations could be grouped in four categories. They called them the "Rational Goal" model, the "Internal Process" model, the "Human Relations" model, and the "Open Systems" model. Each one of these models of organizational management had a specific historical origin: the first two go back to the early years of the twentieth century; the third was a product of the 1920s and 1930s; and the fourth emerged in the 1950s. But each of them keeps recurring regularly in organizational theory and practice. Building on the emerging consensus about organizational paradox, Quinn and Cameron suggested that these various models should not be regarded as alternatives or rivals – among which a choice must be made – but rather as reflecting permanent and necessary features (what Hegel calls "moments") of organizational life. They may be in tension or conflict with each other. But they are also necessary to each other. They are the theoretical expression of the deep paradoxes of organizational life. They embody four poles of organizational life.[8]

Quinn and his colleagues call their approach to the paradoxes of organizational life a "Competing Values Framework" (CVF). They have continued to develop this framework since 1988, and their major exposition of it to date was in a 2006 book, *Competing Values Leadership: Creating Value in Organizations*, and a companion work, *Diagnosing and Changing Organizational Culture: Based on the Competing Values Framework*, as well as in Quinn's textbook for management education, *Becoming a Master Manager: A Competing Values Approach*, the fifth edition of which was published in 2011.[9]

Competing Values Framework

In this chapter, I'm going to use Quinn's Competing Values Framework (CVF) as one of the main vehicles for exploring how the human paradox manifests itself in organizational life. As in the case of Relational Models Theory (RMT) in chapter 11, I'm a strong admirer of the work of Quinn and Cameron and their various colleagues, especially the way in which they have seen the human paradox at work in organizations. I think their work is among of the most interesting in contemporary management theory: it offers many useful tools for organizational and leadership assessment, and for devising and monitoring organizational improvement strategies. I will have some suggestions about ways in which their theoretical perspectives can be widened through an appreciation of the full human paradox. But that doesn't take anything away from the value of their theoretical and practical contributions.

For the purposes of this book, one of the great advantages of the CVF is that, from an early stage, Robert Quinn began to express his paradoxical perspective on organizations in graphical form. One early example is shown in Figure 33 on page 295, in a slightly simplified form.

In their 2006 book, Quinn and his colleagues normally use a rectangular format that is very common in organizational management literature and teaching, as well as in psychometrics. In this approach, two dimensions or axes are contrasted with each other – using high/low or yes/no alternatives or opposites – to yield a 2x2 or four-box diagram, sometimes called a "Boston Box" (apparently because the Boston Consulting Group is said to have popularized it[10]). This pictorial device is very popular in management practice and teaching and in psychometric assessments because it appears to give a complete picture of an organization or problem. Because its two axes can also be used to plot data points in a cluster format, this kind of diagram can yield striking images of the current organization, of other comparable organizations, and of the desired future state. It can show the gap between where things are now and where you want to go. Of course, the usefulness of such assessment instruments is heavily conditioned by the adequacy of the initial assumptions or categories, an issue I'll come back to shortly.

Quinn and his colleagues use the two axes of internal/external and flexibility/control to construct their own 2x2 diagram shown (in a slightly simplified form) in Figure 34 on page 295.

This version of the CVF is helpful because of its simplicity. It displays the two axes that structure the 2x2 boxes, and it shows clearly the four organizational forms and orientations resulting from the interaction of these two pairs of opposites. From the point of view of my exploration of the nature of the human in this book, this image of the core dimensions of organizational life is extremely interesting and encouraging. Three key features of it are particularly important to note right away.

The first is the way it recognizes that basic contradictions or tensions in the nature of the human seem to yield a basic four-part structure. The second is that these contradictions lead to an organizational paradox that mirrors the human paradox. And the third, especially interesting feature of this framework is the way it highlights the contrasting behaviours associated with each of the four organizational modes. The key words here are the four capitalized words in bold, beginning with the letter "C": Create, Compete, Control, and Collaborate.

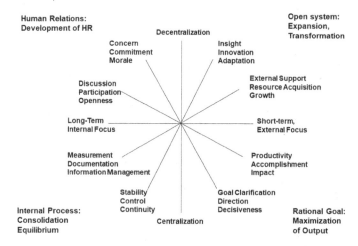

Figure 33. Competing Values Framework (1988)[11]

Figure 34. Competing Values Framework: core dimensions[12]

Quinn and his colleagues call these four concepts or categories "values," and so they call their framework a "competing values" framework. But, as you saw in chapter 3, values are the *inside* of virtues. Values are the inner habits of *feeling* that accompany and nourish our good outward habits of *behaviour*. Western culture has traditionally called those good behaviours "virtues," and that's the term I'm using in this book. In organizational life, as in all other kinds of human life, it's ultimately the behaviours or virtues that really matter and make a difference in the world. The behaviours are the *real* outcomes at which both organizations and individuals aim. The values are merely a step *toward* them. Or, more often, an inner reflection of behaviours that are already present in personal or organizational life. If an individual or an organization *claims* to hold a certain value, but that value isn't reflected in the behaviour of the individual or of the members of the organization, then it isn't a *real* value. It's just an "espoused" value – not one that's really "in-use."[13] A value that may be held somewhere in the head, perhaps, but not in the gut and the feelings, the places that really determine our everyday behaviours, or our virtues.[14]

In order to be translated into *action* in the real world, the "Competing Values Framework" (CVF) must, necessarily, be interpreted as a competing *virtues* framework. From that perspective, it helps confirm and support the use I've been making of the lens of the virtues to explore and rediscover the nature of the human. The apparent congruence between the "Competing Values Framework" and the map of the human I've been developing in this book is even more striking in other versions of the framework. The basic 2x2 image, so valuable for its clarity, lacks some of the detail of Quinn's earliest images. Later versions return to a circular format, like the basic image of the human I've been using in this book. And they reintegrate some of the detail from Quinn's first graphics, including the four management schools or perspectives. The circular version of the Competing Values Framework is shown in Figure 35 on page 297.

At first glance, there appears to be a very close correspondence between this image of the Competing Values Framework (CVF) in Figure 35 and my basic image of the human paradox in, for example, Figures 20 and 25 on pages 200 and 209.

But, on closer inspection, you can detect some differences.

One of the risks with a 2x2 table is that it can appear more complete or more definitive than it really is. Such a table is constructed from dualities or opposites. But what if the opposites aren't of the same kind? As I pointed out in chapter 6, one of the biggest challenges in mapping the nature of the human is discerning whether a pair of contrary virtues is the same as another pair, or whether it occurs at the same level of separative projection. Just because two virtues (or values) contradict each other, that doesn't mean this pair is the same kind of paradox as another one. The paradoxes of justice and mercy, of boldness and prudence, and of passion and self-control are all real paradoxes in the nature of the human. But they didn't belong in my first, highest-level table of opposites.

What if the CVF dualities pictured in Figure 35 don't really occur on the same level in the nature of the human? Then you're comparing

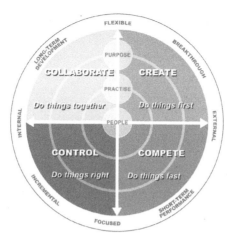

Figure 35. Competing Values Framework[15]

apples and oranges. And the mismatch between opposites could also mean that the framework isn't as complete or comprehensive as it appears, at first, to be.

These are some of the thoughts that begin to occur as soon as you look more closely at the relationship between Figure 35 and Figures 20 and 25. To deepen your grasp of this relationship, look back at Tables 7, 8, and 10 on pages 157–8, 162, and 174–5, for example. You'll notice that the first three of the CVF's three core virtues – Create, Compete, and Control – *all* belong to the family of virtues I there called the virtues of Liberty. They are all virtues that arise in the quadrant I labelled A1. They belong to the corner of the human paradox that's home to what Aquinas (following Plato and Aristotle) called the "irascible" and "concupiscible" appetites.

The fourth virtue – Collaborate – is a little harder to pinpoint because the CVF's language about it is inconsistent. Sometimes the CVF uses words to describe this family of virtues such as concern, compassion, caring, kindness, selflessness, affection – and even love.[16] If you were to take this kind of language at face value, you'd have to link this quadrant of the CVF to the family of virtues I've called Reverence (A2). Or perhaps, more particularly, to one of its sub-families, the virtues of Love (A2b).

But elsewhere the CVF uses more down-to-earth language such as cohesion, consensus, involvement, engagement, community, partnerships, shared objectives, and mutual contribution.[17] And when it comes to measuring this quadrant, the language becomes still more pragmatic. Suggested items for measuring performance outcomes in this

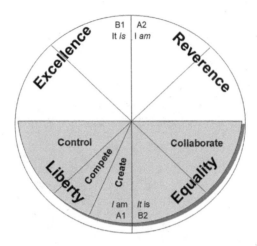

Figure 36. Competing Values Framework and the four families of virtues

area include such things as employee retention rate, measures of employee morale, number of top-quality people attracted and hired, per cent improvement in stress-related health care costs, return on investment in training and education, and reduction in internal grievances/complaints.[18] And a suggested measure for the creation of value in this quadrant is sales per employee![19]

It thus becomes clear the first kind of language is misleading, and that what CVF really has in mind here is something much more practical and more characteristic of life in a business corporation. "Collaborate" designates, in practice, the virtues of reciprocal benefit that belong to what I have called the virtues of Reciprocity (B2b). Cooperation, as Colin Talbot (b. 1952) says, "assumes some form of reciprocal exchange." It "implies an active and willing exchange of resources in some mutually beneficial way."[20]

If Collaborate is a virtue of reciprocity, it becomes possible to plot the four quadrants of the Competing Values Framework against the four quadrants of the human I've been describing in this book. If I adapt Figure 27 on page 222, to develop a similar image for the CVF, you can see that, in the context of the full human paradox, CVF's four quadrants would appear as they do in Figure 36 above.

The obvious thing that strikes you right away in Figure 36 is the number of segments of the four families of human virtues that are blank. The CVF's four families of virtues are all to be found in the bottom half of the figure. They're all virtues of self-assertion. The CVF has been constructed from real paradoxes. But not the most fundamental ones: they are neither first nor even second-level paradoxes.

Nor are the CVF paradoxes at the same level. Control and Collaborate are third level paradoxes: A1a and B2b. Compete and Create, on the other hand, are fourth-level paradoxes. In chapters 8 and 9, as you recall, I did not attempt to develop tables for this fourth level of the virtues. But I suggested it could be done. If you look at Table 10 on pages 174–5 you will see that Compete and Create can both be found in the family of virtues I called the virtues of Pleasure (A1b). So they could easily be used as labels for the families of contrasting virtues at the next or fourth level in this quadrant: that is to say, A1b1 and A1b2. Whether used as labels or not, they would certainly appear in the next two families at this fourth level.

Although the CVF confirms and richly illustrates the role of the human paradox in organizational life, it's also incomplete, and therefore somewhat misleading. Even though it looks at first glance like an image of the human paradox, it is, in reality, only an image of a fairly small subset of the nature of the human.[21]

Competing Values Framework and the Boy Scout Law

You can get some more insight into the nature of the human by looking closely at the Competing Values Framework's revealing discussion of the classic Boy Scout Law.

The traditional Boy Scout Law states that "A scout is trustworthy, loyal, helpful, friendly, courteous, kind, obedient, cheerful, thrifty, brave, clean, *and reverent*." The CVF authors start by mapping these values onto their own 2x2 diagram. The result is shown on Figure 37 on page 300.

You can see that the CVF framework has here produced a rather striking result. The Boy Scout virtues are almost all virtues of reverence. (The Boy Scout Law even makes this explicit – which is why I have taken the liberty of putting that word in italics.) But because the CVF's own four quadrants are a subset of the *opposite* virtues, these virtues of reverence have necessarily been distributed, instead, among the virtues of self-assertion!

Doing the same exercise using all four families of virtues of the full human paradox produces a very different distribution of the same virtues. The result of that exercise is shown in Figure 38 on page 300.

Helpful, friendly, courteous, kind, cheerful, and *reverent* are all clearly virtues of self-giving, where giving is for the *sake* of giving, not because something is due. They therefore belong to the virtues of Reverence (A2). Thrifty and clean are clearly virtues of prudence and temperance, and therefore belong to the virtues of Equality (B2). Brave is the ancient virtue of courage, the key virtue of the "irascible appetite" – the core

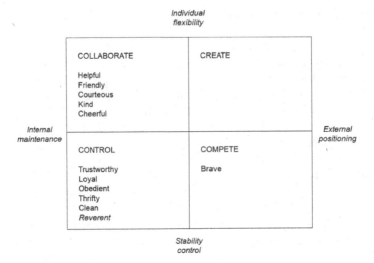

Figure 37. The Boy Scout Law mapped onto the Competing Values Framework[22]

Figure 38. The Boy Scout Law mapped onto the human paradox

virtue of self-assertion – and therefore belongs among the virtues of Liberty (A1). And trustworthy, loyal, and obedient are all virtues where something is due, and so belong among the virtues of Excellence (B1).

Contemporary discussions of "values" often don't distinguish, as they should, between the various modes of certain virtues such as trust, respect, honour, or even freedom. The CVF, like so many others, sometimes uses these terms as if they had only one meaning. But as you saw in the first part of this book (and in Tables 10 and 14, among others), they can all have at least three different meanings, depending on the perspective or attitude that is brought to them.[23] Trust, for example, can mean trust*ing* (A2), trust*worthy* (B1), or trust-*seeking* (B2), just as respect can mean respect*ful* (A2), respect*able* (B1), or respect-*seeking* (B2); and honour can mean honour*ing* (A2), honour-*able* (B1), or honour-*seeking* (A1). In all three examples, the first two terms describe virtues of reverence, but the third describes a virtue of self-assertion. It is common today to use these terms without making such distinctions.[24] Or even to exploit their ambiguity, so that a discussion which appears to be about a virtue of reverence uses sleight-of-hand to substitute a virtue of self-assertion. The speaker or writer wants to hang on to the moral charge that comes with trust*ing* and trust*worthy*, or respect*ing* or respect*able*. But what they *really* mean is that they want to be trusted and respected: that is, what they really mean is trust-*seeking* or respect-*seeking*.[25] In the case of the Boy Scout Law, however, the distinction has been made very clear: it talks about the virtue of being "trust*worthy*" and thus points explicitly to the virtues of Excellence (B1).

The CVF authors recognize, perceptively, that the Boy Scout Law's overwhelming focus on the virtues of reverence is somewhat one-sided. The Law gives relatively short shrift, as they themselves put it, to "*self-assertion* and innovativeness."[26] So they suggest an alternative Boy Scout Law that takes greater account of "the opposite quadrants in the Competing Values Framework." Their recast law reads as follows: "A scout is creative, independent, powerful, self-determining, challenging, strong, questioning, realistic, expansive, wise, engaged and exuberant." The CVF doesn't attempt to plot these alternative virtues on its 2x2 diagram. But if I were to display them in their proper locations in the four families of human virtues, the result would be what you can see in Figure 39 on page 302.

You can see that Figure 39 has yielded almost the reverse image of Figure 37. Whereas almost all virtues of the Boy Scout Law are virtues of reverence – and, of those, most are even virtues of Reverence (A2) – the virtues of the CVF's proposed alternative are, with only one exception, virtues of self-assertion. And of those, all but three are virtues of Liberty (A1), a quadrant which, in Figure 37, held only the single virtue of courage. In fact, to fit in all these new virtues of Liberty, I've even had to reduce the font in the A1 quadrant of Figure 39!

Of course, this was exactly the point. The CVF authors wanted to show that the Boy Scout Law was heavily loaded in favour of one set of

Figure 39. The CVF's revised Boy Scout Law mapped onto the human paradox

virtues. They wanted to show that it didn't give enough attention to the virtues of (as they themselves say) "self-assertion." But, in the process, they have helped show you three things. One is that a complete vision of the nature of the human would have to encompass the virtues both of reverence *and* of self-assertion. It would have to include the virtues shown in Figures 37 and 38, plus all those discussed earlier in this book.

The second thing the CVF discussion of the Boy Scout Law has helped to confirm is that, as the revised Law suggests, the CVF itself (like the contemporary culture it reflects) is biased in the other direction: toward the virtues of self-assertion – and toward the virtues of Liberty (A1) in particular. In fact, it's constructed largely from them.

That's the third thing. The CVF discussion of the Boy Scout Law helps to show you that, in our time, the arrow of virtue has returned not only to the virtues of self-assertion but is now returning – even more precisely – to the virtues of Liberty (A1), where the human began.[27]

Missing virtues: the CVF and the problem of "value"

In my remapping of the four quadrants of the Competing Values Framework (CVF) among the four families of human virtues (Figure 36 on page 298), a striking absence is the blank in B2a. The four CVF quadrants can account, to varying degrees, for the *other* virtues of self-assertion. But even in the bottom half of my image of the human paradox, there is a noticeable lack of anything in the CVF that might correspond to the element I labelled the virtues of Rights (B2a). This suggests that the CVF is perhaps a view of corporations primarily from the perspective of the shareholder, the board of directors, or of senior management. It seems to give somewhat less attention to the perspective of the employees, except in the form of employee engagement. But the latter is addressed primarily as a management concern. (Remember the ultimate proxy measure for engagement and community turned out to be sales per employee.) That might explain the relative lack of references to labour unions or to labour relations, for example.[28] Or the relative lack of emphasis on questions like fairness or the downward accountability of management to employees.[29] It may also suggest why the CVF has sometimes proven less helpful in organizations where the employee perspective is especially critical to outcomes.[30]

The four CVF "values" are all – or largely – virtues of self-assertion. But the CVF also shows it's impossible to talk about anything human, like an organization, without referring, in some way or other, to the virtues of reverence that always accompany them. That's why Quinn and his colleagues can't resist using not only words like concern, compassion, caring, kindness, selflessness, affection, and love but also words like faith, hope, humility, repentance – and even reverence![31] – even though their practical applications show that words like these may be out of proportion to the context and purposes for which they're employed. To describe the human without these kinds of virtues wouldn't be plausible. Without them human beings wouldn't be human. By the use of such words, the CVF points beyond itself and its values, to the genuine virtues of reverence.

In the specific case of the family of virtues the CVF calls Collaboration, there's another reason why it should do so. As you saw in chapter 9, the two sides of any human paradox seem to "lean" in more than one direction at the same time, depending on your perspective. Compared to *another* paradox, the two sides of any paradox seem to lean inward, toward each other. But compared with their partner *within* a paradox, the eight sub-sub-families of virtues (at the third level of separative projection) seem to lean outward: toward *another* duality. We can see that happening again in the CVF. The virtues the CVF calls Collaboration (and that I have called Reciprocity [B2b]) are one half of the virtues of Equality (B2). But compared to the *other* half (Rights [B2a]), Collaboration seems to lean away from them, toward their other neighbour, the virtues of Love (A2b). That's why it's perfectly natural (though potentially misleading) for the CVF to use this kind of language about the virtues of Collaboration/Reciprocity (B2b): the virtues of Love (A2b) are their closest neighbour, and so the former will always carry echoes and overtones from the latter.

Another word used by the CVF that points beyond the virtues of self-assertion – to the missing virtues of reverence – is the very word "value." The CVF uses this word both in the plural – the "competing values" (or virtues) I've been talking about – but also in the singular: as simply "value." These two different uses are present even in the title of one of the CVF books: *Competing Values* [plural] *Leadership: Creating Value* [singular] *in Organizations*. At first glance, the use of "value" in the singular might seem to point us to the "good," or to what I have called the virtues of Excellence (B1). But a closer look at the CVF suggests otherwise.

The CVF defines "value" as what results when the "benefits" an organization "produces" exceed the cost to the organization of producing those benefits.[32] The CVF authors do their best to interpret "benefit" or "value" in the widest possible way. They note, for example, that "what represents value for one organization may not represent value for another." For a private corporation, value may be measured by financial returns to shareholders. But for a school or university value would have to be assessed instead by the quality of the students' experience or their successful preparation for their future life. And, for a hospital, value might be measured instead by the "quality of health care that leads to patient recovery."[33] The CVF also notes that people disagree on "what aspect of value creation is the most important to assess. Some emphasize human concerns, whereas others emphasize environmental sustainability. Some advocate financial capital, whereas others advocate intellectual capital."[34]

In fact, these differences of view make defining value or results in fields like education and health care even more difficult than the CVF suggests.[35] But the CVF authors ultimately resolve the problem of differing ideas about value, at least for their own purposes, by defining value in terms of the CVF itself. Value can be created in an organization, they conclude, in "four ways": "value is created whenever an organization develops competencies in Control, Compete, Create, and Collaborate that collectively generate output that exceeds what individuals (or subunits within the organization) could do on their own."[36] The "key insight" of the CVF is that "value creation requires recognizing the inherent tensions that exist in different forms of value creation, and that focussing on too little or too much in a particular value creation *quadrant* will impede effective value creation."[37] In other words, value (singular) is a product of the four CVF values (plural).

But as you have seen, the four CVF values are only a very limited subset of the human, so the kind of value the CVF is talking about can only be goods associated with this subset. And, in practice, that turns out to be the case. Whenever the CVF grapples concretely with the question of value, it is driven to do so in financial terms: in terms of revenue, return on shareholder equity, and stock price.[38] Nods may be given to the very different meaning of value for not-for-profit organizations, or to alternative definitions of value such as quality of life or community development.[39] But these seem to be mostly *pro forma*. They aren't followed up – nor could they be, within the rather "thin" subset of competing values identified by the CVF.

Despite the CVF's name and its purpose, it does not – and cannot – develop a very "thick" notion of value because, as you can see in Figure 36, its four quadrants are merely a subset of the virtues of self-assertion. As that figure shows, the CVF is a framework primarily for the form of social relations Relational Models Theory (RMT) calls Market Pricing (as you saw in chapter 11). That's where three of the CVF's four quadrants are found.

Because the virtues never stand alone, CVF is also obliged to reach out to other human virtues, especially to some of the other virtues of self-assertion. But the CVF quadrants don't cover the full range even of these virtues. They also make no explicit place for the virtues of reverence or, more particularly (in this case), for the virtues of Excellence (B1). Because these virtues are such a necessary part of the nature of the human, the CVF can't help referring in passing to the virtues such as "justice and goodness" that belong to this family (B1).[40] But these references don't and can't lead anywhere. Because, if the CVF were to grapple with this quadrant (B1) of the full human paradox, it would be required to enquire much more deeply into the nature of the human good and the really profound conflicts which arise between competing notions and components of the good. If it were to do this, the CVF would get bogged down in much deeper and more intractable conflicts between real values or human goods. This would probably make it less useful or practical for its limited, utilitarian, private sector management purposes, related to Market Pricing (A1). But that's exactly the point. Because of its origins and orientation, the CVF has necessarily made a selection of a limited subset of the human virtues.

For that reason, some who have tried to apply the CVF beyond the private sector – in the public sector, for example – have found the results "unsatisfactory."[41] To achieve a larger perspective on the human, it may therefore be helpful to consider the question of competing values in another setting, such as the public sector.

Four families of public service values

Reflection on the role of paradoxes and competing values has been going on in public administration for somewhat longer than in the private sector.

This isn't surprising. The public sector is defined by contestable goods. That's what makes the public sector public. If things were -simpler – if value or the "good" could really be defined as shareholder value – we might not need a public sector at all.

But they aren't. Humans are human. They embody the full nature of the human. And these deep conflicts between competing goods have to be resolved, if at all, in the public sphere. As I pointed out at the beginning of chapter 12, that's what democratic politics is for. It is the civilized alternative to civil war, but also, paradoxically, the moral life of the community. The place where we debate and argue about the relative standing of things, within the hierarchy of goods.

Public organizations necessarily reflect these deep and enduring conflicts between public goods. Their own values have to embrace these tensions as the very essence of work in the public sector. Public organizations are shaped by tensions and conflicts much deeper even than those Quinn and his colleagues have rightly identified in the private sector.[42]

A classic statement of these dilemmas of organizational life was made by the Nobel Prize-winning social scientist, Herbert Simon (1916–2001) in 1946. Simon began by noticing – in the spirit of Francis Bacon, and as Robert Quinn was to do again over forty years later – that the traditional "proverbs" of administration all contradict each other. For every administrative principle or saying you can find its opposite. This led Simon to the conclusion that, in public administration, "[m]utually incompatible advantages must be balanced against each other, just as an architect weighs the advantages of additional closet space against the advantages of a larger living room."[43]

Over the following decades, this insight about the enduring contradictions, dilemmas, and tensions of public organizations was taken up by a variety of scholars and writers.[44] Leading public administration scholars Christopher Pollitt (1946–2018) and Geert Bouckaert (b. 1958) devoted an entire chapter in their widely used comparative study of public management reform to the theme of "trade-offs, balances, limits, dilemmas, contradictions, [and] paradoxes," identifying a potential list of ten such paradoxes or "contradictions."[45]

The paradoxes of public administration have been especially important within a growing literature and practice in the area of public sector value and values.[46] One of the drivers for identifying these public sector paradoxes has been the need (as in the case of the CVF) to make some sense or pattern out of the very long lists of potentially contrasting or competing public sector values. One recent study, for example, identified some 21 possible public values, and the authors noted that, with so many potential and competing values, the key challenge is "sorting out" all these values and "making some sense of their relationships."[47]

The challenge of making sense of the wide and potentially conflicting landscape of public sector values had already been acted upon by some of those who have to concern themselves not just with theory but with practice. In Australia, for example, the Public Service Commission had already found it necessary, in 2003, to "map" the rather long list of public service values included in the Australian Public Service Act (1999) into four "families" of public service values, families which are, necessarily, in some degree of conflict with each other. The four families of public service values identified in Australia are relationship with government and Parliament, relationship with public, workplace relationships, and personal behaviour.[48]

In Canada, a somewhat similar approach was taken to the question of public service values, beginning with the report of a Task Force on Public Service Values in 1996. Faced with the same challenge of making sense of a rather long list of public service values, the Canadian Task Force report (entitled *A Strong Foundation*) grouped them in four families of public service values. These same four families were eventually incorporated by the Canadian government into a *Values and Ethics Code for the Public Service* in 2003.[49] They were retained in a revised *Values and Ethics Code for the Public Sector* in 2012, now summarized in five key words or phrases: respect for democracy, respect for people, integrity, stewardship, and excellence.[50]

Christopher Pollitt has called this Canadian exercise "one of the more thoughtful examples" of the broad international effort by many governments to articulate the values of public service.[51] So I will use it as a framework for exploring some of the ways the human paradox presents itself in public organizations.

The four original Canadian families of public service values were called democratic values, professional values, ethical values, and people values. If I were to show these four Canadian families of public service values (with the five explicatory words or phrases) in relation to the four families of human virtues identified in this book, the result would be something like Figure 40 on page 308.

The "professional" values (A1) of a public service are those it *asserts* as essential to its own professional competence. In this family of values,

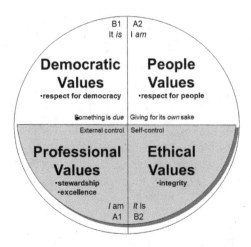

Figure 40. Four families of public service values

public servants demonstrate and value their professional "control" over the resources, information, and tasks committed to their care. In addition to competence itself, the 1996 Task Force and the 2003 and 2012 codes identified other similar and related values, including traditional values such as effectiveness and efficiency, as well as "new" values such as innovation and creativity, also properly highlighted in this quadrant by the CVF.

The so-called "ethical" public service values (B2) are the traditional virtues of prudence and temperance – the virtues of *self*-control – in a public service setting. They are the values that ensure a public service acts "at all times in such a way as to uphold the public trust."[52] In addition to prudence itself, the 1996 report and the 2003 and 2012 codes identified related values such as integrity, honesty, fairness, equity, discretion, and respect for law.[53] *A Strong Foundation* noted that these ethical values are not different from those in other parts of society, but the distinctive form integrity assumes in the public sector is "the ability to hold a public trust and to put the common good ahead of any private interest or advantage."[54] As the 2003 code put it, public servants must "perform their duties and arrange their private affairs so that public confidence and trust in the integrity, objectivity and impartiality of government are conserved and enhanced."[55]

The first two families of public service values are virtues of self-assertion. But they are complemented by two others it seems legitimate to identify with the virtues of reverence. The first of this second pair is what the Task Force and the code called "people" values. In Figure 40 I have taken the liberty of identifying this family with the human virtues I called Reverence (A2).

You will notice that this is a different placement than the one I gave to the family of values the CVF called Collaboration, despite the surprisingly rich language of reverence sometimes deployed by the CVF authors. Why the different treatment here? There are two reasons. The first, as you recall, is that the CVF value turned out, in practice, to have a more pragmatic, utilitarian aim that seemed more aligned with the virtues of mutual benefit or Reciprocity (B2b) – even though the CVF's Collaboration value also "leans" (like all the virtues of B2b) toward Love (A2b).

The second reason is the necessarily different place accorded to "people" in the public sector. Governments deal with two kinds of people: their own employees to be sure, but also the citizens they serve. And the public sector's "people" values apply to both. They apply to its "dealings with both citizens and fellow public servants," as the 2003 Canadian code put it.[56]

The relationship between governments and their citizens cannot be the instrumental one sometimes appropriate for private corporations, with their eye necessarily on the bottom line and on shareholder "value." In the public sector, serving and representing people are the reasons for governments to exist. People are not means to an end. They *are* the ends in themselves. They are the reasons for governments and the public sector to exist. This requires a qualitatively different approach to the human person. As the 2003 Canadian code said about "people" values: "Respect for human dignity and the value of every person should always inspire the exercise of authority and responsibility."[57]

This necessary "valuing" of citizens carries over – or, rather, should carry over – into the valuing of public sector employees by their own organizations. In a public service, "an institution based on relationships of trust," says *A Strong Foundation*, "'people values' – respect for the dignity and recognition of the worth if individuals – take on added importance," even beyond what they should also have in other organizations. After all, public servants are not *just* employees. They, too, are citizens. And a public service whose employees are not treated as citizens should be will not treat citizens that way either. A public service, as the 1996 Task Force report put it, "should display the same values of courtesy, of caring and of concern to its employees that it aspires to offer to other citizens."[58] This added level of caring and concern seems to justify identifying this family of public service values with the virtues of A2.

The fourth family of public service values is the one that distinguishes it most clearly from the CVF framework – and helps to confirm an important gap in the latter. What the Canadians call the "democratic" values identify not only the highest "good" for a public service – "the foundation of all the other public service values"[59] – but also the only legitimate means to discern and balance all the *other* competing and contestable public goods.

This was what was missing from the CVF. It did not have a very "thick" conception of the good. And it did not have a way of reconciling competing goods other than reducing them, ultimately, to the bottom line and to shareholder value. It recognizes that institutions like schools or hospitals have much more complex challenges in identifying and reconciling public goods, but it can offer no insight into how to do it, other than the competing values of the CVF itself, only a subset of human values. The CVF authors quote approvingly the advice of a senior elected official to "make sure that your various constituencies are heard. Make sure they have a say in what is in their best interest." But, for them, this is just another example of "empowerment."[60] The CVF conveys neither the immensity nor the significance of the challenge in the public sector of dealing with the result of such a democratic exercise: a genuine democratic survey of the full range of goods and interests affected by a public choice or policy decision.

The Canadian report on public service values, on the other hand, has a very lively idea of this challenge and sees it as defining one of the highest goods for the public sector. As examples of the "very different and often contradictory purposes or interests" that must be reconciled in the public sector, it mentions the competing interests of "the users of social services and taxpayers, the unemployed and entrepreneurs, developers and preservationists, environmentalists and promoters, union officials and employers, offenders and victims." It is the "sum and balance of these interests, democratically determined," it suggests, "that may add up to something that could be called the public interest, or the common good."[61] And this public interest or common good, it argues, "is for the public service what justice and liberty are for the legal profession, or what healing and mercy are for the medical profession," the highest goods to which each profession aspires.[62] The essence of the "democratic" values, for a public service, is helping elected officials, "under law, to serve the public interest."[63] Flowing from and informing the foundational idea of the public interest are other "democratic" values such as accountability, authority, law, legitimacy, loyalty, impartiality, and trust.[64]

One of the strengths of the Canadian approach to the values of public organizations is its emphasis both on overlap and conflict between values and between families of values. Following Aristotle and Aquinas, the Canadian documents recognize that the four families of public service values are not "fully distinct, but largely overlap or repeat each other." In this sense, the families "are not so much distinct categories but rather lenses or perspectives, through which or from which one can observe and describe the universe of public service values."[65]

At the same time, because of the hierarchy of goods, it is "in the very nature of values to conflict." "Choices in human affairs are not often made between something clearly bad and something clearly good," the Canadians recognize; "they are made instead between competing goods." Values conflict "not just with their opposites but with each other. Even our most cherished values are regularly in tension, and we are constantly having to make trade-offs between them." Liberty (A1) and Equality (B2) may "both be good," as this book has emphasized throughout, "but they also conflict, and any choice where they are at stake will make trade-offs between them. The same is true of public service values. In every choice to be made in the public service, a variety of values is at play, and a weight must be given to each." Learning to live with these tensions, "and seeing them as dynamic rather than necessarily destructive," the Canadians suggest, "is part of learning to be a responsible public servant, and a full human being."[66]

Four families of public values

The Competing Values Framework (CVF), as you saw, uses the word "value" in two ways: both in the plural (values) and in the singular (value). The former is supposed to deliver the latter. The argument is somewhat circular because "value" (singular) is ultimately defined, in practice, largely in terms of the four competing values (plural).

This same distinction between value and values has also been explored in the public sector. Mark Moore (b. 1947), for example, has suggested that public organizations can create public "value" in two ways: through "public sector production," that is to say, using the money and authority entrusted to them "to produce things of value to particular clients and beneficiaries"; and through achieving trust and legitimacy: that is to say, by establishing and maintaining public organizations that meet "citizens' (and their representatives') desires for properly ordered and productive public institutions."[67]

This approach to public sector "value" seems to be even more circular than the CVF's approach. At least the CVF has the ultimate "out" of shareholder value. It has a financial bottom line. But the public value defined by Moore has, and can have, no such bottom line. Performance in the delivery of public services is certainly measurable. But what *kind* of services should be delivered is a matter on which there can be legitimate disagreements. Social outcomes to be achieved are even more contestable. And the sources of trust and legitimacy are also things on which people also can and do differ because of their differing values. These are all matters for public and political debate. "Politics," as Moore admits, "is the answer that a liberal democratic society has given to the (analytically unresolvable) question of what things should be produced for collective purposes with collective resources."[68]

Charles Taylor points out that the search for a basic "value" is circular and, ultimately "incoherent," because it has to draw, implicitly, on the full range of values in order to explain and justify the basic value it proclaims.[69] So the search for public value (singular) seems to bring us back again to the question of values (plural). Public value (singular) can only be defined through the confrontation of competing public values (plural).[70] For that very reason, Colin Talbot, a British public management scholar, has attempted to develop a definition of four families of competing public values. Ultimately finding the CVF unsatisfactory for public organizations, Talbot bases his proposed public values on the four quadrants of Relational Models Theory (RMT) discussed in chapter 11. Inspired by RMT, Talbot's proposed four families of public values are: Autonomy, Equality and Equity, Authority, and Solidarity.

"Autonomy" refers to the public values that focus on personal benefit for individuals (and individual families) especially through choice and competition. "Equality and equity" are the values of being treated equally with due process and reciprocity. They highlight standards, entitlement, and consultation.

"Authority" expresses the values of stability, reliability, regulation, and the enforcement of norms. Talbot rightly recognizes that the essence of this quadrant of the human paradox is not the *imposition* of authority (which belongs elsewhere) but rather the *desire* of humans *for* authority: the authority of excellence. The values of this family are, he suggests, "a fundamental appeal to hierarchical structures to 'take charge' of the collective and impose order."

Finally, "Solidarity" designates the family of the public values that focus on social solidarity, community cohesion, and redistribution. It includes "altruistic motives and self-sacrifice for the good of the collective."[71]

It's easy to see the similarity of Talbot's proposed four families of public values not just with RMT, but with the four families of virtues developed throughout this book. And also with Canada's four families

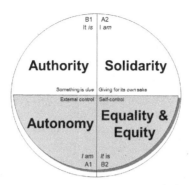

Figure 41. Four families of public values[72]

of public service values. They're identical with the four quadrants of the political paradox discussed in the previous chapter and shown in Figures 30 and 31 on pages 258 and 271. Only the names have been changed. Autonomy is just another word for liberty. Solidarity is one of the dimensions of reverence. And Authority is derived from excellence.

Thus, these four families of public values can be displayed in the form of the basic image of the human paradox I've developed in this book, as in Figure 41 above.

Like the Canadian approach to public service values, Talbot rightly highlights the potential – and even necessary – "tensions" between these four families of values. The values of Autonomy can clash with the values of Authority in differences of view about civil liberties, for example. Or too much emphasis on Autonomy and personal benefit can undermine the values of community Solidarity or Equity. Or they can undermine the values of Authority.[73]

Inspired as they are by Relational Models Theory (RMT), Colin Talbot's four families of public values also share some of the blind spots of RMT. The main one is that neither Talbot nor RMT have anything to say about where these four families come from. They just *are*. They emerge full-blown, as something already given. So there's no hint about the deeper human paradox and the polar structure of being, from which these four families emerge. Nothing about the paradoxical process or dynamic which underlies them, or about their own *internal* paradoxes – the conflicts not just *between* the families but also *within* them.[74] And so there is also no hint about where these four families are *going*. Nothing about the endless series of paradoxes of which these four are just a "moment," a way station or stopping place. Nothing about the kaleidoscopic explosion of conflicting values or virtues of which these four are just a snapshot in time.

The absence of a dynamic perspective also leads Talbot to adopt RMT's suggestion that each of these four families has a "dark side," a potentially negative dimension, not just a positive dimension. He does sense that the "negative" side of each family of virtues has something to do with the "tensions between them." But lacking a dynamic, paradoxical perspective, he doesn't really follow this up and (like RMT) doesn't appear to appreciate fully that the so-called negative features (or "dark side") of each family are the product of both its internal and external conflicts, and of the way self-assertion can block or hijack the virtues of reverence.[75] The challenge here, as in so many other fields, is to gain a deeper awareness of the basic human paradox of self-assertion and reverence, and how its two contrary but inseparable sides play out in every human action.

Organizations and the nature of the human

The Competing Values Framework (CVF), the Canadian approach to public service values, and Colin Talbot's four families of public values all help to show, each in their own way, how organizational life is structured by the nature of the human. Both public and private organizations are shaped – like society and politics before them – by the competing and conflicting virtues of the human paradox.

The Canadian effort to articulate the competing values of public organizations helped you to see the limits of the CVF's attempt to do the same thing, mainly in the context (as it turns out) of private sector organizations. The CVF can't help occasionally using the language of justice and love, of good and reverence, because it's impossible to talk about real human beings and real human life without referring to these essential human virtues of reverence. But they find no place within the architecture of the CVF itself, which is constructed instead from a subset of the virtues of self-assertion.

The public sector frameworks show that these virtues of reverence can't be ignored, however, in public organizations. The public sector serves and represents citizens, not clients or customers. And its employees *are* citizens. The competing values of public organizations have to take account of the full nature of the human and of the human virtues, not just of some portion or subset of them.[76] Public organizations help us to see more clearly how the *full* nature of the human is and must be reflected in organizational life.

But if so, maybe there's a lesson for private organizations in the public sector experience. Based primarily, as they are, on the social relations of Market Pricing and the virtues of Liberty (A1), private corporations may always be limited by the inevitable dominance of the virtues belonging to this pole of the human. As you saw, three of the four CVF values are located there. But private sector companies can never be fully satisfying places for human beings to spend the bulk of their lives unless they consciously reach out to embrace the *full* nature of the human, not just the virtues of Liberty (A1) or some part of the virtues of Equality (B2).[77]

A richer understanding of the full nature of the human might help private sector organizations to develop not only internal cultures that are more democratic and participatory – where there is greater recognition of employee "rights," employee engagement, and the downward accountability of senior management to its employees – but also "thicker" concepts of the good, especially the social good. It may enable a view of its various stakeholders not just as clients, customers, or contractors but as full human beings. That is to say, as citizens – bearers both of rights and of duties, in a framework of democratic community.[78]

Both private and public organizations can benefit by developing a more complete understanding of the nature of the human, and of human psychology – which I will consider more fully in the next chapter.

14

Psychology

In chapter 11, I noted that the social sciences have consistently recognized a basic tension or conflict in human life, though they use a wide variety of words to express this basic human paradox, words such as competition and cooperation, solidarity and dominance, solidarity and power, deference and dominance, interconnection and independence, commitment and individualism, beneficence and reciprocity, and so on. All of these pairs are different labels for the same thing. Each of them reflects or expresses the human response to the two sides of the basic polarity of being. They are the social science vocabulary for reverence and self-assertion.

Not surprisingly, the same polarity has also been recognized in the modern sciences of psychology and psychotherapy. In these fields the same human paradox is inevitably acknowledged and expressed in similar pairs of human psychological needs or impulses, such as "affiliation" (love, friendship) versus "control" (power, status), self versus other, agency versus communion, individualism versus collectivism, independence versus interdependence, and so on.[1] In chapter 6 I already mentioned a contemporary psychotherapist, Irvin Yalom, who recognizes that human life is defined by a necessary relationship (a "dialectic") between these kinds of "diametrically opposed responses to the human situation."[2]

Jung's psychological types

A psychological pioneer who recognized this paradoxical structure of the human and incorporated it into his understanding of the human psyche was the great Swiss psychotherapist Carl G. Jung. As powerfully as any other modern thinker, Jung saw that the nature of the human is a "paradoxical union of irreconcilables," a "synthesis of opposites."[3] He

also saw that this paradoxical structure of the human reflects the underlying polarity of being. It reflects the fundamental duality from which
this book began: the polarity of unity and plurality, of something and
other things, of something and everything, of self and other, of "self
and world."[4] "Both theoretically and practically," says Jung, "polarity
is inherent in all living things."[5] As a result of the fundamental union
of union and non-union within which human beings find themselves –
and which they also find themselves to *be* – the healthy human psyche, as Jung says, "wants both: to divide and to unite."[6] So the human
psyche appears as "a dynamic process which rests on a foundation of
antithesis, on a flow of energy between two poles."[7]

Based on this psychological insight into the human paradox, Jung
developed a theory or inventory of psychological types, first published
in 1921. For a book like this one – about the human paradox – Jung's
inventory of human psychological types is of great interest because he
wasn't content merely to identify a single paradox, or even just a variety of paradoxes. He went beyond this to suggest how these various
dualities might combine and interact to create an expanding variety of
psychological types. The initial polarity of "self and world" explodes
through the addition of further paradoxes to produce the rich diversity
of human psychological types we find in our human world.

For these reasons I'm going to use Jung's architecture of the human
self as an initial framework to explore the psychological dimensions
of the human paradox before looking at some complementary work
in the new fields of cultural, evolutionary, and "positive" psychology. But in this first part of the chapter, I will also go beyond Jung, to
take advantage of how his categories have been incorporated into the
Myers-Briggs Type Indicator (MBTI) which, since the 1960s, has become
one of the most widely used psychometric instruments. The MBTI has
been criticized for its alleged lack of "scientific" rigour and for not adequately reflecting its own theory.[8] But in this book I'm not concerned
with the instrument itself, or the detail of its profiles, but only with the
way in which it employs and extends Jung's psychological categories.
At this level, what's required is not so much "science" as insight and
discernment. In the case of the categories, the insight is mostly Jung's.

One of the reasons the Myer-Briggs typology is useful to me in this
book is that it adds an additional level to the categories, based on a
polarity Jung himself employed but didn't build into the structure of
his own basic inventory. This addition is helpful because it allows me
to take the process of separative projection even further than I normally
do. In chapters 8 and 9, I showed you how the nature of the human can
be traced through three levels of expanding paradox. I suggested this

process could, theoretically, be carried on *ad infinitum*, but I did not try to do it. In a few cases, I hinted that some third-level polarities suggest how further dualities might well be structured at the fourth level. But I didn't do it myself.

In the previous chapter, however, you already saw how, for organizations, the Competing Values Framework (CVF) has, inadvertently, taken the human paradox down to its fourth level, identifying (without realizing it) two sub-components of the virtues of Pleasure (A1b): compete (A1b1) and create (A1b2). Adding a fourth duality to Jung's catalogue of psychological types allows me to go even further. For psychology at least, it allows me to fill out this fourth level. It shows how the same polar logic you have observed throughout this book – the process of separative projection – leads through three further levels, from a simple initial polarity or pair, to an eventual sixteen: an ever-expanding kaleidoscope of human paradoxes. Even these sixteen psychological types probably only scratch the surface of the nature of the human.

Sensation and intuition

A good place to start is with the human function Jung called sensation.[9] Sensation is a good place to start because it's the first way we encounter and know the world. By sensation, Jung means "the sum-total of my awareness of external facts given to me through the function of my senses." Sensation tells us "that something is."[10] As Aristotle says, "the starting point is the fact."[11] And our senses are our first informants about the facts of the world.

But sensation must immediately be paired with another and contrary function. Sensation informs us about things that can be seen, or touched, or physically felt. But that's not the only form of human perception. As I pointed out already, beginning in chapter 2, human beings also perceive things that *can't* be seen. That's a big part of what makes humans human. And for this they need and have another, contrary psychological function. Jung calls this opposite function "intuition." Intuition, he says, "is a sort of perception which does not go by the senses, but it goes via the unconscious." It is a function "by which you see round corners." It takes the form of hunches and "perceptions that somehow work through the subliminal data, such as sense perceptions so feeble that our consciousness simply cannot take them in." A perception of the intuition "creeps up into consciousness": it is "unconscious until the moment it appears."[12] Intuition is a faculty for perceiving the "possibilities" in any human situation. The intuitive person "has a keen

Figure 42. Sensation and intuition

nose for things in the bud pregnant with future promise."[13] For Jung intuition is a natural, normal, and absolutely necessary psychological function "because it makes up for what you cannot perceive or think or feel because it lacks reality."[14]

Sensation and intuition are the two basic functions from which we can begin to explore the psychological dimensions of the nature of the human. They can be represented in the form of the basic image I have been using throughout this book, as in Figure 42 above.

You can see that, in this figure, I have identified sensation with self-assertion and non-union, and intuition with reverence and union. There are many reasons to make these two associations. In the case of intuition and reverence, they're obvious. If the top half of the circle represents the human response to the invisible world of being, it's clear that this half of reality can't be perceived by our senses. It can only be perceived by a faculty like intuition that "looks beyond" the individual facts of the physical world. "When you have an intuitive attitude," says Jung, "you usually do not observe the details. You try always to take in the whole of a situation, and then suddenly something crops up out of this wholeness."[15] The whole background of being *within* which everything exists – and without which nothing *could* exist – is, and must be, entirely invisible to us. Present, but invisible. So it can only be detected by a psychological function that perceives the presence of an absence. "The person who uses only the vision of the eyes is conditioned purely by what he sees," said the Taoist sage Zhuanzi (ca. fourth century BCE). "But it's the intuition of the spirit that perceives reality."[16]

While the connection between intuition and reverence is obvious, the link between sensation and self-assertion is equally strong. In a way, it is even more important because the importance of the physical world for our modern minds helps to explain the dominance of the virtues of self-assertion in our modern world – and even the dominance, in modern culture, of "mind" itself.

As I pointed out in chapter 4 – and again in chapters 7, 8, 10, and 11 – the virtues of self-assertion and our "sensing" of an objective, physical world go hand-in-hand, mutually reinforcing each other. It's our drive to self-assertion and control that makes us encounter a world of individual things. Sensing, Thomas Aquinas says, is "the very application" of self-assertion to some individual thing.[17] And it's the physical encounter of our senses with a concrete, objective world of things that makes us discover our own ego as *itself* an individual, objective thing, separate and distinct from its surrounding environment. The discovery that "*It* is" leads back to the rediscovery of the starting point: to the rediscovery that "*I* am."

Because the world experienced by our senses introduces us to a world of particular, individual things,[18] sensation must also be identified with non-union, whereas intuition is the counterpart of union, the means through which we apprehend the whole. "We see parts of things," says Iris Murdoch, "we intuit whole things."[19]

So sensation belongs in the grey semicircle whose outline is clear and distinct. Intuition belongs instead in the larger encompassing circle, whose circumference is infinite.

Every human being encounters the world through the senses and through intuition. Sometimes these first two psychological functions can be quite evenly balanced. But in almost all of us, one of them is dominant, even if only slightly so. It's our preferred, natural, or most instinctive form of perception. This preferred or dominant function helps give the individual what Jung calls his or her "particular kind of psychology."[20] And the same phenomenon of dominance or preference reoccurs in the other cascading dualities that constitute the human psyche.

Four psychological functions

Sensation and intuition are the starting point for exploring the psychology of the human paradox.

But as soon as these two initial psychological poles go to work, the process of separative projection immediately sets in. Because sensation and intuition are the response of human perception to the polar structure of being, the very same poles begin to make themselves felt *within each side* of this initial paradox. The polar dynamic of "self and world" polarizes these first two poles – and then all the others too.

To begin with, sensation and intuition both bear within themselves two contrasting ways of processing the products of our perception: thinking and feeling. Sensation, for example, may tell us that a thing *is*, but thinking, as Jung says, "tells us *what* that thing is, feeling tells us what it is *worth* to us."[21] Thinking makes judgments about the *truth* of reality. Feeling makes judgments about its *value*.

This is the reappearance of the original human paradox within these first two poles of the psyche. There's a very close connection, for example, between feeling and intuition. In fact, "you can mix up feeling and intuition easily," as Jung admitted.[22] When we intuit things we seem to do so with our feelings. And when we have a feeling about something, it is a kind of inarticulate intuition.[23]

Thinking and sensation are also closely connected. The truth of our human intelligence, says Thomas Aquinas (following Aristotle, as usual), "depends on conformity of thought with thing. ... [T]hings are the measure of our intellect. For by the fact that a thing is so or not, there is truth in what we think and say."[24]

Thinking and feeling are a kind of mirror image of each other, but in different human registers. Love and hate – "pursuit and avoidance" in the sphere of *feeling* – "correspond exactly to affirmation and negation" in the sphere of *thinking*.[25]

Thinking may have a natural affinity with sensation, and feeling with intuition. But these links are not exclusive. The second pair of psychological functions appears as separate poles *within* each of the first two. Thinking and feeling are a second tension or duality of opposites in the human psyche: they are the opposites that reproduce the original polarity of being *within* each of the two poles of the first duality: sensation and feeling. Jung calls these four primary psychological functions – sensation and intuition, thinking and feeling – the "four gates to the world,"[26] and he sometimes pictured them as shown in Figure 43 on page 322.

The capital E at the centre of Jung's diagram represents the human *ego*, the source of human energy and willpower. For Jung, this diagram shows how the ego finds itself at the centre, caught between two pairs of conflicting dualities: sensation (S) and intuition (I) on the horizontal axis, and thinking (T) and feeling (F) on the vertical axis.

But Jung's diagram has several drawbacks. The first is the positioning of the ego. Jung's diagram makes the ego look as if it were something separate from the psychological functions, something they influence or assault *from the outside*. But if these are the four basic psychological functions, they

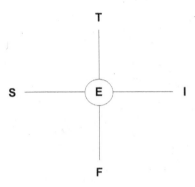

Figure 43. C.G. Jung's image of the four psychological functions[27]

can't be *separate* from the ego: they must somehow *constitute* it. They must somehow be inside it or part of it. Or it must be part of them.

A second drawback to Jung's diagram is that the two pairs of opposites, the two axes, seem to be quite separate. But, as Jung himself says, nobody can "dispose" of any of the four functions.[28] You can't choose not to have some of them. We all use all of them, all of the time. Showing them on separate axes thus misrepresents reality. In reality, the two axes and their four poles must be combined. No one recognized this more clearly than Jung himself. The bulk of his pioneering work on *Psychological Types* was devoted to showing exactly how they do combine to produce the rich variety of human personality types.

A third drawback – related to the second – is that Jung's diagram obscures the process of separative projection whose career you've been following in this book. It's not just that the four functions combine. They do so in ways that keep reproducing the original paradox at each subsequent level. Each new pole produces its own two poles. And these poles produce their own two poles. And so on, *ad infinitum*. Any adequate image for the psychological functions and types, of which Jung was such an important pioneer, needs to show not only how the psychological functions combine but also the organic process through which paradox breeds paradox.

Four psychological profiles

This is where the Myers-Briggs development of Jung's psychological types can help. The functions never stand alone. In each of us, the dominant psychological function on one axis combines with the dominant function on Jung's other axis to produce a new combination. And that new combination forms the core of a distinctive psychological type.

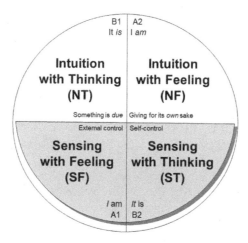

Figure 44. Four basic psychological profiles[29]

This insight allows me to revise Figure 42 to show how the process of separative projection produces the next level of the human paradox: how the two new poles of thinking and feeling polarize the original pair of sensation and intuition to produce four basic psychological combinations.[30] You can see these four in Figure 44 above. In this and subsequent figures I will now often use the Myers-Briggs terminology where it differs from Jung's ("sensing" instead of sensation, for example).

Following the order of the "arrow of virtue," the first (A1) of the four combinations of dominant psychological functions at this second level is the combination of sensing with feeling (SF).[31] Because its purposes are practical and constructive, the Myers-Briggs descriptions of the various personality profiles – while potentially useful in an everyday context – are also rather upbeat. They don't do justice to the deeper, more awesome import of the four corners of the human. As a psychotherapist dealing with psychical disorders in his everyday work, Jung recognized the dark or shadow side of his psychological types, the ways in which these primal forces can go awry and cause great damage to the human person in the form of pathologies and neuroses, especially when the contrasting sides of the human paradox get radically out of balance. But the Myers-Briggs personality profiles normally accentuate the positive. They aim to make people feel good about their own psychological type and to show how all personality profiles can contribute to social and organizational goals and needs. For example, the MBTI describes SFs as normally exhibiting a great deal of personal warmth, and likely to be sociable and friendly.[32] While this description may have some validity in the right context, it doesn't even hint at the darker, primal energies lurking in this corner of the human, the one I have called the virtues of Liberty (A1). The energies of power, pleasure, desire, eros, instrumental control, imagination, and play.

Remember that, in the deeper human paradox, this pole is actually what I called the "engine room" of the human. It's what Aristotle and Aquinas (fully anticipating Jung's linkage of sensation with feeling) called the "sense appetite," home to both the "irascible" and "concupiscible" appetites of Power (A1a) and Pleasure (A1b). It's the original source of all human motivation, desire, drive, and action.[33] It is self-assertion in its purest form and therefore the true home of the ego, as distinct from the complete self. The energies from this quadrant are present in every human being, to some degree or other. But they aren't necessarily dominant in all of us.

The arrow of virtue leads next (A2) to the combination of intuition with feeling (NF), linked to the previous profile by the preference both give to feeling. But in this combination, intuition is now dominant over sensing. Because intuition is now dominant over sensing, people in this category (NF) may be less focussed on immediate facts and circumstances and more preoccupied with imagining new possibilities – new projects or potential intuitive insights.[34] In the following quadrant (B1), intuition is still dominant (as in A2) but is now combined with a preference for thinking instead of feeling (NT).[35] Remember that, in the arrow of virtue, this is the development from the stance of "I *am*" to "It *is*."

The last of the four psychological profiles at the second level of separative projection combines the emphasis on thinking from B1 with the preference for sensing from A1 (sensing with thinking). This is, after all, the movement from the stance of "It *is*" to "*It* is." Like those in the first group, people with this psychological profile (ST) may give primary attention to the immediate facts to be derived from sense perception, but they prefer to process them with more impersonal thinking and logical analysis rather than with feeling.[36]

Eight psychological profiles

It's easy to see the correspondence between these first four psychological profiles and the four families of virtues that define the nature of the human. They aren't exactly the same thing under different names, but because they're both shaped by the underlying dynamic of the polarity of being and the process of separative projection, these first four psychological types resonate in significant ways with the corresponding families of human virtues. They express the same human stances.

But paradox, as you saw in chapter 7, breeds paradox. The process of separative projection ensures that these four profiles will, in turn, generate their own conflicting poles. And for the same reason. The polar structure of being – the paradox of union and non-union, unity and plurality, something and everything, self and other, self and world – again splits these four psychological types into a further eight.

After all, the two poles of self and world obviously offer the potential for two further psychological orientations or preferences: either toward the self or toward the world. Some people are psychologically oriented primarily (but never exclusively) toward the self, toward their own *internal* world. And other people are primarily oriented in the other direction, toward the *external* world. The first type is called "introvert," and the second is called "extravert."

Jung describes an introvert as someone whose attitude is "an abstracting one; at bottom, he is always intent on withdrawing libido* from the [external] object, as though he had to prevent the object from gaining power over him. The extravert, on the contrary, has a positive relation to the object. He affirms its importance to such an extent that his subjective attitude is constantly related to and oriented by the object. The object can never have enough value for him and its importance must always be increased." Introverts tend to be "reserved, inscrutable, rather shy people"; extraverts are "open, jovial, or at least friendly and approachable characters who are on good terms with everybody, or quarrel with everybody, but always relate to them in some way and in turn are affected by them."[37]

The two poles of introversion and extraversion split the four initial psychological profiles into a further eight psychological types, at the third level of separative projection. You can see the result in Figure 45 on page 326.

Jung himself didn't present the eight profiles in exactly this way. I'm using here the MBTI categories derived from Jung. But Jung did recognize that some psychological functions are combined as primary and secondary (or "principal" and "auxiliary"). Beside the primary or

---

* "Libido" is the term often used in psychology and psychotherapy for the source of energy and desire in the human, especially "the striving for pleasure." In that sense it can be identified with that part of the nature of the human I have called the virtues of Liberty (A1), or more specifically, the virtues of Pleasure (A1b). See Sigmund Freud, *A General Introduction to Psychoanalysis*, trans. Joan Riviere (New York: Pocket Books, 1970), 149–50.

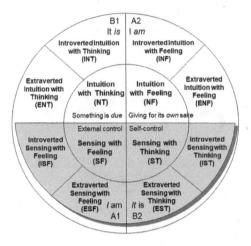

Figure 45. Eight psychological profiles at the third level of separative projection

principal function, another secondary or auxiliary function "is constantly present, and is a relatively determining factor." This insight suggested that thinking, for example, can combine with either sensation or intuition, as a primary or secondary function. And feeling can combine with either of the other pair, in the same two ways.[38]

When the two poles of extraversion and introversion are added to these four combinations, you get the eight psychological types at level three, shown in Figure 45.[39]

Sixteen personality types

Jung himself expressed the distinction between psychological types in which thinking and feeling are dominant and those in which sensation and intuition are dominant as a distinction between "rational" and "irrational" psychological types. By rational, he meant the psychological types who rely primarily on the "rational" or "*judging*" functions such as thinking and feeling.[40] (For Jung – as for Alfred North Whitehead and Max Scheler, as you'll see in the next chapter – feeling has to do with the "function of valuing." It's "a word for the giving of values" – and is therefore, for Jung, a "rational function."[41]) By "irrational" he meant those types that instead rely primarily on the functions of "*perception*," such as sensation and intuition.[42]

Jung's distinction between the "rational" psychological types (who rely primarily on the "judging" functions) and the "irrational" types

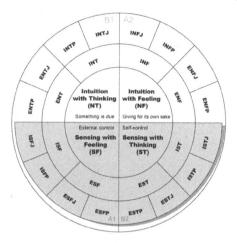

Figure 46. Sixteen personality types at the fourth level of separative projection

(who rely more on the "perceiving" functions) suggested an additional psychological polarity the MBTI calls perceiving and judging.[43] As I mentioned, this fourth polarity allows me to take the evolving picture of the nature of the human down to the fourth level, offering a concrete illustration of the process of separative projection you've been following throughout this book. For psychology, the results at this fourth level are shown in Figure 46 above.

The outer ring of the circle in Figure 46 now shows sixteen "personality types." Because of the limitations of space in the illustration, I have only been able to include the MBTI initials by which these profiles are commonly known. But you can easily interpret them by referring to the longer titles in the outer circle of Figure 45, to which either "judging" (J) or "perceiving" (P) has now been added.[44]

The sixteen personality types in the outer ring of Figure 46 show the process of separative projection in action. The same duality from which the nature of the human unfolds – the original paradox of union and non-union, unity and plurality, something and other things, something and everything, self and other, self and world – keeps working itself out, producing new dualities or paradoxes at every level. The final psychological dichotomy – judging and perceiving – is just another form of it. Perceiving is related outward to the world, and judging is clearly a personal decision of the self. The paradox that began the process is the same one that keeps it going, producing an endless variety in the psychological nature of the human.

Though this is a practical place for me to stop, there's no reason to suppose that the reality of the psyche does so. The identification of only one more form of the original paradox would take this inventory down another level and would then yield thirty-two psychological types.

Freud's psychological architecture

Jung's psychological types (extended by the MBTI) help you get a better idea of what Jung called the "total psychic economy," as illustrated in Figure 46.[45]

You can get another perspective on the richness of Jung's description of psychological types by contrasting it with the psychological architecture of Sigmund Freud (1856–1939). Freud described the psyche as formed by three principal elements: the ego, the *id*, and the super-ego.[46] The ego is the pure self-asserting dimension of the psyche, whose initial drive is simply "self-preservation."[47] This "inclination to aggression is an original, self-subsisting instinctual disposition in man."[48] The ego, in Freud's account, is in tension or some degree of conflict with what Freud originally called the libido – the "striving for pleasure," or the Pleasure Principle: "procuring pleasure and avoiding pain" – which he later also called the "*id*."[49] In its drive for self-preservation the ego learns that the pleasure principle of the libido and the *id* must often be controlled or delayed, and so gradually develops a competing Reality Principle: "which at bottom also seeks pleasure – although a delayed and diminished pleasure, one which is assured by its realization of fact, its relation to reality."[50] For Freud, life consists in the "conflict or interaction between two classes of instincts." On the one hand our "aggressive impulses," and on the other, the "libidinal, sexual or life instincts, which are best comprised under the name of *Eros*." Both "have been in operation and working against each other from the first origin of life."[51]

But both the ego and the *id* stand over against a third psychic element Freud eventually called the super-ego. If the ego is first of all a "bodily ego," ultimately derived from "bodily sensations," the super-ego houses a person's ethical values. In the form of "conscience," the super-ego is "ready to put into action against the ego the same harsh aggressiveness that the ego would have liked to satisfy upon other, extraneous, individuals. The tension between the harsh super-ego and the ego that is subjected to it, is called by us the sense of guilt."[52] In its conflict with the libido and the *id*, "the ego is at bottom following the dictates of its super-ego."[53]

The unfolding of the nature of the human in this book so far makes these three pillars of the Freudian psyche easily recognizable. The

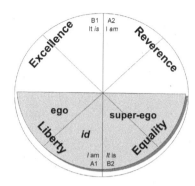

Figure 47. Freud's ego, *id*, and super-ego

Freudian ego corresponds almost exactly to that portion of the nature of the human I've called the virtues of Liberty (A1), more specifically the virtues of Power (A1a). It is the "irascible appetite," already well-known to Plato, Aristotle, and Aquinas long before the modern era. And the libido or the *id* corresponds exactly to the virtues of Pleasure (A1b). It is Aquinas' familiar "concupiscible" appetite, in modern dress.

Freud's super-ego, the home of the conscience, corresponds to the virtues of self-control or what I've called the virtues of Equality (B2). (Possibly even the subset of these virtues I have called the virtues of Rights [B2a].) It is what Aristotle and Aquinas call the rational appetite (or a portion of it). In fact, Freud shows real insight by seeing that the rational appetite or super-ego is an "internalized" form of self-assertion, a self-assertion "sent back to where it came from – that is, it is directed toward his own ego": directed at the self itself, replacing the drive for external or instrumental control with a drive for *self-control*.[54]

So I can readily plot the Freudian psyche on the map of the human paradox. You can see the result in Figure 47 above.

Even if you accept that Freud's super-ego corresponds to the whole of the virtues of Equality (B2) and not just – as it may well be – some subset of them (such as the virtues of Rights [B2a]) – even if you accept this, it's clear that the three elements of what Freud called the "mental apparatus" don't even come close to encompassing the whole nature of the human.[55] As in the case of the Competing Values Framework in chapter 13, displaying these elements on the full map of the human leaves at least half of the map blank. In the Freudian architecture, a mere subset of human dispositions or virtues has been substituted for the whole. Freud's vision of the human is somewhat like a card-player attempting to play bridge or poker with only half a deck of cards.

Freud's insights into the structure of the psyche are certainly useful. But they are not new. And they are not complete. Comparing Figure 47 with Figure 46 illustrates the potential breadth of Jung's contrasting inventory of psychological types. Of course, the two frameworks serve quite different purposes, and describe different realities. Figure 47 is contained within Figure 46: all of the personality types described by Jung possess Freud's "mental apparatus." Figure 46 also meets a higher standard of completeness in two senses: both factually (or empirically) and as an ideal (or normatively).

Factually, Jung's inventory of psychological types offers a fuller portrait of the nature of the human. The very profusion of the sixteen MBTI personality types derived from Jung's typology seems to reflect the diversity of the human psyche, its many corners, possibilities, and aspirations. They offer a fuller picture of all four sides of the nature of the human. They make room not just for the virtues of self-assertion which respond to the visible world of things we can *sense*, but also the virtues of reverence that respond to the invisible world of being we can only *intuit*. Not just the world of "*I* am" (A1) and "*It* is" (B2) – the world of the ego, the *id*, and the super-ego – but also the world of "I *am*" (A2) and "It *is*" (B1).

The paradoxical structure of sixteen psychological types – based on four pairs of conflicting dualities – also accurately reflects the paradoxical structure of reality itself. It shows, again, how the human world is rooted in the polar structure of being: *to* which human life is a response; and *of* which it is a manifestation. The way these dualities cascade down from an initial polarity to sixteen types at the fourth level – and perhaps thirty-two at the fifth? – also shows the polar dynamic of separative projection at work in a human world. Producing the endless paradoxes of the nature of the human: the paradoxes of our psychological nature, just like those of our social and political natures, and of organizational life.

Cultural and evolutionary psychology

C.G Jung's description of human psychological types confirms and provides new insights into the nature of the human I've been exploring in this book. And so do more recent developments in cultural, evolutionary, and "positive" psychology, especially their rediscovery of the virtues as what makes humans human. The gradual revival of interest in "virtue ethics" in the second half of the twentieth century paralleled and helped spark a similar revival of interest in the virtues among contemporary anthropologists and cultural psychologists.[56]

Cultural psychology can be described as "the study of the distinctive mentalities of particular peoples." It is thus distinct from the more general study of mental structures and processes "so widely distributed as to characterize the normal psychological functioning of all human beings," like those proposed by Jung and Freud.[57] Cultural and evolutionary psychologists are in a good position to see that rational reflection on a narrow range of ethical "principles" – to which Western ethics has often been reduced since Kant – doesn't begin to do justice to the range of moral insights and instincts which can be observed across a variety of cultures, much less across the whole span of human evolution. In fact, that narrowness – and its very emphasis on "rationality" or human reason – begin to look like artefacts of the Western mind itself, evidence of its own narrowness and peculiarity. They also begin to look like blinkers or distorting lenses, preventing us Westerners from apprehending the full nature of the human.

In chapter 11 you already encountered the work of Alan Fiske and his Relational Models Theory (RMT), a theory which, I have suggested, comes much closer to reflecting the full nature of the human than many other modern and post-modern frameworks. Fiske himself was influenced by Richard Shweder, another American anthropologist (a "psychological anthropologist and a cultural psychologist"[58]), whose encounters with non-Western cultures (especially the Hindu culture of India) suggested to him that modern Western moral concepts don't come close to capturing the full range of human morality.

As a result of these encounters, Shweder proposes that a more adequate description of human nature needs to take account of three distinct "ethics," which he calls the "big three of morality."[59] The virtues, or "moral goods," don't vary from culture to culture, Shweder suggests, but they tend to "cluster" in what I've called families of virtues, but which Shweder calls "ethics."[60] One of these so-called ethics is, to be sure, the ethics of "autonomy," the ethics of modern Western societies, with its emphasis on the individual and on freedom. But this familiar ethos needs to be augmented, Shweder proposes, by two additional "ethics" less familiar or instinctive to the Western – or at least to the modern and post-modern – mind. These other ethics aren't focussed on the individual, like most Western thinking, but on the surrounding society instead, the society in which individuals are embedded, and by which they are supported and nourished. Shweder calls these two additional ethics the ethics of "community" and the ethics of "divinity." The ethics of "community" recognizes that individuals are always embedded in some larger social unit, like a family or a tribe, and that this embedding calls forth a distinctive range of human virtues, such as respect and loyalty. The ethics of divinity recognizes that, in most cultures and most times, most people feel themselves to be participants not just in a larger social order but also in a larger *sacred* order, and this sense of participation is expressed in yet another range of human virtues, such as sanctity and purity.

You can see that Shweder's work in cultural psychology was feeling its way toward several of the insights about the nature of the human already described throughout this book. His three "ethics" of autonomy, community, and divinity seem, at first glance, to correspond very closely to the three families of virtues I've called the virtues of Liberty (A1), Reverence (A2) and Excellence (B1). It would hence be natural to plot Shweder's three ethics on my map of the human paradox in the way I've done in Figure 48 on page 333.

When you look beneath the names, the picture is a little more complicated because some of the values or virtues Shweder associates with each of his three ethics belong elsewhere, in my view, in the map of the human spirit. For example, Shweder associates the "values" of duty and hierarchy with his ethics of community, whereas I link them with the virtues of Excellence (B1), rather than the virtues of Reverence (A2). Similarly, Shweder associates "justice" with his ethics of autonomy, while I think the virtues of justice are central to the family of Excellence (B1). (See Table 14 on pages 194–5.)

These differences of detail can easily be explained by the spiral staircase and the "double vision" I described in chapters 7 and 10 (Figures 18 and 26). As I mentioned there, Hegel suggests the whole circular or spiral pattern of human development is fully present and visible, in a "simplified" or "abbreviated" form, in any one of the successive stages or cultures (or "moments") which reveal the whole nature of the human.[61] When you look through the lens of any of the families of virtues (Shweder's "ethics"), you see the *whole* human paradox, the whole nature of the human. You see *all* the human virtues, but you see them all through one lens (or maybe more than one), with all the emphasis and coloration that particular lens (or subset of lenses) can give them. So it's not entirely surprising to find virtues of reverence like duty and hierarchy viewed through the equally reverent lens of community (A2). Or even to find a virtue like "justice" (clearly a virtue of reverence [B1]) viewed through the self-assertive lens of autonomy (A1), as it is by John Rawls, for example. What you see, and the way you see it, depend upon where you stand. It depends on your "stance."

In any event, it's clear how much Shweder's "big three" of morality has in common with the nature of the human described in this book.[62] The architecture is similar, even if some of the details differ. He, too, sees the human as a paradox: as a tension or conversation between

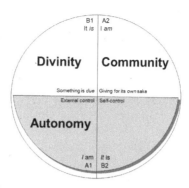

Figure 48. Shweder's three ethics

stances, between distinct and contradictory (but inseparable) poles of the human. And, by and large, his three poles correspond very closely to those I have described here. Shweder also recognizes that his names for the three "ethics" are merely labels for three large clusters (or what I call "families") of related human virtues. When Shweder's three "ethics" are located on the map of the human paradox, as in Figure 48, you can see, at a glance, how the two approaches seem to proceed from very similar intuitions about the nature of the human.

Figure 48 also illustrates some more of the differences. The blank in the bottom right quadrant, for example, suggests Shweder may have missed an important pillar of the human (just like the Competing Values Framework, in chapter 13). But there may also be some good reasons for this omission. For one thing, Shweder locates "rights" with the ethics of autonomy, whereas I think the virtues of "Rights" are one of the key sub-families (B2a) of the virtues of Equality (B2). (Table 10 on pages 174–5.) From Shweder's point of view, the ethics of autonomy may stand, in a sense, for *all* the virtues of self-assertion, not just the virtues of Liberty (A1); they may be the virtues of self-assertion by another name. The blank in the bottom right-hand quadrant of Figure 48 may also have something to do with Shweder's underlying motivation. In chapter 11, I noted that Alan Fiske was so intent upon overturning Western assumptions about individualism and self-interest that he's sometimes led to misinterpret, mislabel, or undervalue the virtues of self-assertion and their role in the nature of the human. It appears that, for similar reasons, the virtues of reverence are, paradoxically, over-represented in Shweder's framework, and the virtues of Equality (B2) overlooked as the necessary polar balance (in the virtues of self-assertion) to the virtues of Liberty (A1).

Moral Foundations Theory

I'll come back to Richard Shweder in chapter 17. But I want to turn now to the work of another cultural psychologist, Jonathan Haidt, a student both of Fiske and of Shweder, where the challenge of achieving an appropriate balance in the description and mapping of the human virtues reoccurs. Influenced by Fiske and Shweder, Haidt and a team of colleagues have set out to identify the "foundations" of human morality – and therefore of human nature itself, since "morality is the key to understanding humanity."[63] The goal is "to find links between virtues and well-established evolutionary theories."[64] They call the result *Moral Foundations Theory*. The theory represents what Haidt calls "educated guesses about what was in the universal first draft of human nature."[65]

Using the same language I've been employing throughout this book, Haidt calls his theory a "*map* of moral space."[66] But the "map" has gone through an "evolution" of its own. In its initial version, Moral Foundations Theory (MFT) posited four basic families of human virtues (Haidt and his colleagues call the families of virtues "moral matrices" or sometimes "modules") which it then labelled Suffering, Hierarchy, Reciprocity, and Purity. Keeping in mind the confusion about hierarchy I already noted in Relational Models Theory (RMT), it's easy to plot these four on my map of the human paradox, as in Figure 49 on page 335.

In this first version of the theory, Haidt and his colleagues correctly intuited two and a half of the four families of virtues, but like RMT, they couldn't express the polar relationships between them. As a result, two of their initial four seem to be components of the virtues of Excellence (B1), and another, Reciprocity (B2b), appears to be only one half of the virtues of Equality (B2), lacking its polar opposite sub-family: the virtues of Rights (B2a).

Once again, as in Shweder's three ethics, one of the four families of human virtues is completely blank. But curiously – given Shweder's influence on Haidt – it's the *other* half of the virtues of self-assertion that have now gone missing. While Shweder's own blank in the virtues of Equality (B2) has now been partly filled in, his "ethic of autonomy" has disappeared, and the virtues of Liberty (A1), the starting place of the human, are, for the time being, completely absent.

The first version of the Moral Foundations Theory, shown in Figure 49, was just another starting point, however. From 2005 to 2009, MFT's families of virtues increased from four to five, and were now

Figure 49. Moral Foundations Theory: version 1 (2004)[67]

Figure 50. Moral Foundations Theory: version 2 (2005–9)[69]

called Care, Fairness/Reciprocity, Loyalty, Authority/Respect and Purity/Sanctity.[68] Again it's easy to locate these five families of virtues in my map of the human paradox, as in Figure 50 above.

As you can see, this second version of Moral Foundations Theory (in Figure 50) loaded up the virtues of Excellence (B1) – perhaps even overloaded them, at least in relation to the other families of values. But it still left one (or perhaps even one-and-a-half) of the four quadrants of the nature of the human completely empty. The challenge of achieving a proper balance between the contending families of virtues still remained to be met.

This challenge was partially addressed in the third version of Moral Foundations Theory, which dates from 2010. In this version the five families were now increased to six by the addition of the virtue of liberty. In this way, Shweder's virtue of autonomy finally found its way back into the "map" of the human offered by Moral Foundations Theory. At the same time, the authors of the theory did some pruning and combining to simplify the list of families of virtues. And they also made consistent a practice (already partially introduced in the second version of the theory) of naming the families by linking a positive virtue with its negative opposite. The new "moral matrix" of Liberty is linked with its opposite: oppression, for example. Similarly, Care is linked (as in the second version of the theory) with "harm," and Loyalty with "betrayal" (instead of the previous negative, "in-group"). For the names of the other three families of virtues, the theory now replaces a pair of positive virtues with a positive and a negative. Fairness is linked with "cheating" (instead of the previous positive virtue, "reciprocity"); Authority with "subversion" (instead of the previous positive virtue, "respect); and Sanctity with "degradation" (instead of the previous positive virtue, "purity").

While I can see the utility of these new pairings for some purposes of psychological research, I don't think they're helpful in constructing a "map" of the virtues. They risk reintroducing the confusion between contradictions and contraries, the confusion Aristotle tried to clear up in the *Metaphysics*. They also risk distorting our understanding of the virtues *as virtues*, by making you focus exclusively on efficient causes and making you forget final causes. By focussing on the "occasion" (Hegel), "affordance" (Webb Keane), or circumstance which may "trigger" a virtue, rather than the structure, dynamic, or *meaning* of the virtue itself. In doing so, they encourage you to understand a virtue from the *outside* rather than from the *inside*: to think about it as something *observed*, rather than something that is actually *lived*.

This risk is increased by Haidt's basic verbal image for the "Moral Foundations." He calls them the "taste buds of the righteous mind."[70] This is a clever rhetorical image, especially if you are trying to get people in a Western culture – who have been learning for three hundred years to think almost exclusively in terms of physical and "efficient" causes – to open their minds again to something that has become as culturally alien to them as the virtues. But it also risks making you think a virtue is something that happens *to* you – a reaction to something external, like the taste of salt or sugar – rather than as something you *do*. It also confuses the form that *doing* takes, and what it requires. In this way you can miss entirely the arduous, demanding effort – the struggle, the defeat, the persistence, experience, and final reward – of a "good habit." Especially a habit of reverence. And where it leads or points you.[71]

So I will take the liberty (as I already did for the second version of the theory, above) of including only the first or positive name for Moral

Figure 51. Moral Foundations Theory: version 3 (2010)

Foundations Theory's six families of virtues. With these deletions, it's easy, once again, to plot these six "moral matrices" or "modules" on my map of the human paradox. You can see the result in Figure 51 above.

Moral Foundations Theory and the families of virtues

One of the strengths of Moral Foundations Theory (like Shweder's three "ethics") is that each of the six virtues that qualify as "foundations" are labels for a much wider family (or "matrix" or "module") of virtues, just like Thomas Aquinas' cardinal virtues, or like the four families in my own map of the human paradox. Thus, the families of "care" and "loyalty" (as devotion[72]) rightly include other virtues of Reverence (A2) such as compassion, kindness, gentleness, self-sacrifice, and "nurturance" (Robert Bellah's "disposition to nurture"). (This seems to be the family of virtues MFT comes closest to describing accurately.) The families of Authority and Sanctity are also rightly said to include other virtues of Excellence (B1), such as deference, respect, chastity, and "cleanliness" (purity).

But questions can and should be asked about whether Moral Foundations Theory has correctly discerned relationships between some of the other virtues. A "map," after all, is only really useful if it helps you to locate things accurately. Should the virtues of justice and trustworthiness, for example, be linked to the family of fairness (B2), as MFT proposes? Or, instead, to the family to which Authority and Sanctity also belong (B1)? Fairness is, after all, merely the form to which justice is reduced in the virtues of Equality (B2), not justice itself, which has a much deeper – and even contradictory – resonance.

And where does "trustworthiness" belong? To the same family as fairness (B2), as MFT suggests? Or to the virtues of Excellence (B1), instead, where meeting a *standard* (like "worthiness") is the test? Trust certainly does have a role to play in the family of virtues to which fairness belongs (B2) – as it also does, for that matter, in the virtues of Reverence (A1). But as a member of the fairness family (B2), it takes the form of trust-*seeking*, rather than trust*worthiness*. (And in the virtues of Reverence [A2], it takes the most virtuous form of all: trust*ing*.)

Similarly, should "temperance" be associated with Sanctity (B1), as MFT suggests? Or with the virtues of "self-control" – the "rational appetite" (B2) – as Aristotle and Aquinas assumed?[73] Can the virtue of Liberty be discussed entirely in the form of *resistance* to bullies and tyrants, as MFT does? Or are the virtues of Liberty (A1) the very ones – the virtues of Power (A1a), the "irascible" appetite, the human disposition to dominate – that also, paradoxically, *create* the tyrants and bullies, in the first place?[74]

As in the case of Relational Models Theory, the terms "authority" and "hierarchy" in the three versions of Moral Foundations Theory are potentially confusing to the unwary. The Western mind is naturally inclined to think of these terms from the top-down: as the *assertion* of hierarchy or authority. But in this form, hierarchy and authority are virtues of self-assertion, *not* of reverence. As I pointed out in chapter 11, this is a blocking or hijacking of reverence by self-assertion, not reverence itself. To his credit, Haidt himself is very clear that this is *not* what he has in mind in using the term authority. For him, the virtue of "authority" refers to "the psychology of the *subordinate* – the psychology of *respect* for authority," not the psychology of the person who asserts authority or hierarchy.[75] This shows that what Haidt and his colleagues have in mind here is indeed a virtue of Excellence (B1), those virtues in which there is a standard to be venerated, where *something is due*.

Two points can be made about loyalty. First, loyalty is one of those virtues which harbour more than one meaning, depending on the use and context (See Table 14 on pages 194–5). Loyalty can be a kind of duty, in which case it belongs in the virtues of Excellence (B1, more specifically the virtues of Goodness [B1b]). Or it can be a kind of devotion, in which case it belongs with the self-giving virtues of Reverence (A2, more specifically, the virtues of Reverence[3] [A2a]). As elsewhere in my discussion of MFT, I have arbitrarily assigned it the second meaning for the purposes of this chapter. Second, as in Relational Models Theory (RMT), it's easy to confuse the virtue of loyalty with its negative consequences, the exclusion of outsiders and the creation of an "in-group." From the point of view of the social and psychological processes, the latter isn't without interest or significance. But from the point of view of the virtues *as virtues*, putting the two together creates potential confusion between two opposite sides of the human paradox. Loyalty is a virtue of union. Exclusion is an act of *non*-union. Exclusion is an act of self-assertion, *not* of reverence. The exclusion of outsiders from an ingroup is, once again, a blocking or hijacking of a virtue of reverence – in this case, the virtue of loyalty – by the virtues of self-assertion.

The challenge of assigning the virtues to appropriate families and explaining the relationships between them shows that, like Relational Models Theory (RMT), Moral Foundations Theory (MFT) still has some distance to go. It can get there by integrating its own insights about the human paradox into a more consistent account of the virtues, and thus of the nature of the human.

Moral Foundations Theory and the human paradox

Moral Foundations Theory gets the basic human paradox exactly right. Following Durkheim, Haidt recognizes that human beings have "a dual nature – we are selfish primates who long to be part of something larger and nobler than ourselves."[76] Except for the negative word "selfish" (which should, properly, be the positive word "self-asserting"), this is an almost perfect summary of the human paradox. It was my own starting point, too, and what the first chapters of this book were designed to show you. We are both x and not-x, at the same time.

But so far, Moral Foundations Theory appears to have made only modest use of this profound insight about the human paradox in its own "map" of the human. Like RMT, MFT normally offers only two forms of explanation for the human virtues: "innateness and social learning."[77] It hasn't yet recognized the deeper role of the polarity of being or the resulting process of separative projection. Nor (like the other social sciences, as you saw in chapter 3) does it have any role for final causes, for the motivating power of the virtues simply "because they are good"[78] – or for what Samuel Johnson calls the "naked dignity" of virtue.[79] So it doesn't yet see how the basic human paradox (which Haidt correctly describes) structures the nature of the human in a polar or paradoxical form, in pairs of opposite families of virtues. MFT does note the rather obvious tension between Liberty (A1) and Authority (B1).[80] But elsewhere it only rarely emphasizes these kinds of paradoxical relations. So it has difficulty identifying appropriate family groupings and their paradoxical contraries. As a result, it doesn't yet have any natural order, structure, or limit.

Relational Models Theory (RMT) had the good fortune to get the basic four poles of the human approximately right. But Moral Foundations

Theory (MFT) started with four families, then expanded to five and then to six, with at least four other potential candidates waiting in the wings.[81] This process is potentially unending. Aristotle identified some eleven virtues and Aquinas mentioned about forty. In this book, I've identified more than 200! There's nothing at all wrong with an expanding list. It faithfully reflects the true nature of the human. But at some point it becomes necessary to put order in the list and to explain it: explain how the virtues relate to each other and how they are structured. What comes "before" what? And why? To do this, it may be necessary to go beyond anthropological and purely psychological explanations to existential and ontological ones. Beyond efficient causes, to final ones.

Taking its own insight about humanity's "dual nature" more seriously will also help Moral Foundations Theory achieve a better balance in its description of the human. Even with the overdue addition of the virtue of Liberty, MFT is still heavily weighted in favour of the virtues of reverence: in fact, two to one. Once again, as in the cases of Alan Fiske and Richard Shweder, this is easy to understand. Like them, Jonathan Haidt and his colleagues are rightly trying to break out of the modern and post-modern Western mindset – its atomism, its focus on the individual rather than the community, its neglect of the virtues, its undue emphasis on the rational mind at the expense of feeling and intuition, and, above all, its denial of the sacred. They're aiming to show the peculiarity and isolation of modern and post-modern Western culture – its *WEIRD*ness – both in the context of contemporary world cultures and, even more, in the light of the "deep past," the long span of human history. They aim to highlight our current Western inability to perceive, describe, and account for the full or complete nature of the human. In the process of doing all this, they've gone overboard, giving the virtues of reverence far more weight than the virtues of self-assertion.

And there's another very good reason why they should do so. If you look again at the basic image of the human I've been using throughout this book, as in Figure 25, on page 209, for example, you'll be reminded that the virtues of reverence are larger and more significant, in a way, than the virtues of self-assertion. The grey semicircle on which I've been presenting the latter is consistently shown as *inside* – floating within and above – the larger background of being to which the virtues of reverence respond and belong. This visual image is intended to convey that the virtues of reverence are, in one sense, prior to – and therefore more important than – the virtues of self-assertion. They create the necessary conditions for both kinds of virtue to flourish or even to exist. Without the "prior" virtues of union, there can be no constructive non-union. Without sound families and communities and nations – without, at the limit, a habitable world, as you will see again in chapter 17 – they both die. Without the virtues of reverence, as Jonathan Haidt himself puts it, "there'd be nothing to divide in the first place."[82]

There are thus some very good or understandable reasons for the remaining imbalance in Moral Foundations Theory.[83] Addressing this imbalance can help Moral Foundations Theory develop into an even more accurate description of human nature, let alone of what I have been calling the nature of the human.

For one thing, this kind of imbalance largely (though not completely) overlooks the deeply paradoxical relationship of reverence and self-assertion: the fact that the virtues of self-assertion are intimately involved in the virtues of reverence, since all human acts – even acts of reverence – are, by definition, acts of self-assertion. It also overlooks the way in which the virtues of self-assertion (like all the virtues) are divided against themselves. As I pointed out, MFT doesn't yet seem to recognize that the virtues of Liberty (A1) often struggle against the very things (such as tyranny and oppression) they themselves create by their assertiveness, their own impulse to domination and control. In the process, these virtues also open the door, paradoxically, to the human experience of reverence.

But I don't want to stress the challenges of Moral Foundations Theory as much as I want to highlight its remarkable contribution to rediscovering of the nature of the human. Most of its basic assumptions and intuitions seem, to me, correct. And its effort to rebalance Western understanding of the nature of the human is long overdue. Its own struggles illustrate how difficult a thing that is to do, for the deep historical, intellectual, and cultural reasons I'll explore in the next chapter.

One of the reasons I've taken you on a tour of the various stages through which MFT has developed is to show you the contemporary Western mind at work, questioning its own assumptions and categories, gradually refining its insights, trying gradually to overcome the limiting presuppositions our own culture has been developing for three thousand years. I wanted to show you how MFT has struggled to rediscover the true nature of the human, buried under centuries of Western intellectual and cultural tradition. The extended birth of Moral Foundations Theory is a case study in the laborious, difficult effort of the Western mind to overcome its own blind spots – especially its very focus on "mind," even the "righteous mind" – and rediscover the full nature of the human.

Moral Foundations Theory helps to demonstrate the urgent need to undertake this exercise of excavation. And it shows that it can, in fact, be done. It shows that all serious explorations of the human ultimately converge in contradictory but mutually necessary insights, when viewed with a wide enough lens.

Above all, the basic intuitions of Moral Foundations Theory confirm and support the assumptions that have guided this book: that human beings have a "dual nature," and that the human virtues are the necessary key for exploring this dual nature and developing a useful "map" of the human paradox.

Positive psychology

The emergence of cultural and evolutionary psychology (rooted in anthropology) has occurred in parallel to another psychological movement called "positive psychology," spearheaded by an American academic psychologist, Martin Seligman. Positive psychology is an equally promising development, which aims to turn psychology away from its negative modern and post-modern preoccupation with mental illness – with the abnormal and the pathological – back toward the traditional concerns of moral philosophy – from Aristotle and the Stoics, to Aquinas and Leibniz – with psychological health, that is, with the psychological foundations of a positive human life and character. It "aims to reclaim the study of character and virtue as legitimate topics of psychological inquiry and informed societal discourse."[84]

Positive psychology sometimes openly refers to the building blocks of a good human life as "virtues." But perhaps because of our postmodern bias against virtue language, it more often calls them "character strengths" or "values in action." As you've seen throughout this book, that is the very essence of a virtue: values are the *inside* of the virtues, the good habits of feeling that support and animate good behaviours. In Seligman's words, they are "what you care about."[85] Virtues are the *outside*, the habits of good behaviour that are supported by and also nourish the internal habits of feeling. A "value in action" *is* a virtue.

Positive psychology has not only rekindled interest in the virtues, it has also approached them in ways that are largely consistent or compatible with the approach described in this book. From my point of view, one of the most helpful features of positive psychology is that it acknowledges (like Richard Shweder and Jonathan Haidt) the tendency (recognized since Aristotle and Aquinas) for the virtues to group themselves naturally into what positive psychology sometimes calls "virtue clusters" (which I've called families of virtues), each of them labelled by a master virtue. Seligman and his colleague Christopher Peterson began by developing an inventory of the virtues, just as I've done in this book (though for different purposes). They mention over sixty virtues, but they focus on twenty-four core virtues, which they group into six basic families or clusters. They call their six families of virtues Wisdom and Knowledge, Courage, Humanity, Justice, Temperance, and Transcendence. You should be able to see, right away, some of the links and parallels between these virtue clusters and the families (and sub-families) of virtues described in this book.

Peterson and Seligman also note the cascading structure of the families of virtues I've described in this book. That feature partly explains their vocabulary. They sometimes reserve the term "virtue" for the highest level, as the name for the families themselves. They call the next level of virtues "character strengths," and the next, "situational themes."[86]

In their initial inventory, Peterson and Seligman explicitly decline to establish any particular relationship between their proposed value clusters, or to suggest any structure to the overall universe of the virtues. They describe their grouping of the virtues into clusters or families as a "classification," but not a "taxonomy." A taxonomy goes further than a classification because it has the structuring "benefits of a good theory." However, the added value of a taxonomy comes, they argue, with a cost or a risk. If the theory's wrong, then the activity or field it's designed to support becomes "self-defeating." Moreover, a taxonomy can be very hard to change. So, in their inventory, Person and Seligman opt for a tentative, unstructured classification that preserves flexibility, while allowing the new field of positive psychology to develop productively. They trust that, as the field develops, theories will emerge to unify their classification.[87]

As you've seen, my objective in this book is complementary, but somewhat different from that of positive psychology. My interest is not so much in the individual virtues as in the architecture of the virtues as a whole, in order to map what Coleridge calls the "structure of our proper humanity."[88] Beginning from the basic polarity of being – unity and plurality, something and everything, self and world – I've shown you how the human response to this universal condition results in two basic human stances and their corresponding families of virtues, recognized (as you saw in chapter 6) by almost all serious thinkers and most of the social sciences – whatever names may be used for the two sides of this initial human paradox. I've called them self-assertion and reverence (but there are many other possible names, as you saw in Tables 5 and 6). And I've also shown you how this basic polarity of being continues to work on these first two families of virtues, splitting them into four, then splitting these four again, and so on, *ad infinitum*, issuing in an endless, cascading series of human paradoxes.

Because you've already discovered the basic architecture of the virtues, I can use it to locate positive psychology's virtue clusters within the nature of the human and display their relationships. Positive psychology's six families of virtues not only seem, at first glance, to fit rather neatly into the four basic families I've already identified, they even seem to correspond quite closely to the eight sub-sub-families described in Tables 10 and 14 on pages 174–5 and 194–5, or to combinations of them.[89] For example, the first virtue cluster, Wisdom and Knowledge, combines the emphasis on wisdom in the virtues of Truth (B1a) with the emphasis on rational knowledge and "critical thinking" more typical of the virtues of Rights (B2a). Positive psychology's second virtue cluster, Courage, including virtues such as bravery, persistence, and vitality, corresponds almost exactly to the virtues of Power (A1a). The family of virtues positive psychology calls "Humanity" includes virtues like love and kindness and so aligns very closely with what I've called the virtues of Love (A2b). Justice is obviously one of the most important virtues of Truth (B1a). The virtue cluster positive psychology calls Temperance, including virtues such as prudence and self-control, is easily identified with what I've called the virtues of Equality (B2b), the virtues of "self-control." And finally, the virtue cluster of Transcendence, including virtues such as awe, wonder, gratitude, and hope, corresponds almost precisely to what I've called the virtues of Reverence[3] (A2a). In fact, as you saw in chapter 9, "Transcendence" is a name I might well have chosen for this sub-sub-family.

By making these initial links between positive psychology's six virtue clusters and some of the eight sub-sub-families of virtues I've already identified, I can show them to you in the format for the nature of the human that I've been using throughout this book, in Figure 52 on page 345.

Positive psychology and the four families of virtues

In Figure 52, you can see that positive psychology's virtue clusters appear to offer a pretty good balance between the virtues of self-assertion and those of reverence. You can also see that, in this format (like the Competing Values Framework, in chapter 13), there seem to be some missing sub-families of virtues, such as the virtues of Pleasure (A1b). Peterson and Seligman state explicitly that these virtues are "not part of our vision of character strengths" – a surprising decision, in view of thousands of years of reflection on them (i.e., the "concupiscible appetite") in the Western tradition – and Seligman's own later frameworks, as you will see.[90]

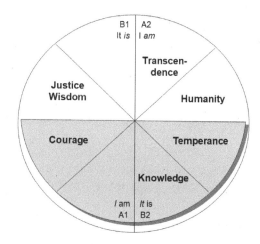

Figure 52. Positive psychology's six virtue clusters

But first impressions can be misleading. In the preceding paragraphs, you may have noticed I used phrases and words like "at first glance" and "almost." That's because the correspondence between positive psychology's six virtue clusters and my sub-sub-families isn't quite as neat as first appears. When you look beneath the surface, some interesting differences begin to emerge. The content of Peterson and Seligman's six virtue clusters doesn't always line up with my sub-sub-families of virtues.

I already noted that the cluster of Wisdom and Knowledge seems to conflate virtues from the two families I've called Truth (B1a) and Rights (B2a). But it also includes creativity and curiosity from the virtues of Pleasure (A1b). Similarly, Peterson and Seligman's cluster of Courage includes integrity, which belongs to the virtues of Goodness (B1b) if your emphasis is on wholeness, or to the virtues of Reciprocity (B2b) if your focus is on ethical self-control. In addition to love and kindness, their cluster of Humanity includes "social intelligence," which seems to link best to the mutual sociality of the virtues of Reciprocity (B2b). In addition to prudence and self-regulation (or self-control), positive psychology's Temperance cluster includes forgiveness and mercy from the virtues of Love (A2b), as well as humility and modesty from the family of virtues I've called Reverence[3] (A2a). In addition to gratitude and hope, the virtue cluster positive psychology calls Transcendence includes beauty, which (as you see in Tables 10 and 14) is a form either of Goodness (B1b) or of Pleasure (A1b); excellence, which is another name for Goodness (B1b); and humour, which belongs with play and playfulness in the family of Pleasure (A1b).

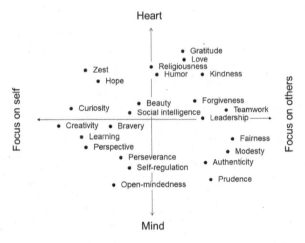

Figure 53. A positive psychology model of the "structure of character"[91]

I can illustrate some of the differences between positive psychology's virtue clusters and my own families of virtues by showing you positive psychology's own ideas about the potential structure of the virtues. I mentioned above that, in their initial inventory, Peterson and Seligman declined to offer any ideas about the relationship between the virtues. They preferred to develop a simple "classification" rather than a "taxonomy." However, Christopher Peterson later developed a model of the structure of the virtues, based on the kind of 2x2 diagram that's also very popular in the literature on organizational management (as you saw in chapter 13). The two axes for Peterson's model are heart versus mind and self versus other. Employing these two axes, Peterson plots the location of positive psychology's 24 virtues (or "character strengths") in relations to his two axes and thus displays what he calls the "structure of character" – that is, what Coleridge calls the "structure of our proper humanity," or what I call the nature of the human or the human paradox. You can see Peterson's depiction of the architecture of the virtues or the "structure of character," in Figure 53 above.

The first thing I want to note about Figure 53 is how much it confirms and is consistent with the map of the human already developed in this book. Three of Peterson's quadrants are just about spot-on in their core spirit or thrust. Bravery, perseverance, and creativity appear in the bottom left quadrant, just where they should be, in what I call the virtues of Liberty (A1).

Fairness and prudence appear, as they should, in the bottom right quadrant, in what I have called the virtues of Equality (B2). Love, gratitude, kindness, and forgiveness all appear where they should, in the top right quadrant, or what I call the virtues of Reverence (A2). "Religiousness" sits right in the middle, between the two top quadrants, straddling the virtues of Reverence (A2) and the virtues of Excellence (B1) – which, as you will see again in chapter 16, is just about where it should be.

The biggest "weakness" in this positive psychology model is in the top left quadrant. Only beauty is correctly located in this quadrant as a virtue of Excellence (B1). The other three virtues in this quadrant of Peterson's model are all misplaced, from my point of view, as are a number of virtues in his other quadrants. No doubt the differences result from differing definitions or interpretations of individual virtues. But I think they also stem from the same problem you saw in chapter 13, where 2x2 diagrams were constructed with mismatched axes, yielding only a piece of reality, not the whole thing. Peterson's horizontal axis of "focus on self" and "focus on others" is an accurate expression of the human paradox of union and non-union. But the same paradox works vertically, too, and Peterson's axis of "heart" and "mind" doesn't properly capture this reality. "Heart" and "mind" are certainly axes, but they aren't vertical axes. They're *diagonal* axes: "heart" signifies the "existential" (I am) paradox of Liberty (A1) and Reverence (A2), while "mind" expresses the "cognitive" or ontological (It is) paradox of Excellence (B1) and Equality (B2).

I think this mismatching of axes results from insufficient development of the basic human paradox of union and non-union. I'll come back to this. But first, you can see how I think positive psychology's twenty-four core virtues are properly located on my map of the human spirit, in Figure 54 on page 348.

Figure 54 shows the first impressions of Figures 51 and 52 were a little misleading. The content of positive psychology's own virtue clusters may not always line up consistently with my families of virtues. But when you look beneath the cluster names and map their virtues onto the human paradox, positive psychology achieves a wider coverage of the eight sub-sub-families of virtues than at first appeared to be the case. In Figure 54, you can see there are no longer any empty segments of my basic image of the human. Positive psychology's virtue clusters now cover all eight sub-sub-families of virtues, at least to some degree.

That doesn't mean the distribution is even, however. There still seem to be some noticeable emphases. The virtues of self-assertion slightly outnumber the virtues of reverence, for example, 14 to 10. This is the

Figure 54. Positive psychology's 24 core virtues mapped onto the human paradox

opposite of Richard Shweder's and Jonathan Haidt's frameworks, where the weighting of the distribution leans the other way – perhaps reflecting anthropology's decisive encounter with non-Western values. Within the virtues of self-assertion, there seems to be a slight bias in favour of the family I've called the virtues of Equality (B2) rather than the virtues of Liberty (A1), 8 to 6.

Despite the overall weighting in favour of self-assertion, Peterson and Seligman still give remarkable prominence – especially for a contemporary framework – to the virtues of reverence. Compared with the Competing Values Framework (CVF) in chapter 13, for example, positive psychology gives a really striking importance to the virtues of Reverence (A2). Within the virtues of reverence, they outnumber the virtues of Excellence (B1), 7 to 3. Even more remarkable is the fact that, at this level, the virtues of Reverence[3] (A2a) slightly outnumber the virtues of Love (A2b), 4 to 3.

When the overall weighting among the virtues of reverence is combined with the weighting among the virtues of self-assertion, another striking fact emerges. The core values on the right-hand side of Figure 54 outnumber the virtues on the left-hand side by almost two to one: 15 to 9. Since the right-hand quadrants are always the more "reverent," within both of the initial families of virtues, and the left-hand quadrants contain the more "assertive" virtues in both families, Figure 54 suggests positive psychology's outlook offers *a reverent take on a basic*

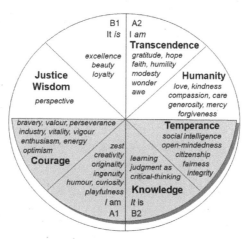

Figure 55. A broader selection from positive psychology's inventory of virtues

stance of self-assertion. If Moral Foundations Theory seems to lean implicitly (in the language of chapter 11) toward a political stance of social conservatism, positive psychology appears to offer something more like a social democratic profile.

I can test these initial impressions by widening the picture. The twenty-four core virtues aren't the only ones mentioned by Peterson and Seligman. In fact, to flesh out their own families of virtues, they actually mention more than sixty virtues. I can't show all of them here. But, if I add a representative selection, it yields a picture something like Figure 55 above.

The overall impression of Figure 54 is largely confirmed by Figure 55. The virtues of self-assertion still outweigh the virtues of reverence. And within the latter, positive psychology still gives a remarkable degree of recognition (especially for a contemporary framework) to the virtues of reverence – and to the virtues of Reverence (A2) in particular, which (in this figure, at least) are now evenly balanced between the virtues of Reverence[3] (A2a, which positive psychology calls Transcendence) and the virtues of Love (A2b, which positive psychology calls Humanity).

Perhaps the most striking feature of Figure 55 is the increased weight given to the virtues of Liberty (A1) – and to the virtues of Power (A1a) in particular (which positive psychology calls Courage). Positive psychology fully recognizes that this corner of the human is what I've called the "engine room" of the human. Without virtues like energy, vitality, vigour, enthusiasm, optimism, zest, perseverance, and so on, the rest of the virtues don't matter because no creative, persistent action whatever can occur. Without these essential virtues, there would be no possibility of any other virtues because there would be no effective, habitual, good action in the world. The virtues of Liberty (A1) are one of the existential keys to the human. That was the great insight of Thomas Hobbes and Friedrich Nietzsche, as you'll see in the next chapter. Positive psychology's lively recognition of this fact confirms the impression that, though it shows a remarkable sensitivity to the virtues of Reverence (A2), the dominant outlook of positive psychology remains rooted in the virtues of self-assertion.

Positive psychology and self-assertion

I can test this impression a little further by looking briefly at what Martin Seligman *does* with the virtues. The use to which he puts them. Seligman hasn't been content to just to talk about the virtues themselves. He's also tried to link them up to larger frameworks. He called his first framework Authentic Happiness.[92] It had three key elements, which he calls positive emotion, engagement, and meaning.[93] It's somewhat unfair to try to link these elements to specific virtues or families of virtues because Seligman cautions that the twenty-four virtues underpin *all* three elements.[94] So, for him at least, they can't really be linked with any one, or any subset of them. But it's very hard to resist doing so, especially since the descriptions of the elements point strongly to one corner of the human or to another.

"Positive emotion," for example, is about pleasure, rapture, ecstasy, scrumptiousness, delicious tastes and smells, sexual feelings, orgasm, delightful sights and sounds, bliss, glee, warmth, comfort, and so on. Seligman calls it the "pleasant life."[95] So, it's pretty hard not to see that this element is a proxy for the virtues of Pleasure (A1b) – which is fascinating, given Peterson and Seligman's explicit exclusion of pleasure from their original classification of the virtues. Similarly, "meaning" is about belonging to and serving something bigger than the self.[96] So this element clearly belongs to the virtues of reverence. But it has a dispassionate or objective element to it, so it belongs to the virtues of "It *is*" (B1), not just "I *am*" (A2). "Meaning" is the very essence of the virtues of Excellence (B1). That's not where it begins in the story of the human, but it's where it first comes into view.[97] Because "meaning" has a high cognitive and mental component (intuitive judgments about meaningfulness), it seems to belong especially to the virtues of Truth (B1a), perhaps even more than to the virtues of Goodness (B1b). Truth (B1a) is where the "meaning" of Goodness (B1b) comes to rational human consciousness.

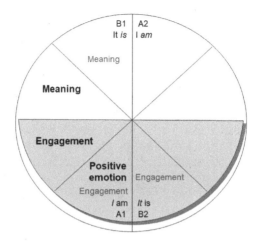

Figure 56. Authentic Happiness and the human paradox

"Engagement" is a little harder to pin down – not least because Seligman has changed his language about it. By engagement, he means a completely absorbing activity, one in which you can "merge with the object." But he points out that this can be a solitary, even solipsistic endeavour, a completely self-absorbing activity or "flow." The term Seligman originally used for engagement was "gratification." It's one side of "positive emotion." The gratifications are "activities we *like* doing." They "absorb and engage us fully." Engagement is perhaps a more "abundant and authentic gratification" than pure pleasure, but it is still a form of self-assertion.[98] The combination of purposefulness, drive, intellect, objectification, and self-absorption implied in Seligman's use of the term "engagement" suggests to me that it spans the virtues of Liberty (A1) and Equality (B2), perhaps especially the virtues of Power (A1a, with their emphasis on agency and primal drive), Pleasure (A1b, the home of "liking" and desire – engagement was, after all, originally a component of "positive emotion"), and Rights (B2a, with their emphasis on the rational, objective intellect).

You can see the elements of Martin Seligman's Authentic Happiness mapped onto the human paradox, in Figure 56 above.

Figure 56 confirms the impression I drew from Figures 51 and 53, that positive psychology spans both the virtues of self-assertion and those of reverence, but tilts toward self-assertion. But Figure 56 also has the surprising result of reversing the emphasis between the right and left-hand sides of the figure. Whereas positive psychology's virtues were over-represented on the right (or more reverential side) before, the elements of Authentic Happiness are grouped mostly on the left (or more self-assertive) side in Figure 56. It's as if the implicit emphasis in the inventory of the virtues were made more explicit in the elements of Authentic Happiness.

Seligman himself eventually recognized that the proposed elements of Authentic Happiness were incomplete and now links the virtues instead to the wider theory of "well-being," or what he sometimes calls "flourishing." For Seligman and some other "well-being" theorists, well-being has five elements – the original three from Authentic Happiness, plus two more: accomplishment and positive relationships.[99]

Accomplishment is, again, very easy to locate on my map of the human. Accomplishment reflects the fact that people pursue success, accomplishment, winning, achievement, and mastery *for their own sakes*. Seligman calls this element of well-being the "achieving life," a life dedicated to accomplishment for the sake of accomplishment.[100] This is the very definition of self-assertion and of the virtues of Power (A1a) in particular – that is, self-assertion merely for the sake of self-assertion itself.

"Positive relationships," like "engagement," is a little trickier to locate. As in the case of the Competing Values Framework (in chapter 13), the language used about this element of well-being can be misleading. It often has overtones of the self-giving characteristic of the virtues of reverence. But the bottom line is how relationships can serve the self. The item used to measure the element of personal relationships in a landmark European well-being study, for example, is: "There are people in my life who really care *about me*."[101] So what's really meant here is a virtue of self-assertion. Personal relationships are important for what you can get out of them, that is, happiness or well-being. What you *get* is just as important as what you give – even the *purpose* of giving. There are overtones of reverence, but the primary focus is on the self. I think the word "relationships" is the key here. A two-way street. The main virtues implied by the "positive relationships" element of well-being are the virtues of Reciprocity (B2b), virtues that can lean toward their close neighbour, the virtues of Love (A2b), but which are firmly located below the line, among the virtues of self-assertion, closely allied to the virtues of Rights (B2a).

With this in mind, you can see how I locate the elements of positive psychology's well-being framework in the nature of the human, in Figure 57 on page 353.

Figure 57 restores some of the balance between the right and left-hand sides of the map of the human, that is to say, between the more

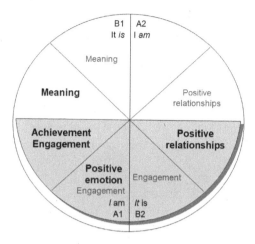

Figure 57. Flourishing: well-being and the human paradox

reverent and more assertive sides of both self-assertion and reverence. But the upper right-hand corner, which was so densely populated in Figure 55, is now comparatively empty, especially the virtues of Reverence[3] (A2a), which received such remarkable attention in positive psychology's initial inventory of the virtues. Above all, Figure 57 confirms the overall impression that positive psychology offers a vision of the human remarkably open to the virtues of reverence but rooted more firmly, nevertheless, in the virtues of self-assertion. In this sense, it perhaps reflects the broader Western, post-modern culture from which it springs. It seems to be the view of the human to which you might come if you found yourself at the top of the spiral staircase pictured in Figure 26 on page 220, with a view out over the whole nature of the human, but from our current vantage point in the virtues of self-assertion – and, within them, increasingly, in the virtues of Liberty (A1). It seems to be a vision of the whole nature of the human but filtered through the lens of self-assertion.

Positive psychology and the human paradox

As I hope you can tell, I'm a big fan of positive psychology, just as I'm a big fan of evolutionary psychology, Moral Foundations Theory, the Competing Values Framework, and Relational Models Theory. Like them, I think positive psychology has enormous potential to turn our Western culture in a much more positive direction – no pun intended. Its greatest value is the rediscovery of the virtues as the building blocks of our humanity and of a good human life. After three hundred years of Western focus on the mind (or on its opposites, the unconscious and the libido), positive psychology unhesitatingly asserts that the definition or nature of the human – the idea of humanity – must be found, instead, in the human virtues.

Positive psychology is yet another important contemporary initiative that restores awareness of the human virtues and their role in the nature of the human – or in what positive psychology calls human "character." It shows us, again, that the condition for nourishing better individual human beings and better human societies is learning again how to cultivate, propagate, and practise the variety of good habits we call virtues. For this reason, positive psychology – together with cultural and evolutionary psychology, Moral Foundations Theory, the Competing Values Framework, and Relational Models Theory – may even represent an important potential turning point in Western culture. The beginning of a wider rediscovery of the full nature of the human.

What would positive psychology require to do that?

Well, one thing it needs – to achieve a more accurate description of the human – is greater awareness of how the virtues interact and reinforce each other across the families of virtues. In its initial classification of the virtues, positive psychology sometimes seems to assume that, if a virtue requires or resembles another virtue, it must belong to the same family. Because integrity requires courage, for example, courage and integrity must belong to the same family of virtues. Or, because prudence and humility both require forms of "self-denial," they too must belong to the same family.[102] I think these assumptions are mistaken and derive from an insufficient sense not only of the subtle contrasts between virtues but also of the unity of the virtues and the way in which the families of virtues interact, influence, and support each other. The virtue of courage, for example, enters not just into integrity but into *every other virtue* because it alone can give them the strength to prevail against obstacles.[103] Even reason requires courage to work properly in the first place and to be effective in the world.[104] No virtue can exist without courage. But that doesn't make them all part of the same family as courage.

Another thing that would enrich positive psychology is even greater awareness of the structuring principle of the human world: the role of paradox and contradiction. Perhaps because they eschewed any organizing principle in their initial classification of the virtues, Peterson and Seligman assembled their initial inventory with little overt acknowledgment of the contradictions between them.[105] Their original inventory gives little hint of the "contradiction between competing values" that gives "ethical life a history"[106] – the kinds of contradictions you saw in the Competing Values Framework, for example, in chapter 13. As you saw in Figure 53, Christopher Peterson does recognize the most basic, inescapable, and universal contradiction – the paradox of self-assertion and reverence, of self-*seeking* and self-*giving* – the basic human paradox Moral Foundations Theory calls our "dual nature." He calls the two sides of the human paradox "focus on self" and "focus on others." His model of the "structure of character" is based on the tension between these two basic poles of the human: where the tension is greater, the virtues are plotted farther apart, and where the tension is less, they're located closer together.[107] (This is similar to my organizing principle that proximate families of virtues "lean" toward each other, while less proximate families "lean" away.)

But elsewhere positive psychology sometimes gives the impression the virtues (or "character strengths") are all aligned. That they're consistent, harmonious, and mutually reinforcing. That you can have them all without too much difficulty, if only you have the right exercises, seminars, education, institutions, or psychological instruments. Consistent with a vantage point in the virtues of Liberty (A1), it can create the overall impression of a drive for instrumental control. Martin Seligman, for example, sometimes seems to imply we can solve most of our human problems with the right measurements, formulas, equations, or training. That, with all these in sufficient abundance, human life can be a "natural progress of win-win."[108]

There's much to be encouraged and applauded about this can-do, positive, up-beat, optimistic attitude. You can't do anything without it – without, that is to say, the virtues of Liberty (A1a). But if positive psychology is going to take us anywhere genuinely human, it needs to be equally aware of the difficulties and obstacles that arise from the virtues themselves, and from their contradictory nature. Even the best ideas, as Hegel says, can descend into "triteness" if they lack "the earnestness, the pain, the patience and the work of the negative."[109] Positive psychology runs this risk. Any approach to the human that doesn't pay enough attention to the paradoxical, self-contradictory character of the virtues is missing out on the pathos, the struggle, the conflict, the ambiguity, the anxiety, the comedy, the nobility, the deep seriousness, and, sometimes, even the tragedy that make human life genuinely human.[110] It is because of their deep understanding of these paradoxes and contradictions that writers like Pascal, Shakespeare, and Tolstoy are among the greatest witnesses to the nature of the human.[111] Greater awareness of the paradoxical nature of the virtues isn't incompatible with the construction of psychological instruments, as Jung's work and

Peterson's own model of the "structure of character" show. Deepening the logic of this model would offer a lens through which to reassess the content of positive psychology's initial virtue clusters.

Above all, greater awareness of the human paradox would help deepen positive psychology's most important discoveries. If you look back at Figure 55 on page 349, you'll see that the two quadrants of the virtues of Liberty (A1) and Reverence (A2) – the two "existential" quadrants of "I am" – are densely populated with important human virtues – even more densely than the virtues of Equality (B2), and, especially, the virtues of Excellence (B1), the two "cognitive" (or ontological) quadrants of "It is." This is a remarkable fact. For almost three thousand years, and especially in the last four hundred years (as you'll see again in the next chapter), Western culture has been increasingly inclined to identify the human with the cognitive and intellectual virtues, with reason and the rational mind. Yet positive psychology implicitly proclaims the central importance of an entirely different set of *existential* virtues, some of which our Western world has almost forgotten.

The contemporary, post-modern Western world might not have much difficulty acknowledging the virtues of Liberty (A1), the virtues of "*I* am." They now provide us with our increasingly dominant cultural lens. But positive psychology implicitly declares the *equal* importance of the *other* family of existential virtues, the virtue of Reverence, or "I *am*" (A2) – including the virtues of Love (A2b, which it calls, significantly, "Humanity"), and even the virtues of Reverence[3] (A2a), which Peterson and Seligman call "Transcendence."

Positive psychology not only rediscovers the virtues as the definition of the human, it also unhesitatingly identifies the virtues of reverence as the key to our humanity and to genuine human happiness, or flourishing. Whereas the virtues of self-assertion are necessary for "achievement," positive psychology affirms that happiness and life satisfaction are more frequently associated with the virtues of reverence: with the virtues found "north of the equator," as Christopher Peterson puts it, in the two top quadrants of the "structure of character" or the human paradox.[112]

In rediscovering the vital importance of the virtues of reverence – the virtues located "north of the equator" in the map of the human – positive psychology links up with the cultural and evolutionary psychology of Richard Shweder and Jonathan Haidt – and, before them, with the insights of C.G. Jung. In the context of contemporary Western social science, this is an extraordinary development. And possibly a harbinger. Maybe this striking convergence is a contemporary sign that the virtues of "*I* am" (A1) ultimately point forward, again, to the virtues of "I *am*" (A2).

Psychology and the educational contract

Richard Shweder's three "ethics," Jonathan Haidt's Moral Foundations Theory, and Christopher Peterson and Martin Seligman's "positive psychology," like the work of C.G. Jung on psychological types, point us to an objective of wholeness or completeness, both for individuals and for social groups.

In groups, as the popularity of the MBTI in contemporary organizations suggests, understanding the enormous variety of human personality types helps us appreciate and value the diversity of the human. It shows how much we need each other in order to achieve anything that can be called fully human.

The social contract that binds us can and should also be understood as what I have been calling an "educational contract." Because we are all constructed in different ways, each one of us can only see a portion of the truth. The world will look quite different to the personality type the MBTI calls an "ESTJ" (Extraverted, Sensing, Thinking, and Judging) than it will to an "INFP" (Introverted, Intuitive, Feeling, and Perceiving) for example. It will look entirely different to someone who cares only for Shweder's ethics of autonomy than it will to those who acknowledge the ethics of community or divinity. It will look very different to someone who gives highest or exclusive importance to what Moral Foundations Theory calls the virtues of Authority or Sanctity than to someone who values only the virtues of Liberty or Fairness. It will also look different to someone whose "signature strengths" are located in the virtue clusters of Courage and Temperance rather than in what Peterson and Seligman call "Humanity" and "Transcendence." It will be, literally, a different world.[113]

So the only way to achieve a more complete or truer picture of reality is to combine the insights to be gained from *all* our different psychological perspectives and families of virtues. Only the combination of all of them – in both their irreducible contradiction and their ultimate complementarity – will yield the full truth about the human or about the human world. "[I]f different points of view could be fully integrated or synthesized," says Richard Shweder, "they would not count as different points of view."[114]

That means we should regard ourselves as bound together by an educational contract, an obligation to achieve, together, a richer, fuller, and more complete vision of reality than we can achieve alone. A society, polity, or organization animated by the spirit of such an educational contract will be a finer, nobler, and ultimately more human place than it could otherwise be. I will return to this theme in my final chapters.

But completeness is an important ideal for individual human beings, too. This was a theme C.G. Jung himself frequently emphasized. "To round itself out," he said, life calls "for completeness."[115] We should "modestly strive to fulfil ourselves," he urged, "and to be as complete human beings as possible."[116] He pointed out that "completeness" and "wholeness" are closely connected to the idea of "healing": "The meaning of 'whole' or 'wholeness' is to make holy or to heal." One of the ways to achieve this kind of psychic wholeness or healing is through the affirmation of the *whole* nature of the human as displayed in Figures 43 to 56 in this chapter. It is the idea of the self as a "psychic totality": "the individual who possesses the four gates to the world, the four psychological functions."[117]

As this suggests, a necessary step to this kind of psychic wholeness or completeness is the discovery that the ego isn't the same thing as the self. As you can see in Figure 47 on page 329, the ego is at best only one half of the self, perhaps even less, perhaps a quarter (A1), or even an eighth (A1a). The ego is merely the self-preserving, self-maintaining, self-asserting core of human dispositions – "the impulse to mastery" – from which all energy proceeds and from which all life begins.[118] It is absolutely essential to human life. "Compared to it," says Jung, "even the external world is secondary, for what does the world matter if the endogenous impulse to grasp it and manipulate it is lacking?"[119]

But important as it is, the ego is not the whole story. It is "part of the personality but not the whole of it."[120] The self, on the other hand, is the "totality of the personality." It is all four poles of the human paradox – with all their cascading paradoxes generated by the polarizing dynamic of separative projection, as depicted in Figures 43 to 56 and elsewhere in this book. The fourfold nature of the human is what Jung himself calls a "magic circle" with "four gates," "where all the split-off parts of the personality are united."[121]

The ego is not the centre of this total or complete self. Or it is not the only one. As all the world's spiritual traditions have recognized, there's also another centre in the psyche, one that Jung refers to as a "non-ego centre."[122] What and where this other non-ego centre is, and what it does, are questions central to all the world religions.[123]

But before I get to this, I need to take you on a tour through the Western philosophical traditions. That may help you to see how we Westerners have lost sight of this other non-ego centre. And how these traditions themselves point us back to it.

15

Philosophy

What has Athens to do with Jerusalem?

That's the famous question posed by Tertullian (ca. 160–225 CE), a second-century Christian writer. Tertullian's question has been interpreted and answered in many ways since he asked it. For a long time it was taken – at least by Christians – to imply the superiority of the spiritual traditions rooted in "Jerusalem." And so their answer often was that the philosophical learning which comes down to us from the Greek culture of ancient Athens could hold little interest for them.

At other times the question has been taken instead to assume the superiority of "Athens." The answer has therefore been the opposite: the philosophical traditions born in Athens have nothing to learn from the spiritual traditions rooted in Jerusalem. At still other times, the answer has been that the traditions stemming from Athens and from Jerusalem are very closely related, perhaps much more closely than many suspect.[1]

From yet another perspective, it might be suggested that Tertullian's question anticipated almost the whole history of Western philosophy and its most important issue.[2] Viewed from this other angle, it can be interpreted instead as a question about the relationship between what David Hume was later to call "is" and "ought." A question about the relationship between sense perception and other kinds of perception: the relationship between reason and morality, between thinking and behaviour, between information and meaning, between thought and action, between thinking and feeling, between mind and heart, between being and love. Between self-assertion and reverence.

In other words, Tertullian's contrast between Athens and Jerusalem confronts us with many of the same dualities you encountered in the previous chapter about the human psyche. C.G. Jung's "four gates" to the human spirit seem to distinguish and to cluster the thinkers and even the periods of what was to become the Western philosophical tradition almost as clearly as they do ourselves and our own individual psyches.

In this chapter I will survey briefly the course of Western philosophy so you can see how each philosopher and philosophical school became a spokesperson for a particular human stance and its corresponding family of human virtues, for some specific aspect or corner of the human paradox.[3] But it may be helpful to begin, as Tertullian's question invites us to do, by considering the prehistory of the Western philosophical traditions. In the Introduction, I mentioned that we need to give due attention both to our "deep past" and our potential "deep future" in order to rediscover the nature of the human. In this chapter the "deep past" will be especially important because getting some perspective on the assumptions about the human our Western philosophical traditions have been gradually building up for us over the last three thousand years or so will require stepping outside them. Looked at from *inside* those traditions, each phase or individual philosopher can be seen to represent some individual strand in the whole nature of the human. But looked at from *outside*, the whole Western philosophical tradition *itself* can be seen, instead, as merely one strand in a larger story about the human.

Understanding that larger story is one of the aims of this book.

Our deep past: the prehistory of Western philosophy

One of the difficulties in any enterprise of thought is the challenge of gaining some perspective on it. The challenge of getting *outside*: outside the reality you want to think about *and* outside the way you think about it. Outside your thought itself.

The first is impossible. We can never get outside the totality of what exists in order to see it as it really is.[4] We're stuck inside. So there will always be something necessarily mysterious and unknown about reality.[5] No explanation could ever include everything, and the details of any explanation would always be influenced by what we have left out. Because we can never get outside the totality of our world to gain some perspective on it, we can never really see it, or understand it, as it is.

But the second challenge – getting outside rational thought – is equally difficult. We're the prisoners of our own thinking process, in at least two ways.

One is that we're time-bound and culture-bound. We're born into an ongoing conversation: the conversation of our family, of our country, and of our own modern and post-modern Western culture. We learn to think in the ways the conversation will allow. In the Introduction, I mentioned Hans-Georg Gadamer's insight that history "does not belong to us, we belong to it."[6] So we can never fully see the assumptions built right into the conversation itself. We can't see what it takes for granted and what it excludes or makes impossible for us to think. We can only think with the tools and assumptions given to us by our time and culture. We can't get outside them. We can change them. But we do so from the *inside*, using the very tools and assumptions given to us by our time and culture. R.G. Collingwood called these assumptions "absolute presuppositions," "absolute" because you can't normally get behind them, or can only do so with very great difficulty.[7]

A second problem – the one I want to explore here – is that we have to think about thought from the *inside* of thought itself. There isn't any other way to think. As soon as you begin to think about something, you're *already* thinking! It's very difficult to think about thought *from the outside*. The only way you can try to get some perspective on rational thought is *by using the tools of thought itself.*[8] This is an obvious self-contradiction. But, unfortunately, it's unavoidable. It's almost impossible to get some perspective on thought from *outside* thought.

Almost impossible. But perhaps not quite.

One way to get at least some perspective on thought itself may be to think about what I called our "deep past." To think about humans *before* they had the tools of what we now think of as rational thought. Or about what humans are like when they *aren't* using those tools. When we're living mainly in some other mode or modes. As we still are, most of the time.

That's one of the reasons the "deep past" is so important. The prehistory of Western philosophy might allow you to get some perspective on what we now think of as rational thought. It might help you to see not just how the thinkers of the Western tradition are spokespersons for the four stances of the human paradox, but also how that tradition itself is only one part of a much larger story about the human. If you could understand what humans were like *before* they had the tools of rational thought, that would help reintroduce you to an earlier and, possibly, deeper nature of the human. The "deep past" can help you get some perspective on human thought: to see it as only one or perhaps several strands in the story of the human, not the story itself, as we Westerners are often tempted to think. And it might also help you to see how those earlier, deeper parts of the human are very much alive in our modern and post-modern world, though we rarely have the eyes to see them. Or ears to hear.

From episodic to mythic culture

The process of rational human thought we associate with the Western philosophical tradition is a relatively recent development in human culture. It goes back less than three thousand years. Plato and Aristotle, the founders of Western philosophy, lived in the Athens of fifth century BCE, only about twenty-four hundred years ago. But by that time, as I pointed out in the Introduction, our hominid ancestors had already been living on this planet for well over two million years, and our own immediate human family – *homo sapiens* – had been evolving for about 500,000 years or so.[9] Over that time they had gradually developed pre-human and human cultures that allowed them not only to survive but also to occupy most of the planet, and develop gradually higher levels of human organization and "civilization." But those cultures had only relatively "recently" developed such distinctive human tools as language. The development of *written* forms of language – the necessary prelude for the kind of developed, rational thinking we associate with Western philosophy – was even more recent.

But even *without written language*, human beings had already developed much of what we now associate with human culture and with the nature of the human. Merlin Donald (b. 1939), a Canadian cultural psychologist and cognitive theorist, suggests that the nature of the human had already evolved through three distinct stages on the road to the culture of ancient Athens, where the Western philosophical tradition was born. None of these earlier stages has been lost from human culture. Each of the successive stages in human evolution encapsulates and retains the earlier ones. In fact, most of our modern and post-modern lives are actually still lived in some of the earliest human modes, *not* in the latest.

The first stage in the evolution of the human is what Merlin Donald calls "episodic" culture. This was the culture humans shared – and still share – with some animals, especially the higher primates. In an episodic culture, life is lived only in the present, as a "series of concrete episodes," and the only things creatures at this level seem to be able hold in their memory are the traces or images of these events.[10]

But even at this stage, the very earliest humans – or those hominids who were to become humans – had already begun to develop some of the key features of human culture. About four million years ago, the primate ancestors of modern humans (known as *australopithecines*) ceased to live in trees and began to move about on two feet. This new form of life would have been extremely dangerous and might have led to their early extinction, were it not for the fact that they began to develop important new social dispositions and skills, including the establishment of campsites, pair-bonding between males and females (which reduced aggression), and a more cooperative approach to the nurture of infants and obtaining food.[11] These new social dispositions were extended by our first clearly hominid ancestors.[12] Between two million and 500,000 years ago, they developed seasonal home bases, social organization, the use of fire and tools, the beginnings of a cooperative approach to hunting, and semi-permanent male-female bonding.[13] These were extremely important developments that distinguished hominids from the higher apes and began to lay the basis of human culture. The disposition of self-assertion was already beginning to be modified by a new disposition of reverence.

Merlin Donald speculates that the link between the episodic culture of our animal origins and later human cultural forms was provided by what he calls "mimetic" culture. The really important turning point for later hominids – including our ancestor *homo sapiens*, who emerged somewhere between 500,000 and 200,000 years ago – was the discovery they could *represent* the episodes of episodic culture – both to themselves and to others – through mimetic techniques. "Mimesis" is the skill of using the body to re-enact or re-present an event or relationship. It's not exactly the same as imitation or mimicry (which are also used by some animals), though it builds on them. It adds a representational and intentional dimension to them: "it involves the *invention* of intentional representations."[14] Mimetic techniques use a wide range of physical actions and modes for purposes of intentional expression – tone of voice, facial expression, eye movement, gestures of all kinds, posture, whole-body movements. And mimesis can put all these together in long sequences for the purpose of representational expression. All of this without any spoken language at all. Voice was already important – especially when combined with facial expressions to communicate a wide range of emotion – but it was still only sound (the "prosodic" aspect of the voice), a kind of rudimentary, non-verbal song.[15]

One of the devices that held all this together was the discovery of rhythm. Rhythm is a uniquely human invention (but one that builds on deep biological processes) and is the "quintessential mimetic skill."[16] It is used to integrate mimetic techniques into the wider social patterns of play, games, dance, song and, especially, ritual. Ritual is a vital part of mimetic culture, integrating the group or tribe into a single social whole through rhythmic collective actions in which individuals play specific roles, and through which they express their social identity. Through ritual humans began to express both their sense of belonging but also their intuitive understanding of the world, their initial sense of meaning and value.

Mimetic culture seems to have reinforced the developing human capacities for working cooperatively. By about 250,000 years ago early *homo sapiens* were banding together to hunt large game on a regular basis, and this required highly developed capacities for cooperation, not just in the hunt but also in the equitable sharing of the spoils.[17] Mimetic culture also supported increased social cooperation in cooking food, expressing social bonding, nurturing children, and teaching skills across the generations within an increasingly stable social structure. Mimetic culture continued and expanded the pattern already initiated in episodic culture for an extended period of child-rearing. Passing on the customs of mimetic culture required even more time, and more intensive and attentive nurture.[18] Our ancestors were developing what Robert Bellah calls a "disposition to nurture," a new human disposition that challenged – or even began to match – the original human disposition to dominate.[19] Deepening of child nurture together with the rhythmic games, dances, and ritual of mimetic culture contributed to developing an increased capacity for emotional expression, including emotive (but still non-linguistic) vocalization. The motive of these early still non-linguistic vocalizations probably wasn't communication, as our post-modern "rational" outlook might lead us to assume, but rather *communion*, a heightened sense of the unity, solidarity, and strength of the band or tribe.[20] Mimesis allowed these early humans to model the emotional aspects of their world, both their own emotions and those of others. Understanding the feelings of others contributed to social bonding but it also, crucially, allowed these human ancestors to break out of the "egocentricity of the episodic mind."[21] The human family was moving even farther along the path from self-assertion to reverence.[22]

The next stage in the evolution of the human, beginning somewhere between 200,000 and 50,000 years ago, was the transition from mimetic culture to what Merlin Donald calls "mythic" culture. Undoubtedly the most important development in this period was the emergence of language, first in the form of oral speech.[23] The cultures of the mimetic period had prepared the way for this development by expanding the range of human perception and feeling. Rituals, for example, led naturally to the development of "emblematic" gestures which were already primitive symbols or perceptual metaphors, and to their corresponding mental models which pushed toward the means for their expression.[24] Northrop Frye (1912–91) developed a theory of "phases" of language that almost exactly corresponds to Merlin Donald's theory of cultural evolution and the arrow of virtue described in this book. He describes the language of this second or mythic culture as "poetic," or the language of metaphor: "In this period there is relatively little emphasis on a clear separation of subject and object: the emphasis falls on the feeling that subject and object are linked by a common power or energy."[25]

Judged by the evidence of surviving Stone Age cultures, it appears that language was invented for purposes we might now consider surprising. It doesn't seem to have emerged for the practical purposes we might expect, like weapon-making or cooking, but for the more *im*practical purposes of *meaning-making*, through storytelling and myth-making, developments that grew directly out of the rituals of the previous mimetic culture. This wasn't a late development in the evolution of language: it seems to have come first.[26] "The primary human adaptation was not language *qua* language," Donald suggests, "but rather integrative, initially mythical thought."[27]

A mythic culture is a narrative culture. It tells stories.[28] Narrative was probably the driving force behind the development of language; language, at this stage of human development, was primarily for telling stories. Narrative was the primary product of the new verbal language, especially in the form of myth, the distilled form of narrative, hammered out over generations and centuries. Mythical stories gave shape and meaning to life and were the dominant organizing force in the new verbal but preliterate societies, controlling all behaviour and even the very perception of reality.[29]

Mythic culture transformed the preceding mimetic culture: not by abolishing it but by embracing it, and by further developing most of its tendencies and potential. The rituals, symbols, songs, dances, and games of mimetic culture were retained and even *strengthened* in their organizing and motivating power by becoming embedded in a narrative, mythic framework that could explain their "origins" and meaning. In this kind of culture, myth penetrates every aspect of daily life. It gives value and significance to every object and event: to clothing, food, and shelter, and to the family and group activities of everyday life. Myth created a new potential for integrating all these disconnected elements into a meaningful whole. Mimetic culture had still been limited to individual episodes. Mythical culture could connect these episodes, drawing out their underlying meaning and significance. Through storytelling, mythic culture infused human life with value and meaning.[30]

By about 50,000 years ago, human moral life was already "basically complete," as Christopher Boehm puts it: "We had both a sense of virtue and a sense of shameful culpritude, and we understood the importance of human generosity well enough to promulgate our predictable golden rules across the face of a then thinly populated planet. We were a people who in important ways had conquered our own abundant selfishness [i.e., self-assertion] – even though that conquest required active vigilance."[31] From that time, these distinctively human virtues began increasingly to be supported, protected, and nourished within a cultural life structured by ritual, stories, symbols, dance, chants, masks, body decoration, and costumes. Starting 50,000 years ago, our human ancestors experienced a cultural explosion. Their physical evolution stabilized, while cultural change accelerated dramatically.[32] Human life was becoming almost entirely ritualized, but now in a much more powerful way. It was becoming what we would now call "religious."[33] Tribal society is "permeated by religion."[34] Religious life and social life were now "inseparable."[35] They were the same thing. They had become what anthropologists call a "total social fact." Social and even "political" life assumed a religious form, giving great importance to the custodians of myth and leaders of ritual activities, such as shamans.[36]

Human culture had come, in Merlin Donald's words, "full circle."[37]

The great reversal

Or perhaps it would be more accurate to say that it had swung around some 180 degrees, to the opposite point from which it had started.

Humans (or pre-humans – those who would become modern humans) had broken out of the "egocentricity" of the episodic outlook so completely that the self was now entirely embedded in a collectivity: the ritual norms and needs of the *whole* group or tribe largely determined *individual* norms and roles. Determined them not in some external way but in a way that was entirely *internalized*: individuals were fulfilled by their *willing* submission to the whole, and to the meaning and value that came from participating in this larger whole.[38]

Self-assertion had not disappeared. But it had now become embedded in a culture of reverence. In this new context, self-assertion could still be employed, against those *outside* the group or tribe for example, as a form of collective self-assertion. And it could also be employed *internally* against bullies, alpha males, and "free riders" who wanted to impose their will on the group from inside.[39] Such "upstarts" were kept in place and controlled by the internal self-assertion of the group or tribe as a whole.[40] Self-assertion could – and would, especially in later cultural phases – also be used as an instrument of reverence itself, to deepen religious individuality within the group.[41] But these very early humans were now living in a culture almost entirely dominated by a disposition to reverence. This is the culture Relational Models Theory (as you saw in chapter 11) calls "communal sharing." It is the natural default culture of all band and tribal societies. Generosity, as Christopher Boehm notes, is a "major virtue" in every hunter-gatherer culture.[42]

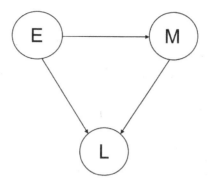

Figure 58. From episodic to mimetic to mythic/linguistic culture[43]

Merlin Donald depicts the development of human culture from epi-sodic to mimetic to mythic culture in a triangular graphic image which you can see in Figure 58 above.

The E in the top left circle stands for episodic and the M in the top right circle for mimetic. The arrow between them indicates that mi-metic culture incorporates and preserves the whole of episodic culture, but not the reverse. The unidirectional arrows from the top circles to the bottom show that all the contents of both episodic and mimetic cultures are directly available to mythic culture (but, again, not the reverse), rep-resented here by a capital L, for language. An L is used here, presum-ably, because another M would have created confusion by duplicating the one at the top standing for mimetic – but also because spoken lan-guage is the crucial enabler for the emergence of mythic culture. And because mythic culture is only the first stage in an evolving linguistic culture, as you will see.

But I can also translate the evolution of the human portrayed in Fig-ure 58 into the basic image I've been using throughout this book. If the first three stages of human evolution are a progression from the "ego-centricity" of episodic culture (*I* am) to a mythic culture saturated with reverence (I *am*) – passing through the middle stage of mimetic culture, the essential bridge from the first to the third – they would then appear as in Figure 59 on page 368.

I could also describe this three-stage evolution of the nature of the hu-man in the language of C.G. Jung, from the previous chapter. If you think about Figure 59 in the terms of Figure 44 (on page 323), for example, it's plausible to think of episodic culture as a culture of "sensing with feel-ing." That's how animals and the higher primates live. But, as you just saw, sensing with feeling led gradually, in human evolution, to intuitions

Figure 59. From episodic to mimetic to mythic culture (2)

about meaning, expressed through symbolic, mimetic acts. So the next stage was a mimetic culture based increasingly on intuition with feeling. But the experience of meaning expressed through the symbols of mimesis eventually led to the discovery of spoken language, and to a mythic culture – now solidly rooted in *intuition with feeling* – in which collective meaning could also be expressed through narrative and storytelling.

Whether expressed in terms of the human virtues or of human psychology, this wasn't the end of the story. The contradictions of the human paradox continued to make themselves felt, ensuring that mythic culture evolved, in turn, into something else. These first three stages in the evolution of the human provide the essential prelude to the subject of this chapter, without which its own story – the career of Western philosophy – doesn't make sense.

The archaeology and architecture of Western philosophy

So far in this chapter, I've been exploring the prehistory of philosophy, not philosophy itself. But this prehistory is essential to understanding the career and structure of the Western philosophical tradition. The first three stages of human culture pose the questions to which the Western philosophical tradition supplies one kind of answer – or answers. Without awareness of this background – without awareness of the questions – these kinds of answers can't be fully understood.

You also need to keep in mind that each stage in the evolution of human culture preserves and encapsulates the previous stages. By the unidirectional arrows in Figure 58, Merlin Donald intends to show the perceptions, practices, and insights of each of the first two stages in human culture continue to be alive in the later ones. You can't fully understand a later stage if you restrict yourself to its own terms alone. You need to understand it from the wider perspective of the full range of the human.

For both these reasons – and because of the underlying nature of the human they reveal and express – these first three stages in human evolution continue to structure the Western philosophical tradition itself. The *archaeology* of the tradition is reflected and preserved in its *architecture*.

From mythic to theoretic culture

The first step in the next phase of Western culture – the shift from the prehistory of philosophy to its history proper – was the invention of *written* language.

In the evolution of the nature of the human, this was, as I said, a remarkably "recent" development. Advanced painting and drawing skills seem to have emerged about 25,000 years ago; the first ideographic writing goes back only 6,000 years; and phonetic writing was invented less than 4,000 years ago.[44]

In the full span of the human, this is only yesterday. By the time the phonetic alphabet was invented, humans had already been using spoken language for at least 45,000 years and possibly much longer. Over a period of some 200,000 years or so, they had developed not only elaborate *spoken* languages but also complex social structures with rich cultures of reverence, deeply infused with ritual and myth.[45]

When a major shift occurs in the evolution of the human, the first result often seems to be, paradoxically, not a challenge to the previous culture but rather its reinforcement. The *new* tools and capabilities are first put to work in service to the *old* paradigm. Before beginning to set off in a different direction, the new stage often takes the previous one to its greatest heights.

We can see this paradox at work in the shift from mythic culture to its successor. The height of mythic culture was reached well after the invention of written language, in what Karl Jaspers calls the "Axial" age, roughly 800–200 BCE.[46] The essence of the Axial age was the full development of the meaning of reverence.[47] As you will see again in the next chapter, this meant working out its deepest implications and requirements. Tribal cultures and – even more – the later hierarchical societies had retained many elements of our primordial self-assertion in their reverent cultures, with various forms of despotism, hierarchy, and violence – even religious violence, including, sometimes, human sacrifice.[48] The great spiritual leaders of the Axial age questioned these remnants of self-assertion and pushed toward even more demanding forms of reverence. They used the new language tools to point toward the potential of an even more radical shift *away* from self-assertion, toward still higher or deeper levels of reverence – toward a self-*giving* that required a kind of *un*selfing, or even, at the limit, the obliteration or complete "extinction" of the self-*seeking* self.[49]

The Axial age turned the idea of sacrifice upside-down.[50] Sacrifice had always played an important role in the religious life of mythic culture, as the giving up of a lower good to a higher good. But, in pre-Axial religious life, that meant the sacrificing of someone or something *else* to benefit yourself or your community. The Axial age discovered that true reverence requires, instead, the sacrifice of your *own* self.[51] It requires an inner "self-transformation" or *un*selfing.[52] In true Axial spirituality the virtues of the highest and lowest classes traded places, in spiritual teaching at least. The "servant" virtues such as humility and self-*giving* became the highest values; the old aristocratic, self-*seeking* values – of power, domination, and social prestige – became the lowest. The spirituality of the Axial age turned human culture upside-down, reversing the hierarchy of the virtues of Liberty (A1) and the virtues of Reverence (A2).[53]

This shift went farthest in the teaching of an Indian sage, Siddhartha Gautama Shakyamuni, later known as the Buddha, but it was also apparent to varying degrees in the other Indian Vedic traditions that developed into the Hindu spiritual tradition; in the Chinese traditions associated with sages such as Confucius, Laozi, and Zhuanzi; and, very prominently, in the prophets of Israel, such as Isaiah, Jeremiah, and Ezekiel.[54]

But even as the Axial age was bringing mythic culture to its highest point – by working out the full implications of reverence – the impact of the new written language, especially the phonetic alphabet, was already preparing the advent of a new stage in human evolution, a stage that was to lead in the opposite direction: to a fuller exploration of the virtues of self-assertion, even – at the extreme – to an obliteration (or submersion, or burial) of the virtues of reverence.

Merlin Donald calls this next stage "theoretic" culture. The difference between the emerging theoretic culture and the previous mythic culture is the distinction between *meaning* and *information*.[55] Whereas the narratives, metaphors, and symbols of mythic culture had aimed to express the *significance* or *value* of events, the new theoretic culture no longer gave such priority to significance or meaning. Its focus instead was now, increasingly, to establish the *facts*.[56] Rather than infusing events

Figure 60. From mythic to theoretic culture

with meaning and *linking them up*, by analogy, into greater wholes that could endow them with significance and value, the new theoretic culture began to *break things down* into discrete, separate units and facts. It started to dissect them and analyse them.[57] Instead of searching for meaning, it began to search instead for laws, formulas, principles, taxonomies, and "procedures for the verification of information."[58]

The central dynamic of mythic culture had been the search for the meaning of being ("I *am*"). The dynamic of the emerging theoretic culture was instead an encounter with the being of an objective *other* ("It *is*"). I can show this next shift in the evolution of the human as in Figure 60 above.

The shift from mythic to theoretic culture – depicted in the top quadrants of Figure 60 – entailed and signalled a number of related shifts I need to underline here. The first was a shift from a *verbal* to a *visual* culture. Written language was both a sign and a driver of this change. Writing is, after all, a *visual* medium of communication. But it was merely the last stage in a process of visuo-graphic invention, over some 200,000 years of human evolution, especially in the previous 40,000 years: from engraved bones and carvings; to cave drawings and paintings (between 37,000 and 10,000 years ago); to cuneiform writing (about 5,000 years ago); to syllabic script (about 2800 BCE); and finally to the Arabic, Hebrew, Aramaic, and Phoenician alphabets. The Phoenician alphabet was especially important because it was transmitted to Greece somewhere between 1100 and 700 BCE and became the basis of the first truly phonetic alphabet.[59]

The shift from a verbal to a visual culture carried implications far beyond written language itself. A verbal/aural culture is a world of the imagination. An interior world, not tied down to prosaic facts. A world of epic poetry and storytelling, of feeling, adventure, and heroic acts. You can listen to a story in the dark or with your eyes closed. A verbal culture isn't limited by the things you can see. You can hear a *voice* speaking to you, inside your head. A verbal culture is a spirit world, a world of mystery, filled with love, value, heroism, and meaning. A world of action and brave deeds. A world defined and encountered, above all, in the human *virtues*.[60]

A visual world, by contrast, is a world of *things*. A material world. A world you can see, study, understand, manipulate, and control. It's a rational world, a world to be approached not by the feelings (or not by the same feelings) but by the rational, controlling *mind*.[61]

The shift from a verbal to a visual culture also heralds the beginning of a gradual shift in the definition of the human. A shift in what is taken to be the centre of the human person. A shift from feeling to thought, from the saying to the said, from voice to word, from heart to head, from spirit to mind, from virtue to reason. From *ought* to *is*.

Henceforth Western culture would increasingly assume that everything important about the human was to be located in thought, in the mind. For the previous mythic culture, rational consciousness was simply one kind of virtue. For the new theoretic culture, virtue would gradually become simply one kind of fact.[62]

Northrop Frye calls the language of this first phase of theoretic culture (B1) "metonymic" because the verbal device of metonymy is a form of analogy ("this stands for that"), similar to the emerging, logical principle of identity (A=A), the flip side of the principle of non-contradiction. In this first phase of theoretic culture,

> language is more individualized, and words become primarily the outward expression of inner thoughts or ideas. Subject and object are becoming more consistently separated, and "reflection," with its overtones of looking into a mirror, moves into the verbal foreground. The intellectual operations of the mind become distinguishable from the emotional operations; hence abstraction becomes possible, and the sense that there are valid and invalid ways of thinking, a sense which is to a degree independent of our feelings, develops into the concept of logic.[63]

Hence, I could also describe this next stage in the evolution of the human in the language of the previous chapter once again. If mythic culture can be described as a culture of *intuition with feeling* – in which collective meaning was expressed through narrative and storytelling – the first stage of the new theoretic culture was a culture of *intuition with thinking*.

Intuition remained, for the time being, the critical *back*ground.[64] Human culture had not yet come "full circle" to its starting point in "sensing," as it would do later, in the second phase of theoretic culture. When this occurred, it would have profound consequences for the nature of the human because the otherness of an objective, material world (as you have already seen) calls on – or calls up – very different virtues than the otherness of the spirit.

But for now, the new theoretic culture was only beginning to emerge from the old mythic culture. The new was still deeply rooted, for the most part, in the old. The *fore*ground of the human, however, was gradually shifting from feeling to thinking.[65]

Greece: the birthplace of theoretic culture

Mythic and theoretic culture are the two poles Tertullian called "Jerusalem" and "Athens." If the height of mythic culture was achieved, in the Axial age, in places such as the Holy Land of Israel, theoretic culture had its birthplace in ancient Greece.[66]

Why Greece? I can only speculate on the reasons why theoretic culture emerged there first. I've already noted that Greek was the first truly phonetic written language, with the flexibility, economy, and power that went with a language not tied to pictures or ideographic symbols. A phonetic alphabet made possible a much wider spread of literacy because it required the learning of only some two dozen symbols instead of hundreds or even thousands.[67] The disconnection from pictorial symbols also allowed the development of less concrete, more abstract concepts and, eventually, "theories."

Another important factor was the evolving religious background of the eastern Mediterranean. Somewhere between 3000 and 2000 BCE, the people of the Mesopotamian region (east of Greece, in what is, more or less, the region of present-day Iraq) had begun to make a distinction between the king and the "god" whom the king served.[68] The king was no longer a "god-king," like the Egyptian pharaoh, but was simply a "tenant-farmer," exercising stewardship over a land that belonged to someone else. At about the same time, new myths also began to appear in which men were created by gods to serve them. The result of these new mythologies was a growing separation between this world and another one, a world *beyond* or outside this one. Joseph Campbell (1904–87) calls this new development "mythic dissociation"[69]: "Man was no longer in any sense an incarnation of divine life, but of another nature entirely, an earthly mortal nature. And the earth was now clay. Matter and spirit had begun to separate."[70]

This separation had many profound implications for human beings' understanding of the world and of themselves.

Because God or the gods were now to be found outside the world, the natural world could be separated from the spiritual world, and looked at objectively, that is to say, as an object, not as an emanation or expression of spirit. Nature was revealed in its neutral "otherness" as a field for exploration, rational understanding, *and control.* "God having become Other to the world," says Marcel Gauchet, "the world now became Other to humans, in two ways: by its *objectivity* at the level of *representation*, and by its ability to be *transformed* at the level of *action*."[71]

In the encounter with what now appeared to them as an "objective" nature, human beings also came face to face with their *own* otherness – both as individual *subjects* and as potential natural *objects* of study.[72] These two developments, as you've already seen, go together. Whereas mythic culture had tended to obliterate the individual in the unity of the whole, "mythic dissociation" allowed both nature and the human individual, paradoxically, to emerge in human culture. This was not completely new, but what occurred in the West went beyond even the Chinese traditions. Western religious culture was now based on a *relationship* rather than *identity* with the "other," so human beings (*half* of the relationship, after all) could take on a separate identity, distinct from the background. They now had a potential existence of their own, a new possibility of "freedom."[73] The emergence of an objective natural world prepared the way for the virtues of self-assertion, and vice versa.[74]

The gradual turn to "naturalism" that resulted from "mythic dissociation" was an important part of the background for the emergence of theoretic culture in ancient Greece. In a naturalized, objective "cosmos," even the gods could become naturalized and "humanized." The Greek gods were much more like human beings than those of the Egyptians or Babylonians further east had ever been.[75] The early – and perhaps legendary – Greek poet known as Homer (from whose works much of Greek culture developed) took this shift of perspective even farther. In his great epic poem the *Iliad*, the primary focus is no longer on the gods but on human beings. In Homer, a "revolution" has already occurred: a "transvaluation of all values in warfare and in life, a substitution of human ideals for the divine ideals that had previously been conventional."[76] For later Greek poets and playwrights it became a commonplace that "man should think the thoughts of man," or "mortal thoughts fit mortal minds."[77]

One reason mythic dissociation went as far as it did in Greece may be that Greek culture didn't participate very fully in the spiritual achievements of the Axial age.[78] With a few exceptions – some aspects of the thought of Plato, for example – Greece didn't share in discovering the complete meaning of reverence or the potential of *un*selfing. Like Vedic and Japanese cultures,[79] Greek culture remained largely aristocratic in outlook, continuing to cherish traditional upper class (even snobbish) values such as honour, courage, ambition, pride, power, hierarchy, wealth, magnificence, liberality, wit, charm, and the other social graces; and finding no place for key Axial values such as humility, modesty, or self-sacrifice.[80] In the Greek hierarchy of values, self-assertion and the "servant" virtues didn't trade places, as they did elsewhere further east. There was no Axial reversal of the virtues of Liberty (A1) and the virtues of Reverence (A2) in Greece. Relatively untouched by the Axial age, Greece remained largely an aristocratic, warrior culture.[81] Instead of the Axial spirit of *un*selfing, the new city states nourished a fierce competitive egotism, an "inherent" spirit of aggression – and tore themselves apart, as a result.[82] Greece remained a culture of self-assertion,[83] and the continuing value attached to self-assertion in Greece prepared the way for the discovery of that *new* form of self-assertion we now know as rational consciousness. It prepared the way for a shift of emphasis from feeling to thought. Aristotle was a warrior and explorer, too. Like Achilles and Odysseus. But a warrior and explorer in a new territory: the territory of the mind.[84]

Another factor preparing the way for the emergence of theoretic culture in Greece was its distinctive geography and political structure. The geography of Greece, its mountainous terrain, its isolation by sea, both as peninsula and archipelago, and the physical dispersion of "Greater Greece" stretching from Italy to Asia Minor, all supported a decentralized political structure with many small kingdoms: city-states small enough for individuals to have an influence on public affairs. In fact, at an early date, most of these city-states had already been transformed into "citizen-states," in which individual "citizens" participated, in various ways, in political decision-making. Greek cities were normally ruled by families of noble landholders who competed with each other, kept each other in check, and helped to maintain a roughly egalitarian society that was conducive to the emergence of the first functioning "democracy" in the Athens of the fifth-century BCE.[85]

Yet another factor was perhaps the climate of Greece and especially its distinctive light. Anyone who has visited Greece will have noticed the astonishing "Greek light" in which, to human sight, objects and landscapes seem to shine with a luminous, shimmering intensity: an almost painful clarity. So it isn't perhaps surprising that ancient Greece should have been the place where *sight* began to replace *voice* as the basis of Western culture.[86] Or where things and facts began to take precedence over feelings, values, and actions.

The culture of "Jerusalem" – the culture of the Axial age – was based on the fundamental insight that "I am"; indeed, it is the name which the people of Israel therefore gave to their God. But as you already saw in chapter 7, the earliest sustained piece of Greek philosophical reasoning – Parmenides' *Way of Truth* – began from the opposite premise: from the assumption that "it is."[87] The "starting point," Aristotle was shortly to say – announcing an entirely new era in human culture – "is the fact."[88]

Plato and Aristotle

Aristotle is the key turning point in the emergence of theoretic culture. But he was only the end of a long process that began with what are usually called the "presocratic" philosophers, such as Parmenides and the Pythagoreans, whom you already met in chapter 2.

The presocratics posed the questions to which the thought of Plato and Aristotle were the answers – or at least the Western tradition's first answers.[89] From the beginning of the sixth century BCE, thinkers located at the extremes of Greek settlement – Asia Minor, northern Greece, Sicily, and Italy – began to develop new ways of thinking about the world that were explicitly critical of the old mythic approaches and aimed instead to understand reality *theoretically*: to explain it, among other things, entirely in terms of the natural world and natural causation. One way they did this, for example, was to suggest that the world was entirely constructed from some basic substance. Thales and Anaximenes of Miletus suggested it might be water or air; Heraclitus of Ephesus suggested fire; Empedocles of Sicily proposed the four "roots" of earth, water, air, and fire; Anaximander of Miletus suggested some other indefinite ("unlimited") substance or nature. Another approach, suggested by Democritus of Abdera in northern Greece (among others), was that the world was constructed from invisible particles or *atoms*, and from the emptiness or void that surrounded them.

These new theories all assumed that the world was no longer to be understood as a site of mysterious powers or heroic deeds. It was instead an immanent "cosmos," an intelligible natural order that can be approached and understood *from inside*, as it were, from its own "natural" elements, principles or "substances" – and through the powers of human reason and thought that can grasp them. Feeling was becoming "objectified." It was building up "a whole objective world of perceptible things and verifiable facts."[90] This was the beginning of rational consciousness. Reality was no longer to be explained narratively or morally, but rather, rationally.[91]

The fundamental shift in human stance accomplished by the presocratics was truly "breathtaking."[92] It opened the door to a new theoretic culture and to a new world of things and facts – the world of "It is" – which can be analysed and subject to purely rational or intellectual judgment. These first stirrings of the new theoretic culture were still often embedded in aspects of the old mythic culture, including religious or quasi-religious cults. The presocratics didn't yet employ the language of detached, rational reflection: they still sounded more like "inspired oracles."[93] But they provided the challenging background to which the thought of the Athenian philosophers Plato and Aristotle aimed to respond in the middle of the fifth century BCE.

The thought of Plato can be interpreted as an attempt to determine what can and should be saved from the old mythic culture of reverence in the new circumstances where it was being challenged by the emerging theoretic culture's "scientific" or naturalistic explanation of nature: "Plato saw it as his task to unite the moral introspection for which [his mentor] Socrates [ca. 470–399 BCE] stood with the scientific knowledge represented by [the presocratic philosophers, such as] the Pythagoreans" you already encountered in chapter 2.[94] In his account of the death of Socrates, for example, Plato's hero explicitly challenges the new "scientific" world view of the presocratics, based exclusively on material causes, arguing that it entirely omits the very causes that are most important to a truly human world: the ideas of the good and the better, and the just and the more just.[95]

In other words, Plato stands as the first important bridge between the moral universe of the old mythic culture and the neutral, scientific outlook of the new theoretic culture which was to shape our modern and post-modern world. He stands in the doorway between them, looking backward as well as forward. His famous emphasis on all learning as a kind of "remembering" can even be interpreted as an implicit recognition that the deepest kind of thinking always reaches back, beyond thinking itself, to the earlier and deeper forms of the human from which theoretic culture was then emerging. Human beings can now "remember" human virtue because they already knew about it "before."[96]

Plato's own approach was rooted in the old mythic culture in many ways. Not only does he reach back to preserve the moral foundation of the mythic world, he often does so in the manner of the older culture, especially the dramatic form of his famous "dialogues." Although, like the presocratics, he explicitly rejected the mythic form employed by Homer, Plato still presented his own thought in a narrative, dramatic, conversational form rather than in discursive, analytic prose. In fact, the dramatic form of the dialogues points even further back: Hans-Georg Gadamer suggests they have a "mimetic character" because the emblematic human "presence" of their hero, Socrates, is ultimately more important – and more persuasive – than Plato's arguments, which, by themselves, are often "unconvincing."[97]

While Plato rejects myth with one hand, he invents it with the other. Some of his most important thought is presented not in a discursive or argumentative form but rather as story and myth. The famous myth of the cave in *The Republic*, for example. Or Aristophanes' story, in the *Symposium*, about the origin of human love in the primeval separation of the three original sexes; or Socrates' own story about his instruction in the higher meaning of love, by the prophetess, Diotima.[98] Whenever Plato has a particularly difficult argument to make, it's often presented in these kinds of narratives.

Plato's famous doctrine of "ideas" was no doubt his response to questions about the relationship between appearance and reality the presocratics' new "scientific" materialism had forced them to pose.[99] But it can also be understood as yet another way in which he tried to preserve the most important values of the old mythic culture against the challenge of the new theoretic one. A world formed exclusively by material causes would be a deterministic world: one in which there was no longer any scope for human striving or human goodness. The suggestion that the visible world is merely the dim reflection of the "eternal" ideas that lie behind it reopens room for human freedom and creativity, and thus for human goodness. The presocratics' new materialistic theories could not and did not remove the need for "thinking beyond the reality of this world."[100]

Plato's roots in the old mythic culture of reverence are also clear in his focus on human behaviour and action, especially virtue, friendship, and love, as well as in his characteristic spirit of "longing." If one wished to describe the fundamental temper that pervades all of Plato's works, it would be this kind of yearning or looking "beyond."[101] These are all linked. What makes humans human is their capacity for love, especially love of the good. The spirit of passionate friendship that runs through Plato – the spirit of *eros* – is, at bottom, a longing for the good. We reach out to our friends because we feel the lack of a good in ourselves. Our longing for the good makes us conscious of our own incompleteness, and we seek to be completed by the good to be found in others. The good person, says Plato, is "always yearning to reach after what is whole and complete, both human and divine."[102] But the lack we feel in ourselves already has a kind of "presence" of its own: a sort of *presence of absence.*[103] Friendship has its basis in this longing for an absent good. And in it the human person goes beyond self-assertion to reverence because such longing already has the "structure of self-transcendence" (or *un*selfing): someone capable of loving the good "transcends himself insofar as he longs for something not there."[104]

Plato and Aristotle represent different stages of the transition from mythic to theoretic culture. Aristotle was more advanced along this road. In fact, he embodies the new theoretic culture in one of its highest forms, the one that would dominate Western culture until the seventeenth century. He is the hinge, the key transitional figure, both announcing and creating the new theoretic world.[105] He rejected the method of his teacher, Plato, in the same way Plato had rejected that of Homer. His thought is now presented in the form of analytic discourse and argument, not in the dramatic, narrative form of Plato's dialogues. He no longer employs myth or story to convey his deepest thought but tries instead to build his arguments logically, rationally, prosaically, starting from the "facts."

Aristotle represents the new triumph of the fact in Western thought. The solution of any difficulty, he says, "consists in the discovery of the facts." Truth must be assessed in the "light" of the facts, according to the "test" of the facts: "if it accords with the facts we can accept it, but if it conflicts with them, we must regard it as no more than a theory."[106]

Reason is now the dominating force, not love. The ardent passion so prominent in Plato and Plato's protagonist, Socrates, has been replaced by a cooler, more distant rationalism. This heralds a new definition of the human. For the dominant current in Western thought, what makes humans *human* was henceforth to be found not in feeling or love but in the intellect. In the mind.[107] For Aristotle, the mind has become "the self of the individual." In his definition of the human, "the thinking part is, or most nearly is, the individual self."[108]

In identifying what is authentically and most fully human with thinking and with thought, Aristotle opened the door to an entirely new era in Western (and human) culture – in fact, to Western culture itself. Because thinking, as he himself recognized, is a "process toward assertion."[109] It is a form of self-assertion. In identifying what is most human with the mind, Aristotle thus played a crucial role in the evolution of the human. He paved the way, in the long run, for our modern and post-modern culture of self-assertion.[110]

And yet, on closer inspection, there turn out to be two Aristotles, not just one.[111] There's the Aristotle who explicitly turns his back on his mentor, Plato. But there's also the Aristotle who remains, in many respects, his pupil. Both of them can be seen, for example, in Aristotle's famous theory of the four kinds of "cause."

In chapters 2 and 3, I already introduced you to Aristotle's distinction between two kinds of cause: efficient and final causes. But I was simplifying the matter there. In fact, Aristotle broke these two down into two more. He identified two different kinds of natural cause, which he called "material" and "efficient" causes. Material cause means the substance from which things are made, such as the silver of a silver bowl. Efficient cause refers to the impact of one thing on another. As I suggested earlier, these are the causes which "push" or make things happen from behind, or below, or before, as it were, by a preceding event. They are the only kinds of cause which are recognized or can be recognized by modern science.

Aristotle fully accepted the emerging views of the "natural" philosophers about natural causation. But in addition to these two types of "natural" cause, he identified two other kinds of cause: those that "pull" us forward into the future, or make things happen from "ahead" or "above." Aristotle called one of them "formal" cause, by which he meant the tendency of all things to achieve their inner "form," the way an acorn seeks to achieve the "form" of an oak tree, or human genes achieve their adult form. The other (as you already saw in chapters 2 and 3) is called "final" cause, which means the goal, purpose, motivation, or "end" for which something is done.[112]

But Aristotle's formal and final causes are perhaps just Plato's *idea* by other names. The *cause* of being, for Aristotle, was its "form," specifically, a particular form combined with particular matter, just like Plato's ideas.[113] And his final cause serves the same purpose as *idea*, opening up room for purposive human goodness and freedom in what would otherwise be a deterministic world, ruled only by material and efficient causes.

Another important way Aristotle remains a disciple of Plato – and is thus still rooted in the mythic culture of reverence – is in the importance he also gave to the human virtues. Though he now located the essence of the human in the rational mind, Aristotle recognized the necessary link between reason and virtue. This works in two directions. Reason is a source of virtue. Indeed, Aristotle's definition of virtue is a "purposive *disposition* … determined by a rational principle."[114] Virtue now means acting in accordance with right reason. But reason itself is also a virtue, an intellectual virtue.[115] And reason can't function properly in the absence of the other virtues. The "eye of the soul," he acknowledged, can't function in the absence of virtue because "what is best … is not evident except to the good man; for wickedness perverts us and causes us to be deceived." Therefore it's impossible to be wise "without being good."[116] This means that "the good man's view is the true one."

And so "the standard by which we measure everything is goodness, or the good man *qua* good."[117]

So, which comes first? Reason or virtue? Mind or heart? Thinking or feeling? Thought or being? Self-assertion or reverence? Is this a vicious circle? Or a virtuous one? Is virtue simply a fact – a fact among other facts? Or is the human reason that knows facts a kind of virtue – one kind of virtue, among many others? The answers to those questions would now determine the whole future course of Western philosophy.[118]

By hanging onto mythic culture's reverence for the "divine," Aristotle put himself on one side of the many answers that could – and would – be given to those questions. Although the founder of theoretic culture, he was himself enough the product of mythic culture to assert that "perfect happiness" was a thing "too high" for purely "human attainment." A human being can only achieve true fulfilment, he argued, "in virtue of something divine within him." In pursuing our various pleasures, that's what we're *really* searching for, and *not* what we think: "because everything contains by nature something divine." Aristotle urged his students and readers not to listen to the poets and playwrights who counselled sticking to purely human thoughts. In words that would echo through the ages – and in many different contexts – he declared, instead, that "we ought as far as in us lies, to put on immortality." The divine element within us is, in fact, "the true self of the individual, since it is the authoritative and better part of him."[119]

That Aristotle thus retained the heart of reverence puts him on one side of a dividing line in the developing Western tradition. That he identified this divine element in us with our minds or intellects – with thinking – puts him on the other side of yet another line. So I can now adapt Figure 60 to show you visually how the two poles of Greek philosophy – Plato and Aristotle – reflect the gradual evolution from mythic to theoretic culture. You can see this in Figure 61, on page 382.

Plato and Aristotle both retained many elements they inherited from the presocratic philosophers, including the encounter with "being" and the cascading opposites this encounter seemed to bring with it: being and becoming, appearance and reality, the One and the many. In Plato these paradoxes were reflected in, among other things, the dialogical form of his work: expressing his assumption that the life of the mind was a continuous process of question and answer. In Aristotle they took the form of wrestling with the contraries and contradictions you already encountered in chapter 2.

But it might also be said – with only a little exaggeration – that Plato and Aristotle each represented or embodied one side of these

Figure 61. From Plato to Aristotle

various pairs of contraries. Plato's thought was taken up with the eternal "being" that must lie, he argued, behind our transitory and deceiving experience of the world; Aristotle's with our "becoming" or doing or activity within that world. Plato thought that "appearances" deceive and must be merely the reflection of the more permanent realities or "ideas" that lie behind the world of appearance. And so he became the father of that permanent current in human thought known as "idealism." Aristotle thought that all thinking must begin from the "facts" of the world. And so he became the father of that permanent tendency in human thought often known as "realism." Plato yearned for the One – we should mount up, he urged, from truths to Truth, from beauties to "Beauty itself"[120] – while Aristotle was firmly rooted in the "many": in the many things and facts from which the world is made, and on which alone our understanding of it can be assured.

If it might be said that Plato looks backward to the old mythic world, then it could equally be said that Aristotle looks forward to the modern world he largely created. But in fact, they both looked forward. Because they embodied two permanent and enduring poles of the human. Two poles of thought or of mind, perhaps. But, more important, two poles of the spirit, and of the virtues. Two poles of the human. The poles of "I am" and "It is."

"Plato and Aristotle!" exclaimed the German poet Heinrich Heine (1797–1856). "These are not merely two systems; they are also types of two distinct human natures, which from immemorial time, under every sort of cloak, stand more or less inimically opposed."[121] Each one of us, says Coleridge, is "born" either a Platonist or an Aristotelian.[122] We are either realists or idealists.[123] We start from the things of this world – and are perhaps content to stop there – or we yearn to look "beyond."[124] "The philosophies of Plato and of Aristotle," says Étienne Gilson, "represent, in their complete generality, the two main attitudes the human mind can adopt with respect to reality."[125]

To tell the truth, Figure 61 is slightly misleading. By the time of Plato, Greek culture had *already* crossed the line, from "I *am*" (A2) to "It *is*" (B1), as Parmenides showed. To be completely accurate, I should really have placed both Plato and Aristotle in the same upper left-hand quadrant, representing sub-families of "It *is*" (B1). But to bring out the differences between them, it's more useful to locate Plato in the way I've done in Figure 61. It's also helpful for a second reason. In a sense, this is the view of Plato, from the point of view of the emerging theoretic culture. Plato stands for "I am" (A2), but he does so *within* a Greek culture whose centre has largely moved on, to "It *is*" (B1).[126] So Figure 61 begins to illustrate the spiral staircase I described in chapters 7 and 10 (Figures 18 and 26). All four families of virtues are present and available in every period of human history (in an "abbreviated" form, as Hegel says). But as the arrow of virtue moves on, from one cultural stage to another, they're viewed and interpreted through the lens of each of those families, in succession. That's what I called "double vision" in chapters 7 and 10. You'll see several more examples of that kind of "double vision" in this book: the whole human paradox viewed through one or more of its four lenses.

Plato and Aristotle were both still rooted in the mythic world of intuition about the good. But Aristotle had moved the centre of the human from feeling to thinking. Intuition was still important. But now it was combined with thinking rather than with feeling. Later, others would take this new emphasis on thinking even further. And since thinking and the mind were becoming the hallmarks of the human for Western culture, the question eventually arose about how to connect them back to the other and earlier dimensions of the human: how to connect "I am" and "It is," value and fact, feeling and thinking, gut and brain, heart and mind, *ought* and *is*.

It was easy to get from *ought* to *is*. Humans had already done it, in the evolution from mythic to theoretic culture. But getting back from *is* to *ought* has proved to be much more difficult.[127]

From ancient to medieval philosophy

If the Western philosophical tradition were a boxing match, I could say that Aristotle won the first round, but Plato won the next two – before Aristotle almost scored a knockout in the fourth.[128]

In the first round, much of the "realist" temper of Aristotelian philosophy was carried forward into the ethical thought of the Stoic
philosophers – such as Epictetus (55–135 CE), Cicero, and Seneca – who
occupied a central position in later Greek and then Roman thought.[129]
The Stoics followed Aristotle closely in their analysis of the human virtues, and in their emphasis on the central role of ethical choice in the
shaping of a genuinely human life. "Consider who you are," said Epictetus. "First of all, you are a human being, that is, one who has nothing
more ruling than choice, and all else subordinate to that."[130] "[N]othing
but honesty and moral good deserves to be admired, wished for, or
striven for," said Cicero.[131] Although sceptical about religious practice
as they understood it, the Stoics nevertheless retained echoes of Aristotle's emphasis on the importance of the divine element in the human.
"The god is near you, with you, inside you," said Seneca. "...[A] holy
spirit is seated within us, a watcher and guardian of our good and bad
actions. As this spirit is treated by us, so it treats us."[132]

But the Aristotelian spirit of the Stoics was soon challenged by a
"neo-Platonic" revival, especially in the form of the later Roman philosopher, Plotinus. Plotinus out-Platoed Plato. He transformed Plato's
own inclination toward the One into a mystical spirituality in which
the One became not just an idea but a World Spirit. For Plotinus, the
universe is constituted on three levels (or hypostases): the One from
which everything else proceeds, and the two further levels of intellect
and soul. The movement of the universe is a procession away from the
One to the many, and – perhaps more important for human life – a
return or ascent of the many back to the unity of the One.[133] It is the
One that "like a light shines through all the virtues."[134] Plotinus announced a radical about-turn from the self-assertive, analytic spirit of
Aristotelian rationalism when he declared that what matters in a truly
human life is not our perception of the many concrete things or facts of
this world but rather a different kind of vision, an internal vision that is
more like a spiritual unselfing: "It is a seeing of a quite different kind,
a self-transcendence, a simplification, self-abandonment, a striving for
union."[135]

Plotinus' mystical Neoplatonism was deeply influential in the
Western philosophical tradition for most of the next thousand years
because it was taken up enthusiastically by the Greek and Roman Fathers of the Church who were seeking to marry Christian spirituality
and revelation with the heritage of classical philosophy. Neoplatonism
provided them with many of the concepts they needed, and a philosophical language that suited their purpose. The Christian doctrine of
the Trinity, for example, hammered out at the Councils of Nicaea (325

CE), Constantinople (381), and Chalcedon (451), was, in part, an appropriation of Plotinus' own three *hypostases* to meet the theological needs of Christianity.

Neoplatonism was deeply influential for the Greek Fathers, such as Gregory of Nyssa (335–394), the most brilliant of the so-called Cappadocian Fathers.[136] But it was equally important for the Western Latin Church because of its powerful echo in the thought of Augustine of Hippo (354–430), the great architect of Western Christianity. For Augustine, his encounter with the thought of Plotinus and the Neoplatonists was a life-changing event and helped prepare his conversion to Christianity. Plotinus helped Augustine to think of God as spirit and gave him a way to understand the message of the Christian scriptures from a theoretical or intellectual perspective. Plotinus and Neoplatonism became the heart of Augustine's theology of love.[137]

Because of his own personal struggles – and, hence, his unparalleled insight into the deep complexity of human psychology and motivation – Augustine fully understood the paradox of self-assertion and reverence that structures the nature of the human – understood it perhaps more clearly and completely than any other thinker in Western history. It was his major and constant theme. Sometimes he called the two sides of the human paradox (like Paul of Tarsus) flesh and spirit, sometimes the "active" and "contemplative" parts of the soul, sometimes transience and eternity, sometimes two "cities," sometimes giving and receiving, sometimes the "lust to dominate" and the acknowledgment of dependence, sometimes intellect and feeling, sometimes knowledge and love, sometimes the two "wills," and sometimes two different kinds of freedom: the freedom simply to assert oneself on the one hand, and on the other, the greater, fuller, or more "perfect freedom" to devote oneself to the service of others. Sometimes he embodied these two sides of the human in biblical figures like Adam and Eve, or Cain and Abel. But whatever he called them, they were always the two opposite but ineradicable poles of the human paradox, "so linked to one another," says Augustine, "that the one cannot exist without the other."[138]

In Augustine's allegorical interpretation, the Christian doctrine of the Fall is simply an expression of our current, direct, personal experience of the "misery" of a world in which the virtues of self-assertion have "fallen away" from or "deserted" the virtues of reverence.[139] The goal and crown of human life, for Augustine, is to heal this fundamental breach in the human. To turn this inherent human discord into concord, into peace and harmony. And the way to do it is to recognize their mutual dependence, to achieve a living, active vision of how they develop and depend upon each other. The highest acts of self-assertion are acts of reverence, and the highest acts of reverence are acts of self-assertion. They go together, indissolubly. The highest kind of self-assertion is, paradoxically, a kind of *unselfing*. A condition of humility and gratitude. It is the recognition that we are ultimately dependent on something we did not create and do not control. Human freedom is not just a matter of making rational choices, because reason alone cannot make us choose well. And, even if it could, it cannot make us *act* on our choices. To choose and to act well, humans must not only *know* the good, they must *love* it. Without love and desire, no action follows. Virtue is simply "rightly ordered love."[140]

Love is higher than knowledge. It comes first. The virtues of Reverence (A2) – and especially the virtues of Love (A2b) – come *before* the virtues of Excellence (B1). To love the good, human beings must already be infused with love itself, a love that is, ultimately, something larger or deeper than ourselves. Acknowledging our dependence on this love, and our grateful participation in it, is not an obligation or a duty. It is a kind of enjoyment or delight. Human beings are moved to act, and to act well, by the sheer, irresistible pleasure of their love for love, in its highest and worthiest forms. By their love for the goodness from which love cannot be separated. The goodness of Love itself.[141] Augustine's greatest work, his *City of God*, is an account of humankind's collective journey into love. His *Confessions*, the story of his own personal spiritual journey – one of the most influential books ever written – is one long love-letter to love.

Together with that of another Neoplatonist theologian (the anonymous fifth-century writer known as "Pseudo-Dionysius") Augustine's theology of love and delight dominated Christian thought – and thus the Western philosophical tradition – for more than six hundred years. However, the growing availability of the works of Aristotle in Latin translation, beginning in the twelfth century BCE, opened a fourth round in the contest between Plato and Aristotle, the two poles of ancient (and of all) thought. Especially in the hands of Thomas Aquinas, access to these works resulted in a dazzling new synthesis between Christian spirituality and Aristotelian rationalism that is one of the highest summits of all human culture. It also marked the re-emerging dominance of theoretic culture, whose growing ascendancy in the West would not again be effectively challenged until the middle of the nineteenth century.

Thomas Aquinas and theoretic culture

Aquinas followed Aristotle in identifying the essence of the human with reason and with the mind. Human beings are a compound of sensing and thinking,[142] but sensing is something humans share with animals. It is their rational nature that defines them as human. "Reason," says Aquinas, "is the principle of human and moral acts."[143] The "cause and root of human good is reason."[144] Man's happiness or fulfilment must therefore be "with respect to his intellect."[145] Human happiness is to be found in a kind of knowledge, "the knowledge of truth."[146]

In making reason the essence of the human, Aquinas also followed Aristotle in his rational reverence for fact and for things. Truth depends, he says, on "conformity of thought with thing"[147]: "The truth of our intellect, if we consider it absolutely, is measured by the thing, for things are the measure of our intellect. For by the fact that a thing is so or not, there is truth in what we think or say."[148]

Here is the triumph of theoretic over mythic culture. But just as there were two Aristotles, there also seem to have been two Aquinases. While, with one hand, Aquinas assures the modern triumph of theoretic culture, with the other he reaches back to preserve, as best he can in this new context, the enduring values and insights of mythic culture. He does this in two ways.

The first way is (like Aristotle) an emphasis on the virtues.[149] The second part of Aquinas' *Summa Theologiæ* – the distillation and summary of his thought[150] – is "perhaps the most comprehensive account ever written of the virtues."[151] While granting theoretic culture's assumption that human fulfilment must be in the mind or thought, Aquinas suggests that perfect happiness could only be achieved by knowledge of ultimate truth, that is to say, "in the vision of the divine essence."[152] But to see *this* kind of perfect truth is "beyond the nature not only of man but of every creature."[153] Since knowledge of ultimate truth is impossible, "true and perfect happiness *cannot* be had in this life."[154] What *is* possible in this life is to gain some insight into ultimate truth "by likeness or participation" in it.[155] Now, for Aquinas, God is Aristotle's "being *as* being." His very essence is to be.[156] But God is not a thing. The essence of God is not to be *something* but to *do* something. In fact, God is the very *act* of being itself. Since "the substance of God is his action, the greatest likeness of man to God is in respect to some operation." Happiness in this world must consist, therefore, not just or even primarily in knowledge, but in an "operation" or activity.[157] In *doing* something, not just in *knowing* something. Happiness must consist in good human action or in what is called virtue. Virtue, says Aquinas, "is the activity happiness consists in."[158]

Even reason or thought, Aquinas points out, agreeing again with Aristotle, is a kind of virtue. And it is the will that "moves the intellect as to the exercise of its act." We only use some human power, like reason, "when we wish to."[159] So without will, the mind cannot function. And without *good* will, it will function badly. Its conclusions or assertions will not be true.

The second way Aquinas tries to hang onto the moral and spiritual achievements of mythic culture is by establishing two hierarchies: a hierarchy *in* the mind and a hierarchy *for* the mind. As to mind itself, he distinguishes, for example, between reason ("ratio") on the one hand, and the higher power of intellect ("intellectus") on the other.[160] What reason can only attain "by means of investigation" or by "a certain discourse," intellect grasps intuitively, or all "at once."[161] He also establishes another mental hierarchy between the virtues of science, understanding, and wisdom. The first depends on the second "as upon something higher, and both depend upon wisdom as upon something highest." Both science and understanding stand lower than wisdom in the hierarchy of virtues because wisdom must ultimately judge "the conclusions of science and the principles on which they are based."[162] Wisdom "directs" and rules the other intellectual virtues and is "architectonic, as it were, with respect to all of them."[163]

However, this introduces a kind of paradox into theoretic culture. Because a virtue which is *"less certain* about higher and greater things" (wisdom) is somehow declared to be "preferable to the virtue which is *more certain* about inferior things" (science or understanding).[164] Obviously this entails a judgment about relative value. Some things are simply more worth knowing about, *even if we can know less about them.* "[T]hat modicum of knowledge we can have of God through wisdom," says Aquinas, "is preferable to all other knowledge."[165]

But *why* is it preferable? Is it just a question of the relative value of two kinds of knowledge? It seems to be even more than that. In fact, thinking and knowledge turn out *not* to be the highest good after all, because knowledge depends on the known being *in* the knower. Whereas love is brought about by the lover being *drawn* to what is loved. But what is "above" human beings is more worthy "in itself," says Aquinas, than it is in us humans. To be *in* us it has to become *like* us (or in the same "mode"), rather than as it really is, *in itself.* This leads Aquinas to a momentous conclusion that seems to overturn the priority he had previously given to reason and to the mind. In the end, Aquinas concludes, "to *love* things above man is more noble than to *know* them."[166]

Here is theoretic culture finally deposed from the pinnacle and mythic culture vindicated. At the very last moment, Aquinas deserts Aristotle – or rather, goes beyond him – and reaches back instead to Augustine and Pseudo-Dionysius, and beyond them to Plotinus and to Plato. And beyond Athens to Jerusalem, and to the prophets of Israel. Despite all the praise heaped on reason and the mind as the hallmarks

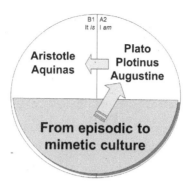

Figure 62. From Plato to Aquinas

of the human, love turns out, in the end, to be more important than knowledge.[167] Human virtue comes before the human mind and is the condition of its success. The achievement of Athens or theoretic culture can only be assured on the prior foundation of Jerusalem or mythic culture, especially the spirituality of the Axial age.[168]

Like Aristotle, Aquinas has crossed one line, but declines to cross another. I can thus augment my previous figure, to include Plotinus, Augustine, and Aquinas, as in Figure 62 above.[169]

As Figure 62 illustrates in graphic form, the career of Western philosophy from Plato to Aquinas not only parallels the evolution from mythic to theoretic culture but also embodies two of the four enduring poles of the human.

The thought of Thomas Aquinas offers another example of something you already saw in the Axial age. The advent of a new mode of being often strengthens something old just before it begins to challenge or replace it with something new. Just as in the Axial age, when the invention of written language brought mythic culture to its highest point before beginning to develop the new theoretic culture, so too Aquinas now used the tools of Greek theoretical culture to take the spiritual insights of the Axial age even further, by explaining and expounding them in the theoretical language of Greek philosophy.

However, this triumphant vindication of theoretic culture masked two potential but opposite dangers. Spiritual life and theoretical life could now be easily confused. Or even separated completely.

And the first danger could become the stepping stone to the second.

Aquinas avoided those dangers, in the end. His writing represents one of the highest points both of theoretic culture *and* of human spirituality.[170] But others would not be so lucky or so wise. By his enthusiastic embrace of the first phase of theoretic culture, Aquinas helped set Western culture on the road that would lead to the second phase. And, beyond that, to our contemporary, post-modern world.[171]

Toward the second phase of theoretic culture

The value given to human reason in medieval Christian philosophy, and its corresponding reverence for facts or things, is the necessary background for the second phase of theoretic culture. The formal starting point of this second phase is usually attributed to the French mathematician and philosopher, René Descartes (1596–1650), in the seventeenth century.

While Descartes' thought may well be considered the beginning of modern theoretic culture, it was also the end of a long process in which the links to mythic culture retained by Aristotle and Aquinas were gradually discarded and the triumph of the mind, of thought and thing, became complete. (Complete in intellectual life, that is. Mythic culture and the virtues of reverence were never discarded by Western culture as a whole because no prior cultural stage is ever superseded but continues, instead, to occupy an important – though often overlooked – place in real human life.)

Just as the thought of Plato and Aristotle was a response to questions posed by the presocratics, the thought of Descartes and his successors was also the result of cultural developments from the fourteenth to the seventeenth centuries.[172]

How the Western cultural tradition got from the first theoretic culture of Aristotle and Aquinas to the second or modern theoretic culture of Descartes and his immediate successors is a very complex story, a story I can only sketch very briefly here.[173] The first strand of this story has something to do with the excesses of success. The very achievements of medieval thought were the seeds of its own undoing.

In the heady atmosphere in which the writings of Aristotle were rediscovered, there was, for example, a temptation to confuse thought with logic, a temptation that has recurred perennially in theoretic culture since that time.[174] One of the results of this confusion was to confuse contraries with contradictions, once again. This was a spur for a linear kind of thinking conducive to the growth of modern science and technology. But it now became increasingly difficult – despite the efforts of Nicholas of Cusa – to hold both sides of the human paradox together or even to see the role of paradox at all. The law of non-contradiction, on which logic is based, seemed to exclude it.

The prestige of logic also encouraged an outlook in later medieval thought in which Aristotle and Aquinas' view that every existing thing in the real world is individual or "particular" was taken to an extreme, and made to yield the conclusion that nothing else has any real existence. Everything else is merely an abstraction or a kind of sign. There are no "universals." They exist only through or in individual things. This altered view of reality was supported and encouraged by medieval developments in canon law, which was abandoning an older corporate conception of society in favour of a new emphasis on individual equality.[175] Thus it became increasingly natural to suggest that reality itself is also ruled "by contingency, and individuality, chance and individual things."[176] Anything else is simply words, or "names."

This so-called "nominalism" (from the Latin word *nomen*, for name) was championed by Franciscan theologians suspicious of Aquinas' revival of Aristotelian rationalism.[177] They sensed that the hierarchical assumptions built into ancient rationalism – even the hierarchy of "goods" – was a potential threat to their own Order's emphasis on humility, poverty, and radical equality. They feared that Athens' emphasis on reason and being might supplant Jerusalem's proclamation of love and mercy. In their pursuit of humility, a core virtue of Reverence (A2), they wanted to be absolutely free to renounce this world's goods, despite all the social and institutional pressure to do otherwise. They therefore also wanted to emphasize God's own absolute freedom, a freedom which reflected and supported their own. So they attacked the Aristotelian foundations of Aquinas' thought, including Aristotle's recognition (following Plato) of the role of "final" causes.[178] To suggest the world is structured by final causes or ideas, the nominalists argued, is to limit the absolute freedom of God the Creator, a freedom on which human freedom depends and which it reflects. A final cause cannot be a real cause, said William of Ockham (ca. 1287–1347), the most influential nominalist thinker, because "it does not exist." To explain the world in terms of final causes is to confuse reasons and causes: to confuse human rationality and culture with the working of the physical world. To explain the latter, only Aristotle's "efficient" causes are needed or can be permitted.[179] Nominalism was thus a kind of materialism or positivism or "crude empiricism" before its time.[180] It looked forward to developments in the second phase of theoretic culture, preparing the ground for a revolution in scientific "method" in the seventeenth and eighteenth centuries. But it also paved the way for a growing inclination to view the world, in the old presocratic way, as "mechanical," without any inherent purpose or meaning.[181] It helped to drive a new wedge between freedom and morality, between "is" and "ought."[182]

This potential was compounded by nominalism's association with a "univocal" concept of being, a concept developed initially by Duns Scotus (ca. 1265/6–1308), and later embraced by William of Ockham. "Univocal" means that being was now conceived in exactly the same way for everything that exists, including God. God's way of being is no different from that of anything else. God's freedom and human freedom are the same.[183] Aquinas had conceived God as *being* itself: the very *act* or source of being, belonging to no category shared by created beings.[184] But for the nominalists, there were no general categories, only particulars or individual things. Conceived "univocally" in this way, the God of nominalism was on the road to becoming just *a* being, among other beings. Maybe the greatest or most powerful of beings, but still just a thing, or entity, among other entities.[185]

This was a momentous change. If God, as Aquinas had described Him, is just another name for being, then the question of his existence can scarcely arise. It would be almost a contradiction in terms to ask whether "being" can *exist*, for they are the same thing. As Pseudo-Dionysius had put it before Aquinas, "There is no kind of thing that God is, and there is no kind of thing that God is not."[186] But if God is a being like other beings, a thing like any other thing, as in William of Ockham's nominalist "univocalism," then the question of his existence can legitimately arise, and can be answered in the negative. No matter how much Ockham might emphasize, for the time being, God's absolute power and his unknowability, nominalism put in place the key intellectual ingredients "for the domestication of God's transcendence and the extrusion of his presence from the natural world."[187]

The nominalists were right. They were right to be suspicious of Aquinas' intellectualism, and any Aristotelian assumption that human fulfilment was something to be achieved in and by the mind.[188] They saw, correctly, that Aquinas' powerful emphasis on human reason – on the mind – could eventually undermine the virtues of reverence. But their solution – with its radical emphasis on liberty and equality – hastened the very result they sought to prevent. It amounted to no less than an attempt to forestall the virtues of self-assertion by appealing to those very virtues! So it didn't push the arrow of virtue backward, from Aquinas' virtues of Excellence (B1) to the Franciscan virtues of Reverence (A2), as they hoped, but forward, instead, to the virtues of Equality (B2).

Nominalism broke up the medieval synthesis into separate parts that became increasingly difficult to reconcile: reason was detached from faith, and knowledge was divorced from virtue. Spiritual life separated into a rationalized theology on the one hand, and a marginalized "mysticism" on the other.[189]

The result was soon seen in the universities, which nearly doubled in number in the fifteenth century, and in their faculties of theology – where nominalism now held sway – which increased almost tenfold.[190] This "academicisation" of theology transformed it and the whole conception of higher learning. Even for Plato and Aristotle, philosophy had remained a kind of spirituality, whose ultimate objective was the inner transformation of the philosopher's own character.[191] The "academicisation" of theology soon turned it into a field of purely abstract or "academic" (in a new sense) learning and dispute, unconnected to the character or virtue of the learner or the teacher. It was now becoming a subject (as a contemporary observer complained) that could be taught to "any one at all, regardless of the moral quality of their lives, on condition of sufficient intelligence."[192] The ideal of neutral, objective "knowledge" and expertise, unconnected to virtue, was beginning to emerge. The founding and growth of the universities pointed straight ahead to the second phase of theoretic culture. Philosophy was no longer the pursuit of a reverent way of life but merely the cultivation of detached, assertive objectivity.[193]

The result of these (and other) developments was a growing scepticism and cynicism in later medieval culture, an outlook that spawned many contrary developments. One was an eagerness for the continued revival of classical learning and culture. An eagerness that became the Renaissance, and inspired a variety of Platonic and Stoic revivals, betraying a hunger for the passion and yearning that seemed to be missing in Aristotle, Aquinas, and much of medieval "scholastic" thought. "I would much rather let all of [Duns] Scotus and other of that [scholastic] sort perish than the books of a single Cicero or Plutarch," said Erasmus of Rotterdam (1466–1536), leader of north-European humanism.[194] It was a Renaissance "humanist" who invented the canard that the scholastics had wasted their energies arguing about how many angels could dance on the head of a pin![195] In the Italian city-states of the fourteenth and fifteenth centuries, the aestheticized cult of individuality spawned by the Renaissance helped to bring about "a rehabilitation of self-assertion."[196]

Another reaction to fifteenth-century scepticism was an eagerness to get back to the primitive essence or living heart of Christianity, uncorrupted by the dry accretions of scholasticism and hierarchy. An eagerness that became the Reformation. The paradox of the Reformation was that, like nominalism and so many later revolutions and protest movements, it actually ended up reinforcing some of the very trends against which it claimed to rebel. And achieved the very result it sought to avoid.[197]

Continuing (rather than challenging) the medieval substitution of theology for religious life, some Protestant traditions focussed everything on the rational "word" of preaching, scripture, and theology, almost eliminating liturgy, metaphor, and symbolism altogether.[198] The pulpit replaced the altar as the focus of worship in many churches, especially those influenced by John Calvin (1509–1564).[199] Calvin himself defined faith as a kind of "knowledge."[200] Doctrine, he said, is "the life of the Church."[201] "Take away assertions," said Martin Luther, "and you take away Christianity."[202] So the late sixteenth century witnessed an avalanche of new "confessions" and formalized statements of belief, "a vast pile of catechisms."[203]

The doctrinal emphasis of the Reformation and the endless proliferation of competing "confessions" led only to disagreements and stalemates for which there was no obvious solution. Worse, it led to religious hatred and violence, and even to wars, and civil wars of religion, which devastated much of Europe for over a century. Exhausted by war and frustrated by endless doctrinal quarrels, Europeans by the middle of the seventeenth century were looking for a new, neutral basis on which to begin all over again.[204]

It was in this fertile soil that "natural religion," deism, and, inevitably, atheism grew.[205] Cities like Geneva and Edinburgh which were strong centres of Calvinism in the sixteenth century became equally strong centres of rationalism only two centuries later.[206] After all, if religion were just a matter of doctrines and "beliefs," why not get them in even more rational – and less conflictual – ways?[207] Intended to save and purify Christianity, the Reformation thus unwittingly prepared the ground for the second phase of theoretic culture that would instead challenge and displace it from the centre of Western culture.[208]

Even Protestantism's more "literal" approach to Biblical interpretation was initially conducive to the development of the natural sciences. Christianity had always regarded God as the author of two books: the Bible and the book of nature. But mainstream Christianity had traditionally been inclined to interpret them both allegorically or symbolically. Protestantism's more literal approach to one was compatible with a more literal or more "natural" approach to the other. The emergence of the natural sciences could be and was regarded as a "reformation," just as much as the religious one.[209]

Supporting these various cultural trends were a number of economic, social, and political developments. The growth of commerce in the late Middle Ages contributed to the emergence of a wealthy, urban merchant class and to the growth of local identities and feeling. In the process, it also gave a new value to individuals and to individualism. These social changes had already supported the earlier intellectual vogue for "nominalism," with its emphasis on freedom and radical equality, an emphasis that flattered the ambitions of an emerging middle class, eager to challenge social structures determined by inherited status.[210] Now the continued strengthening of the urban middle classes did the same for the Reformation, which got its start in the "self-confident" towns and cities of the Holy Roman Empire, such as Nuremberg and Zurich.[211] Martin Luther's doctrine of "justification by faith" could only make sense in a culture that had already been persuaded that the essence of the human is to be found "in the head" or the mind.[212] But it owed its new appeal to – and also reinforced – an emerging sense of individual identity and individual self-sufficiency. It made the relationship to God a purely personal matter. Individual Christians could relate directly to God without depending on anything but themselves.[213] Even reverence now had to express itself in ways more compatible with the growing spirit of self-assertion.

Both economic prosperity and the corresponding mood of self-assertion were further fuelled by the new age of European expansion and global conquest that began in the fifteenth century. The experience of world conquest and occupation spawned an outlook or mood of "limitless" human possibility and power. The dawning era of European colonialism spawned "dreams of unlimited material possibilities," accompanied by "a disregard for moral, customary, or judicious restraints."[214]

This increasingly assertive mood inevitably carried over into other areas of life, even into the appeal of the new natural sciences. The English philosopher and statesman, Francis Bacon, considered the first modern philosopher of science, built on the assumptions of Ockham and the nominalists to develop the concept of modern scientific method, in which nature is not studied speculatively but experimentally, in which nature is "put to the question," rather like a prisoner on an interrogation rack.[215] In setting out the new principles of scientific method, Bacon also revealed the spirit of self-assertion on which they were based. His purpose, he said, was to "lay more firmly the foundations, and extend more widely the limits, of the power and greatness of man."[216] Writing in the heady dawn of the new age of discovery and of European colonialism, Bacon declared that the ambition of the new age of science was even "more noble" than the ambition of those who sought "power" (as he had done) within their own country, or those, like the new European explorers, whose goal was to "extend the power of their country and its dominion among men." The ambition of the new experimental sciences went even farther. It was nothing less, said Bacon, than "to establish and extend the power of the human race itself over the universe." It was, in fact, to establish "the empire of man over things."[217]

In these words Bacon summed up the new spirit of self-assertion that had been developing in European culture from the fourteenth to the seventeenth centuries, preparing the way for René Descartes and the second phase of theoretic culture. This new spirit had already been heralded in 1315 by a decree of the French King Louis le Hutin, which started from the premise that "according to the law of nature each must be born free."[218] It had been heard again, even more clearly, at the end of the next century, in the famous *Oration on the Dignity of Man*, written by a young Italian Platonist philosopher Giovanni Pico della Mirandola (1463–94).[219] Pico's *Oration* offers a new vision of human beings as "constrained by no limits." With complete "freedom of choice" as though they were the "maker and molder" of themselves, human beings are now free to "fashion [themselves]," Pico declared, "in whatever shape [they might] prefer."[220]

Constrained by no limits! In these words you can already hear the modern and post-modern spirit of self-assertion. A spirit echoed, in one register, by Francis Bacon. And, in another, by Niccolò Machiavelli (1469–1527). Machiavelli's famous handbook of *realpolitik*, *The Prince*, is a celebration not just of the virtues of self-assertion, or even of the virtues of Liberty (A1), but, even more specifically, of the virtues of Power (A1a). That is its subject: how to get hold of power, how to hold onto it, and how to expand it. The only thing that counts is "winning" – and the "results" of winning, that is, power. Only the end counts, and to achieve it any means are permissible. The prince should be an expert in deceit and "know how to be a great hypocrite and dissembler." He should break his word whenever it suits his interest to do so. He should know how to be cruel when cruelty is required because "men must either be cajoled or crushed." *The Prince* is a celebration of the virtues of self-assertion, especially the virtues of courage, boldness, ruthlessness, and the disposition to dominate. And, of these, boldness and daring are the most important because "Fortune is a woman and if you wish to master her, you must strike and beat her, and you will see that she allows herself to be more easily vanquished by the rash and violent than by those who proceed more slowly and coldly."[221]

For the purpose of winning and holding onto power, only the virtues of self-assertion are relevant, especially the virtues of – naturally enough – Power (A1). Machiavelli acknowledges the virtues of reverence, but only as something the prince should "seem to have." Not something he should genuinely possess. Hypocrisy is the tribute vice pays to virtue. A prince should "seem" to be merciful, faithful, humane, religious, and upright: he should "seem all charity, integrity, and humanity, all uprightness and piety." But this is only for outward show. Whenever conditions require it, he should know how to "change to the opposite," to the virtues of self-assertion.[222]

Machiavelli's celebration of the virtues of Power (A1a) anticipates one of the most important underground currents of the new theoretic culture, a strand that would emerge even more clearly in post-modern culture, when the second phase of theoretic culture had reached its breaking-point in the nineteenth century.[223] But at the end of the sixteenth century, another closely related strand of future, post-modern self-assertion is also forecast in the *Essays* of Michel de Montaigne (1533–92).

Montaigne's outlook was just as assertive as Machiavelli's but in a very different way. Montaigne was sceptical not just about Christian revelation but about all earnest searching after truth, indeed about all earnestness. Plato had yearned to look beyond the appearances of this world, and even Aristotle had counselled against the ancient poets' advice to stick to purely human concerns. Montaigne, however, was on the side of the poets. Excessive striving for the cardinal virtues – let alone the theological virtues – usually leads to some kind of harmful excess. "Wisdom has its own excesses," said Montaigne, "and is just as much in need of moderation as folly."[224] "The greatness of the soul," he argued, "does not consist so much in yearning upward or striving forward as it does in knowing how to settle yourself down, and set limits to your striving. It defines as great all that is simply enough, and shows its elevation in preferring the average to the outstanding."[225] Humans should aim for much more modest values, the ones Montaigne tried to exhibit in his own essays: values like sincerity, self-knowledge, self-acceptance, personal autonomy, tolerance, friendship, and pleasure. Especially pleasure. Pleasure, he declared, is the real "goal" of life.[226]

In one sense, Montaigne's assertion of the sovereign role of pleasure was not very different from that of Aristotle, Augustine, or Aquinas. It didn't shock his contemporaries. But that wasn't the sense most later readers took from him. If Machiavelli anticipated the role the virtues of Power (A1a) would eventually come to play in our post-modern world, Montaigne foretold the future importance of the virtues of Pleasure (A1b).

These, too, are kinds of self-assertion.[227] Power (A1a) and Pleasure (A1b) would eventually challenge the other theoretic side of self-assertion (B2) from within, pushing the arrow of virtue back toward its starting point. But that was for the future. Because the second phase of theoretic culture was about to begin.

The second phase of theoretic culture

Montaigne and Bacon posed the questions to which Descartes provided the answer. Or rather, an answer. An answer which shaped and continues to shape our modern and post-modern world.

Montaigne's scepticism had moved him to ask the famous question: "*Que sais-je?*"[228] What do I know? What can I know? That was the question for which Descartes found an answer in his celebrated *cogito*.

How do I know I know anything? How do I even know that anything really exists and is not simply some kind of dream? How do I even know that *I* exist? Where can we find some solid starting point, some certainty, from which to move forward, some solid foundation on which human life can be based, free from the endless doctrinal quarrels, conflicts, and wars the Reformation and Counter-Reformation had brought in their wake?

For Montaigne, his *Que sais-je?* was an expression of scepticism, the impossibility of answering these kinds of questions with any certainty, the emblem of an absolute doubt. But Descartes turned Montaigne's doubt inside out. His solution to uncertainty about even these basic questions was to follow the sceptical impulse as far as it can go: to follow it right through to the point where it starts to undermine itself.

Let's doubt everything. Doubt even your own existence. Your own perceptions. Doubt everything you can. But, in the end, there's one thing – and one thing only – that you can't doubt. *You can't doubt that you're doubting.* That, at least, is a certainty. You *are* doubting. And therefore there must be a *you*, to do the doubting.

If I don't exist, I can't doubt. So the fact that I'm thinking these doubts means that I really *do* exist, after all. *Je pense, donc je suis. Cogito ergo sum.* I think, therefore I am. This is the starting point, "the first principle" of the brand new philosophy Descartes was looking for.[229] The solid foundation on which everything human can be built. And the starting point of our modern and post-modern worlds.

It was also the beginning of the second phase of theoretic culture.[230] With his *cogito*, Descartes had moved the centre of Western culture across the line from the virtues of reverence to the virtues of self-assertion. From the stance of "It *is*" and the virtues of Excellence (B1) to the stance of "*It* is" and the virtues of Equality (B2).[231] For one thing, he had, in a stroke, wiped the philosophical slate clean. Some two thousand years of philosophical reflection on human experience – going back to the presocratics – could be swept "completely away."[232] All that was now needed to provide a firm basis for human culture was the individual human mind and its power of thinking: its capacity for doubt, its power of negation. Augustine had already formulated the same *cogito* principle a thousand years earlier.[233] But Descartes made no reference to that earlier discovery; and he now used the same principle to make such a backward reference to the earlier stages of theoretic culture – much less to mythic culture – unnecessary.

Another way Descartes inaugurated the second phase of theoretic culture was his complete identification of the human with the mind and with rational thought. Because of the way he had found his new starting point, his new foundation for certainty, Descartes now defined the nature of the human entirely in terms of the human capacity for thought and for thinking. The *cogito* had assured him that he was real: "I am a real thing and really exist; but what thing? ... [A] thing which thinks."[234] There were two momentous discoveries here. First, human beings are things. Despite Descartes' reassuring discovery that "I am," what he really meant was "*It* is" (B2). The modern world Descartes announces is now constituted of things, of which human beings are only one. And the kind of things they are, are things that think. "I am nothing," says Descartes, "but a *thinking thing*."[235]

Yet another way Descartes heralded the beginning of the modern and post-modern world was in his attitude to the natural world: in his assumptions about what the naked power of human thought can and should be used for. Here he was responding to Bacon rather than to Montaigne. Descartes embraced a new, assertive kind of thinking because it provided knowledge that was "useful" and "practical," unlike the purely "speculative" philosophy of the first phase of theoretic culture. Like Bacon, he rejoiced in the potential of the new science to extend the *power* of man over nature. Understanding the "laws of nature" through the new experimental sciences would "render ourselves," he declared – echoing Bacon's spirit of self-assertion – "the masters and possessors of nature."[236]

In this new era announced by Descartes, humankind would be defined by standing face-to-face with the otherness of the natural world, a world to dominate and control.[237] Not defined by awareness of an otherness of the spirit within. In the first phase of theoretic culture (B1), thinking had still been allied to intuition. Henceforth it was to be allied primarily to sensing (B2).[238]

Descartes was so excited about his own discovery of a fresh starting point for human thought and about the potential of the new sciences for mastering and controlling nature that he proclaimed a new, fool-proof "method" for thinking, based on the procedural model of mathematics, especially geometry.[239] His first and most famous work, published in 1637, was, in fact called *Discours de la méthode* – a "Discourse on the *Method* of Rightly Conducting the Reason and Seeking for Truth in the Sciences." In the old philosophy, Descartes declared, there was nothing that was not the "subject of dispute and in consequence which is not dubious."[240] So the philosophy of the first stage of theoretic culture couldn't provide any kind of solid foundation and was little more than a house to be pulled down and rebuilt using a new method.[241] Only mathematics had so far succeeded in "producing any reasons which are evident and certain." Thus, its methods should now be used in all other areas of human knowledge.

Descartes boiled this mathematical methodology down to four rules. First, "accept nothing as true" which you don't clearly recognize to be so. Second, "divide up the difficulties into as many parts as possible." Third, and most important, carry out the exercise of thinking "in due order, commencing with objects that were most simple and easy to understand, in order to rise little by little, or by degrees, to knowledge of the most complex." And, finally, "make enumerations so complete and reviews so general" that you can be certain you've "omitted nothing."[242]

This method proceeds "one truth" at a time, follows the "true order," enumerates "exactly every term in the matter under investigation [and] contains everything which gives certainty to the rules of Arithmetic." Therefore, it could also be used to establish equal "certainty" in other areas of human thought too. Which Descartes proposed to do, starting with philosophy.[243]

Descartes' so-called "method" has very little to do with real thinking.[244] It was, at best, a caricature of what Aquinas had called "reason" (*ratio*) and had nothing whatever to do with the more subtle, intuitive kind of thinking he had called "intellect" (*intellectus*), the kind required for really deep thinking on difficult matters. And it took no account at all of the contraries or opposites which Aristotle, following the Pythagoreans, had found in all things human. Nor of how the thinking process is embedded in the social process of conversation, as Plato had shown in his dialogues. Descartes' contemporary, Blaise Pascal, saw the limitations of this linear, "geometric" style of thinking, modelled on mathematics, right away. He warned it had little of value to offer unless it was complemented by that other, deeper, intuitive kind of thinking, which he himself called the "heart," or "finesse."[245]

Pascal was right. Descartes' model of reasoning was an illusion. But that didn't matter. It was destined for a long career, as *the* modern model of how the thinking process is supposed to work. It was carried forward on the momentum and growing prestige of the natural sciences and mathematics – and also by the way it embodied the new culture of self-assertion, developing since the fourteenth century.[246] It was destined to cut a wide swath in modern culture not because of its merits alone but because – like nominalism and Luther's doctrine of "justification by faith" – it also appealed to the new spirit of individualism, the growing culture of self-assertion. Truths are much more likely to be discovered, Descartes asserted, "by one man than by a nation."[247] The only source of human self-respect, he said (echoing Pico), is "the use of our free will."[248] The new Cartesian thinkers – like the Lutheran merchants before them – were proud to depend on nothing but themselves and their own individual power of reason.

In Descartes' wake, two seventeenth-century thinkers who developed this assertive individualism influentially in the second phase of theoretic culture were the English thinkers, Thomas Hobbes and John Locke.

Like Descartes (whom he met in Paris in the 1630s), Hobbes dismissed all previous philosophy, especially that of Aristotle and the scholastics. Contrasting the "darkness of School distinctions" with the "clearer light of natural reason," he asserted that earlier philosophers had wasted their time reflecting on the virtues, which "can never be true grounds of any ratiocination," and, as a result, had ended up wallowing in nothing more than a "mediocrity of passions."[249] Following Descartes, Hobbes aspired to establish a "science" of politics based on geometric "method."[250] He did so, in part, by starting, as he thought, from solid and reliable "definitions," the philosophical equivalent of axioms in geometry.[251] And, in part, by going back to the beginning.

For Hobbes, the beginning is "the condition of mere nature" in which human life begins, before civil governments are established (or when they are overthrown): a condition which, he argues, is and was a state of "absolute liberty."[252] Liberty is the natural condition of humans because of who they are: creatures of pure self-assertion. They "naturally love liberty and dominion over others."[253] Humans are power-seeking creatures. The value or worth of a human is simply the extent of his power.[254] The natural human condition is "a perpetual and restless desire of power after power that ceases only in death."[255]

Human happiness, says Hobbes, consists in "continual success in obtaining those things which a man from time to time desires."[256] There is no higher good, no final causes, or "utmost aim" as "the old moral philosophers" had claimed. Happiness is merely the "continual progress of the desire from one object to another."[257] Because human beings are equal in these desires, equality is the other natural condition of humanity. In the state of nature, humans are equal in the hope of obtaining their desires but also equal in their ability to kill each other in pursuit of them. In the state of nature, they must and do become "enemies" to each other. They find themselves in a state of unceasing war: a war which – in one of Hobbes' most celebrated phrases – he called a war "of every man against every man."[258]

The natural state of humankind is "anarchy and the condition of war."[259] In this state of nature, "every man has a right to everything, even to one another's body."[260] But the obvious disadvantages of living always in peril, fear, and chaos – a life Hobbes famously described as "solitary, poor, nasty, brutish and short"[261] – prompt humans to seek to escape from such a lamentable condition. They thus lead to a fundamental law of nature: a wise human being should forego his natural "passions" and should seek peace instead. He should "be willing, when others are too ... to lay down this right to all things, and be contented with so much liberty against other men as he would allow other men against himself."[262] The way human beings have found for "getting themselves out from that miserable condition of war" is by the establishment of civil states: they "agree among themselves to submit to some man or assembly of men voluntarily, on confidence to be protected by him against all others."[263]

There's a fundamental tension between Hobbes' premises and his conclusions. He starts from the principles of liberty and equality, but far from desiring to defend these values in contemporary states, his objective was, on the contrary, to justify authoritarian states.[264] The same contrast can be seen in his treatment of the virtues. His banishing of the virtues as a basis for a theory of the human is more illusion than reality. For as soon as he had established his premise that "the condition of mere nature – that is to say of absolute liberty ... is anarchy and the condition of war," Hobbes' very next step was to promulgate the so-called "laws of nature," or "the precepts by which [men] are guided to avoid that condition" of anarchy and civil war. And these "laws of nature" turn out to be *nothing other than the virtues themselves* – "namely, equity, justice, mercy, humility, and the rest of the moral virtues."[265] In fact, as Hobbes' list shows, his so-called "laws of nature" turn out to be not only the virtues but, even more specifically, the *virtues of reverence* – the "qualities that *dispose* men to peace and obedience"[266] – virtues which can all be summed up, Hobbes says, repeatedly, in the biblical Golden Rule.[267] What Hobbes purported to put out at the front door, he immediately snuck in again through the back door. His contrast between the "laws of nature" and "our natural passions" is nothing more than the contrast between the virtues of reverence and the virtues of self-assertion, or what I have called the human paradox, or the whole nature of the human.[268]

That's not what struck his contemporaries, however. They were more impressed by the bold way in which he now made liberty and equality – the paradox of self-assertion – the starting point or essence of the human. Though he had no intention of doing so, Hobbes inadvertently launched them on their long careers as the quintessentially modern and post-modern values. The emerging modern spirit of self-assertion he so accurately detected behind them – the "perpetual and restless desire of power after power" – ensured that, as soon as he had launched them into the second phase of theoretic culture, liberty and equality were quickly taken up by others and often turned in different directions than Hobbes intended. Including by John Locke.

Building on Hobbes' foundation (but turning many of his conclusions upside down), Locke agreed that human beings are in a state of perfect liberty and equality in what Hobbes had called the "state of nature." And they remain in that condition, he also agreed, until they voluntarily give it up by making a "compact": "till by their own consents they make themselves members of some politic society."[269]

But for Locke, the so-called "state of nature" that precedes organized society is very different than it was for Hobbes. For Hobbes it is a state of war. For Locke, it is instead a state of "living together according to reason," a "state of peace, goodwill, mutual assistance, and preservation."[270] Locke agrees with Hobbes that there is a "law of nature." But for Hobbes the laws of nature do *not* exist in the state of nature: they are the way to get *out* of it. They only exist *after* the state of nature. For Locke, by contrast, the law of nature already exists *in* the state of nature. The only thing lacking in the state of nature is the means to enforce its law.[271] But the law itself exists. It stands as "an eternal rule to all men" which predates organized society, and which civil government is simply the means to "enforce."[272]

Locke's change in the definition of the state of nature prepared the ground for another important step in the evolution from the medieval concept of "right" or law (*jus*) to the modern and post-modern language of "rights."[273] Building on the work of the medieval canonist lawyers, Hobbes had already taken the first two steps. First of all, he redefined "right" no longer as justice but simply as "liberty," a right to everything.[274] Then, when human beings transfer their natural liberty to the sovereign, Hobbes says, they do not transfer all of this right or liberty but "retain" some small portion of it: there are "some *rights* which no man can be understood by any words or signs to have abandoned or transferred."[275] By this means, the medieval "right" (singular) became the modern "rights" (plural).[276]

Locke took the first step through the door Hobbes had opened. For him, the language of "rights" has already become habitual. And because he had redefined the state of nature, these rights were projected backward into it. They were inherent in human beings, as human beings. They already existed in the state of nature. All they acquired in organized society was the opportunity to be protected by "standing laws."[277]

Hobbes may have been the first to say that (what he called "retained") rights were inalienable. But he did not think they were very wide or numerous: they included only such things as the right to save oneself from "death, wounds and imprisonment," and the right not to confess or accuse oneself. But once Hobbes had opened this door of human "rights," a whole modern and post-modern army of rights would march through it, starting with John Locke. By the twenty-first century, as I pointed out in chapter 4, Hobbes' and Locke's language of "rights" had become one of the most typical ways in which the virtues of self-assertion are expressed, almost the only kind of language in which moral issues can be discussed in public discourse today.

Locke had not forgotten the virtues any more than Hobbes. In fact, in the first few paragraphs of his famous *Second Treatise on Civil Government* (as I already noted in chapter 12), the four families of virtues are all explicitly invoked: liberty (A1) and equality (B2), of course, the paradox of self-assertion. But also justice (B1) and charity (A2) – the paradox of reverence.[278] Locke's "law of nature," like Hobbes', is really the virtues of reverence by another name: a law which wills "the peace and preservation of all mankind."[279] The law of nature is "the will of God."[280] Indeed, the virtues of "reverence" are explicitly and prominently acknowledged by that name in much of Locke's writing.[281] But this is the part that looks backward to the mythic and Christian culture from which the second phase of theoretic culture was now emerging. The part that looked forward – to the world Locke was inadvertently creating – was his individualism and his rationalism, the virtues of self-assertion.

For Locke, as for Hobbes, the individual now comes *before* the community. The beginning of political society "depends on the consent of *individuals* to join and make one society."[282] Locke's individualism and his rationalism go together: "[W]e are born free," he says, "as we are born rational."[283] What Hobbes had called the "laws of nature" was, for Locke (like Hobbes), a "law of reason."[284] The individualism of his political philosophy is the flip side of the redefinition of the human as rational consciousness, the essence of this second phase of theoretic culture. "*Reason*," says Locke, italicising his own words, "*must be our last judge and guide in everything.*"[285]

Beginning like Descartes, from the *cogito* – the proof of human existence from the experience of doubt, that is to say, from *thought* – Locke also followed him in rooting the nature of the human in the activity of the *mind.*[286] Indeed, theoretic culture's conception of the world is inevitably so mind-centred that Locke now took it for granted that God is simply "an eternal Mind," "an eternal *cogitative* being."[287] For Locke, as for Descartes, a human being is a "thinking thing"[288] in a world of other things: a "thinking substance" in a world of other substances.[289] Echoing Aristotle and Aquinas, Locke said that human knowledge "is real only so far as there is a conformity between our ideas and *the reality of things.*"[290] But theoretic culture had now passed beyond the world of "*It is*" (B1) and had firmly entered the world of "*It* is" (B2). Locke and his contemporaries had left behind the first phase of theoretic culture – in which thinking was still allied with intuition, the world of Aristotle and Aquinas (B1) – to enter theoretic culture's new, second phase. In this new world, Locke helped reduce truth to a matter only of correct "propositions."[291] And the ideas from which correct propositions are composed now come largely from our senses. Theoretic culture's second phase is based on the new alliance of thinking with "sensing" (B2).[292]

Locke denied that humans have more than a few innate mental endowments and argued that almost all human ideas are put together from simple sense data, which are then assembled into more "complex ideas" by the individual, perceiving ego: a social "atom" just like the tiny atoms or "particles" that make up the substances it perceives.[293] The human, for Locke, is just another individual thing in a world of individual things. And that Lockean, individual self is still our reflex assumption about what it is to be a human being. As I noted in chapter 4, Charles Taylor calls this modern, Lockean self the "punctual" self. Taylor's adjective, "punctual" – also taken from geometry! – is intended to convey the idea that the individual Locke describes is entirely "disengaged," or detached: separated from the surrounding world, from the surrounding society – and even from itself. It stands back, distanced from all three, and seeks to remake them, in the spirit of Bacon and Descartes, through rational control. Like a point in geometry, Locke's new individual is "extensionless": it is "nowhere," except in its power to conceive things – including the self itself – as separate "objects" for the purposes of rational control.[294]

Cartesian rationalism, Hobbesian desire for power after power, Lockean individualism, and Bacon's assertive drive to establish the empire of man over things through science and technology – these four go together and reinforce each other. Together they have fashioned our modern and post-modern world, in which the virtues of self-assertion have taken centre stage.[295]

Northrop Frye calls the second phase of theoretic culture that began with Descartes (B2) the "descriptive phase of language":

> Here we start with a clear separation of subject and object, in which the subject exposes itself, in sense experience, to the impact of an objective world. The objective world is the order of nature; thinking or reflection follows the suggestion of sense experience, and words are the servomechanisms of reflection. Continuous prose is still employed, but all deductive procedures are increasingly subordinated to a primary inductive and fact-gathering process. ... In this phase we return to a direct relation between the order of nature and the order of words, as in the metaphorical phase [mythic culture], but with a sharp and consistent distinction between the two.[296]

The other seventeenth-century thinker, equally influenced by Descartes, who perhaps best embodied all this was Baruch Spinoza.[297] Spinoza presented his thought in a tightly constructed chain of arguments that was a model of the Cartesian "method," leading from an apparently obvious starting point to apparently necessary and inevitable conclusions.[298] From definitions and axioms, Spinoza constructs an expanding series of "propositions," each of which builds on its predecessors and is "proved" by a demonstration. After some of these proofs, Spinoza even adds the concluding notation for mathematical proofs: "Q.E.D." (*quod erat demonstrandum*: which was to be proved). The whole edifice is so seamless that readers are supposed to have the feeling (and often do) of being carried along by an irresistible logic – perhaps even despite themselves.[299]

Carried toward the virtues of self-assertion. Spinoza erected a metaphysical superstructure on the premises already provided by Hobbes. The essence of anything and everything, says Spinoza, is its own self-assertion.[300] Spinoza's vision of human (and all) life as a pure drive for self-assertion has come down to his posterity as the *conatus essendi* (the assertion of being). Descartes' *cogito* and Spinoza's *conatus* – rational thought and naked self-assertion – stand together at the door of the second phase of theoretic culture. They are the two pillars, or charter principles, of modern and (especially the *conatus*) of post-modern Western life.[301]

For philosophy's traditional ideal of the wise or good man, Spinoza substitutes the ideal of the "free" man.[302] A free man is one who "does the will of no one but himself."[303] Goodness is nothing more than "seeking our own profit," and the more a man seeks his own profit the better he is.[304] There are no such things as ends or final causes, and no one asserts himself for the sake of someone or something else.[305] Neither humility, nor compassion, nor shame, nor repentance are virtues. But "self-exaltation" can be, in the right circumstances.[306] Virtue is nothing but "human power itself."[307] "Self-satisfaction" is the "highest thing" we can hope for.[308]

Boiled down to these kinds of propositions, Spinoza can sound rather crude. But just as there were two Aristotles and two Aquinases, there were also two Spinozas. He was excommunicated from his Jewish congregation, but the spirit of reverence lived on in him. Spinoza had a special gift for turning traditional words and concepts inside out. One of them was God, a word that appears constantly in Spinoza's writing and gives it the superficial appearance of an almost religious mysticism. However, for Spinoza, God and Nature are now the same thing. Indeed, the name he frequently uses for God is *"Deus sive Natura"*: God *or* Nature.[309] God is a kind of "substance" indistinguishable from the totality of things.[310] So Spinoza's thought is, technically, a kind of "pantheism," in which humans are defined by their self-assertive stance toward the natural world. But Spinoza's pantheism yields an austere, demanding ethical system – many of the details of which would not have been uncongenial to Aristotle, or even to Aquinas. In order to rise to the intellectual vision of a world in which God is immanent in everything – in which God and the natural world are the same thing – human beings must still overcome and discipline the passions that would otherwise obscure such rational knowledge, just as they were required to do by the greatest thinkers in the first phase of theoretic culture. For Spinoza, the rational appetite, or reason (B2), is still in conflict with the sense appetite, or passions (A1), as it was for them, too.[311] Out of the virtues of self-assertion, Spinoza spins a rational vision of reality which still shimmers with the very spirit of reverence.

It may have been just a rhetorical strategy. In an age when the language of religion still had power, it was a smart move – one that has been repeated many times since, and, to be fair, a move the human paradox makes almost unavoidable (as you saw in the case of John Rawls, in chapter 12) – it was a smart move to dress up the virtues of self-assertion in the language of reverence.[312] If it was a strategy, it was a successful one. Spinoza's new religion of self-assertion initially horrified the seventeenth century. But the eighteenth century was a different story. It became one long "Spinozistic crescendo," a century in which it soon became a challenge to think in any way other than that of Spinoza.[313] Freedom and good became entirely identified – and confused.[314]

Aristotle had seen that reason was a form of self-assertion,[315] so it was perhaps inevitable that the culture of self-assertion, developing since the fourteenth century, should culminate, in the eighteenth-century, in an Age of Reason.

In this century, theoretic culture now identified what it was to be human with the mind. Aristotle and Aquinas had already said something close to this in the first phase of theoretic culture. That is why (following Merlin Donald) I have been calling it theoretic culture in the first place. But there had previously been something *beyond*: something divine, or something like love.[316] Human goodness had always been a kind of virtue.

Now in the second phase, there was no longer anything more. The identification of the human with the mind was complete. Descartes had said: I *think*, therefore I am. It was *thinking* henceforth that defined what it was to be a human being. The happiness of the free man, says Spinoza, is the free exercise of his understanding. But the strength of mind of the free man is not an exercise of the *will*, as the first phase of theoretic culture had conceived it. It is now the "*intellectual* virtue of confronting the facts impassively, without sentiment, and without the intrusion of subjective fears and hopes; it is the virtue of objectivity, an acquiescence in the rationally ascertained truth, however personally disagreeable the truth may seem."[317]

The distinctive feature of the human was, henceforth, the mind.[318] But having identified the human so completely with mind, the challenge for theoretic culture was now to get *outside* the mind and to link it back up with everything else. Now that humans are defined as minds or thinking beings, how can they get back to the insights of mimetic and mythic culture about meaning and value?

This proved to be much more difficult than could have been anticipated. Human reason – especially the radically reduced form of it endorsed by Descartes and Spinoza – is an analytic tool. It is good at breaking things up, or down, in the way Descartes' "method" proposed.[319] But it has much more difficulty putting them back together again.[320] Almost as soon as Descartes' *cogito* and Spinoza's *conatus* had launched the second phase of theoretic culture, things began to fall apart. Into a series of insoluble "problems."

One was the relationship between thinking and being, or between the mind and the world of sense. This problem spawned the endless quarrel between "realism" and "idealism" which has beset philosophy ever since.[321] Another was the so-called "mind/body" problem: how do our minds relate to the bodies in which they find themselves?[322] A third, to which I've already referred, was the relationship between "is" and "ought." How can the rational mind turn its perception and analysis of the "facts" into a recipe for a good life? The way things *are* doesn't really tell us how they *should* be. Or what we should do. Or how we should live. "From facts," Edmund Husserl was later to say, "follow always nothing but facts."[323] There's no obvious way from matter to meaning. From "is" to "ought."[324]

It was the British philosopher David Hume who famously identified this third problem in the eighteenth century.[325] That century and the next were spent in trying vainly to solve it, and the other insoluble dichotomies Descartes and Spinoza had created.[326] One of the most impressive attempts had already been made by the German polymath G.W. Leibniz: mathematician, scientist, historian, public servant, diplomat, librarian, philosopher – perhaps Western culture's last "universal man." Leibniz possessed one of the noblest, most subtle, and most richly furnished intellects in the whole Western tradition. And he had not forgotten the first phase of theoretic culture, even if others wanted to start all over again. He was richly steeped in medieval scholastic thought and tried to transmit its insights to the second phase of theoretic culture inaugurated by Descartes.[327]

Leibniz saw clearly that the banishing of final causes from Western thinking, under the influence of Descartes, Spinoza, and their successors, would lead – and was already leading – to the eclipse of the virtues of reverence.[328] He wanted to recover the reality of final causes and show how they can be reconciled with – are even essential to – the material and mechanical explanations that were beginning to dominate the new phase of theoretic culture, based increasingly, if not exclusively, on efficient causes.[329] To this second phase of theoretic culture, he was (and saw himself to be) what Plato had been to the first: the thinker who reached back to earlier cultures, to save their human values and virtues from the corrosive effect of the new, purely theoretic culture.[330] Foreshadowing Hegel (and this book), he saw the importance of a phenomenology of the spirit that would map the human and moral world into its various "divisions and subdivisions." He even saw that these divisions and subdivisions were based on contraries or "dichotomies," especially among the virtues.[331]

But Leibniz was so much a product of the new age that he could not easily break out of its mind-focussed paradigm. As a fellow mathematician, Leibniz was much taken with Descartes' attempt to apply geometric demonstrations to philosophical questions, and sometimes seemed to believe that it should be possible to establish metaphysical truth "with no less certainty than in the method of Euclid."[332] To Locke's *Essay Concerning Human Understanding* he could only respond, therefore, with a *new* essay on the very same theme: *Nouveaux essais sur l'entendement humain.* The "innate ideas" he stoutly defended against Locke were really (like Hobbes' "laws of nature") the virtues, or "dispositions" to virtue – justice, temperance, self-seeking, self-giving, and so on – by another name. Leibniz' emphasis on inherited "dispositions" was much closer to later evolutionary theory than Locke's notion of the human as a "blank slate," filled up with nothing more than immediate sense data.[333] But not only did Leibniz now conceive these dispositions to virtue as "ideas," he was even willing to concede that most of them should be reduced, by means of definitions, to rational principles and "axioms."[334] His brave attempt to marshal rational argument in defence of traditional religion, in his grand *Théodicée,* almost seemed to concede, by implication, that it was something residing essentially in the mind or thought.[335] He sometimes seemed to conceive God, like Spinoza, as a kind of "substance."[336] And his suggestion that the world was composed of individual "monads" – "windowless" simple substances, "the true Atoms of Nature and, in a word, the Elements of things" – sounded remarkably like Locke's atomistic, "punctual" self.[337] Even the schoolmen of the Middle Ages did not save him because he was often inclined to side with the very "nominalism" that had been their undoing and had paved the way to Descartes and Spinoza.[338] So Leibniz could slip into nominalism's "univocalism," describing God, not (like Aquinas) as being itself or the *act* or source of being, but (like Locke and the deists) as merely *a* being, the greatest of all beings.[339] Perhaps just the original Monad.[340]

Leibniz was too much a child of the new Cartesian world of "*It* is" – with its roots going back to Aquinas and Aristotle – to break out of it. His misguided project of justifying the existence of evil in the world – as part of God's plan for the "best of all possible worlds" – showed how much he remained a prisoner of that world.[341] He could not find his way back from Athens' God of the Cosmos – the Prime Mover – to Jerusalem's God of the heart, despite his own powerful intuition that it was necessary to do so.[342] He could not break the paradigm of theoretic culture.

The splendid "failure" of Leibniz – which was really one of the greatest achievements of the human intellect – this splendid "failure" led to the equally splendid effort of Immanuel Kant. Kant possessed a mind as noble as Leibniz. And, in his own way, he was equally determined to transmit the central moral truths or "commandments" of traditional Christian teaching to the second phase of theoretic culture. But his manner of doing so led him even deeper into the mind-centred vision of the human we have inherited.[343]

Kant's solution to Hume's problem was, in a way (like Plotinus and Plato), to *out-Descartes* Descartes. He first made the mental world entirely autonomous from the unknowable "real" world – the world of what he called "things-in-themselves" – and gave the mind innate principles or categories of judgment by which the external world – a world only of "appearances" or *phenomena* – is mentally constructed.[344] He then made the moral world a purely mental one, derived entirely from and "inexorably commanded by reason," whose strict rules would hold even if the world had never seen any examples of the actions it dictates, or if their feasibility could be seriously doubted, based on human experience.[345]

For Kant, his distinction between "appearances" and "things in themselves" was an attempt to make room for morality in a world ruled increasingly (in the Western mind, at least) by the mechanical determinism of Isaac Newton's "natural laws." It served the same purpose as Plato's "ideas" at the first dawn of theoretic culture. It was a last-ditch attempt to save final causes from the assault they had endured ever since the attack of the medieval nominalists – an assault in which the mechanical universe of Descartes and Newton seemed likely to deliver the final blow. Kant's distinction between appearances and "things in themselves" is the distinction between events and acts. Events are determined entirely by a preceding, external event. Acts, on the other hand, originate to some degree in the actor herself, and so are not determined entirely by material, physical or efficient causes. They fall under the realm of freedom, not of necessity alone. There is an element of *choice*, and therefore of freedom, and of final cause. As "appearances" human beings are part of the world of time and space, and are hence "determined" largely by natural and efficient causes. But, as "things in themselves," they are part of a world beyond time and space, and are hence also "free" to pursue moral "ends," or final causes.[346]

This was a distinction very familiar to Aristotle and to Thomas Aquinas. For them, the virtues were precisely the habits of making good choices. But Kant now largely replaces the virtues with the concepts of "will" and, especially, "duty."[347] Descartes, Hobbes, and Spinoza had recognized self-assertion as the core of this new phase of theoretic culture, and Kant confirms it. Will is the "highest good and the condition of all others."[348] "Nothing in the world," he famously said, "indeed nothing even beyond the world – can possibly be conceived which could be called good without qualification except a *good will*."[349] And a good will is one that knows and does its duty. Indeed, the concept of duty "contains that of a good will."[350] Every other motive of human action must now give way to duty, "because duty is the condition of a will good in itself, whose worth transcends everything."[351] Empathy and even love itself are explicitly ruled out as sources of morality.[352]

To have any moral worth, an action must be done strictly from a sense of duty, which is the "necessity of an action executed from respect for law."[353] In the Newtonian world of "*It is*," for which Kant was consciously trying to invent a compatible moral theory, law now rules everything: "Everything in nature works according to laws."[354] And like Newton's law of gravity, the moral law is known by the mind, by human reason. For Aquinas the human "will" had been a "rational appetite."[355] For Kant it has become a "practical *reason*."[356] The adjective has become a noun. The contained has become the container. Human beings are now defined entirely by reason and locked up in their minds. They can find the formula for Hume's elusive "ought" – which Kant called the "categorical imperative" – *in the very concept of ought itself*.[357] The ground of moral obligation cannot be found, says Kant, in the nature of the human or in any empirical circumstances, but "solely in the concepts of pure reason."[358] "Ought" is simply the "connection" that reason makes between its own "subjective" motives to action (as efficient causes) and moral principles, or "Ideas," as final causes.[359] Humans are moral in following the principles they find in their rational minds "prior to all experience" (i.e., *a priori*), and in their implacable, inner, rational sense of duty.[360]

Like Aquinas, Kant sees the nature of the human as a field of conflict. But for Aquinas, it was largely a conflict between the virtues, between goods. For Kant, it is a conflict between reason and duty on the one hand, and human "needs" and "inclinations" on the other. We are usually in conflict with ourselves in following the stern dictates of conscience.[361] For Kant the "perplexity of opposing claims" is not between competing goods but between reason and the other human inclinations, which reason "despises" or "holds in contempt" – an "opposition of inclination to the precept of reason."[362]

Charles Taylor suggests you can sum up Kant's whole ethical theory "something like this: live up to what you really are, viz., rational agents."[363] But the real life of virtue is not something in the mind: it is an education of the internal feelings and of external behaviour. It is an "*éducation sentimentale*."[364] For Aquinas, how we act outwardly comes from "how we feel inwardly." Virtues are good habits of *outward* behaviour that reflect and express our *inward* habits of feeling. So good actions depend on "well-tempered emotions."[365] In the world of the virtues, desire and duty coincide and reinforce each other. For Kant they no longer do so. Duty "does not rest at all on feelings, impulses, and inclinations;

it rests merely on the relation of rational beings to one another."[366] For Aquinas, self-assertion is "perfected" by virtue. Kant sees it, instead, as "constrained" or "*restricted* by the moral law to agreement with the law."[367] In fact, we aren't really being good if we are influenced by any psychological "inclination," or even by the moral worth of the goal (actions of this kind have "no true moral worth") – or by anything other than reason and duty themselves.[368] After Kant, moral life is no longer a training in virtuous habits (as it still had been for Leibniz – and even for Locke[369]) but becomes instead a rational process of applying appropriate moral "principles" or "maxims" or laws to concrete situations – "even if it thwarts all my inclinations."[370] A virtuous person, by contrast, only rarely has to reflect on a course of action: she is carried forward, instead, by the feeling structure and habit of virtue itself. To perform a bad action would be not only wrong but even distasteful: contrary to her "second" nature.[371] But in the new Kantian world – which has become our own – good action must now be achieved instead through some kind of conscious moral or ethical "reasoning."[372]

Though intended to save traditional morality and even religion, this is, in some important ways, their opposite.[373] It is light years away from Augustine's psychology of "delight," or Aquinas' view that the will is rooted, first and above all, in love.[374] On the contrary, says Kant, moral action flows "from duty and from respect for the law, and not from love or for leaning toward that which the action is to produce."[375] For Kant, "respect for a law that orders love" seems to be more important than love itself.[376] He seems to put respect for the law *ahead even of the law, or what it orders.*[377]

This left Kant with what even he seems to have regarded as a serious – perhaps insoluble – problem about moral motivation, about the *incentive* for acting morally. Through reason alone, Kant thinks, we can *know* the good. We can know what we should do. *But what would make us do it?* For Kant, this seems to be largely a mystery. "[A]n explanation of how and why the universality of the maxim as law (and hence morality) interests us," he says, "is completely impossible for men. ... [H]ow the mere principle of the universal validity of all its maxims as laws ... can furnish an incentive and produce an interest which could be called purely moral; or, in other words, how pure reason can be practical – to explain this all human reason is wholly incompetent ... *An incentive must here be wholly absent* unless this idea of an intelligible world itself be the incentive or that in which reason primarily takes an interest. But to make this conceivable is precisely the problem we cannot solve."[378]

The only way we can make Kant's so-called moral laws of reason binding for us, as he himself says, is by an *arbitrary decision to act as if they were so*: an existential decision "to conduct ourselves according to the maxims of freedom *as if* they were laws of nature."[379] But how or why should we make such a radical, existential decision to act *as if*? Kant's own mind-centred theory is largely powerless to tell us. The best he can do is to suggest that the idea of the moral law is so "sublime" that it produces a kind of "reverence" – even a "reverential awe" – which, though it may be a "reluctant reverence," nevertheless moves our will to act: "through respect for the law and reverence for its duty. No other subjective principle must be assumed as incentive."[380]

But this only presents us with yet another problem. If the motivating power of the moral law is ultimately a kind of reverence, doesn't that mean it depends on a prior virtue of reverence? If we didn't already have habits of respect and of reverence, how or why would we feel reverence *for anything*, let alone for Kant's moral law?[381] There seems to be something missing here. Maybe reason isn't the whole story, after all.[382] Maybe reason is only a "moment," or stage, or element in a bigger story about the nature of the human. Maybe, without reverence, reason itself cannot even be reasonable, and can only be a self-assertive rationalism.[383]

Kant's solution to Hume's problem was magnificent. It was one of the most heroic efforts ever made, through reason alone, to find a way back from *is* to *ought*: back to the meaning and value – the self-giving – from which reason itself emerged. He reaffirmed that an authentically human freedom cannot be simply *negative* freedom, the unconstrained will, but must instead be a positive freedom, *freedom from* natural and "efficient" causes, so we can embrace truly human "ends," or "final" causes. His rediscovery that self-seeking (or *freedom to*) is ultimately just a kind of slavery – a slavery to desire, impulse, fate, or "mechanical" determinism – is one of the most powerful and eternal moral insights. His "categorical imperative" has much in common, in its practical import, with Paul, Augustine, and the whole Christian tradition.[384] It is one more version of the biblical Golden Rule, the same "do unto others" that had been the starting point of Gratian's medieval *Decretum*, and the end point for Thomas Hobbes in his so-called "laws of nature."[385] So Kant didn't get it from reason, as he claimed. He "rationalized" something that came to him from quite another source.[386] In its various formulations, Kant's version of the rule continues to inspire.[387] But it was purchased at the price of another series of disconnects: between the real world and the mind; between mind and body; between nature and morality; between feeling and reason; between reason and action; between the individual and society.[388] And the problems it left unsolved led to the third and final great effort to solve the dilemmas created by Descartes and Spinoza. It led, at the beginning of the nineteenth century, to the great speculative synthesis of G.W.F. Hegel.

If anyone possessed a mind equal to that of Leibniz, it was Hegel. He was the modern Aristotle. His capacious mind roamed over the whole field of human endeavour, from law to art to history to religion. Like Leibniz, he had a rich acquaintance with the whole philosophical tradition beginning with the presocratics, whom he rightly saw as distant precursors. He challenged the exclusive reign of the law of non-contradiction by resurrecting (with Kant's inadvertent help) the Platonic concept of "dialectic,"[389] and by pointing out that "every actual thing involves a coexistence of opposed elements."[390] "Instead of speaking by the maxim of Excluded Middle [i.e., the law of non-contradiction]," he argued, "... we should rather say: Everything is opposite. ... Contradiction is the very moving principle of the world."[391]

In this way, among others, Hegel showed that philosophy cannot be just an abstract analytic exercise but must always be, in a sense, the history of philosophy.[392] He enlarged Kant's rationalist morality by rooting ethical life, not in the abstract principles of an individual, rational mind, but rather in the specific demands of a concrete history and culture, or what – as you already saw, in chapter 12 – he called *sittlichkeit*.[393] For Hegel, only the custom, habit, and "second nature" of a living culture of virtue or *sittlichkeit* can solve Hume's problem of the relationship between "is" and "ought," the problem Kant's rational morality had only made worse.[394] Hegel recognized the "fury of destruction" wrought in the eighteenth century by the way in which a one-sided spirit of self-assertion – a purely "negative freedom," a "freedom of the void" – had freed itself entirely from the virtues of reverence.[395] And as you saw in chapter 2, he tried to reconcile the enduring tension between them by proclaiming a "logic" of human life in which these two poles of the human – the opposites of union and non-union (or identity and non-identity, or particularity and universality) – are finally united.[396]

In fact, with one decisive difference, Hegel's theory of the human and of Western cultural development – based on four "fundamental categories" – is very close to the one developed in this book so far. He recognized that the *history* of Western culture is shaped by the inner *structure* of human nature. And *vice versa*: that very history is still reflected in the enduring and eternal nature of the human. In Hegel's scheme, the human story begins with the "natural man" who first emerges from animal life. The characteristic feature of this aspect of the human, Hegel says, is "appetite" and "self-seeking," so you can easily recognize it as the part of the human I have called the virtues of Liberty (A1). In the development of the human, it is succeeded, Hegel says, by another "category" of the human he calls "immediate knowledge" or "innocence." This second category involves a sudden shift from the "lowest" to all the "finest" and "noblest" human virtues, such as trust, love, fidelity, simplicity, benevolence, sympathy, and faith. You can easily recognize this second stage as the corner of the human I have called the virtues of Reverence (A2). In Hegel's narrative, these first two elements or phases of the human are then succeeded by two more categories, in which the insights of "immediate knowledge" are gradually worked out in human consciousness. Hegel (following Kant) calls these next two stages or aspects of the human Understanding and Reason. Like Kant, Hegel reverses the customary meanings of these words. But in their normal meanings, they are easily recognizable as what I have called the virtues of Excellence (B1) and Equality (B2).[397] Hegel says these stages or "shapes of experience" form a *"circle of necessity* whose moments [i.e., the four stances and families of virtues, and their modes of expression in everyday life] are the ethical powers which regulate the life of individuals."[398] Virtue, says Hegel, is just this "ethical order reflected in the individual character."[399] So I can picture Hegel's whole system in a new version of the basic image I have been using throughout this book, as in Figure 63 on page 417.

As you can see, Hegel had a clear grasp of the nature of the human as it has been described in this book – one of the clearest in the whole Western tradition of thought – including what I have called the arrow of virtue, which Hegel himself calls "the 'procession' of spirit."[400] In fact, Figure 63 looks very like Figure 15 in chapter 7 (on page 143), where you saw how paradox breeds paradox.

What Hegel means by his concept of the Absolute Idea – the crowning pinnacle of his whole system – seems to be what I have called the human paradox or the whole nature of the human.[401] Hegel explains the Absolute Idea as simply "the unity of the idea of *life* [A1 & A2] with the idea of *cognition* [B1 & B2]." Both life and cognition, he says, are "one-sided." The first is merely "natural," and the second merely "conscious." The "unity and truth of these two is the Absolute Idea."[402] The "nature" of the human is an "absolute dialectic" or paradox, a paradox which "forms a circle" – a circle which "returns upon itself" – or even a "circle of circles" because every part or member of the circle is also the "beginning of a new member," that is to say, the beginning a new process of separative projection, leading to its own internal series of cascading paradoxes.[403] For Hegel, the Idea is *not* an "abstract thought": it's a "process."[404] Its "content" is simply the sum total of the various stages or "moments" in its historical development. The Absolute Idea

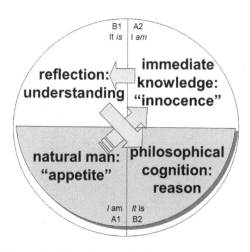

Figure 63. Hegel's four fundamental categories

is the whole "system" or "movement," the whole "procession of spirit," the whole human paradox.[405]

But as I already pointed out in chapters 7 and 10, the flat form of Figure 63 could give you an incorrect notion of Hegel's Absolute Idea. As I mentioned in the Introduction, Hegel thinks the development of Western civilization has taken a form similar to a spiral staircase. Each of the stages – "moments" or landings on the staircase – is an image of the *whole* pattern, the whole nature of the human.[406] The whole circular or spiral pattern of human development is fully present and visible, in a "simplified" or "abbreviated" form, in any one of the human stages or cultures.[407] So, for a really accurate idea of Hegel's Absolute Idea, I now need to show you Figure 63 in the same 3D format as Figures 18 and 26, with all four of Hegel's categories implicitly present and available at *each* of the stages in the explicit unfolding of the Absolute Idea. Because the "procession of spirit" has progressively made them explicit and present to consciousness, the "modern world" has, "for the first time" in history, given all four corners "of the Idea their due." Because we stand at the top of the spiral staircase – and hence can see, understand, and internalize all the earlier stages – all four, according to Hegel, "are now coming into their right."[408]

You can see Hegel's Absolute Idea in a 3D format, in Figure 64, on page 418.

In Figure 64, you are "peering into the heart of Hegel's speculative thought." It gives you a visual representation of what Hegel means by what he calls the Absolute Idea, "a circular movement which

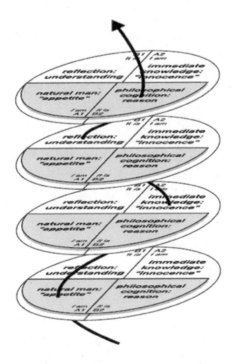

Figure 64. Hegel's Absolute Idea

produces an organic whole."[409] But as I said, there's one decisive – even monumental – difference between Hegel's fourfold picture of the human and mine. He was not at all unaware of or insensitive to the importance of the virtues.[410] But what ultimately counts for Hegel is not so much the virtues themselves as the rational concepts or thoughts which, he assumes, lie behind them and explain them. The rational concepts that make the virtues virtuous.[411] For Hegel, the four fundamental categories aren't just families of virtues. They are, more fundamentally, categories of thought, "thought-forms," or "thought-types." The "procession of spirit" represented by the arrows in Figures 62 and 63 signified for Hegel not just an arrow of virtue but – more deeply, and more importantly – different stages, or "moments," or "grades in the self-determination of thought."[412] It's not merely that the human is entirely defined by thought – "a being that thinks." For Hegel, thought is the very "heart and soul of the world," "the constitutive substance of external things," "the basis of everything."[413]

In the end, Hegel's impressive achievement brought the second phase of theoretic culture to a close by stretching it to its breaking point. For Hegel, the reconciliation between the two sides of the human paradox – between union and non-union, between life and cognition, between reverence and self-assertion – is something that is achieved by and in the rational mind. It is "found in thought and thought only."[414] Rather than putting human reason back into perspective, he saw the march of history as nothing but the triumph of reason itself. It is nothing other than reason unfolding itself or mind knowing itself. It is a "march of mental development," a progress in "self-consciousness," the "building of reason into the real world," mind giving itself "actuality in the process of *World-History*," "clothing itself with the form of events."[415] At the basis of reality is conceptual necessity, and history is just the working out or unfolding of this inner concept that was already there from the beginning. The real is rational, and the rational is the real.[416] "Reason governs the world and has consequently governed its history."[417] The ultimate destination of this kind of absolute reason or mind is not just human action in the world but some kind of completely clear and explicit conceptual statement, or proposition.[418]

This is the sense in which Hegel represents the highest or most extreme point of theoretic culture, the point at which it begins to break down. He represents the extreme development of that emphasis on reason and the rational mind – as the definition of the human – that had begun with Aristotle and reached one its previous summits in Thomas Aquinas.[419] But for them (and even for Leibniz) there had remained something important beyond the reach of mind, something unknowable toward which the mind is continually striving, through means that must go beyond the mind alone. For Hegel, like Kant, all of this disappears.[420] In his description of the human, reason is not only central: it is no longer trying (as Charles Taylor puts it) "to render a reality whose foundations can never be definitively identified, nor is it the thought of a subject whose deeper instincts, cravings and aspirations can never be fully fathomed. On the contrary, at the root of reality, as in the depths of himself, the subject ultimately finds clear conceptual necessity."[421]

Farther than this, theoretic culture cannot go. The process that began with Aristotle has, in Hegel, reached its own outer limits.[422] So now I am finally in a position to expand Figure 62 to include the second phase of theoretic culture, the one that began with Descartes. You can see this expanded picture in Figure 65 on page 420.

You will notice that (with the exception of Hobbes, Machiavelli, and Montaigne, who anticipate the next phase) I've located most of the thinkers of the second phase of theoretic culture in the quadrant of the

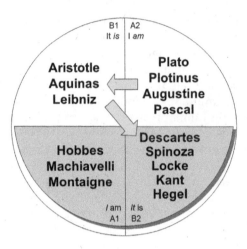

Figure 65. From Plato to Hegel

human stance I call "*It* is" (B2). One of the unifying themes of this second phase of theoretic culture (and of theoretic culture still today) is the way its leading thinkers – whatever their differences – all confront the otherness of what Kant now calls a "phenomenal" world: a world of separate, controllable things, or *phenomena*, distinguished by their very *thingness*, or "itness," rather than (as in the first phase) by the mystery of being.[423] Human beings' relation to the world is now primarily a mental, cognitive, or rational relationship. Something that takes place in the mind. It is a form of knowing. And what humans know, through the data of their senses, are "objects."[424] "Philosophy," says John Locke (echoing Aristotle and Aquinas), "is nothing but the true knowledge of things."[425] For Locke and his successors, all knowledge is "founded in particular things" – that is, in the stance of "*It* is" (B2).[426] The "concept of the *thing*," says Kant, "is the foundation of all determination of existence." Even for Hobbes and Locke, the "laws of nature" were still the traditional human virtues by a new name. But for Kant, they have become merely the relationship between two kinds of laws or rules: the laws of things or objects of experience on the one hand – "the laws of their connection" – and the rules for knowing things on the other: the rules of cognition "in us." Kant even reinvents the concept of community – a critical foundation for the virtues of reverence – as merely a "community of *things*," "parts which constitute together a total possible *cognition*."[427]

Philosophy, says Hegel, echoing Locke and Kant, is nothing more than the "*thinking study of things*."[428] Neither Locke nor Hegel invented the new philosophical primacy of "things." Aristotle and Aquinas had already said something very similar. They were the precursors who had shaped theoretic culture and prepared the way for this new world of things, the world of "*It* is" (B2). However, in the first phase of theoretic culture, they had remained much more alive to the impenetrable mystery that things *are*. Hence Aristotle's definition of metaphysics: the science of being *as* being.[429] The first question that must be asked, says Leibniz – vainly defending the pre-modern stance of "It *is*" (B1) – is: why is there anything at all, rather than nothing?[430] Behind the reality of things lies the ultimate mystery that there *are* any things at all.[431]

Mystery doesn't have much of a place in this new Cartesian, mind-centred, knowledge-focussed world of "*It* is" – of "sensing with thinking" – where human beings are characterized primarily by their capacity for "objective" thought rather than by their potential for virtue. The goal now is clarity and certainty. Better the modest things you can know *and control* than worrying or speculating – as the medieval scholastics were now said dismissively to have done – about things you can't. Where mystery survives at all, it is, as in Hegel's vision, unfolding itself through the historical process into the truth of a perfectly clear, mental concept. For Hegel, the mystical is no longer something "thought cannot both reach and comprehend" but "merely" something that "lies beyond the compass of understanding" – in his reduced sense, that is, beyond purely analytic reason. But not beyond "reason" (in his sense), or the human mind.[432]

The emphasis on mind and the confrontation with the neutral otherness of a "phenomenal" world go together. They are held together by the virtues of self-assertion that underlie them both. Reason itself, as Aristotle had noticed, is a virtue of self-assertion. As soon as we begin to think analytically or critically – as soon as we begin to exercise what we think of as rational consciousness – we are already *asserting* ourselves by "demanding" an explanation for things, even when we can offer no justification for our own demanding.[433] The very "principle of identity" ("this is that," or A=A) – which, together with its flip-side, the law of non-contradiction, is the foundation of all rational logic, and all logical rationalism – is itself an *assertion*, and a form of self-assertion.[434]

Since the seventeenth century, two central ideas – the ideas of freedom and free will on the one hand, and the domination and subjection of nature through science and technology on the other – these two ideas have been held together by a common stance toward the world and by a common moral outlook. The stance is the stance of "*It* is," the stance of disengaged reason, standing back from the world, viewing it objectively – as an "object" – and seeking to master it through instrumental control. The moral outlook is that of the virtues of self-assertion, which express themselves both in the assertive human drive for liberation and freedom from constraint, and in the equally assertive drive to understand and master nature, and subject it to our control.[435] Behind both the stance and the outlook is the culture of individualism and self-assertion that has been gradually developing since the late Middle Ages or even (in canon law, for example) since the beginning of the Christian era.

Thought can sometimes seem to lead the way in cultural evolution. We live differently, we assume, because we have new ideas, a new vocabulary, new categories of thought. But very often the new ideas appeal to us, the new categories make sense, and we intuitively respond to the new words because we are already living or beginning to live – or wanting to live – in the ways they describe or capture. If we were not, the new ideas would fall among thorns, or on stony ground, and they would bear no fruit.[436] How many people have put forward ideas in this untimely way and received no response? Thus, thought doesn't always – or even usually – lead the way in cultural evolution. Or at least it seems to be a two-way street. Ideas can certainly change the world. But we also respond to or take up new ideas and words because we're already living, or want to live, or need to live, in the ways they describe. "Practices cultivate intuitions, intuitions about what is decent," or desirable or worthy, and the intuitions then support or stimulate the development of concepts that explain or justify the practices.[437] The practices often "carry" the understanding, which is embedded in, and implicitly – even unconsciously – justified by, the practices.[438] Modern and post-modern Western societies, for example, tend to be secular, relativist, pragmatic, and materialistic "by virtue of what they *do*," as Terry Eagleton (b. 1943) puts it, "not just of what they *believe*. As far as these attitudes go, they do not have much of a choice."[439] Self-assertion creates a "first language" for modern and post-modern Western culture, so the virtues of reverence, when they survive, are reduced to the status of a "second language."[440]

In the second phase of theoretic culture, the drive to self-assertion that fuelled it still remained largely hidden or disguised. Hobbes came closest to revealing it by recognizing the fundamental human disposition to dominate, our primal drive for "dominion over others."[441] But he quickly took this insight back, in his "laws of nature," which were the virtues of reverence under a new name. Even Spinoza's *conatus*, his self-assertive reductionism, had somehow contrived to present itself, in its practical consequences, as an austere ethos, comparable in its inspiring nobility to those of Aristotle and Aquinas. Even more so, those of Kant and Hegel, which consciously reached back to mythic culture, aiming to preserve its vision of meaning, significance, and value in the new mind-centred world of "*It* is." They had tried to retrace the path from Athens to Jerusalem: to get back to "ought" from the new world of "*It* is."[442] Many would follow them in this effort and still do today. But when Hegel stretched theoretic culture to the breaking point, the self-assertive impulses lodged at its core were ready to emerge in their own right.[443]

Power and pleasure: toward post-modern culture

Like mimetic and mythic culture, theoretic culture in both its forms – modern (B2) and pre-modern (B1) – continues to play an important role in contemporary, post-modern life.

No cultural form, as you have seen, is ever lost from the human repertoire. We still use theoretic culture for many purposes, especially those requiring analysis, research, critical thought, abstract theorizing, and intellectual or policy debates. It has high prestige, and many of us would like to think we live by it, and in it, exclusively, or almost exclusively: that we are, above all, creatures of dispassionate reason. We sometimes use that as an excuse for not embracing or even considering other cultural modes or options, such as religious practice. Some professions, such as academic scholars, use theoretic culture for their work. And since university professors write many of the books we read, they are sometimes inclined to think the work they do shows theoretic culture still provides the "dominant" frame for contemporary life.[444]

Because of what philosophers do and how they do it, the corner of the human I've identified with the virtues of Equality (B2) is the default mode for most philosophers since the Cartesian revolution. Thus, in the nineteenth century, Western philosophy continued to be written largely in the mode of theoretic culture (as it still does today). Germany witnessed a neo-Kantian revival in the second half of the century, while in Britain the influence of Hegel continued to be felt in creative ways. Benjamin Constant, Auguste Comte, John Stuart Mill, T.H. Green, F.H. Bradley, Hermann Cohen, Henri Bergson, and Edmund Husserl all wrote and thought in ways that are recognizably consistent with those of their predecessors in the second phase of theoretic culture, from Descartes to Hegel. Whether they were "realists" or positivists, who emphasized the primacy of material fact over thought, or "idealists," who emphasized the primacy of thought over things, they were all alike prisoners of the virtues of Equality (B2), the virtues of sensing with thinking – emphasizing *either* sensing *or* thinking, or trying in vain to unite them but rarely escaping from the exclusive, binary embrace of "*It* is" (B2).[445]

However, while the philosophers of the nineteenth century continued by and large in this groove of the second phase of theoretic culture, the stance of "*It* is" was gradually ceasing to be the leading edge of the wider Western culture. The arrow of virtue seemed to be moving on behind their backs. It was moving on from one side of the paradox of self-assertion to the other: from the stance of "*It* is" to "*I* am," from sensing with thinking to sensing with feeling, from the virtues of Equality (B2) to the virtues of Liberty (A1) – for which Mill became the classic spokesman. He declared that "self-assertion" is just as much a part of the nature of the human as "self-denial," and "self-development" is just as important as self-control.[446]

We don't yet have an agreed upon name for the new Western cultural condition that began to develop in the nineteenth century. Since it comes in the wake of the second phase of "theoretic culture," it could perhaps be called, simply, "post-theoretic."[447] Alternatively, since "post-theoretic" culture gives a new importance to art, it could also be called (as Richard Rorty suggests) "literary culture."[448] But "literary" is a rather narrow term to capture the broad range of cultural expression and individual expressiveness released in this new phase by the virtues of Liberty (A1). To capture them better, I could instead call the culture of this next phase – following the insights of Charles Taylor – a culture of "expressivism" and "authenticity."[449] Or, following Terry Eagleton, an "aesthetic" culture.[450] Or, combining all these hints, I could call it simply, with deliberate redundancy, "*cultural* culture." But even this largest notion seems to capture only *one* side of the new paradox of "post-theoretic culture." It captures the virtues of Pleasure (A1b), but not those of Power (A1a).

Another name that could be used to describe our contemporary cultural condition is "post-modern." The concept of the "modern" is a very flexible one, to say the least. In everyday speech we often use the word "modern" as a synonym for contemporary. To say that something is modern is to say that it is of today, it is current, it is happening now.

However, the Western tradition has been using the word "modern" in this very way since at least the thirteenth century, when the "nominalism" triumphant in medieval universities was sometimes called the "modern way" (*via moderna*) in contrast to the "old way" (*via antiqua*) of Thomas Aquinas. And the new "mysticism" (that emerged in reaction to nominalism) was sometimes called a "modern" spirituality (*devotio moderna*).[451] The word "modern" was used again, in exactly the same way, in seventeenth-century France, in the great cultural debate between the "ancients" and the "moderns" (*querelle des anciens et des modernes*), who promoted learning from antiquity and creating art to suit the present day, respectively. About the same time, it was also used in music to distinguish the new *stile moderno* of Baroque composers like Monteverdi from the *stile antico* of their Renaissance predecessors, such as Palestrina.

So "modern" is a term we Westerners have been using for almost a thousand years to describe the emerging culture that has shaped our world, the culture of self-assertion.[452] For close to ten centuries, it has meant simply, "contemporary," or "belonging to today, or to the recent past." That makes it rather imprecise, to say the least. It has no end point but just goes on, indefinitely, into the present. Both the imprecision and the endlessness are encouraged by the implicitly positive spin we give – and have been giving, through all those centuries – to the word modern. To call something "modern" is not just to describe something as belonging to today, but also to imply that it is somehow better, or more relevant, or more up-to-date, than something else, than anything that is *not* modern.

The imprecision of the word "modern," and its implicit, positive bias, make it somewhat less than helpful for thinking about the evolution of our Western culture. So I propose to make it a little more precise by putting some kind of reasonable time limit on its use. In this book, I will use – and have already been using – "modern" to designate the second phase of theoretic culture. For my purposes, the "modern" era begins with Descartes, and it comes to an end with Hegel and his stretching of human reason to the point where it begins to break down. In that case then, the culture that comes after it – the culture of the break-down – could legitimately be called "post-modern."

Since there is no agreed upon name for "post-theoretic" culture into which we are currently evolving, I will often use the neutral term "post-modern," in order to make room for *both* sides of this new cultural paradox: both pleasure (A1b) *and* power (A1a). Thus I can now update Figures 58 and 59 to show our post-modern condition on the map of the human. You can see the result in Figure 66 on page 426.

You may think I'm being a bit premature in labelling post-Hegelian culture as "post-modern." We're accustomed to using the term "postmodern" (without a hyphen) to designate cultural currents that don't arise until somewhere in the middle or later decades of the twentieth century, in the 1960s, or 1970s, or even in the 1980s. For most of the nineteenth and twentieth centuries, the term modern or "modernist" is often used. But, apart from the fact that, as I pointed out, "modern" has been used to mean "current" or "contemporary" since at least the Middle Ages, Terry Eagleton argues, plausibly, that the cultural currents of the last two centuries

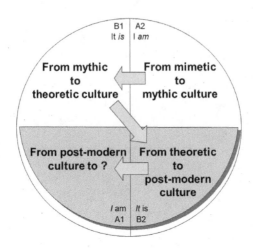

Figure 66. From mimetic to post-modern culture

are all symptoms of transition, from theoretic culture to whatever comes
after it: to post-theoretic or post-modern culture. "Modern*ism*" isn't
"modern," he suggests, it's a sign of transition to the postmodern.[453] Since
I'm using the term "post-modern" to describe the Western cultural shift
that follows the overreaching of Hegel, I will hyphenate it, to distinguish
it from the usual, narrower meaning of "postmodern."

It sometimes makes sense to continue talking about the "modern" as
something "contemporary," when referring, for example, to the ways in
which the Enlightenment reverence for analytic reason continues to manifest itself in our culture today – the many ways we still live in a theoretic
culture. In that sense, we can be said to be living in both a modern *and* a
post-modern world at the same time. That's why I've already been linking those two terms throughout this book, and why I'll continue to do
so, as appropriate. But, for historical purposes, in this book, the modern
era comes to an end with Hegel, and is succeeded by the post-modern.[454]

The second phase of theoretic culture had the effect – not always
intentional – of shifting the centre of Western culture from the virtues
of reverence to the virtues of self-assertion (specifically, from the virtues
of Excellence [B1] to the virtues of Equality [B2]). The cultural work of
the next two centuries was therefore largely devoted to working out the
consequences of that transition, at a time when Western culture was still
overshadowed by awareness – sometimes even a painful awareness – of
how much had been lost in the process. In the nineteenth and much of
the twentieth century, the new virtues of self-assertion tried very hard to

take over the key functions formerly performed by the virtues of reverence. Scientific rationalism, as Terry Eagleton points out, took over their role as the standard of truth; radical politics took on their role as a force of social transformation. "Culture," in the broadest sense, inherited reverence's communitarian impulse, while (in the narrower sense) art and the arts did their best to replicate its "spiritual depth."[455] They do so still. But none of these efforts have fully panned out, and self-assertion has gradually lost its need to look backward: to masquerade as reverence. In the twenty-first century, thanks largely to technology, it grows more and more at home, just being itself.[456] As the virtues of self-assertion carry us forward, beyond theoretic culture, these nineteenth and twentieth century cultural developments (often called "modernism") can now perhaps be seen as a transition phase: a transition from theoretic to post-theoretic culture, to the post-modern, the condition in which we find ourselves in the first half of the twenty-first century.

The two pillars of this developing post-modern culture are exactly those this new corner of the human paradox would lead you to expect. In chapter 8, you saw that the paradox of Liberty (A1) arises from two conflicting families of virtues, the virtues of Power (A1a) and of Pleasure (A1b) (Table 8 on page 162). These two families, with their own cascading, *internal* paradoxes – and the continuing *external* tension between Liberty (A1) and Equality (B2), the *other* side of the paradox of self-assertion (Table 7 on pages 157–8) – now furnish the leading edge of contemporary, post-modern culture. Sensing is still the foreground, as in the second phase of theoretic culture. But in post-modern culture, it has become allied, increasingly, with feeling rather than with thinking, yielding Charles Taylor's "expressive individualism" and a form of contemporary life Terry Eagleton describes as "aestheticized from end to end."[457]

The values of Power (A1a) had, of course, been implicit in the emerging culture of self-assertion since the thirteenth century. That's what self-assertion means, after all: the eternal human disposition to dominate. Aristotle and Aquinas had long ago identified this family of virtues, and Aquinas had called them (without any pejorative intention) the "irascible" virtues. But they also saw that, while these virtues are the indispensable engine room of the human – the source of all energy and accomplishment – they are also (for that same reason) the primary source of evil and need to be fenced-in and guided (or "perfected") by all the other virtues of the human paradox. But when mind replaces virtue at the core of the human, then virtue, as Spinoza himself had candidly recognized, becomes nothing but "human power itself."[458]

Spinoza was by no means the first to see this. As you have seen, the naked role of power in a mind-centred world had already been foreshadowed by Machiavelli and Thomas Hobbes. But Hobbes had fudged the issue with his so-called "laws of nature," which were really the old virtues of reverence in disguise. When the second phase of theoretic culture came to an end, however, Spinoza's *conatus*, the pure doctrine of self-assertion, already implicit in the assertive rationalism of the Enlightenment, was ready to step forward in its own right.

Kant himself had already proclaimed "the absolute worth of the will alone."[459] His disciple J.G. Fichte and two of Fichte's students, F.W.J. Schelling and Arthur Schopenhauer (1788–1860), went further: all developed philosophies of the ego and of the will.[460] For Fichte, the ego and everything else outside the ego – and our consciousness of both of them – are all merely the products of the ego's own "first original act" of self-assertion.[461] "My will, directed by no foreign agency in the supersensual world but by myself alone," said Fichte, "is [the] source of true life and of eternity."[462] "[E]verything is only in the Ego and for the Ego," said Schelling. True philosophy is "nothing other than a continuing elaboration of the Ego; its whole method consists in leading the Ego from one step of self-realization to another."[463] For Schopenhauer, will was nothing less than the reality behind Kant's "phenomenal" world. It was the elusive thing-in-itself: "the being-in-itself of every thing in the world, and ... the sole kernel of every phenomenon."[464]

Friedrich Jacobi (1743–1819) – one of the few eighteenth-century thinkers who resisted the self-assertive outlook of the second phase of theoretic culture – described the philosophy of Kant's offspring as a "speculative Egotism," a "second Spinozism."[465] "A Spinozism," as Étienne Gilson puts it, "of the will."[466] But that's what Spinozism had always been from the start, even in the hands of Spinoza himself. Kant's successors only made explicit the spirit of self-assertion that had been the underground, driving force of the second phase of theoretic culture all along.

The nineteenth-century thinker who articulated the virtues of Power (A1a) with the greatest flair was Friedrich Nietzsche. Many other nineteenth century thinkers also developed philosophies of power. Karl Marx (1818–83) and the Communists, for example.[467] Or at the other end of the political spectrum, Herbert Spencer and the other Social Darwinists he helped to spawn.[468] Spencer took Charles Darwin's (1809–82) theory of the "struggle for life" (just an alternative translation of Spinoza's *conatus essendi*[469]) and turned it into the more sinister concept of the "survival of the fittest."[470] Somewhere in the middle between these two extremes, even John Stuart Mill endorsed the view that the end of human life is the "individuality of power and development."[471] But Nietzsche outdid them all in penetration of thought and power of expression. He understood as clearly as any previous philosopher that *all* human action is a form of self-assertion, that without self-assertion there is no action of any kind. That everything human begins and ends in self-assertion.

For Nietzsche, self-assertion – or what he calls "the will to power" – is "the most fundamental fact" of both the natural and human worlds, from which everything else – all "becoming and affecting" – result.[472] He expressed this conviction more boldly, more dramatically, and with more rhetorical flourish than any previous writer.[473] In his most famous work, *Thus Spoke Zarathustra*, and in all his subsequent books, he declared that the will to power is the central driving force, the essential core of the human. "Only where life is, there also is will," says Nietzsche's Zarathustra: "not will to life, but – so I teach you – will to power!"[474]

The fierceness and provocative bravado with which Nietzsche proclaimed the "will to power" as the essence of the human turned his books into source material for people like Oswald Spengler (1880–1936) and the twentieth-century Nazis, who were glad to mine them for quotes that would serve their own purposes.[475] Swaggering, bombastic declarations, taken out of context – declarations such as: "You say it is the good cause that hallows even war? I tell you: it is the good war that hallows every cause." Or: "War and courage have done more great things than loving your neighbour." – provided them with ample ammunition.[476] Nietzsche's rhetoric did more than a little to fuel an appetite for violence and death that has become an important part of the post-modern anti-Enlightenment culture of self-assertion.[477]

This interpretation of Nietzsche was enhanced by the form of his work: a form that confirms the impression theoretic culture was now beginning to be left behind. Nietzsche was as much artist as philosopher, and the form of his work was no longer the discursive, analytic prose of philosophers from Aristotle to Hegel but – like Plato, at the previous frontier of theoretic culture – self-consciously literary composition: dramatic, declamatory, prophetic, aphoristic, and often fragmentary or non-linear – even poetic – like the new, more impressionistic works of visual art.

Though himself an artist – and though his own work is a "sustained celebration of creativity"[478] – Nietzsche himself insisted that work and power come nevertheless before the pleasures of art, imagination, creativity, and play that are central to the *other* side of the paradox of Liberty (A1): the virtues of Pleasure (A1b). "Of what account is pleasure?" asks Zarathustra. "… I have not aspired after pleasure, I aspire after my work."[479] "Not for pleasure does man strive," says Nietzsche in an outline for *The Will to Power*: "but for power."[480] A powerful nature has no "interest in pleasure," he says in the book itself (a posthumous work compiled by his sister from his notebooks), "it is strength and action."[481]

But in the emerging post-modern or post-theoretic culture, there were many voices ready to champion this *other* side of the paradox of Liberty (A1): to proclaim, instead, the priority of pleasure, play, creativity, and imaginative experience (A1b). This outlook was one of the important strands in the Romantic movement at the beginning of the nineteenth century, and its roots went back even further: to Herder, Goethe, and Rousseau in the eighteenth century. Dissatisfied with the atomistic, mechanistic, reductionist world they felt was being prepared by the rationalism of the Enlightenment, the poets, thinkers, and artists of the Romantic movement argued instead for a more organic, holistic, expressive world view, more respectfully attuned to nature, to community, and to the inner urgings of the human heart. They especially highlighted nature and art as sources that could provide an antidote to the dehumanizing rationalism of the Enlightenment. In the post-theoretic culture of self-assertion, imagination begins to take the place of religious life: it "stands in for soul."[482] Consistent with the movement beyond theoretical culture, many of these voices came from beyond the philosophical community.

A representative figure in the second half of the nineteenth century was the English cultural historian Walter Pater (1839–94). Pater exalted the momentary "mood of passion or insight or intellectual excitement" as the highest goal of human life. The end of human life, he suggested, is *not* "the fruit of experience," as most traditional human wisdom had assumed, but rather "experience itself." From the perspective of the self-assertive virtues of Pleasure (A1b), the traditional objective of human wisdom – to develop human virtues – seems now to be a kind of "failure." Because "habits" – even virtuous habits – are an obstacle to the higher objective of cultivating the spontaneity and "great passions" of the ecstatic life. Only a limited number of "pulses" are available to any human being, in a single human life. So the objective of life must be simply "getting as many pulsations as possible into the given time." Because of its "awful brevity," life should become simply "one desperate effort to see and touch": "To burn always with this hard, gemlike flame, to maintain this ecstasy, is success in life." For this kind of life, "the poetic passion, the desire of beauty, the love of art for art's sake, has most" to offer, says Pater, "for art comes to you proposing frankly to give nothing but the highest quality to your moments as they pass, *and simply for those moments' sake*."[483]

These sentiments were to have a powerful echo in the remainder of the nineteenth century – in the "art for art's sake" or "aesthetic" movement in Swinburne, Baudelaire, Verlaine, Rimbaud, Mallarmé, Wilde, and many others in England and France; in the artistic movement of "impressionism"; and on into the many "modernist" cultural movements of the twentieth century.[484] The young German poet Hugo von Hofmannsthal (1874–1929) described this same quest for the intensity of momentary experience in 1902 as the aesthetic pursuit of "something entirely unnamed, even barely nameable, which, at such moments, reveals itself to me, filling like a vessel any casual object of my daily surroundings with an overflowing flood of higher life." Moments of heightened aesthetic perception and awareness like these, von Hofmannsthal said, are "the Present, the fullest, most exalted Present."[485]

The aesthetic and other virtues of Pleasure (A1b) thus found exponents beyond the philosophical community. But as they were becoming so central to the new post-modern culture, it was inevitable that they should also find support in the philosophical world. A year after von Hofmannsthal's story appeared, the English philosopher G.E. Moore (1873–1958) published *Principia Ethica*, a work which was to influence the philosophical, literary, and wider social worlds of the coming century, beginning with John Maynard Keynes, Virginia Woolf, and the rest of the culturally influential Bloomsbury group. Moore proposed to resolve the age-old problem of human ethics by asserting (among other things) that "personal affections and aesthetic enjoyments include *all* the greatest, and *by far* the greatest goods we can imagine." This, Moore concluded, is "the ultimate and fundamental truth of Moral Philosophy." It is only for the sake of these two things "– in order that as much of them as possible may at some time exist – that any one can be justified in performing any public or private duty." They are, in fact, "the *raison d'être* of virtue."[486] Although Moore's conclusion seems to evacuate the very notion of virtue, the virtues of Pleasure (A1b) could scarcely have found a more forthright philosophical champion.

Thus, post-modern culture in the nineteenth century already exhibited the two sides of the paradox of Liberty (A1): the virtues of Power (A1a) and of Pleasure (A1b).[487] And, as you saw in chapter 4, these two have gradually come to define the public culture of the twentieth and twenty-first centuries. But they are not the only new avenue opened up in the aftermath of theoretic culture. Another option also began to emerge in the nineteenth century, one that points beyond this post-modern paradox. And this third option could be discerned – paradoxically! – even in the thought of Friedrich Nietzsche himself.

Nietzsche's deliberately provocative language obscures the ambiguity of his meaning, which is far more complex than the surface language often suggests. The "will to power" he exalted was a form of self-assertion, certainly.[488] But it was a self-assertion that, for Nietzsche, often seems to be turned *not* against others, but, like Kant, against the self itself. When he uses the rhetoric of "war," for example, Nietzsche seems to mean the contradictions and conflict between the virtues: not a war against others but a "war against oneself, that is to say self-control."[489] Nietzsche's will to power, in its highest form, turns out to be a kind of "self-overcoming."[490] His "highest idea" is that "Man is something that should be overcome."[491] Life, for Nietzsche, is "that *which must overcome itself again and again.*"[492] When he talks about his human ideal, the so-called "superman" – or, more properly translated, "*overman*" – that's what he appears to mean.[493] The person whose will to power has learned to "will backwards." Who has learned to "surrender," to "practise obedience." Who has learned that real power is "sacrifice and service and loving," even the "love that bears all punishment but also all guilt!"[494] Far from despising the self-giving virtues, Nietzsche reserves his highest praise for the person who "always gives and will not preserve himself."[495] The "*overman*" is the person who has learned to "*overcome*" *the self* through heroic self-assertion. The only kind of self-giving Nietzsche denounces is the self-giving inspired by weakness, cowardice, or self-hate – the form of self-giving he associated with Christian morality. For Nietzsche, the praiseworthy form of self-giving must be, instead, a genuine expression of self-assertion. He thus rediscovered one of the main themes of this book: that the highest form of self-assertion is a form of reverence. But, also, that the highest acts of reverence require the highest kind of self-assertion.[496]

Though he despised what he thought of as Christianity, Nietzsche – at least in these moods – was returning implicitly to something not unlike the *unselfing* perspective of Augustine and Thomas Aquinas, even to the virtues of (what Nietzsche himself refers to as) "reverence."[497] His "will to power" therefore points *beyond* the "I am" (A1) of his warrior *rhetoric* to the "I am" (A2) of its potential *meaning.*[498]

The nineteenth century thinker who opens up this third possibility for post-theoretic (or perhaps post-post-theoretic!) culture most strikingly is the Danish philosopher, Søren Kierkegaard (1813–55). No one saw more clearly than Kierkegaard how far Hegel had stretched the limits of theoretic culture, stretched them even to the breaking point, by confusing the realms of life and thought. The truth about life is not found, as Hegel assumed, in the mind or in thought, Kierkegaard said. It can only be found in real life. In thought, you may be able to hold two contradictory truths in your mind at the same time, as Hegel's dialectical logic had shown. But in real life you can't do two contradictory things at the same time. You have to choose. So real truth, the truth about real, lived existence, can only be found in "the reality of the act of choice," an "absolute either/or" with which "philosophy has nothing to do."[499]

In a world where existence, *not* thought, is the ultimate truth about reality, the only appropriate human response, says Kierkegaard, is a religious "faith." But in contrast to Calvin, Kierkegaard doesn't confuse faith with doctrine.[500] It is *not* a set of ideas or propositions. It is a *decision* – a "decision in existence"[501] – a decision about the right attitude or stance to adopt toward the mystery, the "objective uncertainty" that surrounds human life. Faith is precisely the decision to "embrace" this mystery or uncertainty with true reverence, "with the passion of the infinite."[502] It is a "paradox": a contradiction "between the infinite passion of the individual's inwardness and the objective uncertainty."[503] It is even, says Kierkegaard – in language that was to have many echoes in the twentieth century – "absurd."[504] But it is also the only path to truth and reality because the real, in a world of human beings, is "an inwardness that is infinitely interested in existing."[505] The truth is *in the reverence*. It is not in a "what" but in the "how" or the "mode" of relationship. Therefore even someone who worships a false God but "prays with the entire passion of the infinite … prays in truth to God though he worships an idol."[506] True reverence is a kind of *un*selfing, "a dying away from the self."[507] It shows itself in actions, in behaviour, in the virtues of reverence such as humility, in the "small events and ordinary humdrum activities of life."[508] The "glory of being human" is the glory of combining the virtues of self-assertion – such as care and work – with the virtues of reverence. God is Spirit. And human beings are most like God when they too are spirit. That is to say, when they go beyond "exercising dominion" – "which is also glorious and for which we are suited" – to humility and reverence, which are "most glorious of all."[509]

Kierkegaard's escape hatch from the dead end to which Hegel had brought the second phase of theoretic culture was not – like Nietzsche and Moore – to power or to pleasure, the virtues of Liberty (A1), the next stage in the arrow of virtue. Rather, he moved past them, or beyond them, to the virtues of Reverence (A2). With the addition of Kierkegaard to the story of post-modern culture, I can now update Figure 65 to include some of the thinkers from post-theoretic or post-modern culture, up to the beginning of the twentieth century. You can see this new map of the human paradox in Figure 67 on page 434.

Kierkegaard, like Nietzsche, was to have immense influence on the thought of the twentieth century. His rediscovery of the reality and mystery of existence, or being, would inform one of its main philosophical currents. And his challenge to the excesses of theoretic culture suggests one of the possible escape routes from our current post-modern condition. That's a possibility I'll come back to.

But now we need to look briefly at the next phase of the post-modern, in the twentieth and twenty-first centuries.

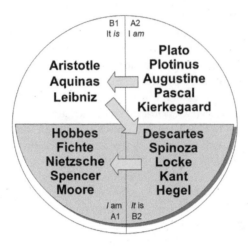

Figure 67. From Plato to G.E. Moore

The twentieth and twenty-first centuries

I obviously can't do justice here to all the currents of Western philosophy in the twentieth and twenty-first centuries (so far), any more than I could for previous periods. So, I will limit myself to four main categories or currents of thought, each of which can be identified with a specific region and culture. The first is the stream that began as "realism" (in opposition to the remnants of Hegelian "idealism") or "logical positivism," and later became known as "analytic" philosophy. A second, closely connected to the first, is called phenomenology; a third, existentialism; and a fourth, pragmatism.

The first stream is a largely (but not exclusively) English-speaking – even British or "Oxbridge" – phenomenon. In addition to G.E. Moore, it includes philosophers such as Bertrand Russell, Ludwig Wittgenstein, Rudolf Carnap, A.J. Ayer, Gilbert Ryle, Richard Hare, J.L. Austin, Stuart Hampshire, P.F. Strawson, W.V. Quine, and others. The link between logical positivism and analytic philosophy seems to be Wittgenstein, whose about-face in the 1930s was the hinge between the first and the second.[510] Analytic philosophy took a "linguistic turn" after the Second World War, focussing for several decades on the analysis of "ordinary language."[511] Though it began the twentieth century in quite a dogmatic mood – filled with the hubris of mathematical logic – this outlook ended it in a much more modest frame of mind, aspiring to little more than minor linguistic clarifications in everyday speech.[512] In neither mood did it have much appetite for the large traditional questions of philosophy about the meaning of life and the nature of the human. Indeed, this brand of twentieth century philosophy tended to see such questions as fundamentally misguided – as merely "linguistic" errors – and reduced its own ambition correspondingly, aiming to be little more than a handmaid to science, helping to tidy it up around the edges.[513] Since neither analytic reason nor empirical observation can get you from "is" to "ought," analytic philosophy normally steers away from constructive or substantive views about "ought" altogether.[514]

One exception to this English-speaking trend was the British mathematician Alfred North Whitehead, co-author (with Bertrand Russell) of *Principia Mathematica* (1910–13), one of the foundational texts of logical positivism. In later years, however, Whitehead turned his attention to metaphysics and aimed to develop a philosophical outlook that can reconcile realism and idealism, or Locke and Hume's "sensationalism" with Kant's "subjectivism."[515] In the process, he developed a vision of the human largely consistent with this book. In Whitehead's account, human beings are "constituted" by four "categories" or "phases" of feeling: four stages or phases of "experience," or "four modes of functioning."[516] "In the place of the Hegelian hierarchy of categories of *thought*," Whitehead rediscovers and substitutes the prior "hierarchy of categories of *feeling*."[517]

Whitehead uses a variety of labels for his four categories. He sometimes calls his first category the "dative phase" of feeling. It is the "primitive experience" of a physical, external world, in which "feeling, and reference to an exterior world pass into appetition."[518] This is the phase of sense appetite and sensing with feeling (A1). The second category is called "conformal feeling." This is a subsequent (but still largely "physical") stage of "*sympathy*, that is, feeling the feeling *in* another and feeling conformally *with* another." This is clearly the phase of intuition with feeling and the virtues of Reverence (A2).[519] Whitehead calls his third category or stage "conceptual feeling." While there is "mentality" in this stage, it doesn't yet take the form of "conscious intellectuality." Instead, it takes the form of "vision." It's closer to the "aesthetic" than to the "intellectual." It's an "aesthetic synthesis," or a vision of "loveliness."[520] This is not yet "conceptual analysis," but only "conceptual valuation."[521] A "conceptual feeling has the character of a '*valuation.*'"[522] It is thus, obviously, the stance I've called "It *is*" or the virtues of Excellence (B2), where goodness and truth arise. Whitehead calls his fourth and last category "comparative feeling." This is the "analytic phase," the stage of conscious intellectuality and "propositional feelings."[523] Clearly, this is the stance of "*It is*," the virtues of rationalism and Equality (B2).

Whitehead recognizes that the categories of feeling are structured by paradox or by what he calls "contrasts."[524] He also recognizes the inherent dynamism of the four poles of the human, the way they pulse forward, each family preparing for the next and shedding light on its predecessors: "Each stage carries in itself the promise of its successor, and each succeeding stage carries in itself the antecedent out of which it arose."[525] This dynamic movement takes place both at the level of the universe and the level of the individual.[526] This forward movement – which I've called the "arrow of virtue" (and which Hegel calls the "procession of spirit") – Whitehead calls simply "process."[527] Process is "a process of 'feeling.'"[528] In his philosophy, knowledge and the knowing mind are no longer on top in the nature of the human. They are merely an "intermediate phase of process."[529] In fact, mental activity itself is simply "one of the modes of feeling."[530] So, process is a broader "becoming of experience": it is "the growth and attainment of a final end."[531] It is the path by which the four categories of feeling – the four corners of the human – are blended to achieve the "actual unity" of an actual individual.[532] For Whitehead (as for Hegel), process "constitutes the character" of its product, and, conversely, "analysis of the product discloses the process."[533] Through process, human beings discover and develop their own nature: "This is the whole point of moral responsibility."[534] The nature of the human is defined by its own final causes. The goal or ideal "defines what 'self' shall arise." The thinker is the "final end whereby there is the thought." The feeler is "the unity emergent from its own feelings." The knowable is "the *complete nature of the knower.*"[535]

As this brief overview suggests, I can easily show you Whitehead's "process" and his four "categories of feeling" in the same format I've been using throughout this book to map the nature of the human. You can see Whitehead's version of the human paradox in Figure 68, on page 437.

Figure 68 shows Whitehead's philosophy was a big step forward in the rediscovery of the human.[536] But it ultimately falls somewhat short of its own goal. Though it aims to marry idealism and realism, I think it may fairly be said that, in the end, realism wins.[537] Whitehead wants to shift the attention of Western philosophy back from things or "objects" to "feelings." But Whitehead's feeling is still largely feeling about *things*. He re-emphasizes the character of feeling as "valuation." But his feeling remains more a valuation of *givenness* than of goodness. It isn't yet valuation of values themselves or of their embodiment as virtues. For Whitehead, even values become things or "eternal objects."

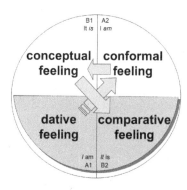

Figure 68. Whitehead's "process": four "categories of feeling"

Despite all his effort to escape from the "sensationalist" empiricism of Locke and Hume on the one hand, and from Kant's phenomenal world – separated by an unbridgeable gulf from the knowing self – on the other, Whitehead's metaphysics seems to remain, at heart, a revised and improved kind of realism or phenomenalism.[538]

With the exception of Whitehead (and some others, such as R.G. Collingwood and Michael Oakeshott), in the twentieth century the traditional questions of philosophers about the nature of the human were largely the province of European philosophers, or what, from the English-speaking perspective, was often referred to as "continental" philosophy. The philosophers of continental Europe also began the twentieth century by exploring the issues of perception raised, in the second phase of theoretic culture, by its philosophy of "things," its background stance of "*It* is" (B2). This philosophical current, known as "phenomenology" – and associated with Edmund Husserl, for example – began with the ambition to develop detailed analyses of human perceptions of Kant's "phenomena": to develop a "science of phenomena."[539] Husserl sought the same certainty of knowledge that had been Western philosophy's goal since Descartes. His goal was still "a philosophy which, to repeat the Kantian phrase, 'will be able to present itself as science.'"[540] For him, as for Hegel, knowing isn't simply one kind of behaviour. Behaviour is, at bottom, a kind of knowing. And leads to knowing. Knowing is still what defines the human.[541]

But phenomenology could be taken in quite different directions than simply the perception of the visible or phenomenal world. In the hands of Maurice Merleau-Ponty (1908–61), for example, it moved toward

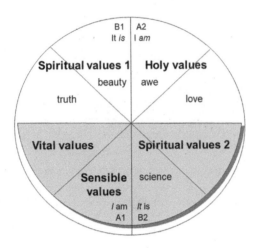

Figure 69. Scheler's four "value-modalities"

a philosophy of language.[542] In the hands of Max Scheler, it became instead a phenomenology of values. Scheler went down the road that Whitehead, for all his insight into the human, had narrowly missed. He discovered what Whitehead overlooked: that the feeling of *values* actually precedes and determines feelings about *objects*.[543] Scheler developed a "phenomenology of emotive life," an "a priori phenomenology of values" and a "theory of ordered ranks of values," which, like Whitehead's "process," support and help confirm the nature of the human described in this book.[544] They were based on his discovery of four basic families of human values, which Scheler calls "value-modalities." His four value-modalities largely mirror the four corners of the human described in this book, with a couple of important differences. You can see how I think Scheler's four "value-modalities" correspond to my own map of the human in Figure 69 above.

As you can see in Figure 69, Scheler slightly reconfigures the four corners of the human identified in this book, by dividing one, and combining two others. For his first two families or "modalities," he splits the two sides of what I have called the virtues of Liberty (A1) into what Scheler calls "vital" values, including courage and "ire" – Aquinas' "irascible virtues" (i.e., the virtues of Power [A1a]) – and what he calls "sensible" values, or "values ranging from *the agreeable to the disagreeable*," or "pleasure and pain" (i.e., the virtues of Pleasure [A1b]).

Scheler calls his third modality "spiritual values." They combine what I've called the virtues of Excellence (B1) with some of the virtues of

Equality (B2): Scheler describes the former as the values of the beautiful, the "objective order of right," and the "pure cognition of truth," and distinguishes them (within the same modality) from the values of "positive 'science' which is guided by the aim of controlling natural appearances." Scheler says the latter are "consecutive values" of the former – which, as I have argued, is entirely correct: the virtues of Equality (B2) depend on, and follow from, the virtues of Excellence (B1). Scheler's fourth family or modality (called values of "the *holy*") exactly corresponds to what I have called the virtues of Reverence (A2), including the values of awe, that is, Reverence³ (A2a), and the values of Love (A2b).[545]

Like C.G. Jung (in chapter 14), Scheler thinks each family of virtues (or "value-modality") can be identified with a specific personality type, archetype, or "pure types of persons." He identifies the "saint" with "holy values," or the virtues of Reverence (A2); the "hero" with "vital values," or the virtues of Power (A1a); the "bon vivant" with "sensible values," or the virtues of Pleasure (A1b); and the "genius" with "spiritual values," or the virtues of Excellence (B1) and Equality (B2).[546] Like Whitehead, Scheler also recognizes what I call the "arrow of virtue." For him, it is "the central history *in* all history." That is to say, the families of virtues (or "different forms of ethos") "unfold historically," according to the laws of the "cosmos of values and its order of ranks."[547] And (like Whitehead again) he even identified the need for the kind of "double vision" that I suggested is required for the four families of virtues: viewing them as *both* historical *and* current (or contemporary), at the same time.[548]

Obviously, from my point of view, Scheler's configuration of his "value-modalities" is very close to the truth about the human but makes the same mistake you already saw in earlier chapters of confusing the second and third levels of separative projection (mixing two families on the third level with two families on the second), and also overlooking an essential distinction at the second level. Because it comes so close to the goal, Scheler's map of the "objective" human values was immensely significant for the future, including for the objective of this book.[549] But in the shorter term, Scheler's influence was mainly in other areas.[550] With exceptions, such as Scheler's friend Dietrich von Hildebrand (1889–1977) and the American philosopher John Dewey (1859–1952), reflection on human values seemed "largely to dry up," until the post-war revival of philosophical interest in the virtues.[551] For the time being, the influence of Husserl and phenomenology went mainly in another direction – a direction equally important for the kind of vision of the human I'm trying to develop in this book.

Husserl's painstaking exploration of the phenomenal world only led him, as you saw in chapter 3, to the discovery of "intentionality," the way in which our intentions and purposes in the world shape what we can know and say about that world. The world-in-itself can only be known through the lens and purposes of the ineradicable knowing subject. So the Western search for certainty of perceptual knowledge comes to a kind of dead-end in the intentionality of the perceiving subject.[552] Husserl stated forthrightly his ultimate conclusion that every form of philosophical realism is "in principle absurd."[553] The conclusions of this first kind of phenomenology – the last gasp of the Enlightenment project of knowing the objective otherness of the world – put paid to logical positivism. Thus, twentieth-century Western philosophy split in two directions: toward the purely analytic – and eventually "linguistic" – philosophy, described above, which has given up on the project of actually knowing anything. Or toward the issues raised by Kierkegaard and Nietzsche in the initial phase of post-modern culture, especially the mysterious "existence" of things. In a way, this second, "existential" option was a return – beyond the philosophy of "things" that dominated the second phase of theoretic culture – to the central place that "being" had held in the thought of Thomas Aquinas in the first phase: an attempted return from the modern stance of "*It* is" (B2) to the earlier, pre-modern stance of "It *is*." (B1)

One of the primary sources for this new development was the German philosopher Martin Heidegger, a student of Husserl.[554] Like Hegel, Heidegger came to many conclusions and perspectives you've already encountered in this book, including a view of the human as a paradox. He calls the two sides of the human paradox "building" (self-assertion) and "dwelling" (reverence); or "challenging" (self-assertion) and "granting" (reverence); or "the revealing that brings forth" (reverence) and the "revealing that challenges" (self-assertion); or "ordering" (self-assertion) and "restraint" (reverence); or "nearness" (reverence) and "distance-less" (self-assertion); or "theoretical" (self-assertion) and "commemorative" (reverence) thought; or some other pairs of terms, the two sides of which always stand for what I've called self-assertion and reverence. Heidegger sometimes calls this initial human paradox the "twofold structure of thrown project" or "thrown possibility" – reflecting the contrasting realities that we are both "thrown" arbitrarily into an existing world but also remain an unfinished project, open to all the inner possibilities of our paradoxical nature, open to making them a reality in our world "by choosing to make this choice."[555]

As in Hegel, Whitehead, and Scheler (and this book), Heidegger's initial twofold human paradox expands, by its own logic, into what Heidegger calls a "fourfold" nature of the human, a fourfold which remains nevertheless a "*primal* oneness" or unity.[556] "None of the four hardens itself toward its own separate peculiarity," says Heidegger. Rather they reflect, embrace, and infuse each other in what Heidegger playfully calls a "mirror-game," a "ring," or "round" of simplicity. Together, the four create what "we call the world." But this kind of truly human world is never fully "explainable nor fathomable" because things like "causes and reasons remain unsuited to it." A genuinely human or humane world needs to be approached in a very different way.[557] In fact, the assumptions of modern theoretic culture must be turned upside-down. The invisible background of *being* the four corners of the modern and post-modern human now "encircle must itself be transformed into the encircling circle and ground of all [that is]."[558] What the Western mind has turned into the contained must be transformed, once again, into the container.

Sometimes Heidegger describes the four poles of the human "fourfold" (*das Geviert*) in highly poetic and mythological language ("to save the earth, to receive the sky, to await the divinities, to initiate mortals").[559] Sometimes he describes them as four "fundamental structures" or "structural moments" of human existence: being a self (A1); being with others (A2); being-in-the-world as such ("the being of all possible beings," "the being of the 'there,'" "the pure 'that it is'") (B1); and being together with things (B2).[560] He also offers a "temporal interpretation" of the same four "essential structures of the fundamental constitution of Dasein" – Heidegger's word for what I call the nature of the human. In this second, "different way" of articulating the same "analysis," he calls them: entanglement (A1), attunement (A2), understanding (B1), and discourse (B2).[561] Elsewhere, Heidegger calls them four "distinctions," oppositions, or "limitations of being": becoming, the ought, thinking, and appearance. Heidegger says these four "permeate" all human "knowledge, action and discourse."[562]

Heidegger himself offers a visual representation of the human "fourfold," and its relationship to the background of being, within which we exist. You can see his own image of the fourfold in Figure 70 on page 442.

I think Heidegger's own image of his "fourfold" has some of the same disadvantages you already saw in Jung's image of the four "psychological functions," in Figure 43 on page 322. Like Jung's ego, Heidegger's "being" in Figure 70 seems to be separated from, and stand outside, the four "distinctions." But as Heidegger himself says, being is the "encircling circle and ground of all [that is]." A more accurate image should show it, therefore, as surrounding and "encircling" the fourfold, not standing apart from it. Like Jung's image again, Heidegger's doesn't have the potential to display the process of separative projection: the way the four corners of the human will expand or explode into a cascading series of their own internal paradoxes.

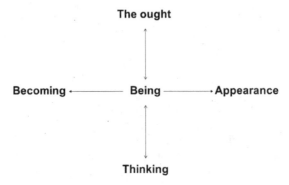

Figure 70. Heidegger's four "distinctions" or limitations of being[563]

Heidegger (like Hegel, Whitehead, and Scheler) also gives an account of Western cultural history very similar to what I've called the "arrow of virtue." Heidegger sometimes calls it the "way," or the "way of revealing," or "destining."[564] This dynamic process, like the arrow of virtue, is the one that, according to Heidegger, has driven Western civilization forward, from its origins in ancient Greece to the eighteenth-century Enlightenment and finally to the post-modern, industrial civilization of the twentieth century.[565] From what I call the virtues of Excellence (B1) to the virtues of Equality (B2) and of Liberty (A1). But Heidegger's own image doesn't lend itself very well to depicting the dynamic process he describes.

For all these reasons, I think the figure of the human paradox I've been using in this book is better suited to display Heidegger's fourfold. In Figure 71 on page 443 you can see how I think Heidegger's "fourfold" relates to the four stances and families of virtues, and to the arrow of virtue, described in this book.[566]

Heidegger himself wouldn't have related the four corners of the human in the order of Figure 71. In his view, the correct order – "the order in which they are internally linked and … the historical order in which they were shaped" – is, instead: becoming, appearance, thinking, and the ought.[567] But that's because he thinks the story of the human begins in ancient Greece.[568] If you take the longer view of our "deep past," as I have done in this book, it's obvious that "the ought" begins long before – perhaps even hundreds of thousands of years before! – the culture of ancient Greece began to develop our Western theoretic culture. Indeed, developing "the ought" ("I am") in mimetic and mythic culture was the crucial stage (A2) at which humans became human, the essential link between our animal (A1) and our rational selves (B1 and B2).[569] If Aristotle was able to take the

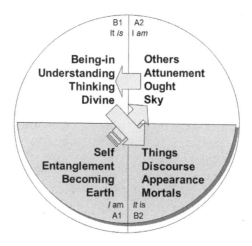

Figure 71. Heidegger's "fourfold"

virtues for granted, as a matter for rational reflection, it was because our hominid ancestors had been gradually developing them – as the definition of the human – ever since they ceased to live in trees and began to walk about on the ground. When Heidegger says "the ought" belongs "essentially to the modern era" (i.e., since Descartes), what he really means is that the modern era is the period when "thought becomes dominant" as the definition of the human, and, as a result, "the ought" *begins to break down* – when the relationship between "is" and "ought" can no longer be established, as Hume pointed out – and becomes a prominent and permanent problem for Kant, and for all his successors.[570]

Similarly, Heidegger is right to identify the distinction between being and "appearance" as rooted in ancient Greece. Aristotle, as you've seen, initiated the Western inclination to attach importance to "things" themselves. But it's in the modern era, with Descartes, Newton, and Kant, that "appearances" – or Kant's "phenomena" – really come into their own as the definition of truth and reality. That's the assumption from which positivism, modern "realism," and phenomenology all began.[571] That's what it means to say "*It* is," instead of the "It *is*" of ancient wisdom and understanding, where human thinking began (B1) – before it declined into modern, calculating "reason" with its focus on things and "appearances" (B2), "a world full of separate objects rather than relationships."[572] So, just as I reversed Hegel's definitions of understanding and reason, I've also reversed Heidegger's placement of "appearance" and "ought," in the arrow of virtue, in Figure 71.

Like Hegel, Whitehead, and Scheler, Heidegger thinks the "internal" structure of the human spirit replicates the "historical order" in which the four corners of the human were "shaped," – and the historical order reflects the structure. But unlike Hegel, Heidegger doesn't view this historical process simply as a story of progress. He doesn't think, as Hegel did, that modern "reason" is an advance upon ancient understanding and wisdom. In fact, he thinks the "assertive" and instrumental character of modern "reason" poses a serious "danger" to the human spirit because its reductive, assertive disposition to dominate risks turning the world into nothing more than an "inventory" of exploitable resources, and humans themselves into mere objects or "instruments."[573] It also obscures the real nature of the human.

Human truth and freedom are both rooted, originally and fundamentally, Heidegger argues, not in the arrogant clarity and certainty at which modern, calculating "reason" aims, but rather in a humbler *revelation*: in the "revealing" that takes place when the curtain of mystery, by which being is concealed, is momentarily drawn back, and a corner of the truth thus becomes "disclosed" or "unconcealed." The modern idea of freedom, that is, "freedom to," is necessarily and permanently rooted in an earlier kind of freedom, "freedom from": freedom not only from the vices that block human virtue or freedom from the self itself – from the self's own self-assertion – but also freedom from the mystery that necessarily envelopes being, freedom from the cloud of unknowing, the freedom of revelation, "disclosing" or "unconcealment."[574] This kind of "freedom *from*" is also a "freedom *for*": a freedom "for one's ownmost possibilities," freedom for the whole nature of the human.[575] Heidegger sometimes calls this place or moment of unconcealment the "opening" or "clearing," like a clearing in a dark forest, where a shaft of light breaks through the overhanging canopy of the forest and illuminates a small patch of ground in the surrounding gloom.[576] In disclosing or unconcealment, human beings can achieve momentary insight – through "attuned understanding" (B1) – into their true nature, their full, fourfold potentiality: they can "see it all."[577] What disclosing discloses is the nature of the human.[578] But the concealment, darkness, and mystery which surround the clearing are as essential to it as the clearing itself. Without them, humans wouldn't be human. The nature of the human is to hear the "call" or the "pull" of the unseen being that underlies and surrounds all beings. "We are who we are," says Heidegger, "by *pointing* in that direction ... man is the pointer."[579]

Heidegger's greatest achievement was his insight that our modern and post-modern Western world is the product of self-assertion, the self-assertion inherent in our distinctive Western theoretic culture.[580]

Modern science and technology are simply the ultimate expression of self-assertion, the self-assertion that began with Aristotle's brand of reason and logic.[581] But now their self-assertion, the self-assertion of this technological world, Heidegger argues, is destroying humans themselves.[582] Thinking of ourselves as "lord[s] of the earth," post-modern human beings no longer encounter our real selves. We no longer know the real nature of the human because we're no longer alert to, or listening to, the revelation or deep wisdom and understanding from which modern, instrumental "reason" emerged.[583] The virtues of self-assertion now obscure the revelation that is the historical and permanent foundation of the nature of the human. They hide our own "fundamental characteristic ... namely, this revealing as such." Self-assertion "not only conceals a former way of revealing ... it conceals revealing itself and with it that wherein unconcealment, i.e., truth, comes to pass."[584] Heidegger therefore thinks the "salvation" of humankind from the reductionism of modern "reason" lies in finding our way back, or forward, to the "clearing": to a renewed awareness of being, a new "nearness" to the hidden background and precondition of all our doing and becoming. The hidden background of being in which beings exist and without which they could not exist.

In rediscovering this prior half of the human from which modern Western rationalism developed, Heidegger made an immeasurable contribution to contemporary Western civilization. He called into question the assumptions – about the nature of the human – that Western culture has been developing since Descartes, since the beginning of the second phase of theoretic culture. But at the same time, Heidegger overlooked or denied that Aristotle and Aquinas had already developed insights very similar to his own in theoretic culture's first phase.[585] In a distinctive reading of his two great predecessors, Heidegger claimed that traditional metaphysics had only been able to think about "being as beings."[586] His new brand of philosophy, he said, aimed to "overcome" this kind of metaphysics by recalling that which gives beings their being: by "recalling Being itself."[587]

Heidegger's distinctive reading of Aristotle and his neglect of Aquinas greatly limited his potential achievement.[588] The result was that he failed to grasp one of their greatest insights. He seems never to have appreciated the role the virtues played in their thought. Discussion of the human virtues occupies over two-thirds of the *Summa Theologiæ*, but "virtue" doesn't merit even a single entry in the analytical index of Heidegger's unfinished magnum opus, *Being and Time*.[589] Aquinas had understood that we can only approach the mystery of being *indirectly*. He had seen that we can only come to understand something about the nature of being through our own stances toward it: through its "effects" in our own behaviour, our own virtues. Thinking about being must be a reflection on human goodness.[590] Heidegger often comes very close to this insight. In his painstaking, linguistic exploration of the beginning of Western thought in the Presocratics, especially Parmenides and Heraclitus – "the inaugurators of all philosophy"[591] – he is always trying to push back through "the barriers that cut us off from the realm where the manifestation of being-human first occurred."[592] He wants to "recapture, to repeat, the beginning of our historical-spiritual existence, in order to transform it into a new beginning."[593] He seems to recognize that existence is a kind of "gift" or "grant," that needs to be met by a similar human response of gratitude, trust, and self-giving.[594] The primary characteristics of being truly "at home" with being, he says, are human behaviours like "care" (*sorge*, a favourite word[595]), "concern," "sparing," "safeguarding," "preserving," "sheltering," "tending," "husbanding," "watchfulness," "protective heed," and "letting-be."[596] "[A]ll willing [i.e., self-assertion]" says Heidegger, "should be grounded in letting be."[597]

Grounded, that is to say, in the virtues of reverence. Or even the virtues of Reverence (A2).[598] In the end, Heidegger is forced to acknowledge, like Immanuel Kant, that achieving the highest potential of the human depends (as he himself says) on "reverence" for the four "possibilities of existence," the four human stances.[599] But like Kant again, he nowhere makes explicit provision even for the virtues themselves, let alone for the virtues of reverence, on which his whole system ultimately depends. Because he takes for granted that the human project starts with Greek philosophical thought, he never seems to let his own insights lead him as far – backward or forward – as they might. He assumes the barrier he is trying to break down is the barrier between the modern stance of "*It* is" (B2) and the ancient Greek stance of "It *is*" (B1). He doesn't see that the real barrier blocking us from the realm where the human first occurred is even further back: it is the boundary between the virtues of Excellence (B1) and the virtues of Reverence (A2).[600]

Heidegger correctly intuited the fourfold nature of the human. But his description and interpretation of the fourfold were limited by his premises. In the end, Heidegger remains largely a captive of the very theoretic culture he strove so hard to escape.[601] Like the medieval nominalists (and their Enlightenment and Romantic successors), he tries to cure self-assertion *by means of self-assertion*: he tries to rescue the modern and post-modern culture of self-assertion by locking it deeper in its own mental prison.[602] He recognizes that the original meaning of the Greek *logos* wasn't "thought" – much less "logic" – as the later Western tradition universally assumed, but rather speaking, or voice or conversation or gathering or *relationship*.[603] But like Aristotle, Kant, and Hegel, he still thinks that it is "by thinking" that human beings are "who we are," that thinking is "the distinctive characteristic of the human."[604] Being may well be revealed to us in feeling – feelings such as anxiety, dread, pleasure, fear, hope, and care[605] – but Heidegger still seems to assume that it's in thinking "that man comes face to face with being."[606] He wants human beings to "step back from one thinking into another," into an "authentic thinking," a "more radical, stricter thinking," the "thinking that is of another sort than that of calculation."[607] But it still seems to be *thinking* at which he aims.[608] He assumes, like Parmenides (the ancient herald of "It is"), that thinking and being are two sides of the same coin.[609] Like Plato, he seems to think everything can be accomplished through "understanding" (B1).[610] His project is always to *think* his way back into the "truth of Being."[611]

But thinking, by itself, can't get you there.[612] The farthest it can get you, if you're lucky, is from the virtues of Equality (B2) back to the virtues of Excellence (B1), from the stance of "*It* is" to the stance of "It *is*" – which seems to be where Heidegger aims.[613] Thinking is, at best, only one half of the human. It is the contained, *not* the container. It is only one form of human virtue and depends, for its very *life*, upon another. For thought alone, being is only an emptiness or a Nothingness, as Hegel had already said.[614] Heidegger struggled hard to escape from the domination of "things" and of "thingness" that had radically impoverished Western thought and culture, at least since Descartes. He rediscovered the prior reality of being (already well-known to Aristotle and Aquinas) through which things exist: which alone gives life and existence to everything, including thought. But he could not use this insight to solve the problem that had eluded so many of his predecessors since Descartes: he could not use it to find the way back from *is* to *ought*.[615] So Heidegger's project – trying to *think* his way back into the truth of being – for all its value and promise, is, ultimately, another kind of dead-end. It points the way. But it can't get you all the way there.[616]

Heidegger called his philosophy the "way back" into the hidden or "concealed ground" of traditional metaphysics.[617] Many others called it "existentialism" – one of the most influential currents of thought in the twentieth century. The existentialist philosophers who followed in Heidegger's wake came in many flavours, from Marxist atheists like Jean-Paul Sartre (1905–80), at one end of the spectrum, to a variety of religious existentialists at the other end, including Karl Jaspers, Gabriel Marcel (1889–1973), Martin Buber, Emmanuel Levinas, and Paul Ricœur. Heidegger himself was rather coy about his place on this spectrum, normally declining to use the word "God" but using "Being" in ways that often seemed to put it in the place of the traditional term, even equating it with the "holy."[618] Existentialism can be seen as a first attempt to recover the pre-rational foundation of the human – the reality of being – that Cartesian rationalism had obscured and replaced with a focus on the things, and the "thingness" of Kant's phenomenal world.[619] But like Heidegger himself, it was constantly tempted to fall back into the very rationalism it struggled to escape.[620]

In the wake of existentialism, many post-war continental philosophers did just that, following its Sartrean (or "neo-Nietzschean") spirit into various forms of critical "structuralism," reminiscent of Husserl's phenomenology, and then "deconstruction," which shared some of the linguistic focus of post-war analytic philosophy. Philosophers such as Michel Foucault (1926–84) and Jacques Derrida (1930–2004) often end up, like Sartre, simply celebrating self-assertion itself, "the potential freedom and power of the self."[621]

Both analytic philosophy and deconstruction feed into a fourth stream of twentieth and twenty-first century thought, called "pragmatism." Interestingly, this stream is largely American and, to the non-American, can sometimes sound almost pugnaciously or assertively American – as if pragmatism were somehow bound up with the defence of a distinctive American identity or culture. This fourth stream uses tools and language from the other three but rejects many of their assumptions. Launched in the late nineteenth century by the American philosopher Charles Peirce (1839–1914), it was developed in the twentieth century by two more Americans, William James and John Dewey, and reformulated at the end of the century by Richard Rorty, among others. Pragmatists, as the name suggests, tend to argue that there is no such thing as absolute truth or truths. Truth is simply "what works" or what "pays," not in the abstract but in concrete, historical situations.[622] It is simply what people agree to, in the here and now. For someone like Rorty, pragmatism even seems to bring philosophy itself to an end, dissolving it into the wider cultural sphere and issuing in a "post-philosophical culture."[623] "Post-philosophy" is a concept entirely appropriate for (perhaps even to be expected in) a post-theoretic or post-modern era.

The fact that Rorty's brand of pragmatism no longer aims to make a substantive or "constructive" contribution to human understanding, only a "therapeutic" one, helps confirm pragmatism is one of the logical, even inevitable, places to end up in a post-theoretic culture.[624] The "triumph" of the therapeutic mindset seems to be one of the distinctive traits of post-modern culture.[625] As if to underline the natural fit between pragmatism and post-modern culture – between pragmatism and the paradox of Liberty (A1) – Rorty repositions philosophy not only as a form of aesthetic or artistic expression but even as a kind of "play" (A1b).[626] This is exactly what you would expect, when the arrow of virtue is moving on – or perhaps already has moved on – from the stance of "*It* is" (B2) to "*I* am" (A1).

Each of these broad currents in twentieth and twenty-first century philosophy – analytic, phenomenological, existential, pragmatic – gives expression to some part of the nature of the human. Phenomenology, logical positivism, and analytic philosophy continue to work in the "*It* is" spirit of the second phase of theoretic culture (B2). Existentialism, by its very nature, points back, instead, toward the stance of "It *is*," toward the earlier awareness of being characteristic of theoretic culture's first phase (B1), or even to the stance of "I *am*" (A2), from which theoretic culture first arose. And pragmatism (together with some existentialists, structuralists, and deconstructionists) sometimes seems to leave theoretic culture behind altogether, reasserting the primacy of the original human stance of "*I* am" (A1).

One of the striking things about the contemporary philosophical landscape – as of our wider culture – is that, as Charles Taylor says, it's "uncapturable by any one range of views." While the gravitational centre of our Western culture, as a whole, seems to be moving gradually into the post-theoretic, post-modern mode – gradually crossing the line, from the virtues of Excellence (B2) back to the virtues of Liberty (A1) – all four corners of the human paradox are now almost equally available to individual human beings. The "salient feature of the modern cosmic imaginary," as Taylor puts it, is that "it has opened a space in which people can wander between and around all these options without having to land clearly and definitely in any one."[627]

This shouldn't surprise you. After all, every human being is a manifestation of the human paradox. So all four dimensions of the nature of the human are present *in* all of us, to some degree, and permanently available *to* us – though the way we express them may often disguise them, or hide them, even from ourselves. Remember, too, that all four dimensions of the human are available in every age. The arrow of virtue may move on, carrying the centre or critical mass of Western culture to a new point on the human compass. But even within that new cultural condition or stance, all four corners of the human are still present, and find expression, though shaped and limited by the cultural "imaginary" of their time. That's the "double vision" I illustrated in Figures 18 and 26 (in chapters 7 and 10). They helped you to visualize one of Hegel's main themes: the *whole* nature of the human is present, in an "abbreviated" form, in each of the historical eras or stages (or "moments") through which it develops (Figure 64 on page 418). Even when one family (or sub-family) of virtues is dominant, all the others are still there, in the background, waiting to be rediscovered or reinvented.[628]

Furthermore, no cultural mode is ever lost. We go on living in all of them, even when we don't recognize it. Even in a theoretic culture, for example, most human life is still carried on in the episodic, mimetic, or mythic modes[629] – even if we can't normally see it and lull ourselves with the story that we are exclusively creatures of reason. And *vice versa*: in a *post*-theoretic culture, the theoretic still remains a major and indispensable mode of the human, even as the cultural centre of gravity moves implicitly away from it.

Rorty's kind of pragmatism doesn't cover even the full range of the virtues of Liberty (A1). It speaks primarily to certain virtues of Pleasure (A1b), especially the virtues of art, creativity, imagination, and play. But the other virtues of pleasure, including sexual pleasure, have found many spokespersons in post-modern culture, especially artists, poets, and novelists such as D.H. Lawrence, Ezra Pound, or Georges Bataille; also occasionally philosophers such as Moore, Bertrand Russell, Herbert Marcuse, or Simon Blackburn; psychologists such as Wilhelm Reich; and, in popular culture, a spokesman like Hugh Hefner.[630] The other side of the paradox of Liberty – the virtues of Power (A1a) – finds support from a philosopher such as Robert Nozick[631] but also from ethnologists such as Konrad Lorenz, and free market economists or ideologists such as Friedrich Hayek, Milton Freedman, Ayn Rand, and Irving Kristol.

In our post-modern culture, all the other quadrants of the human now seem to be available, too. Twentieth-century philosophers such as Étienne Gilson, Jacques Maritain, and Bernard Lonergan continued to explore the enduring relevance of the thought of Thomas Aquinas, especially the reality of being ("It *is*") beneath or behind the world of things ("*It* is"). Others, such as Alasdair MacIntyre, Iris Murdoch, and Bernard Williams helped rediscover the virtues that were so important for Aquinas and Aristotle in the first phase of theoretic culture. Still others, such as Alfred North Whitehead, go back beyond Aristotle (B1) to Plato's world of forms (A2), aiming to reconcile Platonic "idealism" with the "sensationalist empiricism" (sensing with thinking, B2) of the seventeenth century, which lies at the root of modern philosophy, to achieve a "restatement of Platonic realism."[632] And some others seek to explore the depths that open up under the human when experience of the human stance of "I *am*" (A2) makes claims upon us that seem to go beyond theory, beyond thinking, perhaps even beyond being. Because they are pushing back *beyond* theoretic culture, thinkers like Charles Péguy, Rudolf Steiner, Martin Buber, Franz Rosenzweig, Lev Shestov, Simone Weil, and Emmanuel Levinas often write in a poetic, prophetic, allusive, aphoristic, non-linear form that

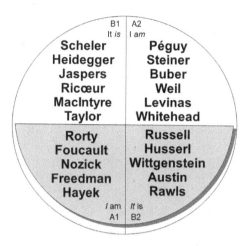

Figure 72. Some twentieth & twenty-first century thinkers

can be suggestive and inspirational rather than purely argumentative. It often points rather than shows. The *voice* is once again as important as the *word*. The *saying* is as important as *what is said*.[633]

With this brief survey, I'm now in a position to update my map of the human paradox once again, showing how the nature of the human is reflected in some of the philosophical outlooks of the twentieth and twenty-first century. You can see the result in Figure 72 above.

You should keep in mind, once again, that I've assigned these thinkers to the four quadrants of the human paradox for illustrative purposes only: arranging them by emphasis or import, not because they can be identified exclusively with only one of the four corners of the human. You should also remember that, in the twentieth and twenty-first centuries, all four families of virtues are now seen through the lens of self-assertion. The arrow of virtue is currently moving somewhere across the frontier between the virtues of Equality (B2) and the virtues of Liberty (A1). That's where the centre or critical mass of our Western culture – our cultural "imaginary" – now seems to be found. In the first decades of the twenty-first century, we're *all* liberals now, no matter what we call ourselves. We Westerners all now think, live, and work within the virtues of self-assertion. All of those included above (or mentioned in the text) would uphold the primal importance of both liberty and equality, would consider them central to their lives and to their culture. Both of those values, and their related families of virtues, are central to the outlook of all the contemporary thinkers I've mentioned.[634]

Incidentally, this may be another good illustration of the "double vision" I've described (Figures 18, 26, and 64). If you look back at Figure 26 (on page 220), you can see that, at the top level, the arrow of virtue is returning to the virtues of Liberty (A1), *but all the other families of virtues are still available*, at that level. The whole nature of the human is still present and accounted for. We Westerners seem to be coming back to where we started as a human race, in the virtues of Liberty (A1). But we're coming back there *at a different level* from where we started out two million years ago. We've been through all the intervening stages in the arrow of virtue, and we've acquired those virtues, too. We have a higher perspective now, a view looking back over the whole human paradox. While we're returning to the starting point, we can view it now from a higher level, from a higher rung on the spiral staircase of the human.

You need to look at Figure 72 *as if it were the top level in* Figure 26. If I've assigned contemporary or recent philosophers elsewhere than the two quadrants of the virtues of self-assertion, it's simply because of the way they embody or emphasize some *other* values, especially in comparison with their colleagues. But all four poles of the human are now filtered through the lenses of the virtues of self-assertion. All four corners of the human are still available to us, and always will be. But at the beginning of the twenty-first century, *all four* are now seen from the perspective of the virtues of Equality (B2) and, increasingly, the virtues of Liberty (A1), the corner of the human through which the arrow of virtue is now passing, in the top level of Figure 26.

You should also remember that each of the four families of virtues is itself a paradox, and has its own internal poles, each of which has, in turn, its own internal tension, and so on *ad infinitum*. Each family is subdivided, again and again. In theory, we could assign to each thinker the *philosophical* equivalent – and, remember, I do mean *philosophical* – of a psychological profile. That means philosophers identified with one family of virtues might have significant philosophical *differences* with others in the same family and also much *in common* with those in an immediately adjacent segment of an adjoining family. Because of his emphasis on the political value of equality, a philosopher like Rorty, for example, is obviously very close to the boundary between Pleasure (A1b) and Rights (B2a), and might have more in common with a philosopher – say, Rawls – rooted in the latter than he or she might have with another philosopher, say Nozick, who clearly belongs to the same paradox of Liberty (A1), but finds a primary home in Power (A1a) rather than Pleasure (A1b).

The archaeology of philosophy and the architecture of the human

In the first half of the twenty-first century, we clearly have a wide variety of philosophical options available to us. And the very richness of these options presents us with a number of dilemmas or questions.

What are we to make of this diversity? What does it tell us? There seem to be at least two possible responses to this question, and they are diametrically opposed.

One possible answer is to say that the very diversity of philosophical opinion shows that the philosophical enterprise is a failure and should be given up. If, after three thousand years, philosophers are still unable to agree on even the most basic truths, then philosophy isn't useful, and should be replaced by something else. That's the conclusion Richard Rorty comes to. Embarrassed (like Descartes, Hobbes, and Kant before him) by the inability of philosophers to achieve the same kind of (at least temporary) consensus as the natural sciences, he concludes that the vain pursuit of "objective truth" or "rational certainty" should be abandoned. In fact, the philosophical game should be given up altogether, and philosophy – or "post-philosophy" – should simply be folded back into the other literary arts, or should become a kind of "therapy," or cultural history, or imaginative enterprise.[635]

As it happens, I agree with many of Rorty's diagnoses and conclusions about modern and post-modern philosophy in the second or post-Cartesian phase of theoretic culture, including his emphasis on philosophy as history and as literature. But I think the lack of philosophical consensus he rightly points to can lead you to a very different conclusion. Instead of seeing it as proof of the bankruptcy of philosophy, you might instead view it as one of the most important truths or insights philosophy has to offer. If all the great philosophers were (as Leibniz and John Stuart Mill suggested) "right in what they affirmed, though wrong in what they denied," then the sum of their – admittedly contradictory – assertions may add up, instead, to a vision of the full or complete nature of the human.[636] Taken as a whole, the very diversity of philosophical perspectives may be one of your best guides to the infinitely complex *reality* of the human paradox. That's what Figures 65 and 72 seem to suggest. The *archaeology* of philosophy may be one of your strongest clues to the *architecture* of the human.[637]

But if that possibility were to be taken seriously, then other things should follow. One of them – as Rorty also rightly suggests – is that we will need to free ourselves from the post-Cartesian (or even post-Aristotelian) assumption that the essence of the human is to be found in the "mind," "thought," or "knowledge." Or in them alone. But where, then, can it be found? Or can it be found at all? Rorty and people like him think not. But surely the very diversity reviewed in this chapter must tell us *something* about ourselves. If we want to find the truth about the nature of the human, maybe we should look more carefully at the full range of human behaviours, or modes of being, or dispositions, that lie behind the riotous diversity of our philosophical ideas. After all, theoretic culture – especially its second, post-Cartesian phase, the bankruptcy of which Rorty now proclaims ⊥ is merely the expression or reflection of certain human stances or modes of being: certain families of human behaviours or virtues which, together, foster such a theoretic culture. If we are to get beyond it, we will need to pay more attention to the virtues themselves. And to where they lead us.

And where *do* they lead us? Where does the arrow of virtue go next? This is where the concept of the "deep future" I mentioned in the Introduction becomes so important. I began this chapter by describing our "deep past," all the deep human time before theoretic culture emerged in ancient Greece: all our pre-rational and even pre-linguistic time, when the human virtues were forged, and human evolution slowly developed all that makes humans truly human. Now it's time to start thinking about our "deep future," the hundreds of millions of centuries ahead of us. Where will the arrow of virtue take us in our "deep future"?

Rorty thinks it leads us into a "literary culture," or what I earlier called a "cultural" or "post-theoretic culture," in which the dominating ideal will no longer be objective truth but merely "aesthetic enhancement." A culture in which there is no seriousness beyond play, and we will all be self-creating selves, entirely "at liberty to rig up a self to suit oneself."[638] This seems to be a good description of the "expressive individualism" I pointed out in chapter 4, one of the most prominent ways the virtues of self-assertion are exhibited in our contemporary Western culture.

But as a description of our probable – much less of our *desirable* – future, it doesn't seem very plausible, for at least four reasons. The first is the very fact that it seems to be a good (if partial) description of where we've now arrived: on the threshold of the paradox of Liberty (A1). In that sense, it's static. The future, it implies, will be an indefinite extension of what we already know, and where we already are. But this is most unlikely. If history shows anything, it seems to suggest the human paradox – precisely because it *is* a paradox – moves on. The tensions and conflicts inherent in the nature of the human (and therefore in any culture) guarantee that it will do so.[639] Especially in a "deep future" that will be vastly longer even than all our "deep past."

Second, if we were to remain stuck in the post-modern paradox of Liberty (A1), pleasure (A1b) would remain alone with power (A1a), the other side of the same paradox. "Expressive individualism" would find itself alone with (among other things) the "possessive individualism" Rorty deplores, and that is such a powerful contemporary obstacle to social justice. But that's not the worst prospect. If pleasure remains alone with power, the result could be even more sinister. The fate of the Weimar Republic, for example, suggests that, in a contest between power and pleasure, power wins. And pleasure, as we know, can also be perverse. It can even be *pleasurable* for pleasure to submit to power. Thomas Hobbes certainly thought so: "Desire of ease and sensual delight," he says, "disposes men to obey a common power."[640] That was Tocqueville's great fear about the appetite for pleasure in modern democracies: that it would ultimately render them incapable of resisting authoritarian power.[641] In a world now dominated by the economic power of an authoritarian (even dictatorial or totalitarian) state like China, it would be premature to say his fears were unjustified.[642]

Third, if pleasure is to resist or, rather, harness power successfully, it will have to call on other human dispositions beyond itself. That is, in fact, what Rorty (like Rawls) ends up doing in practice. In order to give some moral content to pragmatism, he's compelled to appeal repeatedly to the permanent human virtues: to our "obligations to other people," to our "ability to sympathize with the pain of others," to tolerance, to decency, to justice, to hope, to love. These are certainly human goods. But where do they come from? And what do they tell us about the nature of the human?

In order to rescue itself from the void it would otherwise create, pragmatism, like analytic philosophy before it, has to fall back on moral sources it doesn't itself provide.[643] It brings certain assumptions to the table. It adopts an implicit view of the human. But "declines the task of stating it."[644] In order to get from "is" to "ought," contemporary philosophy is obliged to reach back, surreptitiously, not only to Athens, but even from Athens to Jerusalem. From the theoretic culture a philosopher like Rorty now seeks to overcome, to the mythic and mimetic cultures he rejects. The fact that thinkers like Rorty and Rawls find themselves obliged, in the end, to appeal to certain basic human virtues seems to confirm Bernard Williams' conclusion that our human social and ethical life must ultimately be rooted "in people's dispositions."[645] That is to say: in the nature of the human.

Fourth, a vision of the human future limited to the "aesthetic" contradicts the very history of philosophy from which it's derived. If it shows anything, the cacophony of Western philosophical voices from

Plato to Rorty suggests the nature of the human is too complex for human beings to allow themselves to be locked up for long in only one of its corners. We want and need the aesthetic virtues of pleasure and play (A1b), certainly. But we also need the virtues of work and of power (A1a), the other side of the paradox of Liberty (A1). And all the virtues of Liberty aren't enough, either. Even *all* the virtues of self-assertion – both Liberty (A1) *and* Equality (B2) – probably won't be enough. The kind of human flourishing they make possible would still leave us feeling unfulfilled, looking beyond, yearning for something more, for a fuller kind of fullness. Because they leave so much out. *So much of the human.* We humans have a "dual nature," as Jonathan Haidt puts it. We are certainly self-asserting. But we also "long to be part of something larger and nobler than ourselves."[646] A purely "cultural" culture diminishes us and would soon make us hunger and thirst after something nobler and more demanding. More complete. More adult. Pragmatism, as G.K. Chesterton remarks, is "a kind of verbal paradox. Pragmatism is a matter of human needs; and one of the first human needs is to be something more than a pragmatist."[647]

A philosophy that doesn't want to get serious – that even wants to "set aside" seriousness, clinging instead to the realm of "play" – is, self-evidently, not a serious philosophy. It explicitly declines seriousness.[648] It declines to grow up, to put away childish things. Play is essential to human life. It is the root of all that is truly valuable in human life and an indispensable clue about how and where to find it. It is "the foundation and beginning of all real life." But all play, "even the most splendid," is still "only play."[649] It isn't enough. It points beyond itself.

But where *does* it point, in the "deep future" ahead?

Well, it may help to go back to the original meaning of "philosophy" itself. In its original Greek, philosophy meant the "love of wisdom." Philosophy wasn't an "academic" pursuit, aiming at some kind of neutral, "objective" knowledge or truth. It wasn't a technique for solving intellectual problems. It was a way to transform its practitioners and their lives by developing the love of wisdom, and the human virtues that go with it.

But love itself is a virtue. Perhaps the highest of them all. You can't have a love of wisdom without, first, having the virtue of love. So, before you can discover the love of wisdom, you must first discover or experience the wisdom of love.

That's the subject of the next chapter.

16

Religious Life

One of the potential benefits of rediscovering the nature of the human – as you've been doing in this book – is the rediscovery of how and where religion fits into the architecture of the human spirit.

This isn't the time or place for a full-scale exploration of the nature of religion.[1] My purpose in this chapter is much more limited. I want to use the map of the human I've been constructing in this book so far simply to suggest why the human phenomenon we Westerners now call "religion" emerges – naturally and inevitably – from the nature of the human, and how it expresses permanent and necessary features of the human paradox. The map of the human virtues also helps explain some of the features and language of religious life that are otherwise puzzling to the post-modern Western mind.

Unlike the other chapters in the second part of this book, I won't need any new figures or tables to map this part of our nature. Figure 25 on page 209, and Tables 10 and 14 on pages 174–5 and 194–5, are already quite sufficient to show why religious life is likely to be a permanent feature of human life.

This is something that's grown more and more obscure – increasingly difficult to see or understand – over the last four or five centuries. As the arrow of virtue moved on from the virtues of reverence to the virtues of self-assertion – as theoretic culture challenged and then largely buried mimetic and mythic cultures (at least from consciousness, though not from real life) – the meaning of religious life in Western culture was changed. It was reinvented by theoretic culture – naturally enough – as a kind of theory. As something in the mind or the head. As a set of beliefs. Religious life was reinvented by theoretic culture as "religion."

"Religion" (in the sense in which we normally use that word today) is a concept of "Athens" or rather, of the modern and post-modern Western mind, rooted in Greek culture. It's a notion belonging primarily to the culture of self-assertion, to the corners of the human I've called Liberty (A1) and Equality (B2). It was largely invented by the thinkers of the Renaissance, the Enlightenment, and the nineteenth century.[2] In fact, it was invented by the very thinkers who were trying carve out a new, *non*-religious space in Western culture, thus aiming to "quarantine" what they called "religion": to confine it within the institutional Church and the private domain of personal belief and morals.[3] The invention of "religion" (in the sense in which we use that word today) was the Enlightenment's way of quarantining many of the virtues of reverence and expelling them to the margins of organized life. Now that you're familiar with the arrow of virtue and how mimetic and mythic cultures were the necessary condition for theoretic culture, how the virtues of reverence paved the way for the virtues of self-assertion, and Reverence (A2) prepared for Excellence (B1) – it may also be possible to rediscover what we Westerners call "religion": not as a state of mind or as a set of propositions or convictions, but as a kind of virtue or virtues. As a lived expression of the human paradox. Not just something in the head or that you have or "believe." But something you *do*.

The map of the virtues I've been using to explore the human paradox can thus help you rediscover what we call "religion" for what it really is: simply a developed form of human life, or what, in this chapter, I'm going to call (in a concession to our modern and post-modern Western usage) a religious life. Whether or not you think a religious life is for you, I hope the human paradox will help you understand better why and how religious people do what they do, as well as some of the characteristic features and forms of religious life.

I will look at each of these in turn, in this chapter. After considering why our Western culture now has such difficulty understanding the nature and source of what it calls "religious" life, I'll review some of the reverent actions or virtues this kind of life often entails, before looking at other ways a map of the human virtues – both the initial human paradox of self-assertion and reverence, and its sub-paradoxes at the second and third levels of separative projection – can help explain some of the features, language, and varieties of religious life. Finally, I'll consider where this form of human life – this corner of the human paradox – leads or points: where the next stage in the arrow of virtue might take us in the "deep" future ahead.

Paradigm shift: from "religion" to "religious life"

What is a "religion," or what do we mean by that word? And where does it fit in the nature of the human?

Of course, a "religion" can be many things and can have many features or dimensions. For example, Luke Timothy Johnson (b. 1943) identifies "four 'ways' or 'types' of religiosity," four modes or forms of religious "sensibility," which he calls the way of participating in divine benefits, the way of moral transformation, the way of transcending the world, and the way of stabilizing the world.[4] Similarly, Jared Diamond (b. 1937) identifies five "attributes" of religions (belief in the supernatural, shared membership in a social movement, costly and visible proofs of commitment, practical rules for one's behaviour, and "belief that supernatural beings and forces can be induced to intervene in worldly life"), and seven major "functions" religion performs (explanation, defusing anxiety, providing comfort, standardized organization, preaching political obedience, regulating behaviour toward strangers, and justifying wars.)[5] Craig Martin inventories numerous categories or definitions of religion, and William P. Alston (1921–2009) defines religion as having some or most of nine different features.[6] José Casanova (b. 1951) notes you can distinguish between individual and group religiosity at the "interaction level of analysis," between "religious community" and "community cult" at the "organizational level of analysis," and between "religion" and "world" at the societal level.[7]

There's much truth in categories and descriptions like these, especially from a historical and anthropological point of view, from the standpoint of the social sciences. Approaches like these can explain a lot. But many of them seem to share a common characteristic, which is that, by and large, they look at religion from the *outside*, from the point of view of an external, supposedly "neutral" or objective observer. Such approaches sometimes seem to view religion with distorting modern and post-modern Western glasses, emphasizing things or perspectives (like "beliefs") that we Westerners (not recognizing our own exceptionalism) expect to find in a "religion," but which other cultures or traditions may experience in very different ways. For the most part, such approaches consider religion – as the social sciences (to qualify as sciences) must do – from the point of view of efficient causes, rather than of final causes. As a result, they often seem to miss the heart or core of religious life, that which makes it religious, and which explains what and why religious people do what they do, *from the inside*. Social science descriptions of religion can seem to miss the enduring human goods and virtues – the ends and *final* causes – that humans have sought and found in religious life: the way in which it responds to, expresses, and establishes their own humanity.

For a dimension of human life that is concerned with the most "ultimate" things – the meaning of life, and the highest human good or goods – explanation by efficient causes alone seems singularly inappropriate. In fact, it seems likely to betray, or even to destroy, that which it purports to explain, as so many modern and post-modern explanations aim, explicitly or implicitly, to do. Explanations of religion by efficient causes have much to contribute to the understanding of religion as a social, historical, and evolutionary phenomenon. But on their own, they seem unlikely to contribute a great deal to the understanding of religion itself, as religious *life*: the kind of life someone – or a culture – might choose to lead or live.

Jared Diamond notes that "[v]irtually all known human societies have had 'religion' or something like it." To him, that shows religion "springs from some part of human nature common to all of us."[8] The nature of the human I've been exploring in this book suggests he's right.[9] The map of the human paradox I've developed here (look again at Figure 25 on page 209) suggests another way of approaching the nature of religion. It suggests the human traditions we now call "religions" may actually be various configurations and patterns of the human virtues, especially the virtues of reverence – the virtues of Excellence (B1) and Reverence (A2) – but not omitting the other families, either. From this point of view, leading a religious life is not so much a way of being "religious" as a way of being *human*.

In fact, the image of the human in Figures 25 and 27 – a circle divided into four (or eight) parts – has been called "perhaps the oldest religious idea there is." As I already mentioned in chapter 10, it can be traced back to the Mesolithic and Palaeolithic ages, before the invention of the wheel.[10] It is embodied in the "medicine wheel," a spiritual symbol still used by almost all the Indigenous people of North and South America, which takes the same form as Figure 25: a circle divided into four quadrants. The four quadrants of the medicine wheel have many names, expressions, and images. But they are all ways of expressing the four corners of the human: the four poles of a good human life. The medicine wheel at the core of Indigenous American culture helps confirm that what we now call "religion" is really a developed form of the human virtues, viewed and practised through the lens of reverence.[11]

Our English word "religion" comes from the Latin word *religio* which, in Roman culture, expressed the virtues of reverence, respect, and "piety" displayed "in the family and between friends." It was only later adopted to express, by analogy, the reverence due to the highest good or to "God."[12] It meant the "practices" of reverence. As I pointed out in chapter 5, Thomas Aquinas still used the word "piety" primarily for the virtues we owe to our family or community, not for religious piety, as we now do.[13] The original reverence was "family reverence."[14] So "religion," in its original and primary sense, is simply the highest development of the ordinary virtues we learn first in our families and communities.[15] It isn't just a set of convictions and beliefs, as our Western culture has no doubt led you to assume. If you look back at Table 10 on pages 174–5, you'll see that convictions and beliefs are actually, paradoxically, virtues of *self-assertion*, not reverence![16]

Now look back at Table 14 on pages 194–5. You'll see that the human virtues in the two sub-families of the paradox of reverence – and in its four sub-sub-families – sum up the main features of what it is to be a religious person.[17] In an authentic religious life, the practice of virtues like these comes long before dogma and doctrine, which really belong, as I said, to the virtues of self-assertion.[18] Or at least to the more assertive side (B1) of the virtues of reverence. Contrary to what we Westerners now assume, what we call "religion" isn't just a set of beliefs, but rather a specialized, structured, and focussed form of the virtues of reverence. It is, primarily, a form of virtue, or behaviour, or practice.[19] A reverent way of *living*.[20]

The nature of the human you've explored in this book suggests that we Westerners need to shift our paradigm from the concept of "religion" to that of "religious life." This shift in religious assumptions is similar to what Wade Keane argues for in our ethical thinking. He suggests we need to shift ethical thinking from the concept of "ethics" to the concept of "ethical life." Much, if not most, modern and postmodern ethical theory assumes that "ethics" is about individual cases of "decision-making carried out by self-conscious agents." But ethical life isn't really made up of isolated, individual reasoning processes and decisions. It's "not just a matter of knowing the rules of the game, something any idle bystander might accomplish as well. It is being committed enough to that game to care how it turns out." To be ethical, Keane suggests, "is to be invested in a way of life and to live up to some vision of what a good person ought to be."[21]

The nature of the human suggests we need to make the same shift in our thinking and assumptions about "religion": from something that is particular and mental, to something that is continuous and involves the whole person, and the living of a whole life. That's what we mean by the words "spiritual" and "spirituality": a form of action or way of living with your "whole being" – not just with your mind but with your body, feelings, and deepest needs and purposes, too.[22] Spirituality isn't just something in the mind: it is "something that one *does*."[23] Living reverently, in all aspects of your life. Spirituality is merely a developed form of the everyday virtues of reverence. Anyone can be spiritual, or experience life spiritually, and almost everyone does, at some points in their life because everyone is a whole person, if they chose to recognize it, or when they encounter their wholeness in the depth of moving or traumatic life events. As a result, many people to-day call themselves "spiritual" but not religious.[24] This partly reflects our modern and post-modern confusion about "religion." But it also suggests you can distinguish between what might be called "general" and "specific" spirituality. "General" spirituality is that which is lived by many if not most people, whenever they're actively practising or experiencing the virtues of reverence, not just with their minds but with the whole person.[25] "Specific" spirituality is the same thing but within a specific framework or tradition.

Just as spirituality is a developed form of the virtues of reverence, a religious life is a developed form of spirituality: a reverent life, lived within a specific, historical tradition of reverence, within a "corporate spirituality."[26] Religious life isn't a set of rational convictions or propositions. It isn't just something in the mind. It is to be "invested in a way of life and to live up to some vision of what a good person ought to be." A life involving *all* the virtues, but in which (reversing the priority of post-modern Western culture) the virtues of reverence take the lead.[27] From this perspective, many of the attributes and functions by which social scientists define religion may turn out, instead, to be simply "affordances" – concrete causes, conditions, occasions, or opportunities which call upon and nourish the virtues of reverence, which create opportunities for them to flourish or decay – but *not* the virtues themselves.

How did Western culture become so confused about the nature of "religion," and why have we come to equate it, mistakenly, with belief or with something in the mind? How have we come to take for granted "the false idea that faith is a matter of believing in the truth of a system of propositions"?[28] The short answer seems to be Christianity – its evolution over the last two thousand years, and also the Western reaction against it in the seventeenth and eighteenth centuries. For the ancient world, religious life wasn't primarily about convictions and beliefs, much less doctrines. It was a form of action or activity through which adherents could participate in an "experience of power" greater than themselves.[29] Even for the first philosophers such as Plato and Aristotle, as I already noted in the previous chapter, philosophy was a kind of spirituality, a "transformative" way of life, not just a purely theoretical exercise, as it would become in the modern world.[30] For the later Epicurean and Stoic thinkers, philosophy was still "a way of life rather than a set of ideas."[31]

Even Judaism, the religious tradition from which Christianity developed, doesn't possess anything resembling a creed, a catechism, or a theology. Jewish faith, like the other ancient religions, is something you *do*. Its focus isn't on metaphysical speculation or on dogma but on human action.[32] The "five pillars" of Islam are also mainly forms of virtuous, reverent action.[33] Nor do the Eastern religious traditions, such as the Buddhist, Taoist, or Hindu traditions, have many of the things the Western mind would expect to find in a "religion." (As a result, some Western scholars even debate whether these traditions *are* "religions." Whether they qualify!)

It was Christianity that changed all this. But the Christian confusion about the nature of "religion" traces its roots further back, to the Axial age I described in the previous chapter. The significance and the pathos of the Axial age, as you saw there, was that it witnessed *both* the breakthrough to the highest *un*selfing forms of spirituality – in Israel and in Buddhism, Confucianism, and the tradition of the Tao – *and, at the same time*, it witnessed the beginning of the way *out* of the reverent modes of being from which that great insight emerged. Self-assertion began to challenge reverence again, in the assertive rationalism of Greek thought, especially Aristotle.

Christianity inherited both of these developments from the Axial age. It was a mixture of Jewish spirituality and Greek rationalism.[34] It sought to express the deepest spiritual insights of the people of Israel but in the new language of Greek philosophy. As a set of ideas, or propositions, a kind of *belief*. Eager to convert the Hellenistic world of Asia Minor, the earliest Christian Fathers aimed to make the Jewish scriptures and spiritual outlook "relevant to educated Greeks."[35] So they developed a "science of Dogmatics" modelled on the Greek thought familiar to the communities they were addressing.[36] As a result, Christians were gradually led to think of religion or "faith" as a kind of thought or conviction, as something that occurs in the mind. This distinctive Christian emphasis on dogma and "beliefs" may also have been strengthened by the idea that Jesus of Nazareth was a revelation of both God and man, at the same time. As a "religion of Incarnation," Christianity had an additional incentive to become a "religion of interpretation" because dogma and "belief" helped solve the "enigma" of the "unnatural union" of the human and divine in Christ.[37] The creeds developed by the Christian church at its early councils helped to sort these difficult matters out, or at least developed a formula on which everyone could agree. As a result of both these influences, among others, Christianity became an ortho*doxy* – a shared set of *beliefs* – rather than (like almost all other "religious" traditions) an ortho*praxy* – a shared set of spiritual *practices* or virtues of reverence.[38]

This emphasis on creeds and "beliefs" was already strong in medieval Western Christianity. In fact, the "organized exploration" known as "theology" was itself an invention of the Western Christian Church. As you saw in the Introduction, the word "theology" goes back at least to Aristotle. But as the name for a new intellectual, religious discipline – a new "intellectual" way of being religious – it was first made fashionable in the 1120s by Peter Abelard.[39] By the fourteenth century, this new emphasis on theology was already becoming dominant in Western Christianity. Theology and spirituality began to split apart, and "religion" became associated more and more with theology or with something in the mind or intellect.[40] This trend was heightened even more after 1400 by the Protestant and Catholic Reformations, and by the new humanism of the Renaissance. As you saw in the last chapter, these three movements had the long-term effect of emphasizing the doctrinal aspect of "religion" and downplaying religious life, practice, or action.[41]

As you also saw in chapter 15, this Christian rationalism prepared the way for the full-blown rationalism of the second phase of theoretic culture, beginning in the seventeenth century with Descartes. In this new cultural condition, the Western world was increasingly inclined to identify the nature of the human with the mind. This broader cultural rationalism reinforced the growing Christian inclination to define religious "faith" as a state of mind or a "confession," a kind of mental conviction or belief. By the eighteenth century, these two currents combined to cement their common assumption that a "religion" is something "that one believes or does not believe, something whose propositions are true or are not true, something whose *locus* is in the realm of the intelligible, is up for inspection before the speculative mind."[42] This view was never unanimous. But on the whole, it has become the prevailing popular Western view of religion in the twentieth and twenty-first centuries.[43] Religious faith is now often defined, mistakenly, as "belief in something unbelievable."[44] The essence of being a religious person, in this widespread view, is to give assent to some religious statements, propositions, or ideas.[45]

In describing the Christian roots of contemporary Western assumptions about "religion," I don't mean to imply for a moment that the Christian emphasis on thinking and the mind is a defect in Christianity. On the contrary. The Christian intellectual tradition, with its roots in ancient Greek thought, is one of the very highest achievements of Western, and even of global, culture. Most of our Western civilization and thought, even post-modern secular thought, are rooted in these achievements, even when they reject or ignore them. They're often just secularized versions of Christian ways of thinking.[46] But a strength can have – and often does have – its corresponding weakness. The very intellectual strength of the Christian tradition – its emphasis on belief, on rational thought and the mind – has helped to obscure the nature of religious life itself, the very thing about which the mind was to think. For the post-modern Western world, it has obscured the root nature of "religion" as a kind of human *life, not* just a form of thought or belief but a form of human behaviour or actions, a set of habits or virtues. As a developed form of the everyday "ordinary" human virtues, especially the virtues of reverence.

Even medieval Christianity still used the word "faith" in at least three different ways: for something that is believed, but also for an *act*, and for a *habit*.[47] After the Renaissance, the two Reformations, the doctrinal conflicts of the sixteenth and seventeenth centuries, and the eighteenth-century Enlightenment, the first meaning gradually squeezed out the second and third. If you want to understand religious life – and where it fits in the nature of the human – the challenge is to recover them.

Religious life and the virtues

The map of the human paradox suggests you need to reconceive religion as religious *life* – as a developed form of the human virtues. That means "religion" is best understood, not just as a kind of knowledge or belief (our normal Western assumption), but rather as a kind of good *behaviour*: as a type of good human action or actions. A kind of virtue.

Virtue doesn't exhaust the content of religious life. Every religious tradition has its own ideas, concepts, and discourse. Every tradition has its own explicit ethos, doctrines, or perhaps even theology. But these are always secondary and "external" to the "real basic phenomenon of spirituality."[48] Only the virtues can make a religious life a religious *life*: a way of living, a form of behaviour, a way of acting and being. Theology stands to religious life somewhat in the way a music critic stands to music: as a commentary, analysis, or theory *about* something, but not the thing *itself*.[49] Ideas, doctrines, concepts, and theories remain simply self-assertive assertions unless they are put into reverent practice. To become real, and really reverent, they must become virtues, or reverent actions and habits.[50]

Moreover, what do religious teachings teach, in the end? *They teach the virtues.* They teach what the Anglican Book of Common Prayer calls "all virtuous and godly living."[51] Or what Psalm 23 calls "the paths of righteousness."[52] They are all "for training in righteousness."[53] They teach a "new" world in which virtue can be "at home."[54] The closest thing to a definition of "God" you can find in the Jewish scriptures or the Christian Old Testament is "A God merciful and gracious, slow to anger, and abounding in steadfast love and faithfulness."[55] The two descriptors for God used at the beginning of all but one chapters of the *Qur'an* are "the Mercy, the Merciful," or "the Compassion, the Compassionate."[56] In other words, what the scriptures call God is *defined by the virtues*: especially virtues of reverence, such as mercy, generosity, faithfulness, and love. We meet God face-to-face, Psalm 17 says, "in righteousness," in the virtues.[57] The Lord, Jeremiah says twice, "*is* our righteousness."[58] "Blessed are they," says Jesus of Nazareth, "who hunger and thirst after righteousness."[59] The "kingdom of God (or of heaven)," about which he teaches, is always located in the human virtues, especially the virtues of reverence, the virtues of love, compassion, mercy, generosity, gratitude, and so on.[60] The *Qur'an* teaches "charity, kindness, and peace among men."[61] The *Bhagavad Gita* teaches "selfless service" to others.[62] The tradition of the Tao teaches that "loving people and aiding things is goodness."[63] "Be self-controlled! Give! Be compassionate!" says the Hindu *Brhadaranyaka Upanishad*.[64] The "fruit of the spirit," says Paul of Tarsus, is love, joy, peace, patience, kindness, goodness, faithfulness, gentleness, and self-control.[65] Everything else is a means, exercise or preparation for this.[66] "God's commandments," as Thomas Aquinas says, "*are about virtues*."[67] Explicit religious doctrines (and even dogmas) are like all religious language, symbolism and story: they are a *clothing for the virtues*, especially (but not only) for virtues of reverence such as justice, mercy, humility, compassion, kindness, meekness, patience, forgiveness, peace, gratitude, wisdom, and love.[68] If you want to understand religious doctrines or dogmas, you must go through them, and beyond them, to the human virtues which are both their source and goal, their inspiration and their purpose.[69] In the case of Christianity, for example, each of its doctrines or "beliefs" – whatever else it may be – can be interpreted as an expression, emblem, and *enabler* of a crucial human virtue or virtues.[70] The virtue – the lesson for human living – is the *ultimate point of them all*.[71] How could it be otherwise? Even when they point *beyond* life – or proclaim that the meaning of life isn't exhausted by life itself – this crucial insight can only be put into practice *within* life, and by the human virtues.[72]

The four sub-sub-families of reverence: a review

In the next two sections, I'm going to sketch briefly some reverent actions and habits typical of the kind of human life we now call "religious" before looking at other ways a map of the human virtues can help you understand some of the features, language, and varieties of this way of being human.

To set the stage, let me first recall the specific contribution of each of the four sub-sub-families of reverence, at the third level of separative projection. (See Table 14 on pages 194–5.) The virtues of Love (A2b) are the highest of the virtues of reverence and the "engine room" of reverence, just as the virtues of Liberty (A1) are the "engine room" of the human.[73] In fact, they are the inverted form of the latter, the virtues of Liberty (A1) turned upside down: the initial human stance of "*I* am" transformed into "I *am*." Transformed into the pure spirit of self-*giving* – compassion, mercy, generosity, and so on – just as the virtues of Power (A1a) are the purest form of self-*seeking*. Just as the nature of the human draws all its energy, drive, and life from the virtues of Liberty (A1), every form of reverence finds its root in the virtues of Love (A2b) and draws its life and spirit from them.

But the virtues of Love (A2b) – the purest form of reverence – lead inevitably to the virtues of Excellence (B1), where awareness of the goodness or excellence inherent in the self-giving virtues of Reverence (A2) breaks through into human consciousness: not yet as a fully rational consciousness but as conceptual *feeling*, a proto-rational sense or intuition (intuition with thinking) that something is due – due both to goodness and to truth. The virtues of Goodness (B1b) bring out the goodness already inherent in the virtues of Love (A2b). The virtues of Truth (B1a) proclaim the truth of that goodness. The virtues of Reverence[3] (A2a) are the bridge between the virtues of Love (A2b), on the one hand, and the virtues of Goodness (B1b) and of Truth (B1a). They are where the virtues of Love (A2b) begin to turn into the kind of life we now call "religious."

Some actions and habits of religious life: external

With this background in mind, let's consider some of the actions and behaviours typical of a religious *life*. The behaviours in this kind of human life have two forms – internal and external – each of which has two subtypes of its own. I'll start with the two kinds of *external* actions in this section before turning to the *internal* actions of religious life in the next.

You can think of the two kinds of *external* actions of religious life as concentric circles.[74] In the *inner* circle are the virtues of Reverence[3] (A2a) and in the outer circle are the virtues that engage with the world (more on that in a moment). The virtues of Reverence[3] (A2a) – in the inner circle – look both backward and forward along the path of the arrow of virtue. They look backward to the more reverential virtues of Love (A2b), from which they draw all their life, and which they help to support and nourish. They look forward to the slightly more assertive virtues of Excellence (A2), where the otherness already implicit in the virtues of Reverence (A2) emerges into the first level of rational consciousness (intuition with thinking): where "I *am*" turns into "It *is*." In the virtues of Reverence[3] (A2a), the otherness implicit in the virtues of Love (A2b) begins to emerge into consciousness and begins to be consciously cherished and reverenced.[75] But it isn't until the virtues of Excellence (B1) that the idea of "God," or the ultimate goal of reverence, fully comes to "mind."[76] The virtues precede and give rise to the ideas, not the other way around.

The virtues of Reverence[3] (A2a) are rooted in the previous virtues of Love (A2b) and are part of the same family of virtues. But they are subtly different. If the virtues of Love (A2b) are pure, active, self-giving, unselfing love – giving for the very sake of giving – the virtues of Reverence[3] (A2a) are an expression of the same impulse, but no longer purely self-giving. In this other side of the same family, giving is now mingled with the joy, gratitude, and humility of *receiving*, making the virtues of Reverence (A2) as a whole a continuous, loving exchange between giving (A2b) and receiving (A2a).[77] The virtues of Reverence[3] (A2a) are the virtues of the person who not only loves but *experiences* that same love: who also feels herself *to be loved*. The virtues of awe, humility, trust, hope, gratitude, faith, and all the other virtues of Reverence[3] (A2a) are the "love of the beloved." They are the love of the person who is an "object of love," who is "borne" up by love and "sheltered in it." This kind of love is now "requited love: the faith of the beloved in the lover."[78] And the longing to "return love for love."[79]

The beloved "keeps faith" and gives thanks.[80] Consistent with these virtues, Reverence[3] (A2a) includes the "formal" virtues of reverence, sometimes called "worship." As I noted in chapters 5 and 9, all acts of reverence acknowledge superior worth. Even a handshake or a simple "hello" is an act of reverence, acknowledging the value of another person and your potential obligations to them. That's the root meaning of "worship." Worship simply means "the assigning or acknowledging of worth."[81] The English word "worship" (like the word "religion" itself) has secular roots. Its original, secular use for acknowledging worth can still be seen in the honorary title of address, "Your Worship," used for mayors in some English-speaking countries.[82] So, "worship" is the way humans have traditionally expressed respect and reverence, especially for what is most important and valuable to them. Worship, in its religious sense, has been called "the summit of the heart habits we call virtue," because it aims at what is *most* valuable, the deepest or highest kind of excellence and worth – which is the *source* of human excellence and worth themselves, in the virtues of Love (A2b).[83]

Human forms of "worship" are actions or behaviours that acknowledge the highest good, or greatest worth – and express the stance or attitude human beings should exhibit toward this kind of goodness:

reverent virtues such as admiration, love, devotion, humility, and unselfing.[84] But you shouldn't think of reverence as being just for something "else" – some good outside itself. That would be the "instrumental" outlook characteristic of the virtues of self-assertion. Reverence itself *is* a good. All the virtues of Reverence (A2) are expressions of giving *for their own sake*. The goodness and truth proclaimed by the virtues of Excellence (B1) are simply the goodness and truth of this very self-giving, already present in the virtues of Reverence (A2) themselves. When Christians, for example, say that "God is Love," that's what they mean: "God" *is* the spirit of self-giving love, the spirit at the heart of the virtues of Reverence (A2). The virtues of Reverence[3] (A2a), expressed in "worship," aren't just *for* something else: they exhibit, express, embody, or participate in the very thing they revere. They are still a form of giving *for the very sake of giving*.

Consistent with the reverent human impulse to union or attachment – the spirit of *union* at the heart of reverence – the reverent actions of "worship" usually take place in groups or communities. And these virtues are often expressed through the modes and forms best suited to express feelings in general, and feelings of communion and reverence in particular: mimetic forms that engage not just the mind but the *whole* human person, such as ritual, ceremony, symbolism, physical gesture, narrative, singing, dancing, rhythm, and music.

As you can see in Table 14 on pages 194–5, ritual is a virtue of Reverence[3] (A2a). Self-assertion seeks freedom, spontaneity, innovation, and informality. Reverence naturally reveres dignity, solemnity, and formality because they convey the seriousness or importance of that for which reverence is expressed. Because they *express* reverence, and so are, themselves, *forms* of reverence. You can see this kind of reverence at work in any non-religious ritual or ceremony, too, such as a graduation ceremony, a presidential inauguration, or the opening of parliament. Because they are *both* a key mode of expression for reverence, *and* a way to develop and explore it more deeply, the virtues of Reverence[3] (A2a) are at the core of a "religious" life.[85] They serve as a bridge between the four families of reverence.

In the previous chapter, you saw how our modern, rational, or theoretic culture developed out of earlier mimetic and mythic cultures. These earlier cultures were the source (or expression) of most human virtues and of the deepest human intuitions about meaning and value, the intuitions on which theoretic culture builds its theories. Religious life is a product of those earlier mimetic and mythic cultures. So it employs their distinctive resources, which have much older roots in human culture than our modern and post-modern rational consciousness, and which go much deeper into the human psyche and motivation. To the extent that religious life has a rational or mental basis, that basis is initially mimetic and narrative in character. Its "theoretic" elements come much later and are always "secondary" to, or derivative from, the first.

Religious traditions tell stories. They tell many stories, including stories of their own mythic origins, and preserve the links with those founding stories, those primal encounters.[86] And they tell the stories of the encounters *with* those encounters. They tell them over and over again, so the encounters can be continually re-experienced and renewed. That's one of the many reasons religious life naturally takes the form of a religious "tradition."[87] But religious stories aren't just about the past. They are also stories about the future, or about the world we are trying – or should be trying – to create.[88] Like the more formal teachings and doctrines – and prior to them – religious stories are emblems and enablers for the human virtues, especially the virtues of reverence. In Islam, for example, the Prophet provides a "mimetic means to virtue,"[89] just as, in Christianity, Jesus is the "archetype" of the human, the "mediator" who shows the way to pure, "self-forgetting" Love or "God."[90]

The mimetic and narrative roots of religious life also help explain the nature of religious language. The core language of religious *practice* rarely takes the form of rational or discursive prose. It doesn't take the form of statements or propositions. Instead, it takes the form of myth, symbol, storytelling, and poetry: the original, and still the natural human way to discover the human meaning and value so elusive to rational thought alone.[91] And what religious language strives to reveal, with all the devices of poetry and symbol, is not just something beyond or outside this world, but also the full, complete or true nature of the human – a nature that, to be complete, must include the self-giving virtues of reverence, not just the self-seeking virtues of self-assertion.[92]

Religious language is "constitutive" rather than "designative."[93] It doesn't just point to something or point something out (*It* is): it brings it into being (I *am*). Its primary verbal mood isn't the indicative (A=A), characteristic of theoretic culture, but rather, other verbal moods such as the exclamatory, the declaratory, the imperative, the vocative, the hortative, and so on. It often takes the form of declaratory statements and commands – such as "Thou shalt not kill," or "Honour thy father and thy mother," or "Let there be light" – which give voice to the "voice" already "heard" or present, in the human virtues.[94] Religious language is also a language of paradox, reflecting the contradictory nature of the virtues.[95] In religious language, words and symbols don't just represent or signify: they somehow *are*, or constitute, the very thing they're pointing to.[96] That's because religious language is primarily a language of virtue: a language of good *actions*, including acts of worship, ritual, prayer, meditation, and so on.[97] In this context of reverent action, words don't just signify: they also *transmit* or serve as a gateway to the very realities reverence itself expresses and embodies. They're a way for people to *participate* in something.[98] In this kind of language, the understanding of words and the feeling of participation in the reality to which the words refer "merge into one."[99]

Religious language and story are products of mythic culture, but religious rituals are a product of the even earlier mimetic culture I described in the previous chapter. Their primary target isn't the conscious, rational mind but rather the imagination, feelings, and intuition; the deepest, subconscious dimensions of the personality; and all the senses of the body, including movement, gesture, smell, sight, hearing, taste, voice, and so on.[100] Religious ritual can often move people more than purely rational discourse does because it moves *more* of them.[101] Participants can, and often do, feel these practices bring them into a kind of empowering presence because that presence is present *in their own reverence*,[102] and in the patterns of symbols from which the rituals are constructed. Rituals are a physical enactment of the myths and narratives, and of the virtues of reverence they express. But in telling stories about past and future events, rituals of worship are also "revelations here and now, of what is always and forever."[103] The stories and events may be "eternal in nature," but for that reason, they are also "living and present."[104] Religious traditions may tell stories about the past and future, but the virtues they carry are expressed and achieved *in the present*.[105]

The role of places of worship is to generate the *feeling* of union in every self-asserting individual "even before this unification itself has been established."[106] Together with their symbols and ceremonies, they foster feelings and virtues of reverence, especially the virtues of Reverence (A2), such as awe, "humility, mercy and soft-heartedness."[107] Wherever they occur – in the home, or in the community – rituals allow people to express their deepest impulses of reverence by focusing and concentrating them, by giving them shape. They make reverent feelings and states of mind available, not just for deeper experience and reflection, but also to deepen and strengthen them in a human life. Ritual religious practices serve as a source of spiritual and moral energy.

The rituals and other concrete, reverent practices of a religious tradition can be thought of as a kind of "language." A *behavioural* language for deep things that can't be said in any other way, things that are too deep for words.[108] From this perspective, trying to lead a "spiritual" life without the rituals, practices, and demands of a specific religious tradition may be a little like trying to talk without using any particular language. Not impossible, perhaps, but hard to do![109] And without the unselfing demands of a tradition, the pursuit of bare spirituality – in secular "meditation," for example – also risks becoming a self-regarding and self-absorbing exercise, a kind of narcissism, a hidden form of self-assertion.[110] The regular, daily demands of religious ritual can be, instead, a school of *unselfing*, preparing and strengthening participants for other kinds of self-giving.[111]

The role of reverent practices in religious life may perhaps be compared to the role of propositions and theories in theoretic culture. Alfred North Whitehead suggests that in theoretic culture, the role of propositions and theories is to serve as "lures for feeling," the feeling that can become the "germ of mind."[112] Religious practices such as ritual and prayer play a similar role in religious life, as lures for feeling. But their role isn't cognitive, as in theoretic culture, but rather, *existential*. The feelings for which religious actions, like ritual, can serve as a lure are the germ of a human *life*.[113] They are a lure for the habits of feeling that are the inside of the virtues (or habits of behaviour). The role of ritual, says the Confucian thinker Xunzi (third century BCE), "is to nurture."[114] That is to say, nurture the virtues of reverence. *Nurture the disposition to nurture!*

And that's where the outer concentric circles of "external" religious life come in. External religious practices, such as ritual and worship, don't occur just for their own sake. They're also intended to be sources of empowerment for other tasks and challenges, especially for practising the virtues of the other three sub-families of reverence, but all the virtues of self-assertion, too. External religious practices, such as worship, are at the heart of something wider than themselves – which is the role of reverence in life itself, in the *whole* of life. Formal religious practices, such as ritual, ceremony, liturgy, and sacraments, nourish and support the virtues of reverence for their everyday use and expression.[115] They energize, motivate, and equip participants for reverent and transforming action, both within themselves and in the wider world. The *inner* concentric circles of external religious life (especially the virtues of Reverence[3] [A2a]) nourish reverence; the *outer* circles (especially the virtues of Love [A2b], Goodness [B1b], and Truth [B1a], and all the virtues of self-assertion, too) put it to work in the world.[116]

In the outer circles, then, are the other virtues of reverence that flow from the first: everyday virtues of reverence such as kindness, generosity, and mercy (A2), but also virtues of self-assertion, such as courage (A1) and self-control (B2).[117] The circles of reverent action widen out, from the inner core, to influence the behaviours of a religious person, first, in her personal life (diet, dress) or family life (e.g., respect for spouse and parents, the loving nurture of children, [A2b]); second, in her community (honesty, charity, and care for those in need, for example [B1a, A2b]); third, in society as a whole (the pursuit of political and social justice [B2a, B2b]); and finally, toward the whole natural world and universe.

A life of religious reverence therefore has a necessary rhythm of back-and-forth, or to and fro, between the formal practices of reverence, such as ritual and worship, where reverence is nourished, and the wider application of reverence to the tasks of the world.[118] In ritual and worship, the spirit of reverence "is kindled ever new." In the world, "this spark is to be proved."[119]

The conventional, post-modern Western idea of "religion" normally assumes that religious people participate in the formal practices of a religious life, such as worship, for the benefit or gratification of that which is worshipped. That's what Sigmund Freud assumed, for example.[120] But looking at religious life through the lens of the virtues allows you to turn that assumption on its head. Since reverence is a virtue, those who are benefited by participating in religious practices such as worship aren't the worshipped *but the worshippers*.[121] Those who benefit by giving praise are those who *give* it, not that which is praised. Those who benefit from giving thanks are the *thankful*. Those who pray do so in order to be trusting.[122] These virtues are ends in themselves. Giving for its own sake. You could almost say the essence of true thankfulness, for example, is gratitude simply for the opportunity to be grateful![123]

In fact, the activity of participating in religious practices such as worship can be thought of – in a contemporary analogy – as somewhat like going to the "reverence gym": a way of developing spiritual muscles and reflexes for the long-distance run of a whole life through regular "exercise."[124] In the "reverence gym," all the virtues are nourished and kept strong. Without the virtues of Reverence[3] (A2a), the virtues of Love (A2b) on the one hand, and the virtues Truth (B1a) and of Goodness (B1b) on the other, may be at risk of withering or becoming arrogant and assertive. The virtues of the "temple" are the irrigating spring for the virtues of "life" – that is, life beyond the temple. But the latter are the test of the former: the test of their authenticity and sincerity.

The special role of the virtues of Reverence[3] (A2a) in the kind of life we now call "religious" is the constant, regular, disciplined cultivation of *all* the virtues, but the virtues of reverence in particular. This kind of unceasing effort is necessary because of the equally unceasing pull of the virtues of self-assertion in the other direction. The virtues of self-assertion were the starting point, and remain the default position for the human, the one we slide back to unless we're constantly pulling in the other direction, developing the virtues, habits, and stance we need for a genuinely *human* life. Religious "practice" thus has at least two meanings: the doing *of* an action, here and now, but also "practicing" *for* the action, just as in physical exercise or piano practice. As in all exercise, the important thing is the regularity and the discipline of the practice, which develop the sinews, courage, devotion, and reflexes of reverence for daily life.[125]

Some actions and habits of religious life: internal

The *external* actions of a religious life – both the inner core and the outer application in the world – are just one side of religious life. The other side is the *internal* actions – which are supported and nourished by the external actions, and in turn, support them. Like the external, the *internal* actions of religious life also take two forms. The first kind are reverent forms of thinking, or states of mind, such as prayer and meditation. Prayer, meditation, and other spiritual exercises (such as yoga) are techniques of reverence, to achieve its core impulse of union. They explore the depths of the spirit – that is, the whole human person – and connect body, feeling, and mind, both to each other *and* to something else. To other people, and to the whole of reality, of course: to both the other grey circles and the larger circle you saw in Figure 3 on page 32. But as a spirit of union, these internal practices of reverence seek to go even farther: they aim to link the whole human person not just to all beings, but to the ultimate source or ground of all being, as pictured in Figures 7 and 8 (on pages 41 and 75). And even this may not be far enough. There is still that *otherness* of the spirit, the otherness of goodness, excellence, or love we encounter in all moral action, in the depth of the virtues. The light that seems to shine through all of them. This kind of otherness is *really* transcendent because it seems to exist *beyond even being itself*. And the true spirit and practices of reverence yearn to link humans to this as well. Perhaps to this above all.

Prayer, says William James, is "the very soul and essence of religion."[126] Franz Rosenzweig agrees it is the "highest," the "ultimate" form of reverence, "an overflow of the highest and most perfect trust [A2a]."[127] Prayer, like other religious practices, serves as an infusion of spiritual and moral energy, a reaching out to the source of moral energy, and a channelling of its power, through longing, desire, humility, and resolve.[128] The way in which this power calls to you, attracts you, motivates you, and energizes you – almost seems to reach out to you – is part of what Christians call "grace."[129] In prayer, human beings can come face-to-face with the pure power of Love (A2b), feeling both their own inadequacy and distance from its standard of goodness, but also its potential transforming power.[130]

That's where the second kind of internal action of a religious life comes in. In a number of religious traditions, this second kind of internal action is called a gradual *turning of the heart*. The turning of the heart is a metaphor for a gradual reorientation of the human toward this mysterious otherness of the spirit, the source of moral energy, and a reaching out to embrace it.[131] In Christian liturgies, one of the earliest and oldest elements is the *sursum corda*, the opening dialogue of the eucharist, in which the priest says: "Lift up your hearts." And the congregation responds: "We lift them up unto the Lord." This is a public enactment of this second kind of internal religious action. This kind of internal action is central to many traditions because this deepest, most unselfing form of reverence is the summit and key to all the other virtues.[132] A Jewish Rabbinical teaching says, for example, that what really matters in a life is whether a person "directs his heart toward heaven."[133] "Heaven" is a metaphor here for whatever is the highest or most important thing for which reverence can be expressed, the source of all goodness, the otherness at the heart of the virtues. Maimonides aims at the same idea when he says, "the Lord desires the heart, and ... the intention of the heart is the measure of all things."[134]

Why is this "turning of the heart" so important in many religious traditions? It appears to have something to do with the human paradox and the way the virtues of self-assertion – especially the virtues of Power (A1a) and Pleasure (A1b) – continually put up barriers and limits to the virtues of Love (A2b). The turning of the heart is essential because our default virtues of self-assertion make the bottomless demands of the virtues of Love (A2b) very hard for us. Maybe too hard. We can't meet their call to endless self-giving head-on. Other people just aren't that lovable – maybe not even likable, much of the time. To really love them – to be really self-*giving* – in the way the virtues of Love (A2b) call on us to do, human beings have often found they need to make a detour through the love of goodness and love *themselves*. Through a turning of the heart to the "voice of love itself."[135] Through ascending the "ladder of charity" to the embrace of Love itself, before descending "by the same ladder to the love of one's neighbour."[136] Only this other kind of love can achieve the *unselfing* needed to overcome the virtues of self-assertion and harness them, instead, to the virtues of reverence, especially to the virtues of Love (A2b). "Show me, if you can," says John Calvin, "an individual who, unless he has renounced himself [through reverence], is disposed to do good *for its own sake*. ... How difficult it is to perform the duty of seeking the good of our neighbour! Unless you leave off all thought of yourself and in a manner *cease to be yourself*, you will never accomplish it."[137]

The human traditions we Westerners now call "religions" assume that only unselfing, through devotion and reverence for the highest good – for goodness and love themselves, or what some traditions call "God" – can get over the hump of self-assertion and the unlovableness of others. Only a continual practice of the virtues of reverence – and the virtues of Reverence[3] (A2a) in particular – can transform self-*seeking* into self-*giving*.[138] Thomas Aquinas seems to reserve the religious word "faith" specifically for this kind of inner transformation: a reorientation of the will that not only "enlightens" the mind but "also warms the affections."[139] Many religious traditions warn that, without this kind of inner transformation or reorientation, other religious activity – especially some of the external kinds – will be worthless, or possibly even harmful, encouraging instead feelings of self-satisfaction and pride.

To sum up: what we now call a "religious" life is a life of regular habits of reverence that work in two directions: habits of reverent feeling express themselves as habits of behaviour (or virtues), and habits of reverent behaviour (internal and external) nurture habits of feeling (or values). A "religious" life can establish a "practical ritual and moral 'structure'" that orders human self-assertion and shapes it into virtues of reverence, shapes it into something like "habits of the heart."[140] And all of these habits and language have one goal and one goal only: to "induce reverence in ourselves and others."[141]

A "religious" life, as John of the Cross puts it, is an "obscure habit of union."[142] You already understand the importance of words like "habit" and "union," for the nature of the human. But why "obscure"? I'll come back to that in a moment.

The religious paradox

To understand what it now calls "religion," the Western world needs to rediscover it as religious *life*. As a kind of virtue. A way of being human.

That's the first insight from the lens of the virtues and the map of the human. And religious virtues, like all the rest, are something you *do*: a kind of action or behaviour – *good habits*, not just a set of propositions or beliefs.[143] Not just something you think or that is in your mind – though it may and usually does include these – but a developed form of the virtues of reverence.

From this point of view, it's not surprising that for most people throughout history – and for a majority of the world's population today – this fundamental part of their own nature draws them to ways of living in which these important human virtues are fully expressed and nourished. It draws them to the kind of life the West now calls "religious." In fact, the only kind of world where this would *not* happen is a world like the one we Westerners are now living in, a world where – for a variety of environmental, historical, and cultural reasons – the virtues of self-assertion have assumed such an overwhelming presence that the virtues of reverence – or even virtue itself – have become almost completely invisible. Invisible but not absent. In any other kind of world, the virtues of reverence would, and did, lead to their expression in the kind of life we now call "religious." In our post-modern Western world, the question about religious life is "why?" But in any other kind of world or culture, the question is "why not?"

But that's only the first insight. In the rest of this chapter, I want to explore a few other ways the nature of the human described in this book can help you understand some of the features, language, and varieties of religious life, especially some of those that might otherwise be puzzling to the post-modern mind.

The first puzzle the human paradox can help you unravel is the paradoxical character of religious life. The initial human paradox and its sub-families of virtues (such as the paradox of reverence) determine many of the characteristic features of religious life, including its own internal paradoxes – which have levels of their own, just like the human paradox itself.

The initial human paradox – the paradox of self-assertion and reverence – has a religious form which (like the "political paradox" I described in chapter 12) I'll call simply the "religious paradox." At this level, the religious paradox is simply the fact that *reverence can't be expressed without self-assertion*. All action is self-assertion, by definition. To act is to assert yourself or the self. There's no action of any kind without self-assertion. Even the highest religious or spiritual virtues have to be set in motion by self-assertion, whose function, as Thomas Aquinas says, is "to move all powers to act."[144]

Hence, as you already saw in chapter 7, reverence isn't an *alternative* to self-assertion. It's a *kind* of self-assertion. It's a quality added to actions of self-assertion which, depending on the degree of its presence, gradually turns these actions into their opposite.[145] The virtues of reverence are added to, and modify, the virtues of self-assertion. The self can assert itself with very little reverence. But there can't be any virtues of reverence *at all* without self-assertion.[146]

So the first paradox of religious life – as of life itself – is that it's a marriage of reverence with self-assertion, even – or perhaps especially – when reverence strives to purify or "perfect" self-assertion. In the Hindu *Bhagavad Gita*, the Lord Krishna explains this spiritual form of the human paradox to the young prince Arjuna: "He who knows that the way of renunciation and the way of action are one, he verily knows."[147] The Chinese tradition of the Tao calls this paradox "action-less action," or *wu-wei*.[148] The Arabic word *jihād*, sometimes translated as "holy war," really means this highest form self-assertion: self-assertion that turns into reverence, through unselfing.[149] A famous Islamic *hadīth* (or sacred saying) expresses this spiritual form of the human paradox: "The most excellent self-assertion (*jihād*) is that of the conquest of self."[150] The highest acts of self-assertion are acts of reverence. And the highest acts of reverence are heroic acts of self-assertion.[151]

The self-assertive heroism required for the highest forms of unselfing reverence is the quality we're describing when we call someone a "saint" or, in the eastern and Jewish traditions, a "sage." Saints and sages are people spiritually empowered to perform heroic feats of reverent self-assertion.[152] "The sage," says Xunzi, "is a man who has arrived where he has through the accumulation of good acts."[153] In other words they are a hero of virtue. Even *non*-action can be a kind of heroic action of reverence. The person who refuses to save himself or herself, in order to save others, for example. Or someone who endures ferocious torments or temptations without being moved. Siddhartha Gautama Shakyamuni's heroically impassive spurning of repeated onslaughts from Mara, the Lord of Desire, Death, and Duty, for example, turned him into the Buddha. Buddhist monks (and others) who imitate him are overcoming self-assertion through similar heroic acts of reverence. But precisely because these are *acts*, they're also acts of reverent *self-assertion*.[154]

Religious life, like everything else that's human, is a form of self-assertion. It's a kind of self-assertion that strives to *overcome* self-assertion. But it isn't just to establish self-*control*. That would still be a form of self-assertion – a virtue of Equality (B2). In religious life, self-assertion strives instead to overcome self-assertion by transforming self-*seeking* into self-*giving*. In a religious life, self-assertion aims to nourish, support, and promote the virtues of self-giving or of reverence.

The virtues of self-assertion and reverence are inseparable, even, or especially, in religious life.

The role of doubt in religious life

Understanding this basic human and religious paradox – the role of self-assertion in reverence – can also help you appreciate the necessary role of doubt in religious life.

If you think religious "faith" is the same thing as cognitive belief, then doubt seems entirely alien to religious life – even its opposite or enemy. If you think religious "faith" is just "belief in something unbelievable," then doubt looks like the enemy of that kind of belief. But as soon as you begin to appreciate that "religious" life is a form of human virtue – a high form or expression of the *whole* nature of the human – then doubt can and must be reframed as an essential part of religious life. Ecclesiastes, the biblical book "full of corroding doubt" is traditionally read, for example, at Sukkot, or the Jewish Feast of Booths: thus "disenchantment ... in all its old unbroken strength ... is included in the festival itself."[155]

Doubt is the expression, in religious life, of a permanent and necessary side of the human paradox. Religious doubt is simply one of the spiritual expressions of self-assertion. Rational consciousness is a virtue of self-assertion. It demands explanations for everything. It wants to understand. And this self-assertive demand is almost as important to religious life as reverence itself. It's an essential reflection of the human paradox in religious life.[156]

Remember that reverence is a virtue. It's something you *do*. Most people don't come to the religious or high form of the virtues of reverence through a process of rational reflection and decision. It's not very much like joining a political party, where you check out the platform and decide, rationally and consciously, whether you agree with the ideas and whether, as a result, you want to sign up. Or not.

Actually, joining a political party isn't really very much like that either! Like most important human actions, it's much more likely to occur because of some encounter or experience in your life. The rationalization often takes place later. And that's what religious life is like, too. A religious life normally begins through some kind of encounter – with a person[157], or a book,[158] for example – or some kind of event or experience in your life.

Most people in non-Western cultures, and many people in the West, learn the practices of reverence associated with religious life in the same way they learn most of their other basic habits: they encounter them in their families. Their families engage them as children in the everyday religious practices of the home and the community, and perhaps also take them to a synagogue, mosque, church, or temple. In this way, they encounter the reverent activities and practices of religious life: they come to know these actions from the inside and the inner habits of feeling that accompany them. If they discover some of the fullness or fulfilment the virtues of reverence promise, they may want to continue seeking it through these same practices of reverence. That's why, if she maintains a religious life at all, someone who grows up in a Christian family stands a good chance of remaining a Christian. A Jew is very likely to remain a Jew. And a Muslim a Muslim. It's because they have encountered and developed a *habit* of reverence, rooted in their own family and culture.[159]

That means a person leading a religious life normally arrives in the middle of the party, long after it began. They're usually already *doing* something before they start to think about it in a deep way.[160] In fact, they probably wouldn't even bother thinking about it deeply, if they weren't already doing it. They already know or sense its truth. But now they want to understand that truth, in a more conscious or rational way. They want to be able to explain it to themselves.

And the something they're now doing brings its *own* load of ideas and concepts, too. They've arrived even later than you may think. Maybe thousands of years late, in fact! Other people have been practising these same virtues in which they're now engaged for a very long time and have been reflecting on them. Many of these practices, ideas, and concepts have been incorporated into the religious tradition. That's what makes a spiritual tradition so valuable and necessary. It can incorporate the insights and practices of many centuries, even thousands of years. But now a person leading a religious life needs to take stock of these ideas, too.

Some of them will be good ideas, sound or helpful ways of expressing or interpreting the virtues of reverence they're now practising. But some of them won't be. They'll be well-intentioned errors, distortions, or misunderstandings, perhaps reflecting another time or culture, or some hidden assumptions that don't really have anything to do with the truth of the virtues they're now practising. As Aquinas, Maimonides, Kierkegaard, and many others have pointed out, an authentic religious life can be – and usually is – a mixture of true reverence and false belief.[161] True reverence can, and often *does*, go together with false ideas about what that reverence means or represents. And that's where self-assertive doubt comes in. While the habit of reverence keeps religious people practising its virtues, rational doubt "remains restless, and picks at and turns over" the ideas or statements about them or the standard formulations: it chips away at them, helping to separate the false ideas from the true.[162]

In a religious life, doubt helps to sort the wheat from the chaff, the good stuff from the bad stuff. And even the good stuff isn't straightforward, either. Even if you accept the truths of a spiritual tradition, that isn't necessarily the same thing as "believing" them in the normal, cognitive sense. Belief, in the religious sense, means belief *in*, not belief *that*, a virtue of self-assertion.[163] It means something more like *trust*, a virtue of Reverence (A2).[164] You trust that these truths are true. This isn't so different from other areas of life because all learning begins with trust: the learner in any field must begin by taking things on trust.[165] But it's even more appropriate in a religious life because trust itself *is* a virtue of reverence. Those who "practice" a religious tradition do not so much "believe" its truths (in the cognitive sense) as take them on trust or take them for granted – and then get on with the really important thing, which is putting them into practice.

The most important question about religious truths is not whether they are "true" – in a religious life, that's normally taken for granted, as a premise – but rather: *what do they mean*? That isn't self-evident, even to those who "accept" them as "true." What a religious truth at first *appears* to mean on the surface may not be what it really means at all. And usually isn't. An entire lifetime isn't enough to reveal the true or full meaning of religious truth. That's one reason a religious life inevitably takes the form of a spiritual "pilgrimage" or journey, a lifetime quest to discover what religious truth "really" means. Not just in an abstract, mental, or intellectual sense, but in an even more important sense: what it means for *living*, as a real and whole human being.[166] Religious truth is "performative," not informative, or propositional.[167] It isn't found in propositions, or even in the mind, but in actions. Actions of worship, reverence, love, and service.[168] Actions which are true – true to the truth: the truth of the human – and where truth is found and known, primarily, in the action itself.[169]

Here, too, self-assertive doubt plays an essential role in a religious life, helping to winnow out and clarify the "truth" which has, initially, been taken on trust, or taken for granted. The truth known, or sensed, in the action itself. Religious or reverent doubt is like a refiner's fire, burning away the impure from the pure, the inessential from the essential, the apparent or surface meaning from the deep or genuine meaning, the inner meaning from the outer form or symbol, the half-truth from the whole truth, the superstition from the genuine reverence, the wrong path from the right one, the false from the true. The human paradox is alive and active in this aspect of religious life, as in all other dimensions of human life.

The role and language of "mystery" in religious life

The basic human and religious paradox can also help you understand the role and language of mystery in religious life – as in life itself.

Self-assertion wants clarity. It demands an explanation for everything – with an ultimate objective of control. But reverence is the human disposition for union. And at the limit, that means communion or community with *all that is*. If you look back at Figures 5, 8, 11, and 25 (on pages 34, 75, 115, and 209), you'll be reminded that the virtues of reverence are the human response to the encounter with everything and with the mystery of being. The virtues of reverence can't and don't lead to clarity or certainty (that's where some forms of self-assertion – especially the virtues of Rights [B2a] – aim) but rather, to feelings of dependency and mystery. That's why a "habit of union" is, almost by definition (as John of the Cross says), "obscure."

Self-assertion is the disposition for non-union. It breaks things down into chewable chunks. Analysis makes things sharper and clearer. But reverence knits things up instead, into greater wholes, wholes that – precisely because they *are* wholes – inevitably exceed our understanding. That happens whether the totality reverence seeks to embrace is *out*side us, or *in*side us.

Externally, in our relations with other people and things, our disposition for union with all that *is* leads to mystery because (as I already put it) every individual thing you can perceive or control is always surrounded by a totality that can never be grasped by our understanding. You can't get outside it to see it or explain it, as a whole. No explanation could ever include everything, and so the explanation would always be compromised by what you've left out.

Internally, within ourselves, something similar occurs. First of all, the disposition for union points toward all the forces, emotions, instincts, and visions of our own internal, psychic landscape,[170] the vast realm of feeling that connects the biological life of our physical bodies to the conscious life of our rational minds.[171] It wants to knit them up into some kind of whole. But most of this realm of feeling is unknown and unknowable to our conscious mind. It's just as much a mystery to us as the external universe and carries on its own subterranean life, revealed to us in surprising forms, such as dreams. And in any creative activity, including deep or serious thinking, where words, forms, and insights often emerge spontaneously and unbidden, from some preconscious realm of feeling and intuition.

But those are just the "efficient" causes or sources of the person, those that push from "below," as it were. The totality of "final" causes – those that pull us from "above," or ahead – is just as vast and mysterious as the human psyche. As you've seen throughout this book, the universe of the virtues – the behaviours that make us human and define our "humanity" – is a vast, exploding, kaleidoscopic universe, in which every virtue is in some degree of tension or conflict with every other virtue. Although the virtues define the very "idea of humanity," we can never fully grasp or comprehend them all, let alone know with any certainty how to "apply" them – how to resolve all those conflicts – in our daily lives and in the life of our communities and nations. As if the vastness and contradictions of the virtues weren't enough to put limits on our rational comprehension, some of them, as you've seen, have an unfathomable depth of their own, a limitless, infinite quality that takes them well beyond ordinary human understanding.[172]

Moreover, as you saw in chapter 10, a virtue is always something located more in the future than in the past. It is always something we are trying to achieve, but of which we usually fall short. It is not something that pushes us from behind or from the past, like an efficient cause, but something that pulls or "calls" us forward, into the future, like a final cause. For that reason, the virtues about which religious teachings teach can never have the precision and clarity of our knowledge about the physical world or about the past. Because they are eternal *possibilities* – something potential, always yet to come, always shrouded in the unknowable future. Traditions of reverence that teach "all virtuous and godly living" must therefore always have an element of unknowing and the "mysterious."[173]

So human life is surrounded on all sides by deep and impenetrable mystery, the other side of doubt. And since reverence necessarily leads, in (at least) these four ways, to mystery, genuinely religious people have a great deal in common, surprisingly, with many non-religious people, especially those we now called agnostics. "Agnostic" is a term coined by Thomas Huxley (1825–95) in 1869 to describe people who admit they cannot be certain, one way or another, about ultimate reality.[174]

Agnostics are different from atheists because the latter think they know things that agnostics think they can't know. In their certainty, atheists have a great deal in common, paradoxically, with religious dogmatists, now often called "fundamentalists."[175] Atheists and fundamentalists are at opposite extremes. But they're united by a shared certainty that they *know* something. They know opposite things. But they both think they know them. They are the *negative and positive poles of religious dogmatism*: that is, the two poles of religious life reconceived by theoretic culture as "religion," as a kind of knowledge, belief, or certainty.[176]

Agnostics and authentically religious people, on the other hand, both know that they *don't know*. They know that life is ultimately surrounded by mystery, the mystery conveyed by the outside circle I've been using in all the figures in this book. (Look back again at Figures 5, 6, and 7 on pages 34, 38, and 41, for example.) Religious people and agnostics are thus united by their *un*knowing, by acknowledging the ultimately *un*knowable mystery of life. The only thing that divides them, therefore, is the proper attitude to adopt *toward* the mystery, by which they both agree they are surrounded.

For agnostics, self-assertion remains, by and large, the appropriate response to mystery – though (like all human beings) they can't help practising at least some of the virtues of reverence in the everyday life of their families and communities. For religious people, on the other hand, the right stance to adopt toward this mystery is a posture of the deepest reverence. That's what makes them what we now call "religious." The difference between them and agnostics is thus *not* a difference about knowledge or belief. It's a difference *about virtue*.[177]

To people who lead the kind of human life we Westerners now call "religious," experience suggests that genuine human fullness or fulfilment ultimately depends upon the virtues of reverence (virtues that account, after all, for half their nature). They have therefore chosen to put reverence and its practices at, or somewhere near, the centre of their lives.[178] The degree of importance religious people give to the virtues of reverence, and the ways they express them, vary widely, and this variety accounts, among other things, for the different roles provided in each tradition (clergy, laity, etc.), and different ways of defining or dividing time (holy days, seasons, etc.). But for most "religious" people, the deepest truth about life – what makes human beings most fully human – is to be found hidden in the practices of reverence. And they usually haven't discovered this in some concepts, propositions, or ideas. They've discovered it, instead, in the practice and experience of the virtues of reverence themselves.

If reverence leads only to greater and greater mystery, it doesn't make sense to say that people become reverent persons because they already "know" something called "God" – or *nirvana*, or *Brahman*, or *dharma*, or the Tao – or because of their "belief," as the contemporary Western world normally assumes. It must be the other way around. It's only *in and through* the virtues of reverence that humans can encounter the focus or goal of reverence, to which the religious traditions give names like God or *Brahman*, or any of the other terms I mentioned. You can't know *nirvana*, or "enlightenment," or the Tao in advance. But you can learn "the way" to seek them. Human beings are led toward these goals – if they are led to them at all – by reverence, *not the reverse*. It's "the reverent attitude of mind," Augustine says, "which leads them to choose God for their support."[179] In authentic religious life, "God" or the equivalent isn't given content by definitions or formulas. In fact, that's the very thing most religious traditions refuse to do. They refuse to define whatever is at the centre or apex or goal of their reverence. They *show* it, instead, *by the reverence itself*. By the way God (or whatever else the "highest" kind of value, goal or virtue may be called) is given reverence, that is to say, worshipped, served, or sought.[180]

The meaning of the "mystical" in religious life

Although they're not exactly the same thing, the inevitable role of mystery in human life is connected to the features or experiences of religious life sometimes called "mystical." The human paradox can help you understand these, too.

The so-called "mystical" dimensions of religious life are very hard to talk about intelligently or accurately because our own Western culture has distorted our understanding of them. The split between theology and religious practice that occurred in Western Christianity after 1400 has encouraged us to think of the "mystical" as a special kind of ecstatic, psychological "experience." Those kinds of special experiences occur, of course, but they aren't necessarily the heart or the truth of the mystical. They may sometimes be a kind of distortion or betrayal of it. Or even its opposite.

So we need to be very careful when we talk about the "mystical" dimension of religious life. And this is another area where the map of the human paradox I've been constructing in this book can help you sort things out. Understanding the nature of the human can give you a deeper appreciation of what's behind the so-called "mystical" dimension of religious life. Understanding the "mystical" can, in turn, give you greater insight into some of the key features of religious life, more broadly. Understanding both of these can also shed light back on the nature of the human itself.

Much that's obscure or incomprehensible about "religion" when approached though the lens of the mind – when it's assumed to be a kind of thought, a set of propositions, or a "theology" – becomes clearer when "religion" is approached instead through the lens of the virtues and from the perspective of the human paradox, as a way of being human.

I can begin to sort this out by noting that the so-called "mystical" kinds of religious encounters seem to occur at several levels. At a most basic level, the "mystical," properly so-called, is simply the encounter with mystery I discussed in the previous section. In this sense, the so-called "mystical" experience is merely a heightened form of the common religious (and human) encounter with the unknowable character of being and ultimate reality. This is what early Christian theologians (like the anonymous fifth-century writer known as "Pseudo-Dionysius") meant when they talked about "mystical" theology, for example. They simply meant the mystery – the *un*knowing – to which the virtues of reverence – and all human experience – inevitably lead.[181]

But beyond this basic meaning of mystical – as simply the encounter with the necessary mystery of ultimate reality – lies another level of meaning, rooted in a certain kind of deep moral experience. A genuine experience of the virtues – and of trying to lead a virtuous life – can bring you into an encounter with the spirit of the virtues themselves and with the powerful claims they make on us. And with our often unavoidable response to them. Something shines *through* all the virtues, almost like a light, as Plotinus said.[182] The light by which "we see light."[183] An otherness, embedded in the virtues themselves, an otherness that seems to carry with it an unquestionable moral authority. An "absolute above us."[184] An authority to which you simply can't say no.[185] This kind of ethical experience is like an encounter with something *in* yourself *but not only* yourself, an undeniable inner but also "external *other*."[186] Our response can also seem to come from somewhere beyond ourselves: it can seem to be "in us but not of us."[187] The virtues often seem to "call" on us in ways we can find difficult to resist.

Maimonides calls this kind of moral experience the "first degree of prophecy."[188] It has a "mystical" character because – although it's very difficult to describe or account for – the call to certain kinds of self-giving behaviours can be very compelling, almost like an external "voice" that is calling on us or speaking to us. Calling us – or even *commanding* us, irresistibly – to act in certain ways. A voice we hear inside or "behind" us saying "This is the way, walk in it."[189] Almost every human being has had some experience of this kind, when we feel *compelled*, almost in spite of ourselves, to a good or moral action of some kind. And that seems to be what "God" is actually like in the Jewish and Christian scriptures. Or where their idea of "God" – or the experience of what they call "God" – comes from: from that inner moral impulse, call or "voice," from the word that "is very near to you," the word that is "in your mouth and in your heart *for you to do it*."[190] Trying to lead a good or virtuous life can bring human beings into this kind of "mysterious," that is, intuitive, encounter with an otherness of the spirit that seems to be present in the virtues themselves.

This moral experience of being "called" by the virtues, of hearing the "voice" of the virtues which calls upon us – and thus encountering an otherness present *in* the virtues – is a second meaning of "mystical" and the first level of mystical "experience" in religious life. But it can also lead on to another level. It can lead to a second kind of mystical "experience," the kind assumed in the popular conception of "mysticism." At this level, the experience of the internal "call" (which is somehow also external) may be transformed into dreams, visions, or states of rapture and transport. In some cultures such experiences are more common than in the Western traditions. But even in the Christian tradition, there's a long history of visionary encounters, beginning with Paul of Tarsus' conversion experience on the road to Damascus, and other visions he related in his second letter to the Corinthians.[191]

These kinds of dream-like "visions" play an important role in the history of religious life because they allow a direct, intuitive perception of human truth and reality – the truth *about* our human reality.[192] They can express deep insights that conscious human reason (as Maimonides says) "could not comprehend by itself; thus they tell things which men could not tell by reason and ordinary imagination alone."[193] The problem with these visionary encounters, however, is that they don't tell us much on their own.[194] They can be expressions of mental disturbance as easily as anything else.[195] In fact, the visions of the mentally disturbed sometimes bear striking resemblance to encounters of this "visionary" kind. Visionary encounters can also be brought on by deliberate techniques of physical deprivation, as they often are in both Indigenous and Eastern spiritualities.

Hence these kinds of dreamlike or visionary experiences can't really be evaluated by themselves. We can only assess them by their results or consequences, or by the stature of those who have them, and the meaning they attach to them: by the way such encounters influence their whole lives, or how their whole lives and thought illuminate or give meaning to the experience.[196] These "visionary" experiences are either psychological phenomena, which can be explained by purely physical or psychical causes, or else they're simply "very intensive" cases of encountering the call or otherness of the virtues, especially the unselfing virtues of reverence, an experience that's actually available to *every* sincere religious person – in fact, to every human being.[197]

Another kind of experience available to everyone, but which can have what might be called a "mystical" character, is the encounter *with the human paradox itself*: with the paradox of reverence and self-assertion. This kind of "mysticism" is simply an encounter with the tension *between* reverence and self-assertion. An encounter with the conflict between the virtues.

As the spirit of union, reverence naturally seeks a kind of "purity." It wants to unify *completely*. It wants its own reverence to be "pure," uncorrupted by the wrong kind – a selfish or self-regarding kind – of self-assertion.[198] That's why the concept of "purity" is important in most religious traditions. It doesn't mean cleanliness, though it can be symbolized or expressed in that way, and thus become a value in its own right.[199] At a deeper, spiritual level, it means that self-assertion always threatens to dilute, contaminate, or pollute – or even destroy – the reverence essential for human goodness.[200] The "general object" of religious "laws concerning clean and unclean," Maimonides explains, is to induce "respect and reverence."[201] Thomas Aquinas has exactly the same thing in mind when he talks about the higher virtues "perfecting" (or *cleansing*) the lower virtues.[202] Reverence always aims at "purifying" self-assertion as much as possible, that is to say, *integrating* it into the whole nature of the human, and thus harnessing it as support and strength for the virtues of reverence. It aims at what I've called *un*selfing.[203]

And that's what another level of the so-called "mystical" (especially the ascetic) element in religious life is all about. It's a striving toward a "purer" reverence, or toward more complete forms of *un*selfing. In fact, for that reason, it can occur on several more levels. As you saw in chapter 4, reason or rational consciousness are themselves forms of self-assertion, expressions of the human spirit's spontaneous, assertive demand to understand and to control everything. Reducing, harnessing, purifying or "perfecting" self-assertion can also mean gradually taming the self-assertion inherent in rational consciousness, and the analytic, rational speech that goes with it.

Thus, like the simple encounter with mystery or with the otherness of the virtues, some other experiences reported by those yearning for this kind of pure self-giving or unselfing don't involve the kind of "visions" commonly associated with the mystical. That would still be too much a form of self-assertion. It would be incompatible with the yearning itself. If these kinds of mystical encounters can be described at all, they're expressible only indirectly, through images and symbols.[204] That's another thing – like mystery – that makes them "mystical." The psychological experience itself can be described but what's encountered cannot.[205]

But it's still a genuine experience, nevertheless, whose description still requires analytic or rational speech. And even this degree of self-assertion can still seem too much for a genuine striving after "pure" reverence. So, another kind or level of the mystical seeks the gradual elimination even of this last element of self-assertion, the elimination of human speech itself. It leads to silence and darkness.[206] If this kind of "pure" reverence finds expression at all, it will be in non-verbal forms, such as music or silent contemplation.

In this final form, the mystical encounter – that of the Spanish mystic John of the Cross, for example – can no longer even be properly described as an "experience." Because the striving for pure reverence – and the consequent harnessing of self-assertion to the virtues of reverence – gradually take this kind of religious seeker beyond language, beyond even the "self" that could have or could report such experiences. If the first kinds of mystical encounter are an encounter with a mysterious otherness hidden deep in the virtues themselves – that is, a sort of experience of absence – the last is more like an "absence of experience." It's a form of *un*knowing or non-knowing, the final shape of humility. This kind of mystical encounter can even seem like a critique or repudiation of the other kinds – a sort of "anti-mysticism" – because from this perspective, the others are still too assertive, too much contaminated by self-assertion.[207]

For this same reason, however, the mystical (and also the ascetic) impulse can never reach its final goal. It must always remain an unfinished project, or an only partially fulfilled desire. The mystical impulse is ultimately self-defeating, or rather, self-limiting, because the very effort to eliminate self-assertion remains a form of self-assertion.[208] Some mystical traditions try to get around this by striving to eliminate all striving. That's what both Eastern and Western spiritual traditions mean when they talk – as they so often do – about the ultimate spiritual goal as a kind of "emptiness": "refraining from the desire to see or feel anything."[209] But even the striving to eliminate striving remains a kind of striving! And thus, necessarily, a form of self-assertion.[210]

Thus, the human paradox – the paradox of reverence and self-assertion – helps you to understand the necessary mystical and ascetic elements of religious life. Indeed, the "mystical" turns out to *be* that very paradox in one of its most extreme forms: the ultimate striving of reverence to tame, purify, or harness self-assertion. An impulse destined ultimately to fail – or to fall short of its goal – because of the paradox itself.

"Salvation" and "redemption" in religious life

The human and religious paradox – the paradox of self-assertion and reverence – can also help you understand the religious language of "salvation" or "redemption." Many religious traditions talk a lot about something they call "salvation" or "redemption."[211] Some of them also personify this concept by talking about a Saviour or Redeemer.

But why do so many religious traditions think human beings might need to be "saved" or "redeemed"? And what do we need to be saved *from*?

The human paradox should help make this clearer. What we human beings need to be saved from, it turns out, is ... ourselves! From our own restless, thrusting, insatiable egos. From our own virtues of self-assertion.[212]

As I've emphasized throughout this book, the virtues of self-assertion are absolutely essential to a human life. They're what I've called the "engine room" of the human. They are the source of all human action and endeavour. Nothing human happens except through the virtues of self-assertion. All human action – even, paradoxically, the virtues of reverence! – is a form of self-assertion. Even our physical, bodily life is an ongoing series of biological acts of self-assertion taking place below the level of consciousness. The virtues of self-assertion are at the core of what it is to be human, the natural default position of the human, as permanent and necessary a part of the nature of the human as the virtues of reverence.

But the very centrality or primacy of the virtues of self-assertion – the fact that they come first, that everything human is, ultimately, a form of self-assertion – is the danger, the peril, from which the religious traditions assume humans need to be "saved." Because the virtues of self-assertion come first, they have a natural tendency to squeeze out everything else. They are *assertive*, after all! They would like to rule alone.[213] They have a natural disposition to dominate. Indeed, they are nothing more than that very disposition itself in action.

And that's our human problem. Self-assertion allied with reverence is the source of all human goodness. But self-assertion, *on its own*, is the source of all human evil. All evil comes, ultimately, from self-assertion. From the pure disposition to dominate. From the assertion of our own egos, from the sheer desire to be ourselves, and to achieve our own selfish desires of power (A1a) and pleasure (A1b).[214] Evil has its source, says Plotinus, "in self-will."[215] That's the great insight at the heart of many eastern religious traditions. "The reason we have a lot of trouble," says the *Tao Te Ching*, "is that we have selves."[216] But it's at the heart of the Western traditions, too. Isaiah (eighth century BCE) symbolizes the devastation of rapacious human self-assertion in his image of "all the boots of the trampling warriors and all the garments rolled in blood," and in animal images of wolf, leopard, and lion.[217] The Pythagoreans and Plotinus called this primal force of self-assertion *tolma*.[218] Thomas Hobbes called it the war of every man against every man. Nietzsche called it the "will to power." Christians call it "original sin." The force within ourselves, from which we cannot (but also should not, must not) free ourselves, but from which we – and the world we make – need to be "saved."

But the self-assertion from which human beings need to be "saved" or "redeemed" must be understood in a variety of ways. It means aggression and domination, certainly. And selfishness. But also isolation, loneliness, insufficiency, alienation, suffering.[219] By themselves, the virtues of self-assertion, can bring us no peace. On their own, as I already pointed out (in chapter 6), they're "empty."[220] They can't tell you what to use your self-assertion *for*. To answer that question, they need help from somewhere else, from a different kind of virtue. But even worse, the virtues of self-assertion, by definition, are at war with each other. In their conflict, they can help make you a fretful, unquiet, unhappy person. But they're assertive. So, they can also tear you apart. In fact, as I also pointed out (in chapters 6 and 10), the warring virtues of self-assertion even threaten to dissolve the self itself – dissolve it into conflicting, contradictory acts of self-assertion.[221] The best symbolic images for the virtues of self-assertion, on their own, I suggested, are the symbol of pure hunger placed over the doors of some temples dedicated to the Hindu God Shiva, or Shakespeare's image of pure self-assertion as a "universal wolf": both eating themselves up.

One of the central goals of human wisdom has always been to try to bring peace to the internal battleground of the human paradox.[222] That's one of the chief tasks of reverence: to connect, to harmonize, and to *unify* these psychic forces – thus allowing the individual human personality to find inner peace and serenity. It does so by "saving" us from our own self-assertion: by taming, containing, or harnessing self-assertion. Salvation from self-assertion comes from the virtues of reverence. The power of salvation, says Psalm 98, comes from righteousness, mercy, faithfulness, joy, praise, thanksgiving, and justice. In other words, from the virtues of reverence. They are what can break (what Isaiah calls) the yoke of our burden, the bar across our shoulders, the rod of oppression that comes from our own self-assertion.[223]

The Stoics sought to achieve a condition of serenity they called *apatheia*, the taming or elimination of the self-assertive "passions" that tear the self apart. The eastern traditions aim to achieve salvation, or what some of them call *nirvana*, through serene detachment or even the extinction of the ego and its merger with a greater "Whole." The "salvation" at which the various religious traditions aim is a kind of *healing* – which is one of the root meanings of the English word "holy." And healing must be achieved through "wholeness" – which is another root meaning of "holy." It must be achieved by recovering the full nature of the human: reverence as well as self-assertion, self-giving as well as self-seeking.

Because of the harm or evil self-assertion can cause, reverence always strives to keep it in its proper place. To give it a positive rather than a negative role. To harness, entrain, or "perfect" it, as Thomas Aquinas puts it. Reverence begins, as I noted in chapter 5, in humility, the very opposite of self-assertion. But humility isn't just a door to "salvation."

It's a key to the human. Only humans can have humility. That's what makes them human. Any creature can be assertive. That's what makes them creatures, not just inert or vegetable matter. But only humans can deliberately *unself* themselves. Only humans can show reverence to another. To say that humility is not just a door to "salvation" but a key to the truly human is to say exactly the same thing.

The "salvation" or "redemption" the various religious traditions seek to achieve is an answer to a "radically secular question": the salvation of our true humanity. It offers "life in all its *fullness*."[224] Through our *salvation from self-assertion*: the "saving" of human beings from the irreverent and potentially destructive side of their own selves.[225]

Reverence is always a form of *unselfing*.

Sacrifice in religious life

As you already saw, in my discussion of the Axial age in chapter 15, the human paradox can also shed some light on the meaning of the closely related idea of "sacrifice," a universal concept in religious life.

To a secular mind, the very idea of "sacrifice" can seem horrible or even barbaric.[226] It conjures up cruel images of animal and even human sacrifice, images that can make you shudder. Such revulsion is entirely justified. But sacrifice is a good example of how long it can take for the meaning of religious practices and images to emerge: how long it can take for humans to penetrate, from the outer form of something, to its inner spirit or idea.[227]

The basic meaning of sacrifice is that of giving up a lesser good for a greater one. The idea of sacrifice implies that there's a hierarchy of goods – some things are simply better, higher, or "more good" than other things – and it's appropriate to give up (or sacrifice) the lesser good in order to obtain or achieve the greater. You can see this principle at work in something as simple as a diet. You want to lose weight, so you give up (or sacrifice) a bowl of ice cream (a lesser good) today for a greater or higher good: achieving your weight target in the future. That example involves a time delay. You sacrifice something now for a future pay-off. But sometimes the point of the sacrifice is more immediate, as in daily family life, for example. You give up (or sacrifice) your grumpy mood, your golf game, or your new car (lesser goods) in order to cheer up your partner, spend time with an ailing aunt, or pay for your kids' education (higher goods). You give up (or sacrifice) something to help someone else right now. But not just to help *them*. You also do it in order to be *a better you*. To be the kind of person who would make those kinds of choices or sacrifices. The kind of person who would practise those virtues.[228]

In early human cultures, sacrifice often meant giving up or "sacri-ficing" something that was precious to the community – an animal or even a human being – to a greater or even the highest good, that is, to a "god." As you saw in the previous chapter, one of the breakthroughs of the Axial age was the insight that, while these early practices of sacrifice may have been cruel, they embodied or symbolized a deep spiritual truth: the truth of what I have called the human paradox.[229] They sym-bolized that, to be the best they can be, human beings do need to "sacri-fice" something very precious. But the something they need to sacrifice is *themselves*: they need to sacrifice *their own self-assertion*. They need to tame, harness, or subordinate their own primal virtues of self-assertion to the virtues of reverence.[230]

In this spiritual sense, sacrifice means much the same thing as what Thomas Aquinas meant by "perfection": that is to say, it refers to rever-ence's role in "perfecting" the virtues of self-assertion. The real sacrifice of spiritual life is the sacrifice of the self itself. In this kind of spiritual sacrifice, the self becomes its *own* "reasonable, holy, and living sacri-fice."[231] That's why the characteristic figure of the Axial age – the "Axial individual" – is the "renouncer," the person who leaves the organized social world (including its rituals and formal "sacrifices"), to wander the world as a homeless, spiritual pilgrim.[232] In the figure of the re-nouncer, the Axial age discovered that the real, spiritual meaning of sacrifice is the sacrifice of the self.[233] The sacrifice of what you *are* to what you *love*.[234] It is *un*selfing. It's the sacrifice or "perfection" of the virtues of self-assertion for and by the virtues of reverence.[235]

The paradox of mercy and justice in religious life

In its initial form then, the human and religious paradox – of self-assertion and reverence – helps to explain many features of religious life that might otherwise be puzzling if approached exclusively through the cognitive lens of modern and post-modern culture, including the heroic virtue of saints and sages, the religious role of doubt, but also of mystery, the mystical, and sacrifice.

But the initial human paradox of self-assertion and reverence is only the starting point of the human, as this book has shown you. Paradox breeds paradox. Because of the polarity of being and the resulting process of separative projection, the two sides of the first human paradox have their own two poles or internal paradoxes, and those poles have their own paradoxes, and so on, *ad infinitum*. The second and third levels of separa-tive projection can help you understand some other features of religious life, including why the religious traditions are so diverse and divided. I'll come back to the third level in the next section. But I'd first like to point out how the paradox of reverence at the second level (Table 11 on page 179) helps explain some of the basic tensions and outright contradictions always found in religious life. And how these tensions and contradictions have contributed to bringing "religion" into disrepute – sometimes deservedly – in our modern and post-modern world.

Remember, first, that (as you saw in chapter 7) the virtues of reverence involve a necessary tension between the stances of "I *am*" (A2) and "It *is*" (B1). The stance of "I *am*" (A2) is the purest form of self-*giving*, in which the self is given up for others in spontaneous acts of nurture, love, and generosity, not because of any external standard or requirement or because anything is due, but simply for the giving itself, for the sake of giving. However, the virtues of "I *am*" (A2) can't remain forever in this simple, undivided condition because they have their own internal polarity (Table 13 on page 190). But also because this mode of self-*giving* inevitably draws human attention to the very *goodness* of the giving and to the goodness of that for which, or to which, the self is given.[236] Self-giving can't help making us think about the absolute standards – the goodness or excellence – by which our very giving, and its objects or recipients, are to be judged, or which they imply or express.[237] In some ancient Jewish prayers, for example, the faithful begin by saying "Thou," but finish by saying "He" or "It": "as if, in approaching the 'thou,' a transcendence were encountered in the form of 'it' [or 'him']." Emmanuel Levinas calls this transition – from "I *am*" (A2) to "It *is*" (B1) – an encounter with the "Itness" ("*l'illéité*") or *otherness* of the "Infinite": the otherness (It *is*) of that infinite, endless, or bottomless quality of self-giving discovered in the virtues of Reverence, or "I *am*" (A2).[238]

A reverent or religious life isn't, and never can be, merely pure acts of self-giving love (A2). It also, inevitably, requires acts of judgment, decisions about goodness, about standards, and about how they should be applied, both to ourselves and others. It involves judgments about truth, including the truth of the standards themselves, or the truth they may reveal or represent (B1). There's a side to religious life (A2) that is accepting and forgiving. But there's another side (B1) that places *demands* on us, demands we cannot shirk. In religious life, humans encounter not just the human capacity for self-giving (A2), but also its inherent goodness (B1). They encounter not only a primordial responsibility for others that seems to precede and ground all rational thought about it (A2), but also the otherness (or "Itness") of those obligations (B1). Or rather, humans encounter these things not in *religious* life, but in their own *human* life – and that's what can *make* their life what we Westerners now call a "religious" life.[239]

Together with the virtues of "I *am*" or Reverence (A2), religious life (like human life) must also make room for the virtues of "It *is*" or Excellence (B1). And these two "families" of reverence – at the second level of separative projection – are in permanent tension or conflict, a conflict that can be found in all the religious traditions. A conflict between mercy and justice, for example, or between truth and love. Between judging and *not* judging.[240] Between what is given because it's *due* and what is given even though it's *not* due, simply for the sake of the giving itself. [241]

The necessary but difficult marriage between these conflicting virtues can be heard in the language of all authentic religious traditions. It echoes throughout the Psalms of David, the great treasury of religious poetry belonging to all three Western religious traditions. Psalm 85, for example, memorably expresses the deep human yearning to reconcile the two sides of the paradox of reverence: "Mercy [A2] and truth [B1] have met together," the psalmist declares; "righteousness [B1] and peace [A2] have kissed each other. Truth [B1] shall spring up from the earth, and righteousness [B1] shall look down from heaven. ... Righteousness [B1] shall go before [the Lord], and peace [A2] shall be a pathway for his feet."

The paradox of reverence can also be heard in the famous opening verses of Isaiah, chapter 11. They begin by a recitation of the contradictory virtues of the paradox of reverence: wisdom, knowledge, and understanding (B1); but also "fear of the Lord," a biblical expression for the virtues of Reverence (A2), especially Reverence[3] (A2a); judgment, equity, and righteousness (B1); but also meekness and faithfulness (A2). Then, in an image of enduring, prophetic power, Isaiah proclaims the indestructible *unity* of all these contradictory virtues, the unity of the human paradox: "The wolf shall also dwell with the lamb, and the leopard shall lie down with the kid; and the calf and the young lion and the fatling *together*; and a little child shall lead them. And the cow and the bear shall feed; their young ones *shall lie down together*."[242]

The difficulty of accomplishing the reconciliation, for which Psalm 85 and Isaiah so eloquently yearn, explains many of the tensions and contradictions of religious life – including the tensions between tolerance and intolerance. In the contemporary, post-modern world, where one side of self-assertion – the virtues of Equality (B2) – has made "tolerance" an absolute value, an end in itself, it can seem an "intolerable" contradiction that religious traditions preaching peace, love, forgiveness, and mercy can also make judgments – sometimes stern judgments – about conduct or behaviour or social conditions. And it *is* a real contradiction. But also an inevitable and *necessary* one, a contradiction built right into the nature of the human.[243]

This religious contradiction – the spiritual form of the paradox of reverence – is inevitable, an inevitable part of the human, because the virtues of reverence have two conflicting sides: the virtues of Reverence (A2), certainly, but also, and equally, the virtues of Excellence (B1) (Table 11 on page 179). Without *both* sides of this paradox the virtues of reverence wouldn't be complete. And they wouldn't really be reverent either, only a shadow or facsimile of reverence. They wouldn't reflect the full nature of the human. Religious life – like life itself – has an inescapable element of judgment or discrimination about excellence and justice. Indeed, justice *is* a kind of excellence.[244]

The religious traditions are condemned therefore (like human beings) to be both tolerant and *in*tolerant. To be merciful, charitable, generous, and forgiving (A2). But also striving for goodness, justice, truth, and all the other virtues of Excellence (B1). They must preach love but also the absolute goodness or excellence that love implies. Mercy (A2) must season justice (B1).[245] But, without justice, mercy might no longer be a virtue.[246]

The painful conflict between these two sides of the paradox of reverence has been one of the most challenging balancing acts in the religious life of the West. As theoretic culture redefined "religion" as a kind of conviction or belief rather than as a kind of human virtue, the Western religious traditions haven't always succeeded in getting the balance right. They've often been tempted to put the emphasis on truth, and justice, and right, rather than on the mercy, compassion, and benevolence from which these virtues must flow. They have sometimes been tempted to forsake the spirit for the letter, emphasizing dogmatic convictions and judgments rather than compassion and love – even to the point of wars of religion. Wars in the name of love![247] In the twenty-first century, violent religious fanaticism rages again, as fiercely as ever. But it's still an *unholy* alliance between the virtues of Excellence or "It is" (B1), and the virtues of self-assertion. An alliance from which the virtues of Reverence (A2) are largely excluded.[248]

Indeed, one of the most important contributions the virtues of self-assertion – especially the virtues of Equality (B2) – have made to Western civilization over the last three centuries or so has been to call the virtues of reverence *back* to the primacy of the virtues of Reverence (A2), to the practical primacy of mercy, compassion, and love in human life.[249] Their role in reclaiming these highest virtues of reverence is one of the explanations for the puzzling fact I noted earlier in this book: that the modern and post-modern culture of self-assertion has often succeeded, paradoxically, in delivering a more humane and merciful life for large numbers of people than preceding cultures that were more explicitly centred in reverence.[250] Modern self-assertion has delivered some of the very goods of reverence that reverence, alone, was unable to deliver.[251] Yet another paradox, in a book crammed with paradox! From this point of view, modern and post-modern self-assertion can almost be called "providential," even – or especially – from the point of view of the very virtues of reverence it rejects![252]

However, this is also a two-way street. If the virtues of Equality (B2) have been able to make headway in the past century – especially in the form of the virtues of Rights (B2a) – it's partly because they were able to draw on the accumulated moral capital of the virtues of reverence, especially the virtues of Reverence (A2).[253] If they are to sustain their role as agents of mercy in modern life, the virtues of self-assertion may now need to learn that they are trading on the moral capital of reverence. It is by no means clear that they'll be able to continue playing their merciful role if this capital is too far diminished. Western civilization may need to rediscover the virtues of reverence, *in their own right*, if merciful benevolence – the virtues of reverence, in disguise, or in action – is to persist as a driving force in our Western societies.[254]

This is especially true as the arrow of virtue carries us over from the virtues of Equality (B2), back to those of Liberty (A1), where the human story began. That's one of the most important challenges for us in twenty-first century, and I'll come back to it in the final chapters.

The varieties of religious life

At the third level of separative projection, the two poles of the paradox of reverence – Excellence (B2) and Reverence (A2) – each spawn their own two poles of Truth (B1a) and Goodness (B1b) on the one hand, and Reverence[3] (A2a) and Love (A2b) on the other (Table 14 on pages 194–5).

This third level of separative projection suggests why the religious traditions are so diverse and so frequently given to schism. In their diversity, and in their own divisions, the world's religious traditions seem to reflect the kaleidoscopic complexity and contradictions of the nature of the human. The four sub-families of reverence (and all their potential further sub-families) are reflected in the differences and divisions between the various religious traditions, divisions both within and between themselves. It's almost as if the religious traditions themselves exhibit the paradoxes of reverence, both internally and externally.

Externally – *between* and among the different religious traditions – each of them seems to reflect or represent some distinctive feature or dimension of the paradoxes of reverence. The virtues of Reverence (A2) – especially Reverence[3] (A2a) – were the birthplace and product of all polytheistic cultures – the cultures Relational Models Theory (RMT) calls "communal sharing." In these cultures, "life" is the model of all things, "life confronts life," and humans are "porous," open, and vulnerable to a living, spirit world.[255] These remain the core virtues of tribal and Indigenous cultures, where the spirit of reverence pervades every aspect of life, including all those aspects of daily and community life we Westerners have segregated into a "secular" world. They are also at the core of the Eastern religious traditions. The Buddhist, Hindu, and Taoist traditions, for example, remain largely rooted in the virtues of Reverence (A2), while the Western traditions are more at home in the virtues of Excellence (B1). The virtues of Excellence (B1) are the special home of the great Western monotheisms, whose "God," as the embodiment of goodness and truth, replaces the gods and spirits of an enchanted world – where the religious practices of earlier cultures begin to be seen as superstitious and even "idolatrous."

Theology, dogma, and law belong mainly (though not exclusively) to the virtues of Excellence (B1). Spirituality belongs mainly (but not exclusively) to the virtues of Reverence (A2). The Eastern religious traditions focus mainly (though not exclusively) on an *inward* journey of spirituality. For the Eastern traditions, it is as if the arrow of virtue never left Reverence (A2): these traditions look entirely, or largely, *within*. Their motto might well be "I *am*." With the emphasis on *being*, not the ego.[256] So they might be described as religious traditions of "pure" reverence, or pure "union," that is to say, religions in which the virtues of self-assertion have comparatively little role (though somewhat more so in their Far Eastern forms). Indeed, in most of these traditions, the self is the problem, and curbing, restraining, or even dissolving the self is the goal. The objective is normally some form of "detachment" from this world and its cares. This can lead, as in Buddhism, even to the obliteration of the individual as such, and her absorption into a larger unity. When someone understands that his whole being "is something that ought to be extinguished," the Buddha taught, "then he has the correct vision."[257]

While they don't neglect the "inward" spiritual journey, the Western traditions usually emphasize an "outward" one.[258] The Western mind normally sees ultimate reality not just as *inner* but also as *other*. For Eastern spirituality, the essence of spiritual life is found in some kind of identity or *union* with the ground of all being ("I *am*"). But Western spirituality seeks it in terms of *non*-union, or *relationship*, with a "God" somehow found *outside* the world as well as within it ("It *is*"). In religious language, the one fosters religions of *immanence*, the other of *transcendence*. While the Eastern traditions seem to express especially the purest, unselfing spirit of reverence (A2), the Western traditions seem to make more room for the virtues of self-assertion, especially the more assertive side of reverence: the virtues of Excellence (B2).

The Western traditions (Judaism, Christianity, and Islam) draw their initial inspiration and primal energy from the same source as the Eastern, in the virtues of Reverence (A2). But for them, the implicit goodness of these virtues reveals an objective otherness they call "God." Their motto might thus be "It *is*." They look outward as much is inward. Even though that "outward" may well be found *within*. The "transcendence" characteristic of the Western religious traditions is an experience that begins in the virtues of Reverence[3] (A2a) but is completed in the virtues of Excellence (B1), as the self-giving of "I *am*" reveals an otherness, an "It *is*," implicit or embedded in the virtues of self-giving and of love. While the Eastern religious traditions often seek to "extinguish" the self, the Western traditions attach more value to the individual self, to whom they usually give important responsibilities for achieving conditions of justice and mercy here on earth.[259] The arrow of virtue has moved the Western traditions to a new centre of gravity within the virtues of reverence: while not forsaking "I *am*" (A2), the Western traditions exhibit a strong new attachment to the virtues of Excellence (B1), the virtues of Goodness (A2b) and Truth (A2a), with all their fateful, assertive, dogmatic consequences.

Internally – *within* the religious traditions themselves – you can see the same differences and divisions, ultimately rooted in the contending virtues of the human paradox, especially the paradoxes of reverence. It's remarkable how often all the religious traditions divide, and then divide again, into contending streams, which emphasize different poles of the paradoxes of reverence, or different aspects of the nature of the human. Catholic and Protestant Christians. Sunni and Shiite Muslims. Orthodox and Reform Jews. Theravada and Mahayana Buddhists. Each one of these divisions reflects some different combinations or emphases among the various contending virtues of reverence. Each of them might be given the *spiritual* equivalent of a psychological profile – based on its specific recipe of the paradoxes of reverence!

Christianity, for example, is stretched between the radical Axial teachings of Jesus of Nazareth about self-giving love (A2b) on the one hand, and the rational cosmology and theology it inherited from Greece (B1) on the other. The Protestant Christian tradition, with its emphasis on literal scriptural truth and the rational word, is strongly rooted in the virtues of Truth (B1a) – rooted so strongly that Protestantism inadvertently became Western culture's royal road to the secular rationalism of the modern and post-modern world. Protestant Christianity was the vehicle and expression of Western culture's transition from the stance of "It *is*" to the stance of "*It* is": from the virtues of Excellence (B1) to the virtues of Equality (B2), from the first to the second phase of theoretic culture. But the Protestant (especially Calvinist) emphasis on predestination, the elect, and personal moral goodness also pulls those traditions back toward the emphasis on merit and the hierarchy of goods in the virtues of Goodness (B1b). Catholicism's emphasis on hierarchy and dogma roots it strongly in the same virtues of Truth (B1a) and Goodness (B1b), but its emphasis on ritual pulls it equally strongly toward the virtues of Reverence[3] (A2a), and the extreme demands of renunciation and self-giving it requires of its clergy and religious orders pull the tradition even further back, to the virtues of Love (A2b). The Anglican and Lutheran traditions seem to seek a middle way between Calvinism and Catholicism, combining Protestant rationalism with Catholic hierarchy and ritual.

The world's great traditions that we Westerners call "religious" complement and complete each other. Each is unique, with its own distinctive insights, practices, and modes of expression. Yet they're all complementary parts of the same human whole. Each one reflects or emphasizes some distinctive corner of the human paradox, some significant human virtue or virtues. And together, they help to tell a more complete story about the nature of the human.

Religious life and public life: contemporary controversies

Taking a fresh look at what the Western world calls "religion" through the lens of the four families of reverence and the human paradox can also shed some light on our current Western debates about secularism, multiculturalism, and what is sometimes called "reasonable accommodation."

In fact, these controversies are in part the result of our Western confusion and misunderstandings about religious life and its place in the nature of the human. Adopting the post-Reformation Christian and post-Christian view that religious "faith" is something in the mind – a "confession" or "creed," a set of beliefs and convictions – secularists (most of whom probably also assume that these kinds of "beliefs" are beliefs about something unbelievable) sometimes take it for granted, as self-evident, that there's no need for any kind of overt religious reverence in everyday life. Since "religion" is something in the mind, it can be safely locked away in private, without injustice, and hidden from the public sphere. Religion and the signs of religion can be made invisible, without any discrimination against anybody. Everyone, in this kind of secular state, is on an equal footing because their religious "beliefs," if they have any, are all equally private.[260]

It's easy to see how the assumptions Western culture has been developing about religion since the sixteenth century would lead to this conclusion. In fact, it was partly to *get* to this very conclusion that the category of "religion" was invented in the first place. But it's equally easy to see that this way of framing the issue is misleading and unfair. As this chapter has emphasized, a religious life is, in reality, a form of human behaviour, a particular, historically rooted development of the universal human virtues of reverence. It's something you *do*, internally and externally, a way of being human, a kind of *life*, not simply an intellectual conviction or "belief" – something cognitive – as a theoretic culture assumes. Without realizing it, secularists therefore distort the whole nature of the issue by first inventing the concept of "religion," then defining what "religion" is, defining the terms of the debate, and finally imposing them dogmatically on their religious fellow citizens.

If religious life isn't just something in the mind, if it's a reverent way of living – something you do with your whole life – it obviously can't be locked away in private, or it ceases to be what it is. In fact, it ceases to be.

In chapter 12, you saw Michael Sandel's answer to those (like Richard Rorty) who think religious convictions can be "bracketed" and banished from the public square. Put on the side, as it were. Safely ignored and left out of consideration in everything else, except purely private life. Sandel suggests that's like asking someone to dismember themselves, to cut away half of who they are – what they themselves may consider the most important half – and leave it at home whenever they enter the public realm or public debate. He argues that the demand is unjust and a form of discrimination by non-religious people against those who lead a religious life. It asks some citizens to take part in public life as if one arm were tied behind their back. That's anything but a level playing field!

If that argument is plausible in the case of religious convictions and principles, it obviously has even greater force in the case of public expressions of religious reverence, in things like dress, head coverings, symbols, or daily rituals and prayers. These aren't ideas or beliefs *about* reverence. These are the very substance of reverence *itself*. They are some of the key actions through which (so-called) "religious" people express their reverence and nurture it. They are the acts and gestures through which, and by means of which, they hope to turn themselves into genuinely reverent persons. To ask them to forego these actions doesn't respect their religious freedom. On the contrary, it makes them, in their own eyes, *ir*reverent.

Now obviously there might be some circumstance in which this kind of societal demand could be justified. If some group mistakenly thought religious reverence required them to sacrifice animals or abuse children – as some aberrant sect or cult might do – most of us would think the state fully justified to prohibit such practices. But consider the reasons why you might think this. You would do so because you would judge that the practices in question were *not* genuinely reverent, that is, not respectful, caring, nurturing, merciful, loving, just, or good (Table 3 on page 106). You would use – and would have to use – the authentic virtues of reverence as a standard to judge and constrain the inauthentic.[261] Whether you recognized it or not, your judgment and social action would thus implicitly acknowledge and employ the virtues of reverence as a standard of humanity. And, in doing so, it would confirm them as essential to the nature of the human.

For that reason, among others, our potential collective power to constrain the religious reverence of fellow citizens should be used only rarely, and in specific cases, where there is some real and demonstrable possibility of injury or injustice. Prohibiting citizens from exercising the virtues of reverence as they understand them, in a very broad way, without being able to demonstrate some real injury, injustice, or threat, would be unjustified and unjustifiable. It would be an injustice greater than whatever alleged wrong it claimed to remedy. Instead of rescuing the human from some alleged threat, it would mutilate and demean a legitimate expression of what it is to be a full human being. It certainly wouldn't meet the test of the virtues of reverence like those mentioned in the previous paragraph – virtues such as respect, concern, mercy, love, justice, and goodness. Nor the test of other important virtues of reverence even secular states like to endorse, such as fraternity. But it would fail to meet the tests of the virtues of self-assertion, also. It obviously wouldn't pass the test of liberty because it would be a clear infringement of freedom of religion. And it would fail the test of equality, too. "Our cherished ideals of tolerance (including the ideal of having a 'choice') would not amount to much," says Richard Shweder, "if we were merely willing to eat each other's foods and to grant each other permission to enter different houses of worship for a couple of hours on the weekend."[262]

That's something this chapter should help clarify. Justifying such an arbitrary measure on the ground that you're treating everyone equally because you aren't interfering with anyone's religious *beliefs* – that everyone is equally entitled to hold whatever beliefs they like in private, and that therefore you are only putting everyone on the same footing – won't wash. This kind of argument is based on the mistaken Western assumption – a post-Reformation and post-Christian assumption – that religious "faith" is something cognitive, something that takes place in the mind: a confession or creed.[263] Once you understand that a religious life is something else altogether, that it's just that, a *life* – a form of life centred in and based on the virtues of reverence – then you can begin to see that arbitrary or wholesale legal restrictions on the practice of those virtues offers anything but equality. It would be a form of tyranny – a tyranny by those who centre their lives in one half of the human paradox over those who choose to centre their lives in the other.

What next?

Understanding the nature of the human can help you understand the *nature* of religious life and many of its potentially puzzling features.

But understanding religious life can also help to understand the human, and so it may also point you to where we humans are headed, or could be headed. Or should be headed. It may give you an idea of where the arrow of virtue might go next.

Those, like Richard Rorty, who think that religious life can and should be "bracketed" and ignored in contemporary post-modern culture may well turn out to be right.[264] That's certainly a real possibility. Human beings can do whatever they want, if they pay the price. And they could do this, too. But the nature of the human you've been rediscovering in this book suggests why that appears unlikely in the "deep future" ahead.

The virtues of reverence (of which religious life is a developed human form) are a permanent and necessary part of the human – just as indelible as the virtues of Equality (B2), of which John Rawls is a distinguished representative, or the "post-philosophical" virtues of pleasure and play (A1b), for which Richard Rorty is an able spokesperson. They are no more likely to disappear from a human world than the virtues of self-assertion represented by Rawls and Rorty. And if the virtues of reverence are unlikely to disappear – in fact, *couldn't* disappear from a genuinely *human* world – their expression in the form of "religious" life is probably unlikely to disappear, either.

The lens of the virtues suggests that "religion," properly conceived, is not – at least not at first – something you have, or hold, or think, or believe, or assert. For one thing, those would be virtues of self-assertion. It is, instead, something you *do*. It's a developed form of the virtues of reverence, especially the virtues of Reverence (A2) but also those of Excellence (B1) with which they are inseparably linked (See Table 14 on pages 194–5.). It's a kind of *life* – a reverent way to be *human*.

That means religious life is one expression of a permanent and necessary nature of the human, as Jared Diamond concluded. It's part of the structure of the human, not just a phase in our history.[265] Without the virtues of reverence, human beings wouldn't be complete. They wouldn't be fully human. They would only be a shadow or a partial facsimile of the human.

Even if religious life were to be "bracketed" somehow and held apart from the rest of human culture, the virtues of reverence themselves wouldn't disappear from a human world. As you saw in the case of Thomas Hobbes, when you try to put some part of the nature of the human out the front door, it inevitably sneaks back in, when you aren't looking, through the back door.

The virtues of reverence don't disappear, just because they're denied. They go underground. In at least two ways.

They can go underground positively, continuing to nourish loving human relations in family and private life. In the public and community life as well, providing the energy for actions of benevolence, social reform, and improvement. Charles Taylor has suggested that the value of "universal benevolence" – a secularized form of the virtue of "charity" (A2) – provides the moral energy that fuels the impulses to improvement and reform that are such a big part of modern and post-modern world, and of which we can be justly proud.[266] Michael Ignatieff and Hans Joas both suggest that the advancement of "human rights" in the post-modern world has secretly drawn upon the moral energies of the virtues of reverence.[267] Secular liberal reformers, like Rawls and Rorty, surf on a reverent energy, without recognizing or acknowledging it.

But religious energies can also go underground negatively. In fact, they often do, not just in cults and ersatz "religions," but also in secular ideologies and movements like communism, Nazism, libertarianism, populism, or nationalism. Capitalism, atheism, secularism, the nation-state, the market, consumerism, private property, "science," and other such concepts can – and do – become everyday "gods" in the post-modern world.[268] If you try to get rid of "religion" in the name of these goods, you'll probably end up "worshipping" some of them instead. They can be invested with the kind of numinous, self-evident, transcendent value that comes from the virtues of reverence. Unless we recognize that it does, they can take dogmatic, intransigent forms in which even human goods can become sources of great evil.

Religious energies can also take cultural forms. As I noted in chapter 5, rock concerts, mosh pits, and raves are all expressions of a hungry search for connectedness and ritual that aren't satisfied in other ways. The starving of reverence can even manifest itself in a taste for violence. In fact, death, violence, and other forms of degradation may be some of the places where the ineradicable human impulse to reverence goes when it's "stifled."[269]

"Primitivism," says Terry Eagleton, "is the flip side of rationalism."[270] A human reason that can't bend to worship something like Love might well find itself condemned – or even drawn, irresistibly – to worship the reverse.[271] The experience of modern culture since the mid-nineteenth century – especially the steady coarsening of popular Western culture in the second-half of the twentieth and the first decades of the twenty-first centuries – seems to make this possibility quite plausible. There's lots of evidence all around us, if we choose to turn our eyes, to see it – in our changing environment, in our prisons, on our streets, in our schools, in our homes, in our entertainment, films and music, in our all-pervasive electronic media, especially social media and electronic games. The world of much contemporary popular culture is, as Susan Neiman says, a world "never graced by a shadow of reverence."[272]

Reason itself might turn out to be one of the first victims in a world from which reverence has been banished. Since reason is one of the virtues of self-assertion – a "self-assertive spontaneity" – it's not likely to be able, by itself, to control its own inner spirit of self-assertion. A world in which nothing is "sacred" may well turn out to be a very irrational world. In a world devoid of reverence, reason itself might become a self-devouring monster.[273]

A civilization in which reverence isn't acknowledged and nourished as one half of the human doesn't seem likely to be a very human (or humane) one, a place where you'd really want to live. If that's the case, rediscovering the nature of the human – in all its dimensions – is going to be one of the most important challenges for Western societies, in the deep future ahead of us.

In the first half of the twenty-first century, the arrow of virtue seems to be bringing Western culture back to where the human journey began: to the virtues of Power (A1a) and Pleasure (A1b), the old "irascible" and "concupiscible" virtues, the two sides of the paradox of Liberty (A1). The question is: where will it go now?

The fate of Western – perhaps even human – civilization may well hang on the answer.

17

Civilization

In this chapter, I want to come back to the questions I raised in the Introduction about the future of Western and human civilization.

At the beginning of this book, I suggested our lack of a shared idea of the nature of the human is an obstacle to developing greater human civility and may even threaten the idea of civilization itself. What's at stake in understanding who we are as human beings, I said, may not be just our own lives, or the fate of our own societies, but even the future of Western and human civilization. Their future, too, may hang upon rediscovering the nature of the human.

Now that I've developed a map of the human and tested it in six areas of human life, it's time to "apply" it again to those large questions I raised at the start.

To begin to answer them, you need several things. You need to know what we mean or should mean by "civilization," for example. You also need to know where we find ourselves, in the first half of the twenty-first century, and what the options or prospects for that kind of civilization may be. And to assess those options, you need to be sure not just about the nature of the human but also about its order and hierarchy.

In the nature of the human, what comes before what? And equally important: what do we mean by "before"?

These questions can be answered in at least two different ways. They can be answered either genetically or teleologically: according to efficient causes, or to final causes. That is to say, they can be answered either historically on the one hand, or morally and metaphysically on the other. They can be answered from the point of view of our human origins or of our human destination. Where we came from; or where we're going – or might *choose* to go.[1]

The answer will be different in the two cases. Genetically and historically, the nature of the human shows us a different pattern, hierarchy, or progression than it does teleologically or morally. In fact, the pattern or progression in the first case is almost the reverse of the second.

In this chapter I'm going to look at both ways of answering these fundamental questions, and their implications for the rediscovery of the human and for the future of Western and human civilization. Everything seems to hang on the answer to the question of what comes "before" what. If you get it wrong, you won't have a good yardstick to assess our current situation or the options and potential directions for the future. You won't even be able to identify the goal, or "civilization," itself. You need to ask yourself, therefore, whether what you *take* to be the root of our humanity really *is* what makes humans human – or only looks like it.[2]

It's no help finding your way back to our human root if it turns out that, like Martin Heidegger, you're looking in the wrong place. Or for the wrong thing.

Because that question's so important, I'm going to tackle the three needs I mentioned in reverse order in this chapter. I'll start with the two possible answers – genetic and teleological – to the question of what comes "before" what in the nature of the human. That will give me an opportunity to review what this book has shown you so far about the nature of the human, the structure of the virtues, and the "arrow" of virtue. It will help situate where Western culture finds itself in the middle of the twenty-first century, and the potential options or directions for the future. And it will also help me explore the simultaneous equality and hierarchy of the virtues. That will provide a good basis to explore the potential meanings of "civilization" and some of the challenges Western civilization faces in our time. These challenges – or even "crises" – might help us to grow beyond the categories in which the Western world has become accustomed to think, so we can learn to think again in the ways we actually live.

What comes before what? The historical or genetic answer

For our Western culture, the answer to the question of what comes before what is obvious. The root or essence of the human is reason, the life of the mind. Since Aristotle, Western culture has normally identified the self with intellect or reason, with the "thinking part" of the human. For Descartes, Hegel, and modern culture – even for our post-modern culture – the human being is, essentially, a "thinking thing."[3] It's reason or rational thought, we assume, that can sort out all our human contradictions and lead us toward our human destination.[4]

But this view has been challenged, and from more than one side. On one side are all those like Blaise Pascal, David Hume, Karl Jaspers,

Herbert Simon, or Richard Rorty who call reason's bluff: who say that reason can't really deliver on its promises. It can't get you from *is* to *ought*. It's useful as a tool to help you get somewhere. But it can't, by itself, tell you where to go.[5] That has to come from something or somewhere else.

On the other side are those like Paul of Tarsus, Augustine of Hippo, or Hans Joas who say that even if reason *could* deliver on its promises, it's powerless to get you where you want to go.[6] It just doesn't have enough purchase on the human. Because it's a *form* of self-assertion, it can't *cure* self-assertion. We can *think* one thing and *do* another. In fact, the more we think we *ought* to do something, the more difficult it can be to *do* it. Because something in us delights in doing the very opposite, just for the sheer pleasure of self-assertion. Just for the hell of it.

If there's any force in this two-sided criticism of the primacy of reason, taking it as the core or starting point of the human – as our Western culture has done increasingly since Aristotle and, especially, since Descartes – won't solve the problem of human wholeness or fulfilment, let alone the question of human "civilization." To meet these challenges, there has to be something deeper in the human than our modern and post-modern rationality. Something else that comes first. To find the roots of the human, you may have to begin somewhere else.

In chapter 15, you saw that Martin Heidegger reversed Hegel's optimistic assessment of modern rationalism. In the rational form Western thought has assumed since Aristotle, Heidegger argues, it's actually a kind of self-assertion. And our single-minded identification with it is destroying both our planet and ourselves. If we are to save ourselves and our world, we need to find our way back to the "clearing" where being first appeared, first became "unconcealed" to humans. Back to a different, less assertive kind of thinking. Back from our modern stance of "*It* is" (B2) to something more like the premodern stance of "It *is*" (B1).

But for Heidegger, that still means thinking. He may seek a different kind of thinking, but it's still a kind of thinking at which he aims. He wants to get back beyond the virtues of Equality (B1), but thinking only takes him as far as the virtues of Excellence (B1).

But is that far enough to solve the problems of human wholeness and our human destiny? Don't we need to push further back, beyond the virtues of Excellence (B1) – which are still *cognitive* virtues – to the *existential* virtues from which they themselves emerged, and on which they still surf? On which they depend for their very existence? Thinking depends on life itself.[7] If there's anything that holds the endless contradictions of our being in some kind of primitive unity, it doesn't come initially from thought but from being itself. From the primal existential *act* of our being. From the reality that we *are*, that I *am*.[8]

Thus, the starting point for the human can't be the rational mind, even if the Western intellectual tradition usually puts it first. The back and forth of rational discourse – between or within human minds – already depends on a prior *life*. And it also depends on specific features of that life, such as its prior moral commitments or orientation. It depends on prior virtues of honesty, loyalty, trustworthiness, and so on, without which the rational mind can't do its work or do it well. Without these prior virtues, you can't have any kind of conversation at all, internal or external. Even if you could, reason focuses on thought, on the output or product of the rational mind. It focuses on *what* is said. But *before* the said comes the *saying* itself.[9] Before *what* is said comes the *act* of speech. And the *saying* is quite different in nature and import from the *said*. Saying is always *for another*.[10] It's a kind of self-*giving*[11] – not the self-*seeking* of rational consciousness that demands explanations for everything.

Furthermore, saying or speaking is only one half of human dialogue. Genuine conversation requires not just the self-*giving* act of speech but the *receiving* act of listening.[12] Not just any kind of listening: a listening sufficiently humble, patient, grateful and caring – sufficiently self-giving – to really, truly *hear*, and inwardly digest, what is being said.[13] Reverent giving (A2b) and receiving (A2a) are inseparably linked in the action of genuine human dialogue that is prior to the resulting thought.[14]

Before the self-seeking *thought* comes self-giving *virtue*. Behind and before the rational virtues of Equality (B2), and even those of Excellence (B1), lie the prior virtues of pure self-giving, the virtues of Reverence (A2). To put this in historical and anthropological language, I could say that behind the theoretic culture, of which Western civilization is so proud, lie the earlier mythical and mimetic cultures. But as I've already noted, this isn't just a historical reality. It's a permanent fact about the human. Those are still the modes in which we largely live our everyday lives, even if we don't recognize them for what they are.

The virtues of "It *is*" (B1) toward which Heidegger wants to lead us point even further back. They point beyond themselves to the virtues of "I *am*," the virtues of Reverence (A2). But is this far enough? Do even the virtues of Reverence (A2) go back far enough? Do they stand at the beginning? Heidegger's virtues of "It *is*" (B1) may well be rooted in the prior, self-giving virtues of Reverence (A2). But for self-giving to occur, there first has to be a self to be given up.[15] And there also has to be a self to do the giving.[16] Even self-*giving* is a kind of self-*assertion* because any act, of any kind, is, by definition, an act of self-assertion. It may be the kind – like self-giving – that turns self-assertion into its opposite. But it's still, at bottom, a kind of self-assertion.[17]

To find the historical or genetic answer to the question of what comes before what, the clue to all the rest, you have to go *even farther back*. You have to go back, beyond even the virtues of Reverence (A2), to the virtues of Liberty (A1).

Of course, you could go even farther back. The virtues of self-assertion occur within a still larger frame, the frame of being itself.[18] If you look back at Figures 7 and 8 (on pages 41 and 75), for example, you'll be reminded that the grey shape from which I began is located within a larger, unknowable reality of being.[19] The being without which we humans wouldn't even exist. The human response to that larger reality is what eventually takes us forward to the virtues of reverence.[20] But if your quest is for the nature of the human, you're not looking for the beginning of everything. You're just looking for the beginning of the human.

Our historical and genetic starting point has to be pure self-assertion, without which there can be no human activity of any kind. The genetic starting point of the human has to be the virtues of Liberty (A1). In the archaeology and architecture of the human, they stand right back at the beginning: the beginning of human life. Without them, there wouldn't even be any human (or animal) breathing, or digestion, or gesture, or movement. As I put it in chapter 8, there wouldn't be anything we could call *life*.[21]

One of the reasons this genetic or historical starting point is so hard to find, is that (as you saw in chapters 7 and 15) the shift from what I've called the virtues of Liberty (A1) to the virtues of Reverence (A2) takes place so early, both in our individual human lives (ontogenesis) and in the history of the human race (phylogenesis). It takes place in earliest infancy and at the prehistoric dawn of hunting band and tribal culture. When you're looking for our roots, it's easy to stop too soon. It's easy to overlook the fact that, though we reach the virtues of Reverence (A2) *almost* at the beginning, they aren't really our starting point.

The genetic beginning of the human is to be found instead in the prior virtues of Liberty (A1). At the "deepest" – or earliest – level of the human, self-*seeking* comes *before* self-*giving*.[22]

The great reversal: what makes humans human

It's easy to overlook something else, too.

The early *shift* from the virtues of Liberty (A1) to the virtues of Reverence (A2) – early both in our individual human lives and in the evolution of the human race – is *the most crucial transition in the historical and genetic construction of the human*.[23] It's where humans stop being mere animals and begin to be *human* animals. It's what makes humans human.[24] If you want to understand the nature of the human, you need to understand this very early shift of values – from the human stance of "*I* am" (A1) to the stance of "I *am*" (A2).

Now that you're familiar with the four families of virtues, let's review what you've learned about how this shift works in the metaphysics of the human, and how it may have worked in human evolution.

The virtues of Liberty (A1), you recall, are the home of the contradictory, self-assertive impulses of Power (A1a) and Pleasure (A1b) (Tables 8 and 10, on pages 162 and 174–5). The virtues of Power are the "purest" virtues of self-assertion because they're the ones that enable humans to confront and overcome all the obstacles and opposing forces in a life.[25] They are absolutely necessary virtues because they enable human beings to carve out a place for themselves and survive in a hostile world. Aggression is the oldest and deepest of our animal dispositions, without which survival would have been impossible.[26] And when, later, these first, "irascible" virtues become allied to others, they are what give force and determination to them. They are what allow us to persevere in any undertaking, and especially in virtue. Without the virtues of Power (A1), we could never develop the strength of character we need to become consistently virtuous people, let alone to display the heroic virtue of those who undertake great or courageous acts of mercy, or who stand up to oppression and injustice.[27] The virtues of Power (A1a) are even an essential support to reason itself: they serve as its "bodyguard," the force that makes it prevail (when it does) in our lives.[28] They're the pure and natural human "disposition to dominate," as Robert Bellah puts it.[29]

Already, in these initial virtues of Power (A1a), there lies buried an implicit assertion of value that can and does lead on to new perspectives that can balance and modify – even reverse – the initial starting point of pure self-assertion. The simple initial assertion "*I* am," for example, can be translated as "I am worthy" or "I have *value*."[30] At the start, this may be just an assertion of my *own* value. But the perception of value has now entered the human universe. Under the right circumstances or influences, it can later be extended to others, as the condition and recognition of my *own* value.[31]

One thing that starts human beings on a journey beyond themselves is their own bodies. Remember the virtues of Liberty (A1) are the virtues of sensing with feeling. The two are closely connected. Our senses can start us on a journey of feeling which takes us beyond ourselves, into the feelings of others: feeling their feelings as if they were our own. Contemporary science has confirmed the old biblical insight that human compassion starts in the body, in the guts or even in the "bowels." The sight of another's pain activates the pain-related areas of our own brains. The emotions we read in another's face affect our own.[32]

These initial bodily connections are supported and developed by the virtues of Pleasure (A1b), the other side of the paradox of Liberty (A1), the partner and contrary of Power (A1a). As you can see in Table 10 (on pages 174–5), one of the virtues of Pleasure (A1b) is the virtue of imagination. This is one of the virtues through which the perception of my own value can be imaginatively transformed or "transferred" into the value of *others*.[33] Empathy may not start in the imagination: it may start in the body and our bodily connections to others.[34] But the natural empathy of the body can be nourished and developed into a consistent human virtue by the moral imagination. You can enter into the thoughts, feelings, situation, and perspective of someone else through your moral imagination. Someone who can't do this at all is very likely to prove *in*human in important ways.[35]

Another virtue of Pleasure (A1b) that can influence the shift from "*I* am" (A1) to "I *am*" (A2) is the virtue of play. Play is something you do, not for any external purpose, but merely for its own sake, for the sheer pleasure of playing. And for the pleasure of the human relationships play allows, and even requires, if it is to remain sheer play. By sharing in the experience of a human relationship that has no good beyond itself, in which the good is in the doing, the virtues of play prepare human beings (both children and early humans) for the shift from self-assertion to a kind of giving that has no end beyond itself and is merely for the sake of giving.[36] The shift from the virtues of Liberty (A1) to the virtues of Reverence (A2).

A third virtue of Pleasure (A1b) that helps to shift the human stance from "*I* am" (A1) to "I *am*" (A2) is the virtue of desire. Desire is just as assertive and self-seeking as Power, but instead of domination it seeks its own enjoyment. The self-seeking desire of Pleasure (A1b) can be purely for the enjoyment of the activity itself – in which case it is a form of play. Or like Power (A1a), it can be for the sake of obtaining something else. But instead of seeking external, instrumental control as Power does, Pleasure seeks an object purely for its own sake, to enjoy it. This outward movement of desire is what the Greeks called *eros*, the root of all human longing.

This outward movement or reaching of *eros* helps to make a breach in primordial self-assertion – in the virtues of Liberty (A1), from which we began – and from which we still begin. It fuels the critical human transition from the virtues of Liberty (A1) to the virtues of Reverence (A2), the shift that makes humans really human.[37] If the instinct of Power is for aggression, the basic impulse of *eros* is, instead, "to form living substance into ever greater unities."[38] The pleasure-seeking impulse of *eros* reaches out toward some "good" it longs to possess, purely for the sake of the thing, for its own enjoyment.[39] This is the first expression of what can eventually be called "love." All human action is motivated by the desire of something perceived as "good." The perception may be wrong, of course. The something in question may not turn out to be good at all. It may only be a counterfeit. It often is. But that's not how it looks at the time of the action. To the person who acts, it always looks like some kind of good to be desired and attained. All human action is thus for the "love" of something "good." So it might be said that, in this sense at least, all human action is rooted in love.[40] In this same sense, the first outward impulse can be seen as the pattern and foundation of all subsequent human virtue[41] because the notion of what is good or desirable can change.

This initial, primitive experience of love and desire contains within itself the seeds of its own transformation. But the change isn't inevitable or ever complete. The initial outward arc of desire can fall back upon itself. *Eros* can become or remain purely narcissistic, continuing to seek merely its own pleasure. In this case, it becomes the kind of desire we call "erotic."[42]

But the outward trajectory can also carry *eros* beyond its starting point. The experience of "good" and "love" can transform them both. *Eros* can and does normally *reshape* desire into the new forms of bonding and attachment found in family and friendship, where relationships are not purely self-serving but more reciprocal: where self-*giving* begins to balance – or even to exceed – self-*seeking*. A friend or family member can be considered almost "another self," to be treated just like yourself.[43] The Greek word for this altered form of *eros* was *philia*, usually translated as "friendship." Aristotle defined *philia* as "wishing for [a friend] what you believe to be good things, not for your own sake but for his, and being inclined, as far as you can, to bring these about."[44]

Obviously, when self-giving begins to enter the picture in the way Aristotle describes, we've already begun to move beyond the virtues of Liberty (A1), toward the virtues of reverence. But *philia* is just a halfway point between *eros* and something else.[45] In *philia*, there is still something calculating or self-regarding. An "as far as you can." There's an assumption of reciprocity. A desire to get something back, in return. But the initial outward arc of *eros* can and does take human beings well beyond this halfway point, to a form of attachment or relationship that's much more one-sided, but in the opposite direction to that of the virtues of Liberty (A1), the initial starting point of self-assertion. It takes human beings to the virtues of Reverence (A2), in which self-*giving* has completely – or rather, *almost* completely (as completely as is compatible with still being human) – replaced self-*seeking*.[46]

In the history of human evolution, the crucible in which this transformation eventually occurred seems to have been the experience of prehistoric family life and especially the nurturing responsibilities of parenthood. This experience has roots deep in our animal past, especially in the higher primates. The empathy animal and human parents feel for their offspring goes back more than a hundred million years. It seems to be the necessary step that enabled animals to form the first social groups and exhibit the initial patterns of bonding human beings later recognized as friendship.[47] But the capacity to merge self and other, and to feel the feelings of others, imaginatively, as if they were your own, became much more fully developed in human beings, beginning about 250,000 years ago (as you saw in chapters 7 and 15). This was when the first large hunting bands were formed and began to evolve toward the tribal cultures in which mimetic culture evolved into mythic culture. The culture of Reverence (A2) is the default culture of all tribal societies, what Relational Models Theory calls "communal sharing."

The nurturing experience of parenthood – and perhaps especially mothering – seems to be the historical and cultural door through which human beings were later introduced to a new human disposition, one that balanced – or even challenged and transformed – their initial disposition for self-assertion.[48] The bond between mother and offspring, as Frans de Waal says, "provides the evolutionary template for all other attachments, including those among adults."[49] In the self-sacrificing depth of maternal devotion, human beings encountered the model of an entirely different order of being – an order of being that, once discovered, seems to have a compelling authority for *all* of human life, well beyond its original root in parental care.[50] Through the experience of parental nurture, humans were brought into a new universe of values (A2) – values that are the reverse or mirror image of the starting point in self-*seeking* (A1).[51] To their initial, animal disposition to dominate, they developed and greatly enhanced the *other* animal disposition they also inherited, a disposition James Q. Wilson calls "a disposition to attachment," and Robert Bellah calls a "disposition to nurture."[52] They discovered the reality and meaning of self-*giving*.

The ancient Greek word for this third, self-giving form of *eros* – to which its outward-reaching arc eventually leads, beyond *philia* – was *agape*. Because the culture of Greece was largely untouched by the great spiritual discoveries of the Axial age, *agape* does not appear to be a word widely used in ancient Greek philosophical writing, which usually reflected, instead, the Greek culture of self-assertion that gave birth to rational discourse and to theoretic culture. *Agape* is a concept more of Jerusalem than of Athens. It was a Greek word adapted to express a fundamentally *non-Greek* concept. It came into its own in the original Greek versions of the Hebrew scriptures and the Christian New Testament, where it expressed the *un*selfing, self-giving love discovered by the Axial age.[53] *Agape* was eventually translated into Latin as *caritas* and then into English as "charity."

In discovering self-giving, human beings also discovered a new "self." The self revealed by self-*giving* seems to have a depth that is quite different from the assertive self of self-*seeking*, where we humans began. As a result, most of the great spiritual traditions rooted in the Axial age also found it necessary to distinguish between a particular self – identified with the body and the senses, with pleasure and power, and the "fever of the ego" – and a different, "eternal" self, the "Self of all beings, living within the body," a self that is "everlasting, infinite, standing on the motionless foundations of eternity."[54] The existence of these two distinct "selves" within the human has also been rediscovered by modern psychology. C.G. Jung calls them the "ego centre" and the "non-ego centre" of the human personality.[55]

The distinction I've drawn between the stances of "*I* am" (A1) and "I *am*" (A2) helps make clear what these two different selves are, and where they're located in the nature of the human. The particular or ego self is the expression of "natural detachment" or the virtues of Liberty (A1). It *is* these virtues in action. And the non-ego self of the psyche, the "eternal" self of the Axial traditions, is not some mysterious, immaterial, spiritual entity. It is simply the expression of our "natural solidarity of connexion" or the corresponding virtues of Reverence (A2).[56] It *is* those virtues in action.[57]

If there's anything mysterious about this second family of virtues – and about the non-ego self they constitute – it's their special character and the unique place they occupy in the map of the human.[58] As I noted in chapter 5, the virtues of Reverence (A2) have a distinctive quality, one that makes them quite unlike the three other families of virtues. For the other virtues, there seems to be a natural kind of limit. You can have too much of them or too little. Both Confucius and Aristotle expressed this limit through the image of a "mean." The aim of virtue in these other families often seems to be to hit the right "mean" between two extremes.

But for the virtues of Reverence (A2), there doesn't seem to be the same kind of mean or limit. They seem, instead, to be limit*less*.[59] You can never have enough of them. In fact, the more you have of them, the better you are.[60] The more you do them, the more remains to be done. Practising the virtues of Reverence (A2) is a little like falling into a bottomless pit: you never hit bottom. Because nothing is really "due" in these virtues, *everything* is due. Because self-giving is for the *sake* of giving, *you can't ever give enough*. The more you give, the more you have to give. You can never pay off the debt you owe. You can never be quits. You can never fully acquit yourself of your obligations to others.[61]

The limitless or bottomless character of the virtues of Reverence (A2) is what makes them seem "infinite," or gives them the quality sometimes called "eternal."[62] Reverence (A2) is like a trap-door, though which you fall, endlessly. Infinitely. Or eternally. You never stop falling. And this tumble into infinity or eternity can almost seem, therefore, to take you "outside" being itself – as if the solid floor of being suddenly opened up and pitched you into a different realm altogether. Into something that, because it has no limits, is "outside" ordinary space and time, outside being itself: transcendent rather than immanent. Infinite. And eternal. This encounter with the limitless, boundless character of the virtues of Reverence (A2) seems to be one of the experiences that gave rise to the Axial idea of "God" and of what He might be like or unlike.[63]

But here there is yet another paradox. This encounter with "infinity" or "eternity" – or with something that seems to lead or point "outside" being or "beyond" it – seems, nevertheless, to take place *within* being or *through* it. It occurs, for one thing, in the practice and experience of the human virtues. And the human virtues not only are practised (necessarily) *within* being (within all that *is*), they are the human *response* to it, in its various forms, both visible and invisible. The infinite and eternal – though they seem somehow to take you "outside" being – also seem to be discovered *in and through* being itself. It's almost as if being contained something "more or better or other" than itself. Or as if the "in" in infinite has to be interpreted in *two* ways: as meaning both "not" *and* "in," at the same time.[64] As if "every attempt to achieve timeless validity must always remain a temporal phenomenon."[65] As if transcendence isn't something to be discovered *outside* or *beyond* immanence, but rather, *in and through* immanence itself.[66]

Yet another distinctive feature of this second family of virtues is the *way* they're encountered. Because they require such a complete, 180° reversal of the initial virtues of self-assertion (A1) – an "inversion of defiance"[67] – the virtues of Reverence (A2) are often encountered or expressed in oracular, pre-rational prohibitions or commands, of which "Thou Shalt Not Kill" is the archetype in Western culture. These aren't arguments, or concepts, or propositions. They aren't yet even laws. They're simply orders, or commands.[68] Given the radical about-turn in the nature of the human they require, maybe it isn't surprising they should take this form. These sharp orders are like sudden "Stop" signs, halting the initial forward momentum of the human toward Power (A1a) and Pleasure (A1b). Stopping it in its tracks. And sending it in an entirely different direction.[69]

But this is just the start. The negative orders and commands eventually turn out to be just the flip side of much more positive requirements.[70] "Thou Shalt Not Kill" turns out to be just the leading edge and bottom line of a larger, even "infinite" responsibility, not merely for the life but even for the well-being of others.[71] That was another great discovery of the Axial age. "Any human face is a claim on you," is the way Marilynne Robinson puts it.[72] Every human face speaks to you, silently, and gives you unspoken orders and commands.[73] It speaks to you of a self-giving responsibility for others – modelled on parenthood, and especially motherhood.[74] A moral responsibility that turns out to be as much a part of what it is to be human as our original starting point, in pure self-assertion and self-seeking. In fact, the ability to see or "hear" the moral claim in someone else's face is ultimately what makes humans human and distinguishes them from animals or intelligent machines.[75] It's a form of intuition with feeling. But the fact that this new dimension of the human often comes to us in the form of pre-rational orders or commands means that the urgent imperative for these virtues is, in a metaphorical sense, "heard."

It's heard long before it can be given any rational content, or explanation, or justification. Or even before it can be verbally expressed. It's simply heard. Heard, like a "voice." A voice speaking *in and through the virtues of reverence themselves* – in the way they seem to "call" upon us.[76] The voice of love itself.[77] A voice to which we respond – anachronistically – even before it's heard.[78] A voice heard *in* our response, as it were.[79]

A voice that can even be called – as the people of Israel were inclined to do – the "voice of God."[80]

From "I *am*" to "It *is*": toward the virtues of Excellence (B1)

As soon as they reach this point, however, the virtues of Reverence (A2) have already begun to move or point beyond themselves – to the virtues of Excellence (B1).

Each human stance seems to play a vital role as a "hinge" between the family of virtues that precedes it and the family of virtues that follows it. The virtues of Reverence (A2) are the vital hinge between the virtues of Liberty (A1) and the virtues of Excellence (B1). They play this hinge role in several ways. In order for certain questions to form in the human mind, for example – in order for there to be "mind," in the full sense of that word – there must first be a moment or movement of *humility*, the humility that is the hallmark of Reverence (A2). A hesitation in self-assertion, an "I don't know," a moment of wonder. There must be a stage at which the "meaning of life" isn't obvious, or not as obvious as you thought, allowing for the beginning of a deeper search.[81]

The humility of Reverence (A2) is a necessary stage on the road from one kind of self-assertion to a later kind. But it also provides the vital clues that point beyond itself to the virtues of Excellence (B1).

As you saw in chapter 7, practising the virtues of reverence seems to lead to the recognition that these virtues possess an inherent quality of "otherness," an otherness that's just as real as the otherness of the physical world that confronts the ego. An otherness of the spirit. An "objective" quality of goodness. Something found *in* the human but which – once encountered in the human virtues – also seems to stand over *against* the human.[82] Separate and authoritative in its own right, exhibiting or showing forth an absolute standard of "excellence," "rightness," or "goodness" humans can only acknowledge or discover – not invent – and to which they owe a necessary deference or allegiance. To which something is *due*. The mark or trace of something infinite *in* the finite.[83] Not just the self-giving love of Reverence (A2) – in which giving is for its own sake, simply for the sake of giving – but also the truth and goodness that are *in* or revealed by that love. Not just the mercy and forgiveness inseparable from such a love, but also the truth and justice without which they would have no meaning. Not just the friendship and generosity of family and community life, but the justice inherent in them, without which a shared human life wouldn't be possible. Not just the life-giving virtue of trust*ing*, but also its inseparable, reverse side, the virtue of being trust*worthy*. And so on.[84]

In chapter 7, I called this "objective" side of the virtues of reverence the stance of "It *is*" (B1), in contrast to the stance of "I *am*" of the virtues of Reverence (A2).[85] But the virtues of Excellence (B1) retain the accent on the verb rather than the subject (i.e., "It *is*"). That's the hallmark of reverence, without which the stance wouldn't be reverent. The virtues of Excellence (B1) look backward to the virtues of Reverence (A2). They build on them and draw all their content and energy, as it were, from the previous family of virtues.

This is vitally important to recognize. By the time the virtues of Excellence (B1) can go to work – building on them and drawing out their inner content – the virtues of Reverence (A2) are *already there*, providing the fuel and the light that will fill all that comes after them with meaning and urgency.[86] This meaning can be carried *forward*, as a foundation for human life. But it can't be constructed later, as a superstructure of human thought. When Aristotle, for example – the original spokesperson for Excellence (B1) in the Western tradition – begins to reflect on the nature of the human, he is naturally led to reflect on the human virtues. But he can't and doesn't *invent* them, through some process of thought. He doesn't posit them, as principles or propositions, or something in the mind. He *discovers* them already existing in the world around him. They are *already there*: products of the previous mimetic and mythic cultures he's in the process of transforming into theoretic culture.[87] You can't reason *to* the virtues: you reason *from* them. The virtues are the building-blocks of the nature of the human. The axioms or facts of the human world.

But, as soon as they become observable "facts," they have already begun to turn into something else. Or rather, the human that perceives them this way is already beginning to move on, toward something new.[88] The inner "voice" has begun to give way to the observable, phenomenal world. "Seeing" has begun to displace "saying." And in "seeing," there is already a renewed impulse toward domination and control, a new kind of self-assertion.[89]

Because of the growing awareness of an otherness discovered in the practices of reverence – something separate, to which something is due – the third family of virtues (B1) shifts the subject fatefully, from "I" to "It." It shifts the focus from the self and its existence to something external to the self, something other. And this important shift prepares the way for another subsequent shift in outlook that is the decisive turning-point for our modern and post-modern Western culture. The fateful shift from the stance of "I *am*" to the stance of "It *is*" eventually opens the door to yet another shift. The stance of "It *is*" (B1) looks back toward the stance of "I *am*" (A2). But it also looks forward, preparing the way for the later stance of "*It* is" (B2). The virtues of Excellence (B1) point forward to the virtues of Equality (B2).

Just as Reverence (A2) is a hinge between Liberty (A1) and Excellence (B1), the virtues of Excellence (B1) are a vital hinge between Reverence (A2) and Equality (B2). How this works can be seen, for example, in the key virtue of justice, one of the four so-called "cardinal" virtues (Figure 21 on page 203).

The unselfing, self-giving love of Reverence (A2) knows no limits. It is, as I just pointed out, infinite. And its bottomless character points us toward the infinite and the eternal, to something that seems greater or deeper or other than being itself. This works fine as long as only two people are involved. I can give myself completely to another. To a child, for example, or a husband. But what happens when a third

person turns up? Or a fourth, or a fifth, or more? What are my obligations then? I can't give myself completely to all of them.[90] So living in
any kind of kin group, tribe, or society inevitably raises questions about
proportionality, comparability, and precedence. It raises questions of
justice. As human communities become larger and more complex, it
raises them more urgently. What do I owe to other people? Living in
human society inevitably means a development from the virtues of
Reverence (A2) to the virtues of Excellence (B1), from the saying to the
said, from giving for its own sake to giving because something is *due*.
From love to justice.[91]

But the question of justice arises with urgency only because of the
moral energy, the sense of responsibility and concern that have their
roots in the prior virtues of Reverence (A2).[92] The quest for justice and
the other virtues of Excellence (B1) "surf," as it were, on the momentum
and power of the previous virtues (a characteristic I will come back to
shortly). In that sense the virtue of justice looks backward just as much
as it looks forward.[93]

Justice also shows its roots in the virtues of Reverence (A2) because,
unlike the other three "cardinal" virtues, it is always "for another."
Prudence, temperance, and courage are directed at the self. They are
virtues that make you a better self, *for yourself*. They are self-controlling
and self-serving, which is why they are virtues of self-assertion. But the
virtue of justice is about what you owe to someone *else*. Justice is "the
good of others."[94] This marks it out as an authentic virtue of reverence.

But unlike the virtues of the previous family in the arrow of virtue
(A2), an "objective" element now enters into consideration. That's what
makes it a new family of virtues (B1), distinct from the virtues of Reverence (A2). There is now an "impersonal objective interest."[95] Previously, nothing was due: the virtue was in the giving itself. However,
with justice, something *is* due, and the virtue of justice has to do with
finding out what it is and rendering it appropriately.[96]

Rendering justice introduces a new requirement for rational thought
and argument. If justice involves new "objective" considerations of
facts and interests, you have to reason and argue about what those are.
The virtues of Reverence (A2) aren't naturally articulate. They can be
happy with silence. When they enter into language, they are likely to do
so initially as commandments, proclamations, stories, poetry, hymns,
or praise. But the virtues of Justice (B1) are argumentative. They need
reasons and facts. In fact, one of the virtues of Excellence (B1) is Truth
(B1a) itself. Unlike the virtues of Reverence (A2), the virtues of Excellence (B1) push human beings toward the development of reason and
rationality.[97] Not yet the exclusive focus on reason. That will come later.

For the time being the rationality of the virtues of Excellence (B1) is still rooted in the prior virtues of Reverence (A2). It is still a form of intuition. But intuition has become linked to thinking, rather than to feeling alone. It is now *conceptual* feeling. It has begun its course forward to the virtues of Equality (B2).

Rendering what is due appropriately also involves judgments about proportion or proportionality. Justice is "a sort of proportion."[98] The question of appropriate proportion, in the long run, introduces additional considerations, such as fairness and equity. But it's important to emphasize that these are *not* the original starting point for justice. When they become the dominant considerations, the arrow of virtue will already have moved beyond the virtues of Excellence (B1) to the virtues of Equality (B2). For the time being, justice instead means rendering what is due to excellence, to rightness and to goodness. Rendering what is due to the "objective" truth or goodness that was first encountered or revealed in the virtues of Reverence (A2).

This doesn't immediately involve or require equality. In fact, it requires the reverse. It requires *in*equality.[99] The virtue of justice, initially and fundamentally, is the virtue of rendering what is due to goodness and to truth themselves. This requires humility, not self-assertion. Not the self-assertion that demands equality and fairness. In a biblical context, for example, "justice" means rendering what is due to absolute goodness and to absolute truth, or the reverence and trust that are due to God alone. Or to God above all.[100]

In its initial form, the virtue of justice is necessarily a virtue of hierarchy, *not* equality. It's a virtue of hierarchy because it reflects the hierarchy of goods to which justice and reverence are due. This explains why the virtues of Excellence (B1) are so often confused with authority and domination, as they are in Relational Models Theory (RMT), for example. But while hierarchy and domination often go together, it's essential to distinguish them.[101] The virtues of Excellence (B1) necessarily involve hierarchy. But not just because authority is imposed from above, as it were. That's a holdover from the virtues of Liberty (A1), the virtues of domination and power. The virtues of Excellence (B1) are the reverse side of this equation: the human impulse to *acknowledge what is due.* What is due to goodness. To truth. To justice. To others. In this family of virtues, something is due. But the debt isn't yet an equal or reciprocal debt because that to which something is due is so much greater than the debtor. In this family of virtues, reverence is *willingly* offered – *eagerly* offered – to what is above, or what is prior in importance to the self.[102]

The virtues of Excellence (B1) necessarily involve the notion of right ("jus").[103] Right is the "objective interest" of justice, the thing it is seeking to achieve.[104] But at this stage, right is the thing the virtues of Excellence (B1) seek to acknowledge, manifest, or exhibit, the standard they are seeking to achieve. It is the source of "righteousness." It has not yet become *my* right or rights. If rights in this modern sense enter into the righteousness of the virtues of Excellence (B1), they are not yet *my* or *our* rights. They are *your* rights or the rights of *others*. They are what we *owe* to other people – not yet something we claim for ourselves.[105]

From Excellence (B1) to Equality (B2): toward the second phase of theoretic culture

The notions of rationality, proportionality, equity, and right embedded in the idea of justice are some of the things that eventually carry the virtues of Excellence (B1) beyond themselves, to the virtues of Equality (B2).

The perception of an objective otherness that pushes the virtues of Reverence (A2) across the line to the virtues of Excellence (B1) keeps on developing and pushing, until the virtues evolve, once again, into something else. Rational thinking emerges from reflection on the "objective" goodness encountered in the virtues of Reverence (A2). But, once set in motion, its own nature, its own dynamic, carries it beyond its roots in reverence, back into the realm of self-assertion, where the human began.

What carries the arrow of virtue beyond the virtues of Reverence (B2) is the growing perception of an "objective" otherness, separate from the self, and a desire – a potentially assertive desire – to understand or explain the nature of this objective otherness. In the virtues of Excellence (B1), these two developments were still harnessed to the prior virtues of Reverence (A2). But their own momentum eventually sets them free from their initial root, free to discover all the assertive potential implicit in themselves.[106]

Thinking can become an end in itself. The human can be defined not by reverence – nor even by virtue – but by the mind alone. The human can become (as for Descartes and Hegel) a "thinking thing." That's what happens in the virtues of Equality (B2).

In this transition from the virtues of Excellence (B1) to those of Equality (B2), the objective "otherness" confronting the mind begins to change identity. No longer the objective goodness implicit in the virtues of reverence, it becomes instead the otherness of the phenomenal world, the world of "facts." Conceptual feeling and valuation give way to conceptual analysis. Reverence for the *being* of what is – for the mystery of being itself ("It *is*") – gradually gives way to a focus on *that* which is ("*It* is"). And confronted by the otherness of the physical world, human beings discover the reality and separateness of their own self-assertive egos.

As I noted in chapters 4 and 5, these developments are all circular and mutually reinforcing. The growing otherness of the physical world reinforces the separate otherness of the individual ego. And the growing assertiveness of the individual ego reinforces the separate otherness of the physical world. A world no longer to revere but to understand and to control.[107]

The virtues of Equality (B2) are the virtues of the modern (but not yet the post-modern) world. They are the virtues of individualism and scientific rationalism. They are the virtues of the Enlightenment. This corner of the human paradox is the home of the free individual, freely contracting with other free and equal individuals to form purely voluntary societies. In the ideal world of these values, free individuals only agree to surrender a portion of their freedom in order to secure the benefits of living in society. The portion of their freedom they are prepared to surrender is based on a cost-benefit calculation, or, at best, a calculation of reciprocal benefit. The virtues of reverence were *non-*reciprocal, by definition. They were about *giving*: either for the sake of giving itself (A2) or because something was due (B1). But the virtues of self-assertion are about *getting* – or at least getting back as much as you give. They demand reciprocity.[108]

In this self-assertive, Lockean world, the proportionality and equity of justice now insist on becoming full equality. Nothing else will do. Self-assertion resists deference and insists on its own equal place in the sun. Justice becomes simply fairness. Right turns into rights. And rights are no longer primarily the rights of others. They are now just as likely to be *our* rights. Or even *my* rights. Rights to be claimed, or even *demanded*.[109]

The virtues of Equality (B2) are those of the purely thinking person, the human being now defined, above all, as mind. Equality and rationality are joined at the hip from the start because rational thinking aims at a kind of equality, or equivalence, between the thought and the thing thought about. For thought to be rational, thought and thing need to be the *same*. The kind of rational thought the modern world spontaneously recognizes is based on indicative statements or propositions: a subject and predicate, linked and equated by a verb. That is to say, it starts from the principle of identity (A=A), the flip side of the law of non-contradiction.[110]

But the pursuit of equality and sameness introduces a paradox that haunts the virtues of Equality (B2) and pushes them forward – or back, again – toward the virtues of Liberty (A1). Self-assertion seeks individual freedom and individuality. But the more it seeks equality, the more it necessarily embraces *sameness*. In other words, the more it pursues equality, the less it achieves or allows for individuality or difference. In the virtues of reverence, the individual could achieve individuality because each person is *unique*. Unique because of the reverence shown to them.[111] The way in which they are cherished, for who they are. But each person is also *morally* unique in their responsibility for the welfare of others. Nobody can replace you or relieve you of your own moral burdens and obligations toward others. You are morally unique. Irreplaceable.[112] But in the family of Equality (B2), such individuality and uniqueness are constantly threatened by the pursuit of equality itself. Everyone is now, or should be, the *same*.[113]

This paradox of individuality and sameness is one of the internal tensions that eventually push the virtues of Equality (B2) beyond themselves.[114] Related to it are other paradoxes, such as the paradoxes of objectivity and subjectivity. Both of these concepts, so critical for the virtues of self-assertion, now find themselves in a highly ambiguous situation.

The virtues of Equality (B2), by definition, aim to enhance the equal dignity of the individual subject. That's the core of their self-assertive agenda. But the objective, scientific rationality of these same virtues also constructs a world of separate objects. In the process, the subject risks becoming, paradoxically, just another object in a world of objects. Rational consciousness makes you a separate object, an object among innumerable other objects. A fact among facts. Just one more fact in "the great intellectually mastered factual wealth of the cognitive world."[115] A thing among things. A cipher entry in a bureaucratic program. A data point for a search engine.

This is the opposite of being a genuine subject. We can only truly become a subject in ceasing to be merely an object. Interestingly, the very word or concept of subject seems to come from a time and condition when "subject" meant the opposite of equality. Constitutionally and legally, a subject became a subject by being *subject to* someone else. Maybe you can only become a real subject when you become subject to others – when you embrace them and your moral responsibility for them. Like individuality and uniqueness, the dignity of being a genuine subject seems to depend on acknowledging the priority of others, and the primacy of your duty or loyalty toward them. *Subjecting* yourself to them. That is to say, embracing them, in reverence. While self-assertion makes you a separate *object*, reverence seems to make you a true *subject*, in binding you, paradoxically, to others.[116]

Objectivity turns out to be similarly ambiguous. It is central to scientific rationality. But how truly "objective" is this new scientific kind of rational objectivity? On closer inspection, it seems have an agenda – a very assertive agenda – of its own. In two senses: negative and positive.

Negatively, our very pursuit of rational objectivity is already a kind of self-assertion – a negative kind – a distancing of the self from the world, a withdrawal, a refusal to be engaged, connected, or responsible for what we observe. A refusal dictated by the need not to compromise the "objectivity" of the very rational truth we demand. Scientific rationality creates a new gulf between the subject and the object, a gulf its own method both generates and requires.[117]

Positively, so-called "objective" rationality has an assertive agenda of its own, an agenda implicit in rational thought from the start. As I pointed out in chapter 4, rational consciousness is a self-assertive demand to explain everything. So assertive, in fact, that it doesn't feel required to justify its own demanding.[118] The demand seems to be sufficient unto itself. But the implicit, assertive demand is for far more than understanding. It's also for control.[119] That's what rational knowledge is for. Rational consciousness implies "a confrontational posture toward things as they are," "a transformative non-acceptance of things." By its very nature, it involves a "refusal to suffer one's bequeathed lot, the concern to control its mysteries and functions, and the attempt to maximize its capabilities and resources. To understand, to master, and to increase ... an endless reworking of the entire terrestrial condition ... the uncontrollable necessity to innovate ... an imperative to create a new maximizing transformative relation to the given."[120]

How truly "objective" is either of these two sides of rational objectivity? The one stands back, deliberately distancing itself from the observed, allegedly (though often disingenuously) declining to get emotionally involved. The other seeks to use the knowledge so obtained for control and for mastery. In either case, they turn out not to be genuinely objective, as they claim, but to have their own implicit, assertive agenda.

In contrast to this kind of ersatz objectivity, the self-giving of the virtues of reverence can almost seem more truly "objective" or respectful of the object, allowing it simply to *be* what it is. And cherishing it for its being.[121] The "practice of detachment" characteristic of both Eastern and Western spirituality doesn't entail the severing of the subject's relation to the object but rather the "restoration of desire to a proper relation of objectivity; [that is to] say, of *reverence* for its object."[122] John of Damascus (676–749) called this kind of reverence *proskynesis*. "I salute all ... matter," he said, "with reverence."[123]

In reverence, there is always something passive – a necessary corollary of its distinctive attitude to otherness, in its various forms.[124] The passivity of listening or hearing. An element of receptivity or openness.[125] Or patience or endurance, or suffering or sacrifice.[126] Or simply letting go, or letting be. "[A]ll willing [i.e., self-assertion]" says Martin Heidegger, "should be grounded in letting be."[127] In contrast to this kind of reverence, the virtues of self-assertion are active, urgent, and often in a hurry. In a hurry to understand. To get things done in the world. To make things happen. To make things different. And to have their own way.

It's very important for us to recognize the assertiveness implicit in rational thought from the very beginning. Because it means that, left to themselves – unleashed from their roots in reverence – our rational minds have their own inherent control agenda. We're inclined to think of our human reason as a neutral instrument, with no agenda or bias of its own, merely a transparent tool for recording and analysing reality. To be used by humans for good or ill, but not, by its own nature, orienting human beings in any particular way. But locating reason in the nature of the human and in the arrow of virtue, as I've done in this book, helps you to see that isn't so. Reason has a powerful agenda of its own, an agenda of self-assertion and control. In the virtues of Equality (B2), where it reaches its apogee, this may mean primarily *self*-control and scientific rationality. They are the home of the cardinal virtues of prudence and temperance, the home of reason and science. Aristotle and Aquinas called this part of the human the rational appetite. *But appetite it is.* And without support from reverence, its own inherently assertive character eventually will out. The arrow of virtue will cross yet another line, taking it back to its starting point in the virtues of Liberty (A1).

Where we are now: back to the beginning?

That brings me back to the virtues of Liberty (A1), where our Western culture has arrived – or is arriving – again. And another step closer to the question of civilization.

At the beginning of the twenty-first century, the arrow of virtue has brought – or is in the process of bringing – the centre or fulcrum of Western culture back to the virtues of Liberty (A1), where human life started. The Enlightenment thought we could stop the clock at the age of Reason. But it overlooked the fact that rational consciousness is a form of self-assertion. In fact, self-assertion is the very "keystone" of our rational minds. That may be one of the main reasons we feel such a powerful need to make rational assertions: for the very sake of asserting ourselves. In any rational assertion there is "a double and invisible affirmation. In affirming anything the mind affirms itself. And even further: it is for the sake of thus affirming itself that it makes any affirmation at all."[128] Every rational assertion thus has a "double function": affirming not just our own idea but also *ourselves*. And in the process, reassuring ourselves about our own "power."[129]

When the virtues of Equality (B2) (the virtues of pure "reason") lose touch with their partner in rationality (the virtues of Excellence [B1], the virtues of wisdom and understanding), their self-assertive character becomes ever more apparent. Seventeenth-century Western thought spent much of its time consigning Aristotle and Aquinas – the representative thinkers of the virtues of Excellence (B1) – to the garbage heap of history. So, the underground assertiveness of the virtues of the Enlightenment eventually took control and moved the arrow of virtue again, beyond Kant's virtues of self-control (B2) back toward the starting point of the human, back to the virtues of Power (A1a) and of Pleasure (A1b).

In addition to the forward impulse of the human paradox itself – the way the unstable contradiction in every human stance pushes and pulls it forward to the next one – the arrow of virtue is also carried forward by four "bridges." Feeling is the first bridge that leads forward from sensing to intuition (see Figure 44 on page 323): from the stance of "*I* am" and the virtues of Liberty (A1) to the stance of "I *am*" and the virtues of Reverence (A2). Intuition is the second bridge that leads forward from feeling to thinking: from the stance of "I *am*" and the virtues of Reverence (A2) to the stance of "It *is*" and the virtues of Excellence (B1). Thinking is the third bridge that leads back from intuition to sensing: from the stance of "It *is*" and the virtues of Excellence (B1) to the stance of "*It* is" and virtues of Equality (B2). And sensing is the fourth bridge which is now leading back from thinking to feeling: from the stance of "*It* is" and the virtues of Equality (B2) to the stance of "*I* am" and the virtues of Liberty (A1). From theoretic culture to whatever follows it.

Nothing is ever lost completely, however. Just as we still live most of our daily lives in mimetic and mythic culture, we also live, much of the time, in the modern theoretic culture of the Enlightenment, especially in our professional and public lives. We still appeal to their values in our public debates and in our conscious, private thoughts, especially when we want to hide certain realities from ourselves or avoid certain human possibilities.

All four families of human virtues are still open to us – and we live in all of them, sometimes without knowing it. That was the point of Figures 18 and 26 (in chapters 7 and 10). One of the distinctive features

Figure 73. Institutional homes of the four families of virtues

of our contemporary Western culture is that, as Charles Taylor says, it "has opened a space in which people can wander between and around all these options without having to land clearly and definitely in any one."[130] All four stances and families of virtues are still available to us and we can move around among them, depending on the circumstances or the different parts or areas of our lives in which we're engaged. In Figure 73 above, I suggest some of the institutional settings in which we practise the four families of virtues today and where each one of them is, in a sense, most "at home."[131]

Though we don't recognize them for what they are, family life – and the *informal* community life of our friendships (Tönnies' *gemeinschaft*) – are still lived largely in the virtues of Reverence (A2), with necessary reference to the other three quadrants, especially the virtues of Excellence (B1). The latter were the traditional virtues of the State, and still are, to a large degree, because of the core role of the state in maintaining justice, one of the key virtues of Excellence.

But much of our public and democratic life is now also carried on in the virtues of Equality (B2) – the quadrant of human rights, the dominant public language of our time – with some acknowledgment of the claims of the other families, especially Liberty (A1). The virtues of Equality (B2) – the virtues of Rights (B2a) and Reciprocity (B2b) – are the dominant values of civil society, scientific and intellectual debate, public policy and administration, and the more *formal* life of our communities (Tönnies' *gesellschaft*). However, business, financial, cultural, artistic, entertainment, sport, and recreational life all take place largely within the virtues of Liberty (A1), with its competing poles of Power (A1a) and Pleasure (A1b) – but not without some reference to the other three poles of the human, especially the other virtues of self-assertion, the virtues of Equality (B2).

It's partly the central role of business, consumerism, communications, social media, entertainment, art, fashion, music, and recreation in our contemporary lives that makes – or is now making – the virtues of Liberty (A1) the main reference point for our Western culture in the first decades of the twenty-first century. This corner of the human paradox is home to three of the five main contemporary forms of self-assertion I mentioned in chapter 4: both possessive and expressive individualism, as well as the cultivation of the body and of physical pleasure.

The virtues of Liberty (A1) are gradually pushing aside the virtues of Equality (B2), which are the other main legacy of the Western Enlightenment. We still appeal to these other values of the Enlightenment for much of our public debates, but we do so with increasing awkwardness and insincerity because they fit less and less with how we now live and how we want to live. As participants in a culture of consumption, we are motivated more and more by the self-indulgence, self-expression, private satisfactions, and instrumental control characteristic of the virtues of Liberty (A1), and less and less by the rational *self*-control and public virtue central to the virtues of Equality (B2), or what Aristotle and Aquinas call the *rational* appetite. When psychologists Christopher Peterson and Martin Seligman conducted focus groups to identify contemporary attitudes to the virtues, young American adults reacted negatively to the concept of "rationality," because they "juxtaposed it with emotion and intuition," and saw it as a "strategy for denying authentic feelings." As Peterson and Seligman put it, these young Americans "did not *own* rationality."[132]

A big factor in this shift seems to be the role of technology, especially communications and information technology. Of course, technology *per se* enhances our instrumental control over the physical (and, increasingly, the human) world, thus supporting the natural inclinations of the virtues of Liberty (A1). But we also seem to be reshaped by technology ourselves, especially communications technology, including information and computing technology, artificial intelligence (AI), the internet, and social media.

The impact of technology on culture isn't anything new. Scholars such as Harold Innis and Marshall McLuhan have long drawn our attention to the way in which communications technology has continually reshaped human culture throughout history. Indeed, the cultural evolution I have called the arrow of virtue may well be partly the reflection of that very historical process. But it now appears to have entered a critical new phase, in which the impact of communications technology on human culture seems both profound and greatly speeded up. It may also be at odds with the some of the highest forms of human flourishing, even with some of the key values of the Enlightenment itself.[133]

As far as Western democratic political cultures are concerned, for example, new communications technologies seem to have disrupted them in at least two ways or waves since the middle of the twentieth century. First, television made us more passive, turning us inward and away from our concrete attachments to real communities, robbing us of civic engagement and social capital, and transforming us into political consumers and observers rather than responsible citizens, into a fickle audience rather than an engaged citizenry.[134] It also stoked our fears: although, in reality, life was generally growing safer, many people felt more anxious and insecure. Then, the internet and social media dramatically intensified those trends, while organizing and deepening the fears, creating communities and sub-communities of fear and anger, and giving their negative, hate-filled rhetoric a public presence and voice that traditional, more responsible media (even the major television networks) had previously been able to filter out of the public conversation.[135] The algorithms of social media don't just supply sources to meet individual preferences: they actually reshape the individuals themselves, driving them into increasingly extreme and polarized communities.[136]

We comfort ourselves, consciously, with the assumption that we are still living according to the Enlightenment ideal of reason.[137] But more and more of our public and popular culture, and even of our private lives – especially our virtual lives on the internet and social media – now appeals instead to anti-Enlightenment values of power, domination, control, violence, pleasure, and ecstasy, both individual and collective.[138] Though the language of human rights still dominates much of Western public discourse for the time being, it often takes the form of asserting *my* rights or *our* rights rather than the rights of others – *my* right to do whatever I want, including, or especially, with my body.[139] In much of the Western world, this emphasis on my rights or our rights is again beginning to challenge the rights of strangers or of "others" (something I'll come back to in a moment).[140] The appeal to reason is now made, most plausibly and successfully, only when the contemporary world wants to protect or insulate itself against any of the competing claims of the virtues of reverence. We have shifted – or are in the process of shifting – from a culture of "*It* is," of rights and reciprocity (B2), to a culture of "*I* am," a culture of power and of pleasure (A1).

The centre of our Western culture seems to be moving on, for better or for worse, past the virtues of Equality (B2). Over the past half-century, it has undergone what Mark Lilla calls a "subliminal revolution," resulting in "a hyperindividualistic culture in which personal choice and self-definition have become idols."[141] We are now beginning to live in a post-Enlightenment, post-modern, even anti-Enlightenment world. In what Richard Rorty calls a "literary culture" and Terry Eagleton calls an "aesthetic" culture or what, in chapter 15, I called a "cultural culture." A world in which the dominant values are again (or are in the process of becoming) the virtues of Liberty (A1).

This can be a very exciting place to be. But it can also be a scary and menacing one. It's full of innovation, creativity, and change, consistent with these virtues. But it's also not without the dangers and risks of excess, self-indulgence, inequality, and potential injustice – or even oppression. How great a threat do these dangers and risks pose to the future of "civilization"? Can a culture centred in the virtues of Liberty (A1) make enough room for the other human virtues? Or will their own self-assertive stance seek to dominate the rest or stand alone?

Can virtues stand alone? Conflict and "completeness"

Can virtues stand alone? Can you have one, or a few, without the others? That's an important question for you, not only in your personal life but also in considering the future of your own society and of Western civilization. Since the natural impulse of the virtues of self-assertion is, by definition, to assert themselves and thus to deny the importance – perhaps even the existence – of other virtues, we need to ask what the impact of such a denial or rejection would be, for the nature of the human. Are the virtues necessary to each other and mutually self-supporting? Or can they stand alone? Can you have some and not others?[142]

Obviously, in our individual lives, only having some seems possible, and even normal. At least up to a point. None of us is likely to think that we have all the virtues. Or that other people do. We're more likely to think we have very few than that we have many or most of them. Our personalities are determined, in part, by the peculiar mixture of virtues that defines us. The very idea of a psychological type takes for granted that each of us has a distinctive pattern of virtues, a distinctive, though recognizable character, or psychological identity.

But what about someone who lacked one set of virtues entirely? If someone is consistently dishonest, rude, or violent, would we say that they were virtuous? Wouldn't the absence of one set of virtues affect the whole person?[143]

And what about a community or society? Or a civilization? At this level, can you discard one virtue entirely, and still expect the others to operate normally? Can a whole society throw away the virtue of chastity, for example, as an ideal, and still expect people to be honest, loyal, trustworthy, or willingly pay their taxes, or serve on juries, or volunteer to serve their community and their fellow citizens? Perhaps even lay down their lives for them? Are these things completely separate? Or are they ultimately connected?

Some recent commentators have deplored the disappearance of a sense of "shame" from contemporary public and political life.[144] Is it plausible to think this is entirely *unconnected* to the deliberate discarding of shame in our private lives?[145] When opinion leaders advocate and celebrate a world in which "you can let yourself be ruled entirely by desire" in your private life, why shouldn't these same behaviours and values be exhibited in public and political life?[146]

Isn't it more plausible to think that the presence or absence of one set of virtues strengthens or weakens other virtues?[147] Burke and Hegel certainly thought the virtues were connected.[148] And it's not easy to think them wrong. Even a liberal like Alan Wolfe is forced to agree. "Morality, alas, is not so easily divisible," Wolfe admits. "If the state studiously avoids telling a teenager that promiscuous sexuality is a bad thing, how can it make the case that obligations to the poor and needy are a good thing? For Western societies to achieve greater equality, let alone hold onto the equality they have already achieved, they need to insist that the fate of every person is tied to the fate of every other person, and that cannot be done if we claim that, when it comes to matters of sexuality and the family, every person is an island after all."[149] As Steven D. Smith (b. 1952) puts it, "what we do in private will almost certainly have a gradual and subtle, but very real, influence on the sort of community all of us experience."[150]

For what it's worth, those who have thought most deeply about the virtues have all argued that they are necessary to each other and mutually supportive, that the presence of one kind of virtue strengthens them all, and the weakness or absence of a virtue weakens the others.[151] Confucius, Plato, Aristotle, and Aquinas all agreed that the virtues are "connected," and that, if they aren't connected, they can't really be virtuous, or certainly not perfect virtues.[152] That every kind of virtue strengthens every other kind. That the virtues, while distinct, are also "one and the same," a "unity," as Plato put it.[153] For that reason, Plato and Aristotle (like C.G. Jung) argued that human being's highest spiritual aim must be for a kind of "completeness": a wholeness that does justice to all the virtues, all four poles of the human.[154]

Today, one of the obstacles to embracing such an ideal of "complete-ness," is that the nature of the human is a paradox. Though the virtues are necessary to each other, they aren't consistent. They conflict and contradict each other.

Our post-modern culture – with its assumptions about the law of non-contradiction – assumes that if the virtues exist at all, they should all be aligned and should readily be made to cohere.[155] If some virtues are in conflict with other virtues, then they can't really be virtues, can they? It seems more likely they're just a holdover from some earlier stage of human life. Something we can now do without. Or maybe even the enemy of the good – something we should oppose or fight, if the good, as we now conceive it, is to prevail. After all, we can't be both x and non-x, at the same time, can we?

Or can we?

If this book has shown you anything, it should have suggested to you that x and non-x are exactly what human beings seem to be at the very same time. Self-assertion and reverence are opposites. But we can't be assertive without being reverent because self-assertion can only take place within a larger whole. And we can't be reverent without being assertive because all action, even reverence, is a form of self-assertion. Whenever you do anything at all, *both* of these virtues – *opposite* virtues – are always present in your action, whether you can see it or not. In the virtues, opposites don't cancel each other out. Every virtue has its opposite, which, though opposite, is also a virtue. You can't have one without the other. They're mutually necessary to each other. The one suggests and points to the other. To its opposite. "[C]omplete freedom and complete union do not cancel each other out," as N.T. Wright puts it (in the spirit of Khomiakov), "but rather celebrate each other and make each other whole."[156]

Reconciling all these contradictory virtues, in the concrete circum-stances of everyday life, can be very difficult. It sometimes requires great judgment and discernment. But you don't always have time for deep thought. So, more often, it requires well-developed *habits* of virtue – habits both of feeling and behaviour, developed not by rational argu-ment but by experience, example, and apprenticeship. By practice and exercise.

Contrary to the modern emphasis – inherited from Kant and the En-lightenment – on the observance of rationally derived rules, the foun-dation of moral life is not just the cultivation of moral reasoning but, more important, the cultivation of virtuous habits.[157] Without these prior habits, there's no guarantee you'll even recognize a moral choice when you come to it, let alone resolve it easily and well.[158] "A moral life is perfected by practice more than by precept," says James Q. Wilson; "children are not taught so much as habituated."[159] Robert Bellah and his colleagues call these kinds of habits the "habits of the heart," a phrase borrowed from Tocqueville – "les habitudes du cœur" – that goes back to Pascal, St. Paul, and the Old Testament.[160] "Heart," in this sense, encompasses all the vital dimensions of what it means to be a human being, not just the mind or intellect, but will, intention, and feeling, too.

The habits of the heart are learned from "example as much as training."[161] You learn by watching, observing, and imitating. Learning virtue is a kind of *doing*. It's not like following a recipe or a book of rules. It's more like learning to swim or to play the piano.[162] The primary place you do this is in your family, as a child. But later, you go through the same learning process in your school, community, workplace, and profession. The moral education of family, work, and community life is more like an apprenticeship – a long apprenticeship in reverence – than it is like cramming for a formal exam.[163] It is the long accumulation of gut feeling, practical competence, and habit, rather than the accumulation of knowledge in the head or the brain. Under the watchful eyes of those more skilled in the virtues, you practise over and over again until the virtues become second nature, and you can perform them consistently on your own. Until they become "part of the fabric of the trainee."[164]

That's how we normally learn to act virtuously, on a daily basis, without stopping to ponder things deeply or at great length.

But reflective judgment and habitual virtue must both begin by recognizing the force of the competing claims. You can't "reconcile" them simply by cancelling out one of the opposites, by pretending it doesn't – or shouldn't – exist. You have to treat each one of the virtues as an "axiom," as Max Scheler and Iris Murdoch put it.[165] As something that has an independent force and claim, regardless of the contradictions and complications in which it may ensnare you. The language of "axiom" is intended to emphasize the "separateness" and irreducibility of each of the virtues. Even if they are part of a larger human whole, the virtues have to be conceived as sufficiently "independent" from each other "in order to be able to fight each other *and to go on existing in defeat*."[166]

One fairly innocent shortcut to resolving the contradictions of the human paradox is to acknowledge the different values but to reinterpret them, using only one lens: viewing them all from your own perspective alone, from the perspective of only one half (or some portion) of the human. Even if the diversity of the virtues is recognized, their deep contradictions are minimized because most people start from the mistaken assumption that all good things must somehow be aligned or be compatible. All the good must somehow be on *my* side of the human paradox.

Alan Wolfe, for example, offers a quick tour through the four families of human virtues but views them all through the lens of self-assertion. "We need liberalism," he argues, "because without its politics, we are less free [A1] and less equal [B2]. But we also need liberalism because without its morality [B1], we are less fair [B2], and because without its psychology, we are less generous [A2]. Our goal should be the recovery of liberalism in full."[167] Edmund Fawcett exhibits the same temptation to view the whole human paradox through a single lens (equating everything "good" with "liberal"), even turning the quintessential conservative notion of the "common good" into a liberal "test," and the eternal human tension between "the progress of society as a whole" and "civic respect one by one" into merely a "liberal tension," "rival longings in the liberal breast."[168] Similarly, when Deirdre McCloskey gets around to defining the "bourgeois virtues," they turn out to be *all seven* classical virtues. In other words, the so-called "bourgeois virtues" are simply *all* the virtues, as they are "exercised in a commercial society."[169] Adam Gopnik, too, wants to claim core virtues of reverence such as community, connection, sympathy, empathy, kindness, compassion – "a compassionate connection to other people" – and even love as principles and practices of liberalism.[170] Wolfe's, Fawcett's, McCloskey's and Gopnik's conclusions aren't wrong. But instead of "liberalism" or the "bourgeois virtues," they could have said, "the full nature of the human." (In a moment I'll look at other examples, viewing all four families of virtues through the lens of reverence, instead.)

Actually, these are good examples of how cultures work, throughout history, on the kind of spiral staircase of human development I described in chapters 7 and 10. The whole human paradox is present and available in every era or culture. But it's viewed and interpreted through the dominant lens of that culture, the dominant family or families of virtues. That's why, in Figures 18 and 26, I offered you an image of the human paradox in 3D: to suggest how the arrow of virtue moves through the four families of virtues, while each of them serves, in turn, as the primary or dominant lens for *all* of them, at each new cultural turn of the spiral. The virtues provide the consistent ingredients, but the cultures provide the recipes (or "preos," as Relational Models Theory calls them). They combine and recombine the virtues in different proportions, and different ways, and with different emphases. So it's entirely to be expected that, in a liberal and self-assertive culture, the whole human paradox would be viewed and filtered through liberal or market lenses, as Wolfe, Fawcett, McCloskey, and Gopnik do.

But trying to solve the contradictions between the virtues too easily or quickly – through some shortcut of this kind – can lead to less innocent results. It can lead to the assumption that, if all the good is on your side, then those who oppose you must be mistaken, wrongheaded, perverse, or even evil. It can encourage you to see your opponents not as legitimate representatives of some other family of virtues – as essential to the human conversation as you are yourself – but rather, as enemies. Through some utilitarian calculus, you may even be led to a very inhumane conclusion that some individual or group can or should be sacrificed for some kind of supposedly greater good.[171]

The contradictions are simply contradictions and can't be wished away. We have to give each of the virtues its due, its own separate, independent force, even in the face of its contradictory – and equally important – opposite. Courage and boldness are essential, but also prudence and self-control. Perseverance is another necessary virtue, but so are its contraries: spontaneity and creativity. Merit and excellence too, but also humility. Righteousness, but also forgiveness. Mercy embracing justice. Love – but not without truth and judgment.[172]

These contradictions define the very nature of the human. And they explain why paradox, not logic, is the real language of human truth. "Instead of speaking by the maxim of Excluded Middle [the law of non-contradiction]," says Hegel, "… we should rather say: Everything is opposite. … Contradiction is the very moving principle of the world."[173] The deepest kind of truth "can come forth out of the moulds of the understanding only in the disguise of two contradictory conceptions, each of which are partially true," says Coleridge, "and the conjunction of both conceptions becomes the representation or expression (the exponent) of a truth beyond conception and inexpressible."[174]

The nature of the human is an unbreakable partnership between opposites. In Adam Gopnik's splendid words, it is "a knot tied between competing decencies."[175] It's a paradox: a human paradox. And to advance the cause of civilization, all the voices in the conversation, all the human virtues, are important.

Are the families of virtue equal? Axioms and hierarchies

They're all important. But are they all equal?

That's another tricky question. Isaiah Berlin suggests Machiavelli successfully destroyed the idea there's any rational way to arbitrate among the virtues. However much human beings profess one set of virtues, Machiavelli showed, they act according to another. The virtues of reverence and humility are simply incompatible with the virtues of self-assertion necessary to build and maintain successful states and organizations, which often require ruthless or even cruel actions.

For Machiavelli, the virtues of self-assertion were clearly superior to the virtues of reverence. But Berlin suggests an alternative reading of his achievement. He thinks Machiavelli's cynicism destroyed the idea that the virtues (and the values they express) can be made compatible. However, he puts a positive spin on this result. He suggests it opened the path "to empiricism, pluralism, toleration, compromise." In short, to the Enlightenment and to modern liberalism. We simply have to accept that all contradictory values are equally valid, and there's no rational way to arbitrate between them.[176] Berlin isn't a complete relativist. As you saw in chapter 3, he believes there's a world of "objective" values shared by all human beings and by which we're all bound. In that sense, he's a universalist. His view of the human condition – defined by conflicting values to be found inside each one of us – isn't very different from the nature of the human described in this book. But he still doesn't think there's any way to arbitrate between these admittedly universal values.

There is, no doubt, much truth in this. In fact, up to a point, that's one of the arguments of this book. But a darker reading of Berlin's argument is also possible. Machiavelli was certainly not the first to show the necessity of making agonizing choices between starkly contradictory alternatives. That was a commonplace of previous moral thinkers. But he was one of the first moderns to celebrate resolving such dilemmas through pure self-assertion, through an arbitrary act of will. In other words, a world in which there's no way to rank or choose between virtues other than through arbitrary self-assertion can lead back to arbitrary solutions, imposed by power, not to "dialogical" ones – based on dialogue, and on an "educational contract."

In one sense, it's essential for us to think of the virtues as equal. There's no easy calculus by which one virtue automatically trumps another or all the rest. There's no consistent way to prioritize the virtues (or the values, which are the inside of the virtues).[177] In reference to those thinkers, like John Rawls, who want to set up one or more virtues (such as justice) into a priority or basic standard by which to judge and rank all the others, Charles Taylor points out (as I mentioned in chapter 13) that such an approach is circular and, "on the deepest level incoherent," because it has to draw, implicitly, on the full range of values in order to explain or justify "intuitions" about the priority or basic reasons it craves. What it purports to put out the front door must sneak in again, secretly, through the back door. Attempts to simplify or unify the "moral domain" around a "basic reason" or reasons ("thus cramming

the tremendous variety of moral considerations into a Procrustes bed")
have the "paradoxical effect of making us inarticulate on some of the
most important issues of morality."[178]

In every concrete situation, we need to feel the full force of all the
relevant virtues, the whole nature of the human. That's the meaning
of the human paradox. Each one of the virtues must make a powerful
claim on us, at all times. If we lose sight of any of them or fail to give
them their due weight, we will also lose sight of the full nature of the
human, and will end up with a solution or action that is, in some sense
or degree, inhuman, or *inhumane*. When Iris Murdoch urges that the
virtues should all be thought of as independent "axioms," that seems
to be one of the things she's driving at.

But if the virtues are all equal and contradictory, how then are decisions to be made in a civilizing manner, rather than through Machiavelli's arbitrary self-assertion, through the self-assertion either of a tyrant,
or of a democratic faction that wants to impose its own definition of the
good on others? If the virtues are all equal, how are their contradictory
claims to be reconciled in the concrete circumstances of everyday life?
In our own private lives and actions, and in social and political life?

Some contemporary thinkers, like Richard Rorty, suggest the only
standard is democracy. Majority rules.[179] That is a good answer, as far
as it goes. But it doesn't go far enough. Democracy isn't just voting. If
it were just a matter of voting, democracy would be little more than
another form of tyranny: an electoral tyranny. To be genuinely democratic, a democracy requires democratic deliberation. A democratic
culture must be based on dialogue and the sincere, mutual search for
agreement. A political culture of conversation. But in this kind of deliberative democracy, what arguments can be put forward, and how
are they to be weighed, in the discussion? How do we strive for genuine agreement, not just the victory of one side of our nature, or of a
majority?

Part of the answer is that we need to sift, weigh, and consider the
circumstances themselves – the unique circumstances for our action
– just as in the common law. All acts take place in specific, concrete
circumstances. And those very circumstances are among the most important factors that determine which of the virtues should prevail in
a specific case.[180] Our decision about the appropriate virtue, or combination of virtues, will depend upon the circumstances of each case
or action. And *every* case is specific or particular, with its own unique
combination of facts and implications. So the educational contract of a
democratic society will and should include debate about the nature of

the circumstances, and about which virtue, or combination of virtues, is most appropriate in the circumstances – just the way common law judges reason about how to apply the law, in the concrete conditions of a particular case.[181]

But is that enough to solve our dilemma? The circumstances will tell us a great deal about which virtues are most appropriate for a specific case. But will they tell us everything we need to know in our discussion? Even in the consideration of specific circumstances, we will eventually need to consider the consequences of our action on these specific circumstances. Some people think you can stop there. They think you can actually avoid making moral judgments by simply evaluating the *consequences* of decisions, instead.[182] But how can you evaluate consequences without appealing to values and a hierarchy of values? What would make one kind of result *better* than another? What standard should be used to determine the best result? What does "best" mean in this kind of discussion?

To evaluate the consequences of a decision – or even the circumstances in which it's made – won't you eventually need to know how to weigh one good against another, all other things being equal? Won't that be an inevitable part of the debate? When all is said and done, doesn't the debate of a democratic society have to refer to some kind of hierarchy of goods, in order for the debate to proceed? For there to be something by which to persuade the other side? Or some hope for an eventual agreement on the right course of action? If everything is equal to everything else, how would argument work? If we can't weigh goods against each other, what would persuasion mean? Or how could we hope, eventually, to agree?[183]

A democracy is certainly a better way to make decisions than a dictatorship because it's closer to the ideal of the educational contract, the ideal of dialogue in which all the virtues can make their case. But unless we assume the democratic decision is our best possible approximation – in the current circumstances – to some kind of ultimate good, toward which we are all striving (the moral equivalent of Paul Ricœur's "unified" truth), it's just as arbitrary as the decision of a tyrant and will not have as strong a claim on our loyalty as it otherwise should.

And once a decision has been made, how do you know whether it was good one? Or the "best" one in the circumstances? If all values are equal, how can you assess the goodness or worth of a decision and of its consequences? Surely democracies can be wrong, or even evil? In a world of "illiberal" democracies, they clearly can be, and are. But so can the decisions or preferences of your own "internal" democracy, the democracy of your own mind and spirit. You may be under a duty to resist or even fight against the decisions and preferences of an external or (even your own) internal democracy. If all virtues (or values) are equal, how do you know when you're obliged to do so? How do you know when you're morally obligated to take a stand *against* a democratic decision?

And what about the future? It may well be true (as Isaiah Berlin argues) that we can never achieve the perfect or ideal society. But unless we *aim* to achieve it (while knowing that it's beyond our reach), what would lead us to devote ourselves to the betterment of human society? We would just accept, as the Greeks and Romans did, that the world goes round in circles or cycles, without getting anywhere.[184] One of the biggest advances in the development of the human was the Western, providential view of history, in which we are all pilgrims toward some future destination, striving to make God's "will be done on earth, as it is in heaven." This doesn't have to take the form of the crude nineteenth and twentieth-century ideology of "progress," an assumption of continual and inevitable betterment, a myth that can be used to justify any current abomination. We can and should be alert to that kind of temptation.

The arrow of virtue isn't a record of continual advance, as in the modern and post-modern myth of "progress." It necessarily involves losses as well as gains, decline as well as growth because the discovery (or rediscovery) of "new" values naturally casts other contrary values into the shadows and causes them to be overlooked, forgotten, or denied. The Western recovery of the virtues of self-assertion since the fourteenth century, for example, is a gain for humankind. But the corresponding decline of the virtues of reverence is a grave loss.[185] The challenge for the future is to rediscover the latter, while not losing the former. To do that, we need to recognize when – and in what ways – we're actually moving *backwards*.

But if we need to discard the false myth of progress, we also need to hang on to the idea Ernst Troeltsch calls "movement toward what ought to be."[186] If we want to hang onto the idea of *this* kind of human progress or improvement, don't we need some idea of the goal? Or shouldn't we at least assume that there is one?[187] Some standard we're trying to achieve on earth?[188] What then, are the virtues (or values) that should drive our notion of the goal? If they're all equal, there's no forward dynamic, only conflict, power, and stasis. Without some kind of hierarchy of virtues, how would you know what to strive for? Or where to go next?[189]

What comes before what? The moral or teleological answer

This is where you have to make the shift in perspective I referred to at the beginning of this chapter: the shift from a genetic and historical explanation to a teleological or moral one.

To find a standard or direction, you need to ask whether there's a moral order or hierarchy of the virtues that's not the same as the genetic or historical order. For what it's worth, almost all of the greatest thinkers about the virtues concluded that there *is* a hierarchy among them. That there *is* a hierarchy of goods. They didn't always agree about the ranking. But they thought it could, should, and would ultimately have to be done.[190]

How can you think about a hierarchy of goods without destroying the equality of the virtues or surrendering to the reductionist calculus against which Iris Murdoch and Charles Taylor rightly warn? Is there no way between the pure-self-assertion of Machiavelli and the "universalist" relativism of Isaiah Berlin?

Well, one way to approach this problem is to consider two different kinds of hierarchy.

In the first kind of hierarchy, the higher virtues simply win. They cancel out the lower ones. They trump them and take them off the table. This, by and large, seems to be the approach of our modern and post-modern world, with its assumption about the law of non-contradiction. The modern and post-modern virtues of self-assertion simply trump the premodern virtues of reverence and consign them to the waste bin of history. But obviously this first kind of hierarchy won't do. It won't solve our problem. In fact, it makes the problem worse. It leads to the very reductionism that all the exploration of the nature of the human in this book encourages you to avoid.

But maybe there's another kind of hierarchy you could consider. In this second kind of hierarchy, by contrast, the higher virtues wouldn't cancel out the lower virtues. On the contrary, they would strengthen and preserve them, *and make them even more virtuous*.[191]

This second kind of hierarchy would seem to square my circle: it would allow for the kind of hierarchy of goods we need for our civilizing dialogue but without threatening any of the endless variety of other virtues. It has the added advantage of giving you a means for deciding on the hierarchy itself. It gives you a criterion for deciding on the order of priority, all other things being equal. It opens the door to a debate *about* the hierarchy. The higher or more virtuous virtues will be those that preserve and enhance the others.[192] The lower or less virtuous virtues will be those that put the others at risk.

This is, in fact, the approach that Thomas Aquinas took to the virtues. He suggested there are some virtues that embrace and enhance the other virtues, that make them even more virtuous. The absence of these virtues makes the others less virtuous. He uses two words, two metaphors, to express this idea. One is the verb "perfect." And the other is the verb "overflow." Some virtues, he argues, "perfect" the other virtues. That is to say, they embrace them, enfold them, improve them, and make them even more virtuous. They "overflow": cascading downward, like "the gentle rain from heaven upon the place beneath," nourishing the other virtues, and making them grow even stronger and more vigorous.[193]

Aquinas uses the words "perfect" and "overflow" to express almost exactly the same reality Susanne Langer tries to convey with her verb "entrain." Langer invented the English word "entrain" (from the French verb "entraîner") to describe the way individual human acts form themselves into clusters of larger acts. You will recall that, in chapter 7, I noted that the biological world of living things (including human beings) is structured by hierarchies of biological "acts," in which a lead act draws a cluster or clusters of other acts after it, just as a locomotive pulls other boxcars and railway carriages. Langer uses the verb "entrain" to express how this biological process works: how a lead act "entrains" other acts.[194]

But virtues are also acts. Aquinas' words "perfect" and "overflow" convey exactly the same idea as Langer's word "entrain." Virtue itself is said to "perfect" all the other human powers.[195] It links them up – like railway cars, or magnets – to a good habit. It draws them into a growing cluster of good habits. And within the virtues themselves, the higher virtues "perfect" the others. They "overflow" into them (or "entrain" them), so that "the lower powers attend the movement of higher powers." For example, the challenge of the virtues is to manage the feelings or "passions" of the psyche in a constructive way, to make sure they strengthen the self, not weaken or harm it. But true virtue doesn't destroy the feelings. It doesn't stamp them out. It nourishes and strengthens them, making them flow *into* the virtue, giving it energy and power. In fact, "the more perfect has been a virtue *the more passion it causes.*"[196]

Aquinas' concepts of "perfecting" and "overflowing" give us a way to reconcile both the equality and the hierarchy of the virtues, as well as a criterion for determining the order of priority. They suggest that, if there is any kind of order or priority in the virtues, it can only be determined by considering which virtues are more or less compatible with the other virtues. Which virtues nourish and support the others? And which put the others at risk? Or, to put it the other way around: which virtues are a necessary prior condition for the other virtues – if the latter are to be genuinely virtuous?[197]

If you apply this test, what order or hierarchy does it seem to suggest? The genetic and historic construction (or revelation) of the nature of the human in Western culture began with the virtues of Liberty (A2). It then proceeded through the virtues of Reverence (A2), the virtues of Excellence (B1), the virtues of Equality (B2), and finally returns (or is returning) to the virtues of Liberty (A2).[198] A teleological or moral perspective on the human seems to follow the same path as this "arrow of virtue." *But in reverse order.*[199]

Like the genetic, the moral explanation has to start at the beginning. In other words, you must start in the same place, with the virtues of Liberty (A1), with what Aquinas calls the "sense appetite." Without these virtues there can be no virtue. In fact, there can be nothing human at all because any kind of human action is a form of self-assertion. The virtues of Power (A1a) and Pleasure (A1b) are the basic virtues, from which the human begins, the virtues of our animal origins and nature. They're the necessary foundation, at the bottom of the hierarchy.

But they can't really be virtuous on their own.[200] In fact, without something else to complete them and make them virtuous, they will quickly get us into trouble. Without something to direct and control them, we will become psychopaths or depraved, or both. The virtues of Liberty (A1) need the virtues of Equality (B2) to make them virtuous. The "sense appetite" needs the other side of the paradox of self-assertion, the other side of "natural" appetite. It needs the self-control of the virtues of Equality (B2), the "rational appetite." The ego (A1a) and the *id* (A1b) need the super-ego (B2). Together, these two sides of the virtues of self-assertion begin to make human beings recognizably human and potentially virtuous. The virtues of Equality (B2) "perfect" the virtues of Liberty (A1).

But they still aren't enough. The combined virtues of self-assertion are important, essential virtues. But, by themselves, as Hegel says, they're still "empty."[201] As I already noted in chapter 6, self-assertion by itself can't tell you what to use your self-assertion for. Freedom to do what? Equality for what? The answer can't come from self-assertion alone. The "unattached will" can't serve as "a prime source of value" for us.[202] To have any value content, self-assertion needs something beyond itself. Without that something else, the calculating, analytic reason of the virtues of Equality (B2) won't even be reasonable. It will descend, instead, into "rationalism," "the old enemy of reasonableness."[203]

In order to be fully rational, the pure, analytic reason of the virtues of Equality (B2) needs to be completed or "perfected" by the deeper, more intuitive wisdom and understanding of the virtues of Excellence (B1), the other side of the dual faculty Karl Jaspers calls "Reason." It needs what Whitehead calls "conceptual feeling" or "valuation," or what Heidegger calls "commemorative thought" or "attuned understanding," by way of contrast to the "hidden greed" of the objective, explanatory, "calculating" thought that goes with the virtues of Equality (B2).[204] The latter kind of thought needs to be grounded in a deeper intuitive sense of justice and of right. It needs to be animated and inspired by the virtues of Truth (B1a) and Goodness (B1b). It needs awareness not just of technical excellence (B2) and instrumental control (A1) but of the deepest kinds of human goodness and truth (B1), an intuitive wisdom about the whole nature of the human.[205] These first virtues of reverence are essential to give content and value to the "emptiness" of the virtues of self-assertion. The virtues of Excellence (B1) "perfect" the virtues of Equality (B2). They make them even more virtuous.

But even the virtues of Excellence (B1) still aren't enough. As you already saw, earlier in this chapter, our deepest intuitions about justice, right, and goodness always hark back (or point forward, in the arrow of virtue) to the lovingkindness and mercy of the virtues of Reverence (A2).[206] To our deepest sense of responsibility for others and the self-giving virtues of charity and generosity that go with it. They are, ultimately, what give meaning to meaning. Without these virtues as their source and inspiration, justice can't be truly just.[207] The virtues of Reverence (A2) complete and "perfect" the virtues of Excellence (B1). They embrace them, enhance them, and make them even more virtuous than they would otherwise be.

The virtues of Reverence (A2) must stand at the top of the hierarchy of virtues.[208] Not in the sense that they rule or dictate. But only in the sense that they complete, enhance, and "perfect" all the others.[209] They "overflow" onto all the other virtues, making them all more virtuous.[210]

Whenever they raise their head or make their claim, the virtues of Reverence (A2) don't automatically trump or cancel out the other virtues.[211] They are only one of four voices in the human conversation. There's no simple calculus for decision-making, either habitual and reflexive, or conscious and deliberate. Each of the virtues must be considered an "axiom," as Max Scheler and Iris Murdoch put it, with its own equal power and claim that can never be ignored or overlooked for long without grave danger to the nature of the human. The virtues all have equal roles to play in the human conversation and in the educational contract, both external and internal.

But without the virtues of Reverence (A2) as a pole star, or ultimate reference point, or inspiration, none of the other virtues could be wholly virtuous.[212]

And we would have no compass to guide us toward our ultimate destination.[213] We would have nothing to which we could appeal – no values we could use to persuade – in the debates and discussions of our deliberative democracy, as we attempt, together, to discern the good in a particular time or context. Nothing to tell us what we should ultimately be striving for. Or where we should go next.[214]

The meaning and challenge of civilization

My review of the virtues and their structure in the previous sections prepares you to consider the question of civilization. How much is this new world of the virtues of Liberty (A1) compatible with what I called "civilization"? Does it nourish truly civilized values? Or does it open the door to what might be called a new barbarism?

To answer these questions, as I said at the beginning of the chapter, you need to know what these terms mean. What do we mean by words like "civilization" and "barbarism"?

You can approach such words from several angles. One approach is purely functional. Robert Bellah, for example, uses the term civilization simply to describe "societies that have states."[215] But would we describe any society that had a state as "civilized"? Isn't it possible to identify societies from the past or present – or imagine societies from the future – that we might describe as profoundly "uncivilized"? Nazi Germany, for example. Or the Soviet Union under Stalin? Or Saddam Hussein's Iraq?

Joseph Tainter (b. 1949), Niall Ferguson (b. 1964), and Ian Morris (b. 1960) use the term "civilization" in similarly functional ways. Tainter defines civilization as "the cultural system of a complex society."[216] Ferguson defines civilization as "the single largest unit of human organization." But what really counts for him, as the measure of civilization, is the ability of one civilization to "dominate" and "trump" others, as his sub-title ("The West and the Rest") also makes clear.[217] In the same spirit, Morris defines civilization (in the shorter of two definitions) as "social groups' abilities to master their physical and intellectual environments and get things done in the world."[218]

These are really fascinating definitions because they confirm, in spades, our current location in the arrow of virtue. With their emphasis on mastery, domination, efficacy, and external, instrumental control, they are exactly the definitions of civilization you would expect to receive from the point of view of the virtues of self-assertion, especially in a culture which is crossing the line from Equality (B2) to Liberty (A1). "Getting things done in the world" is the virtue of "agency," a virtue of Liberty (A1). These definitions explicitly embrace the view that civilization is an expression or achievement of the virtues of self-assertion, especially the virtues of Liberty (A1).[219]

But the same question can still be asked. Are these definitions good enough? Would they not fit perfectly well with states we would want to describe as *uncivilized*? Are power, mastery, and success in the world really enough to qualify you as "civilized"? Can you not imagine states or cultures that might lose the struggle for power, but which you would want to describe as more "civilized" than their conquerors? Were the Macedonians more civilized than the Greeks? Or the Visigoths than the Romans of the West? What if the Nazis had been the victors in the Second World War? Or the Soviet Union in the Cold War? Would that qualify them as civilized? Or more civilized than their victims?[220]

It seems to me that our word "civilization" comes with a built-in value judgment these purely functional definitions seem to overlook or obscure. As Terry Eagleton remarks, the very word "civilization" seems to denote "both moral qualities and material achievements."[221] When we say something or someone is "civilized," surely we are making a statement about some kind of value or worth – value judgment that goes beyond power, effectiveness, and worldly success. You could have or enjoy all of these and yet still be "uncivilized." Or less civilized than someone else. This qualitative dimension of civilization is highlighted when you contrast it with its opposite, with barbarism. Barbarism is worse than civilization, *even if the barbarians turn out to be better at "getting things done in the world."* Even if they triumph and take over.[222]

Civilization, in this second normative sense, implies an evaluative standard other than power or success. A standard you can meet to a greater or lesser degree. Something you can get closer to or farther away from. Civilization, in this sense, can be thought of not as a state of affairs or a condition but as a *process*. Not a noun as much as a verb or a participle. Civilization is the process by which you become more civilized, by which you approach closer to the normative standard of being civilized. If barbarism is the opposite of civilization, it's the process by which you get farther away from that same standard.

I will call this standard or ideal "civility." Civilization is, then, the process by which a culture or state or person approaches closer to the condition of civility. And barbarism is the process by which they get farther away from it.[223]

What are the characteristics of civility? What are the features of the evaluative standard that should be at the heart of our concept of civilization? How can we identify a culture or state – or person – as being farther advanced in the process of civilization than another? Farther advanced on the road toward civility? Or farther advanced, instead, on the road to barbarism?

R.G. Collingwood was confronted by this very question in the darkest days of the Second World War. When the outcome of that terrible contest was still uncertain, he recognized that the fate of "civilization" hung in the balance, and it looked as if a new kind of barbarism might well triumph. So he looked for the essence of what was at stake in that awful struggle. He tried to identify the essence of civilization or "civility."

The contrasting ideals of the Nazi and Allied combatants inspired Collingwood to define civility by reference to Plato's distinction between *dialectic* and *eristic*.[224] For Plato an "eristic" discussion is one in which the participants aim not for agreement but for victory. In a "dialectical" discussion, by contrast, "you aim at showing your own view is one with which your opponent agrees, even if at one time he denied it; or conversely that it was yourself and not your opponent who began by denying a view with which you really agree."[225] In identifying the search for agreement as one of the defining characteristics of civility, Collingwood was reaching back not just to Plato but also to Hegel, among others. For Hegel, the search for agreement is the very "root of humanity."[226] "[T]he *nature of humanity* is to impel men to *agree* with one another," he argued, "and its very existence lies simply in the explicit realization of a *community* of conscious life."[227]

For Collingwood (as for Plato and Hegel), the ideal of civility is one in which human relations and human politics are "dialectical." A civil community is a *conversation*: a conversation in which the different points of view of the participants are recognized as legitimate and even necessary to the conversation itself. The ultimate objective of this conversation is understanding and agreement between the different perspectives, a recognition of their complementarity and ultimate consistency. It's not the crushing of your opponent, in a war of all against all. A civilized or rather civilizing community is one which changes you and changes others. "We can think which we will do," says Collingwood, "live eristically, or live dialectically. Here ... begins the process of civilization."[228]

The educational contract of civilization (as a process) involves both agreement *and* disagreement: both the agreement at which civilizing discourse aims – that which makes it civil and civilizing – and the *dis*agreement inherent in dialogue, that without which there would be no dialogue. The disagreement also inherent in the human paradox, without which it would not be *human*. Yet another example of the union of union and non-union: the union of agreement/union and disagreement/non-union.

Collingwood's definition of civility – as an ethos of living "dialectically" – was intended as guidance for social practice, for a living community, not just for thought. But it also had implications for thought itself. It was an implicit – and explicit – rejection of the view, so powerful since Descartes, Hobbes, and Spinoza, that mathematics and scientific method provide the model for thinking about the nature of the human. Even today, many people still take for granted, as they did, that any "rational argument must begin with axioms, foundations from which an argument can progress and proceed to conclusions on which all concur." Empirical "evidence," it is still widely assumed, "serves as axioms from which inductive proofs are made."[229]

But nothing about the nature of the human lends itself to these kinds of methods. Even for thinking, let alone for real life – for living. The temptation of this kind of thinking is its drive for clarity and simplicity, its impatience with ambiguity and paradox, and its hostility to contradiction. But the human drive for "rationality and clarity is itself deeply irrational," as Merlin Donald acknowledges. It comes from "deep psychic drives" within us, "drives that we have tried to lock in the attics and cellars of cognitive science." It comes from our initial primary drive to dominate and control our world. That is to say, it comes from what I have called the virtues of self-assertion and is therefore "potentially dangerous." In the wrong time and the wrong place, the drive for rational clarity and certainty can sweep us, as Donald says, into "barbarism."[230]

Among those who have developed an alternative view of human rationality is the German philosopher Hans-Georg Gadamer. Strongly influenced by Collingwood,[231] Gadamer suggested that human understanding is not at all like this modern mathematical or pseudo-scientific model. It is much more like a process of conversation and communion than like a process of induction or deduction from evidence and axioms to self-evident truths. For Gadamer the human condition is like a conversation into which we have stumbled long after – ages after – it began.[232] We can't see where or how the conversation started. And we can't see where it will end. It's as if we came in during a performance and will leave long before it's over. The premises of the conversation are obscure and difficult, if not impossible, to uncover. We are enclosed within a horizon we can neither see, nor see beyond. We are the prisoners of assumptions of which we are unaware, and of the "prejudices" – another word for assumptions or presuppositions – of our culture and our time. The things we simply take for granted, as self-evident. Much of what we take for "reason" is simply the manipulation of these kinds of prejudices.

In this condition, genuine human thought can't be anything like the mathematical or scientific models Descartes, Spinoza, and their successors have tried to imitate. Human understanding must advance, instead, through "a dialectic of question and answer." And this kind of dialectic "makes understanding appear to be a reciprocal relationship of the same kind as conversation."

But this view of human thought – not as linear deduction or induction but as conversation and communion, as a "reciprocal relationship" – this view has moral implications, implications that go well beyond thought itself.

For one thing, the "conversation that we ourselves are" involves a "fusion of horizons." In a successful conversation, Gadamer argues, the partners in dialogue are transformed into a moral communion, bound to each other by the *moral contract of conversation*. They "come under the influence of the truth of the object and are thus bound to each other in a new community. To reach an understanding in a dialogue is not merely a matter of putting oneself forward and successfully *asserting* one's point of view, but being transformed into a communion *in which we do not remain what we were*."[233] To achieve any kind of insight, you can't simply remain stubbornly within your own starting assumptions and categories.[234] In the human conversation that we are, you have to have both the humility and the will to change – even change yourself. There's "no understanding the other without a change of understanding of self." Real understanding has an "identity cost."[235] So the virtues of self-assertion aren't enough, even for successful human thought.

But the moral bond perhaps goes even farther back than Gadamer suggested, to the very conditions of the human conversation itself. Long before the power of the truth or reality for which we are all searching has begun to transform the participants in dialogue, as Gadamer described, the virtues of reverence have already started to play their necessary part in making dialogue possible at all.

As a twentieth-century French Jew, Emmanuel Levinas had even more urgent reason than Collingwood to reflect on the meaning of barbarism and civilization.[236] But he came to very similar conclusions – which he took further, however, in directions parallel to Gadamer's analysis of the moral conditions of conversation and dialogue.

Even for the human conversation to begin, Levinas points out, there must already be mutual obligations, a moral relationship between the participants in the conversation – between question and answer, between the statement and the response – or no such exchange can occur, even within the mind of the questioner, let alone between different individuals and groups. The human conversation entails shared virtues, shared habits of the heart, virtues of reverence such as caring, commitment, honesty, trust, sincerity, and faithfulness among others.[237] Taken as a whole, such shared values constitute a kind of implicit moral contract, a pre-existing contract, one that is presupposed by the other one.[238] The "educational contract" is necessarily and inescapably. a *moral* contract.[239]

But Levinas goes even farther "back." The act of speech itself, he suggests – the *saying*, rather than *what is said* – is always "for another." It is already an act of self-giving, an act of reverence, even *before* it acquires any substantive content.[240] Before the self-assertion of rational consciousness comes the social bond of speech, *the pure act of speaking*, which is always *for* someone else.[241] And this self-giving quality of speech is also what ultimately gives meaning to the speech. It is the source of the very human meaning and value the speech itself seeks to articulate. The said is always trying to bring into rational consciousness a moral value that was already present in the saying itself.[242] Historically, socially, and morally, *the saying comes before the said*.[243]

This takes us back to the meaning of civilization, in both senses of the word: both functional (or empirical) and value-laden (or normative). As you saw in chapter 15, the emergence of human speech was one of the things that enabled the transition from mimetic to mythic culture and laid the groundwork for civilization in the first or functional sense. Even in this purely functional, genetic, or historical sense, civilization is ultimately rooted in the virtues of reverence – the virtues of self-giving, of concern and of attachment – already implicit in the "saying" which must come before the "said." Virtues waiting only to be articulated by human speech.

Furthermore, in the second sense – as a "final cause," that is, as an ideal and a process of developing civility – civilization *is* that very articulation. It is the expression of this prior condition, "underside" or foundation of civilization – the self-giving virtues of reverence – as a conscious (or unconscious) goal, ideal, or standard. The aim or essence of civilization, in this second normative sense, is not the technical power or the disposition to dominate and control – so important to the first or functional definition – but rather the habits and virtues of a generous human heart.[244] When everything else has been swept away, the heart of civility is ultimately to be located (or rooted) in the everyday virtues of self-giving highlighted by Kierkegaard.

Levinas draws inspiration here from the Russian novelist Vasily Grossman (1905–64). Grossman's *Life and Fate*, one of the twentieth century's greatest novels, offers an overwhelming meditation on human evil, brought to its lowest depths in the killing machines of both the Soviet and Nazi systems, mirror images of each other in their common devotion to violence and hatred: class hatred in one case, ethnic and racial hatred in the other. The puzzle, for Grossmann, is how so much evil could be brought about in the name of what its perpetrators called Good. Through the voices of his characters, Grossman rejects "this terrible Good with a capital G," typical of totalitarian systems and ideologies, in favour of what he calls "everyday human kindness. The kindness of an old woman carrying a piece of bread to a prisoner, the kindness of a soldier allowing a wounded enemy to drink from his water-flask, the kindness of youth towards age, the kindness of a peasant hiding an old Jew in his loft. ... The private kindness of one individual towards another: a petty, thoughtless kindness; an unwitnessed kindness. Something we could call senseless kindness. A kindness outside any system of social or religious good." This "everyday" kindness, Grossman's novel argues, "this stupid kindness, is *what is most truly human in a human being*. It is what sets man apart, the highest achievement of his soul. ... This dumb, blind love is man's meaning."[245]

Inspired by Grossman, Emmanuel Levinas calls these everyday virtues of self-giving "the little goodness" – "la petite bonté." For him, this "little goodness," this "crazy goodness," this "poor goodness" is "eternal." It is what is "most human in the human." It holds its own, unvanquished, against all the cruelty and horrors of the twentieth and all other centuries.[246] Civilization is thus, ultimately, a process for developing the self-giving virtues of kindness, mercy, generosity, caring, compassion, and concern: the virtues of Reverence (A2). Without them, all the technical power in the world will still be a kind of barbarism – like the barbarisms of the Nazi and Soviet systems.

Collingwood's, Grossman's, and Levinas' reflections on the meaning of civilization and the nature of the human have been carried forward in another remarkable contemporary novel, *The Dream of Scipio*, by the British author Iain Pears (b. 1955). Interweaving three separate stories, each separated by a thousand years – the last of which is set in Nazi-occupied France in the early 1940s, the darkest years of the twentieth century that also inspired Collingwood's, Grossman's, and Levinas' own meditations – Pears' narrative explores the different potential meanings of civilization: what is lost when it is threatened, and what can be done to protect it? Is civilization a heritage of thought, or of art or literature, or of cultivated refinement? Is it really just human beings' ability to "master their physical and intellectual environments and get things done in the world"?

Pears' answer is that it is none of these. It is not great ideas or great buildings or great technical achievements or great luxuries. It is not in science, or industry or public administration. It isn't the ability to "get things done in the world." Indeed, all of these can be instruments of barbarism if they aren't animated by something else. It's not an abstract otherness "lying outside the individual." It isn't to be found in the external world, and not even in the mind or the understanding. There's a crucial "difference between clever patterns of words, and the answers of the soul." In fact, it may sometimes be necessary to "protest against great ideas for the sake of a small humanity."

The true source of civility, Pears concludes, is really detected in "the impulsions of the heart." What gives the human spirit its nobility may well be an otherness, but it isn't the otherness of Kant's phenomenal world. It's an otherness discovered deep in the human heart. This kind of otherness is encountered in simple "kindheartedness" and selflessness. Civilization may indeed be the "exercise of friendship manifested through conversation," as one of Pears' characters affirms. But, if so, such friendship and conversation have imperatives that go way beyond reciprocity. A commitment to the truth. A faithfulness to obligation. A lovingkindness and mercy. A self-giving reverence for others. An openness to suffering or need, and a readiness to respond. A refusal to do wrong or to do harm or to betray. And a willingness to pay the price of such a refusal. A willingness even to the point, if necessary, of laying down one's life for one's friends.[247]

In a study of those brave few who rescued and sheltered persecuted Jews in Nazi-occupied Europe, Michel Terestchenko (b. 1956) captures Grossman's "everyday kindness," Levinas' "little goodness" and Pears' "impulsions of the heart" in the image of a village pastor's wife who opened her door one evening, in the winter of 1940–1, to find a trembling, cold, frightened Jewish woman, timidly asking for help. The response of the pastor's wife was immediate and spontaneous: "*Naturellement, entrez, entrez* – Of course, come in, come in." From this spontaneous gesture grew an extraordinary story of heroism, in which more than 5,000 Jews were saved and protected by a rural community that itself numbered barely 3,300 residents. For Terestchenko, the first spontaneous response that started it all – "*Naturellement, entrez, entrez* – Of course, come in, come in." – becomes an emblem for the virtues of reverence (or altruism). He calls this simple gesture the "banality of goodness."[248] This banality of goodness is the living heart and core of a genuine civilization, without which a technologically advanced society can – and did – quickly descend into what Hannah Arendt (1906–75) famously called the "banality of evil."[249]

The virtues of self-assertion – both the virtues of Liberty (A1) and the virtues of Equality (B2) – are real virtues. We could not do without them. No virtue would be a real virtue in their absence. In fact, there would be nothing human at all – and therefore no human virtues – without the virtues of self-assertion because every human action, of any kind, is a form of self-assertion. Even the virtues of reverence. The moral heroes who rescued or protected persecuted Jews in Nazi-occupied countries – those who didn't just *feel* the compassion and charity that Levinas, Grossman, and Pears identify as the essence of civilization, but who *acted* on it: that is, turned mere *values* into real, active *virtues* – these just and compassionate people were not just heroes of reverence but also heroes of self-assertion: it was their very strength and independence of character that made it possible for them to act as they did.[250]

The problem with the virtues of self-assertion isn't their existence. It is, instead, their potential to be uncoupled from the virtues of reverence and to become pure assertiveness. The problem isn't only their inherent potential for human aggression, violence, exploitation, and degradation inherent in the "irascible" and "concupiscible" virtues of Power (A1a) and Pleasure (A1b). It's also the unsatisfactory, unfulfilling human results they bring in the midst of all this apparent human flourishing – not just oppression and exploitation, but also isolation, loneliness, meaninglessness, insufficiency, alienation, and suffering.[251]

More deeply, the issue lies in the inherent tendency of the virtues of self-assertion – because they are self-assertive – to resist, deny, or reject anything but themselves. The virtues of self-assertion are the virtues of non-union. By themselves, they naturally resist or deny the other virtues. By their very nature, they want to rule alone. This inherent resistance to anything other than themselves heightens the already existing tensions between the four families of virtues, gradually diminishing both our image of the human and the way we realize it in human culture and civilization.

The essence and measure of civilization, in other words, is not the mastery and control offered by the virtues of self-assertion – essential though they are, even to goodness – but rather the self-giving virtues of reverence.[252] Without them, no increase in capacity to master our physical and intellectual environments and get things done in the world will save us from a growing barbarism.[253]

No matter what we may call it, or how we may dress it up.

Where next? Deeper into Pleasure (A1b) and Power (A1a)?

Where is the arrow of virtue likely to go next?

In the middle of the twenty-first century, is our Western culture well fitted for advancing the process of civilization, the process of increasing human civility? Or is it more likely to lead in the other direction, toward some form (or forms) of increasing barbarism?

As I mentioned in my Introduction, there's a perennial human temptation to think that there can be an "end of history," that humankind has evolved as far as it is likely to go, and that no further change in the human is to be expected. That we have gone about as far as we can go. If history were not there to tell us otherwise, the human paradox would do so. The very contradictions and tensions that structure the nature of the human – and each of its stances and sub-families of virtues – ensure that it's very unlikely to remain exactly where it is forever.[254] The contradictions of the human paradox – and the polar structure of being they reflect – help ensure that change, not stasis, is a law of human life, and that nothing ever remains the same. As soon as one state of affairs has been achieved, it is already turning into something else.[255]

Richard Rorty suggests and hopes that it's possible to embrace the post-modern culture of the virtues of Liberty (A1), as he does, while reaching back, politically and socially, to the ideals of equality, fairness, and redistribution advocated by the previous modern culture of the virtues of Equality (B2), for which John Rawls is a representative spokesperson. Rorty would like to stop the clock somewhere on the frontier between Liberty (A1) and Equality (B2), combining the cultural outlook and temper of the first (A1), of which he is such a representative figure (the "literary" or "cultural" or "aesthetic" culture of post-modernity), with the social policies and moral outcomes more characteristic of the second (B2).[256]

This may be possible. So far at least, it seems to be working, though the evidence is mixed, to say the least. The increasing violence of our popular culture and game culture doesn't yet seem to be bleeding over into real life.[257] But much of its unbridled sexuality certainly is. And our retreat into private pleasures and into the virtual world of the media does seem to be reducing civic engagement in Western countries and slowly eating into their social capital.[258] Nevertheless, if the delicate balance between Liberty (A1) and Equality (B2) Rorty hopes for can be maintained, it would be far from an unhappy outcome.

However, over the long haul – in the "deep future" ahead – it seems a risky bet.

For one thing, this hope seems greatly to underestimate the dominating power of the virtues of Liberty (A1), once they have got the virtues of Equality (B2) all alone, isolated within the virtues of self-assertion, entirely detached from their sustaining source in the virtues of Excellence (B1) and, beyond them, in the virtues of Reverence (A2). The virtues of Power (A1a) and Pleasure (A1b) – the irascible and concupiscible appetites – are enormous human forces. They are the first root and source of all our being, from which all human action of any kind ultimately flows. And it is far from certain that the virtues of Equality (B2) – the "rational" appetite – will be any kind of match for them once the power of naked reason has been shown to be as weak as Rorty admits it to be. When you have given up on the Enlightenment project of a rational world as Rorty has – a world whose truth can be revealed by reason, and on whose truth humans can at least hope to agree – what is left to make the rational appetite rational? Or to give it any restraining power on appetite, period?

Richard Rorty thinks we can sort all this out simply through democracy. But when you have given up on the joint search for meaning in the world, what's left to appeal to in a democracy, other than naked self-interest? In this kind of world, the "motive of self-interest not only is, but must be, and ought to be, the mainspring of human conduct."[259] There's a half-truth in this, as the human paradox shows us. Everything does, and must, start with self-assertion. But if you take it for the whole truth, if you think self-assertion equates to self-interest, if that's all you can appeal to, why should we expect democracy to last for long? Doesn't a democracy depend for its survival on the devotion and the civic virtues of its citizens? On their sense of shared values and devotion to something more than themselves, something more than their own self-interest?

A world where the virtues of self-assertion rule alone stands a good chance, instead, of adopting the view that "we aren't here for long, and when we go, that's that. Finish. So, for God's sake, enjoy yourself now – and sod anyone who tries to stop you."[260] In this kind of world there's no reason to stick with your fifty-one-year marriage if you think it's getting in the way of "life, liberty, and the pursuit of happiness."[261] Or stick with anything else either, for that matter. If there's no good but yourself, why should you be loyal at all? Why should you even be loyal to the good, since there's no good to be loyal to?

Why would you reach back to hang onto the values of Equality (B2), as Richard Rorty wants you to do, if you're busy pursuing power and pleasure?

In a world where the virtues of self-assertion rule alone, a more likely long-term (perhaps very long term) scenario is some kind of further advance into the virtues of Liberty (A1), with Power (A1a) and Pleasure

(A1b) becoming ever more dominant forces in human life. While power and pleasure are certainly in tension – in the "paradox of Liberty" I discussed in chapter 8 – they're also partners and can work together, in surprising ways.

We shouldn't assume, for one thing, that the forces which are currently accumulating enormous power in our world will wear a hostile or negative face. Evil isn't the opposite of good, as we too readily assume. It's the counterfeit of good. It always *looks* like a good to us. That's why we desire it.[262] Or desire to submit to it. Power is likely to wear, and already does wear, a benign and attractive face. It offers us something we desire. Perhaps convenience and speed, as Google and Amazon do, when we give away all the details of our lives to them. Or the gratification of our vanity, as Facebook and other social media do, when we do the same. Perhaps security, as governments do, when they dramatically increase surveillance of our daily lives, undoing, in a lifetime, all the liberties we have achieved in the thousand years since Magna Carta.

Perhaps it will offer simply freedom from care, or effort, or from the arduous, burdensome duties of citizenship. That's another way power and pleasure can work together. As we retreat into our virtual, electronic worlds and into our private bubbles of consumption and domestic pleasures, the responsibilities of citizenship (the duties we inherited from the Enlightenment culture of Equality [B2]) can seem tiresome or even irrelevant. A distraction from our real lives and our real interests, from the pursuit of our private pleasures and our private gain. A University of Michigan study found that American college students were 40 per cent less "empathetic" – less responsive to the distress and perspectives of others – in 2009 than they had been in 1979. And the biggest drop came after 2000, after the emergence of social media.[263] This shift in outlook is reflected in the steady decline of civic engagement in Western countries over the last forty years and the detachment of so many people, born after 1970, from involvement in public and community affairs, including the decline in voter turnout. These things are simply irrelevant to their real lives. And they are happy to have someone else look after them. They can't be bothered. Although Americans born in the 1930s or 1940s "overwhelmingly" say they take an active interest in politics, less than half of young Americans now do. Some 71 per cent of Americans born in the 1930s believe democracy is "essential," but only 29 per cent of those born in the 1980s agree. The picture isn't very different in the UK and Australia, and only slightly better in Canada.[264]

In this mood, authoritarian styles of government can almost begin to seem welcome because they get rid of the distractions and demands of democratic politics.[265] From this point of view, some in the West are even beginning to see China's autocratic form of state capitalism as a potential model for the future because of its allegedly greater "effectiveness" – the perfect blend of public and private power with private pleasure.[266] On the pretext that democracies no longer allow the emergence of "great" leaders with long-term visions, even a former president of France (one of the birthplaces of liberalism and democracy) has endorsed Chinese President Xi Jinping's (b. 1953) move to transform his autocratic rule into a permanent dictatorship.[267] Almost a quarter of American millennials think democracy is a bad form of government. Nearly half of them would prefer strongman rule. One sixth of all Americans favours military rule and support rises to almost a quarter among those aged 18–24.[268]

If our democracies survive in this kind of world, they may be democratic in name only. We might be slavishly free: free to acquire, to consume, to buy things, to entertain ourselves, to have Facebook "friends," and to gratify our appetites. But we would not be genuinely free members of a political community or enjoy authentic democratic rights. Thomas Hobbes rightly foresaw that commerce can easily be married with absolutism, and that, in this kind of state (which he favoured), the only liberties would be those of consumers and of consumption: "the liberty to buy and sell and otherwise contract with another; to choose their own abode, their own diet, their own trade of life, and institute their children as they see fit; and the like."[269]

Peter Thiel, the co-founder of PayPal, argues that the term "capitalist democracy" has become an "oxymoron." Politics is about "interfering with other people's lives." As a libertarian, he therefore opts for capitalism *over* democracy and seeks to escape from "the terrible arc" of democratic politics. Thiel thinks you can do that by escaping from society into outer space or by settling the oceans, or by living in the unregulated space of the internet. But because those places would be human too, they will need to be governed. And if government is not to be political and democratic, it will be authoritarian and dictatorial. So those places might be safe for capitalism but not for much else that's genuinely human. You can already see that possibility in Thiel's yearning for the "single person" who will make the world "safe for capitalism."[270] Of course, Thiel thinks he means some great entrepreneur. But his "single person" will turn out to be something much more sinister. A Napoleon, a Hitler, a Mussolini, a Stalin, a Saddam Hussein, a Deng Xiaoping, a Putin, a Xi Jinping. This kind of future might be safe for capitalism and consumers. But not for much else that's genuinely human. Safe for a small subset of the virtues of Liberty (A1). But not for all the rest of what makes humans human.

Power (A1a) and Pleasure (A1b) aren't always in tension. They can also be mutually reinforcing.[271] They're two sides of the same thing: two sides of the human virtues of Liberty (A1). And they could work together to draw us further into a culture based largely, if not exclusively, on those virtues, a culture in which even the other assertive virtues of Equality (B2) take a very back seat. And in which the virtues of reverence disappear altogether.[272]

This would not be an advance in civilization, no matter how much the inner drive of the virtues of Liberty (A1) for instrumental control allowed us to "master" our physical and intellectual environments and "get things done in the world." It would be a mixture of decadence and oppression. A new kind of barbarism. What's our stock image of a barbarian, after all, if not a person who lives only for power and pleasure?

This second scenario is at least as plausible as Richard Rorty's assumption that you can embrace the culture and spirit of the virtues of Liberty (A1) – the spirit of "play" – yet still hang onto the social goals of the virtues of Equality (B2).[273] In a struggle between power and pleasure alone, power is the stronger and is very likely to win, as the ancient barbarians showed.[274]

Another possible scenario: beyond self-assertion?

But are these the only two possibilities for the future of Western civilization? Or the most likely? Don't the human paradox and the arrow of virtue suggest yet another possibility? [275] The one to which Søren Kierkegaard already pointed forward in the middle of the nineteenth century?[276]

In chapters 7, 10, and 15, I explored Hegel's idea that the arrow of virtue isn't linear but rather more like a spiral staircase (Figures 18, 26, and 64). As I mentioned there, Hegel's vision raises the question of what happens when the arrow of virtue has passed through all four families of virtues. Does the whole spiral process start all over again? Or does it come to an end? Hegel himself is ambiguous on this point. At times his language could give you the impression he thinks the process "begins all over again."[277] But at others, he seems to think that Reason and mind are the end of the story. Once human beings have reached this stage, the spiral stops advancing. The only thing left to achieve is an expansion of the rational mind: from the individual to the "national mind," and then, from the national mind to the "universal world mind whose right is supreme."[278]

Maybe we don't have to choose between these two different visions of the future. Maybe the first could be the way you get to the second.

Maybe the continued, upward movement of the spiral is the way you get closer to what Hegel (or rather his translator) calls the "universal world mind." (Though "mind" may not be quite the right word here.) That possibility is prompted by a question you can't help asking: is it really plausible to think the spiral might stop advancing? If the nature of the human is really a paradox – structured by its own contradictions and by the process of separative projection – is it really plausible that the process would just *stop* somewhere? Isn't it more probable the arrow of virtue will keep moving on, in its characteristic spiral pattern, driven forward by the very same contradictions that have brought us to where we are now?[279] As long as human beings exist, there will be no "end of history." If that's true, wouldn't you expect the story of Western (and human) cultural development to continue as it has until now? In that case, it might also be reasonable to expect that, because of its spiral progress through the four families of virtues, it will keep returning to the same place or places on the spiral – though each time from a different and "higher" perspective.

If something like this were true – or at least possible – we shouldn't assume our current advance into the virtues of Liberty (A1) is the end of the story, or that we will simply carry on, into the deep future, on the same trajectory we've been on for the last four hundred years.[280] Perhaps our current post-modern Western culture is merely one more step on the spiral staircase. We seem to be coming back to where we started, at the virtues of Liberty (A1). But we're at a higher level on the staircase now and can view it from a different perspective, a perspective given to us by all the other steps along the way, including the other three families of virtues our Western culture has explored so far. We can now look back over all the previous landings on the spiral staircase and survey all the corners of the human through which we've come – and which are now available to us, as our full human repertoire. The full nature of the human.[281]

If so, we can't exclude the possibility that the arrow of virtue will continue its upward climb and the same process – or something like it – will happen this time around, as it did the first time. That is to say, the virtues of Liberty (A1) – especially the concupiscible virtues of Pleasure (A1b) – will again propel us forward. Not merely deeper and deeper into themselves, or into their partner (in the paradox of Liberty), the virtues of Power (A1A). But to the next step on the spiral staircase.

Of course, I don't want to turn Hegel's spiral vision of human development into another historical determinism, a kind of moral determinism that would be just as suspect as Hegel's own rationalist determinism or the materialist determinism Karl Marx spun from

Hegel's spiral. Any theory of the human, and of human development, has to give full scope to contingency, chance, and the unexpected. It has to acknowledge the reality of human freedom and choice.[282]

In confronting the challenge that contingency and freedom pose to any theory of the human and of human development, you encounter a paradox of history that's one of the deepest of all the human paradoxes I've been exploring in this book. On the one hand, you have to think of history as open-ended and contingent: without its *in*determinacy, history wouldn't be history. But on the other hand, unless you look for some pattern or structure in history, it becomes incomprehensible. It becomes just one damn thing after another, as in "episodic culture" – without any meaning or truth.[283]

In fact, Paul Ricœur points out that this paradox of history is merely one aspect of a deeper paradox of truth itself. Every person who thinks must be free to think the truth as they see it. But in seeking for such truth, each person implicitly invokes the authority of truth itself, a single, unified truth that must be the same for all of us. Or else there could be no "truth" at all: no standard by which to test and weigh our individual truths. Hence no communication and dialogue, no conversation in which we share and reconcile the truths we see. No educational contract. The *plurality* of our truths is inseparable from the *unity* of the truth we all seek. One more example of the paradox of the one and the many, or the union of union and non-union!

It's the same thing with history, Ricœur says. Without contingency, it isn't history. But without the search for some kind of unified meaning, it's meaningless.[284] Acknowledging and respecting the open-ended contingency of reality doesn't exclude seeking for the pattern, meaning, or truth of human experience. You don't have to give up the search for the overall meaning of human experience, but rather "transform it in light of a radical awareness of historical contingency."[285] In fact, without the search for a pattern, contingency may become simply meaningless or even incomprehensible. When you've fully acknowledged both the reality and the power of human freedom, it remains a legitimate exercise to ask yourself whether the pattern of the human paradox, through which Western culture has evolved so far, suggests anything about our potential human future. If determinism is to be ruled out in human affairs, is there a pattern in human life that may be more like "emergence"? From this perspective, contingency and pattern don't have to be alternatives or opposed: contingency may be the very way in which pattern becomes creative and emerges.[286]

Are there any reasons to think contingent human freedom might eventually encounter the limits of the virtues of self-assertion – and rediscover that the other side of "*I* am" (A1) is the equal reality that "I *am*" (A2)?[287] That the virtues of self-assertion and of reverence can't be separated, no matter how much we may try to do so?

Rediscovering reverence?

That seems like a tall order.

Because, as I described in chapter 15, our Western culture has spent the last four centuries gradually burying half of the virtues or removing them from our public conversation. One of the (not always intended) consequences of the Enlightenment was to reduce the Western conversation, almost entirely, to the internal dialogue between the virtues of self-assertion, between the virtues of Liberty (A1) and of Equality (B2). That's a very important dialogue and raises difficult issues and riddles of its own. But it's not the only one. There's also the prior and larger dialogue between the virtues of self-assertion and the virtues of reverence. A dialogue which has fallen largely silent, in our modern and post-modern Western culture, or is carried on awkwardly, partially, or under different names, without recognizing the two basic sides of the human paradox or how it works.

So the educational contract of civilization can't function properly now because one of the key partners is missing in action. Perhaps the most important partner – if there really is a hierarchy of virtues, with the virtues of Reverence (A2) at its apex. The virtues of reverence are absent from the table, admitted only implicitly, lurking in the background. They are always present in our real lives but unacknowledged in our conscious minds and in our public conversation, except under other names, or in disguise.[288]

The process of civilization – understood as dialogue in search of agreement – requires completeness. It requires the participation of both sides of the human paradox and all four poles of the human. Developing a greater, more humane, more "civil" civilization means rediscovering the identities of the necessary participants in the human conversation. Continuing the process of civilization – developing, enhancing, and deepening civility – means rediscovering the nature of the human, moulded, as it is, by two contrasting families of human virtues – and all their cascading sub-families and sub-sub-families you've encountered in this book. It means rediscovering who we are. We Westerners must awake from our "millennial sleep," as Lev Shestov puts it, and decide to think in the categories in which we actually live.[289]

In the twenty-first century dominated by the virtues of self-assertion – or even by the virtues of Liberty (A1) – that means rediscovering the nature of the human must begin by rediscovering the virtues of reverence: both the virtues of Excellence (B1) and the virtues of Reverence (A2).[290]

This seems, as I said, like a very tall order. But maybe it isn't quite as tall an order as it first appears. Let's consider a few reasons why Western culture could eventually encounter the limits of self-assertion and rediscover that the other side of the human stance of "*I* am" (A1) is the reality that "I *am*" (A2) – rediscover that the virtues of self-assertion and reverence can't be separated, no matter how hard we try to do so.

One of them is the importance our post-modern culture now attaches to the body. Of course, our post-modern preoccupation with the body – its shape and size, its decoration and adornment, its many sources of pleasure, in food, drink, sex, and so on – has more than a whiff of decadence about it. It could, as I just suggested, lead us into new kinds of slavery, both moral and real. In the long run, it seems incompatible with the kind of civic virtue and self-control necessary to sustain healthy democracies.[291]

But – if we pay closer attention than we are yet doing – it can also liberate us from our exclusive equation of the human with the mind, an equation that has dominated Western culture since Aristotle. Theoretic culture was and is based on the assumption that the human is a "thinking thing," and that we meet the essence of our nature, of who we are, in our minds, in rational thought. Post-modern culture has abandoned that assumption in practice but not yet consciously. We hang onto it, reflexively, even when, like Richard Rorty, we have given up on the Enlightenment project of making rational sense of the world. We hang onto it partly because, as I suggested, it offers a handy shield to protect ourselves from the disturbing claims of virtues other than those of self-assertion. It also soothes our consciences to think that, as we plunge deeper into the virtues of Power (A1a) and Pleasure (A1b), we're still acting as reasonable beings.

But to be fair, we also hang onto the definition of human beings as "thinking things" – as mind – mainly because we don't yet have any alternative definition of the nature of the human to replace it.

Because we don't have an alternative, when we do let it go, we let it go completely. We go to the opposite extreme, as in much of our contemporary drug, entertainment, recreation, media, and internet culture, identifying the human with the body or with the non-rational. Or in the assumption that the only alternative to a mind-centred definition of the human is its opposite: a definition rooted in the unconscious forces of the Freudian psyche.[292] Or in the contemporary fascination with sociobiology and neuroscience, our obsession to find the explanation for everything human in the evolutionary biology of the body, in the chemistry and physics of the brain. Or in the quest of contemporary social science to find "natural" sources of human virtue in efficient causes, such as gene pools and genetic selection, or the innate moral capacities and propensities of toddlers and very young children, rather than in the rightness and goodness of the virtues themselves, rather than in the "naked dignity" of virtue.[293] We go to these extremes instead of seeing the nature of the human as *embodied* spirit, as a spiritual *totality*.[294]

But the contemporary emphasis on the body could be at least a first step in liberating us from an exclusive definition of the nature of the human as mind. It can liberate us from the long tyranny of the stances of "It is." It can open the door to a rediscovery of the parallel and prior "existential" reality that "I am." And the discovery that "I am" makes possible the further discovery not just that "*I* am," but also that "I *am*."

The rediscovery of our embodied condition could set us off again, on the voyage we took three thousand years ago in the Axial age, from *eros* to *agape*. As Frans de Waal and the Jewish and Christian scriptures emphasize, bodily connections and feelings come first: virtues like pity, kindness, or charity follow. They don't emerge first from the mind or the brain – as we often take for granted – but rather from the body itself, or even from the guts or the bowels.[295] Once we have rediscovered our common human condition, the physical being we share with all other beings, we may eventually be ready to move on, again, beyond the self-*seeking* virtues of Liberty (A1) – beyond Power (A1a) and Pleasure (A1b) – to the self-*giving* virtues of Reverence (A2).

You can see a glimmer of this potential already, even in a thinker like Richard Rorty. While dismissing all previous claims about the nature of the human, Rorty argues that human beings do, nevertheless, have obligations to each other. But such obligations don't come, he suggests, from "anything other than the *ability* to sympathize with the pain of others." There is nothing behind our moral obligations other than "the gradual spread of the sense that the pain of others matters, regardless of whether they are of the same family, tribe, color, religion, nation, or intelligence as oneself." This sense or "ability" can't be "shown to be *true* by science, or religion, or philosophy." It can only be made "*evident*" to people. A sense of moral obligation of this kind is "a matter of *conditioning* rather than of *insight*."[296]

This is a fascinating place for such a distinguished representative of the virtues of Liberty (A1) to end up. For one thing, Rorty invokes nothing new here, but rather a human quality well-known to most of the deepest thinkers about the nature of the human. Aquinas called it "a certain sweetness of feeling which abhors anything which can afflict another," and he, too, thought it was the source of important human virtues.[297] By embracing it as his source of all moral goodness, Rorty looks back over the previous three families of virtues through which we have travelled on our way to this second round of the spiral staircase. That's where he got it.

Rorty's discovery that this is not so much a "truth" as a human "ability" or disposition – something that can't be *shown* to be "true" but only made "evident" through practice and "conditioning" – is exactly what Aristotle and Aquinas would have said. And so would almost every important thinker about the nature of the human before Kant. They would have called this kind of "ability," power, or disposition – developed through habit and conditioning – a "virtue." That's what a virtue is. A good habit. In other words, what Rorty rediscovered, implicitly, is that we shouldn't start looking for the nature of the human in the mind or in rational thought – as theoretic and modern culture wanted to do – but in the human virtues. The essence of the human lies not in something we can think, or know, or believe, but in something we *do*. And can learn to do better. Not just by thinking about it, but by exercise and practice. Empathy, like other virtues, depends on regular exercise. "People who are low in empathy," says the lead author of the Michigan study, "are a little bit out of shape, and people who are high in empathy are practicing it a lot." What our culture needs to do is spend a lot more time in the reverence "gym," exercising and practising the virtues of reverence, such as empathy.[298]

Rorty leaves out something important from his sources. Sympathizing with the pain of others is a very good thing. But by itself, it may not do very much. As I pointed out in chapter 3, it can even be a kind of egoism or narcissism. Merely a value, a kind *feeling*, that hasn't yet turned into a virtue, into a habitual *action* or behaviour.[299] Nevertheless Rorty's rediscovery that the capacity to feel the pain of others can't be shown to be "true" by human reason but can only be made "evident" by practice rather than by "insight" – this rediscovery is the first or negative half of something far more profound, to which it also looks forward. It's the entry point to an even deeper virtue, the self-giving love of the virtues of reverence. It opens the door, once again, from the virtues of Liberty (A1) to the virtues of Reverence (A2).

How the virtues of Liberty (A1) can point forward, in this way, to the virtues of Reverence (A2) is also suggested by one of their distinctive current manifestations, the one that, in chapter 4, I called "expressive individualism." You will recall that expressive individualism is a set of common contemporary behaviours based on the assumption that each person has a unique core of feeling and intuition that must be expressed, in their own special way, if their true individuality is to be realized.[300] Expressive individualism is a form of the virtues of Pleasure (A1b). It emphasizes personal "feelings," and so many people assume or hope that it can balance or remedy the dehumanizing downsides of the other side of the virtues of Liberty (A1) I called "possessive" individualism, a form of the virtues of Power (A1a). Expressive individualism is visible on our streets every day, in dress and adornment (tattoos, body piercings, unusual hairstyles, and so on), but it has many deeper, more positive forms of expression, including the very wide popularity today of secular spiritual practices, such as yoga and meditation. If the virtues of Equality (B2) emphasized what (in chapter 14) I called "sensing with *thinking*" (*It* is), the virtues of Liberty (A1) emphasize, instead, "sensing with *feeling*" (*I* am). By reintroducing the importance of feeling, expressive individualism points forward to another form of feeling: the "*intuition* with feeling" of the virtues of Reverence (A2). David Martin suggests there's a sense in which we Westerners may already be living in a new "Age of the Spirit," a mixture of the "pre- and post-modern," which yearns beyond the "verbalism and moralism" of Western culture since the Reformation and the Enlightenment, beyond its emphasis on "clarity and explanation," toward forms of experience and practice that reach "the parts of the soul the others don't reach."[301] The spirituality of expressive individualism may often be little more than a form of self-regarding "therapy." It may be another illustration of the "triumph of the therapeutic" in contemporary life.[302] But even in this diminished form, it betrays a deep spiritual hunger, a sense of absence or disquiet, that points forward to the real thing.[303] To the rediscovery of the genuine virtues of reverence.[304]

Our contemporary culture of expressive individualism, with its emphasis on feeling, its longing to close the gap between subject and object, and its underground spiritual hunger – may point us forward from the virtues of Liberty (A1) toward the virtues of Reverence (A2). Just like the first time around – on the first turn of the spiral staircase of the arrow of virtue – from episodic to mimetic and mythic culture. "The thought suggests itself," says Northrop Frye, "that we may have completed a gigantic cycle of language from Homer's time, where the word evokes the thing, to our own day, where the thing evokes the word, and are now about to go around the cycle again, as we now seem to be confronted with an energy common to subject and object which can be expressed verbally only through some form of metaphor. ... [W]e may be entering a new phase altogether."[305]

And maybe our heritage from the European Enlightenment doesn't have to be as great an obstacle as it first appears. After all, the moderate Enlightenment emphasized some of the key virtues of reverence –

hope, gratitude, justice, and reverence itself – just as much as reason, freedom, and the other virtues of self-assertion.[306] As you saw in
chapter 15, even Immanuel Kant was ultimately obliged (like Martin
Heidegger) to root respect for the moral law in the virtue of reverence.
Our way forward could begin by recovering some of the neglected elements of our own Western Enlightenment.

This is all the more important because the achievement of the Enlightenment is not something we should ever underestimate, or devalue, or
seek to undo. On the contrary, it needs to be carefully protected against
the forces of unreason or potential new forms of tyranny in its own creations: the unregulated market and its opposite, the unfettered, authoritarian, all-intrusive, or even proto-fascist state. The Enlightenment's
discovery and promotion of the virtues of self-assertion – the virtues of
Liberty (A1) and Equality (B2) – were an enormous step forward in the
development of civilization, in the process of developing greater civility – just as important as rediscovering the virtues of reverence has now
become.[307] In recovering the full nature of the human, what we should
aim for is certainly not the rejection of the achievements of the Enlightenment but rather a new *dual Enlightenment*, one in which the virtues
of reverence once again assume their equal place beside the virtues of
self-assertion. After all, what many spiritual traditions – especially the
Eastern traditions such as Buddhism – propose as a goal for spiritual
seekers is called "enlightenment," too. So, what we can and should aim
for is "a culture where both kinds of enlightenment [are] respected and
cultivated together."[308]

This objective is all the more plausible and desirable because the
Western Enlightenment hasn't yet fully delivered on some of its own
key promises of a more human, more *humane* civilization. And it is currently at risk of drifting further from that goal, betraying some of its
own key values. Perhaps partly for that reason, it has also spawned a
potentially destructive *anti*-Enlightenment, which now drives much of
our popular Western culture. Both of these can be redeemed by recalling the full range of values and virtues which, together, constitute the
nature of the human. The precious heritage of the Enlightenment must
now be salvaged from its own assertive, self-destroying potential, by
reaching back to sources older than itself: by a rediscovery of the virtues in general – and the virtues of reverence in particular.[309] The virtues
of self-assertion can't achieve their own full potential and may even
create new forms of tyranny unless they're balanced and animated by
the virtues of reverence. Without reverence, modern and post-modern
self-assertion could end up – like the Hindu demon or Shakespeare's
"universal wolf" of pure self-assertion – being "devoured by the

inflexible, inhuman logic of its own creations."[310] By reasserting the full range of the moral and spiritual claims upon us, and the urgent way in which they "call" upon our humanity – by reasserting the very "idea of humanity"[311] – the virtues of reverence can help redeem both the Enlightenment and the anti-Enlightenment and maybe even salvage "the unfinished project of modernity."[312]

Constructing the ego – and letting it go: the role of crisis

There are at least two more reasons to think Western culture might eventually move on, past the virtues of Liberty (A1) to the next turn on the spiral arrow of virtue. But to set the stage for this discussion, let's first consider where we are now as a civilization – or where we may be. To do this, it may help to draw an analogy between our Western civilization and our own individual lives.

Richard Rohr (b. 1943) suggests that one of the most important turning points in a well-lived, individual life is the transition between the "two halves of life."[313] In the first half, our task is to construct an individual ego. In the second half, Rohr suggests, our task is the opposite: to let it go. The first half of life is about striving, achieving, and developing a strong sense of self and of self-worth. The second half of life is about learning that the ego we have built isn't enough for a full life – and even stands in the way of fullness. You have to build your own ego if you're going to do anything worthwhile, especially anything courageous or difficult. You can't do anything without learning to assert yourself. But eventually you must learn the limits of self-assertion. And by then, if you're lucky, your ego has become strong enough to do the difficult work of the second half of your life, which is to move beyond itself. The battles of the first half of our lives "solidify the ego." The battles of the second half, says Rohr, "defeat the ego."[314]

Maybe this trajectory of our individual lives can serve as an image or metaphor for our collective life as a human civilization. Using this analogy, we could think of Western civilization as only now beginning to reach "adulthood." After all – from the perspective of the life cycle of our planet, as I mentioned in the Introduction – the "deep future" ahead of us may be far longer than all the "deep past" behind us. If Western civilization were a "person," we could think of her as no more than a teenager, perhaps not even a young adult. And she could be expected to exhibit many of the same rebellious, self-assertive, self-regarding, and egotistical impulses we associate with adolescence and early adulthood.

From this metaphorical point of view, it's entirely to be expected that the arrow of virtue should have brought us back to the virtues of Liberty

(A1). Emerging from the pure self-assertion of the higher primates (A1), human civilization first developed the virtues of Reverence (A2) that are the basis of all tribal cultures, and then the virtues of Excellence (B1), which formed the heart of the succeeding archaic, hierarchical societies, culminating in the classical cultures of Greece and Rome. These two stages correspond to the stages of infancy and childhood, with which they share many characteristics.[315] But their internal paradoxes carried the arrow of virtue forward from classical culture into the specifically Western culture (an amalgam of Greco-Roman culture with Judeo-Christian and Islamic traditions), culminating in the virtues of Equality (B2), the hallmark of the Western Enlightenment – which strikingly parallel the peer-oriented culture of the early teenage years, with their emphasis on fairness, equality, sameness, and peer approval.[316] But the arrow of virtue has now carried us, beyond the Enlightenment, back toward the virtues of Liberty (A1), into the post-Enlightenment or post-modern culture: into what Richard Rory calls "literary culture," Terry Eagleton calls "aesthetic" culture, and what I earlier called "post-theoretic" or "cultural culture." This culture exhibits all the narcissistic and ego-centred characteristics we spontaneously associate with the later teenage years, with their emphasis on pleasure (A1b) and power (A1a).

If this kind of narrative arc makes any sense – as an analogy – we could say that Western civilization is still only in the "first half of life." The tasks of the "second half of life" still lie ahead of us. We have spent the last three thousand years developing and nurturing the virtues of self-assertion until they've become the core of our Western civilization, the only virtues we now spontaneously recognize. We have spent the first part of our life – as a human civilization – developing the cultural equivalent of an "ego."

But life isn't yet over. In fact, it's just begun. The tasks of the "second half of life" still lie ahead. We've spent the last three thousand years developing the "ego." And now, if we are to continue to grow – as individuals, and as a human civilization – we need to learn to let it go. Or to put it back in its proper place. In the "deep future" ahead, the arrow of virtue now beckons us forward from the virtues of Liberty (A1), to which we seem to be returning, toward the virtues of Reverence (A2), the possible next step on the spiral staircase. It's not a step backward, but a step forward: in which all the best virtues of our self-assertive modern and post-modern culture are preserved and deepened, in some future, unforeseeable synthesis of reverence and self-assertion.[317] As Hegel says, the "return to the beginning is also an advance."[318]

In Rohr's account, what brings the first half of an individual human life to an end is often some kind of crisis, in which an individual discovers that her conception of life, and of herself, was inadequate or incomplete. The second half of life often begins with some kind of "fall" or failure. In our personal lives, it may be the loss of a job, a reputation, a fortune, a marriage, or a dream. It may be an illness or a death. We "hit the wall" in this crisis, and it makes us recognize, often unwillingly, that the ego we have built isn't enough. It's not the whole story about us or about the human. It's not even the *true* story about the human. While we can't do without it, it's not what makes humans really *human*. If we can't move beyond them, the virtues of self-assertion can even destroy us.

Perhaps something similar happens to civilizations, too.

The crisis of climate change

One of the most powerful reasons for thinking that the world is ripe for rediscovering the full nature of the human is our current environmental crisis, especially global climate change, and its looming threat to human civilization, in both senses of the word.[319]

Since the 1750s, the overall temperature of the earth's atmosphere has risen by about 0.6°C (1.1°F). But because of a slight decline in the nineteenth century, this actually understates our current problem. In fact, the rise in average temperature in the twentieth century has been even faster, from about 13.5°C (56.3°F) to about 14.5°C (58.1°F), or about 1.0°C (1.8°F). This represents almost a quarter of the total rise in global temperature since the last Ice Age. This global warming is mainly due to an increase of CO_2 in the atmosphere, from a little less than three parts per 10,000 to almost four, largely (though not exclusively) as a result of the burning of fossil fuels.[320] The accumulation of CO_2 and some other gases in the earth's atmosphere has a "greenhouse effect," which traps incoming heat from our sun, preventing it from being expelled back into space, and gradually warming our planet as a result. If the rise in CO_2 emissions continues, to, say, double the pre-industrial level (which, at the current rate of fossil-fuel burning, is predicted to occur midway through this century), global temperature will also rise by at least 3.0°C (5.4°F) over the pre-industrial level by the end of the century.[321]

This kind of climate change would eventually have disastrous consequences for the natural world and for human life. Continued global warming would cause droughts in many middle latitude regions – bringing desert-like conditions to much of North America and Australia – and extreme weather events, rainfall, and flooding in other parts of the globe, as we are already beginning to see. The melting of the Arctic and Antarctic icecaps could submerge coastal cities around the world and displace hundreds of millions of people. The melting of the Greenland ice sheet alone would be enough to submerge most of New York City and Boston.[322] Even the most ambitious emission targets (limiting global warming over the twenty-first century to 2°C [3.6°F]) would still mean a rise in sea level of half a metre (1.6 ft) or more by 2100.[323] As the temperature rises, the impacts on human health, natural ecosystems, biodiversity, species extinction, water, and food production will grow.[324] Mass migrations of displaced populations, food and water shortages and starvation, and the spreading of diseases might be too much for our current national and international systems and could lead to major conflicts over territory and borders, as they are already doing in Europe and Central America.[325]

But climate change isn't the only environmental threat to human civilization. It's only the leading edge or indicator. One of its background causes is the sheer rate at which human beings – especially those of us in the West – are consuming the world's resources. In 2019, by one estimate, humans had already used up all the resources the world can produce or renew in a year by 29 July. In a developed country like the United States, they had already done so as early as March. For the rest of the year, human beings are living on "credit," running down the world's environmental "capital." To consume at the rate we are now doing, we would need a world more than half again as large as the one we have. And if we go on as we are, the problem will only get worse. By 2030, we will have already exceeded the world's annual renewable environmental assets by 28 June. By 2050, we may annually be using up resources equivalent to *two earths*, not just one. If the whole world consumed resources at the rate the US now does, we would need almost *five earths*. This sounds like a recipe for human destruction.[326]

In November 2017, a manifesto signed by 15,364 scientists from 184 countries warned that we are "jeopardizing our future by not reining in our intense but geographically and demographically uneven material consumption ... Soon it will be too late to shift course away from our failing trajectory, and time is running out. We must recognize, in our day-to-day lives and in our governing institutions, that Earth with all its life is our only home."[327] In March 2018, the UN-sponsored Intergovernmental Science-Policy Platform on Biodiversity and Ecosystem Services (IPBES) – established in 2012 to monitor the planet's ecological health – published the most comprehensive assessments of global ecosystem health to date, warning that vanishing biodiversity and continued land degradation are endangering economies, livelihoods, food security, and human well-being across the globe. "The best available evidence, gathered by the world's leading experts, points us now to a single conclusion," said Sir Robert Watson, chair of IPBES: "we must act to halt and reverse the unsustainable use of nature – or risk not only the future we want, but even the lives we currently lead."[328] A year later, the follow-up IPBES Global Assessment report confirmed that the health of global ecosystems is deteriorating more rapidly than ever. "We are eroding the very foundations of our economies, livelihoods, food security, health and quality of life worldwide," Sir Robert warned again.[329]

Over a decade ago, Tim Flannery (b. 1956), an Australian biologist and author of best-selling books on climate change, warned that if we human beings are unable to alter our habits – and therefore, our nature – over the next few decades, and the rate of global warming remains what it is today, then "the collapse of civilization due to climate change becomes inevitable."[330] Ten years later, he tries to be more upbeat, mainly in order to encourage young people, to let them "know there is hope."[331] His professed optimism is based mainly on two things: first, that the UN's Deep Decarbonization Pathways Project report has developed a roadmap to achieve steep carbon emissions reductions; second, that because of the new social media, individuals are now "immeasurably more powerful than they were a decade ago." The communities of interest fostered by social media are now "capable of altering the policies of institutions and corporations." So now we have the tools to avoid a climate disaster: "Between deep, rapid emissions and third-way technologies, we can do it."[332]

But it isn't easy to share Flannery's new optimism. A decade ago, most climate scientists warned that we could not allow global temperature to rise more than 2°C (3.6°F) over pre-industrial levels without devastating consequences. But ten years later, through inaction, we have probably already lost the chance to keep the global temperature increase below that level and are now tacitly committed, as Flannery himself admits, to "a world 3°C warmer, or even more."[333] Even the most conservative climate change scenario, with the most aggressive carbon emissions mitigation efforts, now offers only 50/50 odds of staying below the 2°C ceiling.[334] But we aren't coming even close to the effort required to achieve that objective. The Paris Climate Accord of 2015 may have seemed to offer hope. But in the following years, the UN Environmental Program reported that the commitments by the signatories represent barely one-third of the emission reductions required to meet the 2°C ceiling. If countries fully meet their commitments in the Accord (which is by no means certain), global temperature will rise by at least 3.0°C (5.4°F) by the end of the twenty-first century.[335] The five-year period from 2015–19 was the warmest of any equivalent period on record and saw an increase of about 0.2°C over the previous five years.[336] In September 2019 the

UN Development Program confirmed that current commitments "fall far short" of what is needed to slow climate change, and instead set the world on track for a rise in emissions of about 10.7 per cent above 2016 levels by 2030.[337] Even the US government Global Change Research Program warns that it would take "significant" reductions in emissions to keep global temperature increase below 2°C (3.6°F). Without major reductions, the increase could even reach as high as 5°C (9°F) or more by 2100.[338] However, in 2020, despite the commitments in the Paris Accord, and a global pandemic (which caused a slight drop in fossil fuel emissions), the concentrations of greenhouse gases in the Earth's atmosphere hit new highs.[339] "At the current rate of increase in greenhouse gas concentrations," said the secretary-general of the World Meteorological Organization in October 2021, "we will see a temperature increase by the end of this century far in excess of the Paris Agreement targets of 1.5 to 2 degrees Celsius above pre-industrial levels."[340] A *Climate Action Tracker* report, presented to the UN's Glasgow climate summit in November 2021, said government emissions reductions commitments for 2030 are only half what is required to meet the Paris target, and estimated end-of-century warming, under current policies, will be 2.7°C.[341]

If Tim Flannery is now reassuring, David Wallace-Wells is justifiably alarmed about what these numbers mean for the future of the planet and of human civilization. In fact, he says, "the facts are hysterical." Even the difference between global warming of 1.5°C and 2°C (neither of which there is as yet even the slightest sign of achieving) would be the death of at least 150 million people, possibly hundreds of millions. To dramatize what this means, he points out this is the equivalent of twenty-five Holocausts, twice the death toll of the Second World War, and three times the death toll of the Great Leap Forward. Even higher levels of warming (toward which we are currently heading) "would unleash suffering beyond anything that humans have ever experienced through many millennia of strain and strife and all-out war." The path we are now on threatens to make large parts of the planet uninhabitable for humans, even by the end of this century.[342] Wallace-Wells describes us as "collectively walking down a path of suicide." Our contemporary industrial, technological civilization is a "civilization enclosing itself in a gaseous suicide, a running car in a sealed garage."[343] As UN Secretary-General Antonio Guterres puts it: "Wake up world. We are killing our planet."[344] "Making peace with nature," he rightly says, "is the defining task of the 21st century. It must be the top, top priority for everyone, everywhere."[345]

This stark threat to civilization is rooted in the virtues of self-assertion our Western culture has been developing and valuing for almost three thousand years, ever since the time of Aristotle.[346] But especially since the beginning of the second phase of theoretic culture I described in chapter 15. In chapter 4, you saw how thinkers like Francis Bacon and René Descartes – who laid the foundation for our modern and post-modern worlds – celebrated the growing, assertive "power" of human beings, power that promised to establish "the empire of man over things" and to make human beings "the masters and possessors of nature."[347]

These were the assumptions that shaped the modern and then the post-modern world. Our contemporary world has been constructed largely upon three closely related sets of values: the ideals of freedom, liberation, and free-will (A1); the ideal of disengaged reason, standing back from the world, viewing it objectively – as an "object" (B2); and the domination and subjection of nature, through science and technology (B2), seeking to "master" it through instrumental control (A1). As you can see, these three clusters of values are all different forms of one common master set of virtues: the virtues of self-assertion. These virtues have brought most of the benefits of our modern and post-modern cultures. But they have also encouraged us to adopt an aggressive, assertive, domineering attitude to the natural world, an outlook that now threatens our survival.[348]

However, the virtues of self-assertion, as you now recognize, are only one half of the nature of the human. Lurking behind them, and behind our current crisis of global climate change, is another invisible reality: the gradual eclipse of the virtues of reverence over the last four or five centuries. Having exploited nature and her resources to build up greater technological and industrial "power" than Bacon or Descartes could ever have dreamt of, we now discover that self-assertion unconstrained by reverence has brought us to the verge of global self-destruction. It is, as Tim Flannery says, "a reductionist world view that has brought the present state of climate change upon us."[349]

The starkness of the global climate and environmental crises makes suddenly clear to us what the last five hundred years of western expansion have often obscured: why the virtues of reverence must, in the end, take priority over, or come before, the virtues of self-assertion.[350] Not just historically. But also mentally, morally, and in our own behaviour, today. As human virtues. In our real, everyday lives. Because self-assertion can only take place within a larger whole. And our first obligation is, therefore, to ensure the health and well-being of the larger whole, without which self-assertion is pointless, or impossible, or suicidal.

The virtues of reverence are the virtues of "union," the habits of human feeling and behaviour associated with a deep awareness of the unity and connectedness of all things. The virtues of self-assertion are the virtues of "non-union," the habits of feeling and behaviour associated with the impulse to freedom, expansion, and self-development. Both are necessary to life, even to biological life, and especially to human life. Without the virtues of self-assertion, we do not have anything worthy to be called life. Without both sides of the human paradox, it would not be a human world.

But only the impulse to union, by definition, can provide a ground to link and nurture them both. That's why, both logically and in reality, the virtues of reverence must take priority over the virtues of self-assertion, why they must come first. They establish the frame. Self-assertion can only take place within a larger frame. Without that larger frame – without, at the extreme limit, a habitable world – reverence and self-assertion both die.[351]

Rediscovering the full nature of the human isn't just something that would be nice to do, if we had the time or the inclination. It isn't a luxury or a taste. It isn't something we can opt out of or leave to others. It's urgent and unavoidable because it's now a question of survival.

And we will eventually have to make this discovery, whether we choose to or not.

That's another reason to think that the arrow of virtue won't get stuck forever in the virtues of Liberty (A1), but will eventually have to take the next turn on the spiral staircase, toward the virtues of reverence.[352] Even if our minds are slow to follow, our behaviours and our actions will have to go in that direction. Eventually our minds will follow, as they always do.

In the twenty-first century – or the twenty-second – we will have to learn again to live within some kinds of limits, limits which must be respected if we are to survive. And the experience of living within those limits, and in a spirit of respect for the larger whole on which we depend, is almost certain to reshape our way of relating to the world, our moral and spiritual outlooks, just as the great age of European expansion fostered the virtues of self-assertion that shaped the modern and post-modern Western world.

When everything around you encourages – or even forces – you to look in one direction, you eventually turn your head to look in that direction, whether you want to or not. Once you begin to govern all your decisions and your conduct by respect for the larger whole on which your life depends, you will find you're already on the road to reverence. Once you recognize that, in the global environment, "everything is connected to and influences everything else," as Tim Flannery puts it, you're already halfway to seeing the world with reverent eyes once again.[353]

Because that's what reverence means.

The crisis of democracy and human rights

Another major challenge – not yet a full-blown crisis but heading that way – seems now to be developing in the Western world in the fields of democracy and human rights.[354] In chapter 12, and again in this chapter, I discussed the how our Western democracy is now under attack from populism, nationalism, and authoritarianism. Because of the stresses of racial and cultural diversity brought about by immigration and population migration, even the contemporary Western world seems to be reaching a point at which the Enlightenment virtues of Equality (B2) are running out of steam and losing some of their power to substitute for, or secretly invoke, the virtues of Reverence (A2), the virtues of mercy, compassion, and self-giving love. Instead, much of the Western world now seems to be reverting back to the virtues of Liberty, the default human stance of "*I* am" (A1) – the "engine room" of the human – in which the starting point for moral decision-making is the "us-versus-them distinction." This is the exclusion/inclusion dynamic Relational Models Theory (RMT) associates with its model of "communal sharing" (A2), but whose *inc*lusive dynamic comes from reverence and whose *exc*lusionary side comes from self-assertion, especially the virtues of Liberty or the stance of "*I* am" (A1). In this stance of primal self-assertion, the first question to be asked of another is: "Is he/she one of us or one of them?" This outlook (A1) "accepts no general obligation to tolerate anyone." When self-assertion turns away from reverence, it becomes quite possible, once again, to claim equality *for yourself* (*I* am) "without assuming that equality must imply duties to everyone else."[355]

This is yet another indication that, in our Western culture, the arrow of virtue is moving, or has moved, across the frontier from the virtues of Equality (B2) to the virtues of Liberty (A1). These, too, are real virtues. So not all is bad in a renewed emphasis on self-identity and self-preservation. There has to be a self, a sturdy and effective self – including a collective self of local and national community – in order to do good in the world. All sides of the human paradox must be given their due. That's why most human virtue remains "local" – limited to our own families and communities.[356] It remains local because we're human, a composite of self-assertion and reverence, and the "non-union" of self-assertion usually "hijacks" (as I put it earlier) or puts limits on the "union" of reverence. Even in reverence, the best we can normally do (as I noted in chapter 5) is to kick our own self-assertion up a notch or two: to our family, our culture, our country, our *own*.[357]

So rediscovering the rights of democratic majorities in the first half of the twenty-first century could turn out to be just as healthy and necessary as the recognition and protection of minority rights in the second half of the twentieth.[358] That's something the proper concern for minorities over the past fifty years has sometimes obscured and needs to be rediscovered. The rights of minorities cannot, do not, and should not cancel out the rights of majorities – a democratic majority is the only means, after all, through which minority rights can be recognized and protected, in the first place. While it's essential to protect the basic human and democratic rights of all citizens, native-born and newcomer alike, it's perfectly reasonable for a democratic society to debate the rate and level at which it can and should admit immigrants, for example. Debate about the rate at which a society can welcome and absorb newcomers, especially from very different cultural backgrounds, and still remain adequately cohesive, is legitimate and necessary, a debate our admirable, contemporary concern for human rights has too often silenced or even censured. And it's also both reasonable and inevitable to decide this kind of question by a democratic majority. Similarly, it's entirely legitimate for a democratic majority to determine the role religion shall have or not have in public life, or the ways in which the state shall recognize or authorize the use of national or other languages. These are not matters that can or should be ruled out of democratic debate *a priori*, or decided, one way or the other, by some abstract judicial fiat. They are properly the matter of reasonable democratic debate and decision by democratic majorities.

The test is whether both the debate and the decision are properly respectful of all citizens and make adequate, generous provision for minorities affected by majority decisions. The self-assertive virtues of Liberty (A1) are not enough by themselves. In fact, on their own, they would take us back to a frightening past. Not the distant one of our tribal ancestors because they were already living in the virtues of Reverence (A2). But something more like the fascist political cultures of the 1930s – the ultimate expression of the virtues of Power (A1a) – from which the Western world only narrowly escaped, and which are rearing their ugly heads once again, all over the Western and non-Western worlds.[359]

A return to the virtues of Liberty (A1) can only be redeemed if we view it as one more step on the spiral staircase of the arrow of virtue. One more step, from which we can look back over *all* the families of virtues through which we have come so far – over all the families which have played their part in the revelation and development of the human. Not just the virtues of self-assertion of which our Western culture is so proud, but also the virtues of reverence from which they emerged, and without which the virtues of self-assertion would turn again into instruments of great evil. One more step, from which we can look back to see *all* the virtues – both of self-assertion *and* of reverence – not just as part of our Western past, but as part of our human present, too. They're an essential part of our human future, without which humans would not be human.

Look again at the virtues of Love (A2b), in the right-hand column of Table 14 on pages 194–5. I doubt you'll have any difficulty recognizing these behaviours as virtues as good habits, without which our culture and communities wouldn't be recognizably human. In fact, these virtues – compassion, pity, generosity, and so on – have often been the *real*, unspoken virtues underpinning our Western achievements in human rights. Maybe even more than the virtues of Equality (B2) themselves. Michael Ignatieff suggests the human rights revolution in the last half of the twentieth century can be best understood as a "rational thought experiment" to force these virtues of reverence "to enlarge and expand their circle of moral concern."[360] In other words, it was a thought experiment to kick the virtues of reverence up another notch or two: to widen their circle of concern from family, culture, and nation to include other races, religions, peoples, and so on. It was an attempt (in Adam Gopnik's words) to "systematize compassion."[361]

As the arrow of virtue moves on, we can perhaps see more clearly now, how much claims for Equality (B2) draw implicitly upon the moral energies of the prior virtues of reverence, toward which they silently point. In fact, Hans Joas argues our post-modern concern for human rights actually involves a new "sacralization" of the human person.[362] Just as the environmental movement expresses a "sacralization" of the environment. Though we don't usually express it that way, both the environmental and the human rights movements involve new perceptions of *sacredness*. That is to say, they involve perceptions of self-evident, even transcendent importance, combined with intense feeling, and the self-giving behaviours of awe, humility, sacrifice, and devotion. Something becomes sacred for us by and in the reverent behaviours we display toward it. Regarding something as "sacred" (implicitly or explicitly) and behaving toward it with awe and reverence are the same thing – or two sides of the same coin. Like the body and expressive individualism, the environmental and human rights movements may be nudging us back – or rather, forward – to the virtues of reverence.

Without which civilization would not be civilized.

Remember that, as virtues of self-assertion, the virtues of Equality (B2) *claim* rights. But only the self-*giving* virtues of reverence can *give* rights.[363] All the protections for minority and human rights in Western countries, since the Universal Declaration of Human Rights in 1948, have been put in place, ultimately, by self-*giving* democratic *majorities*.

But the self-giving virtues of reverence are at odds with the virtues of Liberty (A1) (the left-hand columns of Table 10 on pages 174–5), which are now becoming dominant again in Western societies. How are these two now to be reconciled, in a way that redeems the re-emerging self-assertion of national communities and makes them worthy of our true humanity, the whole nature of the human? A democracy transformed into an instrument of exclusion rather than inclusion is no democracy at all. It is tyranny by another name: an electoral tyranny. A tyranny of the "majority" – which may not even be a real majority at all, just an artifact of propaganda and institutional manipulation. The tyranny of a faction masquerading as the so-called "people," from which everyone else is excluded.[364] How can we reconcile the desire for safety, control, and identity with the virtues of compassion, kindness, and generosity, the virtues of reverence without which our Western communities would not deserve to be called human?

How are the virtues of Love (A2b) to be sustained in the "deep future" ahead, not just as private but as public virtues? No doubt courts, governments, and public leaders can do a lot. They can remind us of our highest human virtues, the standards by which our humanity is judged. They can model these virtues themselves and call us, implicitly and explicitly, back to our true humanity. The competence and effectiveness of public institutions can also create a climate of trust and confidence in which it's easier for ordinary people not only to practise the highest virtues, but also to endorse them in public policies.[365] But will that be enough? If leaders and institutions aren't sustained and supported by political cultures – by a critical mass of ordinary people – that endorse and practice those values, how successful can they be in the long run, especially in an age of social media? Won't they be supplanted – as in too many Western countries they already are supplanted – by populist demagogues who appeal not to our highest virtues, but to our deepest fears and to our primal instincts of self-assertion?

In the past, the virtues of Love (A2b) were sustained by their close alliance with the virtues of Reverence[3] (A2a) (in the column immediately to the left in Table 14), of which they are just the flip side of the same reverent coin. The practice of the virtues of Reverence[3] (A2a) sustained, supported, and nourished the virtues of Love (A2b), and linked them outward to the virtues of Truth (B1a) and Goodness (B1b), the other virtues of reverence.[366] Indeed, the virtues of Reverence[3] (A2a) are often simply a practice, exercise, dress-rehearsal, or workout for practising the virtues of Love (A2b). If they were to be eclipsed, how would all the other virtues fare in the deep future? What other resources or opportunities will we have to nourish the virtues of reverence, without which our virtues of self-assertion can destroy our humanity – and maybe us as well? If it doesn't destroy us first, the climate change crisis may be one of those learning opportunities. The crisis of democracy and human rights may be one as well. What other levers or opportunities may be out there on the road to our deep future? As I said at the end of the previous chapter, that's one of the most important questions for us in twenty-first century.

Establishing a "system of rights" is necessary but not sufficient. It points beyond itself, as Anthony Kronman (b. 1945) says, "to something of still greater value."[367] It's just a first step, toward the rediscovery of the virtues of reverence.

Beyond post-modernity: the lesson of the Axial age

The question for contemporary culture is whether the crisis of global climate change – or some other challenge, like the challenges of democracy, human rights, human migration, and cultural diversity – will serve like an adolescent crisis or a crisis of the first half of life and force our Western civilization to "grow up," to put the "ego" it has spent the last three thousand years developing back in its proper place. Force it to move beyond the virtues of self-assertion and to rediscover the virtues of reverence. Or to put it another way: will such a crisis will help us to rediscover the lesson of the Axial Age, that the highest form of self-assertion is a kind of *un*selfing?

Greece and Rome largely skipped the Axial Age. Although Platonic, Aristotelian, Neoplatonic, and Stoic morality owed a great deal to it, the rational bias of Greco-Roman civilization was really a culture of self-assertion in a new form. If you wanted one word to sum up this culture, it would be (as Bart Ehrman suggests) "dominance" – the disposition to dominate.[368] The opposite self-*giving* insights of the Axial age were powerfully reborn, however, in the Christian and Islamic civilizations that emerged from the Roman empire, blended with Neoplatonism. But they soon began to be challenged from within by the rationalism Christianity absorbed from its Greco-Roman heritage, a rationalism that later flowered in medieval scholasticism, the Reformation and counter-Reformation, and the Renaissance, before triumphing in the Western Enlightenment.

The Axial age was also a response to crisis, to social breakdown and warfare in the ancient "archaic" civilizations of India, China, and the Middle East. It forced spiritual leaders to reach back, beyond mythic culture and the virtues of Excellence (B1), to the earlier moral lessons of mimetic and tribal cultures: to the virtues of Reverence (A2). In doing so they took these virtues to greater depth – or height – than ever before.

The question for us is whether the insights of the Axial age are gone for good, as Nietzsche hoped. Or whether our current challenges will once again cause humanity to rediscover the virtues of reverence. And in so doing, rediscover the whole and complete nature of the human.

Modernity – the modern culture of rationalism, shaped by thinkers from Descartes to Hegel – has given way to the post-modernity of Marx, Nietzsche, Freud, Moore, Rorty, and their successors. This post-modern culture is shaped increasingly not by the Enlightenment's virtues of Equality (B2), but by the virtues of Liberty (A1): the post-modern virtues of Power (A1a) and of Pleasure (A1b). But post-modernity doesn't give us "a new home," as N.T. Wright puts it, or "a place to stay." Settling down in the virtues of Power (A1a) and Pleasure (A1b) wouldn't be consistent with the nature of the human. Nor can we go backward. We can't go back to modernity, to the second phase of theoretic culture – much less to the first. Our only choice is to "pioneer a way through postmodernity and out the other side ... into a new world, a new culture." Maybe the way through, into this new world, is to discover, in the heart of the contemporary virtues of Liberty (A1), the road that leads on, as it did long ago, to the virtues of Reverence (A2), "a way through, not to a reconstruction of an arrogant modernist Self, but to a new way of being human."[369]

Not back to Descartes' *cogito*: I *think* therefore I am. But forward, to the reverse[370] – with a twist: I *am*, therefore I love.

Shifting lenses: the four poles of the human through the lens of reverence

Rediscovering the nature of the human will require us to rethink all four families of virtues. But this time, through the lens of reverence.

Since it's been missing from our Western toolkit for so long, we have to rediscover what the four poles of the human look like when you turn the telescope around and look at them from the other end. Earlier in this chapter, you saw how Alan Wolfe, Edmund Fawcett, Deirdre McCloskey, and Adam Gopnik view all four families of virtues through the lens of self-assertion, as our modern and post-modern culture does. But only a little less than two hundred years ago, Johann Wolfgang Goethe (1749–1832) viewed them all the other way around – through the lens of reverence.

Goethe isn't the deepest thinker about reverence.[371] He was too much a child of the Enlightenment for that.[372] But, in his late work, *Wilhelm Meister's Travels*, he developed an account of fourfold reverence which had a strong influence on his first translator, Thomas Carlyle, and through him, on Emerson, Melville, Tennyson, and many other thinkers of the nineteenth and twentieth centuries, including Charles Horton Cooley, George Herbert Mead, Rudolf Steiner (and through him, on

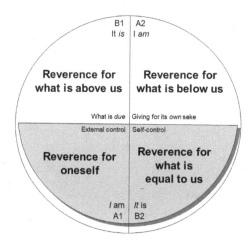

Figure 74. Goethe's four kinds of reverence

the Waldorf School movement), and Albert Schweitzer, whose ethic of "reverence for life" can be traced back to Goethe.

In Goethe's novel, Meister and his companions travel through a strangely fertile and well-ordered country tended by young men and boys. It turns out that the young people are being educated, and their education takes the form of instruction in "reverence." The travellers are told that reverence is the "one thing that no one brings with him into the world, and yet it is this on which everything depends and *by which man becomes human in the full sense*."[373] The reverence in which they are being educated takes four forms: reverence for what is "above us," reverence for what is "below us," reverence for what is "equal to us," and finally, "reverence for oneself," or self-reverence, which, Meister is told, is the "highest" form of reverence.[374]

You can easily see how Goethe's theory of fourfold reverence fits with the four families of virtues that define the nature of the human. It helps you to see how the four corners of the human might look, when they're *all* viewed through the lens of the virtues of reverence, rather than (like Alan Wolfe, Edmund Fawcett, Deirdre McCloskey, and Adam Gopnik) through our normal, current lens of self-assertion. Goethe's four kinds of reverence can even be displayed on the map of the human paradox, as shown in Figure 74 above.

In reverence for what is "below us," Goethe clearly has in mind the virtues of Reverence (A2) because he includes the self-denying virtues of humility and generosity in this type of reverence – "to acknowledge lowliness and poverty, scorn and contempt, humiliation and misery, suffering and death as divine," to show reverence for "the repulsive, the hated, the shunned" – and says it is the "an ultimate to which humanity could and had to attain."[375] Significantly (in the light of the preceding discussion of climate change), he also links this kind of reverence with the disposition to "regard the Earth carefully and serenely," conscious that we depend on the Earth for nourishment but (as we are now relearning, from global warming) "it also produces disproportionate suffering."[376]

Reverence for "that which is above us" corresponds to the virtues of Excellence (B1) because these virtues "testify that there is a God above, who is reflected in ... parents, teachers, superiors," consistent with the eager, willing devotion to a "higher" good that is typical of this family of virtues, where self-giving is stirred because it is "due."[377]

In reverence for what is "equal to us," Goethe is obviously thinking of the virtues of Equality (B2). He links it with philosophy and the search for rational truth – truth "in the cosmic sense."[378]

Perhaps Goethe's most interesting category is the concept of "reverence for oneself" or self-reverence. The focus on the self clearly links this fourth kind of reverence to the virtues of Liberty (A1). But Goethe invites us to turn them inside-out or to rethink them at a higher level: at a higher turn on the spiral staircase. At this highest level, he says, self-reverence no longer has anything to do with presumption, arrogance, or "self-centredness." "Reverence for oneself" is the highest reverence only if it "springs from," unites, and gives birth "once again" to the other three kinds of reverence. Reverence "reaches its greatest strength only when it flows as one and forms a whole."[379]

Herman Melville was so struck by Goethe's idea of "self-reverence" that he wrote a poem about it.

> Wandering late by morning seas
> When my heart with pain was low –
> Hate the censor pelted me –
> Deject I saw my shadow go.
> In elf-caprice of bitter tone
> I too would pelt the pelted one:
> At my shadow I cast a stone.
> When, lo, upon that sun-lit ground
> I saw the quivering phantom take
> The likeness of Saint Stephen crowned:
> Then did self-reverence awake.[380]

Nietzsche, too, was impressed by Goethe's concept of "reverence for oneself" and by the way Goethe himself seemed to embody this spirit. For Nietzsche, Goethe was the image of a human being "who, keeping

himself in check and having reverence for himself … [is] a man of tolerance, not out of weakness, but out of strength," a human being who
lives "in the *faith* that only what is separate and individual may be rejected, that in the totality everything is redeemed and affirmed." For
Nietzsche, Goethe was the very model of "self-overcoming."[381]

As Melville and Nietzsche help to emphasize, the self-reverence
Goethe had in mind isn't anything like a celebration of the self. It isn't
a kind of preening, narcissism, or self-regard. It's not "the gratifying
experience of the self as an entity," so typical of our post-modern culture.[382] Quite the reverse. It's a tender, respectful, cherishing, *reverent*
attitude to the self that both *heals* and makes *whole* (two of the linguistic roots of "holy") a self that, by definition, is divided against itself.
Self-reverence goes beyond self-respect, and perhaps even beyond
self-love, because it conveys a spirit of awe and veneration – even
humility – for, or toward, a self that is something much larger and
more significant than the mere ego.[383] Self-reverence implies a stance
toward your "self" which treats it not just as your "own" – to do with
as your wish – but almost as something "other," something for which
you have a deep moral responsibility: for which you are, in a sense,
merely the trustee.[384] It entails acting toward your *own* self with the
same reverence and care you would show to something else or to another person.

Goethe's concept of "reverence for oneself" helps show why reverence was the right word to choose (in chapter 5) to describe the second
family of virtues, which, together with the virtues of self-assertion, constitute the whole nature of the human. Neither altruism nor fraternity –
much less "prosociality" – would ring true here. Sympathy and empathy wouldn't work, either. None of these would properly or accurately describe the other non-assertive stance we can and should adopt,
not just toward others or to the surrounding environment, but toward
our own selves. Even love wouldn't strike quite the right note.[385] Only
something like reverence can really do the job.

Self-reverence is a virtue which recognizes the deep seriousness of
being a self. Because Goethe here introduces the virtue of reverence
even into the very heart of self-assertion – even into the virtues of Liberty (A1) themselves – the self itself must change. The self for which one
can feel reverence must be a different and much deeper, more complex,
but also more complete or unified self.

You can get some more insight into the larger kind of self revealed by
"reverence for oneself" – and what Goethe's four kinds of reverence can
tell us about the nature of the human – by comparing them to another
similar but more recent attempt to look at the whole human paradox

Figure 75. Shweder's three metaphors

through the lens of reverence. In chapter 14, I introduced you to Richard Shweder, the anthropologist and cultural psychologist who describes the nature of the human in terms of three "ethics," which he calls the ethics of autonomy, community, and divinity. I mapped those three ethics onto my own map of the human paradox, suggesting that the ethic of autonomy corresponds to the virtues of Liberty (A1) (or alternatively to the virtues of self-assertion as a whole), the ethics of community to the virtues of Reverence (A2), and the ethics of divinity to the virtues of Excellence (B1) (Figure 48 on page 333). I suggested Shweder's three ethics go a long way to confirm the reality of the four families of virtues. But Shweder and his colleagues also offer their own "translation" of these three ethics. They suggest three "metaphors" intended to "translate" the three ethics for the contemporary Western (or American) "moral imagination."

You can see Shweder's three "metaphors" in Figure 75 above.

The ethics of autonomy is translated as "sacred self"; the ethics of divinity is "sacred world." I don't think you should get hung up on the word "sacred" here. It doesn't come loaded with some hidden ideology or any specific set of "beliefs." It doesn't have to be associated with "religion."[386] It doesn't have to mean "divine."[387] Even secular things can have the quality of sacredness. Hans Joas suggests that, to become "sacred," something merely has to have two characteristics: self-evident importance or value for a person or a community, combined with intense feeling.[388] Consider what we mean when we say: "Is nothing sacred?" We're implying that some things are so important, or of such high value or worth, that they shouldn't be approached casually or instrumentally, but with appropriate respect and reverence. Remember that in chapter 5 I said that acts of reverence (either physical or mental) acknowledge superior worth, our relationship with it, and our obligations and responsibility toward it. I think Shweder means sacred in this sense – the sense in which even sociobiologist Edward O. Wilson (b. 1929) refers to human nature as a "sacred trust," or psychologist Martin Seligman describes a meaningful life as "sacred."[389] I think Shweder chose it to express the luminous or "numinous" quality that things have for us when we relate to them with and through the virtues of reverence rather than through the virtues of self-assertion.[390]

Shweder says these are metaphors for contemporary Americans. But I think the metaphors also have the advantage of viewing and interpreting the poles of the human through the single lens of reverence, just like Goethe's four kinds of reverence.[391] The "sacred" self is the self you encounter, perceive, or experience when you practise Goethe's virtue of "reverence for oneself" or self-reverence. It's the virtues of Liberty or "I am" (A1), viewed through the lens of reverence. The metaphor of the "sacred self" expresses the fact that "there is a kind of specialness or even privilege to personal intuitions of right and wrong," that every individual has a "particular course of spiritual development, something that no one else can fully know." It emphasizes the distinctiveness and particularity of each individual, and their personal duty to know or discover their own "individuated" moral obligations.[392]

A "sacred world" is the world you encounter, perceive, or experience when you practise Goethe's virtue of reverence for what is "above us." It's the virtues of Excellence or "It *is*" (B1), viewed through the lens of reverence. Perception of a "sacred world" points to an objective "order in which every entity is entitled to be what it is and has its proper place in the order of things." In other words, it's the foundation for the very individuality and individuation of the virtues of Liberty (A1). The metaphor of a "sacred world" opens up "possibilities for heroic expression of God-like personhood through concern with the ultimate aims of human existence and the disengagement from momentary temptations and sufferings."[393]

For Western ears, Shweder translates the ethics of community as "feudal ethics."[394] This third metaphor may sound odd to you at first, but it expresses an important idea. He chose the word "feudal" to evoke non-Western or premodern social systems (like the Western medieval feudal system), in which everyone feels obligations to everyone else within a "feudal" hierarchy of mutual loyalties. The word "feudal" is intended to emphasize the duties we owe to those who are *less* advantaged than we are, to those who are younger, older, weaker, or comparatively disadvantaged in some other way. A successful feudal lord, as Shweder puts it, "tries to do more for others than they have done for him." This is the spirit captured in the familiar phrase *noblesse oblige*. In other words, "feudal ethics" is the practice of Goethe's reverence for what is "below us," reverence for everything and everyone that is somehow subject or vulnerable to us, and to our very presence in the world. Vulnerable to the very *Da* of our *Dasein* – the very "there" of our "being-there."[395] "Feudal ethics" is the virtues of Reverence or the stance of "I *am*" (A2), viewed through the lens of reverence. It expresses our infinite responsibility for other people and other things, our human condition of *"asymmetrical* reciprocity, noblesse oblige, and ecological interdependence."[396]

In Figure 75, you can see that one quadrant of my map of the human paradox is still blank, just as it was in Figure 48, on page 333, my earlier map of Shweder's three ethics of autonomy, community, and divinity. But Shweder's own description of his three metaphors suggests some ways in which I could evolve and expand them, drawing on his insights to deepen your understanding of the nature of the human.

His metaphor of "sacred world," for example, has an ambiguous or dual quality I ignored, for the time being, in making my initial identification with the virtues of Excellence (B1), just as I had previously done for the ethics of divinity in Figure 48. In addition to the reference to "what is above us," Shweder's metaphor of sacred world (and the ethics of divinity it "translates" from Hindu culture) also emphasizes the degree to which the sacred is fully present *in* the world, not just *above* it. Pre-modern and non-Western cultures normally don't recognize a distinction between the secular and the sacred. In fact, the idea of a separate "secular" domain is an invention of our modern and post-modern Western culture of self-assertion. In a culture where the virtues of reverence are the primary lens through which all the other virtues are interpreted and practised, everything in the world is a sign of the sacred, participates in the sacred, or points to it. In a sacred world, "sacred law and natural law are the same thing." In a world experienced through the virtues of reverence, divine order penetrates everything: matter, mind, and everyday social, domestic, and working life. You experience or encounter the sacred through reverent actions *"in* the world."[397]

This means the metaphor of "sacred world" isn't straightforward. It includes two related but distinct orientations. The expression "sacred world" is composed, after all, of two words. So it makes a difference, once again, which word you emphasize, implicitly or explicitly: the adjective or the noun. If you emphasize the adjective – "sacred" – you implicitly refer to a world of being that encompasses more than merely Kant's "phenomenal" world, more than the world of things and of material reality. You can mean a world that is, in some metaphorical sense, "above us." But if you emphasize the noun – "world" – instead,

Figure 76. Four metaphors for the human

then you may also be referring to the material, visible, and social world *around us*.

These two different potential emphases make it possible to expand or complete Shweder's three helpful metaphors, as I've done in Figure 76 above.

The distinction between *sacred* world and sacred *world* is exactly the same as the important difference between the stances of "It *is*" and "*It* is" which I used to construct my initial map of the human in chapter 6. In that earlier contrast, emphasizing the subject or the verb helped me to distinguish the virtues of Excellence (B1) from the virtues of Equality (B2). It's the same thing here.

Emphasizing the adjective connects "sacred world" to one family of human virtues; emphasizing the noun connects it to another. A "*sacred* world," as I said, is the world you encounter when you're practising "reverence for what is above us." It's the virtues of Excellence or "It *is*" (B1), viewed through the lens of reverence. But a "sacred *world*" is what you encounter when you're practising Goethe's virtue of reverence for what is "equal to us." It's the virtues of Equality or "*It* is" (B2), viewed through the lens of reverence. The possibility of a "sacred *world*" explains why some configurations of reverence can have a high degree of "worldliness."[398] When all four families of virtues are seen and lived in a spirit of reverence, the mundane world ("what is around us") becomes sacred too and reverence can (indeed must) have a quality of "worldliness" (B2) quite as much as "otherworldliness" (B1).

Teasing out the distinction between the two potential emphases hidden in "sacred world" helps me to extend Shweder's three metaphors, to reflect all four families of human virtues as viewed through the lens of reverence. But in this form, I'm still left with Shweder's rather awk-ward metaphor of "feudal ethics." It's a good metaphor for its purpose, as I explained. The "feudal" metaphor helps flesh out and make concrete Goethe's concept of reverence for what is "below us," reverence for the vulnerable or less powerful, reverence for all those for whom we are, or should be, responsible. "Feudal ethics" in the sense in which Shweder uses it – reverence for others but especially subordinates – is a very im-portant concept for the contemporary world. Especially for the world of organizations, where, as you saw in chapter 13, even the best manage-ment frameworks (like the Competing Values Framework) rarely give enough emphasis to "downward accountability," the deep moral respon-sibility superiors have, or should have, for their employees. But, despite its strengths, "feudal ethics" is still an awkward term, one that requires explanation. As Shweder himself says, most of us Westerners instinc-tively "recoil at the idea of feudal ethics."[399] That very recoil is significant and part of its rhetorical point. But partly for that reason, the metaphor doesn't perhaps convey its core meaning as clearly or directly as it might.

To make the meaning clearer, I'd like to translate Shweder's trans-lation! The core idea at the heart of the ethics of community – and of the metaphor of "feudal ethics" which translates it – is the idea of our deep moral responsibility for others. In a sacred world, everything is sacred, including the world itself and all the people in it. The ethics of community and "feudal ethics" express our "obligatory responsibility for others."[400] *Because they too are sacred.*

The ethics of community – and the accompanying metaphor of "feudal ethics" – are intended to express something not very different from the metaphor of sacred world or sacred self. They aim to express – and do express – the idea of the "sacred *other.*" The *other* for whom, or for which, you have a potentially bottomless, obligatory, moral responsibility. As I mentioned in my earlier discussion of human rights, Hans Joas calls this shift to seeing other people as sacred the "sacralization of the person." He suggests this kind of sacralization has been going on now for some three or four hundred years and is the necessary cultural background to the rise of human rights as a central preoccupation of Western and even global cul-ture.[401] From this perspective, the centrality of human rights in the contem-porary world isn't just an inevitable result of the steady rise of the virtues of self-assertion over the past three or four centuries. It may also herald a subtle, new form taken by the virtues of reverence – a new way the virtues of reverence are expressed – in our contemporary world. The virtues that are rights-*giving*, not just rights-*seeking*. The "sacredness of the person" – that is to say, of *other* people – is just another way of describing the virtues of Reverence (A2), as viewed through the sole lens of reverence.

Figure 77. Four metaphors for the human (2)

Taking all this into account, I can perhaps revise my expanded version of the metaphors for the human, as in Figure 77 above.

Of course, what Joas calls the "sacralization" of the person could easily be or become a new form of idolatry, a glorification and even "worship" of our individual human self, just as the vision of a sacred world could easily descend into just another pantheism. There are certainly links between *this* kind of sacredness and the post-modern culture of self-assertion, especially the narcissism of the virtues of Liberty (A1). But the phenomenon Joas calls "sacralization" often seems to be linked, instead, to a new, *unselfing* global vision, in which the *personal* self can be and often is "relativized" – or lowered in priority – in relation to other selves or to humanity *as a whole*. Similarly, membership in our own national society can be "relativized" in relation to a global society.[402] In this second kind of linkage, the other doesn't just remain *other* – even a *sacred* other – but can become as important, or sometimes even more important, than our own personal self.

Equating the other with our own self suggests a final change I can make to the metaphors I've evolved from Goethe and Richard Shweder. Figure 77 takes you a long way toward a vision of the four corners of the human, as seen through the lens of reverence. It helps to describe the kind of world human beings inhabit when they're practising Goethe's four kinds of reverence. But the concept of "sacred other" suggests one last twist I can give to this image I've extrapolated from Shweder's metaphors: to bring it back "full circle" to where I began developing the four families of virtues, in chapter 6.

To make this last twist, I invite you to consider what the "other" is when it becomes truly *sacred* for us. That is to say, when we act toward another human being with the virtues of Reverence (A2). When we act in ways that deserve to be called virtues of Reverence (A2) – especially virtues of Love (A2b) – does the other person remain just an *other*? Or does the other become almost like another kind of *self*? Even Aristotle (as you saw, earlier in this chapter) said that a good man's relationship toward a friend is "the same relation that he has toward himself (for a friend *is* another self)."[403] The traditional Christian commandment to "love thy neighbour *as thyself*" also suggests that when you love in a truly reverent way, the other doesn't remain simply an *other*, but instead becomes something more like another self, or another way of conceiving or loving the self. When you are fully living the virtues of reverence, your self is no longer a "discrete entity" but rather "incorporated," as David Martin puts it, so that you find your self "*in* the other."[404] And the other in you. "[B]y unconsciously merging self and other," says Frans de Waal, "the other's experiences echo within us. We feel them *as if they're our own*."[405] Samuel Taylor Coleridge captures this when he compares self-reverence and reverence for another: "[T]o love our future Self is almost as hard," he says, "as to love our Neighbour – it is indeed only a difference of Space and Time – my Neighbour is my *other* Self, *othered* by Space – my old age is to my youth an other Self, *othered* by Time."[406] The person toward whom you act with virtues of Reverence (A2) is *your other self, othered simply by space*. That was Hegel's constant theme and the core of his whole doctrine: that the other is in reality a "second self." In the other, "one meets one's self."[407] All independence is ultimately an illusion. Truth is always the unity of relation to another: "for each is *through its Other* what it is *in itself*, the totality of the Relation." What appears to the virtues of self-assertion like an external relation (or "Reflection") is really, from another angle, an *internal* relation (or "intro-Reflection").[408]

So the other toward whom you act with virtues of Reverence (A2) – the sacred *other* – can perhaps be justifiably described as another sacred form of the self, but with the emphasis altered: no longer just a sacred *self*, but rather, a truly *sacred* self.[409] If you can see the possibility of this equation, it yields the resulting image of the human in Figure 78, on page 591.

As I said, you shouldn't allow any reflex aversion to the word "sacred" to get in the way of your understanding here. "Sacred" isn't an arbitrary word that comes loaded with a hidden agenda. It may eventually lead you in new directions, or to new virtues and realities. But at this stage, it's purely factual or empirical. "Sacred" is simply the best description for the quality things have for us when we approach them through the human virtues of reverence. Sacred self and sacred world are the way the basic polarity of being – unity and plurality, something and other, something and everything, self and world – appears to us when we practise these essential human virtues.[410]

Figure 78. Sacred self and sacred world

As Figure 78 shows, sacred self and sacred world reproduce the internal duality or paradox you already saw in the two basic human stances of "I am" and "It is" in chapter 7. The sacred *self* is the reverent version of "*I* am," the reverent version of the virtues of Liberty (A1). The *sacred* self is the reverent form of "I *am*" or of the virtues of Reverence (A2). A *sacred* world is what you encounter, from the human stance of "It is," when you live the virtues of Excellence (B1) in a spirit of reverence. A sacred *world* is the world you inhabit, from the stance of "*It* is," if you practise the virtues of Equality (B2) in the same spirit. Just because you approach these four corners of the human in a spirit of reverence or union, rather than from a stance of self-assertion or non-union, doesn't mean the tensions and conflicts between them disappear. They remain, as the four permanent, paradoxical poles of the human.[411]

Because the virtues of reverence aren't going to go away – because they are permanent and necessary features of the human – Goethe's four kinds of reverence and Shweder's related metaphors can and should help you think about our post-modern condition and challenges – both personal and societal – with some new and useful lenses. "[A]s we search around for postmodern ways to rethink our responsibilities to society and nature," Shweder says, "it would not be surprising if we began to acknowledge the intuitive appeal of ideas such as sacred self, sacred world … It would not be surprising if we began to worry a lot about how those ideas are to be reconciled with the individualism that we value."[412] That is to say: how they are to be reconciled with the virtues of self-assertion, in the world of today, the world of climate change, human rights, democracy, human migration, diversity, and globalization.

Rethinking the four families of virtues

The lenses of reverence we can borrow from premodern and non-Western cultures should help and encourage you to rethink all four families of human virtues, from our post-modern (or even postmodern) perspective on the next turn of the spiral staircase, in the first half of the twenty-first century.

At this point in Western civilization and in human evolution, even the virtues of Liberty (A1) don't have to be – can't be – merely raw self-assertion. At this stage, self-assertion – even the pursuit of Power (A1a) and Pleasure (A1b) – can and should incorporate all the other insights the arrow of virtue has revealed to us, up to this point in Western cultural evolution. Each family of virtues can now embrace and reflect the other three. At the highest level, true self-assertion can and should now be the self-assertion of the *whole* self – the *whole* nature of the human – not just some part of it. Not just Power (A1a) and Pleasure (A1b), for their own sake. In fact, animated by the spirit of reverence, even the virtues of Power and Pleasure are transformed. Under the influence of self-reverence, you can rediscover that, although human beings seem at first to be pursuing an enormous variety of different pleasures, they may really, at bottom, be pursuing "the same pleasure," as Aristotle says, "and not that which they think, and would assert."[413]

Rethinking Liberty (A1) from the perspective of reverence can also help you to discover that, as long as these virtues insist on staying within the virtues of self-assertion alone, they can't lead to a true kind of freedom. Left to themselves, they assert a world of efficient and material causes, the objective world standing over against their own self-assertion. They discover and proclaim a deterministic world, ruled by necessity, contingency, accident, fortune, and fate.[414] This was the dead end from which Augustine helped to rescue the ancient world.[415] And the problem isn't solved if we simply update our vocabulary and call these same things sociobiology, evolutionary gene pools, neuroscience, econometrics, or something else instead. True liberty can only come from final causes, which set us free to choose the good.[416] And final causes begin only when one human being opens up a space for freedom and the good (in an otherwise deterministic world) by accepting responsibility for another and embracing the disposition to nurture rather than the disposition to dominate, in the virtues of Reverence (A2).[417] That's what some traditions mean when they talk about a "service that is perfect freedom." The virtues of Liberty (A1), by themselves, are subject not only to the whole weight of physical determinism, but also to the whole weight of history. Only reverence acknowledges the full weight of the past while freeing us from it.[418]

Rethinking Liberty (A1) should thus remind you that there are four different kinds of freedom. The "freedom to" of our modern and post-modern virtues of Liberty isn't the only kind of freedom. There's also the "freedom of" (B2), so characteristic of the Enlightenment. The freedom *of* the self. But we shouldn't assume these two appeared out of nowhere. Or that the pre-modern world didn't talk a lot about freedom also. Because it did. Behind these two modern kinds of freedom stand two other kinds of freedom, those which appears so frequently in the ancient authors and the great religious traditions. These other kinds of freedom take the forms of "freedom from" and "freedom for."

The virtues of reverence also promise freedom. But this kind of freedom starts with liberation *from* the determinism of the body, the psyche, our appetites, the material world, efficient and material causes, or the potentially crippling and paralyzing burden of our past deeds. But that's just the beginning. Because this first reverent liberation also sets us free *for*: free for others, free for the good, free for all four stances and families of virtues, freedom for self-*giving*, not just the freedom to seek something for ourselves alone.[419] Without these other kinds of freedom, promised by the virtues of reverence, the freedom offered by the virtues of Liberty (A1) is an illusion. It turns out, in fact, to be a kind of slavery.

Rethinking Equality (B2) from the perspective of reverence should remind you that, despite their embrace of scientific and analytic rationalism, these virtues may not be able, by themselves, to achieve the very "objectivity" they endorse because reason and science come with their own built-in agenda of domineering self-assertion and control. They're a manifestation of the virtues of self-assertion. That's what we want knowledge for. Only reverence can be truly "objective," that is to say, cherishing and "letting be."

Without reverence, the virtues of self-assertion may not really be able to make good on their promise of individuality either because equality makes us all the same. It achieves an equality of ... *equals* or sameness. To achieve truly unique individuality, the virtues of Equality (B2) may thus have to be completed by reverence. This kind of genuine individuality comes instead from the moral demands of the virtues of the virtues of Reverence (A2). To which you and I must respond – because no one else can do it for us. We are morally unique. No one can answer the call for us. No one can take our place.[420] This kind of *genuine individuality* actually calls for "inequality," but in the sense *opposite* to authority, tyranny, or oppression. It means putting others first. It means unselfing and service to others.[421]

Rethinking Excellence (B1) means going beyond the "excellence" hyped in so many contemporary books and speeches. This kind of excellence is simply the excellence of technique. The excellence of technical competence, of utility, and of instrumental control. That is certainly a kind of goodness. But the utilitarian kind of excellence points beyond itself, to a deeper, more authentic goodness: the good of goodness itself, the goodness of all the human virtues and the whole nature of the human. The deep goodness of justice, righteousness, and truth. The absolute goodness that was first revealed in the goodness of self-giving (A2). It is brought to consciousness in the intuitive wisdom and understanding of the virtues of Excellence (B1) before it comes into the searchlight of analytic rationality, in the virtues of Equality (B2). As you saw in chapter 9, the justice of the virtues of Excellence (B1) is much more than the equality, fairness, and reciprocity of Equality (B2) and may even require *in*equality. Or it may inspire a self-giving that goes "way beyond" reciprocity.[422]

Rethinking Reverence (A2) means going beyond the prejudices of our contemporary Western culture, to rediscover this family of virtues for what it is: a permanent and essential cornerstone of the human. The virtues in which we still live most of our family and personal lives and the source of most of what we truly value. It means rediscovering them for the virtues and behaviours that they are and ceasing to confuse them with "beliefs" or "principles."[423]

These virtues aren't derived from religious "beliefs" or even from our religious traditions. It's the other way around. It was the practice and experience of these virtues – and of their partner in reverence, the virtues of Excellence (B1) – that gave rise to the religious traditions in the first place. If we rediscover the virtues, we might begin to understand what those traditions are all about. But that's not the first or most important step. The urgent question for our contemporary world isn't "Who is God?"

It's a prior question: "Who are we?"[424]

The nature of the human: four families of virtues

Surprisingly, one thinker who helps to answer this question is David Hume. In fact, one of those who "solved" Hume's problem – about how to get from "is" to "ought" – was Hume himself. If he didn't completely solve it, at least he found the key that can help you to do so. He found it almost as soon as he framed his famous problem.

Just as Aristotle overrode his own law of non-contradiction only pages after stating it – by showing that everything is a contrary or composed of contraries – Hume did much the same thing. Only one page after stating his own famous problem, he solved it – or rather, shelved it by turning his back on it as a non-problem, wrongly posed. You can't get from "is" to "ought," he said, because "is" is an indicative, empirical statement of the rational mind. There's no direct way from matter – from "the relations of objects" (i.e., "It is") – to meaning or value. There's no purely rational way to "ought." The moral qualities that define humanity – that make humans truly human – aren't derived from human rationality, Hume argued, but rather from what he variously called the human passions, affections, or sentiments: from human intuitions and feelings about the good.[425] They are "more properly felt than judg'd of."[426] And these feelings about the good develop into "durable" and admirable human habits, "character," or virtues.[427] If you want to get to "ought," you have to start from "ought" itself.[428] You have to start with the human virtues.[429] You can't reason *to* the virtues.[430] You reason *from* them. Virtue is the bedrock of the human, on which reason itself is built.

David Hume's key for solving his own problem was the rediscovery of the virtues.[431] Hume thought modern thinkers since Descartes had been a little too hasty in discarding the virtues and banking everything human on the rational mind.[432] For Hume, human nature is "compos'd of two principal parts" – feeling as well as the rational mind – and two basic families of virtues. His names for these two basic families varied. Sometimes he called them the "interested" and the "disinterested," sometimes "public (or common) interest" and "self-interest," sometimes private duties and public duties, sometimes the "social virtues" (those that are "beneficial to society" and induce human beings to "perform their part in society") and those "other kinds of virtue" that promote the good of the "person possess'd of them": the virtues that "render them serviceable to themselves, and enable them to promote their own interest."[433] In the first category, he put virtues like justice, meekness, beneficence, charity, generosity, clemency, compassion, gratitude, friendship, fidelity, and "humanity." In the second he put prudence, temperance, frugality, industry, assiduity, enterprise, courage, intrepidity, ambition, perseverance, patience, activity, vigilance, application, constancy, and "business dexterity."[434] In other words, whatever Hume called them, his two families of virtues are what I have called the virtues of reverence and the virtues of self-assertion. Hume both reflected and helped establish our modern and post-modern culture by giving pride of place to the virtues of self-assertion.[435] But he had to concede, nevertheless, that the virtues of reverence "bear the greatest figure among the moral qualities."[436] Because they establish the frame: they make the other human virtues possible and make them virtuous.[437]

Jean-Paul Sartre's famous dictum that existence precedes essence – and that therefore human beings are free to choose whatever nature their minds may decide to give themselves – was morally frivolous and factually incorrect.[438] The nature of the human – our essence – is determined by the polarity of being itself and by our encounter with it. And by the stances and families of virtues – and all their sub-sub-families – this encounter reveals to us.[439]

The nature of the human, as David Hume discovered, is a paradox – a human paradox – a permanent, necessary, and unbreakable partnership between two opposite and contradictory dimensions of the human spirit: the virtues of self-assertion and the virtues of reverence. These two families of virtues are the contradictory human responses to the underlying polarity of being: the paradox of unity and plurality, of something and everything, of self and world. But this very polarity means the two contradictory sides of the human must immediately develop their *own* internal poles.

Paradox breeds paradox. So, the initial human paradox of reverence and self-assertion quickly spawns four more. The virtues of self-assertion split into their own paradox of Liberty (A1) and Equality (B2). And reverence finds itself similarly divided between the virtues of Excellence (B1) and those of Reverence (A2). These four families of virtues – Liberty, Equality, Excellence, and Reverence – are the four basic poles of what I've called the nature of the human.

Like the four ventricles of the physical heart, the four families of virtues are the great pump of the human spirit, that which distinguishes a true human being from an intelligent, rational monster, or a soulless, amoral automaton of artificial intelligence (AI). In fact, when we use the word "heart" in its metaphorical sense, like Pascal, this is what we're talking about. The four corners of the human spirit, whose continual, inseparable interaction pumps into our lives what is most deeply and genuinely human about them. The nature of the human is a four-way "conversation made of stance,"[440] a "knot tied between competing decencies."[441]

Because of the polar structure of being, any deep or serious reflection on the nature of the human leads to the discovery of these four families, or some version of them, whatever they may be called. When Samuel Taylor Coleridge set out to discover the "structure of our proper humanity," he came up with these same four families of virtues.[442] When Léon Walras aimed to discern the nature of the human "as he can and should be," he came up with, more or less, the same four.[443] When French jurist René Cassin (1887–1976) was charged with putting order into a long list of liberties and protections found in the world's codes and constitutions (for drafting the UN Universal Declaration of Human Rights), he identified the same four families of human values.[444] C.G. Jung discovered the same four "gates" to the human world, and so does

Christopher Peterson.[445] Hegel, Heidegger, Whitehead, Franz Rosenzweig, and Max Scheler all explicitly identified the four pillars of the human, each in his own way.[446] Emmanuel Levinas identifies the same four families of virtues, implicitly.[447] So does Paul Ricœur.[448] And so, by and large, does Robert Nozick.[449]

We aren't free to choose the nature of the human, as I argued in chapter 3. We're only free to embrace it or reject it, to enhance or pervert it. We are free to discover the virtues or to ignore them. We can choose, combine, emphasize, or reinterpret the virtues. But we can't abolish them. The invention or creation of "new" virtues and values – which occurs at each stage of human development – is also a kind of discovery. Or *re*discovery. A rediscovery of the nature of the human.

The *other* human paradox: the stances of "It is" and "I am"

What does Athens have to do with Jerusalem?

The answer to Tertullian's question, this book suggests, is: *everything*. They cannot live apart.

The human world hangs suspended between the "It is" of Parmenides and the "I am" of Exodus.[450]

"Athens" and "Jerusalem" stand here for two sides of the human paradox. They stand, of course, for the virtues of self-assertion and of reverence – the two great families of virtues Hume rediscovered and all their families and sub-families. But – as the archetypal homes of "It is" and "I am" – Athens and Jerusalem can also stand for another version of the human paradox: another human paradox that's almost as important as the first for understanding the nature of the human. The two poles of self-assertion and reverence aren't the whole story about the human.

The nature of the human can be parsed and combined in more ways than one. Once you've identified the four basic poles of the human I've called Liberty (A1) and Equality (B2) on the one hand, and Excellence (B1) and Reverence (A2) on the other, you can easily see how they might be recombined in ways *other* than the initial basic pair of self-assertion and reverence, just as they are recombined in political life (as you saw in chapter 12). Any adequate description of the nature of the human must take account not just of the paradoxes of self-assertion and of reverence, but also the paradoxes of "It is" and "I am": the linked paradoxes of Liberty (A1) and Reverence (A2) on the one hand, and of Excellence (B1) and Equality (B2) on the other.[451]

The virtues of Liberty (A1) and of Reverence (A2) are linked, first of all, by the fact that they're the first two stages in the genetic, historical, and personal human journey I've called the arrow of virtue. But they're also linked by their common focus on the "first person singular," on the *subject*, herself. By their common emphasis on "I": "*I* am" and "I *am*." That's why I've labelled them A1 and A2: to emphasize that the link between these "diagonal" poles is just as important as the link between the two "horizontal" pairs.

They are also linked by something else or by something that flows or follows from this first link. Liberty (A1) and Reverence (A2) are the source of the primal energies that fuel the human person. They are the virtues of pure or primitive self-*seeking* (A1), on the one hand, and its flip side – pure or primitive self-*giving* (A2) – on the other. They are the virtues both of the hero and of the saint.[452] This first axis of A1 and A2 is the powerhouse of the human. All other virtues are some modification, adaptation, or combination of the energies and motivation flowing from self-*seeking* and self-*giving*.

This is the side of the human which, in chapter 7, I called "existential" because it reflects and expresses the being of the self. Hegel calls it "life," the life without which there isn't anything human at all.[453] Martin Heidegger expresses the inseparable poles of this first "diagonal" axis of the human in the German word "*Dasein*," composed of the words "*sein*" (being) and "*da*" (there). In order for anything – including anything human –to actually exist it must combine *being* (A2) with being *there* or being *here* (A1).[454] Karl Jaspers calls this same combination "*Existenz*."[455] In the nature of the human, these two mutually necessary facets of being are reflected and expressed in the diagonal axis of the virtues of Liberty (A1) and the virtues of Reverence (A2). Together they constitute not only the starting point but also the source, the energy, the very life, and existence of the human.[456]

But the paradox of Liberty (A1) and Reverence (A2) – as you well know by now – is only half of the whole story about the human. A "diagonal" slice of my map of the human paradox, instead of a "horizontal" one. But still only one slice. This first diagonal axis is crossed by another one. In chapter 7, I called this second axis of the human "ontological" because it expresses the inevitable human encounter with the being of the *world*. Human beings' encounter with other things – and with the other beings that surround them – leads them to awareness not only that "I am" but that other things and people *are* too. The recognition that "It is." That I am surrounded by an otherness that confronts and challenges my ego and my understanding. This second diagonal axis of the human exhibits the same polar form as the previous one: the same combination of *being* (B1) with being *here* (B2). The paradox of "It *is*" and "*It* is."[457]

This second "diagonal" slice of the human is expressed and embodied in the virtues of Excellence (B1) and of Equality (B2). Together, these two families of virtues form the axis of the human as a *thinking* being: thinking combined either with intuition (B1) or sensing (B2). No longer just a creature of life and action, of self-seeking and self-giving, of heroism and saintliness, but a creature of perception, reflection, and thought. A rational, thinking animal. Hegel calls this second diagonal axis of the human (B1 and B2) "cognition."[458] Whitehead calls it the "mental pole" of the human.[459] Jaspers calls it "Reason," and he insists that any adequate description of human reason needs to take account of its two contrasting and often antagonistic forms. Not just the calculating, discursive reason of our everyday thinking and of scientific rationality, not just the modern idea of reason as "clear, objective thinking, the transformation of the opaque into the transparent." (B2)[460] But also that other kind of thinking I described in chapter 4, the kind that can never be entirely satisfied, that wants to reach beyond its own limits, reach beyond the clear and the transparent, beyond the knowable to the *unknowable*, in the surrounding cloud of mystery, gesturing toward what it cannot know (B1).[461]

So the nature of the human is structured not just by the basic human paradox of self-assertion (A1 and B2) and reverence (B1 and A2) – a "vertical" paradox in my map or diagram of the human – but also by the "diagonal" paradox of "I am" (A1 and A2) and "It is" (B1 and B2).[462] To rediscover the nature of the human, understanding this second paradox – the paradox of what Hegel calls "life" and "cognition," or what Franz Rosenzweig calls the "life-centred" and "world-centred" stances – is almost as important as understanding the first.[463]

It would be important at any time because this second "diagonal" paradox is one of the fundamental, structural features that shapes the nature of the human.[464] But it's especially important now because this is where much of the dilemma of our post-modern Western civilization lies. If we are to have any chance of rediscovering the basic human paradox of self-assertion and reverence, we must clear away the misunderstanding arising from this *other* human paradox: the paradox of "It is" and "I am."

The problem is twofold. On the one hand, the modern (and even our post-modern) world has increasing difficulty in recognizing the two "internal" poles of "It is" ("*It* is" and It *is*"). On the other hand, it has even more difficulty acknowledging its *external* partner in the nature of the human – that is, "I am" – and the structure of their paradoxical relationship.

I already discussed the first problem in chapter 4. Since the seventeenth century, our idea of reason has become increasingly narrow. In the wake of the Enlightenment, our post-modern culture has been increasingly unable or unwilling to recognize that Reason has not one but two parts: not just the discursive, empirical, scientific rationalism of the virtues of Equality (B2), but also the deeper wisdom, goodness, and justice of the virtues of Excellence (B1), the place where human reason touches the invisible, mysterious background of our being and our virtues, and where intuition thus becomes an essential faculty for perceiving reality.

We have come to rest, almost exclusively, in the clear, rational consciousness of the virtues of Equality (B2) and no longer trust – or even know how to do – the deeper thinking characteristic of the virtues of Excellence (B1): what Whitehead calls "conceptual feeling" or "conceptual valuation" (as opposed to "conceptual analysis"), and Heidegger calls "attuned understanding."[465] We no longer understand the nature and importance of human thinking that goes beyond straightforward discursive, utilitarian rationality, aiming to situate it somehow in the wider, mysterious background of being and of our own being. We no longer acknowledge or even recognize the distinction between the kind of thinking that is "the intuition of things which arises when we possess ourselves, as one with the whole [B1] ... and that which presents itself when ... we think of ourselves as separated beings, and place nature in antithesis to the mind, as subject to object [B2]."[466] This limitation of the thinking horizon is a major problem for us, both because it truncates thought itself – making us both over-confident and overly modest about what human thought can do – and because it misleads us about the nature of the human.[467] As so often in the past, we are now often inclined to think that in Enlightenment rationality – the second phase of theoretic culture – humanity reached some kind of final destination.[468] We are thus unprepared for the inevitable twists and turns in the road ahead. Or even to recognize the road we are now on. And where we are on it.

But the second problem is equally grave. Not only have we largely forgotten the contradictory nature of human beings as thinking creatures (both B1 and B2), but we also overlook the paradoxical relationship between both of these poles and something else, something equally important for the nature of the human. We forget or even deny the roots of human reason in the prior reality of "I am": in the two-sided "existential" paradox Hegel calls life, Heidegger calls Dasein, and Jaspers calls Existenz. Both the virtues of Liberty (A1) and the virtues of Reverence (A2). Not only do we overlook the virtues of Excellence (B1), we are even less able to see that they draw their own substance and power from the prior human experience of the self-giving virtues of Reverence

(A2) – that our deepest notions of justice and goodness always refer, implicitly, even farther back, to the prior human virtues of hope, mercy, trust, generosity, and self-giving love.[469] These are just as much a part of the nature of the human as the virtues of Liberty (A1) from which they themselves emerged. Together with the virtues of Liberty (A1), they form the *existential* pole of our nature (A1 and A2, or "I am"), standing over, together (as *Dasein* or *Existenz*), and against the ontological and "mental pole," the virtues of human reason and cognition (B1 and B2, or "It is").[470]

If reality were nothing more than "It is" – nothing more than the physical, phenomenal world of things and of facts – then the Enlightenment *would* indeed be the last word about the human and the world. The world of Spinoza and the world of Kant would be the whole truth, not just part of it. "Did philosophy commence with an *it is* instead of an *I am*," says Coleridge, "Spinoza would be altogether true."[471]

But neither philosophy nor anything else about the human actually begins with "It is." Before human beings can begin to exercise the virtues of Excellence (B1) and Equality (B2), they have already begun – both in their own individual lives and in the longer history of the race and of human civilization – to exercise the virtues of Liberty (A1) and of Reverence (A2), the virtues of "*I* am" and of "I *am*.'" Episodic, mimetic, and mythic culture came long before theoretic culture. In very many ways, they still come first. "I am" still must come before "It is." Life and existence come before cognition. "In order to understand, observe, deduce [B1 and B2]," says Tolstoy, "man must first be conscious of himself as *alive* [A1 and A2]."[472] Without something *in here*, there is nothing *out there*. "The *existential* nature of man," Heidegger agrees, "is the reason why man can represent beings as such, and why he can be conscious of them."[473] Coleridge said exactly the same thing – using the very language of this book – almost a century and a half earlier. "That which we find in ourselves," he said, "is ... the substance and the life of all our knowledge. Without this latent presence of the 'I am,' all modes of existence in the external world would flit before us as coloured shadows, with no greater depth, root or fixture than the image of a rock hath in a gliding stream or the rain-bow on a fast-sailing rain-storm."[474]

In other words, the two poles of "I am" (A1 and A2) are not only necessary, inescapable, inseparable partners to the two poles of "It is" (B1 and B2). They are actually *prior* to them, just as union is prior to non-union, and being is already prior to self-assertion. In all such cases, one side of the human paradox is the prior condition for the other side.[475]

It was Jerusalem – or the people of Israel – that taught Western civilization the importance of the first (I am). It was Athens – or Greek culture – that taught Western culture the importance of the second (It is). In that sense, our modern and (to a lesser extent) our post-modern culture is still Greek. Since the time of Aristotle, we've been learning to live in a world of things, a world therefore in which human beings are defined by their minds, their capacity to analyse, manipulate, and control a world of things, a world in which human beings are "thinking things," the essence of which is their capacity for the use of objective, analytic reason.[476]

The Achilles heel of our modern and (to some extent) our post-modern world is its assumption that Athens can live without Jerusalem. That reason – even in its extended sense (both B1 and B2) – can live alone. That reason is what defines the nature of the human.[477] As I already pointed out in chapter 7, contemporary thinkers who try to "explain" everything according to material or efficient causes, or assert that Enlightenment rationalism is the final word in human understanding, are simply viewing the human world through one kind of "double vision." They are viewing the *whole* nature of the human – all four families of virtues – through the lens of only *one* of them: the lens of the virtues of Equality or the stance of "*It* is" (B2), sensing with thinking.

The assumption that reason defines the human overlooks two important facts. First, that the virtues of reason ("It is") surf on the energy and sheer *being* of the prior virtues, the virtues of "I am."[478] Without life or existence, there is no cognition.[479] Without feeling and intuition, there is no sensing with thinking.[480] Only through the union of both can we achieve "a world at once *lucid* [It is], and intrinsically of immediate *worth* [I am]."[481]

Second, this assumption also overlooks that, though rooted in the virtues of reverence, reason nevertheless harbours a potential internal impetus toward self-assertion. It is a self-assertive spontaneity.[482] The principle of identity ("this is that," or A=A) – which, together with its flip-side the law of non-contradiction, provides the foundation for ordinary, calculating human reason – is an *assertion* and a pure principle of self-assertion.[483]

As the necessary link between the virtues of Excellence (B1) and the virtues of Equality (B2) grows weaker in the modern and post-modern world, Reason has been gradually reduced simply to reason: to discursive, scientific, empirical rationalism. The virtues of Equality (B2) lost their necessary anchor in the virtues of Excellence (B1), that is, in the virtues of reverence. Without that counterweight, their true character as virtues of self-assertion becomes increasingly apparent. Aristotle and Aquinas' "rational appetite" (B2) became more appetite and less rational, generating the anti-Enlightenment of the nineteenth century and preparing the way for the post-modern culture of today, increasingly centred in the virtues of Liberty or "sense appetite" (A1) – sensing with feeling – the place where the human began. If it loses its original root in reverence, this kind of rationality can become a threat to human civilization.

The problem for our contemporary world is that it has got this relationship backward. Or has forgotten it altogether.[484]

Getting reason into perspective: the cases of AI and l'Arche

That means we need to get reason back into perspective. "Any one who values truth," says Jonathan Haidt wisely, "should stop worshipping reason."[485] We need to put reason back into its proper place in the economy of the human as a whole.

In the first half of the twenty-first century, we are in a better position than ever before to see why – and just how misleading and inadequate it is to equate the human with the rational. We're in a better position to see this for two quite opposite reasons: first, because we can now see the danger – the potential inhumanity – of pure intelligence. Second, because we can now see how very human – perhaps especially human – are those who have intellectual disabilities.

You can see the first in the development of artificial intelligence (AI): super-computers and software programs whose super-intelligent power of calculative reasoning vastly exceed that of their creators. A number of informatics pioneers, thinkers, and scientists have warned about the potential danger AI now poses to the future of the human race. Elon Musk (co-founder of PayPal and CEO of Tesla Motors) warns that, in developing AI, humans are "summoning the demon," and that AI is the "the greatest risk we face as a civilization," the "biggest existential threat" to the human race. Stephen Hawking agrees that AI could "take off on its own, and redesign itself at an ever-increasing rate. Humans, who are limited by slow biological evolution, couldn't compete, and would be superseded." Bill Gates is also in "the camp that is concerned about super intelligence," and doesn't understand "why some people are not concerned."[486] Steve Wozniak, co-founder of Apple, agrees that "the future is scary and very bad for people ... [E]ventually [computers will] think faster than us and they'll get rid of the slow humans to run companies more efficiently." Nick Bostrom, an Oxford University philosopher, has even suggested that "self-improving AI could enslave or kill humans if it wanted to, and that controlling such machines could be impossible."[487] Facing an explosion in artificial intelligence, Bostrom suggests, "we humans are like small children playing with a bomb."[488] Max Tegmark, another leading AI theorist, agrees: "a superintelligent

AI with a rigorously defined goal will be able to improve its goal attainment by eliminating us."[489] So does Yoshua Bengio, scientific director for the *Institut québécois d'intelligence artificielle* (Mila): "If our wisdom doesn't catch up quickly enough with our scientific and technological progress, we are going to destroy ourselves."[490]

For reasons like these, Peter Singer suggests "it is not too soon to ask whether we can program a machine to act ethically."[491] In January 2015, Hawking and Musk joined some 8600 other scientists, computer engineers, and artificial intelligence specialists in signing an open letter advocating "expanded research aimed at ensuring that increasingly capable AI systems are robust and beneficial: our AI systems must do what we want them to do."[492] Musk also calls for "swift and decisive" government intervention to oversee development of AI: "AI's a rare case where we need to be proactive in regulation, instead of reactive. Because by the time we are reactive with AI regulation, it's too late … AI is a fundamental risk to the existence of human civilization, in a way that car accidents, airplane crashes, faulty drugs, or bad food were not."[493]

As human beings grapple with the explosion of artificial intelligence, the challenge we face, says Nick Bostrom, is "to hold onto our humanity." But what, exactly, *is* our "humanity"? That's the key question here. "Will the best in human nature please stand up," Bostrom urges.[494] But what, exactly, *is* the "best" in our nature? What's the "nature" of the human, first of all? And what's the "best" in it? *That's the question on which now hangs the whole future of the human race.* For the purposes of artificial intelligence at least, we are very far from being able to answer it.[495]

At the beginning of 2017, for example, a conference of experts concerned about the urgency of developing "beneficial" or "friendly" AI took place in Asilomar, California. The participants adopted a statement of "principles" to guide future development of AI, to ensure it remains "beneficial" and doesn't become a threat to humanity. The principles stated that AI systems should be designed to "align with human values throughout their operation." And the human values they identified were "human dignity, rights, freedoms, and cultural diversity."[496] To be fair, the Asilomar principles implicitly invoke many other values they don't explicitly recognize, as such. But as far as these explicit Asilomar values are concerned, the tables of virtues in this book have already shown you how far they fall short of describing the full nature of the human and of human values. It also points out how unaware the drafters seem to be of the ambiguity, complexity, and bias even a brief list like this one can entail. Even if you could develop an adequate inventory of the virtues, you could not specify them definitively because every virtue is a lens, and every virtue looks *different* through the lens of every other virtue.[497]

From the stance of self-assertion, self-giving looks like subordination. From the point of view of self-giving reverence, self-assertion looks like domination. Rights and freedoms (as claims) are virtues of self-assertion, and thus express that side of our humanity which – reflected back to us in AI – now poses the very threat the authors of the principles seek to forestall. Dignity is one of those wonderful words which seem to hold the whole human paradox within itself. It can mean (and in the contemporary Western world, usually does mean) dignity as rights-*seeking* (B2a) or dignity as self-control (B2b) – that is, virtues of self-assertion – just as easily as it can mean dignity as worthiness (B1b) or dignity as reverence (A2a), that is, virtues of reverence.[498] Much the same thing could be said about diversity. As words like rights, dignity, and diversity illustrate, human values themselves are not "aligned." They are inherently conflictual, contradictory – or dialogical. We humans are defined by the tensions and dialogue between our virtues, *not* by their alignment.

Toward the end of 2017, another conference (*Forum IA Responsible*) in Montreal, Quebec, adopted the preamble for a "Déclaration de Montréal" on the "responsible" development of artificial intelligence, to be co-developed by interested persons over the following months. The preamble identifies seven values as the foundation for ethical AI development: well-being, autonomy, justice, privacy, knowledge, democracy, and responsibility. It's significant that at least four of these seven values are virtues of self-assertion; one (justice) is a virtue of Excellence (B1); and another (responsibility) can be a virtue belonging to at least three families of contradictory virtues, depending on what is meant (as shown in Tables 10 and 14).[499] The final declaration published a year later proposes ten "principles" to guide future development of AI. In the final list, justice and knowledge have been dropped, but solidarity, equity, diversity, prudence, and sustainable development have been added. In this final list only solidarity is clearly a virtue of reverence, while sustainable development joins responsibility (and maybe well-being) as virtues that can belong to different and even contrasting families, depending on the context and the speaker.[500] The Montreal declaration shows some of the same unconscious biases, ambiguities, and limitations as the Asilomar principles.

Max Tegmark, one of the moving spirits behind the Asilomar principles, recognizes that "to wisely decide what to do about AI development, we human beings need to confront not only the traditional computational challenges, but also some of the most obdurate questions in philosophy. ... To program a friendly AI, we need to capture the meaning of life. What's 'meaning'? What's 'life'? What's the ultimate ethical imperative? ... If we cede control to a super-intelligence before answering these questions rigorously, the answer it comes up with is unlikely to involve us. This makes it timely to rekindle the classic debates of philosophy and ethics, and adds a new urgency to the conversation!"[501]

This is very wise, especially since it frames the challenge dialogically – in the form of "debates" – rather than assuming AI can be rescued by ethical "expertise," as some AI thinkers are tempted to do.[502] The very difficulty of those debates causes some other AI experts, such as Stuart Russell (b. 1962), to give up on the whole contradictory field of values altogether. And to propose instead that the challenge of developing "beneficial" or "friendly" artificial intelligence (AI) can be solved simply through "inverse reinforcement learning" (IRL). IRL is based on the assumption AI can be made humane by observing and imitating actual human behaviours or "preferences."[503] There is no doubt much to be said for this approach. But a potential flaw is its inability to take account of the two different ways of defining the human, identified by both Pascal and Kant: by our aspirations *or* by our actual behaviour.[504] Inverse reinforcement learning might possibly allow AI to imitate our *human nature*. But it seems very unlikely to enable AI to mirror the true *nature of the human*: the virtues to which we aspire *but of which our actual behaviour so often falls short*. As Rosalind Hursthouse puts it: "many human beings are *not* going on 'in the way characteristic of the species.'"[505]

If the AI community hopes to solve the grave problem of "beneficial" or "friendly" AI, it may need to stop framing the problem purely in terms of "intelligence." In order to make AI genuinely "human-centred," it won't be enough to "reflect more of the depth that characterizes our own intelligence," as Fei-Fei Li (b. 1976), another AI specialist takes for granted.[506] Because that which makes humans benevolent or friendly *doesn't come from the intellect*. It comes from somewhere else. You can get a precious insight into where it comes from – the source of our true "humanity" – by looking at the question from the very opposite point of view: not from the point of view of *intelligence*, but rather, from the point of view of persons with intellectual *disabilities*.

L'Arche is an international network of communities for people with intellectual disabilities. The experience of these communities helps show us what it means to be genuinely human. The members of these communities don't have all the human intelligence on which Western culture has put so high a value. And yet they are deeply, intensely human because they are "people of the heart, people of trust." They may not have all the rational virtues, but they are richly able to practise the virtues of reverence, especially the virtues of self-giving love (A2). In recognizing the genuine humanity of people who lack so much of what we normally take to be human, we can begin rediscovering the true nature of the human – and thus "truly becoming human," ourselves.[507]

The case of l'Arche is a mirror image of the case of AI. It shows you, from a reverse perspective, where the core and wellspring of our humanity are to be found. You can have super-intelligence and yet no humanity, perhaps even *in*humanity. But even where intelligence is lacking, there can, nevertheless, be a deep, authentic humanity. If human reason loses its initial root and source in the virtues of reverence – for which those with intellectual disabilities are often so gifted – it gradually degenerates into pure self-assertion. It even loses sight of the fact that it *is* a virtue: that the *act* of reason precedes its content. That the *saying* comes before the *said*. It ceases to see itself as a virtue – as a good or bad action or behaviour – and becomes, instead, just a fact, in a world of facts.

In order to become genuinely "beneficial" or "friendly," AI would have to become virtuous. That's what "beneficial" and "friendly" mean, after all. That's what they *are*: virtues. The virtue of "friendship," for example, is the virtue of acting toward someone else "not for your own sake *but for his*."[508] To become friendly and beneficial, AI will have to learn the human virtues and learn to practise them – including the virtues of *un*selfing.

The cases of AI and l'Arche are fascinating because they show you, in a flash, how mistaken were all those – beginning with Aristotle, but especially the founders of our modern and post-modern world, from Descartes to Hegel – who thought that human beings are defined by their human rationality. That to be rational is to be human, and to be human is to be rational. That humans are "thinking things." Humans are now on the point of creating their own thinking things – whose capacity for calculative, computational thinking vastly exceeds our own – yet which are *not* human, and which even have the potential for a terrible *in*humanity. And the reason they have that potential is that their "intelligence" is purely calculative, computational, and instrumental.[509] It's just a kind of thinking. A kind of *reasoning*. Superintelligent *machines*, as Peter Singer recognizes, "are not superintelligent *beings*." So, teaching ethics to a machine is a "daunting task."[510]

It's more than daunting. It may well prove impossible. Since a machine is *not* a being, artificial intelligence doesn't have – and can perhaps never be "programmed" to have – that capacity for *intuition with feeling* (A2), from which flow all our moral instincts and humanity.[511] There is no "algorithm *for life*."[512] There is no "formula" that can calculate "some kind of quantitative proportionality between demands of self, near and dear, and distant others, or even more crudely, demands of self versus others."

Moral judgments are "qualitative, not quantitative." They are based on a prior life of virtue and a host of subtle, intuitive perceptions and considerations, including "deep and particularistic knowledge of surrounding context."[513] Because AI is a pure product of Pascal's "geometric" mind, it's unlikely to be able to acquire his *"esprit de finesse."* What could teach it his "reasons of the heart" – the reasons *that reason doesn't know?*[514]

As I said earlier, moral education is more like an apprenticeship than like cramming for a formal exam. It's the long accumulation of gut feeling, practical competence, and habit, rather than the accumulation of knowledge in the head or the brain. In the programming of computers or AI, what could replace this social learning of family life – its long apprenticeship in reverence? What could teach it to give and to receive, to help and be helped, to touch and be touched, to hug and be hugged, to cherish and be cherished, to nourish and be nourished, to care for and be cared about, to love and be loved? What could give a computer program or an AI algorithm moral gut feelings and attachments, feeling with intuition, the instincts, reflexes, and habits of reverence?[515]

Even though he wants to give up on the field of values altogether, Stuart Russell cannot, of course, do so. To his credit, he recognizes that, to be genuinely beneficial or "helpful," AI will have to acquire virtues of reverence, such as humility and deference.[516] Humility is one of the keys to the human. It is one of the essential virtues that makes humans human. Any creature can be assertive. That's what makes us creatures, as opposed to inert or vegetable matter. But only humans can deliberately and generously *unself* themselves. Only humans can show reverence to another. What could teach a computer program a virtue of reverence, such as humility?

Artificial intelligence may potentially be inhuman by definition because it is pure intelligence. *Because it does not, and perhaps cannot, practice the virtues of reverence*, especially the virtues of Reverence (A2), the cornerstone of our true humanity, the home and source of both benevolence and friendship.[517] In order to become truly and reliably "beneficial" and "friendly," AI would need to transcend itself. It would need to go beyond pure intelligence. It would need to take the "reverse" (teleological or moral) journey of the arrow of virtue: from "*It* is" (B1) to "*It* is" (B2) to "I *am*" (A2).

Rediscovering the virtues: the *pre*- and *post*-rational, and the non-ego centre of the self

The lesson of AI and of l'Arche is that, to describe the nature of the human, you can't begin with thinking or with thought, or even with things. They come later.

When all is said and done, you have to come back to the human virtues.

We know that from our own lives, if we're honest. Despite what we tell ourselves, rational consciousness plays a relatively modest role in our everyday lives, which are mostly led at a much more instinctive, intuitive, emotional, habitual, ritualized, storytelling level of existence. Especially at the deepest, most painful, or most exhilarating moments of our lives, sorrowful or joyful, where rational thought is normally of little use or comfort, and something quite different is required. Mimetic and mythic culture came before theoretic culture. And they still do, in real life.

But you can also see it in the life of the mind itself. Although Aristotle and Aquinas set the pattern of attaching a very high value to reason and intellect – the pattern that has led to our modern Western definition of the human as mind, as a thinking thing – they both devoted a large portion of their own thinking to the role of the virtues in human life and acknowledged that thinking itself is a kind of virtue, and has its own virtues, the so-called "intellectual" virtues. With their feet planted still in mythic culture, they were also in no doubt that there are other virtues, and that these other virtues must come first. Without the other virtues as their foundation, the intellectual virtues can't do their own proper work or do it well because it's all the *other* virtues that confer on them the quality of virtue.

Even in contemporary thought, when all other avenues or arguments are exhausted, thinkers like John Rawls and Richard Rorty (like Immanuel Kant and Martin Heidegger before them) are still obliged to fall back on the virtues. The virtues seem to be the bedrock, to which even the rational mind eventually recurs, when it runs out of other resources or places to go. When the rational mind finds – as it eventually must – that it can't deliver on its promises without something else to give it meaning and value, it seems to grope its way back to the virtues. If a foundation, a starting point, can be found anywhere for human ethical and social life – and even for the life of the mind – it must be found, as Bernard Williams suggests, "in people's dispositions." [518]

Perhaps that's why there's been such a strong revival of interest recently in the virtues. And not just in so-called "virtue ethics." The last few years have witnessed an explosion of books aiming to rediscover the meaning and relevance of the virtues for contemporary human life. With the exhaustion of twentieth-century analytic philosophy – and its slide into the kind of scepticism represented by Richard Rorty – there seems to be an instinctive, inchoate return to the bedrock. To that, without which, human beings would not be human.

As a result, we now find books on the virtues suddenly pouring from the presses. Books on virtues such as truth, beauty, goodness, honour, integrity, justice, hope, gratitude, kindness, civility, altruism, dignity, fairness, happiness, and so on.[519]

This is a very significant development. It suggests that we may be at a turning point. A time when the impetus from other alternative understandings of the human is running – or has already run – out of steam, and our culture is beginning a confused groping back toward something more reliably and distinctively human. Toward something that better defines the nature of the human.

Toward the human virtues – the "ordinary virtues."[520]

If you want to discover the deepest truth about the human, you need to go back beyond a world of things and beyond a human nature defined, above all, by thinking. By thinking about things. You have to go back, beyond thought and thinking, to the human virtues – of which thinking is only one. An important one. But still only one.

If so, we need to pay more attention both to the *pre*-rational and the *post*-rational: to what comes *before* reason. And what comes *after*.[521]

The pre-rational is the practice and experience of the virtues that precedes and enables the rational, both in the history of our human culture and in our own individual lives. Historically (or phylogenetically) that means, among other things, the evolution from episodic to mimetic to mythic culture I discussed in chapter 15, and the development of the virtues, from the virtues of Liberty (A1) to the virtues of Reverence (A2) to the virtues of Excellence (B2). Without these prior virtues, the life of rational intellect in the classical virtues of Excellence (B2) and the modern virtues of Equality (B2) would not have been possible. Our theoretic culture is a latecomer and derives most of its intuitions of value from mimetic and mythic culture, and from the virtues of reverence.

In our own lives (or ontogenetically), it works much the same way. By the time we develop our rational thought processes, we're already persons. Our own mental capabilities and dispositions depend upon the virtues in which they're rooted. "The searcher after truth must love and be beloved," says Coleridge. Because unless someone pursues truth with humility and love, "he will be precipitant and overlook it; or he will be prejudiced and refuse to see it." All pursuit, all discovery, all recognition or statement of truth – even the truths of geometry – depends upon the movement and condition of our will. So, "in the moral being lies the source of the intellectual."[522] Not the other way around. If we haven't learned to be whole persons, our thinking is likely to suffer from similar limitations. Or something worse.

The *post*-rational is what happens when rational consciousness has done all it can and finds itself at the verge of mystery, when the clear track of rational thought runs out, as it must, and we find ourselves merely gesturing, beyond its limits, toward what we cannot know and cannot say. Where does the human go then?[523] What's the proper human response to this kind of mystery? A posture of defiance? Or indifference? Or adventure? Or conquest? Or … reverence?

Just as the virtues must come first – before the mind – in our definition of the human, the virtues of reverence – contrary to the assumption of our modern and post-modern cultures – have to come before *and after* the virtues of self-assertion. Because the virtues of reverence are the virtues of union. Because they are what makes wholeness possible. The wholeness of our nature, of our lives, of our families, of our communities, of our world. And the wholeness of the virtues, too.

The virtues of self-assertion are the virtues of non-union. They are essential to our nature. Without them there would be no human life at all. But on their own, they divide, separate, dominate, and push their own agendas. Without reverence to bind them and balance them, things fall apart.[524] Without reverence to unite us, we would not have a human world. Indeed, as the cold war showed – even before the crisis of climate change – we might not have a world at all. Without the virtues of reverence, everything dies. Including the virtues of self-assertion. Without reverence, reason cannot even be rational.

Once we have ceased defining human beings as minds or thinking things, or by their "beliefs," and have come to see the nature of the human as defined instead by the human virtues, we will be able see how much of our lives are already lived within the virtues of reverence, and how important they are to us, and to our fulfilment.[525] We will be able to start consciously nourishing them rather than ignoring them, overlooking them, fighting them, or leaving them to survive and flourish as best they can, on their own. Just as we have come to see that consciousness is only a thin crust on the deep, molten mass of the unconscious, we may be ripe for seeing that mind or thought (B1 and B2) is a similarly thin slice of the human, floating on a much wider range of feeling and behaviour (A1 and A2). Mind and thought aren't the self. They're only secondary manifestations of something else within the self. Manifestations of self-assertion (B2). And so, they're all the more inclined – by the very nature of self-assertion, by their link with the pure self-assertion of the ego (A1) – to deny the reality of anything else, to deny the reality of the whole. To deny the whole nature of the human.

But the ego isn't the centre of the self, either. Or not the only one. There's also the non-ego centre (A2). And this other non-ego centre – which is another part of the whole self – isn't accessible to us through thought. Or through the mind.[526] The only road or door to this part of the human is through action or behaviour. Through the virtues. Especially the virtues of Reverence (A2). And through reflection on the meaning of those virtues (B1).

"[T]he very existence of modern anti-humanism," says Charles Taylor, "seems to tell against exclusive humanism."[527] That is to say, it tells against a world bereft of reverence. Without reverence, civilization can't really be civilized, if for no other reason than that one of the partners in the human paradox is missing in action. If civilization must, at a minimum, be a human dialogue, then it needs all of its players to be genuine or complete.

The human conversation will go on. But without the virtues of reverence, it will be distorted because only a few of the *dramatis personae* are in the room. And even if they don't lead to the tyranny and depravity – to the barbarism – that a culture centred in power and pleasure would seem to promise, the rational or intellectual virtues can't, *by themselves*, lead us to greater civility, to the *un*selfing human virtues of kindness, generosity, and self-giving love that Emmanuel Levinas and Iain Pears, among others, find to be the heart of genuine civilization – without which civilization cannot be civilized.

We still live in the afterglow of our old religious and Enlightenment cultures. But the corrosive power of the irascible and concupiscible appetites suggests we can't do so forever unless the experience of desire (as in expressive individualism, for example) starts the arrow of virtue moving again in its spiral progression, from *I* am (A1) to I *am* (A2), back to the virtues of reverence, beginning with Reverence (A2).

Protecting, preserving, and enhancing civilization require us to rediscover two things: why the virtues must come first – before the mind – in our definition of the human, and why the virtues of reverence come first among the virtues.[528]

18
Conclusion

In the Introduction, I said a map of the human should do more than merely improve your understanding. It should help you go beyond understanding to action. It should help you not just to *understand* the dimensions of human life better but – far more important – to *act* within them in ways more consistent with the realities of the human spirit identified in this book. My aim was to go beyond ideas and concepts to practise: beyond a virtues social science or philosophy to a way of *living*. I said I hoped to help you *think* in the categories in which we actually *live* – so you don't have to go on living merely in the limited categories in which the Western world has become accustomed to think.[1]

To conclude, I want to come back to this objective. I want to review the meaning of this book for our world, and also what it can mean for you, and for your own life. I'll review here some of the reasons why rediscovering the full nature of the human is essential to the process which, in the previous chapter, I called "civilization": that is, to the ongoing process of developing greater civility, humaneness, or humanity in human life. In the first section of the chapter, I'll review the meaning of this book for our world, and in the second, what it can mean for you: why rediscovering the full nature of the human may be equally important for your own individual life.

The meaning of this book for our world

In this section, I'll recall some of the key reasons you've already encountered in this book why rediscovering the nature of the human is essential to developing a greater condition of civility and humanity in areas of common life we share – areas such as our political, societal, economic, organizational, cultural, global, and technological life.

Saving democracy and civilizing political life

In political life, understanding the nature of the human is essential to explain, first, why democracy is so important to the progress of human civilization, and second, what needs to be done to ensure not only the survival of democracy but its health and integrity. If it wasn't already obvious to you why a democratic, self-governing community is essential to human well-being – something that isn't obvious, apparently, to large portions of the world – the human paradox described in this book should help make that clearer. A free, open, democratic society is the only kind of political regime in which all the various, contradictory corners of the human I've described here can potentially have their say, can make themselves heard, can have a reasonable chance to participate in the political conversation – a conversation "made of stance" – and can be protected in doing so.[2] Any other kind of political regime will turn out to be a tyranny of some kind – even if it calls itself "libertarian" or, at the other extreme, a "people's republic" or a "national socialism." By virtue of its own non-democratic – and therefore authoritarian – nature, it will trample on some portion or portions of the human and exclude them from the conversation, or even persecute or seek to destroy them.

Of course, even democratic political regimes can do that, and have done it. Democratic majorities can be tyrannical too, as Tocqueville points out.[3] But only a democracy has a built-in corrective mechanism – the democratic political conversation and contest itself – in which, over time, that kind of injustice can potentially be brought to light and corrected. Because only a democracy – and this is the key point – is based on an implicit acknowledgment of the nature of the human, an acknowledgment of what makes humans human. As you saw in chapter 12, the permanent democratic contest between the primary political paradox of liberalism and conservatism – and, in the Western world, between the secondary paradox of socialism and libertarianism – is a contest and conversation between the four pillars of the human. It's a projection into public life of our own internal human dialogue between the four human stances and between their four families of human virtues. Democracy is an acknowledgment that, in human affairs, the law of non-contradiction doesn't apply. It's the only political regime based on acceptance of the fact that the nature of the human is a permanent and necessary contradiction. Not a contradiction to be solved or resolved, but rather, a contradiction that must be nourished and protected if humans are to remain human.[4] For the health of political life – just as much as in the nature of the human – there is, and must always be, a loyal opposition. And only a democracy is structured to provide it, and cherish it.

For the same reason, greater awareness of the human paradox is essential in order to transform political opponents from the "enemies" they're increasingly taken to be in our Western democracies back into the essential partners they really are. In the first half of the twenty-first century, the real challenges of public governance and the resulting fractiousness of political life in Western democracies are fuelling political cultures in which the legitimacy of opposing views is increasingly denied. Political parties are reverting to factions, the state and its instruments are often exploited without self-restraint for the benefit and goals of the ruling faction alone, and political opponents are regarded as enemies rather than as legitimate partners in a larger framework of democratic governance, to which all the participants are equally committed. If you talk literally about waging "war" on your political opponents – or if you boast about not playing by the "rules" – you are, by definition, not a civilizing participant in democratic politics.[5] Your actions and language are designed to destroy democracy, whether you recognize it or not.

Regarding political rivals as enemies and treating them that way is the death of democratic politics in practice, and the denial of democratic politics in principle.[6] The essence of democratic life is the acknowledgment of necessary contradiction: the difficult recognition that your opponent is as necessary to the public interest as you are and has a role to play that is just as important for the public good as your own. Because she or he represents some essential portion of the human – liberty, equality, excellence, reverence, or some part of them – more fully or powerfully than you can do, from your own perspective, that is to say, from your own sense of the current political order of priority among the human values and virtues.

Recognizing that democratic opponents are partners rather than enemies leads to a political version of what, throughout this book, I have called the "educational contract": a mutual bond based on awareness that none of us can grasp the whole truth about the human. Each of us can see only some portion of the truth, some dimension of the whole reality. A portion or dimension that no one else can see. Because we don't share the same perspective or see things the same way. Because I am I, and you are you. The only way we can get a little closer to the real truth, or to a vision of the whole reality, is to put *all* our perspectives together. The combined total of all our insights may not be the full truth about anything. But it will be truer than any partial view.[7] That means we have a moral obligation to share our own perspective with others and to listen carefully to what others are telling us about theirs. That's the educational contract. We're bound to each other by our commitment to assemble the whole truth about the world – or, at least something closer to it – by listening to, and learning from, each other.[8]

From this perspective, it's easy to see why R.G. Collingwood's definition of civilization is so important. It's impossible to imagine such an educational contract working except in a "dialectical" (or "dialogical") culture, one in which the aim is to reach agreement through discussion and dialogue. One in which the partners are willing to enter into a communion where they do not remain the same.[9] Where they allow themselves to be transformed by the experience of conversation, transformed by perspectives differing from their own: different views of the same truth for which all the partners in the conversation are searching.[10] In an "eristical" culture – where the aim isn't agreement, but rather, victory for one perspective and defeat for the others – the educational contract can't work. In fact, it has no relevance because there's no desire for learning and no willingness for self-transformation. The first is a civilizing culture, leading toward greater civility. The second leads in the other direction: toward some greater degree of barbarism. A society, polity, or organization animated by the spirit of an educational contract, I suggested earlier, will be a finer, nobler, and ultimately *more human* place than it could otherwise be.[11]

Each of us, and our political parties, can see or feel only a portion of the whole human paradox. And we therefore need each other. We need to listen to and learn from each other, if the whole truth is to emerge, and its claims are to be recognized in political life, as in life, period. We are bound together by an "educational contract." "[N]othing is really happening in the world," says Northrop Frye, "except the education of the people in it."[12] In chapter 12, the "paradox of politics" showed you that democratic political life isn't just a contest for power. It's also the moral life of the community and therefore a learning process, a political and social learning process, in which, at its best, I'm not just trying to win power so I can impose my views on you, but also listening and learning so that, over time, we – and our whole political society – can, in principle, agree.

The search for agreement – the assumption that, beneath all our apparent disagreements, we are already in agreement, or wish to be – is, as Collingwood argued, one of the key marks of civility, the standard or goal at which the process of civilization aims, without which a civilization would not be civilized or civilizing. The fact that political life is a necessary and permanent contradiction doesn't mean it's condemned to deadlock or is simply a dead end. Because of the value it attaches to deliberation and due process, democratic governments will often be "slower" than autocratic governments. In the short term, they can appear less "effective." In a contest between them, democratic governments can seem to start at a disadvantage, with one-arm tied behind their backs. But the vaunted "effectiveness" of authoritarian governments is illusory. And very short-term. Their immediate effectiveness is purchased at the price of suppressing the very diversity and dialogue essential to the learning process required for genuine, long-term advancement – a learning process without which the journey would not lead to a genuinely human destination. It would not lead to a goal or future compatible with human dignity, or with the full or true nature of the human.

The political paradox is compatible with decision-making and good government. And it's also the condition of genuine political progress. The dialogue and learning process of the political contest are the very ways in which political progress is achieved.[13] The search for agreement – the effort to persuade and convince, the assumption that agreement is both desirable and possible – is also both the starting point and the goal which make progress possible, which drive the political contest forward, toward its goal, and make it civilizing, rather than just a non-violent alternative to civil war. Commitment to the educational contract of political life is a commitment to the conditions of the learning process itself – and to each other.

It would be much easier for political actors to see and feel the bond or partnership with their opponents if they could see the need for the same thing within themselves. If they could see the contradictions of the human paradox alive and at work in their own lives and political views. As I pointed out in chapter 12, one of the sources of uncivilized or uncivil conflict between opposing political (or philosophical) positions or views is the failure of the participants to see the contradictions inherent in their *own* outlook.[14] If it's a legitimate contribution to the political conversation, their own outlook is, by definition, unstable, structured by a tension between its own internal, contrary poles. Because they don't see the inherent contradictions in their own views, political actors also can't see that the "educational contract" between themselves and their opponents is just an external, mirror image of the same contract between the opposing (but overlooked) poles of their *own* position in the political geography of the human, and just as essential.[15]

This suggests, incidentally, why a vision of the human based on both virtues and values is ultimately more promising than one based on values alone. A pure language of values can allow you to distance yourself from someone else's "values." They may be values for *her*, but they don't have to be values for *you*. You can turn your back on them. You may want to resist, oppose, or even fight someone else's values.[16] The language of the virtues doesn't allow you to distance yourself from others quite as easily. When you acknowledge something to be a virtue, you recognize it as good or worthy: an admirable, desirable, maybe even necessary way to be human. When you acknowledge something as a virtue, you recognize that it has some kind of claim, not just on others, but also on you.[17] You acknowledge that it is a good or even essential way to be human, part of what it is to be a full, genuine, or true human being. And therefore it's a kind of behaviour to which you, too, should aspire in some way, or to some degree. Virtues *pull* or *call* us in ways that values alone may not.[18]

Societal life and the nature of the human

Awareness of the full nature of the human is therefore just as important for economic, social, and (in the broadest sense) cultural life as it is for political life, and for many of the same reasons. Only an awareness of the full nature of the human can give us the perspective we need on our current Western cultural situation and dilemmas, on the limits of the cultural assumptions we've been building up for ourselves ever since the time of Aristotle, and especially in the last four hundred years or so. Over all that time, to its great credit, Western culture has vastly enlarged our human awareness of two of the important families of virtues that make humans human. But in doing so, it has gradually lost sight of the other two – while surreptitiously calling on them and building on them, especially in fields such as human rights and social justice. Over the last few centuries, we've been playing the human game with a declining portion of the full deck. We have come to define the human as only half of the full nature of the human.[19] And as we now plunge back into a Western culture centred increasingly in the virtues of Liberty (A1) – in the virtues of Power (A1a) and of Pleasure (A1b) – we find ourselves confused, not knowing how – or even whether – to reconcile these primal energies and all their creative and destructive potential, with the virtues of Equality (B2) and the rational, self-controlling creatures we thought we were. Let alone with the dimly remembered virtues of reverence from which both of these modern and post-modern families emerged.

Civilizing the market

One of the results is our current confusion about the role of the private market in Western countries. The overriding importance given to the freedom of the market and of private enterprise by many in the West today is simply a reflection of the virtues of self-assertion – to which the arrow of virtue has returned in Western culture – and the growing dominance of the virtues of Liberty (A1) in the first decades of the twenty-first century. As Figure 73 (on page 528) shows you, the free market is an essential expression of the human. But it represents only one pole of the human, not the whole. Greater awareness of the full range of values and virtues that define our humanity is an essential condition for achieving a healthy balance between economic and market forces on the one hand, and the proper roles of the state, the family, and civil society, on the other. Though they have powerful defenders and supporters elsewhere (especially in the virtues of Equality [B2], the primary home of intellectual disciplines like economics), market values have their own primary home in the virtues of Liberty (A1). Market values are one way you can view the world when you're practising the virtues of self-assertion, and more specifically, the virtues of Liberty (A1). These virtues are an essential part of the human. But they aren't everything. Market values are in a constant, dynamic tension with the other families of virtues that define the human. As I pointed out in chapters 11 and 12, the instrumental virtues of the market are in tension not only with equality, fairness, and reciprocity – virtues of Equality (B2), the other side of the virtues of self-assertion – but also with all the virtues of reverence – virtues such as care, concern, respect, justice, gratitude, sacrifice, responsibility, sympathy, generosity, thoughtfulness, friendship, love, and the disposition to nurture – virtues that make up at least half the nature of the human.

The market mentality isn't the value-neutral outlook it claims to be, in the contemporary Western world. It's not just that market reasoning needs to be balanced or redeemed by moral reasoning. The values of the free market are, in fact, without recognizing it, a covert *form* of virtue, disguised as value-neutrality. Under the cover of neutrality, they smuggle in their own values and virtues.[20] But they're only one form of human virtue, among many. They're important. But they're rooted in only one of the four families of human values – and don't account even for all the virtues of their *own* corner of the human. They're only a subset of the virtues of Liberty (A1). If allowed to rule alone, the market mentality can crowd out all the other vital dimensions that make humans most human. Even for markets themselves to work effectively, they need to be completed and supported by all the other virtues that constitute the nature of the human, and by the institutions in which these other virtues find *their* primary homes. The human paradox helps you put the market – and the corner of the human where it's most at home – back into necessary moral perspective, within the overall nature of the human. Rediscovering the nature of the human is an important condition for achieving a creative and liberating balance between the institutional expressions of the four corners of the human. The unregulated market is just as great a threat to human good as its opposite, the unfettered, authoritarian, all-intrusive state. If we are to steer safely between the Scylla of the market and the Charybdis of the state, we need to relearn who we are, in our full humanity.

Civilizing organizational life

A richer understanding of the human paradox can also contribute to improving the quality of the organizations in which most of us spend most of our lives.

As you saw in chapter 13, even the very best management frameworks – those that recognize the conflicting nature of the virtues – often don't do justice to the full nature of the human. In fact, they are largely constructed from a narrow subset of the virtues, from the instrumental virtues of Liberty (A1), the virtues of the market. They don't normally recognize this limitation, however, and take their "competing" values to be an adequate description of the dynamics of organizational life. As a result, organizational theories and management practices can make it harder for the places where we live our everyday lives to become more responsive and nourishing. They can make it harder for organizations to enhance not just their own "performance" but also the well-being of their employees and of their surrounding communities and societies.

Because of the limited set of virtues and values they identify, organizations may not always give enough conscious emphasis to virtues of Excellence (B1), such as fairness (as what is due), responsibility and solidarity (as duty), or justice and truth, for example. Let alone to virtues of Reverence (A2), such as communion, loyalty, respectfulness, trust, mutuality, generosity, and benevolence. And they may not recognize that traditional upward accountability to superiors should be matched and balanced by an equal "downward accountability" of management to employees, a deep moral responsibility superiors have, or should have, for their employees. That loyalty is a two-way street.

Although animated in principle by a wider range of values than private organizations, even public organizations have their own distinctive motivations and requirements for an overwhelming focus on "managing upward." The very responsiveness of public organizations to political direction – which is the essential, beating heart of their democratic missions – can make public organizations (especially those closest to the centre of government) even more upward-focussed than private organizations. A wider, richer understanding of the nature of the human can help both private and public organizations develop internal cultures that are more democratic, participatory, and accountable – where there is not just greater recognition of employee "rights," but even reverence for "what is below us" – and it can help to strengthen their focus on employee engagement, organizational well-being, and public responsibility.

Understanding the human paradox can help organizations develop "thicker" concepts of the good, especially the social good, as well as a view of their various stakeholders not just as clients, customers, or contractors but as full human beings. That is to say, as citizens. Bearers both of rights and of duties, in a framework of democratic community. This may be newer ground for private organizations, but public organizations have much to learn, too. Indeed, two key tests for the "public interest" that should be employed in assessing any important policy decision are: first, is the range of values employed in assessing the wisdom of the decision wide enough? Does it reflect the full nature of the human or just some arbitrary subset, maybe just the virtues of Liberty (A1) or the virtues of self-assertion? Second, has sufficient weight been given to the highest virtues, to those at the top of the hierarchy of values, at the top of what, in this book I have called the reverse order of the arrow of virtue?

In these and other ways, rediscovering the nature of the human can help all organizations become both better workplaces and better "citizens," better contributors to the public good.

Human rights and civilization

Current debates about human rights, in many Western countries, are another sign that the vital centre of Western culture may be crossing the line from the virtues of Equality (B2) to the virtues of Liberty (A1), where the story of the human began. If so, this is a time of peril for some of the highest values in Western civilization, and for its noblest achievements.

But the return to the virtues of Liberty (A1) could be an opportunity, as well as a danger. We can turn it into an opportunity if we are able to use this turning point (like the crisis of climate change) as a learning opportunity – an opportunity to rediscover the whole nature of the human and the forgotten families of virtues whose underground energies secretly fuel our legitimate, necessary concern for human rights: not just our own rights, but also the rights *of others*. We can turn this danger into an opportunity if we are able to see it as another turn on a spiral staircase. We can make it a forward step, rather than a backward step in the process of civilization if we use it as an opportunity not just to re-consider the role of majority rights, but also to survey the entire nature of the human. Survey it now, from a higher perspective, from a higher rung on the staircase, a rung from which we can look back over the whole arrow of virtue that has brought to where we are today.

And not just look or survey, but also embrace. It's an opportunity to embrace the full range of human virtues the arrow of virtue reveals to us, and which defines who we are as human beings. Embracing the whole nature of the human opens the door to a kind of social cohesion that goes beyond bare tolerance (B2b) – worthy and desirable though it is – to a vision of solidarity and communion (A2a), in which legitimate difference is not a danger or a threat but a necessary complementarity within the whole human paradox. It leads to the social and cultural version of the "educational contract." And it leads to a renewed cultural confidence based on an unanswerable vision of the necessary and fundamental unity of human life.

Global climate change and the human paradox

The urgency of a renewed awareness of the four poles of the human paradox, and of their meaning and importance for the process of civilization, is, if anything, even more obvious at the global level. First of all, without renewed awareness and – far more important – renewed *practice* of the virtues of reverence, we won't be able to solve the immense challenge of global climate change and all the other environmental challenges waiting behind it, which, taken together, threaten the survival of civilization, even in its purely functional sense, let alone the normative meaning you encountered in the previous chapter. We *will* rediscover those virtues, in one way or another, either consciously or unconsciously, directly or indirectly, willingly or unwillingly, because the behaviours they entail are the ones we will have to adopt if life is to survive in the fragile ecosystem of our planet. Unless we learn them or relearn them, there will be no "deep future" ahead for the human race.

Civilizing AI

The threat to human life from rogue AI and super-intelligence may be just as great as the threat of climate change. This kind of AI would be neither "beneficial" nor "friendly" – but instead, just as inherently self-assertive as its rational programmers and their programs. Unless we can find a way to develop super-intelligent AI that mirrors us *at our best* – as the people we *aspire* to be, not just as we actually *are* – the future of the world won't involve us. Developing AI that mirrors us at our best will require us to rediscover who we really are. Not just thinking things, but *beings*: beings shaped by being and defined by the virtues. Beings whose virtues aren't aligned, however, but contradictory. The challenge isn't just aligning AI with our goals, as some AI thinkers suggest.[21] It's that our goals *themselves* aren't aligned – and can never be aligned if our genuine humanity is to be preserved. If our values could be aligned, we would cease to be human – and would be more like computers or a kind of software. Our virtues are inherently contradictory: both self-assertive *and* reverent. Contradictory – but potentially capable of "perfecting" and "overflowing." Developing "beneficial" or "friendly" AI may require us to find the "reverse" (teleological or moral) path of the arrow of virtue: the path that leads from the "*It* is" (B2) of cybernetics and informatics to the "It *is*" (B1) of wisdom and understanding, and eventually to the "I *am*" (A2) from which even wisdom and understanding draw all their value and meaning. It may require us to rediscover not just the virtues of reason and self-assertion but also unfamiliar virtues like *un*knowing and *un*selfing, and all the other virtues of reverence.

The challenge of religious radicalism

In the twenty-first century, the fate of civilization is also threatened by new forms of religious fanaticism. An illicit alliance between the virtues of Liberty (A1) (the purest, rawest form of self-assertion), the virtues of Equality (B2) (the virtues of conviction and belief), and the virtues of Excellence (B1) – an alliance from which the authentic virtues of Reverence (A2) (the virtues of mercy and compassion) are largely excluded – has spawned a fanaticism that now wreaks violence in many parts of the globe, including within our own Western countries. Combatting this threat effectively also hangs upon a rediscovery of the human paradox because this threat comes to us from sources within the human the Western world has largely forgotten or no longer takes seriously. Sources that challenge and reject many of the assumptions about the human we take for granted. We're right to fight back against this new form of barbarism, militarily and through our domestic security, police, and justice systems. The "ordinary" virtues alone aren't enough to deal with this kind of violent barbarism.[22] Evil armed can only be met by force, by the armoured might of justice.[23] And we're also right to fight back intellectually. We're right to insist that the virtues of Liberty (A1) and Equality (B2) are real virtues, and that their discovery, development, and protection within our Western culture is an enormous step forward for humanity and for human civilization.

But we're unlikely to deal effectively with religious radicalism until we appreciate where it's coming from within the nature of the human. Which is to say, *within ourselves*. As long as we think the deep impulses behind the behaviours we abhor are simply alien, we will have great difficulty understanding or anticipating those behaviours, let alone countering them, even within our own countries. If we're blind to the huge post-modern gap, hole, or void in the nature of the human that religious fanaticism – and angry, proto-fascist populisms in our own countries – seek to fill, how can we combat them effectively? To say nothing of the wider kind of dialogue or conversation necessary for world peace. We're fully justified in defending the virtues of self-assertion and insisting they be respected and protected by others. But how can we expect this message to be heard, if we aren't able to see or acknowledge the equal role the virtues of reverence play in the nature of the human, whether or not they take an explicitly "religious" form? Religious fanaticism may be a distortion or caricature. It is self-assertion masquerading as reverence. But the masquerade is a deadly perversion of something genuine about the human. Something genuine about ourselves. Something without which humans wouldn't be human.

Global dialogue and the nature of the human

Relearning the reality of the human paradox is a first step to engaging effectively with the background cultures from which fanaticism grows. It's also a step toward a unifying, peace-making, global dialogue with the world's diverse cultures, outlooks, and ideologies, all of which have their root in some corner or corners of the human. Continuing the advancement of human rights may require us to recognize the various sources in the human from which they have come, and without which they would not have been established: not just the virtues of Equality (B2) that *claim* rights, but also the virtues of reverence that *give* rights. And within them, not just the virtues of Excellence (B1), the initial source from which that giving comes, but also the virtues of Reverence (A2) – mercy, generosity, kindness, compassion, love, and so on – from which this spirit of *giving* itself comes.

In a world divided by culture, religion, ideology, and self-interest, the virtues can be a unifying force by offering us a common, shared language. The virtues are the common language of humanity because they are the language of our common *humanity*. The language that defines what it means to be human. They are the "best items to form an intercultural language" and offer our best hope for intercultural understanding in a globalized world.[24] Understanding better how they all fit together – how each of them expresses some part of the whole nature of the human – is a necessary condition for the mutual respect required by our global and national communities, as we struggle to achieve social justice and solidarity, and to save the planet from the ecological and technological consequences of our own Western self-assertion. The virtues offer us our best path forward to prepare for our "deep future" and pursue the dialectical, dialogical, or paradoxical process of civilization.

Civilization and the virtues

Reaching the next turn in the staircase of Western civilization – with a view out over the whole arrow of virtue and the whole nature of the human – can give us a renewed sense of what's at stake in the *process* of civilization. It could reacquaint us with the essence of that process and how to protect it. And it could help us see what's currently missing from that process, the voices we no longer hear as clearly as we should, the virtues we've forgotten, but which we neglect at our peril. The virtues without which humans wouldn't be human.

However, above and beyond the role of specific virtues (or specific families of virtues) in the nature of the human, the fate of civilization seems to hang upon a rediscovery of virtue itself and its place in the definition of the human. From Aristotle to the Enlightenment, Western culture gradually learned to define human beings as rational animals, as thinking things. As an exclusive definition, this was always implausible. But for a long time, it was balanced by conscious cultivation of the human virtues derived from earlier mythic and mimetic cultures. When the virtues disappeared from Western culture, with Kant, the definition of humans by their rationality alone began to ring hollow. It rings even more hollow now, as we develop forms of artificial intelligence, and as the critical mass of Western culture begins to cross the line from the Enlightenment virtues of Equality (B2) back into the post-modern, anti-Enlightenment virtues of Liberty (A1). We're clearly not just the thinking things the Enlightenment thought we were, but much more. Unless we wish to drown ourselves in the virtues of Power (A1a) and of Pleasure (A1b), we need to rediscover how *much* more. We need to redefine the nature of the human not just as a rational animal, but as an animal capable of virtue.[25]

There is nothing our Western culture requires more urgently than a renewed discourse about virtue itself. And a new cultural *premise* about virtue.[26] Our political and cultural conversations should start from a premise about the nature of the human, based not just on human rationality but, more fundamentally, on our human capacity for virtue –

of which reason is only one form, or at best, two. There is scarcely any area of contemporary Western life – from child development and education, to human rights, architecture, urban planning, and artificial intelligence – that is not affected, for the worse, by our current silence about the virtues, about human goodness.[27] By our inability or unwillingness to start the conversation from an ideal of human virtue and to say how each aspect of our common life enhances – or weakens – the four basic families of human virtues, and which ones are affected, and in what ways. In every area of public policy and our common life, we should adopt some version of Peterson and Seligman's suggested approach to child development: "Rather than adopting a 'more is better' approach to the activities … we should stop and ask what [virtues] we want the activity to accomplish … and whether the details of this activity indeed accomplish its stated goal vis-à-vis a targeted character strength [i.e., virtue]."[28] If civilization is to remain a genuinely civilizing process – not just an ever-increasing technical competence to "get things done in the world," a capacity that can easily take *in*human forms – our social conversation and our cultural debates should start from the human virtues, and should be about how best to nourish and sustain them in our "deep future" ahead.[29]

Rediscovering the human paradox in the public sphere – at the national and global levels – can also be an opportunity to rediscover our own individual selves.

What this book can mean for you

"Every single one of us is a little civilization," says Marilynne Robinson.[30]

This is an insight of the greatest importance for the conclusion of this book. Marilynne Robinson's equation between civilization and our individual selves brings me back, at the close, to the objective I stated at the beginning: to help you not just to *understand* human life better but also to *act* in ways that are more consistent with the nature of the human.

The process of civilization, the process of developing greater civility and humaneness in human life, isn't just a challenge and objective *out there*, as it were, in the wider world of society, organizations, politics, and global affairs. It's also a challenge *in here*. Inside yourself and in your own individual human life. The two are connected – yet another two-way street. Increasing civility and humanity in the world can certainly help each of us to live in a more civilized and civilizing manner. But it works the other way, too. There can be no process of civilization in the wider world if each of us isn't doing our part, in our own lives and spirits, to advance that same process within ourselves. There can be no democracy without democrats, and no civilization without civilized people.

How can we live our lives in ways that reflect the reality that every single one of us is a little civilization? You can perhaps understand and apply Marilynne Robinson's insight in your own life, in at least two ways. They correspond to the two different but complementary ways (dialogical and moral) of thinking about the teleological meaning (as opposed to the genetic or functional meaning) of civilization.

The first (or dialogical way) is to see yourself as a microcosm of what, in chapter 12, I called the political paradox. As I pointed out in the Introduction, each one of us is like a little democracy.[31] We have conflicting voices and perspectives inside ourselves that are just like the contending parties of political life. That's one of the big lessons from your discovery, or rediscovery, of the human paradox. As you've seen in this book, those contending voices within us are the four families of virtues – and all the sub-families and sub-sub-families into which the process of separative projection divides them, and sub-divides them, *ad infinitum*. In fact, the contending forces of political life are really just an external mirror of the human paradox you can find inside yourself.

Your discovery – or rediscovery – that the nature of the human is defined by four families of virtues (and all their theoretically infinite sub-sub-families) suggests that the educational contract is as important *internally* – within ourselves – as it is *externally*, in society, politics, and organizations. Just as we assemble greater truth by listening to and learning from each other, so too can we assemble the whole truth (or something closer to it) only by listening to and learning from our different selves – listening to and learning from all four families of virtues and all the infinite contradictions that cascade from each of them. The nature of the human also requires an *internal* "educational contract" between all the virtues. The internal dialogue of the human spirit – the human paradox – is just as important as the dialectics or dialogue of public space. And the two are connected. As Plato taught in *The Republic*, they are but two sides, mirror images, of the same thing.[32] Without a rich conversation between the various poles of the human paradox *within* ourselves, we aren't likely to be able to sustain a genuine conversation *between* ourselves. To advance the process of civilization, the conversation has to begin within.

Recognizing the infinite ways in which you, like all other human beings, are necessarily divided against yourself, can be a disturbing discovery at first. But it should also be a potential source of comfort and reassurance. First of all, it can help you to recognize yourself. I hope you've been able to recognize each of the families and sub-families of virtues in yourself. There should be some relief in seeing that all those contradictory impulses you feel inside yourself are a necessary part of being human. A relief and comfort, also, in understanding where they come from and how they're related.

The conflicts you already know are lurking within you – if you're being honest with yourself – aren't something negative, a failing or weakness on your part. They're not something about which you should be ashamed or embarrassed. Instead, they're a necessary part of your humanity. Especially when you're trying to act well, or in the light of your deepest intuitions about goodness, or virtue. The multiple human personality isn't abnormal, and the integrated personality normal. It's the other way around. The conflicting multiplicity of all the potential "you's" inside you isn't just an accident: it's the very nature of the human.[33] We start in diversity. Uniting all that diversity, all those conflicting virtues, into an integrated human being is a high moral challenge, maybe the greatest challenge we face in our lives. It isn't a given. It's a "task," as Paul Ricœur says.[34] A "project" and a solemn "trust," as Martin Heidegger puts it.[35] It's the challenge of achieving integrity or wholeness. Achieving wholeness or "completeness" means we need to have the same kind of ongoing decision-making and good government inside ourselves that's the hallmark of a healthy democratic state. Achieving personal integrity and wholeness is the challenge of establishing "a free and yet absolute government in our own spirits."[36] The challenge of making your own little civilization.

Developing the process of civilization as an individual and in your own individual life means developing your own internal "educational contract." It means deciding to live (in Collingwood's words) "dialectically" rather than "eristically." It means taking all of these contending virtues inside yourself seriously, not dismissing the claims of some from the start, just because it would be convenient and easier to do so. Just because it would be less demanding or disturbing. It means developing what Goethe calls "reverence for oneself." It means thinking of yourself just like *another* person for whom you have a solemn trust. Your self is entrusted to you. Your *whole* self. Reverence for yourself means listening carefully to all of the contrary virtues. Those still, small voices that tug at your sleeve, whisper in your ear, and won't go away. It also means establishing your own respectful, attentive, internal conversation between them. A conversation that aims at agreement. Not an agreement in which some of the virtues are defeated or cast aside. But an agreement that contains, preserves, and cherishes *dis*agreement. An agreement in which the contending virtues are all kept very much in play. As if each one of them were an "axiom" (as Iris Murdoch and Max Scheler put it) that can't be overruled.

The moral necessity of keeping all the virtues in play – treating them as if each one were an "axiom" – is one reason why none of us will ever achieve complete harmony, integration, or integrity. We will all have our own distinctive blend and balance of the virtues, the combination and emphasis that give us our character, and make us who we are – a recognizable, moral individual.

Plato's and Jung's ideal of "completeness" can never be fully achieved. It must always remain a goal or ideal, not an achieved reality.[37] It must remain a quest, an unachieved aspiration, because of the contradictions of the human paradox itself. But not for that reason alone. It will also remain permanently beyond your reach because of the "trap door" of the virtues of Reverence (A2). This corner of the human makes unlimited, infinite demands on us.[38] Because nothing is due, everything is due. Because giving is for the sake of giving, you can never give enough. You can never acquit yourself of your responsibility for others. You can never pay off your debt. These "unreasonable" demands of the virtues of Reverence (A2) continually upset the applecart of life. They break open established patterns and settled habits. They push us on to the next stage or level of life.[39] They make any final balance and reasoned compromise ultimately impossible to achieve.

But, even if "completeness" or "agreement" between the virtues is never quite achieved, *aiming for it is everything*. That's what keeps the conversation going and makes it civilized or civilizing.[40] The "search for the view from *manywheres*" is what makes you, truly, a little civilization.[41] You're much less likely to listen carefully, and with civility, to your neighbour – and even less to your opponent – if you're not doing the same thing inside yourself. If you aren't developing and nourishing a rich, unceasing, internal dialogue between the contending virtues, between your multiple selves. If you haven't established your own internal "educational contract."[42]

The goal of establishing a "free and yet absolute government" in your own spirit can seem, at first, to be at odds with the "educational contract" between the conflicting virtues and the multiple selves they create within you. It *would* be at odds, were it not for the second (or what I called "moral") way you can develop the process of civilization in your own life. This second way is to take seriously Levinas' and Iain Pears' insight that the heart of civility and civilization ultimately lies in those same self-giving virtues of reverence. It can't be found in the mastery and control offered by the virtues of self-assertion – or maybe not even in Collingwood's and Gadamer's "dialectical" conversation, unless it's animated or infused by something else. It can't be found in our human reason or intelligence – *no matter how intelligent* – but rather in the everyday virtues of self-giving, in "the little goodness," "la petite bonté." In the "ordinary virtues" of a generous human heart. In simple kindheartedness, generosity, and selflessness. In a kind of friendship and conversation whose imperatives go way beyond reciprocity. A lovingkindness and mercy. A self-giving reverence for others. Even to the point, if necessary, of laying down one's life for one's friends. The heart of civility and civilization is to be found in the spirit of those simple, spontaneous, emblematic words, uttered in the very depths of human terror: "*Naturellement, entrez, entrez* – Of course, come in, come in."

In other words, becoming a little civilization of your own means rediscovering the critical importance of the virtues of reverence in your life, and especially the virtues of Reverence (A2), the vital missing link between our animal origins and our human rationality. It means rediscovering how the virtues of reverence overflow into the virtues of self-assertion, how they "perfect" or "entrain" them. The virtues of Reverence (A2) are ultimately what make humans human.[43] Whenever we value our "humanity," we "presuppose" these virtues and values. And it is *only* in presupposing them that human beings can become truly worthy of their own humanity.[44] The inability to exercise these virtues – to put others first – would condemn artificial intelligence never to be genuinely human or humane. This *in*ability would guarantee that, the more intelligent AI becomes, the more *in*human it may well be. In contrast, the often rich *ability* of people with intellectual disabilities to exercise these same self-giving virtues is what allows them to be so profoundly human. What makes humans human isn't just a kind of thinking, but a capacity for moral intuition with feeling (A2). This kind of intuition and feeling leads to reverent behaviour, to reverent actions, or virtues, and lays the foundation for all good thinking.

Thinking is essential. It allows us to refine and deepen our intuitions. We can't get along without it. But without the prior virtues of reverence, it leads nowhere. At least, nowhere human.[45] Reverence is the "one thing," as Goethe says, "on which everything depends and *by which man becomes human in the full sense.*"[46] "We are, as we always have been, dangerous creatures, the enemies of our own happiness," says Marilynne Robinson. "But the only help we have ever found for this, the only melioration, is in mutual reverence."[47]

Rediscovering the self-giving virtues of reverence – and especially the virtues of Reverence (A2) – can lead you to another important discovery: that there's more than one kind of happiness.[48] There's no question more "ultimate" for human beings than "what's the meaning or goal of life?" What if our post-modern Western pursuit of happiness were looking for the wrong kind of goal, or looking for it in the wrong place? The happiness our modern and post-modern world normally pursues is what's called "flourishing," a kind of contentment, the satisfaction of all our wants and desires – or as many of them as may be possible and reasonable.[49] This kind of happiness is a virtue of self-assertion.[50] The pursuit of this kind of happiness has brought many good things to our modern and post-modern world. It's part of what Charles Taylor calls the "affirmation of ordinary life."[51] It has carved out a new and necessary space, in modern and post-modern Western culture, for the virtues of self-assertion.

But this kind of happiness, as David Brooks says, is "insufficient."[52] It can't really bring you what you're truly looking for in your life.[53] And it's not the only kind of happiness, either.[54] Modern notions of "flourishing" or "happiness" (what Aristotle calls, in Greek, *eudaimonia*) usually don't make enough room for the disquiet or anxiety that must go with a mature, adult awareness of the surrounding mystery, and of the deep, inexhaustible human obligations toward others we discover in the virtues of reverence.[55] We're responsible for others not because they are lovable, or desirable, or beautiful. They may be inconvenient, tiresome, or even threatening. We're responsible for them simply because they *are*. And because they are *other*. Because they are human.[56] The other can be unwelcome or disturb us. We might be glad to get rid of our responsibility if we could. But we can't. Because we're human. In our relationship with other human beings, we're sometimes almost like hostages or prisoners. Against our will. Or at least against our own self-assertion.[57]

Accepting your deep responsibility for others leads to a different kind of happiness. Awareness of the deep seriousness of our situation turns flourishing into something more like "fullness" or fulfilment. Fullness brings a kind of fulfilment that's more like "joy." Joy makes room for the gravity and seriousness of life – for "sober anxiety" – in a way that the modern and post-modern meaning of "happiness" does not.[58] It's the "quiet sense of gratitude and tranquility that comes [not as a goal but simply] as a byproduct of successful moral struggle." The truly human life isn't just the pursuit of happiness but a larger "moral drama": the drama of your own personal struggle to be virtuous, which is the "central drama of life."[59] "[N]othing in life is of any value," says Iris Murdoch, "except the attempt to be virtuous."[60] If "happiness" is a virtue, value, or good of self-assertion, the corresponding good of the virtues of reverence is *goodness itself*. Which brings with it not happiness or human flourishing, but a kind of human fulfilment or fullness.[61] The "fullness of eternity."[62] The fullness of doing what is right or good, whether or not it leads to anything that could be called "happiness."[63] Even if it causes you to lay down your life – in one sense or another – for others.[64] Emmanuel Levinas uses the biblical word "glory" to express this other kind of human fulfilment, the fullness that lies *beyond* happiness and flourishing: the moral grandeur of our human predicament, and the way in which our limitless responsibility for others seems to open us out to infinity.[65]

Some contemporary thinkers like Richard Rorty want even thinking to be a form of "play," just as so many contemporary adults assume that life is supposed to be "fun."[66] But someone who wants to remain at the stage of play simply refuses to get serious or to grow up.[67] Play is an essential stage and component of life – in individual lives and in the life of the human race. It allowed the earliest humans to open a space for meaning, for the virtues of reverence, and, eventually, for civilization.[68] As something that is done for its own sake, and not for the sake of something else, it was essential to developing the nature of the human.[69] It helped prepare the original human transition, the "great reversal" – in prehistoric hunting bands and tribal cultures – from the virtues of Liberty (A1) to the virtues of Reverence (A2). So maybe the contemporary enthusiasm for "play" – and for the other virtues of Liberty (A1) – could go beyond the frivolous and prepare us for a similar transition. Perhaps they could prepare us to rediscover the meaning of joy and of glory, prepare us to rediscover the seriousness and fulfilment of true adult reverence.[70] A self-giving that goes "way beyond" the reciprocity or cooperation of the virtues of Equality (B2), "a self-giving not bounded by some measure of fairness."[71]

Fullness doesn't promise contentment or satisfaction.[72] The quest for it may mean "failing utterly on the scales of human flourishing."[73] In fact, such a quest can sometimes be to your "own hurt."[74] It can even make for a "hard, laborious, troubled life."[75] It can, at the limit, cause you to lay down your life for your friends or for others. Or to risk doing so, by opening your door to a stranger. But it's a truer kind of happiness, a nobler kind of happiness, more worthy of a human and of the whole nature of the human: the virtues of reverence as well as the virtues of self-assertion.[76] This is the "deep happiness of the entirely self-abandoned [i.e., *unselfing*], not the easy shallow satisfaction of those who live to express themselves and enjoy themselves."[77] Happiness as fullness includes a kind of self-giving that isn't just self-seeking. A giving *for the sake of giving*. From which flows everything that makes us genuinely human, not just rational animals.

But here's yet another paradox. This kind of self-giving also turns out, paradoxically, to be the highest and most fulfilling kind of self-seeking. Because self-giving leads you to the kind of self that's genuinely *worth* seeking. In this sense, fullness might be said to "entrain" happiness, just as reverence "perfects" self-assertion.[78] Paul of Tarsus describes it as "having nothing, and yet possessing everything."[79] Those who don't set out in pursuit of what we conventionally call "happiness," but seek, instead, to serve others (we sometimes call them "saints") often find a kind of wisdom and fulfilment – a kind of "humanness" – that makes them an inspiration for others.[80]

The highest form of self-assertion turns out to be a kind of reverence; just as the highest form of reverence is, by definition, self-assertion.[81] In his study of those who resisted Nazi terror to rescue or protect persecuted Jews, Michel Terestchenko discovered that their heroic actions were not rooted in some kind of negation, destruction, or immolation of the self, but instead, in an almost joyful self-fulfilment. They did not have to *overcome* the self to act as they did. They acted to *fulfil* the self. To act otherwise, they felt, would have been untrue to their true self. And so, they *asserted* their true selves, *their whole selves* – the *whole* nature of the human. They performed their deep acts of reverence and compassion with the deepest and truest kind of self-assertion. They acted spontaneously, with energy, resolution, courage, and even a kind of quiet joy.[82]

In this higher vision of happiness – a happiness that's fullness, and not just flourishing – giving is also a kind of receiving. And receiving is a kind of giving. It is in giving that we receive.[83] And it is in receiving that we give. Without receivers there can be no givers. The response of the beloved "affirms" the love of the lover. The self-giving love of the lover is "recreated anew in the trust of the beloved."[84] Only when you truly receive something as a gift can you really learn to recognize the giver and the spirit in which the giver gives.[85] Received in this way, a gift arouses feelings of love for the giver "and a desire to express these feelings by making a reciprocal gift of one's own."[86] Learning to receive reverently is almost as important as developing a habit of giving. Perhaps this is the ultimate human paradox: the paradox that our separateness and our unity – our union and our non-union – are ultimately united and preserved in both the giving *and* the receiving of human reverence.[87] In this kind of vision of the human, giving and receiving "merge," or blend into each other.[88] Together they keep "the gift in motion through self-perpetuating cycles of giving and receiving."[89] "It is a proof of the regard of God for the happiness of mankind," says Samuel Johnson, "that the means by which it must be attained, are obvious

and evident."[90] And what is this secret of human happiness that Johnson says is so "obvious"? "To receive and communicate assistance," he
says, "constitutes the happiness of human life."[91]

Waking up – to the *other* freedom

Maybe our post-modern idea of "happiness" is a little like being asleep –
a kind of "sleeping to death."[92] Maybe the rational consciousness
on which modern Western culture prided itself – and which we
post-moderns still assume defines the nature of the human, at least
when it suits us to do so – maybe rational consciousness isn't as conscious – as aware, or as alert – as we think it is. Maybe it's actually a
kind of drowsiness or slumber, the sleepiness of self-assertion.

Maybe the self-assertion at the heart of modern and post-modern culture means that we are wilfully "asleep" to some important realities.
Asleep to the fact that, in our daily lives and preferences, we're increasingly betraying the rational consciousness on which we still claim to
pride ourselves. Asleep to the fact that, even if we were more faithful to it,
rational consciousness floats and surfs on something else: on life itself, on
the prior appetites and moral energies that make humans human. Asleep
to the fact that our modern and post-modern virtues of self-assertion
developed – and ultimately depend – upon a necessary foundation of human reverence. Asleep to the very "humanity" of our humanity. Asleep
to the fact that others are suffering – perhaps even suffering because of
our own actions, or the place that we occupy in the world, the very space
we take up in the world (the very *Da* of our *Dasein*).[93] Asleep to our responsibility for them and to the claim they make on us. Asleep to the fact
that the world itself is dying: dying because of our own self-assertion and
its cumulative impact on global climate and the ecosphere.

Recognizing all these things more clearly – and accepting our responsibility for them, the responsibility to do something about them –
would be a kind of "waking up."[94]

Not just waking up to a new kind of *knowledge*, but to a different
kind of *virtue*. To the virtues of reverence. Reverence calls on us to stay
awake and be watchful. To keep the watch. The long, slow watches of
the night.[95]

Maybe desire could take us to the farthest edge of desire again, as it
did long ago. Not just erotic desire, or the desire for pleasure and for
play. But desire reaching out beyond itself. To that which it cannot see
and cannot name.[96] To the desire beyond desire. To that without which
desire can never be slaked. Without which desire will remain – or become – a scorching, all-consuming, self-consuming inferno.[97]

Maybe desire could be the next step on the spiral staircase of the arrow of virtue. Maybe it could serve, again, like a refiner's fire.[98] Burning and *purifying* itself. Taking us beyond the virtues of self-assertion to the virtues of reverence. To the rediscovery that they, too, are part of the nature of the human, as much a part of our nature as the virtues of self-assertion so familiar to our modern and post-modern Western culture. Perhaps desire might even take us to the rediscovery that the virtues of reverence are the more important part of our nature. At least more important for defining the human. For defining what makes us most human – in the noblest, most *civilized* meaning of that word.[99]

Maybe the twenty-first century – or the twenty-second – could be the beginning of a new Axial age.

As far as freedom is concerned, at any rate, our modern and post-modern world has got it backward. Or sees only half – perhaps the less important half – of its own central truth. The final liberation is not just the liberation *of* the self, as we now take for granted.

It is also the liberation *from* the self. The freedom *for* others.

Notes

A list of main works cited is available online: https://downloads.utorontopress.com/pdf/TheHumanParadox_MainWorksCited.pdf.

Epigraphs

1 *Isaiah*, 11:6.
2 Plato, *The Republic*, 486A. I have combined two translations. The first words and the last are from *The Republic of Plato*, trans. A.D. Lindsay, 6th rev. ed. (London: J.M. Dent, 1932), 202. The words "a soul which is always yearning" are from *Great Dialogues of Plato*, trans. W.H.D. Rouse (New York: Mentor, 1956), 283.
3 Aristotle, *Metaphysics* 4.2.1005a4, trans. W.D. Ross, in *The Basic Works of Aristotle*, ed. Richard McKeon (New York: Random House, 1941), 735.
4 Confucius, *The Analects*, trans. D.C. Lau (London: Penguin Books, 1979), 75.
5 Saint Augustine, *Confessions*, bk. 4, chap. 14, trans. R.S. Pine-Coffin (Harmondsworth: Penguin, 1961), 84.
6 "[C]reaturae vero visibili debetur quaternarius." Thomas Aquinas, *Summa Theologiæ* 2–2.147.5 (Cambridge: Cambridge Univ. Press, 2006), vol. 43 ("Temperance"), trans. Thomas Gilby, 106. My translation.
7 G.W. Leibniz, "À Foucher," in *Les deux labyrinthes: textes choisis*, ed. Alain Chauve (Paris: Presses Universitaires de France, 1973), 24.
8 G.W.F. Hegel, "Fragment of a System," trans. Richard Kroner, in *Early Theological Writings*, trans. T.M. Knox (Chicago: Univ. of Chicago Press, 1948), 312.
9 Samuel Taylor Coleridge, quoted in Crabb Robinson, *Diary*, i, 399–401, in Thomas McFarland, *Coleridge and the Pantheist Tradition* (Oxford: Oxford Univ. Press, 1969), 254.
10 Friedrich Nietzsche, *Thus Spoke Zarathustra*, trans. R.J. Hollingdale, rev. ed. (Harmondsworth: Penguin Books, 1969), 84–6. Revised to use Walter Kaufmann's translation of *Güter* as "virtues" rather than Hollingdale's translation as "values." See Walter Kaufmann, *Nietzsche: Philosopher,*

Psychologist, Antichrist, 3rd rev. ed. (New York: Vintage Books, 1968), 211. As I explain in chapter 3, values are the *inside* of virtues: they are good habits of *feeling* that accompany and support – and are nourished by – good habits of *behaviour*, or virtues.

11 F.H. Bradley, *Appearance and Reality* (Oxford: Oxford Univ. Press, 1930), 130.

12 G.K. Chesterton, *Orthodoxy* (New York: Dodd Mead, 1924), 177, 209–10.

13 Alfred North Whitehead, *Process and Reality* (New York: Free Press, 1969), 74.

14 Martin Heidegger, "Bremen Lectures: Insight into That Which Is," in *The Heidegger Reader*, ed. Günter Figal, trans. Jerome Veith (Bloomington: Indiana Univ. Press, 2009), 260.

15 Étienne Gilson, *God and Philosophy* (New Haven: Yale Univ. Press, 1941), 69.

16 Simone Weil, "L'amour de Dieu et le malheur," in *Pensées sans ordre concernant l'amour de Dieu* (Paris: Gallimard, 2013), 67.

17 Bernard Williams, *Ethics and the Limits of Philosophy* (Cambridge, MA: Harvard Univ. Press, 1985), 483.

18 Iris Murdoch, *Metaphysics as a Guide to Morals* (London: Vintage, 2003), 483.

19 Emmanuel Levinas, *Entre nous: Essais sur le penser-à-l'autre* (Paris: Livre de Poche, 2010), 39.

20 Paul Ricœur, *Histoire et vérité* (Paris: Points Essais, 2001), 404.

21 Charles Taylor, *A Secular Age* (Cambridge, MA: Belknap Press of Harvard Univ. Press, 2007), 374, 636.

22 Ali Smith, *How to Be Both* (Toronto: Penguin Books, 2015), 88, 304.

23 Robin Wall Kimmerer, *Braiding Sweetgrass: Indigenous Wisdom, Scientific Knowledge, and the Teachings of Plants* (Minneapolis: Milkweed Editions, 2013), 151.

24 William Shakespeare, *Measure for Measure*, in *The Complete Works*, ed. Alfred Harbage (Baltimore: Penguin Books, 1969), 1.1.32–5. References are to act, scene, and line.

Preface

1 Ralph Heintzman, *Rediscovering Reverence: The Meaning of Faith in a Secular World* (Montreal: McGill-Queen's Univ. Press, 2011).

2 F.H. Bradley, *Appearance and Reality* (Oxford: Oxford Univ. Press, 1930), 400.

3 Ralph Heintzman, "The Dialectic of Mind: Some Thoughts on Reason and Civility," *Journal of Canadian Studies* 6, no. 3 (February 1971), 1–2, 63–4. See also: "Mr. Stanfield's Failure," *Journal of Canadian Studies* 9, no. 1 (February 1974) 1–2, 66–7; "The Virtues of Reverence," *Journal of Canadian Studies* 12, no. 1 (February 1977), 1–2, 92–5; "The Sympathy of the Whole," *Journal of Canadian Studies* 12, no. 2 (Spring 1977), 1–2, 93; "The Meaning of Monarchy," *Journal of Canadian Studies* 12, no. 4 (Summer 1977), 1–2, 115–17; "Liberalism and Censorship," *Journal of Canadian Studies* 13, no. 4 (Winter 1978–9), 1–2, 120–2; "The Educational Contract," *Journal of Canadian Studies*

14, no. 2 (Summer 1979) 1–2, 142–5; "The Other Daemon," *Journal of Canadian Studies* 14, no. 4 (Winter 1979–80), 1–2, 151–2; "Two Solitudes," *Journal of Canadian Studies* 15, no. 1 (Spring 1980), 1–2, 123–4.

4 Immanuel Kant, *Critique of Practical Reason*, Conclusion, trans. Lewis White Beck (Indianapolis: Bobbs-Merrill, 1956), 166. Kant here echoes Aristotle's teaching that humans derived the philosophical idea of god from two sources: their own souls and the motions of the stars. Aristotle, "Fragment 12," in *Aristotelis Opera* (Berlin, 1870), 1475 -6, cited in Étienne Gilson, *God and Philosophy* (New Haven: Yale Univ. Press, 1941), 32. Both Aristotle and Kant are anticipated by Psalm 19 which links the "glory" of the heavens and the stars to the laws and commandments of righteousness. The first manifests and symbolizes the second.

5 Aristotle, *The Nicomachean Ethics* 9.4.1166a30–5, trans. J.A.K. Thomson, rev. Hugh Tredennick (London: Penguin Books, 2004), 237.

6 Samuel Johnson, *The Idler*, no. 65, Saturday, 14 July 1759, in *The Idler and The Adventurer*, ed. W.J. Bate, John M. Bullitt, and L.F. Powell (New Haven: Yale Univ. Press, 1963), Yale Edition of the Works of Samuel Johnson, 2:204.

7 Whitehead, *Process and Reality*, ix.

8 Samuel Johnson, *The Rambler*, no. 203, Tuesday, 25 February 1752, ed. W.J. Bate and Albrecht B. Strauss (New Haven: Yale Univ. Press, 1979), Yale Edition of the Works of Samuel Johnson, 5:292–3.

Introduction

1 "[P]hilosophically there is a huge gap, at present unfillable as far as we are concerned, which needs to be filled by an account of human nature, human action, the type of characteristic a virtue is, and above all of human 'flourishing.'" G.E.M. Anscombe, "Modern Moral Philosophy," in *Virtue Ethics*, ed. Roger Crisp and Michael Slote (Oxford: Oxford Univ. Press, 1997), 43–4.

2 Richard Rorty, for example, suggests that human beings have no essence: the self has "no center, no essence" and is merely "a concatenation of beliefs and desires." Richard M. Rorty, "The Priority of Democracy to Philosophy," in *The Rorty Reader*, ed. Christopher J. Voparil and Richard J. Bernstein (Chichester: Wiley-Blackwell, 2010), 248n24. See also David L. Hull, "On Human Nature," 24–34; and David J. Buller, "Adapting Minds: Evolutionary Psychology and the Persistent Quest for Human Nature," in *Arguing about Human Nature: Contemporary Debates*, ed. Stephen M. Downes and Edouard Machery (New York: Routledge, 2013), 35–63.

3 The quotation is from Merlin Donald, *A Mind So Rare: The Evolution of Human Consciousness* (New York: W.W. Norton, 2001), 1–8, 28–45. Donald uses the term to refer, especially, to a specific group of cognitive theorists, but it can be usefully applied to a wider range of neo-Darwinian

theorists, among whom Donald himself mentions Daniel Dennett, Steven Pinker, and Richard Dawkins. Among others, see: Michael T. Ghiselin, *The Economy of Nature and the Evolution of Sex* (Berkeley: Univ. of California Press, 1974); *Metaphysics and the Origin of Species* (Albany, NY: State Univ. of New York Press, 1997); Edward O. Wilson, *Sociobiology: The New Synthesis* (Cambridge, MA: Harvard Univ. Press, 1975), *On Human Nature* (Cambridge, MA: Harvard Univ. Press, 2004), *The Meaning of Human Existence* (New York: Liveright, 2014); Richard Dawkins, *The Selfish Gene* (New York: Oxford Univ. Press, 1976); Daniel C. Dennett, *Consciousness Explained* (Boston: Little, Brown, 1991), *Darwin's Dangerous Idea: Evolution and the Meaning of Life* (New York: Simon & Schuster, 1995); Robert Wright, *The Moral Animal: Why We Are the Way We Are: The New Science of Evolutionary Psychology* (New York: Vintage Books, 1994); Matthew Ridley, *The Origins of Virtue: Human Instincts and the Evolution of Cooperation* (New York: Penguin Books, 1996); Steven Pinker, *The Blank Slate: The Modern Denial of Human Nature* (New York: Viking, 2002). Frans de Waal observes that the clouding of the distinction "between genes and motivations" (or between what I will call efficient and final causes) has led some sociobiologists to "an exceptionally cynical view of human and animal behavior." He mentions Michael Ghiselin and Robert Wright in particular. Frans de Waal, *The Age of Empathy: Nature's Lessons for a Kinder Society* (New York: Three Rivers Press, 2009), 43.

4 Alan Wolfe, *The Future of Liberalism* (New York: Vintage Books, 2010), 30.

5 Donald, *A Mind So Rare*, 8. See also: 25, 202, 281, 290. This view of human nature, as "defined" by consciousness, appears early in Donald's second major book. But in the course of it, he seems to have a change of heart. By the end, he recognizes that the human mind is the product of "deep psychic drives," and that our drive for "rationality and clarity is itself deeply irrational and unclear in its final destination." Donald, 288, 290.

6 Wilson, *On Human Nature*; *The Meaning of Human Existence*; Christopher Berry, *Human Nature* (Oxford: Oxford Univ. Press, 1984); Leslie Stevenson, *Seven Theories of Human Nature*, 2nd ed. (New York: Oxford Univ. Press, 1987); Downes and Machery, *Arguing about Human Nature*; Roger Scruton, *On Human Nature* (Princeton: Princeton Univ. Press, 2017). Edouard Machery suggests theories of human nature can be grouped in two categories: essentialist (which look for a "set of properties that are necessary and jointly sufficient for being a human") and "nomological" (which seek "the set of properties that humans tend to possess as a result of the evolution of their species"). "A Plea for Human Nature," in *Arguing about Human Nature*, ed. Downes and Machery, 64–70.

7 "[L]es sciences humaines ... ne pourraient atteindre à quelque positivité, se prévaloir d'une utilité quelconque, que si le travail ontologique qui

doit leur fournir un fondement et un sens était accompli et ses résultats préservés." Michel Henry, *L'essence de la manifestation* (Paris: Presses Universitaires de France, 2017), 862.

8 "[T]he question as to what man is can only be asked as part of the inquiry about being. ... [T]he definition of the essence of man ... cannot be the product of an arbitrary anthropology that considers man in basically the same way as zoology considers animals." Martin Heidegger, *An Introduction to Metaphysics*, trans. Ralph Manheim (New York: Doubleday, 1961), 121, 171. "To think the truth of Being at the same time means to think the humanity of *homo humanus*." "Letter on Humanism," trans. Frank A. Capuzzi, in collaboration with J. Glenn Gray, in *Basic Writings*, ed. David Farrell Krell (New York: HarperCollins, 1977), 231.

9 The objective of this book might thus be described, in the words of Martin Heidegger, as "a *radical phenomenological anthropology*." Martin Heidegger, "Indication of the Hermeneutical Situation," trans. Michael Baur and Jerome Veith, in *The Heidegger Reader*, ed. Figal, 59. Emphasis in original. Or as what Charles Taylor and Paul Ricœur both call a "philosophical anthropology," defined by Taylor as a "study of the basic categories in which man and his behaviour is [*sic*] to be described and explained." *The Explanation of Behaviour* (London: Routledge, 1970), 4. Or, additionally, in Ricœur's words, as "une anthropologie philosophique qui voulait rassembler les résultats épars des sciences humaines." *Le conflit des interprétations: Essais d'herméneutique* (Paris: Éditions du Seuil, 2013), 354. Or, as what Elizabeth Anscombe calls a "philosophy of psychology." "Modern Moral Philosophy," 26, 30, 40. Or, as what Iris Murdoch calls a "philosophical psychology," something that can "connect modern psychological terminology with a terminology concerned with virtue." *The Sovereignty of Good* (London: Routledge, 1980), 46. Or, what Michel Henry calls a "philosophie de l'affectivité," a "psychologie phénoménologique," "une élucidation systématique de l'essence de l'affectivité," or "le développement d'une phénoménologie et d'une philosophie phénoménologique de l'expérience vécu, de l'ego, de la connaissance de soi, de la vie intérieure et de la temporalité qui lui appartient en propre, de la structure de l'expérience en général et de ses formes essentielles." *L'essence de la manifestation*, 796, 841, 862. Or, in Max Scheler's words, the book's objective might be described as "the structuration of an a priori non-formal ethics." *Formalism in Ethics and Non-Formal Ethics of Value*, trans. Manfred S. Frings and Roger L. Funk (Evanston: Northwestern Univ. Press, 1973), 64. Or, alternatively, in the words of Edmund Husserl, to set out "as its *a priori* the indissoluble essential structure of transcendental subjectivity ... drawn from real, general intuition of essential Being, and described accordingly." *Ideas: General Introduction to Pure Phenomenology*, trans. W.R. Boyce Gibson (New York: Collier Books, 1962), 5–6.

10 "[J]e voudrais bien savoir comment nous pourrions avoir l'idée de l'être,
si nous n'étions pas des êtres nous-mêmes, et ne trouvions ainsi l'être en
nous. … [L]a connaissance de l'être est enveloppée dans celle que nous
avons de nous-mêmes." G.W. Leibniz, *Nouveaux essais sur l'entendement
humain* (Paris: Garnier-Flammarion, 1966), bk. 1, chap. 1, §24, p. 70; chap.
3, §3, p. 83. "The existential nature of man is the reason why man can
represent beings as such, and why he can be conscious of them." Martin
Heidegger, "The Way Back into the Ground of Metaphysics," trans. Walter Kaufmann, in *Existentialism from Dostoevsky to Sartre*, ed. Walter Kaufmann (Cleveland: World, 1956), 214.

11 Yet another related paradox running through our nature – and this book! –
is that true human "fullness" can only be achieved by a kind of "emptiness": that you must "lose" your life, in some sense, in order to "save" it.

12 Credit for launching the post-war revival of interest in the virtues is
sometimes also given to the 1958 paper by Elizabeth Anscombe cited in
note 33 above: "Modern Moral Philosophy," 26–44. On virtue ethics, in
addition to the anthology edited by Crisp and Slote, see also (among others): Rosalind Hursthouse, *On Virtue Ethics* (Oxford: Oxford Univ. Press,
2010); Christine Swanton, *Virtue Ethics: A Pluralistic View* (Oxford: Oxford
Univ. Press, 2003); Robert Merrihew Adams, *A Theory of Virtue: Excellence
in Being for the Good* (Oxford: Oxford Univ. Press, 2013); Julia Annas, *Intelligent Virtue* (Oxford: Oxford Univ. Press, 2013); Paul Bloomfield, *The
Virtues of Happiness: A Theory of the Good Life* (New York: Oxford Univ.
Press, 2014); Stephen M. Gardiner, ed., *Virtue Ethics, Old and New* (Ithaca:
Cornell Univ. Press, 2005); Timothy Chappell, ed. *Values and Virtues: Aris-
totelianism in Contemporary Ethics* (Oxford: Oxford Univ. Press, 2006); Dan-
iel C. Russell, ed., *The Cambridge Companion to Virtue Ethics* (Cambridge:
Cambridge Univ. Press, 2013); Stan van Hooft, ed., *The Handbook of Virtue
Ethics* (Durham: Acumen, 2014); Kevin Timpe and Craig A. Boyd, eds.,
Virtues and Their Vices (Oxford: Oxford Univ. Press, 2014). On the impact
of virtue ethics on psychology, see Everett L. Worthington Jr., Caroline Lavelock, Daryl R. Van Tongeren, David L. Jennings II, Aubrey L.
Gartner, Don E. Davis, and Joshua N. Hook, "Virtue in Positive Psychology," in *Virtues and Their Vices*, ed. Timpe and Boyd, 433–57, and chapter
14 of this book. On the links between virtue ethics and anthropology and
evolutionary theory, see Richard Hamilton, "Naturalistic Virtue Ethics
and the New Biology," in *The Handbook of Virtue Ethics*, ed. Van Hooft,
42–52, and chapter 14 of this book.

13 For Aristotle the word "ethics" has a very broad meaning. He uses it to
designate one half of the universe of human virtues. He distinguishes
between *intellectual* virtue, which can be conveyed through teaching,
and *moral* virtue (or "ethics") which is formed not by teaching but by

"habit." He points out that the word "ethics" is a slight variation of the Greek word "ethos," which he took to mean "habit." For Aristotle this derivation underlines the fact that we learn the virtues "by first exercising them ... [W]e learn by doing them." *Nicomachean Ethics* 1103a14–b2, trans. W.D. Ross, in *The Basic Works of Aristotle*, ed. Richard McKeon (New York: Modern Library, 1968), 952. Martin Heidegger, on the other hand, argues that "ethos" means abode or dwelling place: "the open region in which man dwells." He links it to Heraclitus' saying (Fragment 119) *ēthos anthropōpōi daimōn*, which he translates, freely, as meaning: "Man dwells, insofar as he is man, in the nearness of god." So, for Heidegger, ethics "ponders the abode of man," and, as a result, "that thinking which thinks the truth of Being as the primordial element of man ... is in itself the original ethics." "Letter on Humanism," in *Basic Writings*, edited by Krell, 233–5. But, perhaps because of the enduring, subterranean influence of Immanuel Kant, ethics has a much narrower meaning in our contemporary, everyday usage in the Western world, especially in organizational and public life. It has come to be identified as a specialized set of (often professional) values, those having to do predominantly with rule-following and rule-breaking. In contemporary usage, values, as a whole, express the aspirations of a community, while ethics, as a subset of values, often emphasizes the values of compliance with rules and laws. If you were to see a website, social media, or newspaper headline about some "ethical" lapse today, the story would probably be about a conflict of interest or a failure of integrity in the use of resources, such as financial and human resources. In ordinary usage, "ethics" today usually implies "compliance" with some set of rules or laws, or with some code. Wim Vandekerckhove, "Virtue Ethics and Management," and Paul Kaak and David Weeks, "Virtuous Leadership: Ethical and Effective," in *The Handbook of Virtue Ethics*, ed. Van Hooft, 341–51, 352–64. See also the Ethics and Compliance Initiative, the leading US research organization on workplace integrity. https://www.ethics.org/home. Anthropologist Webb Keane reverses this common sense or everyday usage once more and wants to give ethics the widest possible meaning, equivalent to what Aristotle and Aquinas meant when they talked about the virtues. *Ethical Life: Its Natural and Social Histories* (Princeton: Princeton Univ. Press, 2016), 18. Keane's choice to make ethics the wider concept (the good life), and morality the narrower (rule-following), has broad support from contemporary philosophers, especially those strongly influenced by Kant. See, for example, Williams, *Ethics and the Limits of Philosophy*, 174–96; Paul Ricœur, *Lectures 1*, in *Ricœur: Textes choisis et présentés*, ed. Michaël Fœssel and Fabien Lamouche (Paris: Éditions Points, 2007), 311–12. However, I don't think the attempted reversal of the meanings of ethics and morality works very well in the English language. Morality still has the wider meaning, in ordinary and literary English, and ethics the narrower. In ordinary English, morality and moral are the containers, and ethics and ethical the contained. That, presumably, is why David Hume called the third book of his *Treatise of Human Nature* "Of Morals," and why James Q. Wilson called his book on the virtues *The Moral Sense*. As James Laidlaw remarks, the attempted distinction between ethics and morality is unlikely to govern how ordinary people and scholars "use the words 'ethics' and 'moral' generally. Nor should they. It would be a very bad sign for scholars to detach themselves from natural language to that extent." *The Subject of Virtue: An Anthropology of Ethics and Freedom* (Cambridge: Cambridge Univ. Press, 2014), 114.

14 What I am looking for in this book is what Paul Ricœur calls *"l'ensemble des structures* d'un être qui n'existe que sur le mode de la reprise ou sur celui de l'omission *de ses propres possibilités." Le conflit des interprétations*, 314. Emphasis added.

15 Clifford Geertz, *The Interpretation of Cultures* (New York: Basic Books, 1973), 20.

16 Jonathan Haidt, *The Righteous Mind: Why Good People Are Divided by Politics and Religion* (New York: Pantheon Books, 2012), 92. This book is thus part of "the quest for a realistic moral psychology." Laidlaw, *The Subject of Virtue*, 90. Contemporary cognitive theorists such as George Lakoff (b. 1941) and Mark Johnson (b. 1949) also see themselves as developing a "geography of human experience." Mark Johnson, *The Body in the Mind: The Bodily Basis of Meaning, Imagination, and Reason* (Chicago: Chicago Univ. Press, 1987), xxx–xxxviii; George Lakoff and Mark Johnson, *Philosophy in the Flesh: The Embodied Mind and Its Challenge to Western Thought* (New York: Basic Books, 1999); Edward Slingerland, *Effortless Action: Wuwei as Conceptual Metaphor and Spiritual Ideal in Early China* (New York: Oxford Univ. Press, 2003), 21–4.

17 Paul Ricœur points out that a phenomenology of the spirit seeks the source of meaning "non plus à l'arrière du sujet [i.e., in the efficient causes studied by the sciences and social sciences], mais en avant de lui. … Ainsi une téléologie du sujet s'oppose à une archéologie du sujet." *Le conflit des interprétations*, 46–7. It is a significant fact about our modern and post-modern theoretic culture that it has been ambivalent about how to translate Hegel's own term – *Geist* – and has often mistranslated it as "mind." See, for example, G.W.F. Hegel, *The Phenomenology of Mind*, trans. J.B. Baillie (New York: Harper & Row, 1967); *Philosophy of Right*, trans. T.M. Knox (Oxford: Oxford Univ. Press, 1967); Peter Singer, *Hegel: A Very Short Introduction* (Oxford: Oxford Univ. Press, 2001), 60–2. The question of whether "mind" or "spirit" is the better term to describe the nature of

the human is one of the most important questions raised in and by this book.

18 In this book the word "Western" (with a capital) will normally be used in a cultural sense to refer to cultures with roots in Western Europe which can now also be found in North America and Australasia, among other places. However, when the word is used specifically in discussion of the religious traditions, it also includes Islam, which is clearly part of the religious world of the West rather than of the East.

19 This kind of "mapping across domains of experience" has an important place in contemporary theory about the role of metaphor in human cognition, in which "mapping" is understood as "a correspondence between two sets that assigns to each element in the first a counterpart in the second." Johnson, *The Body in the Mind*, 7; Gilles Fauconnier, *Mappings in Thought and Language* (Cambridge: Cambridge Univ. Press, 2003), 1–9; Slingerland, *Effortless Action*, 21. The second part of this book is devoted to a parallel kind of "mapping across domains of experience."

20 "L'ontologie ne saurait donc demeurer à l'état de théorie ... Assurément la science, ici comme partout ailleurs, ne se substitue pas à la pratique, ni la pratique à la science. Mais, autant et plus qu'ailleurs, la liaison doit se marquer et se réaliser dans une intimité vraiment dynamique et singulière." Maurice Blondel, *L'Être et les êtres* (Paris: Presses Universitaires de France, 1963), 345.

21 Lev Shestov, *Athens and Jerusalem*, trans. Bernard Martin, 2nd ed. (Athens: Ohio Univ. Press, 2016), 64, 205.

22 The objective of this book is therefore exactly the same as Martin Heidegger's *Being and Time*: i.e., to discern the "ontological structure" of the nature of the human, or what Heidegger calls "Dasein." *Being and Time*, 182, trans. Joan Stambaugh (Albany: State Univ. of New York Press, 2010), 176. Heidegger elsewhere says the "goal of all ontology is a doctrine of categories." *An Introduction to Metaphysics*, trans. Manheim 156. Whitehead agrees that the "proper object" of philosophy is the "gradual elaboration of categorial schemes." And for him, as for this book, the "final summary" must be the "diverse categories of existence." Whitehead, *Process and Reality*, 11, 410, 29. What Whitehead calls "categories of existence," Iris Murdoch calls "areas of experience." These areas are what, for her, are named by the virtues. *The Sovereignty of Good*, 57, 74. What I have called here a virtues ontology, Paul Ricœur calls "l'ontologie de l'agir." *Amour et justice* (Paris: Éditions Points, 2008), 9.

23 If you were to replace the single word "concepts" with the word "virtues" in the following sentence, you would have a pretty good description of what I'm trying to do in this book: "In order that as a science metaphysics may be entitled to claim, not mere fallacious plausibility

but insight and conviction, [it] must exhibit the whole stock of *a priori*
concepts, their division according to their various sources (sensibility,
understanding, reason), together with a complete table of them ... all in
a complete system." Immanuel Kant, *Prolegomena to Any Future Metaphysics*, trans. Lewis White Beck et al. (Indianapolis: Bobbs-Merrill, 1950),
114. Similarly, if you were to replace the word "appearances" with the
word "virtues" in the following sentence, you would have another good
description of my objective here: "To survey the field of appearances, to
measure each by the idea of perfect individuality, and to arrange them in
an order and in a system of reality and merit – would be the task of metaphysics." Bradley, *Appearance and Reality*, 433.

24 "People do not like metaphysics, they do not believe in it, they are
ashamed of it and flee from it." Shestov, *Athens and Jerusalem*, 292.

25 Alan Ryan acknowledges "one of the temptations to which philosophy
fell prey quite recently [1965] – a temptation to eliminate metaphysics
and substitute pseudophysics." *The Making of Modern Liberalism* (Princeton: Princeton Univ. Press, 2012), 48.

26 Rudolf Carnap, *Philosophy and Logical Syntax* (London: Kegan Paul,
Trench, Trubner, 1935) in *20th-Century Philosophy: The Analytic Tradition*,
ed. Morris Weitz (New York: Free Press, 1966), 215–16. Emphasis in
original. A year after Carnap, the young A.J. Ayer similarly asserted that
moral arguments are merely "ejaculations and commands" and "pure
expressions of feeling" that have "no objective validity whatsoever." *Language, Truth and Logic* (New York: Dover, 1946), 108, quoted in James Q.
Wilson, *The Moral Sense* (New York: Free Press, 1993), 3.

27 Sidney Hook, *John Dewey* (New York: John Day, 1939), 34–5, cited in Richard M. Rorty, "Dewey's Metaphysics," in *The Rorty Reader*, 72.

28 Stuart Hampshire, *Spinoza* (Harmondsworth: Penguin Books, 1967),
218–20.

29 As a contemporary historian puts it, history is "a construct, necessarily
subjective, no less so indeed than all the other spheres of reality in which
we humans navigate, move and act. It is a hypothesis whose plausibility
is conditioned by unprovable premises, our own subjective experiences,
and familiar structural patterns. There can be no such thing as a generally
binding history, any more than 'my' reality could be 'your' reality, even
though both are indisputably forms of reality." Johannes Fried, *The Middle Ages*, trans. Peter Lewis (Cambridge, MA: Belknap Press of Harvard
Univ. Press, 2015), ix.

30 "The past opens itself only according to the resoluteness and force of illumination that a present has available to it. ... Not only is this reading-into
not contrary to the sense of historical knowing, but it is the basic condition for bringing the past to expression." Heidegger, "Indication of the

Hermeneutical Situation," trans. Baur and Veith, 39–40. Bradley points out the dialogical structure of history is merely an instance of the wider dialogical character of memory, which "depends absolutely upon that which at the moment we are." Bradley, *Appearance and Reality*, 315.

31 The phrase (*wie es eigentlich gewesen*) is from the great German historian Leopold von Ranke (1795–1886). See Fritz Stern, ed., *The Varieties of History: From Voltaire to the Present* (Cleveland: Meridian Books, 1966), 57.

32 "L'historien écrit au present, dans son temps et au cœur de sa culture, meme s'il fait tous les efforts pour atteindre en méthode la plus grande objectivité possible." Robert Muchembled, "Préface à la deuxième edi-tion: Le temps de l'historien," in *Culture populaire et culture des élites dans la France moderne (XVe–XVIIIe siècle)* (Paris: Flammarion, 1991), ix.

33 Hans-Georg Gadamer, *Truth and Method*, trans. and rev. Joel Weinsheimer and Donald G. Marshall, 2nd ed. (New York: Continuum, 2002), 276, 270. "Philosophy will never seek to deny its 'presuppositions,' but neither may it merely admit them. It conceives them and develops with more and more penetration both the presuppositions themselves and that for which they are presuppositions." Heidegger, *Being and Time*, 310, trans. Stambaugh, 297. "[I]f you have no starting point in life you will never get started … it is our prejudgments, sometimes disparaged as prejudices, that make it possible for us to see." Richard A. Shweder, *Why Do Men Barbecue? Recipes for Cultural Psychology* (Cambridge, MA: Harvard Univ. Press, 2003), 330.

34 "Whatever happens, every individual is a child of his time … It is just as absurd to fancy that a philosophy can transcend its contemporary world as it is to fancy that an individual can overleap his own age, jump over Rhodes." Hegel, *Philosophy of Right*, trans. Knox, 11. See also Hans Joas, *The Sacredness of the Person: A New Genealogy of Human Rights*, trans. Alex Skinner (Washington, DC: Georgetown Univ. Press, 2013), 121.

35 R.G. Collingwood, *An Essay on Metaphysics* (London: Oxford Univ. Press, 1966), 3–4; Jean Grondin, *Introduction à la métaphysique* (Montreal: Les Presses de l'Université de Montréal, 2004), 21–2. Immanuel Kant seems to have assumed that the linguistic derivation of "metaphysics" meant, instead, "knowledge lying beyond experience." This helps, perhaps, to explain his own intellectual or cognitive bias in metaphysics: his assump-tion that metaphysics is a form of "*a priori* knowledge, coming from pure understanding and pure reason." *Prolegomena to Any Future Metaphysics*, trans. Beck et al., 13.

36 Aristotle, *Metaphysics* 1.2.982a5–983a25, 6.1.1025b–1026a35, trans. Ross, 691–3, 778–9.

37 Whitehead describes metaphysics (or "speculative philosophy") as "the endeavour to frame a coherent, logical, necessary system of general ideas

in terms of which every element of our experience can be interpreted." *Process and Reality*, 5. For Jean Grondin, "toute philosophie est métaphysique dans l'exacte mesure où elle porte sur un étant, un sujet ou un objet qu'elle tient pour plus fondamental que tous les autres." *Introduction à la métaphysique*, 13, 18. See also *Du sens des choses: L'idée de la métaphysique* (Paris: Presses Universitaires de France, 2013). For a very traditional, almost scholastic, view of metaphysics, see Michael J. Loux, *Metaphysics: A Contemporary Introduction* (London: Routledge, 1998).

38 One of F.H. Bradley's definitions of metaphysics is "the effort to comprehend the universe, not simply piecemeal or by fragments, but somehow *as a whole.*" *Appearance and Reality*, 1. Emphasis added. Martin Heidegger largely agrees: "Metaphysics is an enquiry over and above what-is, with a view to winning it back again as such *and in totality* for our understanding." "What Is Metaphysics?" trans. R.F.C. Hull and Alan Crick, in *Existence and Being* (Chicago: Henry Regnery, 1949), 344. Emphasis added. See also "The End of Philosophy and the Task of Thinking," trans. Joan Stambaugh, in *Basic Writings*, ed. David Farrell Krell (New York: HarperCollins, 1977), 374.

39 "Most of us have views, however inchoate, about human nature and social structure, and we use them to justify our moral and political views." Ryan, *The Making of Modern Liberalism*, 96–7.

40 R.G. Collingwood, *An Essay on Philosophical Method* (London: Oxford Univ. Press, 1965), 140–7. "[L]a plupart des idées et des thèses prétendues positives ou positivistes recouvrent des idées et des thèses métaphysiques mal dissimulées." Charles Péguy, *Zangwill*, in *Une éthique sans compromis*, ed. Dominique Saatdjian (Paris: Pocket, 2011), 176. "Les negations métaphysiques sont des operations métaphysiques, au même titre que les affirmations métaphysiques." Charles Péguy, *Pensées* (Montreal: Les Éditions Variétés, 1943), 37. "Linguistic analysis claims simply to give a philosophical description of the human phenomenon of morality without making any moral judgements. In fact the resulting picture of human conduct has a clear moral bias. ... [W]ould-be neutral philosophers merely take sides surreptitiously." Murdoch, *The Sovereignty of Good*, 49, 78.

41 G.W.F. Hegel, *Encyclopaedia of the Philosophical Sciences*, §98, in *Hegel's Logic*, trans. William Wallace (London: Oxford Univ. Press, 1975), 144. "That the human mind will ever give up metaphysical researches is as little to be expected as that we, to avoid inhaling impure air, should prefer to give up breathing altogether. There will, therefore, always be metaphysics in the world; nay, everyone, especially every reflective man, will have it and, for want of a recognized standard, will shape it for himself after his own pattern." Kant, *Prolegomena to Any Future Metaphysics*, trans. Beck et al., 116.

42 "Reality-testing is a metaphysical act which relies on various aspects of the imagination, including category systems, background assumptions, metaphors, and so on." Shweder, *Why Do Men Barbecue?*, 315.

43 "[W]hoever tries to think philosophically, and to some extent succeeds, must find and does find, when he reflects upon it, that his thought takes shape as a system." Collingwood, *An Essay on Philosophical Method*, 193.

44 "[U]n livre reste une écriture morte tant que ses lecteurs ne sont pas devenus grâce à lui ... les lecteurs d'eux-mêmes." Ricœur, *Amour et justice*, 51. In the tradition of Schleiermacher, Dilthey, and Bultmann, Ricœur calls the act of rethinking "appropriation." *Du texte à l'action*, in *Ricœur: Textes choisis et présentés*, 89–90.

45 Paul Ricœur notes "le caractère *dialectique* de la lecture." *Temps et Récit 3*, in *Ricœur: Textes choisis et présentés*, 98. Emphasis added.

46 "With philosophical research that has become past, the possibility of its having an effect upon its future can never lie in the results as such, but is instead grounded in the primordiality of questioning that has been achieved and concretely developed, and through which such research – as a model that raises problems – is able to become the present ever anew." Heidegger, "Indication of the Hermeneutical Situation," trans. Baur and Veith, 40.

47 "[I]t is only the completed system which in metaphysics is the genuine proof of the principle." Bradley, *Appearance and Reality*, 403.

48 "The more they are coherent and wide – the more fully they realize the idea of a system – so much the more at once are [truths] real and true." Bradley, 477. See also Blondel, *L'Être et les êtres*, 351–2n1.

49 "'Who we are,' morally speaking, is a significant ethical issue and one which [as you will see in chapter 17] has considerable bearing on the global environmental tragedy." Stephen M. Gardiner, *A Perfect Storm: The Ethical Tragedy of Climate Change* (New York: Oxford Univ. Press, 2013), 4.

50 Heather Horn, "Where Does Religion Come From?" *Atlantic*, 17 August 2011, https://www.theatlantic.com/entertainment/archive/2011/08/where-does-religion-come-from/243723/.

51 "Ce penchant un peu métaphysique m'a toujours habité, presque harcelé." Jean-Louis Servan Schreiber, *C'est la vie! Essais* (Paris: Albin Michel, 2015), 16. For a striking example of the contemporary metaphysical impulse, see Anthony T. Kronman, *Confessions of a Born-Again Pagan* (New Haven: Yale Univ. Press, 2016).

52 J.L. Schellenberg suggests that "it's too early" in human evolution to put forward a "comprehensive or deep picture of reality ... with any confidence." *Evolutionary Religion* (Oxford: Oxford Univ. Press, 2013), 52.

53 A human being, says Hegel, is "a born metaphysician." *Encyclopaedia*, trans. Wallace, 144. Immanuel Kant agrees that the metaphysical impulse

"is placed in us by nature itself." It "is an unavoidable need of human reason, as it finds complete satisfaction only in a perfectly systematic unity of its cognitions." *Prolegomena to Any Future Metaphysics*, trans. Beck et al., 102; *Critique of Practical Reason*, trans. Lewis White Beck (Indianapolis: Bobbs-Merrill, 1956), pt. 1, chap. 3, p. 94. Bradley makes the same point: "I must suggest to the objector that he should open his eyes and should consider human nature. Is it possible to abstain from thought about the universe? ... Metaphysics takes its stand on this side of human nature, this desire to think about and comprehend reality. And it merely asserts that, if the attempt is to be made, it should be done as thoroughly as our nature permits. There is no claim on its part to supersede other functions of the human mind; but it protests that, if we are to think, we should sometimes try to think properly." Bradley, *Appearance and Reality*, 3.

54 My consciousness of restating, or, preferably, reformulating what others have already said before me, explains the liberal use of endnotes in this book, and the liberal use of quotation in the endnotes. They are intended to show the ideas put forward here are not arbitrary but rather what the greatest Western thinkers have always known, and already said, in their own way.

55 Chesterton, *Orthodoxy*, 18–19.

56 In that sense, this book could fairly be said to fall into the category mordantly described by Immanuel Kant as "antiquated knowledge produced as new by taking it out of its former context and fitting it into a systematic garment of any fancy pattern with new titles." Kant, *Prolegomena to Any Future Metaphysics*, trans. Beck et al., 9.

57 R.G. Collingwood, *Speculum Mentis or the Map of Knowledge* (Oxford: Oxford Univ. Press, 1963), 38. This book may thus be considered the kind of work Iris Murdoch describes as "a footnote in a great and familiar philosophical tradition." *The Sovereignty of Good*, 45. As Étienne Gilson puts it: "Le métaphysicien n'a pour ainsi dire jamais le sentiment de découvrir quelque chose de nouveau; il éprouve plutôt l'impression que la vérité qui est une découverte pour lui, puisque chacun doit le découvrir pour son propre compte, a toujours été là, sous les yeux de tous et que même ceux d'entre eux qui l'ont méconnue, parfois niée, en ont pourtant fait usage." *Constantes philosophiques de l'être* (Paris: Vrin, 1983), 12.

58 "To give up the idea that there is an intrinsic nature of reality ... is to give up the search for an accurate account of human nature, and thus a recipe for leading the good life for man. ... [We should stop] thinking that the human imagination is getting somewhere." Richard M. Rorty, "Philosophy as a Transitional Genre," in *The Rorty Reader*, 486–8. From a diametrically opposed position, Brad Gregory nevertheless agrees that

the modern philosophical enterprise has completely failed in its ambition "to articulate universal truths based on reason alone." *The Unintended Reformation: How a Religious Revolution Revolutionized Society* (Cambridge, MA: Belknap Press of Harvard Univ. Press, 2012), 378–9. For Alfred North Whitehead, on the other hand, this perception of the "failure" of philosophy – or the lack of philosophical "progress" – arises merely from the degree to which philosophy has been "vitiated by the example of mathematics." Once the proper method of philosophy – "descriptive generalization" – has been adequately distinguished from the method of mathematics – i.e., "deduction" – it becomes possible to appreciate "the very considerable success of philosophy." *Process and Reality*, 10–14.

59 "[A]ll thinkers throughout history have said fundamentally the same thing." Heidegger, *An Introduction to Metaphysics*, trans. Manheim, 82. "Of course they say it only to him who undertakes to think back on them." "Letter on Humanism," trans. Capuzzi with Gray, 241.

60 "[J]'ai trouvé qu'ordinairement dans les combats entre des gens de mérite insigne … la raison est de part et d'autre, mais en différents points, et qu'elle est plutôt pour les défenses que pour les attaques." G.W. Leibniz, Préface to *Essais de Théodicée* (Paris: Garnier-Flammarion, 1969), 47. "[J]'ai remarqué aussi assez souvent que dans leurs disputes de spéculation sur des matières qui sont du ressort de leur esprit, ils ont tous raison de deux côtés, excepté dans les oppositions qu'ils font les uns aux autres." Leibniz, *Nouveaux essais*, bk. 3, chap. 10, §4, p. 297.

61 John Stuart Mill, "Coleridge," in *Mill on Bentham and Coleridge*, ed. F.R. Leavis (Cambridge: Cambridge Univ. Press, 1980), 105.

62 "[N]o philosophy has been refuted, nay, or ever can be refuted. … Thus the history of philosophy, in its true meaning, deals not with a past, but with an eternal present: and, in its results, resembles not a museum of aberrations of the human intellect, but a Pantheon of godlike figures." Hegel, *Encyclopaedia*, §86, in *Hegel's Logic*, trans. Wallace, 126. On this theme, see also Samuel Taylor Coleridge, *The Friend*, ed. Barbara E. Rooke (London: Routledge, 1969), 1:337; Heidegger, "Letter on Humanism," trans. Capuzzi with Gray, 216; "What Calls for Thinking?," trans. Fred D. Wieck and J. Glenn Gray, in *Basic Writings*, 354.

63 "[N]o one is able to obtain the truth adequately, while, on the other hand, we do not collectively fail, but everyone says something true about the nature of things, and while we contribute little or nothing to the truth, by the union of all a considerable amount is amassed." Aristotle, *Metaphysics* 2.1.993a30–b5, trans. Ross, 712. "Every individual being is some one aspect of the idea … It is only in them altogether and in their relation that the notion is realized. … The purpose of philosophy has always been the intellectual ascertainment of the Idea; and everything deserving the name

of philosophy has constantly been based on the consciousness of an absolute unity where the understanding [in Hegel's sense: i.e., reason] accepts
only separation." Hegel, *Encyclopaedia*, §213, in *Hegel's Logic*, trans. Wallace, 275–6. Paraphrasing Gadamer, Charles Taylor calls this the "ideal
of the most comprehensive account possible" and suggests that it should
replace the "old ideal of a point-of-view-less nomothetical science that
grasps all of humanity under one set of explanatory laws." *Dilemmas and
Connections: Selected Essays* (Cambridge, MA: Belknap Press of Harvard
Univ. Press, 2011), 32.

64 "[T]he thinking that thinks into the truth of Being is, as thinking, historical. There is not a 'systematic' thinking and next to it an illustrative history of past opinions. ... Thought in a more primordial way, there is the
history of Being to which thinking belongs as recollection of this history
that unfolds of itself." Heidegger, "Letter on Humanism," trans. Capuzzi
with Gray, 215. "[T]he philosopher, in constructing a system, has his
place in a scale whose structure is such that every term in it sums up the
whole scale to that point ... [T]he entire history of philosophy is the history of a single sustained attempt to solve a single permanent problem,
each phase advancing the problem by the extent of all the work done on
it in the interval, and summing up the fruits of this work in the shape of a
unique presentation of the problem." Collingwood, *An Essay on Philosophical Method*, 191–2, 195.

65 On Aquinas' project of "developing the work of dialectical construction
systematically, so as to integrate the whole previous history of enquiry,
so far as he was aware of it, into his own," see Alasdair MacIntyre, *Whose
Justice? Which Rationality?* (Notre Dame, IN: Univ. of Notre Dame Press,
1988), 206–7; Étienne Gilson, *The Elements of Christian Philosophy* (New
York: Mentor, 1963), 97–8. "[T]he true system cannot have the relation
to [another system] of being merely its opposite; for then this opposite
would itself be one-sided. Much rather, being superior, it must contain
the subordinate. ... True refutation must engage the force of the opponent
and must place itself within the compass of his strength; the task is not
advanced if he is attacked outside himself and the case is carried in his
absence. Hence the refutation of Spinoza's system can consist solely in
this, that his standpoint be first recognized as essential and as necessary,
but that secondly this standpoint be raised *out of itself* to a higher." G.W.F.
Hegel, *Science of Logic*, vol. 2, trans. W.H. Johnston and L.G. Struthers
(London: George Allen & Unwin, 1951), 2:215. Emphasis in original. F.H.
Bradley calls this dialectical process of understanding and inclusion "the
road of indefinite expansion." *Appearance and Reality*, 145. For Whitehead,
it represents "the positive value of the philosophical tradition. One test of
success is the adequacy in the comprehension of the variety of experience

within the limits of one scheme of ideas." *Process and Reality*, ix. Paul Ricœur agrees. *Soi-même comme un autre* (Paris: Éditions du Seuil, 1990), 346–7.

66 Plotinus, *Enneads* 6.9.11, in *The Essential Plotinus*, ed. Elmer O'Brien (New York: Mentor Books, 1964), 87.

67 "Un grand philosophe nouveau, un grand métaphysicien nouveau, n'est nullement, un homme qui arrive à démontrer que chacun de ses prédécesseurs séparément et tous ensemble, et notamment le dernier en date, était le dernier des imbéciles. C'est un homme qui a découvert, qui a inventé quelque aspect nouveau, quelque réalité nouvelle, de la réalité éternelle; c'est un homme qui entre à son tour et pour sa voix dans l'éternel concert." Charles Péguy, *Cahiers de la quinzaine*, 8:xi, in *Une éthique sans compromis*, ed. Dominique Saatdjian (Paris: Pocket, 2011), 229. "The bickerings of philosophical sects are an amusement for the foolish; above these jarrings and creakings of the machine of thought there is a melody sung in unison by the spirits of the spheres, which are the great philosophers. The melody, *philosophia quaedam perennis*, is not a body of truth revealed once and for all, but a living thought whose content, never discovered for the first time, is progressively determined and clarified by every genuine thinker." Collingwood, *Speculum Mentis*, 13.

68 Franz Rosenzweig, *The Star of Redemption*, trans. William W. Hallo (Notre Dame, IN: Univ. of Notre Dame Press, 1985), 68, 126, 354.

69 Rorty, "The Priority of Democracy to Philosophy," in *The Rorty Reader*, 239–58.

70 John Locke, *The Second Treatise on Civil Government*, §222, in *On Politics and Education* (Roslyn, NY: Walter J. Black, 1947), 188–90.

71 Gadamer, *Truth and Method*, trans. Weinsheimer and Marshall, 377–9; Northrop Frye, *Spiritus Mundi: Essays on Literature, Myth, and Society* (Bloomington: Indiana Univ. Press, 1976), 42; Ralph Heintzman, "The Educational Contract," *Journal of Canadian Studies* 14, no. 2, Summer 1979, 1–2, 142–5. What I call the "educational contract" is sometimes called "dialogic ethics" by virtue ethicists. Swanton, *Virtue Ethics*, 266–72. Paul Ricœur calls it (quoting Karl Jaspers) "le 'combat amoureux' de la vérité." *Amour et justice*, 50. Obviously, in referring to an "educational contract," I do not mean something that anyone could be said to have agreed to, but rather a primordial moral condition that underlies all human society, something to be discovered as much as created. I am using the term "contract" here rather in the sense of Edmund Burke's "great primeval contract of eternal society." *Reflections on the Revolution in France*, ed. William B. Todd (New York: Holt, Rinehart & Winston, 1965), 117. Ricœur says this kind of contract is not chronological or historical:

it is a "commencement transcendental ... le commencement de la vie en société." *Le conflit des interprétations*, 349.

72 "Everyone has a range of possibilities and characters in themselves, and the process of arriving at a common policy is curiously complex. A bit like a Cabinet making decisions in fact. ... There's a sort of democracy going on inside each one of us. ... It's not that one chooses freely among all the possibilities. But neither is it that one is forced into choosing one possible life among so many others. The point is that one is, in oneself, all those possibilities." Michael Frayn, quoted in Neal Ascherson, "What made Günther Grass?" *The Observer Review*, 7 September 2003, 6. See also Michael Frayn, *Democracy* (New York: Faber & Faber, 2004).

73 "L'esprit peut même user de l'adresse des *dichotomies* pour faire prévaloir tantôt les unes, tantôt les autres, comme dans une assemblée on peut faire prévaloir quelque parti par la pluralité des voix, selon qu'on forme l'ordre des demandes." Leibniz, *Nouveaux essais*, bk. 2, chap. 2, §40, pp. 164–5. Emphasis in original.

74 Webb Keane notes that "stances" or virtues, or clusters of virtues "can take the form of 'voices,'" which are "inherently dialogic." The "clash of voices" within us (and externally) contributes to "ethical self-formation" through the "struggle for dominance among those voices and the ethical positions they index," as we "consider them and adjudicate between them." *Ethical Life*, 136–49. Keane quotes the last words from Michael Lempert, *Discipline and Debate: The Language of Violence in a Tibetan Buddhist Monastery* (Berkeley: Univ. of California Press, 2012), 110–11. See also R.M. Adams, *A Theory of Virtue*, 208–9.

75 "It is commonplace to locate Western cultural origins in Greece, Rome and Judaeo-Christianity." Larry Siedentop, *Inventing the Individual: The Origins of Western Liberalism* (London: Allen Lane, 2014), 8. For Martin Heidegger, for example "the beginning of our spiritual-historical existence ... is the onset of Greek philosophy." "Rectorship Address: The Self-Assertion of the German University," trans. William S. Lewis, in *The Heidegger Reader*, ed. Figal, trans. Veith, 110. See also "The Question Concerning Technology," trans. William Lovitt, in *Basic Writings*, ed. David Farrell Krell (New York: HarperCollins, 1977), 315; *Introduction to Metaphysics*, trans. Manheim, 169.

76 Henri Frankfort, H.A. Frankfort, John A. Wilson, and Thorkild Jacobsen, *Before Philosophy: The Intellectual Adventure of Ancient Man* (Harmondsworth: Penguin Books, 1949).

77 Richard G. Klein, *The Human Career: Human Biological and Cultural Origins*, 2nd ed. (Chicago: Univ. of Chicago Press, 1999), 186, 579–86.

78 As Edward O. Wilson says, we need "a much broader definition of history than is conventionally used. ... The whole of it, biological and

cultural evolution, must be explored in seamless unity for a complete answer to the mystery [of human nature]." *The Meaning of Human Existence*, 16–18.

79 Jared Diamond traces our human ancestry even farther back, to the time when "the proto-human and proto-chimpanzee evolutionary lines diverged from each other," some six million years ago. *The World Until Yesterday: What We Can Learn from Traditional Societies* (New York: Viking, 2012), 5–7.

80 "[L]'humanité a toujours pensé qu'elle était la dernière et la meilleure humanité … [C]'est justement dans la plus vieille erreur humaine que [le monde moderne] est tombé." Charles Péguy, *Zangwill*, in *Une éthique sans compromis*, 176–7.

81 Herbert Butterfield, *The Whig Interpretation of History* (New York: W.W. Norton, 1965). On the same theme, see Leo Tolstoy, *War and Peace*, trans. Richard Pevear and Larissa Volokhonsky (New York: Vintage Classics, 2008), vol. 3, pt. 2, chap. 7, p. 709; David Martin, *On Secularization: Towards a Revised General Theory* (Farnham: Ashgate, 2005), 138; Iain Pears, *Arcadia* (New York: Vintage Books, 2017), 15.

82 John Thorp, "Ethics, Sex, and Religion: A Tectonic Shift," Lecture delivered at Trent University, December 2013.

83 Fred Adams reports the current scientific consensus that the future brightening of our sun will sterilize earth's biosphere, bringing all earthly life to an end, in about 3.5 billion years. By approximately 7 billion years from now, the earth itself will be absorbed into our expanding sun. Fred C. Adams, "Long-Term Astrophysical Processes," in *Global Catastrophic Risks*, ed. Nick Bostrom and Milan M. Ćirkovović (Oxford: Oxford Univ. Press, 2012), 34–5. See also Schellenberg, *Evolutionary Religion*, 13–14. Schellenberg cites work by Richard W. Pogge, D.O. Gough, K.P. Schroeder, and Robert Cannon Smith, and a team of scientists at Caltech.

84 Edward O. Wilson notes that "the average geological life span of a mammal species is about five hundred thousand years." *The Meaning of Human Existence*, 112. Stephen Hawking is even more pessimistic. Because of unsustainable resource depletion, and because of the increasing certainty of a global "disaster" over time, he estimates the planet Earth will only be habitable for another 1,000 to 10,000 years. By then, the survival of the human race will depend on its ability to "spread out into space, and to other stars." Peter Holley, "We Have 1,000 Years to Leave Planet Earth," *Ottawa Citizen*, 18 November 2016. David Wallace-Wells suggests the "natural lifespan of a civilization may be only several thousand years long, and the lifespan of an industrial civilization conceivably only several hundred." *The Uninhabitable Earth: Life after Warming* (New York: Tim Duggan Books, 2019), 221.

85 "[I]l ne faut point juger de l'éternité par quelques années. … [N]ous ne savons pas jusqu'où nos connaissances et nos organes peuvent être portés dans toute cette éternité qui nous attend. " Leibniz, *Nouveaux essais*, bk. 2, chap. 9, §14, p. 117; chap. 21, §40, p. 165.

86 G.W.F Hegel, *Preface to the Phenomenology of Spirit*, trans. Yirmiyahu Yovel (Princeton: Princeton Univ. Press, 2005), 99, 132–3.

87 "Each of the stages … is an image of the absolute, but at first in a limited mode, and thus it is forced onward to the whole." Hegel, *Encyclopaedia*, §237, in *Hegel's Logic*, trans. Wallace, 292–3.

88 Hegel, *Preface to the Phenomenology of Spirit*, trans. Yovel, 105, 123, 130, 154. 168–9. "What we have done here [in the *Phenomenology*] … is simply to gather together the particular moments, *each of which in principle exhibits the life of spirit in its entirety.*" Hegel, *The Phenomenology of Mind*, trans. Baillie, 797. Emphasis added.

89 Hans Joas comments, perceptively, that Heidegger's deliberate use of a "self-created private language" implicitly expresses his "will to dominate," or what, in this book, I will call the virtues of self-assertion, and, more particularly, the virtues of Liberty (A1) – especially the virtues of Power (A1a). *The Genesis of Values*, trans. Gregory Moore (Cambridge: Polity Press, 2000), 202n51.

90 Though, from this point of view, he was not always a model, I would gladly make mine the words of Immanuel Kant about theoretical jargon: "To make up new words for accepted concepts when the language does not lack expressions for them is a childish effort to distinguish one's self not by new and true thoughts but by new patches on old clothes. If any reader of [this] work can show that he knows more common expressions which are as adequate to the thoughts as the ones I used seemed to me, or can demonstrate the nullity of the thoughts themselves and therewith of the terms used to express them, he should do so. The first would greatly oblige me, for I only want to be understood; the second would be a service to philosophy itself." *Critique of Practical Reason*, Preface, 11.

91 Thomas Gilby, *Phoenix and Turtle: The Unity of Knowing and Being* (London: Longmans, 1950), x. No doubt thinking of Kant (see following note), Hegel also warned against any approach to the polarity of being that "reduces scientific organization to a table," which he described as a "skeleton," because "the flesh and blood have been removed from the bones." Hegel, *Preface to the Phenomenology of Spirit*, trans. Yovel, 160, 163. Merlin Donald, on the other hand, defends the use of images as visual aids to theoretical argument as "a time-saving concession to our archaic analogue mode" of mind! *A Mind So Rare*, 157.

92 And also to Immanuel Kant's tables of four "antinomies" (conflicting "transcendental ideas") of pure reason; his tables of "judgments,"

"categories," and "principles"; his 2x2 table of four false families of morality; and his "Table of Categories of Freedom With Reference to the Concepts of Good and Evil." See *Critique of Pure Reason*, trans. Norman Kemp Smith (London: Macmillan, 1968), 396–421, 107, 113, 196; *Critique of Practical Reason*, trans. Beck, pt. 1, chap. 1 and 2, pp. 41, 68–9. Kant said, rather boldly, that his table of "principles" of the science of nature "shows an inherent perfection" and "we can be sure that there are no more such principles." *Prolegomena to Any Future Metaphysics*, trans. Beck et al., 55. I would make no such claim for the tables in this book, which are certainly open to correction and improvement. As mentioned in the Preface, I subscribe, instead, to Alfred North Whitehead's dictum: "In philosophical discussion, the merest hint of dogmatic certainty as to finality of statement is an exhibition of folly." *Process and Reality*, ix.

93 Hegel, *Encyclopaedia*, §3, in *Hegel's Logic*, trans. Wallace, pp. 6–7. On the same problem of "abstract" concepts, Immanuel Kant said, rather condescendingly, that if any reader found even the simplified version of his "critique" of pure reason presented in this *Prolegomena*, "still obscure, let him consider that not everyone is bound to study metaphysics; that many minds will succeed very well in the exact and even in deep sciences more closely allied to the empirical, while they cannot succeed in investigations dealing exclusively with abstract concepts. In such cases men should apply their talents to other subjects." *Prolegomena to Any Future Metaphysics*, trans. Beck et al., 11. While there is no doubt some truth in this, it seems to me too dismissive and condescending. I have preferred to follow Hegel's hint and use figures and tables to make metaphysical ideas more readily comprehensible to the general reader.

94 John Locke said that "Diagrams drawn on paper are copies of ideas in the mind, and not liable to the uncertainty that words carry in their signification." But he did not think that this can be "done in moral ideas" because of the ambiguity of words. John Locke, *An Essay Concerning Human Understanding*, bk. 4, chap. 3, §19 (New York: Dover, 1959), 2:209. In response to Locke, Leibniz pointed out that there had, in fact, been a number of useful attempts to present moral ideas in graphic images, including the medieval scholastics' tables of predicaments, and the work of his own teacher, Erhard Weigel. Leibniz thought the task of "ordering" moral ideas into their proper families and levels was "very useful," and an important support to moral judgment and memory. Leibniz, *Nouveaux essais*, bk. 4, chap. 3, §19, p. 339; bk. 3, chap. 3, §9, pp. 249–50; bk. 3, chap. 6, §42, p. 285; bk. 3, chap. 10, §14, p. 299. Though I certainly agree with Locke about words, I hope that, in this book, I have been able to show Leibniz at least partly right about diagrams.

95 In a sense, I have tried to supply what Paul Ricœur (following Roman Ingarden) calls "l'activité imageante," the activity by which the reader of any text tries to create a mental image (*"se figurer"*) of its content and meaning. Ricœur, *Temps et Récit 3* in *Ricœur: Textes choisis et présentés*, 95. Italics in original.

Chapter 1. Where to Begin?

1 G.W. Leibniz, *Nouveaux essais sur l'entendement humain* (Paris: Garnier-Flammarion, 1966), bk. 4, chap. 2, §13, p. 19; G.W.F. Hegel, *Science of Logic*, vol. 1, bk. 2, §1, chap. 2, trans. W.H. Johnston and L.G. Struthers (London: George Allen & Unwin, 1951), 2:42, 65–6.

2 Martin Heidegger, "The Principle of Identity," trans. Joan Stambaugh and Jerome Veith, in *The Heidegger Reader*, ed. Günter Figal (Bloomington: Indiana Univ. Press, 2009), 284–94.

3 Brad S. Gregory, *The Unintended Reformation: How a Religious Revolution Revolutionized Society* (Cambridge, MA: Belknap Press of Harvard Univ. Press, 2012), 317.

4 Aristotle, *Metaphysics* 4.3.1005b15–25, 4.6.1011b15–20, trans. W.D. Ross, in *The Basic Works of Aristotle*, ed. Richard McKeon (New York: Random House, 1941), 737, 749.

5 Thomas Aquinas, *Summa Theologiæ* 1–2.65.2, in *Treatise on the Virtues*, trans. John A. Oesterle (Notre Dame, IN: Univ. of Notre Dame Press, 1984), 143.

6 Moses Maimonides, *The Guide for the Perplexed*, trans. M. Friedländer (New York: Dover, 1956), 128, 279. Also, 69, 139.

7 Thomas Hobbes, *Leviathan* (Indianapolis: Bobbs-Merrill, 1958), pt. 1, chap. 12, p. 102.

8 G.W. Leibniz, "Animadversiones," in *Les deux labyrinthes: textes choisis*, ed. Alain Chauve (Paris: Presses Universitaires de France, 1973), 22.

9 John Locke, *An Essay Concerning Human Understanding*, bk. 4, chap. 1, §3 (New York: Dover, 1959), 2:169. Also: Locke, bk. 4, chap. 7, §4, pp. 269–71. While Locke acknowledged the importance of the law of non-contradiction (and its flip side, the principle of identity) for avoiding error in reasoning – and that therefore they "cannot be laid aside" – he did not actually think they were "of much use to the discovery of unknown truths, or to help the mind forwards in its search after knowledge. … [F]or that we are left to our senses to discover to us as far as they can." Locke, §§11–20, pp. 288, 283, 287.

10 Immanuel Kant, *Critique of Pure Reason*, trans. Norman Kemp Smith (London: Macmillan, 1968), 190. Kant distinguished between "analytical" judgments (which "depend wholly" on the law of non-contradiction)

and synthetical judgments, which require additional principles. But even in the case of synthetical judgments, the law of non-contradiction "must never be violated." *Prolegomena to Any Future Metaphysics*, trans. Lewis White Beck et al. (Indianapolis: Bobbs-Merrill, 1950), 14–5. Hegel, on the other hand, said "that no mind thinks or forms conceptions or speaks in accordance with this law, and that no existence of any kind whatever conforms to it." G.W.F. Hegel, *Encyclopaedia of the Philosophical Sciences*, §115, in *Hegel's Logic*, trans. William Wallace (London: Oxford Univ. Press, 1975), 167.

11 F.H. Bradley, *Appearance and Reality* (Oxford: Oxford Univ. Press, 1930), 120. Bradley's statement is misleading, however, as he stood the law of non-contradiction somewhat on its head. Instead of allowing it to rule out anything self-contradictory, as it normally does, he took the "law" to mean exactly the opposite: i.e., that all apparent contradiction is ultimately reconciled in the harmony of absolute reality.

12 Étienne Gilson, *The Elements of Christian Philosophy* (New York: Mentor, 1963), 322n34.

13 Graham Priest, *Beyond the Limits of Thought* (Oxford: Oxford Univ. Press, 2006), 4–5. Priest's Quine reference is: W.V.O. Quine, *Philosophy of Logic* (n.p.: Prentice-Hall, 1970), 81. Quine was certainly not unfamiliar with paradox. But for him, paradoxes were not the fundamental, unresolvable contradictions of human life explored in this book, but simply the kind of intellectual puzzle or word game into which paradox degenerated at the end of the Renaissance, under the assault of the law of non-contradiction. Like most logicians, he thought the contradictions of paradox are merely something to be solved or got rid of, by exposing their underlying fallacy, or avoiding or revising a particular way of talking. W.V. Quine, *The Ways of Paradox and Other Essays* (New York: Random House, 1966), 3–20.

14 For a recent use of the law of non-contradiction to show that God is a "necessarily non-existing entity," see John R. Shook, *The God Debates: A 21st Century Guide for Atheists and Believers (and Everyone in Between)* (Chichester: Wiley-Blackwell, 2010), 24. Shook calls this the "dialectical non-existence proof." For an equally thoroughgoing use of the law of non-contradiction to argue exactly the opposite, see Gregory, *The Unintended Reformation*. See also Dietrich von Hildebrand, *What Is Philosophy?* (Steubenville, OH: Hildebrand Press, 2021), 77–9.

15 "[A]bout the truth of this Law [of Non-Contradiction], so far as it applies, there is in my opinion no question. The question will be rather as to *how far the Law applies and how far therefore it is true*." Bradley, *Appearance and Reality*, 506. Emphasis added.

16 Aristotle, *The Nicomachean Ethics* 8.12.1162a15–20, trans. J.A.K. Thomson, rev. Hugh Tredennick (London: Penguin Books, 2004), 222.

17 Martin Heidegger famously uses the image of "thrown" to express the arbitrariness of "being," or what he calls *Dasein*. See, for example, "The Problem of *Being and Time*," trans. Michael Heim, rev. Jerome Veith, in *The Heidegger Reader*, ed. Figal, 65. Also, *Being and Time*, trans. Joan Stambaugh (Albany: State Univ. of New York Press, 2010), almost throughout, including: 161, 181, 189, 191–2, 259, 265, 383. "Vivre, c'est être *déjà* né, dans une condition que nous n'avons pas choisie, une situation où nous nous trouvons, un canton de l'univers où nous pouvons nous sentir *jetés*, égarés perdus." Paul Ricœur, *Du texte à l'action*, in *Ricœur: Textes choisis et présentés*, ed. Michaël Fœssel and Fabien Lamouche (Paris: Éditions Points, 2007), 389. Emphasis added.

18 The family, as Hegel says, is "the source of obligation." G.W.F. Hegel, *Philosophy of Right*, addition to §181, trans. T.M. Knox (Oxford: Oxford Univ. Press, 1967), 266. See also James Q. Wilson, *The Moral Sense* (New York: Free Press, 1993), 226.

19 "It could be sound advice to say to a woman in strife with herself and tied to a demanding parent, 'You ought to consider yourself, and so break away now, hard as it may be on your parent.' One is then saying more than simply, 'If you wanted to, you would have a right to.' One is saying, 'I know you are shrinking away from it, but this is what you ought to do, and above all else.' In form this is an ought through and through, and an overriding one at that, but its ground is not other-regarding. ... One cannot love one's neighbor as oneself if one has not learned to accept one's own wishes as a proper object of respect and care, as one's own wishes are the paradigm of all wishes." W.D. Falk, "Morality, Self and Others," quoted in Paul Bloomfield, *The Virtues of Happiness: A Theory of the Good Life* (New York: Oxford Univ. Press, 2014), 32, 35.

20 "Individuality is cherished and nurtured, because in order for the whole to flourish, each of us has to be strong in who we are and carry our gifts with conviction, so they can be shared with others." Robin Wall Kimmerer, *Braiding Sweetgrass: Indigenous Wisdom, Scientific Knowledge, and the Teachings of Plants* (Minneapolis: Milkweed Editions, 2013), 134.

21 Hegel defines a dialectic as "a concrete unity of opposed determinations" or "opposite determinations in one relation." Hegel, *Encyclopaedia*, §48, in *Hegel's Logic*, trans. Wallace, 78; *Science of Logic*, vol. 2, §3, chap. 3, trans. Johnston and Struthers, 2:477. As noted later in this book, you should beware of thinking of a "dialectic" as simply a duality – the two sides of an opposition – as many contemporary writers do. Hegel emphasized, correctly, that a dialectic is *not* a duality but a *trinity*, a triad or "triplicity" (or even a "quadruplicity"). Because it includes both sides of a contradiction *and their unity*. See chapter 10, note 1. For Hegel, dialectic always has a dynamic character: its contradictory character is a source of momentum

and change, in thought and in the affairs of the world. It is the "moving principle" of the "concept," "which alike engenders and dissolves the particularization of the universal." It is not just a contradiction, but a positive "development and an immanent progress." Hegel, *Philosophy of Right*, trans. T.M. Knox, 34.

22 Rosalie L. Colie, *Paradoxica Epidemica: The Renaissance Tradition of Paradox* (Princeton: Princeton Univ. Press, 1966), 206. For a general introduction to the meaning and pre-modern history of paradox, especially as a literary device, see "Introduction: Problems of Paradoxes," in Colie, 3–40.

23 "[I]n a family, one's frame of mind is to have self-consciousness of one's *individuality within this unity* as the absolute essence of oneself, with the result that one is in it *not* as an independent person but *as a member*." Hegel, *Philosophy of Right*, §158, trans. Knox, 110. Emphasis added.

24 Francis Bacon, *Of the Dignity and Advancement of Learning*, cited in Michael Bilig, Susan Condor, Derek Edwards, Mike Gane, David Middleton, and Alan Radley, *Ideological Dilemmas: A Social Psychology of Everyday Thinking* (London: Sage, 1988), 15–16. Hegel also notes the paradoxical (or "dialectical") character of many "common proverbs." Hegel, *Encyclopaedia*, §81, trans. Wallace, 118. Anthony Trollope offers a droll list of antithetical proverbs in *Phineas Redux* (Oxford: Oxford Univ. Press, 2011), 13–14. For another modern list of paired proverbs, see Robert E. Quinn, *Beyond Rational Management: Mastering the Paradoxes and Competing Demands of High Performance* (San Francisco: Jossey-Bass, 1988), 30.

25 James Q. Wilson observes that human beings "are not born into a state of nature. They are born into a social compact that has long preceded them and without which their survival would not have been possible." *The Moral Sense*, 234.

26 "Only in the continuous encounter with other persons does the person become and remain a person." Paul Tillich, *The Courage to Be* (New Haven: Yale Univ. Press, 1952), 91.

27 Whitehead suggests the law of non-contradiction only works at the level of inorganic matter, at the level of "things" (It is). As soon as life (I am) begins to emerge from inorganic matter, "incompatibilities" (contradictions) are replaced by "contrasts" (paradox), perceived initially in feeling. Alfred North Whitehead, *Process and Reality* (New York: Free Press, 1969), 101, 113, 119, 125.

28 "Most biological processes are, in fact, dialectical; that is to say, they go forward as an interplay of opposed but mutually determined phases." Susanne K. Langer, *Mind: An Essay on Human Feeling*, vol. 2 (Baltimore: Johns Hopkins Press, 1972), 16–17. Hegel makes the same point about the dialectic of organic life, or the "process of the Living Individuality."

Hegel, *Science of Logic*, vol. 2, §3, chap. 1, trans. Johnston and Struthers, 2:407.

29 "In order to have a correct foundation of the science of biology (and especially physiology), one must always begin with the basic relation of an organism to its environment. This relation constitutes the essence of a life process. ... One should conceive of each as a dependent variable of the processes of life." Max Scheler, *Formalism in Ethics and Non-Formal Ethics of Value*, trans. Manfred S. Frings and Roger L. Funk (Evanston: Northwestern Univ. Press, 1973), 154–5.

30 "Individuation goes on all the time, but it can proceed only in a framework of active involvements with the generating stock and the nourishing substrate of an ambient that is a small detail in the whole vast biosphere. Often, indeed, *the very means of individuation*, being chiefly powers of *aggression* against other individuals, *lead to new involvements* which become paramount, as with organisms that exploit others to the point of becoming entirely dependent on them. ... *Individuation and involvement* are the extremes of the great rhythm of evolution, which moves between them in a direction of its own, always toward more intense activity and gradually increasing ambients of the generic lines that survive." Langer, *Mind: An Essay on Human Feeling*, vol. 1 (Baltimore: Johns Hopkins Press, 1967), 354–5. Emphasis added. My comment about the outer surface of animals is based on Langer, 1:420. Hegel makes the same point, about the "pure mistake" of supposing the particular can be the "determining principle," when "the necessity of the link between particulars [i.e., union/reverence] remains the primary and essential thing." Hegel, *Philosophy of Right*, addition to §181, trans. Knox, 266.

31 "[T]he sum total of all possibility ... serves as the condition of the complete determination of each and every thing." Kant, *Critique of Pure Reason*, trans. Kemp Smith, 489. "[T]he true 'sum of conditions' must completely include all the contents of the world at a given time. ... The cause is not the true cause unless it is the whole cause; and it is not the whole cause unless in it you include the environment, the entire mass of unspecified conditions in the background." Bradley, *Appearance and Reality*, 57, 297.

32 "Ne faut-il pas plutôt passer par des structures dialectiques impliquant une logique qui ne soit pas celle de la non-contradiction?" Paul Ricœur, *Politique, Économie et Société: Écrits et conférences* 4 (Paris: Seuil, 2019), 85.

Chapter 2. Union and Non-union

1 In thinking about things like the principle of contradiction, we have to distinguish, as Maurice Blondel says, between "ce qui est pensé" and "ce qui semble être la loi de la pensée." *Premiers écrits*, 2:128–32, in Jean

Lacroix, *Maurice Blondel, sa vie, son œuvre* (Paris: Presses Universitaires de France, 1963), 115.

2 On one occasion, Martin Heidegger began from a piece of chalk! *Introduction to Metaphysics*, trans. Ralph Manheim (New York: Doubleday, 1961), 24–5.

3 "We find the world's contents grouped into things and their qualities." F.H. Bradley, *Appearance and Reality* (Oxford: Oxford Univ. Press, 1930), 16.

4 Joseph Henrich, Steven J. Heine, and Ara Norenzayan, "The Weirdest People in the World?" In *Arguing about Human Nature: Contemporary Debates*, ed. Stephen M. Downes and Edouard Machery (New York: Routledge, 2013), 198–216.

5 Jonathan Haidt, *The Righteous Mind: Why Good People Are Divided by Politics and Religion* (New York: Pantheon Books, 2012), 96. Jared Diamond uses the same WEIRD acronym to highlight the singularity of Western culture, in *The World Until Yesterday: What We Can Learn from Traditional Societies* (New York: Viking, 2012), 8–9.

6 Aristotle, *Metaphysics* 7.3.1029b3–10, trans. W.D. Ross, in *The Basic Works of Aristotle*, ed. Richard McKeon (New York: Random House, 1941), 786.

7 "The acts of cognition which underlie our experience posit the Real in *individual* form, posit it as having spatio-temporal existence, as something existing in *this* time-spot." Edmund Husserl, *Ideas: General Introduction to Pure Phenomenology*, trans. W.R. Boyce Gibson (New York: Collier Books, 1962), §2, p. 46. Emphasis in original. "[T]he being of things initially at hand is passed over, and beings are first conceived as a context of things (*res*) objectively present. *Being* acquires the meaning of reality. Substantiality becomes the basic characteristic of beings." Martin Heidegger, *Being and Time*, 201, trans. Joan Stambaugh (Albany: State Univ. of New York Press, 2010), 193. Emphasis in original.

8 Husserl, *Ideas*, trans. Gibson, §27, p. 92. Emphasis in original. Also: 106–7, 124–5, 180–1, 220. See also G.W. Leibniz, *Nouveaux essais sur l'entendement humain*, Préface (Paris: Garnier-Flammarion, 1966), 38–9; Max Scheler, *Formalism in Ethics and Non-Formal Ethics of Value*, trans. Manfred S. Frings and Roger L. Funk (Evanston: Northwestern Univ. Press, 1973), 139–40, 147–8.

9 "All actual experiences [*sic*] refers beyond itself to possible experiences, which themselves again point to new possible experiences, and so in *in-finitum*." Husserl, trans. Gibson, §47, p. 135.

10 Husserl, §84, p. 223.

11 "This is certain: things, however absolute and entire they seem in themselves, are but retainers to other parts of nature ... and we must not confine our thoughts within the surface of any body, but look a great

deal further, to comprehend perfectly those qualities that are in it." John Locke, *An Essay Concerning Human Understanding*, bk. 4, chap. 6, §11 (New York: Dover, 1959), 2:262. "As existing, Dasein never relates to a particular object; if it relates solely to one object, it does so by turning away from other beings that always appear prior to, and along with, the object." Martin Heidegger, "The Problem of *Being and Time*," trans. Michael Heim, in *The Heidegger Reader*, ed. Günter Figal, trans. Jerome Veith (Bloomington: Indiana Univ. Press, 2009), 64.

12 "Every thing that exists stands in correlation, and this correlation is the veritable nature of every existence." G.W.F. Hegel, *Encyclopaedia of the Philosophical Sciences*, §135, in *Hegel's Logic*, trans. William Wallace (London: Oxford Univ. Press, 1975), 191.

13 "[I]l y a deux vérités générales absolues, c'est-à-dire qui parlent de l'existence actuelle des choses … [D'une part] nous sommes, de l'autre … il y a quelque autre chose que nous …" G.W. Leibniz, "À Foucher," in *Les deux labyrinthes: textes choisis*, ed. Alain Chauve (Paris: Presses Universitaires de France, 1973), 24. Franz Rosenzweig suggests "I" always involves a "contradiction." "I" is always an "I, however" or a "Thus and not-otherwise," meaning "not otherwise than everything": "For when we designate something as 'thus and not otherwise,' we mean to delimit it as against 'everything' pure and simple." *The Star of Redemption*, trans. William W. Hallo (Notre Dame, IN: Univ. of Notre Dame Press, 1985), 173–4.

14 "The World is the totality of objects that can be known through experience." Husserl, *Ideas*, trans. Gibson, §1, p. 46.

15 Husserl, §27, p. 92. Emphasis in original. Martin Heidegger expands Husserl's phenomenological "horizon" in some four ways, incuding the "transcendental" horizon of time. *Being and Time*, trans. Stambaugh, 441–2. See also Scheler, *Formalism in Ethics*, trans. Frings and Funk, 520.

16 "Pas plus que nous ne pouvons concevoir le monde sans le mettre en morceaux et sans le particulariser, nous ne saurions voir et penser les parties sans les solidariser et les mettre en rapport avec l'univers." Blondel, *La Pensée*, 1:13, in Lacroix, *Maurice Blondel*, 43.

17 "[L]a chose visée entretient des rapports potentiels avec toute autre chose sous l'horizon d'un monde total, lequel ne figure jamais comme objet de discours." Paul Ricœur, *Temps et Récit 1*, in *Ricœur: Textes choisis et présentés*, ed. Michaël Fœssel and Fabien Lamouche (Paris: Éditions Points, 2007), 137.

18 Karl Rahner, *The Practice of Faith: A Handbook of Contemporary Spirituality*, trans. various (New York: Crossroad, 1983), 57.

19 "[L]a connexion réelle de toutes choses … [I]l n'y a point de terme si absolu ou si détaché qu'il n'enferme des relations et dont la parfaite analyse

ne mène à d'autres choses et *même à toutes les autres.*" Leibniz, *Nouveaux essais*, bk. 2, chap. 26, §§5, 10, p. 194–5. Emphasis added.

20 In a striking metaphor, Bradley suggests every individual thing should really appear to us with "*edges which are ragged* in such a way as to imply another existence from which it has been torn, and without which it really does not exist." Bradley, *Appearance and Reality*, 156. Emphasis added. "Toute apparition d'une chose particulière suppose le monde." Emmanuel Levinas, *En découvrant l'existence avec Husserl et Heidegger*, 4th corrected ed. (Paris: Vrin, 2010), 90.

21 Aristotle, *Metaphysics* 1.5.986b1–10, trans. Ross, 699; G.S. Kirk and J.E. Raven, *The Presocratic Philosophers* (Cambridge: Cambridge Univ. Press, 1964), 236–62; Charles H. Kahn, *Pythagoras and the Pythagoreans: A Brief History* (Indianapolis: Hackett, 2001).

22 Martin Heidegger discusses the concepts of "limit" and "unlimited" in early Greek philosophy in *An Introduction to Metaphysics*, trans. Manheim, 46–50. Edmund Husserl also uses the terminology of "limitlessness" to describe the unseen horizon, fringe, or background behind all actual perceptions: "*the stream of experience as a unity.*" *Ideas*, trans. Gibson, §83, p. 220. Emphasis in original.

23 Quoted in Kahn, *Pythagoras and the Pythagoreans*, 24–5. Similarly, Heraclitus said that "what is at variance agrees with itself" through an "attunement of opposite tensions, like that of the bow and the lyre." Fragment 45 in J. Burnet, *Early Greek Philosophy*, 4th ed. (London, 1930), cited in H. and H.A. Frankfort, "Conclusion: The Emancipation of Thought from Myth," in Henri Frankfort, H.A. Frankfort, John A. Wilson, and Thorkild Jacobsen, *Before Philosophy: The Intellectual Adventure of Ancient Man* (Harmondsworth: Penguin Books, 1949), 256.

24 The paradox of the one and the many is central to many traditions. The Sufi Muslim concept of *hayrat* or perplexity, for example, results from the paradoxical attempt "to see the One in the Many and the Many in the One, or rather to see the Many as One and the One as Many." Kātib Çelebī, *The Balance of Truth in Choosing the Most True*, cited in Shahab Ahmed, *What Is Islam? The Importance of Being Islamic* (Princeton: Princeton Univ. Press, 2016), 278.

25 Hans-Georg Gadamer, *Dialogue and Dialectic: Eight Hermeneutical Studies on Plato*, trans. P. Christopher Smith (New Haven: Yale Univ. Press, 1980), 88, 131, 147, 119–20, 204.

26 Aristotle, *Metaphysics* 9.5.1062b34-1063b35, trans. Ross, 856–60.

27 Aristotle, *Metaphysics* 4.2.1005a4, trans. Ross, 735. Aristotle explained that "contradiction and contrariety are not the same," but this distinction is not easy to grasp and seems to have been lost on much of the history of later thought. Aristotle, *Metaphysics*, 9.4.10055b1–10, trans. Ross, 842. On

the distinction between contraries and contradictions, see also Thomas Aquinas, *Summa Theologiæ* 1–2.64.3, in *Treatise on the Virtues*, trans. John A. Oesterle (Notre Dame, IN: Univ. of Notre Dame Press, 1984), 136; Maurice Blondel, *L'Être et les êtres* (Paris: Presses Universitaires de France, 1963), 470; *Premiers écrits*, 2:128–32, in Lacroix, *Maurice Blondel*, 117–19; Alfred North Whitehead, *Process and Reality* (New York: Free Press, 1969), 113; Emmanuel Levinas, *Autrement qu'être ou au-delà de l'essence* (Paris: Le Livre de Poche, 2008), 20.

28 The paradox of the one and the many, of unity and plurality, became the starting point and core of all subsequent Western metaphysics. See, for example, Bradley, *Appearance and Reality*, 416, 460; Whitehead, *Process and Reality*, 168–9.

29 Plotinus, *Enneads*, 5.1.4, in *The Essential Plotinus*, ed. Elmer O'Brien (New York: Mentor Books, 1964), 95–6.

30 Denys Turner, *The Darkness of God: Negativity in Christian Mysticism* (Cambridge: Cambridge Univ. Press, 1995), especially 36–8, 129, 247, 255.

31 Larry Siedentop, *Inventing the Individual: The Origins of Western Liberalism* (London: Allen Lane, 2014), 242, 250, 298. "[I]t was in the formal organization of the debates and disagreements recorded as *quaestiones disputatae* and *quaestiones quodlibetales*, and in the elaboration of both the theological and the secular *distinctiones* which these involved, that enquiry at last found the means to become simultaneously comprehensive and systematic." Alasdair MacIntyre, *Whose Justice? Which Rationality?*, (Notre Dame, IN: Univ. of Notre Dame Press, 1988), 206. "The *summa* is a genre of which Aquinas' is only one example [which] ... exemplifies ... the imperative to listen to opposing viewpoints and to engage in dialectical commerce with them." John W. O'Malley, *Four Cultures of the West* (Cambridge, MA: Harvard Univ. Press, 2004), 96.

32 Nicholas of Cusa, *On the Vision of God*, in *The Essential Writings of Christian Mysticism*, ed. Bernard McGinn (New York: Modern Library, 2006), 352; Ernst Cassirer, *The Individual and the Cosmos in Renaissance Philosophy*, trans. Mario Domandi (Philadelphia: Univ. of Pennsylvania Press, 1972), 8, 13–45, 52, 60, 87, 179. Shahab Ahmed notes that the principle of *coincidentia oppositorum* (in Arabic: *jam' al-aḍdād*) is at the "conceptual heart" of the "Sufi-philosophical amalgam of the Balkans-to-Bengal complex." Paradox is "perhaps *the* definitive conceptual device" in its discourses. *What Is Islam?*, 398.

33 O'Malley, *Four Cultures of the West*, 60.

34 "[P]aradox either turned into a trifling amusement ... or was submerged back into figurative language, where paradoxes always silently dwell. Paradox ceased to inform imaginative literature. ... [I]n a world increasingly dedicated to the pursuit of exact knowledge ... paradoxy lost its

transcendent sense of 're-creation' to become mere 'recreation,' trivial
diversions ... With increasing distrust of 'words,' paradoxes degenerated
into mere puzzles, whose answers were no longer expected to lead into
the experience of real truth." Rosalind L. Colie, *Paradoxica Epidemica: The
Renaissance Tradition of Paradox* (Princeton: Princeton Univ. Press, 1966),
508–9.

35 Colie, 509.

36 Immanuel Kant, *Critique of Pure Reason*, B110–11, trans. Norman Kemp
Smith (London: Macmillan, 1968), 116.

37 G.W.F. Hegel, "Fragment of a System," trans. Richard Kroner, in *Early
Theological Writings*, trans. T.M. Knox (Chicago: Univ. of Chicago Press,
1948), 312. This formula has been called Hegel's whole future philosophical system "in a nutshell." Richard Kroner, "Introduction: Hegel's Philosophical Development," in Hegel, *Early Theological Writings*, 14. Although
his youthful formula seems to me both clearer and more useful, Hegel's
own mature formula for expressing this dialectic states that the "Absolute" is "the identity of Identity and Non-Identity" or "the identity of the
Identical and the non-Identical." *Science of Logic*, vol. 1, bk. 1, trans. W.H.
Johnston and L.G. Struthers (London: George Allen & Unwin, 1951), 1:86;
History of Philosophy, trans. E.S. Haldane (London: Kegan Paul, Trench,
Trubner, 1892–5), 2:80, cited in Emil J. Fackenheim, *The Religious Dimen-
sion of Hegel's Thought* (Boston: Beacon Press, 1967), 247. Charles Taylor
has called this "perhaps the central and most 'mind-blowing' idea of the
Hegelian system." *Hegel* (Cambridge: Cambridge Univ. Press, 1975), 49.

38 Hegel, *Science of Logic*, vol. 1, bk. 2, §1, chap. 2, trans. Johnston and Struthers, 2:67.

39 "Unity is the belonging together of antagonisms. This is original oneness." Heidegger, *An Introduction to Metaphysics*, trans. Manheim, 117.

40 "Being-with as an authentic comportment to existence is possible only on
the basis that each co-existing Dasein can be, and is, authentically itself."
Heidegger, "The Problem of *Being and Time*," trans. Heim, rev. Veith, 65.
"[U]nity and multiplicity are fundamentally in dialectical relationship to
each other." Hans-Georg Gadamer, *Truth and Method*, trans. and rev. Joel
Weinsheimer and Donald G. Marshall, 2nd ed. (New York: Continuum,
2002), 427.

41 Whitehead points out that "all potential objectifications" (somethings)
find their "niche" within "one extensive continuum" (everything). Whitehead, *Process and Reality*, 82.

42 R.G. Collingwood, *Speculum Mentis or the Map of Knowledge* (Oxford: Oxford Univ. Press, 1963), 197. "[L]'être est originairement dialectique." Paul
Ricœur, *Histoire et vérité* (Paris: Points Essais, 2001), 404. Ricœur points
out that all human narrative and storytelling, for example, are based

on the union of union and non-union and are thus a "concordance discordante." *Soi-même comme un autre* (Paris: Éditions du Seuil, 1990), 168–9.

43　Kirk and Raven, *The Presocratic Philosophers*, 247–50; H. and H.A. Frankfort, "Introduction: Myth and Reality," in H. Frankfort et al., *Before Philosophy*, 11–36.

44　Aristotle, *Physics* 2.3, trans. R.P. Hardie and R.K. Gaye; *Metaphysics*,
5.2.1013a20–35, 8.4.1044a30–5, trans. Ross, in *The Basic Works of Aristotle*,
ed. McKeon, 240–1, 752–3, 817. Final causes are only one of four types
of cause Aristotle identified. I'll come back to the other three in chapters
3 and 15. On the four types of cause, see also Thomas Aquinas, "Commentary," *V Metaphysics, lect. 2*, in *Philosophical Texts*, selected and trans.
Thomas Gilby (London: Oxford Univ. Press, 1956), 43–6.

45　"[L]a première question qu'on a droit de faire, sera, Pourquoi il y a plus
tôt quelque chose que rien." G.W. Leibniz, *Les principes de la nature et de
la grâce fondés en raison*, §7, in *Principes de la nature et de la grâce fondés en
raison – Principes de la philosophie ou Monadologie*, ed. André Robinet (Paris:
Presses Universitaires de France, 1986), 45.

46　Karl Jaspers, *Reason and Existenz*, trans. William Earle, in *Existentialism
from Dostoevsky to Sartre*, ed. Walter Kaufmann (Cleveland: World, 1956);
Way to Wisdom, trans. Ralph Manheim (New Haven: Yale Univ. Press,
1960).

47　Aristotle says unity and being are virtually interchangeable terms,
the one implying the other. Aristotle, *Metaphysics* 4.2.1003b20–30,
11.3.1061a15–20, trans. Ross, 732, 855. Thomas Aquinas agrees: "[W]hat-
ever we apprehend we refer to it as being, and consequently as one and
good, which are convertible with being." *Summa Theologiæ* 1–2.55.4, in
Treatise on the Virtues, trans. Oesterle, 56. On the transcendentals of being
(which are "convertible" with being), see Étienne Gilson, *The Elements of
Christian Philosophy* (New York; Mentor, 1963), 149–78.

48　"'[E]verything' implies 'the All.' It can only be that which is identical
with the 'Being' of the All and of each individual object." Rosenzweig,
The Star of Redemption, trans. Hallo, 174.

49　Aristotle, *Metaphysics* 9.6.1048a30–9.8.1050a25. trans. Ross, 826–30.

50　"*Dictum esse ipse actus essentiae*," quoted in Étienne Gilson, *God and Philosophy* (New Haven: Yale Univ. Press, 1941), 64.

51　"The knowledge which is the start or immediately our object can be nothing else than just that which is immediate knowledge, knowledge of the
immediate, of what *is*. ... The bare fact of [sensuous] *certainty*, however,
is really and admittedly the abstractest and the poorest kind of *truth*. It
merely says regarding what it knows: it *is*; and its truth contains solely
the *being* of the fact it knows. ... The Universal is therefore in point of fact
the truth of sense-certainty, the true content of sense-experience. ... It is

as a universal ... that we give utterance to sensuous fact. What we say is 'This', i.e. the universal this; or we say: 'it is', i.e. being in general." G.W.F. Hegel, *The Phenomenology of Mind*, trans. J.B. Baillie (New York: Harper & Row, 1967), 149–52. Emphasis in original.

52 This fourth meaning can open the door to still other questions. Is the source or ground of being something (or some act or action, some verb) that can be found only inside the universe? Or do we need to say that the source of being is also, in some sense, *outside* time and space, outside physical reality? And what do people mean when they say this? While these are important questions, in themselves, they aren't important for this book. So, in this book, I will set this fifth issue aside.

53 G.W.F Hegel, *Preface to the Phenomenology of Spirit*, trans. Yirmiyahu Yovel (Princeton: Princeton Univ. Press, 2005), 130. Franz Rosenzweig describes the "I" as "Nay become audible." *The Star of Redemption*, trans. Hallo, 174.

54 " [L]'individualité enveloppe l'infini ... [Le] principe d'individuation d'une telle ou telle chose ... vient de l'influence ... de toutes les choses de l'univers les unes sur les autres." G.W. Leibniz, *Nouveaux essais*, bk. 3, chap. 3, §6, pp. 248–9.

55 "Dans l'expiation, sur un point de l'ess[a]nce pèse – jusqu'à l'en expulser – le reste de l'ess[a]nce." Levinas, *Autrement qu'être*, 200.

56 What, in this book, I call the polarity of being, Maurice Blondel calls the "normative de l'être" or "la dialectique de l'être," the structure or "concrete logic" of the *real* world – "la dialectique réelle des actions humaines" – which he contrasts to the "logic of thought," with its exclusionary principles of contradiction and identity. *L'Être et les êtres*, 256–8, 271, 289, 470–1.

Chapter 3. The Lens of the Virtues

1 Thomas Aquinas, *Summa Theologiæ* 1.2.2, in *Philosophical Texts*, trans. Thomas Gilby (London: Oxford Univ. Press, 1956), 42. See also G.W. Leibniz, *Essais de Théodicée* (Paris: Garnier-Flammarion, 1969), §§44, 184, pp. 77, 228; William James, *The Varieties of Religious Experience* (New York: Collier Books, 1961), 399–400.

2 William Shakespeare, *Hamlet*, in *The Complete Works*, ed. Alfred Harbage (Baltimore: Penguin Books, 1969), 1.3.78.

3 For Hegel, this is the only genuine, authentic, or useful meaning of truth. A thing is "true" for him only when it conforms to its inner concept, when it's true to what makes it real. For Hegel, the common meaning of truth – a subject conforming to a predicate, as in the logical principle of identity (i.e., A=A) – is simply trivial, banal, and tautological. G.W.F. Hegel, *Encyclopaedia of the Philosophical Sciences*, §138, in *Hegel's Logic*,

trans. William Wallace (London: Oxford Univ. Press, 1975), 191. Martin Heidegger agrees with Hegel: the true or "primordial" meaning of truth is the truth about the nature of the human. The truths about the world, or "factual" truths, are only true "in a secondary sense." And are therefore, on their own, a kind of "untruth." To be truly true, they must be rooted in the wider truth about the human, of which they are only one expression. What is "primarily" true is the truth about the nature of the human, or "Dasein": *"Dasein is 'in the truth.'" "[A]ll truth is relative to the being of Dasein." Being and Time*, 220–1, 256–7, 226–7, trans. Joan Stambaugh (Albany: State Univ. of New York Press, 2010), 211–12, 245–6, 217. Emphasis in original. As you will see later in this book, the common meaning of truth is a product of the stances of "It is." It expresses only the conformity of thought with thing. But truth can take on its full meaning only when the stances of "It is" are united with the stances of "I am." Then it means something more like being "true" to the whole nature of the human, to all four stances of the human paradox, and their related families of virtues.

4 "[H]e who is moved neither by reason nor pity to be of any service to others is properly called inhuman; for he seems to be unlike a man." Baruch Spinoza, *Ethics*, pt. 4, Proposition 50, trans. W.H. White, in *Spinoza Selections*, ed. John Wild (New York: Scribner's, 1958), 331. "Je suis homme, et rien de ce qui est inhumain ne m'est concitoyen." Charles Péguy, *Encore de la grippe*, in *Une éthique sans compromis*, ed. Dominique Saatdjian (Paris: Pocket, 2011), 285. "Though in the heat of battle or the embrace of ideology many of us will become indifferent to suffering or inured to bloodshed, in our calm and disinterested moments we discover in ourselves an intuitive and powerful aversion to inhumanity." James Q. Wilson, *The Moral Sense* (New York: Free Press, 1993), 2. "We all can fairly easily tell the difference between humane and inhumane treatment, and all, even the [egoists], will acknowledge that morality points us in the direction of the humane and that this moral concept is clearly tied to the human condition, though it is hard to see how to derive it from pure rationality or agency." Paul Bloomfield, *The Virtues of Happiness: A Theory of the Good Life* (New York: Oxford Univ. Press, 2014), 67.

5 Immanuel Kant, *Critique of Pure Reason*, A318, trans. Norman Kemp Smith (London: Macmillan, 1968), 313. "[H]umanity, in this sense, is a value. ... [T]here lies within us a desire for humanity ... To aspire to virtue means to try not to be unworthy of what humanity has made us, individually and collectively." André Comte-Sponville, *A Small Treatise on the Great Virtues*, trans. Catherine Temerson (New York: Henry Holt, 2001), 3.

6 "[T]he definition – which ... gained currency in the West and which remains unshaken in the dominant opinion and attitude – of *man as the*

rational animal." Martin Heidegger, *An Introduction to Metaphysics*, trans. Ralph Manheim (New York: Doubleday, 1961), 147. Emphasis added.

7 "For the subjective will, the good and the good alone is the essential, and the subjective will has value and dignity only in so far as its insight and intention accord with the good." G.W.F. Hegel, *Philosophy of Right*, trans. T.M. Knox (Oxford: Oxford Univ. Press, 1967), §131, p. 87.

8 "Being ethical is what makes you human." Webb Keane, *Ethical Life: Its Natural and Social Histories* (Princeton: Princeton Univ. Press, 2016), 12.

9 The Latin word for "virtue" was itself a translation of a Greek word, *aretē*, meaning goodness or excellence. But this word also came loaded with similar, snobbish, self-regarding, "self-satisfied," and assertive overtones of the superior Greek citizen, looking down on non-citizens and slaves, priding himself on his "magnificence," aristocratic "liberality," charm, and manly courage, who "likes his own company" and for whom "modesty is not a virtue." Aristotle, *The Nicomachean Ethics* 2.6.1107b1–1108a35, 9.4.1166a10–b10, trans. J.A.K. Thomson, rev. Hugh Tredennick (London: Penguin Books, 2004), 43–5, 237–7. Even in Roman law, as Hegel notes, "a man is reckoned a person only when he is treated as possessing a certain status." Hegel, *Philosophy of Right*, trans. Knox, §40, p. 39. John Calvin exaggerates, but he correctly discerns the self-assertive core of Greek and Roman virtue, when he says: "The philosophers who have contended most strongly that virtue is to be desired on her own account, were so inflated with arrogance as to make it apparent that they sought virtue for no other reason than as a ground for indulging in pride." *The Institutes of the Christian Religion* 3.7.2, trans. Henry Beveridge (Peabody, MA: Hendrickson, 2012), 450. Hence Anthony Kronman appropriately entitles his overview of Greek and Roman thought "Pride." Anthony T. Kronman, *Confessions of a Born-Again Pagan* (New Haven: Yale Univ. Press, 2016), pt. 2, 115–226.

10 "Virtue has acquired a bad name. To young people it is the opposite of having fun, to older ones it is a symbol of lost virtue that politicians now exploit for partisan purposes, and to young and old alike it is a set of rules that well-meaning but intolerant bluenoses impose on other people." James Q. Wilson, *The Moral Sense*, vii. "[À] une époque comme la nôtre, où règne souvent le cynisme, ou un hédonisme sans frein, celui qui se propose de chanter la vertu n'a pas forcément le beau rôle; il court le risque de se montrer plus ou moins naïf. De nos jours en effet, lorsqu'on dit de quelqu'un qu'il est vertueux, on ne le fait pas sans un certain ton de condescendance, comme si l'on voulait signifier qu'il s'agit là d'une personne un peu contrainte, un peu rigide, qui ne sait pas tout à fait profiter des avantages et plaisirs qu'offre la vie." François Cheng, *Œil ouvert et cœur battant: Comment envisager et dévisager la beauté* (Paris: Desclée de

Brouwer, 2011), quoted in Jean Leahey, "Du spleen à la confiance," *Le Devoir*, 5 January 2017, A7.

11   Wilson, *The Moral Sense*.

12   Christopher Peterson and Martin E.P. Seligman, *Character Strengths and Virtues: A Handbook and Classification* (New York: Oxford Univ. Press, 2004).

13   Christopher Peterson and Nansoon Park, "Classifying and Measuring Strengths of Character," in *The Oxford Handbook of Positive Psychology*, ed. Shane J. Lopez and C.R. Snyder, 2nd ed. (New York: Oxford Univ. Press, 2011), 32.

14   David Brooks, *The Road to Character* (New York: Random House, 2015).

15   James Davison Hunter, *The Death of Character: Moral Education in an Age Without Good and Evil* (New York: Basic Books, 2000).

16   "[T]he good is co-extensive with approbation ... in its widest sense." F.H. Bradley, *Appearance and Reality* (Oxford: Oxford Univ. Press, 1930), 361.

17   Max Scheler, *Formalism in Ethics and Non-Formal Ethics of Value*, trans. Manfred S. Frings and Roger L. Funk (Evanston: Northwestern Univ. Press, 1973), 16–20, 288, 355–6.

18   Comte-Sponville, *A Small Treatise*, trans. Temerson, 3–4.

19   Aristotle, *Nicomachean Ethics* 2.5.1106a10–24, trans. W.D. Ross, in *The Basic Works of Aristotle*, ed. Richard McKeon (New York: Random House, 1941), 957, and in Aristotle, *The Nicomachean Ethics,* trans. Thomson, rev. Tredennick, 39–40.

20   2 Corinthians 6:7.

21   Thomas Aquinas, *Summa Theologiæ* 1–2.55.3, 1–2.58.4, in *Treatise on the Virtues*, trans. John A. Oesterle (Notre Dame, IN: Univ. of Notre Dame Press, 1984), 54, 86.

22   Hegel, *Philosophy of Right*, trans. Knox, §150, pp. 107–8.

23   Scheler, *Formalism in Ethics*, trans. Frings and Funk, 85, 205. Scheler more often speaks of virtue in the singular than in the plural. Another plural definition is: "the areas of the ideal ought which are differentiated by basic [moral] value qualities," i.e., the families of virtues described in this book. Scheler, 28.

24   Bernard Williams, *Ethics and the Limits of Philosophy* (Cambridge, MA: Harvard Univ. Press, 1985), 9.

25   Alasdair MacIntyre, *After Virtue*, 2nd ed. (Notre Dame, IN: Univ. of Notre Dame Press, 1984), 191.

26   Robert Merrihew Adams, *A Theory of Virtue: Excellence in Being for the Good* (Oxford: Oxford Univ. Press, 2013), 31–5.

27   Roger Scruton, *On Human Nature* (Princeton: Princeton Univ. Press, 2017), 103.

28   Julia Annas, *Intelligent Virtue* (Oxford: Oxford Univ. Press, 2013), 9, 109.

29 Christine Swanton, *Virtue Ethics: A Pluralistic View* (Oxford: Oxford Univ. Press, 2003), 19.

30 N.T. Wright, *After You Believe: Why Christian Character Matters* (New York: HarperCollins, 2010), 21.

31 Comte-Sponville, *A Small Treatise*, trans. Temerson, 3–4.

32 Bloomfield, *The Virtues of Happiness*, 173.

33 My concern, in this book, is primarily with virtues (plural), rather than with virtue (singular). I want to uncover the structure or architecture of the virtues as a whole – or what Peterson and Seligman call "character strengths" – rather than the "persisting character" or virtue (singular) they may produce in a particular individual, although the two are closely linked. R.M. Adams, *A Theory of Virtue*, 164.

34 "Les puissances véritables ne sont jamais de simples possibilités. Il y a toujours de la tendance et de l'action." G.W. Leibniz, *Nouveaux essais sur l'entendement humain* (Paris: Garnier-Flammarion, 1966), bk. 2, chap. 1, §2, p. 93.

35 "Each power of the soul is a form or nature and has a natural inclination to something." "A power as such is directed to an act." "[A]ny aptitude by which a man is disposed to an act … may be both by a power and by a habit, for by a power man is, as it were, empowered to do the action, and by the habit he is apt to act well or ill." Thomas Aquinas, *Summa Theologiæ* 1.80.1, 1.77.3, 1.83.2, in *Introduction to St. Thomas Aquinas*, ed. Anton C. Pegis (New York: The Modern Library, 1948), 351, 317, 372. See also Aristotle, *Metaphysics* 5.12.1019a15–1020a7, 9.1.1045b30–9.10.1052a15, trans. W.D. Ross, in *The Basic Works of Aristotle*, ed. Richard McKeon (New York: Random House, 1941), 765–6, 820–34. On Aquinas' concept of "powers," see Robert Pasnau, *Thomas Aquinas on Human Nature* (Cambridge: Cambridge Univ. Press, 2002), 143–57; Étienne Gilson, *The Elements of Christian Philosophy* (New York: Mentor, 1963), 225–6.

36 Christopher Boehm, *Moral Origins: The Evolution of Virtue, Altruism, and Shame* (New York: Basic Books, 2012), 234–5, 289–90, 292, 326, 339; Keane, *Ethical Life*, 3–6.

37 Merlin Donald, *A Mind So Rare: The Evolution of Human Consciousness* (New York: W.W. Norton, 2001), 146.

38 Aristotle, *The Nicomachean Ethics* 3.5.1114b30–1115a5, 7.10.1152a30–2, trans. Thomson, rev. Tredennick, 65, 190. "[T]he habitual practice of ethical living [*sittlichkeit*] appears as a second nature which, put in the place of the initial, purely natural will, is the soul of custom permeating it through and through." "Education is the art of making men ethical. It begins with pupils whose life is at an instinctive level and shows them the way to a second birth, the way to change their instinctive nature into a second, intellectual, nature, and makes this intellectual level habitual to

them." Hegel, *Philosophy of Right*, trans. Knox, §151, and addition to §151, pp. 108, 260.

39 A virtue, says Aquinas, is the "perfection of a power." *Summa Theologiæ* 1–2.55.1, in *Treatise on the Virtues*, trans. Oesterle, 51. Jacques Maritain describes this as "la primauté métaphysique de l'acte sur la puissance." *Humanisme intégral*, new ed. (Paris: Éditions Aubier-Montaigne, 1946), 54.

40 "We are never to consider any single action in our enquiries concerning the origin of morals; but only the quality of character from which the action proceeded. These alone are *durable* enough to affect our senti-ments concerning the person. Actions are, indeed, better indications of a character than words, or even wishes or sentiments; but 'tis only so far as they are such indications, that they are attended with love and hatred, praise or blame." David Hume, *A Treatise of Human Nature* 3.3.1, ed. L.A. Selby-Bigge (London: Oxford Univ. Press, 1968), 575. Emphasis in original.

41 Donald, *A Mind So Rare*, 57–9, 194–5, 228–31. Max Scheler emphasizes the superiority of "automatized" over conscious "life-activities." In fact, to the degree they have to be performed consciously and are accompanied by conscious selections and attention," he suggests, they "become dis-turbed and diseased." *Formalism in Ethics*, trans. Frings and Funk, 286.

42 For Bradley, a "disposition" means "the probable course of psychical events," "capacities of the soul," or forms of "potential existence." Brad-ley, *Appearance and Reality*, 277, 339–40.

43 Susanne K. Langer, *Mind: An Essay on Human Feeling*, vol. 1 (Baltimore: Johns Hopkins Press, 1967), 288. "In every moral individual act of posi-tive value the ability for acts of the same kind increases." Scheler, *Formal-ism in Ethics*, trans. Frings and Funk, 537.

44 "[W]e resolve to do right, we hope to keep our resolutions, we declare them to confirm our own hope, and fix our own inconstancy by calling witnesses of our actions; but at last habit prevails, and those whom we invited to our triumph, laugh at our defeat. Custom is commonly too strong for the most resolute resolver, though furnished for the assault with all the weapons of philosophy." Samuel Johnson, *The Idler*, no. 27, Saturday, 21 October 1758, in *The Idler and The Adventurer*, ed. W.J. Bate, John M. Bullitt, and L.F. Powell (New Haven: Yale Univ. Press, 1963) Yale Edition of the Works of Samuel Johnson, 2:85.

45 Aristotle, *The Nicomachean Ethics* 3.5.1114b30–1115a5, 7.10.1152a30–2, trans. Thomson, rev. Tredennick, 65, 190. "[T]o a large extent the soul is itself its own laws [i.e., habits]." Bradley, *Appearance and Reality*, 314.

46 Christine Swanton calls the habits of feeling that are the "inside" of the virtues "fine inner states": "all virtue expresses fine inner states." *Virtue Ethics*, 26–9, 128.

47 As Max Scheler says, values "correspond" to acts. Values are "clearly feelable phenomena," "true" or "ideal objects." A pure "value quality is given only insofar as it reveals a good as a good of its specific kind" with its specific "value-nuances ... differentiated in their feelable whatness." "Every increase in positive value ... of a being that executes acts is accompanied by an increase in pleasure as a reaction at the corresponding stratum of feeling." *Formalism in Ethics*, trans. Frings and Funk, 288, 16–20, 355–6. Contemporary definitions of "values" often place too much emphasis on the cognitive dimension and overlook that what makes a value a value is a habit of *feeling*, not something cognitive like conviction or "belief." As Hans Joas puts it, values are "objects of intentional feeling." *The Genesis of Values*, trans. Gregory Moore (Cambridge: Polity Press, 2000), 92–3; *The Sacredness of the Person: A New Genealogy of Human Rights*, trans. Alex Skinner (Washington, DC: Georgetown Univ. Press, 2013), 176, 128. Jung distinguishes feeling from emotion: feeling is a "rational function of discriminating values." Emotion is a "condition characterized by physical innervations." As a "function of valuing," feeling has "no physical or tangible physiological manifestations, while emotion is characterized by an altered physiological condition." C.G. Jung, *Analytical Psychology: Its Theory and Practice* (New York: Vintage Books, 1970), 25–7, 31–2. You can be just as emotional about a cognition, a conviction, or a belief as about a value feeling.

48 Perhaps because of the contemporary bias against the word "virtue," the "positive psychology" movement (discussed in chapter 14) often refers to the virtues as "character strengths" or "values in action" – which is the essence of a virtue. Peterson and Seligman, *Character Strengths and Virtues*; Martin E.P. Seligman, *Flourish: A Visionary New Understanding of Happiness and Well-being* (New York: Simon & Schuster, 2013), 36–7. See also: http://www.viacharacter.org/; https://www.authentichappiness.sas.upenn.edu/.

49 Aristotle, *The Nicomachean Ethics* 2.3.1104b10–15, 2.8.1108b15–2.9.1109a30, 3.1.1109b29, trans. Thomson, rev. Tredennick, 35, 46–8, 50. "[L]e sentiment est la réalité de l'acte. ... [L]'affectivité détermine l'action, non comme un antécédent détermine un conséquent, non comme une cause, un motif ou un mobile, mais comme son essence." Michel Henry, *L'essence de la manifestation* (Paris: Presses Universitaires de France, 2017), 811, 814–15. The way Dietrich von Hildebrand puts this is that "the backbone of every virtue is a super-actual value response." (By "super-actual," Hildebrand means states or attitudes which "are by their very nature able to subsist in the depth of our soul, even when we are focused on something else," as opposed to those which are "restricted in their existence to actually being consciously experienced.") *Ethics* (Steubenville, OH: Hildebrand Press, 2020), 377.

50 When evolutionary theory distinguishes between "altruism at the level of *action* and altruism at the level of *thoughts and feelings*," it is making precisely the distinction between the outside and the inside of a virtue, i.e., between virtues and values. David Sloan Wilson, *Does Altruism Exist? Culture, Genes, and the Welfare of Others* (New Haven: Yale Univ. Press, 2015), 7–17. Emphasis added.

51 I disagree with a conception of virtue as "a disposition to a type of psychological processing rather than directly to a type of behavior." R.M. Adams, *A Theory of Virtue*, 133. It is true that a type of psychological processing "shapes behavior only in interaction with other appetitive states [i.e., self-assertion], and with cognitive states, as well as with situations." Adams, 133. But a virtue *qua* virtue combines both the inside and the outside, both the external habit of behaviour and the internal habit of feeling. Without the habit of behaviour, it is not, or not *yet* a virtue. Only a habitual feeling.

52 Evelyn Underhill captures the distinction between a value and a virtue when she suggests the real test is whether it "is just a feeling [i.e., a value] or a fact [i.e., a virtue]." *The Fruits of the Spirit*, ed. Roger L. Roberts (Harrisburg, PA: Morehouse, 2010), 17. Tolstoy expresses the distinction between a merely espoused value and a real virtue, when he notes that the servants in Nikolai Rostov's household were the "most reliable judges of their masters, because they judge not by *conversations and expressions* of feelings, but by *acts and manner of life*." Leo Tolstoy, *War and Peace*, trans. Richard Pevear and Larissa Volokhonsky (New York: Vintage Classics, 2008), Epilogue, pt. 1, chap. 12, p. 1160. Emphasis added. On the other hand, Hans Joas argues: "We cannot understand a human being if we are unfamiliar with his values and judge him only by his actions, which will never represent the total realization of his ideals." *The Sacredness of the Person*, trans. Skinner, 109. Dietrich von Hildebrand agrees: "affective responses are endowed with a moral value of their own." *Ethics*, 365.

53 "There exists in fact no obligatory connection between empathy and kindness." Frans de Waal, *The Age of Empathy: Nature's Lessons for a Kinder Society* (New York: Three Rivers Press, 2009), 45. Samuel Taylor Coleridge points out that "a constitutional quickness of sympathy with pain and pleasure" (or what he calls "sensibility") "proves little more than the coincidence or contagion of pleasurable or painful sensations in different persons" and is "not even a sure pledge of a good heart": "Sensibility is not necessarily benevolence. Nay, by rendering us tremblingly alive to trifling misfortunes, it frequently prevents it, and induces an effeminate selfishness instead." Samuel Taylor Coleridge, *Aids to Reflection* (Port Washington, NY: Kennikat Press, 1971), 88–9. On the same point, see Scheler, *Formalism in Ethics*, trans. Frings and Funk, 298.

54 "My sympathy with another may give me the sentiment of pain and dis-
approbation, when any object is presented, that has a tendency to give
him uneasiness; tho' I may not be willing to sacrifice any thing of my
own interest, or cross any of my passions for his satisfaction." Hume, *A
Treatise of Human Nature* 3.3.1, p. 586. On the reality that emotions of sympathy alone are no guarantee of right action, and may even be a kind of
egoism, see also Rosalind Hursthouse, *On Virtue Ethics* (Oxford: Oxford
Univ. Press, 2010), 102; Michel Terestchenko, *Un si fragile vernis d'humanité: Banalité du mal, banalité du bien* (Paris: La Découverte, 2007), 257;
Keane, *Ethical Life*, 83; Michael Ignatieff, *The Ordinary Virtues: Moral Order
in a Divided World* (Cambridge, MA: Harvard Univ. Press, 2017), 213.

55 Frans de Waal makes this point by distinguishing between empathy and
sympathy. For him, sympathy is the virtue of which empathy is only the
internal feeling, or value. Empathy is "spontaneous" and reactive, but
sympathy is "proactive." It reflects a genuine "concern about the other
and a desire to improve the other's situation." *The Age of Empathy*, 88–9.
Michel Terestchenko argues that, for a *value* of empathy to become a
virtue of empathy, the virtues that (in chapter 5) I will call virtues of reverence must be strongly supported by (what in chapter 4, I will call) the
virtues of self-assertion. *Un si fragile vernis d'humanité*, 228.

56 "Overt actions … are the indispensable pivot and spur of the inner scene.
The inner, in *this* sense, cannot do without the outer." Iris Murdoch, *The
Sovereignty of Good* (London: Routledge, 1980), 43. Emphasis in original.
Max Scheler suggests that values are first encountered or discovered *in*
the performance or execution of virtues. In a characteristic phrase, he
says they "flash out" of our virtuous "acts," through an "intuiting of essences of acts." *Formalism in Ethics*, trans. Frings and Funk, 65, 68, 288–9,
294.

57 "[E]very preferring of a higher value to a lower one makes a later similar
preferring easier, and, conversely … every preferring of a lower value to
a higher one makes a later similar preferring easier." Scheler, *Formalism in
Ethics*, trans. Frings and Funk, 357.

58 "[Human beings] need character to provide a backdrop of habit and authority. Living well involves good character, because only if one has good
character does it become effortless and natural to act rightly. But this
effortlessness and naturalness comes [*sic*] from being happy to conform
one's behaviour to the patterns laid down by one's character." Swanton,
Virtue Ethics, 284–5.

59 By means of a rather amusing but telling example, Bernard Williams
illustrates the critical role – in ethical life – of these inner habits of feeling: "One does not feel easy with the man," he remarks with delicious
understatement, "who in the course of a discussion of how to deal with

political or business rivals says, 'Of course, we could have them killed, but we should lay that aside right from the beginning.'" *Ethics and the Limits of Philosophy*, 185. Elizabeth Anscombe makes the same point, more directly: "[I]f someone really thinks, *in advance*, that it is open to question whether such an action as procuring the judicial execution of the innocent should be quite excluded from consideration – I do not want to argue with him; he shows a corrupt mind." "Modern Moral Philosophy," in *Virtue Ethics*, ed. Roger Crisp and Michael Slote (Oxford: Oxford Univ. Press, 1997), 42. Emphasis in original. For the view that some things should not even arise as possibilities but should be ruled out by deep-rooted, habitual virtue, and by "gut" reactions rather than through "ethical reasoning," see Charles Taylor, *A Secular Age* (Cambridge, MA: Belknap Press of Harvard Univ. Press, 2007), 741; James Q. Wilson, *Moral Sense*, 7–8; Terestchenko, *Un si fragile vernis d'humanité*, 227.

60 Samuel Johnson, *Preface to Shakespeare*, in *Lives of the Most Eminent English Poets* (London: Frederick Warne, n.d.), 507. Similarly, Aristotle asserted that "what everyone believes is so" and therefore moral truth is likely to have been demonstrated when "received opinions [are] left validated." Aristotle, *The Nicomachean Ethics* 9.3.1173a1–2, 7.1.1145b5–10, trans. Thomson, rev. Tredennick, 257, 168. Hegel and Bradley agreed. Hegel, *Encyclopaedia*, §22, trans. Wallace, 35; Bradley, *Appearance and Reality*, 437.

61 The "genesis" of values is explored in two of Hans Joas' works: *The Genesis of Values*, and *The Sacredness of the Person: A New Genealogy of Human Rights*.

62 What, in this book, I am going to call a "family" of virtues can perhaps be linked to what contemporary virtue theorists sometimes call the "modularity" of virtues. The name for a virtue often stands for a much wider "family" of diverse and contrasting or even conflicting virtues. That is to say, they are "traits that are really rather heterogeneous groups of dispositions." R.M. Adams, *A Theory of Virtue*, 128.

63 Maritain, *Humanisme intégral*, 64, 82, 145–6.

64 Ernst Troeltsch, *Historicism and Its Problems*, quoted in Joas, *The Sacredness of the Person*, 132.

65 Maurice Blondel calls these permanent and necessary features of the nature of the human "une norme": "une réalité présente et nécessaire à la constitution même de tous les êtres." *L'Être et les êtres* (Paris: Presses Universitaires de France, 1963), 254.

66 Swanton, *Virtue Ethics*, 34–41. "[V]irtue is good itself, both in spirit and actuality. But there is no Absolute Good or good-in-itself that can be known and then applied. Good is not something to contemplate; it is someting to be done. And so with virtue, too; it is the effort to act well

and in that very effort itself *virtue defines the good.*" Comte-Sponville, *A Small Treatise*, trans. Temerson, 3–4. Emphasis added. "'[L]'idéal' vers lequel [le projet d'action] est orienté, le contenu dont il poursuit la réalisation et qui sert d'étalon à celle-ci trouve … son origine dans l'immanence absolue de la vie affective. … [C'est] l'affectivité qui détermine originellement et fonde l'être même des valeurs." Henry, *L'essence de la manifestation*, 809–10. For the opposite view – that value is found in the goodness of "objects" – see Bloomfield, *The Virtues of Happiness*, 167.

67 "[L]a connaissance … est un dérivé de l'action où elle trouve sa justification et sa réalité." Maurice Blondel, *Lettres philosophiques*, 32–6, in Jean Lacroix, *Maurice Blondel, sa vie, son œuvre* (Paris: Presses Universitaires de France, 1963), 94.

68 Thomas Hobbes, *Leviathan* (Indianapolis: Bobbs-Merrill, 1958), pt. 2, chap. 27, p. 242. "[T]he scholar should be wary of defining 'ethics' simply in terms of values that he or she happens to agree with. … [T]here will always be some values some people hold that others will find repugnant." Keane, *Ethical Life*, 100.

69 Denys Turner, *Thomas Aquinas: A Portrait* (New Haven: Yale Univ. Press, 2013), 30.

70 Dorothea Frede, "The Historic Decline of Virtue Ethics," in *The Cambridge Companion to Virtue Ethics*, ed. Daniel C. Russell (Cambridge: Cambridge Univ. Press, 2013), 124–48.

71 R.M. Adams, *A Theory of Virtue*, 115–232.

72 James Laidlaw describes "the idea of 'relativism' as the anthropologists' ex officio stance on moral life and as a sort of disciplinary membership badge." *The Subject of Virtue: An Anthropology of Ethics and Freedom* (Cambridge: Cambridge Univ. Press, 2014), 23–32. The quote is on page 23. Max Scheler lists four "errors" of moral relativism: "(1) the confusion of changes in values with changes in the estimations of the units of goods and actions bearing these values, (2) the false inference of changes in values from changes in norms, (3) the erroneous inferences of deficient objectivity and insight from deficient universality, (4) the failure to see that it is in the moral value-estimation of 'willing' and 'action' (in contrast to being) and of norms of duty (in contrast to virtue) that there is a truly non-formally variable moment." *Formalism in Ethics*, trans. Frings and Funk, 296n66, 304.

73 Keane, *Ethical Life*, 158, 122–3. Keane resists the suggestion that this makes him a moral relativist. But he seems to escape from relativism only by ceasing to be a social scientist: "Does this then condemn us to some kind of amoral relativism? I think not, because no one is *only* a natural or social scientist and no one inhabits solely the third-person perspective." Keane, 260.

74 "Cultural relativity may be one of the most important contributions an-
    thropology can make to the social and historical sciences, *and to the public
    at large.*" Joseph A. Tainter, *The Collapse of Complex Societies* (Cambridge:
    Cambridge Univ. Press, 2017), 84. Emphasis added.

75 Jared Diamond, *The World Until Yesterday: What We Can Learn from Tradi-
    tional Societies* (New York: Viking, 2012), 21, 216.

76 Elinor Ochs and Carolina Izquerdo, "Responsibility in Childhood: Three
    Developmental Trajectories," *Ethos* 37, no. 4, (December 2009): 397, cited
    in Keane, *Ethical Life*, 260–1.

77 James Q. Wilson, *The Moral Sense*, 173.

78 For Merlin Donald, the distinctive feature of the human (as opposed to
    animal) consciousness is its condition of "enculturation." *A Mind So Rare*,
    150–1.

79 R.G. Collingwood, *An Essay on Metaphysics* (Oxford: Oxford Univ. Press,
    1966). Hans-Georg Gadamer, *Truth and Method*, trans. and rev. Joel Wein-
    sheimer and Donald G. Marshall, 2nd ed. (New York: Continuum, 2002).

80 Max Scheler suggests moral relativism results from mistaking "val-
    ue-symbols" for the "values themselves." "[T]he *fullness* and *variety* of the
    types of moral ideas of life that we find in peoples and nations are by no
    means objections to the *objectivity* of moral values." *Formalism in Ethics*,
    268–9, 215–17, 297, 492. Emphasis in original.

81 Diamond, *The World Until Yesterday*, 21, 214–17.

82 Richard A. Shweder, *Why Do Men Barbecue? Recipes for Cultural Psychology*
    (Cambridge, MA: Harvard Univ. Press, 2003), 180–2.

83 "Thus in Roman law, for example, there could be no definition of 'man',
    since 'slave' could not be brought under it – the very status of slave in-
    deed is an outrage on the conception of man." Hegel, *Philosophy of Right*,
    trans. Knox, §2, p. 15.

84 Annas, *Intelligent Virtue*, 61. Annas explains how virtue brings about
    social progress through the tensions which can develop between "two
    communities": the "natural community" of family and nation into which
    we are born and "another community," the community of the virtuous
    with which we can come to identify. The abolition of slavery occurred
    because "membership of a community bonded by commitment to acting
    virtuously did detach people from the traditional roles involved in their
    original contexts of family and culture." Annas, 52–65. The words quoted
    are on page 63.

85 Aristotle, *Physics* 2.3.194b15–195a25, trans. R.P. Hardie and R.K. Gaye;
    Metaphysics, 5.2.1013a20–35, 8.4.1044a30–5, trans. W.D. Ross, in *The Basic
    Works of Aristotle*, ed. Richard McKeon, 240–1, 752–3, 817. In chapter 15,
    you'll see that Aristotle actually identified four types of cause: material,
    efficient, formal, and final. For the purposes of simplicity, I've conflated

material with efficient cause here, and formal with final, as is often done. On the four types of cause, see also Thomas Aquinas, "Commentary," V *Metaphysics, lect. 2,* in *Philosophical Texts,* trans. Gilby, 43–6.

86 The evolution of the word "science" in Western cultural history is deeply paradoxical. When all thinkers from the seventeenth to the nineteenth centuries – from Descartes to Kant, Fichte, and Hegel – use the words "scientific" and "science," they still mean them in the classical, Aristotelian sense of certainty derived, deductively, from first principles, not in the sense of probabilities derived, inductively, from observation, experience, and experiment, which they called "natural philosophy." Because of the linguistic shift in the late nineteenth century – when the term "science" became the name for the second rather than the first – contemporary, experimental "science" inherited the aura of certainty from the classical meaning of "science," even though it still deals only in probabilities.

87 "A scholar trained in anthropology learns early on that [value judgements] are *scientifically inadmissible,* detrimental to the cause of understanding, intellectually indefensible and simply unfair. ... One is either an impartial social scientist or a social critic, and the latter should not masquerade as the former." Tainter, *The Collapse of Complex Societies,* 85. Emphasis added.

88 Laidlaw, *The Subject of Virtue,* 1–10.

89 Francis Bacon said that physics should be based on efficient and material causes alone and that, in physics, "the inquisition of final causes is barren and like a virgin consecrated to God produces nothing." *De Dignitate & Augmentis Scientiarum,* quoted in David Deming, *Science and Technology in World History: The Black Death, the Renaissance, the Reformation and the Scientific Revolution* (Jefferson, NC: McFarland, 2012), 3:200. Similarly, Spinoza asserted "things" must be explained only by the efficient causes of their own internal dynamism and not by any external end. A so-called final cause is "really an efficient cause," misunderstood "because men are usually ignorant of the causes of their desires." *Ethics,* 3, Proposition 7, and 4, Preface, trans. W.H. White, in *Spinoza Selections,* 215–16, 284. "The great achievement of the seventeenth-century scientific revolution was to develop a language for nature that was purged of human meanings." Charles Taylor, *Dilemmas and Connections: Selected Essays* (Cambridge, MA: Belknap Press of Harvard Univ. Press, 2011), 28.

90 On the "hostility to Ideas" in the empirical sciences, see Edmund Husserl, *Ideas: General Introduction to Pure Phenomenology,* trans. W.R. Boyce Gibson (New York: Collier Books, 1962), §18, p. 72. On the "widespread" view ("believed to be virtually a self-evident truth by many thinkers") that "concepts which involve consciousness or intentionality ... cannot

belong to a satisfactory data language" and are therefore "untestable," see Charles Taylor, *The Explanation of Behaviour* (London: Routledge, 1970), 73.

91 "The future is the driving power … [It] originates, so to speak, not in a thrust but in a pull. The present passes not because the past prods it on but because the future snatches it toward itself." Franz Rosenzweig, *The Star of Redemption*, trans. William W. Hallo (Notre Dame, IN: Univ. of Notre Dame Press, 1985), 328. Martin Heidegger argues the nature of the human is "grounded in the future," that it comes into being "primarily out of the future." *Being and Time*, 327, 426, trans. Stambaugh, 312, 405. Paul Bloomfield is typical of current intellectual culture in wanting to deny the future can "pull" us forward in this way. *The Virtues of Happiness*, 66, 160–1.

92 Hegel calls the "end" or final cause the "soul of the action," "what is purposed in an actual concrete action," "the end which actuates its effort." Hegel, *Philosophy of Right*, trans. Knox, §§121, 140, 142, pp. 82, 93, 105. Max Scheler calls the "motivation" inspired by final causes a "causality of attraction." *Formalism in Ethics*, trans. Frings and Funk, 344.

93 On the necessity of final causes for understanding human meanings and an intentional world, see G.W. Leibniz, "On Geometrical Method and Method of Metaphysics," trans. Philip P. Wiener, in *Leibniz Selections*, ed. Philip P. Wiener (New York: Scribner's, 1951), 89; Bradley, *Appearance and Reality*, 312; Alfred North Whitehead, *Process and Reality* (New York: Free Press, 1969), 101; Taylor, *Dilemmas and Connections*, 28–9; Richard Shweder, *Thinking Through Cultures: Expeditions in Cultural Psychology* (Cambridge, MA: Harvard Univ. Press, 1991), 74; Martin E.P. Seligman, Peter Railton, Roy F. Baumeister, and Chandra Sripada, *Homo Prospectus* (New York: Oxford Univ. Press, 2016).

94 Immanuel Kant notes the distinguishing feature of human beings is that their actions are *not* just events – "not dynamically determined in the chain of natural causes through either outer or inner grounds antecedent in time." Instead, human action is "the power of *originating* a series of events." *Critique of Pure Reason*, A554/B582, trans. Kemp Smith, 476. Emphasis added. On the distinction between events and actions, see also Bradley, *Appearance and Reality*, 54, 250–1, 260; Scheler, *Formalism in Ethics*, trans. Frings and Funk, 384; Blondel, *L'Action*, 467–70, in Lacroix, *Maurice Blondel*, 109; Paul Ricœur, *Soi-même comme un autre* (Paris: Éditions du Seuil, 1990), 78–85.

95 "Meanings, intentions, ideas, values, emotions … are not the kind of things … that science was designed to study." Shweder, *Why Do Men Barbecue?*, 313.

96 Keane, *Ethical Life*, 6.

97 "[W]e belong to [the region in which our ideal impulses originate] in a more intimate sense than that in which we belong to the visible world, for we belong in the most intimate sense wherever our ideals belong." James, *The Varieties of Religious Experience*, 399.

98 "If you are a mind/body monist ... then the voluntariness of voluntary actions must be an illusion." Shweder, *Why Do Men Barbecue?*, 303. Edward O. Wilson, the founder of sociobiology, illustrates Shweder's point. His assumption that everything is ultimately just the product of the "laws of physical cause and effect" requires him to conclude that free will is just an illusion, even if a necessary one. It doesn't really exist "in ultimate reality." But human belief in it is "biologically adaptive" because otherwise humans would fall into "fatalism." So, the illusion of human freedom is "necessary for sanity and thereby for the perpetuation of the species." *The Meaning of Human Existence* (New York: Liveright, 2014), 37, 170. As Paul Ricœur notes, an ontology of "events" goes necessarily and inevitably with an ontology of "things." *Soi-même comme un autre*, 118.

99 D.S. Wilson, *Does Altruism Exist?*, 62–71; Elliott Sober and David Sloan Wilson, *Unto Others: The Evolution and Psychology of Unselfish Behavior* (Cambridge, MA: Harvard Univ. Press, 1998), 199–201, 304–8, 334. Though he doesn't call them by name, Edward O. Wilson does seem to recognize the distinction between efficient and final causes. But he thinks the first are "broader" or "vastly larger," as if efficient causes enclosed, or could ultimately account for, final causes. *The Meaning of Human Existence*, 12–14, 173–4. As James Laidlaw remarks, with charming directness, much contemporary social science aims to show "the impression that there are reflective, intentional, self-responsible persons is no more than a useful device for the reproduction of the system. It is therefore a relentlessly watertight explanation of a world in which it would be a miracle if anything were ever to change, one from which cruelty, pride, and jealousy are quite as absent as love, and *in which, I am pleased to report, we do not in fact live.*" *The Subject of Virtue*, 9. Emphasis added.

100 Christopher Boehm rigorously avoids any suggestion that the virtues might actually be goods in themselves and owe some of their attractive power to that very goodness. But at the same time, he cannot help noticing that, in hunter-gatherer cultures, human virtues like generosity were intentionally "boosted" because early humans already recognized these virtues as goods or final causes to be pursued for their very goodness, "actively and purposefully reinforced by social communities that believe[d] in things like social harmony and the Golden Rule." This reintroduction of final causes (or "a certain purposive element") back into a social "science" from which they are supposed to be banished – the necessary acknowledgment that intentions "do make a difference," that

"it seems to be the thought or more properly the feeling that counts" – all this seems to make Boehm uneasy. So he does his best to downplay this heresy and transform purposes, intentions, and goods back into the efficient causes of mainstream evolutionary theory, such as gene pools and natural selection: "[C]ulturally based purposeful inputs are both part of natural selection and a product thereof," he argues. "Thus, their effects have gone beyond shaping everyday group life prosocially, for *they have helped to shape our gene pools in prosocial directions that are similar.*" Boehm is still obliged, nevertheless, to admit that evolution has turned human beings into moral creatures, who can be fully explained only through final causes: "[O]ne major and totally unintentional side effect has been the conscience that originally made us a moral species. Another has been our unusual propensity to practice generous behaviour outside the family, which evolved through a variety of mechanisms and which, I propose, humans have deliberately amplified to facilitate better cooperation." He also concludes his book with his own sermon about "right and wrong," thus demonstrating that a world without final causes is not a human world. *Moral Origins*, 280, 331–2, 302, 333, 359. Emphasis in original.

101 For the drive to explain the virtues through the "natural," unformed reflexes of toddlers and young children, see, for example, Paul Bloom, *Descartes' Baby: How the Science of Child Development Explains What Makes Us Human* (New York: Basic Books, 2004); Keane, *Ethical Life*, 39–73; Amrisha Vaish, Malinda Carpenter, and Michael Tomasello, "Young Children Selectively Avoid Helping People with Harmful Intentions," *Child Development* 81, no. 6 (Nov.–Dec. 2010): 1661–9.

102 Samuel Johnson, *The Rambler*, no. 208, Saturday, 14 March 1752, ed. W.J. Bate and Albrecht B. Strauss (New Haven: Yale Univ. Press, 1979), Yale Edition of the Works of Samuel Johnson, 5:316. Even a virtue ethicist like Paul Bloomfield assumes the "truth about teleology will not require anything beyond what is required by the truth about biology." *The Virtues of Happiness*, 161.

103 Peterson and Seligman, *Character Strengths and Virtues*, 84. "[W]e have to understand that goodness itself is precisely the *raison d'être* of this being ordered to the good." Hildebrand, *Ethics*, 232.

104 Robert Nozick, *The Examined Life* (New York: Simon & Schuster, 1990), 172.

105 "[I]f ever there was any thing, which could be call'd natural [in the sense of common, frequent, or universal], the sentiments of morality certainly may; since there never was any nation of the world nor any single person in any nation, who was utterly depriv'd of them, and who never, in any instance, shew'd the least approbation or dislike of manners. These sentiments are so rooted in our constitution and temper, that without entirely

confounding the human mind by disease or madness, 'tis impossible to extirpate and destroy them." Hume, *A Treatise of Human Nature* 3.1.2, p. 474.

106 Keane, *Ethical Life*, 122–3. As already noted in chapter 2, what Webb Keane calls an "affordance" Hegel calls an "occasion." G.W.F. Hegel, *Science of Logic*, vol. 1, bk. 2, §2, chap. 3, trans. W.H. Johnston and L.G. Struthers (London: George Allen & Unwin, 1951), 2:196.

107 "In every end of a self-conscious subject, there is a *positive* aspect necessarily present because the end is what is purposed in any actual concrete action." Hegel, *Philosophy of Right*, trans. Knox, §140, p. 93. Emphasis in original.

108 Coleridge, *Aids to Reflection*, 70. Emphasis added.

109 "The distinction between the End or *final cause* and the mere *efficient cause* (which is the cause ordinarily so-called) is of supreme importance." Hegel, *Encyclopaedia*, §204, trans. Wallace, 268. Emphasis added. Alfred North Whitehead calls this the "ontological principle" – the reality that any action must be explained by final as well as by efficient causes. *Process and Reality*, 29, 54, 61.

110 "[L]'agir spécifiquement humain … doit relier sa motion primitive à son terme ultime." Blondel, *L'Action*, 2:110–15, in Lacroix, *Maurice Blondel*, 125.

111 Seligman, *Flourish*, 105. Emphasis in original. See also Seligman et al., *Homo Prospectus*.

112 Keane, *Ethical Life*, 181.

113 de Waal, *The Age of Empathy*, 41. Emphasis in original. As Steven Pinker puts it, we need to "distinguish the *process* [efficient and evolutionary causes] from the *product* [human values or final causes and free will]." "A Biological Understanding of Human Nature," in *Science at the Edge*, ed. John Brockman, updated ed. (New York: Union Square Press, 2008), 43. Emphasis added.

114 David Hume calls this development (from efficient to final cause) the "progress of the sentiments." *A Treatise of Human Nature* 3.2.2, 5, pp. 500, 523. But Hume rejects the reality of final cause. So, for him, this "progress" is, presumably, a purely efficient one. James A. Harris, *Hume: An Intellectual Biography* (Cambridge: Cambridge Univ. Press, 2015), 52–3.

115 "It is our dividedness that defines the human race. … But it is also the case that we share the ordinary virtues, and we recognize them across all our differences. They are ordinary because they are concerned with the recurrent essentials of our common life, because they express our learned instincts about what moral life requires of us if we are to survive and reproduce the life of family, neighborhood, kith and kin. We are moral beings because we have no choice – our survival and success as social

beings depends on virtue. It is not an option, but a necessity." Ignatieff, *The Ordinary Virtues*, 222.

116 "Without its social histories, ethical life would not be ethical; without its natural histories, it would not be life." Keane, *Ethical Life*, 262.

117 "Cultures differ in the degree to which one or other of the ethics [families of virtues] and corresponding moral goods predominates in the development of social practices and institutions and in the elaboration of a moral ideology." Shweder, *Why Do Men Barbecue?*, 102.

118 In his *Aklāq-i Nāṣirī*, the most influential book of political theory and ethics in Islamic history before the modern period, Naṣīr-ud-Dīn Ṭūsī (d. 1274) said the virtues are based on "the understanding of people of insight and the experiences of men of sagacity, unvarying and unchanging with the variation of the ages or the revolutions in modes of conduct and traditions." He distinguished them from "manners and customs" established by "convention." Quoted in Shahab Ahmed, *What Is Islam? The Importance of Being Islamic* (Princeton: Princeton Univ. Press, 2016), 214

119 "[T]he individual values of autonomy, strength of character, determination, dignity, virtue and truthfulness, along with the social values of mutual respect and fairness, and finally, in the common relationship of all people to the society that overarches them, the values of solidarity and mutual interconnection … these values … possess a universal, rationally necessary validity." Troeltsch, *Historicism and Its Problems*, quoted in Joas, *The Sacredness of the Person*, trans. Skinner, 104. George Lakoff and Mark Johnson suggest the virtues – justice, empathy, nurturance, strength, uprightness, "and so forth" – "are very good candidates for universal moral concepts." *Philosophy in the Flesh: The Embodied Mind and Its Challenge to Western Thought* (New York: Basic Books, 1999), 325.

120 Shweder, *Why Do Men Barbecue?*, 38; Joas, *The Sacredness of the Person*, trans. Skinner, 105.

121 Shweder, *Why Do Men Barbecue?*, 6.

122 "For example, benevolence and respect are constrained to varying degrees, according to the objective requirements of a culture." Swanton, *Virtue Ethics*, 280.

123 "[V]alues and principles are objective only to the extent they are kept abstract and devoid of content." Shweder, *Why Do Men Barbecue?*, 38. See also Hegel, *Philosophy of Right*, trans. Knox, §150, pp. 107–8.

124 Jean Grondin points out that Plato's so-called "idea" and Aristotle's "form" both come from the Greek word εἶδος, meaning form. *Introduction à la métaphysique* (Montreal: Les Presses de l'Université de Montréal, 2004), 59n5. It might perhaps be argued that Platonic, Aristotelian, and Kantian teleological "idealism" is a "degraded" form of the spiritual

reality of the virtues: an important and valuable attempt to capture the truths of human life, but in a cognitive form, a form of the mind, rather than in the form of actual, lived life – truths of the stances of "I am" reduced to the truths of the stances of "It is."

125 "[I]f anyone is held up as a pattern of virtue, the true original with which we compare the alleged pattern and by which alone we judge of its value is to be found only in our minds. This original is the idea of virtue, in respect of which the possible objects of experience may serve as examples (proofs that what the concept of reason commands is in a certain degree practicable), but not as an archetype." Kant, *Critique of Pure Reason*, A315/B372, trans. Kemp Smith, 311.

126 One of Aquinas' constant themes is that moral judgments should never be made in the abstract but only in a specific context, when all the particular circumstances are taken into account. "Commentary," *Ethics, 2, lect. 2*, in *Philosophical Texts*, trans. Thomas Gilby, 285.

127 As Christine Swanton puts it, the virtues are "contoured" to make them "applicable to concrete situations." The simple naming or definition of a virtue doesn't suffice to exhaust its content, its complex relationship and integration with the other virtues, or to determine whether behaviour in specific circumstances constitutes a virtue or its opposite, a vice. For this you need what Martha Nussbaum and Christine Swanton call a "thicker" idea of virtue. It's not enough to "look at what is done, what is achieved, or what are the outcomes." You also need to make "fine judgments" about "what is going on inside the individual," and all the surrounding circumstances. To determine whether an action is indeed virtuous, you need a "sophisticated understanding of the relationships between the individual's own psyche, the facts of her behaviour in a specific context, the social milieu in which she operates, and her attitudes toward that milieu." *Virtue Ethics*, 279–80, 207–8, 155–9. On this theme, see also R.M. Adams, *A Theory of Virtue*, 115–43.

128 "Every culture hedges in this potentially universal morality in a specific way by defining its field and conditions of application." Joas, *The Sacredness of the Person*, trans. Skinner, 105.

129 Exodus 13:21–2.

130 Kant, *Critique of Pure Reason*, A838/B866, trans. Kemp Smith (London: Macmillan, 1968), 657; Hegel, *Science of Logic*, vol. 2, §3, chap. 3, trans. Johnston and Struthers, 2:466; Troeltsch, *Historicism and Its Problems*, quoted in Joas, *The Sacredness of the Person*, 109. "[B]eing fully virtuous does seem to be an ideal that we aspire towards but can never achieve." Annas, *Intelligent Virtue*, 64. Iris Murdoch calls this "the magnetic non-representable idea of the good which remains not 'empty' so much as mysterious": "The idea of perfection is … the true sense of the

'indefinability' of the good ... It lies beyond, and it is from this beyond that it exercises its *authority*." *The Sovereignty of Good*, 62–3. Emphasis in original.

131 Leibniz, *Nouveaux essais*, bk. 2, chap. 30, §§1, 4, pp. 225–6; bk. 4, chap. 4, §1, p. 345. On stances, virtues, and values as forms of eternal possibility, "eternal objects," "protypes," and so on, see Bradley, *Appearance and Reality*, 339–43; Husserl, *Ideas*, trans. Gibson, §3, p. 48; Whitehead, *Process and Reality*, 173, 300, 103, 106; Heidegger, *Being and Time*, 12, trans. Stambaugh, 11; Blondel, *L'Être et les êtres*, 475, 349–50n1; Henry, *L'essence de la manifestation*, 826, 834–5, 838; Swanton, *Virtue Ethics*, 275–85.

132 Because they are forms of "eternal possibility," the virtues, like other final causes, are always characterized by a certain "indefiniteness." They are "certain and yet indefinite." Their indefiniteness is "always determined only in a resolution with regard to the actual situation." Heidegger, *Being and Time*, 298, 308, trans. Stambaugh, 285–6, 295. As Whitehead puts it, "their own natures do not in themselves disclose in what actual entities this potentiality is realized." "The actualities *have* to be felt, while the pure potentials *can* be dismissed. So far as concerns their functioning as objects, this is the great distinction between an actual entity and an eternal object. The one is stubborn matter of fact; and the other never loses its 'accent' of potentiality." Whitehead, *Process and Reality*, 35, 280. Thus the capacity for virtue is a "capacité toute formelle, en ce sens qu'il appartient à l'expérience quotidienne et en commun de lui donner un contenu." Paul Ricœur, *Amour et justice* (Paris: Éditions Points, 2008), 109.

133 Shweder, *Thinking Through Cultures*, 153.

134 William Shakespeare, *Measure for Measure*, in *The Complete Works*, ed. Alfred Harbage (Baltimore: Penguin Books, 1969), 1.1.32–5.

135 "La nature de l'homme se considère en deux manières: l'une selon sa fin, et alors il est grand et incomparable; l'autre selon sa multitude, comme on juge de la nature du cheval et du chien, par la multitude, d'y voir la course ... ; et alors l'homme est abject et vil. Et voilà les deux voies qui en feront juger diversement, et qui feront tant disputer les philosophes. Car l'un nie la supposition de l'autre, l'un dit : 'Il n'est pas né à cette fin; car toutes ses actions s'y répugnent'; l'autre dit : 'Il s'éloigne de la fin quand il fait ses basses actions.'" Pascal, *Pensées* (Paris: Garnier-Flammarion, 1973), §242, p. 96. "[W]hereas, so far as nature is concerned, experience supplies the rules and is the source of truth, in respect of the moral laws it is, alas, the mother of illusion! Nothing is more reprehensible than to derive the laws prescribing what *ought to be done* from what *is done*, or to impose upon them the limits by which the latter is circumscribed." Kant, *Critique of Pure Reason*, A319, trans. Kemp Smith, 313. Similarly, Maurice Blondel notes that, "par une option mauvaise," human beings can turn

away from "leur fin véritable." *L'Être et les êtres*, 259. Jacques Maritain calls this the difference between "les lois statistiques de la nature humaine" and "la nature de l'être humain," structured "dans les profondeurs de sa nature," by the paradox of love and liberty. *Humanisme intégral*, 294, 200, 97, 199. Hence, Rosalind Hursthouse rightly notes that any adequate ethical theory of human nature cannot be "just a statistical notion." It must be "avowedly normative" and must "give up with a vengeance any idea that most human beings do what it is 'characteristic' of human beings to do." *On Virtue Ethics*, 223.

136 A currently popular approach to developing "beneficial" or "friendly" artificial intelligence (AI), called "inverse reinforcement learning" (IRL), is based on the hope that AI can be made humane by observing and imitating actual human behaviours. The flaw in this approach (as discussed again in chapter 17) is its inability to take account of the distinct ways of defining the human, identified by both Pascal and Kant. Inverse reinforcement learning might possibly allow AI to imitate our *human nature*. But it's very unlikely to enable AI to mirror the true *nature of the human*. Max Tegmark, *Life 3.0: Being Human in the Age of Artificial Intelligence* (New York: Alfred A. Knopf, 2017), 261–2; Stuart Russell, *Human Compatible: Artificial Intelligence and the Problem of Control* (New York: Penguin 2020), 178–9, 190–2.

137 "That no one of us will ever act in a way which is adequate to what is contained in the pure idea of virtue is far from proving this thought to be in any respect chimerical. For it is only by means of this idea that any judgment as to moral worth or its opposite is possible." Kant, *Critique of Pure Reason*, A315/B372, trans. Kemp Smith, 311. The UN Universal Declaration of Human Rights presumed "that rights were recognized rather than conferred." Edmund Fawcett, *Liberalism: The Life of an Idea* (Princeton: Princeton Univ. Press, 2014), 292.

138 "[P]ossibility as an existential is the most primordial and the ultimate ontological determination of Dasein … As an existential, possibility does not refer to a free-floating potentiality of being in the sense of the 'liberty of indifference' (*libertas indifferentiae*). … Dasein has always already got itself into definite possibilities. As a potentiality for being which it *is*, it has let some go by; it constantly adopts the possibilities of its being, grasps them, and sometimes fails to grasp them. But this means that Dasein is a being-possible which is entrusted to itself … Dasein is the possibility of being free *for* its ownmost potentiality of being." Heidegger, *Being and Time*, 143–4, 264, 299, trans. Stambaugh, 139–40, 253, 286. Emphasis in original.

139 Heidegger, *Being and Time*, 242–3, trans. Stambaugh, 233–4. "[I]f taking care [B2] and being concerned [A2] fail us, this does not, however,

mean that these modes of Dasein [stances and families of virtues] have been cut off from its authentic being a self. As essential structures [stances] of the constitution of Dasein they also belong to the condition of the possibility of existence in general. Dasein is authentically itself only insofar as it projects itself, *as* being-together with things taken care of [B2] and concernful being with … [A2], primarily upon its ownmost potentiality of being [A1]." Heidegger, 263, trans. Stambaugh, 252.

140 "[A]ll ethical cognition must be based on *'value-experience' that occurs in feeling and preferring*, just as all theoretical thinking must be based on sensory experiences." Scheler, *Formalism in Ethics*, trans. Frings and Funk, 326. Emphasis in original.

141 Dietrich von Hildebrand suggests this "ultimate 'yes' or 'no'" is "the deepest point of man's freedom." *Ethics*, 336.

142 Plato, *Meno* 81B–82D, in *Great Dialogues of Plato*, trans. W.H.D. Rouse, ed. Eric H. Warmington and Philip G. Rouse (New York: New American Library, 1956), 42; Scheler, *Formalism in Ethics*, trans. Frings and Funk, 244. Tolstoy gives an excellent description of this process of the "recognition" of a virtue, in his account of how, in his wife's own moral distress at his actions, Nikolai Rostov recognizes the need to cease beating his serfs. Tolstoy, *War and Peace*, trans. Pevear and Volokhonsky, Epilogue, pt. 1, chap. 8, p. 1147.

143 Charles Taylor, *Sources of the Self: The Making of the Modern Identity* (Cambridge: Harvard Univ. Press, 1989), 54, 59–60, 68–9, 90, 257. "Any view which will not explain, and also justify, an attitude essential to human nature, must surely be condemned." Bradley, *Appearance and Reality*, 218. Whitehead calls this "the metaphysical rule of evidence." Whitehead, *Process and Reality*, 175–6.

144 "The end … is also the principle. Present from the first it supplies the test of its inferior stages, and as these are included in fuller wholes, the principle grows. … Every sphere of experience would be measured by the absolute standard, and would be given a rank answering to its own relative merits and defects." Bradley, *Appearance and Reality*, 440–1.

145 Scruton, *On Human Nature*, 49. Emphasis added.

146 Leibniz, *Nouveaux essais*, bk. 2, chap. 31, §3, p. 229; bk. 4, chap. 4, §5–10, pp. 345–6.

147 Hume, *A Treatise of Human Nature* 3.2.1, p. 484.

148 Hegel, *Encyclopaedia*, §§138, 213, trans. Wallace, 191, 276.

149 Husserl, *Ideas*, trans. Gibson, §27, p. 93.

150 Isaiah Berlin, *The Crooked Timber of Humanity: Chapters in the History of Ideas*, ed. Henry Hardy (London: Fontana Press, 1991), 11.

151 James Q. Wilson, *The Moral Sense*, 235–7.

152 Blondel, *L'Être et les êtres*, 239, 284–5, 304. Daniel Harrington points out that practically all the ethical teachings in the New Testament, for example, have ancient parallels and are not entirely new or extreme departures "from the noblest social norms of the Jewish and Greco-Roman worlds." D.J. Harrington, "Biblical Perspectives: Problem Areas," in Daniel J. Harrington and James F. Keenan, *Jesus and Virtue Ethics: Building Bridges between New Testament Studies and Moral Theology* (Lanham, MD: Rowman & Littlefield, 2002), 12.

153 Taylor, *A Secular Age*, 589. The virtues might thus be described as "transcendental," in the Kantian sense. That is to say, any discussion or description of a human world would presuppose them, or require them as a starting point, as "*a priori* representations constituting the condition under which [the world is] given to us." Kant, *Critique of Pure Reason*, A12–16, trans. Kemp Smith, 59–62.

154 Maurice Blondel suggests the "invention" of new values doesn't take the form of "fabrication" but rather of "discernment" of new duties and generosities. *L'Être et les êtres*, 275. Similarly, Max Scheler suggests invention and discovery come together through the "differentiation of feeling." Through the increasing discrimination of our feelings, we can discover "new" virtues, which were already implicit in a human world, only waiting for us to encounter or perceive them. *Formalism in Ethics*, trans. Frings and Funk, 157. Later in this book (beginning in chapter 7), I will call the process Scheler describes the "arrow of virtue."

155 Paul Ricœur suggests that, in the end, the pre-theoretic language of poetry and myth abolishes the distinction between creation and discovery. Paul Ricœur, *La Métaphore vive*, in *Ricœur: Textes choisis et présentés*, ed. Michaël Fœssel and Fabien Lamouche (Paris: Éditions Points, 2007), 135. The Western concept of God is perhaps the archetypal case of something that can be at once an invention *and* a discovery. The idea of "God" is clearly a human invention – a product of our social and cultural history – but this invention also has the character of a discovery, or an encounter. See Thomas Römer, *L'invention de Dieu* (Paris: Éditions du Seuil, 2014).

156 "The concept of genesis ... aims to identify the genuine historical innovation ... while at the same time preserving the self-evident character that such innovation may also exhibit for those involved. ... The metaphor of birth might be another appropriate way of expressing how something historically new may take on an unconditional quality." Joas, *The Sacredness of the Person*, trans. Skinner, 3. See also *The Genesis of Values*, trans. Moore.

157 Troeltsch, *Historicism and Its Problems*, quoted in Joas, 108.

158 Heidegger, *Being and Time*, 243, trans. Stambaugh, 234. Emphasis in original.

159 Heidegger, 339, 145, trans. Stambaugh, 324, 141. Without acknowledging the source, Heidegger here paraphrases Augustine's Sermon 272, "On the Holy Eucharist": "Be what you see; receive what you are," often remembered and quoted as "Behold what you are, become what you receive." https://earlychurchtexts.com/public/augustine_sermon_272_eucharist.htm.

160 Plato, *Symposium* 204D–207A, in *Great Dialogues of Plato*, trans. Rouse, 101. Hegel says exactly the same thing as Diotima when he argues freedom and necessity are not, as so many people mistakenly assume, "mutually exclusive": "[F]reedom presupposes necessity ... A good man is aware that the tenor of his conduct is essentially obligatory and necessary." Hegel, *Encyclopaedia*, §158, trans. Wallace, 220. "[L]e sens de l'expérience humaine se fait à travers nous, mais pas par nous: nous ne dominons pas le sens, mais le sens nous fait en même temps que nous le faisons." Paul Ricœur, *Politique, Économie et Société: Écrits et conférences* 4 (Paris: Seuil, 2019), 91.

161 Jonathan Haidt, *The Righteous Mind: Why Good People Are Divided by Politics and Religion* (New York: Pantheon Books, 2012), 92.

162 Peterson and Park, "Classifying and Measuring Strengths of Character," 32.

163 Coleridge, *Aids to Reflection*, 91. What Coleridge calls the "structure of our proper humanity," Maurice Blondel calls "la norme qui est la forme même de la personne." *L'Être et les êtres*, 277.

164 "If we reflect upon the nature of the virtues we are constantly led to consider their relation to each other. The idea of an 'order' of virtues suggests itself, although it might of course be difficult to state this in any systematic form." Murdoch, *The Sovereignty of Good*, 57. The aim of this book is to construct Murdoch's proposed "order" of virtues in the "systematic form" she thought would be difficult to achieve.

165 "[T]he daily discourse of ordinary people is filled with oblique references to morality. We talk constantly about being or not being decent, nice, or dependable; about having or not having character; about friendship, loyalty, and moderation or fickleness, insincerity and addiction. ... This preoccupation, like the adjectives with which we express it – loyal, kind or nice; disloyal, selfish, or rude – is with the language of morality, even though we often disguise it in the language of personality. It is the language of virtue and vice." James Q. Wilson, *The Moral Sense*, vii. Webb Keane also emphasizes "how saturated ordinary exchanges are with the ongoing business of establishing one's ethical worth in the eyes, or ears, of others, the everyday task of giving an account of oneself." *Ethical Life*, 138.

166 Aristotle notes that words such as malice, shamelessness, envy, adultery, theft, and murder are "names that directly connote depravity," just as words like temperance or courage directly express the opposite. *The*

Nicomachean Ethics 2.6.1107a10–15 trans. Thomson, rev. Tredennick, 42.
See also Williams, *Ethics and the Limits of Philosophy*, 129–30. Also: 143,
145, 147, 152, 154, 163, 200.

167 Scheler, *Formalism in Ethics*, trans. Frings and Funk, 198–9. Scheler argues
that *"value*-ception" (Wert*nehmung*) always *precedes* perception (Wahr*nehmung*). Scheler, 197. Alfred North Whitehead agrees. For him, "individual
facts" are created through the "breath of feeling" which comes from the
"ingression of eternal objects into the actual occasion," thus generating
"values." *Process and Reality*, 102–3.

168 Iris Murdoch, *Metaphysics as a Guide to Morals* (London: Vintage, 2003),
155, 315; Husserl, *Ideas*, trans. Gibson, §88, p. 238.

169 "Whatever we might identify as a fundamental common human nature,
the possible object of an ultimate experience-transcending science is
always and everywhere mediated in human life through culture, self-
understanding, and language." Taylor, *Dilemmas and Connections*, 26–7.
Taylor paraphrases Gadamer.

170 Gadamer, *Truth and Method*, trans. Weinsheimer and Marshall, 370–9; R.G.
Collingwood, *An Autobiography* (London: Oxford Univ. Press, 1939), 29–
43; Samuel Taylor Coleridge, *The Friend*, ed. Barbara E. Rooke (London:
Routledge, 1969), 1:466.

171 Husserl, *Ideas*, trans. Gibson, §36–7, pp. 108–9. Emphasis added. Also §84,
pp. 222–6.

172 Scheler, *Formalism in Ethics*, trans. Frings and Funk, 302.

173 Aristotle, *The Nicomachean Ethics* 9.5.1176a15–20, 7.8.1151a15–20, trans.
Thomson, rev. Tredennick, 267, 186–7.

174 On how the virtues determine and condition knowledge and what it is
possible to know, especially the deepest metaphysical and moral truth,
see Moses Maimonides, *The Guide for the Perplexed*, trans. M. Friedländer
(New York: Dover, 1956), 47–8; Aquinas, *Summa Theologiæ* 1–2.57.1, in
Philosophical Texts, trans. Gilby, 7; Aquinas, *Summa Theologiæ* 2–2.60.1
(Cambridge: Cambridge Univ. Press, 2006), vol. 37 ("Justice"), trans.
Thomas Gilby, 69; Hegel, *Philosophy of Right*, trans. Knox, addition to §4,
p. 227; Coleridge, *The Friend*, 1:115, 336; Rosenzweig, *The Star of Redemp-
tion*, trans. Hallo, 387–8; Scheler, *Formalism in Ethics*, trans. Frings and
Funk, 318.

175 Williams, *Ethics and the Limits of Philosophy*, 51.

176 Williams, 201. "The sociology of culture is necessarily a sociology of
morals." David Martin, *On Secularization: Towards a Revised General Theory*
(Farnham: Ashgate, 2005), 185.

177 Ignatieff, *The Ordinary Virtues*, 203.

178 "[J]ust as defining the virtues helps us to deliberate, understanding better as we do what it is good to be, so this understanding can be further

aided by clarifying the constitutive goods. We help to clarify what it is good to be by getting clearer on just what is noble or admirable about the human potential. [These are] two facets of the same exploration. On one, we are defining the virtues, the qualities of life we want to have; on the other, we are looking at what is, the human being endowed with its potential in the world, and taking inspiration from what we find worthy in this. ... We are in some way *moved* by human powers; this forms part of the moral meanings of our world, along with our sense of what it is good to be, and what we ought to do." Taylor, *Dilemmas and Connections*, 11.

179 Williams, *Ethics and the Limits of Philosophy*, 51.

180 "Neither in moral nor mathematical science is the knowledge of first principles reached by logical means: it is virtue, whether natural or acquired by habituation, that enables us to think rightly about the first principle." Aristotle, *The Nicomachean Ethics* 7.8.1151a15–20, trans. Thomson, rev. Tredennick, 186–7.

181 Thomas Aquinas, *Theological Texts*, selected and trans. Thomas Gilby (London: Oxford Univ. Press, 1955), 219n1.

182 Comte-Sponville, *A Small Treatise*, trans. Temerson, 4.

183 Peterson and Seligman sometimes distinguish between "virtues," "character strengths," and "situational themes," reserving the first for their six large categories, the second for the twenty-four components of the first six, and the third for other virtues. Peterson and Seligman, *Character Strengths and Virtues*, 12–14.

184 Rosalind Hursthouse suggests "our list of generally recognized virtue terms is, I think, quite short." *On Virtue Ethics*, 41. On the contrary, as this book illustrates, it seems to me almost endlessly long. I agree with Christine Swanton that the distinction between a short list of "truly moral" virtues and all the other "good habits" required for everyday life is artificial and mistaken. As she says (and as I hope this book helps to show), the "moral virtues are legion." *Virtue Ethics*, 70–1.

185 In the last century several psychological scholars have in fact read through a dictionary to establish long lists of character traits and virtues. This is known as the *lexical approach* to personality. Peterson and Seligman, *Character Strengths and Virtues*, 68–9.

186 "The concepts of the virtues, and the familiar words that name them, are important since they help to make certain potentially nebulous areas of experience open to inspection." Murdoch, *The Sovereignty of Good*, 57. For Murdoch, the very number and "complexity" of the virtues is an advantage because it reflects the "multifarious cases of good behavior." But she also insists on the relatedness of the virtues, and their ultimate "unity and interdependence." Murdoch, 48, 54, 61, 66, 76, 95.

187 Plato, *The Laws*, 1.631, 12.963–4, trans. Trevor J. Saunders (Harmondsworth: Penguin Books, 1970), 55, 521–2. See also, *Symposium* 196C–198D, in *Great Dialogues of Plato*, trans. Rouse, 92.

188 Aristotle, *The Nicomachean Ethics* 4.1.1119b20–9.1128b35, trans. Thomson, rev. Tredennick, 82–111.

189 Aquinas, *Summa Theologiæ* 1–2.57.6, in *Treatise on the Virtues*, trans. Oesterle, 77–9.

190 "It may well be that being particularly well endowed with respect to some virtues inevitably involves being not very well endowed in others." Hursthouse, *On Virtue Ethics*, 213.

191 "All the good things in life cannot be simultaneously maximized. When it comes to implementing true values, there are always trade-offs, which is why there are different traditions of values (cultures) and why no one cultural tradition has ever been able to honor everything that is good." Shweder, *Why Do Men Barbecue?*, 38, 350.

192 Rosalind Hursthouse points out that most Western parents' child-rearing practices *implicitly* assume the virtues are the "best way to achieve a good life," even if they *explicitly* deny it. *On Virtue Ethics*, 176–7.

193 "True, to lack entirely any one of the virtues on the standard list is necessarily to be on the way to possessing a corresponding vice, but it may be that there are some less familiar ones of which this is not true. ... Possession of such a virtue would count towards an overall assessment of an individual human being as a good one, but the lack of it in a different individual would not necessarily count against their being good." Hursthouse, 213–14.

194 Shweder, *Why Do Men Barbecue?*, 27–8, 217–73. Hegel suggests that chastity and modesty are expressions of the "ethical aspect of love." Hegel, *Philosophy of Right*, trans. Knox, §163, pp. 113–14.

195 "[I]n a postmodern world eager for any ironic turn, we should be willing to revalue certain aspects of premodern thought." Shweder, *Why Do Men Barbecue?*, 335. On the need for anthropology to "[take] seriously the forms of life we describe ... as something we learn from as well as about," see also Laidlaw, *The Subject of Virtue*, 45–6.

196 Hegel, *Philosophy of Right*, trans. Knox, §130, p. 87; Rosenzweig, *The Star of Redemption*, trans. Hallo, 228; Peterson and Seligman, *Character Strengths and Virtues*, 84.

197 Terestchenko, *Un si fragile vernis d'humanité*.

198 Hume, *A Treatise of Human Nature* 3.3.1, p. 578.

199 In Alfred North Whitehead's language, virtues and values are both immanent *and* transcendent: "as a realized determinant [a virtue or value] is immanent; as a capacity for determination it is transcendent." *Process and Reality*, 280.

200 Clifford Geertz' influential definition of culture is: "an historically trans-mitted pattern of meanings embodied in symbols, a system of inherited conceptions expressed in symbolic forms by means of which men com-municate, perpetuate, and develop their knowledge about and attitudes toward life." *The Interpretation of Cultures* (New York: Basic Books, 1973), 89. Western anthropology's "most exquisite and straightforward" defini-tion of culture is Robert Redfield's 1941 version: "shared understandings made manifest in act and artefact." A more recent one is: "a reality lit up by a morally enforceable conceptual scheme or subset of meanings in-stantiated in practice." Shweder, *Why Do Men Barbecue?*, 10, 238.

201 Hegel, *Science of Logic*, vol. 1, bk. 2, §2, chap. 3, trans. Johnston and Stru-thers, 2:196; Keane, *Ethical Life*, 122–3.

202 "It is a supposition of cultural psychology that when people live in the world differently, it may be that they live in different worlds." Shweder, *Thinking Through Cultures*, 23.

203 A "stance" has been described as "a way of categorizing or judging expe-rience particular to a group or individual." Paul Kockelman, "Stance and subjectivity," *Journal of Linguistic Anthropology* 14, no. 2 (December 2004): 129, quoted in Keane, *Ethical Life*, 136. Keane comments, significantly, that "stances can take the form of 'voices' that embody ... recognizable types of ethical persons or actions." Keane, 136. Thinkers have many different names for what, in this book, I call "stances" (and their related families of virtues). F.H Bradley, for example, calls them "modes" or "attitudes" or "aspects of experience." *Appearance and Reality*, 403–14. Martin Heidegger's terms for stance include "standpoint" (*standpunkt*), "attitude," "modes of being," "ways of being," "manners of being," "structural moments," "structural factors," "constitutive moments," "constitutive factors," the "fundamental possibilities" of human being (or of *Dasein*). For Heidegger, each of the four human modes of being has its own distinctive "modes of behaviour." *Being and Time*, 5, 19–21, 24–5, 180, 190–1, 193, 200, 203, 206, 208–9, 211, 220, trans. Stambaugh, 4, 19–21, 24, 175, 184, 186–7, 193, 198, 200–1, 203, 211. Maurice Blondel's names for the stances include "centres de perspectives sans lesquels aucun classe-ment, aucune formule de relation ne seraient possibles," "des systèmes contrastants de fins," "synthèses antagonistes," "groupes hétérogènes," systèmes antagonistes," "états antagonistes," and "diverses tendances antagonistes." *L'Être et les êtres*, 257, 375; *L'Action*, 110–15, in Lacroix, *Maurice Blondel*, 97–102. Paul Ricœur's terms for "stance" include "circuit de sens," "points de départ," "point de vue, " "angle de vue," "signifi-ant-clés," "sphères de sens," "régions de significations humaines," "fig-ures de l'homme," "figures des vertus," "figures de l'Esprit," "sphères de culture." "mode d'être," "structures ontiques." *Soi-même comme un autre*,

109, 107n1; *Le conflit des interprétations: Essais d'herméneutique* (Paris: Édi-tions du Seuil, 2013), 96, 160–3, 171–3, 176–7, 243–4, 331–2, 358. A stance can also be described as a "hermeneutic," a way of "interpreting" the world. So, the nature of the human described in this book might also be called, in Ricœur's language, a "conflict of interpretations," "un conflit des herméneutiques rivales," or, better still, "la complémentarité des her-méneutiques rivales." *Le conflit des interprétations*, 44, 244. Iris Murdoch calls the stances "contexts of attention": "the reasons for the divergence of one moral temperament from another." *The Sovereignty of Good*, 33, 45. Richard Shweder uses the term "stand" instead of "stance" but means the same thing. *Thinking Through Cultures*, 23. On the concept of "stance," see also Scheler, *Formalism in Ethics*, trans. Frings and Funk, 139–40, 147–8; Nozick, *The Examined Life*, 151 61.

204 "[J]e *suis* est un axiome ... une vérité primitive ... c'est-à-dire que c'est une des énonciations premières connues, ce qui s'entend dans l'ordre na-turel de nos connaissances, car il se peut qu'un homme n'ait jamais pensé à former expressément cette proposition, qui lui est pourtant innée." Leib-niz, *Nouveaux essais*, bk. 4, chap. 7, §7, p. 362. On "I am" as the implicit "first truth" or "first statement," the reality that underlies every other hu-man reality and truth, see also Kant, *Critique of Pure Reason*, A405, trans. Kemp Smith, 367; *Prolegomena to Any Future Metaphysics*, trans. Lewis White Beck et al. (Indianapolis: Bobbs-Merrill, 1950), 85; Johann Gottlieb Fichte, *The Science of Knowledge*, trans. A.E. Kroeger (London: Trubner, 1889), in *The Age of Ideology: The Nineteenth Century Philosophers*, ed. Henry D. Aiken (New York: Mentor, 1956), 61–3; F.W.J. Schelling, *Werke*, i, 209, quoted in *Hegel's Logic*, trans. William Wallace (London: Oxford Univ. Press, 1975), 320; Edmund Husserl, *Cartesian Meditations*, §§6 and 9, cited in Emmanuel Levinas, *Entre nous: Essais sur le penser-à-l'autre* (Paris: Livre de Poche, 2010), 93–4; Heidegger, *Being and Time*, 211, trans. Stam-baugh, 203; "Modern Science, Metaphysics and Mathematics," trans. W.B. Barton, Jr. and Vera Deutsch, in *Basic Writings*, ed. David Farrell Krell (New York: HarperCollins, 1977) 278–9; Ricœur, *Le conflit des interpréta-tions*, 440; *Soi-même comme un autre*, 371.

205 Aristotle, *Metaphysics*, 5.7.1017a30-35, trans. Ross, *The Basic Works of Aristotle*, ed. McKeon, 761; Thomas Aquinas, *Summa Theologiæ*, 1.1.1, in *Introduction to St. Thomas Aquinas*, ed. Pegis, 4. On the transcendentals of being (which are convertible with being), see Étienne Gilson, *The Elements of Christian Philosophy*, 149–78.

206 Franz Rosenzweig calls this first human stance the "accented I" (as distinct from the "unemphatic I") and says it is the "actual root word" of humanity. *The Star of Redemption*, trans. Hallo, 201. Martin Heidegger does so too, implic-itly: "*I* am always this being. The 'I' seems to 'hold together' the wholeness of

the structural whole [i.e., all four stances and families of virtues]." Heidegger, *Being and Time*, 317, trans. Stambaugh, 303. Emphasis in original.

207 "Being-human defines itself out of a relation to what is as a whole." Heidegger, *An Introduction to Metaphysics*, trans. Manheim, 142. "The paradox of existence, then, is that the choice in which the self originates is itself possible only within a given situation." Louis Dupré, *Transcendent Selfhood: The Loss and Recovery of the Inner Life* (New York: Seabury Press, 1976), 36.

208 "[S]i l'existence se substitue au sujet, l'idée de l'être prend une nouvelle signification. ... [A]ntérieurement à la représentation [l'esprit humain] est engagé d'une façon saisissante dans l'être. ... Conscience confuse, conscience implicite précédant toute intention – ou revenue de toute intention – elle n'est pas acte mais passivité pure. ... Dans sa non-intentionnalité en deçà de tout vouloir ... l'identité recule devant son affirmation ... Mise en question de l'affirmation et de l'affermissement de l'être." Levinas, *Entre nous*, 59, 61, 138. Emphasis in original.

209 "Fragile et gratuit, l'être, en commençant avec le nôtre, aurait pu ne jamais voir le jour. Mais on n'y peut rien, il est, il y a de l'être, et nous en sommes, le temps d'un soupir. C'est ce mystère, et notre perplexité face à lui, face à nous-mêmes, qui est à l'origine de la philosophie ou de la métaphysique, la pensée de l'être. " Grondin, *Introduction à la métaphysique*, 19.

210 Maurice Blondel calls this "la polarisation psychique." *L'Action*, 110–15, in Lacroix, *Maurice Blondel*, 95.

211 Hegel, *Science of Logic*, vol. 2, bk. 3, chap. 1A, trans. Johnston and Struthers, 2:406–7; *Philosophy of Right*, §§158, 278, trans. Knox, 110, 180.

212 Paul Ricœur calls this basic human paradox (among other things) "[le] rapport de la liberté à l'obligation." *Le conflit des interprétations*, 569.

213 "[U]ne sorte d'indépendance dépendante." Paul Ricœur, *Le Volontaire et l'Involontaire*, in *Ricœur: Textes choisis et présentés*, 273.

214 "Being-there [Dasein] is itself by virtue of its essential relationship to being in general." Heidegger, *An Introduction to Metaphysics*, trans. Manheim, 24.

Chapter 4. The Virtues of Self-Assertion

1 G.W.F Hegel, *Preface to the Phenomenology of Spirit*, trans. Yirmiyahu Yovel (Princeton: Princeton Univ. Press, 2005), 130. "[I]individuality essentially implies negation." G.W.F. Hegel, *Philosophy of Right*, trans. T.M. Knox (Oxford: Oxford Univ. Press, 1967), addition to §324, p. 295. Franz Rosenzweig says the human stance of "*I* am" (or the "accented I") is "the Nay become audible." *The Star of Redemption*, trans. William W. Hallo (Notre Dame, IN: Univ. of Notre Dame Press, 1985), 201.

2 Hegel refers to the "need of the particular to *assert itself* in some distinctive way." Hegel, *Philosophy of Right*, trans. Knox, §193, p. 128. Emphasis added. On "Man" as "the violent one," whose "powers of language, of understanding, of temperament, and of building are themselves mastered (bewältigt) in violence," see Martin Heidegger, *An Introduction to Metaphysics*, trans. Ralph Manheim (New York: Doubleday, 1961), 126, 132.

3 Aristotle, *Metaphysics* 14.3.1091a15–20, trans. W.D. Ross, in *The Basic Works of Aristotle*, ed. McKeon (New York: Random House, 1941), 920; G.S. Kirk and J.E. Raven, *The Presocratic Philosophers* (Cambridge: Cambridge Univ. Press, 1964), 250–3.

4 N. Joseph Torchia, *Plotinus, Tolma, and the Descent of Being: An Exposition and Analysis* (New York: Peter Lang, 1993), 14–18. On *tolma* in Greek and Neoplatonic thought, see also Albrecht Dihle, *The Theory of Will in Classical Philosophy* (Berkeley: Univ. of California Press, 1982), 22–4, 114–16. Dihle famously argues that there was no concept of "will," in the Christian and modern sense, in classical philosophy. But this does not apply to more basic self-assertion.

5 Plotinus' stages or levels in the descent of being are the One, *Nous* (or Intellect, or the Intellectual Cosmos), and Soul (composed of its own three distinct levels: All-Soul, World-Soul, individual souls).

6 Torchia, *Plotinus*, 14–18. Also: Plotinus, *Enneads* 5.1.1–12, in *The Essential Plotinus*, ed. Elmer O'Brien (New York: Mentor Books, 1964), 90–104.

7 Plotinus, *Enneads* 6.9.3, in *The Essential Plotinus*, 78.

8 Torchia, *Plotinus*, 96–8.

9 Thomas Aquinas, *Summa Theologiæ* 1–2.58.1, in *Treatise on the Virtues*, trans. John A. Oesterle (Notre Dame, IN: Univ. of Notre Dame Press, 1984), 81. Aristotle's and Aquinas' term for self-assertion is "appetite" (*orexis*) or the "appetitive power." For Aristotle and Aquinas on "appetite," see chapter 8, note 2.

10 "[E]vil ... has its source in self-will." Plotinus, *Enneads* 5.1.1, in *The Essential Plotinus*, ed. O'Brien, 91. O'Brien indicates that by his translation "self-will" he means self-assertion: "By our weak, English 'self-will,' the Pythagorean *tolma* is meant – the instinct for self-affirmation that is at the origin of the complex universe." O'Brien, 91n2. On self-assertion as the source of all injustice and violence, as of all morality and reverence, see also David Hume, *A Treatise of Human Nature*, 3.2.1, ed. L.A. Selby-Bigge (London: Oxford Univ. Press, 1968), 480; Hegel, *Philosophy of Right*, trans. Knox, §139, p. 92; Rosenzweig, *The Star of Redemption*, trans. Hallo, 170.

11 Thomas Hobbes, *Leviathan* (Indianapolis: Bobbs-Merrill, 1958), pt. 1, chap. 11, p. 86; Baruch Spinoza, *Ethics*, pt. 3, Propositions 6 and 7, in *Spinoza Selections*, ed. John Wild (New York: Scribner's, 1958), 215–16.

12 G.W.F. Hegel, "The Spirit of Christianity and its Fate," in *Early Theological Writings*, trans. T.M. Knox (Chicago: Univ. of Chicago Press, 1948), 186. Emphasis added.

13 "Now we are all supposed to be conscious primarily of our assertive selves." Robert N. Bellah, Richard Madsen, William M. Sullivan, Ann Swidler, and Steven M. Tipton, *Habits of the Heart*, updated ed. (Berkeley: Univ. of California Press, 1996), 111.

14 "What is universal in the modern world is the centrality of freedom as a good." Charles Taylor, *Sources of the Self: The Making of the Modern Identity* (Cambridge: Harvard Univ. Press, 1989), 395. "[L]exercice de la liberté … est bien la référence majeure de la pensée morale des Modernes." Paul Ricœur, *Lectures 3*, in *Ricœur: Textes choisis et présentés*, ed. Michaël Fœssel and Fabien Lamouche (Paris: Éditions Points, 2007), 322.

15 Bellah et al., *Habits of the Heart*, 127; Charles Taylor, *A Secular Age* (Cambridge, MA: Belknap Press of Harvard Univ. Press, 2007), 171.

16 In using "self-assertion" as a name for the family of virtues of "non-union," I'm following the usage of T.H. Green, *Lectures on the Principles of Political Obligation* (London: Longmans, Green, 1927), 10; John Stuart Mill, *On Liberty* (Harmondsworth: Penguin Books, 1974), 127; and F.H. Bradley, *Appearance and Reality* (Oxford: Oxford Univ. Press, 1930), 367–80, among others. Dietrich von Hildebrand does not recognize the virtues of self-assertion as genuine values. He dismisses them as "merely subjectively satisfying goods," and criticizes his mentor, Max Scheler, for including them in his hierarchy of values. *Ethics* (Steubenville, OH: Hildebrand Press, 2020), 36–51. But, in this area, Scheler was nearer the truth than Hildebrand.

17 "In accordance with [the fundamental attitude of the Western spirit], being is defined from the standpoint of thinking and reason. This is true even where the Western spirit shuns the domination of reason by seeking the 'irrational' and 'alogical.'" Heidegger, *An Introduction to Metaphysics*, trans. Manheim, 122. See also Max Scheler, *Formalism in Ethics and Non-Formal Ethics of Value*, trans. Manfred S. Frings and Roger L. Funk (Evanston: Northwestern Univ. Press, 1973), 371.

18 Emmanuel Levinas emphasizes the character of perception and rational consciousness as "grasping" and "seizing." *Altérité et transcendance* (Paris: Le Livre de Poche, 2010), 128; *Éthique comme philosophie première* (Paris: Rivages poche, 2015), 69. Martin Heidegger also uses the verb "grasp" as a synonym or image for the action of assertive, analytic, and conceptual reason. See, for example, *Being and Time*, 149–50, trans. Joan Stambaugh (Albany: State Univ. of New York Press, 2010), 144–5.

19 Aristotle, *The Nicomachean Ethics* 6.9.1176a15–20, 7.8.1142b10–15, trans. Thomson, rev. Tredennick, 158.

20 Bernard J.F. Lonergan, *Insight: A Study of Human Understanding* (London: Darton, Longman & Todd, 1973), 332. Paralleling Lonergan's definition of reason as a self-assertive spontaneity, Paul Ricœur describes the virtues of Reverence (A2) ("la sollicitude") as "*une spontanéité bienveillante.*" *Soi-même comme un autre* (Paris: Éditions du Seuil, 1990), 222. Emphasis in original.

21 Harold C. Goddard, *The Meaning of Shakespeare* (Chicago: Univ. of Chicago Press, 1962), 2:79. Emphasis in original.

22 Hegel denies that reason is a form of self-assertion and argues that it is in fact a form of "humility" because it involves "letting slip all our individual opinions and prejudices, and submitting to the sway of fact. ... [W]hen we think, we renounce our selfish and particular being, [and] sink ourselves in the thing ..." G.W.F. Hegel, *Encyclopaedia of the Philosophical Sciences*, §23–4, in *Hegel's Logic*, trans. William Wallace (London: Oxford Univ. Press, 1975), 36, 39. There is some truth in this. As you will see again in chapter 17, one of the poles of self-assertion (what Hegel calls "philosophical cognition" or Reason [B2]) is less assertive and more reverent than the *other* side of self-assertion (what Hegel calls the "natural man" or "appetite" [A1]). But reason is still a form of self-assertion (as Hegel's own spontaneous linking of reason to "fact" and to "thing" makes clear). Even the initial, more reverent form of reason (what Hegel calls "reflection" or Understanding [B2]) is more assertive and less reverent than the other deeper side of reverence (what Hegel calls "immediate experience" or "innocence" [A2]). Its initial appearance in the "arrow of virtue" was what prepared the way for the human journey back out of reverence into self-assertion. As Hegel himself says: "To think is in fact *ipso facto* to be free." Hegel, 36. Emmanuel Levinas sees clearly this essentially assertive character of reason: "Le rationnel se réduit ... au *pouvoir sur l'objet ... La raison est ... domination* où la résistance de l'étant comme tel est surmontée ... comme par une ruse de chasseur ... Accéder au rationnel, c'est saisir. ... La perception, le saisir ... demeure et le premier mouvement de l'âme naïve [A1] ... et l'ultime geste du philosophe réfléchissant [B2]." *Entre nous: Essais sur le penser-à-l'autre* (Paris: Livre de Poche, 2010), 19, 88, 90. Emphasis added.

23 "The impulse of the mind is derived from a very strong interest." Hume, *A Treatise of Human Nature* 3.2.10, p. 556. "Interest" is Hume's frequent term for self-assertion or appetite. Martin Heidegger expresses the self-assertiveness of human reason with words like "wrested," "torn," and "robbery": "Truth (discoveredness) must always first be wrested [abgerungen] from beings. Beings are torn from concealment. Each and every factical discoveredness is, so to speak, always a kind of *robbery.*" *Being and Time*, 222, trans. Stambaugh, 213. Emphasis in original. See also *An Introduction to Metaphysics*, trans. Manheim, 132.

24 What, in this book, I will call a sub-family (or sub-sub-family) of virtues, Dietrich von Hildebrand calls a "section of morality" or a "sphere [or realm] of goods." He recognizes that these sub-families combine into larger families (or "general attitudes"), which finally combine into two "ultimate fundamental responses," "the deepest basis of all our other attitudes," which I will call self-assertion and reverence. *Ethics*, 377–84.

25 "My rights enhance my *power*. They increase my *self-control*. ... The citizens of every modern Western state possess an ever-growing arsenal of rights. ... More of the benefits that once were left to chance or charity are today viewed as *entitlements* to which their recipients have an enforceable *claim*. ... The growth of a realm of rights is motivated by a longing for *control*. Luck and love are forms of vulnerability. Each is a kind of dependence. Their conversion to rights represents an increase in our *independence* or *autonomy*. This is something that humans have always desired. But the hypertrophic expansion of the sphere of entitlements in the modern world is motivated by a *desire for control* of a peculiarly exaggerated kind." Anthony T. Kronman, *Confessions of a Born-Again Pagan* (New Haven: Yale Univ. Press, 2016), 20–1. Emphasis added to highlight the virtues of self-assertion embedded in claims for human rights.

26 "The notion of 'rights' has achieved an unnatural predominance in the language of politics." Roger Scruton, *The Meaning of Conservatism*, 3rd rev. ed. (South Bend, IN: St. Augustine's Press, 2002), 42.

27 Brad S. Gregory, *The Unintended Reformation: How a Religious Revolution Revolutionized Society* (Cambridge, MA: Belknap Press of Harvard Univ. Press, 2012), 228. Emphasis added. Gregory's own quote is from Mary Ann Glendon, *Rights Talk: The Impoverishment of Political Discourse* (New York: Free Press, 1991).

28 Kronman, *Confessions of a Born-Again Pagan*, 68.

29 Edmund Fawcett, *Liberalism: The Life of an Idea* (Princeton: Princeton Univ. Press, 2014), 348. "The discourse of rights encouraged the spread of entitlement claims into ever wider areas. Soon virtually any political issue became posable as an issue of rights." Fawcett, 297. That the language of "rights" is now almost the only language in which social goods can be described, let alone discussed, is illustrated by the declaration of Antonio Tajani, the European Union's commissioner for enterprise and industry, that "Travelling for tourism is a right." Bojan Pancevski, "Tourism a Human Right, EU Decides," *Ottawa Citizen*, 19 April 2010, 1–2.

30 Hans Joas, *The Sacredness of the Person: A New Genealogy of Human Rights*, trans. Alex Skinner (Washington, DC: Georgetown Univ. Press, 2013); Taylor, *Sources of the Self*, 305; Michael Ignatieff, *The Rights Revolution* (Toronto: Anansi, 2000).

31 Alexis de Tocqueville, *L'ancien régime et la Révolution* (Paris: Gallimard, 1967), 203.

32 An interesting recent milestone in the contemporary pursuit of physical pleasure was the licensing of Addyi, or "Pink Viagra," a Viagra-type pill for women. Unlike Viagra, which works on the physical mechanics of the penis to improve erections, Addyi adjusts the brain chemicals of women to *increase* sexual desire. A product of this kind symbolizes a fundamental, contemporary shift in the cultural and ethical presuppositions of Western culture: a shift from reverence to self-assertion. "'Pink Viagra' Gets Nod from Feds," *Ottawa Citizen*, 30 March 2018, NP1–2.

33 Michael J. Sandel, *What Money Can't Buy: The Moral Limits of Markets* (New York: Farrar, Straus & Giroux, 2012).

34 C.B. Macpherson, *The Political Theory of Possessive Individualism: Hobbes to Locke* (Oxford: Oxford Univ. Press, 1962). Robert Bellah and his colleagues use the term "utilitarian individualism" to describe the contemporary expression of this outlook, but Macpherson's historical term seems to me more readily comprehensible to the general reader. See Bellah et al., *Habits of the Heart*, 27.

35 Charles Taylor developed the term "expressivism" under the influence of Isaiah Berlin's term "expressionism," originally used to describe the influence of Herder on the post-Enlightenment. But Taylor alters the noun to avoid confusion with the twentieth-century artistic movement also called "expressionism." For Taylor, the expressivist impulse is "an aspiration to escape from a predicament in which the subject is over against an objectified world, to overcome the gap between subject and object, to see objectivity as an expression of subjectivity, or in interchange with it." Charles Taylor, *Hegel* (Cambridge: Cambridge Univ. Press, 1975), 13, 29; *Sources of the Self*, 374–6.

36 Christopher Lasch, *The Culture of Narcissism: American Life in an Age of Diminishing Expectations* (New York: W.W. Norton, 1978).

37 Bellah et al., *Habits of the Heart*, 333–4. Also 27, 33–5, 47. For a critical view of expressive individualism, see Carl R. Trueman, *The Rise and Triumph of the Modern Self: Cultural Amnesia, Expressive Individualism, and the Road to Sexual Revolution* (Wheaton, IL: Crossway, 2020).

38 Philip Rieff, *The Triumph of the Therapeutic: Uses of Faith after Freud* (Chicago: Univ. of Chicago Press, 1987).

39 Taylor, *A Secular Age*, 473–5.

40 Donald T. Campbell, "How Individual and Face-to-Face Group Selection Undermine Firm Selection in Organizational Function," in *Evolutionary Dynamics of Organizations*, ed. J.A.C. Baum and J.V. Singh (New York: Oxford Univ. Press, 1994), 23, quoted in David Sloan Wilson, *Does Altruism Exist? Culture, Genes, and the Welfare of Others* (New Haven:

Yale Univ. Press, 2015), 51. See also, Elliott Sober and David Sloan Wilson, *Unto Others: The Evolution and Psychology of Unselfish Behavior* (Cambridges, MA: Harvard Univ. Press, 1998), 329–30; Joseph Heath, "Methodological Individualism," Stanford Encyclopedia of Philosophy, ed. Edward N. Zalta (Spring 2015 edition), updated 21 January 2015, https://plato.stanford.edu/archives/spr2015/entries/methodological-individualism.

41 Heidegger, *Being and Time*, 263, trans. Stambaugh, 252.

42 Maurice Blondel, *L'Action*, 37, in Jean Lacroix, *Maurice Blondel, sa vie, son œuvre* (Paris: Presses Universitaires de France, 1963), 25.

43 Frans de Waal, *The Age of Empathy: Nature's Lessons for a Kinder Society* (New York: Three Rivers Press, 2009), 203. de Waal's own word here is "aggressiveness."

44 When Christine Swanton says "creativity" is "part of the profiles of all virtues," she implicitly expresses the fact that all virtue is a form of self-assertion. *Virtue Ethics: A Pluralistic View* (Oxford: Oxford Univ. Press, 2003), 99. As you will see later in this book, creativity is a virtue of Pleasure (A1b), which is a sub-family of the virtues of Liberty (A1), one of the two sub-families of the virtues of self-assertion.

45 "In this element of the will is rooted my ability to free myself from everything. Man alone can sacrifice everything, his life included." Hegel, *Philosophy of Right*, trans. Knox, addition to §5, p. 227.

46 "Sciences of experience are *sciences of 'fact.'*" Edmund Husserl, *Ideas: General Introduction to Pure Phenomenology*, trans. W.R. Boyce Gibson (New York: Collier Books, 1962), §2, p. 46. Emphasis in original.

47 Mark Johnson gives a good description of the "objectivist" assumptions which have dominated modern and post-modern Western thought since the eighteenth century, and are commonplace in contemporary culture: "The world consists of objects that have properties and stand in various relationships independent of human understanding. The world is as it is, no matter what any person happens to believe about it, and there is one, correct 'God's-Eye-View' about what the world really is like. In other words there is a rational structure to reality, independent of the beliefs of any particular people, and correct reason mirrors this rational structure." Mark Johnson, *The Body in the Mind: The Bodily Basis of Meaning, Imagination and Reason* (Chicago: Chicago Univ. Press, 1987), x.

48 "The word *I* is always connected with a 'thou' on the one hand and an 'outer world' on the other." Scheler, *Formalism in Ethics*, trans. Frings and Funk, 389.

49 "[T]he formal will of mere self-consciousness [i.e., pure self-assertion] ... finds an external world confronting it. ... As *immediate* individuality, a person in making decisions is related to a world directly confronting him,

and thus the personality of the will stands over against this world, as
something subjective." Hegel, *Philosophy of Right*, trans. Knox, §§8, 39, pp.
24, 38. Emphasis in original. On "things" and "externality" as expressions
of self-assertion, see also *The Phenomenology of Mind*, trans. J.B. Baillie
(New York: Harper & Row, 1967), 149–50, 791–2; *Science of Logic*, vol. 2,
bk. 3, chap. 1, trans. W.H. Johnston and L.G. Struthers (London: George
Allen & Unwin, 1951), 2:410–13.

50 "[L]a monstration du monde et la position [i.e., positing, or self-assertion]
d'un *ego*, sont symétriques et réciproques. Aussi bien ne saurait-il y avoir
de visée du réel, donc de prétention à la vérité, sans *l'auto-assertion* d'un
sujet qui se détermine et s'engage dans son dire." Paul Ricœur, *Le conflit
des interprétations: Essais d'herméneutique* (Paris: Éditions du Seuil, 2013),
352. Emphasis added.

51 Hegel, *Philosophy of Right*, trans. Knox, §256, p. 154; Alfred North Whitehead, *Process and Reality* (New York: Free Press, 1969), 76, 83, 89.

52 John Locke, *The Second Treatise on Civil Government*, in *On Politics and Education* (Roslyn, NY: Walter J. Black, 1947).

53 Taylor, *Sources of the Self*, 160–72.

54 Marcel Gauchet, *The Disenchantment of the World: A Political History of Religion*, trans. Oscar Bruge (Princeton, NJ: Princeton Univ. Press, 1997), 22.
On consciousness and thinking as "negation," see Hegel, *Encyclopaedia*,
§12 & §91, trans. Wallace, 17, 135; Whitehead, *Process and Reality*, 187.
Alan Ryan captures this essentially negative side of self-assertion when
he says that "liberalism is well defined in negative terms. Its central commitment, liberty, is in general a negative notion." *The Making of Modern
Liberalism* (Princeton: Princeton Univ. Press, 2012), 28.

55 "Resistance characterizes the being of innerwordly beings." Heidegger,
Being and Time, 210, trans. Stambaugh, 202.

56 Blondel, *La Pensée*, 2:41, in Lacroix, *Maurice Blondel*, 45–6. For a brief
survey of the two kinds of human reason in the whole history of Western thought, see the translator's note for §45, p. 73, in *Hegel's Logic*,
trans. William Wallace, 310–12. Étienne Gilson suggests that, from at
least one point of view, "the state of mind of the scientist very much
resembles that of plain common sense." *The Elements of Christian Philosophy* (New York: Mentor, 1963), 180. But Max Scheler makes the case
for a third kind of everyday rationality of "effective experience," an
"'intermediate sphere' lying between our perceptual content and its
objects on the one hand and those objectively thought objects on the
other." *Formalism in Ethics*, trans. Frings and Funk, 139–40. Whitehead
and Bradley agree with Scheler that the scientific world view "diverges
from common sense." Whitehead, *Process and Reality*, 88; Bradley, *Appearance and Reality*, 232.

57 Herbert A. Simon points out, however, that what we now think of as human reason depends on premises, on so-called "facts" (that are themselves the products of hidden premises and values), and on rules of inference, none of which reason itself can supply. As a result, this kind of reason can be helpful in deciding on means to achieve certain ends, but "it has little to say about the ends themselves." All this modern kind of reason can do, Simon says, "is help us reach agreed-on goals more efficiently." The goals themselves have to come from somewhere else. *Reason in Human Affairs* (Palo Alto: Stanford Univ. Press, 1983), 7, 106.

58 Aristotle, *The Nicomachean Ethics* 9.7.1177a10–9.8.1179a35, trans. Thomson, rev. Tredennick, 270–6.

59 Aquinas, *Summa Theologiæ* 1–2.57.2, 1–2.66.5, in *Treatise on the Virtues*, trans. Oesterle, 70–1, 156–8. On the concept of "intellect" in medieval thought, see Denys Turner, *Faith, Reason and the Existence of God* (Cambridge: Cambridge Univ. Press, 2004), xiv–xvi, 75–88, 232–3.

60 Pascal, *Pensées* (Paris: Garnier-Flammarion, 1973), §§224, 909–11, pp. 92, 307–9. "[C]e sont les calculs qui sont dans la réalité, et non la réalité qui sont dans les calculs. ... [L]a réalité n'est point dans le calcul. Elle n'est pas au cœur du calcul. ... Corneille, Racine, Pascal, Molière lisaient toute psychologie à venir. Autrement mais ils lisaient. Car ils pouvaient et savaient lire dans ce que nos Français ont si proprement nommé le cœur humain." Charles Péguy, *Notes pour une thèse*, in *Une éthique sans compromis*, ed. Dominique Saatdjian (Paris: Pocket, 2011), 189–90. On the "heart," see also Dietrich von Hildebrand, *The Heart: An Analysis of Human and Divine Affectivity* (South Bend, IN: St. Augustine's Press, 2007).

61 Immanuel Kant, *Critique of Pure Reason*, trans. Norman Kemp Smith (London: Macmillan, 1968), 300–4; Hegel, *Encyclopaedia*, §28, trans. Wallace, 48; Samuel Taylor Coleridge, *Aids to Reflection* (Port Washington, NY: Kennikat Press, 1971), 223.

62 For Heidegger, there are many "interim stages" between these two poles, but the shift from understanding (B1) to reason (B2) always involves a "dimming down," a "dwindling," or a "leveling down," through which "what is manifest [can] be seen in its determinable, definite character." Heidegger, *Being and Time*, 137–8, 150–8, 260, trans. Stambaugh, 133–4, 145–53, 249; "Bremen Lectures: Insight into That Which Is," in *The Heidegger Reader*, ed. Günter Figal, trans. Jerome Veith (Bloomington: Indiana Univ. Press, 2009), 266.

63 Samuel Taylor Coleridge, *The Friend*, ed. Barbara E. Rooke (London: Routledge, 1969), 1:520–2. Emphasis added.

64 Heidegger, *Being and Time*, 150–8, trans. Stambaugh, 145–53.

65 "En l'un [l'esprit de géométrie], les principes sont palpables, mais éloignés de l'usage commun; de sorte qu'on a peine à tourner la tête de

ce côté-là, manque d'habitude; mais pour peu qu'on l'y tourne, on voit les principes à plein; et il faudrait avoir tout à fait l'esprit faux pour mal raisonner sur des principes si gros qu'il est presque impossible qu'ils échappent. Mais dans l'esprit de finesse, les principes sont dans l'usage commun et devant les yeux de tout le monde. On n'a que faire de tourner la tête, ni de se faire violence; il n'est question que d'avoir bonne vue, *mais il faut l'avoir bonne*: car les principes sont si déliés et en si grand nombre, qu'il est presque impossible qu'il n'en échappe. Or, l'omission d'un principe mène à l'erreur; ainsi, il faut avoir la vue bien nette pour voir tous les principes, et ensuite l'esprit juste pour ne pas raisonner faussement sur des principes connus. ... On les voit à peine, *on les sent plutôt qu'on les voit*; on a des peines infinies à les faire sentir à ceux qui ne les sentent pas d'eux-mêmes; ce sont des choses tellement délicate et nombreuses, qu'il faut un sens bien délicat et bien net pour les sentir, et juger droit et juste selon ce sentiment ... Il fait tout d'un coup *voir la chose d'un seul regard* et non pas par progrès de raisonnement." Pascal, *Pensées*, §§909–10, pp. 307–8. Emphasis added.

66 Turner, *Faith, Reason and the Existence of God*, xv, 121. "La dernière démarche de la raison est de reconnaître qu'il y a une infinité de choses qui la surpassent." Pascal, *Pensées*, §373, p. 134. On the demand of the intellect "to pass beyond itself" and thus discover " a whole beyond thought, a whole to which thought points and in which it is included," see Bradley, *Appearance and Reality*, 508; Blondel, *La philosophie et l'esprit chrétien*, 1:30–1, in Lacroix, *Maurice Blondel*, 134; Levinas, *Altérité et transcendance*, 28. Although he didn't always approve of the results, Kant gave a good description of the unstoppable impulse of the human spirit to push beyond the boundaries of ordinary reason. Immanuel Kant, *Prolegomena to Any Future Metaphysics*, trans. Lewis White Beck et al. (Indianapolis: Bobbs-Merrill, 1950), 81, 100.

67 Karl Jaspers, *Reason and Existenz*, trans. William Earle, in *Existentialism from Dostoevsky to Sartre*, ed. Walter Kaufmann (Cleveland: Meridian Books, 1956), 196.

68 Martin Heidegger's term for the self-assertion that transcends itself in reverence is "care." "Care" is a two-faced or two-sided term, reflecting the human paradox. Its "pre-scientific" meanings are instances of self-assertion – "seeking shelter, sustenance and livelihood." But its "ontological" meaning describes the human stance that has encountered the potentiality of the whole nature of the human and embraces it. It "projects" these "potentialities" – all four human stances – upon itself as real, "definite" possibilities it wants to enact, and does so with "anticipatory resoluteness," the self-assertion that has become a form of reverence. *Being and Time*, 57, 297–8, 322–5, trans. Stambaugh, 57, 285, 308–10.

Chapter 5. The Virtues of Reverence

1 Aristotle, *The Nicomachean Ethics* 8.12.1162a.18–19, trans. J.A.K. Thomson, rev. Hugh Tredennick (London: Penguin Books, 2004), 222.

2 "Young men should always show their elders the respect due to their age by rising at their approach, and giving up their seats to them, and similar courtesies." Aristotle, *The Nicomachean Ethics* 9.2.1165a25–30, trans. Thomson, rev. Tredennick, 233.

3 "We are justified in acknowledging to ourselves and to others the value of our individual lives and the respect this properly *demands*." Paul Bloomfield, *The Virtues of Happiness: A Theory of the Good Life* (New York: Oxford Univ. Press, 2014), 112. Emphasis added. When Ted Honderich says "no one possesses respect in the entire absence of freedom," he is (consciously or unconsciously) placing himself in the position of the person claiming, seeking, or "possessing" respect, *not* the person exercising the *virtue* of respect. *Conservatism: Burke, Nozick, Bush, Blair?* (London: Pluto Press, 2005), 87.

4 Anthony Kronman notes that the self-*giving* virtues discussed in this chapter (such as gratitude) are good not just for those to whom they are given but also – and especially – for those *who give*. Anthony T. Kronman, *Confessions of a Born-Again Pagan* (New Haven: Yale Univ. Press, 2016), 50, 59. This insight can also be turned around: the lack of such virtues is harmful to those who lack them. Bloomfield, *The Virtues of Happiness*, 4.

5 Marcel Gauchet, *The Disenchantment of the World: A Political History of Religion*, trans. Oscar Bruge (Princeton, NJ: Princeton Univ. Press, 1997), 178.

6 David Sloan Wilson, *Does Altruism Exist? Culture, Genes, and the Welfare of Others* (New Haven: Yale Univ. Press, 2015), 3.

7 In Auguste Comte's own list of ten "affective forces," seven correspond to egoism and only three to altruism. Michel Bourdeau, "Auguste Comte," trans. Mark van Atten, Stanford Encyclopedia of Philosophy; article first published 1 October 2008, updated 16 October 2014, https://plato.stanford.edu/entries/comte.

8 Christopher Boehm, *Moral Origins: The Evolution of Virtue, Altruism, and Shame* (New York: Basic Books, 2012), 367n31, 294, 339. Boehm cites S.A. West, A.S. Griffin, and A. Gardner, "Social Semantics: Altruism, Cooperation, Mutualism, Strong Reciprocity, and Group Selection," *Journal of Evolutionary Biology*, 2007, 20:415–32.

9 D.S. Wilson, *Does Altruism Exist?*, 22.

10 Elliott Sober and David Sloan Wilson, *Unto Others: The Evolution and Psychology of Unselfish Behavior* (Cambridges, MA: Harvard Univ. Press, 1998), 17. "Human behaviour ... is the circuitous technique by which human genetic material has been and will be kept intact. Morality has *no*

other demonstrable ultimate function." Edward O. Wilson, *On Human Nature* (Cambridge, MA: Harvard Univ. Press, 2004), 167. Emphasis added.

11 Paradoxically, altruism turns out to be the wrong word for almost the opposite reason, too. Starting as it does from a baseline of self-assertion, contemporary social science normally assumes altruism must therefore be the *opposite* of self-assertion (as Comte intended), i.e., an action that entails at least the possibility of either no benefit or loss to the actor. Because such a definition lacks a dialectical or paradoxical perspective, it misses the complementarity of the virtues and the way in which they entrain or "perfect" each other, leading, in their complementarity, to human fullness or fulfilment. Thus, it turns out, not surprisingly, that none of the world's religious traditions actually endorse or promote altruism, in this modern formulation. D.S. Wilson, *Does Altruism Exist?*, 75–91.

12 Christine Swanton points out that, as a virtue, benevolence cannot be just promoting the good of others, as in utilitarianism, but "requires the promotion of good *with love* in various manifestations, ranging from parental love to humane concern." *Virtue Ethics: A Pluralistic View* (Oxford: Oxford Univ. Press, 2003), 23. Emphasis added.

13 Webb Keane, *Ethical Life: Its Natural and Social Histories* (Princeton: Princeton Univ. Press, 2016), 6.

14 This absence is strikingly illustrated in a 2x2 figure David Sloan Wilson developed to "map" certain religious virtues and vices (his own interpretation of the "Hutterite Worldview"). Two of Wilson's four quadrants are completely empty. *Does Altruism Exist?*, 85, fig. 6.1.

15 "Every word causes the whole of the language to which it belongs to resonate and the whole world-view that underlies it to appear. Thus every word, as the event of a moment, carries with it the unsaid, to which it is related by responding and summoning. The occasionality of human speech is not a casual imperfection of its expressive power; it is, rather, the logical expression of the living virtuality of speech that brings a totality of meaning into play, without being able to express it totally." Hans-Georg Gadamer, *Truth and Method*, trans. and rev. Joel Weinsheimer and Donald G. Marshall, 2nd ed. (New York: Continuum, 2002), 458. On "la polysémie," the reality that words have multiple meaning and are capable of acquiring new meanings without losing the older ones, see also Paul Ricœur, *Le conflit des interprétations: Essais d'herméneutique* (Paris: Éditions du Seuil, 2013), 139. Ricœur points out that the meaning of words is circumscribed *not* by definitions but by the way they bump up against other words, and, indeed, against *all* the other words of the language. This is a striking, linguistic illustration of the paradox of the one and the many, or the structuring principle I have called (following Hegel) the union of union and non-union.

16 "[F]inding a word which stands while its meaning gradually changes has an essential function in the development of philosophical thought. The right word for a difficult concept is often recognized as such before the concept is defined; the definition grows up under the constant suggestion of the word, by virtue of its etymology and all its linguistic relations, its traditional ambiguities, its poetic and even slangy uncommon uses. The thinker who leans on a promising word hopes to find his apt and enlightening concept as a possible meaning for that word; where logical invention flounders the term with its suggestiveness holds him to his line of thought." Susanne K. Langer, *Mind: An Essay on Human Feeling*, Vol. 1 (Baltimore: Johns Hopkins Press, 1967), 108–9. On the "right word," the word whose rightness can't be explained in terms of its functional or instrumental result but rather, the result of which needs to be explained by its very "rightness" – which "allows what we are striving to encompass to appear" – see Charles Taylor, *The Language Animal: The Full Shape of the Human Linguistic Capacity* (Cambridge, MA: Belknap Press of Harvard Univ. Press, 2016), especially 25–34, 61–3, 178.

17 F.W. Farrar, *The Witness of History to Christ: Five Sermons Preached before the University of Cambridge, Being the Hulsean Lectures for the Year 1870* (London: Macmillan, 1871), 144.

18 Thomas Aquinas explains that what constitutes a "family" of virtues is that all the virtues that can be grouped under, or associated with, it "strike the same note and reproduce the tone and measure for which it is mainly admired and from which it gets its name." *Summa Theologiæ* 2–2.157.3 (Cambridge: Cambridge Univ. Press, 2006), vol. 44 ("Well-Tempered Passion"), trans. Thomas Gilby, 43.

19 On sympathy, see, for example, David Hume, *A Treatise of Human Nature*, ed. L.A. Selby-Bigge (London: Oxford Univ. Press, 1968). On sympathy and empathy, see, for example, Frans de Waal, *The Age of Empathy: Nature's Lessons for a Kinder Society* (New York: Three Rivers Press, 2009), 88–93.

20 Léon Walras' other two "principles" of human morality are "justice" and "association." As noted in chapter 17, Walras anticipated the four families of virtues described in this book. "Théorie de la propriété," in *Revue Socialiste* (Tome 23, no. 138, 15 juin 1896, 668–81 and Tome 24, no. 139, 15 juillet 1896, 23–35), trans. Guido Erreygers, Marylène Pastides, and Peter Vallentyne, in *The Origins of Left Libertarianism: An Anthology of Historical Writings*, ed. Peter Vallentyne and Hillel Steiner (Palgrave, 2000). https://klinechair.missouri.edu/docs/theory_of_property_trans.pdf.

21 "Only to the man possessing reverence does the world of religion open itself; only to him will the world as a whole reveal its meaning and value. So reverence as a basic moral attitude stands at the beginning of all

religion." Dietrich von Hildebrand, *Fundamental Moral Attitudes*, trans. Alice M. Jourdain (New York: Longmans, Green, 1950), 15.

22 Saint Augustine, *City of God*, trans. Henry Bettenson (London: Penguin Books, 2003), 373–4. The Islamic scripture, the *Qur'an*, also illustrates how religious practice is a deepening of the practice of reverence originally encountered in the family: it urges the devout to "remember God as you remember your forefathers, or *with deeper reverence*." *The Koran* 2:199–200, trans. N.J. Dawood (London: Penguin Books, 2003), 30. Emphasis added.

23 Augustine, *City of God*, trans. Bettenson, 330. On "primal trust" as the necessary precondition for "the conscious formulation of this primal trust in the direction of God," see Karl Rahner, *The Practice of Faith: A Handbook of Contemporary Spirituality*, trans. various (New York: Crossroad, 1983), 61.

24 Based on the work of Fustel de Coulanges, Larry Siedentop emphasizes that all ancient religion was originally family based: "it spoke to and through the family. ... The ancient family was itself a religious cult." Even when, in archaic societies, religious practice was extended to cities and to hierarchical communities and governments, it retained its original family base and orientation. *Inventing the Individual: The Origins of Western Liberalism* (London: Allen Lane, 2014), 351, 7–32. Also: Rahner, *The Practice of Faith*, 61.

25 Thomas Aquinas, *Summa Theologiæ* 1–2.60.3, in *Treatise on the Virtues*, trans. John A. Oesterle (Notre Dame, IN: Univ. of Notre Dame Press, 1984), 101.

26 On "family piety," see G.W.F. Hegel, *Philosophy of Right*, trans. T.M. Knox (Oxford: Oxford Univ. Press, 1967), §166, p. 114.

27 See, for example, John Locke, *Some Thoughts Concerning Education*, §§99–100, 107, in *On Politics and Education* (Roslyn, NY: Walter J. Black, 1947), 287, 291.

28 "[I]t is the business of philosophy to preserve the *power of the most elemental words* in which Dasein expresses itself and to protect them from being flattened by the common understanding to the point of unintelligibility, which in its turn functions as a source of illusory problems." Martin Heidegger, *Being and Time*, 220, trans. Joan Stambaugh (Albany: State Univ. of New York Press, 2010), 211. Emphasis in original.

29 Richard A. Shweder, *Why Do Men Barbecue? Recipes for Cultural Psychology* (Cambridge, MA: Harvard Univ. Press, 2003), 335; Michael J. Sandel, *What Money Can't Buy: The Moral Limits of Markets* (New York: Farrar, Straus & Giroux, 2012), 187.

30 In using "reverence" as a name for the family of virtues of "union," I'm following the usage of Goethe, Nietzsche, G.K. Chesterton, Albert Schweitzer, Rudolf Steiner, and Dietrich von Hildebrand, among others. I will come back to Goethe in chapter 17. See Johann Wolfgang von Goethe,

Wilhelm Meister's Journeyman Years or The Renunciants, trans. Krishna Winston, in *Goethe: The Collected Works*, ed. Jane K. Brown (Princeton: Princeton Univ. Press, 1995), 10:203–10; Friedrich Nietzsche, *Beyond Good and Evil*, trans. R.J. Hollingdale (London: Penguin Books, 2003), §§260, 263, 287, pp. 194–215; G.K. Chesterton, *Orthodoxy* (New York: Dodd Mead, 1924), 177, 209–10; Albert Schweitzer, *Reverence for Life: The Ethics of Albert Schweitzer for the Twenty-First Century*, ed. Martin Meyer and Kurt Bergel (Syracuse: Syracuse Univ. Press, 2002); *Reverence for Life: The Words of Albert Schweitzer*, ed. Harold E. Robles (Anna Maria, FL: Maurice Bassett, 2017); Rudolf Steiner, *Metamorphoses of the Soul: Paths of Experience*, vol. 1, Lecture 4: "The Mission of Reverence," https://rsarchive.org/Medicine/GA058/English/RSP1983/19091028a01.html; Hildebrand, *Fundamental Moral Attitudes*, 1–15.

31 "[C]et instinct général *de société*, qui se peut appeler *philanthropie* dans l'homme." G.W. Leibniz, *Nouveaux essais sur l'entendement humain* (Paris: Garnier-Flammarion, 1966), bk. 1, chap. 2, §9, p. 76. "If attachment and sympathy are as fundamental as proposed, we had better pay close attention to them in any discussion of human nature." de Waal, *The Age of Empathy*, 68.

32 Alfred North Whitehead, *The Aims of Education* (New York: Free Press, 1967), 14. On the "temporal horizon" (similar to the spatial horizon) of "now," "infinite in both direction[s]," an essential feature of "the reality which immediately surrounds me," see Edmund Husserl, *Ideas: General Introduction to Pure Phenomenology*, trans. W.R. Boyce Gibson (New York: Collier Books, 1962), §27, p. 92. Karl Jaspers calls this "eternity in time." "On My Philosophy," trans. Felix Kaufmann, in *Existentialism from Dostoevsky to Sartre*, ed. Walter Kaufmann (Cleveland: World, 1956), 154. Charles Taylor calls it "gathered time." *A Secular Age* (Cambridge, MA: Belknap Press of Harvard Univ. Press, 2007), 56–9, 714, 720, 750.

33 "Reverence is *the* attitude which can be designated as the mother of all moral life, for in it man first takes a position toward the world which opens his spiritual eyes and enables him to grasp values." Hildebrand, *Fundamental Moral Attitudes*, 5. Emphasis in original.

34 "To neglect my parents in old age is not an act of [in]justice but an act of impiety [i.e., irreverence]. Impiety is the refusal to recognize as legitimate a demand that does not arise from consent or choice. And we see that the behaviour of children toward their parents cannot be understood unless we admit this ability to recognize a bond that is 'transcendent,' that exists, as it were, 'objectively,' outside the sphere of individual choice." Roger Scruton, *The Meaning of Conservatism*, 3rd rev. ed. (South Bend, IN: St. Augustine's Press, 2002), 23.

35 Dietrich von Hildebrand calls this aspect of reverence "the disposition to recognize something superior to one's arbitrary pleasure and will, and to be ready to subordinate and abandon oneself." *Fundamental Moral Attitudes*, 10–11. See also *Ethics* (Steubenville, OH: Hildebrand Press, 2020), 41, 225, 371, 481; *The Heart: An Analysis of Human and Divine Affectivity* (South Bend, IN: St. Augustine's Press, 2007), 10–13. "[A] separation of worth from reality and truth would mutilate our nature." F.H. Bradley, *Appearance and Reality* (Oxford: Oxford Univ. Press, 1930), 331.

36 From a letter of Nahmanides to his son, in Israel Abrahams, *Hebrew Ethical Wills* (Philadelphia: Jewish Publication Society, 1948), 95–8, in *Judaism*, ed. Arthur Hertzberg (New York: Washington Square Press, 1963), 186. On the importance of humility to genuine goodness, see also Hume, *A Treatise of Human Nature* 3.3.2, p. 595; Hildebrand, *Fundamental Moral Attitudes*, 9–10, 56; Iris Murdoch, *The Sovereignty of Good* (London: Routledge, 1980), 103–4; David Brooks, *The Road to Character* (New York: Random House, 2015), 262.

37 "Dans la déposition par le moi de sa souveraineté de moi … signifie l'éthique et aussi probablement la spiritualité même de l'âme, mais certainement la question du sens de l'être." Emmanuel Levinas, *Éthique comme philosophie première* (Paris: Rivages poche, 2015), 96. On "le dé-saisissement du soi humain, dans sa volonté de maîtrise, de suffisance, d'autonomie," see also Paul Ricœur, *Lectures 3*, in *Ricœur: Textes choisis et présentés*, ed. Michaël Fœssel and Fabien Lamouche (Paris: Éditions Points, 2007), 210. Simone Weil goes too far, but she is going in the right direction when she calls this side of human virtue "[l]a mort de ce qui en nous dit 'je.'" *Pensées sans ordre concernant l'amour de Dieu* (Paris: Gallimard, 2013), 28.

38 Paul Bloomfield, for example, characterizes the unselfing virtues – the "humbler set of traits" – taught by the world's great spiritual traditions as "a servile lack of self-respect" and dismisses them as "flights of moral nobility" – a *"reductio ad absurdum"* – the truth of which "defies philosophical comprehension," and which are incompatible with true "happiness." *The Virtues of Happiness*, 82–3, 96, 123–4. In so doing, Bloomfield perhaps illustrates and demonstrates that humility "is a scandal and foolishness for natural morality." Dietrich von Hildebrand, *Ethics* (Steubenville, OH: Hildebrand Press, 2020), 486.

39 Michel Terestchenko, *Un si fragile vernis d'humanité: Banalité du mal, banalité du bien* (Paris: La Découverte, 2007). Paul Ricœur says the "effacement de soi" which is one side of the authentic human paradox, requires "estime de soi" and excludes "haine de soi." *Soi-même comme un autre* (Paris: Éditions du Seuil, 1990), 198.

40 "[L]'élan spirituel [reverence], même quand il paraît refréner ou mortifier l'élan vital [self-assertion], ne fait que l'élever, le perfectionner." Maurice

Blondel, *L'Être et les êtres* (Paris: Presses Universitaires de France, 1963), 270–1.

41　On "how much human life requires prosociality [i.e., reverence]," see D.S. Wilson, *Does Altruism Exist?*, 128–9; Bloomfield, *The Virtues of Happiness*, 145. Bloomfield calls this point of view "objective," but I think it has more to do with reverence or draws upon the prior virtues of reverence. As an "objective" stance (B2), it is (by definition) a calculating, rational reciprocity, and not an impulse of giving *for its own sake*. The contemporary crises of democracy and human rights discussed in chapter 17 show how much the virtues of Equality (B2) secretly draw upon the self-giving of the virtues of Reverence (A2).

42　John Calvin is one of the great prophets of unselfing and humility in the Western tradition: "How difficult it is to perform the duty of seeking the good of our neighbour! Unless you leave off all thought of yourself and in a manner cease to be yourself, you will never accomplish it." *The Institutes of the Christian Religion* 3.7.2, 4, 5, trans. Henry Beveridge (Peabody, MA: Hendrickson, 2012), 450–2.

43　What I call unselfing may be similar to the "millennium-old" Persian/Urdu concept of *bī-khwudi* ("without-Self-ness" or "Self-lessness") which, together with its opposite, *khwudī* ("Self-ness" or "Self-hood"), was "(re-)mobilized" by philosopher, poet, and reformer Muhammad Iqbal "as the seminal concepts for the (self-)creation of a new twentieth-century species of Muslim capable of meeting the challenges of modernity." Shahab Ahmed, *What Is Islam? The Importance of Being Islamic* (Princeton: Princeton Univ. Press, 2016), 340.

44　Martin Heidegger reminds us that there is a kind of "unselfing" that is the *opposite* of what I am talking about in this paragraph: not the self-*giving* unselfing of reverence but the self-*seeking* "self-forgetting" of self-assertion, the self-asserting self that has "forgotten" its true nature, "forgotten" the whole nature of the human, reverence as well as self-assertion. This kind of self-assertive "self-forgetting" is a "confused backing away from one's own factical potentiality-of-being," i.e., from the four stances and their families of virtues. *Being and Time*, 341–2, trans. Stambaugh, 326. Obviously, the whole purpose of this book is not to endorse, but to remedy *this* kind of self-forgetting.

45　Hegel, *Philosophy of Right*, trans. Knox, §181, p. 122.

46　What, in this book, I will call the "hijacking" of reverence by self-assertion, Dietrich von Hildebrand calls "the *interference* of pride [A1a] or concupiscence [A1b]." *Ethics*, 446. Emphasis added.

47　Wilson's word for reverence here is, again, "prosociality." Elsewhere it's usually altruism. D.S. Wilson, *Does Altruism Exist?* 138. Wilson gives a good description of how this hijacking works at the levels of the family, clan, ethnic group, or nation. D.S. Wilson, 137. On the hijacking of the virtues of reverence by self-assertion to fuel some of the most powerful forces in the modern and post-modern world, such as ethnic loyalty and nationalism, see also James Q. Wilson, *The Moral Sense* (New York: Free Press, 1993), 226–7; Keane, *Ethical Life*, 236–7; Michael Ignatieff, *The Ordinary Virtues: Moral Order in a Divided World* (Cambridge, MA: Harvard Univ. Press, 2017), 208–12. David Hume had already said much the same thing. *A Treatise of Human Nature* 3.2.2, p. 487.

48 "The intensity of private attachments encourages, not prevents, universal Benevolence." Samuel Taylor Coleridge, *The Friend*, ed. Barbara E. Rooke (London: Routledge, 1969), 1:336.

49 Max Scheler, *Formalism in Ethics and Non-Formal Ethics of Value*, trans. Manfred S. Frings and Roger L. Funk (Evanston: Northwestern Univ. Press, 1973), 94.

50 Bernard Lonergan, "Variations in Fundamental Theology," 10, cited in Frederick E. Crowe, "Editors' Preface" in Bernard Lonergan, *Verbum: Word and Idea, Collected Works of Bernard Lonergan*, ed. Frederick E. Crowe and Robert M. Doran (Toronto: Univ. of Toronto Press, 1997), 2:viii. On the way "the boundaries of love exhibited by humans extend outwards from the familiar terrain of one's children, parents, lovers, and very close friends, to strangers, criminals, animals, and even to nonsentient natural objects," see also Swanton, *Virtue Ethics*, 124. Lonergan's and Swanton's vision of the outward movement of reverence may be compared to the ancient Stoic "circles of concern" which widen out from concern for self, to concern for family, extended family, "fellow tribesmen" or neighbours, fellow citizens, and, ultimately, for the whole human race. Anthony A. Long and David A. Sedley, eds., *The Hellenistic Philosophers* (Cambridge: Cambridge Univ. Press, 1987), 1:349, cited in Bloomfield, *The Virtues of Happiness*, 15.

51 Charles Taylor, *Sources of the Self: The Making of the Modern Identity* (Cambridge: Harvard Univ. Press, 1989), 6. See also David Goodhart, *The Road to Somewhere: The New Tribes Shaping British Politics* (London: Penguin Books, 2017), 109.

52 The Jewish and Christian scriptures often seem to locate the source or home of pity, kindness, and mercy in the bowels! Alexander Cruden, *Cruden's Complete Concordance to the Old and New Testaments* (Peabody, MA: Hendrickson, n.d.), 54. See also Taylor, *A Secular Age*, 741; Ricœur, *Soi-même comme un autre*, 386; Terestchenko, *Un si fragile vernis d'humanité*, 262; de Waal, *The Age of Empathy*, 48, 66; Keane, *Ethical Life*, 44–5, 251.

53 Langer, *Mind*, 2:312–13.

54 Paul Ricœur calls this "la signification absolument irréductible du corps propre": "Posséder un corps, c'est ce que font ou plutôt c'est ce sont les personnes." *Soi-même comme un autre*, 71, 46.

55 "[S]eul un *égo* incarné, c'est-à-dire un *égo* qui est son propre corps, peut
    faire couple avec la chair d'un autre *égo*." Ricœur, 385. Italics in original.
    Also: *Du texte à l'action*, in *Ricœur: Textes choisis et présentés*, 390.
56 Sandel, *What Money Can't Buy*, 128.
57 Aristotle notes that Greek warriors were motivated to be courageous by
    their desire for civic honour and to avoid civic disgrace, thus confirming
    that honour-*seeking* is a virtue that belongs with courage (A1) and the
    other similar virtues of self-assertion. *The Nicomachean Ethics* 3.8.1116a15–
    3.9.1117b20, trans. Thomson, rev. Tredennick, 70–4.
58 "[I]n duty the individual finds his liberation; first, *liberation from* depend-
    ence on mere natural impulse ... secondly, *liberation from* the indetermi-
    nate subjectivity, which ... remains self-enclosed and devoid of actuality.
    In duty the individual acquires his substantive freedom." Hegel, *Philoso-
    phy of Right*, trans. Knox, §149, p. 107. Emphasis added.
59 Heidegger, *Being and Time*, 298, 308, 312, 315, 344, 385, trans. Stambaugh,
    285, 294–5, 299, 301, 329, 367.
60 See, for example, Alan Ryan's "negative" definition of freedom (follow-
    ing Thomas Hobbes) as the absence of constraint on our *freedom to* be the
    exclusive "master" of our own actions, in *The Making of Modern Liberal-
    ism* (Princeton: Princeton Univ. Press, 2012), 9–11, 16, 28, 45, 52, 60–2. To
    which Hegel replies that the definition of freedom as the "ability to do
    what we please ... contains not an inkling of the absolutely free will, of
    right, ethical life, and so forth. ... [I]t may indeed be called an illusion."
    Hegel, *Philosophy of Right*, trans. Knox, §15, pp. 27–8.
61 "Alors que la croyance doxique s'inscrit dans la grammaire du 'je-crois-
    que,' l'attestation relève de celle du 'je-crois-en.' Par là elle se rapproche
    du témoignage, comme l'étymologie le rappelle, dans la mesure où c'est
    en la parole du témoin que l'on croit." Ricœur, *Soi-même comme un autre*,
    33. The etymological root of *fido* (I have faith) is the same as the Greek
    peithomai (I have confidence, I trust). In Roman culture, *fides*, the Latin
    word for "faith," acquired its full meaning in the context of the law,
    where it implied good faith, loyalty, keeping one's word, etc. Jean Gron-
    din, *Introduction à la métaphysique* (Montreal: Les Presses de l'Université
    de Montréal, 2004), 138n11; Hildebrand, *Fundamental Moral Attitudes*, 30.
    In other words, as a virtue of reverence, the meaning of belief is most
    clearly rendered by words like trust and confidence, or words like loyalty
    and faithful*ness*.
62 David Sloan Wilson dismisses efforts "to tease apart the subtle differ-
    ences in thoughts and feelings that have largely the same behavioural
    manifestations." *Does Altruism Exist?*, 73, 142. But if you really want to
    understand the nature of the human, everything depends on the difficult
    work of "teasing" out these subtle but decisive distinctions between the

virtues. Consider, for example, Aristotle's ancient virtues of "liberality." It can seem, at first glance, to be much the same as the virtue of generosity. But there is a whole world of difference between them. Considered more carefully, liberality turns out to have overtones of pride and vanity, the aristocratic snobbishness and self-regard of the "free" citizen of a Greek *polis*, looking down on slaves, rural dwellers, foreigners, and others. Liberality is an honour-*seeking* virtue, not a truly honour*able* one. Much less an honour*ing* virtue, like generosity. Similarly, consider the subtle, ambiguous relationship between "seeking" and "dwelling," two manifestations of the virtues of self-assertion and of reverence. Seeking can be a restless, self-assertion, but it can also be a hungering and thirsting after righteousness. Dwelling can be an abiding in righteousness and reverence, but it can also be a self-assertive complacency. In chapter 10, I discuss a similar ambiguous and paradoxical relationship between attachment and detachment. Teasing out the differences between apparently similar but, in reality, very *different* moral concepts and virtues becomes even more important in cross-cultural comparisons. See Shweder, *Why Do Men Barbecue?*, 134–67.

63 "[R]everence is evident in justice toward others, in consideration for the rights of another, for the liberty of another's decisions, in limiting one's own lust for power, and in all understanding of another's rights. Reverence for our neighbors is the basis of all true community life." Hildebrand, *Fundamental Moral Attitudes*, 13.

64 Hans Joas, *The Sacredness of the Person: A New Genealogy of Human Rights*, trans. Alex Skinner (Washington, DC: Georgetown Univ. Press, 2013).

65 Hume, *A Treatise of Human Nature* 3.2.6, p. 529.

66 Paul Ricœur calls the paradox of reverence "une dialectique de l'amour et de la justice." Or, "la convergence des deux pédagogies du genre humain : celle de l'amour et de la justice." Ricœur, *Soi-même comme un autre*, 37; *Histoire et vérité* (Paris: Points Essais, 2001), 282; *Amour et justice* (Paris: Éditions Points, 2008). On the paradox of reverence – the paradox of mercy and justice – in Genesis Rabbah 12:15 (Rabbinic theology), see Franz Rosenzweig, *The Star of Redemption*, trans. William W. Hallo (Notre Dame, IN: Univ. of Notre Dame Press, 1985), 427.

67 Maureen Mancuso, Michael M. Atkinson, André Blais, Ian Greene, and Neil Nevitte, *A Question of Ethics: Canadians Speak Out*, rev. ed. (Toronto: Oxford Univ. Press, 2006), 44. Charles Taylor cites similar French data from studies by Jean-Louis Schlegel and Sylvette Denèfle in *A Secular Age*, 824n23.

68 "Gratuité du *pour l'autre*, réponse de responsabilité qui sommeille déjà dans la salutation, dans le *bonjour*, dans le *au revoir*." Emmanuel Levinas, *Entre nous: Essais sur le penser-à-l'autre* (Paris: Livre de Poche, 2010), 172. On the

implicit virtues of reverence hiding in everyday actions such as cheerful greetings, politeness, invitations, presents, deal-making, cheering on a sports team, and so on, see Deirdre N. McCloskey, *The Bourgeois Virtues: Ethics for an Age of Commerce* (Chicago: Univ. of Chicago Press, 2006), 128; Joas, *The Sacredness of the Person*, 159; Robert N. Bellah, *Religion in Human Evolution: From the Paleolithic to the Axial Age* (Cambridge, MA: Belknap Press of Harvard Univ. Press, 2011), 278; Rahner, *The Practice of Faith*, 58.

69 "[L]e *donner* est en quelque façon le mouvement originel de la vie spirituelle." Emmanuel Levinas, *Difficile liberté*, 3rd corrected ed. (Paris: Le Livre de Poche, 2010), 100. Jacques Maritain suggests "ce qui dans l'homme vivifie l'homme" is "l'Amour même et le Don." *Humanisme intégral*, new ed. (Paris: Éditions Aubier-Montaigne, 1946), 97. One of Paul Ricœur's names for the virtues of reverence (and sometimes for what I will later call the virtues of Reverence (A2)) is "l'économie du don." *Amour et justice*, 9, 22, 33–5; *Lectures 3*, in *Ricœur: Textes choisis et présentés*, 323–5.

70 "The Olympics as a Kind of Religion," *The Economist*, 7 August 2016, https://www.economist.com/erasmus/2016/08/07/the-olympics-as -a-kind-of-religion.

71 "[S]ports stadiums are the cathedrals of our civic religion, public spaces that gather people from different walks of life in rituals of loss, hope, profanity and prayer." Sandel, *What Money Can't Buy*, 172.

72 With the rise of the virtues of self-assertion, imagination "stands in for soul." Thomas McFarland, *Originality and Imagination* (Baltimore: The Johns Hopkins Univ. Press, 1985), 199.

73 As Terry Eagleton remarks, the arts provide "an ersatz sort of transcendence in a world from which spiritual values have been largely banished." *Reason, Faith, and Revolution: Reflections on the God Debate* (New Haven: Yale Univ. Press, 2009), 83.

74 In the consumption of cultural and artistic products, they seek to meet a need that "used to be assuaged more surely and more often by sacred objects and offices." Susanne K. Langer, *Feeling and Form* (New York: Scribner's, 1953), 405.

75 It might be said that, since the eighteenth century, we have evolved from a "culture of religion" to a "religion of culture." The two terms of this contrast are from Charles Norris Cochrane, *Christianity and Classical Culture* (New York: Oxford Univ. Press, 1976), 29. But he used them in the *opposite* direction: to describe the evolution from the pagan to the Christian empire of Rome.

76 Denys Turner, *Faith, Reason and the Existence of God* (Cambridge: Cambridge Univ. Press, 2004), 114–15; David Martin, *On Secularization: Towards a Revised General Theory* (Farnham: Ashgate, 2005), 9; de Waal, *The Age of Empathy*, 63–4. See also Diarmaid MacCulloch's eloquent, closing

meditation on music and reverence in *Christianity: The First Three Thousand Years* (New York: Viking, 2010), 1014–15.

77 For a striking expression of the virtues of reverence inspired by encounter with the natural world, see Robin Wall Kimmerer, *Braiding Sweetgrass: Indigenous Wisdom, Scientific Knowledge, and the Teachings of Plants* (Minneapolis: Milkweed Editions, 2013).

78 Martha Nussbaum, *Upheavals of Thought: The Intelligence of the Emotions* (Cambridge: Cambridge Univ. Press, 2001), 54. "Wonder and awe are akin, but distinct: wonder is outward-moving, exuberant, whereas awe is linked with bending or making oneself small. In wonder I want to leap or run, in awe to kneel." Nussbaum, 54n53.

79 Hans Joas argues that empathy alone was not enough to trigger the concern for human rights that's a hallmark of modern and post-modern culture. To become a real source of motivation to action, empathy had to be augmented by other virtues of reverence, such as awe, which perceived the human person as sacred, or of supreme value. *The Sacredness of the Person*, 59–60.

80 Paul Woodruff, *Reverence: Renewing a Forgotten Virtue* (New York: Oxford Univ. Press, 2001), 36–7.

81 Robert N. Bellah, Richard Madsen, William M. Sullivan, Ann Swidler, and Steven M. Tipton, *Habits of the Heart*, updated ed. (Berkeley: Univ. of California Press, 1996), 154–5, 210, 334–5.

82 Rosenzweig, *The Star of Redemption*, trans. Hallo, 287.

83 Lionel Trilling, *Sincerity and Authenticity* (Cambridge, MA: Harvard Univ. Press, 1972), 41.

Chapter 6. The Human Paradox

1 "Human cultural evolution could not have progressed very far ... without some means of subdividing working memory into at least two fields: self and other." Merlin Donald, *A Mind So Rare: The Evolution of Human Consciousness* (New York: W.W. Norton, 2001), 257.

2 Thomas Aquinas, *Summa Theologiæ* 1–2.57.1, in *Treatise on the Virtues*, trans. John A. Oesterle (Notre Dame, IN: Univ. of Notre Dame Press, 1984), 68.

3 Friedrich Schleiermacher, *On Religion: Speeches to Its Cultured Despisers*, trans. John Oman (New York: Harper & Row, 1958), 4.

4 G.W.F. Hegel, *Philosophy of Right*, trans. T.M. Knox (Oxford: Oxford Univ. Press, 1967), §264, addition to §156, pp. 163, 261. Elsewhere, Hegel says that true "individuality" is the union of "particularity" and "universality." Hegel, §§7, 272, 278, addition to 259, pp. 23, 175, 180, 279.

5 Comte identifies ten "affective forces," of which seven correspond to egoism and three to altruism. Michel Bourdeau, "Auguste Comte," trans.

Mark van Atten, Stanford Encyclopedia of Philosophy; published 1 October 2008, updated 16 October 2014. https://plato.stanford.edu/entries/comte.

6 "The first leave my autonomy and personality almost intact. ... When I act under the influence of the second, by contrast, I am simply a part of a whole, whose actions I follow, and whose influence I am subject to." Émile Durkheim, "Review of Guyau's *L'irreligion de l'avenir*," trans. A Giddens, in *Emile Durkheim: Selected Writings*, ed. A. Giddens (New York: Cambridge Univ. Press, 1992), 219–20, cited in Jonathan Haidt, *The Righteous Mind: Why Good People Are Divided by Politics and Religion* (New York: Pantheon Books, 2012), 225–6.

7 F.H. Bradley, *Appearance and Reality* (Oxford: Oxford Univ. Press, 1930), 367–79.

8 William James, *The Varieties of Religious Experience* (New York: Collier Books, 1961), 92, 102, 398–9.

9 Friedrich Nietzsche, *Thus Spoke Zarathustra*, trans. R.J. Hollingdale, rev. ed. (Harmondsworth: Penguin Books, 1969), 84–6. Revised. I have preferred Walter Kaufmann's translation of *Güter* as "virtues" rather than Hollingdale's translation as "values." See Walter Kaufmann, *Nietzsche: Philosopher, Psychologist, Antichrist*, 3rd rev. ed. (New York: Vintage Books, 1968), 211. As I explained in chapter 3, values are the *inside* of virtues: they are good habits of *feeling* that accompany and support – and are nourished by – good habits of *behaviour* or virtues.

10 G.K. Chesterton, *Orthodoxy* (New York: Dodd Mead, 1924), 177, 209–10.

11 Max Scheler, *Formalism in Ethics and Non-Formal Ethics of Value*, trans. Manfred S. Frings and Roger L. Funk (Evanston: Northwestern Univ. Press, 1973), 137, 278–81.

12 Martin Buber's names for the two sides of the human paradox are "individuality" and the "person." *I and Thou*, 2nd ed., trans. Ronald Gregor Smith (New York: Charles Scribner's Sons, 1958), 116, 62–5.

13 Franz Rosenzweig, *The Star of Redemption*, trans. William W. Hallo (Notre Dame, IN: Univ. of Notre Dame Press, 1985), 398, 325, 403.

14 Alfred North Whitehead, *Process and Reality* (New York: Free Press, 1969), 397–402.

15 Maurice Blondel, *L'Être et les êtres*, 270–1, 275, 280–1, 327. My translation. Blondel also calls these two sides of the human paradox "l'élan vital" (self-assertion) and "l'élan spirituel" (reverence).

16 Jacques Maritain, *Humanisme intégral*, new ed. (Paris: Éditions Aubier-Montaigne, 1946), 24, 82, 84, 87, 199–200. Maritain uses love and "grace" interchangeably.

17 "[U]ne dualité s'inscrivant dans sa propre essence. ... [C]ontradictions qui déchire l'humanité mais qui ont leur source dans la nature de

l'humanité et dans la Nature tout court." Emmanuel Levinas, *Difficile liberté*, 3rd corrected ed. (Paris: Le Livre de Poche, 2010), 61, 95. "[S]imultanéité d'une position dans la totalité et d'une réserve à son égard ou séparation." *Entre nous: Essais sur le penser-à-l'autre* (Paris: Livre de Poche, 2010), 25. My translation.

18 Paul Tillich, *The Courage to Be* (New Haven: Yale Univ. Press, 1952), 86.

19 Susanne K. Langer, *Mind: An Essay on Human Feeling*, vol. 1 (Baltimore: Johns Hopkins Press, 1967), 324, 355.

20 Iris Murdoch, *Metaphysics as a Guide to Morals* (London: Vintage, 2003), 295, 324–6, 350.

21 "[D]eux directions fondamentales de l'imaginaire social. La première tend vers l'intégration, la répétition, le reflet. La seconde, parce qu'excentrique, tends ver l'errance. Mais l'une ne va pas sans l'autre." Paul Ricœur, *Du texte à l'action*, in *Ricœur: Textes choisis et présentés*, ed. Michaël Fœssel and Fabien Lamouche (Paris: Éditions Points, 2007), 381. See also *Soi-même comme un autre* (Paris: Éditions du Seuil, 1990), 198, 254; *Amour et justice*, 77–8; *Ricœur: Textes choisis et présentés*, 41, 296–7, 300, 387.

22 Ernest Becker, *The Denial of Death* (New York: Free Press, 1973), 203–4.

23 Irvin D. Yalom, *Love's Executioner* (New York: HarperCollins, 1990), 7.

24 Frans de Waal, *The Age of Empathy: Nature's Lessons for a Kinder Society* (New York: Three Rivers Press, 2009), 5.

25 Richard Shweder, *Thinking Through Cultures: Expeditions in Cultural Psychology* (Cambridge, MA: Harvard Univ. Press, 1991), 153.

26 James Q. Wilson, *The Moral Sense* (New York: Free Press, 1993), 121, 123, 128, 245–6.

27 Marcel Gauchet, *The Disenchantment of the World: A Political History of Religion*, trans. Oscar Bruge (Princeton, NJ: Princeton Univ. Press, 1997), 11–12.

28 Susan Neiman, *Moral Clarity: A Guide for Grown-Up Idealists* (Orlando: Harcourt, 2008), 12–13.

29 Joseph Soloveitchik, *Lonely Man of Faith*, cited in David Brooks, *The Road to Character* (New York: Random House, 2015), xi–xii.

30 Jean Vanier, *Becoming Human* (Toronto: House of Anansi Press, 1998), 18–19.

31 Roger Scruton, *On Human Nature* (Princeton: Princeton Univ. Press, 2017), 79, 111.

32 Christine Swanton, *Virtue Ethics: A Pluralistic View* (Oxford: Oxford Univ. Press, 2003), 58–9.

33 Christopher Boehm, *Moral Origins: The Evolution of Virtue, Altruism, and Shame* (New York: Basic Books, 2012), 52. Elsewhere Boehm expands this duality to a trinity: egoism, nepotism, and altruism. But the last two

describe degrees of generosity, or to whom the generosity is shown. See: 83, 205, 226, 234, 267, 270–5, 289–90.

34 Haidt, *The Righteous Mind*, 220.

35 David Martin, *On Secularization: Towards a Revised General Theory* (Farnham: Ashgate, 2005), 11–12.

36 Robert N. Bellah, Richard Madsen, William M. Sullivan, Ann Swidler, and Steven M. Tipton, *Habits of the Heart*, updated ed. (Berkeley: Univ. of California Press, 1996); Robert N. Bellah, *Religion in Human Evolution: From the Paleolithic to the Axial Age* (Cambridge, MA: Belknap Press of Harvard Univ. Press, 2011). In his Surjit Singh Lecture (2012), Bellah says the terminology of reverence and self-assertion used in this book is an "improvement" on the two terms (the "culture of separation" and the "culture of coherence") he used in the conclusion to *Habits of the Heart*. See Robert N. Bellah, "Can Religion Meet the Challenge of Human Evolution?" Surjit Singh Lecture, Graduate Theological Union, Berkeley, 28 February 2012, 18. https://gtu.edu/sites/default /files/docs/gtu-old/R.%20Bellah%20Surjit%20Singh%20Lecture %202.28.12%20PDF.pdf.

37 Brooks, *The Road to Character*, 4–8.

38 The "immanence perspective" "sees our highest goal in terms of a certain kind of human flourishing, in the context of mutuality, pursuing each his/her own happiness on the basis of assured life and liberty, in a society of mutual benefit." The "transformation perspective" aims instead at "a transformation of human beings that takes them beyond or outside what is normally understood as human flourishing, even in a context of reasonable mutuality (that is, where we work for each other's flourishing)." Charles Taylor, *A Secular Age* (Cambridge, MA: Belknap Press of Harvard Univ. Press, 2007), 430–5.

39 Aristotle, *Metaphysics* 1.5.986a20–30, 11.9.1066a13–17, 12.7.1072a30–5, trans. W.D. Ross, in *The Basic Works of Aristotle*, ed. Richard McKeon (New York: Random House, 1941), 698, 865, 879; *The Nicomachean Ethics* 1.6.1096b5–10, 2.6.1106b29–31, trans. J.A.K. Thomson, rev. Hugh Tredennick (London: Penguin Books, 2004), 11, 41; G.S. Kirk and J.E. Raven, *The Presocratic Philosophers* (Cambridge: Cambridge Univ. Press, 1964), 238–41; Charles H. Kahn, *Pythagoras and the Pythagoreans: A Brief History* (Indianapolis: Hackett, 2001), 65; Parmenides of Elea, *Fragments*, trans. David Gallop (Toronto: Univ. of Toronto Press, 1984), 89; Jean Grondin, *Introduction à la métaphysique* (Montreal: Les Presses de l'Université de Montréal, 2004), 35.

40 Aristotle, *Metaphysics* 4.2.1005a4, trans. Ross, 735.

41 Aristotle, *Metaphysics* 11.3.1060b30–1061b16, trans. Ross, 854–6.

42 Aristotle, *Metaphysics* 10.4.1055b1–10, trans. Ross, 842.

43 "[T]o *be* and *not to be* are not opposed as contraries but as contradictories." Aquinas, *Summa Theologiæ* 1–2.64.3, in *Treatise on the Virtues*, trans. Oesterle, 136.

44 "As a fact and given we have in feeling diversity and unity in one whole, a whole implicit and not yet broken up into terms and relations. This immediate union of the one and the many is an 'ultimate fact' from which we start ... These facts or truths, as they are offered, I find my intellect rejects, and I go on to discover why it rejects them. It is because they contradict themselves." Bradley, *Appearance and Reality*, 508–11.

45 Aristotle, *Metaphysics* 12.10.1075a34–5, trans. Ross, 886. "Statements opposed as affirmation and negation belong manifestly to a class which is distinct, for in this case, *and in this case only*, it is necessary for the one opposite to be true and the other false. Neither in the case of contraries, nor in the case of correlatives, nor in the case of 'positives' and 'privatives' is it necessary for one to be true and the other false." Aristotle, *Categories* 10.13b1–10, trans. E.M. Edghill, in *The Basic Works of Aristotle*, ed. McKeon, 32. Emphasis added.

46 Thomas Aquinas, *Summa Theologiæ* 1.77.4, in *Introduction to St. Thomas Aquinas*, ed. Anton C. Pegis (New York: The Modern Library, 1948), 318; *Summa Theologiæ* 1–2.54.2, in *Treatise on the Virtues*, trans. Oesterle, 46.

47 Leibniz explains the difference between contradictions and contraries as a distinction between two kinds of "truths": truths of "reason" and truths of "fact." Truths of reason are "necessary," and their opposite is "impossible." But truths of fact are "contingent," "et leur opposé est possible." G.W. Leibniz, *Les principes de la philosophie ou la Monadologie*, §33, in *Principes de la nature et de la grâce fondés en raison – Principes de la philosophie ou Monadologie*, ed. André Robinet (Paris: Presses Universitaires de France, 1954, 1986), 89. Alfred North Whitehead expresses the difference between contradictions and contraries as a distinction between "incompatibilities" and "contrasts." *Process and Reality*, 101, 113, 119, 125.

48 Aristotle, *Metaphysics* 14.4.1091a30–14.5.1092a15, trans. Ross, 920–2.

49 Aristotle, *Metaphysics* 12.10.1075b30–3, trans. Ross, 887.

50 Dietrich von Hildebrand identifies four different types of contradiction (or "exclusiveness"), ranging from "contradictory exclusiveness" at one end, to the "complementary polarity" of "positive values" at the other. This polarity is "not only compatible with the inner unity of the values but even implies it." *Ethics* (Steubenville, OH: Hildebrand Press, 2020), 147–151. See also: Pascal, *Pensées* (Paris: Garnier-Flammarion, 1973), §229, p. 93; Philippa Foot, "Virtues and Vices," in *Virtue Ethics*, ed. Roger Crisp and Michael Slote (Oxford: Oxford Univ. Press, 1997), 163–77; T.H. Irwin, "Do Virtues Conflict? Aquinas' Answer," in *Virtue Ethics, Old and New*, ed. Stephen M. Gardiner (Ithaca: Cornell Univ. Press, 2005), 60–77.

51 "[C]ertaines corrélations sont probablement décelables, entre certains aspects et à certains niveaux, et il s'agit pour nous de trouver quels sont ces
aspects *et où sont ces niveaux*." Claude Lévi-Strauss, *Anthropologie structur-
ale* (Paris: Plon, 1958), 95, cited in Paul Ricœur, *Le conflit des interprétations:
Essais d'herméneutique*, 68n4. Emphasis added. On both the importance
and the difficulty of "classification" – sorting matters of thought or of
being into their correct categories and equivalent levels (genus, species,
etc.) – as one the principal challenges of human thinking, see Aristotle,
Posterior Analytics 2.13–19, trans. G.R.G. Mure, in *The Basic Works of Aristotle*, ed. McKeon, 175–86; G.W. Leibniz, *Nouveaux essais sur l'entendement
humain* (Paris: Garnier-Flammarion, 1966), bk. 3, chap. 3, §9–10, pp. 249–
51; chap. 6, §§14, 41–2, pp. 267–9, 285; chap. 10, §14, p. 299; G.W.F. Hegel,
Science of Logic, vol. 2, §3, chap. 2A(b)1–2, trans. W.H. Johnston and L.G.
Struthers (London: George Allen & Unwin, 1951), 2:436–47; Whitehead,
Process and Reality, 11; Edward O. Wilson, *The Meaning of Human Existence*
(New York: Liveright, 2014), 125.

52 James Q. Wilson, *The Moral Sense*, xiii. Later in this book you will see that
these virtues all belong to specific families of virtues (which constitute
the nature of the human), as follows: the virtues of Liberty (A1) (courage); the virtues of Reverence (A2) (modesty, sympathy); the virtues of
Excellence (B1) (duty, integrity); and the virtues of Equality (B2) (fairness,
self-control).

53 André Comte-Sponville, *A Small Treatise on the Great Virtues*, trans. Catherine Temerson (New York: Henry Holt, 2001), 4. In Comte-Sponville's
list of eighteen virtues, interestingly, thirteen are virtues of reverence and
only five are virtues of self-assertion. Even more interesting, fully nine or
ten of Comte-Sponville's thirteen virtues of reverence (depending on the
meaning of fidelity) are virtues of Reverence (A1); and in his five virtues
of self-assertion, he does not include even a single virtue of Rights (B2a),
not even the quintessential contemporary virtue of respect(-seeking).

54 William J. Bennett, *The Book of Virtues: A Treasury of Great Moral Stories*
(New York: Simon & Schuster, 1993). Bennett's virtues include three from
what I will later call the virtues of Liberty (A1) (courage, perseverance,
work); three from the virtues of Reverence (A2) (compassion, faith,
friendship); one from the virtues of Excellence (B1) (honesty); one from
the virtues of Equality (B2) (self-discipline); and two virtues that belong
to different families, depending on the nuance or overtone that is emphasized (loyalty, responsibility).

55 N.T. Wright, *Broken Signposts: How Christianity Makes Sense of the World*
(New York: HarperCollins, 2020). The words quoted are on page 3.

56 Deirdre N. McCloskey, *The Bourgeois Virtues: Ethics for an Age of Commerce*
(Chicago: Univ. of Chicago Press, 2006), 408.

57 "How could man ever have invented the power which pervades him, which alone enables him to *be* a man?" Martin Heidegger, *An Introduction to Metaphysics*, trans. Ralph Manheim (New York: Doubleday, 1961), 131.

58 This consistent left-right arrangement of the virtues has the inconvenience that, in chapter 14, libertarianism and right-wing populism will appear on the left side of my figures, while socialism and left-wing populism will appear on the right. However, for my purposes, this inconvenience is more than compensated by the fact that, in all the tables of this book, the virtues of self-assertion will appear first, in alphabetical order, on the left side. Since, in the Western world, we read from left to right, and since, in our post-modern world, the virtues of self-assertion always come first – and are the reference point for other virtues – it is appropriate that the virtues of self-assertion should always appear first to the reader, on the left side, and the contrasting virtues of reverence should be related to them, on the right.

59 "Connection comes before action." Adam Gopnik, *A Thousand Small Sanities: The Moral Adventure of Liberalism* (New York: Basic Books, 2019), 71. In philosophical language, this might be called "the transcendental necessity of holism." Taylor, *A Secular Age*, 157. Leibniz calls it "la connexion réelle de toutes choses." Leibniz, *Nouveaux essais*, bk. 2, chap. 25, §5, p. 194. Martin Buber calls it "the *a priori* of relation." *I and Thou*, 69.

60 Lionel Trilling, *Sincerity and Authenticity* (Cambridge, MA: Harvard Univ. Press, 1972), 44–7, 76–80. "In one respect the self vanished with the restricting bond to both God and the other." Marcel Gauchet, *The Disenchantment of the World: A Political History of Religion*, trans. Burge, 171.

61 G.W.F. Hegel, *The Phenomenology of Mind*, trans. J.B. Baillie (New York: Harper & Row, 1967), 543. For Hegel, the self of pure self-assertion is just a "medley and multiplicity of impulses," and if "given free rein in every direction to satisfy its needs, accidental caprices, and subjective desires, destroys itself and its substantive concept in this process of gratification." *Philosophy of Right*, trans. Knox, §§12, 17, 185, pp. 26, 28, 123. Franz Rosenzweig also recognizes that, if unbalanced by other virtues, the pure self-assertion of the virtues of Liberty (A1) (or "caprice") simply dissolves the self in random acts of self-assertion. *The Star of Redemption*, trans. Hallo, 117–18. Martin Heidegger's term for what Hegel calls the "disintegrated" self of pure self-assertion is "unself-constancy," as opposed to the "self-constancy of Dasein," the unified self of the whole nature of the human. *Being and Time*, 322–3, trans. Joan Stambaugh (Albany: State Univ. of New York Press, 2010), 308–9.

62 Karl Jaspers, *Way to Wisdom*, trans. Ralph Manheim (New Haven: Yale Univ. Press, 1960), 113. See also John of the Cross on the same theme, in

Denys Turner, *The Darkness of God: Negativity in Christian Mysticism* (Cambridge: Cambridge Univ. Press, 1995), 237–8.

63 William Shakespeare, *Troilus and Cressida*, in *The Complete Works*, ed. Alfred Harbage (Baltimore: Penguin Books, 1969), 1.3.119–24. José Casanova suggests that, "if it does not enter into a creative dialogue with the other, with those traditions [of reverence] which are challenging its identity," Western modernity rooted in the virtues of self-assertion "may end up being devoured by the inflexible, inhuman logic of its own creations." *Public Religions in the Modern World* (Chicago: Univ. of Chicago Press, 1994), 234. Michel Terestchenko calls the self of pure self-assertion "une hypostase démonique ... que l'on ne peut identifier à la subjectivité ... [Ce moi] ne peut jamais se trouver *parce qu'il n'est ici aucune dialectique à l'œuvre.*" *Un si fragile vernis d'humanité: Banalité du mal, banalité du bien* (Paris: La Découverte, 2007), 40. Emphasis added.

64 Hegel, *The Phenomenology of Mind*, trans. Baillie, 607–10; *Philosophy of Right*, trans. Knox, §§5, 135, pp. 21–2, 89–90.

65 "Liberalism has always been about giving people the ability to control their lives, not about telling them how to lead them." Alan Wolfe, *The Future of Liberalism* (New York: Vintage Books, 2010), 75.

66 Hegel, *Philosophy of Right*, trans. Knox, §148, pp. 106–7; Iris Murdoch, *The Sovereignty of Good* (London: Routledge, 1980), 42; Bernard Williams, *Ethics and the Limits of Philosophy* (Cambridge, MA: Harvard Univ. Press, 1985), 12, 117–18; Casanova, *Public Religions in the Modern World*, 229.

67 Gopnik, *A Thousand Small Sanities*, 13. First emphasis in the original, second emphasis added.

68 Murdoch, *Metaphysics as a Guide to Morals*, 507.

69 Karl Rahner, *The Practice of Faith: A Handbook of Contemporary Spirituality*, trans. various (New York: Crossroad, 1983), 146, 212–14.

70 One of Hegel's ways of stating the human paradox is as a "clash" between "empty, abstract freedom" (i.e., self-assertion) and the "content which fills that void" (i.e., reverence). Hegel, *Philosophy of Right*, trans. Knox, §336, p. 214.

71 "[C]e que nous croyons être notre moi est un produit aussi fugitif et aussi automatique des circonstances extérieures que la forme d'une vague de la mer." Simone Weil, *Pensées sans ordre concernant l'amour de Dieu* (Paris: Gallimard, 2013), 89.

72 Murdoch, *Metaphysics as a Guide to Morals*, 507.

73 Karl Jaspers calls this (in language similar to Martin Heidegger's) "the command of my authentic self to my mere empirical existence. I become aware of myself as that which I myself *am*, because it is what I *ought* to be." *Way to Wisdom*, 55. Emphasis added.

Chapter 7. Paradox Breeds Paradox

1 G.W.F. Hegel, *Encyclopaedia of the Philosophical Sciences*, §93, in *Hegel's Logic*, trans. William Wallace (London: Oxford Univ. Press, 1975), 137. This pithy, enigmatic sentence is quite typical of the *Encyclopaedia*, which Yirimiyahu Yovel describes as a "series of concise, compressed (and 'frozen') paragraphs which are to be further developed by the lecturer." G.W.F Hegel, *Preface to the Phenomenology of Spirit*, trans. Yirmiyahu Yovel (Princeton: Princeton Univ. Press, 2005), 161. Elsewhere (in the "Greater Logic") Hegel expands upon this condensed formula: "The Existent, then, being determined as Whole, has Parts, and the Parts constitute its existence … Now in so far as this Existent is Part, it is not Whole, nor composite but simple. But the relation to Whole is external to it, and therefore does not concern it; thus the independent entity is not Part even in itself, for it is Part only through this relation. But now, since it is not Part, it is Whole; for the only relation which is given is this Relation of Whole and Parts, and the independent entity is one of the two. But when it is Whole it is again composite; it again consists of Parts, and so to infinity." G.W.F. Hegel, *Science of Logic*, vol. 1, bk. 2, §2, chap. 3, trans. W.H. Johnston and L.G. Struthers (London: George Allen & Unwin, 1951), 2:148.

2 Hegel, *Science of Logic*, vol. 1, bk. 2, §1, chap. 2, trans. Johnston and Struthers, 2:51, 60, 484. Hegel uses the term "intro-Reflection" to distinguish it from purely "External Reflection," in which something is dialectically related to something "which is other to it," but "remains *external to it.*" In "intro-Reflection," by contrast, the same something is "Other to that which is *in itself.*" Hegel, 113–14, 29–30. But in External Reflection, the "distinctness" of anything results only from its *relation* to its Other, so Reflection and intro-Reflection turn out, in the end, to be the same thing. Because the two initial, external things are "not distinct entities" as they at first appear, External Reflection is really "an attitude of the Thing-in-itself only to itself: it is essentially intro-Reflection. … Reflection into other is intro-Reflection." Hegel, 115, 142.

3 F.H. Bradley, *Appearance and Reality* (Oxford: Oxford Univ. Press, 1930), 157, 26–7, 259.

4 Whitehead's "coordinate division" expresses the "indefinite coordinate divisibility of each atomic individuality." Alfred North Whitehead, *Process and Reality* (New York: Free Press, 1969), 336, 334, 293.

5 The source of this term is somewhat ambiguous. Owen Barfield uses it consistently as the descriptive name for Coleridge's polar theory of life or metaphysics. And he consistently puts it in quotation marks, as if to indicate that he is quoting Coleridge. Owen Barfield, *What Coleridge Thought*

(Middletown, CT: Wesleyan Univ. Press, 1971), 53, 76, 79–80, 111, 147, 164, 185, 216n3, 249n9, 253n22. But Barfield doesn't ever seem to give a specific reference for the term, and I have so far been unable to discover it in any of the obvious sources. Coleridge speaks of "progressive individuation" and "projective reproduction," but I have not yet found him to use the specific term "separative projection." Samuel Taylor Coleridge, *The Theory of Life* (*Hints Towards a More Comprehensive Theory of Life*) in *Selected Poetry and Prose of Samuel Taylor Coleridge*, ed. Donald Stauffer (New York: Random House, 1951), 596, 598. So, I conclude, provisionally, that the term is Barfield's. However, I will use it in this book to designate Coleridge's vision of the dynamic process that underlies "life," the same process Hegel calls "intro-Reflection," whereby every particularity divides and subdivides unendingly into its contrary, internal polarities, which nevertheless retain their original unity or wholeness. "Separative projection" echoes right back to the presocratic philosopher Anaximander (a pupil of Thales), who said that, at the origin of the world, "the *oppositions* in the substratum [the Boundless or the Infinite (or being)] ... were *separated* out." Quoted in H. and H.A. Frankfort, "Conclusion: The Emancipation of Thought from Myth," in Henri Frankfort, H.A. Frankfort, John A. Wilson, and Thorkild Jacobsen, *Before Philosophy: The Intellectual Adventure of Ancient Man* (Harmondsworth: Penguin Books, 1949), 254. Emphasis added.

6 Coleridge, *The Theory of Life*, 578. Maurice Blondel calls this "la persistence des contraires dans l'une et l'autre des alternatives réalisées." *L'Être et les êtres* (Paris: Presses Universitaires de France, 1963), 259.

7 "[P]articularity is always duality." G.W.F. Hegel, *Philosophy of Right*, trans. T.M. Knox (Oxford: Oxford Univ. Press, 1967), §139, p. 93.

8 The term "projection" happily links the concept of separative projection to Martin Heidegger's concept of "project" (*Entwurf*) as a key human way of being and understanding: the way that understands the nature of the human as forms of "potentiality" or "possibility." In its "fundamental structures," stances, or families of virtues, a human being can "understand itself in terms of possibilities." In its mode of "projecting," the nature of the human "*is* its possibilities as possibilities. ... It is existentially that which it is *not yet* in its potentiality of being." And only because it gets its "constitution" from "its character of project, only because it *is* what it becomes or does not become, can it say understandingly to itself: 'become what you are!'" *Being and Time*, 145, trans. Joan Stambaugh (Albany: State Univ. of New York Press, 2010), 140–1. Emphasis in original.

9 Coleridge, *The Theory of Life*, 591. "EVERY POWER IN NATURE AND IN SPIRIT *must evolve an opposite as the sole means and condition of its manifestation:* AND ALL OPPOSITION IS A TENDENCY TO RE-UNION. This is

the universal Law of Polarity or essential Dualism, first pronounced by Heraclitus, 2000 years afterwards republished and made the foundation both of Logic, of Physics, and of Metaphysics by Giordano Bruno. The principle may be thus expressed. The *Identity* of Thesis and Antithesis is the substance of all *Being*; their *Opposition* the condition of all *Existence*, or Being manifested; and every *Thing* or Phænomenon is the Exponent of a Synthesis as long as the opposite energies are retained in that Synthesis." *The Friend*, ed. Barbara E. Rooke (London: Routledge, 1969), 1:94. Hegel agrees this "same dynamic lies at the root of every natural process, and, as it were, forces nature out of itself." *Encyclopaedia*, §81, trans. Wallace, 118. Robert Nozick calls the ever-deepening combination of diversity and unity (i.e., union of union and non-union) "organic unity" and suggests it is the source of "value" in the world. *The Examined Life* (New York: Simon & Schuster, 1990), 164. Contrary to popular (and even scholarly) assumptions, the thesis-antithesis-synthesis formula comes from Fichte rather than from Hegel, whose triadic "logic" is "different, freer, and without a priori formulaic limitations." Yirmiyahu Yovel, "Introduction," in Hegel, *Preface to the Phenomenology of Spirit*, 29n18. Hegel comments on the formalistic and "vapid misuse" of triplicity, in *Science of Logic*, vol. 2, §3, chap. 3, trans. Johnston and Struthers, 2:479.

10 R.G. Collingwood, *Speculum Mentis or the Map of Knowledge* (Oxford: Oxford Univ. Press, 1963), 197.

11 Hegel, *Encyclopaedia*, §119, trans. Wallace, 173; *Science of Logic*, vol. 1, bk. 2, §2, chap. 2, trans. Johnston and Struthers, 2:139. Hegel also uses the "trivial" examples of above and below, right and left, and father and son as examples of "intro-Reflection": "contain[ing] Contradiction in one term." Hegel, vol. 1, bk. 2, §1, chap. 2, trans. Johnston and Struthers, 2:68.

12 "We must admit kinds and degrees and different levels of virtue." Bradley, *Appearance and Reality*, 387. Alfred North Whitehead notes that because life is structured by cascading paradoxes, a "higher" paradox "involves unplumbed potentiality for the realization of depth in its lower components." *Process and Reality*, 132.

13 As the Lord Krishna explains to the young prince Arjuna in the Hindu *Bhagavad Gita*, "Even to maintain your body, Arjuna, you are forced to act." *The Bhagavad Gita* 3.8, trans. Eknath Easwaran (New York: Vintage Books, 2000), 18. See also 25, 90, 94.

14 "[T]he immediate or natural will ... i.e., as the impulses desires, inclinations, whereby the will finds itself determined in the course of nature ... has for me the general character of being *mine*." Hegel, *Philosophy of Right*, trans. Knox, §11, p. 25. Emphasis added. "Dasein is in each instance always *mine*." Heidegger, *Being and Time*, 221, trans. Stambaugh, 212. Emphasis added.

15 "[T]he good, as self-sacrifice, is clearly in collision with itself. For *an act of self-denial* is, no less, in some sense a self-realization, and it inevitably *includes an aspect of self-assertion.*" Bradley, *Appearance and Reality*, 375. Emphasis added. "[I]l nous faut rejeter une perspective qui définit conceptuellement l'altruisme comme le *contraire* de l'égoïsme." Michel Terestchenko, *Un si fragile vernis d'humanité: Banalité du mal, banalité du bien* (Paris: La Découverte, 2007), 18. Emphasis in original.

16 Robert Nozick calls this the "egoistic stance." *The Examined Life*, 151–2.

17 Susanne Langer points out that, even in the womb, a fetus must already "muster its strength and carry through the winning act," which is a "*vigorous piece of self-assertion*" prior to birth. Susanne K. Langer, *Mind: An Essay on Human Feeling*, vol. 3 (Baltimore: Johns Hopkins Press, 1982), 134. Emphasis added.

18 Jerome Kagan, *The Nature of the Child* (New York: Basic Books, 1984), 111.

19 Sigmund Freud, *Civilization and Its Discontents*, trans. James Strachey (New York: W.W. Norton, 1962), 13–15; Jean Piaget and Barbel Inhelder, *The Psychology of the Child* (New York: Basic Books, 1969), 22, cited in Robert N. Bellah, *Religion in Human Evolution: From the Paleolithic to the Axial Age* (Cambridge, MA: Belknap Press of Harvard Univ. Press, 2011), 13. Bellah reports, however, that George Butterworth argues this "unitive" period should be pushed back to the prenatal stage: that "a boundary exists in infant perception between infant and the world," although "the very young infant has no objective, reflective self-awareness." George Butterworth, "Some Benefits of Egocentrism," in *Making Sense: The Child's Construction of the World*, ed. Jerome Bruner and Helen Haste (London: Methuen, 1987), 70–1, cited in Bellah, 614n21.

20 Bradley calls this the "pre-relational stage of existence": "There was a time when the separation of the outer world, as a thing real, apart from our feeling, had not even been begun." Bradley, *Appearance and Reality*, 461, 231.

21 Webb Keane, *Ethical Life: Its Natural and Social Histories* (Princeton: Princeton Univ. Press, 2016), 81. Among other references, Keane cites: Elinor Ochs, *Culture and Language Development: Language Acquisition and Language Socialization in a Samoan Village* (Cambridge: Cambridge Univ. Press, 1988); Bambi B. Schieffelin, *The Give and Take of Everyday Life: Language Socialization of Kaluli Children* (Cambridge: Cambridge Univ. Press, 1990); Michael Tomasello, *The Cultural Origins of Human Cognition* (Cambridge, MA: Harvard Univ. Press, 1999), 81.

22 Frans de Waal, *Good Natured: The Origins of Right and Wrong in Humans and Other Animals* (Cambridge, MA: Harvard Univ. Press, 1996); *The Age of Empathy: Nature's Lessons for a Kinder Society* (New York: Three Rivers Press, 2009).

23 Frans de Waal gives a colourful description of the culture of domination among the primates, and the intimidating rage of an alpha male. He explicitly contrasts this culture with the natural human instincts of fairness and equality, emphasizing the different attitudes of humans and apes "toward social hierarchy." *The Age of Empathy*, 159–63.

24 Hegel, *Encyclopaedia*, §24, trans. Wallace, 39, 43–5. Paul Ricœur calls this "le côté sauvage de notre existence pulsionnelle." *Le conflit des interprétations: Essais d'herméneutique* (Paris: Éditions du Seuil, 2013), 330. See also Max Scheler, *Formalism in Ethics and Non-Formal Ethics of Value*, trans. Manfred S. Frings and Roger L. Funk (Evanston: Northwestern Univ. Press, 1973), 578.

25 Edward O. Wilson acknowledges that evolution through "multilevel selection" (the process of natural selection both between individuals and between groups) has "hardwired" two conflicting dispositions into our "biological human nature," "two vectors" that define the "essence of the human character": the self-seeking disposition I call self-assertion and the self-giving (or altruistic) disposition I call reverence. The eternal conflict between these two is therefore not a "personal irregularity but a timeless human quality." Edward O. Wilson, *The Meaning of Human Existence* (New York: Liveright, 2014), 27–33, 60, 75, 117–18, 178–80. Max Scheler recognized all this as long ago as 1916: *Formalism in Ethics*, trans. Frings and Funk, 279–80.

26 Christopher Boehm, *Moral Origins: The Evolution of Virtue, Altruism, and Shame* (New York: Basic Books, 2012), 154–5, 177, 163–4.

27 C.G. Jung, *Analytical Psychology: Its Theory and Practice* (New York: Vintage Books, 1970), 46, 157. On the "identity of participation" in tribal societies, see also Bellah, *Religion in Human Evolution*, 117–74; Emmanuel Levinas, "Lévy-Bruhl et la philosophie contemporaine," in *Entre nous: Essais sur le penser-à-l'autre* (Paris: Livre de Poche, 2010), 49–63.

28 "Being-there [Dasein] is *itself* by virtue of its essential relationship to being in general." Martin Heidegger, *An Introduction to Metaphysics*, trans. Ralph Manheim (New York: Doubleday, 1961), 24. Emphasis in original. From Avicenna to Thomas Aquinas to Heidegger, one of the constants in Western thought is that the first awareness of the human being is an awareness of *being*. Jean Grondin, *Introduction à la métaphysique* (Montreal: Les Presses de l'Université de Montréal, 2004), 149, 153.

29 H. and H.A. Frankfort, "Introduction: Myth and Reality," in H. Frankfort et al., *Before Philosophy*, 19, 14. Emphasis added. Paul Ricœur calls this "la position [i.e., positing] de l'existence par l'existence, de l'existence de l'autre comme condition de mon existence pleine et entière." *Histoire et vérité* (Paris: Points Essais, 2001), 400.

30 "It is not the *I*, then that is given up, but that false self-asserting instinct." Martin Buber, *I and Thou*, 2nd ed., trans. Ronald Gregor Smith (New York: Charles Scribner's Sons, 1958), 78.

31 "Resoluteness [A1] brings the self right into its being together with things [B2] at hand, actually taking care of them, and pushes it toward concerned being-with [B1] with the others [A2]." Heidegger, *Being and Time*, 298, trans. Stambaugh, 285.

32 "That which from the point of view of the finite world appears as self-negation is from the point of view of ultimate being the most perfect self-affirmation, the most radical form of courage." Paul Tillich, *The Courage to Be* (New Haven: Yale Univ. Press, 1952), 158. Karl Rahner calls this highest form of self-assertion "a radical self-positing of the subject in an unconditional surrender." *The Practice of Faith: A Handbook of Contemporary Spirituality* (New York: Crossroad, 1983), 77.

33 "In all immanent trends to unfold our nature, our attitude has the character of self-*affirmation*; whereas in every value-response our attitude has the basic feature of self-*donation*." Dietrich von Hildebrand, *Ethics* (Steubenville, OH: Hildebrand Press, 2020), 230–1. Emphasis added.

34 "Nothing is so impossible, for instance, as this, that *I am*: for 'I' is *at the same time* simple *self-relation* [*I* am: A1] and, as undoubtedly, *relation to something else* [I am: A2]." Hegel, *Encyclopaedia*, §143, trans. Wallace, 204. Emphasis added.

35 Both Hegel and Levinas call this second stage in the development of the human – the stage of "I *am*" – a stage of "innocence." Levinas suggests – correctly, as I will argue – that it occupies an "intermediate ontological status" between purely biological life ("*I* am," or the stance of the nature of the human I will later label A1) and thought ("It is," or the stances I will later call B1 and B2). Hegel, *Encyclopaedia*, §24, trans. Wallace, 42; Levinas, *Entre nous*, 25–6.

36 "In this process the subjective will further determines what it recognizes as its own in its object (*Gegenstand*), so that this object becomes the will's own true concept, becomes objective (*objektiv*) as the expression of the will's own universality." Hegel, *Philosophy of Right*, trans. Knox, §107 p. 76. See also Bradley, *Appearance and Reality*, 229; Whitehead, *Process and Reality*, 280.

37 Paraphrasing Jean Nabert, Paul Ricœur calls this human move (the movement I call the "arrow of virtue"), from the stance of "I *am*" to the stance of "It *is*," from the virtues of Reverence (A2) to the virtues of Excellence (B1), a "glissement du prédicat de valeur [i.e., a virtue] – courageux, généreux – à l'essence du courage, de la bonté ... [U]ne essence [B1] naît lorsque l'acte créateur [A1 & A2] se retire de ses créations, de ses rythmes d'existences intimes, offerts désormais à la contemplation [B1]." It is the "'transfert' du sujet de l'action [I am] vers le pôle d'entendement ou de raison [It is] qui donne à l'idéal son apparente extériorité." *Le conflit des interprétations*, 301–2, 298.

38 "[W]e say of what is necessary, 'It is.' We thus hold it to be simple self-relation, in which all dependence on something else is removed." Hegel, *Encyclopaedia*, §147, trans. Wallace, 208. "Hast thou ever raised thy mind to the consideration of EXISTENCE, in and by itself, as the mere act of existing? Hast thou ever said to thyself thoughtfully, IT IS! heedless in that moment whether it were a man before thee, or a flower, or a grain of sand? Without reference, in short, to this or that particular mode or form of existence? If thou hast indeed attained to this, thou wilt have felt the presence of a mystery, which must have fixed thy spirit in awe and wonder." Coleridge, *The Friend*, 1:514. The German translation of "It *is*" is "*Es gibt*," which is Martin Heidegger's term for "It *is*." The literal meaning of "*Es gibt*," i.e., "It gives," gives Being an implicit overtone of a primal "gift" or "grant," a primal giving to which Heidegger thinks there must be an appropriate human response (of self-giving). Heidegger, *Being and Time*, 212, 230, 316, trans. Stambaugh, 203, 220, 302; "Letter on Humanism," trans. Frank A. Capuzzi, in collaboration with J. Glenn Gray; "Modern Science, Metaphysics, and Mathematics," trans. W.B. Barton, Jr. and Vera Deutsch; "The Question Concerning Technology," trans. William Lovitt; "What Calls for Thinking?," trans. Fred D. Wieck and J. Glenn Gray; and "The End of Philosophy and the Task of Thinking," trans. Joan Stambaugh, in *Basic Writings*, ed. David Farrell Krell (New York: Harper-Collins, 1977), 214–15, 251, 316, 345, 385, 391–2. Alfred North Whitehead implicitly makes a similar linguistic point in English – paralleling Heidegger's German *es gibt* – when he says that, in the initial human perception of physical realities, an "eternal object" (i.e., Plato's "form") is "functioning *datively*." *Process and Reality*, 191. Emphasis added.

39 "By thus cancelling individuality ... the inherent nature of the world's process [the 'arrow of virtue'] merely gets room, as it were, to enter real existence independently on its own account (*an und für sich selbst*). The general content of the actual course of the world has already made itself known. Looked at more closely, it is again nothing else than the two proceeding movements of consciousness. From them have come virtue's shape and mould, for since they originate it, virtue has them before it; its aim, however, is to supersede its source and origin, and realize itself, or be 'for itself,' become objectively explicit." G.W.F. Hegel, *The Phenomenology of Mind*, trans. J.B. Baillie (New York: Harper & Row, 1967), 403.

40 "Even what is within him is for him, because it '*is*,' something *external*, something upon which he must first call." Franz Rosenzweig, *The Star of Redemption*, trans. William W. Hallo (Notre Dame, IN: Univ. of Notre Dame Press, 1985), 232. Emphasis added.

41 In patristic and scholastic Christian theology, the category in which "something is due" was sometimes called the "befitting" or *honestum*,

"that which deserves to be loved, desired and pursued for the sake of its own intrinsic perfection." Étienne Gilson, *The Elements of Christian Philosophy* (New York: Mentor, 1963), 170–1. On the "the general principle" of "dueness," see also Dietrich von Hildebrand, *Ethics*, 255–67.

42 Emmanuel Levinas' term for the stance of "It *is*" (B1) is "l'Illéité." *Autrement qu'être ou au-delà de l'essence* (Paris: Le Livre de Poche, 2008), 28, 184, 196, 230–1, 234, 240, 247, 252, 261; *Dieu, la mort et le temps* (Paris: Le Livre de Poche, 2010), 231, 234, 236, 240, 257. Robert Nozick calls this "third stance" (of "It *is*" [B1]) the "absolute stance" or "absolutist stance." In this stance, he says, "we relate to valuable things (and characteristics) or gain them *because* they are independently valuable." *The Examined Life*, 152–5. Emphasis in original.

43 Exodus 3:14. While Exodus proclaims the "*I am*" (A2) of reverence, Isaiah recognizes the "*I am*" (A1) of self-assertion, symbolized by "Babylon": "Now therefore hear this, you lover of pleasures, who sit securely, who say in your heart, 'I am, and there is no one besides me.' ... Your wisdom and your knowledge led you astray ... But evil shall come upon you, which you cannot charm away." Isaiah 47:8–11.

44 The fact that the "*I am*" of the God of the people of Israel is actually revealed to them at the *next* stage of "It *is*" is reflected in the Hebrew name for this God – Yahweh (or the tetragram Yhwh) – which resembles the third person form of the Hebrew word (*haya*) which means "to be." So Yahweh means "He is." "Names of God," Jewish Encyclopedia, https://www.jewishencyclopedia.com/articles/11305-names-of-god. Robin Wall Kimmerer points out that the biblical Yahweh is phonetically very close to the Indigenous North American Ojibwe or Anishinabemowin word *yawe*, meaning "to be." "To speak of those possessed with life and spirit we must say *yawe*. By what linguistic confluence do Yahweh of the Old Testament and *yawe* of the New World both fall from the mouths of the reverent? Isn't this just what it means to be, to have the breath of life within, to be the offspring of Creation?" *Braiding Sweetgrass: Indigenous Wisdom, Scientific Knowledge, and the Teachings of Plants* (Minneapolis: Milkweed Editions, 2013), 56. Thomas Römer suggests that, in the biblical context of Exodus 3, where God declares himself to Moses, Yahweh "est d'abord 'celui qui est avec,' qui promet assistance." *L'invention de Dieu* (Paris: Éditions du Seuil, 2014), 43.

45 Charles Freeman, *The Closing of the Western Mind: The Rise of Faith and the Fall of Reason* (London: Pimlico, 2003), 11; Grondin, *Introduction à la métaphysique*, 29.

46 Parmenides of Elea, *Fragments*, trans. David Gallop (Toronto: Univ. of Toronto Press, 1984), 55; G.S. Kirk and J.E. Raven, *The Presocratic Philosophers* (Cambridge: Cambridge Univ. Press, 1964), 266–9; Grondin, *Introduction à la métaphysique*, 21. Emphasis added.

47 "The fundamental difference between the attitudes of modern and ancient man as regards the surrounding world is this: for modern, scientific man the phenomenal world is primarily an 'It'; for ancient – and also for primitive – man it is a 'Thou.'" H. and H.A. Frankfort, "Introduction: Myth and Reality," in Henri Frankfort et al., *Before Philosophy*, 12. See also Richard Shweder, *Thinking Through Cultures: Expeditions in Cultural Psychology* (Cambridge, MA: Harvard Univ. Press, 1991), 153; Kimmerer, *Braiding Sweetgrass*, 55.

48 Robert Nozick calls this the "relational stance." In this stance (as in the first, "egoistic stance" [A1]), "value is *somehow connected to the self*, either within it or between it and something else." *The Examined Life*, 152. Emphasis added. In other words, the "relational" stance of "*It* is" (B2) is a second stance of self-assertion, a stance of rights (B2a) and reciprocity (B2b).

49 Martin Heidegger distinguishes the "factuality" of the stance of "*It* is" (B2), the "factuality of something objectively present within the world," from the "facticity" of the previous human stance of "It *is*" (B1). In the latter, the nature of the human "does not encounter itself as something objectively present within the world," but rather "as a being that has to be as it is and can be." In the first stance of "It *is*" (B1), "*that-it-is* has itself" already been "disclosed," before it can be objectively present within the world, in the later stance of "*It* is" (B2). There is a decisive difference between the "disclosedness of world" (It *is*) and the "discoveredness of innerworldly beings belonging to the disclosed" (*It* is). *Being and Time*, 276, 420, trans. Stambaugh, 265, 400.

50 Emmanuel Levinas' term for the stance of "*It* is" is "l'il y a." He emphasizes "le caractère désertique, obsédant et horrible de l'*être*, entendu selon l'*il y a* … son inhumaine *neutralité*." *De l'existence à l'existant* (Paris: Vrin, 2013), 10. Emphases in original.

51 Marcel Gauchet, *The Disenchantment of the World: A Political History of Religion*, trans. Oscar Bruge (Princeton, NJ: Princeton Univ. Press, 1997), 73.

52 Whitehead, *Process and Reality*, 301. Paul Ricœur calls this the "capture du *qui?* par le 'quelque chose.'" *Soi-même comme un autre* (Paris: Éditions du Seuil, 1990), 77, 118.

53 Martin Heidegger says Parmenides' "doctrine of Being" was the "crucial step that decided the sense and destiny of Western ontology and logic." "Indication of the Hermeneutical Situation," trans. Michael Baur and Jerome Veith, in *The Heidegger Reader*, ed. Günter Figal (Bloomington: Indiana Univ. Press, 2009), 58. "Something is present to us. It stands steadily by itself and thus manifests itself. *It is*. For the Greeks 'being' basically meant this standing presence." *An Introduction to Metaphysics*, trans. Manheim, 50. Emphasis added.

54 "[T]he process constitutes the character of the product, and ... conversely analysis of the product discloses the process." Whitehead, *Process and Reality*, 298.

55 What, in this book, I call the "whole" or "full" nature of the human – both self-assertion *and* reverence – Jacques Maritain calls "un *humanisme intégral*." *Humanisme intégral*, new ed. (Paris: Éditions Aubier-Montaigne, 1946), 12–15. Emphasis in original.

56 Paul Ricœur calls this "la structure double du corps propre." He calls this "dialectic of the person" a dialectic of "selfness" (ipséité) and "sameness" (mêmeté), or a dialectic of "concordance discordante." *Soi-même comme un autre*, 71–2, 77, 159, 167–8, 176–9.

57 Robert Nozick also identifies four basic human "stances" largely consistent with the four outlined in this chapter. *The Examined Life*, 151–61.

58 Hegel, *Encyclopaedia*, §220, trans. Wallace, 282.

59 Emmanuel Levinas also uses the word "procession" for what I call the "arrow of virtue." *Entre nous*, 171–3. Martin Heidegger calls it, among other things, "destining." Heidegger, "The Question Concerning Technology," trans. Lovitt, 306–15. Alfred North Whitehead calls it simply "process." *Process and Reality*, 240–8. Franz Rosenzweig calls it "the path to human existence," the "inner direction" of human "volition," "the path of us," the "path of creation," and so on. *The Star of Redemption*, trans. Hallo, 67, 87–9, 119. Paul Ricœur's names for it include "le système des figures tirées en avant," "le parcours des figures," "parcours signifiant," "le parcours des figures de l'Esprit," "la dialectique ascendante des figures de l'esprit," "construction progressive des figures de l'esprit," and "un arrangement prospectif des figures de l'esprit et un enchaînement progressif des sphères de culture." *Le conflit des interprétations*, 163, 171–3, 243–4, 331–2.

60 Although not inspired by it, my image of the "arrow of virtue" has the happy advantage of linking up with Thomas Aquinas' image of being moving toward an end "as the arrow is directed by the archer." *Summa Theologiæ* 1.2.3, in *Introduction to St. Thomas Aquinas*, ed. Anton C. Pegis (New York: The Modern Library, 1948), 27. Paul Ricœur also uses the image of an "arrow" that leads in language to "un référant possible," and in culture to "une construction progressives des figures de l'esprit" (Hegel's "moments" and my stances or families of virtues). *Le conflit des interprétations*, 343, 331. Max Scheler suggests the movement of the arrow of virtue results from the "differentiation of feeling," especially the "act of love." Through the increasing discrimination of our feelings we discover "new" virtues, which were already implicit in a human world, only waiting for us to encounter or perceive them. *Formalism in Ethics*, trans. Frings and Funk, 157, 261. What I call here the arrow of virtue may be contrasted

with the arrow of cognition, which works in the opposite direction. See chapter 17, note 199, below.

61 Maurice Blondel calls them "les phases aussi bien simultanées que successives d'une dialectique de la civilisation." *L'Être et les êtres*, 483.

62 Shahab Ahmed captures this point (and what I mean by "double vision") when he argues that many values we associate with Western modernity and post-modernity – including self-assertion, individual autonomy, and the affirmation of ordinary life – were "amply present in pre-modern societies of Muslims where they constituted fundamental components of notions of the Self." My "double vision" is also analogous to the distinction Ahmed makes between "Con-Text *in toto*" (the entire, accumulated Islamic repertoire) and "Con-Text *in loco*" (its partial manifestation in a specific time and place): "[T]o the extent that the universal lexicon of Con-Text *in toto* remains in circulation and is available for consultation and exploration, all of its elements ... are potentially available at any given moment to be taken on as Con-Text *in loco*." *What Is Islam? The Importance of Being Islamic* (Princeton: Princeton Univ. Press, 2016), 329–30n68, 362. In my language: all the dimensions of the nature of the human were (and are) fully present in pre-modern societies but viewed *there* mainly through the lens of the virtues of reverence – just as they are all still present in our post-modern (and postmodern) Western cultures, but viewed *here* mainly through the lens of self-assertion.

63 Hegel, *Preface to the Phenomenology of Spirit*, trans. Yovel, 99, 132–3. As Hegel puts it, the arrow of virtue (or "procession of spirit") is a manifestation of the "pure unrest of life," a kind of "Bacchanalian whirl" in its spiral forward movement, both phylogenetic and ontogenetic. But "the whirl is equally a simple and transparent rest." That is to say, the human paradox is *both* a historical process *and* the whole nature of the human in any age or individual, which is simply "the whole movement taken as rest." Hegel, 152–4. Max Scheler notes that the human paradox can be known at three distinct levels: (1) at the level of the whole nature of the human ("that can be known by all at any time"), as in this book, for example; (2) in the specific configurations of virtues that distinguish each individual and establish their distinctive moral character ("that suit only individuals"); and (3) in the specific historical cultures at each "new stage of development," when "new values" and virtues are revealed and "become visible." *Formalism in Ethics*, trans. Frings and Funk, 494.

64 Hegel, *The Phenomenology of Mind*, trans. Baillie, 808. On the spiral shape of human experience, se also C.G. Jung, *Individual Dream Symbolism in Relation to Alchemy: A Study of the Unconscious Processes at Work in Dreams*, trans. R.F.C. Hull, in *The Portable Jung*, ed. Joseph Campbell (New York:

The Viking Press, 1971), 450; Emmanuel Levinas, *Difficile liberté*, 3rd corrected ed. (Paris: Le Livre de Poche, 2010), 52.

65 "Each of the stages … is an image of the absolute, but at first in a limited mode, and thus it is forced onward to the whole." Hegel, *Encyclopaedia*, §237, trans. Wallace, 292–3. Also: *Preface to the Phenomenology of Spirit*, trans. Yovel, 105, 123, 130, 154. 168–9.

66 Hegel, *Preface to the Phenomenology of Spirit*, trans. Yovel, 105, 123, 130, 154. 168–9. "What we have done here [in the *Phenomenology*] … is simply to gather together the particular moments, *each of which in principle exhibits the life of spirit in its entirety*." Hegel, *The Phenomenology of Mind*, trans. Baillie, 797. Emphasis added. What I have called "double vision" can also be compared to Aquinas' principle of "analogy," according to which "les idées les plus hautes se réalisent dans l'existence d'une manière essentiellement diverse, tout en gardant intacte leur formalité propre." Maritain, *Humanisme intégral*, 144–5.

67 When you try to think about the nature of the human – when you try to turn the whole "movement" and its constituent "moments" (or families of virtues) into "an object of consciousness," into "the simple self-overviewing whole" – as I have been trying to do in this book – Hegel says that effort is like "an abbreviated birthgiving," "a shape reduced to its abbreviation." Hegel, *Preface to the Phenomenology of Spirit*, trans. Yovel, 134–5, 168, 130, 123.

68 "Each [of thinking (B1 & B2), feeling (A1 & A2) and volition (A1 & B2)] is one element in the whole, or *the whole in one of its aspects*; and hence, *when you get an aspect or element, you have the whole with it*. But because, given one aspect (whatever it may be), we find the whole universe, to conclude that in the universe there is nothing beyond this single aspect, seems quite irrational." Bradley, *Appearance and Reality*, 154. Emphasis added.

69 Edward O. Wilson, *Consilience: The Unity of Knowledge* (New York: Alfred A. Knopf, 1998); Steven Pinker, *Enlightenment Now: The Case for Reason, Science, Humanism, and Progress* (New York: Viking, 2018); *Rationality: What It Is, Why It Seems Scarce, Why It Matters* (New York: Viking, 2021). Paul Ricœur describes the Wilson/Pinker stance as "aspirée par une ontologie du *quelque chose en général* [It is]." *Soi-même comme un autre*, 118. Emphasis in original. He points out that the same kind of "double vision" is at work in other contemporary paradigms, such as Freudian psychoanalysis, which is limited by the "angle de vue [stance]" through which it views "la totalité du phénomène humain." *Le conflit des interprétations*, 177.

70 Alfred North Whitehead expresses this cascading hierarchy of polarities in human (and biological) life – resulting from "separative projection" (or "intro-Reflection") – when he says that the "higher contrasts [polarities]

depend on the assemblage of a multiplicity of lower contrasts." *Process and Reality*, 113.

71 "In practice certainly we leave out of the account the whole background of existence; we isolate a group of elements, and we say that, whenever these occur, then something else happens; and in this group we consider ourselves to possess the 'sum of the conditions.' ... But the background is never exhausted by this object, and it never could be so." Bradley, *Appearance and Reality*, 57, 153. Karl Jaspers calls this limitless horizon *within* which humans exist the "Encompassing" or the "Comprehensive" (depending on the translation). *Reason and Existenz*, trans. William Earle, in *Existentialism from Dostoevsky to Sartre*, ed. Walter Kaufmann (Cleveland: World, 1956), 184–6; *Way to Wisdom*, trans. Ralph Manheim (New Haven: Yale Univ. Press, 1960), 28–38. Martin Heidegger calls it the "concealed," within which the illumination of the "clearing" creates a space of "unconcealment," where the human and Being meet in the "appropriative event" of "Ereignis." *Being and Time*, 133, 170, 350–1, trans. Stambaugh, 129, 164, 334; "The End of Philosophy and the Task of Thinking," trans. Stambaugh, 373–92; "The Principle of Identity," trans. Joan Stambaugh and Jerome Veith, in *The Heidegger Reader*, 291–4.

72 Rahner, *The Practice of Faith*, 3, 6, 42.

73 "[A]reality which is always present ... even though unrecognized." Jaspers, *Reason and Existenz*, trans. Earle, 196. Martin Heidegger calls the invisible background of being the "upon-which ... that underlies all *being* of beings." *Being and Time*, 324–5, trans. Stambaugh, 309–10. Emphasis in original.

74 Grondin, *Introduction à la métaphysique*, 19–20.

Chapter 8. The Paradoxes of Self-Assertion

1 "The standpoint of consciousness is to know the object-like things as standing opposite it, and to know itself as standing opposite them." G.W.F Hegel, *Preface to the Phenomenology of Spirit*, trans. Yirmiyahu Yovel (Princeton: Princeton Univ. Press, 2005), 116–7.

2 Aristotle's and Aquinas' term for self-assertion is "appetite" (*orexis*) or the "appetitive power." Aristotle distinguishes between the sense appetite (A1) and the rational, intellectual, or calculative appetite (B2). Aristotle, *De Anima* 3.10.433a1–433b30, trans. J.A. Smith in *The Basic Works of Aristotle*, ed. Richard McKeon, 597–9; *The Nicomachean Ethics* 6.2.1139a15–b5, trans. J.A.K. Thomson, rev. Hugh Tredennick (London: Penguin Books, 2004), 146–7. Aristotle's rational appetite became what Aquinas also calls the will, a subset of the appetitive power, and the source of all virtue "because the will moves to their acts all other powers that are in

some way rational." *Summa Theologiæ* 1–2.56.3, Question 58.1, in *Treatise on the Virtues*, trans. Oesterle, 60, 81. Aquinas calls the form of intellect of the rational appetite or will the "agent intellect" (B2), as distinct from the "possible intellect" (B1). *Summa Theologiæ* 1.84.6, in Étienne Gilson, *The Elements of Christian Philosophy* (New York: Mentor, 1963), 354n10. On the subdivision of the sense appetite into the "irascible" and "concupiscible" appetites, see notes 24 and 29 below. On self-assertion as appetite and impulse, see also G.W. Leibniz, *Nouveaux essais sur l'entendement humain* (Paris: Garnier-Flammarion, 1966), bk. 2, chap. 21, §36, p. 161; G.W.F. Hegel, *Philosophy of Right*, trans. T.M. Knox (Oxford: Oxford Univ. Press, 1967), §150, p. 108. Merlin Donald refers to "the deep psychic drives that we have tried hard to lock in the attics and cellars of cognitive science," recognizing "they are the principal forces that energize our entire cultural universe." As Donald himself acknowledges, our drive for "rationality and clarity is itself deeply irrational." Merlin Donald, *A Mind So Rare: The Evolution of Human Consciousness* (New York: W.W. Norton, 2001), 285, 288, 290.

3 Charles Taylor, *Sources of the Self: The Making of the Modern Identity* (Cambridge: Harvard Univ. Press, 1989), 395. As Iris Murdoch points out, freedom is "itself a moral concept, and not just a prerequisite of morality." *The Sovereignty of Good* (London: Routledge, 1980), 38.

4 My names for the families of virtues (like the names for the virtues themselves) are simply "moral labels" which can help "our pattern sensitive brains to isolate morally salient patterns." Andy Clark, "Word and Action: Reconciling Rules and Know-How in Moral Cognition," cited in Christine Swanton, *Virtue Ethics: A Pluralistic View* (Oxford: Oxford Univ. Press, 2003), 278.

5 Hegel describes the paradox of self-assertion: "the demand for equality [B2] of satisfaction with others," on the one hand. Yet, on the other, "the need of the particular to assert itself in some distinctive way [A1]." See Hegel, *Philosophy of Right*, trans. Knox, §193, p. 128.

6 Paul Ricœur also uses "liberty" as a synonym or metaphor for pure self-assertion (A1), in *Philosophie de la volonté 2: Finitude et culpabilité*, in *Ricœur: Textes choisis et présentés*, ed. Michaël Fœssel and Fabien Lamouche (Paris: Éditions Points, 2007), 285–92. "A living man knows himself not otherwise than as wanting [i.e., appetite], that is, he is conscious of his will. And his will, which constitutes the essence of his life, man is conscious of and cannot be conscious of otherwise than as free." Leo Tolstoy, *War and Peace*, trans. Richard Pevear and Larissa Volokhonsky (New York: Vintage Classics, 2008), Epilogue, pt. 2, chap. 8, p. 1201.

7 Henry Sidgwick, *The Methods of Ethics* (Indianapolis: Hackett, 1981), 420–1, in Michel Terestchenko, *Un si fragile vernis d'humanité: Banalité du mal,*

banalité du bien (Paris: La Découverte, 2007), 249. "La volonté [Aristotle's "rational appetite" and Aquinas' "will" (B2)], c'est l'énergie [A1a] même du désir [A1b] qui a été *contredit par les autres* [It is], par les valeurs, par le devoir, mais qui à travers ces péripéties a gardé son énergie [self-assertion]." Paul Ricœur, *Politique, Économie et Société: Écrits et conférences 4* (Paris: Seuil, 2019), 85. Emphasis added. See also Paul Bloomfield, *The Virtues of Happiness: A Theory of the Good Life* (New York: Oxford Univ. Press, 2014), 103–4.

8 When eighteenth-century thinkers such as David Hume and Adam Smith routinely invoke the distinction between "interests born of calculation [B2], and passions, based on impulse [A1]," they refer, implicitly, to the paradox of self-assertion. J.A.W. Gunn, "Interests Will Not Lie: A Seventeenth-Century Political Maxim," *Journal of the History of Ideas* 29, (1968), 558, quoted in Stephen Holmes, *Passions and Constraints: On the Theory of Liberal Democracy* (Chicago: Univ. of Chicago Press, 1995), 45.

9 From this point of view, "immorality" can be attributed, by some, to a "lack of development": "We can understand immoral people as being stuck at a certain level of maturational development and who have a hard time seeing, or are incapable of seeing, what is good for them." Bloomfield, *The Virtues of Happiness*, 149.

10 This corner of the human may thus be related to the ancient Greek concept of *dunamis*, the "originative source of change in another thing or in the thing itself," "the potency of acting and being acted upon." Aristotle, *Metaphysics* 9.1.1046a10–20, trans. W.D. Ross, in *The Basic Works of Aristotle*, ed. Richard McKeon (New York: Random House, 1941), 820–1.

11 "L'action est l'existence elle-même et son essence, elle est le pouvoir qui la constitue, originellement éprouvé et vécu dans le Je peux, et son exercice." Michel Henry, *L'essence de la manifestation* (Paris: Presses Universitaires de France, 2017), 811. "In life, we must act, and our acts will inevitably be performed from the first-person-singular point of view [A1]." Bloomfield, *The Virtues of Happiness*, 145.

12 "The basic metaphysical essence of metaphysically isolated Dasein is centred in *freedom*." Martin Heidegger, "The Problem of *Being and Time*," trans. Michael Heim, rev. Jerome Veith, in *The Heidegger Reader*, ed. Günter Figal, trans. Jerome Veith (Bloomington: Indiana Univ. Press, 2007), 65–6. Emphasis in original.

13 Thomas Hobbes, *Leviathan* (Indianapolis: Bobbs-Merrill, 1958), pt. 1, chap. 8, p. 68.

14 For Aristotle and Aquinas on appetite, see notes 2 above, 24 and 29 below.

15 Plato, *The Laws* 1.631, trans. Trevor J. Saunders (Harmondsworth: Penguin Books, 1970), 55.

16 The way Hegel puts it is that self-assertion's pursuit of its own needs and wants (A1) brings the self-asserting self up against needs and wants themselves, i.e., against something real, "something which has being for others by whose needs and work satisfaction for all alike is conditioned." This "social moment ... directly involves the demand for equality of satisfaction with others [B2]." Hegel, *Philosophy of Right*, trans. Knox, §192–3, pp. 127–8.

17 Aristotle, *The Nicomachean Ethics* 6.1.1139a1–6.2.1139b15, trans. Thomson, rev. Tredennick, 145–7.

18 "Now the subject (in so far as, determinate in its need, it relates itself to the external, and therefore is itself external or instrument) exerts *force* upon the object. Its particular character and its finitude in general fall within the more definite appearance of this relation. – The external aspect of this is the Process of Objectivity in general." G.W.F. Hegel, *Science of Logic*, vol. 2, §3, chap. 1, trans. W.H. Johnston and L.G. Struthers (London: George Allen & Unwin, 1951), 2:411–12.

19 Sigmund Freud, *Civilization and Its Discontents*, trans. James Strachey (New York: W.W. Norton, 1962), 70. "[T]he more a man controls [B2] his aggressiveness [A1], the more intense becomes his ideal's [his super-ego's] inclination to aggressiveness against his ego. It is like a displacement, a turning round upon his own ego." *The Ego and the Id*, trans. Joan Riviere, rev. James Strachey (New York: W.W. Norton, 1962), 44. David Hume agrees that the only way to control self-assertion is by "this very affection itself, by an alteration of its direction. ... [I]tself alone restrains it." David Hume, *A Treatise of Human Nature* 3.2.2, ed. L.A. Selby-Bigge (London: Oxford Univ. Press, 1968), 492. Some virtue ethicists contrast virtue and self-control, on the ground that, to be fully virtuous, virtue must include the *desire* for good behaviour, and therefore excludes the necessity for self-*control*. If self-control is necessary, then the behaviour is not genuinely virtuous. See, for example, Swanton, *Virtue Ethics*, 26, 29, 67. Although this view goes back to an old distinction Aristotle and Aquinas made between temperance (a virtue) and continence (not fully virtuous), it overlooks that fully one-quarter of the virtues are characterized by versions and dimensions of self-control.

20 "La possession totale de soi dans la réflexion [B2] n'est que l'envers de la liberté [A1]." Emmanuel Levinas, *En découvrant l'existence avec Husserl et Heidegger*, 4th corrected ed. (Paris: Vrin, 2010), 55.

21 Following many other scholars of the Enlightenment, José Casanova notes that freedom of religion and of conscience "is chronologically 'the first freedom' as well as the precondition of all modern freedoms." *Public Religions in the Modern World* (Chicago: Univ. of Chicago Press, 1994), 40.

22 Susanne K. Langer, *Mind: An Essay on Human Feeling*, vol. 1 (Baltimore: Johns Hopkins Press, 1967), 354.

23 "[E]very determination, every concrete, every concept is essentially a union of distinguished and distinguishable moments, which pass over through determinate and essential difference into contradictory moments." Hegel, *Science of Logic*, vol. 1, bk. 2, §1, chap. 2, trans. Johnston and Struthers, 2:70. "That is to say, particularity is always duality." *Philosophy of Right*, trans. Knox, §139, p. 93. Whitehead says the same thing, in other language: "[A]ctual entities ... arise out of a potentiality for division, which in actual fact is not divided." Alfred North Whitehead, *Process and Reality* (New York: Free Press, 1969), 93.

24 "The sensitive appetite [A1] is one generic power, but is divided into two kinds, namely the concupiscible [A1b] and the irascible [A1a]. By the former the soul works according to the pain-pleasure principle, by the latter it deals with emergency reactions. The irascible is, as it were, the champion of the concupiscible, attacking what hinders pleasure or inflicts harm, which respectively the concupiscible desires and shrinks from. Anger starts from desire and leads to it." Thomas Aquinas, *Summa Theologiæ* 1.81.2, in *Philosophical Texts*, trans. Thomas Gilby (London: Oxford Univ. Press, 1956), 254. Also in *Introduction to St. Thomas Aquinas*, ed. Anton C. Pegis (New York: The Modern Library, 1948), 356–7. See also *Summa Theologiæ* 1–2.56.4, in *Treatise on the Virtues*, trans. Oesterle, 61–3. For the sources of Aquinas' irascible (A1a), concupiscible (A1b), and rational (B2) appetites, in Plato and Aristotle, see: Plato, *The Republic*, bk. 7, 434D–441D, 579A–582C, 585C–587A, in *Great Dialogues of Plato*, trans. W.H.D. Rouse, ed. Eric H. Warmington and Philip G. Rouse (New York: New American Library, 1956), 235–41, 379–80, 387; Aristotle, *De Anima* 3.9.432a15–3.10.433b30, trans. Smith, in *The Basic Works of Aristotle*, ed. McKeon, 596–9. Hegel's terms for Aquinas' concupiscible and irascible appetites are "sensibility" and "irritability." Hegel, *Science of Logic*, 2.3.1A, trans. Johnston and Struthers, 2:409. Dietrich von Hildebrand follows Aquinas in calling the "two different centers" of the ego self "pride" (A1a) and "concupiscence" (A1b). *Ethics* (Steubenville, OH: Hildebrand Press, 2020), 436, 455–76.

25 Paul Ricœur, *Le conflit des interprétations: Essais d'herméneutique* (Paris: Éditions du Seuil, 2013), 45, 203, 290, 440. Ricœur recognizes that, together, they are "l'affirmation la plus originaire." Ricœur, 203. Maurice Blondel calls these two sides of primal self-assertion "domination" (A1a) and "jouissance" (A1b). *L'Être et les êtres* (Paris: Presses Universitaires de France, 1963), 282.

26 Franz Rosenzweig suggests the name "defiance" for this primal form of self-assertion. *The Star of Redemption*, trans. William W. Hallo (Notre Dame, IN: Univ. of Notre Dame Press, 1985), 67–9.

27 Aquinas, *Summa Theologiæ* 1–2.58.1, in *Treatise on the Virtues*, trans. Oesterle, 81.

28 "We want to be important in some way, to count in the world and make a difference to it. Importance is an additional, separate dimension of reality. ... The best sort of importance also has value and meaning. Yet making a difference does have a claim on its own; it is a separate evaluative notion." Robert Nozick, *The Examined Life* (New York: Simon & Schuster, 1990), 170–1. Nozick suggests that power has "two modes": "the having of effect" ("involves being a causal source *from which* effects flow") and "being taken account of" ("involves being a place *toward which* responses flow"). Nozick, 174–5. Emphasis added.

29 The "object [of the irascible appetite] is something arduous, because its tendency is to overcome and rise above obstacles." Aquinas, *Summa Theologiæ* 1.81.2, in *Introduction to St. Thomas Aquinas*, 356. See also: 1–2.67.4, 2–2.58.4, 2–2.141.2, 2–2.141.4, 2–2.146.1, in *Treatise on the Virtues*, trans. Oesterle, 168; *Summa Theologiæ*, (Cambridge: Cambridge Univ. Press, 2006), vol. 43 ("Temperance"), trans. Thomas Gilby, 9, 19, 85. Aquinas' notion of the "arduous" good echoes Cicero's view that morally good actions "are extremely arduous and laborious and fraught with danger both to life and to the many other goods that make life worth living." Cicero, *De officiis* [On Public Responsibility], quoted in John W. O'Malley, *Four Cultures of the West* (Cambridge, MA: Harvard Univ. Press, 2004), 133. See also Leibniz, *Nouveaux essais*, bk. 2, chap. 20, §12, p. 142; Martin Heidegger, *Being and Time*, 297–301, trans. Joan Stambaugh (Albany: State Univ. of New York Press, 2010), 284–8; Ricœur, *Histoire et vérité* (Paris: Points Essais, 2001), 268.

30 Aquinas, *Summa Theologiæ* 1.81.1, in *Introduction to St. Thomas Aquinas*, 355.

31 Michael Oakeshott, *Rationalism in Politics and Other Essays* (London: Methuen, 1962), 172, 170, 173.

32 Oakeshott, 177. Emphasis added. Consciously or unconsciously, Oakeshott seems to have paraphrased Augustine of Hippo's observation that "to enjoy a thing is to rest with satisfaction in it for its own sake." *On Christian Doctrine*, chap. 4, §4, in *Late Have I Loved Thee: Selected Writings of Saint Augustine on Love*, ed. John F. Thornton and Susan B. Varenne (New York, Vintage Books, 2006), 77.

33 Aristotle, *The Nicomachean Ethics* 7.13.1153b25–35, trans. Thomson, rev. Tredennick, 195–6.

34 Pascal, *Lettres écrites à un provincial* (Paris: Garnier-Flammarion, 1967), 255. "[L]a volonté ne se porte jamais qu'à ce qu'il lui plaît le plus et ... rien ne lui plaît tant alors que ce bien unique qui comprend tous les autres biens."

35 Aquinas, *Summa Theologiæ* 1–2.56.3, in *Treatise on the Virtues*, trans. Oesterle, 61. "[T]he one who loves is drawn by affection to a *union* with what is loved." Aquinas, *Summa Theologiæ* 1–2.66.6, trans. Oesterle, 159. Emphasis added.

36 Aquinas, *Summa Theologiæ* 1.81.2, in *Introduction to St. Thomas Aquinas*, 357.

37 Aquinas, 357.

38 As Robert Nozick puts it, the "very notion of freedom" is "a concept rooted in the egoist stance [A1]." *The Examined Life*, 161.

39 The greatness of Thomas Hobbes in the history of Western thought is his uniquely clear-sighted understanding that the core of the virtues of Liberty (A1) is the natural human pursuit of power (A1a) and domination over others. *Leviathan*, pt. 2, chap. 17, p. 139.

40 "[E]ffort et résistance formant une unité indivisible." Paul Ricœur, *Soi-même comme un autre* (Paris: Éditions du Seuil, 1990), 372.

41 President Recep Erdogan of Turkey seems to be only the latest of these radical reformers whose only object is the elimination of all obstacles to their own self-assertion. As early as 1996, he admitted democracy was, for him, only a means to gain power, a means which could be discarded once power was secured. Christian Desmeules, "Erdogan, le despote que cachait le démocrate," *Le Devoir*, 14 March 2018, A1–8. This article is a review of Guillaume Perrier, *Dans la tête de Recep Tayyip Erdogan* (Arles: Actes du Sud, 2018). Populists are "against institutions only when they are in opposition," as Jan-Werner Müller puts it. "Populists in power are fine with institutions – which is to say with *their* institutions." *What Is Populism?* (London: Penguin Books, 2017), 62. Emphasis in original.

42 "Whatever has a price can be replaced by something else as its equivalent; on the other hand whatever is above all price, and therefore admits of no equivalent, has a dignity." Immanuel Kant, *Foundations of the Metaphysics of Morals*, trans. Lewis White Beck (Indianapolis: Bobbs-Merrill, 1959), §2, p. 53.

43 Paul Ricœur places competition midway between conflict (A1a) and cooperation (B2). *Soi-même comme un autre*, 184–5. On competition as "sociability seen from the standpoint of individualism," and team-play as the "high point in the development of play … at which individualism is beginning to be transcended," see R.G. Collingwood, *Speculum Mentis or the Map of Knowledge* (Oxford: Oxford Univ. Press, 1963), 105–6.

44 "To have power is to dominate." Gilson, *The Elements of Christian Philosophy*, 294.

45 "The unbridled law of the market breeds monopoly – or if not monopoly, business oligarchy – which not only stifles competition, but which may also set up an independent corporation or cartel in rivalry to the state."

Roger Scruton, *The Meaning of Conservatism*, 3rd rev. ed. (South Bend, IN: St. Augustine's Press, 2002), 103. In November 2015, Anheuser-Busch InBev SA reached an agreement to buy SABMiller PLC for $112 billion, creating a company which produces almost one-third of the world's beer; Pharmaceutical giant Pfizer purchased rival Allergan for $160 billion, aiming to create the world's largest pharmaceutical company (the deal later fell apart); and hotel giant Marriott acquired the Starwood hotel group for $12.2 billion to create the world's largest hotel group. These kinds of mergers and acquisitions appear to be driven more by the disposition to dominate than by an appetite for competition. "£71-Billion Megabrew Deal Finalized," *Globe and Mail*, 12 November 2015, B1 & 11; "Le traitement anti-impôts de Pfizer," *Le Devoir*, 24 November 2015, B3; "Marriott Deal a Game Changer," "Pfizer, Allergan Deal Creates Global Behemoth," *Ottawa Citizen*, 24 November 2015, C6–7.

46 Taylor, *Sources of the Self*, 101, 384, 413, 503.

47 "Men being naturally selfish [A1], or endow'd only with a confin'd generosity, they are not easily induc'd to perform any action for the interests of strangers, except with a view to some reciprocal [B2b] advantage, which they had no hope of obtaining but by such a performance." Hume, *A Treatise of Human Nature* 3.2.5, p. 519. Equality (B2) ultimately "sees our highest goal in terms of a certain kind of human flourishing, in the context of mutuality [i.e., reciprocity], pursuing each his/her own happiness on the basis of assured life and liberty, in a society of mutual benefit." Charles Taylor, *A Secular Age* (Cambridge, MA: Belknap Press of Harvard Univ. Press, 2007), 430–1. On the distinction between reciprocity and mutuality, see note 50 below.

48 "[T]he conditions of individuality are called *rights* [B2a]. As surely as [an individual] *affirms* its individuality [A1], so surely does it affirm such a sphere [B2] – the two conceptions indeed are convertible." J.G. Fichte to Friedrich Jacobi, in Jacobi's *Briefwechsel*, ii, 208, cited in *Hegel's Logic*, trans. William Wallace (London: Oxford Univ. Press, 1975), 305. Emphasis added.

49 "My entitlements of course depend on other people. If I am to receive what belongs to me, they must be willing and able to honor my rights. ... If my entitlements are to be honored, I need to depend on the enlightened self-interest of others, joined in a *system of reciprocal respect driven by the egoistic desire of each* to secure the possession of what he or she is owed." Anthony T. Kronman, *Confessions of a Born-Again Pagan* (New Haven: Yale Univ. Press, 2016), 65–6. Emphasis added.

50 Despite their more "reverent" content in comparison to the virtues of Rights (B2a), the virtues of Reciprocity and cooperation (B2b) remain nevertheless very much virtues of self-assertion. Their self-assertive character

is what accounts for their insistence on reciprocity. As Webb Keane notes: "[C]ooperation for mutual benefit might be just an intelligent form of self-interest, to which benefiting others is secondary." Webb Keane, *Ethical Life: Its Natural and Social Histories* (Princeton: Princeton Univ. Press, 2016), 46. Similarly, Hans Joas refers to "the ever-present threat of the reduction of justice [B1] to mere utilitarian reciprocity [B2b]." *The Genesis of Values*, trans. Gregory Moore (Cambridge, Polity Press, 2000), 186. That's why Paul Ricœur distinguishes between mutuality and reciprocity. In the "mutuality" of the virtues of reverence (A2), *giving* comes first; in the "reciprocity" of the virtues of self-assertion (B2), *receiving* comes first. *Parcours de la reconnaissance* (Paris: Gallimard, 2013), 245–56, 350–77, 400–1. Mutuality does *not* "imply or require equality [B1]." James Laidlaw, *The Subject of Virtue: An Anthropology of Ethics and Freedom* (Cambridge: Cambridge Univ. Press, 2014), 124. In my language, reciprocity is the form mutuality takes in the virtues of self-assertion; mutuality is the form reciprocity takes in the virtues of reverence.

51 Aquinas describes the permanent contest between the two sides of the paradox of self-assertion: the rational appetite or will (B2) seeks to control the sense appetite or passions (A1a and A1b) which do "not just obey spontaneously but with a certain power of opposition" – an opposition entirely to be expected in what are, after all, the virtues of self-assertion! *Summa Theologiæ* 1–2.58.3, in *Treatise on the Virtues*, trans. Oesterle, 82–3.

52 Hume, *A Treatise of Human Nature* 2.3.8, 3.2.2, 3.3.1, pp. 437, 492, 583; Heidegger, *Being and Time*, 138, trans. Stambaugh, 134; "The Environmental Experience," trans. Ted Sadler and Jerome Veith, in *The Heidegger Reader*, ed. Figal, 35–6.

53 This is the "existential concept of science" (as opposed to the "logical concept") which "understands science as a mode of existence." Heidegger, *Being and Time*, 357, trans. Stambaugh, 340.

54 "[T]here is a Wisdom [B1] higher than Prudence [B2], to which Prudence stands in the same relation as the Mason and Carpenter to the genial and scientific Architect." Samuel Taylor Coleridge, *The Friend*, ed. Barbara E. Rooke (London: Routledge, 1969), 1:118.

55 On "capitalism" as an expression of the virtues of Liberty (A1) ("un esprit d'exaltation des puissances actives et inventives, du dynamisme de l'homme et des initiatives de l'individu"), see Jacques Maritain, *Humanisme intégral*, new ed. (Paris: Éditions Aubier-Montaigne, 1946), 121.

56 John O'Malley notes that "pleasure" and "play" (A1b) are key words that come close to "capturing the essence of [artistic] culture." O'Malley, *Four Cultures of the West*, 180.

57 Iris Murdoch, *Metaphysics as a Guide to Morals* (London: Vintage, 2003), 408; Plotinus, *Enneads* 1.6.5, in *The Essential Plotinus*, ed. Elmer O'Brien

(New York: Mentor Books, 1964), 38. Dietrich von Hildebrand also refers to the "inner light" of the virtues. *The Heart: An Analysis of Human and Divine Affectivity* (South Bend, IN: St. Augustine's Press, 2007), 10. He calls this the "intrinsic relation of the moral values to an absolute above us." *Ethics*, 481.

Chapter 9. The Paradoxes of Reverence

1 Webb Keane, *Ethical Life: Its Natural and Social Histories* (Princeton: Princeton Univ. Press, 2016), 6. Keane also references James Laidlaw's remark that people "are evaluative." *The Subject of Virtue: An Anthropology of Ethics and Freedom* (Cambridge: Cambridge Univ. Press, 2014), 3. "It is not possible to eliminate the reference to value, meaning, or some evaluative dimension." Robert Nozick, *The Examined Life* (New York: Simon & Schuster, 1990), 172.

2 "Every valuing, even where it values positively, is a subjectivizing. It does not let beings: be. Rather, valuing lets beings: be valid – solely as the objects of its doing." Martin Heidegger, "Letter on Humanism," trans. Frank A. Capuzzi, in collaboration with J. Glenn Gray, in *Basic Writings*, ed. David Farrell Krell (New York: HarperCollins, 1977), 228.

3 Dietrich von Hildebrand calls this judgment of merit or excellence a "value-response": "Only in the value-response do we find that such a response is objectively *due* the object." *Ethics* (Steubenville, OH: Hildebrand Press, 2020), 201–54. The words quoted are on page 228. Emphasis in original. On "the general principle" of "dueness," see also Hildebrand, 255–67.

4 David Hume captures this dimension of the paradox of reverence: "Love [A2] and esteem [B1b/A2a] are at bottom the same passions, and arise for the same cause [i.e., reverence]. The qualities, that produce both, are agreeable, and give pleasure. But where this pleasure is severe and serious; or where its object is great, and makes strong impression; or where it produces any degree of humility [A2a] and awe [A2a]: In all cases, the passion, which arises from the pleasure, is more properly denominated esteem [B1b/A2a] than love [A2b]. Benevolence [A2b] attends both: But is connected with love [A2b] in a more eminent degree." David Hume, *A Treatise of Human Nature* 3.3.4, ed. L.A. Selby-Bigge (London: Oxford Univ. Press, 1968), 608n1. Hume's analysis confirms that what (later in this chapter) I will call the virtues of Reverence[3] (A2a) are the necessary bridge between the virtues of Love (A2b), on the one hand, and the virtues of Excellence (B1), on the other. Dietrich von Hildebrand makes the same contrast between esteem and love in *Ethics*, 374–5.

5 Charles Taylor describes this shift from the stance of "I *am*" (A2) to the stance of "It *is*" (B1): "We sense in the very experience of being moved

by some higher good that we are moved by what is good *in it* rather than that it is valuable because of our reaction. We are moved by seeing its point as something infinitely valuable." *Sources of the Self: The Making of the Modern Identity* (Cambridge, MA: Harvard Univ. Press, 1989), 74. Emphasis added.

6 Dietrich von Hildebrand calls this second side of self-giving, that is a giving of the self to something objectively important, "reverent submission to something greater than ourselves." *Ethics*, 225. See also *The Heart: An Analysis of Human and Divine Affectivity* (South Bend, IN: St. Augustine's Press, 2007), 10.

7 Paul of Tarsus enumerates many of the virtues of Excellence (B1): "[W]hatever is *true*, whatever is *honourable*, whatever is *just*, whatever is *pure*, whatever is *lovely*, whatever is *commendable*, if there is any *excellence* and if there is anything *worthy of praise*, think about these things." Philippians 4:8. I have substituted the Authorized Version's "lovely" for the RSV's "pleasing."

8 As already noted in chapter 5, Paul Ricœur calls the paradox of reverence "une dialectique de l'amour [A2] et de la justice [B1]." Or, "la convergence des deux pédagogies du genre humain : celle de l'amour et de la justice." *Soi-même comme un autre* (Paris: Éditions du Seuil, 1990), 37; *Histoire et vérité* (Paris: Points Essais, 2001), 282; *Amour et justice* (Paris: Éditions Points, 2008). Franz Rosenzweig captures the two sides of the paradox of reverence when he notes that rabbinic theology formulates the "concept of the divine power of creation in the question whether God created the world in righteousness [B1] or rather in love [A2]." *The Star of Redemption*, trans. William W. Hallo (Notre Dame, IN: Univ. of Notre Dame Press, 1985), 117.

9 "There is no justice [B1] in love [A2], no proportion in it, because in any specific instance it is only a glimpse or parable of an embracing, incomparable reality. It makes no sense at all because it is the eternal breaking in on the temporal. So how could it subordinate itself to cause or consequence?" Marilynne Robinson, *Gilead* (Toronto: HarperCollins, 2004), 238. In his description of Sufism, Shahah Ahmed implicitly discerns the same frontier between the two families of the virtues of reverence: "Sufism seeks a truth more profound [A2] than the truth of the law [B1], and it seeks that truth in the exploration of the vast depths of God's Ocean of Truth [A2] where the law [B1], standing safely at the shore, does not venture." *What Is Islam? The Importance of Being Islamic* (Princeton: Princeton Univ. Press, 2016), 289.

10 Christine Swanton expresses the paradoxes of reverence and of Reverence (A2) when she says (quoting Kant) "*love* as a form of '*coming close*' [A2] must be tempered by *respect* as a form of '*keeping one's distance*'

[A2a/B1]." When she says love must be "delimited by respect," she is expressing the lines *both* between the virtues of Love (A1b) and Reverence[3] (A1a) (respect*ful*), *and* between the virtues of Reverence (A1) and the virtues of Excellence (B1) (respect*able*). Love (A2), as she says "must satisfy standards of excellence [B1]." Much of what I call the virtues of Excellence (B1) (where "something is due"), Swanton calls "status morality," which is "basically a respect morality, and is characterized by a variety of behaviours which signify and acknowledge status of various sorts." *Virtue Ethics: A Pluralistic View* (Oxford: Oxford Univ. Press, 2003), 23, 43–7, 99–100, 103–10. Emphasis added. Swanton cites (among others) Geoffrey Cupit, *Justice as Fittingness* (New York: Oxford Univ. Press, 1996). The Kant reference is to *The Doctrine of Virtue: The Metaphysics of Morals*, trans. Mary Gregor (Cambridge: Cambridge Univ. Press, 1996), §24, pp. 198–9.

11 In untangling the distinction between reverence and respect, Max Scheler overlooks this crucial distinction between the different kinds or modes of respect. But he correctly captures the cooler, more judgmental tone of the virtues of Excellence (B1), where respect must be deserved or earned, compared to the warmer, non-judgmental, generous, spontaneous self-giving of the virtues of Reverence (A2), where respect is accorded regardless of the merits of the receiver: "There can be *reverence* … only if … the value … is feelably given [A2]. If, on the other hand, there is only assessment and nothing else … there is only *respect* [B1]." Max Scheler, *Formalism in Ethics and Non-Formal Ethics of Value*, trans. Manfred S. Frings and Roger L. Funk (Evanston: Northwestern Univ. Press, 1973), 224n53. Emphasis added.

12 Like so many biblical passages, Psalm 85 expresses the deep human yearning for the spiritual wholeness achieved by uniting the two sides of the paradox of reverence: "Mercy [A2] and truth [B1] have met together; righteousness [B1] and peace [A2] have kissed each other. Truth [B1] shall spring up from the earth, and righteousness [B1] shall look down from heaven. The Lord will indeed grant prosperity and our land will yield its increase. Righteousness [B1] shall go before him, and peace [A2] shall be a pathway for his feet." Psalm 85:10–13.

13 As noted in chapter 5, the Jewish and Christian scriptures often seem to locate the source or home of pity, kindness, and mercy in the bowels! Alexander Cruden, *Cruden's Complete Concordance to the Old and New Testaments* (Peabody, MA: Hendrickson, n.d.), 54.

14 Martin Heidegger calls this pre-rational awareness "apprehension" (*Vernehmung*). He describes it as "ac-cepting anticipation" or "a receptive attitude toward the appearance of [what is]," but emphasizes one should "avoid lumping it together with the activity of thought or with judgments," which follow it. *An Introduction to Metaphysics*, trans. Ralph

Manheim (New York: Doubleday, 1961), 140–1. Whitehead also uses the term "direct apprehension" or, more frequently, "prehension" to designate preconscious awareness. Alfred North Whitehead, *Process and Reality* (New York: Free Press, 1969), 283, 66, 71–2. Max Scheler calls these prerational perceptions "conation" (*Streben*), which for him "designates the most general basis of experiences." Scheler suggests conations already have a "goal," or the quality of intentionality: they are already directed toward or away from something. *Formalism in Ethics*, trans. Frings and Funk, 30n24, 40–1; Hans Joas, *The Genesis of Values*, trans. Gregory Moore (Cambridge: Polity Press, 2000), 90–1. Paul Ricœur calls them "aperception": "l'aperception, distincte de toute représentation objectivante," "la certitude non représentative," "prélinguistique." *Soi-même comme un autre* (Paris: Éditions du Seuil, 1990), 371–2, 376. Merlin Donald uses the word "awareness" to designate a form of consciousness which includes the pre-rational, and which is one of the bridges between animal and human life. *A Mind So Rare: The Evolution of Human Consciousness* (New York: W.W. Norton, 2001), 94–5. Tolstoy makes a similar distinction between "reason" and "consciousness." Leo Tolstoy, *War and Peace*, trans. Richard Pevear and Larissa Volokhonsky (New York: Vintage Classics, 2008), Epilogue, pt. 2, chap. 10, p. 1210.

15 Martin Heidegger distinguishes between the two different meanings of "understanding" in the two cognitive stances of "It *is*" (B1) and "*It* is" (B2): "[U]nderstanding ... as 'explaining' [B2] must be interpreted ... as an existential derivative of the primary understanding [B1] which constitutes the being of the there in general [It *is*]. ... In understanding as an existential [B1], the thing we are able to do is not a what [*It* is], but being [Sein] as existing [It *is*]." For Heidegger, what understanding (B1) understands is the nature of the human, the "potentiality" of the four poles (or "structures") of the human paradox. Understanding (B1) is the human potentiality "to see it all." This explains why "understanding" (B1) does not and cannot have the clarity of analytic reason (B2) because it is concerned primarily with "possibilities" (the four stances and their families of virtues) rather than with things. And possibilities, because only possible, cannot have the definiteness and precision of things. They cannot be "grasped": "Such a grasp precisely takes its character of possibility away from what is projected [B1], it degrades it to the level of a given, intended content [B2]." *Being and Time*, 143–8, 167, trans. Joan Stambaugh (Albany: State Univ. of New York Press, 2010), 138–9, 141, 144, 161.

16 "[T]he starting point is the fact." Aristotle, *The Nicomachean Ethics* 1.4.1095b5–10. Also, 1.8.1098b10–15, 7.2.1146b5–10, 10.1.1172a35–b6, 10.8.1179a20–5, trans. J.A.K. Thomson, rev. Hugh Tredennick (London: Penguin Books, 2004), 8, 18, 171, 255, 276; *Metaphysics*, bk. 12, trans. W.D.

Ross, in *The Basic Works of Aristotle*, ed. McKeon (New York: Random House, 1941), 872–88. Thomas Aquinas echoes Aristotle, as usual, in asserting that "things are the measure of our intellect." *Summa Theologiæ* 1–2.64.3, in *Treatise on the Virtues*, trans. John A. Oesterle (Notre Dame, IN: Univ. of Notre Dame Press, 1984), 135.

17 Aristotle, *The Nicomachean Ethics* 5.3.1131a25–30, trans. Thomson, rev. Tredennick, 119; Michael J. Sandel, *Justice: What's the Right Thing to Do?* (New York: Farrar, Straus & Giroux, 2009), 187.

18 "'[G]ood!' means '*it is* good.' … [O]nly after the the work has been done can the craftsman say 'Good!' to himself '*as his due.*'" Rosenzweig, *The Star of Redemption*, trans. Hallo, 129–31. Emphasis added.

19 Truth and goodness (together with unity or union) are the so-called "transcendentals" of being that Aquinas (following but modifying Aristotle) identified as "convertible" with being. On the transcendentals, see Étienne Gilson, *The Elements of Christian Philosophy* (New York: Mentor, 1963), 149–78. Maurice Blondel captures the paradox of Excellence (B1) when he refers to the "principe de vérité [B1a] et de bonté [B1b]." *L'Être et les êtres* (Paris: Presses Universitaires de France, 1963), 290.

20 David Hume holds that loyalty or allegiance is "an original obligation and authority independent of all contracts." Hume, *A Treatise of Human Nature* 3.2.8, p. 542.

21 Dietrich von Hildebrand, *Fundamental Moral Attitudes*, trans. Alice M. Jourdain (New York: Longmans, Green, 1950), 16–25.

22 Hildebrand, 33–46.

23 "[L]e sujet du droit [law-*abiding*] est le même que le sujet digne de respect [respect*able*]." Paul Ricœur, *Le Juste 1*, in *Ricœur: Textes choisis et présentés*, ed. Michaël Fœssel and Fabien Lamouche (Paris: Éditions Points, 2007), 359. Ricœur argues that, whereas "respectable" goes with the deontological "morality" of law-abiding (B1a), admirable ("*estime*") belongs instead to the teleological "ethics" of the virtues of Goodness (B1b). Two names Ricœur sometimes uses for the two sides of the paradox of Excellence (B1) are "respect de soi" (B1a) and "estime de soi" (B1b). Together they define "l'homme comme sujet d'imputation éthico-juridique [B1]." Ricœur, 357–8; *Lectures 1*, in *Ricœur: Textes choisis et présentés*, 311–15. Like Hume, Ricœur notes the very close ties between the virtues of Goodness (B1b) and the virtues of Reverence (A2): "Estime de soi [B1b] et sollicitude [A2] ne peuvent se vivre et se penser l'une sans l'autre." Ricœur, 313.

24 Aquinas, *Summa Theologiæ* 1–2.66.5, in *Treatise on the Virtues*, trans. Oesterle, 157–8.

25 Aristotle, *The Nicomachean Ethics* 5.1.1130a5–15, trans. Thomson, rev. Tredennick, 115.

26 Aristotle, *The Nicomachean Ethics* 5.6.1134b5–10, p. 129.
27 Aristotle, *The Nicomachean Ethics* 5.5.1133b20–5, 5.10.1137b20–35, pp. 127, 140–1.
28 Étienne Gilson says beauty is a "forgotten transcendental" of being, which suggests it is properly located in the virtues of Excellence (B1), together with truth and goodness. *The Elements of Christian Philosophy*, 174–8.
29 Anthony T. Kronman, *Confessions of a Born-Again Pagan* (New Haven: Yale Univ. Press, 2016), 116. Kronman makes rich use of Melanie Klein's discussion of gratitude and generosity in "Envy and Gratitude," in *The Writings of Melanie Klein*, vol. 3, *Envy and Gratitude and Other Works, 1946–1963* (New York: Delacorte, 1975), 176–235, in Kronman, 49–59.
30 Charles Taylor, *A Secular Age* (Cambridge, MA: Belknap Press of Harvard Univ. Press, 2007), 702.
31 As you will see in chapter 14, "Transcendence" is the name Peterson and Seligman use for this family of virtues (A2a). They suggest it is the "most 'implicit'" of (what I call) the sub-sub-families of virtues. It "infuses" all of the great cultural traditions and is usually "taken for granted." Christopher Peterson and Martin E.P. Seligman, *Character Strengths and Virtues: A Handbook and Classification* (New York: Oxford Univ. Press, 2004), 50, 517–622.
32 "Knowledge of values, the understanding of them as values [B1], already presupposes a basically reverent attitude [A2]." Dietrich von Hildebrand, *Ethics* (Steubenville, OH: Hildebrand Press, 2020), 242.
33 George Eliot, *Scenes of Clerical Life* (London: Dent, 1976), 251.
34 Hildebrand calls this "category of importance" (A2a) the "objective good for the person" or *bonum mihi* (good for me), a third category distinct from the important-in-itself to which a value-response is "due" (B1) and from the "merely subjectively satisfying" (A1). He identifies gratitude, hope, and joy with it, correctly. Hildebrand, *Ethics*, 52–63, 223–4, 415–16.
35 Max Scheler distinguishes the virtues of Reverence[3] (A2a) from the virtues of Love (A2b) as follows: "In contrast to love [A2b], whose movement involves the immediate feeling of the (qualified) height of a value, 'reverence' [A2a] *presupposes* the feeling of a given value and an *assessment* of its object, which obviously is not the case with love." *Formalism in Ethics*, trans. Frings and Funk, 223n53. Emphasis in original. It is clearly the assessment which is crucial here, and it suggests how Reverence[3] (A2a) links Love (A2b) with the virtues of Truth (B1a) and Goodness (B1b) by "leaning" toward these virtues of Excellence (B1) – by anticipating their inner spirit to give "what is due."

36 Martha Nussbaum, *Upheavals of Thought: The Intelligence of the Emotions* (Cambridge: Cambridge Univ. Press, 2001), 54n53.
37 For an exploration of each of the seven "classical" virtues (as well as a few others), and many of their corresponding vices, see Kevin Timpe and Craig A. Boyd, eds., *Virtues and Their Vices* (Oxford: Oxford Univ. Press, 2014). See also Peterson and Seligman, *Character Strengths and Virtues*.
38 Thus, I could say, as Martin Heidegger says of *Being and Time*, "this phenomenological interpretation is not a cognition of existent *qualities* of beings, but rather a determination of the *structure* of their being." *Being and Time*, 67, trans. Stambaugh, 67. Emphasis added.
39 "[T]he cultures [i.e., stances and their families of virtues] are neighbors to one another, almost touch one another. They almost hold hands. … The cultures meld into one another." John W. O'Malley, *Four Cultures of the West* (Cambridge, MA: Harvard Univ. Press, 2004), 32.
40 "If one sees the moral domain through the prism of virtue, one will see it as a rich kaleidoscope, complex and multifaceted." Swanton, *Virtue Ethics*, 76.
41 Michael Bilig, Susan Condor, Derek Edwards, Mike Gane, David Middleton, and Alan Radley, *Ideological Dilemmas: A Social Psychology of Everyday Thinking* (London: Sage, 1988), 163.
42 Konrad Lorenz, *On Aggression* (New York: Bantam, 1966), quoted in Christopher Boehm, *Moral Origins: The Evolution of Virtue, Altruism, and Shame* (New York: Basic Books, 2012), 291.
43 Donald, *A Mind So Rare*, 92, 94.
44 Shahah Ahmed says Islam, too, is constituted by "the conceptual and practical production and accomodation of *internal contradiction*." *What Is Islam?*, 302. Emphasis in original. Paul Ricœur argues religious language describes human experience, and the ultimate reference for all religious parables, proverbs, and sayings is not so much the Kingdom of God as "la réalité humaine dans sa totalité." Ricœur, *L'Herméneutique biblique*, in *Ricœur: Textes choisis et présentés*, 207.
45 Both Alfred North Whitehead and Robert Nozick want to use this combination of diversity and unity (i.e., the union of union and non-union) as the source of "value" in the world. Whitehead, *Process and Reality*, 412; Nozick, *The Examined Life*, 164. But I think that's going too far. The overcoming of duality is not *in itself* a value, or source of value. The polarity of being is only an "affordance" that enables value to appear and structures it. You can't derive genuine value from things or facts, but only from the human *response* to the "affordance" of the polarity of being: i.e., from all the human virtues, and from the self-giving virtues of reverence, in particular – which is the human activity of acknowledging superior worth.

Chapter 10. Four Families of Virtues

1 Hegel expresses this same dynamic process in the following manner: "A living being is a syllogism, of which the very elements are in themselves systems and syllogisms. They are however active syllogisms or processes; and in the subjective unity of the vital agent make only one process." G.W.F. Hegel, *Encyclopaedia of the Philosophical Sciences*, §217, in *Hegel's Logic*, trans. William Wallace (London: Oxford Univ. Press, 1975), 280. Hegel also calls this same "syllogism of syllogisms" a "circle of circles," to express the dynamic progression I have called the "arrow of virtue." G.W.F. Hegel, *Science of Logic*, vol. 2, §3, chap. 3, trans. W.H. Johnston and L.G. Struthers (London: George Allen & Unwin, 1951), 2:484. Hegel uses the threefold image of the syllogism because for him the two sides of a paradox (or dialectic) are always united, in their unity. Life is the union of union and non-union. "Everything is a Syllogism." *Encyclopaedia*, trans. Wallace, §181, p. 244. So a paradox, properly conceived, is a *trinity*, not a duality. Reverence and self-assertion are not only a *duality*, but also, in the nature of the human, a *unity* – making, by their combination, a "triad" or a "triplicity." Hegel, §85, p. 123; Hegel, *Preface to the Phenomenology of Spirit*, trans. Yirmiyahu Yovel (Princeton: Princeton Univ. Press, 2005), 159–60. In fact, Hegel also points out that because the first term of a dialectic (or syllogism) must already contain an implicit negative – it must already be "internally differentiated" and "inherently defective and must be endowed with the impulse of self-development" – and can therefore be "counted as a duality," "the third term may be counted as fourth, and the abstract form of it may be counted as a *quadruplicity* in place of triplicity." Hegel, *Science of Logic*, vol. 2, §3, chap. 3, trans. Johnston and Struthers, 2:471–2, 478. Emphasis added.

2 John O'Malley, for example, identifies four "cultures" or "styles" of the West, three of which are primarily (but not exclusively) rooted in one or another of the four human stances and families of virtues, and one seems constituted by a mixture of sub-families of virtues. O'Malley himself recognizes that *his* four cultures are not *the* four cultures of the West. *Four Cultures of the West* (Cambridge, MA: Harvard Univ. Press, 2004), 5–6. It is striking that, for a work largely about the Christian culture of the West, O'Malley is completely silent about the virtues of Reverence (A2).

3 "Le 'merci' n'est pas un véritable remerciement *que s'il n'était pas dû.*" Michel Terestchenko, *Un si fragile vernis d'humanité: Banalité du mal, banalité du bien* (Paris: La Découverte, 2007), 58. Emphasis added. Terestchenko paraphrases Francis Hutcheson.

4 Thomas Aquinas, *Summa Theologiæ* 1.21.3, in *Theological Texts*, trans. Thomas Gilby (London: Oxford Univ. Press, 1955), 41.

5 Hegel calls these two diagonal axes of the human "life" and "cognition"; Karl Jaspers calls them *existenz* and reason. Hegel, *Encyclopaedia*, §236,

trans. Wallace, 292; Karl Jaspers, *Reason and Existenz*, trans. William Earle, in *Existentialism from Dostoevsky to Sartre*, ed. Walter Kaufmann (Cleveland: World, 1956), 197–8.

6 "[A] 'doctrine of virtues' … will be a natural history of [the human spirit]." G.W.F. Hegel, *Philosophy of Right*, trans. T.M. Knox (Oxford: Oxford Univ. Press, 1967), §150, p. 108. I have changed Knox's translation from "mind" to the "human spirit" because he consistently (mis)translates Hegel's term *"geist"* (spirit) as "mind."

7 Plato, *The Laws* 1.631, 12.963–4, trans. Trevor J. Saunders (Harmondsworth: Penguin Books, 1970), 55, 521–2. See also, *Symposium* 196C–198D, in *Great Dialogues of Plato*, trans. W.H.D. Rouse, ed. Eric H. Warmington and Philip G. Rouse (New York: New American Library, 1956), 92.

8 David Martin suggests Christianity's "primary virtues are faith, hope and love, and its supporting ancillary virtues patience, prudence, wisdom, humility, sincerity, judgement, mercy and care for the brethren." *On Secularization: Towards a Revised General Theory* (Farnham: Ashgate, 2005), 173.

9 Thomas Aquinas, *Summa Theologiæ* 1–2.61.2, in *Treatise on the Virtues*, trans. John A. Oesterle (Notre Dame, IN: Univ. of Notre Dame Press, 1984), 110–1. Aquinas explains that what constitutes a "family" of virtues is that all the virtues that can be grouped under or associated with it "strike the same note and reproduce the tone and measure for which it is mainly admired and from which it gets its name." Aquinas, *Summa Theologiæ* 2–2.157.3 (Cambridge: Cambridge Univ. Press, 2006), vol. 44 ("Well-Tempered Passion"), trans. Thomas Gilby, 43.

10 C.G. Jung, *Memories, Dreams, Reflections*, trans. Richard and Clara Winston, rev. ed. (New York: Pantheon Books, 1973), 348–9.

11 "Prudence is an active principle, and implies a sacrifice of self, *though only to the same self* projected, as it were, to a distance." Samuel Taylor Coleridge, *Aids to Reflection* (Port Washington, NY: Kennikat Press, 1971), 88. Emphasis added. Emmanuel Levinas points out that even courage can, in a sense, be considered a virtue of self-control: "Le courage n'est pas une attitude en face de l'autre, mais à l'égard de soi." *Liberté et commandement* (Paris: Le Livre de Poche, 2008), 45.

12 "[P]rudence keeps life safe, but does not often make it happy. The world is not amazed with prodigies of excellence but when wit tramples upon rules, and magnanimity breaks the chains of prudence." Samuel Johnson, *The Idler*, no. 57, Saturday, 19 May 1759, in *The Idler and The Adventurer*, ed. W.J. Bate, John M. Bullitt, and L.F. Powell (New Haven: Yale Univ. Press, 1963), Yale Edition of the Works of Samuel Johnson, 2:177–8.

13 Aquinas, *Summa Theologiæ* 1–2.61.2, in *Treatise on the Virtues*, trans. Oesterle, 110–1. On prudence, see W. Jay Wood, "Prudence," in *Virtues*

and Their Vices, ed. Kevin Timpe and Craig A. Boyd (Oxford: Oxford Univ. Press, 2014), 37–58.

14 Aristotle, *The Nicomachean Ethics* 5.6.1134b1–10, trans. J.A.K. Thomson, rev. Hugh Tredennick (London: Penguin Books, 2004), 129. "The duties prescribed by justice [B1] must be given precedence over everything else, including the pursuit of knowledge [B2], for such duties concern the welfare of other human beings, and nothing ought to be more sacred in our eyes than that." Cicero, *De officiis* [On Public Responsibility], quoted in O'Malley, *Four Cultures of the West*, 133.

15 Aquinas, *Summa Theologiæ* 1–2.64.2, 1–2.66.4, in *Treatise on the Virtues*, trans. Oesterle, 134, 155.

16 Aristotle, *The Nicomachean Ethics* 5.1.1129b25–1130a10, trans. Thomson, rev. Tredennick, 115.

17 "[D]istinguer de l'idée de justice, qui est première, fondamentale, morale, universelle, obligatoire, l'imagination grossière d'égalité qui n'est le plus souvent qu'une contrefaçon vile." Charles Péguy, *Bernard-Lazare*, in *Une éthique sans compromis*, ed. Dominique Saatdjian (Paris: Pocket, 2011), 336.

18 Aristotle, *The Nicomachean Ethics* 3.1131a10–b25, trans. Thomson, rev. Tredennick, 118–20; Aquinas, *Summa Theologiæ* 1–2.60.3, in *Treatise on the Virtues*, trans. Oesterle, 101.

19 Aquinas, *Summa Theologiæ* 2–2.57.1, vol. 37 ("Justice"), trans. Gilby, 5.

20 Aquinas, *Summa Theologiæ* 1–2.68.1, in *Treatise on the Virtues*, trans. Oesterle, 161. "The call [of conscience] comes *from* me, and yet *over* me." Martin Heidegger, *Being and Time*, 275, trans. Joan Stambaugh (Albany: State Univ. of New York Press, 2010), 265. Emphasis in original. Most premodern cultures were shaped by deep feelings of distinction and hierarchy, but also of fairness. However, what fairness meant in such premodern cultures was usually *giving people their due*, in accordance with their rank and clan. Caroline Humphrey, "Inequality," in *A Companion to Moral Anthropology*, ed. Didier Fassin (Malden, MA: Wiley-Blackwell), 302–19, cited in Webb Keane, *Ethical Life: Its Natural and Social Histories*, 254. "The idea of *social* hierarchy in terms of Truth is embedded in the idea of *cosmological* hierarchy in terms of Truth." Shahab Ahmed, *What Is Islam? The Importance of Being Islamic* (Princeton: Princeton Univ. Press, 2016), 376. First emphasis in original, second added.

21 Aquinas, *Summa Theologiæ* 1–2.54.3, 1–2.62.1, in *Treatise on the Virtues*, trans. Oesterle, 47, 119. Emphasis added. "[W]e become like the divinity by our own virtues even though the divinity posseses them not." Plotinus, *Enneads* 3.8.8, in *The Essential Plotinus*, ed. Elmer O'Brien (New York: Mentor Books, 1964), 111.

22 "[Le] souci d'autrui l'emportant sur le souci de soi. C'est cela que j'appelle 'sainteté.' Notre humanité consiste à reconnaître cette priorité de l'autre." Emmanuel Levinas, *Les Imprévus de l'histoire* (Paris: Le Livre de Poche, 2007), 179.

23 Ahmed, *What Is Islam?*, 469, 471–5, 481, 485, 502.

24 Ahmed, 478–85.

25 *Dīn* is central to Muslim thought and culture but isn't easy to translate. Sometimes it's translated narrowly as simply worship or worshipful, or sometimes more broadly as "religion." But it's also the "key for the ultimately successful living of a virtuous Muslim life," an essential quality for "rulership" and good government. Or even a "whole way of life … which permeates the whole fabric of society." Ahmed, 480, 488–9, 465, 187–8. Like reverence, *dīn* seems to be an expansive, "telescopic," or "scalable" concept that can signify the virtues of Reverence[3] (A2a), Reverence (A2), or reverence – or even, more broadly still, virtue itself: all four families of virtues. For my purposes, I tentatively conclude the most accurate identification is with the virtues of reverence as a whole. (The expansive or scalable quality of *dīn* shows why the similarly expansive term, reverence, was the right one for these cascading families of virtues.)

26 The identification of "life" with self-assertion is relatively straightforward. Even bodily acts of breathing and the pumping of the heart are forms of self-assertion. The identification of "welfare" with self-assertion is a little more tentative. But, in context, "welfare" is the "empirical test" of good government "in the context of the needs of the time and place." It is "welfare in the here and now." Ahmed, 470–1, 504. So "welfare" could signify the virtues of Equality (B2) or even of Rights (B2a). But I tentatively conclude the most appropriate linkage is with the virtues of self-assertion as a whole.

27 Some versions of the Seven Grandfathers substitute generosity (*migwe'aadiziwin*) for honesty, for example: "The Gifts of the Seven Grandfathers," Ojibwe.net, https://ojibwe.net/projects/prayers-teachings/the-gifts-of-the-seven-grandfathers/.

28 The English words used as equivalents for the Seven Grandfathers are imperfect translations. For example: the Anishinaabe word usually translated as "honesty" apparently can also mean "good character" or "righteousness," that is, to live correctly and with virtue. https://ojibwe.lib.umn.edu/main-entry/gwayakwaadiziwin-ni; https://idvc.ca/seven-grandfather-teachings/; https://en.wikipedia.org/wiki/Teachings_of_the_Seven_Grandfathers.

29 "Truth is to know all these Teachings [of the Seven Grandfathers]." David Bouchard and Joseph Martin, *Seven Sacred Teachings* (North Vancouver: More Than Words, 2009), 21, http://www.btgwinnipeg.ca

/uploads/5/2/4/1/52412159/the_seven_sacred_teachings_.pdf. See also
Tanya Talaga, *Seven Truths* (Toronto: Audible, 2020), https://www
.audible.ca/pd/Seven-Truths-Audiobook/B08N5JMLSY.

30　"[A] giving of ourselves to it instead of a consuming of it." Dietrich von
Hildebrand, *Ethics* (Steubenville, OH: Hildebrand Press, 2020), 225.

31　Aristotle, *The Nicomachean Ethics* 1.1.1095b25–1096a5, 4.3.1123a35–
4.4.1125b25, trans. Thomson, rev. Tredennick, 8–9, 93–100; Aquinas,
Summa Theologiæ 1–2.60.5, in *Treatise on the Virtues*, trans. Oesterle, 106.
In his otherwise insightful discussion of La Rochefoucauld, Michel
Terestchenko fails to distinguish between the self-assertive virtue of
"honour-seeking" (A1) and the more properly "aristocratic" virtue of
"honourable" (B1). *Un si fragile vernis d'humanité*, 36–7.

32　Heidegger, *Being and Time*, 145–8, trans. Stambaugh, 140–3.

33　Aristotle, *The Nicomachean Ethics* 7.3.1139b15–7.10.1143b20, trans. Thomson, rev. Tredennick, 147–60; Aquinas, *Summa Theologiæ* 1–2.57.2, 1–2.57.4,
1–2.65.1, in *Treatise on the Virtues*, trans. Oesterle, 69–71, 73–4, 139–42.

34　Whitehead expresses the difference between these two types of thinking –
associated with the stances of It *is* (B1) and *It* is (B2) – as a distinction
between "conceptual *valuation*" (B1) and "conceptual *analysis*" (B2). Alfred North Whitehead, *Process and Reality* (New York: Free Press, 1969),
289. As mentioned in chapter 4, Heidegger makes a similar distinction
between "undifferentiated," "heedful," or "attuned understanding"
(B1) (which first "discloses" a "totality of relevance" or a "totality of significance") and "thematic interpretation" or "theoretical propositional
statements" (B2) (by which the relevance can be "made explicit" or its
"conceptuality" can be "explicitly grasped"). Heidegger, *Being and Time*,
137–8, 150–8, 260, trans. Stambaugh, 133–4, 145–53, 249.

35　When Yuval Noah Harari suggests human happiness may depend on
"whether people know the truth about themselves," he implicitly adopts
a stance of "It is." But it could be the stance of "*It* is" (B2) or of "It *is*" (B1),
depending whether he means a scientific truth (B2) about human biology
or behaviour, or a truth of wisdom (B1) about the whole nature of the
human. *Sapiens: A Brief History of Humankind* (Toronto: Penguin Random
House, 2016), 396.

36　Aristotle, *The Nicomachean Ethics* 10.8.1178a10–25, trans. Thomson, rev.
Tredennick, 273; C.G. Jung, *Analytical Psychology: Its Theory and Practice*
(New York: Vintage Books, 1970), 12, 25–7, 31–2.

37　Charles Taylor, *A Secular Age* (Cambridge, MA: Belknap Press of Harvard
Univ. Press, 2007), 741.

38　Pascal, *Pensées*, §224, p. 92; Charles Péguy, *Notes pour une thèse*, in *Une
éthique sans compromis*, ed. Dominique Saatdjian (Paris: Pocket, 2011), 190.
On the "heart," see also Dietrich von Hildebrand, *The Heart: An Analysis*

of Human and Divine Affectivity (South Bend, IN: St. Augustine's Press, 2007).

39 Hope and optimism are explicitly conflated, for example, by "positive psychology," to be explored in chapter 14. See Christopher Peterson and Martin E.P. Seligman, *Character Strengths and Virtues: A Handbook and Classification* (New York: Oxford Univ. Press, 2004), 569–82.

40 "I've noticed that the more optimistic people are, the more petty and egotistical they tend to be. ... The more sorrow there is in a man, the less hope he has of survival – the better, the kinder, the more generous he becomes. ... I've realized now that hope almost never goes together with reason. It's something quite irrational and instinctive." Vasily Grossman, *Life and Fate*, trans. Robert Chandler (New York: New York Review Books, 2006), 87–8.

41 Paul Ricœur, *Esprit*, Special edition, July–August 1988, in *Ricœur: Textes choisis et présentés*, ed. Michaël Fœssel and Fabien Lamouche (Paris: Éditions Points, 2007), 282–3.

42 "All of these [four] dimensions of freedom subsist together and flow into each other. One or another dimension may assume ascendancy in a particular life, but together they describe the integral potentiality of each person's freedom." Roger Haight, *Spirituality Seeking Theology* (Maryknoll, NY: Orbis Books, 2014), 31–2.

43 Iris Murdoch, *Metaphysics as a Guide to Morals* (London: Vintage, 2003), 351, 355–60, 365–9, 379, 390, 483, 492–3; Max Scheler, *Formalism in Ethics and Non-Formal Ethics of Value*, trans. Manfred S. Frings and Roger L. Funk (Evanston: Northwestern Univ. Press, 1973), 64.

44 "Beauty [B1b], truth [B1a], pleasure [A1b], and sensation [A1] are all things that are good. ... [E]ach possesses a character of its own; and in order to be good, the other aspects of the universe must also be themselves." F.H. Bradley, *Appearance and Reality* (Oxford: Oxford Univ. Press, 1930), 362–3.

45 Murdoch, *Metaphysics as a Guide to Morals*, 367.

46 Julia Annas' notion of virtuous activity "'flowing' effortlessly from the person's overall harmoniously arranged goals" is contradicted not only by Murdoch's and Scheler's visions of the virtues as irreducible, contending "axioms," and by the human paradox described in this book, but also (as Annas herself admits) by "the normal course of our lives." *Intelligent Virtue* (Oxford: Oxford Univ. Press, 2013), 76, 79.

47 C.G Jung, Martin Buber, and Paul Ricœur agree the two sides of the human paradox cannot ultimately be reconciled in the mind or in thought but only by being *lived*, in a real human life. C.G. Jung, *Psychological Types*, trans. H. Godwin Baynes (London: Routledge, 1964), 64–8; Martin Buber, *I and Thou*, trans. Ronald Gregor Smith, 2nd ed. (New York:

Charles Scribner's Sons, 1958), 95–6; Paul Ricœur, *Amour et justice* (Paris: Éditions Points, 2008), 42. Even Hegel, despite his own confidence in the power of thought, noted: "It is said that contradiction cannot even be thought: but in the pain of the Living Entity it is even an actual existence." Hegel, *Science of Logic*, vol. 2, §3, chap. 1, trans. Johnston and Struthers, 2:411.

48 "The natural man, whose motions follow the rule of his appetites, is not his own master. ... [H]is freedom is merely formal." Hegel, *Encyclopaedia*, trans. Wallace, §24, p. 39.

49 G.W.F. Hegel, *The Phenomenology of Mind*, trans. J.B. Baillie (New York: Harper & Row, 1967), 543.

50 Karl Jaspers, *Way to Wisdom*, trans. Ralph Manheim (New Haven: Yale Univ. Press, 1960), 113. See also John of the Cross on the same theme, in Denys Turner, *The Darkness of God: Negativity in Christian Mysticism* (Cambridge: Cambridge Univ. Press, 1995), 237–8.

51 Hegel, *The Phenomenology of Mind*, trans. Baillie, 607–10; *Philosophy of Right*, trans. Knox, §§5, 135, pp. 21–2, 89–90.

52 Murdoch, *Metaphysics as a Guide to Morals*, 507.

53 "[L]e mal est contraire à soi-même ... il s'embarrasse et se détruit par sa propre malice." Blaise Pascal, *Lettres provinciales* (Paris: Garnier-Flammarion, 1967), 231.

54 Iris Murdoch, *The Sovereignty of Good* (London: Routledge, 1980), 65.

55 Turner, *The Darkness of God*, chap. 7, 168–85. Emphasis added.

56 Murdoch, *Metaphysics as a Guide to Morals*, 373.

57 Murdoch, *The Sovereignty of Good*, 66–7.

58 Coleridge, *Aids to Reflection*, 223. The Sufi Muslim tradition calls the ultimately unresolvable – and therefore inexpressible – conflict of goods and virtues *hayrat* or "perplexity." Ahmed, *What Is Islam?*, 278. On the theme of contradiction and the limits of human thought, see Graham Priest, *Beyond the Limits of Thought* (Oxford: Oxford Univ. Press, 2006).

59 Aristotle, *The Nicomachean Ethics* 2.7.1107a30–2.9.1109a25, trans. Thomson, rev. Tredennick, 43–9; Confucius, *The Doctrine of the Mean*, in *Confucian Analects, The Great Learning & The Doctrine of the Mean*, trans. James Legge (New York: Dover, 1971), 382–434.

60 "As soon as we come to moral values [B1], this principle [of the mean] no longer applies." Hildebrand, *Ethics*, 397.

61 Robert Merrihew Adams, *A Theory of Virtue: Excellence in Being for the Good* (Oxford: Oxford Univ. Press, 2013), 190.

62 Thomas Aquinas suggests we cannot really go too far in virtues like these but only in their "exterior expression," which should always be marked by "discretion" and by "loving kindness." Aquinas, "Commentary," *Romans, xii, lect. 1*, in *Theological Texts*, trans. Gilby, 183.

63 Bernard Williams agrees that a virtue of Excellence (B1) such as justice is not subject to a "mean" and Paul Bloomfield agrees wisdom isn't subject to it either. Bernard Williams, "Justice as a virtue," in *Essays on Aristotle's Ethics*, ed. Amélie O. Rorty (Berkeley: Univ. of California Press, 1980), 189–200, cited in Paul Bloomfield, *The Virtues of Happiness: A Theory of the Good Life* (New York: Oxford Univ. Press, 2014), 185.

64 Aquinas, *Summa Theologiæ* 1–2.64.4, in *Theological Texts*, trans. Gilby, 182.

65 In the virtues of Reverence (A2), such as hope and love, "eternity has already come – even in the midst of time." These virtues are "the unearthly in earthly life." Franz Rosenzweig, *The Star of Redemption*, trans. William W. Hallo (Notre Dame, IN: Univ. of Notre Dame Press, 1985), 332, 326, 204. Maurice Blondel says the virtues "incarnent l'universel et l'infini dans nos existences singularisées." *L'Être et les êtres* (Paris: Presses Universitaires de France, 1963), 294–5.

66 "[T]he categories emerge ... in a manner identical with the actual process they categorize. ... [T]he individual point ... reveals to us the whole course of the orbit." Rosenzweig, *The Star of Redemption*, trans. Hallo, 150–1.

67 "Du haut, on voit le bas, du bas on ne voit vraiment pas le haut." Maurice Blondel, *Itinéraire philosophique*, 24, in Jean Lacroix, *Maurice Blondel, sa vie, son œuvre* (Paris: Presses Universitaires de France, 1963), 135.

68 As Max Scheler puts it: once a "new" value or virtue has been discovered (or rediscovered), and "become visible" – through the work of a specific, historical culture – it "remains in existence." *Formalism in Ethics*, trans. Frings and Funk, 494. Similarly, Goethe says that the Christian ethic of reverence for "that which is below us" (A2) "having once made its appearance, can never vanish again." Johann Wolfgang von Goethe, *Wilhelm Meister's Journeyman Years or The Renunciants*, trans. Krishna Winston, in *Goethe: The Collected Works*, ed. Jane K. Brown (Princeton: Princeton Univ. Press, 1995), 10:205.

69 What Christine Swanton calls a "pluralistic" view of virtue ethics may be accounted for by the four families of virtues (and their sub-families) and by what I call "double vision." *Virtue Ethics: A Pluralistic View* (Oxford: Oxford Univ. Press, 2003), 21–30, 42–9, 53, 93, 99. The same thing could perhaps be said about the virtue categories Robert Adams calls the "structural" virtues, especially courage (A1), and the "motivational" virtues, especially benevolence (A2). R.M. Adams, *A Theory of Virtue*, 33–4, 133, 171–99.

70 "[L]'homme pourra entrer plus avant dans les profondeurs de sa nature, sans mutiler ni défigurer celle-ci." Jacques Maritain, *Humanisme intégral*, new ed. (Paris: Éditions Aubier-Montaigne, 1946), 97.

71 John O'Malley notes that each of his "four cultures of the West" (or what I call stances and families or sub-families of virtues) is a "paradox":

"Each has two aspects or manifestations, which can seem to be in opposition to each other." O'Malley, *Four Cultures of the West*, 26.

72 C.G. Jung, *Analytical Psychology: Its Theory and Practice* (New York: Vintage Books, 1970), 42.

73 Phil Lane Jr., Judie Bopp, Michael Bopp, Lee Brown, and elders, *The Sacred Tree: Reflections on Native American Spirituality*, 4th ed. (Twin Lakes, WI: Lotus Press, 2012). Commenting on the medicine wheel, Robin Wall Kimmerer sums up the whole argument of this book: "[A]t the intersection of these four directions, is right where we stand as humans, trying to find balance among them." *Braiding Sweetgrass: Indigenous Wisdom, Scientific Knowledge, and the Teachings of Plants* (Minneapolis: Milkweed Editions, 2013), 151.

74 Ali Smith, *How to Be Both* (Toronto: Penguin Books, 2015), 304.

75 "[L]e 'à faire' de la valeur et le 'qu'il soit' de l'existence d'autrui sont strictement réciproques." Ricœur, *Histoire et vérité* (Paris: Points Essais, 2001), 399.

76 What, in this book, I'm calling the whole nature of the human, Iris Murdoch calls "the whole of excellence … the full extent of what virtue is like." *The Sovereignty of Good*, 102–3.

Chapter 11. Society

1 "[J]e ne peux saisir l'acte d'exister ailleurs que dans les signes épars dans le monde. C'est pourquoi une philosophie réflexive doit inclure les résultats des méthodes et de présuppositions de toutes les sciences qui tentent de déchiffrer et d'interpréter les signes de l'homme." Paul Ricœur, *Le conflit des interprétations: Essais d'herméneutique* (Paris: Éditions du Seuil, 2013), 441.

2 "In the final, the positive state, the mind has given over the vain search after Absolute notions, the origin and destination of the universe and the causes of phenomena, and applies itself to the study of their laws … [T]he ultimate perfection of the Positive system would be (if such perfection could be hoped for) to represent all phenomena as particular aspects of a single general fact; – such as Gravitation, for instance." Auguste Comte, *The Positive Philosophy of Auguste Comte*, trans. Harriet Martineau (London: Trübner, 1875), 1:1–17, in *Nineteenth-Century Philosophy*, ed. Patrick L. Gardner (New York: Free Press, 1969), 134.

3 "Sociology itself emerged as part of the process of secularization because it represented the autonomous study of Man in Society." David Martin, *On Secularization: Towards a Revised General Theory* (Farnham: Ashgate, 2005), 18.

4 John Stuart Mill, *A System of Logic, Ratiocinative and Inductive*, cited in Stefan Collini, Donald Winch, and John Burrow, *That Noble Science of Politics* (Cambridge: Cambridge Univ. Press, 1983), 127.

5   Alan Page Fiske, *Structures of Social Life: The Four Elementary Forms of Human Relations* (New York: Free Press, 1991), 185, 195.

6   Comte identifies ten "affective forces," of which seven correspond to egoism and three to altruism. Michel Bourdeau, "Auguste Comte," trans. Mark van Atten, Stanford Encyclopedia of Philosophy, published 1 October 2008, updated 16 October 2014, https://plato.stanford.edu/entries/comte.

7   "The first leaves my autonomy and personality almost intact. ... When I act under the influence of the second, by contrast, I am simply a part of a whole, whose actions I follow, and whose influence I am subject to." Émile Durkheim, "Review of Guyau's *L'irreligion de l'avenir*," trans. A Giddens, in *Emile Durkheim: Selected Writings*, ed. A. Giddens (New York: Cambridge Univ. Press, 1992), 219–20, cited in Jonathan Haidt, *The Righteous Mind: Why Good People Are Divided by Politics and Religion* (New York: Pantheon Books, 2012), 225–6.

8   Fiske, *Structures of Social Life*, 28, 66–7, 84, 90, 414n7.

9   Georg Simmel, *Die Religion*, in *Essays on Religion* (New Haven: Yale Univ. Press, 1997), 170, 186, quoted in Hans Joas, *The Genesis of Values*, trans. Gregory Moore (Cambridge: Polity Press, 2000), 73.

10   Fiske, *Structures of Social Life*, 38, 391.

11   Fiske, 36–7, 85, 91, 95–6, 103, 374.

12   As far as reverence is concerned, for example, George H. Mead (sometimes called the "father" of "symbolic interactionism" in sociology and social psychology) described this side of the nature of the human as a "religious attitude of kindness, helpfulness, universal neighborliness, and sympathetic assistance to those in distress," in which there is a complete "fusion of the 'me' [of social relationships] with the 'I'" of self-assertion. George H. Mead, *Mind, Self and Society from the Standpoint of a Social Behaviourist*, ed. Charles W. Morris (Chicago: Univ. of Chicago Press, 1934), 274, cited in Fiske, *Structures of Social Life*, 85.

13   Fiske, *Structures of Social Life*, 26–7.

14   Fiske, 96.

15   Fiske. See also Nick Haslam, ed., *Relational Models Theory: A Contemporary Overview* (Mahwah, NJ: Lawrence Erlbaum Associates, 2004).

16   I prefer to use Fiske's original descriptions of the four "models" rather than his updated versions (in, for example, "Relational Models Theory 2.0," in *Relational Models Theory*, ed. Haslam, 3–25). One of the attractions of the original formulation was the simplicity of language employed.

17   Fiske, *Structures of Social Life*, 13–14.

18   Fiske, 14.

19   Fiske, 14–15.

20   Fiske, 15.

21 Fiske, 23–4.

22 Alan Page Fiske, "Four Modes of Constituting Relationships: Consubstantial Assimilation; Space, Magnitude, Time, and Force; Concrete Procedures; Abstract Symbolism," in *Relational Models Theory*, ed. Haslam, 61–146.

23 Fiske, *Structures of Social Life*, 25. More recently Fiske seems to have discovered some other models which "cross-cut or intersect" with the original four and with each other, and also some "meta-relational" models that "shape how people construct, evaluate, motivate and cognize combinations of relationships." But the original four are still claimed to be the only ones "that structure social coordination in all domains of human activity." Fiske, "Relational Models Theory 2.0," 12.

24 Fiske, *Structures of Social Life*, 52, 87, 226, 211, 88. See also "Relational Models Theory 2.0," and "Four Modes of Constituting Relationships: Consubstantial Assimilation; Space, Magnitude, Time, and Force; Concrete Procedures; Abstract Symbolism," in *Relational Models Theory*, ed. Haslam, 4, 82, 125.

25 Fiske, *Structures of Social Life*, 388–91.

26 José Casanova, *Public Religions in the Modern World* (Chicago: Univ. of Chicago Press, 1994), 4. On the tendency of cultures to "fence" in the "potentially universal morality by defining its areas and conditions of application," thereby "excluding people of different nationalities, ethnic groups, races or religions, of another sex or age, or of other mentalities and moralities," see Joas, *The Genesis of Values*, trans. Moore, 174.

27 Hegel had already described how self-assertion produces the exclusionary dimension of family, community, or national life: "For the community, the whole, is a nation, it is itself *individuality* [A1], and really only is something for itself by other individualities being for *it*, by *excluding* them from itself and knowing itself independent." G.W.F. Hegel, *The Phenomenology of Mind*, trans. J.B. Baillie (New York: Harper & Row, 1967), 497. Emphasis added.

28 C.G. Jung uses the expression "taken in tow" to describe a case like this, where one psychological function is hijacked by, or subordinated to, another. *Psychological Types*, trans. H. Godwin Baynes (London: Routledge, 1964), 445.

29 Fiske, *Structures of Social Life*, 402, 211, 103–6, 89, 117.

30 Fiske, "Relational Models Theory 2.0," 7–8.

31 Shakespeare enumerates the "kingly" virtues as "justice [B1a], verity [B1a], temperance [B2b], stableness [B2?], bounty [A2b], perseverance [A1a], mercy [A2b], lowliness [A2a], devotion [A2a], patience [A2b], courage [A1a], fortitude [A1a]." None of these are virtues of dominance, and most of them are virtues of service or reverence. William

Shakespeare, *Macbeth*, in *The Complete Works*, ed. Alfred Harbage (Baltimore: Penguin Books, 1969), 4.3.91–4.

32 Nick Haslam, "Research on the Relational Models: An Overview," in *Relational Models Theory*, ed. Haslam, 38. This natural human "eagerness" to give reverence where reverence is *due* is the reverse or positive side of the *libido dominandi* described by David Hume and Adam Smith. Stephen Holmes, *Passions and Constraints: On the Theory of Liberal Democracy* (Chicago: Univ. of Chicago Press, 1995), 55. On the "natural human disposition" for "obedient service" and "inner reverence" for authority, see also Hegel, *The Phenomenology of Mind*, trans. Baillie, 525–7; David Hume, *A Treatise of Human Nature* 3.2.10, ed. L.A. Selby-Bigge (London: Oxford Univ. Press, 1968), 555; Friedrich Nietzsche, *Beyond Good and Evil*, trans. R.J. Hollingdale (London: Penguin Books, 2003), §263, pp. 202–3. See also the following note.

33 Robert N. Bellah, *Religion in Human Evolution: From the Paleolithic to the Axial Age* (Cambridge, MA: Belknap Press of Harvard Univ. Press, 2011), 178. With the insight of his genius, Tolstoy gives a precise analysis of the world of difference between "hierarchy" and "dominance" in his description of three characters on the eve of the battle of Austerlitz. As if to drive home the distinction (and the dialectical relationship) between "hierarchy" and "dominance," the sentiments of the three are interleaved, like layers in a cake, or the contrasting harmonies of counterpoint, in succeeding chapters of Volume 1, Part 3. Rostov's reverent feelings of "self-forgetfulness" and "self-denial" are described in chapters 8, 10, and 13. Drubetskoy's and Bolkonsky's self-assertive disposition to dominate is described in chapters 9 and 12. Later, in Volume 3, on the eve of the battle of Borodino, Tolstoy draws another similar contrast between Drubetskoy's self-assertive careerism (A1) and Pierre Bezukhov's unselfing readiness to "sacrifice everything" (the virtues of Reverence [A2]). Leo Tolstoy, *War and Peace*, trans. Richard Pevear and Larissa Volokhonsky (New York: Vintage Classics, 2008), vol. 1, pt. 3, chaps. 8–10, 12–13, pp. 245–56, 264–5; vol. 3, pt. 1, chap. 23, p. 681; pt. 2, chaps. 18 and 22, pp. 752–3, 765–6.

34 "Authority [B1] differs from mere power [A1] or force in that a person can possess authority only over one who knows by evidence that this person possesses a deeper and wider moral insight than he does. Moral 'trust' in an authority is based on this insight, and authority is based on this trust [i.e., reverence]. If this trust is removed, authority becomes non-moral power [A1] and force." Max Scheler, *Formalism in Ethics and Non-Formal Ethics of Value*, trans. Manfred S. Frings and Roger L. Funk (Evanston: Northwestern Univ. Press, 1973), 328.

35 The confusion between reverence and rank is very common in Western political thought. See, for example, Robert Nisbet, *Conservatism: Dream and Reality* (New Brunswick, NJ: Transaction, 2008), 64.

36 Fiske, *Structures of Social Life*, 218; "Relational Models Theory 2.0," 3, 6.

37 Fiske, *Structures of Social Life*, 133.

38 Fiske, 19–20, 30, 34, 38, 79, 91–2, 94, 99, 106, 133, 144, 182, 370, 398–400, 431; "Relational Models Theory 2.0," 11.

39 Fiske, *Structures of Social Life*, 30, 38, 91, 94.

40 Henry A. Murray, *Explorations in Personality* (Oxford: Oxford Univ. Press, 1938), quoted in Fiske, 106. Murray's classic definition of achievement motivation uncannily echoes Aquinas' definition of virtue in general and of the virtues of the "irascible appetite" (or what I have called the virtues of Power [A1a]) in particular. On the "irascible" appetite and virtues, see chapter 8, notes 24 and 29 above.

41 Fiske, *Structures of Social Life*, 94, 106–110, 7, 118–19, 134, 174.

42 Fiske, 396–8, 18–20; Fiske, "Relational Models Theory 2.0," 3, 6.

43 Fiske, *Structures of Social Life*, 398.

44 Fiske, "Relational Models Theory 2.0," 20–1.

45 Fiske, *Structures of Social Life*, 398, 111.

46 Fiske, 387.

47 Fiske, "Relational Models Theory 2.0," 38, 44; Nick Haslam and Alan Page Fiske, "Social Expertise: Theory of Mind or Theory of Relationships?" in *Relational Models Theory*, ed. Haslam, 148–9, 153.

48 Fiske, "Relational Models Theory 2.0,", 15.

49 Fiske, *Structures of Social Life*, 25, 205–6, 183, 391–2, 119.

50 Fiske, "Relational Models Theory 2.0," 15.

51 Fiske, *Structures of Social Life*, 163, 185–6, 194, 199, 210, 224, 228, 400–7. Merlin Donald agrees, up to a point. *A Mind So Rare: The Evolution of Human Consciousness* (New York: W.W. Norton, 2001), 208, 266. The relationship between Donald's four stages of human culture and the four families of virtues is discussed in chapter 15.

52 Thomas Aquinas, *Summa Theologiæ* 1–2.58.1, 1–2.58.2, 1–2.66.3, in *Treatise on the Virtues*, trans. John A. Oesterle (Notre Dame, IN: Univ. of Notre Dame Press, 1984), 81, 83, 153.

53 It is therefore astounding that Rosalind Hursthouse declares the "irrelevance to ethical naturalism of the human ethological fact that human beings (male human beings?) are characteristically aggressive." *On Virtue Ethics* (Oxford: Oxford Univ. Press, 2010), 222. On the contrary, this is the starting point and foundation of the nature of the human and of all virtue.

54 Johan Huizinga, *Homo Ludens: A Study of the Play Element in Culture* (Kettering, OH: Angelico Press, 2016); Bellah, *Religion in Human Evolution*, 89–97,

569–90; R.G. Collingwood, *Speculum Mentis or the Map of Knowledge* (Oxford: Oxford Univ. Press, 1963), 102–7; Jung, *Psychological Types*, trans. Baynes, 82.

55 H. and H.A. Frankfort, "Introduction: Myth and Reality," in Henri Frankfort, H.A. Frankfort, John A. Wilson, and Thorkild Jacobsen, *Before Philosophy: The Intellectual Adventure of Ancient Man* (Harmondsworth: Penguin Books, 1949), 19.

56 Shahab Ahmed points out, for example, that "questions about the meaning and constitution of Self have been central to the discourses of Muslims from very early in history." Shahab Ahmed, *What Is Islam? The Importance of Being Islamic* (Princeton: Princeton Univ. Press, 2016), 329–31. The same could be said about the whole Christian tradition. See, for example, Larry Siedentop, *Inventing the Individual: The Origins of Western Liberalism* (London: Allen Lane, 2014).

57 On the gradual emergence of "the principle of freedom of property" from the "universal principle" of "freedom of personality" embedded in Christianity, see G.W.F. Hegel, *Philosophy of Right*, trans. T.M. Knox (Oxford: Oxford Univ. Press, 1967), §62, p. 51.

58 Modern Western capitalism "constitutes a sharp departure from most of human history and most human cultures." Brad S. Gregory, *The Unintended Reformation: How a Religious Revolution Revolutionized Society* (Cambridge, MA: Belknap Press of Harvard Univ. Press, 2012), 483n27, referencing Joyce Appleby, *The Relentless Revolution: A History of Capitalism* (New York: W.W. Norton, 2010). Webb Keane notes that, in premodern cultures, where the virtues of self-assertion are rarely dominant, "[t]he ethics of interaction overwhelm the dictates of profit-seeking." *Ethical Life: Its Natural and Social Histories* (Princeton: Princeton Univ. Press, 2016), 115.

59 On "the pursuits of commerce" as virtues of self-assertion, see Samuel Taylor Coleridge, *The Friend*, ed. Barbara E. Rooke (London: Routledge, 1969), 1:508; Martin Heidegger, "Bremen Lectures: Insight into That Which Is," in *The Heidegger Reader*, ed. Günter Figal, trans. Jerome Veith (Bloomington: Indiana Univ. Press, 2009), 271; *An Introduction to Metaphysics*, trans. Ralph Manheim (New York: Doubleday, 1961), 149.

60 Michael J. Sandel, *What Money Can't Buy: The Moral Limits of Markets* (New York: Farrar, Straus & Giroux, 2012), 103.

61 Fiske, *Structures of Social Life*, 92, 199, 122, 400–1, 405. Colin Talbot appears to make this same error in his admirable book, *The Paradoxical Primate* (Exeter: Imprint Academic, 2005), 58–9.

62 Fiske, 160, 199.

63 Fiske, 128, 186.

64 Webb Keane notes that research on child development "seems to push against any strong form of innateness or neurophysiological determinism …

That is, we should not draw from this evidence a conclusion that humans, as individual self-contained biological organisms, are genetically predisposed to ethics or morality." *Ethical Life*, 71.

65 Fiske, "Relational Models Theory 2.0," 13–15. Reference to natural selection was not entirely absent from the first version of the theory. *Structures of Social Life*, 199.

66 Fiske, *Structures of Social Life*, 81, 86, 126, 129, 195, 382.

67 Haslam, *Relational Models Theory*, 13–15, 48, 62, 67, 90, 92, 94, 101, 103, 109, 122, 153.

68 Fiske, "Relational Models Theory 2.0," 14.

69 Aquinas, *Summa Theologiæ* 1–2.49.2, in *Treatise on the Virtues*, trans. Oesterle, 6.

70 Fiske, *Structures of Social Life*, 167.

71 Fiske, 199.

72 "[L]es conflits internes du social, pour être surmontés, devraient être eux-mêmes compris et pénétrés *en esprit*." Jacques Maritain, *Humanisme intégral*, new ed. (Paris: Éditions Aubier-Montaigne, 1946), 294. Emphasis in original.

Chapter 12. Politics

1 As José Casanova puts it, "liberal categories of thought ... permeate not only political ideologies and constitutional theories but the entire structure of modern thought." *Public Religions in the Modern World* (Chicago: Univ. of Chicago Press, 1994), 215. Yuval Noah Harari calls liberalism "the dominant religion of our age." *Sapiens: A Brief History of Humankind* (Toronto: Penguin Random House, 2016), 392.

2 This chapter could be described as an exercise in what Roger Crisp and Michael Slote call "virtue politics," in distinction from "virtue ethics." "Introduction," in *Virtue Ethics*, ed. Roger Crisp and Michael Slote (Oxford: Oxford Univ. Press, 1997), 25. On the virtues and one strand of political thought, see Christie Hartley and Lori Watson, "Virtue in Political Thought: On Civic Virtue in Political Liberalism," in *Virtues and Their Vices*, ed. Kevin Timpe and Craig A. Boyd (Oxford: Oxford Univ. Press, 2014), 415–32.

3 Paul Ricœur, *Histoire et vérité* (Paris: Points Essais, 2001), 269; David Martin, *On Secularization: Towards a Revised General Theory* (Farnham: Ashgate, 2005), 185.

4 Stephen Holmes points out that the defence (or even advocacy) of "self-interest" in classical liberal theory was motivated, in part, by the assumption that a focus on private self-interest could help to damp down the destructive human impulses vividly on display in (among other

places) Europe's wars of religion. *Passions and Constraints: On the Theory of Liberal Democracy* (Chicago: Univ. of Chicago Press, 1995), 4, 42–68. In other words, self-assertion (B2) was called upon, once again, to "bridle" self-assertion (A1).

5 David Hume emphasizes the role of politicians in the moral education of the democratic citizenry: their role in fostering "an esteem for justice and an abhorrence of injustice." *A Treatise of Human Nature* 3.2.2, 6, ed. L.A. Selby-Bigge (London: Oxford Univ. Press, 1968), 500–1, 533–4.

6 "Power and authority seek each other. Their search is the process of politics." Roger Scruton, *The Meaning of Conservatism*, 3rd rev. ed. (South Bend, IN: St. Augustine's Press, 2002), 148.

7 Paul Ricœur identifies this same paradox of politics ("le paradoxe politique"), and describes it as a distinction between "*le* politique" and "*la* politique." *Histoire et vérité*, 295–6, 303. Emphasis added.

8 Jacques Maritain calls the political struggle "la plus connaturelle au monde des formes d'activité." *Humanisme intégral*, new ed. (Paris: Aubier, Éditions Montaigne, 1946), 290.

9 "If democracy has an advantage over authoritarianism, it is that the struggles of interest, power, and ego that are the unavoidable stuff of human life take place in the open. The attempt to suppress them runs the risk that they will break out sooner or later, and that kind of upheaval can be hugely destructive." Andrew J. Nathan, "China: The Struggle at the Top," *New York Review of Books* 64, no. 2 (9 February 2017), 36.

10 Quoted in Yuen Yuen Ang, "Autocracy with Chinese Characteristics: Beijing's Behind-the-Scenes Reforms," *Foreign Affairs* 97, no. 3 (May/June 2018), 40.

11 "The key liberal idea has ... been self-mastery: a good society, from a liberal perspective, is one in which people get to decide the kinds of lives they want to lead." Alan Wolfe, *The Future of Liberalism* (New York: Vintage Books, 2010), 246. Wolfe's use of the term "self-mastery" is misleading here. As the second clause shows, what he means is self-*assertion*, or mastery *by* or *for* the self, not mastery *of* the self, a virtue of reverence.

12 Edmund Fawcett disagrees. He argues instead that liberalism has four pillars: conflict, resistance to power, progress, and respect. But Fawcett himself acknowledges that "protection from arbitrary, undue power is what people, immemorially, had spoken of in banner terms as liberty. Such protection for everyone was what, immemorially, they had spoken of as equality." *Liberalism: The Life of an Idea* (Princeton: Princeton Univ. Press, 2014), 10–16.

13 Adam Gopnik, *A Thousand Small Sanities: The Moral Adventure of Liberalism* (New York: Basic Books, 2019), 25.

14 Leo Strauss, *Liberalism: Ancient and Modern* (New York: Basic Books, 1968), 8. Even the third meaning of "liberal" – generous or open-handed, as in the Aristotelian virtue of "liberality" – can be traced to the same root meaning of freedom: "the most common opportunities for showing whether one has the character of a free man or of a slave are afforded by one's dealings with one's possessions." Strauss, 28.

15 John W. O'Malley, *Four Cultures of the West* (Cambridge, MA: Harvard Univ. Press, 2004), 155.

16 Northrop Frye, *By Liberal Things* (Toronto: Clarke Irwin, 1959), 18.

17 John Locke, *The Second Treatise on Civil Government*, chap. 2, in *On Politics and Education* (Roslyn, NY: Walter J. Black, 1947), 76–7. Locke was only following the views already put forward by Thomas Hobbes, who, though certainly no liberal, inadvertently established the intellectual premises on which liberalism would be built. But Hobbes (like the later American Declaration of Independence) actually puts equality *before* liberty: it is the natural equality of men, he argues, that, in the absence of "civil states" leads to a "war of every man against every man," and therefore to a natural right of liberty. *Leviathan* (Indianapolis: Bobbs-Merrill, 1958), pt. 1, chaps. 13 and 14, pp. 104–9.

18 "The point of the liberal act is to expand freedom while also expanding equality." Gopnik, *A Thousand Small Sanities*, 78.

19 Paul Ricœur calls this human disposition "l'ambition de dominer sur la nature et sur les autres hommes." *Le conflit des interprétations: Essais d'herméneutique* (Paris: Éditions du Seuil, 2013), 262. Shakespeare expresses the human disposition to dominate when the future Richard III confesses "this earth affords no joy to me but to command, to check, to o'erbear." *Henry VI, Part 3*, in *The Complete Works*, ed. Alfred Harbage (Baltimore: Penguin Books, 1969), 3.2.165–6.

20 As Paul Ricœur puts it, "effort et résistance form[e]nt une unité indivisible ... exister, c'est résister." *Soi-même comme un autre* (Paris: Éditions du Seuil, 1990), 372. "[T]he history of liberalism is the history of a concern to protect individual liberty against a succession of threats. ... [I]f what I do flows from what I choose to do rather than what someone else dictates, I am to that extent free. ... A man is free when he is master of his actions; he is master of his actions if nobody else is master of his actions." Alan Ryan, *The Making of Modern Liberalism* (Princeton: Princeton Univ. Press, 2012), 9–11.

21 Thomas Hobbes' "second law of nature" is that, when a state of peace is possible, a man should lay down his "right to all things, and be contented with so much liberty against other men as he would allow other men against himself." *Leviathan* (Indianapolis: Bobbs-Merrill, 1958), pt. 1, chap. 14, p. 110.

22 "[S]elf-interest is an intrinsically egalitarian and universalist principle. All human beings have interests, and, from a political point of view, their interests are of equal worth." Holmes, *Passions and Constraints*, xii.

23 On liberty and equality as the core "substantive commitments" of liberalism, see Wolfe, *The Future of Liberalism*, 10–15. Wolfe makes a case for two other liberal dispositions: a temperamental liberalism of openness and generosity, and a procedural liberalism which values due process. But these two look more like virtues of reverence, seen from a liberal perspective. They confirm humans cannot help viewing the full nature of the human through the lens of their own stance, by what I have called "double vision." Stephen Holmes acknowledges liberals advocate "the priority of liberty" but interprets it to mean "psychological security and personal independence for all, legal impartiality within a single system of laws applied equally to all, the human diversity fostered by liberty, and collective self-rule through elected government and uncensored discussion." Holmes, *Passions and Constraints*, 13, 16.

24 John Rawls, *A Theory of Justice* (Cambridge, MA: Belknap Press of Harvard Univ. Press, 1971), 17–22, 118–92. This is remarkably like Thomas Hobbes' second law of nature mentioned in note 21 above.

25 Rawls, 60–5, 150–61.

26 Rawls, 61.

27 Rawls, 75.

28 Rawls, 101.

29 Rawls, 101–2.

30 Michael J. Sandel, *Justice: What's the Right Thing to Do?* (New York: Farrar, Strauss & Giroux, 2009), 224.

31 Sandel. Emphasis added.

32 G.W.F. Hegel, *Philosophy of Right*, trans. T.M. Knox (Oxford: Oxford Univ. Press, 1967), Third Part, §§142–360, translator's note 142, pp. 105–223, 346.

33 Charles Taylor, *Hegel* (Cambridge: Cambridge Univ. Press, 1975), 376.

34 "[L]es trois termes de la devise républicaine, liberté, égalité, fraternité, ne sont pas sur le même plan … par la fraternité nous sommes tenus d'arracher à la misère nos frères les hommes; c'est un devoir préalable; au contraire l'égalité est un devoir beaucoup moins pressant." Charles Péguy, *De Jean Coste*, in *Une éthique sans compromis*, ed. Dominique Saatdjian (Paris: Pocket, 2011), 278.

35 Rawls, *A Theory of Justice*, 105.

36 Paul Ricœur, Alan Page Fiske, and Anthony Kronman all note, in their own ways, that Rawls' appeal for sharing (the sharing required for equality) implicitly depends on the virtues of reverence – and especially the virtues of Reverence (A2) – but declines to acknowledge this dependence.

Paul Ricœur, *Amour et justice* (Paris: Éditions Points, 2008), 40–1; Alan Page Fiske, *Structures of Social Life: The Four Elementary Forms of Human Relations* (New York: Free Press, 1991), 119. Anthony Kronman, *Confessions of a Born-Again Pagan* (New Haven: Yale Univ. Press, 2016), 42.

37 Rawls, *A Theory of Justice*, 560.

38 Sandel, *Justice*, 251.

39 Charles Taylor, *Sources of the Self: The Making of the Modern Identity* (Cambridge, MA: Harvard Univ. Press, 1989), 89.

40 Scruton, *The Meaning of Conservatism*, 73.

41 Seyla Benhabib, "Models of Public Space: Hannah Arendt, the Liberal Tradition and Jürgen Habermas," in *Habermas and the Public Sphere*, ed. Craig Calhoun (Cambridge, MA: MIT Press, 1991), 82, quoted in Casanova, *Public Religions in the Modern World*, 65.

42 Wolfe, *The Future of Liberalism*, 181. "Our cherished ideal of tolerance (including the ideal of having a 'choice') would not amount to much if we were merely willing to eat each other's foods and to grant each other permission to enter different houses of worship for a couple of hours on the weekend." Richard A. Shweder, *Why Do Men Barbecue? Recipes for Cultural Psychology* (Cambridge, MA: Harvard Univ. Press, 2003), 216.

43 Sandel, *Justice*, 243.

44 Michael J. Sandel, *What Money Can't Buy: The Moral Limits of Markets* (New York: Farrar, Straus & Giroux, 2012), 13.

45 Sandel, *Justice*, 261. "[C]ommon norms cannot be presupposed as the premise and foundation of a modern social order but, rather, as the potential and always fragile outcome of a process of communicative interaction. ... By going 'public,' religion as well as other normative traditions can, therefore, contribute to the vitality of such a public sphere." Casanova, *Public Religions in the Modern World*, 230–1.

46 G.W.F. Hegel, *The Phenomenology of Mind*, trans. J.B. Baillie (New York: Harper & Row, 1967), 607–10; *Philosophy of Right*, trans. Knox, §§5, 135, pp. 21–2, 89–90.

47 "[W]hat a mistake it is to regard freedom and necessity as mutually exclusive ... [F]reedom presupposes necessity ... A good man is aware that the tenor of his conduct is essentially obligatory and necessary. ... [M]an is most independent when he knows himself to be determined." G.W.F. Hegel, *Encyclopaedia of the Philosophical Sciences*, §158, in *Hegel's Logic*, trans. William Wallace (London: Oxford Univ. Press, 1975), 220. Michael Bilig et al. note that even in ordinary, everyday discourse (in health care or education, for example) "the language of freedom includes within itself the language of necessity." Michael Bilig, Susan Condor, Derek Edwards, Mike Gane, David Middleton, and Alan Radley, *Ideological Dilemmas: A Social Psychology of Everyday Thinking* (London: Sage, 1988), 144.

Hans Joas expresses Hegel's dialectic of freedom and necessity as the experience of "the feeling of 'I can do no other' which accompanies a strong
value commitment not as a restriction, but as the highest expression of
our own free will." *The Genesis of Values*, trans. Gregory Moore (Cambridge, Polity Press, 2000), 5.

48 "[C]omme un moindre mal est une espèce de bien, de même un moindre
bien est une espèce de mal, s'il fait obstacle à un bien plus grand." G.W.
Leibniz, *Essais de Théodicée* (Paris: Garnier-Flammarion, 1969), §8, p. 108.
My translation.

49 "Equality is the general shaping form of justice." Thomas Aquinas,
Summa Theologiæ 2–2.61.2 (Cambridge: Cambridge Univ. Press, 2006), vol.
37 ("Justice"), trans. Thomas Gilby, 93.

50 Aquinas, *Summa Theologiæ* 1–2.67.1, in *Treatise on the Virtues*, trans.
Oesterle, 161; Emmanuel Levinas, *Éthique et Infini* (Paris: Le Livre de
Poche, 1984), 96, 101.

51 Sandel, *Justice*, 261.

52 Aristotle, *Politics*, 3.12.1282b.15–3.13.1284a.2, trans. Benjamin Jowett, in
The Basic Works of Aristotle, ed. Richard McKeon (New York: Random
House, 1941), 1192–5.

53 Locke, *The Second Treatise on Civil Government*, §5, p. 77.

54 Jacques Maritain calls this "political paradox" "l'antinomie qui crée l'état
de tension propre à la vie temporelle de l'être humain." *Humanisme intégral*, new ed. (Paris: Éditions Aubier-Montaigne, 1946), 142.

55 Thus Adam Gopnik, for example, wants to claim core virtues of reverence
such as compassion, community, sympathy, empathy, kindness, and even
love as liberal values. *A Thousand Small Sanities*, 6, 13, 18–20, 25, 80, 113.
For this reason, Stephen Holmes is right to deplore the "tyranny of false
polarities." Because of what I have called "double vision" (seeing the
whole human paradox from each of its stances) so-called "binary" opposites such as "individualism vs. community, self-interest vs. virtue, negative liberty vs. positive liberty, limited government vs. self-government,"
can and do and must go together, even within liberalism itself. *Passions
and Constraints*, 28.

56 Edmund Fawcett inventories representative nineteenth-century liberals
who can stand for some of liberalism's various strands. *Liberalism*, 118,
134.

57 "It is allegiance [i.e., reverence] which defines the condition of society,
and which constitutes society as something greater than the 'aggregate of
individuals' that the liberal mind perceives." Scruton, *The Meaning of Conservatism*, 24. Robert Nisbet captures this premodern character of conservatism, somewhat awkwardly, when he refers to the "innate feudalism of
the conservative ethic." *Conservatism: Dream and Reality* (New Brunswick,

NJ: Transaction, 2008), 63. When Edmund Fawcett says "Resisting modernity lies indeed at the conservative core," he is not entirely wrong, but views conservatism through distorting liberal lenses and misses the point. *Conservatism: The Fight for a Tradition* (Princeton: Princeton Univ. Press, 2020), 102.

58 Adam Gopnik nicely captures the roots of liberalism in the new stance of "*It* is" (B2) when he suggests "*the* foundational liberal instinct" – even more foundational than liberalism's commitment to "freedom of debate" – is the conviction that "there's no escaping the specificities of the world." *A Thousand Small Sanities*, 189. Emphasis in original.

59 Democracy depends, for example, on virtues of reverence such as "friendship," which are older than democracy – and at the root of genuine conservatism: "Justice is a primary condition for the existence of the body politic, but Friendship is its very life-giving form." Jacques Maritain, *Man and the State* (Chicago: Univ. of Chicago Press, 1956), 10. Michael Oakeshott suggests conservatism is the disposition for friendship in political form. *Rationalism in Politics and Other Essays* (London: Methuen, 1962), 177–96.

60 "Now one's will is not right in willing some particular good unless it refers to the common good as to an end, since the natural appetite of any part is ordered to the common good of the whole. ... [A]nyone living in a society is in some way a part and member of the whole society. ... [T]he common good surpasses the individual good of one person." Thomas Aquinas, *Summa Theologiæ* 1–2.19.10, 1–2.21.3, 2–2.58.12, in *Treatise on Happiness*, trans. John A. Oesterle (Notre Dame, IN: Univ. of Notre Dame Press, 1983), 191, 206, and in *Summa Theologiæ*, vol. 37 ("Justice"), trans. Gilby, 51.

61 Leo Tolstoy, *War and Peace*, trans. Richard Pevear and Larissa Volokhonsky (New York: Vintage Classics, 2008), Epilogue, pt. 1, chap. 14, p. 1169.

62 Hegel, *Philosophy of Right*, trans. Knox, §§255–71, pp. 154–74; Scruton, *The Meaning of Conservatism*, 29–30, 39–40, 43, 76. Scruton suggests a conservative can and will therefore favour public ownership of enterprises that are "indispensable to the life of the community." Scruton, 104. A good litmus test to distinguish authentic conservatives from those who only call themselves "conservative" (i.e., neoliberals in disguise) is whether they are open to this kind of public enterprise. Stephen Holmes is right to describe "collective ownership" as a "classically illiberal arrangement." *Passions and Constraints,* 16.

63 John W. Gardner, *Excellence: Can We Be Equal and Excellent Too?* (New York: Harper & Brothers, 1961).

64 Scruton, *The Meaning of Conservatism*, 9.

65 Hegel, *The Phenomenology of Mind*, trans. Baillie, 525. On "reverence *for* the established order," see also *Philosophy of Right*, trans. Knox, addition to §138, p. 255. Emphasis added.

66 Anthony Trollope, *The Prime Minister* (Oxford: Oxford Univ. Press, 2011), 143.

67 Although he confuses conservatives and neoliberals, Robert Nisbet's description of Ronald Reagan's 1980s coalition in the US gives an idea of the variety of outlooks that can parade (even falsely) under the "conservative" banner. *Conservatism*, 111.

68 Rawls, *A Theory of Justice*, 107, 525.

69 Rawls, 520.

70 Martin Heidegger, *Being and Time*, 285, trans. Joan Stambaugh (Albany: State Univ. of New York Press, 2010), 273.

71 "J'appelle pouvoir sur la société l'être, quel qu'il soit, qui *veut* la conservation de la société et qui *fait* pour sa conservation; l'être qui manifeste une *volonté* et commande une action conservatrice de la société ..." Louis de Bonald, *Essai analytique sur les lois naturelles de l'ordre social* (Paris: Adrien Le Clere, 1817), 37, cited in Marcel Gauchet, "Préface," in Benjamin Constant, *Écrits politiques* (Paris: Gallimard, 1997), 57–8. Emphasis in original. In the wake of the dissolution of medieval Christianity, the new, absolute monarchies of the Ancien Régime were an attempt to employ, as Jacques Maritain puts it, "des moyens humains, des moyens d'État, des moyens politiques, pour essayer de sauver *l'unité* tout à la fois spirituelle et politique du corps social." *Humanisme intégral*, 161. Emphasis added. That was the spirit carried forward by the new "conservatism" in nineteenth century democracy.

72 Pierre Reboul, *Chateaubriand et Le Conservateur* (Lille: Presses universitaires, 1973).

73 J.R. Derré, "Chateaubriand et Bonald," *Cahiers de l'Association internationale des études françaises* 21, no. 20 (1969), 147–66, https://www.persee.fr /web/revues/home/prescript/article/caief_0571-5865_1969_num _21_1_933.

74 Anthony Trollope captures this side of nineteenth century British conservatism when he puts into the mouths of Conservative MP's – opposed to their own leader's proposal to disestablish the Church of England – the despairing cry: "Was nothing to be conserved by a Conservative party?" *Phineas Redux* (Oxford: Oxford Univ. Press, 1983, 2011), 59.

75 Fawcett, *Conservatism*, 21.

76 Viscount Bolingbroke, *The Idea of a Patriot King* (1738), cited in Jeffrey Hart, *Viscount Bolingbroke: Tory Humanist* (London: Routledge, 1965), 106. Hegel also argued that "man must ... venerate the state as a secular deity." Hegel, *Philosophy of Right*, trans. Knox, addition to §270, p. 285.

77 Aquinas, *Summa Theologiæ* 2–2.58.5–6, vol. 37 ("Justice"), trans. Gilby, 31–7.

78 Edmund Burke, *Reflections on the Revolution in France*, ed. William B. Todd (New York: Holt, Rinehart & Winston, 1965), 117.

79 George H. Sabine, *A History of Political Theory*, 3rd ed. (New York: Holt, Rinehart & Winston, 1961), 607. "It would be fair to say, I think, that the main task of political conservatism, as represented by Burke, Maistre, and Hegel, was to put obligations of piety [i.e., reverence] back where they belong, at the centre of the picture." Roger Scruton, *On Human Nature* (Princeton: Princeton Univ. Press, 2017), 126.

80 Robert Peel, "The Tamworth Manifesto," The Victorian Web, last updated 22 July 2002, https://www.victorianweb.org/history/tamworth2.html.

81 Quoted in Nisbet, *Conservatism*, 31.

82 Paul Smith, *Disraelian Conservatism and Social Reform* (London: Routledge, 1967), 2–3; Fawcett, *Liberalism*, 125.

83 Fawcett, *Conservatism*, 87.

84 Fawcett, 175–8.

85 During the Thatcher administration from 1979 to 1990, the share of national income going to the poorest fifth of the British population declined from 10 to 6 per cent, while the share going to the wealthiest fifth rose from 37 to 45 per cent. Michael Meacher, "Worse Than Under Thatcher," *Guardian*, 15 July 2003, cited in Ted Honderich, *Conservatism: Burke, Nozick, Bush, Blair?* (London: Pluto Press, 2005), 28.

86 James Farney and David Rayside, eds., *Conservatism in Canada* (Toronto: Univ. of Toronto Press, 2013).

87 "[C]onservatives will seek to uphold all those practices and institutions – among which, of course, the family is pre-eminent – through which the habits of allegiance [i.e., virtues of reverence] are acquired. … Conservatives believe in the power of the state as necessary to the state's authority, and will seek to establish and enforce that power in the face of every influence that opposes it." Scruton, *The Meaning of Conservatism*, 23–4.

88 British Conservative Jacob Rees-Mogg, for example, says the "great virtue of Toryism is focusing on the individual." Conservatives, he argues, "basically believe that people should make decisions over their own lives, that they should be as free as possible to do that." Quoted in Dan Hitchens, "The Individualist," *First Things*, no. 299 (January 2020), 54.

89 "Does Canada Need the Conservatives?" *Globe and Mail*, 30 December 2015, A8. Similarly, a respected Canadian national columnist simply assumes that "conservatives see people as individuals" and that a conservative party is therefore a "party of free markets, limited government and equal opportunity." Andrew Coyne, "Michael Cooper Could Have Said This," *Ottawa Citizen*, 6 June 2019, NP4.

90 For recent (very different) attempts to articulate a conservatism that goes beyond small-government neoliberalism, see, for example: Mark Lilla, "Two Roads for the New French Right," *New York Review of Books* 65, no. 20 (20 December 2018), 42–6; Yoram Hazony, "Conservative Democracy,"

First Things, no. 289 (January 2019), 19–26; Daniel McCarthy, "A New Conservative Agenda," *First Things*, no. 291 (March 2019), 19–25; Sohrab Ahmari, "The New American Right," *First Things*, no. 296 (October 2019), 27–31; R.R. Reno, Mary Eberstadt, Joshua Mitchell, and Ryszard Legutko, "National Conservatism," *First Things*, no. 296 (October 2019), 43–55; Sohrab Ahmari, Jeffrey, Blehar, Patrick Dineen et al., "Against the Dead Consensus," *First Things*, 21 March 2019, https://www.firstthings.com /web-exclusives/2019/03/against-the-dead-consensus; R.R. Reno, "A New Fusionism," *First Things*, no. 302 (April 2020), 59–61.

91 The ersatz "conservative" attempt to marry anti-state libertarian neoliberalism with an interventionist moral commitment to traditional values is sometimes called "fusionism" and attributed to (among others) the American political writer Frank Meyer (1909–72). Frank S. Meyer, *In Defense of Freedom: A Conservative Credo* (Chicago: Henry Regnery, 1962); Ben Sixsmith, "The Fusionism That Failed," *First Things*, no. 294 (June/July 2019), 11–13; R.R. Reno, "A New Fusionism," *First Things*, no. 302 (April 2020), 59–61.

92 Alain Rey, ed., *Dictionnaire historique de la langue française* (Paris: Dictionnaires Le Robert, 2006), 2012.

93 R.R. Palmer and Joel Colton, *A History of the Modern World*, 2nd rev. ed. (New York: Alfred A. Knopf, 1961), 392, 432; Wolfe, *The Future of Liberalism*, 18; Fawcett, *Liberalism*, 7.

94 "Libéralisme," Wikipedia, last updated 20 October 2021, http://fr .wikipedia.org/wiki/Lib%C3%A9ralisme; Fawcett, *Liberalism*, 7.

95 Roy Jenkins, *Gladstone* (London: Macmillan, 1996), 204–5.

96 Fawcett, *Liberalism*, 118.

97 Fawcett, 124.

98 Crane Brinton, John B. Christopher, and Robert Lee Wolff, *A History of Civilization, Vol. Two: 1715 to the Present*, 2nd ed. (Englewood Cliffs, NJ: Prentice-Hall, 1960), 162; Norman Davies, *Europe: A History* (London: Pimlico, 1997), 802.

99 For this reason, Adam Gopnik is wrong to suggest that what we now call neoliberalism – "the belief that free-market solutions will solve everything" – is "not part of the liberal genetic line at all." *A Thousand Small Sanities*, 197–8. On the contrary, this kind of liberalism is one of the original starting points in the *history* of liberalism, and a core strand in the permanent *metaphysics* of liberalism: the virtues of Liberty (A1) shorn of the virtues of Equality (B2), their necessary and permanent partner in the overall paradox of liberalism, without whose two sides liberalism can never be truly liberal.

100 Ryan, *The Making of Modern Liberalism*, 33.

101 Oscar Douglas Skelton, *Life and Letters of Sir Wilfrid Laurier* (Toronto: McClelland & Stewart, 1965), 1:43.

102 Honderich, *Conservatism*, 6–31; Scruton, *The Meaning of Conservatism*, 11.

103 T.H. Green, *Lectures on the Principles of Political Obligation* (London: Longmans Green, 1927), 39. Green was building on Hegel, who had already anticipated a wider role for the state in social welfare, and in the promotion of "broader freedoms." Hegel, *Philosophy of Right*, trans. Knox, §§241–5, pp. 148–50.

104 Green, 39.

105 Herbert Spencer, "The New Toryism," in *The Man versus the State*, ed. Donald MacRae (Harmondsworth: Penguin Books, 1969), 63–81. Originally published in 1884.

106 Fawcett, *Liberalism*, 46.

107 Jenkins, *Gladstone*, 218.

108 Fawcett, *Liberalism*, 133.

109 Fawcett, 162.

110 Palmer and Colton, *A History of the Modern World*, 583–4.

111 Mark Lilla suggests the key values of the New Deal were justice (B1) and solidarity (A2), from the two core families of "conservative" values. *The Once and Future Liberal: After Identity Politics* (New York: HarperCollins, 2018), 103.

112 "We are governed by parties that no longer know what they want in a large sense, only what they don't want in a small sense. Republicans don't want the programs and reforms that are the legacy of the New Deal, the New Frontier, and the Great Society. Democrats don't want Republicans to cut them." Lilla, 97–8.

113 Edmund Fawcett suggests this new liberalism of "conservation" could also be called a "liberalism of melancholy, if that did not sound worldweary and over-Western." *Liberalism*, 407. For an example of this contemporary liberalism of "conservation," see Canadian Prime Minister Justin Trudeau's warning that political leaders who think they can "turn back the clock are wrong," in his speech to the Italian parliament, on 30 May 2017. Robert Fife, "Trudeau Warns World Leaders Can't 'Turn Back the Clock' on Progress," *Globe and Mail*, 30 May 2017, https://www.theglobeandmail.com/news/politics/trudeau-warns-world-leaders-cant-turn-back-the-clock-on-progress/article35153177/.

114 "Starting in the late nineteenth century … liberals left behind their once-strong commitments to laissez-faire in favor of reliance on government. … Conservatives in the United States and to a lesser degree Great Britain did the opposite: they abandoned their conviction that government could play an important role in strengthening the social order in favor of the libertarian ideal that government should be kept as far removed from people's lives as possible." Wolfe, *The Future of Liberalism*, 219.

115 Fawcett, *Liberalism*, 380–1.

116 In 1884, Herbert Spencer predicted "[T]he laws made by Liberals are so greatly increasing the compulsions and restraints exercised over citizens, that among Conservatives who suffer from this aggressiveness there is growing up a tendency to resist it. ... So that if the present drift of things continues, it may by and by really happen that the Tories will be the defenders of liberties which the Liberals, in pursuit of what they think popular welfare, trample underfoot." "The New Toryism," 81.

117 "Liberals want government to be large enough, for instance to enforce gun control laws, but not intrusive enough to have anything to do with women and their reproductive choices." Gopnik, *A Thousand Small Sanities*, 91. "Let the question be one of free speech or freedom of religion, and liberals can be as libertarian as any conservative denouncing occupational health and safety measures; but should the question be one of funding elementary schools or offering food stamps, liberals can be as pro-government as conservatives are when talking about fighting crime or supporting the troops." Wolfe, *The Future of Liberalism*, 227.

118 Fawcett, *Liberalism*, 133.

119 Paul Ricœur recognizes the very close ties between the virtues of Reciprocity (B2b) and the virtues of reverence in general – and between the virtues of Reciprocity (B2b) and the virtues of Love (A2b), in particular. But, also, the very real differences between them. *Amour et justice*, 31. See also *Lectures 1*, in *Ricœur: Textes choisis et présentés*, ed. Michaël Fœssel and Fabien Lamouche (Paris: Éditions Points, 2007), 314.

120 Richard Hofstadter, *Social Darwinism in American Thought* (Boston: Beacon Press, 1992), 45.

121 Alan Wolfe notes that libertarianism has "two poles," but he suggests they are "big government" which is bad, and "small government" which is good. But these are what Aristotle called "contradictions," not the "contraries" which structure all things. The two poles or "contraries" of libertarianism are Liberty (A1) and Excellence (B1). *The Future of Liberalism*, 242.

122 This is a very different configuration than that of Robert Nisbet, for example, who imagines a simple continuum, with socialism at one end, conservatism at the other, and liberalism in the middle. *Conservatism*, 38. But see note 123, immediately below.

123 "Traditional conservatives have, and will continue to have, a good deal in common with socialists in the democracies." Nisbet, 117. "[I]t is as deep an instinct in a conservative as it is in a socialist to resist the champions of 'minimal' government." Scruton, *The Meaning of Conservatism*, 41.

124 In response to the implicit cruelty and selfishness of Whig laissez-faire, an old Tory like Samuel Johnson urged a more generous, compassionate

approach to social policy. "From a Review of Soame Jenyns' *A Free Enquiry into the Nature and Origin of Evil*," in *"Rasselas" and Essays*, ed. Charles Peake (London: Routledge, 1967), 162. The difference between a Tory like Johnson and a Whig like Burke can be measured by Burke's contrasting answer (in *Thoughts and Details on Scarcity*) to Prime Minister Pitt's question about what government should do in the event of a famine. Burke's answer amounted to, nothing. Nisbet, *Conservatism*, 51, 70. It is also interesting to contrast Burke's laissez-faire approach to public welfare with Hegel's emphasis on the primary role and responsibility of the state. Hegel, *Philosophy of Right*, trans. Knox, §§241–5, pp. 148–50.

125 Scruton, *The Meaning of Conservatism*, 99.

126 Palmer and Colton, *A History of the Modern World*, 587. Robert Nisbet denies that the policies of Disraeli and Bismarck show any genuine conservative commitment to communitarian social welfare. *Conservatism*, 71–3.

127 Gad Horowitz, "Conservatism, Liberalism and Socialism: An Interpretation," *Canadian Journal of Economics and Political Science* 32, no. 2 (1966), 143–71; Hugh Segal, *The Right Balance: Canada's Conservative Tradition* (Vancouver: Douglas & McIntyre, 2011); Ben Woodfinden, "The Enduring Appeal of Red Toryism," *C2C Journal*, 18 January 2020, https://c2cjournal.ca/2020/01/the-enduring-appeal-of-red-toryism/.

128 Peter Thiel, "The Education of a Libertarian," Cato Unbound, 13 April 2009, http://www.cato-unbound.org/2009/04/13/peter-thiel/education-libertarian. Thomas Aquinas well understood the mentality of social Darwinists and libertarians like Rockefeller, Carnegie, and Peter Thiel with their excessive devotion to "excellence" that turns self-styled libertarians into elitists and closet aristocrats. He called it "pride": "[P]ride is a craving for excellence out of reason. ... [I]t hates being equal with our fellows ... but wills to dominate them." Aquinas, *Summa Theologiæ* 2–2.162.1, vol. 37 ("Justice"), trans. Gilby, 119.

129 Leszek Kolakowski, *Main Currents of Marxism*, Vol. 1: *The Founders* (Oxford: Oxford Univ. Press, 1985), 182–233.

130 One of the first to use the term in its modern sense seems to have been Leonard Read, who established the Foundation for Economic Education in 1946 to promote libertarian ideas. "Leonard Read," Wikipedia, last updated 11 October 2021, https://en.wikipedia.org/wiki/Leonard_Read.

131 Robert Nozick, *Anarchy, State, and Utopia* (New York: Basic Books, 1974). To this kind of view, Hegel responded: "[I]t is one of the commonest blunders of abstract thinking to make private rights and private welfare count as *absolute* in opposition to the universality of the state." Hegel, *Philosophy of Right*, trans. Knox, §126, p. 85. Emphasis in original.

132 Barrie McKenna, "In Canada, unlike the U.S., the American Dream Lives On," *Globe and Mail*, 15 January 2012, https://www.theglobeandmail.com/report-on-business/rob-commentary/in-canada-unlike-the-us-the-american-dream-lives-on/article4171456/; Miles Corak, Lori Curtis, and Shelley Phipps, "Economic Mobility, Family Background, and the Well-Being of Children in the United States and Canada," IZA Discussion Paper, no. 4814, March 2010, https://ftp.iza.org/dp4814.pdf. The World Economic Forum ranks Canada 14th out of 82 countries for social mobility, and the United States 27th. *The Global Social Mobility Report 2020: Equality, Opportunity and a New Economic Imperative* (Geneva: World Economic Forum, January 2020), 58–9, 196–7. https://www3.weforum.org/docs/Global_Social_Mobility_Report.pdf.

133 Aristotle, *The Nicomachean Ethics* 5.3.1131a25–30, trans. J.A.K. Thomson, rev. Hugh Tredennick (London: Penguin Books, 2004), 119.

134 "[H]onour is not truly due save to virtue. ... [H]onour is due to excellence...and a man's excellence is gauged by his virtue above all." Aquinas, *Summa Theologiæ*, 2–2.143.2, 2–2.145.1 (Cambridge: Cambridge Univ. Press, 2006), vol. 43 ("Temperance"), trans. Thomas Gilby, 63, 73.

135 Julian Borger, "The Anti-Democratic Alliance," *The Guardian Weekly* 197, no. 25 (24–30 November 2017), 1, 12.

136 Alexis de Tocqueville, *L'ancien régime et la Révolution* (Paris: Gallimard, 1967), 51, 53, 260, 318–19.

137 "[I]ndividual strengths of mind and body being different from birth, all efforts to compensate through law and government for this diversity of strengths can only cripple the liberties of those involved; especially the liberties of the strongest and most brilliant. This is, in brief, the view which conservative writers have unfailingly taken, from Burke on, on the relation between liberty and equality." Nisbet, *Conservatism*, 60.

138 Hegel, *Philosophy of Right*, trans. Knox, §§49, 200, pp. 44, 130.

139 "The idea is to redress the bias of contingencies in the direction of equality. ... [A]s far as possible the choice of a conception of justice should not be affected by accidental contingencies." Rawls, *A Theory of Justice*, 102, 530.

140 Christopher Boehm, *Moral Origins: The Evolution of Virtue, Altruism, and Shame* (New York: Basic Books, 2012), 149–50, 177, 204, 308, 319; Robert N. Bellah, *Religion in Human Evolution: From the Paleolithic to the Axial Age* (Cambridge, MA: Belknap Press of Harvard Univ. Press, 2011), 178–9, 260–2. Bellah refers to "a U-shaped curve of despotism – from the despotic apes to the egalitarian hunter-gatherers to the re-emergence of despotism in complex societies." Bellah, 178.

141 David Goodhart, *The Road to Somewhere: The New Tribes Shaping British Politics* (London: Penguin Books, 2017), xi.

142 David Goodhart suggests that, "[s]horn of the Hard Authoritarians" (a very significant qualification), so-called "decent" populism is a "fundamentally mainstream worldview representing a large part of the centre ground of British politics." Goodhart's "decent populists" accept many features of the "great liberalisation on issues of race, sexuality and gender," but they "reject mass immigration, place a high value on national citizenship, are hostile to non-contributory welfare, and do not like multiculturalism (at least in its separatist form)." Goodhart, 220, 57.

143 Goodhart, x, 6, 55, 57, 71, 219–20. Goodhart's so-called "decent populism" seems to be a rather flexible category and includes not only Italy's Five Star Movement and the German Alternative für Deutschland but also Jarosław Kaczyński's Law and Justice party (PiS) in Poland, and Viktor Orbán's Fidesz party in Hungary. Goodhart, 71. Yet, in power, the latter two have used most of the tools for totalitarian oppression from the standard neofascist toolkit. This kind of populism seems very far from "decent."

144 Jan-Werner Müller, *What Is Populism?* (London: Penguin Books, 2017), 23, 70, 98.

145 What I call right-wing populism, Edmund Fawcett often refers to as the "hard right." Fawcett, *Conservatism*, 339–54.

146 Jan-Werner Müller defines populism (in the sense I am using in this chapter) as anti-elitist, antipluralist, and an "exclusionary form of identity politics." Müller, *What Is Populism?*, 2–4, 19–25. Populism advances a claim · to exclusive representation of the popular will "understood in a moral, as opposed to empirical, sense." The "core claim" of populism is that "only some of the people are really the people." *What Is Populism?*, 20–1.

147 Müller, 69.

148 Jan-Werner Müller suggests that, when they achieve power, populists' approach to governance exhibits three main features: "[1] attempts to hijack the state apparatus, [2] corruption and 'mass clientelism' (trading material benefits or bureaucratic favours for political support by citizens who become the populists' 'clients'), and [3] efforts systematically to suppress civil society." Müller, 4, 44–9.

149 K. Marx and F. Engels, *Manifesto of the Communist Party* (Moscow: Progress, 1965), 62.

150 Leszek Kolakowski, *Main Currents of Marxism*, Vol. 2: *The Golden Age*, trans. P.S. Falla (Oxford: Oxford Univ. Press, 1985), 485–91, 497–509.

151 Jennifer Levitz, Jeffrey Ng, Jeremy Page, "Son of Fallen Communist Party Official Escorted from U.S. Home by Guards," *Globe and Mail*, 16 April 2012, A11.

152 "National Socialism and Italian Fascism need to be understood as populist movements." Müller, *What Is Populism?*, 93. Vasily Grossman notes

that, "rather than peering haughtily at the common people through a monocle," National Socialism "talked and joked in their own language. It was down-to-earth and plebeian. And it had an excellent knowledge of the mind, language and soul of those it deprived of freedom." *Life and Fate*, trans. Robert Chandler (New York: New York Review Books, 2006), 23.

153 Hobbes, *Leviathan*, pt. 1, chap. 11, p. 86.

154 On the "irascible" appetite and virtues, and their tendency "to overcome and rise above obstacles," see chapter 8, notes 24 and 29.

155 On right-wing populism and right-wing populist leaders, see Federico Finchelstein, *From Fascism to Populism in History* (Oakland: Univ. of California Press, 2019); *A Brief History of Fascist Lies* (Oakland: Univ. of California Press, 2020); Ruth Ben-Ghiat, *Strongmen: Mussolini to the Present* (New York: W.W. Norton, 2020).

156 Nick Haslam, "Research on the Relational Models: An Overview," in *Relational Models Theory: A Contemporary Overview*, ed. Nick Haslam (Mahwah, NJ: Lawrence Erlbaum Associates, 2004), 38; Fiske, *Structures of Social Life*, 52, 87, 226, 211, 88; "Relational Models Theory 2.0," and "Four Modes of Constituting Relationships: Consubstantial Assimilation; Space, Magnitude, Time, and Force; Concrete Procedures; Abstract Symbolism," in *Relational Models Theory*, ed. Haslam, 4, 82, 125.

157 In 1939, C.G. Jung said the Nazi movement came "as near to being a religious movement as anything, since A.D. 622," the year of the prophet Muhammad's flight to Medina, and the birth of Islam. C.G. Jung, "The Difference between Eastern and Western Thinking," in *The Portable Jung*, ed. Joseph Campbell, trans. R.F.C. Hull (New York: Viking Press, 1971), 495. Léon Brunschwicg also described the Nazi Nuremberg rallies as religious events. Steven Lukes, *Émile Durkheim: His Life and Work* (London: Penguin Press, 1973), 399n71, cited in Joas, *The Genesis of Values*, trans. Moore, 199n43. José Casanova notes the close connection between theocracy and fascism. *Public Religions in the Modern World*, 219. On theocracy and tyranny, see also Hegel, *Philosophy of Right*, trans. Knox, addition to §270, pp. 284–5.

158 Paul Mozur, "Inside China's Dystopian Dreams: AI, Shame and Lots of Cameras," *New York Times*, 8 July 2018, https://www.nytimes .com/2018/07/08/business/china-surveillance-technology.html.

159 Müller, *What Is Populism?*, 11, 20, 101.

160 Palmer and Colton, *A History of the Modern World*, 430–43.

161 "Liberalism is individualistic, and the ideal-typical liberal believes that individuals should be rewarded for personal achievement and merit." For a true liberal, concessions to "nonindividualistic institutions" such

as the family and community are a "compromise with irrational human passions." Holmes, *Passions and Constraints*, 38, 40.

162 Locke, *The Second Treatise on Civil Government*, §106, p. 128. Paul Ricœur, *Le Juste 1* (Paris: Éditions Esprit, 1995), in *Ricœur*, ed. Fœssel and Lamouche, 360.

163 Ryan, *The Making of Modern Liberalism*, 106.

164 Adam Gopnik nicely describes the liberal idea of community as "an idea of *shared choices.*" *A Thousand Small Sanities*, 39. Emphasis added.

165 "[Conservatism] arises directly from the sense that one belongs to some continuing pre-existing social order, and that this fact is all-important in determining what to do. … [C]onservatives are committed, in this way, to the pursuit and upkeep of an underlying social unity." Scruton, *The Meaning of Conservatism*, 8, 10, 14–15. See also Nisbet, *Conservatism*, 37–8, 55, 59, 85–101, 115–17; Mark Lilla, "Republicans for Revolution," *New York Review of Books* 59, no. 1 (12 January 2012), 14; Edmund Fawcett, *Conservatism*, 144.

166 Paul Ricœur gets this conservative view exactly right: "Sans la médiation institutionnelle, l'individu n'est qu'une esquisse d'homme, son appartenance à un corps politique est nécessaire à son épanouissement humain et, en ce sens, elle n'est pas digne d'être révoquée." *Le Juste 1*, in Fœssel and Lamouche, eds., *Ricœur*, 360. However, instead of attributing the second view to conservatism, Ricœur attributes it instead to a "distinction entre deux versions du libéralisme." This may have something to do with the differences in political vocabulary between France and the English-speaking world. But it also has to do with the fact that conservatism, properly so-called, is a premodern outlook that explicitly embraces the modern and post-modern commitment to what can be called the *liberal* political order. In that sense, Ricœur is right: the contemporary debate between conservatism and liberalism is a debate between two kinds of liberalism.

167 "There is no autonomy that does not presuppose the sense of a social order." Scruton, *The Meaning of Conservatism*, 66.

168 Thomas Aquinas, *Summa Theologiæ* 3.8.3, in *Theological Texts*, trans. Thomas Gilby (London: Oxford Univ. Press, 1954), 338.

169 Robert N. Bellah, Richard Madsen, William M. Sullivan, Ann Swidler, and Steven M. Tipton, *Habits of the Heart*, updated ed. (Berkeley: Univ. of California Press, 1996), 219–49, 275–96.

170 Alasdair MacIntyre, *After Virtue*, 2nd ed. (Notre Dame, IN: Univ. of Notre Dame Press, 1984), 223.

171 Edmund Burke, "Speech on the Representation of the Commons in Parliament" (1782), in *Selected Writings and Speeches*, ed. Peter J. Stanlis (New York: Doubleday Anchor, 1963), 330.

172 G.K. Chesterton, *Orthodoxy* (New York: Dodd Mead, 1924), 85.

173 Charles Taylor, *A Secular Age* (Cambridge, MA: Belknap Press of Harvard Univ. Press, 2007), 56–9, 714, 720, 750.

174 Nisbet, *Conservatism*, 40; Scruton, *The Meaning of Conservatism*, 17.

175 Scruton, 47–8.

176 Thomas J. Peters and Robert H. Waterman Jr., *In Search of Excellence: Lessons from America's Best-Run Companies* (New York: Warner Books, 1984).

177 "One-sided development of the individual mind … that is the meaning of Whiggism in England. That is the meaning of Whiggism in any country." A.S. Khomiakov, "On Humboldt," in *Russian Intellectual History: An Anthology*, ed. Marc Raeff (New York: Harcourt, Brace & World, 1966), 217.

178 Interview 23 September 1987, quoted in Douglas Keay, *Woman's Own*, 31 October 1987, 8–10. *Wikiquote* says that a transcript of the interview at the Margaret Thatcher Foundation website "differs in several particulars, but not in substance." https://en.wikiquote.org/wiki/Margaret_Thatcher. Consciously or not, Thatcher was paraphrasing Nozick: *Anarchy, State, and Utopia*, 32–3.

179 Shweder, *Why Do Men Barbecue?*, 2. "We are able to see precisely because we have a standpoint." Martin, *On Secularization*, 18.

180 John F. Helliwell, Richard Layard, and Jeffrey D. Sachs, *World Happiness Report 2018* (New York: Sustainable Development Solutions Network, 2018), 20–1. https://s3.amazonaws.com/happiness-report/2018/WHR_web.pdf.

181 "Every essential form of spiritual life is marked by ambiguity." Martin Heidegger, *An Introduction to Metaphysics*, trans. Ralph Manheim (New York: Doubleday, 1961), 8.

182 Roger Scruton, for example, appears to think that the "paradox of liberalism," (the "tension in liberalism" between the "demand for equal treatment" [B2] and the "emphasis on the free, self-fulfilling individual" [A1]) is a fatal flaw, rather than seeing it for what it is: the paradox self-assertion (Liberty [A1] and Equality [B2]), without which liberalism would have neither integrity nor authenticity, as a genuine reflection of one half of the human paradox. *The Meaning of Conservatism*, 182–94. Patrick J. Dineen makes the same error about the contradictions of liberalism, in *Why Liberalism Failed* (New Haven: Yale Univ. Press, 2018).

183 Müller, *What Is Populism?*, 77.

184 John Rawls' schematic, hierarchical "tree" of "principles" can't help including virtues of reverence (justice, beneficence, mercy, fidelity, not to injure, not to harm) together with virtues of self-assertion (efficiency, courage, fairness). Rawls, *A Theory of Justice*, 109. This tree seems to stand the nature of the human on its head, and to put reason ahead of virtue

instead of virtue before reasoning. It makes virtue derivative of reason instead of the reverse. It assumes what I elsewhere call the arrow of cognition rather than the arrow of virtue. See chapter 17, note 199, below.

185 Sandel, *What Money Can't Buy*, 81.

186 Gilles Paquet notes Karl Polanyi, François Perroux, and Kenneth Boulding (among others) all subscribed to a multifaceted view of human society in which market exchange (A1) must be combined with public authority (B1), solidarity (A2) and reciprocity (B2), in (among other places) *Tableau d'avancement: Petite ethnographie interprétative d'un certain Canada français* (Ottawa: Presses de l'Université d'Ottawa, 2008), 149.

187 "We are all liberals now ... [A]ll in the West are universalists now in the sense that almost everyone ... accepts that all human lives are of equal worth." Goodhart, *The Road to Somewhere*, 11, 109. "The modern ideal has triumphed. We are all partisans of human rights." Taylor, *A Secular Age*, 419; *Sources of the Self*, 6, 395. See also Casanova, *Public Religions in the Modern World*, 220.

188 Kronman, *Confessions of a Born-Again Pagan*, 37–8.

189 Lilla, *The Once and Future Liberal*, 26. Emphasis added.

190 Roger Scruton notes the "near-universal agreement among American moral philosophers that individual autonomy [A1] and respect for rights [B2] are the root conceptions of moral order." *On Human Nature*, 114–15.

191 Goodhart, *The Road to Somewhere*, xix.

192 Goodhart, 233.

193 Joas, *The Genesis of Values*, trans. Moore, 186; Amitai Etzioni, *The New Golden Rule: Community and Morality in a Democratic Society* (New York: Basic Books, 1996), xviii.

194 Maritain, *Humanisme intégral*, 217, 245; Scruton, *The Meaning of Conservatism*, 182–94.

195 Khomiakov, "On Humboldt," 215, 212.

Chapter 13. Organizations

1 On the virtues in organizations and organizational leadership, see Wim Vandekerckhove, "Virtue Ethics and Management," and Paul Kaak and David Weeks, "Viruous Leadership: Ethical and Effective," in *The Handbook of Virtue Ethics*, ed. Stan van Hooft (Durham: Acumen, 2014), 341–51, 352–64.

2 Manfred Kets de Vries, *Organizational Paradoxes: Clinical Approaches to Management* (London: Tavistock, 1980).

3 Thomas J. Peters and Robert H. Waterman Jr., "Managing Ambiguity and Paradox," in *In Search of Excellence: Lessons from America's Best-Run Companies* (New York: Warner Books, 1984), chap. 4, pp. 89–118.

4 Paul Evans and Yves Doz, "The Dualistic Organization," in *Human Resource Management in International Firms*, ed. Paul Evans, Yves Doz, and André Laurent (New York: St. Martin's Press, 1990), 219–42; Paul Evans, "Balancing Continuity and Change: The Constructive Tension in Individual and Organizational Development," in *Managing the Paradoxes of Stability and Change*, ed. S. Srivastva and R.E. Fry (San Francisco: Jossey-Bass, 1992), 253–8; Dave Ulrich and Dale Lake, *Organizational Capability: Competing from the Inside Out* (New York: John Wiley, 1990), 17–18; James C. Collins and Jerry I. Porras, *Built to Last: Successful Habits of Visionary Companies* (New York: HarperCollins, 1994), 44; Charles Handy, *The Age of Paradox* (Boston: Harvard Business School Press, 1994); Barry Johnson, *Polarity Management: Identifying and Managing Unsolvable Problems* (Amherst, MA: HRD Press, 1996); John Storey and Graeme Salaman, *Managerial Dilemmas: Exploiting Paradox for Strategic Leadership* (Chichester: Wiley, 2009); Nina Rosoff, *The Power of Paradox: The Protean Leader and Leading in Uncertain Times* (New York: Routledge, 2011); Thomas E. Cronin and Michael A. Genovese, *Leadership Matters: Unleashing the Power of Paradox* (London: Routledge, 2012).
5 Richard Tanner Pascale, *Managing on the Edge: How the Smartest Companies Use Conflict to Stay Ahead* (New York: Simon & Schuster, 1990), 53.
6 Handy, *The Age of Paradox*, x.
7 Even a small sample of the enormous recent scholarly output on organizational dualities and paradox over the last two decades would run to dozens or possibly even hundreds of scholarly articles. For reasons of space, I have omitted such a selection here.
8 Robert E. Quinn, *Beyond Rational Management: Mastering the Paradoxes and Competing Demands of High Performance* (San Francisco: Jossey-Bass, 1988); Robert E. Quinn and Kim S. Cameron, eds., *Paradox and Transformation: Toward a Theory of Change in Organization and Management* (Cambridge, MA: Ballinger, 1988).
9 Kim S. Cameron, Robert E. Quinn, Jeff DeGraff, Anjan V. Thakor, *Competing Values Leadership: Creating Value in Organizations* (Cheltenham: Edward Elgar, 2006); Kim S. Cameron and Robert E. Quinn, *Diagnosing and Changing Organizational Culture: Based on the Competing Values Framework*, 3rd ed. (San Francisco: Jossey-Bass, 2011); Robert E. Quinn, Sue R. Faerman, Michael P. Thompson, Michael R. McGrath, and Lynda S. St. Clair, *Becoming a Master Manager: A Competing Values Approach*, 5th ed. (Hoboken, NJ: John Wiley & Sons, 2011). Quinn and Cameron have also linked up with Martin Seligman's "positive psychology" movement, discussed in chapter 14, and adopted the language of the "positive organization." See, for example, Kim S. Cameron, Jane E. Dutton, and Robert Quinn, *Positive Organizational Scholarship: Foundations of a New Discipline*

(San Francisco: Berrett-Koehler, 2003); Kim Cameron, *Positive Leadership: Strategies for Extraordinary Performance*, 2nd ed. (San Francisco: Berrett-Koehler, 2012). But, even in this alternative form, Quinn has retained the insight into the "organizational tensions" generated by competing values, and the need for organizational leaders to be "bilingual," or capable of seeing and managing both sides of all the resulting organizational paradoxes. Robert E. Quinn, *The Positive Organization: Breaking Free from Conventional Cultures, Constraints, and Beliefs* (San Francisco: Berrett-Koehler, 2015), 11–16, 136.

10 Colin Talbot, *The Paradoxical Primate* (Exeter: Imprint Academic, 2005), 15.

11 Adapted from Quinn, *Beyond Rational Management*, 51.

12 Adapted from Cameron et al., *Competing Values Leadership*, 7.

13 Chris Argyris and Donald Schon, *Organizational Learning: A Theory of Action Perspective* (Reading, MA: Addison-Wesley, 1978); Chris Argyris, *Overcoming Organizational Defenses: Facilitating Organizational Learning* (Needham Heights, MA: Allyn & Bacon, 1990); *Knowledge for Action: A Guide to Overcoming Barriers to Organizational Change* (San Francisco: Jossey-Bass, 1993).

14 Thomas Aquinas, *Summa Theologiæ* 2–2.141.3 (Cambridge: Cambridge Univ. Press, 2006), vol. 43 ("Temperance"), trans. Thomas Gilby, 14–15.

15 Cameron et al., *Competing Values Leadership*, cover.

16 Cameron et al., 79–82.

17 Cameron et al., 38–9.

18 Cameron et al., 130.

19 Cameron et al., 96.

20 Talbot, *The Paradoxical Primate*, 64.

21 Leibniz notes that, in sorting out the different categories of the human and of the human world, there is a constant risk of getting things misaligned at the wrong level, mistaking the contained for the container. G.W. Leibniz, *Nouveaux essais sur l'entendement humain* (Paris: Garnier-Flammarion, 1966), bk. 3, chap. 3, §9, pp. 249–51; chap. 4, §16, p. 257; chap. 6, §14, pp. 267–8; bk. 4, chap. 6, §4, p. 354; chap. 9, §12, p. 382. See also G.W.F. Hegel, *Encyclopaedia of the Philosophical Sciences*, §32, in *Hegel's Logic*, trans. William Wallace (London: Oxford Univ. Press, 1975), 52.

22 Slightly modified from Cameron et al., *Competing Values Leadership*, 57. Emphasis added.

23 Paul Ricœur notes that many values which parade under the same name have, in fact, quite distinct – or even "opposite" – meanings. *Le conflit des interprétations: Essais d'herméneutique* (Paris: Éditions du Seuil, 2013), 110.

24 Paul Bloomfield, for example, says that respect is "univocal. Respect is respect." But, in the same paragraph, he refers to at least three different

kinds of respect: as a virtue of Reverence (A2) (honouring, deference); as a virtue of Excellence (B1) (respecting the "value" or "attributes" of something to which respect is "due"); and as a virtue of Equality (B2) (treating "equals as equals"). *The Virtues of Happiness: A Theory of the Good Life* (New York: Oxford Univ. Press, 2014), 59–60.

25 See the references to trust, for example in Cameron et al., *Competing Values Leadership*, 136. Michael Ignatieff makes the same point about the ambiguity of contemporary claims for "dignity" that I make here about claims for "respect": "[D]ignity might be too focussed on the self … Dignity is a defense of 'me,' or my group's claims." *The Ordinary Virtues: Moral Order in a Divided World* (Cambridge, MA: Harvard Univ. Press, 2017), 203.

26 Cameron et al., *Competing Values Leadership*, 58.

27 David Brooks makes exactly the same point, using the example of the Girl Scouts instead. David Brooks, *The Road to Character* (New York: Random House, 2015), 8. Brooks cites James Davison Hunter, *The Death of Character: Moral Education in an Age Without Good or Evil* (New York: Basic Books, 2000).

28 One of the rare references to unions and labour relations occurs in a quote from a manager. But Cameron et al. interpret this only as a lesson in "empowerment." Cameron et al., *Competing Values Leadership*, 139.

29 Fairness and equity are mentioned in Cameron et al., 136–7.

30 Christian D. Helfrich, Yu-Fang Li, David C. Mohr, Mark Meterko, and An E. Sales, "Assessing an Organizational Culture Instrument Based on the Competing Values Framework: Exploratory and Confirmatory Factor Analyses," *Implementation Science* 2, no. 13 (2007). https://www.ncbi.nlm .nih.gov/pmc/articles/PMC1865551.

31 Cameron et al., *Competing Values Leadership*, 72–8.

32 Cameron et al., 21.

33 Cameron et al., 22.

34 Cameron et al., 22.

35 The CVF authors suggest organizations "must be very clear to their employees and to the shareholders what their core definition of value is," but they do not appear to recognize that for many public sector organizations, like health and educational institutions, this will be very difficult, if not impossible, to achieve. Because "value" or the good, in those sectors, is an inherently contestable concept, involving all the contradictions of the nature of the human. Cameron et al., 152.

36 Cameron et al., 29.

37 Cameron et al., 156. Emphasis added.

38 Cameron et al., 93, 150–1.

39 Cameron et al., 150, 152.

40 Cameron et al., 136.

41 Colin Talbot, *Theories of Performance: Organizational and Service Improvement in the Public Domain* (Oxford: Oxford Univ. Press, 2010), 211. Talbot's assessment applies to his earlier attempts to apply the CVF in the public sector, including *Measuring Public Value: A Competing Values Approach* (London: Work Foundation, 2008); "Competing Public Values and Performance," in *Holy Grail or Achievable Quest? International Perspectives on Public Sector Performance Management* (n.p.: KPMG International, 2008), 141–52.

42 There is a certain irony here, in that many of Quinn's initial insights about paradox were developed in the public sector, and with public sector funding: see Quinn et al., *Becoming a Master Manager*, xii.

43 Herbert A. Simon, "The Proverbs of Administration," *Public Administration Review* 6, no. 1 (Winter 1946), 62.

44 Charles Perrow, *Complex Organizations* (Glenview: Scott Foreman, 1972); Jeffrey L. Pressman and Aaron Wildavsky, *Implementation* (Berkeley: Univ. of California Press, 1973); Christopher Hood, *The Limits of Administration* (Chichester: John Wiley, 1976); *The Art of the State: Culture, Rhetoric, and Public Management* (Oxford: Oxford Univ. Press, 1998); Peter Aucoin, "Administrative Reform in Public Management: Paradigms, Principle, Paradoxes and Pendulums," *Governance: An International Journal of Policy and Administration* 3, no. 2 (April 1990), 115–37; Vincent Wright, "The Paradoxes of Administrative Reform," in *Public Management and Administrative Reform in Western Europe*, ed. W. Kickert (Cheltenham: Edward Elgar, 1997), 7–13; B. Guy Peters, "What Works? The Antiphons of Administrative Reform," in *Taking Stock: Assessing Public Sector Reforms*, ed. B. Guy Peters and Donald Savoie (Montreal: McGill-Queen's Univ. Press, 1998), 78–107; Andrew Gray and Bill Jenkins, "Government and Administration: Paradoxes of Policy Performance," *Parliamentary Affairs* 56, no. 2 (2003), 170–87; John Halligan, "Accountability in Australia: Control, Paradox, and Complexity," *Public Administration Quarterly* 31, no. 3 (2007), 453–79; Eva M. Witesman and Charles R. Wise, "The Centralization/Decentralization Paradox in Civil Service Reform: How Government Structure Affects Democratic Training of Civil Servants," *Public Administration Review* 69, no. 1 (2009): 116–27; Talbot, *The Paradoxical Primate*; *Measuring Public Value*; "Competing Public Values and Performance," 141–52; *Theories of Performance*, chap. 6, pp. 123–38; Helen Margretts, Perri 6, and Christopher Hood, eds., *Paradoxes of Modernization: Unintended Consequences of Public Policy Reform* (Oxford: Oxford Univ. Press, 2010).

45 Christopher Pollitt and Geert Bouckaert, *Public Management Reform: A Comparative Analysis*, 2nd ed. (Oxford: Oxford Univ. Press, 2004), 159–81.

46 Talbot, *Theories of Performance*, chap. 6, pp. 123–38.

47 T.B Jorgenson and B. Bozeman, "Public Values: An Inventory," *Administration and Society* 39, no. 3 (May 2007), 377, cited in Talbot, 128.

48 Australia, *Embedding the APS Values* (Canberra: Australian Public Service
     Commission, 2003), http://www.apsc.gov.au/publications-and-media
     /current-publications/embedding-the-aps-values.

49 Canada, Canadian Centre for Management Development, *A Strong Foun-
     dation: Report of the Task Force on Public Service Values and Ethics* (Ottawa:
     Canadian Centre for Management Development, 2000); Canada, Treasury
     Board of Canada Secretariat, *Values and Ethics Code for the Public Service*
     (Ottawa: Treasury Board of Canada Secretariat, 2003).

50 Canada, Treasury Board of Canada Secretariat, *Values and Ethics Code for
     the Public Sector* (Ottawa: Treasury Board of Canada Secretariat, 2011),
     http://www.tbs-sct.gc.ca/pol/doc-eng.aspx?id=25049. The new Code
     came into effect on 2 April 2012.

51 Christopher Pollitt, *The Essential Public Manager* (Maidenhead: Open
     Univ. Press, 2003), 147.

52 Treasury Board of Canada Secretariat, *Values and Ethics Code* (2003), 9.

53 Interestingly, the 2012 Code requires that public servants act "in such
     a way as to maintain their employer's trust." Which would make it a
     trust-*seeking* virtue, a virtue of self-assertion. Treasury Board of Canada
     Secretariat, *Values and Ethics Code* (2011), 5.

54 Canadian Centre for Management Development, *A Strong Foundation*, 56.

55 Treasury Board of Canada Secretariat, *Values and Ethics Code* (2003), 9.

56 Treasury Board of Canada Secretariat, 10.

57 Treasury Board of Canada Secretariat, 10.

58 Canadian Centre for Management Development, *A Strong Foundation*, 57.

59 Canadian Centre for Management Development, 54.

60 Cameron et al., *Competing Values Leadership*, 139.

61 Canadian Centre for Management Development, *A Strong Foundation*, 32.

62 Canadian Centre for Management Development, 37.

63 Treasury Board of Canada Secretariat, *Values and Ethics Code* (2003), 7.

64 Treasury Board of Canada Secretariat, 7; Canadian Centre for Manage-
     ment Development, *A Strong Foundation*, 53–4.

65 Canadian Centre for Management Development, *A Strong Foundation*, 53;
     Treasury Board of Canada Secretariat, *Values and Ethics Code* (2003), 7.

66 Canadian Centre for Management Development, *A Strong Foundation*, 30,
     63, 2, 63, 30. For Canadian examples of conflicting public service values
     in specific cases, see also Canadian Centre for Management Develop-
     ment, *Building on a Strong Foundation – The Dialogue Continues: A Case
     Study Approach to Values and Ethics in the Public Service* (Ottawa: Canadian
     Centre for Management Development, 2000).

67 Mark H. Moore, *Creating Public Value: Strategic Management in Government*
     (Cambridge, MA: Harvard Univ. Press, 1995), 53.

68 Moore, 54.

69 Charles Taylor, *Sources of the Self: The Making of Modern Identity* (Cambridge: Harvard Univ. Press, 1989), 89.
70 Montgomery van Wart, *Changing Public Sector Values* (New York: Garland, 1998).
71 Talbot, *Theories of Performance*, chap. 10, pp. 211–13.
72 Talbot, 212.
73 Talbot, 213.
74 The four quadrants in some of Robert Quinn's figures are divided (similar to Figure 27 on page 222), with labels for each side. But on closer inspection, these divisions are not poles or contraries, but simply distinct "criteria" within each quadrant. They are "additional," not paradoxical. Quinn, *Beyond Rational Management*, 48; Quinn et al., *Becoming a Master Manager*, 13, 15.
75 Talbot, *Theories of Performance*, chap. 10, p. 212.
76 The way Hegel puts this is that a civil service is "universal in character and so has the universal explicitly as its ground and as the aim of its activity," whereas the private sector is "essentially concentrated on the particular." G.W.F. Hegel, *Philosophy of Right*, trans. T.M. Knox (Oxford: Oxford Univ. Press, 1967), §250, p. 152. Martin Seligman makes the same point when he compares business students with officer cadets: "The Wharton MBAs care about making money. The West Point cadets care about serving the nation." Martin E.P. Seligman, *Flourish: A Visionary New Understanding of Happiness and Well-Being* (New York: Simon & Schuster, 2013), 231.
77 Tom Peters seems to be pushing in that direction with his concepts of "extreme employee engagement" and "radical humanization." Thomas J. Peters, "Extreme Humanization/Extreme Employee Engagement – Observations on Excellence 2019: 'People First' (Still) Works," 23 January 2019, https://tompeters.com/wp-content/uploads/2019/01/012319 _ExtremeHumanization.pdf.
78 Martin Seligman's vision of "positive business" comes closer to articulating a conception of corporate life more consistent with the full nature of the human: "The new bottom line of the positive corporation in this view is profit ... plus meaning ... plus positive emotion ... plus engagement ... plus positive human relations." Seligman, *Flourish*, 231.

Chapter 14. Psychology

1 Leonard M. Horowitz, "On the Cognitive Structure of Interpersonal Problems Treated in Psychotherapy," *Journal of Consulting and Clinical Psychology* 47, no. 1 (February 1979), 5–15; Leonard M. Horowitz and John Vitkus, "The Interpersonal Basis of Psychiatric Symptoms," *Clinical*

Psychology Review 6, no. 5 (1986), 443–69, cited in Alan Page Fiske, *Structures of Social Life: The Four Elementary Forms of Human Relations* (New York: Free Press, 1991), 134; Christopher Peterson, *A Primer in Positive Psychology* (New York: Oxford Univ. Press, 2006), 183.

2 Irvin D. Yalom, *Love's Executioner* (New York: HarperCollins, 1990), 7.

3 C.G. Jung, *Individual Dream Symbolism in Relation to Alchemy: A Study of the Unconscious Processes at Work in Dreams*, trans. R.F.C. Hull, in *The Portable Jung*, ed. Joseph Campbell (New York: Viking Press, 1971), 394–5, 399.

4 C.G. Jung, *Psychological Types*, trans. H. Godwin Baynes (London: Routledge, 1964), 478.

5 C.G. Jung, *Memories, Dreams, Reflections*, trans. Richard and Clara Winston, rev. ed. (New York: Pantheon Books, 1973), 346.

6 C.G. Jung, *Answer to Job*, trans. R.F.C. Hull, in *The Portable Jung*, ed. Campbell, 633.

7 Jung, *Memories, Dreams, Reflections*, 350.

8 Merve Emre, *The Personality Brokers: The Strange History of Myers-Briggs and the Birth of Personality Testing* (New York: Doubleday, 2018), especially xv–xvi, 204–22, 248–9, 267–8. Not all the criticisms seem well founded, however. One of the early critiques of the MBTI asserted that its "S-N" dimension is "merely conservatism versus liberalism." Emre, 218. As you saw in chapter 12, there is more than a little truth in this, but it is not a ground for criticism.

9 C.G. Jung, *Analytical Psychology: Its Theory and Practice* (New York: Vintage Books, 1970), 11.

10 Jung, 11.

11 Aristotle, *Nicomachean Ethics* 1.41095b10–24, trans. J.A.K. Thomson, rev. Hugh Tredennick (London: Penguin Books, 2004), 5–10.

12 Jung, *Analytical Psychology*, 14–15.

13 Jung, *Psychological Types*, trans. Baynes, 463–4. Jung's linking of intuition with "possibility" echoes Leibniz' view that "ideas" are forms of eternal "possibility," and Heidegger's view that the nature of the human "is primarily being possible": the four corners of the human are "definite possibilities" which human beings can grasp or "fail to grasp." G.W. Leibniz, *Nouveaux essais sur l'entendement humain* (Paris: Garnier-Flammarion, 1966), bk. 2, chap. 30, §§1, 4, pp. 225–6; bk. 4, chap. 4, §1, p. 345; Martin Heidegger, *Being and Time*, 143–4, trans. Joan Stambaugh (Albany: State Univ. of New York Press, 2010), 139. Thomas Aquinas calls the intellect of the stance of "It *is*" (B1) the "possible intellect," as distinct from the "agent intellect" (B2). *Summa Theologiæ* 1.84.6, in Étienne Gilson, *The Elements of Christian Philosophy* (New York: Mentor, 1963), 354n10.

14 Jung, *Analytical Psychology*, 14–15. "Moral facts, as opposed to the sphere of meanings, are facts of non-formal intuition ... A value must be caught in intuition." Max Scheler, *Formalism in Ethics and Non-Formal Ethics of*

Value, trans. Manfred S. Frings and Roger L. Funk (Evanston: Northwestern Univ. Press, 1973), 166.

15 Jung, *Analytical Psychology*, 17–18.

16 *The Book of Chuang Tzu*, in *The Tao: Finding the Way of Balance and Harmony*, ed. Mark Forstater (New York: Plume, 2003), 216.

17 Thomas Aquinas, *Summa Theologiæ* 1–2.15.1, in *Treatise on Happiness*, trans. John A. Oesterle (Notre Dame, IN: Univ. of Notre Dame Press, 1983), 136. As discussed in chapters 4 and 8, Aquinas' word for self-assertion (following Aristotle) is "appetite."

18 "The apprehending by sense ... attains ... some particular good." Aquinas, 1–2.2, in *Treatise on Happiness*, trans. Oesterle, 43.

19 Iris Murdoch, *Metaphysics as a Guide to Morals* (London: Vintage, 2003), 1.

20 Jung, *Analytical Psychology*, 16.

21 Jung, 13.

22 Jung, 13.

23 "[T]he intuitive judgment in its subjective form conforms to what there is to feel in its datum." Alfred North Whitehead, *Process and Reality* (New York: Free Press, 1969), 316.

24 Thomas Aquinas, *Summa Theologiæ* 1–2.57.5, 1–2.64.3, in *Treatise on the Virtues*, trans. John A. Oesterle (Notre Dame, IN: Univ. of Notre Dame Press, 1984), 76, 135. See also Aristotle, *Metaphysics* 1.1.980a22–980b25, 10.1.1053a30–5, trans. W.D. Ross, in *The Basic Works of Aristotle*, ed. Richard McKeon (New York: Random House, 1941), 689, 837.

25 Aristotle, *The Nicomachean Ethics* 6.2.1139a20–5, trans. Thomson, rev. Tredennick, 146.

26 Jung, *Analytical Psychology*, 137–8.

27 Jung, 17. © 2007 Foundation of the Works of C.G. Jung, Zürich. Reprinted with permission of the Foundation.

28 Jung, 16.

29 Isabel Briggs Myers with Peter B. Myers, *Gifts Differing* (Palo Alto: Consulting Psychologists Press, 1980), 5–7.

30 "There are thus three stages, the stage of pure physical purpose [A1], the stage of pure intuition [A2], and the stage of intellectual feelings [B1 & B2]. But these stages are not sharply distinguished." Whitehead, *Process and Reality*, 326.

31 Bradley argues that all human experience starts from an undifferentiated unity of "feeling," and that unified feeling remains the necessary but unseen, experiential "background" to each of (what I call) the families of virtues. F.H. Bradley, *Appearance and Reality* (Oxford: Oxford Univ. Press, 1930), 413. At this first, or "individualizing phase" (A1) of feeling and experience, Whitehead says, "sensa" are "experienced emotionally ... vague feeling-tone differentiates itself into various types of sense – those of touch, sight, smell, etc." Whitehead, *Process and Reality*, 136, 141.

32 Briggs Myers and Myers, *Gifts Differing*, 5–6.
33 "La concupiscence [A1b] et la force [A1a] sont les sources de toutes nos actions." Pascal, *Pensées* (Paris: Garnier-Flammarion, 1973), §187, p. 84.
34 Briggs Myers and Myers, *Gifts Differing*, 6–7.
35 One of Martin Heidegger's names for "intuition with thinking" is "attuned understanding." For him it is the critical or foundational "structural moment" (i.e., stance) of the nature of the human because it is where all its "possibilities" (i.e., stances and families of virtues) are "disclosed" or "unconcealed" and can become a "project" for human beings. "Attunement" is Heidegger's word for feeling, intuition, emotion, "mood": "being affected or moved." Thus his "attuned understanding" is exactly the same, and plays the same role (B1), as Whitehead's "conceptual feeling" where "valuation" begins. *Being and Time*, 260, 137–8, trans. Joan Stambaugh (Albany: State Univ. of New York Press, 2010), 249, 133–4; Whitehead, *Process and Reality*, 287–90.
36 Briggs Myers and Myers, *Gifts Differing*, 5.
37 Jung, *Psychological Types*, trans. R.F.C. Hull, in *The Portable Jung*, ed. Joseph Campbell, 179.
38 C.G. Jung, *Psychological Types*, trans. Baynes, 513–17.
39 For the purposes of displaying the eight new profiles at the third level of separative projection, I have been obliged to decide how to place each new pair around the circumference of the circle. I have done so here on the assumption (based on Jung's definitions above) that extraversion is more closely connected to sensing than to intuition; and that introversion is more closely connected with intuition than with sensation. This explains why the E-profiles are to be found at the bottom of each half of the circle, and the I-profiles are found at the top of both halves.
40 Jung, *Psychological Types*, trans. Baynes, 452–6.
41 Jung, *Analytical Psychology*, 25, 31.
42 Jung, *Psychological Types*, trans. Baynes, 468–71.
43 Briggs Myers and Myers, *Gifts Differing*, 22–4.
44 As in Figure 45, I have again been obliged to decide on the placement of these profiles around the circumference. As in the previous case, I have concluded that "perceiving" is more closely connected with sensing than with intuition and that "judging" is more closely connected to intuition than to perceiving. So, the profiles ending in P are placed closer to the bottom of the circle and the profiles ending in J are placed closer to the top.
45 Jung, *Psychological Types*, trans. Baynes, 507.
46 Sigmund Freud, *The Ego and the Id*, trans. Joan Riviere, rev. James Strachey (New York: W.W. Norton, 1962), 7–29.

47 Sigmund Freud, *A General Introduction to Psychoanalysis*, trans. Joan Riviere (New York: Pocket Books, 1970), 360.

48 Sigmund Freud, *Civilization and Its Discontents*, trans. James Strachey (New York: W.W. Norton, 1962), 69.

49 Freud, *The Ego and the Id*, trans. Riviere, rev. Strachey, 12–14.

50 Freud, *A General Introduction to Psychoanalysis*, 149, 361–6.

51 Sigmund Freud, "The Libido Theory," in *General Psychological Theory: Papers on Metapsychology* (New York: Simon & Schuster, 2008), 183. Freud's account of the relationship between libido and the id is somewhat confusing and seems to have shifted over time. At the time of the *The Ego and the Id* (1923) he asserted that "[a]t the very beginning, all the libido is accumulated in the id," and is later drawn on by the ego. Freud, *The Ego and the Id*, trans. Riviere, rev. Strachey, 36. In his *Outline of Psycho-Analysis* (1940), he asserted instead that "at first the whole available quota of libido is stored up [in the ego]. We call this state the absolutely primary narcissism. It lasts till the ego begins to cathect the ideas of objects with libido, to transform narcissistic libido into object-libido." See James Strachey, "The Great Reservoir of Libido," in Freud, *The Ego and the Id*, 53–6. The later formulation seems more consistent with the account of the relationship between the two primary forms of self-assertion (A1a and A1b) offered in this book.

52 Freud, *Civilization and Its Discontents*, 70; Peter Gay, *Freud: A Life for Our Time* (New York: W.W. Norton, 1988), 412–16.

53 Sigmund Freud, "Neurosis and Psychosis," trans. Joan Riviere, in *General Psychological Theory*, 186.

54 Freud, *Civilization and Its Discontents*, 70. "[T]he more a man controls his aggressiveness [self-assertion], the more intense becomes his ideal's [his super-ego's] inclination to aggressiveness against his ego. It is like a displacement, a turning round upon his own ego." *The Ego and the Id*, 44.

55 Freud, "Neurosis and Psychosis," 189.

56 Jonathan Haidt, *The Righteous Mind: Why Good People Are Divided by Politics and Religion* (New York: Pantheon Books, 2012), 369n68; Jonathan Haidt and Craig Joseph, "The Moral Mind: How 5 Sets of Innate Intuitions Guide the Development of Many Culture-Specific Virtues, and Perhaps Even Modules," in *The Innate Mind*, ed. P. Carruthers, S. Laurence, and S. Stich (New York: Oxford Univ. Press, 2007), 3:367–91, cited in Haidt, *The Righteous Mind*; James Laidlaw, *The Subject of Virtue: An Anthropology of Ethics and Freedom* (Cambridge: Cambridge Univ. Press, 2014), 47–91.

57 Richard A. Shweder, *Why Do Men Barbecue? Recipes for Cultural Psychology* (Cambridge, MA: Harvard Univ. Press, 2003), 27. See also "Cultural Psychology: What Is It?," in *Thinking Through Cultures: Expeditions in Cultural Psychology* (Cambridge, MA: Harvard Univ. Press, 1991), 73–110.

58 Shweder, *Why Do Men Barbecue?*, 292.
59 Richard A. Shweder, Nancy C. Much, Manamohan Mahapatra, and Lawrence Park, "The 'Big Three' of Morality (Autonomy, Community, Divinity) and the 'Big Three' Explanations of Suffering," in Shweder, *Why Do Men Barbecue?*, 74–133. See especially figure 2.2 ("The 'Big Three' of Morality") on page 98.
60 Shweder, *Why Do Men Barbecue?*, 162.
61 G.W.F Hegel, *Preface to the Phenomenology of Spirit*, trans. Yirmiyahu Yovel (Princeton: Princeton Univ. Press, 2005), 105, 123, 130, 154. 168–9. "What we have done here [in the *Phenomenology*] … is simply to gather together the particular moments, *each of which in principle exhibits the life of spirit in its entirety.*" Hegel, *The Phenomenology of Mind*, trans. J.B. Baillie (New York: Harper & Row, 1967), 797. Emphasis added.
62 Although Shweder explicitly identifies a threefold nature of the human, he also implicitly acknowledges both the human paradox and its four sub-families. For example, in his description of the Hindu culture in the Indian town of Oriya, he says: "In contrast to the premises of modern liberal [i.e., A1 and B2] thought, the view of the world espoused by Oriya women and men is built on a logic of difference [B1] and solidarity [A2] rather than on equality [B2] and domination [A1]." Shweder, *Why Do Men Barbecue?*, 241.
63 Haidt, *The Righteous Mind*, 199.
64 Haidt, 122.
65 Haidt, 153.
66 Haidt, 92.
67 Jonathan Haidt and Craig Joseph, "Intuitive Ethics: How Innately Prepared Intuitions Generate Culturally Variable Virtues," *Daedalus* 133, no. 4 (Fall 2004), 55–66, cited in Haidt, *The Righteous Mind*, 341n36.
68 In the second version of Moral Foundations Theory, Haidt and his colleagues began the practice of employing pairs of names for each of the "moral matrices" or families of virtues. At this stage three of the pairs still linked positive virtues. But two others linked a virtue with its negative opposite: care was linked with "harm," and loyalty with "in-group." This practice was made consistent in the third iteration of the theory, as discussed below. Because I am interested in the virtue rather than its opposite, I have taken the liberty of eliminating "harm" and "in-group" in this list, as I will do consistently for the third version of the theory.
69 Haidt and Joseph, "The Moral Mind," cited in Haidt, *The Righteous Mind*, 341n34.
70 Haidt, *The Righteous Mind*, especially 112–27.
71 This is especially evident in Haidt's discussion of religion, whose value and significance are described as merely the creation of community, or

as that of a team sport. Haidt, 149, 273. This is, of course, backward. It's the experience of tribal, family, and community life that leads to religious life and to its truths, not the reverse. For similar accounts of religion see David Sloan Wilson, *Does Altruism Exist? Culture, Genes, and the Welfare of Others* (New Haven: Yale Univ. Press, 2015), 79–80, 89, 91; Yuval Noah Harari, *Sapiens: A Brief History of Humankind* (Toronto: Penguin Random House, 2016), 24–39. These seem to be good examples of mistaking the causes, conditions, and occasions of our becoming aware of certain truths and realities for the truths and realities themselves.

72 As you saw in chapter 5 (Table 14), loyalty can have several meanings. As devotion, it belongs to the virtues of Reverence (A2), as duty, it belongs to the virtues of Excellence (B1). By the associations Haidt gives it, he appears to have loyalty in mind here as devotion, a virtue of Reverence (A2).

73 On temperance, see Robert C. Roberts, "Temperance," in *Virtues and Their Vices*, ed. Kevin Timpe and Craig A. Boyd (Oxford: Oxford Univ. Press, 2014), 93–111.

74 Haidt, *The Righteous Mind*, 123–7, 170–6. Also: http://www.moralfoundations.org.

75 Haidt, 341–2n36. Emphasis added.

76 Haidt, 220.

77 Haidt, 26.

78 Christopher Peterson and Martin E.P. Seligman, *Character Strengths and Virtues: A Handbook and Classification* (New York: Oxford Univ. Press, 2004), 84.

79 Samuel Johnson, *The Rambler*, no. 208, Saturday, 14 March 1752, ed. W.J. Bate and Albrecht B. Strauss (New Haven: Yale Univ. Press, 1979), Yale Edition of the Works of Samuel Johnson, 5:316. This was Johnson's final *Rambler* essay.

80 Haidt, *The Righteous Mind*, 173. See also: http://www.moralfoundations.org.

81 A list of potential future additions includes honesty, ownership, self-control, and waste. Haidt, 350n53.

82 Haidt, 212.

83 In light of the current balance in Moral Foundations Theory, it's fairly easy to see why Jonathan Haidt has found himself shifting from largely liberal sympathies to more social-conservative sympathies. Haidt, 289–94.

84 Peterson and Seligman, *Character Strengths and Virtues*, 3.

85 Martin E.P. Seligman, *Flourish: A Visionary New Understanding of Happiness and Well-Being* (New York: Simon & Schuster, 2011), 229. Curiously, Seligman suggests there is "no philosophical discipline concerned with what we care about." Seligman, 229. On the contrary, in the form of the virtues,

this was a central – if not *the* central – preoccupation of philosophy from Plato and Aristotle to Leibniz, and, in other forms, from Hegel to Heidegger and Paul Ricœur (as you will see in the next chapter).

86 Peterson and Seligman, *Character Strengths and Virtues*, 13–14.

87 Peterson and Seligman, 6–7. For a view of the positive psychology movement from the point of view of virtue ethics, see Everett L. Worthington Jr., Caroline Lavelock, Daryl R. Van Tongeren, David L. Jennings II, Aubrey L. Gartner, Don E. Davis, and Joshua N. Hook, "Virtue in Positive Psychology," in *Virtues and Their Vices*, ed. Timpe and Boyd, 433–57.

88 Samuel Taylor Coleridge, *Aids to Reflection* (Port Washington, NY: Kennikat Press, 1971), 91.

89 This correspondence is not surprising, since Peterson and Seligman's classification strategy explicitly relies on "the history of moral and religious theorizing to identify broad classes of virtues." Peterson and Seligman, *Character Strengths and Virtues*, 80.

90 Peterson and Seligman, 75.

91 Peterson, *A Primer in Positive Psychology*, 158. The term "structure of character" for this image is employed in Christopher Peterson and Nansoon Park, "Classifying and Measuring Strengths of Character," in *The Oxford Handbook of Positive Psychology*, ed. Shane J. Lopez and C.R. Snyder, 2nd ed. (New York: Oxford Univ. Press, 2011), 32.

92 Martin E.P. Seligman, *Authentic Happiness: Using the New Positive Psychology to Realize Your Potential for Lasting Fulfilment* (New York: Free Press, 2002).

93 Actually, this is his later explanation. See Seligman, *Flourish*, 11–14. In *Authentic Happiness* the usual term for what Seligman later called engagement is "gratification." *Authentic Happiness*, 248–9, 262–3.

94 Seligman, *Flourish*, 24.

95 Seligman, 11; *Authentic Happiness*, 262.

96 Seligman, *Flourish*, 12, 17. *Authentic Happiness*, 250–63.

97 As noted above (note 35) and in the next chapter, Alfred North Whitehead calls this corner of the human "conceptual feeling," and Martin Heidegger calls it "attuned understanding." *Process and Reality*, 287–90. *Being and Time*, 260, 265–6, trans. Stambaugh, 249, 254.

98 Seligman, *Flourish*, 11–12, 16–17; *Authentic Happiness*, 248–9, 262. Emphasis added. Martin Heidegger recognizes this completely self-absorbing activity or "flow," when "one is 'really' busy with something and totally immersed in it," but notes this is *not* the self-*giving* unselfing of reverence but the self-*seeking* "self-forgetting" of self-assertion. This kind of "self-forgetting" can actually be a "confused backing away from one's own factical potentiality-of-being" – i.e., from the whole nature of the human. *Being and Time*, 354, 341–2, trans. Stambaugh, 337, 326.

99 Seligman, *Flourish*, 14–29. For an overview of well-being theory, Seligman cites E. Diener, E.M. Suh, R.E. Lucas, and H.L. Smith, "Subjective Well-Being: Three Decades of Progress," *Psychological Bulletin* 125, no. 2 (March 1999), 276–302. Also: J.F. Helliwell, "How's Life: Combining Individual and National Variables to Explain Subjective Well-Being," *Economic Modelling* 20, no. 2 (March 2003), 331–60; E. Diener and W. Tov, "Well-Being on Planet Earth," *Psychological Topics* 18, no. 2 (December 2009): 213–19; Derek Bok, *The Politics of Happiness: What Governments Can Learn from New Research on Well-Being* (Princeton: Princeton Univ. Press, 2009). Seligman himself distinguishes between three kinds of well-being theories: wanting, liking, and needing theories – which, as Seligman's words themselves make clear, are all forms of self-assertion. Seligman, *Flourish*, 275, 277–8, 317–19.

100 Seligman, *Flourish*, 18–19.

101 T. So and F. Huppert, "What Percentage of People in Europe Are Flourishing and What Characterizes Them?" (23 July 2009), cited in Seligman, *Flourish*, 26–7. Emphasis added.

102 Peterson and Seligman, *Character Strengths and Virtues*, 36–8.

103 Thomas Aquinas, *Summa Theologiæ* 1.81.2 in *Introduction to St. Thomas Aquinas*, ed. Anton C. Pegis (New York: Modern Library, 1948), 356. See also: 1–2.67.4, 2–2.58.4, 2–2.141.2, 2–2.141.4, 2–2.146.1, in *Treatise on the Virtues*, trans. Oesterle, 168; *Summa Theologiæ* (Cambridge: Cambridge Univ. Press, 2006), vol. 37 ("Justice"), trans. Thomas Gilby, 29, and vol. 43 ("Temperance"), trans. Thomas Gilby, 9, 19, 85.

104 Thomas Aquinas, *Summa Theologiæ* 2–2.158.1, (Cambridge: Cambridge Univ. Press, 2006), vol. 44 ("Well-Tempered Passion"), trans. Thomas Gilby, 55.

105 Words like paradox, contradiction, conflict, or dialectic don't appear in the analytical index of the original inventory. A few hints may be found in the text but are not followed up in the classification of the virtues (though they are expanded in Peterson's later model of the "structure of character"). Peterson and Seligman, *Character Strengths and Virtues*, 87–8, 51.

106 Webb Keane, *Ethical Life: Its Natural and Social Histories* (Princeton: Princeton Univ. Press, 2016), 183.

107 Peterson and Park, "Classifying and Measuring Strengths of Character," 31. See also Peterson, *A Primer in Positive Psychology*, 182.

108 Seligman, *Authentic Happiness*, 260.

109 Hegel, *Preface to the Phenomenology of Spirit*, trans. Yovel, 100–1. Whitehead agrees with Hegel that insufficient emphasis on the structuring role of paradox leads to "vagueness" and "triviality." Whitehead, *Process and Reality*, 131–3.

110 Max Scheler calls the human inability to live all the contradictory human virtues equally or "simultaneously" "*the essential tragic of all finite personal being ... equally justified provinces* of duty clash." *Formalism in Ethics*, trans. Frings and Funk, 590, 593. Emphasis in original.

111 Charles Péguy makes a similar point about Corneille, Racine, Pascal, and Molière. *Notes pour une thèse*, in *Une éthique sans compromis*, ed. Dominique Saatdjian (Paris: Pocket, 2011), 190.

112 Peterson and Park, "Classifying and Measuring Strengths of Character," 31.

113 "It is a supposition of cultural psychology that when people live in the world differently, it may be that they live in different worlds." Shweder, *Thinking Through Cultures*, 23.

114 Shweder, 301.

115 Jung, *Individual Dream Symbolism*, trans. Hull, 406. See also *Answer to Job*, 561. In his search for completeness, however, Jung sometimes fell back into the Pythagoreans' ancient error of confusing contradictories – good and evil, for example – with contraries, the error Aristotle tried to correct in his *Metaphysics*.

116 Jung, *Analytical Psychology*, 149.

117 Jung, 137.

118 Sigmund Freud, "Instincts and Their Vicissitudes," trans. Cecil M. Baines, in *General Psychological Theory*, 77–93.

119 Jung, *Memories, Dreams, Reflections*, 348–9.

120 C.G. Jung, *Aion: Researches into the Phenomenology of the Self*, trans. R.F.C. Hull, in *The Portable Jung*, ed. Campbell, 143.

121 Jung, *Analytical Psychology*, 138.

122 Jung, 187, 195.

123 "[I]l peut y avoir un *moi* qui n'est pas *moi-même*." Emmanuel Levinas, *Difficile liberté*, 3rd corrected ed. (Paris: Le Livre de Poche, 2010), 24.

Chapter 15. Philosophy

1 Tertullian, *De Praescriptione Hereticorum*, 7, cited in Luke Timothy Johnson, *Among the Gentiles: Greco-Roman Religion and Christianity* (New Haven: Yale Univ. Press, 2009), 1.

2 On this theme, see also Lev Shestov, *Athens and Jerusalem*, trans. Bernard Martin, 2nd ed. (Athens: Ohio Univ. Press, 2016); John W. O'Malley, *Four Cultures of the West* (Cambridge, MA: Harvard Univ. Press, 2004), 1–36.

3 The objective of chapter 15 might thus be described in the words of Martin Heidegger: "to point out, *in a pictorial manner*, the different currents and tendencies ... to highlight the central ontological and logical structures within each of the decisive turning points of Western anthropology

by way of a primordial return to the sources. ... In this way *the being that is in movement becomes visible according to its categorial structure.*" "Indication of the Hermeneutical Situation," trans. Michael Baur and Jerome Veith, in *The Heidegger Reader*, ed. Günter Figal (Bloomington: Indiana Univ. Press, 2009), 58, 60. Emphasis added.

4 "[W]e can never survey the actual world except from the standpoint of an immediate concrescence which is falsifying the presupposed completion." Alfred North Whitehead, *Process and Reality* (New York: Free Press, 1969), 244.

5 Karl Jaspers calls this limitless horizon *within* which humans exist the "Encompassing" or the "Comprehensive" (depending on the translation). *Reason and Existenz*, trans. William Earle, in *Existentialism from Dostoevsky to Sartre*, ed. Walter Kaufmann (Cleveland: World, 1956), 184–6; *Way to Wisdom*, trans. Ralph Manheim (New Haven: Yale Univ. Press, 1960), 28–38.

6 Hans-Georg Gadamer, *Truth and Method*, trans. and rev. Joel Weinsheimer and Donald G. Marshall, 2nd ed. (New York: Continuum, 2002), 276.

7 R.G. Collingwood, *An Essay on Metaphysics* (Oxford: Oxford Univ. Press, 1966).

8 "[O]n ne saurait rendre relative une relation logique que dans un discours logique." Emmanuel Levinas, *Dieu, la mort et le temps* (Paris: Le Livre de Poche, 2010), 145. See also Paul Ricœur, *Le conflit des interprétations: Essais d'herméneutique* (Paris: Éditions du Seuil, 2013), 33.

9 Richard G. Klein, *The Human Career: Human Biological and Cultural Origins*, 2nd ed. (Chicago: The Univ. of Chicago Press, 1999), 186, 579–86.

10 Merlin Donald distinguishes between episodic and "procedural" memory which is "quite different and structurally more archaic." *Origins of the Modern Mind: Three Stages in the Evolution of Culture and Cognition* (Cambridge, MA: Harvard Univ. Press, 1991), 149–50. Leibniz had already noted the episodic nature of consciousness in animals and some humans. The striving for a kind of pure empiricism, he suggests (perhaps ironically), is actually a regression to a form of episodic consciousness. G.W. Leibniz, *Nouveaux essais sur l'entendement humain* (Paris: Garnier-Flammarion, 1966), bk. 2, chap. 11, §11, pp. 119–20; bk. 4, chap. 27, §3, p. 422.

11 Edward O. Wilson, *The Meaning of Human Existence* (New York: Liveright, 2014), 21.

12 For several decades, the conventional account of early human evolution referred to three successive species: from *homo habilis*, to *homo erectus*, to *homo sapiens*. More recent evidence has suggested to some anthropologists that *homo erectus* was an Asian branch, descended from an intermediate species now called *homo ergaster*, the first hominid species "whose anatomy and behaviour fully justify the label human." *Homo ergaster* is

also now proposed as the ancestor of the subsequent African and European hominid species: first, *homo heidelbergensis*, and, second, *homo sapiens*. Klein, *The Human Career*, 255–7, 364–6.

13 Klein, 237–8, 292, 325–8, 350–4, 364–6; Donald, *Origins of the Modern Mind*, 105, 114, 122, 148.

14 Donald, *Origins of the Modern Mind*, 169. Emphasis in original. Leibniz also notes higher mammals and humans deprived of speech can nevertheless communicate general ideas through mimesis. Leibniz, *Nouveaux essais*, bk. 2, chap. 11, §10, p. 119.

15 Donald, 182.

16 Donald, 186. On the biology of rhythm, see Susanne K. Langer, *Mind: An Essay on Human Feeling*, vol. 2 (Baltimore: Johns Hopkins Press, 1972), 16–17.

17 Christopher Boehm, *Moral Origins: The Evolution of Virtue, Altruism, and Shame* (New York: Basic Books, 2012), 146–7, 151–2. On large-game hunting, Boehm cites the work of archaeologist, Mary Stiner.

18 Donald, *Origins of the Modern Mind*, 176–7.

19 Robert N. Bellah, *Religion in Human Evolution: From the Paleolithic to the Axial Age* (Cambridge, MA: Belknap Press of Harvard Univ. Press, 2011), 191; Frans de Waal, *The Age of Empathy: Nature's Lessons for a Kinder Society* (New York: Three Rivers Press, 2009), 11, 67.

20 Langer, *Mind*, 2:301–3.

21 Donald, *Origins of the Modern Mind*, 171, 174, 189.

22 In May 2016, archeologists reported finding an underground cave near Bruniquel, in southwestern France, in which Neanderthals, a hominid species distinct from *homo sapiens* (and later replaced by them in Western Europe), appear to have arranged broken stalagmites, carefully shaped into similar lengths (between 2.1–2.4 tons of material), in a large circular pattern, about 30 metres across. Modern carbon-dating techniques indicate the arranged materials in the cave date from more than 100,000 years earlier than the well-known prehistoric cave paintings in the same region, which date between 37,000 and 22,000 years ago. Camille Gévaudan, "Le Néanderthal, ce spélologue," *Le Devoir*, 26 May 2016, A1, A8.

23 Klein, *The Human Career*, 348–9, 514–17, 590–1.

24 Donald, *Origins of the Modern Mind*, 216–33. On the beginning of thought and language in "the symbolic finishing of excessive nervous impulses within the nervous system itself ... which eventuate in wild expressions, dance, magic, then the wishing of curses and blessings on other creatures and investing implements such as arrows, fishhooks and weapons with potency and luck by solemn rites and hallowing the places for dancing or feasting with sacrificial bloodshed" and *not* "as a signalling device," see Langer, *Mind*, 2:314, 324.

25 Northrop Frye, *The Great Code: The Bible and Literature* (Toronto: Academic Press Canada, 1982), 6. See also Paul Ricœur, *Amour et justice* (Paris: Éditions Points, 2008), 55–9. Max Scheler agrees "the large families of language form value-units." *Formalism in Ethics and Non-Formal Ethics of Value*, trans. Manfred S. Frings and Roger L. Funk (Evanston: Northwestern Univ. Press, 1973), 302n77.

26 Donald, *Origins of the Modern Mind*, 213.

27 Donald, 215.

28 "Our minds consist of story-telling. ... Conscious mental life is built entirely from confabulation. It is a constant review of stories experienced in the past and competing stories invented for the future." Wilson, *The Meaning of Human Existence*, 167–8.

29 Donald, *Origins of the Modern Mind*, 256–8.

30 Paul Ricœur argues human narrative or storytelling is fundamentally and essentially moral. Stories carry ethical meaning, by definition. You can't have an ethically neutral story. Storytelling serves as the "propadeutique à l'éthique." *Soi-même comme un autre* (Paris: Éditions du Seuil, 1990), 139, 167.

31 Boehm, *Moral Origins*, 314.

32 Richard Klein calls this "the most dramatic behavioral shift that archeologists will ever detect." *The Human Career*, 514.

33 "Historically, religion has been ... the core of culture." José Casanova, *Public Religions in the Modern World* (Chicago: Univ. of Chicago Press, 1994), 63.

34 Merlin Donald, *A Mind So Rare: The Evolution of Human Consciousness* (New York: W.W. Norton, 2001), 316.

35 Edward Evan Evans-Pritchard, *Theories of Primitive Religion* (Oxford: Oxford Univ. Press, 1965), 65, cited in Shahab Ahmed, *What Is Islam? The Importance of Being Islamic* (Princeton: Princeton Univ. Press, 2016), 208.

36 "Everything intermingles in them, everything constituting the strictly social life of societies that have preceded our own. ... In these 'total' social phenomena ... all kinds of institutions are given expression at one and the same time – religious, juridical, and moral, which relate to both politics and the family." Marcel Mauss, *The Gift: The Form and Reason for Exchange in Archaic Societies* (New York: Routledge, 1990), 3, quoted in Webb Keane, *Ethical Life: Its Natural and Social Histories* (Princeton: Princeton Univ. Press, 2016), 207; Donald, *Origins of the Modern Mind*, 211, 258.

37 Donald, *Origins of the Modern Mind*, 268.

38 "[T]he ancient individual loses himself in the community not in order to find himself but rather, quite simply, in order to construct the community; he himself disappears." Franz Rosenzweig, *The Star of Redemption*, trans. William W. Hallo (Notre Dame, IN: Univ. of Notre Dame Press, 1985), 55.

39 Boehm, *Moral Origins*, 149–50, 177, 204, 308, 319.

40 Based on Boehm's work, Robert Bellah observes that hunter-gatherer societies usually succeed in controlling the "upstarts" who were more successful in dominating later archaic human societies, when bands and tribes gave way to larger chiefdoms, kingdoms and states: "Reverse dominance hierarchy is a form of dominance [i.e., self-assertion]: egalitarianism is not simply the absence of despotism, it is the active and continuous elimination of despotism." *Religion in Human Evolution*, 177–8. See also: David Sloan Wilson, *Does Altruism Exist? Culture, Genes, and the Welfare of Others* (New Haven: Yale Univ. Press, 2015), 111; G.W.F. Hegel, *Philosophy of Right*, trans. T.M. Knox (Oxford: Oxford Univ. Press, 1967), §93, p. 67.

41 José Casanova suggests Bronislaw Malinowski showed conclusively that "even in primitive societies the heightening of emotions and the lifting of the individual out of himself are by no means restricted to gatherings and to crowd phenomena." Bronislaw Malinowski, *Magic, Science and Religion* (Garden City, NY: Doubleday, 1954), 57, quoted in Casanova, *Public Religions in the Modern World*, 45.

42 Boehm, *Moral Origins*, 300.

43 Donald, *Origins of the Modern Mind*, 270. Copyright © 1991 by the President and Fellows of Harvard College.

44 Donald, 278.

45 Donald, 206, 237.

46 Jaspers, *Way to Wisdom*, 99–103. Hans Joas explains that, by "Axial," Jaspers means the "axis" of history: "the one point in history that allows a dichotomous distinction between everything that came before or after it." "The Axial Age Debate as Religious Discourse," in *The Axial Age and Its Consequences*, ed. Robert N. Bellah and Hans Joas (Cambridge, MA: Belknap Press of Harvard Univ. Press, 2012), 10.

47 There is a rich, scholarly debate on the nature and significance of the Axial age. Some of the issues (such as which cultures were truly Axial and which were not) can be illuminated if the Axial breakthrough is defined from the point of view of the virtues it entailed or emphasized, rather than focusing on more cognitive aspects, such as the concept of "transcendence." I believe the core of the Axial breakthrough was the deepening of the insights of the human stance of "I *am*" at the heart of the virtues of Reverence (A2), and the consequent reversal of the aristocratic and servant virtues. This only occurred in certain cultures (especially Israel and India), and distinctly *not* in Greece – which is one of the keys to understanding our modern and post-modern Western (and now global) culture. On the Axial age, see Bellah and Joas, *The Axial Age*.

48 Bellah, *Religion in Human Evolution*, 197–264. Based on the work of Egyptologist Jan Assman, Bellah refers to the "culture of the 'violent-hearted'"

in archaic, hierarchical societies: "because upstarts rule by force and survive only by military victory." The growth of larger, more complex societies and states served to "free the disposition to dominate [self-assertion] from the controls previously placed upon it" in smaller, tribal societies. Bellah, 236, 261.

49 José Casanova describes the Axial age as a "wave of world renunciation" or "world rejection." Casanova, *Public Religions in the Modern World*, 49. This is correct, as Robert Bellah's comment in note 53 below confirms. But it misses the critical Axial attitude to the self.

50 David Martin, "Axial Religions and the Problem of Violence," in *The Axial Age*, ed. Bellah and Joas, 303–5.

51 "What to me is the multitude of your sacrifices? says the Lord. I have had enough of burnt offerings of rams and the fat of fed beasts ... Wash yourselves; make yourselves clean; remove the evil of your doings from before my eyes; cease to do evil, learn to do good; seek justice, rescue the oppressed, defend the orphan, plead for the widow." Isaiah 1:11, 16–17. "Rend your hearts and not your clothing." Joel 2:13. "Sacrifice and offering thou didst not desire; mine ears hast thou opened: burnt offering and sin offering hast thou not required. Then said I, Lo, *I come*: in the volume of the book it is written of me, I delight to do thy will, O my God; yea thy law is within my heart." Psalm 40:6–8. Emphasis added.

52 I believe this is consistent with Charles Taylor's definition of the Axial age, which he describes, in part, as "a shift from a mode of religious life which involved 'feeding the gods,' where the understanding of human good was that of prospering or flourishing ... to a mode in which ... there is [a] notion of a higher, more complete good, a notion of complete virtue, or even of a salvation beyond human flourishing ... an escape through self-transformation." "What Was the Axial Revolution?," in *Dilemmas and Connections: Selected Essays* (Cambridge, MA: Belknap Press of Harvard Univ. Press, 2011), 368, 372.

53 "It is only with the *renouncer*, who leaves the world of [elaborate, formal religious ceremonies of] sacrifice and [social] status, that we find the axial individual." Bellah, *Religion in Human Evolution*, 508. Emphasis added.

54 The Axial reversal of values reached a later height in the Christian idea that God Himself had entered history in the "form of a slave," and in formulas such as: "He hath put down the mighty from their seats and hath exalted the humble and meek." Philippians 2:7; Luke 1:52.

55 Contemporary information technology and theory crown the journey of theoretic culture from meaning to information: "Cybernetics transforms language into an exchange of news. The arts become regulated-regulating instruments of information." Martin Heidegger, "The End of Philosophy and the Task of Thinking," trans. Joan Stambaugh, in *Basic Writings*, ed.

David Farrell Krell (New York: HarperCollins, 1977), 376. The culmination of theoretic culture's emphasis on "information" rather than meaning is the "computational theory of mind" (CTM), according to which "mental life consists of information-processing or computation." In this "notion of mechanical rationality," intelligence is a "computational system," in which "knowledge and goals are represented as patterns in bits of matter," and, in pursuit of a goal, "new accurate beliefs are derived from old ones" through some "normatively valid systems like logic, statistics or laws of cause and effect in the world." Steven Pinker, *Language, Cognition and Human Nature* (New York: Oxford Univ. Press, 2015), 270. One of the challenges for this theory is how the notion of "goal" – which is a kind of meaning, value, or good – fits into it. "Merely to have information, however abundant, is not to know." Martin Heidegger, *An Introduction to Metaphysics*, trans. Ralph Manheim (New York: Doubleday, 1961), 17.

56 Paul Ricœur describes the distinction between mythic and theoretic culture as "la poétique de l'amour et la prose de la justice." *Amour et justice*, 32.

57 "The Intelligence does not contemplate unity, for, even when it comtemplates The One, it does not contemplate it as a unity. Otherwise there would be no intelligence. It begins by being one but does not remain one. Unconsciously it becomes multiple, as if pressed down by its own weight." Plotinus, *Enneads* 3.8.8, in *The Essential Plotinus*, ed. Elmer O'Brien (New York: Mentor Books, 1964), 170.

58 Donald, *Origins of the Modern Mind*, 274–5.

59 Donald, 275–98.

60 The difference between a visual and an oral culture is dramatically expressed in the biblical account of Elijah's despairing journey to Mount Sinai, fleeing the wrath of Jezebel. When he encounters God on the mountain, scripture emphasizes that God is not in anything physical – he is emphatically *not* in the wind, or earthquake, or fire – but only in a "still small *voice*," which questions Elijah's behaviour and points out the way of duty to him. 1 Kings 19:11–18. Shakespeare expresses the same difference when an awakened King Lear – awakened to the world's sorrows and injustices – cries out to an unfeeling world: "Look with thine ears … Hark in thine ear." *King Lear*, in *The Complete Works*, ed. Alfred Harbage (Baltimore: Penguin Books, 1969), 4.6.149–50.

61 Jean-François Billeter notes the decisive difference between the "ocular" or vision-based metaphors that underpin Western thought and the action-based metaphors of traditional Chinese thought, whose goal is performative rather than propositional, i.e., mastery of the human virtues rather than abstract reasoning about an objective world. "Pensée occidentale et pensée chinoise: le regard et l'acte," in *Différences, valeurs, hiérarchie*

(Paris: École des Hautes Études en Sciences Sociales, 1984), 25–51, cited in Edward Slingerland, *Effortless Action: Wu-wei as Conceptual Metaphor and Spiritual Ideal in Early China* (New York: Oxford Univ. Press, 2003), 4–5. On the link between vision and rational intellect, see also Emmanuel Levinas, *Entre nous: Essais sur le penser-à-l'autre* (Paris: Livre de Poche, 2010), 165. Anyone who is old enough, as I am, to have listened, as a child, to the Lone Ranger on the radio, and then to have watched him on television, is in a position to appreciate just how much the interior imagination of an aural world exceeds the power of external images in a visual culture. Daniel C. Richardson, author of *Measuring Narrative Engagement: The Heart Tells the Story*, has found that, measured by physical symptoms such as pulse, body temperature, and ectodermic activity, audiobooks are more cognitively and emotionally stimulating than videos of the same works. Catherine Lalonde, "Trouver sa voix," *Le Devoir*, 8 March 2019, B5.

62 Modern philosophy, as Alfred North Whitehead puts it, draws a "phenomenal veil" between persons and "action and evaluation." However, there are "no rational principles which penetrate from the veil to the dark background of reality." *Process and Reality*, 165.

63 Frye, *The Great Code*, 7. Paul Ricœur calls the language of the first phase of theoretic culture (B1) "le langage argumentatif." *Amour et justice*, 55–9.

64 Even Aristotle, the founder of theoretic culture, recognizes that thinking both begins and ends in intuition. *The Nicomachean Ethics*, bk. 6, chaps. 6–11, 1141a 5–10, 1142a25–30, 1143a35–b1, trans. J.A.K. Thomson, rev. Hugh Tredennick (London: Penguin Books, 2004), 152, 156, 161.

65 "[W]hat is culturally *backgrounded* in contemporary North America ... is culturally *foregrounded* in contemporary South Asia and in the sensibilities of many premodern peoples in various regions of the world." Richard A. Shweder, *Why Do Men Barbecue? Recipes for Cultural Psychology* (Cambridge, MA: Harvard Univ. Press, 2003), 133. Emphasis added.

66 Levinas, *Dieu, la mort et le temps*, 144–5, 193.

67 Donald, *Origins of the Modern Mind*, 297.

68 Marcel Gauchet dates the "bifurcation" from around 3000 BCE. *The Disenchantment of the World: A Political History of Religion*, trans. Oscar Bruge (Princeton, NJ: Princeton Univ. Press, 1997), 10, 16. Joseph Campbell places the beginning of the process about 2000 BCE. *The Masks of God: Occidental Mythology* (Harmondsworth: Penguin Books, 1976), 72–5.

69 J. Campbell, *The Masks of God*, 72–5, 78, 106, 114.

70 Joseph Campbell, *Myths to Live By* (New York: Bantam Books, 1973), 74–5.

71 Gauchet, *The Disenchantment of the World*, 95. Emphasis added.

72 In Marcel Gauchet's words, "as soon as the world was attributed to a separate subject, it became possible to separate humans from the cosmos." Gauchet, 73.

73 Marcel Gauchet calls this the "fundamental paradox" of Western religious history: "the growth in the gods' power, which might reasonably
   be expected to be detrimental to humans, proves to be to their ultimate
   advantage." Gauchet, 30.

74 Martin Buber, *I and Thou*, 2nd ed., trans. Ronald Gregor Smith (New York:
   Charles Scribner's Sons, 1958), 18–23. Martin Heidegger calls this process
   the "secession of the logos," the "separation between being and thinking": it "became the starting point for the domination of reason. This
   secession of the logos which started logos on its way to becoming a court
   of justice over being occurred in Greek philosophy itself." *An Introduction
   to Metaphysics*, trans. Manheim, 150.

75 H. and H.A. Frankfort, "Conclusion: The Emancipation of Thought from
   Myth," in Henri Frankfort, H.A. Frankfort, John A. Wilson, and Thorkild
   Jacobsen, *Before Philosophy: The Intellectual Adventure of Ancient Man* (Har-
   mondsworth: Penguin Books, 1949), 248–9.

76 John S. Dunne, *The City of the Gods: A Study in Myth and Morality* (New
   York: Macmillan, 1965), 33.

77 Aristotle, *The Nicomachean Ethics* 10.7.1177b30–1178a1, trans. Thomson,
   rev. Tredennick, 272.

78 José Casanova agrees it's important to distinguish the truly "religious"
   character of the Axial age revolution in Israel from the more humanist and
   "protoscientific" cultural developments in Greece in the same period. "Religion, the Axial Age, and Secular Modernity in Bellah's Theory of Religious
   Evolution," in *The Axial Age*, ed. Bellah and Joas, 207–10.

79 Bellah, *Religion in Human Evolution*, 523.

80 Aristotle, *The Nicomachean Ethics* 4.1.1119b20–9.1128b35, trans. Thomson,
   rev. Tredennick, 82–111. Contrast Aristotle's still self-assertive approach
   to virtue with the – far more "reverential" – value given to the virtues
   of modesty and humility in Thomas Aquinas, *Summa Theologiæ* 2–2.160,
   2–2.161 (Cambridge: Cambridge Univ. Press, 2006), vol. 44 ("Well-
   Tempered Passion"), trans. Thomas Gilby, 83–115.

81 John W. O'Malley suggests "[t]he ideals held up for emulation [in Hel-
   lenic education] were those of the noble warrior." *Four Cultures of the
   West*, 128. Charles Taylor discusses the "warrior *agōn*" of Greek culture,
   challenged by Plato. *Sources of the Self: The Making of the Modern Identity*
   (Cambridge, MA: Harvard Univ. Press, 1989), 20–1.

82 Karen Armstrong, *The Great Transformation: The Beginning of Our Religious
   Traditions* (New York: Alfred A. Knopf, 2006), 103–4. Armstrong references Jean-Pierre Vernant, *Myth and Society in Ancient Greece*, 3rd ed.,
   trans. Janet Lloyd (New York: Zone Books, 1996), 29–32, 90. Edith Hall
   identifies "ten particular qualities" of Greek culture, seven of which are
   clearly virtues of self-assertion. And the other three probably qualify as

assertive too. *Introducing the Greeks: From Bronze Age Seafarers to Navigators of the Western Mind* (New York: W.W. Norton, 2014), 1.

83 Heidegger, *An Introduction to Metaphysics*, trans. Manheim, 112.

84 Edith Hall's subtitle (*From Bronze Age Seafarers to Navigators of the Western Mind*) nicely captures the analogy I've drawn here between Odysseus and Aristotle. H. and H.A. Frankfort also compare the early Greek philosophers to "conquistadors." "Conclusion: The Emancipation of Thought from Myth," 254.

85 Bellah, *Religion in Human Evolution*, 334–41.

86 "[W]e prefer seeing to everything else." Aristotle, *Metaphysics* 1.1.980a25, trans. W.D. Ross, in *The Basic Works of Aristotle*, ed. Richard McKeon (New York: Random House, 1941), 689. See also Saint Augustine, *Confessions*, bk. 10, chap. 35, trans. R.S. Pine-Coffin (Harmondsworth: Penguin Books, 1961), 241. Aquinas, *Summa Theologiæ* 2–2.167.2, vol. 44 ("Well-Tempered Passion"), trans. Gilby, 209.

87 Parmenides of Elea, *Fragments*, trans. David Gallop (Toronto: Univ. of Toronto Press, 1984), 55; G.S. Kirk and J.E. Raven, *The Presocratic Philosophers* (Cambridge: Cambridge Univ. Press, 1964), 266–9; Charles Freeman, *The Closing of the Western Mind: The Rise of Faith and the Fall of Reason* (London: Pimlico, 2003), 11.

88 Aristotle, *The Nicomachean Ethics* 1.4.1095b5–10, trans. Thomson, rev. Tredennick, 8.

89 Hans-Georg Gadamer, *The Beginning of Knowledge*, trans. Rod Coltman (New York: Continuum, 2002), 105.

90 Langer, *Mind: An Essay on Human Feeling*, vol. 1 (Baltimore: Johns Hopkins Press, 1967), 241. Max Scheler suggests this "objective" world emerges from feeling because feeling begins to develop "a cognitive function" in the "feeling of values" which are the distinctive, original "objects" of feeling. In this process of "intentional feeling, the world of objects 'comes to the fore' by itself, but only in terms of its *value*-aspect." *Formalism in Ethics*, trans. Frings and Funk, 257–9. Emphasis in original. F.H. Bradley agrees: "Nature is but one part of a feeling whole, which we have separated by our abstraction … And then we set up this fragment as self-existing." *Appearance and Reality* (Oxford: Oxford Univ. Press, 1930), 236. Alfred North Whitehead calls the process, by which *feelings* are gradually transformed into objective *data*, "transmutation." *Process and Reality*, 292–7, 67, 103.

91 Patricia Curd, "Presocratic Philosophy," in *The Stanford Encyclopedia of Philosophy*, ed. Edward N. Zalta (*Spring 2012 Edition*), http://plato.stanford.edu/archives/spr2012/entries/presocratics/.

92 H. and H.A. Frankfort, "Conclusion: The Emancipation of Thought from Myth," 251.

93 H. and H.A. Frankfort, 251.

94 Hans-Georg Gadamer, *Dialogue and Dialectic: Eight Hermeneutical Studies on Plato*, trans. P. Christopher Smith (New Haven: Yale Univ. Press, 1980), 21, 23.

95 Explaining everything on the basis of efficient or material causes, as the presocratics had begun to do, would be, Socrates argues, like explaining the fact that he now finds himself condemned to death by the people of Athens by reference to his biochemistry, rather than by reference to the "real causes" of his immanent death, which are that the people of Athens thought it "better" to condemn him, and he thought it "better and more just" to submit to their sentence. Plato, *Phaedo* 95D–100A, in *Great Dialogues of Plato*, trans. W.H.D. Rouse, ed. Eric H. Warmington and Philip G. Rouse (New York: New American Library, 1956), 501–3.

96 Plato, *Meno* 81B–82D, in *Great Dialogues of Plato*, trans. Rouse, 42.

97 Gadamer, *Dialogue and Dialectic*, 21–2.

98 Plato, *The Republic*, bk. 7, 514A–519C, in *Great Dialogues of Plato*, trans. Rouse, 312–17; *Symposium* 189D–194B, 200C–213D, in *Great Dialogues of Plato*, trans. Rouse, 87–9, 97–107.

99 Plato, *The Republic*, bk. 10, 595B–598C, in *Great Dialogues of Plato*, trans. Rouse, 394–6.

100 Gadamer, *Dialogue and Dialectic*, 37–8.

101 Samuel Taylor Coleridge said that the essence of the Platonic tone is the "thirst for something not attained." *Philosophical Lectures*, quoted in Thomas McFarland, *Coleridge and the Pantheist Tradition* (Oxford: Oxford Univ. Press, 1969), 299.

102 Plato, *The Republic*, bk. 6, 484D–486B, in *Great Dialogues of Plato*, trans. Rouse, 283.

103 "Desire imports something absent: and a need of what is absent." Thomas Traherne, *Centuries of Meditations*, ed. Bertram Dobell (New York: Cosimo, 2009), 28.

104 Gadamer, *Dialogue and Dialectic*, 14–15.

105 Bellah, *Religion in Human Evolution*, 593–5.

106 Aristotle, *The Nicomachean Ethics* 7.2.1146b5–10, 10.8.1179a15–25, trans. Thomson, rev. Tredennick, 171, 276.

107 "Aristotle is the founder not only of the positive sciences but also of the positive philosophy." Shestov, *Athens and Jerusalem*, 74, 77.

108 Aristotle, *The Nicomachean Ethics* 9.4.1166a15–25, trans. Thomson, rev. Tredennick, 236.

109 Aristotle, *The Nicomachean Ethics* 6.9.1142b10–15, trans. Thomson, rev. Tredennick, 158.

110 "[T]he great age of Greece was a single creative *self-assertion*." Heidegger, *An Introduction to Metaphysics*, trans. Manheim, 90. Emphasis added.

111 Étienne Gilson, *L'être et l'essence*, 2nd ed. (Paris: Vrin, 1987), 60.

112 Aristotle, *Physics* 2.3.194b20–195a20, trans. R.P. Hardie and R.K. Gaye; *Metaphysics* 1.2.983a25–b5, 5.1.1013a20–35, 8.4.1044a30–b2, trans. W.D. Ross, in *The Basic Works of Aristotle*, ed. Richard McKeon, 240–1, 693, 752, 817. On the four types of cause, see also Thomas Aquinas, "Commentary," *Metaphysics, lect. 2*, in *Philosophical Texts*, selected and trans. Thomas Gilby (London: Oxford Univ. Press, 1956), 43–6.

113 Aristotle, *Metaphysics* 9.6.1048a30–9.8.1050b25, 12.7.1072b10–30, trans. Ross, 880; Gilson, *L'être et l'essence*, 53, 114, 328; Bernard J.F. Lonergan, *Insight: A Study of Human Understanding* (London: Darton, Longman & Todd, 1973), 367–71; *Verbum: Word and Idea in Aquinas*, The Collected Works of Bernard Lonergan, ed. Frederick E. Crowe and Robert M. Doran (Toronto: Univ. of Toronto Press, 1997), 2:37–8.

114 Aristotle, *The Nicomachean Ethics* 2.6.1107a1–5, trans. Thomson, rev. Tredennick, 42. Emphasis added.

115 Aristotle, *The Nicomachean Ethics* 6.1.1138b20–13.1145a10, trans. Thomson, rev. Tredennick, 144–66.

116 Aristotle, *The Nicomachean Ethics* 6.12.1144a30–7, trans. W.D. Ross, in Richard McKeon, ed., *Introduction to Aristotle* (New York: Modern Library, 1947), 440. "Bad will makes truth unwelcome, and unwelcome truth tends to be overlooked." Lonergan, *Insight*, 561.

117 Aristotle, *The Nicomachean Ethics* 10.5.1176a15–20, trans. Thomson, rev. Tredennick, 267.

118 "[T]he crucial question is whether we can and ought to regard our lives as mere fact. … Even the most trivial gifts of our everyday social existence are more than just factual circumstances; they always contain within them a sense of obligation to which mere facts cannot give rise." Hans Joas, *The Sacredness of the Person: A New Genealogy of Human Rights*, trans. Alex Skinner (Washington, DC: Georgetown Univ. Press, 2013), 158–9.

119 Aristotle, *The Nicomachean Ethics* 10.6.1177b25–1178a5, 7.13.1153b30–5, trans. Thomson, rev. Tredennick, 272, 196.

120 Plato, *Symposium* 209C–213D, in *Great Dialogues of Plato*, trans. Rouse, 105–6.

121 Heinrich Heine, *Deutschland*, i, quoted in C.G. Jung, *Psychological Types*, trans. H. Godwin Baynes (London: Routledge, 1964), 9.

122 Samuel Taylor Coleridge, *Table Talk*, 2 July 1830, cited in McFarland, *Coleridge and the Pantheist Tradition*, 58.

123 "La division entre *platonici* et *aristotelici* se maintiendra, en effet, jusqu'à la fin du Moyen Âge, sinon jusqu'à nos jours, selon qu'une pensée se reconnaîtra davantage dans l'idéalisme des dialogues de Platon ou dans le réalisme plus analytique du Stagirite [Aristotle]." Jean Grondin, *Introduction à la métaphysique* (Montreal: Les Presses de l'Université de Montréal, 2004), 115.

124 On the "irrepressible need of the human heart" to look "beyond," see
    Charles Taylor, *A Secular Age* (Cambridge, MA: Belknap Press of Har-
    vard Univ. Press, 2007), 638. Walter Kaufmann calls this the "ontolog-
    ical interest" of humankind: the "yearning for another state of being
    ... another life, as it were, richer and stronger; a rebirth in beauty and
    perfection." Walter Kaufmann, *Nietzsche: Philosopher, Psychologist, An-
    tichrist*, 3rd rev. ed. (New York: Vintage Books, 1968), 254–5.
125 Étienne Gilson, *The Elements of Christian Philosophy* (New York: Mentor,
    1963), 107. "Aristotle and Aristotelians write books on politics, whereas
    Plato and Platonists always write Utopias." *Unity of Philosophical Experi-
    ence* (New York: Scribner's, 1965), 68.
126 "Greek philosophy ... evolved the generalization that the actual world
    can be conceived as a collection of primary substances qualified by uni-
    versal qualities." Whitehead, *Process and Reality*, 184.
127 "Le subjectif et son Bien ne sauraient se comprendre à partir de l'ontol-
    ogie. Par contre à partir de la subjectivité du Dire, la signification du Dit
    pourra s'interpréter." Emmanuel Levinas, *Autrement qu'être ou au-delà de
    l'essence* (Paris: Le Livre de Poche, 2008), 77.
128 Charles Freeman gives a useful but one-sided account of these four
    "rounds" in *The Closing of the Western Mind*. An insightful account of the
    first three remains Charles Norris Cochrane's classic *Christianity and Clas-
    sical Culture* (New York: Oxford Univ. Press, 1976).
129 "On a parlé, à juste titre, d'une 'philosophie de l'immanence' pour quali-
    fier toute la pensée de l'hellénisme: immanence du *logos* universel pour le
    stoïcisme, qui commande un stoïcisme moral vis-à-vis de tout ce qui est,
    immanence du bonheur pour l'épicurieme, et mise en question de la tran-
    scendance, sinon de toute visée de vérité, pour le scepticisme." Grondin,
    Introduction à la métaphysique, 116.
130 Epictetus, *Discourses* 2.10.1–2, quoted in Martha Nussbaum, *The Ther-
    apy of Desire: Theory and Practice in Hellenistic Ethics* (Princeton: Prince-
    ton Univ. Press, 1994), 326. For Aristotle, see *The Nicomachean Ethics*
    3.2.1111b5–1112a17, 6.2.1139a15–b15, 10.4.1175a15–20, trans. Thomson,
    rev. Tredennick, 54–6, 146–7, 264.
131 Cicero, *De officiis* 1.20.66, in O'Malley, *Four Cultures of the West*, 133.
132 Seneca, *Moral Epistles* 41.1–2, in Nussbaum, *The Therapy of Desire*, 326.
133 N. Joseph Torchia, *Plotinus, Tolma, and the Descent of Being: An Exposition
    and Analysis* (New York: Peter Lang, 1993), 3–4.
134 Plotinus, *Enneads* 1.6.5, in *The Essential Plotinus*, 38.
135 Plotinus, *Enneads* 6.9.11, in *The Essential Plotinus*, 88. Emphasis added.
    Lev Shestov suggests Plotinus "lost confidence in philosophic thought ...
    he seeks salvation outside of knowledge." *Athens and Jerusalem*, 222.

136 John Meyendorff, "Preface," and Abraham J. Malherbe and Everett Ferguson, "Introduction," in Gregory of Nyssa, *The Life of Moses*, trans. Abraham J. Malherbe and Everett Ferguson (New York: Paulist Press, 1978), xiii, 3–5.

137 "The personal philosophical thought of Augustine is to Plotinus as the personal philosophical thought of Thomas Aquinas is to Aristotle." Gilson, *The Elements of Christian Philosophy*, 17.

138 Peter Brown, *Augustine of Hippo: A Biography* (London: Faber & Faber, 1990), 151–2, 205, 246, 320–1, 327, 366, 369, 373–4. The words quoted are on page 374n2. Also: Saint Augustine, *City of God*, trans. Henry Bettenson (London: Penguin Books, 2003), 568, 584, 599, 874, 891; Saint Augustine, *Confessions*, bk. 8, chaps. 5–10, trans. Pine-Coffin, 164–75.

139 Augustine, *City of God*, trans. Bettenson, 568, 572, 1065, 1070, 1073.

140 Augustine, *City of God*, trans. Bettenson, 637.

141 Brown, *Augustine of Hippo*, 154–5, 178, 238, 373–5. Also: Augustine, *City of God*, trans. Bettenson, 196, 310, 425, 590, 604, 637, 870, 872, 1023, 1090.

142 "[T]here is a twofold nature in man, intellectual and sensitive." Thomas Aquinas, *Summa Theologiæ* 1–2.10.3, in *Treatise on Happiness*, trans. John A. Oesterle (Notre Dame, IN: Univ. of Notre Dame Press, 1983), 105.

143 Aquinas, *Summa Theologiæ* 1–2.19.1, in *Treatise on Happiness*, trans. Oesterle, 178.

144 Aquinas, *Summa Theologiæ* 1–2.66.1, in *Treatise on the Virtues*, trans. John A. Oesterle (Notre Dame, IN: Univ. of Notre Dame Press, 1984), 149.

145 Aquinas, *Summa Theologiæ* 1–2.4.5, in *Treatise on Happiness*, trans. Oesterle, 48.

146 Aquinas, *Summa Theologiæ* 1–2.66.3, in *Treatise on the Virtues*, trans. Oesterle, 154. "[T]he doctrine of Thomas Aquinas is thoroughly intellectualist in its inspiration." Gilson, *The Elements of Christian Philosophy*, 278.

147 Aquinas, *Summa Theologiæ* 1–2.57.5, in *Treatise on the Virtues*, trans. Oesterle, 76.

148 Aquinas, *Summa Theologiæ* 1–2.64.3, in *Treatise on the Virtues*, trans. Oesterle, 135.

149 Of the 2668 articles in Aquinas' great *Summa Theologiæ*, some 1535 (or almost 60 per cent) appear in the second part dealing with human acts (especially the virtues), which almost seems to "submerge" the two other parts dealing with God and Christ. And almost half of the first part (dealing with God) is itself devoted to understanding human nature, in the range of other creatures. Bernard McGinn, *Thomas Aquinas's* Summa Theologiae: *A Biography* (Princeton: Princeton Univ. Press, 2014), 44–5, 69, 93. Thus Aquinas' theology is also, or even primarily, *an anthropology*, rooted in an analysis of the nature of the human: i.e., of the human virtues. Robert Pasnau examines Aquinas' so-called "Treatise of Human

Nature," which covers fifteen questions from the first part of the *Summa theologiæ*, or some 3 per cent of the whole *Summa*. But Pasnau does not get to Aquinas' discussion of the virtues which takes up the second part of the *Summa*, and vastly overshadows the rest of it. *Thomas Aquinas on Human Nature* (Cambridge: Cambridge Univ. Press, 2002), 3.

150 Robert Pasnau points out that, by "a *summa* of theology, Aquinas does not mean the pinnacle of his work but merely a summary." *Thomas Aquinas on Human Nature*, 5.

151 Denys Turner, *Thomas Aquinas: A Portrait* (New Haven: Yale Univ. Press, 2013), 187. Philippa Foot suggests Aquinas' *Summa Theologiæ* is "one of the best sources we have for moral philosophy." "Virtues and Vices," in *Virtue Ethics*, ed. Roger Crisp and Michael Slote (Oxford: Oxford Univ. Press, 1997), 164.

152 Aquinas, *Summa Theologiæ* 1–2.3.8, in *Treatise on Happiness*, trans. Oesterle, 39.

153 Aquinas, *Summa Theologiæ* 1–2.5.5, in *Treatise on Happiness*, trans. Oesterle, 61.

154 Aquinas, *Summa Theologiæ* 1–2.5.3, in *Treatise on Happiness*, trans. Oesterle, 57. Emphasis added. See also *Summa Contra Gentiles*, chap. 48, in *Introduction to St. Thomas Aquinas*, ed. Anton C. Pegis (New York: Modern Library, 1948), 463–7.

155 Aquinas, *Summa Theologiæ* 1–2.5.6, in *Treatise on Happiness*, trans. Oesterle, 63.

156 Gilson, *The Elements of Christian Philosophy*, 146.

157 Aquinas, *Summa Theologiæ* 1–2.55.2, in *Treatise on the Virtues*, trans. Oesterle, 53.

158 Aquinas, *Summa Theologiæ* 1–2.5.5, in *Treatise on Happiness*, trans. Oesterle, 60.

159 Aquinas, *Summa Theologiæ* 1–2.9.1, in *Treatise on Happiness*, trans. Oesterle, 93.

160 It was apparently common among medieval scholastics to assume that "*intellectus*" came from *intus legere*, or to read within. In other words, *intellectus* can grasp, directly and intuitively, the innermost essences of things, hidden within their external, accidental properties. Pasnau, *Thomas Aquinas on Human Nature*, 169.

161 Aquinas, *Summa Theologiæ* 1–2.5.1, in *Treatise on Happiness*, trans. Oesterle, 55.

162 Aquinas, *Summa Theologiæ* 1–2.57.2, in *Treatise on the Virtues*, trans. Oesterle, 70–1.

163 Aquinas, *Summa Theologiæ* 1–2.66.5, in *Treatise on the Virtues*, trans. Oesterle, 157.

164 Aquinas, *Summa Theologiæ* 1–2.66.5, in *Treatise on the Virtues*, trans. Oesterle, 157. Emphasis added.

165 Aquinas, *Summa Theologiæ* 1–2.66.5, in *Treatise on the Virtues*, trans. Oesterle, 158.

166 Aquinas, *Summa Theologiæ* 1–2.66.6, in *Treatise on the Virtues*, trans.
    Oesterle, 159. Emphasis added. "Note this difference: things known are
    in the knower, not after their own manner of existence, whereas desire
    goes out to things just as they are in themselves, and the lover in a sense
    is changed into them." "Exposition," *de Divinis Nominibus, 2, lect. 4*, in
    Aquinas, *Theological Texts*, selected and trans. Thomas Gilby (London:
    Oxford Univ. Press, 1954), 32. "[W]ith respect to divine things, higher
    than the soul: now thus it is better to love them than to understand them;
    it is better to love God than to know about him, for the divine goodness
    is most perfectly in God, which is how it is desired by the will, than it is
    as shared in us or conceived by the mind." "Disputations," 22 *de Veritate*,
    11, in Aquinas, *Philosophical Texts*, trans. Gilby, 257. See also Gilson, *The
    Elements of Christian Philosophy*, 283–5.
167 On how Aquinas uses Augustine to correct Aristotle, and Aristotle to cor-
    rect Augustine, see Alasdair MacIntyre, *Whose Justice? Which Rationality?*
    (Notre Dame, IN: Univ. of Notre Dame Press, 1988), 205.
168 On the very last pages of his *Guide for the Perplexed*, Maimonides – in an
    arc very similar to Aquinas – finally puts aside his Aristotelian assump-
    tions and recognizes that the love of God is *not* a kind of knowledge
    after all, but rather a kind of "act" or "actions": "to seek loving-kindness,
    judgement, and righteousness and thus to imitate the ways of God." Mo-
    ses Maimonides, *The Guide for the Perplexed*, trans. M. Friedländer (New
    York: Dover, 1956), 396–7.
169 Charles Taylor captures why Augustine can be categorized as a thinker of
    "I *am*" (A2) and Aquinas as a thinker of "It *is*" (B1), in the following way:
    "[W]e can contrast the temper of these Augustinian proofs [of the existence
    of God] with those that Thomas formulated. The latter argue to God from
    the existence of created reality (or what the proofs show to be created re-
    ality). They pass, as it were, *through objects* [It *is*]. The Augustinian proofs
    move *through the subject* [I *am*] and through the undeniable foundations of
    his presence to himself." *Sources of the Self*, 141. Emphasis added.
170 Robert Barron, *Thomas Aquinas: Spiritual Master* (New York: Crossroad,
    2008).
171 "Thomas Aquinas revived the Aristotelian approach to knowing things
    so successfully that he unwittingly laid the foundation of the scientific
    revolution that was to transform western thought." Freeman, *The Closing
    of the Western Mind*, 333. "Aristotle won a complete victory over Plato,
    and what he established and constructed has remained standing to our
    day. ... [T]he Middle Ages could not and would not break with the tradi-
    tion of Greek philosophy. ... Modern philosophy merely continued and
    perfected the work of Scholasticism." Shestov, *Athens and Jerusalem*, 105,
    266, 278.

172 Franz Rosenzweig suggests Western culture has been shaped by three
     "enlightenments," not just one: the first enlightenment of Aristotle and
     ancient Greek culture (i.e., the first phase of theoretic culture) which
     "directed its criticism against the dreams of mythology [i.e., mythic
     culture]"; a second enlightenment of the Renaissance which directed its
     critique against the purely rational knowledge and "webs of intellect"
     spun by medieval scholasticism; and a third enlightenment – the En-
     lightenment of the seventeenth and eighteenth centuries "which we are
     accustomed to designate by that name" (i.e., the second phase of theoretic
     culture) – which directed its critique "against the gullibility of experi-
     ence" and thus became "slowly but surely a historical critique." *The Star
     of Redemption*, trans. William W. Hallo (Notre Dame, IN: Univ. of Notre
     Dame Press, 1985), 97–9. Rosenzweig's so-called second enlightenment
     of the Renaissance is thus the essential bridge from the first to the second
     phase of theoretic culture, and (from the nominalists to Francis Bacon)
     "proves ever more clearly a scientific one." Rosenzweig, 98.
173 José Casanova sums up "four related and simultaneously unfolding
     developments" which, together, helped to undermine the medieval re-
     ligious system: "the Protestant Reformation; the formation of modern
     states; the growth of capitalism; and the early modern scientific revolu-
     tion." *Public Religions in the Modern World*, 21. A standard reference on
     the early part of this transition is Steven Ozment, *The Age of Reform 1250–
     1550: An Intellectual and Religious History of Late Medieval and Reformation
     Europe* (New Haven: Yale Univ. Press, 2020). Ozment's account has been
     criticized for its bias and omissions: see Eamon Duffy, "Why Was There a
     Reformation?" *The New York Review of Books* 68, no. 3 (25 February 2021),
     41–2. An impressive recent attempt to tell the theoretical part of this story
     is Robert Pasnau, *Metaphysical Themes 1274–1671* (Oxford: Oxford Univ.
     Press, 2013). A broader but equally impressive historical overview is Brad
     S. Gregory, *The Unintended Reformation: How a Religious Revolution Revolu-
     tionized Society* (Cambridge, MA: Belknap Press of Harvard Univ. Press,
     2012). For a longer view, which emphasizes how modern individualism
     and rationalism are outgrowths of Christianity itself, see Larry Siedentop,
     Inventing the Individual: The Origins of Western Liberalism (London: Allen
     Lane, 2014). Charles Taylor's two major works – *Sources of the Self* and *A
     Secular Age*, especially the first – are important explorations of this tran-
     sition from the ancient and medieval to the modern and post-modern
     condition, which emphasize the gains as well as the losses. For an older,
     philosophical account, see John Herman Randall Jr., *The Career of Philoso-
     phy: From the Middle Ages to the Enlightenment* (New York: Columbia Univ.
     Press, 1962). On the roots of individualism and rationalism in medieval
     Christianity, see also Johannes Fried, *The Middle Ages*, trans. Peter Lewis

(Cambridge, MA: Belknap Press of Harvard Univ. Press, 2015), and Kevin Madigan, *Medieval Christianity: A New History* (New Haven: Yale Univ. Press, 2015).

174 On the centrality of logic in the curriculum of the medieval universities, see O'Malley, *Four Cultures of the West*, 94; Macintyre, *Whose Justice?*, 206. On the way logic "has vitiated thought and procedure from the first discovery of mathematics and logic by the Greeks," see Whitehead, *Process and Reality*, 69.

175 Siedentop, *Inventing the Individual*, 218–19, 229; Gregory, *The Unintended Reformation*, 197–8.

176 Fried, *The Middle Ages*, 357–8.

177 Robert Pasnau argues that "nominalism" is "an historical fiction" – invented in the fifteenth century – but one that is "not without some basis in reality," and helps "to get scholars into the right territory, even while obscuring the overall narrative" because William of Ockham's views, especially about "material substances," "often foreshadow the eventual rejection of scholasticism in the seventeenth century." He suggests that "the status of universals was just one and not the most important of the issues that came to be seen as distinctive of nominalism." *Metaphysical Themes 1274–1671*, 83–8.

178 Shestov, *Athens and Jerusalem*, 223–4.

179 Siedentop, *Inventing the Individual*, 310, 313, 318–19.

180 Gilson, *Unity of Philosophical Experience*, 76, 86.

181 Taylor, *Sources of the Self*, 82.

182 For C.G. Jung, the medieval controversy between nominalism and realism is a prime illustration of the fundamental human paradox: it expressed a permanent and necessary human contradiction. Abelard's failed attempt to bridge the divide between them through his "conceptualism" makes him an iconic figure for Jung, living proof that the human paradox can never be resolved by the intellect alone, but only in the "living reality" of real human life. *Psychological Types*, trans. Baynes, 52–69.

183 On Duns Scotus, univocalism, and nominalism, see Gilson, *L'être et l'essence*, 132–6; Grondin, *Introduction à la métaphysique*, 165–71.

184 "It is impossible for a term to be predicated univocally of God and creatures." Aquinas, *Summa Theologiæ* 2–2.81.1, in *Philosophical Texts*, trans. Gilby, 93

185 Thus, Whitehead, for example, embraces univocalism when he says: "God's existence is not different from that of other actual entities, except that he is 'primordial.'" *Process and Reality*, 91.

186 Pseudo-Dionysius, *Divine Names* in *Pseudo-Dionysius: The Complete Works*, trans. Colm Luibheid and Paul Rorem (NJ: Paulist Press, 1987), 98, quoted in Denys Turner, *Faith, Reason and the Existence of God* (Cambridge:

Cambridge Univ. Press, 2004), 157, 188. As often the case, Pseudo-Dionysius adapts Plotinus: "The One is absent from nothing and from everything." *Enneads* 6.9.4, in *The Essential Plotinus*, 79.

187 Gregory, *The Unintended Reformation*, 38.

188 Aquinas, *Theological Texts*, trans. Gilby, 404n3.

189 Denys Turner describes this process as "the disintegration of a unified 'mystical theology' into the fragments of a theology no longer 'mystical' and a theologically irrelevant 'mysticism.'" *The Darkness of God: Negativity in Christian Mysticism* (Cambridge: Cambridge Univ. Press, 1995), 225.

190 Gregory, *The Unintended Reformation*, 38.

191 "In antiquity teachers of philosophy generally tried to create an atmosphere in the classroom that seems almost religious, *filled with reverence* for the texts and conducive to reflection and a life lived in conformity with the teaching of the texts. In its avowed practitioners philosophy meant first of all *a way of life*, a way dedicated to the truths upon which they discoursed. ... This existential aspect of philosophy would remain strong in Christianity *until the founding of the universities*." O'Malley, *Four Cultures of the West*, 81. Emphasis added.

192 Denys the Carthusian, *De Contemplatione*, cited in Turner, *The Darkness of God*, 218.

193 O'Malley, *Four Cultures of the West*, 102.

194 Erasmus, "The Godly Feast," in *Colloquies, Collected Works of Erasmus*, ed. Craig R. Thompson (Toronto: Univ. of Toronto Press, 1997), 40:1.192, in O'Malley, *Four Cultures of the West*, 161.

195 Diarmaid MacCulloch, *Christianity: The First Three Thousand Years* (New York: Viking, 2010), 582.

196 Siedentop, *Inventing the Individual*, 334. Siedentop here summarizes the classic account of the Renaissance by Jacob Burckhardt, an account with which he does not entirely agree.

197 "The irony is that ... the 'world' won after all. Perhaps the contradiction lay in the very idea of a disciplined imposition of the Kingdom of God. The temptation of power was, after all, too strong, as Dostoevsky saw in the legend of the Grand Inquisitor. Here lay the corruption." Taylor, *A Secular Age*, 158.

198 Marilynne Robinson, *The Death of Adam: Essays on Modern Thought* (New York: Picador, 2005), 215–16; Alister McGrath, *Christianity's Dangerous Idea: The Protestant Revolution – A History from the Sixteenth Century to the Twenty-First* (New York: HarperCollins, 2007), 291–2.

199 John Bowden, ed., *Christianity: The Complete Guide* (Toronto: Novalis, 2005), 483.

200 "[F]aith is a knowledge of the divine favour toward us, and a full persuasion of its truth. ... [T]he term faith is justly extended to the whole sum

of heavenly doctrine." John Calvin, *The Institutes of the Christian Religion* 3.2.1–15, trans. Henry Beveridge (Peabody, MA: Hendrickson, 2012), 355–65. The words quoted are on pages 362–4. Also: Alister E. McGrath, ed., *Theology: The Basic Readings* (Oxford: Blackwell, 2008), 8–9; Alister E. McGrath, *Theology: The Basics*, 2nd ed. (Oxford: Blackwell, 2008), 17–19; Bruce Gordon, *Calvin* (New Haven: Yale Univ. Press, 2009), 60.

201 Calvin, *The Institutes of the Christian Religion* 4.12.1, trans. Beveridge, 813. Elsewhere Calvin said doctrine was the "soul of the church": Calvin to Protector Somerset, 22 October 1548, cited in Gordon, *Calvin*, 60, 255.

202 O'Malley, *Four Cultures of the West*, 63. One of Luther's favourite words for faith, however, was the Latin word "fiducia" which means confidence or trust. McGrath, *Theology: The Basics*, 10–13.

203 Patrick Collinson, "The Late Medieval Church and its Reformation: 1400–1600," in *The Oxford Illustrated History of Christianity*, ed. John McManners (Oxford: Oxford Univ. Press, 1990), 266, 263.

204 "Doctrinal disagreement – along with its multiple social, moral, and political effects – is the most fundamental and consequential fact about Western Christianity since 1520 ... As things turned out, not only did no one win in early modern Europe, but Catholics, Lutherans, Reformed Protestants, and Western Christianity in general all lost. ... They made religion as such memorably associable with coercion, oppression and violence, and thus provided ballast for the still widespread conviction that emancipation, autonomy, freedom, and modernity as such imply the supersessionist rejection of religion." Gregory, *The Unintended Reformation*, 45, 160.

205 "[A]theism resulted from the inner dynamics of our own believing culture and not from extrinsic influence." Louis Dupré, *Transcendent Selfhood: The Loss and Recovery of the Inner Life* (New York: Seabury Press, 1976), 14.

206 McGrath, *Christianity's Dangerous Idea*, 264.

207 "Because reliance on ecclesiastical authorities and biblical interpreters had led to so many competing Christian truth claims, some protagonists understandably surmised that only reason divorced from religion could hope to establish a neutral, solid, foundation for truth." Gregory, *The Unintended Reformation*, 114. See also David Martin, *On Secularization: Towards a Revised General Theory* (Farnham: Ashgate, 2005), 4–5.

208 Hegel, *Philosophy of Right*, trans. Knox, 12.

209 McGrath, *Christianity's Dangerous Idea*, 372–9.

210 Siedentop, *Inventing the Individual*, 311–12.

211 MacCulloch, *Christianity*, 615.

212 Taylor, *A Secular Age*, 8–14, 293–4, 613–14.

213 McGrath, *Christianity's Dangerous Idea*, 251.

214 John C. Weaver, *The Great Land Rush and the Making of the Modern World* (Montreal: McGill-Queen's Univ. Press, 2003), 348.

215 Quoted in R.G. Collingwood, *The Idea of History* (New York: Oxford Univ. Press, 1956), 269. Deirdre McCloskey (citing Macaulay) notes that, as Lord Chancellor (the rough equivalent of the modern prime minister), Bacon was the last man in England to use the torture rack for official purposes! Deirdre N. McCloskey, *The Bourgeois Virtues: Ethics for an Age of Commerce* (Chicago: Univ. of Chicago Press, 2006), 369.

216 Francis Bacon, *The New Organon*, in *The Complete Essays of Francis Bacon* (New York: Washington Square Press, 1963), 250.

217 Bacon, 262–3.

218 Siedentop, *Inventing the Individual*, 312.

219 "The ideas of this oration proved to be enormously influential in the late Renaissance, and in the longer term they can be seen as setting the scene for the Enlightenment assertion of human autonomy in the eighteenth century." McGrath, *Christianity's Dangerous Idea*, 34.

220 Pico della Mirandola, *Oration on the Dignity of Man*, in *The Renaissance Philosophy of Man*, ed. E. Cassirer, P.O. Kristeller, and J.H. Randall (Chicago: Univ. of Chicago Press, 1948), pp. 224–25, quoted in Taylor, *Sources of the Self*, 199–200. Recent research suggests the "traditional" modern interpretation of Pico as anticipating modernity is anachronistic and that Pico looks backward more than he looks forward. Anthony Grafton, "Thinking Outside the 'Pico Box,'" *The New York Review of Books* 67, no. 17 (5 November 2020), 37–9; Brian P. Copenhaver, *Magic and the Dignity of Man: Pico della Mirandola and His Oration in Modern Memory* (Cambridge, MA: Harvard Univ. Press, 2019).

221 Niccolò Machiavelli, *The Prince*, trans. Christian E. Detmold (New York: Washington Square Press, 1966), 78, 77, 76–7, 38–9, 7, 114.

222 Machiavelli, 77–8.

223 On the "truth" of Machiavelli as a revelation of the virtues of self-assertion, see Jacques Maritain, *Humanisme intégral*, new ed. (Paris: Éditions Aubier-Montaigne, 1946), 218–19.

224 Michel de Montaigne, *Essais* (Paris: Livre de Poche, 2001), bk. 3, chap. 5, p. 1314. "La sagesse a ses excès, et n'a pas moins besoin de modération que la folie." My translation.

225 Montaigne, bk. 3, chap. 13, p. 1731. "La grandeur de l'âme n'est pas tant, tirer à mont, et tirer avant, comme savoir se ranger et circonscrire. Elle tient pour grand, tout ce qui est assez. Et montre sa hauteur, à aimer mieux les choses moyennes, que les éminentes." My translation.

226 "Toutes les opinions du monde en sont là, que le plaisir est notre but ... Quoiqu'ils disent, en la vertu même, le dernier but de notre visée, c'est la volupté. ... Cette volupté pour être plus gaillarde, nerveuse, robuste,

virile, n'en est que plus sérieusement voluptueuse. Et nous lui devions donner le nom du plaisir." Montaigne, bk. 1, chap. 19, p. 125.

227 See the excellent essay by Mark Lilla, "The Hidden Lesson of Montaigne," *New York Review of Books* 58, no. 5 (24 March 2011), 19–21. For a more admiring view, which shows, inadvertently, how much the spirit of Montaigne is aligned with the post-modern sensibility, see Tim Parks, "Montaigne: What Was Truly Courageous?" *New York Review of Books* 63, no. 18 (24 November 2016), 59–61.

228 Montaigne, *Essais*, bk. 2, chap. 12, p. 821.

229 René Descartes, *Discourse on Method*, trans. Elizabeth S. Haldane and G.R.T. Ross, in *The Philosophical Works of René Descartes*, ed. Elizabeth S. Haldane and G.R.T. Ross (Cambridge: Cambridge Univ. Press, 1969), 1:101. "With the '*cogito sum*' Descartes claims to prepare a new and secure foundation for philosophy. But what he leaves undetermined in this 'radical' beginning is the manner of the being of the *res cogitans*, more precisely *the meaning of the being of the 'sum'* [I am]." Martin Heidegger, *Being and Time*, 24, trans. Joan Stambaugh (Albany: State Univ. of New York Press, 2010), 23. Emphasis in original.

230 G.W.F. Hegel, *Encyclopaedia of the Philosophical Sciences*, §64, in *Hegel's Logic*, trans. William Wallace (London: Oxford Univ. Press, 1975), 100; Whitehead, *Process and Reality*, 184, 186; Paul Ricœur, *Parcours de la reconnaissance* (Paris: Gallimard, 2013), 150; Shestov, *Athens and Jerusalem*, 290–1.

231 Analyzing the emergence and changing meanings of certain English words in the seventeenth century, Webb Keane suggests they illustrate that it was "the moment that the balance between the values of hierarchy [B1] and equality [B2], respectively, began to shift (for a heterogeneous set of reasons). As that shift of balance continued … the value of equality [B2] came to trump that of hierarchy [B1]." *Ethical Life*, 180.

232 Descartes, *Discourse on Method*, trans. Haldane and Ross, 89.

233 Augustine, *City of God*, bk. 11, chap. 26, trans. Bettenson, 460.

234 René Descartes, "Meditation 2," in *Meditations on First Philosophy*, trans. Elizabeth S. Haldane and G.R.T. Ross, in *The Philosophical Works of René Descartes*, 1:152.

235 Descartes, "Meditation 3," trans. Elizabeth S. Haldane and G.R.T. Ross, in *The Philosophical Works of René Descartes*, 1:169. Emphasis added. It was only a very small step from Aquinas' definition of human souls as "intellectual substances" to Descartes' "thinking thing." On Aquinas, see Gilson, *The Elements of Christian Philosophy*, 224–8.

236 Descartes, *Discourse on Method*, trans. Haldane and Ross, 119.

237 Echoing Bacon and Descartes, Hegel took for granted "the absolute right of appropriation which man has over 'things.'" *Philosophy of Right*, trans. Knox, §44, p. 41.

238 All our knowledge, Montaigne had said, comes to us from our five senses. Montaigne, *Essais*, bk. 2, chap. 12, p. 913.

239 In his pursuit of a "geometric" method for thinking, Descartes was pursuing an ambition that went back to Aquinas and even to Boethius in the fifth century. O'Malley, *Four Cultures of the West*, 87.

240 Descartes, *Discourse on Method*, trans. Haldane and Ross, 86.

241 Descartes, 95, 99.

242 Descartes, 92–3.

243 Descartes, 94.

244 Hegel was one of those who later rejected the mathematical model proposed for philosophy by Descartes and Spinoza and embraced even by Leibniz. G.W.F. Hegel, *Preface to the Phenomenology of Spirit*, trans. Yirmiyahu Yovel (Princeton: Princeton Univ. Press, 2005), 147. Alfred North Whitehead (himself a great mathematician) agrees that philosophy has been "vitiated" by the model of mathematics. *Process and Reality*, 13–14, 69–70.

245 Pascal, *Pensées* (Paris: Garnier-Flammarion, 1973), §§224, 910–11, pp. 92, 307–9.

246 Stephen Holmes notes that the celebration of self-assertion ("the pursuit of personal advantage") was "a distinctive innovation of the modern humanism to which all [later] liberals subscribed." *Passions and Constraints: On the Theory of Liberal Democracy* (Chicago: Univ. of Chicago Press, 1995), 27.

247 Descartes, *Discourse on Method*, trans. Haldane and Ross, 91.

248 René Descartes, *The Passions of the Soul*, pt. 3, Article 52, trans. Elizabeth S. Haldane and G.R.T. Ross, in *The Philosophical Works of René Descartes*, 1:401; also, *The Principles of Philosophy*, pt. 1, Principle 37, trans. Haldane and Ross in *The Philosophical Works*, 233–4.

249 Thomas Hobbes, *Leviathan* (Indianapolis: Bobbs-Merrill, 1958), pt. 2, chap. 29, p. 258, pt. 1, chap. 4, p. 45, pt. 1, chap. 15, p. 131.

250 "[T]he only science it has pleased God hitherto to bestow on mankind." Hobbes, pt. 1, chap. 4, p. 41.

251 Hobbes, pt. 1, chap. 5, pp. 47–50.

252 Hobbes, pt. 2, chap. 31, p. 277.

253 Hobbes, pt. 2, chap. 17, p. 139.

254 Hobbes, pt. 1, chap. 10, p. 79.

255 Hobbes, pt. 1, chap. 11, p. 86.

256 Hobbes, pt. 1, chap. 7, p. 61.

257 Hobbes, pt. 1, chap. 11, p. 86.

258 Hobbes, pt. 1, chap. 13, pp. 104–6.

259 Hobbes, pt. 2, chap. 31, p. 277.

260 Hobbes, pt. 1, chap. 14, p. 110.

261 Hobbes, pt. 1, chap. 13, p. 107.

262 Hobbes, pt. 1, chap. 14, p. 110.

263 Hobbes, pt. 2, chap. 17, pp. 139–43.

264 Once human beings have entered into a "contract" – explicitly or implicitly – to establish a civil state, everything changes, Hobbes argues. Or turns upside down. By this very contract, they have given up most of their original liberty and equality for good because the law is "made by the sovereign power, and all that is done by such power is warranted and owned by every one of the people." Hobbes, pt. 2, chap. 18, chap. 30, pp. 146, 271–2.

265 Hobbes, pt. 2, chap. 31, pp. 277, 281; pt. 1, chap. 15, pp. 119–32; pt. 2, chap. 17, p. 139; pt. 2, chap. 26, p. 212.

266 Hobbes, pt. 2, chap. 26, p. 212. Emphasis added.

267 Hobbes, pt. 1, chap. 15, p. 130; pt. 2, chap. 17, p. 139; pt. 2, chap. 26, p. 215; pt. 2, chap. 27, p. 231.

268 Hobbes, pt. 2, chap. 17, p. 139.

269 John Locke, *The Second Treatise on Civil Government*, §§14–15 in *On Politics and Education* (Roslyn, NY: Walter J. Black, 1947), 82–3.

270 Locke, §19, p. 84.

271 Without an "umpire" or "common judge," every man must enforce the law of nature for and by himself: in the state of nature "everyone has the executive power of the law of nature." That is the "inconvenience" of the state of nature, for which the establishment of civil government is the remedy. Locke, §13, pp. 81–2.

272 Locke, §135, p. 145.

273 For Thomas Aquinas, "right" (*jus*) was normally a singular word expressing the objective interest of justice. He usually expressed what we now call "rights" (plural) as "being at liberty or having the ability to do so and so." Aquinas, *Summa Theologiæ* 2–2.57, vol. 37 ("Justice"), trans. Gilby, 2–3, note c.

274 Hobbes, *Leviathan*, pt. 1, chap. 14, p. 109.

275 Hobbes, pt. 1, chap. 14, pp. 109–12, 117–18; pt. 1, chap. 15, pp. 127–8; pt. 2, chap. 21, pp. 175–7.

276 Basil Willey suggests "it was the idea of a controlling *Law* [jus] of Nature which officially dominated the Middle Ages, rather than that of the liberating *Rights* of Nature; and that in passing into the seventeenth and eighteenth centuries, 'Nature' ceases to be mainly a regulating principle and becomes mainly a liberating principle." *The Eighteenth Century Background* (London: Penguin, 1965), 23, quoted in David Cameron, *The Social Thought of Rousseau and Burke: A Comparative Study* (London: Weidenfield & Nicolson, 1973), 44. Emphasis in original. The modern notion of "rights" thus turns the medieval notion of "right" (jus) upside down: the

latter was about "what is rightly owed to another"; the former is about what is owed to the *self*. MacIntyre, *Whose Justice?*, 198–9.

277 Locke, *The Second Treatise on Civil Government*, §136, pp. 145–6.

278 Locke, §§4–5, pp. 76–7.

279 Locke, §7, p. 78.

280 Locke, §135, p. 145.

281 Locke, §§67, 74, 232–5, pp. 107, 111, 195–7; *Some Thoughts Concerning Education*, in *On Politics and Education* (Roslyn, NY: Walter J. Black, 1947), §§99–100, 107, pp. 287, 291; *A Letter Concerning Toleration*, in *On Politics and Education*, 21–3.

282 Locke, *The Second Treatise on Civil Government*, §106 in *On Politics and Education*, 128. Emphasis added.

283 Locke, §61, p. 104.

284 Locke, §57, p. 101.

285 John Locke, *An Essay Concerning Human Understanding*, bk. 4, chap. 19, §14 (New York: Dover, 1959), 2:438. Alexander Campbell Fraser observes this sentence "might be taken for a motto" to the whole *Essay*. Locke, 438n3.

286 "[I]f I know I doubt, I have as certain perception of existence of the thing doubting, as of that thought which I call doubt." Locke, bk. 4, chap. 9, §3, 2:305.

287 Locke, bk. 4, chap. 10, §12–13, 2:316–17. Emphasis added.

288 Locke, bk. 4, chap. 10, §18, 2:320.

289 Locke, bk. 2, chap. 27, §13, 1:453–4.

290 Locke, bk. 4, chap. 4, §3, 2:228. Emphasis added. Locke's text puts "conformity" in italics.

291 "[T]ruth properly belongs only to propositions." Locke, bk. 4, chap. 5, §2, 2:244; chap. 6, §3, 2:252.

292 "This great source of most of the ideas we have, depending wholly upon our senses, and derived by them to the understanding, I call SENSATION." Locke, bk. 2, chap. 1, §3, 1:123. Whitehead calls the philosophy of Locke and Hume a "sensationalist empiricism." Locke "assumes that the utmost primitiveness is to be found in sense-perception." Whitehead, *Process and Reality*, 72, 134.

293 Locke, bk. 4, chap. 3, §25, 2:216–17.

294 Taylor, *Sources of the Self*, 160–72. Paul Ricœur points out that this "punctual" character of the Lockean self was already implicit in Descartes' *cogito*. *Soi-même comme un autre*, 18.

295 On the links between modern individualism, rationalism, and the technological mastery of nature, see also Paul Ricœur, *Lectures 1*, in *Ricœur: Textes choisis et présentés*, ed. Michaël Fœssel and Fabien Lamouche (Paris: Éditions Points, 2007), 370; Dupré, *Transcendent Selfhood*, 4; O'Malley, *Four Cultures of the West*, 119.

296 Frye, *The Great Code*, 13. Paul Ricœur calls the language of the second phase of theoretic culture (B2) "le langage démonstratif." *Amour et justice*, 55–9.

297 Paul Hazard, *The European Mind 1680–1715*, trans. J. Lewis May (Harmondsworth: Penguin Books, 1964), 157.

298 Leibniz said that Spinozism was "un cartésianisme outré." *Essais de Théodicée* (Paris: Garnier-Flammarion, 1969), §393, p. 348.

299 Jean-Jacques Mairan to Nicolas Malebranche (1713) in McFarland, *Coleridge and the Pantheist Tradition*, 76–7.

300 "Each thing, in so far as it is in itself, endeavours to persevere in its being. The effort by which each thing endeavours to persevere in its own being is nothing but the actual essence of the thing." Spinoza, *Ethics*, 3, Propositions 6 & 7, trans. W.H. White, in *Spinoza Selections*, ed. John Wild (New York: Scribner's, 1958), 215–16.

301 "[I]l faut se demander si … le *conatus* est l'humanité de l'homme." Levinas, *Dieu, la mort et le temps*, 27.

302 Lewis Samuel Feuer, *Spinoza and the Rise of Liberalism* (Boston: Beacon Press, 1958), 199.

303 Spinoza, *Ethics*, 4, Proposition 66, trans. White, 346.

304 Spinoza, Propositions 24 and 20, trans. White, 303–4.

305 Spinoza, Preface, Propositions 52 and 25, trans. White, 282–6, 332–3, 306–7.

306 Spinoza, Propositions 53, 50, 54, and 58 trans. White, 333–4, 330–1, 337–8.

307 Spinoza, Proposition 20, trans. White, 304.

308 Spinoza, Proposition 52, trans. White, 333.

309 Stuart Hampshire, *Spinoza* (Harmondsworth: Penguin Books, 1967), 36–9.

310 Spinoza, *Ethics*, 1, Definition 6, trans. W.H. White, in *Spinoza Selections*, 94–5.

311 Spinoza called Part 4 of his *Ethics* "Of Human Bondage," and many of the propositions in that part are intended to show how human beings can and should overcome the bondage of the passions through the self-assertion of reason. Spinoza, *Ethics*, 4, trans. White, 282. This confirms that Spinoza's ethics is a philosophy of the virtues of Equality or "self-control" (B2).

312 Leibniz said Spinoza's rhetoric about the intellectual love of God was nothing but "trappings for the people, since there is nothing loveable in a God who produces without choice and by necessity, without discrimination of good and evil. The true love of God is founded not in necessity but in goodness." "Refutation of Spinoza," trans. George Martin Duncan, in *Leibniz Selections*, ed. Philip P. Wiener (New York: Scribner's, 1951), 496.

313 McFarland, *Coleridge and the Pantheist Tradition*, chap. 2, 53–106.

314 Spinoza, *Ethics*, 4, Propositions 67–72, trans. White, 346–51.

315 Aristotle, *The Nicomachean Ethics* 6.9.1142b10–15, trans. Thomson, rev. Tredennick, 158. On thinking and reason as self-assertion, see also Martin Heidegger, "Modern Science, Metaphysics and Mathematics," trans. W.B. Barton Jr. and Vera Deutsch, in *Basic Writings*, ed. Krell, 278–9.

316 "Objectivity had been pursued since antiquity. But in the early Christian and Medieval ages it had largely been balanced by an intensive inward trend which appears in the nature of art, the language of prayer, and, generally, the entire rhythm of life." Dupré, *Transcendent Selfhood*, 15.

317 Hampshire, *Spinoza*, 167–8.

318 "With the *cogito-sum*, reason now becomes explicitly posited according to its own demand as the first ground of all knowledge and the guidelines of the determination of the things." Heidegger, "Modern Science, Metaphysics and Mathematics," trans. Barton and Deutsch, 281.

319 "[L]a voie de l'*analyse*, de la décomposition en unités plus petites, c'est la voie même de la science." Ricœur, *Le conflit des interprétations*, 100. Emphasis in original.

320 "[T]he atomism which is implicit in the mainstream post-Cartesian epistemology … [is] a (partly justified) method which has been illegitimately projected onto ontology." Charles Taylor, *Dilemmas and Connections: Selected Essays* (Cambridge, MA: Belknap Press of Harvard Univ. Press, 2011), 39.

321 On how the "shattering" of the "isolated subject" from the "world" led to a "problem of reality" expressed in the ensuing quarrels between "realism and idealism," see Heidegger, *Being and Time*, 206, trans. Stambaugh, 198–9.

322 "How any thought should produce a motion in body is as remote from the nature of our ideas, as how any body should produce any thought in mind." Locke, *An Essay Concerning Human Understanding*, bk. 4, chap. 3, §28, 2:220–1; Whitehead, *Process and Reality*, 128.

323 Edmund Husserl, *Ideas: General Introduction to Pure Phenomenology*, trans. W.R. Boyce Gibson (New York: Collier Books, 1962), §8, p. 56.

324 "[A]s soon as logos in the sense of statement assumes the rule over being, the moment being is experienced and conceived as *ousia* [substance], already thereness, the distinction between being and the ought is in preparation. … Thus it is in the modern era, when this very same thought becomes dominant in the form of self-sufficient reason, that the distinction between being and the ought really comes into its own. The process is completed in Kant." Heidegger, *An Introduction to Metaphysics*, trans. Manheim, 163–5.

325 "In every system of morality, which I have hitherto met with, I have always remark'd, that the author proceeds in the ordinary way of reasoning, and establishes the being of a God, or makes observations

concerning human affairs; when of a sudden I am surpriz'd to find, that instead of the usual copulations of propositions, *is*, and *is not*, I meet with no proposition that is not connected with an *ought*, or an *ought not*. This change is imperceptible; but is, however, of the last consequence ... [A] reason should be given, for what seems altogether inconceivable, how this new relation can be a deduction from others, which are entirely different from it. ... [T]he distinction of vice and virtue is not founded merely on the relations of objects, nor is perceiv'd by reason." David Hume, *A Treatise of Human Nature* 3.1.1, ed. L.A. Selby-Bigge (London: Oxford Univ. Press, 1968), pp. 469–70.

326 On the problem of "is" and "ought," see Bradley, *Appearance and Reality*, 136.

327 G.W. Leibniz, *Discours de métaphysique*, 11 (Paris: Pocket, 1993), 34; *Nouveaux essais*, bk. 1, chap. 3, §21, p. 82.

328 "[L]a philosophie mécanique des modernes ... s'éloigne trop des êtres immatériels au préjudice de la piété." Leibniz, *Discours de métaphysique*, 18, p. 46.

329 "Les âmes agissent selon les lois des causes finales ... Les corps agissent selon les lois des causes efficientes ou des mouvements. Et les deux règnes, celui des causes efficientes et celui des causes finales sont harmoniques entre elles." G.W. Leibniz, *Principes de la philosophie ou Monadologie*, §79, in *Principes de la nature et de la grâce fondés en raison – Principes de la philosophie ou Monadologie*, ed. André Robinet (Paris: Presses Universitaires de France, 1986), 119.

330 Leibniz, *Discours de métaphysique*, 19–20, pp. 47–50; *Nouveaux essais*, Préface, 33–4.

331 Leibniz, *Nouveaux essais*, bk. 3, chap. 3, §9–10, pp. 249–50. On "maps" of the human spirit, see also: bk. 3, chap. 6, §§14, 41–2, pp. 267–9, 285; chap. 10, §14, p. 299; bk. 4, chap. 3, §19, p. 339; chap. 8, §12, p. 382. On "dichotomies" (especially among the virtues), see also: bk. 2, chap. 21, §§31–5, 39–40, 47, 67, pp. 159–61, 164–5, 167, 177; bk. 3, chap. 6, §32, p. 280.

332 G.W. Leibniz, *De emendatione*, in *Les deux labyrinthes: textes choisis*, ed. Alain Chauve (Paris: Presses Universitaires de France, 1973), 16. Even in his efforts to defend the truth of Christianity, Leibniz did not repudiate Descartes' ambition to apply the geometric or mathematical model to rational argument. *Essais de Théodicée*, §62, p. 86. In fact, he hoped to establish the existence of God "dans la rigueur d'une évidence mathématique." *Nouveaux essais*, bk. 4, chap. 10, §7, p. 387.

333 Leibniz, *Nouveaux essais*, Preface, p. 37; bk. 1, chap. 1, §§5, 11, pp. 64–5; §§21–6, pp. 69–71; chap. 3, §20, p. 86.

334 Leibniz, bk. 1, chap. 2, §21–2, pp. 82–3; bk. 1, chap. 3, §16, p. 86; bk. 4, chap. 8, §11, p. 367.

335 "[N]os fautes, pour la plupart, viennent du défaut ou du mépris de l'art de penser." Leibniz, *Essais de Théodicée*, §31, p. 70. And yet, the other side of Leibniz could readily see that: "La vertu est la plus noble qualité des choses créées." Leibniz, §124, p. 180.

336 G.W. Leibniz, "Au Landgrave," November 1686, in *Les deux labyrinthes: textes choisis*, 15.

337 Leibniz, *Principes de la nature et de la grâce fondés en raison – Principes de la philosophie ou Monadologie*, ed. Robinet, 47, 59, 69–71, 93, 97. My translation.

338 The young Leibniz described the "nominalist sect" as "the most profound of all among the scholastics, and the most consistent with the character of our present-day, reformed philosophy." Pasnau, *Metaphysical Themes 1274–1671*, 87. See also Benson Mates, *The Philosophy of Leibniz: Metaphysics and Language* (New York: Oxford Univ. Press, 1986), 170–88; Leibniz, *Nouveaux essais*, bk. 2, chap. 21, §6, p. 147; *Principes de la philosophie ou Monadologie*, ed. Robinet, 95. On the relationship between Leibniz and Spinoza, see "Excursus Note V: Leibniz and Spinoza," in McFarland, *Coleridge and the Pantheist Tradition*, 271–4.

339 Leibniz, *Discours de métaphysique*, §§1, 35, pp. 23, 69. On Locke's view of God as simply one being among others, merely "the most powerful, and most knowing" of all beings, see Locke, *An Essay Concerning Human Understanding*, bk. 4, chap. 10, 2:306–24.

340 "Thus God alone is the primitive unity or the original simple substance; of which all created or derived monads are the products." G.W. Leibniz, *The Monadology*, §47, trans. various, in *Leibniz Selections*, ed. Wiener, 542.

341 Leibniz, *Discours de métaphysique*; *Essais de Théodicée*.

342 Leibniz, *Essais de Théodicée*, §29, p. 69.

343 "Kant followed Hume in this misconception [his focus on "mental operation"]; and was thus led to balance the world upon thought – oblivious to the scanty supply of thinking." Whitehead, *Process and Reality*, 175.

344 Immanuel Kant, *Critique of Pure Reason*, trans. Norman Kemp Smith (London: Macmillan, 1968).

345 Immanuel Kant, *Foundations of the Metaphysics of Morals*, trans. Lewis White Beck (Indianapolis: Bobbs-Merrill, 1959), §2, p. 24.

346 Immanuel Kant, *Critique of Practical Reason*, trans. Lewis White Beck (Indianapolis: Bobbs-Merrill, 1956), pt. 1, bk. 1, chap. 3, pp. 103–7; *Prolegomena to Any Future Metaphysics*, trans. Lewis White Beck et al. (Indianapolis: Bobbs-Merrill, 1950), 91–5. Franz Rosenzweig makes a crucial point in suggesting Kant's *Ding an sich* is the "one fixed point left standing" from the "chaos" of idealism, though it was "shunted" aside, and wasn't "worked on" by idealism. *The Star of Redemption*, trans. Hallo, 145.

In other words, the *Ding an sich* points back (or forward) – beyond the stance of "*It* is" (B2) to the stances and virtues of "*I am*" (A1 and A2).

347 In the *Critique of Pure Reason*, Kant is still somewhat inclined to defend the virtues (or at least the "concepts of virtue") and moral "laws" (plural); however, in the later works, he is more inclined to describe humans as subject to "the moral law" (singular). But even in the first *Critique*, the moral laws are "purely intellectual" principles. *Critique of Pure Reason*, A315, B430–1, trans. Kemp Smith, 311, 382–3.

348 Kant, *Foundations of the Metaphysics of Morals*, trans. Beck, §1, p. 12.

349 Kant, 9. Emphasis in original.

350 Kant, 15.

351 Kant, 20.

352 Kant, *Critique of Practical Reason*, trans. Beck, pt. 1, bk. 1, chaps. 1 and 3, pp. 35, 84, 87–8. Dorothea Frede, "The Historic Decline of Virtue Ethics," in *The Cambridge Companion to Virtue Ethics*, ed. Daniel C. Russell (Cambridge: Cambridge Univ. Press, 2013), 124–48.

353 Kant, *Foundations of the Metaphysics of Morals*, trans. Beck, §1, p. 16.

354 Kant, §2, trans. Beck, p. 29. Kant attempts, implausibly, to draw a parallel between moral laws and Newton's physical laws of nature. Kant, 55; *Critique of Pure Reason*, B431–2, trans. Kemp Smith, 383; *Critique of Practical Reason*, trans. Beck, pt. 1, bk. 1, chap. 2, pp. 72–3.

355 Aquinas, *Summa Theologiæ* 1–2.6.2, in *Treatise on Happiness*, trans. Oesterle, 71.

356 Kant, *Foundations of the Metaphysics of Morals*, trans. Beck, §2, p. 29. Emphasis added.

357 I have followed Lewis Beck White in translating "categorical imperative" as "ought" here. See "Introduction" in Kant, xii. Kant himself equated "ought" with his "imperative." Kant, §2, pp. 30, 38–9.

358 Kant, 5.

359 Kant, *Prolegomena to Any Future Metaphysics*, trans. Beck and others, 92–3.

360 Kant, *Foundations of the Metaphysics of Morals*, trans. Beck, §2, p. 24.

361 Kant even uses the image of a man "tear[ing] himself" apart, if his action is to have "genuine moral worth." Kant, §1, p. 14. While emphasizing the conflict between reason and inclination, Kant nevertheless denies the possibility of conflict within the reason itself. Kant, §2, p. 55.

362 Kant, §2, pp. 21–2, 27, 42. Hegel calls this "a view of morality as nothing but a bitter, unending struggle against self-satisfaction, as the command: 'Do with abhorrence what duty enjoins.'" Hegel, *Philosophy of Right*, §124, trans. Knox, 84. Hegel's quote is from Schiller.

363 Taylor, *Sources of the Self*, 365.

364 Alasdair MacIntyre, *After Virtue*, 2nd ed. (Notre Dame, IN: Univ. of Notre Dame Press, 1984), 149; James Q. Wilson, *The Moral Sense* (New York: Free Press, 1993), 243–4.

365 "[E]xteriores actus procedunt ab interioribus passionibus; et ideo mod-
    eratio eorum dependet a moderatione interiorum passionum." Aquinas,
    Summa Theologiæ 2–2.141.3, Volume 43 ("Temperance"), trans. Gilby,
    14–15.

366 Kant, *Foundations of the Metaphysics of Morals*, trans. Beck, §2, p. 52.

367 Kant, *Critique of Practical Reason*, trans. Beck, pt. 1, bk. 1, chap. 3, p. 76.
    Emphasis added.

368 Kant, *Foundations of the Metaphysics of Morals*, trans. Beck, §1, p. 14–16.

369 Leibniz, *Nouveaux essais*, bk. 2, chap. 21, §§47–69, pp. 167–78; Locke, *Some
    Thoughts Concerning Education*, §§94–107, in *On Politics and Education*,
    281–91.

370 Kant, *Foundations of the Metaphysics of Morals*, trans. Beck, §1, p. 17. On the
    relationship between what Kant calls maxims, principles and laws, see
    Kant, §2, p. 38n9; *Critique of Practical Reason*, trans. Beck, pt. 1, bk. 1, chap.
    1, §1, p. 17.

371 "[A] man of virtue rightly judges matters relating to that virtue, not from
    scientific theory but from a settled disposition which has become second
    nature to him." Aquinas, "Exposition," *de Divinis Nominibus*, 2, *lect. 4*, in
    Theological Texts, trans. Gilby, 32.

372 To develop powers of moral reasoning in young people, Kant recom-
    mends what we would now call the "case study" method, through
    which, he argues, it is possible "to make judging according to moral laws
    a natural occupation." Kant, *Critique of Practical Reason*, trans. Beck, pt. 2,
    pp. 155–65.

373 "I should seek to further the happiness of others," Kant says, for example,
    "*not* as though its realization was any concern of mine ... I should do so
    merely because the maxim which excludes it from my duty cannot be com-
    prehended as a universal law in one and the same volition." Kant, *Founda-
    tions of the Metaphysics of Morals*, trans. Beck, §2, p. 60. Emphasis added.

374 Max Scheler suggests Kant's philosophy expresses "a basic 'hostility'
    toward, or 'distrust' of the given *as* such, a fear of the given as chaos ...
    Hence this attitude is the opposite of *love* of the world, of trust in and lov-
    ing devotion to the world." *Formalism in Ethics*, trans. Frings and Funk,
    67. As Charles Péguy puts it, so memorably: "*Le kantisme a les mains pures,*
    MAIS IL N'A PAS DE MAINS." *Victor Marie, comte Hugo*, in *Une éthique
    sans compromis*, ed. Dominique Saatdjian (Paris: Pocket, 2011), 247. Italics
    and upper case in original. On love as the necessary basis of all action
    and morality, see Augustine of Hippo, in Brown, *Augustine of Hippo*,
    154–5; Aquinas, *Summa Theologiæ* 1–2.6.4, in *Treatise on Happiness*, trans.
    Oesterle, 44; Levinas, *Entre nous*, 117–18; André Comte-Sponville, *A Small
    Treatise on the Great Virtues*, trans. Catherine Temerson (New York: Henry
    Holt, 2001), 225–6.

375 Kant, *Critique of Practical Reason*, trans. Beck, pt. 1, bk. 1, chap. 3, p. 84. It is not enough to act *"according* to duty." To qualify as genuinely moral, action must be done *"from* duty." Kant, pt. 1, bk. 2, chap. 2, p. 122.

376 Kant, 85–6. Max Scheler calls this "the most extreme nonsense that rationalism ever set forth in ethics." *Formalism in Ethics*, trans. Frings and Funk, 223n53.

377 "[T]he form of universality ... is itself the determining ground of the will. Therefore not the object, i.e., the happiness of others, [is] the determining ground of the pure will but rather it [is] the *lawful form alone.*" Kant, chap. 1, trans. Beck, 35. Emphasis added.

378 Kant, *Foundations of the Metaphysics of Morals*, trans. Beck, §3, p. 80–2. Emphasis added. "[W]e cannot comprehend how the *ought* should determine ... and could become the cause of actions whose effect is an appearance in the sensible world." *Prolegomena to Any Future Metaphysics*, trans. Beck et al., 92. Emphasis in original.

379 Kant, *Foundations of the Metaphysics of Morals*, trans. Beck, §3, p. 82. Emphasis added. Elsewhere, he makes the same point as follows: "In [morality, a realm of ends] is a practical idea for bringing about *that which is not actually real but which can become real through our conduct*, and which is in accordance with this idea." Kant, 55n17. Emphasis added.

380 Kant, *Critique of Practical Reason*, trans. Beck, pt. 1, bk. 1, chap. 3, pp. 81–91. Contrary to his reputation as a dry and abstract writer of impenetrable thoughts, Kant gives us some eloquent and affecting descriptions of how an encounter with goodness, concretely embodied in real moral persons, can prompt involuntary feelings of *reverence*, and so inspire us to imitate them. See, for example, Kant, 79–80; *Foundations of the Metaphysics of Morals*, trans. Beck, §3, p. 73. Kant suggests that moral education should be based on "a vivid exhibition of the moral disposition in examples" like these. *Critique of Practical Reason*, trans. Beck, pt. 2, pp. 164–5.

381 "There can be no 'reverence' for a norm or a moral law that is not founded in reverence for the *person* who posits it – founded ultimately in love for this person as a model." Scheler, *Formalism in Ethics*, trans. Frings and Funk, 573. Emphasis in original.

382 From the point of view of the virtues, the issue of moral motivation is transformed, and almost disappears: human beings act well, not from some kind of abstract reasoning process, but rather from habit and good character. They almost cannot act otherwise. See Rosalind Hursthouse, *On Virtue Ethics* (Oxford: Oxford Univ. Press, 2010), 123; Iris Murdoch, *The Sovereignty of Good* (London: Routledge, 1980), 37; Michel Terestchenko, *Un si fragile vernis d'humanité: Banalité du mal, banalité du bien* (Paris: La Découverte, 2007), 237.

383 "[I]l est remarquable que Kant ne se soit pas posé le problème du rapport entre le caractère de quasi-position de soi par soi de l'autonomie et le caractère virtuel d'affection par l'autre impliqué par le statut du respect en tant que mobile. ... C'est cette *conjonction dans le respect entre autoposition* [self-assertion] *et l'auto-affection* [reverence] qui nous autorisera à remettre en question ... l'indépendance du principe de l'autonomie ... autrement dit, à *mettre en doute l'autonomie de l'autonomie* [self-assertion]." Ricœur, *Soi-même comme un autre*, 249–51. First two italics in original, second two added.

384 Kant's arbitrary declaration ("I say") that "every rational being exists as an end in himself and not merely as a means to be arbitrarily used by this or that will" had nothing to do with the dictates of "pure reason," as he assumed but could not show. It was instead a reflection of the almost two thousand previous years of Christian culture, which Kant merely took for granted. *Foundations of the Metaphysics of Morals*, trans. Beck, §2, p. 46.

385 Kant said the "banal" Golden Rule was "derived" from his own categorical imperative and "restricted by various limitations." So, at least in its negative version ("What you don't want ..."), it "cannot be a universal law because it contains the ground neither of duties to one's self, nor of the benevolent duties to others," nor of "obligatory duties to another." Kant, *Foundations of the Metaphysics of Morals*, trans. Beck, §2, p. 48n14.

386 Paul Ricœur says Kant's categorical imperative is simply a "formalization" of the Golden Rule, which is one of the "notions reçues que le philosophe n'a pas à inventer mais à éclaircir et à justifier." And "behind" the Golden Rule, he suggests, can be heard "la voix de la sollicitude," or the "call" of the virtues of Reverence (A2). *Soi-même comme un autre*, 255–64. On the Golden Rule, see also *Lectures 3*, in *Ricœur: Textes choisis et présentés*, 320–6.

387 Kant seems to have given at least five versions of the categorical imperative. Kant, *Foundations of the Metaphysics of Morals*, trans. Beck, 39, 47, 49–50, 57. The reason for restating it in various forms, Kant says, significantly, is "to bring an idea of reason closer to *intuition* (by means of a certain analogy) and thus nearer to *feeling*." Kant, 54–5. Emphasis added. The italicized words point to some key dimensions of the whole nature of the human which the Kantian vision tends to undervalue.

388 Kant "insists upon a decided and radical dualism, the dualism of the sensuous and intelligible world. For his problem is ... the problem of 'is' and 'ought,' of experience and Idea." Ernst Cassirer, "Kant and the Problem of Metaphysics: Remarks on Martin Heidegger's Interpretation of Kant," trans. Moltke S. Gram, in *Kant: Disputed Questions*, ed. Moltke S. Gram (Chicago: Quadrangle Books, 1967), 148.

389 Hegel, *Encyclopaedia*, trans. Wallace, §81, p. 117.

390 Hegel, §48, p. 78.

391 Hegel, §119, p. 174. Heidegger agrees in *An Introduction to Metaphysics*, trans. Manheim, 21.

392 On "the diversity of philosophical systems as the progressive develop-ment of truth," see Hegel, *Preface to the Phenomenology of Spirit*, trans. Yovel, 65–6. By insisting that philosophy must always be the history of philosophy, Hegel was in a sense, reaching back to reclaim mythic cul-ture for the second phase of theoretic culture: he was insisting that deep thinking must always have a "narrative" character, not just an analytic one.

393 Hegel, *Philosophy of Right*, trans. Knox, §§3, 33, 137, 142–56, 142n1, pp. 16, 36, 91–2, 105–10, 346; Charles Taylor, *Hegel* (Cambridge: Cambridge Univ. Press, 1975), 376.

394 Hegel, Addition to §108, pp. 248–9; §151, pp. 108–9.

395 Hegel, §5, pp. 21–2; *The Phenomenology of Mind*, trans. J.B. Baillie (New York: Harper & Row, 1967), 599–610.

396 G.W.F. Hegel, "Fragment of a System," trans. Richard Kroner, in *Early Theological Writings*, trans. T.M. Knox (Chicago: Univ. of Chicago Press, 1948), 312.

397 Hegel, *Encyclopaedia*, trans. Wallace, §§19, 24, pp. 27, 37, 42–3, 45. For an earlier sketch of the four "principles" at the heart of Hegel's "Absolute Idea," see also *Philosophy of Right*, trans. Knox, §§349–60, pp. 218–23. Following Kant, Hegel reverses the traditional and everyday meanings of reason and understanding, making Understanding (in his sense) the more superficial, analytic kind of thought, and Reason (in his sense) the deeper, more dialectical thinking. But, even with this reversal of meaning, Hegel's ordering of them is *still the correct one*. So I have kept Hegel's *or-der*, but, for understanding and reason, I have *reversed his meaning*.

398 Hegel, *Philosophy of Right*, trans. Knox, §§32, 145, pp. 35, 105. Emphasis added.

399 Hegel, §150, p. 107.

400 Hegel, *Encyclopaedia*, trans. Wallace, §222, p. 282. Some other translations (mistranslating *geist*) call this the "movement of mind." *Philosophy of Right*, trans. Knox, §341, p. 216. Emmanuel Levinas uses the same word "procession" to describe what I have called the "arrow of virtue." *Entre nous*, 171–3.

401 Already, before Hegel, Kant had said that "only the totality of things, in their interconnection as constituting the universe, is completely adequate to the idea." Kant, *Critique of Pure Reason*, trans. Kemp Smith, A318, p. 313.

402 Hegel, *Encyclopaedia*, trans. Wallace, §236, p. 292. On the distinction yet mutual dependency between cognition and truth, see also Samuel Taylor

Coleridge, *The Statesman's Manual* in *Lay Sermons*, ed. R.J. White (London: Routledge, 1972), 78; Maurice Blondel, *L'Être et les êtres* (Paris: Presses Universitaires de France, 1963), 470.

403 G.W.F. Hegel, *Science of Logic*, vol. 2, §3, chap. 3, trans. W.H. Johnston and L.G. Struthers (London: George Allen & Unwin, 1951), 2:483–4. Hegel would later call this "circle of circles" a "syllogism, of which the very elements are in themselves systems and syllogisms." Hegel, *Encyclopaedia*, trans. Wallace, §217, p. 280.

404 Hegel, *Science of Logic*, vol. 2, §3, p. 2:399.

405 Hegel, *Encyclopaedia*, trans. Wallace, §§215, 237, pp. 278–9, 292–3; *Preface to the Phenomenology of Spirit*, trans. Yovel, 65–6, 102, 122.

406 "Each of the stages … is an image of the absolute, but at first in a limited mode, and thus it is forced onward to the whole." Hegel, *Encyclopaedia*, trans. Wallace, §237, pp. 292–3; *Preface to the Phenomenology of Spirit* trans. Yovel, 105, 123, 130, 154. 168–9.

407 Hegel, *Preface to the Phenomenology of Spirit*, trans. Yovel, 105, 123, 130, 154. 168–9. "What we have done here [in the *Phenomenology*] … is simply to gather together the particular moments, *each of which in principle exhibits the life of spirit in its entirety*." Hegel, *The Phenomenology of Mind*, trans. Baillie, 797. Emphasis added.

408 Hegel, *Philosophy of Right*, trans. Knox, additions to §§182, 273, pp. 266, 286. "The absolute idea may in this respect be compared to the old man who utters the same creed as the child, but for whom it is pregnant with the significance of a lifetime." *Encyclopaedia*, trans. Wallace, §237, p. 293.

409 Yirmiyahu Yovel, "Running Commentary," in Hegel, *Preface to the Phenomenology of Spirit*, trans. Yovel, 132–3. Martin Heidegger's terms for what Hegel calls the Absolute Idea include "the complete, authentic occurrence of Dasein," "the movement of occurrence in general," and "the totality of occurrence of Dasein." *Being and Time*, 385, 389–90, trans. Stambaugh, 366, 370–1.

410 Although he defines the human as "a being that thinks" whose "innermost self is thought," when Hegel describes "what is essential and permanent in human nature" or "man as man" he falls back not on thought but on the human virtues: courage, learning, patriotism, justice, "religious truth and the like." Hegel, *Encyclopaedia*, trans. Wallace, §§24, 11, 140, 175, pp. 38, 15, 200, 240.

411 "The good is in principle the essence of the will in its substantiality and universality, i.e., of the will in its truth, and therefore it exists simply and solely in thinking and by means of thinking." Hegel, *Philosophy of Right*, trans. Knox, §132, p. 87. What Whitehead said of Kant applies equally to Hegel: his "act of experience is essentially knowledge. Thus whatever is not knowledge is necessarily inchoate, and merely on its way to knowledge." Whitehead, *Process and Reality*, 179. "Spinoza and Hegel followed

the way opened up by Socrates: throughout their work they never ceased to develop the idea that virtue and knowledge are one and the same thing." Shestov, *Athens and Jerusalem*, 131.

412 Hegel, *Encyclopaedia*, trans. Wallace, §121, p. 176.

413 Hegel, §24, pp. 37–8.

414 Hegel, §24, p. 43.

415 Hegel, *Philosophy of Right*, trans. Knox, §§62, 217, 270, 259, 346, pp. 51, 139, 167, 160, 217.

416 Hegel, 10.

417 G.W.F. Hegel, *The Philosophy of History*, trans. J. Sibree, in *The Age of Ideology: The Nineteenth Century Philosophers*, ed. Henry D. Aiken (New York: Mentor, 1956), 96.

418 For Hegel, the rational concept is the "ultimate spring of all activity, life, and consciousness." Hegel, *Philosophy of Right*, trans. Knox, §7, p. 24. "L'optimisme de Hegel, sa foi dans la puissance de l'Esprit, reposent sur l'affirmation, souvent formulée, qu'il n'y a rien qui ne soit susceptible d'être dit, et que le langage de l'homme est capable de tout exprimer. ... La prétention de lever grâce au langage la contradiction que manifeste la dialectique de l'action ne saurait cependant être prise au sérieux." Henry, *L'essence de la manifestation*, 889.

419 Heidegger, *An Introduction to Metaphysics*, trans. Manheim, 151, 158; Emmanuel Levinas, *Difficile liberté*, 3rd corrected ed. (Paris: Le Livre de Poche, 2010), 352; *Entre nous*, 135.

420 "Kant and Hegel went to seek the final truth in one and the same place. ... Hegel thought Kant through to the end." Shestov, *Athens and Jerusalem*, 117, 119.

421 Taylor, *Hegel*, 569.

422 Whitehead, *Process and Reality*, 133; Rosenzweig, *The Star of Redemption*, trans. Hallo, 144; Henry, *L'essence de la manifestation*, 906.

423 The stance of most thinkers from Descartes to Hegel was, in Michel Henry's words, "un monisme qui identifie la réalité avec l'objectivité en tant que tel." *L'essence de la manifestation* (Paris: Presses Universitaires de France, 2017), 887. Martin Heidegger says the post-Cartesian world is characterized by "a primary orientation to thingliness": "Descartes narrowed down the question of the world to that of the thingliness of nature," and that "Cartesian ontology of the world ... basically is still customary today." *Being and Time*, 99–100, trans. Stambaugh, 96–8. Northrop Frye quotes the seventeenth-century poet Cowley, "hailing Bacon as the Moses who had led modern thought out of the Egypt of superstition":

> From words, which are but pictures of the thought
> (Though we our thoughts from them perversely drew)
> To *things, the minds right object* he it brought.

Frye, *The Great Code*, 13. Emphasis added.

424 Kant, *Prolegomena to Any Future Metaphysics*, trans. Beck et al., 30, 34, 54. Whitehead, *Process and Reality*, 179–80.

425 Locke, "Epistle to the Reader," in *An Essay Concerning Human Understanding*, 1:14.

426 Locke, *An Essay Concerning Human Understanding*, bk. 3, chap. 3, §4, p. 2:15.

427 Kant, *Prolegomena to Any Future Metaphysics*, trans. Beck et al., 54, 66, 58. Emphasis added. For Kant, there is "no intuition at all beyond the field of sensibility," i.e., the data of the five senses. Kant, 63.

428 Hegel, *Encyclopaedia*, trans. Wallace, §1, p. 4. Italics in original. "Hegel n'a pas conçu pour la conscience un mode de présence à soi-même autre que le mode de présence de l'objet." Henry, *L'essence de la manifestation*, 902.

429 Aristotle, *Metaphysics* 4.1.1003a15–25, trans. Ross, 731.

430 "[L]a première question qu'on a droit de faire, sera, Pourquoi il y a plus tôt quelque chose que rien." Leibniz, *Principes de la nature*, 45.

431 "Sans doute est-ce le mérite des philosophies de la négativité depuis Hegel de nous avoir remis sur le chemin d'une philosophie de l'être qui devra décrocher de la chose et de l'essence." Paul Ricœur, *Histoire et vérité* (Paris: Points Essais, 2001), 405.

432 Hegel, *Encyclopaedia*, trans. Wallace, §82, p. 121.

433 Lonergan, *Insight*, 332. Paul Ricœur calls this "le préjugé de la conscience": "cette subtile concupiscence de soi qui est peut-être le rapport narcissique de la conscience immédiate de la vie." *Le conflit des interprétations*, 147, 151. Merlin Donald also recognizes that the human drive for "rationality and clarity is itself deeply irrational." *A Mind So Rare*, 288, 290.

434 Levinas, *Entre nous*, 138, 141, 154; *Éthique comme philosophie première* (Paris: Rivages poche, 2015), 84.

435 "Freedom [A1] and equality [B2] and, even more, the ability to realize them, depend upon the determination of human beings to *govern nature* so that they will not be governed by it." Alan Wolfe, *The Future of Liberalism* (New York: Vintage Books, 2010), 36. Emphasis added.

436 Hans Joas suggests, for example, that the success of eighteenth-century writings against torture "is due to the fact that their readers were already convinced when they were published." *The Sacredness of the Person*, 45.

437 Richard Shweder, *Thinking Through Cultures: Expeditions in Cultural Psychology* (Cambridge, MA: Harvard Univ. Press, 1991), 154.

438 Taylor, *A Secular Age*, 173.

439 Terry Eagleton, *Reason, Faith, and Revolution: Reflections on the God Debate* (New Haven: Yale Univ. Press, 2009), 143. Emphasis added. Marcel Gauchet identifies some of the "practices" of self-assertion that "carry" (or

determine) modern and post-modern "beliefs." *The Disenchantment of the World*, 96–7, 179.

440 Robert N. Bellah, Richard Madsen, William M. Sullivan, Ann Swidler, and Steven M. Tipton, *Habits of the Heart*, updated ed. (Berkeley: Univ. of California Press, 1996), 154–5, 210, 334–5.

441 Hobbes, *Leviathan*, pt. 2, chap. 17, p. 139.

442 Hegel, *Encyclopaedia*, trans. Wallace, §232–5, p. 289–92.

443 "À la liberté du savoir se subordonne, depuis Hegel, toute finalité encore apparemment étrangère au désintéressement de la connaissance; et l'*être*, dans cette liberté, est *dès lors* entendu lui-même comme *affirmation active de cet être même*, comme la *force* et l'*effort d'être*. L'homme moderne persiste dans son être en souverain préoccupé uniquement d'assurer les *pouvoirs de sa souveraineté*. Tout ce qui est possible est permis. ... Merveille de la liberté occidentale moderne que ne gêne aucune mémoire ni remords et qui s'ouvre sur un 'radieux avenir' où tout est réparable." Levinas, *Éthique comme philosophie première*, 73. Emphasis in original.

444 Donald, *Origins of the Modern Mind*, 275, 345–6. Elsewhere Donald acknowledges, however, that "the mimetic and oral-narrative systems normally dominate human consciousness." Donald, 368.

445 Bradley is a fascinating case in point. One often has the feeling that Bradley's metaphysics is actually trying to describe what, in this book, I call the human paradox, or the whole nature of the human. Or what Bradley himself calls "the general state of the total soul." But because he is a prisoner of the stance of "It is" (B2), Bradley seems unable, finally, to break out of a world composed primarily of things, a phenomenal world, determined by the "that" and the "what," the "total universe," or "total world," a world of "sense" and of "thought" (B1), the otherness of the phenomenal world, and the opposing self-assertion of rational consciousness. Bradley, *Appearance and Reality*, 154, 161, 200, 213, 405–14, 422, 466, 485–7, 143, 334–5.

446 John Stuart Mill, *On Liberty* (Harmondsworth: Penguin Books, 1974), 127. Because of the balance of his views, Mill is not an easy figure to place on my notional map of the human. He defended equality with almost the same vigour as liberty. But it seems fair to suggest that he leaned, if anywhere, toward the latter. He asserted that "whatever crushes individuality is despotism." Mill, 128.

447 Merlin Donald himself has speculated on the possibility of a "post-theoretic" culture: "The Digital Era: Challenges for the Modern Mind," *Cadmus* 2, no. 2 (May 2014), 68–79. See also his lecture to the Swedish Collegium for Advanced Study: "The Modern Communications Environment: An Evolutionary Perspective," 18 February 2016, https://vimeo.com/157414065. See also Frye, *The Great Code*, 15.

448 Richard M. Rorty, "Philosophy as a Transitional Genre," in *The Rorty Reader*, ed. Christopher J. Voparil and Richard J. Bernstein (Chichester: Wiley-Blackwell, 2010), 474.

449 Taylor, *Hegel*, 13; *Sources of the Self*, 374–6; *A Secular Age*, 473–5.

450 Terry Eagleton, *Culture and the Death of God* (New Haven: Yale Univ. Press, 2014), 184, 189.

451 MacCulloch, *Christianity*, 565–6; Gregory, *The Unintended Reformation*, 85, 141, 256, 259, 311–12.

452 Robert Pasnau reflects on the thousand-year career of the word "modern" but offers a very different proposal for usage. *Metaphysical Themes 1274–1671*, 1–2.

453 Eagleton, *Culture and the Death of God*.

454 "We have grown into a different civilization from our medieval [B1] and even early modern [B2] forebears. We [post-]moderns [B2/A1] may differ among ourselves as to what happened in this phenomenon we call 'modernity,' but it seems agreed by all that something important has changed. It is as though an earthquake has shifted the fields, and we can no longer enter the forest in the same way." Taylor, *Dilemmas and Connections*, 15.

455 Eagleton, *Culture and the Death of God*, 174.

456 Denys Turner points out the "denial of God" has become "unalarming" to the "practical mentality" of contemporary culture "for which nothing is required except that nothing is required." *Faith, Reason and the Existence of God*, 153. "Whereas modernism experiences the death of God as a trauma, an affront, a source of anguish, as well as a cause for celebration, postmodernism does not experience it at all." Eagleton, *Culture and the Death of God*, 186.

457 Eagleton, *Culture and the Death of God*, 184.

458 Spinoza, *Ethics*, 4, Proposition 20, trans. White, 304.

459 Kant, *Foundations of the Metaphysics of Morals*, trans. Beck, §1, p. 10.

460 Ricœur, *Parcours de la reconnaissance*, 150.

461 Johann Gottlieb Fichte, *The Science of Knowledge*, trans. A.E. Kroeger (London: Trubner, 1889), in *The Age of Ideology*, 68.

462 Johann Gottlieb Fichte, *The Vocation of Man*, trans. William Smith (Indianapolis: Bobbs-Merrill, 1956), 125.

463 F.W.J. Schelling, *Werke*, i, 193; iii, 450, quoted in McFarland, *Coleridge and the Pantheist Tradition*, 104–5. "In the last and highest instance there is no other being but willing." Schelling, 1/7, 350, quoted in Andrew Bowie, "Friedrich Wilhelm Joseph von Schelling," in *The Stanford Encyclopedia of Philosophy* (Winter 2010 Edition), ed. Edward N. Zalta, http://plato.stanford.edu/archives/win2010/entries/schelling/.

464 Arthur Schopenhauer, *The World as Will and Representation*, vol. 1, trans. E.F.J. Payne, in *Nineteenth-Century Philosophy*, ed. Patrick L. Gardner (New York: Free Press, 1969), 97–103.

465 Friedrich Jacobi, *Werke*, ii. 310; *Von den Göttlingen Dingen*, 196, quoted in Mc-Farland, *Coleridge and the Pantheist Tradition*, 98. Richard Kroner agrees that Fichte and Schelling's speculative idealism was "Spinozism worked out on the level of Kant's critical philosophy." "Introduction: Hegel's Philosophical Development," in Hegel, *Early Theological Writings*, trans. Knox, 3.

466 Gilson, *Unity of Philosophical Experience*, 242.

467 Marxism, as Jacques Maritain notes, is a quintessential expression of the modern and post-modern spirit of self-assertion: "il consiste en définitive à revendiquer pour l'homme ... [une] souveraine indépendance dans la maîtrise de la nature et dans le gouvernment de l'histoire." *Humanisme intégral*, 61.

468 With her usual astuteness, Marilynne Robinson remarks: "It is no accident that Marxism and social Darwinism arose together, *two tellers of one tale*," i.e., the tale of the virtues of Power (A1). *What Are We Doing Here?* (Toronto: McClelland & Stewart, 2019), xiii. Emphasis added. On Social Darwinism, see: Richard Hofstadter, *Social Darwinism in American Thought* (Boston: Beacon Press, 1992); Robert C. Bannister, *Social Darwinism: Science and Myth in Anglo-American Thought* (Philadelphia: Temple Univ. Press, 1979); Mike Hawkins, *Social Darwinism in European and American Thought, 1860–1945: Nature as Model and Nature as Threat* (Cambridge: Cambridge Univ. Press, 1997).

469 Max Scheler notes that Darwin's "struggle for life" is just "another formulation" of Spinoza's *conatus*. *Formalism in Ethics*, trans. Frings and Funk, 277, 280.

470 Donald MacRae, "Introduction," in Herbert Spencer, *The Man versus the State*, ed. Donald MacRae (Harmondsworth: Penguin Books, 1969), 29.

471 Mill, *On Liberty*, 121. The views Mill endorsed were those of Wilhelm von Humboldt (1767–1835), the founder of the University of Berlin, the original model for the modern research university.

472 Friedrich Nietzsche, *The Will to Power*, 635, quoted in Kaufmann, *Nietzsche: Philosopher, Psychologist, Antichrist*, 264.

473 Another prophet of the human disposition to dominate, contemporary to Nietzsche, is Émile Zola, of whose twenty-volume novel cycle (*Les Rougon-Macquart*) it is the central theme. Aaron Matz, "Inheriting Hunger," *New York Review of Books* 68, no. 2 (11 February 2021), 36–8.

474 Friedrich Nietzsche, *Thus Spoke Zarathustra*, trans. R.J. Hollingdale, rev. ed. (Harmondsworth: Penguin Books, 1969), 138.

475 Hans Joas, *The Genesis of Values*, trans. Gregory Moore (Cambridge: Polity Press, 2000), 32–3.

476 Nietzsche, *Thus Spoke Zarathustra*, trans. Hollingdale, 74. I have altered Hollingdale's "charity" to "loving your neighbour" to make clear the meaning of the Christian term "charity."

477 Taylor, *A Secular Age*, 374.

478 Kaufmann, *Nietzsche: Philosopher, Psychologist, Antichrist*, 414.

479 Nietzsche, *Thus Spoke Zarathustra*, trans. Hollingdale, 251. Revised to use Walter Kaufmann's translation of "pleasure" rather than "happiness." See Kaufmann, *Nietzsche: Philosopher, Psychologist, Antichrist*, 278.

480 Kaufmann, *Nietzsche: Philosopher, Psychologist, Antichrist*, 262.

481 Nietzsche, *The Will to Power*, 781, quoted in Kaufmann, 277.

482 Thomas McFarland, *Originality and Imagination* (Baltimore: The Johns Hopkins Univ. Press, 1985), 199.

483 Walter Pater, "Conclusion," in *The Renaissance: Studies in Art and Poetry* (1873) (Twickenham: Tiger Books, 1998), 236–9. Emphasis added. Contrast Pater's overtly self-assertive (even self-indulgent) vision of art with Iris Murdoch's contrary claim that what great art offers us is "the austere consolation of a beauty which teaches that nothing in life is of any value except the attempt to be virtuous." *The Sovereignty of Good*, 87.

484 On Pater, Wilde, and the aesthetic movements of the last half of the nineteenth century, see J.E. Chamberlin, *Ripe Was the Drowsy Hour: The Age of Oscar Wilde* (New York: Seabury Press, 1977).

485 Hugo von Hofmannsthal, *The Lord Chandos Letter and Other Writings*, trans. Joel Rotenberg (New York: New York Review of Books, 2005), quoted in Charles Rosen, "Radical, Modern Hofmannsthal," *New York Review of Books* 57, no. 6 (8 April 2010), 85–6.

486 G.E. Moore, *Principia Ethica* (Cambridge: Cambridge Univ. Press, 1962), §113, pp. 188–9. Emphasis in original.

487 Paul Ricœur notes that Spinoza, Leibniz, Schopenhauer, Nietzsche, and Freud all put the virtues of Liberty (A1) ahead even of the virtues of Equality (B2) or Excellence (B1). For all of them, rational consciousness becomes "une fonction seconde de l'effort [A1a] et désir [A1b]." *Le conflit des interprétations*, 289–90. The inclusion of Leibniz in this list is debatable, but the insight for the remainder is critical.

488 As Christine Swanton puts it, Nietzsche's idea of the "will to power" is "connected essentially with the nature of humans as active, growing, developing [i.e., self-assertive] beings." *Virtue Ethics: A Pluralistic View* (Oxford: Oxford Univ. Press, 2003), 134.

489 Nietzsche, *Thus Spoke Zarathustra*, trans. Hollingdale, 64; *Beyond Good and Evil*, trans. R.J. Hollingdale (London: Penguin Books, 2003), §200, p. 122.

490 Nietzsche, *Thus Spoke Zarathustra*, trans. Hollingdale, 136–9.

491 Nietzsche, 75

492 Nietzsche, 138. Emphasis in original.

493 Nietzsche, 164–6.

494 Nietzsche, 163, 138, 94.

495 Nietzsche, 44.

496 For Franz Rosenzweig the importance of Nietzsche lies not so much in the substance of his thought but in his life, and the way – as both prophetic poet and philosopher *at the same time* – he broke the "dichotomy" of theoretic culture between "soul" (I am) and "mind" (It is), and embodied them instead as a "a unity, man [A1 & A2] and thinker [B1 & B2], a unity to the last." As a result of the impact of Nietzsche's personal example, "Man in the utter singularity of his personality [I am] … stepped out of the world which knew itself as the conceivable world [It is]." *The Star of Redemption*, trans. Hallo, 9–10.

497 Nietzsche, *Beyond Good and Evil*, trans. Hollingdale, §§260, 263, 287, pp. 194–215.

498 Hence, I agree with Christine Swanton that "the idea of the will to power, properly understood [i.e., as the virtues of self-assertion], can provide the basis for a rich psychologically informed conception of virtue." "Nietzschean Virtue Ethics," in *Virtue Ethics, Old and New*, ed. Stephen M. Gardiner (Ithaca: Cornell Univ. Press, 2005), 182. See also her article "Can Nietzsche Be an Existentialist and a Virtue Ethicist?" in *Values and Virtues: Aristotelianism in Contemporary Ethics*, ed. Timothy Chappell (Oxford: Oxford Univ. Press, 2006), 171–88.

499 Søren Kierkegaard, *Either/Or*, trans. Walter Lowrie (New York: Anchor Books, 1959), 2:179–80.

500 Søren Kierkegaard, *Concluding Unscientific Postscript to the "Philosophical Fragments,"* trans. David F. Swenson, Lillian Marvin Swenson, and Walter Lowrie, in *A Kierkegaard Anthology*, ed. Robert Bretall (New York: Modern Library, 1946), 230–1.

501 Kierkegaard, 244–5.

502 Kierkegaard, 212. "[A]t the deepest level … there lies an emotional 'Yes!'" Scheler, *Formalism in Ethics*, trans. Frings and Funk, 343.

503 Kierkegaard, 215.

504 Kierkegaard, 220–1.

505 Kierkegaard, 229.

506 Kierkegaard, 211–12, 248, 255–6, 258.

507 Kierkegaard, 200, 240.

508 Kierkegaard, 246, 244.

509 Søren Kierkegaard, *Spiritual Writings*, trans. George Pattison (New York: HarperCollins, 2010), 113–33. The words quoted are on pages 124–5.

510 David Pears, *Wittgenstein* (London: Fontana, 1971).

511 Richard M. Rorty, ed., *The Linguistic Turn: Essays in Philosophical Method*, 2nd ed. (Chicago: Univ. of Chicago Press, 1992).

512 As Iris Murdoch puts it, the second phase merely substituted "an impersonal language-world for the old impersonal atom-world of Hume and Russell." Murdoch, *The Sovereignty of Good*, 25.

513 "First of all, moral values were analyzed down to one thing, along lines
    suggested by Sidgwick and Moore; then even this one thing was proved
    not to be a *thing* at all, but an attitude to things. And so the ethical world
    was made safe for value-free scientific naturalism." Timothy Chappell,
    "Virtue Ethics in the Twentieth Century," in *The Cambridge Companion to
    Virtue Ethics*, ed. Russell, 154. Emphasis in original.

514 "Empiricism, especially in the form given to it by Russell, and later by
    Wittgenstein, thrust ethics almost out of philosophy." Murdoch, *The Sov-
    ereignty of Good*, 48.

515 Whitehead said his metaphysics was a "transformation of some main
    doctrines of Absolute Idealism onto a realistic basis." Whitehead, *Process
    and Reality*, vii, 186.

516 Whitehead, 188–91. Whitehead sometimes combines the first two, as the
    "responsive phase" (or the "physical pole"), and the second two as the
    "supplemental stage" (or the "mental" or "conceptual pole"). Whitehead,
    245–8, 290, 410–11. It is perhaps an indication of Whitehead's fundamen-
    tal realism or phenomenalism that he thinks of the first two as merely the
    "physical" pole of the human, instead of the "existential" pole.

517 Whitehead, 192. Emphasis added.

518 Whitehead, 344, 189, 191.

519 Whitehead, 188–91. Emphasis in original.

520 Whitehead, 245–7.

521 Whitehead, 190–1, 289–90.

522 Whitehead, 281, 326. Emphasis added. "[T]he valuation of the conceptual
    feeling is a 'valuation up' or a 'valuation down.'" Whitehead, 282. Max
    Scheler calls this "preferring."

523 Whitehead, 190–1, 289–90.

524 "Opposed elements stand to each other in mutual requirement. In their
    unity, they inhibit or *contrast*." The "higher" categories of feeling "combine
    the contraries" in "contrasts of higher types," a "chain of contrasts." The
    categories are "specific modes of diversity [non-union] and identity [un-
    ion]." In Whitehead's "process," "diverse feelings [e.g., individual families
    of virtues] pass on to wider generalities of integral feeling [e.g., the whole
    nature of the human]. Such a wider generality is a *feeling of a complex of
    feelings*, including their specific elements of identity [union] and contrast
    [non-union]." Whitehead, 411, 188–9, 325, 191–2, 244. Emphasis added.

525 Whitehead, 191.

526 "[E]ach actual entity ... repeats in microcosm what the universe is in
    macrocosm." Whitehead, 248.

527 In the concept of "organic process," Whitehead expresses what, in this
    book, I've called "double vision": organism and process are combined in
    a "twofold manner." "Process" is the forward movement through which

an organism (and the universe) is developed. But "in any stage" of the process, the organism itself (and the universe) is fully present: it is an "incompletion in process of production." Whitehead, 247–8. Any stage in the process "has the character of a unified feeling of the actual world [the whole nature of the human] from the standpoint of that region [i.e., of a specific family of virtues]." Whitehead, 335.

528 Whitehead, 178.

529 Whitehead, 186.

530 Whitehead, 71. Perhaps without recognizing it, Whitehead echoes Pascal: "Tout notre raisonnement se réduit à céder au sentiment." *Pensées*, §2, p. 2.

531 Whitehead, 193, 174.

532 Whitehead, 174.

533 Whitehead, 298.

534 Whitehead, 297.

535 Whitehead, 174–5, 106, 74. Emphasis added.

536 How big a step Whitehead took toward the rediscovery of the human is suggested by the conclusion to *Process and Reality*, which (if applied to the virtues) could serve equally well as a capsule summary of this book: "The final summary can only be expressed in terms of a *group of antitheses*, whose apparent self-contradiction depend [*sic*] on neglect of the *diverse categories of existence* [i.e., the human stances and families of virtues]. In each antithesis there is a shift of meaning which converts the opposition into a contrast." Whitehead, 410. Emphasis added.

537 Although Whitehead himself thinks his "final outcome is after all not so greatly different" from Bradley, it is also, as he acknowledges, "close to Spinoza." Whitehead, vii, 98.

538 "[T]he expansion of the universe in respect to actual *things* is the first meaning of 'process.'" Whitehead, 248. Emphasis added.

539 Husserl, *Ideas*, trans. Gibson, 37. "La phénoménologie est la science des phénomènes. Cela signifie qu'elle est une description, antérieure à toute théorie et indépendante de toute présupposition, de tout ce qui se propose à nous, en qualité d'existant, dans quelque ordre ou quelque domaine que ce soit." Michel Henry, *L'essence de la manifestation*, 59.

540 Husserl, *Ideas*, trans. Gibson, 19.

541 "[C]ette problématique [dans la philosophie de Husserl] reste, quant à sa *visée* fondamentale, celle de la constitution de toute réalité dans et par la conscience, constitution solidaire des philosophies du *Cogito*." Ricœur, *Soi-même comme un autre*, 373. Emphasis in original.

542 Maurice Merleau-Ponty, "Sur la phénoménologie du langage," in *Éloge de la philosophie* (Paris: Gallimard, 1960), 83–111. Husserl and

phenomenology would continue to influence twentieth-century Western philosophy in other ways. In the hands of Hans-Georg Gadamer and Paul Ricœur, for example, phenomenology moved in the direction of "heremeneutics," the interpretation of meanings buried within various kinds of human experience and expression, including the various interpretive disciplines, such as semantics, semiology, psychoanalysis, history, literary criticism, and so on. In the hands of Emmanuel Levinas, phenomenology led toward a vision of "ethics" or the virtues as "first philosophy," a vision very close to the conclusions of this book.

543 Scheler, *Formalism in Ethics* trans. Frings and Funk, 257–9.

544 Scheler, 64, 109. "Feeling, preferring, and rejecting, loving and hating, which belong to the totality of spirit [*des Geistes*], possess their own a priori contents independent of inductive experience and pure laws of thought." Scheler, 65.

545 Scheler, 104–10. Emphasis in original. Another significant difference between Scheler's four "value-modalities" and the four families of virtues described in this book is the overlap, in Scheler's scheme, between his "vital" values and my virtues of Excellence (B1), especially the virtues of Goodness (B1b). In his "vital" modality, Scheler includes values such as "nobility" and excellence, which I think belong to what I call the virtues of Excellence (B1). This overlap may be more apparent than real, however, because Scheler explains that what he means by "noble" is the "ideal of the hero." Scheler, 502. If so, it is rightly included in the virtues of Power (A1a), the home of courage and the heroic.

546 Scheler occasionally refers to a fifth "value-modality which he calls the "modality of the useful," or the "values of utility." The personality archetype he identifies with this family he calls the "leading spirit." Scheler is not consistent about the values of "usefulness," because elsewhere he says that "a person can never be 'agreeable' or 'useful,'" and that the "value of what is 'useful' is founded in the values of what is agreeable [i.e., the virtues of Pleasure (A1b)]." Scheler, 85, 94, 109–10, 269, 307, 502, 585. On the ways in which "exemplary characters" can serve as "moral exemplars" in anthropology and moral life, see James Laidlaw, *The Subject of Virtue: An Anthropology of Ethics and Freedom* (Cambridge: Cambridge Univ. Press, 2014), 83–7; MacIntyre, *After Virtue*, 27–32, 73–8.

547 Scheler, 303–7, 538n194. Scheler thinks the "arrow of virtue" moves in a "direction" similar to the one described in this book but seems to leave out the important stage of the virtues of Excellence and the "state" (B1). Scheler, 541. On the whole, Scheler thinks "growth of the ethos [i.e., the arrow of virtue] occurs in the movement of *love* and its power," and is a "gradual enlargement and expansion of the domain of the objects of love

and its types (family, tribe, people, nation, etc.)." Scheler, 261, 538, 305–6. Emphasis in original.

548 Scheler, 541–2.

549 Michel Henry suggests, however, that although Scheler's discovery of the role of feeling in human understanding was an "intuition of genius," his phenomenology of human values is still too rationalistic, and does not yet do full credit to the role of human feeling in the identification of human values. For Henry, *every* perception is, by its very nature, a form of *feeling*. In Scheler's lingering rationalism, Henry sees the essential problem of the whole Western philosophical tradition. *L'essence de la manifestation*, 715–35.

550 Scheler was a major contributor to the current of moral and political thought known as "personalism," which had a particularly strong influence in France in the 1930s, especially in the work of Emmanuel Mounier and his periodical *Esprit*, and, through them, on important twentieth-century thinkers such as Jacques Maritain and Paul Ricœur. See Thomas D. Williams and Jan Olof Bengtsson, "Personalism," The Stanford Encyclopedia of Philosophy, ed. Edward N. Zalta (Summer 2016 Edition), https://plato.stanford.edu/archives/sum2016/entries/personalism/.

551 Joas, *The Genesis of Values*, 124. Timothy Chappell, "Virtue Ethics in the Twentieth Century," in *The Cambridge Companion to Virtue Ethics*, ed. Russell, 149–71.

552 Maurice Merleau-Ponty, "Évolution de la phénoménologie," in *Existence et Dialectique: Textes choisis*, ed. Maurice Dayan (Paris: Presses Universitaires de France, 1971), 63–4.

553 Husserl, *Ideas*, trans. Gibson, 12. "C'est le bienfait inestimable, *quoique finalement négatif*, de toute la phénoménologie husserlienne, d'avoir établi que les recherches de 'constitution' renvoient à du prédonné, à du préconstitué." Ricœur, *Le conflit des interprétations*, 151. Emphasis added. Maurice Blondel suggests the search for a "realistic" phenomenology (or phenomenological realism) – the attempt to find the being or reality of the world in the "sum" of phenomena – is somewhat like running after our own shadow in the headlights of a moving automobile. *L'Être et les êtres*, 375–6, 378–9.

554 Paul Ricœur (a disciple of both) describes the shift from Husserl to Heidegger as "le retournement qui, à la place d'une épistémologie de l'interprétation, met une ontologie de la compréhension. ... Comprendre n'est plus alors un mode de connaissance, mais un mode d'être, le mode de cet être qui existe en comprenant." Ricœur, *Le conflit des interprétations*, 28.

555 Heidegger, *Being and Time*, 199, 144, 268. trans. Stambaugh, 192, 139, 258.

556 Martin Heidegger, "Building Dwelling Thinking," trans. Albert Hofstadter, in *Basic Writings*, ed. Krell, 323–39; "The Question Concerning

Technology," trans. William Lovitt, in *Basic Writings*, 311, 314; "Bremen
Lectures: Insight into That Which Is," trans. Jerome Veith, in *The Heidegger Reader*, 259–66. Emphasis in original. Note that Heidegger also refers
to another "fivefold" (*Fünffache*) "in which the unified essence of metaphysics unfolds." "On Nietzsche," trans. Jerome Veith, in *The Heidegger
Reader*, 225. He also refers to a "threefold" of being, unconcealment, and
appearance. *An Introduction to Metaphysics*, trans. Manheim, 92.

557 Heidegger, "Bremen Lectures," trans. Veith, 264–6, 268.

558 Heidegger, *An Introduction to Metaphysics*, trans. Manheim, 170. Like Hegel, Heidegger suggests human beings have an "ontological structure of
the circle." *Being and Time*, 153, trans. Stambaugh, 148–9.

559 Heidegger, "Building Dwelling Thinking," trans. Hofstadter, 336. Heidegger's poetic description of the fourfold as two pairs (earth/sky, divine/
mortals) accurately reflects the two "diagonal" pairs of families of virtues
that establish both the path of the arrow of virtue in time and the internal
structure of the nature of the human: A1/A2 and B1/B2.

560 Heidegger, *Being and Time*, 12–13, 16–17, 41, 130–1, 134, 180–2, trans.
Stambaugh, 11–12, 16–17, 39, 127–8, 131, 175–6.

561 This "temporal" terminology for the four "structural moments" of the
nature of the human helps Heidegger to highlight their dynamic character and also their fundamental unity: "Every understanding [B1] has
its mood [A2]. Every attunement [A2] understands [B1]. Attuned understanding [B1] has the characteristic of entanglement [A1]. Entangled [A1],
attuned [A2] understanding [B1] articulates itself with regard to its intelligibility in discourse [B2]." Heidegger, 331–2, 334–5, trans. Stambaugh,
316–17, 320–1.

562 Heidegger, *An Introduction to Metaphysics*, trans. Manheim, 79–80, 167–8.

563 Heidegger, 164.

564 Heidegger, "The Question Concerning Technology," trans. Lovitt, 305–6.

565 Heidegger, "Bremen Lectures," trans. Veith, 278.

566 Heidegger's poetic "fourfold" (earth/sky, divine/mortals) may also be
the four corners of the human *viewed through the lens of reverence*, similar to Goethe's four forms of reverence discussed in chapter 17. This
is suggested by Heidegger's descriptive language about it, and by the
fact that the "fourfold" seems to be specially associated with "giving"
and with "gift." "Building Dwelling Thinking," trans. Hofstadter, 336,
328. "Bremen Lectures," trans. Veith, 255–60. Heidegger's discussion of
"care" as the "being of Dasein" in *Being and Time* also suggests his vision of fourfold Dasein is already filtered through the lens of reverence,
especially the virtues of Excellence (B1). For Heidegger, Dasein is never
"mere urge" (self-assertion): "it is always already care." Through care, the
self's original concern about its own being evolves into concern about its

"ownmost potentiality-of-being-a-self" (the four stances) and the potentiality of others. *Being and Time*, 191–5, 297–8, trans. Stambaugh, 184–9, 284–5.

567 Heidegger, *An Introduction to Metaphysics*, trans. Manheim, 80, 167–8.

568 "[T]he beginning of our spiritual-historical existence … is the onset of Greek philosophy." Martin Heidegger, "Rectorship Address: The Self-Assertion of the German University," trans. William S. Lewis, in *The Heidegger Reader*, 110. See also "The Question Concerning Technology," trans. Lovitt, 315.

569 "[T]here's an original I-ought which goes with I-exist ["I am" (A2)]." William E. Hocking to P.H. Epps, 14 October 1954, cited in Dupré, *Transcendent Selfhood*, 109n12.

570 Heidegger, *An Introduction to Metaphysics*, trans. Manheim, 80–1, 164–72. "Thus it is in the modern era, when … thought becomes dominant in the form of self-sufficient reason, that the distinction between being and the ought really comes into its own. The process is completed in Kant. … The predominance of the essent ["*It* is"] *endangered the ought* ["It *is*"] in its role as standard and criterion." Heidegger, 165. Emphasis added.

571 See Mark Johnson's description of the "objectivist" assumptions underlying modern, post-modern and contemporary Western culture in chapter 4, note 47.

572 Jonathan Haidt, *The Righteous Mind: Why Good People Are Divided by Politics and Religion* (New York: Pantheon Books, 2012), 96.

573 Heidegger, "Bremen Lectures," trans. Veith, 272, 280, 282.

574 Heidegger, "The Question Concerning Technology," trans. Lovitt, 287–317.

575 Heidegger, *Being and Time*, 188–99, trans. Stambaugh, 182–92. The words quoted are on page 192. Heidegger calls this kind of freedom *for* the whole nature of the human a freedom for the "possibility of existing as a *whole potentiality-of-being*." Heidegger, 264, trans. Stambaugh, 253.

576 Heidegger, 133, 170, 350–1, trans. Stambaugh, 129, 164, 334; "The End of Philosophy and the Task of Thinking," trans. Stambaugh, 373–92. The "appropriative event" through which the human and Being meet in the "clearing" is still a kind of thought, even though it is a "thinking that is of another sort [B1] than that of [self-assertive] calculation [B2]." Martin Heidegger, "The Principle of Identity," trans. Joan Stambaugh and Jerome Veith, in *The Heidegger Reader*, 291–4. The early Heidegger seems to have been readier to acknowledge the role of feeling in this other kind of thinking. Heidegger calls this condition of being affected or moved "attunement." Attunement is the characteristic feature of understanding (B1), the "structure" of being (or stance) in which human beings discover the full "possibilities-of-being," the four "structures," modes of being,

stances, or families of virtues. Understanding [B1] is always "attuned understanding." "Attuned understanding" is, for the Heidegger of *Being and Time*, what "conceptual feeling" or "conceptual valuation" [B1] are for Whitehead. Significantly, the terms are reversed: feeling is a noun for Whitehead but only an adjective for Heidegger. *Being and Time*, 137–8, trans. Stambaugh, 133–4.

577 Heidegger, *Being and Time*, 143–4, trans. Stambaugh, 139.

578 Heidegger, 267–74, trans. Stambaugh, 257–64.

579 Heidegger, "Building Dwelling Thinking," trans. Hofstadter, 326; "What Calls for Thinking?," trans. Fred D. Wieck and J. Glenn Gray, in *Basic Writings*, 350–1. Unlike other deep thinkers from Augustine to Levinas and Ricœur, who hear the "call" or the voice of Being speaking to humans (a call to which they must listen if they are to be "saved") as a "call" to love, or to responsibility for others, Heidegger hears it mainly as a call to "thinking."

580 Grondin, *Introduction à la métaphysique*, 329.

581 "[T]he essence of modern technology, the *Ge-Stell*, began with the fundamentally essential act of besetting [self-assertion]." Heidegger, "Bremen Lectures," trans. Veith, 281.

582 "The human is now the one assailed by and for the besetting [self-assertion]." Heidegger, 272.

583 "[T]he roots of the truth of statement [B2] reach back to the disclosedness of understanding [B1]." Heidegger, *Being and Time*, 223, trans. Stambaugh, 214.

584 Heidegger, "The Question Concerning Technology," trans. Lovitt, 308–9.

585 Aquinas himself merits only three brief references in *Being and Time*. Heidegger, *Being and Time*, trans. Stambaugh, 482. "[O]n se demande quel malheur d'un temps oublieux de la sagesse a bien pu plonger ce métaphysicien de race dans une méconnaissance invincible de sa propre tradition?" Étienne Gilson, *Constantes philosophiques de l'être* (Paris: Vrin, 1983), 131. Heidegger does acknowledge that Aquinas conceived "being as pure act." But he quickly dismisses this discovery as "metaphysics [that] has remained unalterably 'physics' … a mechanical repetition of the question about the essent as such." *An Introduction to Metaphysics*, trans. Manheim, 168, 14–15.

586 Martin Heidegger, "The Way Back into the Ground of Metaphysics," trans. Walter Kaufmann, in *Existentialism from Dostoevsky to Sartre*, ed. Walter Kaufmann (Cleveland: World, 1956), 207.

587 Heidegger, 209.

588 Heidegger's neglect of Aquinas might seem surprising because he had a very Thomistic education and wrote his doctoral thesis on an aspect of medieval philosophy. But after his abandonment of Christianity, one of

his objectives seems to have been to "radically" eliminate "the remnants of Christian theology within the philosophical problematic." Heidegger, *Being and Time*, 229, trans. Stambaugh, 220.

589 Heidegger even dismisses the relevance of "empty 'habitus.'" He does, however, associate a distinctive virtue (or what he prefers to call "attitude") with three of the four "fundamental structures" or "structural moments" of the human. The "special attitude" that "characterizes" Being-in (B1) is "care"; the one related to being with "things" (B2) is "taking care of them"; the one of being with others (A2) is "concern." He says there is no "special attitude" for being a "self" (A1), however, because it "would be a tautology": "in this determination the other two structural moments of care, already being-in [B1] ... and being-together-with [things (B2) and others (A2)] are *co-posited*." *Being and Time*, 300, 193, trans. Stambaugh, 287, 186. Emphasis and elision in original.

590 Heidegger sometimes seems to neglect the point he elsewhere acknowledges (in *Being and Time*, for example) that even reverence must be a form of self-assertion. He therefore later interprets reflection on human values as merely another form of self-assertion. He does not appear to notice that it is the assertive side of *reverence* (B1) – the result of separative projection within the virtues of reverence. Martin Heidegger, "Letter on Humanism," trans. Frank A. Capuzzi, in collaboration with J. Glenn Gray, in *Basic Writings*, ed. Krell, 228; *An Introduction to Metaphysics*, trans. Manheim, 138. Contrast with *Being and Time*, 137–8, trans. Stambaugh, 133–4.

591 Heidegger, *An Introduction to Metaphysics*, trans. Manheim, 104–6.

592 Heidegger, 120, 150.

593 Heidegger, 32.

594 Significantly, "It *is*" translates, in German, as "Es *gibt*" ("It *gives*"). So, for Heidegger, "giving" is built right into the idea of Being and requires an appropriate human response. Heidegger, *Being and Time*, 212, 230, 316, trans. Stambaugh, 203, 220, 302; "Letter on Humanism," trans. Capuzzi with Gray; "Modern Science, Metaphysics, and Mathematics," trans. Barton and Deutsch; "The Question Concerning Technology," trans. Lovitt; "What Calls for Thinking?" trans. Wieck and Gray; and "The End of Philosophy and the Task of Thinking," trans. Stambaugh, 214–15, 251, 316, 345, 385, 391–2.

595 "Care" (*sorge*) is, for Heidegger, what love is for Aquinas: the virtue (or what Heidegger prefers to call "attitude") that is in all other virtues, that makes them virtuous: "it is always already *in* them as an existential *a priori*." Except that, for Heidegger, "care" (sorge) isn't so much a virtue as a family of virtues, or the family of all families of virtues, the stance of all stances. Care is the stance of the whole human paradox, the stance of the whole nature of the human: "care is the ontological term for the

wholeness of the structural totality of Dasein." *Being and Time*, 193, 252, trans. Stambaugh, 187, 242. Emphasis in original.

596 Heidegger, "Building Dwelling Thinking," trans. Hofstadter, 327–9; "What Calls for Thinking?," trans. Wieck and Gray, 367; and "Letter on Humanism," trans. Capuzzi with Gray, in *Basic Writings*, ed. Krell, 222, 228–9, 236–9; "Bremen Lectures," trans. Veith, 266–7.

597 Heidegger, *An Introduction to Metaphysics*, trans. Manheim, 17.

598 Heidegger's interpretation of these words and expressions sometimes seems to smack more of the virtues of self-assertion than of reverence: "the care of livelihood, of profession, of enjoyment," and so on. "Indication of the Hermeneutical Situation," trans. Baur and Veith, 43–4. But these are the self-assertive forms in which "care" makes its first and normal appearance in human life before it is or can be transformed into reverent care. *Being and Time*, 317, 333, 335–7, trans. Stambaugh, 303, 317, 320–2.

599 Heidegger, *Being and Time*, 391, trans. Stambaugh, 372.

600 Heidegger seems to sense the tension between the virtues of Liberty (A1) and the virtues of Reverence (A2) that lies behind the virtues of Excellence (B1) in the arrow of virtue. He calls this tension between A1 and A2 "a reluctant will to mastery." Which shows, perhaps, why he never really seems to penetrate the real content of the virtues of Reverence (A2). He never seems to perceive clearly the role of the virtues of self-*giving* as the essential bridge to the human. But he *does* see clearly that the initial, reverent kind of thinking that lets being and beings be (B1) is quite different from the self-assertive reason (B2) we have inherited from Plato and, especially, Aristotle. Heidegger, *An Introduction to Metaphysics*, trans. Manheim, 104–6, 148.

601 Ironically, Heidegger himself seems to have sensed this danger: "The danger of a relapse into intellectualism persists precisely for those who wish to combat it." Heidegger, 103.

602 "Even those who perceived the dangers in the present development of our society were fully subject to its prejudices and, in their search for a solution, have merely succeeded in radicalizing the problem." Dupré, *Transcendent Selfhood*, 10.

603 Heidegger, *An Introduction to Metaphysics*, trans. Manheim, 104–6, 143.

604 Heidegger, "What Calls for Thinking?," trans. Wieck and Gray, 367; "The Principle of Identity," trans. Stambaugh and Veith, 288.

605 Heidegger's term for the role of feeling in the initial "disclosing" of being is "attunement." Heidegger, *Being and Time*, 134–40, 340–5, trans. Stambaugh, 130–6, 324–30. On Heidegger and feeling, see also Henry, *L'essence de la manifestation*, 735–57.

606 Heidegger, *An Introduction to Metaphysics*, trans. Manheim, 119.

607 Heidegger, "Bremen Lectures," trans. Veith, 266; "The Principle of Identity," trans. Stambaugh and Veith, 294; *An Introduction to Metaphysics*,
trans. Manheim, 103.

608 For Heidegger, the "essential structures" of human being (i.e., the four
stances and families of virtues) are "centred in disclosedness" (B1). "Dasein *is* as an understanding [B1] potentiality-of-being." "Being-with others" (A2) only rarely merits specific mention in *Being and Time* as one of
the four "structures" and is often swallowed up with "things" in encompassing expressions such as "worldly beings," or even simply "world."
Being and Time, 231, 181, 211, 228, 190–1, trans. Stambaugh, 221, 175, 203,
218, 184. Heidegger recognizes the reality of "I am," but for him it is normally the assertive "*I* am" (A1), not the reverential "I *am*" (A2). It is the "I
am" of "certainty," the "I am" who "posits and thinks." "Modern Science,
Metaphysics, and Mathematics," trans. Barton and Deutsch, 279.

609 Heidegger, "The Principle of Identity," trans. Stambaugh and Veith, 286–
7, 293; Parmenides, *Fragments*, trans. Gallop, 57. Heidegger recognizes
that being and thinking are not the same "in the sense of mere equivalence." Their relationship is dialectical: they are one "in a contending
sense," i.e., "the same in the sense of belonging together." *An Introduction
to Metaphysics*, trans. Manheim, 117–18.

610 "The mode of being of Dasein as a potentiality of being lies existentially
in understanding [B1]." Heidegger, *Being and Time*, 143, trans. Stambaugh, 139.

611 Heidegger, "Letter on Humanism," trans. Capuzzi with Gray, 235. Heidegger does sometimes appear to acknowledge that the structures of
thought are a reflection of (or reflection on) an even more "basic experience." "Indication of the Hermeneutical Situation," trans. Baur and Veith,
60; *An Introduction to Metaphysics*, trans. Manheim, 140–1, 118–19, 159–61,
138.

612 Heidegger himself frequently seems to intuit that thinking alone may not
be enough. But in this mood, he is inclined to fall back not so much on
the human virtues as on art, especially poetry, as the means that can help
humans to think their way back into the presence of Being. Heidegger,
"The Question Concerning Technology," trans. Lovitt, 316; *An Introduction to Metaphysics*, trans. Manheim, 21. That seems to be one of the reasons so many of his later essays are devoted to the poetry of Hölderlin.
"*Der Spiegel* Interview with Martin Heidegger," trans. Jerome Veith and
others, in *The Heidegger Reader*, 330.

613 Heidegger's world – like that of Aristotle and Kant – is still a world
of "things." He does, however, distinguish between "things" and "objects." Objects are what are perceived by the modern scientific and technological culture of self-assertion. "Things" are what are perceived by

the eyes of reverence, the spirit of "giving" and "sacrifice." But they are still *things*. Heidegger's thought seems to yearn back from "*It* is" (B2) to "It *is*" (B1). *But no further*. Heidegger, "Bremen Lectures," trans. Veith, 254–67.

614 Hegel, *The Phenomenology of Mind*, trans. Baillie, 676; Heidegger, *Being and Time*, 283–6, trans. Stambaugh, 272–5; *An Introduction to Metaphysics*, trans. Manheim, 169; "Letter on Humanism," trans. Capuzzi with Gray, 238.

615 Paul Ricœur notes Heidegger's failure to show "le chemin inverse: de l'ontologie vers l'éthique" and suggests his reluctance to embrace a perspective based on the virtues of human action was motivated at least in part by their potential challenge to the hegemony of theoretic culture. *Soi-même comme un autre*, 403–4.

616 You can get an idea of where Heidegger stops short in the thought of his contemporary, Franz Rosenzweig. Like Heidegger, Rosenzweig uses the concepts of "concealment" and unconcealment, but for Rosenzweig, what is made "manifest" in what Heidegger calls the "clearing" (or what Rosenzweig calls "revelation") is not just being, but love. Rosenzweig, *The Star of Redemption*, trans. Hallo, 388–90, 417. The word "love" appears to occur only once in *Being and Time*, and there only in a footnote reference to concepts of Christian theology. Heidegger, *Being and Time*, 190, trans. Stambaugh, 184n4. Paul Ricœur suggests Heidegger fell short because he was still too much the prisoner of "It is," prisoner of an implicit ontology of "things" and of "objects." *Soi-même comme un autre*, 379–80. From this point of view, perhaps the same question could be asked about Heidegger that he himself posed about Nietzsche: "[W]as he himself only the last victim of a long process of error and neglect, but as such the unrecognized witness to a new necessity?" Heidegger, *An Introduction to Metaphysics*, trans. Manheim, 30.

617 Heidegger, "The Way Back," trans. Kaufmann, 215.

618 Martin Heidegger, "What Is Metaphysics?," trans. R.F.C. Hull and Alan Crick, in *Existence and Being* (Chicago: Henry Regnery, 1949), 360; "Letter on Humanism," trans. Capuzzi with Gray, 230.

619 Paul Ricœur suggests an authentic existentialist agenda for twentieth and twenty-first century philosophy, towards a true "philosophie de l'acte d'exister." *Histoire et vérité*, 405. Italics in original.

620 Levinas, *Autrement qu'être*, 128.

621 Taylor, *Sources of the Self*, 488.

622 Leibniz had already noted that "le fondement de la vérité des choses contingentes et singulières est dans le succès." But, unlike pragmatists, he recognized there is more than one kind of truth, and even truth about the phenomenal world is dependent on other kinds of truth which find

"leurs archétypes dans la possibilité éternelle des choses." Leibniz, *Nouveaux essais*, bk. 4, chap. 4, §1–5, p. 345; bk. 4, chap. 11, §1–10, p. 393.

623 Richard M. Rorty, "Introduction: Metaphysical Difficulties of Linguistic Philosophy," in *The Rorty Reader*, 64–5.

624 Richard M. Rorty, "Introduction" to *Philosophy and the Mirror of Nature*, in *The Rorty Reader*, 88.

625 Philip Rieff, *The Triumph of the Therapeutic: Uses of Faith after Freud* (Chicago: Univ. of Chicago Press, 1987); Taylor, *A Secular Age*, 618–20.

626 Richard M. Rorty, "From Logic to Language to Play: A Plenary Address to the InterAmerican Congress," in *The Rorty Reader*, 145–51.

627 Taylor, *A Secular Age*, 351.

628 Martin, *On Secularization*, 143–4.

629 Donald, *Origins of the Modern Mind*, 368. Webb Keane points out we normally draw our conclusions about other people from a wide variety of mimetic or "semiotic" signals, including voice, timbre, bodily posture, smell, physical location, and so on. He calls this "everyday semiotics." *Ethical Life*, 82–3, 109. This point had already been made by Edmund Husserl, among others. *Ideas*, 46.

630 Simon Blackburn, *Lust* (New York: Oxford Univ. Press, 2004). Robert C. Solomon defends the claim that erotic love is a virtue in "Erotic Love as a Moral Virtue," in *Virtue Ethics, Old and New*, ed. Stephen M. Gardiner, 81–100. Hefner's column, "The Playboy Philosophy," appeared in *Playboy* magazine in twenty-five instalments from December 1962 to 1966. See Steven Watts, *Mr. Playboy: Hugh Hefner and the American Dream* (Hoboken, NJ: John Wiley, 2008), 472n17. "Like Trumpism, Hefnerian values have prospered in the blue-collar vacuum created by religion's retreat, community's unraveling." Ross Douthat, "A Playboy for President," *New York Times*, 14 August 2016.

631 "No state more extensive than the minimal state can be justified." Robert Nozick, *Anarchy, State, and Utopia* (New York: Basic Books, 1974), 297.

632 Whitehead, *Process and Reality*, vii–ix, 64.

633 "[T]he old type of philosopher, impersonal by profession, a mere deputy of the naturally one-dimensional history of philosophy is replaced by a highly personal type, the philosopher of the *Weltanschauung*, the point of view. ... Its new point of departure is the subjective, the extremely personal self." Rosenzweig, *The Star of Redemption*, trans. Hallo, 105–6.

634 "It is not that modern forms of humanism or faith are unconnected to ideals of order. On the contrary. But they are now connected to the same one. The modern ideal has triumphed. We are all partisans of human rights." Taylor, *A Secular Age*, 419.

635 Richard M. Rorty, "Introduction: Metaphysical Difficulties of Linguistic Philosophy," 61, 63; "Dewey's Metaphysics," 75; "Perspectives on

Richard Rorty, I: From Philosophy to Post-Philosophy: An Interview with Richard M. Rorty," interviewed by Wayne Hudson and Wim van Reijen, 495, 497; and "Trotsky and the Wild Orchids," in *The Rorty Reader*, 501, 504. Brad Gregory agrees the modern philosophical enterprise has completely failed in its ambition "to articulate universal truths based on reason alone," but does so from a position diametrically opposed to that of Rorty. Gregory, *The Unintended Reformation*, 378–9. Alfred North Whitehead disagrees, attributing this perception of failure to the way in which modern philosophy has been corrupted by the "example of mathematics." *Process and Reality*, 10–14.

636 John Stuart Mill, "Coleridge," in *Mill on Bentham and Coleridge*, ed. F.R. Leavis (Cambridge: Cambridge Univ. Press, 1980), 105.

637 Paul Ricœur calls this the "dialectique d'une archéologie et d'une téléologie." *Le conflit des interprétations*, 239.

638 Rorty, "Philosophy as a Transitional Genre," 474; "Introduction: Metaphysical Difficulties of Linguistic Philosophy," 89; "Is 'Cultural Recognition' a Useful Concept for Leftist Politics?" 472; and "The Priority of Democracy to Philosophy," in *The Rorty Reader*, 255.

639 "[I]l n'y a pas pour l'homme d'équilibre statique, mais seulement un équilibre de tension et de mouvement." Maritain, *Humanisme intégral*, 143.

640 Hobbes, *Leviathan*, pt. 1, chap. 11, p. 87.

641 Alexis de Tocqueville, *L'ancien régime et la Révolution* (Paris: Gallimard, 1967), 203. "[A] longing may arise for an objective order in which man gladly degrades himself to servitude and total subjection, if only to escape the torment of vacuity and negation." Hegel, *Philosophy of Right*, addition to §141, trans. Knox, 258.

642 In his famous (or infamous) *Der Spiegel* interview at the end of his life, Martin Heidegger said he was still "not convinced" that democracy was an appropriate system of government for a technological age. *"Der Spiegel* Interview with Martin Heidegger" trans. Veith and others, 324.

643 On the problem of modern moral sources, see Taylor, *Sources of the Self*, 99, 185, 199, 317–19, 348, 498–9, 502, 512.

644 R.G. Collingwood, *An Essay on Philosophical Method* (London: Oxford Univ. Press, 1965), 146.

645 Bernard Williams, *Ethics and the Limits of Philosophy* (Cambridge, MA: Harvard Univ. Press, 1985), 483.

646 Haidt, *The Righteous Mind*, 220.

647 G.K. Chesterton, *Orthodoxy* (New York: Dodd Mead, 1924), 64.

648 Rorty, "Dewey's Metaphysics," 83.

649 R.G. Collingwood, *Speculum Mentis or the Map of Knowledge* (Oxford: Oxford Univ. Press, 1963), 106–7.

Chapter 16. Religious Life

1 For a fuller and somewhat different exploration of religious life, see Ralph Heintzman, *Rediscovering Reverence: The Meaning of Faith in a Secular World* (Montreal: McGill-Queen's Univ. Press, 2011).

2 Wilfred Cantwell Smith, *The Meaning and End of Religion* (New York: Macmillan, 1963).

3 Shahab Ahmed, *What Is Islam? The Importance of Being Islamic* (Princeton: Princeton Univ. Press, 2016), 176–80. Ahmed gives an overview of the contemporary scholarly literature deconstructing the Western concept of "religion." Ahmed, 176–7n2. Among other works, Ahmed cites: Talal Asad, *Genealogies of Religion: Discipline and Reasons of Power in Christianity and Islam* (Baltimore: Johns Hopkins Univ. Press, 1993); Timothy Fitzgerald, *The Ideology of Religious Studies* (New York: Oxford Univ. Press, 2000); Craig Martin, *Masking Hegemony: A Genealogy of Liberalism, Religion and the Private Sphere* (London: Equinox, 2010); Robert Wuthnow, *Meaning and Moral Order: Explorations in Cultural Analysis* (Berkeley: Univ. of California Press, 1987).

4 Luke Timothy Johnson, *Among the Gentiles: Greco-Roman Religion and Christianity* (New Haven: Yale Univ. Press, 2009), 44–9.

5 Jared Diamond, *The World Until Yesterday: What We Can Learn from Traditional Societies* (New York: Viking, 2012), 329–63. After announcing and discussing these seven functions, Diamond than goes on to add an eighth, which he calls "badges of commitment."

6 Martin's definitions include religion as a belief system; as something that specifically concerns supernatural matters; as matters of faith; as concerning the meaning of life; as concerning spirituality or spiritual well-being; as communal institutions oriented around a set of beliefs, ritual practices, and ethical or social norms. Alston's non-mandatory criteria of religion are 1. Belief in one or more supernatural beings. 2. A distinction between sacred and profane objects. 3. Ritual acts focused on these objects. 4. A moral code believed to have been sanctioned by the god(s). 5. Religious feelings (awe, mystery, etc.) that tend to be aroused by the sacred objects and during rituals. 6. Prayer and other communicative conduct concerning the gods. 7. A world view according adherents a significant place in the universe. 8. A more or less comprehensive organization of one's life based on the world view. 9. An organization bound together by 1. William P. Alston, *Philosophy of Language* (Englewood Cliffs: Prentice Hall, 1964), 88, cited in Martin, *Masking Hegemony*, chapter 1, cited in Ahmed, *What Is Islam?*, 179n6.

7 José Casanova, *Public Religions in the Modern World* (Chicago: Univ. of Chicago Press, 1994), 43–4.

8 Diamond, *The World Until Yesterday*, 324.

9 Even Edward O. Wilson concludes that a "predisposition to religious belief" is "an ineradicable part of human nature." *On Human Nature* (Cambridge MA: Harvard Univ. Press, 2004), 169. The only error here is the word "belief."

10 C.G. Jung, *Analytical Psychology: Its Theory and Practice* (New York: Vintage Books, 1970), 42.

11 Phil Lane Jr., Judie Bopp, Michael Bopp, Lee Brown, and elders, *The Sacred Tree: Reflections on Native American Spirituality*, 4th ed. (Twin Lakes, WI: Lotus Press, 2012).

12 Saint Augustine, *City of God*, trans. Henry Bettenson (London: Penguin Books, 2003), 373–4.

13 Thomas Aquinas, *Summa Theologiæ* 1–2.60.3, in *Treatise on the Virtues*, trans. John A. Oesterle (Notre Dame, IN: Univ. of Notre Dame Press, 1984), 101.

14 Aquinas, *Summa Theologiæ* 1–2.100.9, 1–2.121.1, in *Theological Texts*, selected and trans. Thomas Gilby (London: Oxford Univ. Press, 1955), 150, 262.

15 Karl Rahner, *The Practice of Faith: A Handbook of Contemporary Spirituality*, trans. various (New York: Crossroad, 1983), 61.

16 "[P]rofessed belief … is instinctively aggressive." Northrop Frye, *The Great Code: The Bible and Literature* (Toronto: Academic Press Canada, 1982), 229; Alfred North Whitehead, *Process and Reality* (New York: Free Press, 1969), 312.

17 "[L]a religion vise à placer toute experience, y compris l'expérience morale, mais pas seulement elle, dans la *perspective* de l'économie du don." Paul Ricœur *Lectures 3*, in *Ricœur: Textes choisis et présentés*, ed. Michaël Fœssel and Fabien Lamouche (Paris: Éditions Points, 2007), 323. Emphasis in original.

18 Ernst Cassirer, *An Essay on Man* (New York: Bantam Books, 1970), 87.

19 *"Most enduring religions promote altruism* [i.e., reverence] *expressed among members of the religious community, defined in terms of action."* David Sloan Wilson, *Does Altruism Exist? Culture, Genes, and the Welfare of Others* (New Haven: Yale Univ. Press, 2015), 79. Italics in original.

20 Franz Rosenzweig suggests that even "theology itself conceives of its content as event, not as content; that is to say, as what is lived, not as life. As a result its preconditions are not conceptual elements, but rather immanent reality." *The Star of Redemption*, trans. William W. Hallo (Notre Dame, IN: Univ. of Notre Dame Press, 1985), 108.

21 Webb Keane, *Ethical Life: Its Natural and Social Histories* (Princeton: Princeton Univ. Press, 2016), 38, 12. Keane echoes sociologist Georg Simmel's view that the Ought must be rooted in the "whole person" and in an

"entire personal life." Hans Joas, *The Genesis of Values*, trans. Gregory Moore (Cambridge, Polity Press, 2000), 82. Of course the point had also been made long before by Aristotle. On the Aristotelian moral vision, based on the continuous pursuit of the "good life" (what it is good to *be*) versus the Kantian vision based on individual moral decisions or choices (what it is right to *do*), see, among others, Bernard Williams, *Ethics and the Limits of Philosophy* (Cambridge, MA: Harvard Univ. Press, 1985), 174–96; Ricœur, *Lectures 1, Le Juste I* (Paris: Éditions Esprits, 1995), in *Ricœur: Textes choisis et présentés*, 311–20, 357-8; Charles Taylor, *Sources of the Self: The Making of the Modern Identity* (Cambridge, MA: Harvard Univ. Press, 1989), 3; *Dilemmas and Connections: Selected Essays* (Cambridge, MA: Belknap Press of Harvard Univ. Press, 2011), 9–11.

22 "Man lives in the spirit ... if he enters into relation with his whole being." Martin Buber, *I and Thou*, 2nd ed., trans. Ronald Gregor Smith (New York: Charles Scribner's Sons, 1958), 39. "[F]aith is a *total* act of the soul: it is a *whole* state of the mind, or it is not at all! and in this consists its power, as well as its exclusive worth." Samuel Taylor Coleridge, *The Friend*, ed. Barbara E. Rooke (London: Routledge, 1969), 1:315. In spirituality "vitality and intentionality are united." Paul Tillich, *The Courage to Be* (New Haven: Yale Univ. Press, 1952), 84. This is where, as Karl Jaspers puts it, "for the first time there is both impulse and goal." *Reason and Existenz*, trans. William Earle, in *Existentialism from Dostoevsky to Sartre*, ed. Walter Kaufmann (Cleveland: World, 1956), 194.

23 J. Matthew Ashley, "The Turn to Spirituality? The Relationship between Theology and Spirituality," in *Minding the Spirit: The Study of Christian Spirituality*, ed. Elizabeth A. Dreyer and Mark S. Burrows (Baltimore: Johns Hopkins Univ. Press, 2005), 161. Emphasis added.

24 A recent study identifies 18 per cent of Americans as "spiritual but not religious." Art Raney, Daniel Cox, and Robert P. Jones, *Searching for Spirituality in the U.S.: A New Look at the Spiritual but Not Religious*, Public Religion Research Institute, 6 November 2017, https://www.prri.org/research/religiosity-and-spirituality-in-america/.

25 Mary Froelich defines spirituality as "the human spirit fully in act." This means "the core dimension of the human person radically engaged with reality (both contingent and transcendent). It refers to human persons being, living, acting according to their fullest intrinsic potential – thus, ultimately, in the fullness of interpersonal, communal, and mystical relationship." "Spiritual Discipline, Discipline of Spirituality: Revisiting Questions of Definition and Method," in *Minding the Spirit: The Study of Christian Spirituality*, ed. Elizabeth A. Dreyer and Mark S. Burrows, 71. Roger Haight describes spirituality as "a form of behavior," a "way of life," "constructed by the daily activities that shape a person's life."

Spirituality is "prior to" institutions like a "church," and "prior to and the basis of doctrine." *Spirituality Seeking Theology* (Maryknoll, NY: Orbis Books, 2014), x–xi, 1.

26 Haight, *Spirituality Seeking Theology*, 6.

27 Dietrich von Hildebrand, *Fundamental Moral Attitudes*, trans. Alice M. Jourdain (New York: Longmans, Green, 1950), 15.

28 Hans Joas, *The Sacredness of the Person: A New Genealogy of Human Rights*, trans. Alex Skinner (Washington, DC: Georgetown Univ. Press, 2013), 177.

29 L.T. Johnson, *Among the Gentiles*, 43.

30 Karen Armstrong, *The Case for God* (New York: Alfred A. Knopf, 2009), 73. Also: Jean Grondin, *Introduction à la métaphysique* (Montreal: Les Presses de l'Université de Montréal, 2004); Pierre Hadot, *Qu'est-ce que la philosophie antique* (Paris: Gallimard, 1995), Pierre Hadot, *La philosophie comme manière de vivre*, entretiens avec J. Carlier et A.I. Davidson (Paris: Albin Michel, 2001).

31 L.T. Johnson, *Among the Gentiles*, 47. Also: Martha Nussbaum, *The Therapy of Desire: Theory and Practice in Hellenistic Ethics* (Princeton: Princeton Univ. Press, 1994).

32 Arthur Hertzberg, ed., *Judaism* (New York: Washington Square Press, 1963), xiv, xxii; Adin Steinsaltz, *The Essential Talmud*, Thirtieth Anniversary Edition (New York: Basic Books, 2006), 263.

33 Reza Aslan, *No god but God: The Origins, Evolution, and Future of Islam* (New York: Random House, 2005), 150; John L. Esposito, *The Future of Islam* (New York: Oxford Univ. Press, 2010), 42–8. If and when Islam generates "creeds," they tend to be informal, personal, and individual, not a ticket of entry or a condition of membership. Ahmed, *What Is Islam?*, 193.

34 Charles Taylor, *A Secular Age* (Cambridge, MA: Belknap Press of Harvard Univ. Press, 2007), 275–9.

35 John Meyendorff, "Preface," in Gregory of Nyssa, *The Life of Moses*, trans. Abraham J. Malherbe and Everett Ferguson (New York: Paulist Press, 1978), xiii. Also: Diarmaid MacCulloch, *Christianity: The First Three Thousand Years* (New York: Viking, 2010), 30–1, 95–6, 141–3, 196, 211–28. Peter Brown describes this process as the "surprisingly rapid democratization of the philosophers' upper-class counterculture by the leaders of the Christian church." "Late Antiquity," in *A History of Private Life*, vol. 1, *From Pagan Rome to Byzantium*, ed. Philippe Ariès and Georges Duby (Cambridge, MA, Belknap Press of Harvard Univ. Press, 1987), quoted in Casanova, *Public Religions in the Modern World*, 50.

36 Moses Maimonides, *The Guide for the Perplexed*, trans. M. Friedländer (New York: Dover, 1956), 109. See also: Rosenzweig, *The Star of Redemption*, trans. Hallo, 399; Paul Ricœur, *Le conflit des interprétations: Essais d'herméneutique* (Paris: Éditions du Seuil, 2013), 365.

37 Marcel Gauchet, *The Disenchantment of the World: A Political History of Religion*, trans. Oscar Bruge (Princeton, NJ: Princeton Univ. Press, 1997), 76–83; John W. O'Malley, *Four Cultures of the West* (Cambridge, MA: Harvard Univ. Press, 2004), 81–4; MacCulloch, *Christianity*, 30–1, 95–6, 141–3, 196, 211–28; Anthony T. Kronman, *Confessions of a Born-Again Pagan* (New Haven: Yale Univ. Press, 2016), 91-5, 100-105.

38 Even when a non-Christian tradition, such as Islam for example, does talk about orthodoxy, it usually means "correct practices." Talal Asad, *The Idea of an Anthropology of Islam* (Washington: Center for Contemporary Arab Studies, Georgetown Univ., 1986), cited in Ahmed, *What Is Islam?*, 270–4.

39 MacCulloch, *Christianity*, 398. The term but not the discipline of theology goes back to Aristotle and even to Plato, who was the first to use it. Grondin, *Introduction à la métaphysique*, 109.

40 Denys Turner, *The Darkness of God: Negativity in Christian Mysticism* (Cambridge: Cambridge Univ. Press, 1995), 216–25; Robert Barron, *Thomas Aquinas: Spiritual Master* (New York: Crossroad, 2008), 12–13.

41 Heintzman, *Rediscovering Reverence*, 47–8.

42 W.C. Smith, *The Meaning and End of Religion*, 40.

43 Karen Armstrong points out that even the fundamentalist and other such movements that seem to revolt against these modern assumptions often serve to confirm them, both by what they affirm and by what they seek to resist. They are forms of religious positivism, seeking an "absolute certainty" modelled, ironically, on the modern scientific ideal but alien to genuine spirituality, with its necessary emphasis on mystery and unknowing. *The Case for God*, especially 269–75. On experientialist "positivism," see also Turner, *The Darkness of God*, 249, 259, 262.

44 Tillich, *The Courage to Be*, 172. For examples of precisely this view, see Bertrand Russell's definition of faith as "a firm belief in something for which there is no evidence," in *Human Society in Ethics and Politics*, cited in *Lapham's Quarterly* 3, no. 1 (Winter 2010), 213; or A.C. Grayling's definition of faith as "an attitude of belief independent of, and characteristically in the countervailing face of, evidence," in Mick Gordon and Chris Wilkinson, eds., *Conversations on Religion* (London: Continuum, 2008), 3.

45 Alister McGrath, *Christianity's Dangerous Idea: The Protestant Revolution – A History from the Sixteenth Century to the Twenty-First* (New York: HarperCollins, 2007), 429–30. For a recent example, see Thomas Joseph White, "Letter to an Aspiring Priest," *First Things*, no. 291 (March 2019), 29.

46 Martin Heidegger, *An Introduction to Metaphysics*, trans. Ralph Manheim (New York: Doubleday, 1961), 11; "Indication of the Hermeneutical Situation," trans. Michael Baur and Jerome Veith, in *The Heidegger Reader*, ed. Günter Figal (Bloomington: Indiana Univ. Press, 2009), 42–3, 55–8.

47 Aquinas, *Summa Theologiæ* 1–2.55.1, in *Treatise on the Virtues*, trans. Oesterle, 51.

48 Rahner, *The Practice of Faith*, 14, 22, 59–60, 62–5. Roger Haight calls this the "basal character" of spirituality. *Spirituality Seeking Theology*, 6. See also, William James, *The Varieties of Religious Experience* (New York: Collier Books, 1961), 42, 390; J. Matthew Ashley, "The Turn to Spirituality? The Relationship between Theology and Spirituality," in *Minding the Spirit: The Study of Christian Spirituality*, ed. Elizabeth A. Dreyer and Mark S. Burrows, 162–3.

49 William Temple, *Nature, Man and God* (London: Macmillan, 1934), 317, quoted in W.C. Smith, *The Meaning and End of Religion*, 321. "Theology and what arises out of such reflection, doctrines, emerge out of spirituality and reflect the spirituality to which they give expression." Haight, *Spirituality Seeking Theology*, xi.

50 "Dieu veut plus disposer la volonté que l'esprit." Pascal, *Pensées* (Paris: Garnier-Flammarion, 1973), §441, p. 155.

51 Collect for All Saints' Day, *The Book of Common Prayer* (Toronto: Macmillan of Canada, 1959), 299.

52 Psalm 23:3.

53 2 Timothy 3:16.

54 2 Peter 3:13.

55 Exodus 34:6. D.J. Harrington, "Biblical Perspectives: Theological Significance," in Daniel J. Harrington and James F. Keenan, *Jesus and Virtue Ethics: Building Bridges between New Testament Studies and Moral Theology* (Lanham, MD: Rowman & Littlefield, 2002), 81.

56 Bruce Lawrence, *The Qur'an: A Biography* (Vancouver: Douglas & McIntyre, 2006), 197–8.

57 Psalm 17:15.

58 Jeremiah 23:6, 33:14. Emphasis added. Emmanuel Levinas suggests Deuteronomy's declaration that God "loves the stranger" (10:18–19) is not a story about God but a *definition* of God. *Les Imprévus de l'histoire* (Paris: Livre de Poche, 2007), 165.

59 Matthew 5:6.

60 Matthew 5, 13, 18, 20, 22, 25; Mark 4; Luke 6:20, 13, 17:20–1, 18:16–17. "[T]he kingdom of God is righteousness." Søren Kierkegaard, *Spiritual Writings*, trans. George Pattison (New York, HarperCollins, 2010), 146–7. "[T]he kingdom of God is primarily and above all on earth." Gerhard Lohfink, *Jesus of Nazareth: What He Wanted, Who He Was* (Collegeville, MN: Liturgical Press, 2012), 25.

61 *The Koran* 4:114, trans. N.J. Dawood (London: Penguin Books, 2003), 73.

62 *The Bhagavad Gita* 3:1–43, trans. Eknath Easwaran (New York: Vintage Books, 2000), 17–22.

63 *The Book of Chuang Tzu*, in *The Tao: Finding the Way of Balance and Harmony*, ed. Mark Forstater (New York: Plume, 2003), 123.

64 *Bṛhadāranyaka Upanishad*, bk. 5, chap. 2, in *The Upanishads*, trans. and ed. Valerie J. Roebuck (London: Penguin Books, 2003), 82.

65 Galatians 5:22–3. I have combined the translations of the Authorized Version and the NRSV here. Evelyn Underhill suggests the order in which Paul lists the virtues here is not "casual" but rather a "progressive series from one point and that one point is Love ... the budding point from which all the rest [of the virtues] come." *The Fruits of the Spirit*, ed. Roger L. Roberts (Harrisburg, PA: Morehouse, 2010), 14. In other words, Paul follows the order of what I have called the arrow of virtue.

66 "The great art ... of piety, and the end for which all the rites of religion seem to be instituted, is the perpetual renovation of the motives to virtue." Samuel Johnson, *The Rambler*, no. 7, 10 April 1750, ed. W.J. Bate and Albrecht B. Strauss (New Haven: Yale Univ. Press, 1979), The Yale Edition of the Works of Samuel Johnson, 3:40.

67 Aquinas, Disputations, *de Caritate*, 2, in *Theological Texts*, trans. Gilby, 211. Emphasis added.

68 Micah 6:8; Colossians 3:12–17.

69 "[S]pirituality ... provide[s] the meaning and import of objective doctrines and practices." Haight, *Spirituality Seeking Theology*, 169.

70 Étienne Gilson, expounding (but not perhaps entirely reflecting) Aquinas, thinks Christian religious teachings teach sacred "doctrine." *The Elements of Christian Philosophy* (New York: Mentor, 1963), 23–9. But what do the Christian "doctrines" *themselves* teach? What do they ultimately *mean*, for human life? The Christian doctrines of grace and justification by faith, for example, are expressions and enablers of the virtues of gratitude, humility, and unselfing; the doctrines of eternal life and of Providence are enablers of trust and hope; the resurrection of the body is an enabler of hope and of reverence for our physical being; the doctrine of the virgin birth proclaims the virtues of purity, chastity, and unselfing; the doctrine of the Crucifixion is an emblem of obedience, self-sacrifice, unselfing, devotion, self-giving, forgiveness, and love; the doctrines of redemption and salvation are enablers of trust, confidence, faith, and hope; the doctrine of Creation is an enabler of humility, gratitude, joy, thanks, praise, respect, and reverence for the whole physical world; the doctrine of the Incarnation is another symbol of reverence for the physical world of Creation, but also of the virtues of mercy, sharing, self-giving, fellowship, friendship, and love, and it is also an enabler of all these virtues as well as of gratitude, trust, hope, confidence, praise and joy.

71　Rosalind Hursthouse suggests an atheist would be justified in rejecting reverence (or "piety") as a virtue because it is based on "beliefs" that are not rational, and therefore "no reasons at all." *On Virtue Ethics* (Oxford: Oxford Univ. Press, 2010), 232–3. It does not seem to occur to her that the "beliefs" come from and express the virtues, not the reverse.

72　"Le temporel et le matériel y sont et le terrain, et l'objet, et l'une de deux parties. Quand l'éternel livre une bataille temporelle, il faut bien que ce soit une bataille temporelle. Quand le spirituel livre une bataille au matériel il faut bien que ce soit une bataille matérielle." Charles Péguy, *Note conjointe sur M. Descartes et la philosophie cartésienne*, in *Une éthique sans compromis*, ed. Dominique Saatdjian (Paris: Pocket, 2011), 295.

73　The virtues of Reverence (A2) are, in Jacques Maritain's words, "ce qui dans l'homme vivifie l'homme, étant l'Amour et le Don." *Humanisme intégral*, new ed. (Paris: Éditions Aubier-Montaigne, 1946), 97.

74　Thomas Aquinas, *Summa Theologiæ* 2–2.81.1, in *Philosophical Texts*, trans. Thomas Gilby (London: Oxford Univ. Press, 1956), 349–50.

75　"There is … something in the serious attempt to look compassionately at human things which automatically suggests that 'there is more than this.'" Iris Murdoch, *The Sovereignty of Good* (London: Routledge, 1980), 73.

76　Emmanuel Levinas, *De Dieu qui vient à l'idée*, 2nd expanded ed. (Paris: Vrin, 2004).

77　Paul Ricœur, *Soi-même comme un autre* (Paris: Éditions du Seuil, 1990), 220.

78　Rosenzweig, *The Star of Redemption*, trans. Hallo, 167–71. "This love communicates to the beloved [A2a] the very qualities of being that are possessed by the lover [A2b]." Haight, *Spirituality Seeking Theology*, 85. "[W]hen you feel that the earth loves you in return [A2a], that feeling transforms the relationship from a one-way-street [A2b] into a sacred bond." Robin Wall Kimmerer, *Braiding Sweetgrass: Indigenous Wisdom, Scientific Knowledge, and the Teachings of Plants* (Minneapolis: Milkweed Editions, 2013), 124–5.

79　Kronman, *Confessions of a Born-Again Pagan*, 58.

80　Rosenzweig, *The Star of Redemption*, trans. Hallo, 169.

81　Marilynne Robinson, *The Death of Adam: Essays on Modern Thought* (New York: Picador, 2005), 71.

82　James F. White, *Introduction to Christian Worship*, 3rd rev. ed. (Nashville: Abingdon Press, 2000), 27.

83　N.T. Wright, *After You Believe: Why Christian Character Matters* (New York: HarperCollins, 2010), 188.

84　"Worship ordinarily implies respect, even admiration to a high degree, demonstrated by symbolic actions which indicate the asymmetrical relationship – as by reduction of bodily posture by obeisance, kneeling or prostration; or by presentation of objects in offering." Raymond Firth, *Rank and Religion in Tikopia: A Study in Polynesian Paganism and Conversion to Christianity* (London: Allen & Unwin, 1970), 297, cited in Robert N. Bellah, *Religion in Human Evolution: From the Paleolithic to the Axial Age* (Cambridge, MA: Belknap Press of Harvard Univ. Press, 2011), 189. Bradley recognizes a posture of "devotion" to the "utterly good" is "implied in all religion." He calls this posture "moral prostration." F.H. Bradley, *Appearance and Reality* (Oxford: Oxford Univ. Press, 1930), 389n1. Similarly, Franz Rosenzweig argues mimetic "gesture perfects man for his full humanity," and that "prostration" is "the ultimate gesture of all mankind." *The Star of Redemption*, trans. Hallo, 372–3, 324. Shahab Ahmed tells a significant anecdote about his Harvard teaching assistant who remarked "how difficult it is to convey to someone who has never pressed his forehead to the ground in *saidah* what is Islam." *What Is Islam?*, 254.

85 Ritual is the "scaffolding in which all religious thought has taken shape." Susanne K. Langer, *Mind: An Essay on Human Feeling*, vol. 3 (Baltimore: Johns Hopkins Press, 1982), 142. Robert Bellah suggests that ritual "may rival the world of daily life as the paramount reality." Bellah, *Religion in Human Evolution*, 11.

86 Martin Buber calls these primal encounters the "original relational incident." *I and Thou*, 54. "Even events which no historical evidence could ever firmly establish must be *recollected* rather than *construed*. It may well be the case, as Franz Rosenzweig suggests, that no one ascended the mountain and no one descended, yet the Sinai event, though clouded in historical darkness, remains essentially a 'memorable' event." Louis Dupré, *Transcendent Selfhood: The Loss and Recovery of the Inner Life* (New York: Seabury Press, 1976), 76. Dupré's reference is to Rosenzweig, *The Star of Redemption*, trans. Hallo, 319.

87 In Hindu India, "the preferred medium of instruction and transmission of psychological, metaphysical and social thought continues to be the story." Sudhir Kakar, *Shamans, Mystics and Doctors: A Psychological Inquiry into India and Its Healing Traditions* (New York: Alfred A. Knopf, 1982), 1, quoted in Richard A. Shweder, *Why Do Men Barbecue? Recipes for Cultural Psychology* (Cambridge, MA: Harvard Univ. Press, 2003), 238–9.

88 Paul Ricœur notes that the Jewish and Christian Bible normally looks forward to what will come or *should* come. God is not the author of the world so much as the source or support or inspiration for overcoming the evil that is already in the world. The arc of the Bible is an "ascending" or upward movement, in which words like "in spite of" take the place of "because of." In this sense the structure of the Bible resembles the structure of religious life itself. *Esprit*, special issue, July–August 1988, 57–63, in *Ricœur: Textes choisis et présentés*, 277–85.

89 Ahmed, *What Is Islam?*, 374.

90 Barron, *Thomas Aquinas: Spiritual Master*, 49.

91 "Narrative is not only the way we understand our personal and collective identities, it is the source of our ethics, our politics, and our religion. It is, as William James and Jerome Bruner assert, one of our two basic ways of thinking. Narrative isn't irrational – it can be criticized by rational argument – but it can't be derived from reason alone. Mythic (narrative) culture is not a subset of theoretic culture, nor will it ever be. It is older than theoretic culture and remains to this day an indispensable way of relating to the world." Bellah, *Religion in Human Evolution*, 280.

92 "[C]e que le langage religieux fait, c'est redécrire: ce qu'il redécrit, c'est l'expérience humaine. Dans ce sens, nous devons dire que le référant ultime des paraboles, des proverbes, des dires eschatologiques n'est pas le Royaume de Dieu, mais *la réalité humaine dans sa totalité*." Ricœur, *L'Herméneutique biblique*, in *Ricœur: Textes choisis et présentés*, 207. Emphasis added.

93 Charles Taylor, *The Language Animal: The Full Shape of the Human Linguistic Capacity* (Cambridge, MA: Belknap Press of Harvard Univ. Press, 2016), 3–50.

94 "All revelation is summons and sending." Buber, *I and Thou*, 115.

95 "True sayings seem paradoxical." *Tao Te Ching* in *The Taoist Classics: The Collected Translations of Thomas Cleary* (Boston: Shambhala, 2003), 1:46. On this theme in religious language, see also Denys Turner, *Faith, Reason and the Existence of God* (Cambridge: Cambridge Univ. Press, 2004), 106; David Martin, *On Secularization: Towards a Revised General Theory* (Farnham: Ashgate, 2005), 178; Ricœur, *Le conflit des interprétations*, 77; Ahmed, *What Is Islam?*, 285–6, 389.

96 Leszek Kolakowski, *Religion* (New York: Oxford Univ. Press, 1983), 166.

97 "Religious language is not so much theology but rather the exclamations, dialogues, greetings and sequences of liturgy. ... Such acclamations and appraisals are neither functional nor informative. We do not so much understand our words as stand under them; we do not possess them but are possessed by them." Martin, *On Secularization*, 176, 179.

98 "[T]he representations of faith participate in what they disclose and uncover." Martin, 174.

99 Kolakowski, *Religion*, 165.

100 "Ritual is essentially a bodily process." Randall Collins, *Interactive Ritual Chains* (Princeton: Princeton Univ. Press, 2004), 53–4, quoted in Bellah, *Religion in Human Evolution*, 278.

101 Susan Neiman, *Moral Clarity: A Guide for Grown-Up Idealists* (Orlando: Harcourt, 2008), 121.

102 Origen, *Prayer. Exhortation to Martyrdom*, trans. John J. O'Meara (New York: Paulist Press, 1954), in *The Essential Writings of Christian Mysticism*, ed. Bernard McGinn (New York: Modern Library, 2006), 82–3. See also, Maimonides, *Mishneh Torah* (Repetition of the Torah), cited in Joel L. Kraemer, *Maimonides: The Life and World of One of Civilization's Greatest Minds* (New York: Doubleday, 2008), 336; Buber, *I and Thou*, 79; Rahner, *The Practice of Faith*, 70, 83–4, 177, 213, 256–8, 295–6.

103 J. Campbell, *Myths to Live By*, 98.

104 Rosenzweig, *The Star of Redemption*, trans. Hallo, 317.

105 Dupré, *Transcendent Selfhood*, 77.

106 Rosenzweig, *The Star of Redemption*, trans. Hallo, 357.

107 Maimonides, *The Guide for the Perplexed*, trans. Friedländer, 367, 356.

108 Charles Taylor, *Hegel* (Cambridge: Cambridge Univ. Press, 1975), 382; *Sources of the Self*, 91–2; Williams, *Ethics and the Limits of Philosophy*, 114, 146–8, 152–4; Emmanuel Levinas, *Difficile liberté*, 3rd corrected ed. (Paris: Le Livre de Poche, 2010), 19, 284; N.T. Wright, *Surprised by Hope: Rethinking Heaven, the Resurrection, and the Mission of the Church* (New York: HarperCollins, 2008), 263.

109 J.L. Schellenberg suggests that what he calls "evolutionary religion" should aim to get rid of as many of the religious "details" as possible and turn religion instead into a "thin" proposition about ultimate reality, a kind of "ultimism." *Evolutionary Religion* (Oxford: Oxford Univ. Press, 2013), 105–6, 148–9, 152. But this is the opposite of what "religion" actually is: a kind of life, activity or action, a form of virtue. For this kind of life, the more details the better! Each of them creates what Whitehead calls a "lure for feeling" and an opportunity for exercising the virtues of reverence.

110 Rosenzweig, *The Star of Redemption*, trans. Hallo, 207–8, 268, 274; Haight, *Spirituality Seeking Theology*, 55.

111 Levinas, *Difficile liberté*, 38–9.

112 Whitehead, *Process and Reality*, 30, 103–4, 302, 307.

113 What Whitehead calls "lures for feeling," Franz Rosenzweig calls "goals for emotion," the kinds of emotion that, in contrast to mere "theologism," can provide the inner fuel for genuine virtues of reverence, and thus have a real "influence on," or find a "resolution" in, "life itself." *The Star of Redemption*, trans. Hallo, 411–13.

114 Xunzi, bk. 19, in John Knoblock, *Xunzi: A Translation and Study of the Complete Works* (Stanford: Stanford Univ. Press, 1994), quoted in Bellah, *Religion in Human Evolution*, 472.

115 In listing some of the "practices" that constitute a Muslim life, Shahab Ahmed shows how the *inner* circle of formal religious practice blends into the *outer* concentric circles of everyday life. *What Is Islam?*, 357, 78.

116 Thomas Aquinas describes the first kind of religious acts (in the inner circle) as those "conducting to grace," and the second kind (in the outer circles) as those "coming from grace." Aquinas, *Summa Theologiæ* 1–2.108.1, in *Theological Texts*, trans. Gilby, 154.

117 Aquinas, *Summa Theologiæ* 2–2.81.1, in *Philosophical Texts*, trans. Gilby, 349–50.

118 "[H]er path from the miracle of divine love out into the earthly world, gives force and dignity to that which it behooves her to do through the recollection of what was experienced in the magic circle: 'As he loves, so shall you love.'" Rosenzweig, *The Star of Redemption*, trans. Hallo, 204.

119 "There, on the threshold [of the holy place], the response, the spirit, is kindled ever new within him; here, in an unholy and needy country, this spark is to be proved." Buber, *I and Thou*, 52–3. N.T. Wright points out that there is "a to-and-fro in the Old Testament between the presence of God filling, and dwelling in, the Temple, and that same presence eventually filling, and dwelling in, the whole world." *After You Believe*, 84; *Surprised by Hope*, 189–232.

120 Sigmund Freud, *Civilization and Its Discontents*, trans. James Strachey (New York: W.W. Norton, 1962), 21.

121 Augustine, *City of God*, trans. Bettenson, 377, 398; Thomas Aquinas, *III Sentences*, IX, i. 3, sol iii; *Compendium Theologiae*, 248; and *Summa Theologiæ*, 2–2.81.5, in *Theological Texts*, trans. Gilby, 242–3, 388.

122 Rosenzweig, *The Star of Redemption*, trans. Hallo, 184.

123 I believe this insight comes from Emmanuel Levinas, but I haven't yet been able to retrace the source.

124 Aristotle notes the connection between "moral states" and "exercise": "people develop qualities corresponding to the activities that they pursue. This is evident from the example of people training for any competition or undertaking: they spend all their time in exercising." *The Nicomachean Ethics* 3.5.1114a5–10, trans. J.A.K. Thomson, rev. Hugh Tredennick (London: Penguin Books, 2004), 63. Karl Rahner, Ari L. Goldman, and Julia Annas make the same comparison between virtue (including the virtues of reverence) and various other forms of physical or artistic exercise or practice. Rahner, *The Practice of Faith*, 56, 256; Ari L. Goldman, *Being Jewish: The Spiritual and Cultural Practice of Judaism Today* (New York: Simon & Schuster, 2000), 207–8; Julia Annas, *Intelligent Virtue* (Oxford: Oxford Univ. Press, 2013), 1, 14.

125 "La loi rituelle … constitue la sévère discipline qui tend vers cette justice [rendue à l'autre]. Celui-là seul peut reconnaître le visage d'autrui qui a su imposer une règle sévère à sa propre nature. … Aucune puissance intrinsèque n'est accordée au geste rituel. Mais … la voie qui mène vers l'homme nous ramène à la discipline rituelle, à l'éducation de soi. Sa

grandeur est dans sa régularité quotidienne. ... La loi est effort. La quotidienne fidélité au geste rituel demande un courage, plus calme plus
noble et plus grand que celui du guerrier." Levinas, *Difficile liberté*, 38–9.

126 James, *The Varieties of Religious Experience*, 361.

127 Rosenzweig, *The Star of Redemption*, trans. Hallo, 184.

128 Samuel Taylor Coleridge describes prayer as "faith passing into act; a
union of will and the intellect realizing in an intellectual act." The "habit
of prayer" is the habit of "turning your thoughts into acts ... and even so
reconverting your actions into thoughts." "Notes on the Book of Common Prayer: Prayer," in *Selected Poetry and Prose of Samuel Taylor Coleridge*,
edited by Donald Stauffer (New York: Random House, 1951), 553–4. Coleridge is close to Aquinas here, who describes prayer as "a certain kind
of hermeneutic of the human will." *Summa Theologiæ* 3.21.4. in Denys
Turner, *Thomas Aquinas: A Portrait* (New Haven: Yale Univ. Press, 2013),
174.

129 For Thomas Aquinas, grace is a "glow of soul," a "spiritual condition of
being in the soul," a "turning" of the heart or "inward motion," "bending
the human heart to good," the "very movement of free will itself towards
good." *Summa Theologiæ* 1–2.90.3, 1–2.109.6, 1–2.112.2; Disputations, 27
de Veritate, 2, *ad* 7; *I Quodlibets*, 4. 7, c. & *ad* 1, 2, in *Theological Texts*, trans.
Gilby, 165, 159–60, 173. For Karl Rahner, grace is also the attractive power
which *causes* that effect. Haight, *Spirituality Seeking Theology*, 159. Another
part of "grace" is the virtue of humility (A2a). The way the power of love
almost seems to reach out to you, almost seems to take the initiative,
should encourage an appropriate humility. We shouldn't take too much
credit for our own limited goodness. We shouldn't get too puffed up
about it. We should be more modest and recognize that love meets us half
way. Maybe more than halfway. James, *The Varieties of Religious Experience*, 102.

130 Immanuel Kant says the challenge for all non-religious moralities is to
find a comparable source of moral motivation. *Foundations of the Metaphysics of Morals*, trans. Lewis White Beck (Indianapolis: Bobbs-Merrill,
1959), §3, p. 80–2; *Prolegomena to Any Future Metaphysics*, trans. Lewis
White Beck et al. (Indianapolis: Bobbs-Merrill, 1950), 92. Iris Murdoch
agrees ethics requires "a substitute for prayer, that most profound and effective of religious techniques," and also for "the concept of sacrament."
Murdoch, *The Sovereignty of Good*, 69.

131 The image of spiritual "turning" is a richly biblical one. For just three
among many examples, see 2 Chronicles 36:13, Psalm 85:4, and James
1:17. The image of an inward "turning" is also common in traditional
Christian spirituality. See, for example, Evagrius Ponticus, Bernard
de Clairvaux, John Tauler, Johann Arndt, and Nicholas of Cusa in *The*

Essential Writings of Christian Mysticism, 107–9, 150, 279, 349, 436. The way John Calvin puts it is that we are called to "give up" to God "the affections of the heart." *The Institutes of the Christian Religion* 3.7.8, trans. Henry Beveridge (Peabody, MA: Hendrickson, 2012), 454. For a modern Jewish use of the image of "turning," see Buber, *I and Thou*, 57–61, 100–1, 119–20.

132 Aquinas, *Summa Theologiæ* 2–2.81.5, in *Theological Texts*, trans. Gilby, 388.

133 Hertzberg, *Judaism*, 183.

134 Letter of Maimonides to Hasdai Halevi, in *A Treasury of Jewish Letters*, ed. F. Kobler (Philadelphia: Jewish Publication Society, 1954), 1:197–8, quoted in Hertzberg, 16. Maimonides points out that the Hebrew word "satan" conveys the opposite human impulse: it is "derived from the same root as *séteh*, 'turn away' [Proverbs 4:15]; it implies the notion of turning and moving away from a thing." Maimonides, *The Guide for the Perplexed*, trans. Friedländer, 298.

135 Rosenzweig, *The Star of Redemption*, trans. Hallo, 176.

136 Aelred of Rievaulx, *Spiritual Friendship*, in O'Malley, *Four Cultures of the West*, 145.

137 Calvin, *The Institutes of the Christian Religion* 3.7.2, 5, trans. Beveridge, 450–2; Rosenzweig, *The Star of Redemption*, trans. Hallo, 214–15.

138 Rosenzweig, *The Star of Redemption*, trans. Hallo, 213–15.

139 Thomas Aquinas, "Commentary," 2 *Corinthians, ii, lect. 3*, in *Theological Texts*, trans. Gilby, 184.

140 Robert N. Bellah, Richard Madsen, William M. Sullivan, Ann Swidler, and Steven M. Tipton, *Habits of the Heart*, updated ed. (Berkeley: Univ. of California Press, 1996), 137. Confucius agreed: *The Analects*, trans. D.C. Lau (London: Penguin Books, 1979), 1.12, 61.

141 Aquinas, *Summa Theologiæ* 2–2.91.1, in *Philosophical Texts*, trans. Gilby, 350.

142 John of the Cross, *The Ascent of Mount Carmel* 2.3.1, quoted in Turner, *The Darkness of God*, 245. As Max Scheler says, the "essence" of reverence is "to unite and join together." *Formalism in Ethics and Non-Formal Ethics of Value*, trans. Manfred S. Frings and Roger L. Funk (Evanston: Northwestern Univ. Press, 1973), 94.

143 "[L]a foi est, en tant que telle, un *acte* qui ne se laisse réduire à aucune parole, à aucune écriture." Paul Ricœur, *Amour et justice* (Paris: Éditions Points, 2008), 53. Emphasis added.

144 Thomas Aquinas, *Summa Theologiæ* 1–2.58.2, in *Treatise on the Virtues*, trans. Oesterle, 81. As discussed in chapters 4 and 8, Aquinas' word for self-assertion (following Aristotle) is "appetite."

145 Martin Buber contrasts "self-will" with the "grand will" that is its opposite. *I and Thou*, 59–60, 83.

146 "It is not the *I*, then that is given up, but that false self-asserting instinct." Buber, 78.

147 *The Bhagavad Gita* 5.5, quoted in Joseph Campbell, *Myths to Live By* (New York: Bantam Books, 1973), 126.

148 *The Book of Chuang Tzu*, ed. Forstater, 93, 60–1; Edward Slingerland, *Effortless Action: Wu-wei as Conceptual Metaphor and Spiritual Ideal in Early China* (New York: Oxford Univ. Press, 2003). "All the fullness of action springs from this source of in-action." Rosenzweig, *The Star of Redemption*, trans. Hallo, 59.

149 "The greater jihad is the more difficult and more important struggle against one's ego, selfishness, greed, and evil." Esposito, *The Future of Islam*, 48.

150 Seyyed Hossein Nasr, *Islam: Religion, History, Civilization* (New York: HarperSanFrancisco, 2003), 57. Shahab Ahmed argues that, although "the chains of transmission for this Hadith are regarded by the experts of the science of Hadith as weak," textual evidence suggests it belonged to the "vocabulary which constructs and expresses *being Muslim*" in the pre-modern Muslim Balkans-to-Bengal complex. *What Is Islam?*, 318–21.

151 "That which from the point of view of the finite world appears as self-negation is from the point of view of ultimate being the most perfect self-affirmation, the most radical form of courage." Tillich, *The Courage to Be*, 158. Karl Rahner calls this highest form of self-assertion "a radical self-positing of the subject in an unconditional surrender." *The Practice of Faith*, 77.

152 "The steadfast defiance [self-assertion] of the hero was the only possible root for the eruption of the faith of the saint who gives himself to God and faces the world." Rosenzweig, *The Star of Redemption*, trans. Hallo, 224.

153 Xunzi, bk. 23, in *Xunzi: A Translation*, 3:166–7, quoted in Bellah, *Religion in Human Evolution*, 469.

154 Confucian and Taoist philosophers "grappled with the paradox that results from holding both that one should *actively* strive to be virtuous and that the purposeful *effort* contaminates the result." Keane, *Ethical Life*, 22. Emphasis added. See Slingerland, *Effortless Action*.

155 Rosenzweig, *The Star of Redemption*, trans. Hallo, 321.

156 "We are not only not forbidden to examine and propose our doubts, so it be done with humility and proceed from a real desire to know the Truth; but we are repeatedly commanded so to do." Coleridge, *The Friend*, 1:281.

157 Max Scheler suggests it is through encounter with a saintly person "that the idea of the divine is filled with positive, intuitive content which cannot be derived from philosophy and which has the full objectivity that corresponds to this independent type of experience." *Formalism in Ethics*, trans. Frings and Funk, 293.

158 Emmanuel Levinas, *Éthique et infini* (Paris: Le Livre de Poche, 1984), 13; Ricœur, *Amour et justice*, 49–50.

159 Paul Ricœur acknowledges belonging to a spiritual tradition is, at first, a matter of biological, geographic, and cultural chance, but suggests embracing this fate freely "sera compensé au centuple par une surabondance de compréhension de soi-même et de l'autre." *Amour et justice*, 49–50.

160 "The assent is affected by the will, not by taking thought." Aquinas, *Disputations*, 14 *de Veritate*, 1, in *Theological Texts*, trans. Gilby, 197.

161 Thomas Aquinas, *Sermons on the Apostles' Creed*, quoted in Bruce D. Marshall, "*Quid scit Una Vetula*. Aquinas on the Nature of Theology," in *The Theology of Thomas Aquinas*, ed. Rik van Nieuwenhove and Joseph Wawrykow (Notre Dame, IN: Univ. of Notre Dame Press, 2005), 1–35, cited in Bernard McGinn, *Thomas Aquinas's* Summa Theologiae: *A Biography* (Princeton: Princeton Univ. Press, 2014), 223n40; Maimonides, *The Guide for the Perplexed*, trans. Friedländer, 202; Søren Kierkegaard, *Concluding Unscientific Postscript to the "Philosophical Fragments,"* trans. David F. Swenson, Lillian Marvin Swenson, and Walter Lowrie, in *A Kierkegaard Anthology*, ed. Robert Bretall (New York: Modern Library, 1946), 258.

162 Aquinas, *Disputations*, 14 *de Veritate*, 1, in *Theological Texts*, trans. Gilby, 197.

163 "Alors que la croyance doxique s'inscrit dans la grammaire du 'je crois-que, l'attestation relève de celle du 'je crois-en.'" Ricœur, *Soi-même comme un autre*, 33.

164 Lev Shestov denies "faith" can mean "trust." He argues faith is, instead, a "creative power," a power that "determines and forms being," a power "to create the good." *Athens and Jerusalem*, trans. Bernard Martin, 2nd ed. (Athens: Ohio Univ. Press, 2016), 246, 271. Shestov's alternative concept of faith is not wrong, of course. But the two are not at all incompatible.

165 Aquinas, *Summa Theologiæ* 2–2.2.3, in *Theological Texts*, trans. Gilby, 199. Aquinas also cites Aristotle on this same point.

166 Many spiritual traditions (including Bonaventure and Teresa of Avila in the Christian tradition; the Sufi epic, *The Conference of the Birds*; the Mahayana Buddhist *Guide Book to Meditation on Amida*, and Kundalini yoga in the Hindu tradition) describe a spiritual quest or journey with six stages in which the unselfing depth or height of the spirit is achieved, followed by a final seventh stage of illumination. From the point of view of the families of virtues described in this book, this journey could be interpreted as the spiral path of the arrow of virtue through the four families of virtues, leading eventually back to the virtues of Liberty (A1) and then to the unselfing virtues of Reverence (A2) (for a second time), followed by the revelation ("It *is*") of the virtues of Excellence (B1). Bernard McGinn, ed., *The Essential Writings of Christian Mysticism*, 149–79,

460, 451; Turner, *The Darkness of God*, 102–17; MacCulloch, *Christianity*, 439; Aslan, *No god but God*, 206–16; Joseph Campbell, *The Masks of God: Oriental Mythology* (Harmondsworth: Penguin Books, 1976), 236, 282, 310–20; Arthur Avalon (Sir Joseph Woodroffe), *The Serpent Power* (Madras: Ganesh, 1931), 317–478, cited in J. Campbell, *Myths to Live By*, 109–16.

167 Terry Eagleton, *Reason, Faith, and Revolution: Reflections on the God Debate* (New Haven: Yale Univ. Press, 2009), 111. In religious language: "*The informative yields place to the performative.*" Martin, *On Secularization*, 180. Emphasis in original.

168 "The proposition 'God is the truth' ... is the proposition with which we thought we had attained an uttermost knowledge. But if we look more closely into what truth is, we find that ... the apparent knowledge concerning his essence becomes the proximate, immediate experience of his activity: that he is the truth tells us in the final analysis none other than that he – loves." Rosenzweig, *The Star of Redemption*, trans. Hallo, 388–9.

169 Maurice Blondel warns against "la substitution des théories à ce qu'on peut appeler l'expérimentation ontologique, à cet exercice méthodique et ascétique de la vie spirituelle où les certitudes progressivement acquises se fondent moins sur une construction de concepts que sur une possession réelle de *vérités vécues*." *L'Être et les êtres* (Paris: Presses Universitaires de France, 1963), 278. Emphasis added. For Blondel, the virtues (especially the virtues of reverence) "incarnent l'universel et l'infini dans nos existences singularisées." Blondel, 294–5.

170 Karl Jaspers calls this limitless horizon of the *internal* human landscape the "Encompassing which we are." *Reason and Existenz*, trans. Earle, 186–91.

171 R.G. Collingwood, *The New Leviathan* (London: Oxford Univ. Press, 1966), 18–39.

172 The Sufi Muslim tradition calls this unresolvable conflict of goods and virtues *hayrat* or "perplexity." Ahmed, *What Is Islam?*, 278.

173 Martin Heidegger, *Being and Time*, 145–8, trans. Joan Stambaugh (Albany: State Univ. of New York Press, 2010), 140–3.

174 MacCulloch, *Christianity*, 861.

175 "Fundamentalism" traces its name back to a series of twelve volumes of essays, entitled *The Fundamentals*, published between 1910 and 1915 by British and American conservative evangelical Christians. Fundamentalism insists, among other things, on an entirely literal reading of the Bible and its meaning. The term has since been extended, by analogy, to many other forms of dogmatism, both religious and non-religious. MacCulloch, 863, 960, 990–1.

176 R.G. Collingwood, *Speculum Mentis or the Map of Knowledge* (Oxford: Oxford Univ. Press, 1963), 266.

177 For a somewhat similar argument about the religious response to uncertainty, see Alister McGrath, *Through a Glass Darkly: Journeys through
Science, Faith and Doubt – a Memoir* (London: Hodder & Stoughton, 2020).
David Martin also suggests one can be "agnostic as to philosophic arguments about a realist or non-realist account of God" because "the
spiritual landscape [i.e., the four families of virtues, including, especially,
the virtues of reverence] is apodictically [undeniably, self-evidently] present to us all, 'believers' or not." Martin, *On Secularization*, 175.

178 Any authentically religious person could thus descibe herself, like Jean
Larose, as "en quelque sorte un non-croyant pratiquant." *Google Goulag:
Nouveaux essais de littérature appliquée* (Montreal: Boréal, 2015), 81.

179 Augustine, *City of God*, trans. Bettenson, 330. See also Rahner, *The Practice
of Faith*, 61.

180 Collingwood, *Speculum Mentis*, 268–9.

181 A "mystical" theology of the kind associated with Pseudo-Dionysius, for
example, has been described by Denys Turner as "that speech about God
which is the failure of speech." *The Darkness of God*, 19–49. The words
quoted are on page 20.

182 Plotinus, *Enneads* 1.6.5, in *The Essential Plotinus*, 38.

183 Psalm 36:9.

184 Dietrich von Hildebrand, *Ethics* (Steubenville, OH: Hildebrand Press,
2020), 481.

185 "L'hétéronomie d'une autorité irrécusable." Emmanuel Levinas, *Entre
nous: Essais sur le penser-à-l'autre* (Paris: Livre de Poche, 2010), 179.

186 Iris Murdoch, *Metaphysics as a Guide to Morals* (London: Vintage, 2003),
408. Emphasis added.

187 The inner source from which we respond to that voice, "our freedom to
love," as Denys Turner puts it, also seems to be "*in us but not of us … not
'ours' to possess, but ours only to be possessed by.*" *The Darkness of God*,
251. Emphasis added.

188 Maimonides says the moral experience of this "first degree" of prophecy
"consists in the divine assistance which is given to a person, and induces
him to do something good and grand …; he *finds in himself* the cause
that moves and urges him to this deed. This degree of divine influence is
called 'the spirit of the Lord'; and of the person who is under that influence we say that the spirit of the Lord came upon him, clothed him, or
rested upon him, or the Lord was with him, and the like." Maimonides,
The Guide for the Perplexed, trans. Friedländer, 241–2. Emphasis added.

189 "And when you turn to the right or when you turn to the left, your ears
shall hear a word behind you, saying, 'This is the way, walk in it.'" Isaiah
30:21.

190 Deuteronomy 30:14. Emphasis added.

191 2 Corinthians 12:2–4.

192 Jung suggests these second-level, "visionary" experiences are "a particularly vivid experience of the processes of the collective unconscious. Mystical experience is experience of archetypes." Jung, *Analytical Psychology*, 110.

193 Maimonides, *The Guide for the Perplexed*, trans. Friedländer, 230. Maimonides points out that, with the exception of Moses, almost all religious visionary experiences recorded in the Tanakh (the "Old Testament") occur in dreams. Maimonides, 244–5. He calls this kind of visionary experience in dreams "the most perfect development" of the "imagination and intuitive faculty." Maimonides, 225, 229. Like Thomas Aquinas, Blaise Pascal, C.G. Jung, and Alfred North Whitehead, Maimonides thinks intuition is an ability to size up a large body of information or a whole situation "and draw inferences from them very quickly, almost instantaneously." Maimonides, 229. In Islam, too, the prophet is one whose "strong imaginative faculty ... represents in the form of particular, sensible images and verbal modes the universal truth grasped by the prophet's intellect." Falur Rahman, *Prophecy in Islam* (London: George Allen & Unwin, 1958), 36, quoted in Ahmed, *What Is Islam?*, 235.

194 "[S]ome persons ... perceive scenes, dreams, and confused images, when awake, in the form of a prophetic vision. They then believe that they are prophets; they wonder that they perceive visions, and think that they have acquired wisdom without training. They fall into grave errors as regards important philosophical principles, and see a strange mixture of true and and imaginary things. All this is the consequence of the strength of their imaginative faculty, and the weakness of their logical faculty, which has not developed, and has not passed from potentiality to actuality." Maimonides, *The Guide for the Perplexed*, trans. Friedländer, 228.

195 "Religious belief can be very close to madness." MacCulloch, *Christianity*, 13.

196 "[I]n a prophetic vision only allegories are perceived, or rational truths are obtained, that lead to some knowledge in science, such as can be arrived at by reasoning. This is the meaning of the words, 'in a vision I will make myself *known* unto him.'" Maimonides, *The Guide for the Perplexed*, trans. Friedländer, 245. These words no doubt betray Maimonides' own devotion to Aristotelian rationalism. But they also express the important fact that a religious vision is tested not by the vision itself but only by the depth of the spiritual truth it conveys.

197 Rahner, *The Practice of Faith*, 60. "[S]ome people will manage effectively to love their neighbours. I think the 'machinery of salvation' (if it exists) is essentially the same for all. There is no complicated secret doctrine. We are all capable of criticizing, modifying and extending the area of strict obligation we have inherited." Murdoch, *The Sovereignty of Good*, 74.

198 "All virtues are purifications whose term is perfect purity." Plotinus, *Enneads* 1.2.7, in *The Essential Plotinus*, 117.

199 Jonathan Haidt notes this link between physical cleanliness and spiritual purity. *The Righteous Mind: Why Good People Are Divided by Politics and Religion* (New York: Pantheon Books, 2012), 61, 70, 103–4.

200 Paul Ricœur interprets traditional images of defilement, impurity, and uncleannesss as spiritual metaphors for the way in which pure self-assertion can corrupt and "enslave" itself. *Philosophie de la volonté 2: Finitude et culpabilité*, in *Ricœur: Textes choisis et présentés*, 285–92.

201 "Cleanliness in dress and body by washing and removing sweat and dirt is included among the various objects of the Law, but only if connected with purity of action, and with a heart free from low principles and bad habits. ... For the chief object of the Law is to [teach man to] diminish his desires, and to cleanse his outer appearance *after* he has purified his heart." Maimonides, *The Guide for the Perplexed*, trans. Friedländer, 330, 328. Emphasis added.

202 "The Latin for 'perfect' virtues is *purgati animi*, literally, virtues of 'a soul now purged or cleansed.'" John A. Oesterle, translator's note, in Aquinas, *Treatise on the Virtues*, 115n34.

203 From his rationalist perspective, Hegel says the "demand for the *purification* of impulses" means that "impulses should become the rational system of the will's volitions. To grasp them like that, proceeding out of the concept of the will, is the content of the philosophical science of right." G.W.F. Hegel, *Philosophy of Right*, trans. T.M. Knox (Oxford: Oxford Univ. Press, 1967), §19, pp. 28–9. Emphasis in original. Max Scheler suggests that purification "means a continuous falling away (in our value-estimations and spiritual observation) from all that does not belong to our personal essence. It is an ever increasing *clarification* of the center of our existence for our consciousness." *Formalism in Ethics*, trans. Frings and Funk, 348. Emphasis in original.

204 "[M]ost prophecies are given in images, for this is the characteristic of the imaginative faculty, the organ of prophecy." Maimonides, *The Guide for the Perplexed*, trans. Friedländer, 247.

205 In the late medieval Catholic church there was a tradition of meditative practices leading often to "mystical" states or experiences, of which Ignatius of Loyola's "Spiritual Exercises" are among the best known. Ignatius himself (the founder of the Jesuit Order) (1491–1556) had many mystical experiences, as did other "mystics" such as Hildegard of Bingen (1098–1179), Teresa of Avila (1515–82) and Marie de l'Incarnation (1599–1672). See, among others, Dupré, *Transcendent Selfhood*, 92–104.

206 "It is as if they were blinded and struck silent ... Thus the rational soul speaks truth at last about God when it does not speak." Marsilio Ficino,

"On the Mystical Theology of Dionysius the Areopagite," in *On Dionysius the Areopagite*, ed. and trans. Michael J.B. Allen (Cambridge, MA: Harvard Univ. Press, 2015), 1:11.

207 Turner, *The Darkness of God*, especially 226–73. The words quoted are on page 264. Turner suggests John of the Cross implicitly criticizes his mentor, Teresa of Avila, for attaching too much importance to her mystical "experiences." Turner, 250–1.

208 Citing Joel Robbins, James Laidlaw call this the "infinite regress" of self-assertion. *The Subject of Virtue: An Anthropology of Ethics and Freedom* (Cambridge: Cambridge Univ. Press, 2014), 134. Laidlaw's reference is to Joel Robbins, *Becoming Sinners: Christianity and Moral Torment in a Papua New Guinea Society* (Berkeley: Univ. of California Press, 2004), 249.

209 K. Kavanaugh, *St. John of the Cross* (London: SPCK, 1987), cited in Margaret Donaldson, *Human Minds: An Exploration* (New York: Allen Lane, 1993), 153–4. The similarity between the emphasis on "emptiness" in both the Christian spiritual and mystical tradition and the eastern meditative traditions is very striking. Charles Taylor points out the wonderful paradox that in many important forms of religious practice "real fullness only comes through emptiness." *A Secular Age*, 780n8.

210 "[I]n self-control and self-effacement it is, after all, still man who controls and effaces." Rosenzweig, *The Star of Redemption*, trans. Hallo, 75.

211 This phenomenon is sometimes called "soteriology." Douglas Estes, "Soteriology," *The Encyclopedia of Christian Civilization*, 25 November 2011, http://onlinelibrary.wiley.com/doi/10.1002/9780470670606.wbecc1287/abstract.

212 On "salvation" from self-assertion, see Kierkegaard, *Spiritual Writings*, trans. Pattison, 169–70. "[L]e paradoxe d'un libre arbitre captif – le paradoxe d'un *serf-arbitre* – est insupportable pour la pensée. Que la liberté [A1] soit à délivrer, que cette délivrance soit délivrance du propre esclavage, cela ne peut être dit en style direct: c'est pourtant la thématique centrale du 'salut.'" Ricœur, *Philosophie de la volonté 2: Finitude et culpabilité*, in *Ricœur: Textes choisis et présentés*, 286.

213 Self-assertion "obstructs" (as Max Scheler puts it) the "full experience" of all the other human virtues, while reverence "'foreshadows ever richer and higher values." *Formalism in Ethics*, trans. Frings and Funk, 244.

214 "All vices are outgrowths of either pride [A1a] or concupiscence [A1b], or of both together [A1]." Hildebrand, *Ethics*, 398. "[A]ffirmer la liberté [A1], c'est prendre sur soi l'origine du mal. Par cette proposition, j'atteste un lien si étroit entre mal et liberté que ces deux termes s'impliquent mutuellement; le mal a la signification de mal parce qu'il est l'œuvre d'une liberté; je suis l'auteur du mal." Ricœur *Le conflit des interprétations*, 566.

215 Plotinus, *Enneads* 5.1.1, in *The Essential Plotinus*, 91.

216 *Tao Te Ching*, in *The Taoist Classics*, 1:15.

217 Isaiah 9:5, 11:6–7.

218 "Impelled by *tolma*, daring, man comes necessarily to evil as well as to the brave and noble." Heidegger, *An Introduction to Metaphysics*, trans. Manheim, 144.

219 Dupré, *Transcendent Selfhood*, 42–9.

220 G.W.F. Hegel, *The Phenomenology of Mind*, trans. J.B. Baillie (New York: Harper & Row, 1967), 607–10; *Philosophy of Right*, trans. Knox, §§5, 135, pp. 21–2, 89–90.

221 Lionel Trilling, *Sincerity and Authenticity* (Cambridge, MA: Harvard Univ. Press, 1972), 44–7, 76–80. "In one respect the self vanished with the restricting bond to both God and the other." Gauchet, *The Disenchantment of the World*, 171.

222 Hans-Georg Gadamer, *Dialogue and Dialectic: Eight Hermeneutical Studies on Plato*, trans. P. Christopher Smith (New Haven: Yale Univ. Press, 1980), 88.

223 Isaiah 9:4.

224 Haight, *Spirituality Seeking Theology*, 178, 144. Emphasis added.

225 "Délivrance en soi d'un Moi réveillé de son rêve impérialiste ... réveillé à soi." Emmanuel Levinas, *Autrement qu'être ou au-delà de l'essence* (Paris: Le Livre de Poche, 2008), 256. "La mort de ce qui en nous dit 'je.'" Simone Weil, *Pensées sans ordre concernant l'amour de Dieu* (Paris: Gallimard, 2013), 28.

226 From his rationalist stance in the virtues of Equality (B2), Paul Bloomfield, for example, denies that sacrifice plays any role in the moral life. *The Virtues of Happiness: A Theory of the Good Life* (New York: Oxford Univ. Press, 2014), 123.

227 Hegel, *Philosophy of Right*, trans. Knox, addition to §268, p. 282.

228 As Franz Rosenzweig puts it, the truly reverent person "sacrifices his life and receives in return none other than this: to be allowed and able to sacrifice it. ... For him who trusts and hopes, there is no sacrifice that would mean a sacrifice to him." *The Star of Redemption*, trans. Hallo, 284. Webb Keane makes the same point in a more general way: "Deference [i.e., reverence], the regard I display for you, is simultaneously a display of my own character ... I display my respect for [others] and, in the process, *enact my own character*" as the kind of person who practices virtues like respect and deference. *Ethical Life*, 104, 112–13. Emphasis added.

229 "Under these carnal sacrifices," as John Calvin puts it, "there was a reality": "the greater sacrifice with which we dedicate ourselves soul and body ... [A]ll the good works ... are called sacrifices." *The Institutes of the Christian Religion* 4.18.16–17, trans. Beveridge, 943.

230 Maimonides explores the spiritual meaning of sacrifice in the story of Abraham and Isaac. The deep, spiritual meaning of this otherwise

horrifying story is that "man's duty is to love and to fear God, even without hope of reward or fear of punishment." *The Guide for the Perplexed*, trans. Friedländer, 306–7.

231 *The Book of Common Prayer*, 85. The Prayer Book words are adapted from Romans 12:1.

232 Bellah, *Religion in Human Evolution*, 508. The "renouncer" remains the paradigm of spiritual excellence in Eastern traditions, such as Jainism. The role of other good Jains is to support the renouncers. James Laidlaw, *The Subject of Virtue: An Anthropology of Ethics and Freedom*, 126.

233 The Axial figure of the "renouncer" is also emblematic of the paradox of reverence: the virtues of reverence can serve simultaneously for binding and *un*binding – while often serving to integrate the individual *within* a larger group and community, they can also free or separate the individual *from* the community, in pursuit of, or service to, something higher, greater or ultimately more important. Casanova, *Public Religions in the Modern World*, 216.

234 Thomas Aquinas (citing Augustine) explores the meaning of sacrifice in the story of Jesus' *self*-sacrifice on the Cross: "his voluntary enduring of his Passion ... sprang from *the highest charity* [A2b]. Clearly Christ's Passion was a *true sacrifice*." *Summa Theologiæ* 3.48.3, in *Theological Texts*, trans. Gilby, 331–2. Emphasis added.

235 One of the main themes of Michel Terestchenko's study of the moral heroes who saved and protected Jews in Nazi-occupied Europe is a denial that the virtues of reverence involve any kind of "sacrifice." He wants his account to serve as a "critique d'une vision sacrificielle de l'altruisme." His denial is understandable, as he wants to proclaim the human paradox, and to show that self-assertion and reverence are contraries, not contradictions. But the virtues of reverence do necessarily entail an "objective" self-sacrifice, in the sense of giving up a lesser good for a higher good: possibly even giving up your own life. Tereschenko's critique mixes up *how and why* people did what they did – and *how* they viewed themselves – with *what they actually did*. As Terestchenko himself says, the heroes he describes placed their devotion to others, and to their own non-ego centre (A2), "plus haut que la quête du bonheur ou la défense de ses avantages particuliers." Terestchenko, *Un si fragile vernis d'humanité*, 290–3. That is the very definition of sacrifice. But this kind of "sacrifice" is *not* the destruction of the self: it is the very highest and noblest form of self-assertion.

236 Webb Keane notes that one's intial ethical "gut reaction" can be brought into "ones'own field of consciousness," where it can become "explicit" and "objectified." In other words, the virtues of Reverence/"I *am*" (A2) open the door to the virtues of Excellence/"It *is*" (B1), and eventually to

the virtues of Equality/"*It* is" (B2). *Ethical Life*, 68. Max Scheler makes
the same point. Values emerge as objects of feeling. But they are "not
first of all comprehended." They simply "stand before" us, as objective
"value-feelings" or "value-qualities": "A new act of reflection is required
if this 'feeling of' is to become objective, thus enabling us to reflect subse-
quently on *what* we 'feel' in the already objectively given value." Scheler,
Formalism in Ethics, trans. Frings and Funk, 257–9. Emphasis in original.

237 "L'emphase de l'extériorité est excellence. ... Cette hyperbole, cette
ex-cellence [B1] n'est que le 'pour l'autre' [A2] dans son désintéressement." Levinas, *Autrement qu'être*, 281.

238 "[C]omme si, au cours de cette approche du 'toi' survenait sa transcendance en 'il.'" Emmanuel Levinas, *Éthique et Infini*, 102. My translation.
"[U]ne éthique plus vieille que l'ontologie ... la signification même de
l'Infini." *De l'existence à l'existant* (Paris: Vrin, 2013), 11.

239 "[L]a responsabilité pour autrui, jamais assumée, me lie: un commandement jamais entendu est obéi. ...Trace d'une relation avec l'*illéité*
[Levinas' term for "It is" (B1)] ... m'ordonnant à la responsabilité.
Relation – ou religion – excédant la psychologie de la foi et de la perte de
la foi – elle m'ordonne d'une façon an-archique, précisément, sans jamais
se faire – sans s'être jamais faite – présence ni dévoilement de principe."
Levinas, *Autrement qu'être*, 261.

240 Franz Rosenzweig calls this the contradiction between "divine sternness"
and "divine love." Justice (B1) and mercy (A2) have a "ceaseless connection," "an alternating current oscillating" between them. The unity of
"the country labelled God" is "the constant equalization of apparently
opposite 'attributes.'" *The Star of Redemption*, trans. Hallo, 349.

241 "Appeler Dieu *Abba* [as Jesus of Nazareth does] indique l'affection, l'intimité, la proximité [A2], mais aussi le respect et la soumission [B1]. ...
Deux traits caractérisent le bon père. Tout d'abord la sollicitude [A2] ...
Mais en même temps l'autorité [B1] ... On lui doit affection [A2] et
soumission [B1]. Il est *l'idéal du fils*." José-Antonio Pagola, *Jésus: Approche
historique*, trans. Gérard Grenet (Paris: Les Éditions du Cerf, 2019), 332–3.
Emphasis added.

242 Isaiah 11:6–7. Emphasis added. The Talmud (Tractate Rosh Hashanah)
examines the paradox of reverence in a debate between the claims of
justice (B1) in Deuteronomy 10:17 and those of mercy (A2) in Numbers
6:25. Levinas, *Entre nous*, 242–3. Thomas Aquinas explores the paradox
of reverence in the *Summa Theologiæ* 1.21.4 and 1.21.14, concluding that
mercy (A2) comes before justice (B1) and makes it possible. Nicholas
Love's *The Mirror of the Blessed Lyf of Jesus Christ*, written about 140 years
after Aquinas' death, is another debate between Truth and Justice (B1)
on the one hand, and Mercy and Peace (A2) on the other. Denys Turner,

Thomas Aquinas: A Portrait, 199–202. Even Immanuel Kant implicitly acknowledged the paradox of reverence. "I have differentiated," he said, "between the ideas of wisdom [B1] and holiness [A2], although I have shown them to be fundamentally and objectively identical." "Preface," in *Critique of Practical Reason*, trans. Lewis White Beck (Indianapolis: Bobbs-Merrill, 1956), 11.

243 "Norm-seeking [B1] and empathetic [A2] tolerance [B1] can be uneasy companions. The virtues of forthrightness [B1] and humility [A2] are both ethical; so too the often contradictory values of loyalty [B1 & A2] and freedom [A1]." Keane, *Ethical Life*, 100. Here as elsewhere, Keane seems to conflate the virtues of Reverence (A2) ("empathetic") and those of Equality (B2) ("tolerance").

244 Plato, *The Republic*, bk. 1, 347A–353D, in *Great Dialogues of Plato*, trans. W.H.D. Rouse, ed. Eric H. Warmington and Philip G. Rouse (New York: New American Library, 1956), 147–54. "Goodness is a general term, under which justice, and the other virtues, are special headings." Thomas Aquinas, *Expositio de Hebdomadibus* 5, in *Theological Texts*, trans. Gilby, 39.

245 William Shakespeare, *The Merchant of Venice*, in *The Complete Works*, ed. Alfred Harbage (Baltimore: Penguin Books, 1969), 4.1.182–95; "La justice sort de l'amour. ... L'amour doit toujours surveiller la justice." Levinas, *Entre nous*, 117–18. See also Scheler, *Formalism in Ethics*, trans. Frings and Funk, 288; Ricœur, *Amour et justice*.

246 Aquinas, *Summa Theologiæ* 2–2.58.12 (Cambridge: Cambridge Univ. Press, 2006), vol. 37 ("Justice"), trans. Thomas Gilby, 53; Maimonides, *The Guide for the Perplexed*, trans. Friedländer, 341; Rahner, *The Practice of Faith*, 288.

247 "[I]ntellectual humility ... seems to have been in short supply in Latin Christendom, which has been the scene of total, almost obsessive identification with favourite schemes, driven to any wild or repellent consequences, justifying murderous schisms." Taylor, *A Secular Age*, 652.

248 Fanaticisms of all kinds are "a strange mixture of a value-response attitude [B1] and pride [A1a] and concupiscence [A1b]." Hildebrand, *Ethics*, 445. Jung suggests fanaticism is "always a sign of repressed doubt." Jung, *Analytical Psychology: Its Theory and Practice*, 172.

249 "[H]uman rights is best seen as a rational thought experiment, as a critical discourse whose purpose is to force the ordinary virtues to enlarge and expand their circle of moral concern." Michael Ignatieff, *The Ordinary Virtues: Moral Order in a Divided World* (Cambridge, MA: Harvard Univ. Press, 2017), 214.

250 José Casanova notes that "since the eighteenth century the direction of influence has been reversed and ... increasingly modern societal morality has been the one challenging, informing and influencing church morality." "The Contemporary Disjunction Between Societal and Church

Morality," in *Church and People: Disjunctions in a Secular Age*, ed. Charles Taylor, José Casanova, George F. McLean (Washington: The Council for Research in Values and Philosophy, 2012), 127.

251 Maritain, *Humanisme intégral*, 34, 233–4. This paradoxical result may have something to do with self-assertion's greater inclination "to think in terms of generalizations and abstractions." Objectification, generalization and abstraction help to turn "moral intuitions" (i.e., intuition with feeling [A2]) into "potential objects of reflection, criticism, justification, and so forth" (i.e., intuition with thinking [B1], leading to sensing with thinking [B2]). Keane, *Ethical Life*, 66–8. James Q. Wilson agrees. *The Moral Sense* (New York: Free Press, 1993), 236–7. But Hans Joas argues this "generalization" could not have occurred without a parallel or background "sacralization" of the person – that is to say, it could not have occurred without the development of background virtues of reverence. *The Sacredness of the Person*.

252 Taylor, *A Secular Age*, 637.

253 "Human rights universalism [B2] is contemptuous of pity [A2] because it is discretionary, emotional, and highly personal. Yet it is possible that pure pity [A2] has done more real work to save victims than the language of rights [B2]." Ignatieff, *The Ordinary Virtues*, 213.

254 Taylor, *A Secular Age*, 247–51, 572.

255 Taylor, 36–9, 83.

256 "[A]ll creatures have being as their root, being as their home, being as their base." *Chandogya Upanishad*, chap. 8, in *The Upanishads*, ed. and trans. Valerie J. Roebuck (London: Penguin Books, 2003), 176.

257 Edward Conze, ed., *Buddhist Scriptures* (Harmondsworth: Penguin Books, 1969), 113, 115.

258 Dupré, *Transcendent Selfhood*, viii.

259 N.T. Wright, *After You Believe*.

260 Edmund Fawcett, for example, simply takes for granted that "excluding religious reason from public debate ... serves believers and nonbelievers alike: keeping the argumentative peace and allowing for collective decision-making in diverse, conflicted societies." *Conservatism*, 125.

261 The abolition of slavery and many benevolent social reforms of the nineteenth and twentieth centuries were led by people for whom prevailing practices were incompatible with genuine reverence. Annas, *Intelligent Virtue*, 52–65.

262 Shweder, *Why Do Men Barbecue?*, 216.

263 "International law governing religious liberty has tended to assume a distinctly Protestant model of faith ... as a matter of the inner belief of individuals rather than the external rituals of communities." Keane, *Ethical Life*, 255.

264 Richard M. Rorty, "The Priority of Democracy to Philosophy," in *The Rorty Reader*, ed. Christopher J. Voparil and Richard J. Bernstein (Chichester: Wiley-Blackwell, 2010), 243; "Religion in the Public Square: A Reconsideration," in *The Rorty Reader*, 456–62.

265 Mircea Eliade, *A History of Religious Ideas*, Vol. 1: *From the Stone Age to the Eleusinian Mysteries* (Chicago: Univ. of Chicago Press, 1978), xiii.

266 Taylor, *Sources of the Self*, 319, 367, 448, 455, 517. N.T. Wright emphasizes the importance of Christian "eschatology," the "future-oriented" outlook of the Christian New Testament, one that looks forward not so much to life in a future heaven as to the future "transformation" of our own "earth." *Surprised by Hope*, 101. From a Jewish perspective, Franz Rosenzweig makes much the same point about Christianity. *The Star of Redemption*, trans. Hallo, 374–5. Paul Ricœur sees both Judaism and Christianity as future-oriented, in contrast to the focus of earlier mythologies and much rational thought on origins. *Esprit*, special issue, July–August 1988, in *Ricœur: Textes choisis et présentés*, 277–85.

267 Joas, *The Sacredness of the Person*; Ignatieff, *The Ordinary Virtues*, 214.

268 Ahmed, *What Is Islam?*, 180–2. Ahmed cites, among others, Wuthnow, *Meaning and Moral Order*.

269 Taylor, *A Secular Age*, 638.

270 Eagleton, *Reason, Faith, and Revolution*, 90.

271 Thomas Mann, *The Confessions of Felix Krull, Confidence Man* (New York: Signet, 1957), 145.

272 "There's so much trash – sometimes masquerading as a satire of trash – on the airwaves that it's hard to say what's worse: The blunting violence that's called action? The lackadaisical transformation of sex to commodity? The shows that invite people to degrade themselves for a few dollars or minutes of fame? All of them chip away at human dignity." Neiman, *Moral Clarity*, 241.

273 Bernard Williams observes that "in ethics, *reflection can destroy knowledge*." *Ethics and the Limits of Philosophy*, 148, 154, 167–8. Emphasis in original.

Chapter 17. Civilization

1 Paul Ricœur calls this the distinction between "origine 'historique'" and "origine axiologique." *Le conflit des interprétations: Essais d'herméneutique* (Paris: Éditions du Seuil, 2013), 207.

2 "Le problème consiste seulement à se demander si le commencement est au commencement. " Emmanuel Levinas, *Autrement qu'être ou au-delà de l'essence* (Paris: Le Livre de Poche, 2008), 257.

3 René Descartes, "Meditation 3" in *Meditations on First Philosophy*, trans. Elizabeth S. Haldane and G.R.T. Ross, in *The Philosophical Works of René Descartes*, ed. Elizabeth S. Haldane and G.R.T. Ross (Cambridge: Cambridge Univ. Press, 1969), 1:157, 169. Similarly, Hegel says "man is a thinking being." G.W.F. Hegel, *Encyclopaedia of the Philosophical Sciences*, §98, in Hegel's Logic, trans. William Wallace (London: Oxford Univ. Press, 1975), 144.

4 Plato, *The Republic*, bk. 9, 585C–587A, in *Great Dialogues of Plato*, trans. W.H.D. Rouse, ed. Eric H. Warmington and Philip G. Rouse (New York: New American Library, 1956), 387; Aristotle, *Nicomachean Ethics* 9.4.1166a15–25, 9.8.1168b34–1169a5, 10.7.1177a10–20, 1177b25–1178a10, 10.8.1179a20–35, trans. J.A.K. Thomson, rev. Hugh Tredennick (London: Penguin Books, 2004), 236, 244, 270, 272–3, 276; Thomas Aquinas, *Summa Theologiæ* 1–2.61.2, 1–2.66.1, in *Treatise on the Virtues*, trans. John A. Oesterle (Notre Dame, IN: Univ. of Notre Dame Press, 1984), 110, 149. For contemporary rationalist manifestos, see Steven Pinker, *Enlightenment Now: The Case for Reason, Science, Humanism, and Progress* (New York: Viking, 2018); *Rationality: What It Is, Why It Seems Scarce, Why It Matters* (New York: Viking, 2021).

5 "La raison a beau crier, elle ne peut mettre le prix aux choses." Pascal, *Pensées* (Paris: Garnier-Flammarion, 1973), §81 p. 59.

6 Hans Joas argues "rationality is a weak motivator of morality." *The Sacredness of the Person: A New Genealogy of Human Rights*, trans. Alex Skinner (Washington, DC: Georgetown Univ. Press, 2013), 93–4. So do Rosalind Hursthouse and Christine Swanton: Rosalind Hursthouse, *On Virtue Ethics* (Oxford: Oxford Univ. Press, 2010), 235; Christine Swanton, *Virtue Ethics: A Pluralistic View* (Oxford: Oxford Univ. Press, 2003), 66.

7 "[C]onsciousness presupposes experience, and not experience consciousness. It is a special element in the subjective forms of some feelings." Alfred North Whitehead, *Process and Reality* (New York: Free Press, 1969), 67.

8 "[L]'assurance d'être soi-même agissant et souffrant … préservera la question *qui*? [I am] de se laisser remplacer par la question *quoi*? [It is]" Paul Ricœur, *Soi-même comme un autre* (Paris: Éditions du Seuil, 1990), 35. Emphasis in original.

9 Leibniz distinguishes between "le dit en soi" and "l'action même qui le dit": "sans le désir de nous faire entendre nous n'aurions jamais formé le langage." G.W. Leibniz, *Nouveaux essais sur l'entendement humain* (Paris: Garnier-Flammarion, 1966), bk. 2, chap. 27, §13, p. 203; bk. 3, chap. 1, §2, p. 236.

10 "[I]n speech the self-existent singleness of self-consciousness comes as such into existence, so that its particular individuality is something for others. … Language is self-consciousness existing *for others* … and at

the same time fuses directly with others and is *their* self-consciousness."
G.W.F. Hegel, *The Phenomenology of Mind*, trans. J.B. Baillie (New York:
Harper & Row, 1967), 530, 660–1. Emphasis in original.

11 Levinas, *Autrement qu'être*, 44, 47, 81, 101, 125, 127–8, 147–8, 223–5,
249–51, 260–2.

12 Ricœur, *Soi-même comme un autre*, 380.

13 "Listening-to … is the existential being-open of Dasein as being-with
for the other [A2]." Martin Heidegger, *Being and Time*, 163, trans. Joan
Stambaugh (Albany: State Univ. of New York Press, 2010), 158. Elision in
original.

14 Dietrich von Hildebrand, *Ethics* (Steubenville, OH: Hildebrand Press,
2020), 216.

15 Levinas, *Autrement qu'être*, 119, 127, 172.

16 "[N]e faut-il pas, pour se rendre disponible, s'appartenir en quelque
façon? … [L]e soi s'atteste par le mouvement même en lequel il se
démet." Ricœur, *Soi-même comme un autre*, 166, 392.

17 Franz Rosenzweig calls this the "secret prehistory of the soul [A2] in the
self [A1]": "The soul … derives from the self of man. Specifically, it is defiance [A1] which emerges to the fore in the soul [A2], that defiance [A1]
which *asserts* the character in constant surges. *It* is the secret origin of the
soul, *it* provides the soul with the strength to withstand, to stand fast."
The Star of Redemption, trans. William W. Hallo (Notre Dame, IN: Univ. of
Notre Dame Press, 1985), 170. First emphasis added, others in original.

18 "[T]he very being of a thing … precedes an act of willing." Thomas
Aquinas, *Summa Theologiæ* 1–2.10.1, in *Treatise on Happiness*, trans. John A.
Oesterle (Notre Dame, IN: Univ. of Notre Dame Press, 1983), 102.

19 Franz Rosenzweig compares the relationship between being and reasoning, with its "world-centred multiplicity," to a painting hanging on a
wall: "It would be impossible to hang the picture [reason/"It is"] but for
the wall [being/"I am"]." *The Star of Redemption*, trans. Hallo, 13.

20 Building on Kierkegaard, Michel Henry suggests the very first encounter
of human beings with being is a kind of "suffering." *L'essence de la manifestation* (Paris: Presses Universitaires de France, 2017), 839–43, 852–6.
Paul Ricœur builds on Michel Henry's insight to develop an "ontologie
de la chair" and a "phénoménologie du souffrir." He describes human
beings as "agissant et souffrant." *Soi-même comme un autre*, 35, 172, 367–
80. For Martin Heidegger, "anxiety" is what suffering is for Michel Henry
and Paul Ricœur: the experience which first reveals humans to themselves, first introduces them to their own "being." *Being and Time*, 184–91,
trans. Stambaugh, 178–84.

21 "La concupiscence [A1b] et la force [A1a] sont les sources de toutes nos
actions." Pascal, *Pensées*, §187, p. 84. Paul Ricœur calls this "le caractère

originaire de l'affirmation," or "l'antériorité, l'archaïsme du désir," "[l']
antériorité de la pulsion par rapport à la prise de conscience et à la
volition." *Histoire et vérité* (Paris: Points Essais, 2001), 400; *Le conflit des
interprétations*, 358. Emphasis in original. See also Henry, *L'essence de la
manifestation*, 831.

22 "Du 'il y a' [Levinas' term for the human stance of "*It* is" (B2), Kant's
phenomenal world] … émerge la subjectivité … Cette première sortie de
soi, éruption de l'être, s'amorce par la reconnaissance des choses, mais
aussi étape du jouir de la vie, de se suffire à soi-même [A1]. Cet amour
de soi est un égoïsme qui fonde l'être et constitue *la première expérience
ontologique.*" Emmanuel Levinas, *Altérité et transcendance* (Paris: Le Livre
de Poche, 2010), 110. Emphasis added. See also: *Les Imprévus de l'histoire*
(Paris: Le Livre de Poche, 2007), 178–9; *Liberté et commandement* (Paris: Le
Livre de Poche, 1999), 71; *Entre nous: Essais sur le penser-à-l'autre* (Paris:
Livre de Poche, 2010), 10.

23 Emmanuel Levinas calls this crucial shift in human values the "human
inversion": "Et voici que surgit, dans la vie vécue par l'humain – et *c'est
là que, à proprement parler l'humain commence* … – du se vouer à l'autre. …
Tout se passe comme si le surgissement de l'humain dans l'économie de
l'être renversait le sens et l'intrigue et le rang philosophique de l'ontologie: l'en-soi de l'être persistant à être se dépasse dans la gratuité du hors-
de-soi-pour-l'autre, dans le sacrifice ou la possibilité du sacrifice, dans la
perspective de la sainteté." Levinas, *Entre nous*, 221, 10. Emphasis added.

24 "We alone have measured the quality of mercy among our own kind."
Edward O. Wilson, *The Meaning of Human Existence* (New York: Liveright,
2014), 132.

25 On the "irascible" appetite and virtues, and their tendency "to overcome
and rise above obstacles," see chapter 8, notes 24 and 29.

26 Iranäus Eible-Eibesfeldt, *Love and Hate: The Natural History of Behavior
Patterns* (New York: Aldine, 1996), cited in Robert N. Bellah, *Religion in
Human Evolution: From the Paleolithic to the Axial Age* (Cambridge, MA:
Belknap Press of Harvard Univ. Press, 2011), 70–1.

27 Michel Terestchenko, *Un si fragile vernis d'humanité: Banalité du mal, banalité du bien* (Paris: La Découverte, 2007). Self-assertion (or "defiance")
"provides the soul with the strength to withstand, to stand fast." Rosenzweig, *The Star of Redemption*, trans. Hallo, 170.

28 Thomas Aquinas, *Summa Theologiæ* 2–2.158.1 (Cambridge: Cambridge
Univ. Press, 2006), vol. 44 ("Well-Tempered Passion"), trans. Thomas
Gilby, 55.

29 Bellah, *Religion in Human Evolution*, 175, 191, 261, 266.

30 "[U]n 'je suis' [est] strictement égal à un 'je vaux.'" Ricœur, *Histoire et
vérité*, 399.

31 "Par la valeur je me dépasse en autrui. J'accepte qu'il soit, afin que moi aussi je sois, que je sois non seulement comme un vouloir-vivre, mais comme une existence-valeur." Ricœur, 399.

32 Frans de Waal, *The Age of Empathy: Nature's Lessons for a Kinder Society* (New York: Three Rivers Press, 2009), 82.

33 Paul Ricœur calls this a "transfert en imagination." *Parcours de la reconnaissance* (Paris: Gallimard, 2013), quoted in Michaël Fœssel, "Introduction: Paul Ricœur ou les puissances de l'imaginaire," in *Ricœur: Textes choisis et présentés*, ed. Michaël Fœssel and Fabien Lamouche (Paris: Éditions Points, 2007), 9.

34 "[I]magination is not what drives empathy. ... Bodily connections come first – understanding follows." de Waal, *The Age of Empathy*, 72.

35 Whitehead notes that the virtues of "sympathy" (A2) – "that is, feeling the feeling *in* another and feeling conformally *with* another" – are the first stage in the human journey (the arrow of virtue) *beyond* the initial human experience of physical "appetite" (A1). Whitehead, *Process and Reality*, 188–9.

36 R.G. Collingwood, *Speculum Mentis or the Map of Knowledge* (Oxford: Oxford Univ. Press, 1963), 106–7; Bellah, *Religion in Human Evolution*, 89–97.

37 "Rien n'est si *semblable* à la charité [A2] que la cupidité [A1], et rien n'y est si *contraire*." Pascal, *Pensées*, §526, p. 180. Emphasis added.

38 Sigmund Freud, "The Libido Theory," in *General Psychological Theory: Papers on Metapsychology* (New York: Simon & Schuster, 2008), 183. "[T]he main purpose of Eros [is] that of uniting and binding." *The Ego and the Id*, trans. Joan Riviere, rev. James Strachey (New York: W.W. Norton, 1962), 35.

39 "The object arousing the appetite is a good that is apprehended." Thomas Aquinas, *Summa Theologiæ* 2–2.145.2 (Cambridge: Cambridge Univ. Press, 2006), vol. 43 ("Temperance"), trans. Thomas Gilby, 75. "[O]n ne saurait vouloir que ce qu'on trouve bon." Leibniz, *Nouveaux essais*, bk. 2, chap. 21, §17, p. 153.

40 "[T]he initial activity of the appetitive power is loving." Aquinas, 2–2.47.1 (Cambridge: Cambridge Univ. Press, 2006), vol. 36 ("Prudence"), trans. Thomas Gilby, 7.

41 "Charity is thus the mother and root of all virtues insofar as it is the form of all virtues." Aquinas, *Summa Theologiæ* 1–2.62.4, in *Treatise on the Virtues*, trans. Oesterle, 123. Christine Swanton follows Aquinas in suggesting love is "foundational" and "part of the profiles of all virtue." *Virtue Ethics*, 100–1.

42 Paul Ricœur, *De l'interprétation*, in *Ricœur: Textes choisis et présentés*, 226.

43 Aristotle, *Nicomachean Ethics* 9.4.1166a30–35, trans. Thomson, rev. Tredennick, 237.

44 Aristotle, *Rhetoric* 2.3.1380b35–1381a5, trans. W. Rhys Roberts, in *The Basic Works of Aristotle*, ed. Richard McKeon (New York: Random House, 1941), 1386.

45 Actually, it is probably a halfway point *beyond* the next stop. As the kind of reasonable virtue described and praised by Plato and Aristotle, friendship is what self-giving becomes when it begins to evolve *beyond* the virtues of Reverence (A2), toward the virtues of Excellence (B1). For purposes of exposition (as Hegel often does) I have put it *before*, but in human evolution, it almost certainly comes *after*. The first stop is the reversal of original self-assertion that takes place in family and tribal life, i.e., in the virtues of Reverence (A2).

46 "Cette expérience [la première sortie de soi, en la forme de l'amour de soi] appelle à l'ouverture et à la véritable sortie de soi. L'humain passera par une autre étape décisive où le sujet malgré sa satisfaction échoue à se suffire. Toute sortie de soi représente la fissure qui s'instaure dans le Même vers l'Autre. *Désir métamorphosé en attitude d'ouverture à l'extériorité.* Ouverture qui est appel et réponse à autrui. La proximité de l'autre, origine de toute mise en question de soi." Levinas, *Altérité et transcendance*, 110. Emphasis added. David Martin notes the "tension" between "free gift" (A2) and "balanced and symmetrical exchange" (B2b) as one of the "parallel tensions" of a basic "dialectic" (i.e., the human paradox). *On Secularization: Towards a Revised General Theory* (Farnham: Ashgate, 2005), 11.

47 Bellah, *Religion in Human Evolution*, 68–73. Bellah reviews the work of Sarah Hrdy, Irenäus Eible-Eibesfeldt, and Frans de Waal, among others.

48 Levinas, *Autrement qu'être*, 109, 111, 114, 121–4, 126–7, 165, 168, 170.

49 de Waal, *The Age of Empathy*, 11, 67.

50 Dietrich von Hildebrand, *Fundamental Moral Attitudes*, trans. Alice M. Jourdain (New York: Longmans, Green, 1950), 13.

51 James Q. Wilson, *The Moral Sense* (New York: Free Press, 1993), 226; Anthony T. Kronman, *Confessions of a Born-Again Pagan* (New Haven: Yale Univ. Press, 2016), 52.

52 Wilson127–8; Bellah, *Religion in Human Evolution*, 70–4, 191, 261, 266, 472.

53 André Comte-Sponville, *A Small Treatise on the Great Virtues*, trans. Catherine Temerson (New York: Henry Holt, 2001), 270.

54 *The Bhagavad Gita* 2.30, 2.24, trans. Eknath Easwaran (New York: Vintage Books, 2000), 11. See also 13, 20, 24. See also Edward Conze, ed., *Buddhist Scriptures* (Harmondsworth: Penguin Books, 1969), 227; *The Book of Chuang Tzu*, in *The Tao: Finding the Way of Balance and Harmony*, ed. Mark Forstater (New York: Plume, 2003), 192.

55 C.G. Jung, *Analytical Psychology: Its Theory and Practice* (New York: Vintage Books, 1970), 187, 195. William James said these two sides of the

"dual nature" of human beings are "firm facts of human nature, no matter whether we adopt a theistic, a pantheistic-idealistic, or a medico-materialistic view of their ultimate causal explanation." William James, *The Varieties of Religious Experience* (New York: Collier Books, 1961), 92, 102, 398.

56 Martin Buber, *I and Thou*, 2nd ed., trans. Ronald Gregor Smith (New York: Charles Scribner's Sons, 1958), 62–5. Buber's names for the two selves – the particular and eternal selves – are "individuality" and the "person." Paul Ricœur calls them "la mêmeté" and "l'ipséité." *Soi-même comme un autre*, 12–14. Emmanuel Levinas calls these two selves the "Moi" and the "Soi," or the "conscience intentionnelle" and the "conscience non-intentionelle" or "non-réflexive." *Autrement qu'être*, 146, 160–4, 173–7; *Altérité et transcendance*, 39–41. Dietrich von Hildebrand calls them the "free personal center" and the "reverent, humble, loving center" of the human. *Ethics*, 213, 394–5, 436–7, 489.

57 Franz Rosenzweig says the activity of the non-ego self, or soul, is "the sowing of eternity into the living," In these virtues, "eternity has shifted into time." It has "already come – even in the midst of time!" *The Star of Redemption*, trans. Hallo, 378, 369, 325, 332.

58 Georg Simmel calls the non-ego self "a third category [A2] lying beyond the self's present reality [A1] and the unreal, merely demanded idea of value [B1]." *Lebensanschauung* (Munich, 1922), 112, quoted in Hans Joas, *The Genesis of Values*, trans. Gregory Moore (Cambridge, Polity Press, 2000), 80. Iris Murdoch describes the non-ego self as "a substantial and continually developing mechanism of attachments, the purification and reorientation of which must be the task of morals." *The Sovereignty of Good* (London: Routledge, 1980), 71.

59 "There is a mysterious spontaneity in charity; it is as if something were opened ... that superabundantly flows ... without limit." Hildebrand, *Ethics*, 375. "La seule valeur absolue c'est la possibilité humaine de donner sur soi une priorité à l'autre." Levinas, *Entre nous*, 119.

60 Thomas Aquinas, *Summa Theologiæ* 1–2.64.4, in *Theological Texts*, trans. Thomas Gilby (London: Oxford Univ. Press, 1954), 182.

61 "[H]e who has performed one kind of duty will not think himself thereby discharged. ... [T]he only limit to his beneficence is the failure of his means." John Calvin, *The Institutes of the Christian Religion* 3.7.2, trans. Henry Beveridge (Peabody, MA: Hendrickson, 2012), 454. "On n'est jamais quitte à l'égard d'autrui." Emmanuel Levinas, *Éthique et Infini* (Paris: Le Livre de Poche, 1984), 101; *Altérité et transcendance*, 50, 114. "[U]ne quête qui ne peut être épuisée par aucun programme d'action." Paul Ricœur, *L'Herméneutique biblique*, in *Ricœur: Textes choisis et présentés*, 206. See also Terestchenko, *Un si fragile vernis d'humanité*, 261.

62 "[U]n infini qui commande dans le visage de l'Autre." Levinas, *Autrement qu'être*, 155.

63 Levinas, *Altérité et transcendance*, 28–9, 46–7; *Autrement qu'être*, 233, 236, 244, 247, 252.

64 Emmanuel Levinas, *Dieu, la mort et le temps* (Paris: Le Livre de Poche, 2010), 120, 218, 250. Also, *De Dieu qui vient à l'idée*, 2nd expanded ed. (Paris: Vrin, 2004), 106.

65 Joas, *The Sacredness of the Person*, 128.

66 "It is the will whose potentialities have become truly explicit which is the truly infinite ... [T]his will is not mere potentiality, capacity, potency (*potentia*), but the infinite in actuality (*infinitum actu*) ... In the free will the infinite becomes actual and present: the free will itself is this Idea whose nature is to be present here and now." G.W.F. Hegel, *Philosophy of Right*, trans. T.M. Knox (Oxford: Oxford Univ. Press, 1967), §22, p. 30. "Le temporel et le matériel y sont et le terrain, et l'objet, et l'une de deux parties. Quand l'éternel livre une bataille temporelle, il faut bien que ce soit une bataille temporelle. Quand le spirituel livre une bataille au matériel il faut bien que ce soit une bataille matérielle." Charles Péguy, *Note conjointe sur M. Descartes et la philosophie cartésienne*, in *Une éthique sans compromis*, ed. Dominique Saatdjian (Paris: Pocket, 2011), 295. "[L]'œuvre commune n'apparaîtrait plus comme une œuvre divine à réaliser sur terre par l'homme, mais plutôt une œuvre humaine à réaliser sur terre par le passage de quelque chose de divin, *qui est l'amour*, dans les moyens humains et dans le travail humain lui-même." Jacques Maritain, *Humanisme intégral*, new ed. (Paris: Éditions Aubier-Montaigne, 1946), 208. Emphasis added.

67 Rosenzweig, *The Star of Redemption*, trans. Hallo, 167.

68 "Law reckons with times, with a future, with duration. The commandment knows only the moment; it awaits the result in the very instant of its promulgation." Rosenzweig, 177. Following Franz Rosenzweig, Paul Ricœur also distinguishes between a "command" (A2) and a law (B1). The command comes first in the human story and is nothing more than a voice, the voice of love itself (A2b). But in this (mythic or "poetic") form (A2), it already contains a moral imperative, which will and must become a law (B1). *Amour et justice* (Paris: Éditions Points, 2008), 20–2.

69 Martin Heidegger uses terms such as "interrupt," "break," "breach," "jolt," "abrupt arousal" – as well as "stopped" itself – to express what I call the "stop signs" of the "call" or commands that "interrupt" the normal human default mode of self-assertion and send it in a new direction, the direction of reverence. *Being and Time*, 271, trans. Stambaugh, 261. "L'être qui s'exprime, l'être qui est en face de moi me dit *non*, par son expression même. Ce *non* ... est impossibilité de tuer celui qui présente ce

visage, il est possibilité de rencontrer un être à travers une interdiction."
Levinas, *Liberté et commandement*, 52. Also, *Difficile liberté*, 3rd corrected
ed. (Paris: Le Livre de Poche, 2010), 26; *De Dieu qui vient à l'idée*, 246–7.

70 "[A]n (ideal) *ought-not-to-be* ... is the foundation of every imperative
proposition. Throughout history, therefore, proscriptions have always
preceded prescriptions (e.g., the Decalogue)." Max Scheler, *Formalism in
Ethics and Non-Formal Ethics of Value*, trans. Manfred S. Frings and Roger
L. Funk (Evanston: Northwestern Univ. Press, 1973), 211. Emphasis in
original.

71 Levinas, *Dieu, la mort et le temps*, 133–4; *Altérité et transcendance*, 132–3.
"[J]e passe du : tu ne tueras pas, au : tu aimeras, du refus de la guerre à
la construction de la paix, j'entre dans le cycle des actions, que je fais."
Ricœur, *Histoire et vérité*, 275.

72 Marilynne Robinson, *Gilead* (Toronto: HarperCollins, 2004), 66.

73 "Le visage, c'est le fait pour un être de nous affecter, non pas à l'indicatif,
mais à l'impératif." Levinas, *Liberté et commandement*, 52. The theme of
the moral impact of the human "face" is one of the constant, recurring
themes in Levinas' philosophy. Frans de Waal confirms Levinas' emphasis on the moral impact of the "face": "[E]mpathy needs a face." The face
is the "emotion highway." *The Age of Empathy*, 78–83. The quotes are on
pages 82–3.

74 "[I]l suffit qu'un seul homme soit tenu sciemment, ou, ce qui revient au
même, sciemment laissé dans la misère pour que le pacte civique tout entier soit nul; aussi longtemps qu'il y a un homme dehors, la porte qui lui
est fermée au nez ferme une cité d'injustice et de haine." Charles Péguy,
De Jean Coste, in *Une éthique sans compromis*, ed. Saatdjian, 279.

75 "Being ethical is what makes you human. To act without restraint is to
be an animal." Webb Keane, *Ethical Life: Its Natural and Social Histories*
(Princeton: Princeton Univ. Press, 2016), 12.

76 "[A]n ought becomes a moral and genuine ought whenever ... [it] comes
to this person and to him alone as a 'call' ... It is good precisely in the
sense of being 'independent of my knowledge.' ... Yet it is the '*good in
itself*' for '*me*,' in the sense that there is an experienced *reference* to me ...
something that ... points to 'me,' something that whispers, 'For you.'"
Scheler, *Formalism in Ethics* trans. Frings and Funk, 490. Emphasis in original. Hans Joas also notes that values "call" upon us: we experience them
as a "demand" or a "claim," a call and a demand we have to answer in
our action. *The Sacredness of the Person*, 122, 124, 127–8. Following Heidegger, Paul Ricœur also emphasizes the voice of conscience as a "call";
"l'appel du souci." *Amour et justice*, 103–4. Hegel had already described
this call as an "inner voice," a "voice divine." Hegel, *The Phenomenology of
Mind*, trans. Baillie, 663.

77 Rosenzweig, *The Star of Redemption*, trans. Hallo, 176.

78 "Before they call I will answer, while they are yet speaking I will hear." Isaiah 65:24.

79 "I have put my words in your mouth." Isaiah 51:16. "What man hears in his heart as his own human speech is the very word that comes out of God's mouth." Rosenzweig, *The Star of Redemption*, trans. Hallo, 151.

80 Levinas, *Altérité et transcendance*, 49, 54, 105–7, 113–15, 132–3.

81 Levinas, 42–4.

82 "[T]he *transcendence* of man is something *immanent* to man's nature." Hildebrand, *Ethics*, 231. Emphasis in original.

83 What I have called the otherness of the spirit, Jacques Maritain calls "des réalités intérieures mais supra-humaines." *Humanisme intégral*, 87. "[L]a conscience apparaît pour assigner à un effort devenu spirituel un but infini." Maurice Blondel, *L'Être et les êtres* (Paris: Presses Universitaires de France, 1963), 270.

84 With his characteristic insight, Tolstoy captures not only the essence of the virtues of Reverence (A2) – giving for the sake of giving – but also how this "giving for its own sake" reveals or leads on to the more "objective" insights of the virtues of Excellence (B1), about truth and goodness: "Pierre's insanity consisted in the fact that he did not wait, as before, for personal reasons, which he called people's merits, in order to love them, but love overflowed his heart, and, loving people *without reason* [A2], he discovered the *unquestionable reasons* [B1] for which it was *worth* loving them." Leo Tolstoy, *War and Peace*, trans. Richard Pevear and Larissa Volokhonsky (New York: Vintage Classics, 2008), vol. 4, pt. 4, chap. 19, p. 1124. Emphasis added.

85 As already noted in chapters 7 and 16, Emmanuel Levinas' term for "It is" is "*Illéité.*" *Autrement qu'être*, 28, 184, 196, 230–1, 234, 240, 247, 252, 261; *Dieu, la mort et le temps*, 231, 234, 236, 240, 257.

86 Ricœur, *Le conflit des interprétations*, 398–9.

87 Aristotle, *Nicomachean Ethics* 8.1.1155a15–25, trans. Thomson, rev. Tredennick, 200–1. "[I]ntellectual feelings are not to be understood unless it be remembered that they *already find at work* 'physical [existential] purposes' more primitive than themselves. Consciousness follows, and does not precede the entry of the conceptual prehensions of the relevant universals." Whitehead, *Process and Reality*, 318. Emphasis added.

88 "[L]e contenu de cette expérience originelle … n'est pas un monde de choses, mais un monde psychique, un monde de sentiments." Henry, *L'essence de la manifestation*, 783.

89 "[C]ohésion et complicité d'un voir et d'un prendre." Levinas, *Altérité et transcendance*, 128.

90 "Love after all always remains between two people; it knows only of I and Thou, not of the street." Rosenzweig, *The Star of Redemption*, trans. Hallo, 203–4.

91 "Now the Anyone appears, the Indefinite as such … The effect of the love of 'neighbor' is that 'Anyone' and 'all the world' thus belong together … Now they unite in the mighty unison of a 'we.'" Rosenzweig, 236. "Que la visée du vivre-bien enveloppe de quelque manière le sens de la justice, cela est impliquée par la notion même de l'autre. L'autre est aussi l'autre que le *tu*. Corrélativement, la justice s'étend plus loin que le face-à-face. … [L]a visée éthique s'étend à tous ceux que le face-à-face laisse en dehors au titre de tiers." Ricœur, *Lectures 1*, in *Ricœur: Textes choisis et présentés*, 314–15. On justice and "le tiers," see also: Levinas, *Autrement qu'être*, 108, 129, 132, 137, 144, 146, 188, 202, 204, 224, 234, 245–9, 251, 262–3, 278, 281.

92 Levinas, *Autrement qu'être*, 77, 253. "À l'extravagante générosité du pour-l'autre [A2] se superpose un ordre raisonnable, ancillaire ou angélique de la justice à travers le savoir [B1], et la philosophie [B1&2] est ici une *mesure* apportée à l'infini de l'être-pour-l'autre de la paix et de la proximité [A2] et comme la sagesse [B1] de l'amour [A2]." *Altérité et transcendance*, 149–53.

93 "[I]l nous importe … de donner à la sollicitude [A2] un statut plus fondamental que l'obéissance au devoir [B1]. … [L]e sens de la justice [B1] ne retranche rien à la sollicitude [A2]; il la suppose." Ricœur, *Soi-même comme un autre*, 222, 236.

94 Aristotle, *Nicomachean Ethics* 5.1.1130a1–10, 5.6.1134b5–10, trans. Thomson, rev. Tredennick, 115, 129; Thomas Aquinas, *Summa Theologiæ* 2–2.58.12 (Cambridge: Cambridge Univ. Press, 2006), vol. 37 ("Justice"), trans. Thomas Gilby, 51; Ricœur, *La Mémoire, l'histoire, l'oubli*, in *Ricœur: Textes choisis et présentés*, 398.

95 "[F]or justice especially, in comparison with other virtues, an impersonal objective interest is fixed." Aquinas, *Summa Theologiæ* 2–2.57.1, vol. 37 ("Justice"), trans. Gilby, 5.

96 "[J]ustice is the habit whereby a person with a lasting and constant will renders to each his due." Aquinas, *Summa Theologiæ* 2–2.57.4, vol. 37 ("Justice"), trans. Gilby, 21.

97 "[L]'*agape* se déclare, se proclame, la justice argumente." Ricœur, *Parcours de la reconnaissance*, 347.

98 Aristotle, *Nicomachean Ethics* 5.3.1131a30, trans. Thomson, rev. Tredennick, 119.

99 Thomas Aquinas, *Summa Theologiæ* 1.47.2, in *Introduction to St. Thomas Aquinas*, ed. Anton C. Pegis (New York: The Modern Library, 1948), 262–4. Paul Ricœur calls this necessary *in*equality of the virtues of reverence "la verticalité de l'appel [entre l'instance qui appel et le soi appelé], égale à son infériorité." *Soi-même comme un autre*, 394.

100 "[Abraham's] trust in the promise is accordingly of the utmost merit; it is a manifestation, Scripture says, of his justice. By 'justice' in this context,

Scripture would seem to mean, most simply, the willingness to *give God his due*." Thomas Pangle, *Political Philosophy and the God of Abraham* (Baltimore: Johns Hopkins Press, 2003), 142. Emphasis added.

101 Bellah, *Religion in Human Evolution*, 178.

102 "A passion of willingness, of acquiescence, of admiration, is the glowing centre of this state of mind." James, *The Varieties of Religious Experience*, 202. "[L]a justice [B1] découle ... de la prééminence d'autrui [A2]." Levinas, *Altérité et transcendance*, 177. On the human eagerness to show deference in many cultures, see Nick Haslam, "Research on the Relational Models: An Overview," in *Relational Models Theory: A Contemporary Overview*, ed. Nick Haslam (Mahwah, NJ: Lawrence Erlbaum Associates, 2004), 38. For Tolstoy's brilliant portrayal of this aspect of the virtues of Excellence (B1), see chap. 11, n. 33. Iris Murdoch suggests the eagerness of the virtues of Excellence (B1) to acknowledge higher worth is central to the human encounter with great art. *The Sovereignty of Good*, 88.

103 Aquinas, *Summa Theologiæ* 2–2.57, vol. 37 ("Justice"), trans. Gilby, 2–17.

104 Aquinas, 5.

105 "*Le droit de l'homme, absolument et originellement,* ne prend pas sens qu'en autrui, comme *droit de l'autre homme*. Droit à l'égard duquel jamais je ne suis quitte! Responsabilité ainsi infinie pour autrui." Levinas, *Altérité et transcendance*, 133. First emphasis in original, second added. See also Levinas, 149–53.

106 "The main function of [intellectual] feelings [B2] is to heighten the emotional intensity accompanying the valuations in the conceptual feelings [B1] involved, and in the more physical purposes [A1 & A2] which are more primitive than any intellectual feelings [B2]. They perform this function by the sharp-cut way in which they limit abstract valuation to express possibilities relevant to definite logical subjects." Whitehead, *Process and Reality*, 317–18.

107 "La culture peut, d'abord, être interprétée – et c'est la dimension privilégiée de l'Occident gréco-romain (et sa possibilité d'universalisation) – comme une intention de lever l'*altérité* de la Nature qui, étrangère et préalable surprend et frappe l'identité immédiate qui est le *Même* du moi humain. D'où l'humain comme le *je* du 'je pense' et la culture comme *savoir* ... Culture de l'autonomie humaine et probablement, de prime abord, culture très profondément athée. Pensée de l'égal à la pensée. ... [D]éjà dans le savoir même, la contraction musculaire de la main qui saisit et déjà disposant de matière qu'elle enserre ou que le doigt de la main montre. ... La perception est 'prise,' appropriation, acquisition et promesse de satisfaction faite à l'homme; surgissement dans le moi d'un sujet intéressé et actif. ... Dès avant la technologie de l'âge industriel et sans la prétendue corruption dont on accuse cet âge, la culture du savoir

et de l'immanence est l'esquisse d'une pratique incarnée, de la mainmise
et de l'appropriation, et de la satisfaction." Levinas, *Entre nous*, 185–7.

108 Paul Ricœur expresses the difference between the two types of reciprocity – between the "mutuality" of the virtues of Reverence (A2) and the
"reciprocity" of the virtues of Equality (B2) – as the "gap" between "le
couple donner-recevoir" (A2) and "le couple recevoir-rendre" (B2). (And
distinguishes them both from the "equivalence" of "justice" [B1] and the
market [A1].) In the "mutuality" of the virtues of reverence (A2), giving
comes first; in the "reciprocity" of the virtues of self-assertion (or "l'auto-
assertion") (B2), receiving comes first. *Parcours de la reconnaissance*, 375.

109 "[Q]u'est-ce que la Déclaration des droits de l'homme sinon un immense
programme, un immense appareil d'une constante revendication."
Charles Péguy, *L'Argent suite*, in *Une éthique sans compromis*, ed. Saatdjian,
54. On human rights as *demands*, see also Joas, *The Sacredness of the Person*,
18–19; Keane, *Ethical Life*, 112; Kronman, *Confessions of a Born-Again Pagan*, 72.

110 "[C]orrélation et égalité entre le pensé et la pensée." Levinas, *Dieu, la mort
et le temps*, 227. Also, *De Dieu qui vient à l'idée*, 94.

111 "Ce que la sollicitude [reverence] ajoute, c'est la dimension de valeur qui
fait que chaque personne est irremplaçable." Ricœur, *Soi-même comme un
autre*, 226.

112 "[T]here is an experienced *reference* to me … something that … points
to 'me,' something that whispers, 'For you.' And precisely this *content*
places me in a *unique* position in the moral cosmos and obliges me with
respect to actions, deeds and works, etc., which, when I represent them
all call, 'I am for you and you are for me.'" Scheler, *Formalism in Ethics*,
trans. Frings and Funk, 490. Emphasis in original. "In revelation, the
summons goes to the proper name of the individual, the wholly and
solely definite substantive, unique in its way, a way peculiar to it and it
alone." Rosenzweig, *The Star of Redemption*, trans. Hallo, 236. "Unicité
signifie ici impossibilité de se dérober et de se faire remplacer. … irremplaçable et unique dans la responsabilité … mon unicité comme celui à
qui personne ne peut se substituer." Levinas, *Autrement qu'être*, 95–8.

113 "[A]t a basic ontological, metaphysical level, all Homo sapiens are of a
kind, and as such, at bottom, equals, peers, and to that extent, *identical*."
Paul Bloomfield, *The Virtues of Happiness: A Theory of the Good Life* (New
York: Oxford Univ. Press, 2014), 68. Emphasis added.

114 Paul Ricœur calls this paradox "la dialectique de la mêmeté et de l'ipséité." *Soi-même comme un autre*, 33, 176.

115 Rosenzweig, *The Star of Redemption*, trans. Hallo, 11.

116 Hegel's suggests the ego of "pure activity" first develops an awareness
or feeling of being a self in the self-*giving* "love and friendship" of family

life. In the family, the ego gladly "restricts" its own self-assertion, and, in that restriction, "first arrives at the feeling of his own self-hood." Hegel, *Philosophy of Right*, trans. Knox, addition to §7, p. 228.

117 "Le sujet conscient n'est-il pas celui-là même qui n'a aucune alliance avec ce dont il est conscient? Ne ressent-il pas toute parenté avec ce dont il a conscience comme compromettant sa vérité?" Levinas, *Autrement qu'être*, 131. Paul Bloomfield perfectly (but apparently unwittingly) expresses this distancing of the self from the world that occurs in the virtues of Equality, or the stance of "It is" (B2), by suggesting that even acting morally in a given situation "is not to imagine 'standing in another's shoes,' or to apply the Golden Rule," but rather to "stand back from it ... in a way that is abstracted from our personal ends." *The Virtues of Happiness*, 143.

118 Bernard J.F. Lonergan, *Insight: A Study of Human Understanding* (London: Darton, Longman & Todd, 1973), 332.

119 "As soon as human knowledge demands an explanation, it does not exceed the essence of [the "fourfold"] world but rather falls beneath it. ... [O]bjective presentation ... is essentially already an attack upon what concerns us. In the appearance of pure presence that the standing-over-against – the objective – offers us, there lies hidden the *greed* of presentational *calculation*." Martin Heidegger, "Bremen Lectures: Insight into That Which Is," in *The Heidegger Reader*, ed. Günter Figal, trans. Jerome Veith (Bloomington: Indiana Univ. Press, 2009), 265, 268. Emphasis added.

120 Marcel Gauchet, *The Disenchantment of the World: A Political History of Religion*, trans. Oscar Bruge (Princeton, NJ: Princeton Univ. Press, 1997), 22, 96–7, 179.

121 Dietrich von Hildebrand calls this "a reverent distance from the world": "[B]eing is never a *mere* means for the reverent man and his accidental egoistic aims. ... [H]e leaves it the necessary space for its proper unfolding." *Fundamental Moral Attitudes*, trans. Jourdain, 6–10.

122 Denys Turner, *The Darkness of God: Negativity in Christian Mysticism* (Cambridge: Cambridge Univ. Press, 1995), chap. 7, 168–85. Emphasis added. Martin Heidegger calls this reverential attitude toward the things of the world "the thinging of the thing," and he calls the reverence in which things are so thinged "nearness." Nearness is a proximity which "preserves remoteness," i.e., lets things be. "Bremen Lectures," trans. Veith, 263, 266. Max Scheler dismisses the modern pursuit of "objectivity," through the banishing of feeling and value perceptions, as a "specifically modern, bourgeois judgement." For him (like Aquinas), love is a constitutive principle of cognition and makes knowledge itself possible. Joas, *The Genesis of Values*, 88–9.

123 Damascene distinguishes *proskynesis* from *latreia*, the reverence reserved only for God. John of Damascus (John Damascene), *On the Divine Images*.

Three Apologies against Those Who Attack the Divine Images, trans. D. Anderson (New York, 1980) 23, 82–8, cited in Diarmaid MacCulloch, *Christianity: The First Three Thousand Years* (New York: Viking, 2010), 447–8.

124 "[L]a passivité devient l'attestation même de l'altérité." Ricœur, *Soi-même comme un autre,* 368. Ricœur surveys three kinds of "passivity" Ricœur, 368–9.

125 "C'est de cette passivité hors pair que la métaphore de la voix, à la fois intérieur à moi et supérieur à moi, est le symptôme ou l'indice. … [L]a passivité de l'être-enjoint consiste dans la situation d'écoute dans laquelle le sujet éthique se trouve placé par rapport à la voix qui lui est adressée à la seconde personne." Ricœur, 394, 406.

126 "'[S]uprême passivité' … abandon de la subjectivité souveraine et active … la déposition ou la dé-situation du sujet … Plus passive que toute réceptivité." Levinas, *Autrement qu'être,* 81. Also, Ricœur, 272. On suffering and passivity, see also Michel Henry and Paul Ricœur in note 20 above.

127 Martin Heidegger, *An Introduction to Metaphysics,* trans. Ralph Manheim (New York: Doubleday, 1961), 17.

128 "This is not a simple matter of linking concepts, but of a double and invisible affirmation. In affirming anything the mind affirms itself. And even further: it is for the sake of thus affirming itself that it makes any affirmation at all." Daniel Esssertier, *Les formes inférieures de l'explication* (Paris: Alcan, 1927), 57–8, quoted in Susanne K. Langer, *Mind: An Essay on Human Feeling,* Vol. 3 (Baltimore: Johns Hopkins Press, 1982), 20–1.

129 Langer, *Mind,* 3:21–2.

130 Charles Taylor, *A Secular Age* (Cambridge, MA: Belknap Press of Harvard Univ. Press, 2007), 351.

131 With the exception of the "Market" (which he barely recognizes), these are the names Hegel also gives to the stages of the "circle of necessity" by which the human ethical order (or *sittlichkeit*) is developed. Hegel, *Philosophy of Right,* trans. Knox, §§32, 256, pp. 35, 155. Max Scheler also thinks the various forms of human community, including the "community of love," the "life-community," the state, and society can each be identified with one or more of his "value-modalities." *Formalism in Ethics,* trans. Frings and Funk, 109–10.

132 Christopher Peterson and Martin E.P. Seligman, *Character Strengths and Virtues: A Handbook and Classification* (New York: Oxford Univ. Press, 2004), 100. Emphasis added.

133 Harold Innis, *Empire and Communications* (Toronto: Univ. of Toronto Press, 1972); *The Bias of Communication* (Toronto Univ. of Toronto Press, 1968); Marshall McLuhan, *The Gutenberg Galaxy* (Toronto: Univ. of Toronto Press, 1964); *Understanding Media: The Extensions of Man* (New York:

McGraw-Hill, 1966); William J. Bernstein, *Masters of the Word: How Media Shaped History from the Alphabet to the Internet* (New York: Grove Press, 2013); Lisa Gitelman, *Always Already New: Media, History, and the Data of History* (Cambridge, MA: MIT Press, 2006); *Paper Knowledge: Toward a Media History of Documents* (Durham: Duke Univ. Press, 2014); Lisa Gitelman and Geoffrey Pingree, eds., *New Media, 1740–1915* (Cambridge, MA: MIT Press, 2003); Adrian Johns, *The Nature of the Book: Print and Knowledge in the Making* (Chicago: Univ. of Chicago Press, 1998); Friedrich Kittler, *Optical Media* (Cambridge: Polity Press, 2010); *Gramophone, Film, Typewriter* (Stanford: Stanford Univ. Press, 1999); John Durham Peters, *Speaking into the Air: A History of the Idea of Communication* (Chicago: Univ. of Chicago Press, 2001); *The Marvelous Clouds: Toward a Philosophy of Elemental Media* (Chicago: Univ. of Chicago, 2015).

134 Jan-Werner Müller refers to "the 'media democracy' or 'audience democracy' of our time (in which citizens engage in political activity primarily by watching the powerful)." *What Is Populism?* (London: Penguin Books, 2017), 43. Müller cites Bernard Manin, *The Principles of Representative Government* (New York: Cambridge Univ. Press, 1997) and Jeffrey Edward Green, *The Eyes of the People: Democracy in an Age of Spectatorship* (New York: Oxford Univ. Press, 2010). David Goodhart notes that contemporary citizens of Western democracies are now "far less likely to be a member of anything – church group, community group, charity club – they are often people whose social universe has shrunk to work, the family and the virtual reality of television, radio and the internet." *The Road to Somewhere: The New Tribes Shaping British Politics* (London: Penguin Books, 2017), 61.

135 Yascha Mounk, *The People vs. Democracy: Why Our Freedom Is in Danger and How to Save It* (Cambridge, MA: Harvard Univ. Press, 2018), 137–50; Goodhart, *The Road to Somewhere*, 58, 63–4.

136 Stuart Russell, *Human Compatible: Artificial Intelligence and the Problem of Control* (New York: Penguin 2020), 8–9, 105. See also Ned Desmond, "The Threat of Artificial Intelligence," *First Things*, no. 315 (August/September 2021), 39–43; Max Fisher and Amanda Taub, "On YouTube's Digital Playground, an Open Gate for Pedophiles," *New York Times*, 3 June 2019, https://www.nytimes.com/2019/06/03/world/americas/youtube -pedophiles.html; Kevin Roose, "The Making of a YouTube Radical," *New York Times*, 8 June 2019.

137 Steven Pinker, *Enlightenment Now: The Case for Reason, Science, Humanism, and Progress* (New York: Viking, 2018).

138 "Résultat: un 'nous' tribal et jouissant, constamment connecté et cherchant l'union perpétuelle avec les autres, dans une impression de *continuité*, s'oppose désormais au fondateur '*je pense donc je suis*.'" Claudia Attimontelli

and Vincenzo Susca, *Pornoculture: Voyage au bout de la chair*, translated into French by Jean-Luc Defromont (Montreal: Liber, 2017), quoted in Catherine Lalonde, "Je jouis donc je suis," *Le Devoir*, 28 February, 2017, A1, A8.

139 Michael J. Sandel, *What Money Can't Buy: The Moral Limits of Markets* (New York: Farrar, Straus & Giroux, 2012), 47; Louis Bernard, "À qui appartient ma vie?" *Le Devoir*, 30 January 2019, A6.

140 "[T]he more individualistic our society has become and the more assertive Americans have become about their rights, the more narrowly political discussion and legal discourse have revolved around the self." Mark Lilla, *The Once and Future Liberal: After Identity Politics* (New York: HarperCollins, 2018), 121.

141 Lilla, 134.

142 For an overview of the contemporary philosophical debate on the interconnection of the virtues, see the editors' "Introduction," in Kevin Timpe and Craig A. Boyd, eds., *Virtues and Their Vices* (Oxford: Oxford Univ. Press, 2014), 9–11.

143 The fourth-century Abba John the Little of Scetis in the Nile Delta said that "a man should have a little bit of all the virtues." John Colobus, *Apophthegmata Patrum*, 34, quoted in W. Harmless, *Desert Christians: An Introduction to the Literature of Early Monasticism* (Oxford: Oxford Univ. Press, 2004), 199–200, cited in Diarmaid MacCulloch, *Silence: A Christian History* (New York: Viking, 2013), 77.

144 See, for example: Scott Reid, "Have You No Shame? The True Crisis in Politics Is the Loss of Dignity," *Ottawa Citizen*, 14 December 2013, B1–2; Michael Den Tandt, "Mayor Ford Emblematic of the Moral Decline of Politics," *Ottawa Citizen*, 13 December 2013, A12; Stephen Maher, "A New Public Amorality: Ford's Antics Translate into Worldwide Fame," *Ottawa Citizen*, 28 December 2013, A7; Scott Gilmore, "In Praise of Shame," *Maclean's* 133, no. 1 (February 2020), 8–10.

145 At almost exactly the same time some of the columnists cited in the previous note were wringing their hands about the loss of morality and shame in political life, a *Globe and Mail* columnist suggested that a good way to deal with cyber-bullying through sexually explicit images would be for *everyone* to post photos of themselves naked – or even having sex – on the Web. Tabatha Southey, "What If Porn Couldn't Be Used for Revenge?" *Globe and Mail*, 7 December 2013, F3.

146 Angelina Chapin, "Society Slow to Accept Sexual Fluidity for Men," *Ottawa Citizen*, 28 December 2013, B6. Italian sociologist Vincenzo Susca, co-author (with Claudia Attimonelli) of a study of the mainstreaming of pornography in Western culture (*Pornoculture: Voyage au bout de la chair*, translated into French by Jean-Luc Defromont [Montreal: Liber, 2017]), speculates that, by lowering the thresholds of shame and shock, the new

Western "pornoculture" helped prepare the ground for the election of Donald Trump as president of the United States in 2016: "Trump, c'est le triomphe de la pensée du ventre." Lalonde, "Je jouis donc je suis," A1, A8. David Brooks makes the same connection between private and public morality: "Books will someday be written on how Trump, this wounded and twisted man, became morally acceptable to tens of millions of Americans. But it must have something to do with the way over the past decades we have divorced private and public morality, as if private narcissism would have no effect on public conduct." "The Essential John McCain," *New York Times*, 19 October 2017, https://www.nytimes.com/2017/10/19/opinion/the-essential-john-mccain.html?_r=0. On the inevitable "seepage" between public and private morality "and vice versa," see also Kronman, *Confessions of a Born-Again Pagan*, 80–2.

147 Edward O. Wilson notes that the fauna and flora of an ecosystem are "far more than collections of species. They are also a complex system of interactions, where the extinction of any species under certain conditions could have a profound impact on the whole." *The Meaning of Human Existence*, 125–6. Perhaps the same thing can be said about the virtues.

148 Edmund Burke, "Speech on Moving His Resolutions for Conciliation with the Colonies," in *Selected Writings and Speeches*, ed. Peter J. Stanlis (New York: Doubleday Anchor, 1963), 185; Hegel, *Philosophy of Right*, trans. Knox, addition to §268, p. 282.

149 Alan Wolfe, *The Future of Liberalism* (New York: Vintage Books, 2010), 91.

150 Steven D. Smith, *The Disenchantment of Secular Discourse* (Cambridge, MA: Harvard Univ. Press, 2010), 86, quoted in Brad S. Gregory, *The Unintended Reformation: How a Religious Revolution Revolutionized Society* (Cambridge, MA: Belknap Press of Harvard Univ. Press, 2012), 186. Gregory points out that this works in the other direction, too, and that the public influences the personal: "private and public life are inseparable in real life." Gregory, 186.

151 Rosalind Hursthouse reports on an unpublished (and apparently now "lost") paper by Timothy Chappell in which he inventories "(something like) thirty (!) versions of the doctrine of the unity of the virtues." *On Virtue Ethics*, 153n9.

152 Confucius, *The Analects*, trans. D.C. Lau (London: Penguin Books, 1979), 75; Aristotle, *Nicomachean Ethics* 6.11.1143a25–30, 6.13.1145a1–5, trans. Thomson, rev. Tredennick, 160, 166; Aquinas, *Summa Theologiæ* 1–2.65.1, in *Treatise on the Virtues*, trans. Oesterle, 140.

153 Plato, *The Laws*, 12:963–4, trans. Trevor J. Saunders (Harmondsworth: Penguin Books, 1970), 521–2.

154 Plato, *The Republic*, bk. 6, 484D–486B, in *Great Dialogues of Plato*, trans. Rouse, 283; Aristotle, *Nicomachean Ethics* 1.9.1100a5, 1.10.1101a15,

10.7.1177b25–6, trans. Thomson, rev. Tredennick, 21, 24, 272; Jung, *Analytical Psychology*, 149.

155 Even a virtue ethicist like Rosalind Hursthouse assumes the virtues necessarily entail "the idea that human nature is harmonious." *On Virtue Ethics*, 260.

156 N.T. Wright, *Surprised by Hope: Rethinking Heaven, the Resurrection and the Mission of the Church* (New York: HarperCollins, 2008), 102.

157 As Webb Keane remarks, "moral reasons can often be shown to serve the self through impression management or by defending a cultural worldview against challenges." *Ethical Life*, 70.

158 Murdoch, *The Sovereignty of Good*, 56, 67.

159 James Q. Wilson, *The Moral Sense*, 249.

160 Alexis de Tocqueville, *De la démocratie en Amérique* (Paris: Gallimard, 2007), 1:426.

161 Gilles Paquet, *Governance Through Social Learning* (Ottawa: Univ. of Ottawa Press, 1999), 242.

162 "[T]he acquisition and exercise of virtue can be seen to be in many ways like the acquisition and exercise of many mundane activities, such as farming, building or playing the piano ... but the result is not routine but the kind of actively and intelligently engaged practical mastery that we find in practical experts such as pianists and athletes." Julia Annas, *Intelligent Virtue* (Oxford: Oxford Univ. Press, 2013), 1, 14. On practice (or exercise) and virtue, see also Aristotle, *The Nicomachean Ethics* 3.5.1114a5–10, trans. Thomson, rev. Tredennick, 63; Karl Rahner, *The Practice of Faith: A Handbook of Contemporary Spirituality*, trans. various (New York: Crossroad, 1983), 56, 256. Ari L. Goldman, *Being Jewish: The Spiritual and Cultural Practice of Judaism Today* (New York: Simon & Schuster, 2000), 207–8.

163 "Becoming virtuous requires habituation and experience. We encounter habituation first through our education, both in school and in the family. We are not just told what to do but given role models and encouraged to act in ways that promote and show appreciation of loyalty and bravery. ... We are trained and formed through being habituated to act in loyal and brave ways, and to respond positively to presentations of loyalty and bravery." Annas, 12.

164 Paquet, *Governance through Social Learning*, 239.

165 Scheler, *Formalism in Ethics*, trans. Frings and Funk, 64; Iris Murdoch, *Metaphysics as a Guide to Morals* (London: Vintage, 2003), 351–2, 355, 365–9, 379–81, 390–1, 483.

166 Murdoch, *Metaphysics as a Guide to Morals*, 367. Emphasis added. Maurice Blondel calls this the "normative des êtres": "pour elle ce qui est repoussé n'est pas supprimé par là même." *L'Être et les êtres*, 257–8.

167 Wolfe, *The Future of Liberalism*, 23. Wolfe implicitly acknowledges his "two other kinds of liberalism" are really echoes of the *other* side of the human paradox when he recognizes that "temperamental [A2] and procedural [B1] liberalism are as valuable to everyone, whatever their views, as substantive liberalism [i.e., Liberty (A1) and Equality (B2)] is and ought to be contentious." He also acknowledges the virtues of reverence when he recognizes that liberalism "may not contain the whole truth" and that it is therefore necessary to "incorporate ideas from the *other side* if they contain something of value." Wolfe, xviii, 20. Emphasis added.

168 Edmund Fawcett, *Liberalism: The Life of an Idea* (Princeton: Princeton Univ. Press, 2014), 342, 199.

169 Deirdre N. McCloskey, *The Bourgeois Virtues: Ethics for an Age of Commerce* (Chicago: Univ. of Chicago Press, 2006), 507–8.

170 Adam Gopnik, *A Thousand Small Sanities: The Moral Adventure of Liberalism* (New York: Basic Books, 2019), 6, 13, 18–20, 25, 80, 113. The words quoted are on page 19.

171 The moral genius of Charles Péguy could already see, in 1910, that the sacrifice of one man for *raisons d'État*, in the Dreyfus affair, could potentially lead to the sacrifice of a whole people, in the Holocaust. *Notre Jeunesse* (Paris: Gallimard, 1993), 274. See also his horrified comments ten years earlier on the Armenian genocide and the crimes of colonialism. *Encore de la grippe*, in *Une éthique sans compromis*, 286–7.

172 Hildebrand, *Ethics*, 487.

173 Hegel, *Encyclopaedia*, trans. Wallace, §119, p. 174.

174 Samuel Taylor Coleridge, *Aids to Reflection* (Port Washington, NY: Kennikat Press, 1971), 223. "[L]'un-pour-l'autre ... étranger au Dit de l'être, s'y montre comme contradiction." Levinas, *Autrement qu'être*, 213.

175 Gopnik, *A Thousand Small Sanities*, 13.

176 Isaiah, Berlin, "The Question of Machiavelli," *The New York Review of Books*, 4 November 1971, http://www.nybooks.com/articles/archives/1971/nov/04/a-special-supplement-the-question-of-machiavelli/; "The Decline of Utopian Ideas in the West," in *The Crooked Timber of Humanity: Chapters in the History of Ideas*, ed. Henry Hardy (London: Fontana Press, 1991), 31.

177 "Any codification ranking the virtues ... is bound to come up against cases where we will want to change the rankings." Hursthouse, *On Virtue Ethics*, 57.

178 Charles Taylor, *Sources of the Self: The Making of Modern Identity* (Cambridge: Harvard Univ. Press, 1989), 89.

179 Richard M. Rorty, "The Priority of Democracy to Philosophy," in *The Rorty Reader*, ed. Christopher J. Voparil and Richard J. Bernstein (Chichester: Wiley-Blackwell, 2010), 239–58.

180 Thomas Aquinas, *Summa Theologiæ* 1–2.18.5, 1–2.18.9, 1–2.18.11, in *Treatise on Happiness*, trans. Oesterle, 167, 173, 178; Hursthouse, *On Virtue Ethics*, 211–12.

181 "[The] two ideals of perfection which diverge [i.e., self-assertion and "self-sacrifice," i.e., reverence] [are] equally good. It is only the particular conditions which in each case can decide between them." F.H. Bradley, *Appearance and Reality* (Oxford: Oxford Univ. Press, 1930), 370–1. On the need to "take account of the necessary situatedness" of moral, cultural, and institutional claims, see Joas, *The Sacredness of the Person*, 128.

182 This approach to moral decision-making is sometimes called "consequentialism," a form of utilitarianism. See Walter Sinnott-Armstrong, "Consequentialism," The Stanford Encyclopedia of Philosophy, ed. Edward N. Zalta (Winter 2015 Edition), https://plato.stanford.edu/archives/win2015/entries/consequentialism/.

183 "Le monde contemporain, scientifique, technique et jouisseur, se voit sans issue – c'est à dire sans Dieu – non pas parce que tout est permis et, par la technique, possible, mais parce que tout y est *égal*." Levinas, *De Dieu qui vient à l'idée*, 31. Emphasis added. Paul Ricœur suggests that "estime de soi" is necessarily bound up with "la hiérarchisation de nos actions." *Lectures 1*, in *Ricœur: Textes choisis et présentés*, 313.

184 Charles Norris Cochrane, *Christianity and Classical Culture* (New York: Oxford Univ. Press, 1976).

185 "Bien des progrès ont été réalisés ainsi, concernant avant tout le monde de la réflexivité et la *prise de conscience de soi* ... Le malheur de l'histoire moderne a été que ce processus ... s'est accompli non pas sous le signe de l'unité, mais sous le signe de la division." Maritain, *Humanisme intégral*, 34–5. Emphasis in original.

186 Ernst Troeltsch, *Historicism and Its Problems*, quoted in Joas, *The Sacredness of the Person*, 123. On the importance of this kind "progress," see also Martin E.P. Seligman, *Authentic Happiness: Using the New Positive Psychology to Realize Your Potential for Lasting Fulfilment* (New York: Free Press, 2002), 260; Martin, *On Secularization*, 6.

187 "I believe that the very possibility of such a [just] social order can itself reconcile us to the social world. ... [W]e can reasonably hope that we or others will someday, somewhere, achieve it; and we can do something toward this achievement. This alone, quite apart from our success or failure, suffices to banish the dangers of resignation and cynicism." John Rawls, *The Law of Peoples* (Cambridge, MA: Harvard Univ. Press, 1999), 128, cited in Susan Neiman, *Evil in Modern Thought: An Alternative History of Philosophy* (Princeton: Princeton Univ. Press, 2002), 314.

188 Richard Rorty wants to retain Hegel's emphasis on the "irreducible temporality" of culture and thought while jettisoning his assumption that

history has a meaning or direction or goal. Richard M. Rorty, "Trotsky and the Wild Orchids," in *The Rorty Reader*, 505.

189 "A deep understanding of any field of activity … involves an increasing revelation of degrees of excellence. … Increasing understanding of human conduct operates in a similar way. We come to perceive scales, distances, standards … The idea of perfection works thus within a field of study, producing an increasing sense of direction. … As we deepen our notions of the virtues, we introduce relationship and hierarchy." Murdoch, *The Sovereignty of Good*, 61–2, 95. As her title suggests, Murdoch often seems to thinks the virtues of Excellence (B1), especially Goodness (B1b) stand at the apex of the hierarchy of virtues. But occasionally she seems to acknowledge, instead, that the "supreme principle in the united world of the virtues … is love [A2b]." Murdoch, 57.

190 Plato, *The Laws*, 1:631, trans. Trevor J. Saunders, 55; Aristotle, *Nicomachean Ethics* 1.7.1098a15–20, 10.6.1177a1–10.7.1177a25, trans. Thomson, rev. Tredennick, 16, 269–70; Aquinas, *Summa Theologiæ* 1–2.59.2, 1–2.59.5, in *Treatise on the Virtues*, trans. Oesterle, 90–2, 95–6; G.W. Leibniz, *Essais de Théodicée* (Paris: Garnier-Flammarion, 1969), §8, p. 108; Bradley, *Appearance and Reality*, 355; Maurice Blondel, *Itinéraire philosophique*, 24, in Jean Lacroix, *Maurice Blondel, sa vie, son œuvre* (Paris: Presses Universitaires de France, 1963), 135. Max Scheler suggests some five criteria for determining the hierarchy of values. *Formalism in Ethics*, trans. Frings and Funk, 90–100.

191 "Le paradoxe serait résolu si l'on trouvait un principe de hiérarchie tel que les finalités soient en quelque sorte incluses les unes dans les autres, le supérieur étant comme l'excès de l'inférieur." Ricœur, *Soi-même comme un autre*, 203. Ricœur suggests Aristotle's theory of the virtues does not succeed in establishing such a hierarchy.

192 "A higher category [of "contrast," i.e., paradox] involves unplumbed potentiality for the realization of depth in its lower components." Whitehead, *Process and Reality*, 132.

193 The "gentle rain" is, of course, a phrase not from Aquinas but from William Shakespeare, *The Merchant of Venice*, in *The Complete Works*, ed. Alfred Harbage (Baltimore: Penguin Books, 1969), 4.1.183.

194 Susanne K. Langer, *Mind: An Essay on Human Feeling*, vol. 1 (Baltimore: Johns Hopkins Press, 1967), 326.

195 Aquinas, *Summa Theologiæ* 1–2.57.3, in *Treatise on the Virtues*, trans. Oesterle, 72.

196 Aquinas, *Summa Theologiæ* 1–2.59.5, 1–2.61.4, in *Treatise on the Virtues*, trans. Oesterle, 96, 114. Emphasis added. Aquinas' image of overflowing seems to have been borrowed from the Neoplatonism of Pseudo-Dionysius, but given a new meaning. Étienne Gilson, *The Elements of Christian*

Philosophy (New York: Mentor, 1963), 211. Ironically, Friedrich Nietzsche expresses the same idea as Aquinas – the entrainment or perfection of the passions by the virtues – and even uses the same image of "overflowing." *Thus Spoke Zarathustra*, trans. R.J. Hollingdale (Harmondsworth: Penguin Books, 1969), 64; *Beyond Good and Evil*, trans. R.J. Hollingdale (London: Penguin Books, 2003), §260, pp. 195–6.

197 Hegel seems to express exactly the same idea as Aquinas' concept of "perfecting" or "overflowing" when he distinguishes between purely "formal," abstract, and negative freedom on the one hand, and true, positive, or concrete freedom on the other; or when he contrasts merely "natural and finite" subjectivity [A1] with true and "infinite" subjectivity [A2]; or when he talks about the necessary coincidence of freedom and necessity. Or when he says, for example: "A good man is aware that the tenor of his conduct is absolutely necessary. ... [M]an is most independent [A1] when he knows himself to be determined by the absolute idea [the whole human paradox] throughout." Hegel, *Encyclopaedia*, trans. Wallace, §157, p. 220.

198 Emmanuel Levinas sums up the hierarchy (and "arrow") of virtue in a single sentence: "*Sous les espèces* de la relation avec l'autre homme [A2b] ... arrivent une transcendance [A2a], une sortie de l'être [B1] et ainsi l'*impartialité* elle-même [B2b] par laquelle, notamment sera possible la science dans son objectivité [B2a] et l'humanité en guise de moi [A1]." Levinas, *De Dieu qui vient à l'idée*, 26. Emphasis in original. Martin Heidegger also captures the whole flight of the arrow of virtue in one sentence: "Entangled [A1], attuned [A2] understanding [B1] articulates itself ... in discourse [B2]." *Being and Time*, 335, trans. Stambaugh, 321. Hegel does so almost as succinctly. Starting from the "natural man, whose motions follow the rule only of his appetites" (A1), the human spirit, Hegel argues, develops through the stages of "immediate knowledge," which includes "everything which the moralists term innocence as well as religious feeling, simple trust, love, fidelity, and natural faith" (i.e., A2), then "reflection" or understanding (B1), and, finally, "philosophical cognition" or reason (B2). Hegel, *Encyclopaedia*, trans. Wallace, §24, pp. 39, 42.

199 What I am here calling the "reverse" or teleological order of the arrow of virtue (i.e., A1→B2→B1→A2) might also be called the arrow of cognition. In the Western philosophical tradition since Aristotle – and in general Western intellectual culture since Locke and Hume – the "reverse" or cognitive order is the order in which the human mind is assumed to work. In this Western empirical realist tradition, the self-asserting ego (A1) is assumed to encounter and derive sense data from an objective, phenomenal world of things (B2), from which it extracts generalizations, ideas, and universals (B1), of which some of the truths (B1a), may be

truths about goodness (B1b), including, possibly, the truth about the goodness of love and generosity (A2). In the Western arrow of cognition, truth (B1a) is assumed to come *before* goodness (B1b), as it does for Aquinas. But in the arrow of virtue, goodness (B1b) comes before truth (B1a), and founds its very truth in the prior virtues of self-giving love (A2). Paraphrasing Aquinas, Étienne Gilson accurately identifies the contrasting directions of the arrows of virtue and cognition: "In the order of being, the existential act [I am] comes first; in the order of quiddities [It is], what comes first is the intellect, along with intellectual knowledge [B2 & B1]." *The Elements of Christian Philosophy*, 303. The problem for the arrow of cognition (and for the Western intellectual tradition since Locke) is the wide gulf between knowledge and love, which is much more difficult to cross (or is even disdained) in the order of the arrow of cognition than in the order of the arrow of virtue. The "reverse" or cognitive order is the correct, rational, hierarchical order of values. But without the prior impulse and insight of spontaneous, self-giving generosity, it can't supply the motivational power that can turn knowledge into love. Nor teach the goodness and truth revealed by love. The surer way is to start from love (A2b). And from the love of Love (A2a). Perhaps that's why the arrow of virtue, not the arrow of cognition, is the actual genetic and historical order, both in our individual lives (ontogenetic) and in the history of the human race (phylogenetic). A successful childhood is a long apprenticeship in reverence, establishing the emotional and moral base for sound adult cognition.

200 "[The] error does not lie in ... attributing a positive value to pleasure; it lies, rather, in ... putting this value in the wrong rank in the order of values." Scheler, *Formalism in Ethics*, trans. Frings and Funk, 253.

201 Hegel, *The Phenomenology of Mind*, trans. Baillie, 607–10; *Philosophy of Right*, trans. Knox, §§5, 135, pp. 21–2, 89–90.

202 Murdoch, *Metaphysics as a Guide to Morals*, 507. "Freedom, we find out, is not an inconsequential chucking of one's weight about, it is the disciplined *overcoming of self*." *The Sovereignty of Good*, 95. Emphasis added.

203 Marilynne Robinson, *The Death of Adam: Essays on Modern Thought* (New York: Picador, 2005), 91; Terry Eagleton, *Reason, Faith, and Revolution: Reflections on the God Debate* (New Haven: Yale Univ. Press, 2009), 92. "An unthinking reverence for Reason ... helped make all of those overarching systems that claimed to be reasonable but that crushed human beings with them." Gopnik, *A Thousand Small Sanities*, 35. Bernard Williams refers, for example, to William Godwin's "ferociously rational refusal to respect any consideration that an ordinary human being would find compelling." *Ethics and the Limits of Philosophy* (Cambridge, MA: Harvard Univ. Press, 1985), 107.

204 Whitehead, *Process and Reality*, 287–90; Heidegger, "Bremen Lectures," trans. Veith, 266, 268; *Being and Time*, 252, 260, trans. Stambaugh, 244, 249.

205 Ricœur, *Le conflit des interprétations*, 297–8.

206 Paul Ricœur calls this step "un recours aux ressources encore inexplorées de l'éthique [B1], en deçà de la morale [B2]." *Soi-même comme un autre*, 406.

207 "[T]hough justice as a virtue is primarily concerned with respecting status and honouring (legitimate) rules and procedures, rules and procedures have to be made and interpreted, and making and interpreting them with a loving eye will enhance or 'perfect' justice." Swanton, *Virtue Ethics*, 116.

208 Both Coleridge and Franz Rosenzweig present their versions of the four families of virtues in the reverse or teleological order of the arrow of virtue, or the order of the arrow of cognition (i.e., A1→B2→B1→A2) rather than in the genetic order (i.e., A1→A2→B1→B2). Coleridge, *Aids to Reflection*; Rosenzweig, *The Star of Redemption*, trans. Hallo, 242–3, 260, 306.

209 Evelyn Underhill calls this feature of the hierarchy of virtues "the radiance that pours down from the Upper story." *The Fruits of the Spirit*, ed. Roger L. Roberts (Harrisburg, PA: Morehouse, 2010), 39.

210 "Love, therefore, is first … It is the alpha and omega of all virtue. … Had love not preceded morality, would we know anything of morality at all? And what does morality offer that might be better than the love from which it arises, the love that it lacks and that both drives and attracts it? That which makes morality possible is also that toward which it tends and that frees it." Comte-Sponville, *A Small Treatise*, trans. Temerson, 226. "[O]nly love can bring about complete unity, unifying what is different in love and … unifying the personality." Søren Kierkegaard, *Spiritual Writings*, trans. George Pattison (New York, HarperCollins, 2010), 169. Robert Nozick expresses how (what I call) the virtues of Reverence (A2) stand at the top of the hierarchy of value by calling this "fourth stance" (of "I am") the "combined stance." It "unites the previous three stances in a mutually reinforcing way." *The Examined Life* (New York: Simon & Schuster, 1990), 158–61.

211 Christine Swanton agrees that love isn't a virtue which "trumps all other virtues." But she seems to think her view (shared with Aquinas) that love is "a part of the profiles of all virtue" precludes seeing love as a "separate and dominating virtue … at the top of a hierarchy," which "may come into conflict with other virtues." *Virtue Ethics*, 100–1. Neither of these views precludes the other.

212 Max Scheler agrees that the families of virtues (or what he calls "value modalities") have an "a priori order of ranks," and he largely agrees with the teleological or moral order of hierarchy suggested in this

chapter – with one exception: he reverses the order of his first two (A1a and A1b) and puts the virtues of Power (A1a), or what he calls "vital" values, "*higher*" in the hierarchy than the virtues of Pleasure (A1b), or what he calls "sensible" values. *Formalism in Ethics*, trans. Frings and Funk, 110. This does not make sense to me, from either the genetic or the teleological viewpoint. As Dietrich von Hildebrand suggests, "pride" (A1a) is the greatest "antithesis to charity [A2b]," greater even than concupiscence (A1b). *Ethics*, 461.

213 Max Scheler suggests it is the virtues of Reverence (A2), and the virtues of Love (A2b), in particular, that move (what I have called) the "arrow of virtue" forward and disclose or "create" new virtues. Scheler, 261. Adam Gopnik agrees: "The secret truth is that what we are having most of the time is the same reform, over and over again, directed to new places and people ... Our circles of compassion enlarge." *A Thousand Small Sanities*, 47. So does Martin: *On Secularization*, 11.

214 "Nothing is in fact more important for moral growth, for the very moral life of the person, than consideration for the objective hierarchy of values, and the capacity to give priority to that which is ontologically higher." Hildebrand, *Fundamental Moral Attitudes*, 29. Hildebrand suggests the hierarchy is established by the degree of "self-donation" (self-giving) in the virtue. Which is why love stands at the pinnacle of the hierarchy of virtues. *Ethics*, 371–6.

215 Bellah, *Religion in Human Evolution*, 166–7, 224, 531. In a similar vein, Alan Wolfe suggests that "government" is a "synonym for civilization." *The Future of Liberalism*, 229.

216 Joseph A. Tainter, *The Collapse of Complex Societies* (Cambridge: Cambridge Univ. Press, 2017), 41. For a review of classical and contemporary social science approaches to the definition of civilization, see Tainter, 39–90.

217 Niall Fergusson, *Civilization: The West and the Rest* (New York: Penguin Press, 2011), 1–8.

218 Ian Morris, *The Measure of Civilization: How Social Development Decides the Fate of Nations* (Princeton: Princeton Univ. Press, 2013), 3. Morris' longer definition is: "the bundle of technological, subsistence, organizational, and cultural accomplishments through which people feed, clothe, house, and reproduce themselves, explain the world around them, resolve disputes within their communities, extend their power at the expense of other communities, and defend themselves against others' attempts to extend their power." Morris, 5. Morris seems to use "civilization" and "social development" as equivalent terms.

219 Morris comes down "strongly on the materialist side" in the running debate on the relative importance of material and cultural forces in shaping

history. Just as one would expect him to do, from this perspective. Morris, 253.

220 "La question est pour nous de savoir si ces nouvelles civilisations ... méritent ici et là le nom de civilisations *humaines*, c'est-à-dire qui atteignent le cœur même de l'homme ... pour y susciter de stables formations de vertus, et pour créer dans la conscience et dans la société des structures vitales et progressives." Maritain, *Humanisme intégral*, 285. Emphasis in original.

221 Terry Eagleton, *Culture and the Death of God* (New Haven: Yale Univ. Press, 2014), 183. Jacques Maritain also combines both the functional and normative definitions. For him, "civilization" has "two poles," combining both "le développement matériel" and "le développement moral." *Humanisme intégral*, 102–3.

222 Even when it yearns for something more (like altruism), the only standard or test a purely functional or evolutionary perspective can use to assess something (without recourse to final causes or goods) is, in the end, that "it caused some groups to outcompete other groups." David Sloan Wilson, *Does Altruism Exist? Culture, Genes, and the Welfare of Others* (New Haven: Yale Univ. Press, 2015), 114. From the purely evolutionary perspective, winning is everything, and it might well be the barbarians or authoritarians who win the "Darwinian contest," in the end. But being truly human requires another higher standard, one that remains unvanquished, even if they do.

223 R.G. Collingwood, *The New Leviathan* (London: Oxford Univ. Press, 1942).

224 Plato, *Meno* 75B–76D, in *Great Dialogues of Plato*, trans. Rouse, 34.

225 Collingwood, *The New Leviathan*, 181.

226 G.W.F Hegel, *Preface to the Phenomenology of Spirit*, trans. Yirmiyahu Yovel (Princeton: Princeton Univ. Press, 2005), 192.

227 Hegel, *The Phenomenology of Mind*, trans. Baillie, 127. Emphasis added.

228 Hegel, 306. On the priority of the question over the response, see also Levinas, *De Dieu qui vient à l'idée*, 136–8. For Levinas, the priority of the question reveals the priority of the virtues of reverence over rational consciousness: it reveals the birth of the latter in "le Désir de l'Infini." *De l'existence à l'existant* (Paris: Vrin, 2013), 12.

229 Charles Freeman, *The Closing of the Western Mind: The Rise of Faith and the Fall of Reason* (London: Pimlico, 2003), 340. Also: 11–13, 314, 348.

230 Merlin Donald, *A Mind So Rare: The Evolution of Human Consciousness* (New York: W.W. Norton, 2001), 290, 288.

231 Gadamer said Collingwood was "almost the only person I could find a link with here." Hans-Georg Gadamer, *Truth and Method*, trans. and rev. Joel Weinsheimer and Donald G. Marshall, 2nd rev. ed. (New York: Continuum, 2002), 370. Gadamer was especially influenced by the "logic of question

and answer" developed in Collingwood's brief intellectual autobiography. *An Autobiography* (London: Oxford Univ. Press, 1939), 29–43. He was apparently unaware that the same dialectical perspective had been richly developed in Collingwood's unfinished masterpiece, *The New Leviathan.*

232 Webb Keane makes much the same point about ethical life: "Justifications start in media res: they reflect back on an ethical life that is already in motion." Keane, *Ethical Life*, 249.

233 Gadamer, *Truth and Method*, trans. Weinsheimer and Marshall, 377–9. Emphasis added. "Thus commitment to the conversation easily becomes commitment to the other person." Keane, *Ethical Life*, 109. Gadamer's emphasis on the determining influence of culture on the human mind is fully supported by Merlin Donald's theory of human cognition, with its emphasis on "enculturation." *A Mind So Rare*, 150–1.

234 To achieve any real insight, you have to have what George Pattison calls "hermeneutical generosity": "that is, the willingness to enter into worlds of thought and experience other than your own with the assumption that they will prove to be humanly important testimonies." "Foreword," in Kierkegaard, *Spiritual Writings*, trans. Pattison, xvi. "Generosity" is a virtue of Reverence (A2). This means therefore that the cognitive virtues depend on prior virtues of reverence, such as generosity.

235 Charles Taylor, *Dilemmas and Connections: Selected Essays* (Cambridge, MA: Belknap Press of Harvard Univ. Press, 2011), 37.

236 Levinas, "Quelques réflexions sur la philosophie de l'hitlérisme," in *Les Imprévus de l'histoire*, 23–33. Also : "De la déficience sans souci au sens nouveau," in *De Dieu qui vient à l'idée*, 77–89.

237 "Tous les actes de langage … engagent leur locateur, par une clause tacite de sincérité en vertu de laquelle je signifie effectivement ce que je dis." Ricœur, *Du texte à l'action*, in *Ricœur : Textes choisis et présentés*, 393. "[L]a sincérité ou la véracité que l'échange d'informations … suppose déjà. … La sincérité n'est pas un attribut du Dire; c'est le Dire qui accomplit la sincérité, inséparable du donner." Levinas, *Autrement qu'être*, 148, 224.

238 "[T]echnical devices of conversational interaction and coordination seem to involve social commitments. … [M]orality [is] a very basic presupposition of ordinary interaction, the mere expectation that others are cooperative." Keane, *Ethical Life*, 100–1. "The institutionalization of rational argument itself – in parliament, in public political debate, in the scientific seminar or conference – also remains dependent on an emotional commitment to values and practices." Joas, *The Sacredness of the Person*, 57.

239 "[U]ne philosophie du dialogue … ne peut pas ne pas être une éthique." Levinas, *Altérité et transcendance*, 108.

240 "Le Dire qui énonce un Dit est dans le sensible la première 'activité' qui arrête ceci comme cela; mais cette activité d'arrêt et de jugement, de

thématisation et de théorie, survient dans le *Dire* en tant que pur 'pour Autrui,' pur donation de signe à Autrui (langage d'avant le Dit)." Levinas, *Autrement qu'être*, 101.

241 Although Levinas aims to reverse the priority Hegel gave to thought, Hegel himself actually seems to make a very similar point: "[I]n speech the self-existent singleness of self-consciousness comes as such into existence, so that its particular individuality is something *for others.*" Hegel, *The Phenomenology of Mind*, trans. Baillie, 530. Emphasis added.

242 "C'est ma responsabilité pour l'autre qui est le *pour* de la relation, la signifiance même de la signification laquelle signifie dans le *Dire* avant de se montrer dans le *Dit*. *L'un-pour-l'autre* – c'est-à-dire la signifiance même de la signification! ... [S]ignifiance distincte de la fameuse 'donation de sens,' puisque la signification c'est cette relation même avec le prochain, l'un-pour-l'autre." Levinas, *Autrement qu'être*, 158–9.

243 "[L]a subordination de la volonté à l'impersonnelle raison, au *discours en soi* – aux lois écrites, exige le *discours en tant que rencontre d'homme à homme.*" Levinas, *Liberté et commandement*, 57. Emphasis added. From an evolutionary perspective, Merlin Donald agrees: "[T]he emergence of language could not have been an end in itself ... The first priority was not to speak, use words, or develop grammars. It was to bond as a group, to learn to share attention and set up social patterns that would sustain sharing and bonding in the species." *A Mind So Rare*, 253.

244 "Le logos thématisant, le Dire disant un dit ... procède de ce Dire pré-originel, cet antérieure à toute civilisation et à tout commencement dans la langue parlée de la signification. ... Mais d'autre part 'le faire signe' dans le monde où se parle objectivement une langue ... doit percer le mur du sens *dit* pour retourner à cet *en-deçà de la civilisation.*" Levinas, *Autrement qu'être*, 224n1–2. Emphasis in original.

245 Vasily Grossman, *Life and Fate*, trans. Robert Chandler (New York: New York Review Books, 2006), 407–10. Emphasis added.

246 Levinas, *Altérité et transcendance*, 116–18; *Entre nous*, 242.

247 Iain Pears, *The Dream of Scipio* (Toronto: Alfred A. Knopf, 2002), 370–1, 124, 89, 367, 381, 140.

248 Terestchenko, *Un si fragile vernis d'humanité*, 207–22, 255–64, 270–3.

249 Hannah Arendt, *Eichmann in Jerusalem: A Report on the Banality of Evil* (New York: Penguin Books, 1994). "Much existentialist thought relies upon ... a 'thinking reed' reaction which is nothing more than a form of romantic self-assertion. It is not this which will lead a man to unselfish behaviour in the concentration camp." Murdoch, *The Sovereignty of Good*, 73.

250 Terestchenko, *Un si fragile vernis d'humanité*, 225–9. "Quand l'esprit d'un people est perverti au point de nourrir un *Sittlichkeit* meurtrière, c'est finalement dans la conscience morale d'un petit nombre d'individus,

inaccessibles à la peur et à la corruption, que se réfugie l'esprit qui a déserté des institutions devenues criminelles." Ricœur, *Soi-même comme un autre*, 298. Second emphasis added. Ricœur makes the same point by contrasting Husserl and Levinas. For Ricœur, Husserl represents the pole of "*I* am" (A1), the movement that proceeds *from the self*, toward the Other; Levinas represents the pole of "I *am*" (A2) the movement *from the Other* toward the self. The latter is the truly "ethical" pole, the pole that "calls" or *commands*. But the other pole, the pole that responds – and *acts* – is just as important for a truly *human* life. Without a welcoming, effective, self-assertive response, the ethical "call" or command of reverence would be unavailing. It would fall on dry ground and have no result. Ricœur, 198, 382, 390–3.

251 Anxiety disorders are the most common mental illness in the US, affecting 40 million adults in the United States, or 18.1 per cent of the population. Depression is the leading cause of disability in the United States among people ages 15–44. https://adaa.org/about-adaa/press-room /facts-statistics. Other than accidents, suicide is the leading cause of death for Americans between the ages 10–34. https://www.cdc.gov/injury /wisqars/pdf/leading_causes_of_death_by_age_group_2016–508.pdf. In January 2020, the World Health Organization recognized that depression is a leading cause of disability worldwide and a major contributor to the overall global burden of disease. https://www.who.int/news-room /fact-sheets/detail/depression.

252 I think this is actually what an evolutionary theorist like David Sloan Wilson means when he argues for "altruism" and "prosociality" and suggests "we must choose policies with the welfare of the whole world in mind." *Does Altruism Exist?*, 149. However, Wilson's argument involves a hidden but decisive shift (as in so many works by sociobiologists) *from efficient to final causes*. "Intentional" selection is a *final* cause, fundamentally different in kind from the *efficient* cause of "natural" selection on which evolutionary theory is based (although the latter can involve the former, as Wilson, Boehm and others have shown). Therefore "welfare," like all other human goods, is a fundamentally paradoxical and *contestable* concept. In fact, it involves the whole human paradox. The "welfare of the whole world" might even be said to be the ultimate human paradox.

253 "La rencontre de l'autre est la grande expérience ou le grand événement. ... l'apparition possible d'une absurdité ontologique: le souci d'autrui l'emportant sur le souci de soi. ... Notre humanité consiste à pouvoir reconnaître cette priorité de l'autre. ... C'est l'éveil originel d'un 'je' responsable d'autrui, l'accession de ma personne à l'unicité du 'je' appelé et élu à la responsabilité pour autrui. Le 'je' humain n'est pas une unité close sur soi, telle l'unicité de l'atome, mais une ouverture,

celle de la responsabilité, qui est le vrai commencement de l'humain et de la spiritualité. Dans l'appel que m'adresse le visage de l'autre homme, je saisis de façon immédiate les grâces de l'amour: la spiritualité, le vécu de l'humanité authentique. ... Il s'agit là de notre première expérience, celle-là même qui nous constitue, qui est comme le fond de notre existence. D'ailleurs, aussi indifférent qu'on se prétende, on ne peut croiser un visage sans le saluer, ou sans se dire 'Que va-t-il me demander?' Non seulement notre vie personnelle est fondée là-dessus, *mais aussi toute la civilisation.* " Levinas, *Les Imprévus de l'histoire*, 178–83. Emphasis added.

254 Maritain, *Humanisme intégral*, 143. Another reason is that "virtue itself is an essentially developmental notion." Annas, *Intelligent Virtue*, 38–40.

255 "Transition into something else is the dialectical process within the range of Being." Hegel, *Encyclopaedia*, trans. Wallace, §161, p. 224.

256 "So souls must go, but rights must stay ... But there is no reason to think that rights are more than useful fictions if one believes that metaphysical naturalism is true. In this case there are no grounds for believing there is anything to violate, whatever might happen to be illegal." Gregory, *The Unintended Reformation*, 226.

257 Steven Pinker, *The Better Angels of Our Nature* (New York: Penguin, 2012); James R. Flynn, *What Is Intelligence? Beyond the Flynn Effect*, expanded ed. (Cambridge: Cambridge Univ. Press, 2009).

258 Robert D. Putnam, *Bowling Alone: The Collapse and Revival of American Community* (New York: Simon & Schuster, 2000); Robert D. Putnam with Shaylyn Romney Garrett, *The Upswing: How America Came Together a Century Ago and How We Can Do It Again* (New York: Simon & Schuster, 2020); Daniel T. Rodgers, *Age of Fracture* (Cambridge, MA: Harvard Univ. Press, 2011).

259 The words are from swashbuckling MP F.E. Smith's notorious rectorial address to the University of Glasgow on 7 November 1923, quoted in Paul Johnson, "The Age of Stout Hearts and Sharp Swords – and Fun," *The Spectator*, 15 April 2006, 36.

260 The ethos and the words are those of novelist Simon Raven, quoted in Michael Barber, "Simon Raven: Caddish Chronicler of Upper-Class Life," *Guardian Weekly*, 24–30 May 2001, 10.

261 Deirdre Blair, *Calling It Quits: Late-Life Divorce and Starting Over* (New York: Random House, 2007), quoted in Anne Kingston, "The 27-Year Itch," *Maclean's* 120, no. 3 (29 January 2007), 42. https://archive.macleans.ca/article/2007/1/29/the-27year-itch.

262 Aquinas, *Summa Theologiæ* 1–2.1.2–6, in *Treatise on Happiness*, trans. Oesterle, 5–12.

263 Zosia Bielski, "Universe Me," *Globe and Mail*, 1 June 2010, L1 & L3.

264 Mounk, *The People vs. Democracy*, 100, 105–6.

265 Russian novelist Eugene Vodolazkin dresses up the new authoritarianism as an "age of concentration" and a "new Middle Ages." "The Age of Concentration," *First Things*, no. 274 (June/July 2017), 33–8. See also Jason Brennan, *Against Democracy* (Princeton: Princeton Univ. Press, 2016); John Micklethwait and Adrian Wooldridge, *The Fourth Revolution: The Global Race to Invent the State* (New York: Penguin, 2014), 133–66. On the "new authoritarians," see Michael Ignatieff, "Are the Authoritarians Winning?" *New York Review of Books* 61, no. 12 (10 July 2014), 53–5.

266 Daniel A. Bell, *The China Model: Political Meritocracy and the Limits of Democracy* (Princeton: Princeton Univ. Press, 2015). For a review and critical discussion, see Stein Ringen, "Is Chinese Autocracy Outperforming Western Democracy?" Open Democracy, 12 June 2015, https://www .opendemocracy.net/stein-ringen/is-chinese-autocracy-outperforming -western-democracy.

267 6Medias, "Poutine, Chine, la démocratie … La vision de Nicolas Sarkozy," *Le Point International*, 10 March 2018, https://www.lepoint.fr /monde/poutine-chine-democratie-la-vision-du-monde-de-nicolas -sarkozy-10-03-2018-2201298_24.php.

268 Mounk, *The People vs. Democracy*, 109–10. A March 2018 study for the Democracy Fund Voter Study Group found that, while American support for "army rule" has increased steadily over the past 20 years, support for a strong leader actually declined for the first time in 2017, returning to 1995 levels. The authors speculate that the decline in support for a strong leader may reflect the fact that "Donald Trump has personified authoritarian leadership in a way many Americans found distasteful." Lee Drutman, Larry Diamond, and Joe Goldman, *Follow the Leader: Exploring American Support for Democracy and Authoritarianism*, Washington: Democracy Fund Voter Study Group, March 2018, https://www.voterstudygroup .org/publications/2017-voter-survey/follow-the-leader.

269 Thomas Hobbes, *Leviathan* (Indianapolis: Bobbs-Merrill, 1958), pt. 2, chap. 21, p. 173.

270 Peter Thiel, "The Education of a Libertarian," Cato Unbound, 13 April 2009, http://www.cato-unbound.org/2009/04/13/peter-thiel/ education-libertarian.

271 Ian Buruma remarks that the example of China shows that "individual hedonism can be successfully combined with political authoritarianism." "Why Rock n' Roll Is the Music of Dictatorships," *Globe and Mail*, 8 April 2016, A12.

272 Iain Pears evokes this possibility in the dystopian version of two alternative human futures, in his novel *Arcadia* (New York: Vintage Books, 2017).

273 Bryan Caplan, "The Totalitarian Threat," in *Global Catastrophic Risks*, ed. Nick Bostrom and Milan M. Ćirkovović (Oxford: Oxford Univ. Press, 2012), 504–19.

274 "Nous nous demandons si l'humain, pensé à partir de l'ontologie comme liberté [A1], comme volonté de *puissance* [A1a] ... si cet humain est encore à la mesure de ce qui, dans la déficience humaine, frappe l'intelligence moderne. Intelligence moderne, celle qui, à Auschwitz, vit l'aboutissement de la loi et de l'obéissance – découlant de l'acte héroïque [A1a] – dans les totalitarismes, fasciste et non-fasciste, du XXᵉ siècle. ... Et le phénomène du stalinisme et les résurgences des conflits nationalistes entre États entrés dans la voie du socialisme, donnèrent aux possibilités de la dégradation humaine une signification différente de celle qu'elle pouvait recevoir à partir d'une *innocente barbarie*, des fautes originelles ou non originelles et du *divertissement* [A1b]." Levinas, *De Dieu qui vient à l'idée*, 83–4. Emphasis added.

275 As David Martin notes, conceptions about possible futures for Western civilization are inevitably "related to one's understanding of the status and staying power of varying modes of being [i.e., the four stances and families of virtues]." *On Secularization*, 142.

276 In Kierkegaard, Michel Henry finds an implicit ontology "radicalement différente de celle des Grecs et de Hegel comme de Heidegger lui-même": "une ontologie positive de la subjectivité, ontologie qui joue à l'égard de la philosophie de l'existence le rôle d'un fondement essentiel et l'empêche en conséquence de dégénérer dans la littérature et le verbalisme ou ... dans le vide et la confusion d'un quelconque 'irrationalisme.'" *L'essence de la manifestation*, 851n1, 519n1.

277 Hegel, *The Phenomenology of Mind*, trans. Baillie, 808.

278 Hegel, *Philosophy of Right*, trans. Knox, 36.

279 "The elements themselves must harbor the potential whence movement originates and the reason for the order in which they enter the current." Rosenzweig, *The Star of Redemption*, trans. Hallo, 87–8.

280 Scheler, *Formalism in Ethics*, trans. Frings and Funk, 542–3.

281 "[T]he creation of civil society [B2] is the achievement of the modern world which has for the first time given all the determinations of the Idea [i.e., all four stances and families of virtues] their due." Hegel, *Philosophy of Right*, trans. Knox, addition to §182, p. 266. At the next step on the spiral staircase, therefore, the virtues of Reverence (A2) would no longer be "la sollicitude en quelque sorte 'naïve' ... mais une sollicitude 'critique.'" Ricœur, *Soi-même comme un autre*, 318.

282 Hans Joas remarks that Ernst Troeltsch regarded "inadequate reflection on the relationship between historical teleology and unanticipatable historical innovation as Hegel's crucial and irremediable failing." *The Sacredness of the Person*, 106.

283 Hans Joas calls this "the risk of historical episodism": "If, in contrast to notions of progress and the work of Hegel, there is no universal historical context, then history may fragment into disconnected parts: it may be possible to compare these parts, but no connecting thread runs through them." Joas, 118.

284 "Le paradoxe de la notion d'histoire est, que, d'une part, elle devient incompréhensible si elle n'est pas une *unique* histoire, unifiée par un sens, mais que, d'autre part, elle perd son historicité même si elle n'est pas une aventure *imprévisible*." Paul Ricœur, *À l'école de la phénoménologie* (Paris: Vrin, 2004), 57–60. Emphasis in original. Elsewhere Ricœur calls this paradox "l'antinomie de la structure et de l'événement" or "du systématique et de l'historique." *Le conflit des interprétations*, 130, 133.

285 Joas, *The Sacredness of the Person*, 128. "The thesis of the end of metanarratives ... itself represents a metanarrative ... [T]he abandonment of teleological and evolutionist interpretations of history does not spare us the effort of placing ourselves in an historically reflective relationship to the origin of our ideals and to the fate of their realization. A limited justification for teleological or evolutionist ways of thinking then becomes perfectly possible." *The Genesis of Values*, 8.

286 Maritain, *Humanisme intégral*, 64, 245.

287 "If time is a turning circle, there is a place where history and prophecy converge – the footprints of First Man lie on the path behind us and on the path ahead. ... If time does in fact eddy back on itself, maybe the journey of the First Man will provide footsteps to guide the journey of the Second." Robin Wall Kimmerer, *Braiding Sweetgrass: Indigenous Wisdom, Scientific Knowledge, and the Teachings of Plants* (Minneapolis: Milkweed Editions, 2013), 207.

288 Lionel Trilling, *Sincerity and Authenticity* (Cambridge, MA: Harvard Univ. Press, 1972), 41.

289 Lev Shestov, *Athens and Jerusalem*, trans. Bernard Martin, 2nd ed. (Athens: Ohio Univ. Press, 2016), 205.

290 Richard A. Shweder suggests "community [ie. the virtues of Reverence (A2)] and divinity [i.e., the virtues of Excellence (B1)] are essential goals and must be acknowledged for the sake of individual identity and human progress." *Why Do Men Barbecue? Recipes for Cultural Psychology* (Cambridge, MA: Harvard Univ. Press, 2003), 343. Jacques Maritain agrees Western civilization needs to relearn not just a love of humankind but a love for "ce qui dans l'homme vivifie l'homme, étant l'Amour même et le Don [A2]." *Humanisme intégral*, 97.

291 Alexis de Tocqueville, *L'ancien régime et la Révolution* (Paris: Gallimard, 1967), 203.

292 Michel Terestchenko notes the temptation to assume that the only alternative to "l'idée d'un moi, sujet de la conscience et maître de soi" is the

Freudian deconstructed, psychological self, where there is no genuine "me," merely " une succession d'impulsions psychologiques et organiques qui tour à tour prennent le dessus." *Un si fragile vernis d'humanité*, 37–9.

293 Samuel Johnson, *The Rambler*, no. 208, Saturday, 14 March 1752, ed. W.J. Bate and Albrecht B. Strauss (New Haven: Yale Univ. Press, 1979) Yale Edition of the Works of Samuel Johnson, 5:316. For the contemporary drive to explain human virtue on the basis of gene pools and genetic selection, see, for example, Christopher Boehm, *Moral Origins: The Evolution of Virtue, Altruism, and Shame* (New York: Basic Books, 2012). For the drive to explain it through the moral capacities and propensities of toddlers and young children, see, for example, Paul Bloom, *Descartes' Baby: How the Science of Child Development Explains What Makes Us Human* (New York: Basic Books, 2004); Keane, *Ethical Life*, 40–5.

294 "[A] human whole beyond the contrast of 'body and soul.'" Rosenzweig, *The Star of Redemption*, trans. Hallo, 80.

295 de Waal, *The Age of Empathy*, 72; Alexander Cruden, *Cruden's Complete Concordance to the Old and New Testaments* (Peabody, MA: Hendrickson, n.d.), 54. See also Taylor, *A Secular Age*, 741. Contemporary ethical theory seems to be gradually working its way back to the insights of the Western spiritual traditions: "[V]alues are not some external system of concepts or rules but, rather, a *way of being a person in a body* ... bodily habits may not go all the way down, but they go deep. On the other hand, the ethical values embodied in those habits are inseparable from their concreteness." Keane, *Ethical Life*, 108–9. Emphasis added.

296 Rorty, "Trotsky and the Wild Orchids," in *The Rorty Reader*, 506–7. Emphasis added. In this remarkable passage, Rorty comes very close to grasping why Hegel thought the normal, modern meaning of truth – a subject conforming to a predicate, as in the logical principle of identity (i.e., A=A) – is simply trivial, banal, and tautological. For Hegel, a thing is "true" only when it conforms to its inner concept, when it's *true* to what makes it *real*. Thus, for him, "to be untrue is the same thing as to be bad. A bad man is an untrue man, a man who does not behave as his notion or vocation requires." Hegel, *Encyclopaedia*, trans. Wallace, §§138, 213, pp. 191, 276. Rorty is trying to say the same thing but does not have the language or concepts to do so. I could translate both Hegel's and Rorty's insights into the language of this book, by saying that a "true" human being is one who lives up to the full nature of the human, the whole human paradox. That is also what Heidegger means by "authentic Dasein."

297 "[D]ulcedine affectus, qua quis abhorret omne illud quod potest alium contristare." Aquinas, *Summa Theologiæ* 2–2.157.3, vol. 44 ("Well-Tempered Passion"), trans. Gilby, 42–3.

298 Sara Konrath, quoted in Zosia Bielski, "Universe Me," *Globe and Mail*, 1 June 2010, L3.

299 Samuel Johnson might have been anticipating some contemporary thinkers like Rorty, when he wrote: "Compassion is by some reasoners, on whom the name of philosophers has been too easily conferred, resolved into an affection merely selfish, an involuntary perception of pain at the involuntary sight of a being like ourselves languishing in misery. But this sensation, if ever it be felt at all from the brute instinct of uninstructed nature, will only produce effects desultory and transient; it will never settle into a principle of action, or extend relief to calamities unseen, in generations not yet in being." *The Idler*, no. 4, Saturday, 6 May 1758, in *The Idler and The Adventurer*, ed. W.J. Bate, John M. Bullitt, and L.F. Powell (New Haven: Yale Univ. Press, 1963) Yale Edition of the Works of Samuel Johnson, 2:13–14.

300 Robert N. Bellah, Richard Madsen, William M. Sullivan, Ann Swidler, and Steven M. Tipton, *Habits of the Heart*, updated ed. (Berkeley: Univ. of California Press, 1996), 333–4. Also 27, 33–5, 47.

301 Martin, *On Secularization*, 53–4.

302 Philip Rieff, *The Triumph of the Therapeutic: Uses of Faith after Freud* (Chicago: Univ. of Chicago Press, 1987).

303 "[L]a caricature est une révélation dont il faut dégager un sens; sens qui demande correction, mais que l'on ne peut impunément ni ignorer ni négliger." Levinas, *De Dieu qui vient à l'idée*, 26n5.

304 Webb Keane notes another contemporary source of pressure back toward the virtues of reverence; in the process, he sums up the whole course of the arrow of virtue to date and its related "spiral staircase." In contrast to the original prehistoric cultures in which religion was inseparable from the "total social fact," and social existence was "already thoroughly saturated with ethics prior to any regulating principles" (A2), Keane suggests "scriptural monotheisms tend to objectify ethics [It *is*], exerting pressure on them to become more consistent and cognitively explicit [B1]. But objectification also tends to separate ethics from everyday habits and foster the taking of a third-person perspective on ethical life. This tendency is reinforced by the modern division among what the sociologist Max Weber called 'value spheres.' [B2] Paradoxically, this very division of value spheres [It is], by identifying ethics with a specifically religious domain, can inspire strenuous efforts to break out of that confinement. The result can be the cultivation of piety [reverence] meant to encompass *all* domains of life [A2]. Yet the piety project must still wrestle with the consequences [B2] of that initial objectification [B1], which tend to undermine that very goal." Keane, *Ethical Life*, 208–9. Emphasis in original. In the last sentence, Keane nicely captures the reality

of what I've called the "spiral staircase": we arrive back at the same place in the nature of the human but must view it now from a different or higher perspective, which takes account of all the intervening stages and insights. As Keane says, "history matters." Keane, 207.

305 Northrop Frye, *The Great Code: The Bible and Literature* (Toronto: Academic Press Canada, 1982), 15. Charles Taylor's description of the "expressivist consciousness" makes a point similar to Frye and identifies one of the core impulses of contemporary "expressive individualism" that might eventually carry us beyond the virtues of Liberty (A1), back toward the virtues of Reverence (A2): "an aspiration to escape from a predicament in which the subject is over against an objectified world, to overcome the gap between subject and object, to see objectivity as an expression of subjectivity, or in interchange with it." *Hegel* (Cambridge: Cambridge Univ. Press, 1975), 29. Similarly, William James suggests "the rigorously impersonal view of science might one day appear as having been a temporarily useful eccentricity rather than the definitively triumphant position which the sectarian scientist at present so confidently announces it to be." James, *The Varieties of Religious Experience*, 388n8. Max Scheler hints that the next phase of the "arrow of virtue" might be some kind of "community of persons" (A2), beyond the modern and post-modern "ethos of society" (B2), a "personal-communal existence," in which the essential characteristics of "life-community" (A2) and "society" (B2) are both "cogiven." *Formalism in Ethics*, trans. Frings and Funk, 541, 539.

306 Susan Neiman, *Moral Clarity: A Guide for Grown-Up Idealists* (Orlando: Harcourt, 2008), 215–85. See also David Sorkin, *The Religious Enlightenment: Protestants, Jews, and Catholics from London to Vienna* (Princeton: Princeton Univ. Press, 2008).

307 Neil Postman, *Building a Bridge to the Eighteenth Century: How the Past Can Improve Our Future* (New York: Alfred A. Knopf, 1999).

308 Margaret Donaldson, *Human Minds: An Exploration* (New York: Allen Lane, 1993), 264.

309 Ricœur, *Lectures 1*, in *Ricœur: Textes choisis et présentés*, 371–2.

310 José Casanova, *Public Religions in the Modern World* (Chicago: Univ. of Chicago Press, 1994), 234.

311 Immanuel Kant, *Critique of Pure Reason*, A318, trans. Norman Kemp Smith (London: Macmillan, 1968), 313.

312 Casanova, *Public Religions in the Modern World*, 231, 234. The words cited are a quote from Jürgen Habermas, *The Theory of Communicative Action*, 2 vols. (Boston: Beacon Press, 1987), 143–271.

313 Richard Rohr, *Falling Upward: A Spirituality for the Two Halves of Life* (San Francisco: Jossey-Bass, 2011).

314 Rohr, 26, 47.

315 Alan Page Fiske, *Structures of Social Life: The Four Elementary Forms of Human Relations* (New York: Free Press, 1991), 163, 185–6, 194, 199, 210, 224, 228, 400–7. Donald, *A Mind So Rare*, 208, 266.

316 Webb Keane mentions the tension between the "ethics of pleasure" (A1b) and those of "self-mastery" (B2) in Greek and Roman culture, and the tension between "hierarchy" (B1) and "equality" (B2) in nineteenth-century England, as examples of the "contradiction between competing values" that can give "ethical life a history." Keane, *Ethical Life*, 183.

317 "[T]he ethos of *Western Europe in modern times*, in comparison with the ethos of the Middle Ages and the ethoses of other modern cultures, has been *predominantly societal* [i.e., *gesellschaft*, or the virtues of Equality (B2)] in all special value regions (religion, state, commerce). But it is equally certain that there are visible hints that the *principle of solidarity* [i.e., reverence] which conflicts with this ethos, will win *new reality* in both experience and theory … [T]o expect a simple return to the predominance of the ethos of the life-community [*gemeinschaft*, or Communal Sharing (A2)] is in our view an error." Scheler, *Formalism in Ethics*, trans. Frings and Funk, 542–3. Emphasis in original.

318 Hegel, *Encyclopaedia*, trans. Wallace, §244, p. 296. On the same theme, see Troeltsch, *Historicism and Its Problems*, 763, in Joas, *The Sacredness of the Person*, 126; Rahner, *The Practice of Faith*, 35; Levinas, *Entre nous*, 72; Taylor, *A Secular Age*, 637.

319 This argument is developed more fully in Ralph Heintzman, *Rediscovering Reverence: The Meaning of Faith in a Secular World* (Montreal: McGill-Queen's Univ. Press, 2011), 154–73.

320 Michael E. Mann and Lee R. Krump, *Dire Predictions: Understanding Climate Change*, 2nd ed. (New York: DK, 2015), 43, 84, 116. This book is a summary and distillation of the UN Intergovernmental Panel on Climate Change (IPCC) Fifth Assessment Report. See also Jeffrey Bennett, *A Global Warming Primer: Answering Your Questions about the Science, the Consequences, and the Solutions* (Boulder, Colorado: Big Kid Science, 2016); Joseph Romm, *Climate Change: What Everyone Needs to Know* (New York: Oxford Univ. Press, 2016). In February 2019, a US-led study (with researchers in Canada and Scotland) concluded that scientific confidence that human activities are responsible for rising temperatures at the Earth's surface has now reached "five-sigma" level of certainty in all of three satellite data sets widely used by climate researchers. Alister Doyle, "Scientists Give Evidence for Man-Made Global Warming a 'Gold Standard,'" *Globe and Mail*, 26 February 2019, A5.

321 Mann and Krump, 34, 47, 121.

322 Mann and Krump, 110–11, 122–3, 158–9.

323 Mann and Krump, 116–17.

324 Mann and Krump, 121, 130–1, 163.

325 Mann and Krump, 138–9.

326 Gabriel Laurence-Brook, "Tout avoir consommé dès le 29 juillet," *Le Devoir*, 30 July 2019, A7; Alexandre Shields, "Dès mercredi l'humanité aura épuisé les ressources de la planète pour 2018," *Le Devoir*, 31 July 2018, A3; "L'humanité vivra 'à crédit' dès lundi," *Le Devoir*, 4 August 2016, A4. These articles report on information from the Global Footprint Network, the World Wildlife Fund and the annual *State of the Climate* report.

327 William J. Ripple, Christopher Wolf, Thomas M. Newsome, Mauro Galetti, Mohammed Alamgir, Eileen Crist, Mahmoud I. Mahmoud, and William F. Laurance, "World Scientists' Warning to Humanity: A Second Notice," *BioScience* 67, no. 12 (December 2017), 1026–8, https://doi.org/10.1093/biosci/bix125. See also a follow-up open letter signed by 11,258 scientists from 153 countries published in *BioScience* on 5 November 2019: William J Ripple, Christopher Wolf, Thomas M. Newsome, Phoebe Barnard, William R. Moomaw, "World Scientists' Warning of a Climate Emergency," *BioScience* 70, no. 1 (January 2020), https://doi.org/10.1093/biosci/biz088.

328 "Media Release: Biodiversity and Nature's Contributions Continue Dangerous Decline, Scientists Warn," Intergovernmental Science-Policy Platform on Biodiversity and Ecosystem Services (IPBES). https://www.ipbes.net/news/media-release-biodiversity-nature%E2%80%99s-contributions-continue-%C2%A0dangerous-decline-scientists-warn; Natasha Gilbert, "Top UN Panel Paints Bleak Picture of World's Ecosystems," *Nature*, last updated 28 March 2018, https://www.nature.com/articles/d41586-018-03891-1?sf185681218=1.

329 "Media Release: Nature's Dangerous Decline 'Unprecedented' Species Extinction Rates 'Accelerating.'" Intergovernmental Science-Policy Platform on Biodiversity and Ecosystem Services (IPBES), 6 May 2019, https://www.unenvironment.org/news-and-stories/press-release/natures-dangerous-decline-unprecedented-species-extinction-rates; https://www.un.org/sustainabledevelopment/blog/2019/05/nature-decline-unprecedented-report/.

330 Tim Flannery, *The Weather Makers: How We Are Changing the Climate and What It Means for Life on Earth* (Toronto: HarperCollins, 2006), 209.

331 Tim Flannery, *Atmosphere of Hope* (London: Penguin, 2015), 222. For another upbeat, encouraging view with similar motivations, see Christiana Figueres and Tom Rivett-Carnac, *The Future We Choose: Surviving the Climate Crisis* (New York: Alfred A. Knopf, 2020).

332 Flannery, *Atmosphere of Hope*, 212–13, 216, 223.

333 Flannery, 213.

334 Mann and Krump, *Dire Predictions*, 84–5, 92–5, 98–9.

335 United Nations Environment Programme, *The Emissions Gap Report 2018* (Nairobi: UNEP, 2018), https://wedocs.unep.org/bitstream/handle /20.500.11822/26879/EGR2018_ESEN.pdf?sequence=10.

336 World Meteorological Organization (WMO), *Global Climate in 2015– 2019* (Geneva: WMO, 2019), 3, https://library.wmo.int/doc_num. php?explnum_id=9936.

337 United Nations Development Program (UNDP) and United Nations Framework Convention on Climate Change (UNFCCC), *The Heat Is On: Taking Stock of Global Climate Ambition*, NDC Global Outlook Report (New York and Bonn: UNDP and UNFCCC, September 2019), 6–7, https:// unfccc.int/sites/default/files/resource/NDC%20Outlook.pdf. The NDC Synthesis report published by the UN Framework Convention on Climate Change (FCCC) secretariat on 26 February 2021 confirmed current national commitments are not on track to meet the Paris Agreement goals. In fact, current national goals would reduce emissions by only -1 per cent from 2010 levels in 2030, compared to -45 per cent required to meet the goal of limiting the global temperature rise to 1.5 per cent by the end of the century. UN Framework Convention on Climate Change, *Nationally Determined Contributions under the Paris Agreement*, UN FCCC, 17 September 2021, https://unfccc.int/sites/default/files/resource/cma2021_08E. pdf; https://unfccc.int/news/climate-commitments-not-on-track-to-meet -paris-agreement-goals-as-ndc-synthesis-report-is-published.

338 D.J. Wuebbles, D.W. Fahey, K.A. Hibbard, B. DeAngelo, S. Doherty, K. Hayhoe, R. Horton, J.P. Kossin, P.C. Taylor, A.M. Waple, and C.P. Weaver, "Executive Summary," in *Climate Science Special Report: Fourth National Climate Assesssment*, ed. D.J. Wuebbles, D.W. Fahey, K.A. Hibbard, D.J. Dokken, B.C. Stewart, and T.K. Maycock (Washington, DC: US Global Change Research Program, 2017), 12–34, https://science2017.globalchange.gov /chapter/executive-summary/. Also: U.S. Global Change Research Program (USGCRP), *Impacts, Risks, and Adaptation in the United States: Fourth National Climate Assessment*, vol. 2: *Report-in-Brief*, ed. D.R. Reidmiller, C.W. Avery, D.R. Easterling, K.E. Kunkel, K.L.M. Lewis, T.K. Maycock, and B.C. Stewart (Washington, DC: US Global Change Research Program, 2018), https://nca2018.globalchange.gov/downloads/NCA4_Report-in-Brief.pdf.

339 World Meteorological Organization, *State of Global Climate 2020: WMO Provisional Report*, 5. https://library.wmo.int/index.php?lvl=notice_display &id=21982#.YYRiXfnMLIV. See also United Nations, *United in Science Report 2020* (Geneva: World Meteorological Organization, 9 September 2020), 2–3. https://trello-attachments.s3.amazonaws.com/5f560af19197118edf74cf93 /5f57886a97dc4d4d4a186195/a71f21152f9f6fc88b20e5e3a7482cb8/United _In_Science_2020_Smaller_File_Size.pdf.

340 World Meteorological Organization, "State of Climate in 2021: Extreme Events and Major Impacts," Press Release no. 31102021, 31 October 2021. https://public.wmo.int/en/media/press-release/state-of-climate -2021-extreme-events-and-major-impacts.

341 Climate Action Tracker, *Warming Projections Global Update: November 2021*. https://climateactiontracker.org/documents/997/CAT_2021-11 -09_Briefing_Global-Update_Glasgow2030CredibilityGap.pdf.

342 David Wallace-Wells, *The Uninhabitable Earth: Life after Warming* (New York: Tim Duggan Books, 2019), 28–31, 6, 15. For another dire view, see Mark Lynas, *Our Final Warning: Six Degrees of Climate Emergency* (London: Fourth Estate, 2020).

343 Wallace-Wells, 220–3.

344 Anthony Sharwood, "United Nations Boss Antonio Guterres Says 'We Are Killing Our Planet' after Latest Disastrous Climate Data," *Huffington Post*, 1 November 2017, http://www.huffingtonpost.com.au/2017 /10/31/united-nations-boss-antonio-guterres-says-we-are-killing-our -planet-after-latest-disastrous-climate-data_a_23261461/. Guterres' comments were prompted by an earlier WMO report: see World Meteorological Organization (WMO), "The State of Greenhouse Gases in the Atmosphere Based on Global Observations through 2016," *WMO Greenhouse Gas Bulletin*, no. 13 (30 October 2017), https://ane4bf-datap1.s3-eu -west-1.amazonaws.com/wmocms/s3fs-public/ckeditor/files/GHG _Bulletin_13_EN_final_1_1.pdf.

345 The Secretary General, *The State of the Planet*, Address at Columbia University, 2 December 2020, https://www.un.org/sites/un2.un.org/files /sgspeech-the-state-of-planet.pdf.

346 For reflection on the ethical dimensions of climate change, see Stephen M. Gardiner, *A Perfect Moral Storm: The Ethical Tragedy of Climate Change* (New York: Oxford Univ. Press, 2013).

347 Francis Bacon, *The New Organon*, in *The Complete Essays of Francis Bacon* (New York: Washington Square Press, 1963), 250, 262–3; René Descartes, *Discourse on Method*, trans. Elizabeth S. Haldane and G.R.T. Ross, in *The Philosophical Works of René Descartes*, ed. Elizabeth S. Haldane and G.R.T. Ross (Cambridge: Cambridge Univ. Press, 1969), 1:119.

348 "[T]he fact that we have brought that nightmare eventuality [that large portions of the planet may soon become uninhabitable] into play at all is perhaps the overwhelming cultural and historical fact of the modern era." Wallace-Wells, *The Uninhabitable Earth*, 16.

349 Flannery, *The Weather Makers*, 17.

350 "Depuis que les premières techniques ont protégé la vie contre les cataclysmes naturels et que, renversant la situation, les mortels étendent,

sans heurts, par les sciences, leur empire sur les éléments, ils ne luttent qu'entre eux. L'humanisme commença avec ces guerres où l'on oublia les forces de la Nature. ... Et voilà que la nature revient. ... Il y avait donc quelque chose derrière. ... Pour la première fois les problèmes sociaux et les luttes entre hommes ne révèlent pas l'ultime sens du réel." Levinas, *Les Imprévus de l'histoire*, 141–4.

351   As already noted in chapters 6 and 16, this might be called, in philosophical language, "the transcendental necessity of holism." Taylor, *A Secular Age*, 157. Leibniz calls it "la connexion réelle de toutes choses." Leibniz, *Nouveaux essais*, bk. 2, chap. 25, §5, p. 194. Martin Buber calls it "the *a priori* of relation." *I and Thou*, 69.

352   Jacques Maritain calls this potential next turn of the arrow of virtue "une nouvelle effusion de 'miséricorde.'" *Humanisme intégral*, 245.

353   Flannery, *The Weather Makers*, 160, 17.

354   Freedom House reports fourteen years of steady global democratic decline. More than half of countries rated Free or Not Free in 2009 have suffered a net decline in the past decade. Sarah Repucci, *Freedom in the World 2020: A Leaderless Struggle for Democracy* (Washington: Freedom House, 2020), https://freedomhouse.org/report/freedom-world/2020/leaderless-struggle-democracy.The 2017–18 Rule of Law Index report indicates that human rights have declined in almost two-thirds of 113 countries surveyed. World Justice Project, *Rule of Law Index 2017–18* (Washington: World Justice Project, 2018), https://worldjusticeproject.org/sites/default/files/documents/WJP_ROLI_2017–18_Online-Edition_0.pdf.

355   Michael Ignatieff, *The Ordinary Virtues: Moral Order in a Divided World* (Cambridge, MA: Harvard Univ. Press, 2017), 208–12.

356   Ignatieff, 208. "Our conscience remains local because our ultimate loyalties are local: to kith and kin, our own, our people, our community. The human rights revolution has changed what we believe about the duty of states. I doubt it has changed *us*." Ignatieff, 215–16. Emphasis in original.

357   "[The] universalist ethos must be tempered by moral particularism: all humans are equal but they are not equally important to us; our obligations and allegiances ripple out from family to friends to stranger fellow-citizens in our neighbourhoods and towns, then to nations and finally to all humanity." Goodhart, *The Road to Somewhere*, 109.

358   "If the liberals who dominated in the 1990s were preoccupied with the rights of ethnic, religious, and sexual minorities, the new [illiberal eastern European] consensus is about the rights of the majority." Ivan Krastev, "Eastern Europe's Illiberal Revolution: The Long Road to Democratic Decline," *Foreign Affairs* 97, no. 3 (May/June 2018), 51.

359   Philip Oltermann, "Can a Continent's New Xenophobes Reshape Europe?" *The Guardian Weekly*, 9 February 2018, 6–7.

360 Ignatieff, *The Ordinary Virtues*, 214. "The meeting point between the language of rights and the ordinary virtues is actually the language of compassion, pity and generosity [A2]." Ignatieff, 214.

361 Gopnik, *A Thousand Small Sanities*, 25. Jacques Maritain calls this the ambition to "organize" or "socialize" love. *Humanisme intégral*, 97–8.

362 Joas, *The Sacredness of the Person*. Yuval Noah Harari uses similar language when he suggests that liberalism *"sanctifies* the subjective feelings of individuals." *Sapiens: A Brief History of Humankind* (Toronto: Penguin Random House, 2016), 392. Emphasis added.

363 Levinas, *Altérité et transcendance*, 133, 149–53.

364 "[D]emagogues with paramilitary support who christen themselves 'the representatives of the people' do not thereby become so. ... Without regular elections and open debates in civic forums such as the press, and without the political culture that makes both seem legitimate in the eyes of the people, majoritarianism is purely fictitious." Stephen Holmes, *Passions and Constraints: On the Theory of Liberal Democracy* (Chicago: Univ. of Chicago Press, 1995), 9.

365 Brian Marson and Ralph Heintzman, *From Research to Results: A Decade of Results-Based Service Improvement in Canada* (Toronto: IPAC, 2009), 37.

366 The virtues of Reverence[3] (A2a) (expressed in religious life) are, as Roger Scruton puts it, "both a product of the moral life and the thing that sustains it." *On Human Nature* (Princeton: Princeton Univ. Press, 2017), 143.

367 "[W]e need a system of rights because our powers of self-restraint and sympathy are limited. ... Until such a system is in place, a free, democratic life is impossible. But it is not its highest goal. It is merely a preliminary to that, and the real shortcoming of every political morality that explains the need for a system of rights by appealing to the idea of autonomy [i.e., the virtues of self-assertion], is that it hides this highest goal from view. ... [T]he establishment of even the most perfect system of rights can never be more than a prelude to something of still greater value." Kronman, *Confessions of a Born-Again Pagan*, 44.

368 Bart D. Ehrman, *The Triumph of Christianity: How a Forbidden Religion Swept the World* (New York: Simon & Schuster, 2018), 5. Ehrman underlines that this "commonsense, millennial-old view" was one "that virtually everyone accepted and shared, including the weak and marginalized." Ehrman, 5. This was the really important feature of the culture. Not just that it preserved the initial human "disposition to dominate" or pure self-assertion (A1), but that *everyone eagerly and naturally submitted to this disposition* (B1).

369 N.T. Wright, *Paul* (Minneapolis: Fortress Press, 2009), 172–3.

370 "If the *'cogito sum'* is to serve as the point of departure for the existential analytic, we ... need to turn it around ... Then, the first statement is *'sum'* [I am]." Heidegger, *Being and Time*, 211, trans. Stambaugh, 203.

371 Owen Barfield, "Goethe and the Twentieth Century," in *Romanticism Comes of Age*, new ed. (Middletown, CT: Wesleyan Univ. Press, 1967), 164–83. Jane K. Brown points out there is a strong streak of irony in the second instalment of Wilhelm Meister, and especially in the chapters where Goethe's theory of fourfold reverence is presented. The "Pedagogic Province" is partly a parody of the famous German educators Basedow and Campe, and their relationship to Rousseau. However, despite the irony and parody, Brown acknowledges the concepts of these chapters are "mostly presented as agents for good and for order. So positively are they presented, indeed, that it is easy to overlook the elements of irony and common sense that undermine the superlatively enthusiastic presentations." "Introduction," in *Conversations of German Refugees/Wilhelm Meister's Journeyman Years*, ed. Jane K. Brown (Princeton: Princeton Univ. Press, 1995), Goethe's Collected Works, 10:8–10. It is almost as if Goethe's Enlightenment self wanted or needed to maintain some ironic distance between himself and the convictions to which he had come – perhaps almost in spite of himself – in the last decade of his life.

372 "Goethe is truly the great heathen and the great Christian at one and the same time. ... Goethe's life is truly a hike along the precipice between two abysses ... the two abysses which yawn on each side of the ridge which everyone must nonetheless ascend sooner or later for the sake of vitality of life." Rosenzweig, *The Star of Redemption*, trans. Hallo, 283, 286.

373 Johann Wolfgang von Goethe, *Wilhelm Meister's Journeyman Years or The Renunciants*, trans. Krishna Winston, ed. Jane K. Brown (Princeton: Princeton Univ. Press, 1995), Goethe's Collected Works, 10:203. Emphasis added.

374 Goethe, 204–5. Consciously or unconsciously, Goethe seems to have paraphrased Augustine of Hippo's "four kinds of things which are to be loved," which are almost identical to Goethe's four kinds of reverence: "first, that which is above us; second, ourselves; third, that which is on a level with us; fourth, that which is beneath us." *On Christian Doctrine*, chap. 23, §22, in *Late Have I Loved Thee: Selected Writings of Saint Augustine on Love*, ed. John F. Thornton and Susan B. Varenne (New York: Vintage Books, 2006), 79.

375 Goethe, 205, 210.

376 Goethe, 203.

377 Goethe, 203.

378 Goethe, 205.

379 Goethe, 205, 203.

380 Herman Melville, "Shelley's Vision," in *Till I End My Song*, ed. Harold Bloom (New York: HarperCollins, 2010), 153.

381 Friedrich Nietzsche, "Expeditions of an Untimely Man," in *Twilight of the Idols*, trans. R.J. Hollingdale (Harmondsworth: Penguin, 1968), §§49–51, pp. 102–4.

382 Trilling, *Sincerity and Authenticity*, 122.

383 Self-reverence has overtones of the "humility and awe" that, for David Hume, distinguishes "esteem" (B1) from love (A2). *A Treatise of Human Nature* 3.3.4, ed. L.A. Selby-Bigge (London: Oxford Univ. Press, 1968), 608n1. Self-*reverence* is therefore quite different in character from the contemporary sense of self-*respect*, derived from Kant, which Paul Bloomfield, for example, takes to be the key to what he calls "the Good Life." *The Virtues of Happiness*, 1–7.

384 Heidegger, *Being and Time*, 144, 168, 188, 192, trans. Stambaugh, 139–40, 162, 182–3, 185.

385 In her discussion of Nietzsche, Christine Swanton turns Goethe's self-reverence into self-*love*. *Virtue Ethics*, 11–14, and elsewhere.

386 The concept of the "sacred" as exclusively distinctive of religious life has been criticized and increasingly rejected in recent decades. Stewart Guthrie, for example, suggests the concept of the sacred "can apply to any domain." William E. Paden suggests it is a "potential factor in the constitution of *all* social worlds," even though "religion is one of its primary and prototypical expressions." Stewart Guthrie, "The Sacred: A Sceptical View," and William A. Paden "Sacrality as Integrity: 'Sacred Order' as a Model for Describing Religious Worlds," in *The Sacred and Its Scholars: Comparative Methodologies for the Study of Primary Religious Data*, ed. Thomas A. Idinopolous and Edward A. Yoman (Leiden: E.J. Brill, 1996), cited in Shahab Ahmed, *What Is Islam? The Importance of Being Islamic* (Princeton: Princeton Univ. Press, 2016), 209n71.

387 Peterson and Seligman, *Character Strengths and Virtues*, 39.

388 "Secular content may also take on the qualities of sacrality; namely, subjective self-evidence and affective intensity. Sacredness may be ascribed to new content." Joas, *The Sacredness of the Person*, 5.

389 Wilson, *The Meaning of Human Existence*, 60; Seligman, *Authentic Happiness*, 260.

390 The word "numinous" was invented by Rudolf Otto. *The Idea of the Holy* (Oxford: Oxford Univ. Press, 1973), 36.

391 Perhaps not entirely coincidentally, Shweder describes "three salient measures" of women's well-being in an Indian Hindu culture, as manifested in her relations "with those above, around and below her": i.e., *exactly Goethe's terminology*. Shweder, *Why Do Men Barbecue?*, 260.

392 Shweder, 105.

393 Shweder, 109–11.

394 Shweder, 103–13.

395 "[M]a place dans l'être, le *Da-* de mon Dasein, n'est-il pas déjà usurpa-
     tion, déjà violence à l'égard d'autrui?" Levinas, *Altérité et transcendance,*
     180. Also: *Éthique comme philosophie première* (Paris: Rivages poche, 2015),
     87–8, 97.

396 Shweder, *Why Do Men Barbecue?*, 106–9. Emphasis added.

397 Shweder, 109–12. Emphasis added.

398 Ahmed, *What Is Islam?*, 224–7.

399 Shweder, *Why Do Men Barbecue?*, 107.

400 Shweder, 107.

401 Joas, *The Sacredness of the Person*, 51, 128, 159, 190.

402 Roland Robertson and JoAnn Chirico, "Humanity, Globalization and
     Worldwide Religious Resurgence: A Theoretical Explanation," *Sociological
     Analysis* 46, no. 3 (1985), cited in Casanova, *Public Religions in the Modern
     World*, 226.

403 Aristotle, *The Nicomachean Ethics* 9.4.1166a30–5, trans. Thomson, rev. Tre-
     dennick, 237.

404 Martin, *On Secularization*, 180. Emphasis added.

405 de Waal, *The Age of Empathy*, 65. Emphasis added. de Waal's name for
     what I'm calling the *"sacred* self" is "the foreign self."

406 Samuel Taylor Coleridge, *Coleridge's Notebooks*, ed. Seamus Perry (Oxford:
     Oxford Univ. Press, 2002), 120–1. Emphasis in original.

407 Hegel, *Encyclopaedia*, trans. Wallace, §§24, 159, pp. 39, 222. "[T]he sub-
     stance of individuality necessarily involves other individuals *within it."*
     The Phenomenology of Mind, trans. Baillie, 457. Emphasis added.

408 G.W.F. Hegel, *Science of Logic*, vol. 1, bk. 2, §2, chap. 3, trans. W.H. John-
     ston and L.G. Struthers (London: George Allen & Unwin, 1951), 2:142–59.
     Also *Philosophy of Right*, trans. Knox, addition to §158, p. 261; Bradley,
     Appearance and Reality, 404; Ricœur, *Soi-même comme un autre*, 37.

409 Simone Weil gets at the idea of the *"sacred* self" when she suggests that
     the person of truly good will, "en présence d'un malheureux, ne sent
     aucune distance entre lui et soi-même; *il transporte en l'autre tout son être
     ... La cause est l'identité des êtres humains* à travers toutes les distances ap-
     parentes que met entre eux le hasard de la fortune." *Pensées sans ordre con-
     cernant l'amour de Dieu* (Paris: Gallimard, 2013), 91–3. Emphasis added.

410 When viewed through the lens of reverence rather than self-assertion, the
     "fourfold division of virtue" is revealed as "four forms of love." Hilde-
     brand, *Ethics,* 485.

411 Jacques Maritain calls the four poles of the human viewed through the
     lens of reverence "une *conscience de soi évangélique,"* which includes rever-
     ence for the virtues of self-assertion: "un respect évangélique de la nature
     [A1] et de la raison [B2], de ces structures naturelles que l'humanisme
     moderne à servi à découvrir." *Humanisme intégral*, 82, 84–5. Emphasis

in original. Franz Rosenzweig sums up the four poles of sacred self and sacred world in two sentences: "The soul [*sacred* self/I *am*/A2] demands as object [It *is*], animated with soul by it, an articulated life [*sacred* world/B1]. It then exercises its freedom [sacred *self*/I am/A1] on this life, animating it in all its individual members [sacred *world*/It is/B2], and everywhere inseminating this ground of the living structure with the seeds of name, of animated individuality, of immortality." *The Star of Redemption*, trans. Hallo, 241.

412 Shweder, *Why Do Men Barbecue?*, 133.

413 Aristotle, *The Nicomachean Ethics* 7.13.1153b30–5, trans. Thomson, rev. Tredennick, 196.

414 "Whence ... springs the conviction in all philosophy of all the centuries that it is in mechanism, in *Selbstbewegung* [self-generated movement], in movement in a circle, that we must seek the final mystery of creation? ... But what freedom can there be where everything is 'natural,' where mechanism rules?" Shestov, *Athens and Jerusalem*, 115.

415 Cochrane, *Christianity and Classical Culture*, 478–516.

416 Paul Ricœur calls this "[le] rapport de la liberté à l'obligation." *Le conflit des interprétations*, 569. Webb Keane acknowledges that "to be ethical is to have some freedom of action and, so, to discover the ethical is to reveal some fundamental distinction between the causal determinations of behavior (whether those be biological, psychological, or socioeconomic in origin) and people's capacity to act." *Ethical Life*, 181.

417 "Ce n'est pas parce que Autrui est nouveauté qu'il 'donne lieu' à un rapport de transcendance – c'est parce que la responsabilité *est* transcendance qu'il peut y avoir du nouveau sous le soleil." Levinas, *De Dieu qui vient à l'idée*, 32. Emphasis added.

418 Levinas, *Les Imprévus de l'histoire*, 24–6; Martha Nussbaum, *The Fragility of Goodness: Luck and Ethics in Greek Tragedy and Philosophy* (Cambridge: Cambridge Univ. Press, 1986), 49.

419 See, for example, Galations 5:1, 13–25.

420 "It is in this kind of *ethical unsubstitutability* and not in numerical uniqueness that [Georg] Simmel sees the essence of individuality." Joas, *The Genesis of Values*, 82. Emphasis added.

421 Levinas, *Autrement qu'être*, 272. Hegel agrees with Levinas that it is in self-giving experiences such as friendship and love that the ego of "pure activity" (A1) becomes a genuine self (A2): "[I]t is there that [a man] first arrives at the feeling of his own self-hood." Hegel, *Philosophy of Right*, trans. Knox, addition to §7, p. 228.

422 Taylor, *A Secular Age*, 430.

423 Jared Diamond suggests some five ways contemporary Western societies could learn from the prehistoric band and tribal cultures that Relational

Models Theory calls cultures of "Communal Sharing" (A2), including rediscovering "religion" as "a broader and more complex matter than just adopting metaphysical beliefs that we've decided are true, or rejecting beliefs that we've decided are false." *The World Until Yesterday: What We Can Learn from Traditional Societies* (New York: Viking, 2012), 464.

424 "[C]e que le langage religieux fait, c'est *redécrire*; ce qu'il redécrit, c'est *l'expérience humaine*. Dans ce sens, nous devons dire que le référant ultime des paraboles, proverbes et dires eschatologiques n'est pas le Royaume de Dieu, mais la réalité humaine dans sa totalité." Ricœur, *L'Herméneutique biblique*, in *Ricœur: Textes choisis et présentés*, 207. Emphasis in original.

425 Hume, *A Treatise of Human Nature* 3.1.2, 3.1.5, 3.1.6, 3.1.8, 3.3.1, pp. 470–6, 517, 532, 546–7, 581, 589–90.

426 Hume, 3.1.2, p. 470.

427 Hume, 3.1.2, 3.3.1, pp. 471, 575. "To conform to the ethical order on this or that particular occasion is hardly enough to make a man virtuous; he is virtuous only when his mode of behaviour is a fixed element in his character." Hegel, *Philosophy of Right*, trans. Knox, addition to §150, p. 260.

428 Paul Ricœur makes this point in a criticism of Heidegger. *Amour et justice*, 108–9. See also Levinas, *Éthique comme philosophie première*, 96, 98.

429 "[T]he 'ought-to-be' which is never absent from the moral sphere becomes an 'is' only in ethical life [i.e., in *sittlichkeit*, a culture of habitual, customary virtue]." Hegel, *Philosophy of Right*, trans. Knox, addition to §108, p. 249. "It is only ... *in* preferring and rejecting, *in* loving and hating, i.e., in the course of *performing* such intentional functions and acts, that values and their order flash before us! The a priori content lies in what is given in these manners. A spirit limited to perception and thinking would be absolutely blind to values, no matter how much it might have the faculty of 'inner perception,' i.e., of psychic perception." Scheler, *Formalism in Ethics*, trans. Frings and Funk, 28n18, 68. Emphasis in original.

430 "There is no possibility of 'justifying morality from the outside' by appealing to anything 'non-moral,' or by finding a neutral point of view that the fairly virtuous and the wicked can share. ... It is only from within the outlook of the (at least moderately) virtuous that the truth of 'the virtues benefit their possessor' can be discerned. ... [M]orality can't be justified from the outside." Hursthouse, *On Virtue Ethics*, 179, 181, 187. Hursthouse here summarizes the views of a number of contemporary philosophers (including R.M. Hare) with whom she largely agrees, but whose views she wishes to qualify from the point of view of "ethical naturalism."

431 On Hume and the virtues, see (among others) Paul Russell, "Hume's Anatomy of Virtue," in *The Cambridge Companion to Virtue Ethics*, ed. Daniel C. Russell (Cambridge: Cambridge Univ. Press, 2013), 92–123; Roger Crisp, "Hume on Virtue, Utility, and Morality," in *Virtue Ethics, Old and*

New, ed. Stephen M. Gardiner (Ithaca: Cornell Univ. Press, 2005), 159–78. Crisp suggests Hume's discussion of the virtues ranks "as among the most significant since Aristotle." Crisp, 160.

432 Hume, *A Treatise of Human Nature* 3.2.3, 3.2.12, 3.3.1, pp. 500, 570, 578–9. Hume apparently had Bernard Mandeville especially in mind in these passages. James A. Harris, *Hume: An Intellectual Biography* (Cambridge: Cambridge Univ. Press, 2015), 132.

433 Hume, *A Treatise of Human Nature* 3.2.2, 3.2.5, 3.2.10, 3.3.1, 3.3.6, pp. 490–3, 521–2, 555, 578, 587–8, 618–19.

434 Hume, 3.3.1–3, 3.3.6, pp. 578, 587–8, 599–600, 603, 618. Hume puts justice in the category of the virtues (of reverence) that serve the "public good." But he distinguishes, rather unconvincingly, between "artificial" and "natural" virtues. J.B. Schneewind suggests Hume's distinction between natural and artificial virtues reflects the distinction between perfect and imperfect duties introduced by natural law theorists, such as Hugo Grotius and Samuel Pufendorf, in order to supplant Aristotelian virtues-based moral theory with the kind of law-centred theory that found its culmination in Kant. "The Misfortunes of Virtue," in *Virtue Ethics*, ed. Roger Crisp and Michael Slote (Oxford: Oxford Univ. Press, 1997), 178–200.

435 James Harris notes that Hume's treatment of "greatness of mind" (a subset of the virtues of self-assertion) in the *Treatise* is "more than twice as long" as his treatments of the virtues of reverence, such as goodness and benevolence. Hume, 135–6.

436 Hume, *A Treatise of Human Nature* 3.3.1, p. 578.

437 Hume, 3.2.8, 3.3.3, pp. 546, 604. Roger Scruton argues that what causes humans "to see the world in terms of value" is the "web of attachments" into which they are born: "Their very existence is burdened with a debt of love and gratitude and it is in responding to that burden that they begin to recognize the power of 'ought.' This is not the abstract, universal 'ought' of liberal theory – or at least, not yet – but the concrete, immediate 'ought' of family attachments. It is the 'ought' of piety [i.e., reverence], which recognizes the unquestionable rightness of local, transitory and historically conditioned social bonds. ... Until they have felt that claim, rational beings have no motive to find value in the human world." Roger Scruton, *The Meaning of Conservatism*, 3rd rev. ed. (South Bend, IN: St. Augustine's Press, 2002), 192.

438 Jean-Paul Sartre, "Existentialism is a Humanism," trans. Philip Mairet, in *Existentialism from Dostoevsky to Sartre*, ed. Walter Kaufmann (Cleveland: World, 1956), 289–91. "[C]hez Sartre ... sa philosophie du néant est la conséquence d'une philosophie insuffisante de l'être; en particulier toute sa théorie de la valeur est grevée par une conception pauvre de l'être." Ricœur, *Histoire et vérité*, 401.

439 "La signification précède l'ess[a]nce." Levinas, *Autrement qu'être*, 29.

440 Ali Smith, *How to Be Both* (Toronto: Penguin Books, 2015), 88, 304.

441 Gopnik, *A Thousand Small Sanities*, 13.

442 Coleridge's own names for the four families of virtues described in this book are "sensibility" (A1 – sensing with feeling), "prudence" (B2 – self-control), "morality" (B1 – It *is*), and "religion" (A2 – reverence and love). Coleridge, *Aids to Reflection*, 91.

443 Léon Walras identified three foundational "principles" of human morality: fraternity, justice, and "association." However, as he had already placed these three in a prior context of liberty and the individual, it's fair to say that Walras anticipated the four families of virtues described in this book. Walras' "principles" correspond to the four families of virtues, as follows: liberty/individual (A1), fraternity (A2), justice (B1), and association (B2). "Théorie de la propriété," originally published in *Revue Socialiste* (Tome 23, no. 138, 15 juin 1896, 668–81, and Tome 24, no. 139, 15 juillet 1896, 23–35), and included in pt. 2 of *Études d'Économie Sociale*, 2nd ed. (Paris: R. Pichon et R. Durand-Auzias, 1936) 205–39, trans. Guido Erreygers, Marylène Pastides, and Peter Vallentyne, in *The Origins of Left Libertarianism: An Anthology of Historical Writings*, ed. Peter Vallentyne and Hillel Steiner (Palgrave, 2000), http://klinechair.missouri.edu/docs/theory_of_property_trans.pdf.

444 Cassin's names for the four families of virtues found in this book are dignity (B1), liberty (A1), equality (B2), and brotherhood (A2). Fawcett, *Liberalism*, 291.

445 Jung, *Analytical Psychology*, 137–8; Christopher Peterson, *A Primer in Positive Psychology* (New York: Oxford Univ. Press, 2006), 158, Figure 6.3: "Tradeoffs Among Character Strengths."

446 Hegel calls these four pillars of the human the "moments" of a "circle of necessity" which constitutes the "ethical order": these "moments" (or families of virtues) "are the ethical powers which regulate the life of individuals. … [I]t is in individuals that these powers are represented, have the shape of appearance, and become actualized." Hegel, *Philosophy of Right*, trans. Knox, §145, p. 105. Max Scheler calls his four families of values or "value-modalities" "the inner spiritual structure of all mankind in whose personal centre moral values are originally located." *Formalism in Ethics*, trans. Frings and Funk, 104–10, 517.

447 Levinas, *De Dieu qui vient à l'idée*, 26. See note 198 above.

448 The basic human paradox of self-assertion and reverence is a constant, structuring theme in Ricœur's work. His informal names for the four families of virtues include: liberty (A1), love (A2), justice (B1), and reciprocity (B2). See, for example: Ricœur, *Amour et justice*; *Parcours de la reconnaissance*, 245–56, 350–77, 400–1; *Philosophie de la volonté 2: Finitude et culpabilité*, in *Ricœur: Textes choisis et présentés*, 285–92; *Lectures 1*, in

Ricœur: Textes choisis et présentés, 314. Ricœur also frequently identifies the paradoxes, dialectics, or sub-sub-families of these four families.

449 See Nozick's discussion of the four human "stances," in *The Examined Life*, 151–61.

450 "[L]a nécessité simultanée et de la hiérarchie enseignée par Athènes et de l'individualisme éthique *abstrait* et quelque peu anarchique, enseigné par Jérusalem … Chacun de ces principes, laissés à lui-même, n'accélère que le contraire de ce qu'il veut garantir. Ne pensez-vous pas qu'à notre époque surtout, la valeur de cette protestation contre la hiérarchie doive nous être particulièrement sensible et qu'*elle demande une explicitation métaphysique?*" Levinas, *Liberté et commandement*, 99–100. Emphasis in original.

451 This second pairing is what Whitehead has in mind when he describes the human as "*dipolar*, with its physical [A1 & A2] and mental [B1 & B2] poles." Whitehead, *Process and Reality*, 280, 322. Emphasis added.

452 "[L]es deux grandeurs antiques … la grandeur héroïque et la grandeur de sainteté." Charles Péguy, *L'argent suite*, in *Une éthique sans compromis*, ed. Saatdjian, 212.

453 Hegel, *Encyclopaedia*, trans. Wallace, §236, p. 292.

454 Martin Heidegger, "The Way Back into the Ground of Metaphysics," trans. Walter Kaufmann, in *Existentialism from Dostoevsky to Sartre*, 213–14; *An Introduction to Metaphysics*, trans. Manheim, 23–4.

455 Karl Jaspers, *Reason and Existenz*, trans. William Earle, in *Existentialism from Dostoevsky to Sartre*, 183, 192–3, 197, 203.

456 "Même la noblesse stoïcienne de la résignation au logos tient son énergie déjà de l'ouverture à l'*au-delà de l'Ess[a]nce.*" Levinas, *Autrement qu'être*, 273–4. Emphasis in original.

457 Bradley calls this paradox "the dualism of the 'that' and the 'what'": "bare existence" or that something "should be" on the one hand, and on the other hand, that it should be something "in particular" – "an existence and a content." Bradley, *Appearance and Reality*, 143, 148–9, 403–4.

458 Hegel, *Encyclopaedia*, trans. Wallace, §236, p. 292.

459 Whitehead, *Process and Reality*, 280, 290.

460 Jaspers, *Reason and Existenz*, trans. Earle, 195.

461 "[I]f reason means the pre-eminence of thought … then more is included than mere thinking [B2]. It is then what goes beyond all limits [B1], the omnipresent demand of thought, that not only grasps what is universally valid and is an *ens rationis* in the sense of being a law or principle of order of some process [B2], but also brings to light the Other, stands before the absolutely counter-rational, touching it and bringing it, too, into being [B1]." Jaspers, 195.

462 "[E]n nous, ni la pensée [B1 & B2] n'est la pensée sans la vie, ni la vie [A1 & A2] n'est la vie sans la pensée." Blondel, *L'Être et les êtres*, 470.

463 For Hegel the "Absolute Idea" is "the unity of the theoretical [B1 and B2] and practical [A1 and A2] culture, and thus at the same time the unity of life [I am] with the idea of cognition [It is]." Hegel, *Encyclopaedia*, trans. Wallace, §236, p. 292. Franz Rosenzweig calls these two poles of the human "the contrast of the life-centred [I am] and the world-centred [It is] points of view." *The Star of Redemption*, trans. Hallo, 11–13, 155, 173. Paul Ricœur calls the human stance of "It is" "la question quoi" and the stance of "I am," "la question qui." These two stances or "questions" are expressed in two contrasting "approaches" to the world: "referential" (It is) and "reflexive" (I am). *Soi-même comme un autre*, 35, 56, 71–2, 77, 159.

464 The two sides of this other or "diagonal" human paradox (the contrasting human stances of "I am" and "It is") are what Michel Henry calls the "deux modes spécifiques et fondamentaux conformément auxquels s'accomplit et se manifeste la manifestation de ce qui est. Dans le premier de ces modes ["It is"], l'être se manifeste hors de lui, s'irréalise dans le monde, il est sa lumière, le pur milieu de visibilité où l'étant se manifeste. ["It is": sensing (B2) and intuition (B1) with thinking] ... Dans le second de ces modes, dans le sentiment ["I am"], l'être surgit et se révèle en lui-même, se rassemble avec soi et s'éprouve, dans la souffrance et dans la jouissance de soi, dans la profusion de son être intérieur et vivant ["I am": sensing (A1) and intuition (A2) with feeling]." *L'essence de la manifestation*, 860–1.

465 Whitehead, *Process and Reality*, 289; Heidegger, *Being and Time*, 252, 260, trans. Stambaugh, 244, 249.

466 Samuel Taylor Coleridge, *The Friend*, ed. Barbara E. Rooke (London: Routledge, 1969), 1:520–2.

467 From their different disciplinary perspectives (cognitive, philosophical, and ethical), Merlin Donald, Paul Ricœur, and Webb Keane point out that much contemporary research on the human falsifies that which it studies by its very own methods and analytic bias. Donald, *A Mind So Rare*, 46–91, 149–55; Ricœur, *Soi-même comme un autre*, 74, 200, 206; Keane, *Ethical Life*, 58, 73.

468 Charles Péguy, *Zangwill*, in *Une éthique sans compromis*, ed. Saatdjian, 176–7; *Notre Jeunesse*, 74.

469 Emmanuel Levinas explains how the virtues of Reverence (A2) precede and provide the foundation for the cognitive virtues of Excellence (B1) and Equality (B2), how the latter (especially justice) depend on their roots in the former (especially charity or love): "[C]'est l'ordre éthique de la proximité humaine [A2] qui suscite ou appelle celui de l'objectivité de la vérité et du savoir [B1 & B2]. ... À l'extravagante générosité du pour-l'autre [A2] se superpose un ordre raisonnable, ancillaire ou angélique, de la justice [B1] à travers le savoir [B1 & B2], et la philosophie [B1 & B2] est ici une *mesure* apportée à l'infini de l'être-pour-l'autre de la paix et de

la proximité [A2] et comme la sagesse [B1] de l'amour [A2]. … [Il faut] rejoindre la justice [B1] à partir de ce qu'on peut appeler la charité [A2] … amour désintéressé, sans concupiscence [A2]. … [C]ette obligation initiale [A2], devant la multiplicité des humains, se fait justice [B1]. … [L]'idée de justice [B1] est superposée à cette charité initiale [A2], mais dans cette charité initiale [A2] réside l'humain; à elle remonte la justice elle-même [B2]. L'homme n'est pas seulement l'être qui comprend ce que signifie l'être [B1 & B2], comme le voudrait Heidegger, mais l'être qui a déjà entendu et compris le commandement de la sainteté dans le visage de l'autre homme [A2]." Levinas, *Altérité et transcendance*, 145, 148, 177, 181. Emphasis in original. "[U]ne richesse de signification qui était *déjà là*, qui a toujours déjà précédé l'élaboration rationnelle. … [L]e discours des philosophies est à la fois reprise herméneutique des énigmes qui le précèdent, l'enveloppent et le nourrissent ["I am": A1 and A2], et recherche du commencement, quête de l'ordre, appétit du système ["It is": B1 and B2]." Ricœur, *Le conflit des interprétations*, 399. Emphasis added.

470 "Toute la philosophie de Jaspers atteste l'opposition irréductible de l'être et de la connaissance." Henry, *L'essence de la manifestation*, 518.

471 Samuel Taylor Coleridge, quoted in Crabb Robinson, *Diary*, i, 399–401, in Thomas McFarland, *Coleridge and the Pantheist Tradition* (Oxford: Oxford Univ. Press, 1969), 254. "Le kantisme est la base de la philosophie, si la philosophie est ontologie." Levinas, *Autrement qu'être*, 275.

472 Tolstoy, *War and Peace*, trans. Pevear and Volokhonsky, Epilogue, pt. 2, chap. 8, p. 1201. Emphasis added.

473 Heidegger, "The Way Back," trans. Kaufmann, 214. Emphasis added.

474 Samuel Taylor Coleridge, *The Statesman's Manual*, in *Lay Sermons*, ed. R.J. White (London: Routledge, 1972), 78.

475 "Ce n'est donc pas l'habitude de penser selon les lois de l'extension spatiale et de l'impénétrabilité matérielle qui explique notre logique formelle et notre atomisme intellectuel, c'est cette habitude elle-même qui a besoin d'être expliqué par notre activité morale." Blondel, *Premiers écrits*, 2:128–32, in Lacroix, *Maurice Blondel*, 117.

476 "[O]n se donne au départ une idée étroite et pauvre de l'être, réduit au statut de la *chose*, du donné brut – ou de l'*essence* elle-même." Ricœur, *Histoire et vérité*, 400–1.

477 In this kind of reductionist, mind-centred vision of the human, the brain can often be mistaken, as Paul Ricœur points out, for "l'équivalent substituable de la personne." *Soi-même comme un autre*, 159, 162, 178. This common assumption of contemporary popular culture is illustrated by an article in a Saturday newspaper illustrated by a large image of the brain with the title: "Is This Where the Soul Lives?" Brandy Shillace, "Is This Where the Soul Lives?" *Globe and Mail*, 10 April 2021, O1.

478 Defining the human exclusively in terms of rationality amounts, in Ernst Troeltsch's words, to "the selection of one value from the irreconcilable polytheism of values." *Historicism and Its Problems*, quoted in Joas, *The Sacredness of the Person*, 102.

479 Paul Ricœur calls this "l'antériorité du plan ontique [I am] par rapport au plan réflexif [It is], la priorité du *je suis* [A1 & A2] sur le *je pense* [B1 & B2]." *Le conflit des interprétations*, 330, 358. Emphasis in original. "[A]s Truth [B1 & B2] is the correlative of Being [A1 & A2], so is the act of Being [A1 & A2] the great organ of Truth [B1 & B2]." Coleridge, *The Statesman's Manual*, 78.

480 Whitehead, *Process and Reality*, 134.

481 Whitehead, 401. Emphasis added.

482 Bernard J.F. Lonergan, *Insight: A Study of Human Understanding* (London: Darton, Longman & Todd, 1973), 332.

483 Levinas, *Entre nous*, 138, 141, 154; Blondel, *Premiers écrits*, 2:128–32, in Lacroix, *Maurice Blondel*, 117.

484 "Notre modernité ne tiendrait pas seulement aux certitudes de l'Histoire et de la Nature [B1 & B2 : "It is"], mais à une alternance : Récupération [B1 & B2] et Rupture [A1 & A2 : "I am"], Savoir [B1 & B2] et Socialité [A1 & A2]. Alternance où le moment de la récupération [B1 & B2] n'est pas plus vrai que celui de la rupture [A1 & A2], où les lois [B1 & B2] n'ont pas plus de sens que le face-à-face avec le prochain [A1 & A2]." Levinas, *De Dieu qui vient à l'idée*, 207.

485 Jonathan Haidt, *The Righteous Mind: Why Good People Are Divided by Politics and Religion* (New York: Pantheon Books, 2012), 89.

486 David Z. Morris, "Elon Musk Says Artificial Intelligence Is the 'Greatest Threat We Face as a Civilization," *Fortune Tech*, 15 July 2017. http://fortune.com/2017/07/15/elon-musk-artificial-intelligence-2/; "'Summoning the Devil': Elon Musk Warns against Artificial Intelligence," *RT Question More*, 27 October 2014, https://www.rt.com/usa/199863-artificial-intelligence-dangers-humanity/; Maureen Dowd, "Elon Musk's Billion Dollar Crusade to Stop the A.I. Apocalypse," *Vanity Fair*, 26 March 2017, https://www.vanityfair.com/news/2017/03/elon-musk-billion-dollar-crusade-to-stop-ai-space-x; Dion Dassanayake, "Bill Gates Joins Stephen Hawking in Warning Artificial Intelligence IS a Threat to Mankind," *The Daily Express*, last updated 22 April 2015, http://www.express.co.uk/news/world/555092/Bill-Gates-Stephen-Hawking-Artificial-Intelligence-AI-threat-mankind; Lindsay Bever, "'I Fear I May Not Be Welcome' in U.S.: Hawking," *Ottawa Citizen*, 21 March 2017, NP5.

487 Charles Arthur, "What's Next in Robot Revolution," *The Guardian Weekly*, 1–7 January 2016, 1, 10.

488 Nick Bostrom, *Superintelligence: Paths, Dangers, Strategies* (Oxford: Oxford Univ. Press, 2016), 319.

489 Max Tegmark, *Life 3.0: Being Human in the Age of Artificial Intelligence* (New York: Alfred A. Knopf, 2017), 279.

490 "Si notre sagesse ne rattrape assez rapidement nos progrès scientifiques nous allons nous autodétruire." Karl Rettino-Parazelli, "Une question de confiance: Le président du groupe Thales favorable à des lois pour encadrer l'IA," *Le Devoir*, 25 January 2019, A10.

491 Peter Singer, "As Machines Become Smarter, Can They Also Be Ethical?" *Globe and Mail*, 18 April 2016, A12.

492 "An Open Letter: Research Priorities for Robust and Beneficial Artificial Intelligence," Future of Life Institute, http://futureoflife.org/ai-open-letter/; "Scientists Join Elon Musk & Stephen Hawking, Warn of Dangerous AI," *RT Question More*, 13 January 2015, https://www.rt.com/usa/222015-sc ientists-dangers-artificial-intelligence/. The authors of the open letter do not appear to notice that the language of their letter ("AI systems must do what we want them to do") embodies the very self-assertion – the disposition to dominate – they fear in AI systems. The latter are simply mirroring back to us the self-assertion embedded in our own calculating, human rationality, which we do not recognize for what it is, taking it to be a purely neutral instrument, and overlooking its hidden bias and agenda.

493 D.Z. Morris, "Elon Musk," http://fortune.com/2017/07/15/elon -musk-artificial-intelligence-2/. David Hume almost seems to have anticipated the contemporary debate about AI when he rejected the existence of "eternal rational measures of right and wrong" that could enable "inanimate matter to become virtuous or vicious." *A Treatise of Human Nature* 3.1.2, p. 471.

494 Bostrom, *Superintelligence*, 319–20.

495 "Perhaps there's a way of designing a self-improving AI that's guaranteed to retain human-friendly goals forever, but I think it's fair to say that we don't yet know how to build one – *or even whether it's possible*." Tegmark, *Life 3.0*, 268. Emphasis added.

496 Tegmark, 330.

497 This is similar to Leibniz's point that everything can be "multipliée perspectivement": "il y a comme autant de différents univers, qui ne sont pourtant que les perspectives d'un seul selon les différents points de vue." G.W. Leibniz, *Les principes de la philosophie ou Monadologie*, §57, in *Principes de la nature et de la grâce fondés en raison – Principes de la philosophie ou Monadologie*, ed. André Robinet (Paris: Presses Universitaires de France, 1986), 105. This is one of the reasons "character traits [i.e., virtues] cannot be given a neutral, scientific, specification." Hursthouse, *On Virtue Ethics*, 229. Paul Ricœur notes that science requires "la *clôture* de l'univers signifiant" whereas other forms of expressing human truth require instead "l'éclatement du langage," "son *ouverture*." *Le conflit des*

interprétations, 104–5. Emphasis added. This suggests one of the obstacles to developing benevolent or "friendly" AI may be the technical language of software programming itself, which requires a "clôture" inconsistent with the "ouverture" of real human and moral life.

498 Hegel says the first two (self-assertive) meanings of dignity, emphasized by the modern and post-modern world, ultimately depend upon the second (reverent) two. For him, the individual has "value and dignity" only in so far as her "insight and intention accord with the good." Hegel, *Philosophy of Right*, trans. Knox, §131, p. 87.

499 "Déclaration de Montréal pour un développement responsable de l'intelligence artificielle," Forum IA Responsable, 3 November 2017, https://www.declarationmontreal-iaresponsable.com/la-declaration.

500 "Déclaration de Montréal pour un développement responsable de l'intelligence artificielle," https://www.declarationmontreal-iaresponsable.com/rapport-de-la-declaration. See also "Enjeux et code d'éthique: Pour que la machine reste l'allié de l'homme, " *Le Devoir*, Cahier spécial D, 8 December 2018. Another limitation of the Montreal declaration is that its ten principles are intended to guide the developers and the development of AI, not AI itself. This seems to side-step the real challenge: the virtues that will or will not be *built into AI itself* – and how to do that. *New York Times* articles on how YouTube algorithms enable and even develop pedophiles and political radicals illustrate that the ethical challenge of AI may lie even more in the amoral cognitive imperatives of AI itself than in the ethics of AI developers and programmers. Fisher and Taub, "On YouTube's Digital Playground, an Open Gate for Pedophiles," *New York Times*, 3 June 2019; Roose, "The Making of a YouTube Radical," *New York Times*, 8 June 2019. See also Russell, *Human Compatible*, 8–9, 105; Desmond, "The Threat of Artificial Intelligence," *First Things*, 39–43.

501 Tegmark, *Life 3.0*, 279.

502 Catherine Stinson, "Deep Learning," *Globe and Mail*, 24 March 2018, O1, O6–7. It is an illusion to think you can solve the ethical challenges of AI by piling on so-called ethical "expertise." That's the same instrumental mindset that creates the challenge of AI in the first place. Expertise is the accumulation of information and technique. It is a self-assertive value of Rights (B2a), a value of "sensing with thinking," closely allied with the instrumental outlook of the virtues of Liberty (A1). Information and technique are no guarantors of ethical insight and judgment, let alone character. There are as many fools and knaves among ethics "practitioners" as in any other community. What matters in ethics is not expertise but wisdom and understanding, virtues of Excellence (B1), virtues of "intuition with thinking," closely allied to the "intuition with feeling" of the virtues of Reverence (A2). In ethics, what you should be looking for isn't an "expert" but a sage. See Scheler, *Formalism in Ethics*, trans. Frings and Funk, 326.

503 Russell, *Human Compatible*, 178–9, 190–2. See also Tegmark, *Life 3.0*, 261–2.

504 Pascal, *Pensées*, §242, p. 96; Kant, *Critique of Pure Reason*, A319, trans. Kemp Smith, 313. See also Blondel, *L'Être et les êtres*, 259; Maritain, *Humanisme intégral*, 294, 200, 97, 199.

505 Hursthouse, *On Virtue Ethics*, 223. Emphasis in original. Or, as Jacques Maritain puts it: "Il n'y a rien que l'homme désire autant qu'une vie héroïque; il n'y a rien de moins ordinaire à l'homme que l'héroïsme." *Humanisme intégral*, 9.

506 Fei-Fei Li, "How to Make A.I. That's Good for People," *New York Times*, 7 March 2018, https://www.nytimes.com/2018/03/07/opinion/artificial-intelligence-human.html.

507 Jean Vanier, *Becoming Human* (Toronto: House of Anansi Press, 1998), 2, 5.

508 Aristotle, *Rhetoric* 2.3.1380b35–1381a5, trans. Roberts, in *The Basic Works of Aristotle*, ed. McKeon, 1386.

509 On the "computational theory of mind" (CTM), see Steven Pinker, *Language, Cognition and Human Nature* (New York: Oxford Univ. Press, 2015), 269–71; Donald, *A Mind So Rare*, 153–7.

510 Peter Singer, "As Machines Become Smarter, Can They Also Be Ethical?" *Globe and Mail*, 18 April 2016, A12.

511 One reason computers cannot be "programmed" to have the moral intuitions and feelings of human beings is that the "individual mind cannot be fully described by itself or by any separate researcher." Wilson, *The Meaning of Human Existence*, 169–70. If the structure and processes of the brain cannot even be imagined by the conscious minds they compose, then, by definition, those same conscious minds are unlikely to be able to "program" artificial intelligence to have intuitions and feelings like their own.

512 Onora O'Neill, "Abstraction, Idealization and Ideology in Ethics," in *Moral Philosophy and Comtemporary Problems*, ed. J.D.J. Evans (Cambridge: Cambridge Univ. Press, 1987), quoted in Hursthouse, *On Virtue Ethics*, 54. Emphasis added.

513 Swanton, *Virtue Ethics*, 195.

514 "Le cœur a ses raisons que la raison ne connaît point." Pascal, *Pensées*, §224, p. 92.

515 "[W]hereas children can spend many years in that magic persuadable window where their intelligence is comparable to that of parents, an AI might, like Prometheus, blow through this window in a matter of days or hours." Tegmark, *Life 3.0*, 263. The only problem with this observation is its focus on "intelligence." In what Tegmark calls "value-loading," family life doesn't just shape children's intelligence but, more important, their habits of feeling and behaviour, i.e., virtues, the "set of emotional lessons based on the attunements and upsets in the contacts between infants and caretakers … stored in the amygdala as rough, wordless blueprints for

emotional life." Daniel Goleman, *Emotional Intelligence: Why It Can Matter More than IQ* (London: Bloomsbury, 1996), 22, quoted in Swanton, *Virtue Ethics*, 64.

516   Russell, *Human Compatible*, 175–6, 200. Russell thinks the AI problem can be solved by building machines "whose actions can be expected to achieve *our* objectives" (Russell's emphasis). AI machines "designed in this way will defer to humans: they will ask permission; they will act cautiously when guidance is unclear; and they will allow themselves to be switched off." Russell, 247. See also "How to Stop Superhuman A.I. Before It Stops Us: The Answer Is to Design Artificial Intelligence That's Beneficial, Not Just Smart," *The New York Times*, 8 October 2019. https://www.nytimes.com/2019/10/08/opinion/artificial-intelligence.html. There is much to be welcomed in this approach, but Russell does not appear to recognize the degree to which his own approach is still driven by the instrumental virtues of self-assertion ("achieve *our* objectives") even as it aims to teach computers virtues of reverence, such as humility and "deference." He recognizes the human paradox generates two kinds of human "preferences": "preferences for one's own intrinsic well-being [self-seeking] and preferences concerning the well-being of others [self-giving]." Russell, 228. But his use of words like "preference" and "utility," and his (partial) embrace of "preference utilitarianism," show he views both kinds of conflicting "preferences" through the lens of the first – through the lens of self-assertion.

517   Philosophers Paul Dumouchel and Luisa Damiano disagree. They believe it's possible for AI to develop a kind of "artificial empathy." *Vivre avec les robots: Essai sur l'empathie artificielle* (Paris: Seuil, 2016). For another optimistic view, based on a potential algorithm of the virtues, see Martin Gilbert, *Faire la morale aux robots: Une introduction à l'éthique des algorithmes* (Montreal: Atelier 10, 2020). Mark Zuckerberg, CEO of Facebook (now renamed to Meta), is also an optimist about AI: Jonathan Vanian, "Mark Zuckerberg Argues Against Elon Musk's View of Artificial Intelligence … Again," *Fortune Tech*, 26 July 2017. https://fortune.com/2017/07/26/mark-zuckerberg-argues-against-elon-musks-view-of-artificial-intelligence-again. There seems to be a terrible Catch-22 in this problem. Either AI *cannot* develop the virtues of reverence that make humans human: in which case its inhuman super-intelligence becomes an urgent threat to the human race. Or it *can*: in which case, computers that possessed such virtues must cease to be regarded merely as machines and must instead be regarded as *beings*, with all the rights, duties, and accountability – guilt and innocence – that would entail.

518   Williams, *Ethics and the Limits of Philosophy*, 483.

519   For some recent examples, see: Stephen L. Carter, *Integrity* (New York: HarperPerennial, 1997); *Civility: Manners, Morals and the Etiquette of*

Democracy (New York: HarperPerennial, 1998); Howard Gardner, *Truth, Beauty and Goodness Reframed: Educating for the Virtues in the Twenty-First Century* (New York: Basic Books, 2011); Ruth W. Grant, ed., *In Search of Goodness* (Chicago: Univ. of Chicago Press, 2011); Kwame Anthony Appiah, *The Honor Code: How Moral Revolutions Happen* (New York: W.W. Norton, 2010); Michael J. Sandel, *Justice: What's the Right Thing to Do?* (New York: Farrar, Straus & Giroux, 2009); Amartya Sen, *The Idea of Justice* (Cambridge, MA: Belknap Press of Harvard Univ. Press, 2009); Anthony Scioli and Henry B. Biller, *Hope in the Age of Anxiety: A Guide to Understanding and Strengthening Our Most Important Virtue* (New York: Oxford Univ. Press, 2009); Robert A. Emmons, *Thanks: How Practicing Gratitude Can Make You Happier* (New York: Houghton Mifflin, 2008); Christopher Boehm, *Moral Origins: The Evolution of Virtue, Altruism, and Shame* (New York: Basic Books, 2012); Lee Alan Dugatkin, *The Altruism Equation: Seven Scientists Search for the Origins of Goodness* (Princeton: Princeton Univ. Press, 2006); Oren Harman, *The Price of Altruism: George Price and the Search for the Origins of Human Kindness* (London: Vintage, 2011); Michael Rosen, *Dignity: Its History and Meaning* (Cambridge, MA: Harvard Univ. Press, 2012); Eric Lambin and Teresa Lavender Fagan, *An Ecology of Happiness* (Chicago: Univ. of Chicago Press, 2012); P.M. Forni, *Choosing Civility: The Twenty-Five Rules of Considerate Conduct* (New York: St. Martin's Griffin, 2003); Philip Smith, Timothy L. Phillips, and Ryan D. King, *Incivility* (Cambridge: Cambridge Univ. Press, 2010); Kent M. Weeks, *In Search of Civility: Confronting Incivility on the College Campus* (New York: Morgan James, 2011); Christine Pearson and Christine Porath, *The Cost of Bad Behavior: How Incivility Is Damaging Your Business and What to Do about It* (New York: Portfolio, 2009); Christian Smith and Hilary Davidson, *The Paradox of Generosity: Giving We Receive, Grasping We Lose* (New York: Oxford Univ. Press, 2014); Oliver Sacks, *Gratitude* (Toronto: Knopf Canada, 2015); David Brooks, *The Road to Character* (New York: Random House, 2015). This very partial selection does not include the many recent books on virtue ethics, some of which are mentioned in the Introduction, note 12.

520 Ignatieff, *The Ordinary Virtues.*

521 Whitehead suggests that rational consciousness should be "relegated to the intermediate phase" of human life. It is not "foundational in existence, either as an essential attribute for an actual entity, or as the final culmination whereby unity of experience is attained!" Whitehead, *Process and Reality*, 186–7. See also Bradley, *Appearance and Reality*, 508.

522 Coleridge, *The Friend*, 1:336, 115.

523 "La dernière démarche de la raison est de connaître qu'il y une infinité de choses qui la surpassent; elle n'est que faible si elle ne va jusqu'à connaître cela." Pascal, *Pensées*, §373, p. 134.

524 David Martin notes "one of the major paradoxes of freedom, which is that autonomy [A1] depends on heteronomy [B1] if it is not to disintegrate." *On Secularization*, 145.

525 "[L]a signification éthique signifie non pas *pour* une conscience qui thématise, mais *à* une subjectivité, toute obéissance, obéissant à une obéissance précédant l'entendement." Levinas, *De Dieu qui vient à l'idée*, 126.

526 On the "body-based" ego centre and the "non-conceptual," non-ego centre, see Donald, *A Mind So Rare*, 134–5; Rosenzweig, *The Star of Redemption*, trans. Hallo, 175–6.

527 Taylor, *A Secular Age*, 638.

528 "[L]e surgissement même de *l'humain* dans l'être est l'interruption de l'être persévérant dans l'être [self-assertion] – et de la violence que dénotent un peu cette notion de persévérance et son *conatus essendi* – , le dés-inter-essement possible par l'humain [reverence] éveillant la pensée d'emblée à un *ordre plus haut que le connaître*. Nous sommes *hommes avant d'être savants* et le demeurons encore après avoir beaucoup oublié." Emmanuel Levinas, *Hors sujet* (Paris: Livre de Poche, 2006), 11. Emphasis added, except Levinas' italicization of Spinoza's Latin words.

Chapter 18. Conclusion

1 Lev Shestov, *Athens and Jerusalem*, trans. Bernard Martin, 2nd ed. (Athens: Ohio Univ. Press, 2016), 64, 205.

2 "Democratic politics matches, better than any alternative, the diversity and spontaneity of the human spirit." James Q. Wilson, *The Moral Sense* (New York: Free Press, 1993), 247. On democracy as the political regime that "institutionalizes" conflict and "universal moral rules," see also Paul Ricœur, *Lectures 1*, in *Ricœur: Textes choisis et présentés*, ed. Michaël Fœssel and Fabien Lamouche (Paris: Éditions Points, 2007), 372; Hans Joas, *The Genesis of Values*, trans. Gregory Moore (Cambridge, Polity Press, 2000), 175; Mark Lebar, "Virtue and Politics," in *The Cambridge Companion to Virtue Ethics*, ed. Daniel C. Russell (Cambridge: Cambridge Univ. Press, 2013), 265–89.

3 Alexis de Tocqueville, *De la démocratie en Amérique* (Paris: Gallimard, 2007), 1:375–89.

4 Franz Rosenzweig, *The Star of Redemption*, trans. William W. Hallo (Notre Dame, IN: Univ. of Notre Dame Press, 1985), 333–4; Paul Ricœur, *Soi-même comme un autre* (Paris: Éditions du Seuil, 1990), 300.

5 Jeremy W. Peters and Michael M. Grynbaum, "Steve Bannon, Back on the Outside, Prepares His Enemies List," *New York Times*, 18 August 2017, https://www.nytimes.com/2017/08/18/business/media/bannon-said-to-be-planning-his-return-to-breitbart-news.html; Jim Rutenberg, "Bannon Ready for War with a Long List of Targets," *New York Times*, 20

August 2017, https://www.nytimes.com/2017/08/20/business/bannon-ready-for-war-with-a-long-list-of-targets.html.

6 Steven Levitsky and Daniel Ziblatt, *How Democracies Die* (New York: Crown, 2018), 174–5, 212–31; Yascha Mounk, *The People vs. Democracy: Why Our Freedom Is in Danger and How to Save It* (Cambridge, MA: Harvard Univ. Press, 2018), 116–19.

7 Aristotle, *Metaphysics* 2.1.993a30–993b10, trans. W.D. Ross, in *The Basic Works of Aristotle*, ed. Richard McKeon (New York: Random House, 1941), 712; Thomas Aquinas, *Summa Theologiæ* 1–2.14.3, in *Treatise on Happiness* trans. John A. Oesterle (Notre Dame, IN: Univ. of Notre Dame Press, 1983), 131.

8 "[I]l y a *des* interprétations … [J]e m'oriente toujours par rapport à d'autres qui lisent les choses autrement. Cette situation conflictuelle ne pourra jamais s'apaiser, se réconcilier dans un savoir total. Nous sommes livrés à l'affrontement. Tout ce que nous pouvons tenter, c'est *que cet affrontement se fasse dans l'amitié,* dans ce que Karl Jaspers appelait le *combat amoureux.*" Paul Ricœur, *Politique, Économie et Société: Écrits et conférences 4* (Paris: Seuil, 2019), 92. First emphasis in original, second two added.

9 Christine Swanton identifies an entire category of "virtues of practice" which are necessary to underpin a dialectical or dialogical culture, or what she calls "dialogic ethics." *Virtue Ethics: A Pluralistic View* (Oxford: Oxford Univ. Press, 2003), 249–72.

10 "[A]mong the truths long recognized by Continental philosophers … one is the importance … of antagonistic modes of thought: which, it will one day be felt, are as necessary to one another in speculation, as mutually checking powers are in a political constitution. A clear insight, indeed, into this necessity is the only rational or enduring basis of philosophical tolerance; the only condition under which liberality in matters of opinion can be anything better than a polite synonym for indifference between one opinion and another." John Stuart Mill, "Coleridge," in *Mill on Bentham and Coleridge*, ed. F.R. Leavis (Cambridge: Cambridge Univ. Press, 1980), 104.

11 "Social knowledge arises from the search for agreement. Even the common law, which leans on coercion, involves the attempt to find socially agreed solutions." Roger Scruton, *The Meaning of Conservatism*, 3rd rev. ed. (South Bend, IN: St. Augustine's Press, 2002), 32.

12 Northrop Frye, "The Quality of Life in the Seventies," *University of Toronto Graduate* 3, no. 5 (June 1971), 47. On the "perfectibility and *Education of the Human Race,*" see also G.W.F. Hegel, *Philosophy of Right*, trans. T.M. Knox (Oxford: Oxford Univ. Press, 1967), §343, pp. 216–17. Italics in original.

13 "[L]iberty of public discussion is a technique designed to enlist the decentralized imagination and knowledge of citizens, to expose errors, and to encourage new proposals." Stephen Holmes, *Passions and Constraints: On the Theory of Liberal Democracy* (Chicago: Univ. of Chicago Press, 1995), 34.

14 Edmund Fawcett, *Liberalism: The Life of an Idea* (Princeton: Princeton Univ. Press, 2014), 326.

15 In Hegelian language, perception of the dialectic of external Reflection would be easier if there were greater awareness of the parallel process of intro-Reflection, of which Reflection is just the external form. G.W.F. Hegel, *Science of Logic*, vol. 1, bk. 2, §1, chap. 2; §2, chaps. 1 and 3, trans. W.H. Johnston and L.G. Struthers (London: George Allen & Unwin, 1951), 2:35–70, 115, 142.

16 Paul Bloomfield, *The Virtues of Happiness: A Theory of the Good Life* (New York: Oxford Univ. Press, 2014), 27.

17 "To recognize a character trait as a virtue … is to recognize the … reasons for acting … *as* reasons, to recognize them as reason for oneself." Rosalind Hursthouse, *On Virtue Ethics* (Oxford: Oxford Univ. Press, 2010), 234. Emphasis in original.

18 Hans Joas refers to "the feeling of *captivation* inherent in the experience of value," which he says is "central to a modern theory of value." *The Genesis of Values*, 225n67. Emphasis added.

19 Jacques Maritain, *Humanisme intégral*, new ed. (Paris: Éditions Aubier-Montaigne, 1946), 34–5.

20 Michael J. Sandel, *What Money Can't Buy: The Moral Limits of Markets* (New York: Farrar, Straus & Giroux, 2012), 103.

21 Tegmark, *Life 3.0*, 259–68.

22 Michael Ignatieff, *The Ordinary Virtues: Moral Order in a Divided World* (Cambridge, MA: Harvard Univ. Press, 2017), 221.

23 "[C]oercion is annulled by coercion; coercion is thus shown to be not only right under certain conditions but necessary, i.e., as a second act of coercion which is the annulment of the one that has preceded." Hegel, *Philosophy of Right*, trans. Knox, §93, p. 67.

24 Julia Annas, *Intelligent Virtue* (Oxford: Oxford Univ. Press, 2013), 53n2.

25 "[U]n retour au *pur* idéal de l'*Aufklärung* ne paraît plus aujourd'hui suffisant. Pour libérer cet héritage de ses perversions, il faut le relativiser, c'est-à-dire le replacer sur la trajectoire d'une plus longue histoire enracinée d'une part dans la Torah hébraïque et l'Évangile de l'Église primitive, d'autre part dans l'éthique grecque des Vertus et la philosophie politique qui lui est appropriée." Ricœur, *Lectures 1*, in *Ricœur: Textes choisis et présentés*, 371–2.

26 "Along with the decline in bad discrimination (based on race, gender and class) there has been a decline in good discrimination too – discrimination that helps to reinforce good, virtuous behaviour in everyday life." David Goodhart, *The Road to Somewhere: The New Tribes Shaping British Politics* (London: Penguin Books, 2017), 221–2.

27 Steven Pinker notes how fields ranging from architecture and urban planning to the arts and humanities have been harmed in the twentieth and

twenty-first centuries by flawed assumptions about human nature. "A Biological Understanding of Human Nature," in *Science at the Edge*, ed. John Brockman, updated ed. (New York: Union Square Press, 2008), 51–4.

28 Christopher Peterson and Martin E.P. Seligman, *Character Strengths and Virtues: A Handbook and Classification* (New York: Oxford Univ. Press, 2004), 60–1.

29 Nancy E. Snow, ed., *Cultivating Virtue: Perspectives from Philosophy, Theology, and Psychology* (New York: Oxford Univ. Press, 2015).

30 Marilynne Robinson, *Gilead* (Toronto: HarperCollins, 2004), 197. Robinson's suggestion that each one of us is a little civilization recalls Leibniz' doctrine that every part and portion of the universe, no matter how small, reflects and expresses the whole. G.W. Leibniz, *Textes inédits*, ed. G. Grua, and *Monadologie*, in *Les deux labyrinthes: textes choisis*, ed. Alain Chauve (Paris: Presses Universitaires de France, 1973), 53, 133.

31 Michael Frayn, quoted in Neal Ascherson, "What Made Günther Grass?" *The Observer Review*, 7 September 2003, 6. See also Michael Frayn, *Democracy* (New York: Faber & Faber, 2004).

32 Plato, *The Republic*, bk. 2, 367C–369C, bk. 4, 434D–436C, 439E–441D, bk. 8, 544A–546A, in *Great Dialogues of Plato*, trans. W.H.D. Rouse, ed. Eric H. Warmington and Philip G. Rouse (New York: New American Library, 1956), 165, 234, 241, 342.

33 "La multiplicité des moi's n'est pas le hasard, mais la structure de la créature." Emmanuel Levinas, *Entre nous: Essais sur le penser-à-l'autre* (Paris: Livre de Poche, 2010), 39.

34 "[J]e ne possède pas d'abord ce que je suis … [L]a position du soi n'est pas une donnée, elle est une *tâche*." Paul Ricœur, *Le conflit des interprétations: Essais d'herméneutique* (Paris: Éditions du Seuil, 2013), 439–40. Emphasis in original.

35 Martin Heidegger, *Being and Time*, 143–5, 191–2, trans. Joan Stambaugh (Albany: State Univ. of New York Press, 2010), 139–41, 185.

36 "[T]he dignity of Human Nature will be secured and at the same time a lesson of humility taught to each individual, when we are made to see that the universal necessary Laws, and pure Ideas of Reason, were given us, not for the purpose of flattering our Pride and enabling us to become national legislators; but that by an energy of continued self-conquest, we might establish a free and yet absolute government in our own spirits." Samuel Taylor Coleridge, *The Friend*, ed. Barbara E. Rooke (London: Routledge, 1969), 1:185. "This is that conquest of the world and of ourselves, which has been always considered as the perfection of human nature." Samuel Johnson, *The Rambler*, no. 7, 10 April 1750, ed. W.J. Bate and Albrecht B. Strauss (New Haven: Yale Univ. Press, 1979), Yale Edition of the Works of Samuel Johnson, 3:40.

37 Robert Merrihew Adams, *A Theory of Virtue: Excellence in Being for the Good* (Oxford: Oxford Univ. Press, 2013), 209–10.

38 "[A]n unlimitedness that manifests itself in … boundless, irresistible charity." Dietrich von Hildebrand, *Ethics* (Steubenville, OH: Hildebrand Press, 2020), 487.

39 "[I]n love of neighbour [A2] it is the *ever-new disruption of the permanent mold of character* by the ever-unexpected *eruption* of the act of love. Precisely for this reason one cannot predict what this act will consist of, in any one instance. It must be unexpected. If it were possible to indicate it in advance, it would not be an act of love. … [T]he unforeseen, the unhoped for, the great surprise is … precisely man's act of love. … By completing itself, life now remains in itself, nay, in its *un*completedness, that is to say in its growth." Rosenzweig, *The Star of Redemption*, trans. Hallo, 216, 240, 284. Emphasis added.

40 The way Charles Taylor puts this same idea is that, although the "ideal of the most comprehensive account possible … can in the nature of things never be integrally realized," it remains "nevertheless an important ideal both epistemically and humanly: epistemically, because the more comprehensive account would tell more about human beings and their possibilities; humanly, because the language would allow more human beings to understand each other and to come to undistorted understandings." *Dilemmas and Connections: Selected Essays* (Cambridge, MA: Belknap Press of Harvard Univ. Press, 2011), 32.

41 Richard A. Shweder, *Why Do Men Barbecue? Recipes for Cultural Psychology* (Cambridge, MA: Harvard Univ. Press, 2003), 360. Emphasis added.

42 James Q. Wilson, *The Moral Sense*, 241.

43 "Here is a man, that does many benevolent actions; relieves the distress'd, comforts the afflicted, and extends his bounty even to the greatest strangers. No character can be more amiable and virtuous. We regard these actions as proofs of the greatest humanity." David Hume, *A Treatise of Human Nature* 3.2.1, ed. L.A. Selby-Bigge (London: Oxford Univ. Press, 1968), 478. On humans' "humanity" as defined by our "superhuman" obligations to others, see also: Emmanuel Levinas, *Les Imprévus de l'histoire* (Paris: Le Livre de Poche, 2007), 179; *Éthique comme philosophie première* (Paris: Rivages poche, 2015), 95–7; Paul Ricœur, *Histoire et vérité* (Paris: Points Essais, 2001), 275. Christine Swanton says the virtues of Reverence (A2) (both love [A2b] and respect(ful) [A2a]) are "foundational" in virtue ethics: they play a "pivotal and integrating role in the profiles of the virtues." *Virtue Ethics*, 99–100.

44 Max Scheler, *Formalism in Ethics and Non-Formal Ethics of Value*, trans. Manfred S. Frings and Roger L. Funk (Evanston: Northwestern Univ. Press, 1973), 288–9.

45 The "spiritual core forms the foundation of the human spirit." Psychologists Ken Pargament and Pat Sweeney, quoted in Martin E.P. Seligman, *Flourish: A Visionary New Understanding of Happiness and Well-Being* (New York: Simon & Schuster, 2013), 150.

46 Johann Wolfgang von Goethe, *Wilhelm Meister's Journeyman Years or The Renunciants*, trans. Krishna Winston, ed. Jane K. Brown (Princeton: Princeton Univ. Press, 1995), Goethe's Collected Works, 10:203. Emphasis added.

47 Marilynne Robinson, *What Are We Doing Here?* (Toronto: McClelland & Stewart, 2019), 32.

48 Dietrich von Hildebrand points out "the concept of happiness is not a univocal one" but rather an "analogous one," and that "we use the term for completely different things, having in common only their character of being something positive. The decisive moment from the moral point of view concerns the question of which kind of happiness is at stake." *Ethics*, 318n2.

49 "[T]he complete satisfaction of [his needs and inclinations, man] sums up under the name of happiness." Immanuel Kant, *Foundations of the Metaphysics of Morals*, trans. Lewis White Beck (Indianapolis: Bobbs-Merrill, 1959), §2, p. 21. On "happiness" as the "satisfaction" of "needs, inclinations, passions, opinions, fancies, &c.," see also Hegel, *Philosophy of Right*, trans. Knox, §123, p. 83. In this modern, rationalist spirit, Stuart Russell simply takes it for granted a "perfectly rational entity *maximizes the expected satisfaction of its preferences* over all possible lives it could choose to lead." *Human Compatible*, 232. Emphasis added.

50 Based on data from the Gallup World Poll, the *World Happiness Report* measures individual life evaluations around the globe, using the "Cantril ladder" as the primary measure of "happiness" or "subjective well-being," terms which are used interchangeably in the report. (The Cantril ladder question asks respondents to value their current lives on a 0 to 10 scale, with the worst possible life as a 0 and the best possible life as a 10.) The report identifies six key variables which explain almost three-quarters of the variation in national annual average "happiness" or life evaluations among countries. The six variables are GDP per capita, social support, healthy life expectancy, freedom to make life choices, generosity, and freedom from corruption. I think it's fair to say *five of these six variables are values of self-assertion*. The only exception is generosity. It should be noted that the Gallup World Poll does not have a widely available measure of life purpose (a value, predominantly, of reverence), so the *World Happiness Report* cannot test whether it would play a strong role in support of "happiness," or high life evaluations. However, the authors of the report observe that "newly available data from the large samples of UK data does

suggest that life purpose plays a strongly supportive role, independent of the roles of life circumstances and positive emotions." John F. Helliwell, Richard Layard, and Jeffrey D. Sachs, *World Happiness Report 2018* (New York: Sustainable Development Solutions Network, 2018), 13–17, https://s3.amazonaws.com/happiness-report/2018/WHR_web.pdf. Daniel Kahneman suggests "responses to global well-being questions should be taken with a grain of salt," and concludes that "the word *happiness* does not have a simple meaning and should not be used as if it does." *Thinking Fast and Slow* (Toronto: Doubleday Canada, 2011), 398–407. Emphasis in original.

51 Charles Taylor, *Sources of the Self: The Making of the Modern Identity* (Cambridge: Harvard Univ. Press, 1989), 215–18; *A Secular Age* (Cambridge, MA: Belknap Press of Harvard Univ. Press, 2007), 80, 372.

52 David Brooks, *The Road to Character* (New York: Random House, 2015), 15.

53 "Il suffit de se représenter tous ses désirs satisfaits. Au bout de quelque temps, on serait insatisfait. On voudrait autre chose, et on serait malheureux de ne pas savoir quoi vouloir." Simone Weil, *Pensées sans ordre concernant l'amour de Dieu* (Paris: Gallimard, 2013), 11–12.

54 "Votre bonheur est digne de compassion, et ne peut être enviée que par ceux qui ignorent quel est le véritable bonheur." Blaise Pascal, *Lettres provinciales* (Paris: Garnier-Flammarion, 1967), 250.

55 "[T]out le métaphysique, tout le religieux, tout le philosophique, toute la pensée, tout le sentiment, toute la vie admet en soi, accueille, fomente une inquiétude propre d'où sortira quelque jour la liberté." Charles Péguy, *Bernard-Lazare*, in *Une éthique sans compromis*, ed. Dominique Saatdjian (Paris: Pocket, 2011), 346–7.

56 Franz Rosenzweig points out that, in the original Hebrew and Greek, the word we translate as "neighbour" (as in "Love thy neighbour") means simply the person who is nearest "regardless of what he may have been before or afterward." *The Star of Redemption*, trans. Hallo, 218.

57 "[Ê]tre soi – condition d'otage – c'est toujours avoir un degré de responsabilité de plus, la responsabilité pour la responsabilité de l'autre. ... C'est de par la condition d'otage qu'il peut y avoir dans le monde pitié, compassion, pardon et proximité. Même le peu qu'on en trouve, même le simple 'après-vous-Monsieur.' L'incondition d'otage n'est pas le cas limite de la solidarité, mais la condition de toute solidarité." Emmanuel Levinas, *Autrement qu'être ou au-delà de l'essence* (Paris: Le Livre de Poche, 2008), 185–6. See also Weil, *Pensées*, 93; Iris Murdoch, *The Sovereignty of Good* (London: Routledge, 1980), 40; Paul Ricœur, *Amour et justice* (Paris: Éditions Points, 2008), 83–4. Graham Greene captures Levinas' notion of being a captive or "hostage" of the need in the "face" of the other, and Ricœur's notion of the moral "call" to which we must respond, when he describes a doctor in a Mexican seacoast village getting up to answer a

summons to a dying woman "as though unwillingly he had been summoned to an occasion he couldn't pass by." *The Power and the Glory* (Harmondsworth: Penguin Books, 1967), 16.

58 "Together with the sober anxiety that brings us before our individualized potentiality-of-being [the four stances] goes the unshakable joy in this possibility." Heidegger, *Being and Time*, 310, trans. Stambaugh, 296. See also Maritain, *Humanisme intégral*, 64–5.

59 Brooks, *The Road to Character*, 262–3.

60 Murdoch, *The Sovereignty of Good*, 87. "[M]oral goodness matters more for man than anything else." Hildebrand, *Ethics*, 186.

61 "[D]es expériences culminantes de plénitude." Paul Ricœur, *L'Herméneutique biblique*, in *Ricœur: Textes choisis et présentés*, 207.

62 Rosenzweig, *The Star of Redemption*, trans. Hallo, 228. By "eternity," Rosenzweig means something that is "always yet to come," but also "always already in existence," a future which, "without ceasing to be future, is nonetheless present," a "Today which is, however, conscious of being more than Today." This kind of "eternity" has "no relationship at all to time": "it has entered the once-and-for-all; it has become eternal." Rosenzweig, 224. On this view of eternity, as "not in the past or in the future," but in another realm altogether, "outside time," and therefore already present "within" us "this very day," see also Augustine, *Confessions*, trans. R.S. Pine-Coffin (Harmondsworth: Penguin Books, 1961), 197, 253; Søren Kierkegaard, *Spiritual Writings*, trans. George Pattison (New York: HarperCollins, 2010), 153–63. Dietrich von Hildebrand agrees: "moral values manifest a character of transcendence … they hint at eternity." *Ethics*, 186. Jacques Maritain calls this stance "à la fois éternelle et progressive." *Humanisme intégral*, 78.

63 "[T]he more a cultivated reason deliberately devotes itself to the enjoyment of life and happiness, the more the man falls short of true contentment." Kant, *Foundations of the Metaphysics of Morals*, trans. Beck, §1, p. 11.

64 As Charles Taylor puts it, there is "a good that we might sometimes more appropriately respond to in suffering and death, rather than in fullness and life." *Dilemmas and Connections*, 5.

65 Levinas, *Autrement qu'être*, 149–50, 225–9, 235–7, 252–3; Ricœur, *Amour et justice*, 86–7; David Martin, *On Secularization: Towards a Revised General Theory* (Farnham: Ashgate, 2005), 177. When Moses asks God to "show me your glory," God responds that He will show him "my goodness." Exodus 33:18–19.

66 Richard M. Rorty, "From Logic to Language to Play: A Plenary Address to the InterAmerican Congress," 145–51; and "Dewey's Metaphysics," in *The Rorty Reader*, ed. Christopher J. Voparil and Richard J. Bernstein (Chichester: Wiley-Blackwell, 2010), 83.

67 R.G. Collingwood, *Speculum Mentis or the Map of Knowledge* (Oxford: Oxford Univ. Press, 1963), 106–7.

68 Johan Huizinga, *Homo Ludens: A Study of the Play Element in Culture* (Kettering, OH: Angelico Press, 2016); Robert N. Bellah, *Religion in Human Evolution: From the Paleolithic to the Axial Age* (Cambridge, MA: Belknap Press of Harvard Univ. Press, 2011), 89–97, 569–90; Collingwood, *Speculum Mentis*, 102–7; C.G. Jung, *Psychological Types*, trans. H. Godwin Baynes (London: Routledge, 1964), 82.

69 Webb Keane, *Ethical Life: Its Natural and Social Histories* (Princeton: Princeton Univ. Press, 2016), 41–8.

70 "C'est ce retournement de la crise du sens en irresponsabilité du jeu [A1b] qui est, peut-être, malgré son ambiguïté, la modalité la plus perversement subtile du fiasco humain. … Mais le fiasco de l'humain … ne suggère-t-il pas par cette remise en question même une autre signifiance: un autre sens et une autre façon de signifier? On peut se demander si le désaccord entre le Sens et l'Être … ne rappelle pas à une rationalité qui se passe de la confirmation par l'Être et à qui *le fiasco de la rationalité du Même* [B2] *est une épreuve nécessaire et supportable*? Rationalité nouvelle ou plus ancienne … que la positivité et qui, par conséquent ne se réduit pas à l'aventure ontologique avec laquelle, d'Aristote à Heidegger [B1 & B2], elle coïncide." Emmanuel Levinas, *De Dieu qui vient à l'idée*, 2nd expanded ed. (Paris: Vrin, 2004), 85–6. Emphasis in original.

71 Taylor, *A Secular Age*, 430. Similarly, N.T. Wright notes that the virtues of reverence imply a "vision of a genuinely human existence [that] goes way beyond Aristotle's 'happiness' and into a different sphere altogether." *After You Believe: Why Christian Character Matters* (New York: HarperCollins, 2010), 89.

72 Max Scheler (or his translators) describes fullness or fulfilment (rather unfortunately, in English) as "contentment." But for him, contentment "has nothing to do with *pleasure*." It is "an *experience of fulfillment*; it sets in only if an intention toward a value is fulfilled through the appearance of this value. There is no contentment without the acceptance of objective values." *Formalism in Ethics* trans. Frings and Funk, 96. Emphasis in original.

73 Taylor, *A Secular Age*, 151.

74 Psalm 15:4.

75 John Calvin, *The Institutes of the Christian Religion* 3.8.1, trans. Henry Beveridge (Peabody, MA: Hendrickson, 2012), 458. Paul Ricœur calls this kind of "wisdom" "la voie de la douleur et du renoncement." *Esprit*, special issue, July–August 1988, in *Ricœur: Textes choisis et présentés*, 284.

76 "[I]t is a quite peculiar phenomenon that sensuous enjoyment or a harmless trivial delight (e.g., attending a party or going for a walk) will bring us full 'contentment' *only* when we feel 'content' in the more central

sphere of our life, where everything is 'serious.' It is only against this background of a deeper contentment that a fully content laughter can resound about the most trivial joys." Scheler, *Formalism in Ethics*, trans. Frings and Funk, 96–7. Emphasis in original.

77 Evelyn Underhill, *Light of Christ*, in *Lent with Evelyn Underhill*, ed. G.P. Mellick Belshaw (Harrisburg, PA: Morehouse, 1990), 102.

78 "[S]elf-centered happiness alone can be directly intended. Authentic happiness, on the contrary, by its very nature cannot be the end of our actions, but is definitely a gift bestowed on us when we abandon ourselves to a good endowed with a genuine value." Hildebrand, *Ethics*, 324.

79 2 Corinthians 6:10.

80 "[W]e are glad if some mature agents develop virtues inimical to personal flourishing for the great benefit of the world at large, or portions of that world." A sound view of the virtues "allows for extreme self-sacrifice ... to exhibit the greatest love and strength, and to thereby remain as an ethical ideal of perfection. However, it does not follow from this view that all should strive to attain this ideal." Swanton, *Virtue Ethics*, 86, 153.

81 "[T]he 'gentle' virtues require the expression of strength ... Not only must gentleness be suffused by strength, strength must be tempered by gentleness." Swanton, 154. Jacques Maritain calls this highest form of reverence "l'héroïsme [A1] de l'amour [A2]." *Humanisme intégral*, 127. The way Hegel puts this is that the "form" of freedom (i.e., self-assertion), which is merely "negative," stands in "antithesis" to its "content" (i.e., reverence), by which it is fulfilled. G.W.F. Hegel, *Encyclopaedia of the Philosophical Sciences*, trans. William Wallace (London: Oxford Univ. Press, 1975), §§145, 147, 159, pp. 206, 208, 222.

82 "L'accord avec soi se présente dans l'action altruiste comme une détermination plus essentielle de l'agir que l'obéissance à la loi par pur devoir. Elle est joie et non douleur. ... [L]'acteur altruiste n'agit nullement par une espèce de néantisation de sa volonté, se soumettant aveuglement à la volonté de l'affligé ou de la victime. Sa volonté, loin d'être brisée, défaite, anéantie dans un 'non-vouloir,' est au contraire dans *une tension de l'être tout entier* qui, de ce fait, engendre un vrai bonheur: la plénitude du sentiment d'exister. ... Épiphanie du Bien dans l'acte jaillissant d'une obligation éprouvée au plus intime de soi et qui *engage la totalité des facultés de l'être*." Michel Terestchenko, *Un si fragile vernis d'humanité: Banalité du mal, banalité du bien* (Paris: La Découverte, 2007), 270, 277, 284. Emphasis added. Terestchenko calls this highest kind of self-assertion (the assertion of the whole human person "dans l'unité de ses facultés") "présence à soi," in contrast to an "absence à soi," in which condition humans fail to act on their moral intuitions or fail to stand up against injustice. Terestchenko, 291–2. Rosalind Hursthouse quotes a Dutch woman who was

among those who risked their lives to help Jews during the Holocaust: "I don't think it such a courageous thing to do. For certain people it is a self-evident thing to do." *On Virtue Ethics*, 127n6. Robert Merrihew Adams notes "very many of the rescuers said that helping Jews who came to them was something they 'had' to do. ... [W]hen Jews appeared on their doorstep they judged that not helping them was not an alternative worthy of consideration." *A Theory of Virtue*, 151. This surely illustrates Iris Murdoch's point that a virtuous life is "a small piecemeal business which goes on all the time." The life of virtue is not "a grandiose leaping about unimpeded at critical moments." In fact, "at crucial moments of choice," as the virtuous rescuers of Jews show us, "most of the business of choice is already over." *The Sovereignty of Good*, 37.

83 "[S]elf-sacrifice is also, on the other hand, a form of self-realization." F.H. Bradley, *Appearance and Reality* (Oxford: Oxford Univ. Press, 1930), 369. Émile Durkheim notes that, in acts of "understanding, esteem and affection of his neighbor," a human being receives back a "lift" that "sustains him; the feeling society has for him uplifts the feeling he has for himself." *The Elementary Forms of Religious Life* (New York: Free Press, 1995), 213, quoted in Joas, *The Genesis of Values*, 59–60. Paul Ricœur says that, in virtues of Reverence (A2) such as compassion, "celui qui paraît être seul à donner reçoit plus qu'il ne donne par la voie de la gratitude et de la reconnaissance." Ricœur, *Lectures 1*, in *Ricœur: Textes choisis et présentés*, 314. Christian Smith and Hilary Davidson call this the "paradox of generosity": *The Paradox of Generosity: Giving We Receive, Grasping We Lose* (New York: Oxford Univ. Press, 2014).

84 "The trusting faith of the beloved affirms the momentary love of the lover and consolidates it into something enduring. This is the requited love: the faith of the beloved in the lover. ... The lover who sacrifices himself in love is recreated anew in the trust of the beloved, and this time forever." Rosenzweig, *The Star of Redemption*, trans. Hallo, 171.

85 Rosenzweig, 393.

86 Anthony T. Kronman, *Confessions of a Born-Again Pagan* (New Haven: Yale Univ. Press, 2016), 58.

87 Paul Ricœur calls this dimension of the human paradox "la dialectique de la *dissymétrie* entre moi et autrui et la *mutualité* de leurs rapports ... l'intégration de la dissymétrie à la mutualité dans l'échange de dons. ... [L]a gratitude ... reçoit de la dialectique entre dissymétrie et mutualité un surcroît de sens. ... [L]e recevoir [est] le terme charnière entre le donner et le rendre; dans le recevoir, lieu de gratitude, la dissymétrie entre le donateur et le donataire est deux fois affirmée; autre est celui qui donne et celui qui reçoit; autre est celui qui reçoit et celui qui rend. C'est dans l'acte de recevoir et dans la gratitude qu'il suscite que cette double

altérité est préservée." *Parcours de la reconnaissance* (Paris: Gallimard, 2013), 400–1. Emphasis added.

88 Taylor, *A Secular Age*, 702. In a recent local survey of American public and high school students, those who reported high levels of "prosociality" (reverence or altruism) correlated with the level of social support they received from their family, neighbourhood, church, school, and extracurricular activities: "In plain English, those who reported giving also reported receiving." David Sloan Wilson, *Does Altruism Exist? Culture, Genes, and the Welfare of Others* (New Haven: Yale Univ. Press, 2015), 120.

89 Robin Wall Kimmerer, *Braiding Sweetgrass: Indigenous Wisdom, Scientific Knowledge, and the Teachings of Plants* (Minneapolis: Milkweed Editions, 2013), 165. "We are not born for ourselves alone. ... Everything that the earth produces is created for our use, and we, too, as human beings are born for the sake of other human beings, that we might be able mutually to help one another; we ought therefore to take nature as our guide and contribute to the common good of humankind by reciprocal acts of kindness, by giving and receiving from one another, and thus by our skill, our industry, our talents work to bind human society together in peace and harmony." Cicero, *De officiis* [On Public Responsibility], in John W. O'Malley, *Four Cultures of the West* (Cambridge, MA: Harvard Univ. Press, 2004), 133.

90 Samuel Johnson, "Sermon 1," in *Sermons*, ed. J.H. Hagstrum and J. Gray (New Haven: Yale Univ. Press, 1978), Yale Edition of the Works of Samuel Johnson, 14:4.

91 Samuel Johnson, *The Adventurer*, no. 67, 26 June 1753, in *The Idler and The Adventurer*, ed. W.J. Bate, John M. Bullitt, and L.F. Powell (New Haven: Yale Univ. Press, 1963), Yale Edition of the Works of Samuel Johnson, 2:389. Anthony Kronman agrees with Johnson: "the supreme happiness ... is the joy of loving and being loved." *Confessions of a Born-Again Pagan*, 59. Contemporary psychological research also supports Samuel Johnson: a "master strength" of the nature of the human is not only the capacity to love but also the capacity to *be* loved. D.M. Isaacowitz, G.E. Vaillant, and M.E.P. Seligman, "Strengths and Satisfaction Across the Adult Lifespan," *International Journal of Aging and Human Development* 57, no. 2 (September 2003): 181–201, cited in Seligman, *Flourish*, 21.

92 Samuel Taylor Coleridge, *Aids to Reflection* (Port Washington, NY: Kennikat Press, 1971), 118.

93 "[A]ll societies require interplay with their environment; and in the case of living societies this interplay takes the form of robbery. ... [L]ife is robbery. It is at this point that with life morals become acute. The robber requires justification." Alfred North Whitehead, *Process and Reality* (New York: Free Press, 1969), 124–5. "If we are fully awake, a moral question

arises as we extinguish the other lives around us on behalf of our own." Kimmerer, *Braiding Sweetgrass*, 177.

94 Dietrich von Hildebrand calls this "awareness of responsibility" an "ultimate *awakedness*." *Fundamental Moral Attitudes*, trans. Alice M. Jourdain (New York: Longmans, Green, 1950), 33–46. The words quoted are on page 33. Emphasis in original. See also Levinas, *De Dieu qui vient à l'idée*, 77–89; Maritain, *Humanisme intégral*, 63. Paul of Tarsus uses the same image: "[Y]ou know what time it is, how it is now the moment for you to wake from sleep. For … the night is far gone, the day is near. Let us then lay aside the works of darkness and put on the armour of light." Romans 13:11–12.

95 "[É]veil à une vigilance, originelle et ultime, de la pensée où autrui, encore partie d'un monde objectif dans le savoir est aussi hors le monde." Emmanuel Levinas, *Hors sujet* (Paris: Livre de Poche, 2006), 11. "Give light to my eyes, lest I sleep in death." Psalm 13:3.

96 Despite his own reductionist assumptions, Yuval Noah Harari is on the right track when he concludes "the real question facing us" is: "What do we want to want?" *Sapiens: A Brief History of Humankind* (Toronto: Penguin Random House, 2016), 414.

97 "Désir d'un autre ordre que ceux de l'affectivité et de l'activité hédonique ou eudémonique … un désir qui ne saurait se combler, qui se nourrit de son accroissement même … Désir d'au-delà de la satisfaction et qui n'identifie pas, comme le besoin, un terme ou une fin. Désir sans fin, d'au-delà de l'Etre: dés-int*eressement*, transcendance – désir du Bien." Levinas, *De Dieu qui vient à l'idée*, 111. Emphasis in original.

98 Malachi 3:2.

99 "L'homme est l'être qui reconnaît la sainteté et l'oubli de soi. … L'homme n'est pas seulement l'être qui comprend ce que signifie l'être, comme le voudrait Heidegger, mais l'être qui a déjà entendu le commandement de la sainteté dans le visage de l'autre homme." Emmanuel Levinas, *Altérité et transcendance* (Paris: Le Livre de Poche, 2010), 181. "Thus man's intention beyond himself and all life constitutes his essence. And precisely this is the essential concept of 'man': He is a thing that transcends its own life and all life. The core of his nature – apart from all special organization – is in fact this movement, this spiritual act of transcending himself!" Scheler, *Formalism in Ethics*, trans. Frings and Funk, 289.

Index

Page references in **bold** indicate a table; page references in *italics* indicate a figure.

Index

200–2; sub-sub-families of, 221–3, 222; in teleological order, 907n208; through lenses of reverence, 199–200, 580, 592–4; *vs.* value-modalities, 846nn545–6; Western culture and, 262

fraternity, 100, 262

Freedman, Milton, 450

freedom: autonomy and, 165; definitions of, 716n60, 771n14; egoist stance and, 745n38; equality and, 252; ethical living and, 929n416; in families of virtues, 186, 213; four kinds of, 165, 191, 213, 251, 593, 849n575; Heidegger's idea of, 444; limitations of individual, 252; as necessity, 683n98, 692n160, 773n47; paradoxes of, 82, 700n14, 905n197, 942n524; post-modern ideal of, 155, 635; of religion, 502, 742n21; self-assertion and, 83; as value, 165; as virtue, 105. *See also* liberty

free will, 421, 573, 683n98, 890n66

Freud, Sigmund, 53, 328, 473, 738n69, 742n19, 797n51

friendship, 888n45

Froelich, Mary, 859n25

Frost, Leslie, 265

Frye, Northrop, 364, 372, 406, 565, 616, 837n423

fullness: of action, 871n148; complementarity of the virtues and, 709n11; ego stands in the way of, 567; of eternity, 632; *vs.* flourishing/happiness, 456, 631–3; of giving, 201; of life, 492, 567, 949n64; of nature of the human, xvi, 4, 225, 456, 484; objective values and, 950n72; paradox of emptiness and, 642n11, 877n209;

of relationship, 859n25; of reverence, 479; *vs.* satisfaction, 632

fundamentalism, 483, 861n43, 873n175

future, 682n91. *See also* deep future

Gadamer, Hans-Georg, 7, 361, 378, 548, 549, 846n542, 910n233

Galilei, Galileo, 37

Gates, Bill, 603

Gauchet, Marcel, 119, 374, 810n73

Geertz, Clifford, 5, 696n200

gemeinschaft (informal community), 231

generosity, 187, 947n50

genesis: concept of, 691n156

genuine individuality, 593

Gershwin, Ira, 9

gesellschaft (civil society), 231

Gilby, Thomas, 15

Gilson, Étienne, 20, 383, 428, 450, 705n56, 753n28, 863n70, 906n199

Gladstone, William Ewart, 268

Glorious Revolution, 264

God: absolute freedom of, 392; as *being* itself, 392; Christian idea of, 394, 807n54; as *cogitative* being, 405; definitions of, 465–6; denial of, 840n456; "I *am*" (A2) and "It *is*" (B1) stages of, 734n44; knowledge of, 388; love of, 827n312, 862n58, 868n118; as one being among others, 830n339; as the Other, 374; philosophical idea of, 639n4; proof of existence of, 817n169, 819n185; as truth, 873n168; virtues and, 466; voice of, 517; Western concept of, 691n155

Goethe, Johann Wolfgang: influence of, 580, 583; life of, 926n372; theory of reverence of, *581*, 583, 585, 588, 591, 628, 630, 762n68, 848n566,